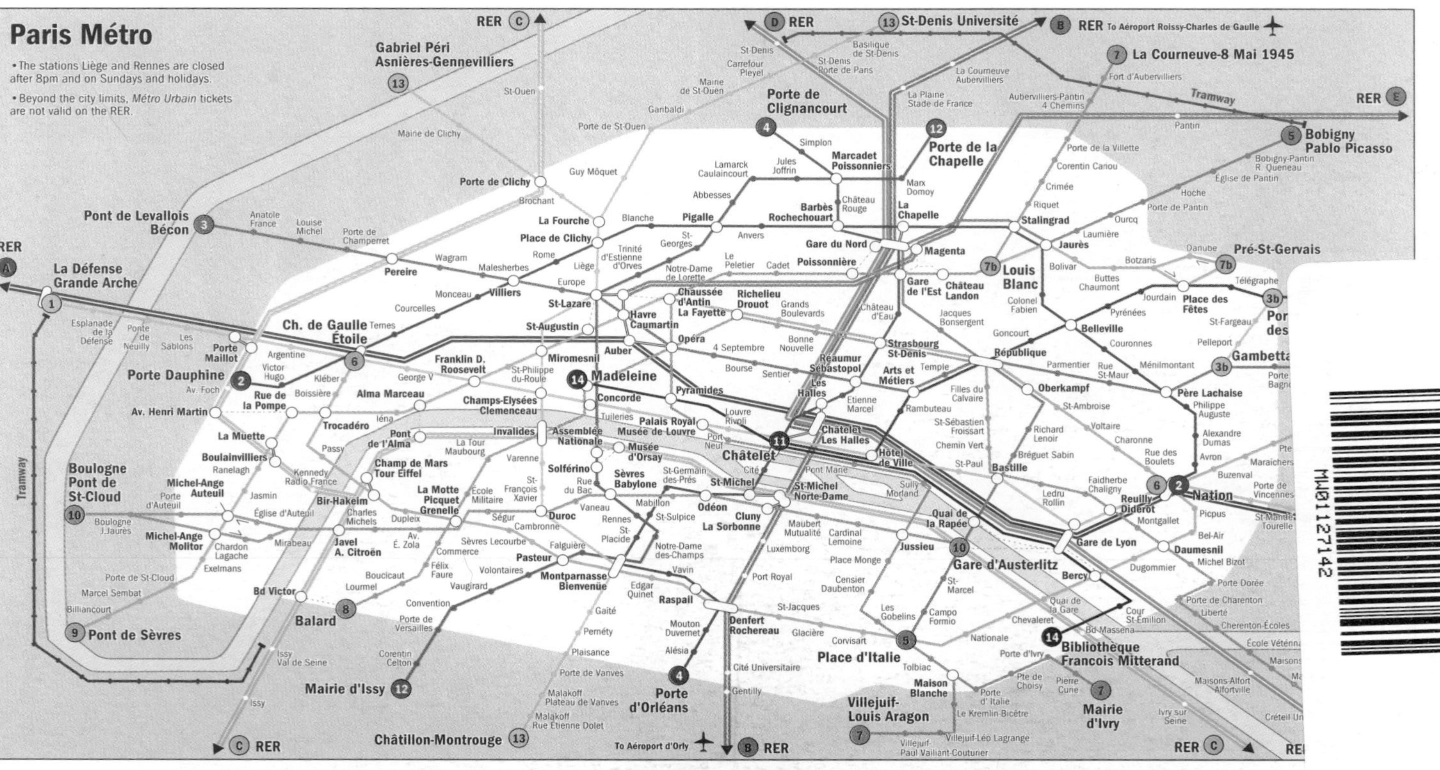
Paris Métro
• The stations Liège and Rennes are closed after 8pm and on Sundays and holidays.
• Beyond the city limits, Métro Urbain tickets are not valid on the RER.
RER A
La Défense Grande Arche
Pont de Levallois Bécon
Gabriel Péri Asnières-Gennevilliers
RER C
Porte de Clignancourt
RER D
St-Denis Université
RER B To Aéroport Roissy-Charles de Gaulle
La Courneuve-8 Mai 1945
Tramway
RER E
Bobigny Pablo Picasso
Porte de la Chapelle
Pré-St-Gervais
Gambetta
Nation
Boulogne Pont de St-Cloud
Pont de Sèvres
Balard
Mairie d'Issy
Châtillon-Montrouge
Porte d'Orléans
To Aéroport d'Orly
Villejuif-Louis Aragon
Mairie d'Ivry
Bibliothèque Francois Mitterand
Place d'Italie
Gare d'Austerlitz
Gare de Lyon
Bastille
République
Châtelet
Châtelet Les Halles
Madeleine
Ch. de Gaulle Étoile
Porte Dauphine
Gare du Nord
Gare de l'Est
St-Lazare
Montparnasse Bienvenüe
Denfert Rochereau
Invalides
Concorde
Opéra
Pigalle
Stalingrad
Belleville
Père Lachaise
Trocadéro
Bir-Hakeim
Pasteur
Raspail
St-Michel
Odéon
Jussieu

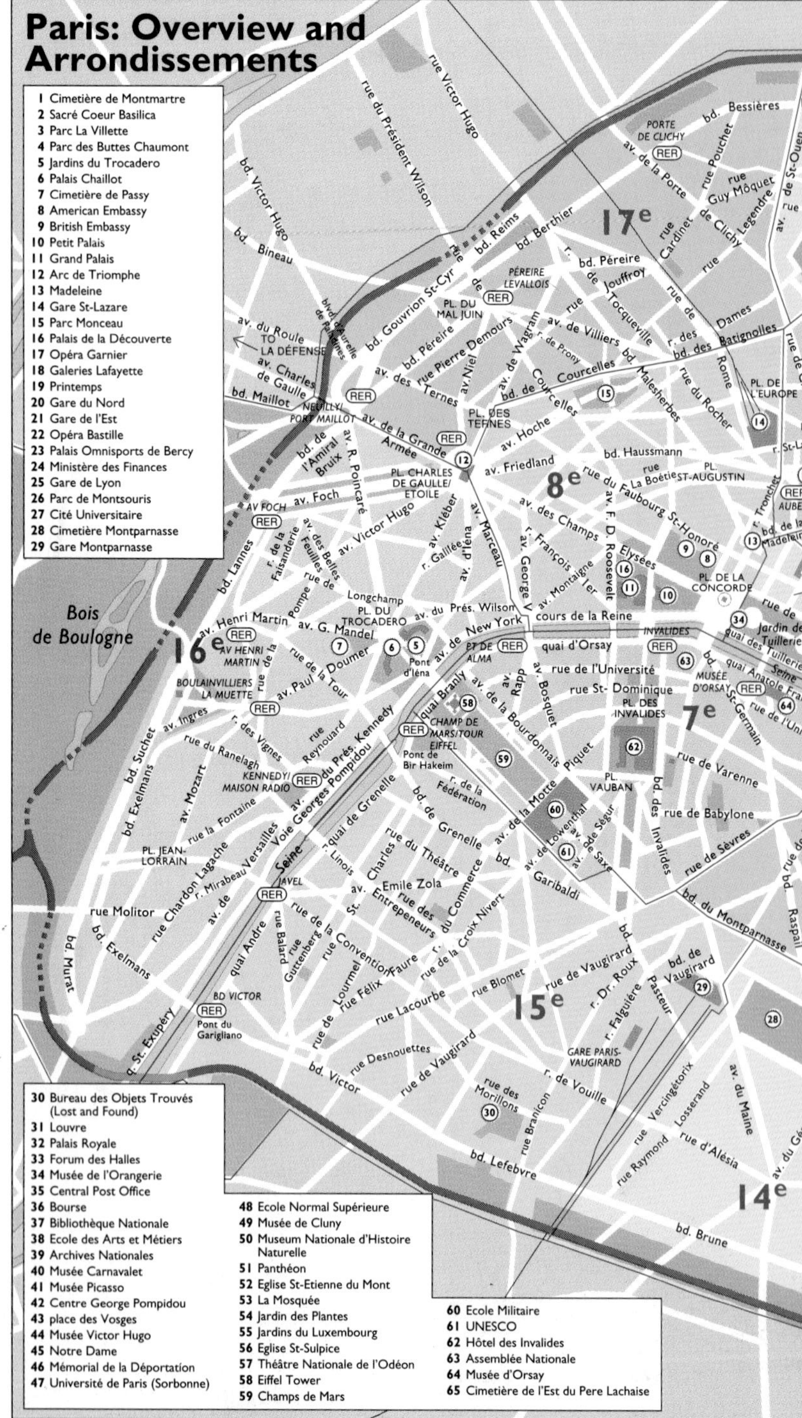
Paris: Overview and Arrondissements
1 Cimetière de Montmartre
2 Sacré Coeur Basilica
3 Parc La Villette
4 Parc des Buttes Chaumont
5 Jardins du Trocadero
6 Palais Chaillot
7 Cimetière de Passy
8 American Embassy
9 British Embassy
10 Petit Palais
11 Grand Palais
12 Arc de Triomphe
13 Madeleine
14 Gare St-Lazare
15 Parc Monceau
16 Palais de la Découverte
17 Opéra Garnier
18 Galeries Lafayette
19 Printemps
20 Gare du Nord
21 Gare de l'Est
22 Opéra Bastille
23 Palais Omnisports de Bercy
24 Ministère des Finances
25 Gare de Lyon
26 Parc de Montsouris
27 Cité Universitaire
28 Cimetière Montparnasse
29 Gare Montparnasse
30 Bureau des Objets Trouvés (Lost and Found)
31 Louvre
32 Palais Royale
33 Forum des Halles
34 Musée de l'Orangerie
35 Central Post Office
36 Bourse
37 Bibliothèque Nationale
38 Ecole des Arts et Métiers
39 Archives Nationales
40 Musée Carnavalet
41 Musée Picasso
42 Centre George Pompidou
43 place des Vosges
44 Musée Victor Hugo
45 Notre Dame
46 Mémorial de la Déportation
47 Université de Paris (Sorbonne)
48 Ecole Normal Supérieure
49 Musée de Cluny
50 Museum Nationale d'Histoire Naturelle
51 Panthéon
52 Eglise St-Etienne du Mont
53 La Mosquée
54 Jardin des Plantes
55 Jardins du Luxembourg
56 Eglise St-Sulpice
57 Théâtre Nationale de l'Odéon
58 Eiffel Tower
59 Champs de Mars
60 Ecole Militaire
61 UNESCO
62 Hôtel des Invalides
63 Assemblée Nationale
64 Musée d'Orsay
65 Cimetière de l'Est du Pere Lachaise
Bois de Boulogne
16e
17e
8e
7e
15e
14e
TO LA DÉFENSE
PORTE DE CLICHY
PÉREIRE LEVALLOIS
PL. DU MAL JUIN
NEUILLY/ PORT MAILLOT
PL. DES TERNES
PL. CHARLES DE GAULLE/ ETOILE
PL. DU TROCADERO
PL. DE L'EUROPE
PL. ST-AUGUSTIN
PL. DE LA CONCORDE
PL. DES INVALIDES
PL. VAUBAN
PL. JEAN-LORRAIN
CHAMP DE MARS/TOUR EIFFEL
KENNEDY/ MAISON RADIO
GARE PARIS-VAUGIRARD
Seine

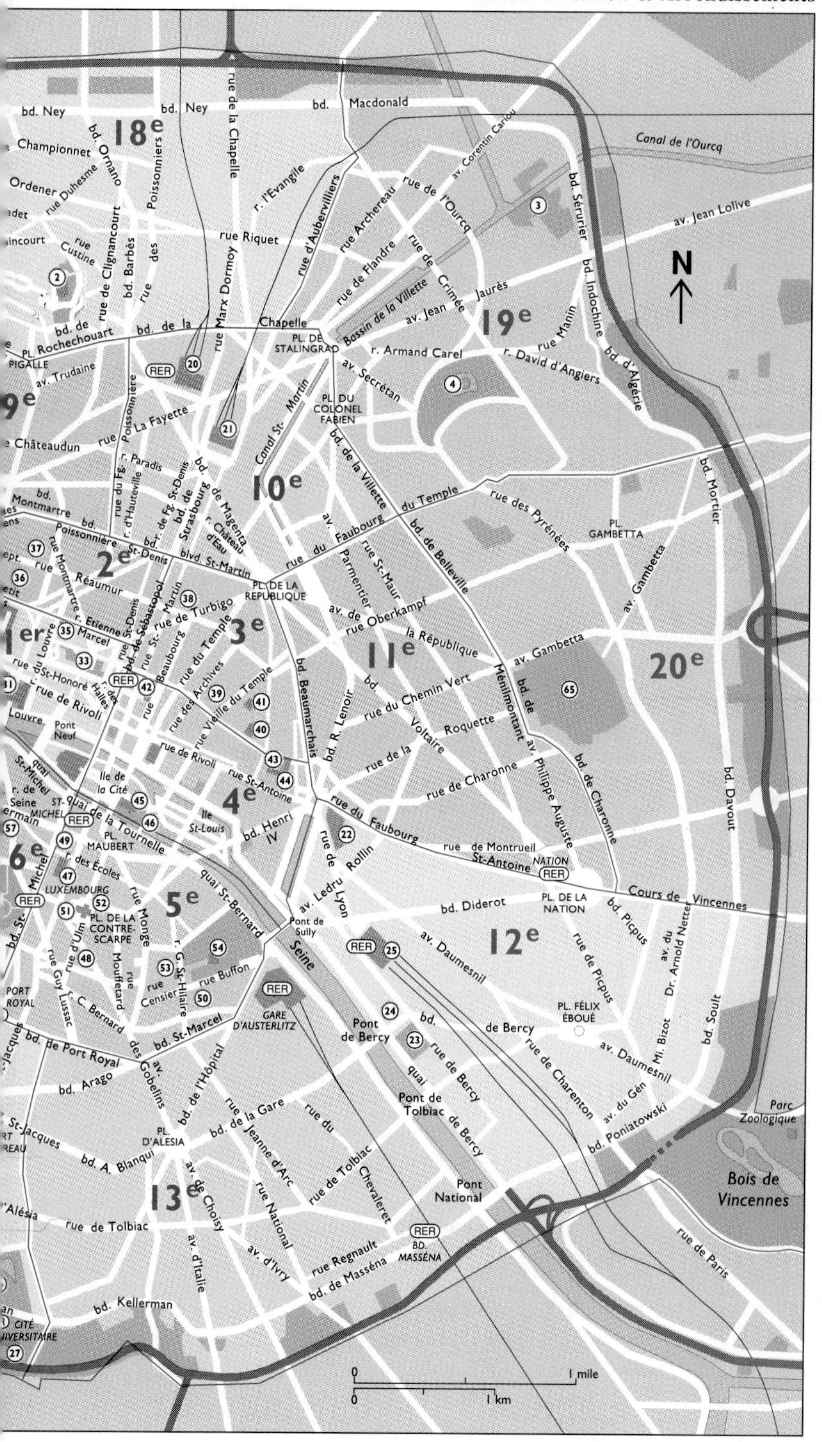

Paris: 1er and 2e

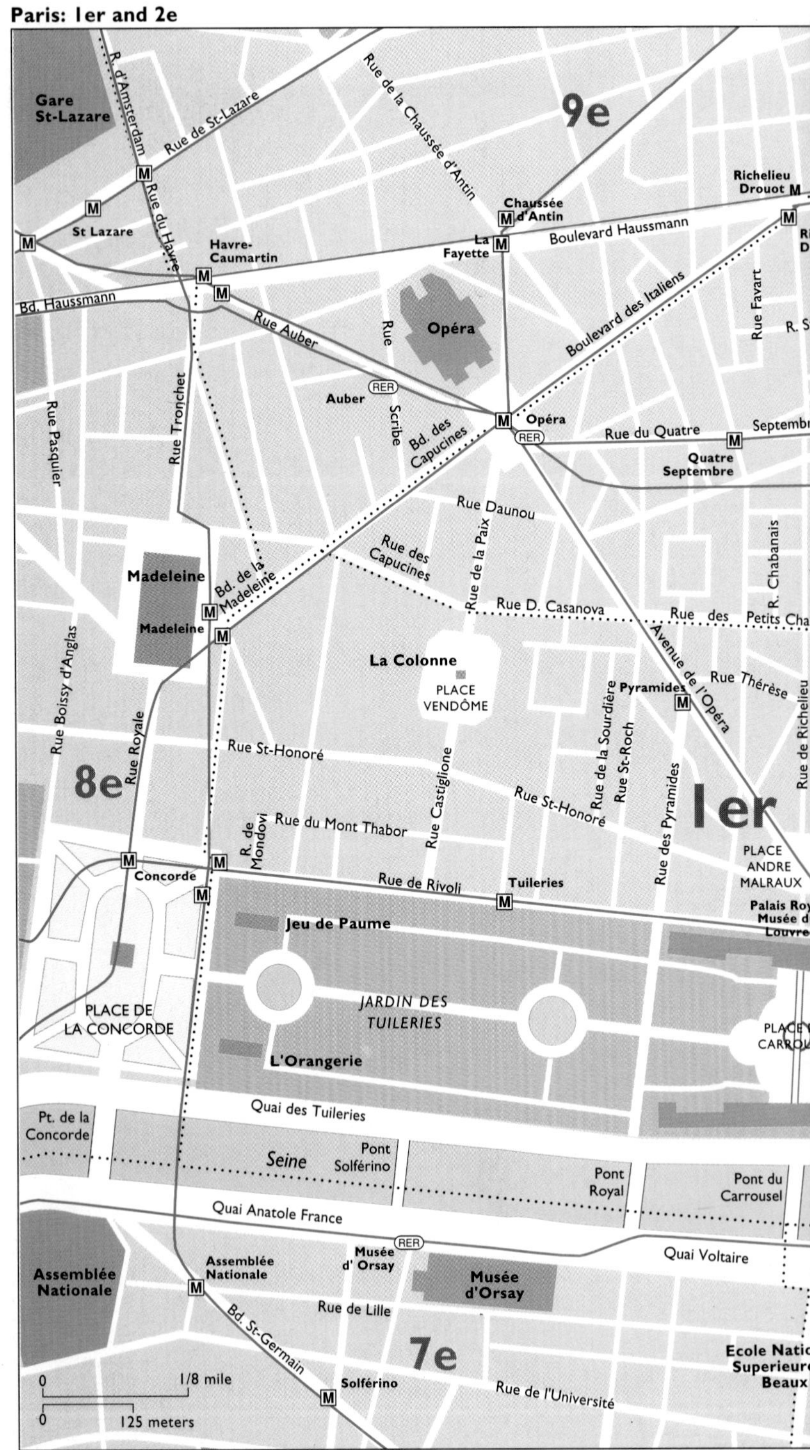

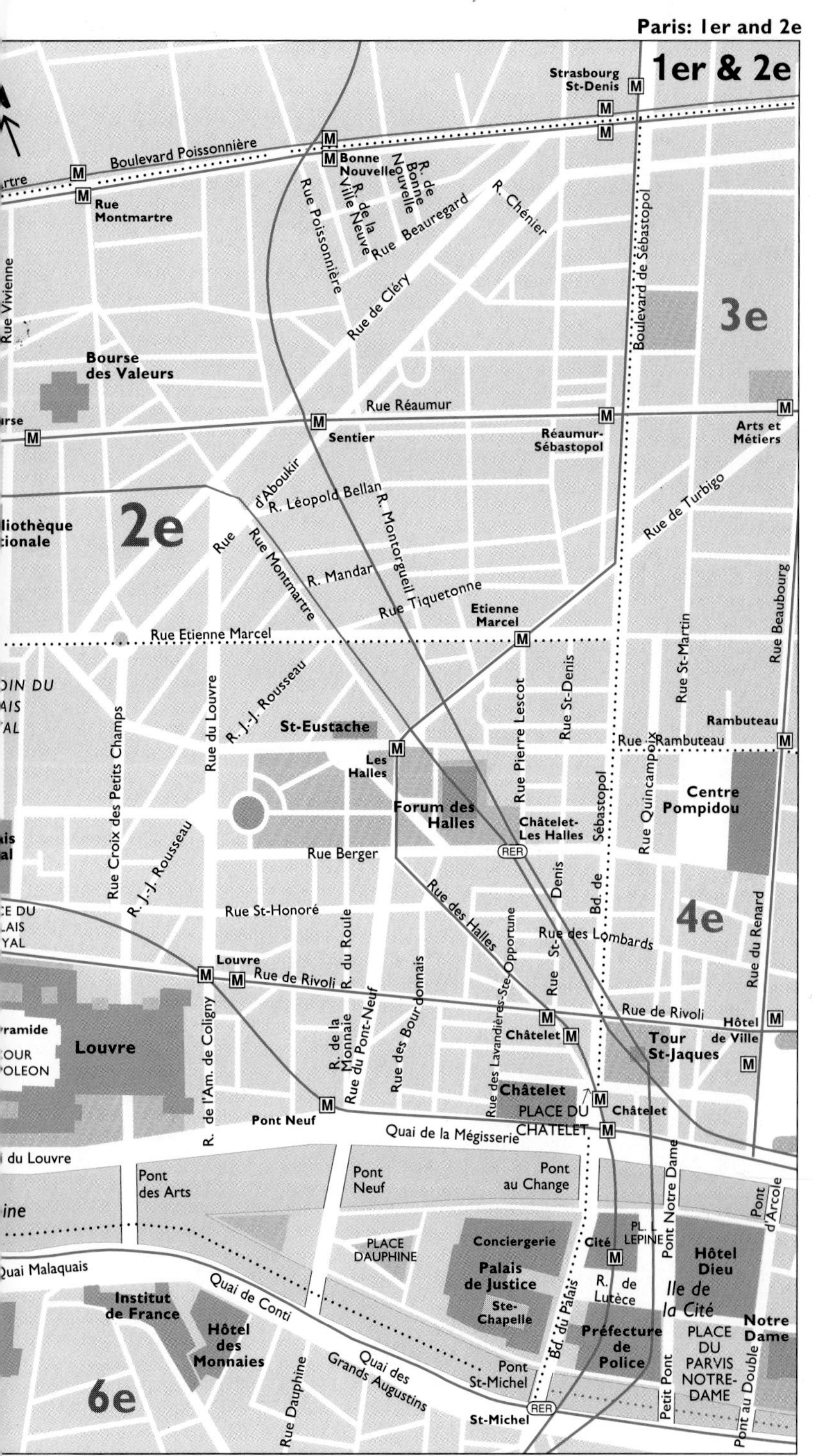
1er & 2e
2e
3e
4e
6e
Boulevard Poissonnière
Bonne Nouvelle
Strasbourg St-Denis
Rue Montmartre
Rue Poissonnière
R. de la Ville Neuve
R. de Bonne Nouvelle
Rue Beauregard
R. Chénier
Rue de Cléry
Boulevard de Sébastopol
Rue Vivienne
Bourse des Valeurs
Rue Réaumur
Sentier
Réaumur-Sébastopol
Arts et Métiers
Rue d'Aboukir
R. Léopold Bellan
R. Montorgueil
Rue de Turbigo
Rue Montmartre
R. Mandar
Rue Tiquetonne
Etienne Marcel
Rue Etienne Marcel
Rue Beaubourg
Rue St-Martin
R. J.-J. Rousseau
St-Eustache
Rue du Louvre
Rue Croix des Petits Champs
Rue Pierre Lescot
Rue St-Denis
Rambuteau
Rue Rambuteau
Les Halles
Forum des Halles
Châtelet-Les Halles
Rue Quincampoix
Centre Pompidou
Rue Berger
RER
Rue des Halles
Bd. de Sébastopol
Rue St-Honoré
Rue des Lavandières-Ste-Opportune
Rue St-Denis
Rue des Lombards
Rue du Renard
R. du Roule
Rue des Bourdonnais
Louvre
Rue de Rivoli
Hôtel de Ville
Châtelet
Tour St-Jaques
Louvre
R. de la Monnaie
Rue du Pont-Neuf
R. de l'Am. de Coligny
Pont Neuf
Châtelet
PLACE DU CHATELET
Quai de la Mégisserie
Pont des Arts
Pont Neuf
Pont au Change
Pont Notre Dame
Pont d'Arcole
PLACE DAUPHINE
Conciergerie
Palais de Justice
Ste-Chapelle
Cité
PL. L LEPINE
Hôtel Dieu
Ile de la Cité
R. de Lutèce
Quai Malaquais
Quai de Conti
Institut de France
Hôtel des Monnaies
Bd. du Palais
Préfecture de Police
Notre Dame
PLACE DU PARVIS NOTRE-DAME
Pont St-Michel
Quai des Grands Augustins
Rue Dauphine
Petit Pont
Pont au Double
St-Michel

Paris: 5e and 6e

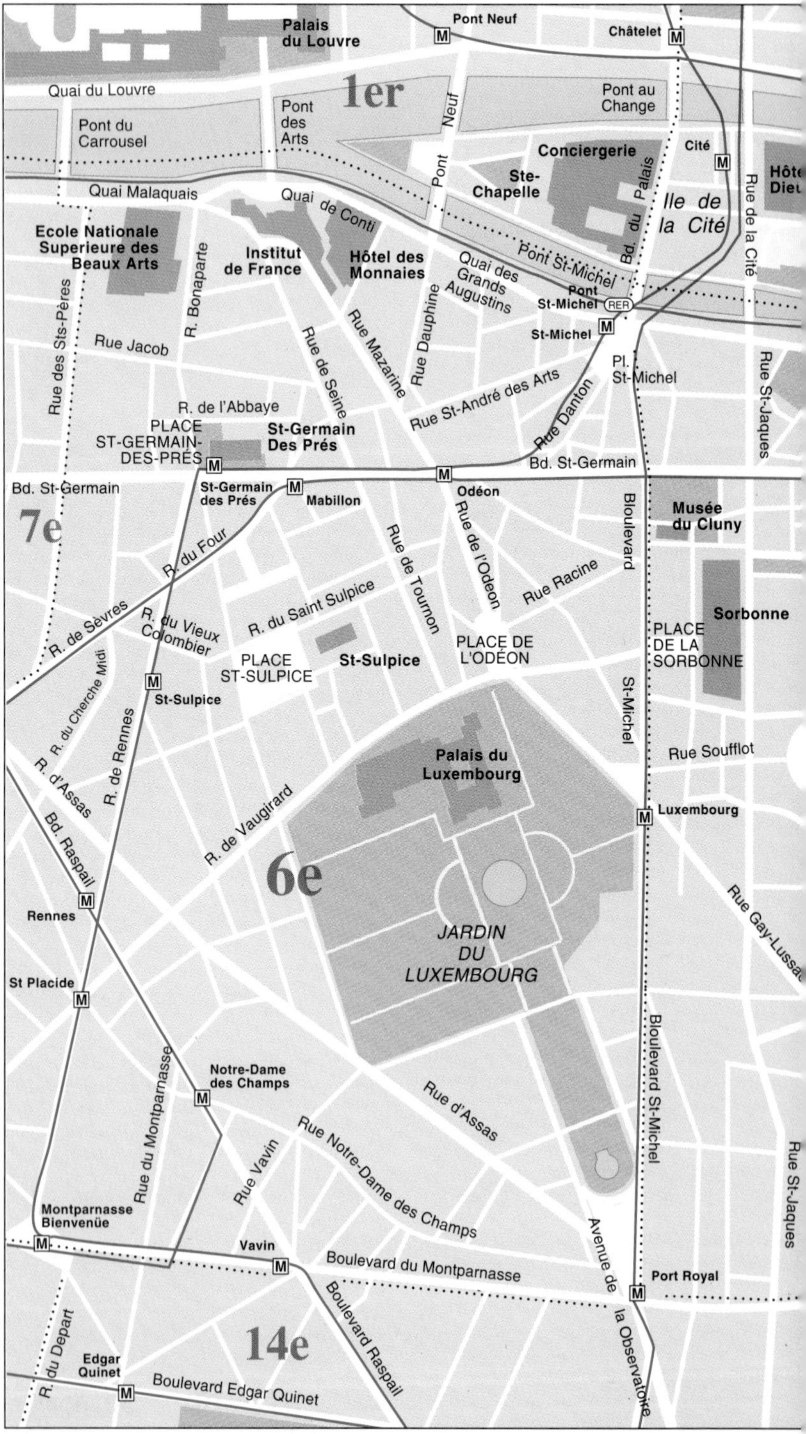

Palais du Louvre
Pont Neuf
Châtelet
1er
Quai du Louvre
Pont du Carrousel
Pont des Arts
Pont au Change
Conciergerie
Cité
Ste-Chapelle
Hôte Dieu
Quai Malaquais
Quai de Conti
Pont Neuf
Bd. du Palais
Ile de la Cité
Rue de la Cité
Ecole Nationale Superieure des Beaux Arts
Institut de France
Hôtel des Monnaies
Quai des Grands Augustins
Pont St-Michel
Pont St-Michel RER
St-Michel
R. Bonaparte
Rue des Sts-Pères
Rue Jacob
Rue de Seine
Rue Mazarine
Rue Dauphine
Pl. St-Michel
Rue St-Jacques
R. de l'Abbaye
PLACE ST-GERMAIN-DES-PRÉS
St-Germain Des Prés
Rue St-André des Arts
Rue Danton
Bd. St-Germain
Bd. St-Germain
St-Germain des Prés
Mabillon
Odéon
7e
Boulevard St-Michel
Musée du Cluny
R. du Four
Rue de Tournon
Rue de l'Odeon
Rue Racine
Sorbonne
R. de Sèvres
R. du Vieux Colombier
R. du Saint Sulpice
PLACE DE LA SORBONNE
PLACE ST-SULPICE
St-Sulpice
PLACE DE L'ODÉON
St-Sulpice
R. du Cherche Midi
R. de Rennes
Palais du Luxembourg
Rue Soufflot
R. d'Assas
Luxembourg
Bd. Raspail
R. de Vaugirard
6e
Rennes
Rue Gay-Lussac
JARDIN DU LUXEMBOURG
St Placide
Boulevard St-Michel
Notre-Dame des Champs
Rue d'Assas
Rue du Montparnasse
Rue Notre-Dame des Champs
Rue Vavin
Rue St-Jacques
Montparnasse Bienvenüe
Avenue de la Observatoire
Vavin
Boulevard du Montparnasse
Port Royal
Boulevard Raspail
14e
R. du Depart
Edgar Quinet
Boulevard Edgar Quinet

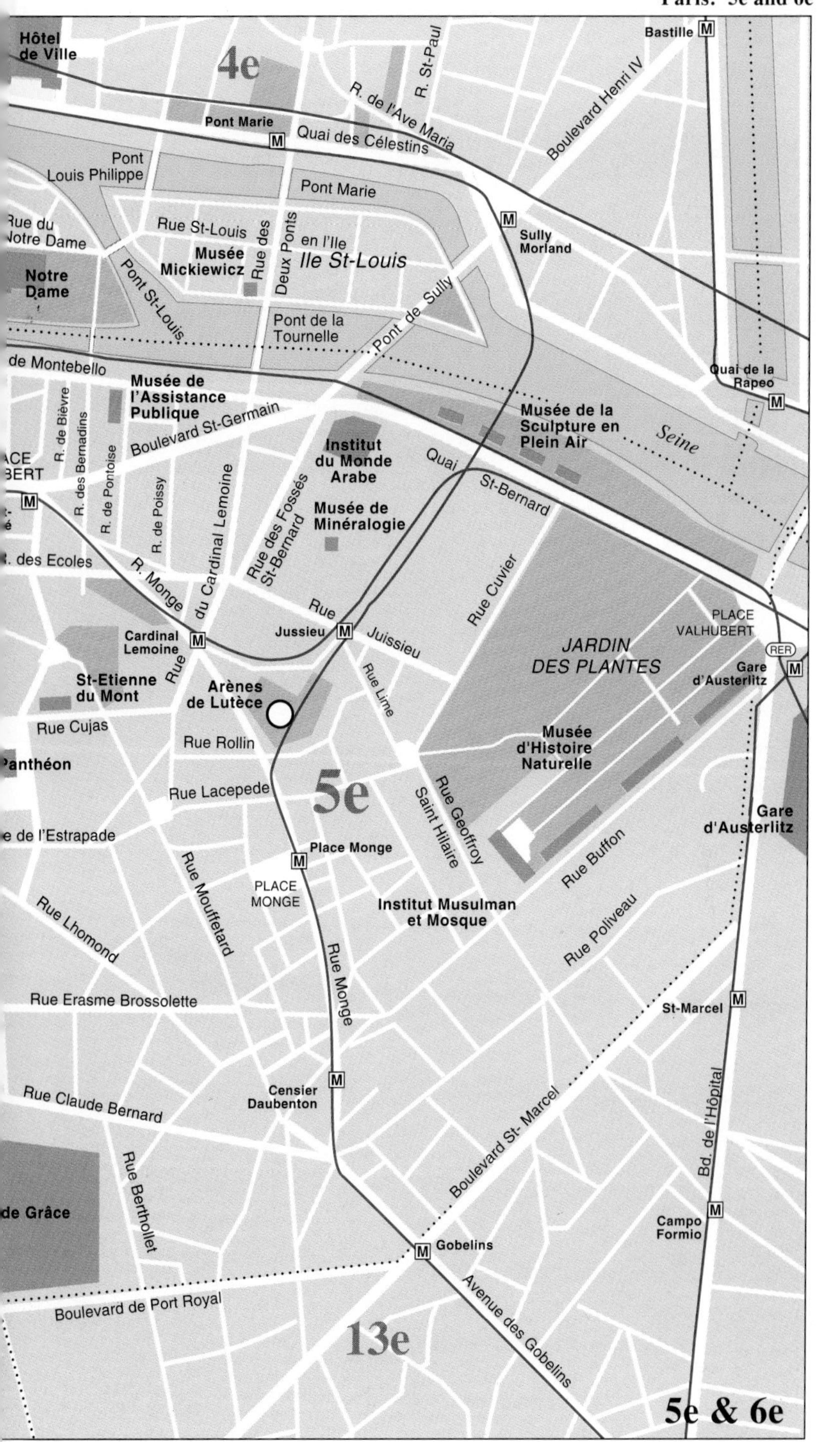

Hôtel de Ville
4e
R. St-Paul
R. de l'Ave Maria
Bastille
Boulevard Henri IV
Pont Marie
Quai des Célestins
Pont Louis Philippe
Pont Marie
Rue du Notre Dame
Rue St-Louis
Rue des Deux Ponts
en l'Ile
Ile St-Louis
Sully Morland
Musée Mickiewicz
Notre Dame
Pont St-Louis
Pont de Sully
Pont de la Tournelle
de Montebello
Quai de la Rapeo
Musée de l'Assistance Publique
Musée de la Sculpture en Plein Air
Seine
Boulevard St-Germain
R. de Bièvre
R. des Bernadins
R. de Pontoise
R. de Poissy
Rue du Cardinal Lemoine
Institut du Monde Arabe
Quai St-Bernard
Rue des Fossés St-Bernard
Musée de Minéralogie
R. des Ecoles
R. Monge
Rue Cuvier
Rue Juissieu
Jussieu
PLACE VALHUBERT
Cardinal Lemoine
JARDIN DES PLANTES
RER
Gare d'Austerlitz
St-Etienne du Mont
Arènes de Lutèce
Rue Lime
Rue Cujas
Rue Rollin
Musée d'Histoire Naturelle
Panthéon
Rue Lacepede
5e
Rue Geoffroy Saint Hilaire
Gare d'Austerlitz
de l'Estrapade
Place Monge
Rue Mouffetard
PLACE MONGE
Rue Buffon
Rue Lhomond
Institut Musulman et Mosque
Rue Poliveau
Rue Monge
Rue Erasme Brossolette
St-Marcel
Censier Daubenton
Rue Claude Bernard
Boulevard St-Marcel
Bd. de l'Hôpital
Rue Berthollet
de Grâce
Campo Formio
Gobelins
Boulevard de Port Royal
Avenue des Gobelins
13e
5e & 6e

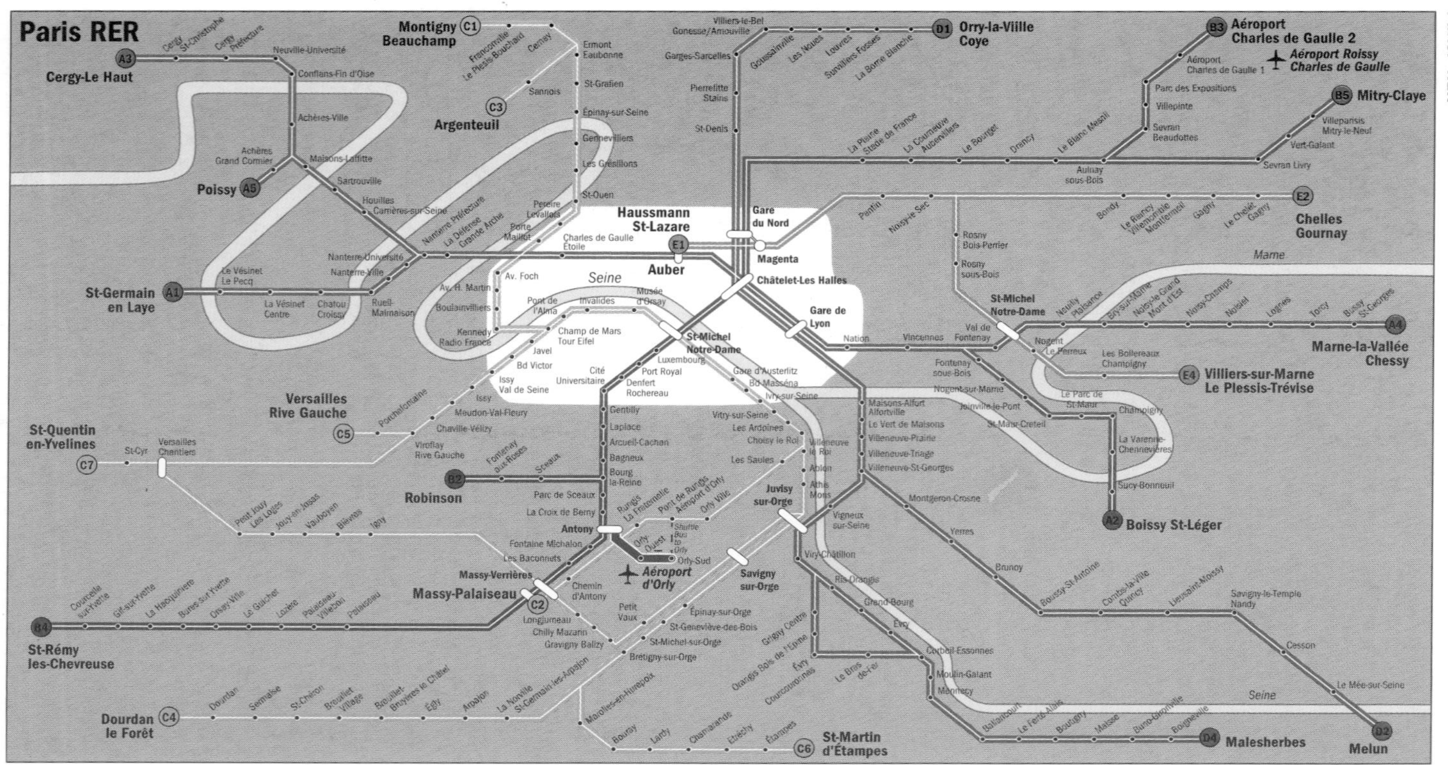

Paris RER
A3 Cergy-Le Haut
Cergy St-Christophe
Cergy Préfecture
Neuville-Université
Conflans-Fin d'Oise
Achères-Ville
Achères Grand Cormier
Poissy A5
Maisons-Laffitte
Sartrouville
Houilles Carrières-sur-Seine
Nanterre Préfecture
La Défense Grande Arche
Nanterre-Université
Nanterre-Ville
St-Germain en Laye A1
Le Vésinet Le Pecq
Le Vésinet Centre
Chatou Croissy
Rueil-Malmaison
Montigny Beauchamp C1
Franconville Le Plessis-Bouchard
Cernay
Ermont Eaubonne
Sannois
C3 Argenteuil
St-Gratien
Épinay-sur-Seine
Gennevilliers
Les Grésillons
St-Ouen
Pereire Levallois
Porte Maillot
Charles de Gaulle Étoile
Haussmann St-Lazare
E1
Auber
Gare du Nord
Magenta
Châtelet-Les Halles
Gare de Lyon
Av. Foch
Av. H. Martin
Boulainvilliers
Kennedy Radio France
Pont de l'Alma
Invalides
Musée d'Orsay
Seine
Champ de Mars Tour Eiffel
Javel
Bd Victor
Issy Val de Seine
Cité Universitaire
St-Michel Notre-Dame
Luxembourg
Port Royal
Denfert Rochereau
Gare d'Austerlitz
Bd Masséna
Ivry-sur-Seine
Versailles Rive Gauche
C5
Porchefontaine
Issy
Meudon-Val-Fleury
Chaville-Vélizy
Viroflay Rive Gauche
St-Quentin en-Yvelines
C7
St-Cyr
Versailles Chantiers
Petit Jouy Les Loges
Jouy-en-Josas
Vauboyen
Bièvres
Igny
B2 Robinson
Fontenay aux-Roses
Sceaux
Gentilly
Laplace
Arcueil-Cachan
Bagneux
Bourg la-Reine
Parc de Sceaux
La Croix de Berny
Antony
Fontaine Michalon
Les Baconnets
Massy-Verrières
Massy-Palaiseau
C2
Rungis La Fraternelle
Pont de Rungis Aéroport d'Orly
Orly Ville
Orly Ouest
Shuttle Bus to Orly
Orly-Sud
Aéroport d'Orly
Chemin d'Antony
Petit Vaux
Longjumeau
Chilly Mazarin
Gravigny Balizy
B4
St-Rémy lès-Chevreuse
Courcelle sur-Yvette
Gif-sur-Yvette
La Hacquinière
Bures-sur-Yvette
Orsay-Ville
Le Guichet
Lozère
Palaiseau-Villebon
Palaiseau
Dourdan le Forêt C4
Dourdan
Sermaise
St-Chéron
Breuillet Village
Breuillet-Bruyères le Châtel
Égly
Arpajon
La Norville St-Germain-lès-Arpajon
Marolles-en-Hurepoix
Bouray
Lardy
Chamarande
Etréchy
Étampes
C6 St-Martin d'Étampes
Vitry-sur-Seine
Les Ardoines
Choisy le Roi
Les Saules
Villeneuve le Roi
Ablon
Athis Mons
Juvisy sur-Orge
Savigny sur-Orge
Épinay-sur-Orge
St-Geneviève-des-Bois
St-Michel-sur-Orge
Brétigny-sur-Orge
Grigny Centre
Orangis Bois de l'Épine
Évry Courcouronnes
Le Bras de-Fer
Vigneux sur-Seine
Viry-Châtillon
Ris-Orangis
Grand-Bourg
Évry
Corbeil-Essonnes
Moulin-Galant
Mennecy
Ballancourt
La Ferté-Alais
Boutigny
Maisse
Buno-Gironville
Boigneville
D4 Malesherbes
Villiers-le-Bel Gonesse/Arnouville
Garges-Sarcelles
Pierrefitte Stains
St-Denis
Goussainville
Les Noues
Louvres
Survilliers Fosses
La Borne Blanche
D1 Orry-la-Viille Coye
La Plaine Stade de France
La Courneuve Aubervilliers
Le Bourget
Drancy
Le Blanc Mesnil
Aulnay sous-Bois
Sevran Beaudottes
Villepinte
Parc des Expositions
Aéroport Charles de Gaulle 1
B3 Aéroport Charles de Gaulle 2
Aéroport Roissy Charles de Gaulle
Sevran Livry
Vert-Galant
Villeparisis Mitry-le-Neuf
B5 Mitry-Claye
Pantin
Noisy-le-Sec
Bondy
Le Raincy Villemomble Montfermeil
Gagny
Le Chénay Gagny
E2 Chelles Gournay
Rosny Bois-Perrier
Rosny sous-Bois
Marne
Nation
Vincennes
Val de Fontenay
St-Michel Notre-Dame
Neuilly Plaisance
Bry-sur-Marne
Noisy-le-Grand Mont d'Est
Noisy-Champs
Noisiel
Lognes
Torcy
Bussy St-Georges
A4 Marne-la-Vallée Chessy
Nogent Le Perreux
Les Boullereaux Champigny
E4 Villiers-sur-Marne Le Plessis-Trévise
Fontenay sous-Bois
Nogent-sur-Marne
Joinville-le-Pont
St-Maur Créteil
Le Parc de St-Maur
Champigny
La Varenne-Chennevières
Sucy-Bonneuil
A2 Boissy St-Léger
Maisons-Alfort Alfortville
Le Vert de Maisons
Villeneuve-Prairie
Villeneuve-Triage
Villeneuve-St-Georges
Montgeron-Crosne
Yerres
Brunoy
Boussy-St-Antoine
Combs-la-Ville Quincy
Lieusaint-Moissy
Savigny-le-Temple Nandy
Cesson
Le Mée-sur-Seine
D2 Melun

Let's Go writers travel on your budget.

"Guides that penetrate the veneer of the holiday brochures and mine the grit of real life."

—The Economist

"The writers seem to have experienced every rooster-packed bus and lunar-surfaced mattress about which they write."

—The New York Times

"All the dirt, dirt cheap."

—People

Great for independent travelers.

"The guides are aimed not only at young budget travelers but at the independent traveler; a sort of streetwise cookbook for traveling alone."

—The New York Times

"A guide should tell you what to expect from a destination. Here *Let's Go* shines."

—The Chicago Tribune

"An indispensible resource, *Let's Go*'s practical information can be used by every traveler."

—The Chattanooga Free Press

Let's Go is completely revised each year.

"A publishing phenomenon...the only major guidebook series updated annually. *Let's Go* is the big kahuna."

—The Boston Globe

"Unbeatable: good sight-seeing advice; up-to-date info on restaurants, hotels, and inns; a commitment to money-saving travel; and a wry style that brightens nearly every page."

—The Washington Post

All the important information you need.

"*Let's Go* authors provide a comedic element while still providing concise information and thorough coverage of the country. Anything you need to know about budget traveling is detailed in this book."

—The Chicago Sun-Times

"*Let's Go* guidebooks take night life seriously."

—The Chicago Tribune

Let's Go Publications

Let's Go: Alaska & the Pacific Northwest 2002
Let's Go: Amsterdam 2002 **New Title!**
Let's Go: Australia 2002
Let's Go: Austria & Switzerland 2002
Let's Go: Barcelona 2002 **New Title!**
Let's Go: Boston 2002
Let's Go: Britain & Ireland 2002
Let's Go: California 2002
Let's Go: Central America 2002
Let's Go: China 2002
Let's Go: Eastern Europe 2002
Let's Go: Egypt 2002 **New Title!**
Let's Go: Europe 2002
Let's Go: France 2002
Let's Go: Germany 2002
Let's Go: Greece 2002
Let's Go: India & Nepal 2002
Let's Go: Ireland 2002
Let's Go: Israel 2002
Let's Go: Italy 2002
Let's Go: London 2002
Let's Go: Mexico 2002
Let's Go: Middle East 2002
Let's Go: New York City 2002
Let's Go: New Zealand 2002
Let's Go: Paris 2002
Let's Go: Peru, Ecuador & Bolivia 2002
Let's Go: Rome 2002
Let's Go: San Francisco 2002
Let's Go: South Africa with Southern Africa 2002
Let's Go: Southeast Asia 2002
Let's Go: Southwest USA 2002 **New Title!**
Let's Go: Spain & Portugal 2002
Let's Go: Turkey 2002
Let's Go: USA 2002
Let's Go: Washington, D.C. 2002
Let's Go: Western Europe 2002

Let's Go *Map Guides*

Amsterdam
Berlin
Boston
Chicago
Dublin
Florence
Hong Kong
London
Los Angeles
Madrid
New Orleans
New York City
Paris
Prague
Rome
San Francisco
Seattle
Sydney
Venice
Washington, D.C.

FRANCE 2002

Emily Jane Griffin editor
Sarah E. Eno associate editor
Sarah Y. Resnick associate editor

researcher-writers
Rebecca Bienstock
Tamar Katz
Catherine Koss
Annalise Nelson
Angela Peluse
Nathaniel Schwartz

Brooks Newkirk map editor
Amélie Cherlin managing editor

St. Martin's Press New York

HELPING LET'S GO If you want to share your discoveries, suggestions, or corrections, please drop us a line. We read every piece of correspondence, whether a postcard, a 10-page email, or a coconut. Please note that mail received after May 2002 may be too late for the 2003 book, but will be kept for future editions. **Address mail to:**

Let's Go: France
67 Mount Auburn Street
Cambridge, MA 02138
USA

Visit Let's Go at **http://www.letsgo.com,** or send email to:

feedback@letsgo.com
Subject: "Let's Go: France"

In addition to the invaluable travel advice our readers share with us, many are kind enough to offer their services as researchers or editors. Unfortunately, our charter enables us to employ only currently enrolled Harvard students.

Distributed outside the USA and Canada by Macmillan.

ISBN: 0-312-27036-4

First edition
10 9 8 7 6 5 4 3 2 1

Let's Go: France is written by Let's Go Publications, 67 Mount Auburn Street, Cambridge, MA 02138, USA.

Printed in the USA on recycled paper with biodegradable soy ink.

HOW TO USE THIS BOOK

Welcome to Let's Go: France 2002! This year, we've tried to restore *Paris et les provinces* each to their full, individual glory, and we've included new detours that will pull you almost magnetically off the beaten path. We've expanded our coverage of daytrips, like Pérouges, outside Lyon, or Cassis, outside Marseille, and given you even more information about the hazy, lazy wine and champagne routes.

ORGANIZATION OF THIS BOOK

INTRODUCTORY MATERIAL. The first chapter, Discover France, provides you with an overview of French travel, including Suggested Itineraries that give you an idea of what you shouldn't miss and how long it will take to see it. The Life & Times chapter provides you with a general introduction to the history, literature, art, music, and popular culture of France. The Essentials section outlines the practical information you will need to prepare for and execute your trip.

COVERAGE. The black tabs in the margins will help you to navigate between chapters quickly and easily. Our book is divided into eighteen regions, beginning with Paris and the Ile de France and moving up to the northwestern coast and then around the nation in a vaguely counter-clockwise way, dipping down to Corsica and back up to the Northeast. At the beginning of each regional section, which correspond loosely to French governmental divisions, as well as the sense of local identity of residents in a given area, you can find a helpful box. It will list short descriptions of each city and town in the area, with a map, and thumbpicks (☒) indicating which ones are really worth your time.

APPENDIX. The appendix contains useful **conversions,** a **climate chart,** a **phrasebook** of handy phrases in French, and a **glossary** of foreign and architectural words. You can also use our inside back cover for information on **measurements, currency,** and as a quick reference for **telephoning** to and from France.

A FEW NOTES ABOUT LET'S GO FORMAT

RANKING ESTABLISHMENTS. In each section (accommodations, food, etc.), we list establishments in order from the best on down. The one exception is in our Paris chapter, where establishments are sometimes listed by location as well, when different *arrondissements* are combined. Our absolute favorites are so denoted by the highest honor given out by *Let' s Go*, the Let's Go thumbs-up (☒).

PHONE CODES AND TELEPHONE NUMBERS. Phone numbers in text are also preceded by the ☎ icon.

GRAYBOXES AND IKONBOXES.
Grayboxes at times provide wonderful cultural insight, at times simply crude humor. In any case, they're usually amusing, so enjoy. Whiteboxes, on the other hand, provide important practical information, such as warnings, helpful hints and further resources.

A NOTE TO OUR READERS The information for this book was gathered by *Let's Go* researchers from May through August of 2001. Each listing is based on one researcher's opinion, formed during his or her visit at a particular time. Those traveling at other times may have different experiences since prices, dates, hours, and conditions are always subject to change. You are urged to check the facts presented in this book beforehand to avoid inconvenience and surprises.

RESEARCHER-WRITERS

Rebecca Bienstock *Côte d'Azur, Corsica, and the Alps*

Rebecca traded in the wilds of off-season New Zealand for the definitely *in* season on the Côte d'Azur, where she sped around in sportscars and mingled with high-society (how many houses did that guy have?), picking up a personal chef along the way. But she always made her weekly phone call, even after long ferry rides. She then returned to the island life on Corsica, alternately hiking and scrounging for Hollywood gossip, before scaling the Alps and their swinging nightlife, leaving no nightclub unturned.

Tamar Katz *Berry-Limousin, Périgord, Poitou-Charentes, and the Loire Valley*

The sleepy towns and châteaux of central and western France had never seen anything like Tamar. Whipping through a grueling itinerary like a pro, Tamar went way beyond the call of duty, revealing new accommodations, establishments, and even a new *digéstif* in the Marais Poitevin. In her weekly calls, Tamar couldn't stop calling France spectacular; we think the same of her.

Catherine Koss *Brittany and western Normandy*

Cait tackled her ancestral home this summer with great enthusiasm and free of the "been there, done that" syndrome. Nearly doubling the hard coverage of these regions with her piles of brilliantly conveyed information, Cait soaked up so much local culture that we thought she'd come back speaking Breton. Besides her travelogue copy, which made us actually feel like we were there, our fearless researcher kept our walls full with weekly postcards.

Annalise Nelson *Champagne, Alsace-Lorraine, Franche-Comté, Flanders, and eastern Normandy*

Never before has quite so charming a history buff tackled the big, bad North. The lovely Anna swooned down the Champagne route, kept running into the prolific military architect Vauban, and spent the better part of a morning in a McDonald's dumpster looking for her wallet. Surviving adventures from the magnitudinous to the microscopic, she managed to send back hysterical, informative dispatches, disdaining Dunkerque and adoring Alsace. *Vachement super*, Anna!

Angela Peluse *Lyon and the Auvergne, Burgundy, and Provence*

A no-nonsense attitude propelled Angie through the kitsch of Provence and the smokestacks of Clermont. Churning out stellar coverage, this adopted *Lyonnaise* improved our tequila-bar coverage and found the most burning nightspots around, but had a zero-tolerance policy for slovenly accommodations. Singing the praises of Magnum bars one minute and stopping crime the next, our super-hero did such great research it practically rendered us extraneous. What up Angie!

Nathaniel L. Schwartz *Aquitaine, Gascony, and Pays Basque, Languedoc-Roussillon, Périgord*

Nate, yearning for the dangers of the developing world, found himself in towns perhaps too quaint for words, but he managed to contain his gag reflex long enough to fall in love with southwestern France, from the Pyrenean mountain towns to central castles and caves. And it with him; Nate charmed many a local, from village mayors to honey-makers. His meticulous documentation of criminal activity left us in stitches; we're still sorry about the honey pot! Nate finally made it down to Morocco after he finished, returning bearded and blissful.

Anne Jump *Editor, Paris*
Valerie de Charette *Researcher-Writer, Paris*
John Hulsey *Researcher-Writer, Paris*
Heidi Morrison *Researcher-Writer, Paris*

ACKNOWLEDGMENTS

The Let's Go 2002 series is dedicated to the memory of Haley Surti

These books don't just put themselves together, you know. They're assembled by machine.

Team France thanks: Our six wonderful researchers. Amélie for being the best frenchies' ME, Brooks, Anne J. for Paris, Anne Chisholm for common sense, Jack, Vicky, and Jessop (aka Team SPAM), for being such…ummm…for being podmates. Just kidding, we love you guys so much it's *sick*. Cody Dydek for "hellos," Fish for action copy and digestive system updates, the Barker Center, Anky-Ank for being the best ever def totes, Leo's Place and Hi-Rise Bakery, the Internet for valuable procrastination, Dire Straits…excuse, PR and the DR…de de de de

Emily thanks: Sarah and Sarah for everything, including their amazing last-minute work, Alayna and Sido for "good times, good times," Dina, Wallach, Heyward, Alex, and Ashley for senior spring. Katie for what will be at the rue du Dragon. Olivia for remembering me in Hanoi. Kate for Coloradan dispatches. Mom and Dad for the first France trip in 1988, for housing me so graciously, and for all the moral support.

Sarah E. thanks: Em my stellar and dedicated editor, Sarah R. for her meticulous hard work, Sofia for "hieeee", George for econ lessons, Jessop for all the love, Fish for backrubs, Caits for Bridgeport and the arboretum, Urbs for garage sales, Claire for tennis and sherwood forest, T for chillin', Ames for shoes e-mails, Lainer for her adventures, Beth for my 1st real diner, Lil for Cali dispatches, Mom and Dad for love, counseling and gossip.

Sarah R. thanks: Emily and Sarah for being fantastic! Sofia for the laughs. Rach, David, Gina, and Tony for being the best for so long. Reggie for homemade cookies. Brady for putting up with me. Crista for bonding over S&TC. The Mmes. Finkelstein for my love of French. Joe for backrubs. Caleb and Sarah for hugs and being so understanding. Mom, Dad, Titch, and Tamar for all their love and unending support.

Editor
Emily Jane Griffin
Associate Editors
Sarah E. Eno, Sarah Y. Resnick
Managing Editor
Amélie Cherlin
Map Editor
Brooks Newkirk

France: Regions

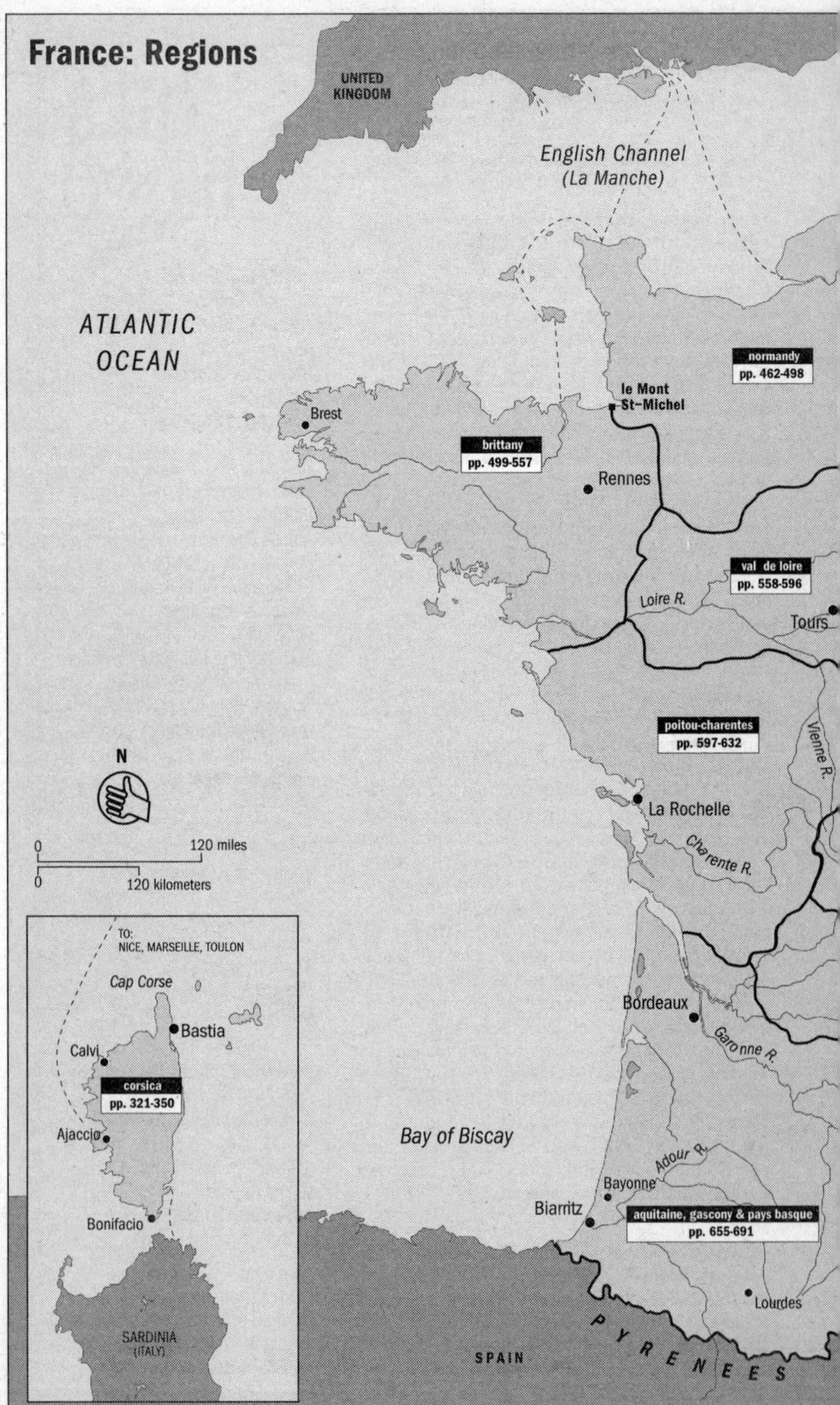

UNITED KINGDOM
English Channel
(La Manche)
ATLANTIC OCEAN
normandy
pp. 462-498
le Mont St-Michel
Brest
brittany
pp. 499-557
Rennes
val de loire
pp. 558-596
Loire R.
Tours
poitou-charentes
pp. 597-632
Vienne R.
N
La Rochelle
Charente R.
0
120 miles
0
120 kilometers
TO:
NICE, MARSEILLE, TOULON
Cap Corse
Bastia
Calvi
corsica
pp. 321-350
Ajaccio
Bonifacio
SARDINIA
(ITALY)
Bordeaux
Garonne R.
Bay of Biscay
Adour R.
Bayonne
Biarritz
aquitaine, gascony & pays basque
pp. 655-691
Lourdes
SPAIN
PYRENEES

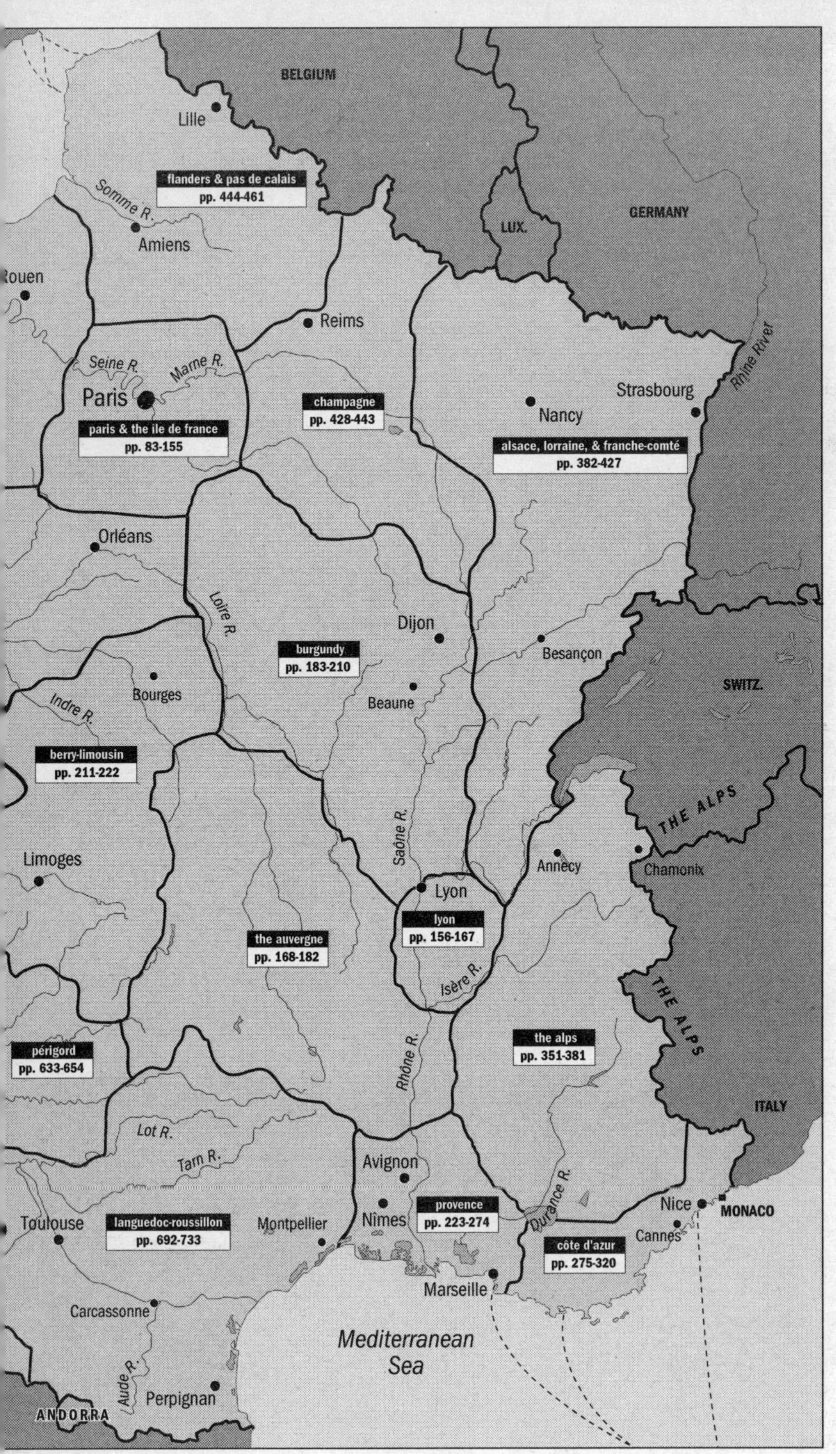

BELGIUM
Lille
flanders & pas de calais
pp. 444-461
Somme R.
Amiens
LUX.
GERMANY
Rouen
Reims
Rhine River
Seine R.
Marne R.
Paris
champagne
pp. 428-443
Strasbourg
Nancy
paris & the ile de france
pp. 83-155
alsace, lorraine, & franche-comté
pp. 382-427
Orléans
Loire R.
Dijon
burgundy
pp. 183-210
Besançon
Bourges
Beaune
SWITZ.
Indre R.
berry-limousin
pp. 211-222
THE ALPS
Saône R.
Annecy
Chamonix
Limoges
Lyon
lyon
pp. 156-167
the auvergne
pp. 168-182
Isère R.
THE ALPS
the alps
pp. 351-381
périgord
pp. 633-654
Rhône R.
ITALY
Lot R.
Tarn R.
Avignon
Durance R.
provence
pp. 223-274
Nice
MONACO
Toulouse
languedoc-roussillon
pp. 692-733
Montpellier
Nîmes
Cannes
côte d'azur
pp. 275-320
Marseille
Carcassonne
Mediterranean Sea
Aude R.
Perpignan
ANDORRA

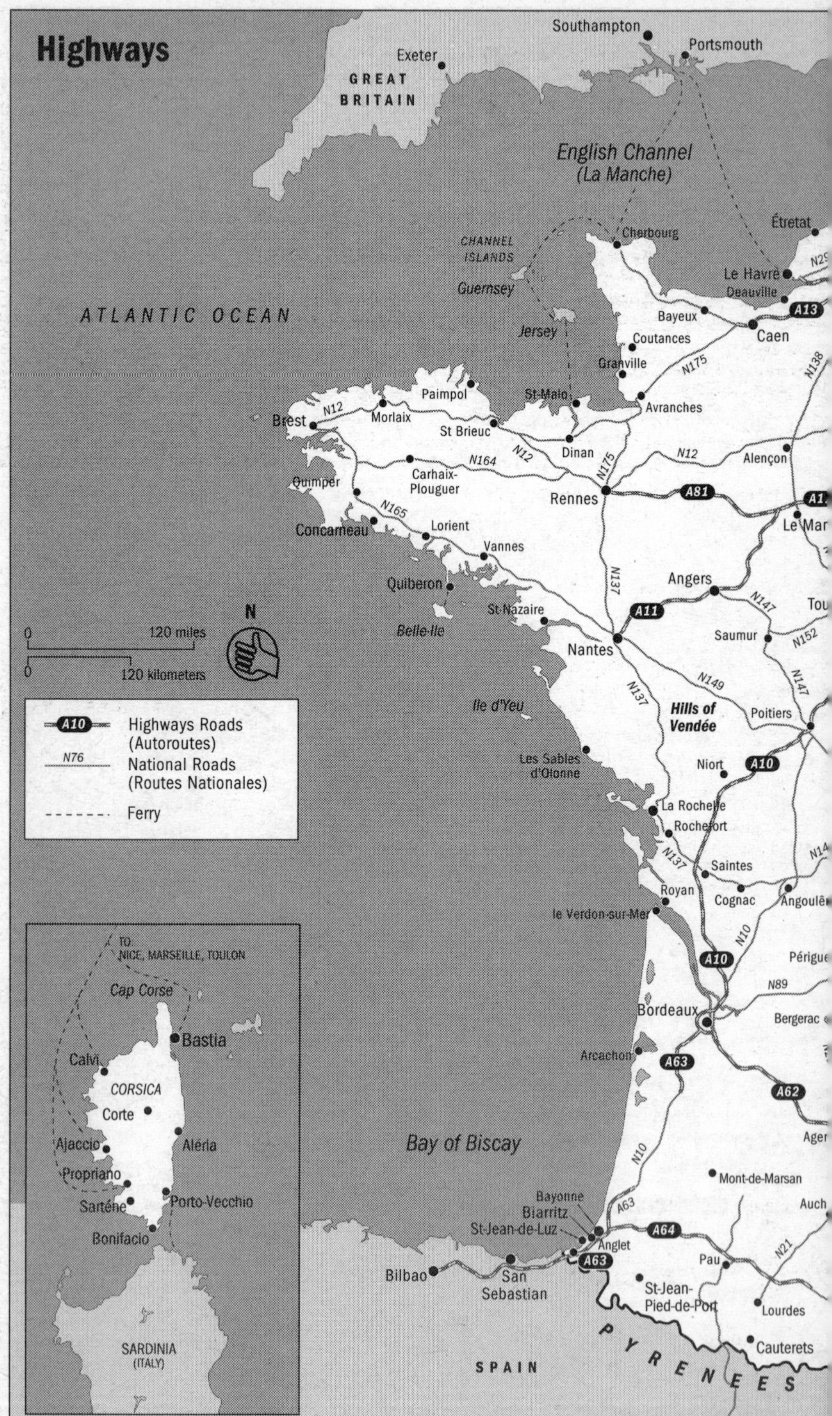

Highways
Southampton
Portsmouth
Exeter
GREAT BRITAIN
English Channel (La Manche)
CHANNEL ISLANDS
Guernsey
Jersey
Cherbourg
Étretat
Le Havre
Deauville
Bayeux
Caen
Coutances
Granville
Avranches
St-Malo
Dinan
Paimpol
Morlaix
Brest
St Brieuc
Quimper
Carhaix-Plouguer
Concarneau
Lorient
Vannes
Quiberon
Belle-Ile
St-Nazaire
Rennes
Alençon
Le Mans
Angers
Saumur
Nantes
Ile d'Yeu
Hills of Vendée
Poitiers
Les Sables d'Olonne
Niort
La Rochelle
Rochefort
Saintes
Royan
Cognac
Angoulême
le Verdon-sur-Mer
Bordeaux
Bergerac
Arcachon
Bay of Biscay
Mont-de-Marsan
Bayonne
Biarritz
St-Jean-de-Luz
Anglet
Pau
Bilbao
San Sebastian
St-Jean-Pied-de-Port
Lourdes
Cauterets
SPAIN
PYRENEES
ATLANTIC OCEAN
N
0 120 miles
0 120 kilometers
A10 Highways Roads (Autoroutes)
N76 National Roads (Routes Nationales)
Ferry
TO NICE, MARSEILLE, TOULON
Cap Corse
Bastia
Calvi
CORSICA
Corte
Aléria
Ajaccio
Propriano
Sartène
Porto-Vecchio
Bonifacio
SARDINIA (ITALY)

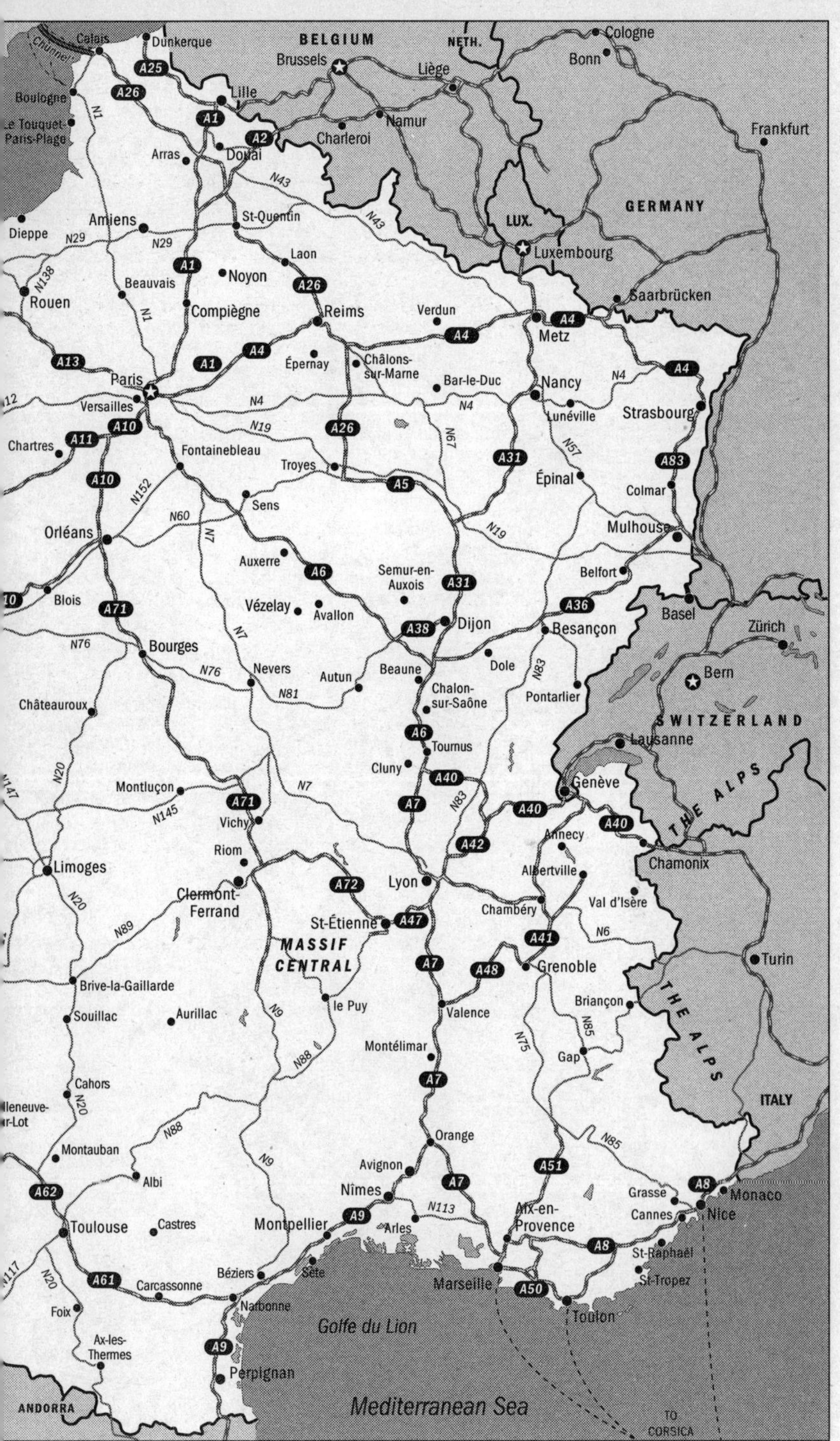
Chunnel
Calais
Dunkerque
BELGIUM
NETH.
Cologne
Brussels
Liège
Bonn
A25
A26
Boulogne
Lille
N1
Le Touquet-
Paris-Plage
A1
Namur
Frankfurt
A2
Charleroi
Arras
Douai
N43
GERMANY
Dieppe
Amiens
St-Quentin
N43
LUX.
N29
N29
Laon
Luxembourg
N138
A1
Noyon
Rouen
Beauvais
A26
Saarbrücken
N1
Compiègne
Reims
Verdun
A4
Metz
A4
A13
A1
A4
Épernay
Châlons-
sur-Marne
A4
Paris
Bar-le-Duc
Nancy
N4
Versailles
N4
N4
Lunéville
Strasbourg
A10
N19
A26
N67
N57
Chartres
A11
Fontainebleau
A31
A83
Troyes
Épinal
A10
A5
Colmar
N152
Sens
N60
N19
Mulhouse
Orléans
N7
Auxerre
A6
Semur-en-
Auxois
A31
Belfort
Blois
Vézelay
Avallon
A36
Basel
A71
Dijon
A38
Besançon
Zürich
N76
N7
Bourges
Dole
N76
Nevers
Autun
Beaune
N83
Bern
Chalon-
sur-Saône
Pontarlier
Châteauroux
N81
SWITZERLAND
A6
Tournus
Lausanne
N20
Cluny
A40
Montluçon
N7
Genève
THE ALPS
N145
A71
A7
N83
A40
A40
Vichy
A42
Annecy
Riom
Limoges
Chamonix
Lyon
Albertville
A72
Clermont-
Ferrand
N20
Chambéry
Val d'Isère
St-Étienne
A47
N89
MASSIF
CENTRAL
N6
A41
Turin
A7
A48
Grenoble
Brive-la-Gaillarde
le Puy
Briançon
Souillac
Aurillac
N9
Valence
THE ALPS
N85
N75
Montélimar
Gap
N88
Cahors
A7
ITALY
N20
N88
Orange
N85
Montauban
N9
Avignon
A51
A7
Albi
A8
A62
Nîmes
Grasse
Monaco
N113
Aix-en-
Provence
Cannes
Nice
Toulouse
Castres
Montpellier
A9
Arles
A8
St-Raphaël
N20
A61
Béziers
Sète
St-Tropez
Carcassonne
Marseille
A50
Narbonne
Toulon
Foix
Golfe du Lion
Ax-les-
Thermes
A9
Perpignan
ANDORRA
Mediterranean Sea
TO
CORSICA

Rail Lines

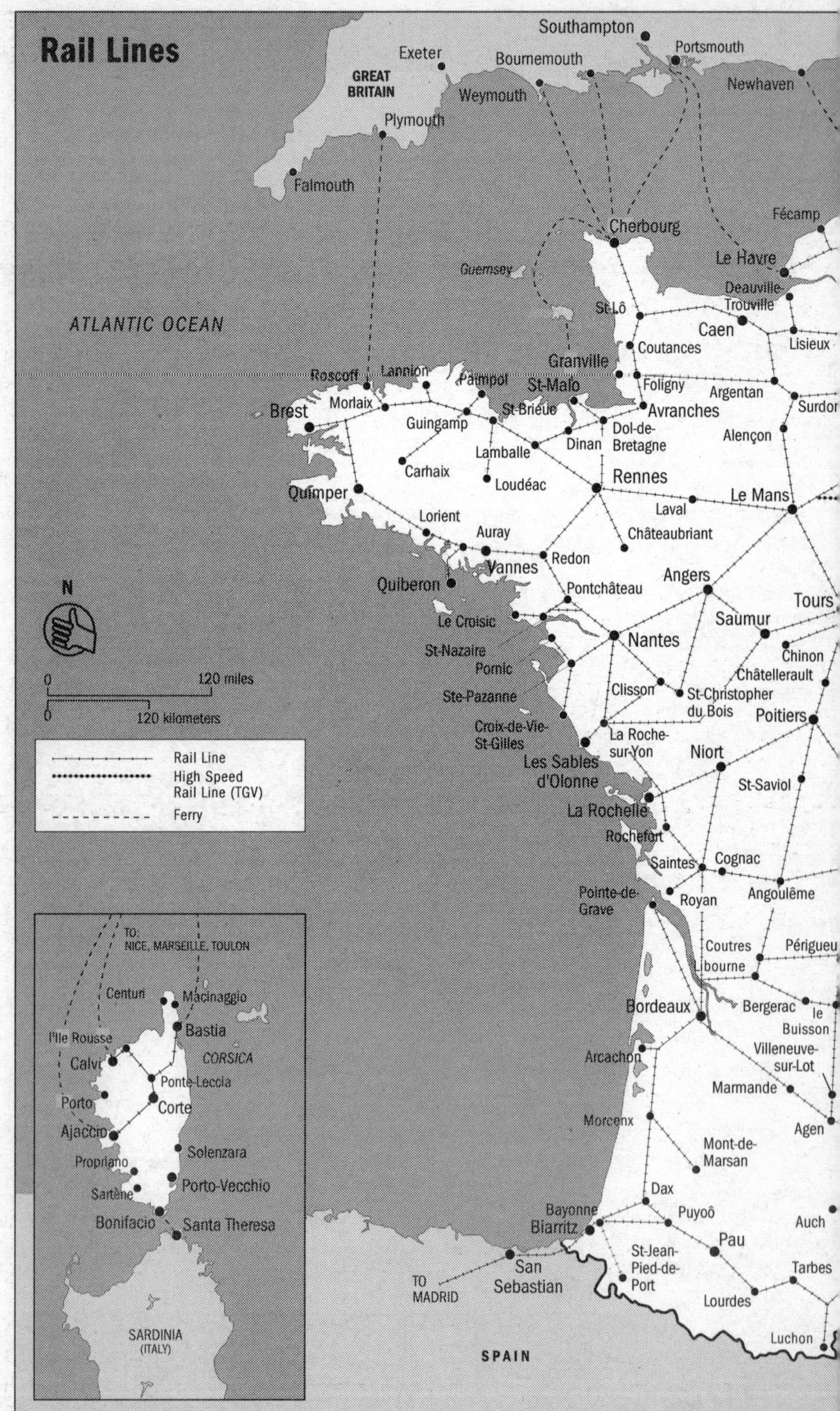

Southampton
Portsmouth
Exeter
Bournemouth
GREAT BRITAIN
Weymouth
Newhaven
Plymouth
Falmouth
Cherbourg
Fécamp
Guernsey
Le Havre
Deauville-Trouville
St-Lô
ATLANTIC OCEAN
Caen
Coutances
Lisieux
Granville
Roscoff
Lannion
Paimpol
St-Malo
Foligny
Argentan
Brest
Morlaix
St-Brieuc
Avranches
Surdon
Guingamp
Dol-de-Bretagne
Dinan
Alençon
Lamballe
Carhaix
Rennes
Loudéac
Quimper
Laval
Le Mans
Lorient
Châteaubriant
Auray
Redon
Vannes
Quiberon
Angers
Pontchâteau
Tours
Le Croisic
Saumur
Nantes
St-Nazaire
Chinon
Pornic
Châtellerault
Clisson
St-Christopher du Bois
Ste-Pazanne
Poitiers
Croix-de-Vie-St-Gilles
La Roche-sur-Yon
Les Sables d'Olonne
Niort
St-Saviol
La Rochelle
Rochefort
Saintes
Cognac
Pointe-de-Grave
Royan
Angoulême
Coutres
Périgueux
Libourne
Bordeaux
Bergerac
le Buisson
Villeneuve-sur-Lot
Arcachon
Marmande
Morcenx
Agen
Mont-de-Marsan
Dax
Bayonne
Puyoô
Auch
Biarritz
Pau
St-Jean-Pied-de-Port
Tarbes
San Sebastian
TO MADRID
Lourdes
Luchon
SPAIN
N
0
120 miles
0
120 kilometers
Rail Line
High Speed Rail Line (TGV)
Ferry
TO: NICE, MARSEILLE, TOULON
Centuri
Macinaggio
Bastia
l'Ile Rousse
CORSICA
Calvi
Ponte-Leccia
Corte
Porto
Ajaccio
Solenzara
Propriano
Porto-Vecchio
Sartène
Bonifacio
Santa Theresa
SARDINIA (ITALY)

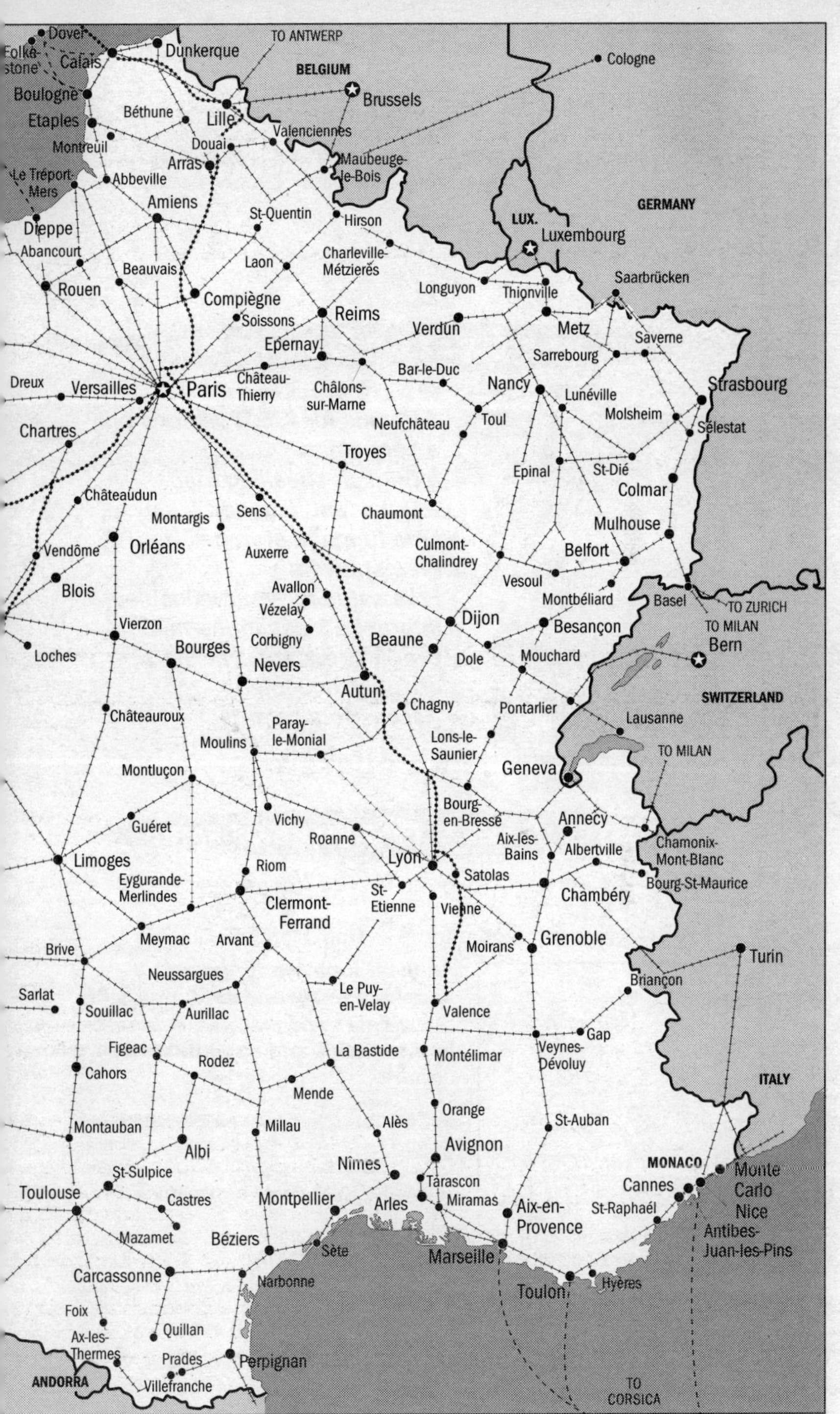
Dover
Folke-
stone
Calais
Dunkerque
TO ANTWERP
BELGIUM
Cologne
Boulogne
Brussels
Béthune
Lille
Etaples
Valenciennes
Montreuil
Douai
Maubeuge-
le-Bois
Arras
Le Tréport-
Mers
Abbeville
GERMANY
Amiens
St-Quentin
Hirson
LUX.
Dieppe
Luxembourg
Abancourt
Charleville-
Métzieres
Laon
Beauvais
Saarbrücken
Rouen
Longuyon
Thionville
Compiègne
Reims
Soissons
Verdun
Metz
Saverne
Epernay
Sarrebourg
Dreux
Château-
Thierry
Bar-le-Duc
Versailles
Paris
Châlons-
sur-Marne
Nancy
Strasbourg
Lunéville
Toul
Molsheim
Chartres
Neufchâteau
Sélestat
Troyes
St-Dié
Epinal
Colmar
Châteaudun
Chaumont
Sens
Montargis
Mulhouse
Vendôme
Orléans
Auxerre
Culmont-
Chalindrey
Belfort
Vesoul
Avallon
Blois
Basel
TO ZURICH
Montbéliard
Vézelay
Vierzon
Dijon
TO MILAN
Besançon
Corbigny
Beaune
Bern
Loches
Bourges
Nevers
Dole
Mouchard
Autun
SWITZERLAND
Chagny
Pontarlier
Châteauroux
Lausanne
Paray-
le-Monial
Moulins
Lons-le-
Saunier
TO MILAN
Montluçon
Geneva
Bourg-
en-Bresse
Annecy
Guéret
Vichy
Roanne
Aix-les-
Bains
Chamonix-
Mont-Blanc
Albertville
Limoges
Lyon
Riom
Satolas
Bourg-St-Maurice
Eygurande-
Merlindes
Clermont-
Ferrand
St-
Etienne
Chambéry
Vienne
Meymac
Arvant
Grenoble
Moirans
Turin
Brive
Neussargues
Briançon
Le Puy-
en-Velay
Sarlat
Souillac
Aurillac
Valence
Gap
Figeac
La Bastide
Veynes-
Dévoluy
Montélimar
Rodez
Cahors
Mende
ITALY
Orange
Montauban
Millau
Alès
St-Auban
Albi
Avignon
Nîmes
MONACO
Monte
Carlo
St-Sulpice
Tarascon
Cannes
Toulouse
Castres
Montpellier
Arles
Miramas
Nice
Aix-en-
Provence
St-Raphaél
Antibes-
Juan-les-Pins
Mazamet
Béziers
Sète
Marseille
Carcassonne
Narbonne
Hyères
Toulon
Foix
Quillan
Ax-les-
Thermes
Prades
Perpignan
ANDORRA
Villefranche
TO
CORSICA

CONTENTS

MAPS

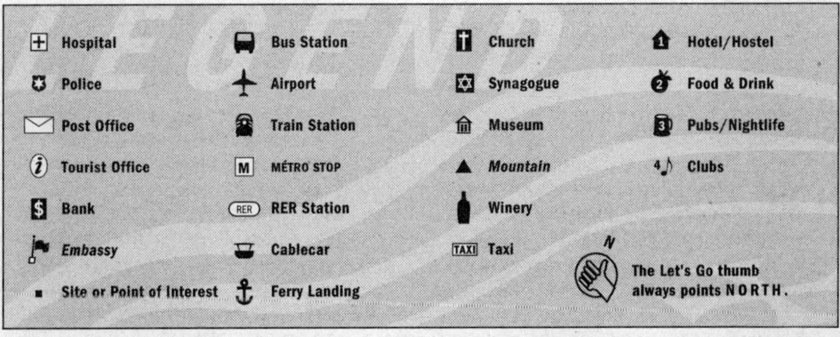

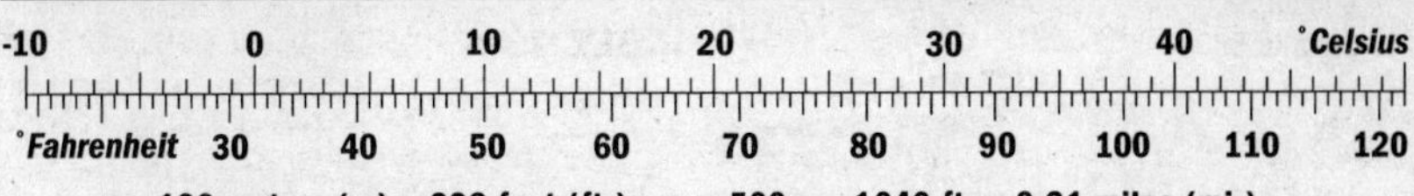

100 meters (m) = 328 feet (ft.) **500m = 1640 ft. = 0.31 miles (mi.)**
1 kilometer (km) = 0.625 mi. **50km = 31.25 mi.** **1 hectare (ha) = 2.47 acres**

DISCOVER FRANCE

So you're going to France. Congratulations; there's nothing like it. France is everything it's cracked up to be and more: jewel of Europe, holder of the patents for sex and fine food, inventor and perpetrator of every art from glaziery to the production of fine lace hats. There is no France but France, and—upon closer inspection—there is, indeed, no France at all. It's a shock to find that a country so supposedly monolithic is in fact being pulled apart at the seams—by myth-crazed, Celtic-speaking Bretons; by perfect-pitch navigating Basques; by hard-accented Alsatians and a host of other regional subgroups rolled up under protest in the large, bumpy crêpe that is France.

To pursue a metaphor slightly too far, France, like any crêpe, can be either sweet or salty—*sucrée* or *salée*. When sweet, it is the best-living country in Europe; one of dark, black, truffle-breeding loam and great purple lawns of lavender, of gaping, ruined châteaux silhouetted against the dusk, and windy flower-covered islands severed from the mainland by the rough Atlantic. Salty, France is a country of intrigue, inventor of the rotating wooden baby-abandonment cupboard, breeder of scandals and infants, forever checking out who's with who and what they're wearing. Finally—we're gonna strain this baby 'til she breaks—France can be the bitterest of crêpes: every inch of it, from the most Teutonic Alsatian town to Paris itself, has been fought over for centuries, and what seems picturesque now is often the product of great destruction and misery: the abandoned castle, say, of a village destroyed by the monarch when its counts got too uppity; or the walled cities of Languedoc, their ramparts insufficient to protect them from a rapacious Church bent on stamping out the theological opposition that threatened its financial base; or again pretty La Rochelle, removed from history (and development) for 300 years by a French naval blockade that killed three-quarters of its 28,000 citizens. Finally, France is marked from the north all the way down by vestiges of invasion; plaques, walls, monuments, and simple wreaths left in memory of the countless Frenchmen killed by invaders from abroad. There are other Frances out there—the star-struck, the intellectual, the glittering financial giant in steel, glass, and concrete—but your best bet may simply be to go there.

FACTS AND FIGURES

OFFICIAL NAME: République Française

POPULATION: 59,329,691

CAPITAL: Paris

GDP—PER CAPITA: US$23,300

PRESIDENT: Jacques Chirac, 1995-2002

AVERAGE NUMBER OF TOOTHBRUSHES PER PERSON: 0.5

NUMBER OF SUBJECTS AT JACQUES CHIRAC'S DINNER TABLE: 3 (soccer, soccer, and soccer, says Mme. Chirac)

MAJOR RELIGIONS: 90% Catholic, 2% Muslim, 1% Protestant, 1% Jewish

AREA: 543,965km^2

HIGHEST PEAK: Mont Blanc (4807m)

LONGEST RIVER: Loire (1024km)

NUMBER OF PRESIDENTS FOUND DEAD IN BED WITH A MISTRESS: 1 (Félix Faure)

NUMBER OF PRESIDENTS FOUND AT THE TOP OF A TREE IN THE MIDDLE OF THE NIGHT IMPERSONATING A MONKEY: 1 (Paul Deschanel)

WHEN TO GO

In July, Paris starts to shrink; in August, it positively shrivels. The city in August is devoid of Parisians, animated only by tourists and the pickpockets who love them. On the other hand, the rest of France fills with Frenchmen during these months; they hop over to the Norman coast, swell the beaches of the western Atlantic coast from La Rochelle down to Biarritz, and move around the shores of rocky Corsica. Backpackers, as if responding to some sort of deep homing urge, all run to Nice. The Côte d'Azur becomes one long tangle of anglophone, halter-topped, khaki-shorted arms and legs from June to September, a constant, exhausting party. Early summer and autumn are the best times to visit Paris—the city has warmed up, but not completely emptied out—while winter there can be abominable, presided over by the terrible *grisaille*—chill "grayness." The north and west of France are prone to wet, though mild, winters and springs, while summers are warm but undependable. The center and east of the country have a more continental climate, with often harsh winters and long, dry summers; these are also generally the least crowded and most unspoiled regions—with some exceptions. From December to February, the Alps provide some of the best skiing in the world, while the Pyrenees offer a less frenetic, if less climatically dependable, alternative.

BRIGHT LIGHTS, BIG CITIES

Though **Paris** (pp. 83-147) is one of the world's great cities, you'll find plenty to do in France's major regional centers. **Lyon** (p. 156), France's second city, has long had a reputation for staid *bourgeoisie.* Don't be taken in by this—the undisputed culinary capital of France was also the center of the Resistance in WWII. In **Marseille's** (p. 223) 2600-year history, this vibrant working city—the third largest in France—has never failed to make itself heard. **Nice** (p. 277) is a party town packed with museums, but be warned—there's no sand on its famous beach. Then again, with the rest of the Côte d'Azur but a pebble's throw away, who cares? The new capital of Europe is **Strasbourg** (p. 395). With a hybrid Franco-German culture, it's an obvious home for the European Parliament. The west of France isn't devoid of cities either. **Montpellier** (p. 727) is both the gay capital of France and the capital of the Languedoc. **Rennes** (p. 500) mixes a medieval *vieille ville* and major museums with a lot of frenzied party kids, while rosy **Toulouse** (p. 693) is the heart of the Languedoc and the French aerospace industry, and home to tons of collegians.

BIG STONE BUILDINGS

French châteaux range from imposing feudal ruins to the well-preserved country homes of 19th-century industrialists. The greatest variety and concentration is to be found in the **Loire Valley** (pp. 558-596). Here the defensive hilltop fortresses of **Chinon** (p. 581) and **Saumur** (p. 583) contrast with the Renaissance grace of **Chenonceau** (p. 579) and **Chambord** (p. 569). The Loire has no monopoly on châteaux, though. Near Paris you can find tributes to the great Louis XIV's even greater ego: **Versailles** (p. 147). In Provence, you'll be hard-pressed to decide whether the Palais des Papes in **Avignon** (p. 241) is a castle or a palace, while nearby the craggy ruins of **Les Baux** (p. 251) will take you back to the age of chivalry. Perhaps the most impressive château is the fortress of **Carcassonne** (p. 705), a medieval citadel which still stands guard over the Languedoc. To find some castles not mobbed by tourists, head to the **Route Jacques Cœur** near **Bourges** (p. 216).

Paris' **Notre Dame** (p. 115) is the most famous Church building in France, but a more exquisite Gothic jewel is the nearby **Sainte-Chapelle** (p. 116). The Gothic style first reached maturity at **Chartres** (p. 150), while other medieval masterpieces await at **Strasbourg** (p. 395) and **Reims** (p. 429). A different and more modern sensibility animates Le Corbusier's masterpiece at **Ronchamp** (p. 420).

THE OUTDOORS

Everyone's heard of the **Alps,** and some of the best hiking and skiing in the world can be found around **Val d'Isère** (p. 376) and **Chamonix** (p. 369). But the Alps are just one of France's four major mountain ranges. Just north of them, you can get into the **Jura** mountains (p. 420) in Franche-Comté, while **Le Mont-Dore** (p. 173), in the **Massif Central,** is a spectacular area in the center of the country. To the southwest, you can climb into Spain from the western **Pyrenees** (p. 686). If snow-capped peaks aren't your thing, lowland pleasures can be found in the flamingo-filled plains of the **Camargue** (p. 260). For advanced hikers, it's possible to trek the length of rugged **Corsica's** interior (p. 321), but the less advanced can find great day and overnight hikes everywhere on the island, including the **Cap Corse** (p. 343).

DRINK

Let's Go was shocked and dismayed to read that France only ranks second in international wine consumption, being trumped by her neighbor Italy. Luckily, the types of inebriants France produces are *certainement* not limited to wine. Start with an *apéritif* of a champagne cocktail from one of **Reims'** spectacular *caves* (p. 429). To try a little bit of everything, check out the red wines in **Bordeaux** (p. 656), **Burgundy** (p. 183), and Alsace's **Route du Vin** (p. 403) or the whites of the **Loire Valley** (p. 558) and environs. Top it all off with an after-dinner drink—either **Cognac** in the eponymous town (p. 609), or Calvados, made throughout **Normandy** (p. 462).

BAKE

The Côte d'Azur attracts two types of people—the stars who make its glamor, and the masses who come looking for it. You'll party among the tanned youth of Europe in **Nice** (p. 277) and **Juan-les-Pins** (p. 302). Surfers should head straight for the big rollers of the Atlantic coast in **Anglet** (p. 666), while if sun and sand are your only desires, try **Porto Vecchio** (p. 345) in Corsica. Some of France's most beautiful beaches await in foggy Brittany, at **Belle-Ile** (p. 544) and **St-Malo** (p. 510).

LET'S GO PICKS

BEST ACCOMMODATIONS: The Alps win first AND second place, with variety and value in both **Val d'Isère** (p. 376) and **Chamonix** (p. 369).

BEST CEMETERIES: Everybody who's been anybody in the last millennium is in Paris' **Père Lachaise** (p. 136); everybody from before is in **Les Alycamps** in Arles (p. 254).

LONGEST SHOTS: The **bar-o-mètre** in Nice's Tapas del Mundo (p. 277); the still-loaded **German artillery** in Longues-sur-Mer (p. 486); your chances at the famous **Monte-Carlo Casino** (p. 295).

BEST INDOOR RAINSHOWERS: at the funky **Maison Satie** in Honfleur (p. 473): each room is a surprise!

MOST TALENTED MIDGET: Henri **Toulouse-Lautrec** whose original posters of high-kicking cabaret dancers grace the walls of the eponymous museum in his hometown of Albi (p. 702).

MOST WHIMSICAL PALACE: Le Palais Idéal in Hauterives (p. 359); assembled stone by stone by the local postman.

BEST CONCRETE: Le Corbusier's astounding **Notre-Dame-du-Haut** in Ronchamp (p. 420) is a heart-wrenching tribute to France's war dead.

MOST CONCRETE: Le Havre (p. 471) was redesigned entirely in big gray blocks, from toilet-bowl theaters to skyscraper churches.

LEAST CONCRETE: The idea of **beauty.**

BEST ISLANDS: White homes with blue shutters cover idyllic **Ile d'Yeu** (p. 629). Sheep and stone crosses are the main inhabitants of **Ile d'Ouessant** (p. 533). Neither one is any larger than a Peugeot.

BEST ISLAND LARGER THAN A PEUGEOT: Out of the Mediterranean rose **Corsica** (p. 321), a paradise of beaches and heather-covered mountains.

BEST REVOLUTION: A tough call, with the Commune and *the* Revolution running neck-and-neck (pun intended). We'll have to go with the Commune (p. 10) for its senseless violence, leftism with a vengeance, and sheer destruction.

SUGGESTED ITINERARIES

The following itineraries are a few of the easiest trips you can take in France. We intend these mostly for use by those who haven't traveled around France very much; however, even frequent visitors will find that our itineraries are an easy way to outline travel in each of these regions. We think each of the trips below introduces the traveler to a different regional identity or two. There are many Frances, however, and these are not the only ones; in fact, we've left out more than half the country. For more ideas, see "other trips" below, or the regional chapter introductions. Finally, our "cream of France" itinerary is exactly what it sounds like.

PROVENCE AND THE COTE D'AZUR

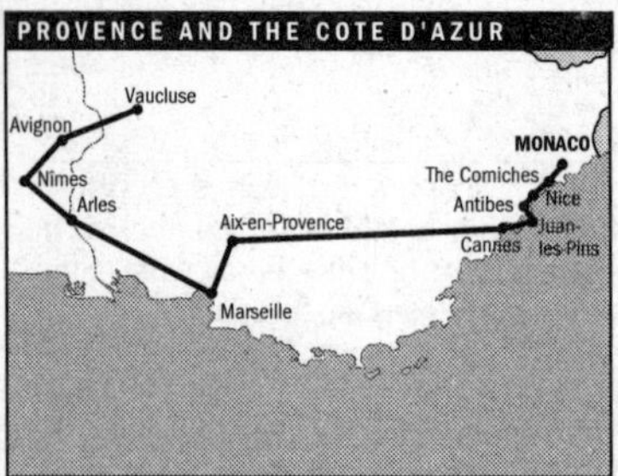

PROVENCE AND THE COTE D'AZUR (2 WEEKS) This is one of the most popular and heavily visited areas of France. Visit the Côte d'Azur for beaches and glamor, and inland Provence for fields of lavender, old stone, and slow sun-drenched villages. **Nice** is the unofficial capital of the Côte d'Azur, a nonstop anglophone beach party with more beaches, nightlife, and budget housing than you can shake a glowstick at (2 days; p. 277). Don't neglect the nearby clifftop villages of the **Corniches** (2 days; p. 288). If you have any money left, you'll want to daytrip east to **Monaco,** which is absolutely the richest place in France (actually its own micro-state) and packed with wealthy idlers, expensive houses, and frivolous attractions (1 day; p. 292). Twin towns **Antibes** and **Juan-les-Pins** have enough beauty and nightlife for ten towns; don't miss them (1 day and at least 1 night; p. 299). **Cannes,** home to the famous and exclusive film festival, is star-packed all year round, and has some of the cheapest housing on the coast (1 day; p. 303). **Aix-en-Provence** is a slow little provençal city full of fountains, twisty streets, and Cézanne paintings (1 day; p. 234). Rough and loud **Marseille** is not for everyone, but nevertheless it's one of the South's most living cities (1 day; p. 223). The aqueduct near **Nîmes** (p. 264) and the great arena at **Arles** (p. 254) are sites that no Rome-phile should skip (1 day each). **Avignon,** city of Popes, hosts a yearly drama festival that theater fans shouldn't miss (1 days; p. 241); besides, it's the closest city to the impossibly lovely **Vaucluse,** a group of sleepy, ruin-dotted, quintessentially provençal little towns (2 days; p. 247).

BRITTANY AND NORMANDY

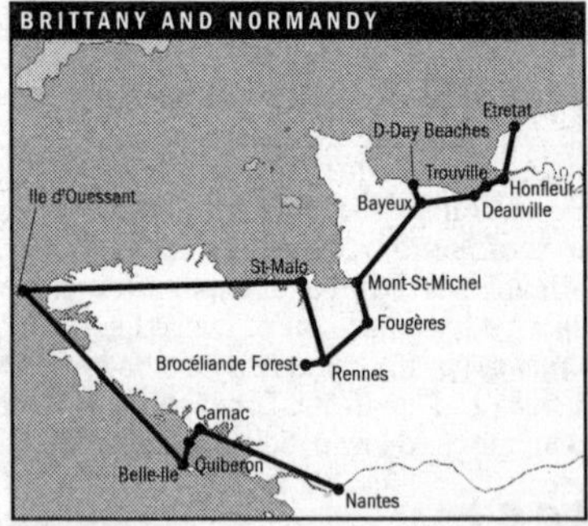

BRITTANY AND NORMANDY (2 WEEKS) These two *départements* have it all, from cities to isolated, ruggedly beautiful coasts and isles. Technically a part of the Loire, medieval **Nantes** is worth a stop for its intact château and tight pedestrian districts (1 day; p. 552). The giant prehistoric stones at **Carnac** are just one vestige of Brittany's prehistoric residents (1 day; p. 546). **Quiberon** and nearby **Belle-Ile** have some of France's most rugged landscapes (2 days; p. 542). One of the best parts of Brittany is its tiny islands, inhabited by equal numbers of fishermen and sheep; spend at least one day at the flower-strewn **Ile d'Ouessant** (p. 533). No visit to Brittany would be complete without seeing the fortified seaside resort of **St-Malo** (2 days; p. 510). **Rennes,** with its fabulous, student-oriented nightlife, makes a perfect base for daytrips, if you can roll out of bed before noon! Nearby **Fougères** is a literary château town, and the **Brocéliande forest,** the ancient haunt of Merlin and Guinevere, is one of Brittany's most legend-steeped sites (2 days total; p. 500). **Mont-St-Michel** is a fortified island monastery shot through with tunnels, passageways, and underground chambers and stuffed with tourists (1 day; p. 494). Visit **Bayeux,** home of the 1000-year-old tapestry that recounts William the Conqueror's invasion of England (1 day; p. 482); then head to the nearby **D-Day beaches,** which memorialize the events of 1944 with striking honesty (1-2 days; p. 484). Choose among seaside towns for your remaining two days: **Deauville** and **Trouville,** are the snootiest sunny spots north of Nice (p. 476); **Etretat** (p. 470) is home to the legendary Falaise d'Aval, or "elephant cliffs," and **Honfleur** (p. 473), which is almost sickeningly charming. Almost.

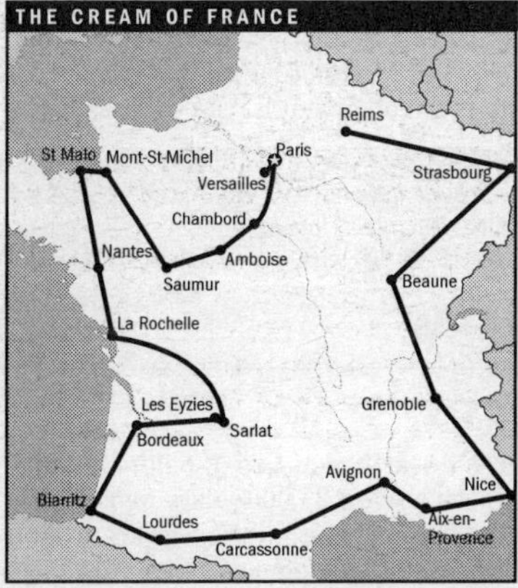

THE CREAM OF FRANCE (1 MONTH) To see everything worth seeing in France in only a few weeks may seem impossible, but you can still try! You'll need at least 4-5 days to see the sights and shops of **Paris** (p. 83)—make sure to make time for a day-trip to **Versailles** (p. 147). Next, slip down to the Loire Valley. The château of **Amboise** (1 day; p. 572) was home to four French kings, while **Saumur** (1 day; p. 583) is famous for its castle, its riding school, and its sparkling wines. Combine a trip here with one to **Chambord** (p. 569), perhaps as grand as Versailles, which also merits a visit, perhaps a night tour. Then travel up to the island abbey of **Mont-St-Michel** (1 day; p. 494). A little farther along the coast is popular **St-Malo** (1 day; p. 510), with ramparts, beaches, and fantastic seafood. Next, head down to **Nantes** (2 days; p. 552) for medieval sights and modern nightlife, before soaking up the sun in beach-blessed, historical **La Rochelle** (1 day; p. 616). For a change of pace, contemplate times past in medieval **Sarlat** (1 day; p. 637), and the 17,000-year-old cave paintings of **Les-Eyzies-de-Tayac** (1 day; p. 639). Test your taste buds in the vineyards of **Bordeaux** (2 days; p. 656) before zipping southward to *basque* on the beach in **Biarritz** or **Bayonne** (2 days; p. 667). From there, follow the pilgrims to miraculous **Lourdes** (1 day; p. 682). Keep heading east to reach the stunning walls of **Carcassonne** (1 day; p. 705), guarding the town as they have done for centuries. No less formidable are the fortifications of the Palais-des-Papes in festive **Avignon** (1 day; p. 241). Students have been partying in elegant **Aix-en-Provence** (1 day; p. 234) for 600 years, but for non-stop action go to **Nice** (2 days; p. 277), undisputed capital of the Riviera. For a change of scenery, climb into the Alps to reach dynamic **Grenoble** (2 days; p. 351). You'll find highs of a different sort in **Beaune** (1 day; p. 190), home of Burgundy's most precious wines, while to the northeast, **Strasbourg** (2 days; p. 395) offers Alsatian wines and a hybrid Franco-German culture. Finally, finish off in style with a tasting at one of the many champagne *caves* in **Reims** (1 day; p. 429).

OTHER TRIPS The **Route du Vin** (p. 410) is a string of medieval Alsatian villages with crooked little vine-covered houses half-drowned in geraniums and petunias—all this near the wineries and First World War memorials of the Germanic northeast. The turreted, many-chimneyed, insanely elaborate castles of the **Loire Valley** (p. 558) are France's greatest Renaissance treasure. France's best hiking and windsurfing are in the rugged, rocky, sun-blasted island of **Corsica** (p. 321), which is ringed with beautiful beaches and crumbling Genoese watchtowers. The **Burgundy region** (p. 183) is known for its great wines and sleepy villages, as are the towns surrounding **Bordeaux** (p. 656) in the southwest. Finally, don't forget the **Alps**—greatest of Europe's mountain ranges, beloved of skiers and mountain bikers alike (p. 351)—or the exquisite **Dordogne,** a river-cut valley of walnut trees, lazy flowing water, and geese with big fat livers (p. 643).

HISTORY AND CULTURE

> But the true travelers are those who only leave
> So as to leave; light hearts, like balloons,
> They are never separated from their fate,
> And, without knowing quite why, always say: Let's Go.
> —Charles Baudelaire, *Les Fleurs du Mal*

A HISTORICAL OVERVIEW

A BRUSH WITH PREHISTORY

In 1868, the skull of an advanced hominid was unearthed at Cro-Magnon, in **Périgord** (p. 633). Cro-Magnon man is thought to have lived 27,000 years ago; 10,000 years later, his descendants were busy leaving bison graffiti in their caves around the **Dordogne valley** (p. 643), and by 4500 BC Neolithic peoples were carving huge stone monuments like those found at **Carnac** (p. 546). These mysterious creations were admired by the Celtic **Gauls,** who arrived from the east around 600 BC. Gauls traded and co-existed peacefully with their new neighbors, the Phocean **Greeks,** who had founded a colony in the 7th century BC at Massilia (present day **Marseille,** p. 223). These tribes flourished for five centuries until an expanding Rome made Provence its favorite province in 125 BC. Though it took Rome less than three years to subdue the South, fierce resistance from France's northern Gauls kept the Romans out of that region until **Julius Caesar's** victory at Alesia in 52 BC. Both parties did well under the occupation; Gaul remained intact and safe from invasion, while Rome bequeathed to France her language and political system.

FROM CHARLES IN CHARGE TO MY THREE SONS

By the time Rome fell in AD 476, Gaul had suffered Germanic invasions for centuries. While many tribes plundered and passed on, the Franks eventually dominated Gaul and the country became known by their name. Under the Romans, the population had been Christianized, but the Franks remained pagan until the baptism of their king **Clovis,** first of the Merovingian dynasty, in 507. Clovis chose the then minor town of Paris as his capital, and extended his rule over most of Gaul. Frankish inheritance laws, which divided territories equally among the king's sons, did nothing to support his legacy and the kingdom rapidly disintegrated.

When the dashing **Charles Martel** (the Hammer) reunited the Frankish domains and defeated the previously unstoppable **Moors** at Poitiers (p. 598) in 732, the way was open for his diminutive son **Pépin le Bref** (the Short) to claim the throne in 754. Pépin was the first monarch to be crowned by a Pope, earning France the nickname "eldest daughter of the Church." Despite his achievements, Pépin was outshined by his son, the magnificent Charlemagne, who gave his name to the Carolingian dynasty. In hopes of recapturing the Roman Empire's glory and breadth, he added what are now Germany, Austria, and Switzerland to his domains, fulfilling his dream in 800 when the pope crowned him Holy Roman Emperor. The territorial squabbles following his death in 814 were only resolved in 843 with the **Treaty of Verdun,** which divided the empire among Charlemagne's three grandsons. The territories thus created have never truly been at peace; Charles the Bald's Francia has always fought Louis the German's eastern third over the middle corridor of Lotharingia—modern day **Alsace-Lorraine** (p. 382).

STORMIN' NORMANS

In the 10th century a new wave of invaders debarked on France's shores. The Scandinavian **Vikings,** no longer content with their centuries-old pastime of harassing France's shoreline, forced the ailing Carolingian **Charles the Simple** to grant them the duchy of **Normandy** (p. 462). When the last Carolingian died in 987, France's nobles elected **Hugh Capet** as king. Surrounded by powerful vassals, the king presided over Paris and the tiny Ile-de-France and relied on the prestige of his position and their own insecurity to keep the nobles in check. But the Duke of Normandy upset the delicate balance between the aristocracy and nobility when he conquered England in 1066, earning himself the epithet **William the Conqueror.** By passing the English succession into Continental hands, this conquest paved the way for centuries of Anglo-French warfare. Things got serious in 1152 after Henry Plantagenêt, Duke of Anjou, married Louis VII's well-endowed ex **Eleanor of Aquitaine.** Now master of more of France than Louis VII himself, Plantagenêt went on to inherit the English crown two years later as **Henry II.** Yet when his chivalrous heir, **Richard the Lionheart,** departed for the Crusades, England fell into the hands of the incompetent younger brother, **John.** When he ignored a summons to the court of French king **Philippe-Auguste** (1180-1223), hence forfeiting by feudal law his French territories, the new king earned himself the nickname **John Lackland.** Once rid of the English threat to his kingdom, Philippe made a series of clever marriages which left him one of the most powerful men in Europe.

OF MONKS AND MEN: THE MEDIEVAL CHURCH

This endless warfare devastated peasant life, and many sought refuge inside the monasteries and convents which had sprung up all over Europe. In addition to the promise of eternal salvation, the Church offered commoners a rare opportunity for advancement outside the feudal hierarchy. Townspeople raised cathedrals to the honor of God, and monasteries and convents swelled with novitiates. Soon the power of the monasteries was as great as that of the aristocracy, and in the 11th century, the abbot of **Cluny** (p. 196) was as influential as any monarch. **Pope Innocent II** proclaimed the first Crusade from **Clermont** (p. 168), hoping to wrest Jerusalem from the Saracens. Thousands, from kings to peasants, flocked to take the cross, swayed by the promise of salvation and the probability of plunder. Though only the first of the eight Crusades launched between 1095 and 1271 had any military success, exposure to the advanced civilizations of the east and a revival of international trade helped stir Europe from her intellectual slumber.

The balance between the papacy and monarchies was tested and then tipped when **Philip IV** challenged **Pope Boniface VIII** at the opening of the 14th century. The king arrested the pope to prevent his imminent excommunication; old Boniface died after the arrest, and his French successor, **Pope Clement V,** moved the pope's court from Rome to church-owned **Avignon** (p. 241). Six more popes held mass in France, increasing French power but spawning the **Black Death** (according to the superstitious and the Italians); the papacy finally returned to Rome in 1377 .

ONE HUNDRED YEARS OF INCERTITUDE

Possession of the French crown was thrown into question in 1328 on the death of **Charles IV,** last of the Capetians. Charles had only daughters, and since French law prohibited a woman from inheriting the throne, the nobles gave the kingship to his distant relation **Philippe de Valois.** When Philippe encroached upon English Aquitaine, Charles IV's English nephew **Edward III** landed his army at Normandy and claimed the throne for himself, starting off a series of wars between France and England known as the Hundred Years War. Decades of inconclusive battling seemed nearly over, as did French sovereignty, when the English crowned their own **Henry VI** king of France following his father's tremendous 1415 victory at **Agincourt** and subsequent domination of Paris. Salvation for the French came in 1429, when a 17-year-old peasant girl claiming divine inspiration forced her way to the makeshift court of the **Dauphin** (Charles VII) in **Chinon** (p. 581). Leading the

French army, **Joan of Arc** won a string of victories before her betrayal and capture by Burgundians, who were at that time allied to the English. They handed her to the English authorities, who convicted her of witchcraft and burnt her at the stake in **Rouen** (p. 463) in 1430. But the tide of war had turned; by 1453 only **Calais** (p. 456) was left in English hands.

HUGUENOTS AND HUNTED HENRIES

With the English confined to their island, the French kings spent the rest of the century consolidating their position, arm-twisting their way into **Provence** (p. 223) and **Burgundy** (p. 183) by the end of the 15th century. This domestic cohesion allowed **François Ier** to set out for Italy; his military forays failed but he returned with the imported glory of the Renaissance. This prosperous tranquility was soon shattered by the religious strife of the Reformation, which developed Protestantism in Europe. As Catholics went toe-to-toe and tenet-to-tenet with the newly reformed Huguenots (Protestants), **Catherine de Medici,** regent for her son **Charles IX,** reluctantly collaborated with the zealously Catholic **Henry de Guise** to retain papal supremacy. De Guise orchestrated the massacre of 3000 guests at the wedding of Henry III's sister to the Huguenot **Henry of Navarre** on St. Bartholomew's Day in 1572; organized slaughter and Huguenot retribution immediately spread through Paris and the rest of the country. A series of assassinations, including those of Henry III and de Guise, prompted Henry of Navarre—now **King Henry IV**—to convert to Catholicism before his 1594 coronation, saying *"Paris vaut bien une messe"* ("Paris is worth a mass").

HERE COMES THE SUN KING

Henry IV, first of the Bourbon line, succumbed to an assassin's dagger in 1610 and was succeeded by **Louis XIII.** Louis' capable and ruthless minister, **Cardinal Richelieu,** consolidated political power in the hands of the monarchy and created the centralized, bureaucratic administration characteristic of France to this day. When Richelieu and Louis died within months of each other in 1642, they were succeeded by another king-and-cardinal combo, **Louis XIV** and **Cardinal Mazarin.** Since Louis was only five years old at the time, the cardinal again took charge, but by 1661 the 24-year-old monarch had decided he was ready to rule alone. Not known for his modesty, Louis styled himself as the Sun King and took the motto *"l'état, c'est moi"* ("I am the state"). Though he kept the nobles in check by drawing them to his new 14,000 room palace of **Versailles** (p. 147) and creatively emptying their pockets, he drained the royal coffers with the ruinous **War of the Spanish Succession** and alienated the public by revoking the **Edict of Nantes** in 1685—effectively declaring open season on French Protestants. As the nobles vegetated at court, most didn't even notice their complete loss of political power. When Louis finally died in 1715, he had outlasted even his grandsons and was succeeded by his two-year old great-grandson **Louis XV.** Coming to its senses, the aristocracy made a grab to reclaim power, as the national debt soared and a series of disastrous wars led to the loss of France's colonies in Canada and India.

BOURBON ON THE ROCKS: REVOLUTION & REGICIDE

When **Louis XVI** ascended to the throne in 1774, the country was in a desperate financial state. While peasants blamed the soon-to-be-*ancien* regime for their mounting debts, the useless aristocrats detested the king for his attempts at reform. In 1789, to get out of this no-win situation, Louis XVI called a meeting of the archaic **Estates General,** an assembly of delegates from the three classes of society: aristocrats, clergy, and everyone else. Unable to secure fair representation, the bourgeois-dominated **Third Estate** broke away and declared itself to be the **National Assembly.** Inviting the other Estates to join it, the National Assembly, now residing in a tennis court, took an **oath** not to disband until the country had a constitution. The king sent in troops to intimidate the Assembly and received the immortal reply "the assembled nation cannot receive orders." As rumors multiplied, the initiative passed to the Parisian mob, known as the *sans-culottes* ("without breeches"—i.e. working class). When they attacked the old royal fortress-prison, storming the **Bastille** (p. 132) on July 14th, a destructive orgy exploded across the nation as peasants burnt the records of their debts and obligations. The encouraged Assembly responded in August with the **abolition of feudal privileges** and the **Declaration of the Rights of Man.** When the petrified king tried to flee the country in 1791 he was arrested and imprisoned; meanwhile, royalist Austria and Prussia mobilized to stamp out this democratic disease. As the revolutionary armies miraculously defeated the invaders, the radical **Jacobin** faction took control of the Assembly, abolished the monarchy, and declared the Republic. In January 1793, the **king was guillotined,** along with his wife, **Marie Antoinette,** and the *ancien régime* was over; here the Revolution should have ended.

TRUNCATING TERROR, EGOCENTRIC EMPEROR

But now the Revolution took a radical turn. When the Church refused to be subjugated to the Assembly, it was abolished and replaced by the oxymoronic **Cult of Reason.** Confusing rationalization with decimalization, they introduced a new calendar with 10-day weeks; though this did not catch on, the Revolutionary metric system is now the international standard. As counter-revolutionary paranoia set in, power lay with the "incorruptible" **Robespierre** and his draconian **Committee of Public Safety.** Any suspicion of royalist sympathy led straight to the gallows, and Dr. Guillotine himself did not escape the vengeance of his fearful invention. The 12-man Committee turned on itself and even Robespierre met with a grisly execution. The **Reign of Terror** was over, and power was entrusted to a five-man **Directory.**

Meanwhile, war continued. A brilliant young Corsican general swept through northern Italy and forced the Austrians to capitulate. Fearful of his rising popularity, the Directory jumped at **Napoleon Bonaparte**'s idea of invading Egypt to threaten the British colonies in India. Though successful on land, his disease-ridden army was marooned in Cairo after the destruction of his fleet at the Battle of the Nile. Ever the pragmatist, Napoleon responded by abandoning it and hurrying back to France to salvage his political career. Riding a wave of public support, Napoleon deposed the despised Directory, declaring himself First Consul in 1799, Consul for Life in 1802, and ultimately Emperor in 1804. When not at war, Napoleon crafted a legal code which would be his longest-lasting achievement; traces of it are discernible in French law today. Though it remained largely faithful to revolutionary ideals, the **Code Napoléon** bears touches of his autocratic approach to life, re-establishing slavery and total marital obedience from wives. Napoleon also made peace with the Church and reformed the education system, but war remained his specialty. After crushing the Austrians at Austerlitz, the Prussians at Jena, and the Russians at Friedland, he left only Britain undefeated, safe in her island refuge after Nelson's destruction of the French fleet at Trafalgar in 1807.

Napoleon's downfall came during the Russian campaign of 1812. The Russians withdrew before the advancing *Grande Armée*, ravaging their own land to deny the enemy food and shelter. After occupying a deserted Moscow, Napoleon was forced to withdraw at the onset of winter. The freezing cold decimated the French ranks and, of the 700,000 men he had led out to Russia, barely 200,000 returned. Napoleon's enemies sensed their time had come and attacked. Though he rose to the challenge with what many consider to be militarily the greatest of his campaigns, he had finally lost the support of his war-weary people. In return for abdicating in 1814, Napoleon was exiled to the Mediterranean island of Elba, and the monarchy reinstated under Louis XVIII, brother of his headless predecessor.

The story has a final twist: Napoleon, having secretly left Elba and landed near Cannes on March 26, 1815, marched northward to a rapturous reception and forced the king to flee back to England. This adventure only lasted **One Hundred Days,** ending three months later on the field of Waterloo in Flanders, where the Duke of Wellington triumphed as much by luck as by skill. The ex-Emperor threw himself on the mercy of the English, who banished him to remote St. Helena in the south Atlantic, where he died in 1821—probably poisoned by royalist French agents. Popularly regarded as a hero in France, Napoleon still commands an empire of thousands who flock to pay their respects at his grandiose tomb in Paris' **Hotel des Invalides** (see p. 128).

ANOTHER DAY, ANOTHER NAPOLEON

Though obliged at first to recognize the Revolution's achievements, France's reinstated monarchy soon returned to its despotic ways. But when **Charles X** restricted the press and limited the electorate to the landed classes, the people spoke up. Following the **July Revolution of 1830,** Charles, remembering the fate of his brother, abdicated quickly, and a **constitutional monarchy** was created under the "citizen king," **Louis-Philippe.** While the middle classes prospered, the industrialization of France created a class of urban poor receptive to the new ideas of socialism. When the king and his bourgeois government refused to reform, the people were well practised: there followed the **February Revolution of 1848** and the declaration of the **Second Republic** with universal male suffrage for the first time. Playing on the myth of his name, the emperor's nephew **Louis Napoleon** got himself elected president. Since the constitution barred him from seeking a second term, he seized power in an 1851 coup, affirmed one year later by a popular referendum declaring him Emperor Napoleon III. During his reign, France revived herself; her factories hummed and **Baron Haussmann** rebuilt Paris, creating the grand boulevards.

PARIS IN THE SIEGETIME

The confident French did not notice the storm clouds gathering across the Rhine, where **Bismarck** had almost completed the unification of Germany. Tricking the French into declaring war, the Iron Chancellor had his troops overrun the country; the emperor was captured and as German armies advanced, the **Third Republic** was declared. Paris held out for four months, though her citizens were reduced to eating rats and communication with the outside world was limited to hot air balloons. Her position was hopeless, though, and the city ultimately capitulated; Germany pulled out after receiving the Alsace-Lorraine territory and an exorbitant occupation indemnity. After this humiliation, the Parisian mob revolted and declared the **Commune,** which was quickly and bloodily crushed as thousands of *communards* died under the rifles of French troops. The Third Republic was further undermined by the **Dreyfus Affair,** a product of the humiliated army's search for a scapegoat. Dreyfus, a Jewish captain in the French army, was convicted in 1894 on trumped-up charges of treason, and exiled. When the army refused to consider the case even after proof of Dreyfus' innocence was uncovered, France became polarized between the Dreyfusards, who argued for his release, and the reactionary right-wing Anti-Dreyfusards, to whom Dreyfus was an unpatriotic traitor regardless of the evidence. Dreyfusard momentum became unstoppable after Emile Zola condemned the army, the government, and society for its anti-semitic prejudice in his dramatic diatribe *J'accuse;* Dreyfus was finally pardoned in 1904.

WAR AND PEACE... AND WAR AGAIN

Germany's 1871 unification had changed the balance of power in Europe. After centuries of conflict, the **Entente Cordiale** brought the British and the French into cooperation in 1904. With the addition of Czarist Russia, Britain, and France formed the **Triple Entente** and faced the **Triple Alliance** of Germany, Italy, and the Austro-Hungarian Empire. When **World War I** erupted in 1914, German armies rapidly advanced on France in a seeming replay of the previous conflict, but a stalemate soon developed as the opposing armies dug trenches along the length of the country. The withdrawal of newly revolutionary Russia in 1917 was balanced by the entry of the USA, and victory for the West came in 1918. It is still possible to visit the fields where Europe lost an entire generation (see **Memorials near Verdun,** p. 394). Devastated by four years of fighting on her territory, and with 1.3 million men dead, France pushed for crippling reparations from Germany; these and accompanying humiliations were often invoked by Hitler in his rise to power.

During the great depression of the 1930s, France was politically paralyzed and incapable of dealing with the rising threat of Nazi Germany. World War II began with the German invasion of Poland in 1939, and France declared war on Germany in response. In May 1940, the German flank swept through Belgium, bypassing a string of fortresses along the German border which had formed France's main defensive position. Allied defenses collapsed, and France capitulated in June. The country was partitioned, with the north under German occupation, and a puppet state in the south ruled from **Vichy** (p. 180) by WWI hero **Maréchal Pétain.** Though evidence indicates that many French people willingly collaborated with the Germans, today France prefers to commemorate the brave men and women of the Resistance; their headquarters in Lyon have now been made into a museum (**Centre d'Histoire,** p. 165). Those French forces that escaped the Germans were commanded by the French government-in-exile, under **General Charles de Gaulle.** It was at his insistence that French troops led the **liberation of Paris** on August 25th, 1944.

AFTER THE WAR: A NEW HOPE FOR EUROPE

The **Fourth Republic** was proclaimed in 1944, but its wartime leader de Gaulle quit in 1946, unable to adapt to the deadlock of democratic politics. Like the Third Republic, France's new state lacked a strong executive to keep the country running when the legislature stalemated; over the next 14 years France saw 25 governments. Despite this chaos, the Fourth Republic witnessed an economically resurgent France, and when the constitution was reformed in 1958, the **Fifth Republic,** under the renewed leadership of the still-revered de Gaulle, inherited a sound industrial base. Fiercely nationalist, de Gaulle's foreign policy was a success, delicately playing the USA against the USSR to France's advantage. But his domestic conservatism brought growing problems at home and, in May 1968, what started as a student protest against the university system rapidly grew into a full-scale revolt as workers struck in support of social reform. The National Assembly was dissolved and things looked to be heading for revolution yet again, averted only when fresh elections returned the Gaullists to power. However, the aging general had lost his magic touch, and he resigned following a referendum defeat in 1969.

During de Gaulle's reign, the structure of France's relations with the world had changed significantly. France's stint as a colonial power ended with her 1954 defeat in present-day **Vietnam,** and the granting of independence to **Algeria** following eight years of civil war between Algerians and French settlers. Meanwhile a new era of European cooperation had begun, designed to put an end to the disastrous cycle of war which had devastated the continent. What began as the European Coal and Steel Community in 1952 became the **European Economic Community (EEC)** after the 1957 **Treaty of Rome.**

MODERN HISTORY

Many feared that the Fifth Republic would collapse after de Gaulle, its founding father, resigned in 1969. It endured, of course, but its tone changed fundamentally. De Gaulle was succeeded by the *Gaulliste* **Georges Pompidou,** who continued his predecessor's stewardship of the economy but had less success in the arena of international politics. Following Pompidou's unexpected death in 1974, his conservative successor **Valéry Giscard d'Estaing** assumed the presidency, while Paris' new, tube-encrusted art museum assumed his name. When D'Estaing's term expired in 1981, the socialist **François Mitterrand** was elected president, a position he would hold until 1995. While Mitterrand began his term with widespread nationalization and expanded benefits, the international climate could not support such generosity. By 1986, the right had control of parliament, and Mitterrand had to appoint the ruthless conservative **Jacques Chirac** as Prime Minister. At the same time, the far right began to flourish under the leadership of **Jean-Marie Le Pen,** who formed the **Front National (FN)** on an anti-immigration platform. The healthy French post-war economy had led to the development of a new working class from North Africa, and Le Pen was able to capitalize on a racism toward these immigrants that is often phrased euphemistically in terms of "cultural difference."

Mitterrand withdrew to control foreign affairs, allowing Chirac to assume a great deal of domestic power. Chirac privatized many industries, but a transport strike and widespread terrorism damaged the right, allowing Mitterrand to win a second term in 1988. Widely publicized scandals in the early 90s involving Mitterrand's ministers led to crushing parliamentary defeats, forcing him to again appoint a conservative prime minister. Mitterrand further lost prestige when the 1991 referendum on the Maastricht Treaty, which would transform the European Community into the more closely integrated **European Union (EU),** scraped through with a 51% approval rating despite massive government support. With the Maastricht Treaty of 1992 the EEC evolved into the EU, and the 1995 Schengen Agreement created a six-nation zone without border controls. 1999 saw both the extension of this zone to the entire EU save the UK, Ireland, and Denmark, and the birth of the European single currency, the **euro,** which is slated to replace the franc in 2002 (see **The Euro,** p. 35).

In the mid-nineties, Mitterrand made two startling confessions. The first was that he had collaborated with the Vichy government before joining the Resistance in 1943. The second, and more shocking, revelation was that he was seriously ill with cancer, and had been so for many years. His death in January 1996, came shortly after the presidency had finally been won by his arch-rival Jacques Chirac.

IN THE NEWS

Though Chirac himself has always polled well, the right has hardly gone unchallenged. 1997 elections returned a socialist parliament, and Chirac was forced to accept one-time presidential rival **Lionel Jospin** as prime minister. As the 2002 presidential campaign approaches, Jospin is enjoying a boost in popularity created by France's lowest unemployment rate since 1991, and his negotiation of a landmark ceasefire with Corsican separatists. Meanwhile, Chirac's Gaullist **RPR party** has been shaken by scandal and high-level instability; Paris Mayor **Jean Tiberi** was implicated in a 1989 ballot-stuffing fraud and the party has burnt through two presidents in the wake of 1999's parliamentary losses. The far right has been in an equally tumultuous state, as two different *Front National* parties compete for the extremist vote following a split between Le Pen and his deputy, **Bruno Mégret.** Political squabbles were temporarily put aside as France assumed the **presidency of the European Union** for the last half of 2000.

A CULTURAL SAMPLER

Frenchmen were making art long before the arrival of the "civilizing" Greeks and Romans. The prehistoric murals of **Lascaux** (p. 641) and **Les Eyzies-de-Tayac** (p. 639), and the huge stone monoliths of **Carnac** (p. 546) testify to the presence of ancient and well-established peoples in both the north and south of France. No such monuments stand to the ancient Gauls, whose legacy was swept away by Roman conquerors. Rome's leavings are most visible in Provence, in the theater at **Orange** (p. 270) and the arena and temple at **Nîmes** (p. 264). Nearby, the golden arches of the **Pont du Gard** aqueduct (p. 268) served up 44 million gallons of water to Nîmes' thirsty citizens every day. While classical civilization left many themes and ideals for French art, Christianity has been the most prevailing topic of and inspiration for French art in its many forms. No scene is more common than the Crucifixion, and no village or town, however tiny, lacks a simple church or grand cathedral.

ARCHITECTURE

THE INCREDIBLE FLYING BUTTRESS. The first distinctively "Western" style emerged during the 9th century, when artists under Charlemagne's patronage combined elements of the Classical legacy with elements of the northern Barbarian tradition to create a highly symbolic art form. The same religious sentiment is conveyed by French churches of the 11th and 12th centuries. Dubbed **Romanesque**

and characterized by round arches and barrel-vaulting, their beauty is one of simple grandeur. These churches, like the **Basilique St-Sernin** in Toulouse (p. 697), and the **Basilique Ste-Madeleine** at **Vézelay (p. 208),** were designed to accommodate large crowds of worshippers. Meanwhile, the great pilgrimages of the period provided both reason and inspiration for the building of cathedrals.

The architecture that characterizes the later Middle Ages is known as the **Gothic** style. One of its first proponents was Abbot Suger of St-Denis, whose rebuilding of the **Basilique St-Denis** (p. 153) in the late 12th century set the stage for later Gothic structures. Gothic architecture utilizes a system of arches that distributes weight outward. Flying buttresses (the stone supports jutting out from the sides of cathedrals) counterbalance the pressure of the ribbed vaulting, relieving the walls of the roof's weight. As a result, the walls of Gothic churches seem to soar effortlessly skyward, and light streams in through enormous stained glass windows. The cathedrals at **Noyon** and **Laon** (p. 453) in northern France embody the early Gothic style, characterized by simplicity in decoration. The high Gothic style of the later Middle Ages embodied more extreme ornamentation as seen in the cathedrals of **Amiens (p. 460), Chartres (p. 150),** and **Reims (p. 429).**

THE GOLD RUSH. François I, who hired Italian artists to improve his lodge at **Fontainebleau,** also commissioned the remarkable **Château de Chambord** (p. 569) and additions to the **Louvre** (p. 136), combining flamboyant French Gothic motifs with aspects of Italian design. But kings were not the only ones building palaces during the Renaissance. As French aristocrats moved away from Paris to the surrounding countryside, they demanded suitably lavish living quarters, and great châteaux began to spring up in the Loire Valley. In the 17th century, **Fouquet,** Louis XIV's finance minister, commissioned **Le Vau, Le Brun,** and **Le Nôtre** to build for him the splendid **Baroque Château de Vaux-le-Vicomte,** which inspired Louis XIV to enhance Versailles. Louis used the same team of architect, artist, and landscaper to expand his mansion at **Versailles** (p. 147). He moved there in 1672, shifting the seat of the French government away from the ancient capital. Here Louis commissioned the world's largest royal residence, an exorbitantly beautiful palace full of crystal, mirrors, and gold, and surrounded by formal gardens.

CITY LIGHTS. The rise of Neoclassicism is exemplified by **Jacques-Germain Soufflot's** grandiose **Eglise Ste-Geneviève** (1757) in Paris, which was deconsecrated during the revolution and rededicated as the **Panthéon** (p. 124). It serves as the resting place of Voltaire and Rousseau. This style ruled from 1804 to 1814.

The 1850s and 60s in Paris saw **Baron Georges-Eugène Haussmann** commissioned to modernize the city and give it light, circulation, and safety. Haussmann's solution was to flatten many of Paris' hills and to tear long, straight boulevards through the clutter of the city's old alleys. These overhauls increased circulation of goods and people, modernized the water, sewer, and gas lines, and made it impossible for Paris' citizens to rebel by barricading the streets. Most importantly, Haussmann's work made Paris a work of art and a splendid capital, transforming it from an intimate medieval city into a bustling metropolis. Wide sidewalks (demolished in the next century to make room for automobiles) encouraged the proliferation of sidewalk cafés, kiosks, crowds, and *flâneurs* (people strolling conspicuously).

Engineering came onto the architectural scene in the latter part of the 19th century, as **Gustave Eiffel** and architect **Louis-Auguste Boileau** designed Le Bon Marché, the world's first department store. Eiffel's later project, the star exhibit of the Universal Exhibition of 1889, was first decried by Parisians as hideous and unstable. The **Tour Eiffel** (p. 127) is now the best-loved landmark in the country.

The ornate style of **Art Nouveau** developed in the late 19th century, though it was not labeled as such until the 20th century. It is perhaps best experienced in Paris, where various Métro stops, designed by **Hector Guimard,** display the vinelike, intricate ironwork that is one characteristic of the movement.

MODERN TIMES. Revolutionary trends in architecture have resulted in a number of controversial building projects in Paris. The advent in the 1950s of **HLMs,** housing projects, on the outskirts of Paris, was met with scorn. World-renowned Swiss **Futurist** architect **Le Corbusier** designed the chapel at **Ronchamp (p. 420)**, outside Belfort in Alsace-Lorraine. The **Centre Pompidou (**p. 121**),** hated by some and adored by others, was built in 1970 by **Richard Rogers** and **Renzo Piano.** Many of these projects began as part of Mitterand's 15-billion-franc endeavor known as the *Grands Projets,* which included the construction of the **Musée d'Orsay,** the **Parc de la Villette,** the **Institut du Monde Arabe,** the **Opéra** at the Bastille, and the **Louvre pyramid,** among others. **I.M. Pei's** glass pyramid, planted smack in the middle of the Louvre courtyard, was blocked for months while the conservative Finance Ministry took its time moving out of the offices in the Richelieu branch of the ancient palace. Conservatives have succeeded, however, in keeping towering urban architecture (except for the Montparnasse tower) out of Paris proper. Skyscrapers are exiled to the business and industrial suburb of **La Défense,** home to the **Grande Arche,** a giant, hollowed-out cube of an office building aligned with the Arc de Triomphe, the smaller arch in the Tuileries, the place de la Concorde, and the Louvre. In recent news, the **ZAC project** (*zone d'aménagement concerte*) aims to build a new university, sports complex, public garden and métro in the 13*ème*.

FINE ARTS

THE MIDDLE AGES AND CHRISTIAN ART. The non-architectural artistic creations of the Middle Ages—manuscript illumination, tapestry weaving, and decorative arts can be viewed in various museum collections, notably the **Musée de Cluny** (p. 138) in Paris and the former seminary in **Bayeux (p. 482), which now houses its famous tapestry.** As the medieval period wore on, Christian themes continued to inform the day's art, but these works slowly began to creep out of the cathedrals and into more secular venues.

THE RENAISSANCE IN FRANCE. A new focus on the human realm, coupled with a nostalgia for the classical past, strongly colored the art of the 16th-century **Renaissance. François I,** who ruled France from 1515 to 1547, was quick to recognize the importance of the new artistic achievements in Italy, but it was Italian artists, not French, who benefited from his patronage. François brought the aging **Leonardo da Vinci** to his court; the fabulous paintings by **Il Rosso** at François' Fontainebleau remain one of the château's greatest attractions.

Under Louis, an indigenous French art flourished and rose to European dominance. Secular themes became more prevalent than religious symbolism. **Nicolas Poussin** elaborated the theory of the "grand manner," with huge, panoramic canvases and mythical and historical subjects. The **French Royal Academy,** founded in 1648, came to value this style above all others, and subsequent French painters had to contend with its weighty "academic" conventions. Drawing on the academic style, two 18th-century artists, **Watteau** and **Boucher,** developed an art to please the aristocracy, a fluffy and extravagant genre since dubbed **Rococo. Elisabeth Vigée-Lebrun,** one of only two women artists in the Academy, also painted Europe's rich and famous; her portrait of Marie Antoinette and her children is on display at Versailles.

POLITICS AND ART CHANGE. Painters espousing bourgeois values began to break with tradition. **Chardin** glorified motherhood and the prosaic details of homemaking. This nascent style soon triumphed, as the austerity of the Revolution of 1789 threw the flamboyant art of the aristocracy into disfavor. The chief painter of the Republic, **Jacques-Louis David,** looked to Rome for subjects that would convey contemporary republican values. His *Oath of the Horatii* (1784) depicts three sons swearing to their father that they will defend the Republic of Rome, and his *Death of Marat* (1793) commemorates one of the martyrs of the Revolution. The Napoleonic period adopted this **Neoclassicism** as its official style.

ROMANTICISM AND ORIENTALISM. The Romantics of the first half of the 19th century relied on vivid color and expressive brush strokes to create an emotional and subjective visual experience. Artists like **Théodore Géricault** and **Eugène Delacroix** took as their subjects the exotic, the violent, the grotesque—anything to provoke spontaneous emotion—while shunning Classical harmony. Consider two of Géricault's titles: *Decapitated Heads* (c. 1818) and *Portrait of a Child Murderer* (1822-23). His gifted contemporary, Delacroix, shared Géricault's interest in great drama; his *Liberty Leading the People* (1830) is a triumphant scene of the bare-breasted Lady Liberty ushering in the new Republic. Delacroix's passionate, swirling brushstrokes and bold use of color influenced the later Impressionists.

The tradition of exoticizing "the other" was ushered in by **Jean-Auguste Dominique Ingres** and **Gérôme**—artists now commonly described as Orientalists. The former's talent for evoking sensual surfaces is apparent in such works as *Odalisque*, in which a woman peers coyly over her shoulder from a luxurious harem couch.

REALISM. If the Revolution of 1789 ushered in an art with a political conscience, the Revolution of 1848 introduced an art with a social conscience. **Realists** like **Gustave Courbet** scrutinized and indeed glorified the "humble" aspects of peasant life. His *Burial at Ornans* (1850), at the Musée d'Orsay (p. 138), caused a scandal when first exhibited because it used the grand scale of history painting to depict a simple village scene. Fellow Realist **Jean Millet** showed the dignity of peasants, the value of their work, and the idyllic simplicity of their lives. Another group of mid-19th-century painters, particularly **Camille Corot** and **Théodore Rousseau,** transformed landscape painting, depicting rural subjects from direct observation while paying close attention to light and atmosphere.

IMPRESSIONISM. In the mid-19th century, an artistic movement developed that sought to capture the very experience of seeing. The rise of **Impressionism,** the fragmentation of color and shape, allowed the viewing of art to be more of a slow revelation than an immediate comprehension. The critics and the public saw this exploration as an attack on staid values and tastes. Perhaps the most shocking of the group was **Edouard Manet,** whose paintings did away with much of the fine shading and modeling of academic art. Manet's *Olympia* (1863), now at the Musée d'Orsay in Paris (p. 138), challenged bourgeois societal dominance; *Olympia* is a naked prostitute who stares down the viewer while receiving flowers from a client. His *Le Déjeuner sur l'Herbe (*1863), depicting a picnic party composed of a nude woman and two men, revolutionized the possibilities of subject matter and perturbed his contemporaries. Lighter and airier than Manet, **Claude Monet** is perhaps the most famous of the Impressionists. His repeated renderings of haystacks and of Rouen's cathedral showed the transformation of a constant subject by light. Toward the end of his life, plagued by cataracts, Monet painted a monumental series of waterlilies (*nymphéas*), notable for their rich colorings and abstract quality. Monet was generally acknowledged by his peers as the head of the group, so it is fitting that his painting *Impression: Soleil Levant (Impression: Sunrise*, now at the Musée Marmottan in Paris, p. 140) of 1872 gave the movement its name (although the name was originally assigned by a mocking critic who hated the style). The Impressionists, once relegated to a "Room of the Rejected," became a huge success and paved the way for 20th-century Western art.

Although Monet's soft style has become synonymous with Impressionism, the group was far from homogeneous in style. **Camille Pissarro** worked with fragmented brushstrokes, while **Gustave Caillebotte** is recognizable for his dramatic use of traditional perspective; looking at his paintings is like being pulled into a vortex. **Pierre Auguste Renoir,** by contrast, painted in a sugary, shimmering manner, while **Bèrthe Morisot,** the group's only woman, and **Alfred Sisley,** a landscape painter, developed their own distinctive styles. **Edgar Degas'** many paintings, sculptures, and innovative pastels of racehorses and dancers demonstrate his lifelong interest in line and movement. **Mary Cassatt,** an American expatriate and a great friend of Degas, was known for her technically stupendous prints and for her scenes of women and children which were revolutionary in their absence of sentimentality. Impressionism's influence extended to sculpture, where **Auguste Rodin** and **Camille Claudel** tried to capture growth instead of light. The **Musée Rodin** and the surrounding gardens in Paris (p. 138) offer ample examples of their affecting and emotional work.

POST-IMPRESSIONISM. The fragmented inheritors of the Impressionist tradition share the label of **Post-Impressionism. Paul Cézanne** worked in Aix-en-Provence and created still-lifes, portraits, and geometric landscapes (among them his many versions of the prominent *Mont Ste-Victoire*, 1885-87), using planes of orange, gold, and green and bold, geometric blocks of color. **Georges Seurat** took this fragmentation of shape a step further with **Pointillism,** a style in which thousands of tiny dots of paint merge to form a coherent picture in the viewer's eye. **Paul Gauguin** used large, flat blocks of color with heavily drawn outlines to paint "primitive" scenes from Brittany, Arles, Tahiti, and Martinique. He had gone to Arles to join his friend **Vincent Van Gogh,** a Dutch painter who had moved to the south of France in search of new light, color, and imagery. The poverty and mental illness that plagued him throughout his short life are reflected in his work. Similarly tortured in his art and life was **Henri de Toulouse-Lautrec,** a man of noble lineage who was disabled by a bone disease and a childhood accident. Toulouse-Lautrec's well-known posters, many of which are displayed in his hometown of Albi (p. 702), capture the brilliant and lascivious nightlife of 19th-century Paris. **Struggling with pointillism during a trip to Collioure in the Languedoc (**p. 713**), Henri Matisse** abandoned the technique and began squeezing paint from the tube directly onto the canvas. Shocked Parisian critics dubbed the artists associated with the expressive style **Fauves** (wild animals), and the name stuck. While **Fauvism** made only a brief splash on the canvas of time, Matisse's art remained a vibrant celebration of life.

CUBISM AND THE SCHOOL OF PARIS. Former Fauve artist **Georges Braque** and Spanish-born **Pablo Picasso** developed **Cubism,** a technique of composing the canvas with shaded planes (not cubes). By converting everyday objects—fruits, glasses, vases, newspapers—into these cross-cutting planes, Braque and Picasso sought to analyze pictorial space as an overlapping system of geometric shapes. It was this basic idea—that a painting could be something other than an "objective" rendering of visual experience—that paved the way for much of modern art.

After developing Cubism in the mid-1910s, Braque's and Picasso's careers diverged. Picasso became arguably the greatest artist of the 20th century, constantly innovating and breaking new artistic ground. His career, spanning many decades and movements, is chronicled at the **Musée Picasso** in Paris (p. 139) and at the beautiful seaside **Musée Picasso** in Antibes (p. 299). In the 1920s and 30s, Picasso was the brightest star in a group of talented artists who came to Paris from all over the world to practice their craft in the exciting, avant-garde atmosphere of inter-war Paris. This **School of Paris** was made up of members such as **Marc Chagall** and **Giorgio de Chirico,** who immigrated to Paris from Russia and Italy respectively. Chagall created Cubist fairytale pictures of Russian villages and Jewish legends, while de Chirico painted strange, often sinister images that became the darlings of the later Surrealist movement.

Dadaism and Surrealism. Marcel Duchamp led the **Dadaists,** a group of artists who focused on utter nonsense and non-art—examples include the drawing of a mustache on a picture of the Mona Lisa, exhibiting a urinal turned upside down, and sculpture consisting of nails stuck onto an iron or a bicycle wheel on a stool.

In 1924, **André Breton** published his Surrealist Manifesto and launched the **Surrealist** movement among a group of former Dadaists. The Surrealists claimed to create an art of the subconscious, seeking out the dream world that was more real than the rational world around them. **René Magritte, Salvador Dalí, Yves Tanguy,** and **Max Ernst** painted and etched their now-playful, now-disturbing images of top hats, castles, angels, misplaced nude bodies, and melting clocks.

LITERATURE

THE BEGINNINGS. Before the 10th century, when the colloquial Latin spoken in Gaul evolved into a form of French, French literature did not really exist. The first text composed in the nascent French language—closer to Latin than to modern French—was the **Serment de Strasbourg,** a contractual oath written on February 14, 842. As the language developed in the 11th century, many literary forms emerged, such as the **chansons de geste,** epic poems celebrating heroic deeds in the age of Charlemagne. The 15th-century **Renaissance** brought not so much a shift in form and style as a transformation of subject matter. The Italian **humanist** movement that had restored secular life as the focus of art and literature quickly swept into France. With the invention of the printing press around 1450, literature addressing the very foundations of human nature was in mass circulation. The greatest literary figures of the 16th century all wrote in prose: **Rabelais,** the moralist, **Calvin,** the reformer, and **Montaigne,** the essayist. While each profoundly affected the literary discipline, Montaigne left to posterity the personal essay, a form of self-exploration that he more or less invented.

CLASSICAL PERIOD. While the 16th century's liberating approach to subject matter persisted into the 17th century, its freedom of style and language did not. The **Académie Française,** founded in 1635, gathered some 40 men to regulate and codify French literature, grammar, spelling, and rhetoric. The standards they set loosely at this time would soon solidify into rigid regulations, giving birth to the **Classical** age of French literature. Heralded by the poetry of **Malherbe,** among others, the age yielded the three most influential **dramatists** in the nation's history: **Corneille, Molière,** and **Racine. Corneille** penned *Le Cid*, a story of love, honor, and family set in Spain and criticized by the Académie for not conforming to its increasingly dogmatic standards. **Racine**'s most important work, *Phèdre* (considered by some to be the greatest work in the French literary canon), recounts the tale of the incestuous love of Phèdre for her stepson Hippolyte. Finally, the irrepressible **Molière** sacrificed a stable career in the family upholstery business for a try at the stage. In a country overrun with furniture and always craving good theater, his decision was undeniably fortunate. His comedies of manners, including *Le Misanthrope*, *Le Bourgeois Gentilhomme*, *Les Femmes Savantes*, and *Tartuffe*, satirize the habits and speech of his time with deadly wit and a faultless sense of comedy.

REBEL WITHOUT A CAUSE Arthur Rimbaud makes most modern bad boys seem as adventurous as Trappist monks. During the Franco-Prussian War of 1870, the 16-year-old Rimbaud ran away from home to start a revolution, but was foiled when he was arrested at the train station for traveling without a ticket. Undeterred, he ran away again a year later to defend the Paris Commune (p. 10), renouncing it just before its bloody suppression. Politically disillusioned, Rimbaud put his trust in the pen rather than the bayonet, and set out to change the world through poetry. By abandoning traditional forms, trusting his visions, and torturing himself to achieve new experiences, he attempted to "derange all the senses." The confident 17-year-old sent some verses to Paul Verlaine, who was so impressed that he invited Rimbaud to stay with him. Arriving in Paris in 1871, Rimbaud seduced the older poet, who left his wife and child; after two years, the two men separated acrimoniously. In 1875, at the ripe old age of 21, Rimbaud discarded poetry and set off to explore the world, traveling to Indonesia and Egypt; he finally settled down to a peaceful career running guns into Ethiopia. When cancer forced him to return to France in 1891, he found himself famous: during his absence, Verlaine, believing him dead, had published the works of "the late Arthur Rimbaud." Rimbaud died in Marseille later that year, and is now recognized as one of France's greatest poets.

In the realm of philosophy, French thinkers reacted to the skepticism that had arisen in the wake of Humanism by establishing the foundations of **Rationalism**—logical thought based on first principles. "Cogito, ergo sum" ("I think, therefore I am") is the motto by which **René Descartes** forced Western thought into the modern age. **Blaise Pascal** was another of the new breed of thinkers. Mathematician, scientist, and Christian philosopher, Pascal wrote a series of *Pensées (Thoughts)*, in which he pondered man's place in an infinite universe.

THE ENLIGHTENMENT. The trend toward Rationalism crescendoed in the 18th century, when thinkers came to believe that they could uncover a set of rational laws to explain human nature and human institutions. No work captures the century's literary mood better than **Denis Diderot's Encyclopédie,** a multi-volume work that sought to catalogue, systematize, and rationalize the whole of human knowledge. Born amid this questioning, the century's creative literature bore a distinctly philosophical tone. **Voltaire's** *Candide* relates the story of a simple young man who travels the world over, convinced that "all is the best in the best of all possible worlds," only to meet misfortune at every turn.

Taking the cynicism of the age to its logical extreme, many thinkers began to question and criticize the French state. One of the more vocal critics, **Jean-Jacques Rousseau,** introduced the concept of the "social contract," an implicit bond between the individual and society, whereby individuals sacrifice a measure of personal freedom in return for the protection of their interests by the state. Unfortunately, he felt, the inhabitants of *ancien régime* France had "negotiated" a very poor contract; some historians believe that his attacks on the state helped to launch the French Revolution. However, despite their attitude of cynicism toward the world as it was, the Enlightenment philosophers believed in the healing power of reason. This faith was shattered by the violent and chaotic Revolution.

19TH CENTURY. Deeply influenced by German Romantics like Goethe, a new literary movement began in the 19th century. Initiated by **Mme de Staël, François-René de Chateaubriand,** and **Benjamin Constant,** and crystallized by **Victor Hugo,** the **Romantic** movement was colored by a preoccupation with the self and emotions, often conveyed through lyric poetry. For the first time, the novel flourished as a primary mode of expression with the penning of masterpieces like Hugo's *Les Misérables*, and *The Red and the Black* and *The Charterhouse of Parma*, both by **Stendhal.**

Romanticism soon fell out of vogue, when writers grew tired of its sugary emotionalism, preferring to focus on the ordinary citizen. **Honoré de Balzac**'s *Comédie Humaine* dealt unflinchingly with the harsh realities of life under Louis-Philippe. **Gustave Flaubert** was another who rejected the ideal**s of the Romantics; his** *Madame Bovary* relates the life of the wife of a bourgeois doctor, detailing her hopes and wishes, both simple and extravagant. As a whole, **Realists** like Flaubert crafted exacting, almost scientific descriptions. **Emile Zola** took realism into journalistic territory, developing social and political themes with impassioned advocacy (see p. 10). At the same time, in 1861, **Charles Baudelaire** published his infamous *Les Fleurs du Mal (The Flowers of Evil)*, ushering in a new age of poetry that focused on the sordid world of contemporary Paris—the alienation and *ennui*.

As the century closed, a new movement known as **Symbolism** emerged, grounded in the experiments of Baudelaire, heralded by **Paul Verlaine** and **Arthur Rimbaud,** and brought to fruition by **Stéphane Mallarmé** and later **Paul Valéry.** Symbolists decried the concern of their predecessors for the world of appearances. Through symbols and carefully crafted language, they attempted to probe a more profound reality. The **Positivism** of **Auguste Comte** aimed to describe human progress in three stages: the theological, the metaphysical, and the positive, the last of which allowed a rational explanation of nature.

20TH CENTURY. Novelist **Marcel Proust** moved beyond Realism in his monumental *A la Recherche du Temps Perdu* (*In Search of Lost Time*), which uses the Belle Epoque as the background for a romanesque investigation of the experience of time, memory, and the nature of art. Proust-philes now visit Illiers-Combray, near Chartres, and Cabourg (p. 476), the Norman seaside resort that served as the model for the author's town of Balbec. After the shock of the First World War, literature moved in new and sometimes radical directions. **Surrealist** poets like **André Breton** attempted to escape the mundane world of bourgeois life by looking to a more exciting, albeit ephemeral, world of dreams. Continuing the trend of profound psychological and ontological questioning, author/philosophers **Jean-Paul Sartre** and **Albert Camus** explored the foundations of human nature in treatises and fictional works. Sartre's philosophy of **Existentialism,** introduced in his tome *L'Etre et le Néant (Being and Nothingness)*, holds that existence has no inherent meaning or value and that it is not being that matters, but becoming. Camus, weaving with Sartre's existential threads, initiated a literature of the absurd. In works such as *L'Etranger (The Stranger)* and *La Peste (The Plague)*, he confronted the fundamentally disorienting experience of being human. Absurdist **Eugène Ionesco** wrote nonsensical plays like *La Cantatrice Chauve (The Bald Soprano)*. **Simone de Beauvoir,** an extremely influential member of the mid-20th-century wave of feminism, applied Existentialism specifically to women in such masterpieces as *Le Deuxième Sexe* (*The Second Sex*).

While Sartre and Camus preserved somewhat traditional literary styles, experimental writing in the 1950s and 1960s produced the **Nouveau Roman** (the New Novel), which challenged the reader by abandoning conventional narrative techniques and embracing subject matter previously considered trivial and mundane. Among its best known exponents are **Alain Robbe-Grillet** and **Nathalie Sarraute,** arch-priestess of stream-of-consciousness writing.

THE POST-AGE. With this new writing came new literary criticism. **Jacques Lacan** wrote of the Mirror Stage—he imagined the moment of division that occurs the first time a child looks in the mirror and realizes that the image both is and isn't himself. **Claude Lévi-Strauss** brazenly suggested that western culture was not the pinnacle of culture itself, holding that every culture ("advanced" or not) develops similar systems of making communities run smoothly. With this premise, he founded the modern school of ethnography, or **cultural relativism.** Initiating the **post-structuralist** school was **Gilles Deleuze,** who rejected the notion that God or Reason or any other Big Thing directs our individual lives. It was **Jacques Derrida** who fully articulated the notion of **deconstruction,** arguing that language itself is not neutral, and could be taken apart to reveal its culture-specific assumptions. Who knew? **Michel Foucault** jumped on this bandwagon as well, explaining that life's events can't be attributed to one first cause, that "cause" is the net effect of the actions of multiple sources. **Luce Irigaray** took on the "phallocentrism" (sort of French for "sexism") in Freudian psychoanalysis, by showing what happens to women when the penis is made the central object of self-identification. **Postmodernist Marguerite Duras** played fast and loose with facts and history (personal and national). According to Duras, there is no unchanging set of biographical facts about a person. Rather, what you write (loosely defined) is who you are. **François Lyotard** examined the changing shape of the institutions of time, memory, and Lycra. For the latest in French writing, check the lists of best sellers in the weekly magazine *Livre*, the monthly magazine *Lire*, or look for reviews in the literary sections of national newspapers (see **Les Journaux,** p. 23).

MUSIC

MEDIEVAL AND RENAISSANCE MUSIC. **Philippe de Vitry** contributed to French musical history with his treatise, **Ars nova,** which examined the theoretical aspects of music in 14th-century France. In approximately the same time period, medieval France spawned its own version of the cliché love song. These were crooned by **troubadours** traveling throughout Provence. Franco–Flemish, **Guillaume Dufay** (1400-1474), of the Burgundian court, and **Jean d'Ockeghem** (1420-1497) exerted a French influence in Renaissance music. However, **Josquin des Prez** (1440-1521) made use of the prospering Italian courts and left France for Milan. **Adrian Willaert** (1490-1562), also a native Frenchman, left for the wealthy courts in Venice, further contributing to the rise of Italian musical influence.

INFERIORITY COMPLEX. This exodus of musical talent led to Italy's musical monopoly during the next 150 years. In fact, one of the next influential French composers began his life as Giovanni Battista Lulli. Later becoming a naturalized French citizen and gallicizing his name to **Jean-Baptise Lully** (1632-87), this adventurous musician and composer brought musical influence back to France. Lully went on to become a court musician, composer, and conductor for Louis XIV and collaborated with Molière on several ballets. In 1687, during a particularly vigorous conducting session, Lully drove his baton through his foot; he died from the subsequent infection. Picking up Lully's (composing, not conducting) style, **Jean-Philippe Rameau** (1683-1764) furthered the development of **music theory.** In spite of Rameau's contributions, the **Classical period** (mid-1700s to early 1800s) in France was not particularly strong, with more domination by France's Germanic neighbors who gave birth to masters such as Haydn, Mozart, and Beethoven.

EXPATS TAKE OVER. Some of the most famous "French" composers were not actually French at all, but spent the majority of their adult lives and musical careers in France. **Frédéric Chopin** (1810-49), Polish by birth, could nearly be considered a Parisian, living much of his life in Paris and becoming involved with French writer **George Sand.** Also in Paris was Hungarian-born **Franz Liszt** (1811-86), who, inspired by Chopin and by the technical virtuosity of the talented Italian violinist **Niccolò Paganini,** extended the possibilities of piano performance technique.

THE OPERATIC BOOM. With the movement into the Romantic period of the mid-to late-19th century, France regained a position of prominence and once again enjoyed its status as a major center of musical influence. The rise of the bourgeoisie in the early part of the 19th century resulted in the spectacle of **grand opera,** as well as the simpler **opéra comique.** These styles later merged and culminated in the *über*-Romantic **lyric opera,** a mix of soaring arias, exotic flavor, and tragedy (usually death). **Major operas of this period include Gounod's** *Faust* (1859), **Saint-Saëns'** *Samson et Dalila* (1877), **Bizet's** *Carmen* (1875), **Offenbach's** *Les Contes d'Hoffmann* (1880), and **Berlioz's** *Les Troyens* (1856-58). Symphonic music also developed substantially in the Romantic era due to French contributions. Berlioz, in particular, is renowned for his *Symphonie Fantastique* (1830), a not-so-subtle semi-autobiographical account of the composer's unrequited love for the Irish actress Harriet Smithson.

TURN OF THE CENTURY. As in other arts, music at the turn of the 20th century began a new period of intense, often abstract invention. One of the most beloved French composers is **Claude Debussy** (1862-1918). His instrumental works *Prélude à l'après-midi d'un faune* (1894) and *La Mer* (1905), as well as his opera *Pelléas et Mélisande* (1902), use tone color and non-traditional scales to evoke moods. His works are often labeled **Impressionistic,** after the artistic movement of the same period. **Erik Satie,** born in Honfleur in 1866, composed in a sarcastic, anti-sentimental spirit, in striking contrast to that of Debussy. **Maurice Ravel** (1895-1937) also composed in the Impressionistic style of Debussy. His platinum-single, mood-enhancing *Bolero* (1928) is one of his best known works.

20TH CENTURY. In the later 20th century, French composers have continued to populate the *avant garde.* The *Création du monde* (1924) of **Darius Milhaud** (1892-1974), a native of Aix-en-Provence, took some of the first tentative steps on the part of European music to come to terms with jazz. The music of **Olivier Messiaen** (born in Avignon in 1908) weaves new sounds, rhythms, and harmonies into complex and powerfully emotional textures. His *Quatuor pour la fin du temps* (Quartet for the End of Time) was first performed by the composer and three fellow prisoners in a German prison camp in 1941. The more electronically minded **Edgar Varèse** (1883-1965) utilized 18 quadrophonic speakers in an enclosed space designed by **Le Corbusier** for the premiere of his *Poème électronique* at the 1958 World's Fair in Brussels. Paris remains a hotbed for composition in the post-electronic European tradition, anchored by the **IRCAM** institute (☎ 01 44 78 47 44) in the Pompidou Museum, under the leadership of **Pierre Boulez** (born 1925).

JAZZ AND CABARET. France has been particularly receptive to **jazz** and recognized its artistic worth sooner than the US. Jazz singer **Josephine Baker** left the US for Paris in 1925, finding the French to be much more accepting than her segregated home. Another style similar to jazz that grew in popularity in the 1930s was **cabaret,** made famous by the iconic voice of **Edith Piaf** (1915-1963). She is famed for ballads such as *Non, je ne regrette rien* and *La Vie en Rose.* Singing, dancing, and acting sensation **Yves Montand,** was Piaf's protégé and lover (and future lover of Marilyn Monroe, among many others). In the 1930s, French musicians copied the swing they heard on early Louis Armstrong sides, but the 1934 Club Hot pair of violinist **Stéphane Grapelli** and stylish Belgian-Romany guitarist **Django Reinhardt** were already innovators. After WWII, a stream of American musicians came to Paris. A jazz festival in 1949 brought the young **Miles Davis** across the pond for a dreamy April in Paris and a **romance** with actress **Juliette Greco.** Pianist **Bud Powell,** drummer **Kenny Clarke,** and others found the respect, dignity, and gigs accorded them in Paris too attractive to leave. The resort culture of southern France has also been good to musicians—**Mingus** shocked listeners in Antibes in 1960 and got paid to do it. The jet set of jazz continues to tour the resorts of Juan-les-Pins, Cannes, and St-Tropez, and now includes some French nationals. Pianist **Jacky Terrasson** has recently taken giant steps to earn the helm of the late and beloved **Michel Petrucciani.** You may catch him at **Au Duc des Lombards** in Paris (see p. 109).

POP MUSIC. France has been afflicted by the girl- and boy-band phenomenon even longer than the US. Also very popular is dance music, whose (mostly foreign) stars appear and disappear faster that you can say "pitch control." Among more music-like music is that of **Patrick Bruel,** who attained Beatles-like status in the late 90s. In the 80s a number of solid groups emerged, like **Téléphone, Indochine,** and **Les Rita Mitsouki.** The oft-married and aging rock star **Johnny Hallyday** still plays sold out shows. In general, France remains more loyal than many nations to its stars of the past, and few weeks go by without a television documentary on "Cloclo" (60s superstar **Claude François**) or **Dalida** (France's disco queen), who both met tragic ends, although Cloclo, who died when he tried to change a lightbulb while in the bath, takes the cake. The talented and controversial **Serge Gainsbourg,** on the other hand, managed to survive years of alcohol and drug abuse to die at age 63. He caused a scandal for, among other things, shooting a video called *Lemon Incest* with his daughter, actress Charlotte Gainsbourg, and for burning a 500F note on live television.

THE NEXT BIG THINGS. In recent years, ethnic hybrids have had a huge influence on French pop music. Check out **Karim Kacel, Cheb Kalad,** and **Manu Chao** (formerly of **Mano Negra**) for examples of African **raï.** For some progressive-syntho fun, expose yourself to **Air.** Another phenomenally successful export has been the French disco house sound, with the 70s-influenced (and occasionally 70s-sampling) tunes of **Daft Punk, Bob Sinclar,** and **Cassius** burning up dance floors. Daft Punk's *Homework* album and Cassius' *1999* album are probably the best embodiment of the sound. Recent pop hits have come from groups like **Les Nubians, Les Négresses Vertes, Louise Attaque,** and soloists like **Axel Renoir and Etienne Daho.** French R&B stars **Native** and **Teri Moïse** top the charts along with rap stars like **MC Solaar, Liaison Dangereuses, Manau, Passithe,** and controversial **NTM** (Nique Ta Mère) and the more recent **KDD** (Kartel Double Dentente), whose lyrics speak out against urban crime, racism, and anti-immigrant prejudice in France.

LISTENING. The bulk of popular music played on French radio will be familiar to anglophone travelers, despite a 1996 law requiring that **francophone music** make up 40% of radio playlists—much of that quota gets filled between 1 and 6am.

FILM

THE ORIGINS. Not long after he and his brother Louis presented the world's first paid screening in a Paris café in 1895, **Auguste Lumière** remarked, "The cinema is a medium without a future." In defiance (or occasional support) of this statement, the French have striven to reveal the broadest possibilities of film. The trick cinema of magician-turned-filmmaker **Georges Méliès** astounded audiences with "disappearing" objects, but by 1908 gave way to an emphasis on narrative. **Max Linder's** physical comedy spoke volumes through the silent medium.

France was the Hollywood of the early days of cinema. However, WWI stunted French growth and allowed the Americans to set their claws in for good. Still, the creative climate in France was fertile: new movements in art engaged with film and yielded the slapstick *Entr'acte* (1924) of **René Clair,** starring that grand-Dada of impertinence, Marcel Duchamp, and **Luis Buñuel's** *Un Chien Andalou* (1928), a marvel of jarring associations featuring Salvador Dalí.

SOUND AND FURY. The 1930s brought the transition to sound and the growth of **Poetic Realism** under **Marcel Carné** and writer **Jacques Prévert** (*Daybreak*, 1939), with its concern for the gritty lives of the working class. **Jean Renoir** balanced social criticism with a gentle humanism, revealing in *The Rules of the Game* (1939) the erosion of the French upper classes and hinting at his country's malaise at the doorstep of war. Censorship during the Occupation led to a move toward nostalgia and escapist cinema. Yet **Carné** and **Prévert**'s epic *Children of Paradise* (1943-5) finds the indomitable spirit of the French.

THE NEW WAVE. After the war, **Jean Cocteau** carried the poetic into the fantastic with *Beauty and the Beast* (1946) and *Orphée* (1950). However, popular French taste went in for lush, well-buffed productions. A group of young intellectuals gathered by critic **André Bazin** for the magazine **Cahiers du Cinéma** took issue with this "cinema of quality." Encouraged by government subsidies, in 1959 they swapped the pen for the camera. **François Truffaut's** *The 400 Blows* and **Jean-Luc Godard's** *Breathless* sounded the clarion call of the **French New Wave.** Other directors associated with the New Wave are **Louis Malle** (*The Lovers*, 1958), **Eric Rohmer** (*My Night with Maud*, 1969), and **Agnès Varda** (*Cléo from 5 to 7*, 1961). Godard emerged as the New Wave oracle through the 60s. His collaborations with actors **Jean-Paul Belmondo** and **Anna Karina,** including *Vivre Sa Vie* (1962) and *Pierrot le Fou* (1965), inspired a generation of filmmakers. *Weekend* (1967), a descent into anarchy and cannibalism which concludes with the Lumière-invoking intertitle, "The End of Cinema," marks the proximity of contemporary film and radical politics and presages the national events of May 1968 (see p. 11).

MODERN FILM. The world impact of French cinema in the 60s brought wider recognition of French film stars in the 70s and 80s, such as the stunning **Catherine Deneuve** *(Belle de jour, Les Parapluies de Cherbourg)*, the alluring **Brigitte Bardot** (*Et Dieu Créa la Femme*), gothic priestess **Isabelle Adjani** (*La Reine Margot*), and the omnipresent **Gérard Depardieu** (*Danton*, *Camille Claudel*), as well as **Juliette Binoche** *(Blue)* and **Julie Delpy** (*Europa, Europa*). Recent comedies like *Les Visiteurs* (1992) and *Sitcom* (1998) poke fun at American B-grade comedies and television sitcoms. *Betty Blue* (1985), *Manon des Sources* and *Jean de Florette* (1986), Louis Malle's WWII drama *Au Revoir les Enfants* (1987), **Krzysztof Kieslowski's** "Three Colors" trilogy, *Blue* (1993), *White* (1994), and *Red* (1994), and **Jean-Pierre Jeunet's** *Le Fabuleux destin d'Amélie Poulain* (2001) have all become popular favorites of recent French cinema.

FILM AND SOCIETY. Some of the most explosive recent French films are the production of *cinéma beur*, the work of second-generation North Africans coming to terms with life in the HLMs (housing projects) of suburban Paris. Rich with graffiti art and rap music, films like **Mehdi Charef's** *Le Thé au harem d'Archi Ahmed* (1986) and **Mathieu Kassovitz's** *La Haine* (1995) expose the horrors of urban racism. Facing up to a history of colonialism is another recent preoccupation, as in **Claire Denis'** *Chocolat* (1987)—to be distinguished from the American film of the same name featuring Juliette Binoche. Art cinema continues to prosper under **Marcel Hanoun** (*Bruit d'Amour et de Guerre*, 1997) and **Jacques Doillon** (*Ponette*, 1997).

GOIN' TO THE MOVIES. France retains a vibrant film culture, with 12 annual festivals in addition to the May **Cannes** event (see p. 303). English-language films marked *version originale (v.o.)* are shown in English with French subtitles (*sous-titres*); those marked *version française (v.f.)* are dubbed into French. A ticket will usually cost around 35-50F/€5.34-7.62, but each film is discounted at its Wednesday premiere. Cinephiles would do well to catch the week-long *fête du cinéma,* in various cities and towns throughout the summer, which offers substantial discounts.

TELEVISION

Much of French television will be familiar to anglophones: a significant portion of sitcoms and dramas are dubbed English-language shows. France has recently jumped on the reality show bandwagon and bested everyone with its *Loft Story*, a show in which 11 men and women share an apartment for ten weeks and are filmed 24 hours a day. A version of the show *Survivor* will premiere in the fall, and the British show *The Weakest Link (Le Maillon faible)* is already on the air. But the gameshow to watch is *Questions pour un champion,* where the questions are actually—gasp—hard, and the prizes dictionaries. In general, French television leaves much to be desired, although news programs are excellent and completely devoid of any tabloid material. In addition, most shows and movies are shown commercial-free.

NEWSPAPERS AND RADIO

LES JOURNAUX. France has relatively few daily papers for its size. Chief among them in readership, though not in prestige, is the slightly right-of-center *Le Figaro. Le Monde* is France's newspaper of record, especially on international affairs. No French newspaper is so widely read, and none so influential; policy-makers both left and right pay close attention to the paper's left-leaning editorials. Despite its prestige, *Le Monde* continues to decline in readership within France and has trailed the less respected *Le Figaro* for 15 years. *Le Parisien,* though read outside Paris in a stripped-down version, depends on the capital for most of its readership. Of the committed left-wing papers, *Libération* ("*Libé*") seems to be doing better than the downright communist *L'Humanité.* Many French avoid newspapers of any stripe and read weekly magazines: the liberal *Nouvel Observateur,* the rightist and less intellectual newsmagazine *L'Express,* or the decidedly frothy *Paris-Match. Le Canard Enchaîné,* virtually unreadable to anyone but a native, delivers the country's best investigative journalism in prose laced with puns and heavy on slang. As for English-language papers, the *New York Times* can be found in Paris and other large cities alongside the *Times of London.* The *International Herald Tribune,* much easier to find, combines coverage from the *New York Times* and the *Washington Post,* with a focus on international news. On the radio, both **Voice of America** and the **BBC World Service** broadcast English-language news; for frequencies, see their websites at www.voa.gov/allsked.html and www.bbc.co.uk/worldservice/index.shtml respectively.

LA RADIO. French radio went commercial in 1984, but large conglomerates have mostly prevented the rise of independent stations. National stations include *Fun Radio*, *NRJ*, and *Skyrock* for teens; *Nostalgie*, an adult-oriented station with emotional music; and *Europe 1* for news. Among France's public stations are *France Inter*, a general interest station, and *France Info* for news. Today, most popular music played on the radio will be familiar to anglophones, despite a 1996 law requiring that francophone music make up 40% of radio playlists; much of the quota gets filled from to 1 to 6am. Frequencies vary from city to city; check www.mobiquid.com/fr/frequence.v22.asp, where you can search by city for any and all radio stations.

SPORTS

Of all Europeans, the French may be alone in loving cycling as much as football. On July 7, 2002, kickstands will go up for the three weeks and over 3500km of the **Tour de France,** which has ended on Paris' Champs-Elysées (p. 129) for the last 26 of its 98 years. The American Lance Armstrong has won for the past three years. Football, *the* European sport, also consumes the French; France recently played international host and king of the world's *footballeurs* at the **Coupe Mondial** (World Cup) in 1998, and stunningly won in the new Stade de France outside Paris. The national team, *Les Bleus*, continued their winning streak in the European Championship at Rotterdam in June, 2000. Finally, *Les Bleus* were once again victorious in June 2001 at the *Coupe des Confédérations*, finishing off their *Triple Historique*. Though its football fanaticism has never been more rabid, France has already seen over half its championship team exported to scissor-kick for other countries. The France team's star **Zinédine Zidane** (nicknamed *Zizou*) was recently lured to Spain's Real Madrid from Italy's Juventus Turin for a record 75 million euros. Loyalty to individual French teams remains high, with RC Lens, Olympique de Marseille, AS Monaco, and Paris St-Germain enjoying the largest fan bases.

Natives of small-town southern France play **pétanque,** a game of concentration and accuracy similar to bocce or bowls and dominated by old men, though this seems to be changing. In the southwest, **rugby** is gaining in popularity, and **golf** continues to grow nationwide. **Tennis** balls bounce in virtually every town; racket-toting tourists can usually get a temporary membership at a local court. The adventurous can hang-glide off the High Normandy coast or in the Mediterranean, and more cost-conscious travelers can go on any number of **hikes,** from the Pyrenees to the Alps and from Corsica to the Atlantic coast. In the winter months **skiing** is immensely popular, and France boasts the self-proclaimed "world's greatest skiing venue" in the Rhône-Alps region. Host to three winter Olympics, the country offers a wide variety of resorts with opportunities for all ski levels at breathtaking locations such as Chamonix, Grenoble, and Albertville.

A FRENCH FOOD PRIMER

Charles de Gaulle complained that no nation with 400 types of cheese could ever be united; watch a pack of ravenous Frenchwomen tearing through a *fromagerie* and you'll agree. Gastronomy remains an important part of French culture and receives world-wide renown. Though *le fast-food* and *le self-service* have thoroughly invaded France, many still shop daily for their ingredients, and restaurants observe the traditional order of courses. One could hardly expect less from the people who coined the term *haute cuisine.*

MEALS. The French ease into their food consumption for the day with a breakfast (*le petit déjeuner*) which is usually light, consisting of bread *(le pain)* or sometimes croissants or *brioches* plus an espresso with hot milk *(café au lait)* or a hot chocolate (*le chocolat*, often drunk from a bowl). The largest meal of the day is lunch (*le déjeuner*) between noon and 2pm. Most shops, businesses, and government agencies close during this time, even in big cities. Dinner (*le dîner*) begins quite late, and restaurants may not serve you if you want to dine at 6 or 6:30pm. Eating at 8pm is much more acceptable. A complete French meal includes an *apéritif* (drink), an *entrée* (appetizer), a *plat* (main course), salad, cheese, dessert, fruit, coffee, and a *digestif* (after-dinner drink, typically a cognac or other local brandy, such as *calvados* in Normandy). *Kir*, white wine with *cassis* (blackcurrant liqueur), and *pastis*, a licorice liqueur diluted with water, are the most common *apéritifs*. The French drink wine with virtually every meal.

MENUS. Most restaurants offer a *menu à prix fixe* (fixed-price meal) that costs less than ordering *à la carte*. The menu may include an *entrée* (appetizer), a main course *(plat)*, cheese *(fromage)*, and dessert (see **Menu Reader,** p. 737). The *formule* is a cheaper, two-course version. Most restaurants are closed between lunch and dinner, but odd-hour cravings can be satisfied at brasseries, the middle ground between the casual café and the structured restaurant.

Bread is served with every meal; it is perfectly polite to use a piece to wipe your plate. Etiquette dictates keeping one's hands above the table, not in one's lap, but elbows shouldn't rest on the table. Mineral water or wine are the typical beverages accompanying a meal. Order sparkling water *(eau pétillante* or *gazeuse)* or flat mineral water *(eau plate)*. Ice cubes *(glaçons)* are rare. To order a pitcher of tap water, ask for *une carafe d'eau*. Finish the meal with espresso *(un café)*, which comes in little cups with blocks of sugar. When *boisson comprise* is written on the menu, you are entitled to a free drink (usually wine) with the meal. The tip *(pourboire)* is always included in the check *(l'addition)*.

A warning to vegetarians: trust no one. The concept is foreign to most waiters and chefs, and even an innocent-sounding salad might hold a slice of ham lurking in the lettuce. You'll probably have most luck at crêperies, ethnic restaurants, and places catering to a younger crowd; if all else fails, order an omelette.

GROCERIES. For an occasional 90F/€14 spree you can have a marvelous meal, but it's easy to find satisfying dinners for under 60F/€9.15 or to assemble inexpensive meals yourself with staples such as cheese, pâté, wine, and bread. Those in a hurry can find anything from smelly cheese to American cereals in the numerous supermarket chains, like Casino, Marchéplus, Monoprix, and Prisunic, but fresher and finer picnics can be assembled at outdoor markets (*Let's Go* lists locations and times in most towns). Start with bread from the boulangerie (bakery), and then proceed to the charcuterie for pâté, *saucisson* (hard salami), *jambon* (ham), or quiches, or buy a delicious freshly roasted chicken from the boucherie (butcher's). Local produce is best found at a *marché* (market). If you want someone else to do the work, boulangeries often sell a variety of fresh sandwiches. Pâtisseries and confiseries will sate nearly any sweet tooth with treats ranging from candy to ice cream to pastries.

CAFES. Cafés in France, legendary as the habitat of writers and intellectuals from Hemingway to Sartre, figure pleasantly in the daily routine. When choosing a café, remember that you pay for its location. Those on a major boulevard can be much more expensive than smaller establishments a few steps down a sidestreet. Prices in cafés are two-tiered, cheaper at the counter *(comptoir)* than in the seating area *(salle)*; outdoor seating *(la terrasse)* may charge a third level. Coffee, beer, and (in the south) the anise-flavored *pastis* are the staple café drinks, but there are other refreshing options. Consider the cool *Perrier menthe*, a bottle of Perrier mineral water with mint syrup. *Citron pressé* (lemonade)—note that *limonade* is a soda—and *diabolo menthe* (peppermint soda) are popular non-alcoholic choices. If you order *café*, you'll get espresso; for coffee with milk, ask for a *café crème*. *Bière à la pression*, or draft beer, is 660ml of either pale *(blonde)* or dark *(brune)* lager; for something smaller ask for a *demi* (330ml). A glass of red is the cheapest wine in a café (4-6F/€0.61-0.91), with white costing about twice as much. Tips are not expected in cafés, except for super chic ones in big cities.

THE ELIXIR OF LIFE

Wine *(le vin)* pervades French culture, and no occasion is complete without a glass or four. The range and variety of wines available are tremendous and therefore terrifying for the uninitiated. Not only does the character and quality of a wine depend on which of the 60 grape varieties it is made from, but the climate and soil type also have a crucial effect. White wine *(vin blanc)* can be made from both white grapes *(blanc de blancs)* or red *(blanc de noirs)*; in the latter case care must be taken to prevent the skins from coloring the wine. Red wine *(vin rouge)* and *rosé* are always made from red grapes.

Wine-producing regions are scattered throughout France, each with its own specialty. On the Dordogne and Garonne rivers, the famous Bordeaux region produces mostly reds, white Pomerol, Médoc and Graves, and sweet white Sauternes. Red Bordeaux is often called claret in English. Burgundy is especially famous for its reds, from the wines of Chablis and the Côte d'Or in the north, to the Beaujolais and Mâconnais in the south. The northeast offers Alsatian whites that tend to be dry and fruity, complementing spicy foods. Delicately-bouqueted whites predomi-

...AND WHICH WINE DOES MADAME DESIRE? Embarrassed that the *garçon* (waiter) will scoff at your inexpert handling of wine? Stop biting your nails and read on to discover all that a wine connoisseur needs to know. First, when the *garçon* presents the wine, nod knowingly and show no fear. Briefly hold your glass to the light and then against a white surface. Check that the liquid is clear. Next hold it to your nose and take a sniff. If it smells sulfurous, vinegary, or moldy, tell the *garçon* *"non."* You are an expert; no one can pull the wool over your eyes. Now swirl the wine several times and smell it again. This scent should be much stronger. To really show off your expertise, sniff the middle of the wine as well by tipping the glass sideways and sticking your nose well over the side. The wine has now passed the initial tests and is ready for tasting. Sip the wine delicately, letting some air enter your mouth with the liquid (this brings the flavor out more). Try to taste the wine on each region of your tongue to distinguish between the bitter, sweet, acidic, and salty sensations. If the smell or taste is not as strong as you would like, ask the waiter to put your wine in a carafe so it can breathe a little more. Ultimately, regardless of your ability to feign expertise, which may be impressive to friends, family, and waitstaff alike, your personal taste matters far more in selecting the perfect glass.

nate in the Loire Valley. Major vineyards are also found in Anjou, Touraine and Sancerre. In Provence, the Côtes de Provence around Marseille are recognized for their *rosés*, while the Côtes du Rhône produce the sweet white *Muscat de Beaumes-de-Venise* and celebrated reds such as the famous *Châteauneuf du Pape.* Although many areas produce sparkling wines *(vins mousseux)*, only those grown and produced in Champagne can legally bear its name.

Other grape-based delights include Cognac and Armagnac, which come from Charente and Gascony respectively. Technically distinguished from brandy by strict government regulations, Cognac is a double-distilled spirit and so has a higher alcohol content than the single-distilled but more flavorful Armagnac. Unlike other wines, Cognac and Armagnac are usually enjoyed as *digestifs*.

A budget traveler in France can be pleasantly surprised by even the least expensive *vins de tables* (table wines), which are what most French drink. When buying wine, look for the product of the region you're in. Don't feel that you have to splurge to drink well; bad wine is virtually unheard of in France, and you can buy a decent red for as little as US$5. Table wines in restaurants can be bought by the liter *(une carafe)*, the half-liter (*une demi-carafe*), and sometimes the quarter-liter. Many cities have wine bars where you can buy vintage wine by the glass; this is a good way to learn about wine without the prices you'd otherwise have to pay. To indulge for absolutely nothing, visit regions with vineyards, like Burgundy and Bordeaux, where wine producers frequently offer free *dégustations* (tastings).

GASTRONOMIC TOUR DE FRANCE

NORMANDY. Norman cuisine is famed for both its apples and dairy products. Creamy, pungent (and some would say downright stinky) *camembert* cheese is best when it's soft in the middle. The apples make the province's traditional *cidre* which Flaubert once referred to saying, "All of us Normans have a drop of cider in our veins." *Calvados*, an apple brandy, ranks with the finest cognacs, while *poire* is to pears as cider is to apples. The local *apéritif* is *pommeau*, which sits halfway between cider and *calvados*.

BRITTANY. The region's trademark crêperies offer savory buckwheat *galettes* wrapped around eggs, mushrooms, seafood, or ham, and dessert crêpes filled with chocolate, fruit, or jam. These are accompanied by *bolées* (earthenware bowls) of dry *cidre brut* or the sweeter *cidre doux.* Brittany's pâtisseries display *kouign amann* (flaky pastry saturated with butter and sugar) and the custard-like *far breton.* Whatever the meal, seafood should be a part of it.

POITOU-CHARENTES. Another region known for its succulent *fruits de mer* (seafood): try Marennes-Oléron *huîtres* (oysters), *moules à la mouclade* (mussels in a wine, cream, and egg sauce), and *fricassée d'anguilles* (eels in a red wine sauce). *Escargots* (snails), known locally as *cagouilles*, are prepared either with a meat-and-spice stuffing *(à la saintongeaise)* or with a red wine sauce *(aux lumas)*. Finally, the celebrated *cabécou*, a tangy goat cheese, is often served warm on a bed of lettuce. The nectar of the region is *cognac*, used liberally in *charentais* cooking, but *Pineau des Charentes*, a more affordable mixture of cognac and grape or pear juice, makes a sublime and sweet *apéritif*.

LOIRE VALLEY. The rich soil nurtures asparagus, strawberries, and sunflowers. In the *caves* once used as quarries for the châteaux, tubs of mushrooms neighbor barrels filled with wine. Well-known whites include Touraine, Montlouis, and Vouvray, while Chinon, St-Nicolas-de-Bourgeuil, and Saumur are predominately red. Saumur is also famous for its sparkling white *crémant de Loire*, which rivals champagne in taste, but certainly not in price.

PERIGORD. This area is famous for its *cèpe* mushrooms and truffles which are used in its traditional meat dishes. These also make use of walnuts, honey, and *chèvre*. Its walnut wines rival the renowned Monbazillac, a syrupy sweet white wine cultivated 6km south of Bergerac.

AQUITAINE, PAYS BASQUE, AND GASCONY. Gascony gives the world culinary specialties such as *foie gras* and *confit de canard* (duck cooked in its own fat), while **Aquitaine**'s glory is its wine. When departing from the staple claret, this region's drink of choice is *armagnac*, a strong brandy. The wines complement food flavored with *cèpes* (porcini mushrooms) and the elusive *truffe noir*. The **Pays Basque** has a distinctly Spanish influence in its cuisine. The *jambon cru* (cured ham) of Bayonne, the *thon* (tuna) of St-Jean-de-Luz, the steaming *moules* (mussels) of Biarritz, and the ubiquitous *piperade* (omelette filled with green peppers, onions, tomatoes, and thyme) are among the most notable of the region's dishes. Basque desserts include the flaky *croustade* pastry, made with plums or apples, as well as the rich, almond-paste-filled *gâteau basque*.

LANGUEDOC-ROUSSILLON. In the **Languedoc,** one popular regional dish is *cassoulet*, a hearty stew of white beans, sausage, pork, mutton, and goose. In **Roussillon**, try *cargolade* (snails stuffed with bacon) or one of the many seafood offerings. The tangy, fermented *roquefort* and *St-Nectaire* cheeses complement the luscious fruits of the Garonne Valley. The region is also known for its full-bodied red wines like Minervois and Corbières, as well as Lunel, Mireval, and St-Jean-de-Minervois, sweet whites which make good *apéritifs* or dessert wines.

PROVENCE. Along the Mediterranean, Provence has simple and fresh food. Regional specialities include *bouillabaisse* (a hearty fish and seafood stew), *soupe au pistou* (a brew of pine nuts, fresh basil, and garlic), *aïoli* (a creamy garlic dip), and fresh seafood. The rough, full reds of the nearby Côte du Rhône and clean, lavender rosés of the Côte de Provence provide lovely accompaniments.

CORSICA. A trip to the island of Corsica affords the opportunity to sample a cuisine that is hearty and fresh. Herbs from the *maquis* (an impenetrable tangle of lavender, laurel, myrtle, rosemary, and thyme growing on Corsica's hillsides) impart a distinct flavor to local specialties. The island's most famous specialties are *sanglier* (wild boar), *brocciu* (ewe's cheese), *gâteau de chataigne* (chestnut cake), and *charcuterie Corse*, free-range pork products including *prisuttu* (ham), *coppa* (backmeat), *lonzu* (filet), *panzetta* (breast), and *saucisson* (hard salami). Other delicacies include *pâté de merle* (blackbird pâté) and *niolo* (a sharp goat cheese), and honeys, nougats, cakes, jams, and spices. Fortunately the fragrant, flavorful Corsican wines are as inexpensive as their mainland cousins.

ALPS. Food in the French Alps has a Swiss twist. Regional specialties include *fondue savoyarde* (bread dipped in a blend of cheeses, white wine, and kirsch), *raclette* (strong cheese melted and served with boiled potatoes and onions), and *gratin dauphinois* (sliced potatoes baked in a creamy cheese sauce). Alpine cheeses are mild and creamy: try *tomme*, *St-Marcellin* (half goat's milk), *beaufort*, and *reblochon*. Regional wines include the whites of Apremont, Marignan, and Chignin, and the rich reds produced in Montmélian and St-Jean-de-la-Porte. If there's room for dessert, try *roseaux d'Annecy* (liqueur-filled chocolates), *St-Genux* (*brioche* topped with pink praline), or *gâteau de Savoie* (a light sponge cake). *Eaux de vie*, strong liqueurs distilled from fruits, are popular here, especially when made from local *framboises* (raspberries).

LYON AND THE AUVERGNE. The city of Lyon reigns supreme in the world of *haute cuisine*. A typical delicacy consists of an unmentionable bull's organ prepared in a subtle, creamy sauce. Other delicacies include organs such as brain, stomach, and intestines. Finish off with *tarte tatin*, an apple tart baked upside-down. Within the heartland of France, the farm kitchens of the **Auvergne** simmer with rich food—pork, cabbage, veal, turnips, and potatoes. Try *potée* (pork stew) or *tripoux* (sheep's feet stuffed with sheep's stomach). Tarts and jams are filled with apricots from local orchards. The acclaimed *cantal* cheese is called *fourme*, a term from which the French derived *fromage*.

BURGUNDY. By learning a few colorful words, you can taste your way to connoisseurship of the finest Burgundian wines. It can be *fruité* (fruity), *moelleux* (mellow), *vif* (lively), or *velouté* (velvety). Châteaux feature whites such as the dry Pouilly-sur-Loire from Nièvre and Chablis from L'Yonne, and full-bodied reds including Vougeot, Gevrey-Chambertin, Nuits-St-George, and Corton from the Côte d'Or and Givry from Saône-et-Loire. Delectable cuisine includes *gougères* (puffed pastry filled with cabbage or cheese), *hélix pomatia* (snails) in butter and garlic, and the esteemed *bœuf bourguignon*. The *jambon persillé* (a gelatin mold of ham and parsley) may be an acquired taste, but the traditional *coq au vin* (chicken in wine sauce) is fantastic from the start. Desserts include *pain d'épices* (gingerbread) and pastries filled with cherries and black currants.

BERRY-LIMOUSIN. While **Berry** produces wines of the highest quality—those of Sancerre, Menetou-Salon, Châteaumeillant, and Valençay are particularly well-known—local specialties such as *soupe au pain* (bread soup) sound less than enticing. Instead, try *poulet en barbouille*, chicken roasted over a fire, cut in pieces, and then simmered in a creamy sauce made of its own blood mixed with cream, egg yolk, and liver. **Limousin** is renowned throughout France for its beef and lamb, often garnished with walnuts, honey, *chèvre*, and local mushrooms. Local fruit-based liqueurs are also highly regarded; try one with *clafoutis*, a pudding-like dessert made of a light, eggy dough baked with black cherries.

ALSACE. Germanic influences are rampant in Alsatian cuisine. Traditional dishes are *tarte à l'oignon* (onion pie), *choucroute garnie* (sauerkraut cooked in white wine sauce and topped with sausages and ham), and *coq au Riesling* (chicken in white wine sauce). Alsace's much-touristed wine route boasts the dry Riesling, one of the world's finest whites. In the **Jura**'s wine route, vineyards stretching from Arbois to Lons-le-Saunier produce respectable *appellations* with a decidedly fruity flair, including the famous *vin jaune*. Cooks in **Lorraine** make up in heartiness what they lack in delicacy; bacon, butter, and cream are key ingredients in artery-hardening dishes like *quiche lorraine*. Desserts include *madeleines* (delicate vanilla biscuit) from Commercy and *macarons* from Nancy.

THE NORTH. Top it all off with some bubbly in **Champagne,** famous for the delicious intoxicant that bears its name. In **Flanders,** beer and *moules* (mussels) swathed in an astounding variety of sauces abound. And finally, in **Picardy,** it's *pâté de canard* (duck pâté), *flamiche aux poireaux* (a creamy quiche-like tart with leeks), and *ficelle Picarde* (a cheese, ham, and mushroom crêpe).

Hungry yet?

ESSENTIALS

DOCUMENTS AND FORMALITIES

ENTRANCE REQUIREMENTS

Passport (p. 30). Required for all non-EU citizens, plus UK and Irish citizens.

Visa (p. 33). For all stays, required of citizens of South Africa. Over 90 days, required of Australian, Canadian, New Zealand, and US citizens.

Work Permit (p. 32). Required for Australian, Canadian, New Zealand, South African, and US citizens.

FRENCH CONSULAR SERVICES ABROAD

Always call ahead, since different services have varying opening hours; those listed are for visa concerns. Most consulates will also receive inquiries in the afternoon, provided you call ahead and make an appointment.

Australia, Consulate General, Level 26 St. Martins Tower, 31 Market St., Sydney NSW 2000. ☎(02) 92 61 57 79; fax (02) 92 83 12 10; cgsydney@france.net.au; www.france.net.au/consulat/index.htm. Open M-F 9am-1pm.

Canada, Consulate General, 1 pl. Ville Marie, 26th floor, Montréal, QC H3B 4SE. ☎514 878 43 85; fax 514 878 39 81; www.consulfrance-montreal.org. Open M-F 8:30am-noon. Consulat général de France à Québec, Maison Kent, 25 rue Saint-Louis, Québec, QC G1R 3Y8. ☎418 694 22 94; fax 418 694 22 97; www.consulfrance-quebec.org. Open M-F 9am-12:30pm. Consulat Général de France à Toronto, 130 Bloor St. West, Suite 400, Toronto, ON M5S 1N5. ☎416-925 80 41; fax (416) 925 30 76; www.consulfrance-toronto.org. Open M-F 9am-12:30pm.

Ireland, French Embassy, Consulate Section, 36 Ailesbury Rd., Ballsbridge, Dublin 4. ☎(1) 260 16 66; fax (1) 283 01 78; www.ambafrance.ie. Open M-F 9:30am-12:30pm.

New Zealand, New Zealand Embassy and Consulate, 34-42 Manners St., P.O. Box 11-343, Wellington. ☎(04) 384 25 55; fax (04) 384 25 77. Open M-F 9am-1pm. French Honorary Consulate in Auckland, P.O. Box 1433, Auckland. ☎(09) 379 58 50; fax (09) 358 70 68; www.dree.org/nouvelle-zelande.

South Africa, Consulate General at Johannesburg, 191 Jan Smuts Ave., Rosebank, mailing address: PO Box 1027, Parklands 2121 (if you live in Gauteng, KwazuluNatal, Free State, Mpumalanga, Northern Province, North West Province or in Lesotho). ☎(011) 778 56 00, visas ☎(011) 778 56 05; fax (011) 778 56 01. Open M-F 8:30am-1pm. If you live in the Northern Cape, Eastern Cape or Western Cape, consult the Consulate General at Cape Town, 2 Dean St., Gardens, mailing address: P.O. Box 1702 Cape Town 8000. ☎(021) 423 1575; fax (021) 424 84 70; www.consulfrance.co.za (for both consulates). Open M-F 9am-12:30pm.

United Kingdom, Consulate General, P.O. Box 520, 21 Cromwell Rd., London SW7 2EN. ☎(020) 7838 2000; fax (020) 7838 20001; www.ambafrance.org.uk. Open M-W 8:45am-3pm, Th-F 8:45am-noon. Visa service: P.O. Box 57, 6a Cromwell Pl., London SW7 2EW. ☎(020) 7838 2050. Open M-F 9-10am and 1:30-2:30pm.

United States, Consulate General, 4101 Reservoir Rd. NW, Washington D.C. 20007. ☎202-944-6195; fax 202-944-6148; www.consulfrance-washington.org. Open M-F 8:45am-12:45pm. Visa service: ☎202-944-6200 (M-F 2-5pm, answering machine 8:45am-12:45pm); fax 202-944-6212. Consulates also located in Atlanta, Boston, Chicago, Houston, New Orleans, Los Angeles, Miami, New York, and San Francisco. See www.info-france-usa.org/america/consulat/consulat.htm for more info.

FOREIGN CONSULAR SERVICES IN FRANCE

Call before visiting any of these embassies, since various services have different hours of availability. Visa services tend to be available only in the morning. If you find yourself in serious trouble, call your country's embassy or consulate; they should be able to provide legal advice, and may be able to advance you some money in a dire emergency. But don't expect them to get you out of every scrape: you must always abide by French law while in France and if you are arrested the consulate can do little but point you toward a lawyer. Dual citizens of France cannot call on the consular services of their second nationality for assistance.

AUSTRALIA. Australian Embassy and Consulate, 4 rue Jean Rey, 75724 Paris Cedex 15 (☎01 40 59 33 00; fax 01 40 50 33 10; after-hours emergency ☎01 40 59 33 01; www.austgov.fr). Open 9:15am-noon and 2-4:30pm.

CANADA. Canadian Embassy and Consulate, 35 Ave. Montaigne, 75008 Paris (☎01 44 43 29 00). Hours: 9am-noon and 2-5pm. General Delegation of **Quebec,** 66 rue Pergolèse, 75116 Paris (☎01 40 67 85 00; www.mri.gouv.qc.ca/paris/).

IRELAND. Embassy of Ireland, 12 Avenue Foch, 75116 Paris (☎01 44 17 67 00; fax 01 44 17 67 60; irembparis@wanadoo.fr). Open M-F 9:30am-noon. Also in Antibes, Cherbourg, Lyon, and Monaco.

NEW ZEALAND. New Zealand Embassy and Consulate, 7 ter rue Leonardo da Vinci, 75116 Paris (☎01 45 01 43 43; fax 01 45 01 26 39; NZEMBASSY.PARIS@wanadoo.fr). Open July-Aug. M-Th 8:30am-1pm and 2-5:30pm, F 8:30am-2pm; Sept.-June M-F 9am-1pm and 2-5:30pm.

SOUTH AFRICA. South African Embassy, 59 Quai d'Orsay, 75007 Paris; mailing address 59 Quai d'Orsay 75343 Paris Cedex 07 (☎01 53 59 23 23; www.afrique-sud.net). Open M-F 8:30am-5:15pm; consular services 8:30am-noon.

UNITED KINGDOM. British Embassy, Consulate Section, 18bis rue d'Anjou, 75008 Paris (☎01 44 51 31 02; www.amb-grandebretagne.fr). Open M-F 9:30am-12:30pm and 2:30-5pm.

UNITED STATES. Consulate General, 2 rue Saint-Florentin 75001. (☎01 43 12 22 22; www.amb-usa.fr). M: Concorde. Open M-F 9am-3pm, notarial services 9am-noon. Don't wait in the long line; go to the right and tell the guard that you are there for American services. Also in **Bordeaux, Marseille, Strasbourg, Lyon, Rennes, Toulouse,** and **Nice,** visa services only in Paris.

PASSPORTS

REQUIREMENTS. Citizens of Australia, Canada, Ireland, New Zealand, South Africa, and the US need valid passports to enter France and to re-enter their own country. France does not allow entrance if the holder's passport expires in under three months after the expected date of departure; returning home with an expired passport is illegal and may result in a fine.

PHOTOCOPIES. Be sure to photocopy the page of your passport with your photo, passport number, and other identifying info, as well as any visas, travel insurance policies, plane tickets, or traveler's check serial numbers. Carry one set of copies in a safe place, apart from the originals, and leave another set at home. Consulates also recommend that you carry an expired passport or an official copy of your birth certificate in a part of your baggage separate from other documents.

LOST PASSPORTS. If you lose your passport in France, immediately notify the local police and the nearest embassy or consulate of your home government. To expedite replacement, you will need to know all info contained in the lost passport and show identification and proof of citizenship. A replacement may take weeks to process and it may be valid only for a limited time. Any visas stamped in your old passport will be irretrievably lost. In an emergency, ask for immediate temporary traveling papers that will permit you to re-enter your home country. Your passport is a public document belonging to your nation's government. You may have to surrender it to a foreign government official, but if you don't get it back in a reasonable amount of time, inform the nearest mission of your home country.

NEW PASSPORTS. Citizens of Australia, Canada, Ireland, New Zealand, the UK, and the US can apply for a passport at the nearest post office, passport office, or court of law. Citizens of South Africa can apply for a passport at the nearest office of Foreign Affairs. Any new passport or renewal applications must be filed well in advance of the departure date, although most passport offices offer rush services for a very steep fee. Citizens living abroad who need a passport or renewal services should contact the nearest consular service of their home country.

Australia: Info ☎13 12 32; www.dfat.gov.au/passports. Apply at a post office, passport office (in Adelaide, Brisbane, Canberra, Darwin, Hobart, Melbourne, Newcastle, Perth, or Sydney), or overseas diplomatic mission. AUS$128 (32-page) or AUS$192 (64-page); valid for 10 years. Children AUS$64 (32-page) or AUS$96 (64-page); valid for 5 years.

Canada: Canadian Passport Office, Department of Foreign Affairs and International Trade, Ottawa, ON K1A OG3 (☎613-994-3500 or 800-567-6868; www.dfait-maeci.gc.ca/passport). Applications available at passport offices, Canadian missions, and post offices. Passports CDN$60; valid for 5 years (non-renewable).

Ireland: Pick up an application at a *Garda* station or post office, or request one from a passport office. Then apply by mail to the Department of Foreign Affairs, Passport Office, Molesworth St., Dublin 2 (☎(01) 671 1633; fax 671 1092; www.irlgov.ie/iveagh), or the Passport Office, Irish Life Building, 1A South Mall, Cork (☎(021) 27 25 25). Passports IR£45; valid for 10 years. Under 18 or over 65 IR£10; valid for 3 years.

New Zealand: Send applications to the Passport Office, Department of International Affairs, P.O. Box 10526, Wellington, New Zealand (☎(0800) 22 50 50 or (4) 474 8100; fax (4) 474 8010; passports@dia.govt.nz; www.passports.govt.nz). Standard processing time is 10 working days. Passports NZ$80; valid for 10 years. Children NZ$40; valid for 5 years. 3 day "urgent service" NZ$160; children NZ$120.

South Africa: Department of Home Affairs. Passports are issued only in Pretoria, but all applications must still be submitted or forwarded to the nearest South African consulate. Processing time is 3 months or more. Passports around ZAR80; valid for 10 years. Under 16 around ZAR60; valid for 5 years. For more info, check out www.usaembassy.southafrica.net/VisaForms/Passport/Passport2000.html.

United Kingdom: Info ☎(0870) 521 0410; www.open.gov.uk/ukpass/ukpass.htm. Get an application from a passport office, main post office, travel agent, or online (for UK residents only) at www.ukpa.gov.uk/forms/f_app_pack.htm. Then apply by mail or in person at a passport office. Passports UK£28; valid for 10 years. Under 15 UK£14.80; valid for 5 years. The process takes about 4 weeks; faster service (by personal visit to the offices listed above) costs an additional UK£12.

United States: Info ☎202-647-0518; www.travel.state.gov/passport_services.html. Apply at any federal or state courthouse, authorized post office, or US Passport Agency (in most major cities); see the "US Government, State Department" section of the telephone book or a post office for addresses. Processing takes 3-4 weeks. New passports US$60; valid for 10 years. Under 18 US$40; valid for 5 years. Passports may be renewed by mail or in person for US$40. Add US$35 for 3-day expedited service.

ONE EUROPE. The idea of European unity has come a long way since 1958, when the European Economic Community (EEC) was created in order to promote solidarity and cooperation between its six founding states. Since then, the EEC has become the European Union (EU), with political, legal, and economic institutions spanning 15 member states: Austria, Belgium, Denmark, Finland, France, Germany, Greece, Ireland, Italy, Luxembourg, the Netherlands, Portugal, Spain, Sweden, and the UK.

What does this have to do with the average non-EU tourist? In 1999 the EU established **freedom of movement** across 14 European countries–the entire EU minus Denmark, Ireland, and the UK, but plus Iceland and Norway. This means that border controls between participating countries have been abolished and visa policies harmonized. While you're still required to carry a passport (or government-issued ID card for EU citizens) when crossing an internal border, once you've been admitted into one country, you're free to travel to all participating states. Britain and Ireland have also formed a **common travel area,** abolishing passport controls between the UK and the Republic of Ireland. This means that the only times you'll see a border guard within the EU are traveling between the British Isles and the Continent and in and out of Denmark.

For more important consequences of the EU for travelers, see **The Euro (p. 35)** and **European Customs** and **EU customs regulations** (p. 34).

VISAS AND WORK PERMITS

French visas are valid for travel in any of the states of the EU common travel area (the entire Union except the UK, Ireland, and Denmark, plus Iceland and Norway); however if the primary object of your visit is a country other than France you should apply to their consulate for a visa. All visitors to France are required to register their presence with the police in the town in which they are staying; this is normally done automatically by hotels and hostels and when signing a lease with a landlord. Double-check on entrance requirements at the nearest French Embassy or Consulate (listed under **Embassies & Consulates,** on p. 29) for up-to-date info before departure. US citizens can also consult the website at www.pueblo.gsa.gov/cic_text/travel/foreign/foreignentryreqs.html.

VISITS OF UNDER 90 DAYS. Citizens of South Africa need a **short-stay visa** (*court séjour*). To apply, your passport must be valid for three months past the date you intend to leave France. In addition, you must submit two passport-sized photos, proof of a hotel reservation or an organized tour or, if you intend to stay with relatives or friends, a certificate of accommodation stamped by the police station or town hall (2 copies) or if you intend to work, a letter from your employer, a return ticket, and proof of medical insurance. A transit visa (1 or 2 entries of 1 or 2 days each) costs ZAR69.79; single/multiple entry visa for 30 days or under costs ZAR174.46; for 31-90 days, the cost is ZAR209.35 for single entry, or ZAR244.24 for multiple entries. Apply for a visa at your nearest French consulate; short-stay visas for South African nationals usually take 2 days to process.

VISITS OF OVER 90 DAYS. All non-EU citizens need a **long-stay visa** (*long séjour*) for stays of over 90 days. Requirements vary according to the nature of your stay; contact your French consulate. The visa itself can take two months to process and costs 650F. US citizens can take advantage of the Center for International Business and Travel (CIBT, ☎800-925-2428), which will secure visas for travel to almost all countries for a service charge. Within 60 days of their arrival, all foreigners (including EU citizens) who plan to stay over 90 days must apply for a **temporary residence permit** (*carte de séjour temporaire*).

STUDY AND WORK PERMITS. Only EU citizens have the right to work and study in France without a visa. Others wishing to study in France must apply for a special student visa. For more info, see **Alternatives to Tourism,** p. 77.

IDENTIFICATION

French law requires that all people carry a form of official identification—either a passport or an EU government-issued identity card. The police have the right to demand to see identification at any time and you risk running a large fine if you do not comply. Minority travelers, especially black and Arab travelers, should be especially careful to carry proof that they are in France legally. In general when traveling it is advisable to carry two or more forms of identification, including a photo ID. A passport combined with a driver's license or birth certificate usually serves as adequate proof of your identity and citizenship. Many establishments, especially banks, require several IDs before cashing traveler's checks. Never carry all your forms of ID together, however; you risk being left entirely without ID or funds in case of theft or loss. It is useful to carry extra passport-size photos to affix to the various IDs or railpasses you may acquire, although photo booths can be found in just about every métro station.

For more info on all the forms of identification listed below, contact the **International Student Travel Confederation (ISTC),** Herengracht 479, 1017 BS Amsterdam, Netherlands (☎+31 20 421 2800; fax 421 2810; www.istc.org).

TEACHER & STUDENT IDENTIFICATION. The **International Student Identity Card (ISIC),** the most widely accepted form of student ID, provides discounts on sights, accommodations, food, and transport. The ISIC is preferable to an institution-specific card (such as a university ID) because it is more likely to be recognized (and honored) abroad. All cardholders have access to a 24hr. emergency helpline for medical, legal, and financial emergencies (in North America call 877-370-ISIC, elsewhere call US collect +1 715-345-0505, UK collect +44 20 8762 8110, or France collect +33 155 633 144), and holders of US-issued cards are also eligible for insurance benefits (see **Insurance,** p. 45). Many student travel agencies issue ISICs, including STA Travel in Australia and New Zealand; Travel CUTS in Canada; usit in the Republic of Ireland and Northern Ireland; SASTS in South Africa; Campus Travel and STA Travel in the UK; Council Travel (www.counciltravel.com/idcards/default.asp) and STA Travel in the US (see p. 57).

The card is valid from September of one year to December of the following year and costs US$22. Applicants must be degree-seeking students of a secondary or post-secondary school and must be of at least 12 years of age. Because of the proliferation of fake ISICs, some services (particularly airlines) require additional proof of student identity, such as a school ID or a letter attesting to your student status, signed by your registrar and stamped with your school seal. The **International Teacher Identity Card (ITIC)** offers the same insurance coverage as well as similar but limited discounts. The fee is US$22.

YOUTH IDENTIFICATION. The International Student Travel Confederation also issues a discount card to travelers who are 26 years old or under, but are not students. This one-year **International Youth Travel Card** (**IYTC;** formerly the **GO 25** Card) offers many of the same benefits as the ISIC. Most organizations that sell the ISIC also sell the IYTC (US$22).

ISICONNECT SERVICE. If you are an ISIC card carrier, you can activate your ISIC's ISIConnect service, an integrated communications service. With ISIConnect, one toll-free access number (☎0800-900-850 in France) gives you access to several different methods of keeping in touch via the phone and Internet, including a 24hr. emergency **help line.** To activate your ISIConnect account, visit the service's website (www.isiconnect.ekit.com).

CUSTOMS

RECLAIMING VALUE-ADDED TAX. Most purchases in France include a 20.6% value-added tax (**TVA** is the French acronym, VAT the English). Non-EU residents (including EU citizens who reside outside the EU) in France for less than six

CUSTOMS IN THE EU. As well as freedom of movement of people within the EU (see p. 32), travelers in the EU member countries (Austria, Belgium, Denmark, Finland, France, Germany, Greece, Ireland, Italy, Luxembourg, the Netherlands, Portugal, Spain, Sweden, and the UK) can also take advantage of the freedom of movement of goods. This means that there are no customs controls at internal EU borders (i.e. you can take the blue customs channel at the airport) and travelers are free to transport whatever legal substances they like as long as it is for their own personal (non-commercial) use–up to 800 cigarettes, 10L of spirits, 90L of wine (60L of sparkling wine), and 110L of beer–that's more than enough you lush! You should also be aware that duty-free was abolished in 1999 for travel between EU member states; however, travelers between the EU and the rest of the world still get a duty-free allowance when passing through customs.

months can reclaim 17.1% of the total price on purchases over 1200F made in one store. Only certain stores participate in this **vente en détaxe** refund process; ask before you buy. You must show a non-EU passport or proof of non-EU residence at the time of purchase and ask the vendor for a *bordereau de détaxe* form in triplicate; make sure that they fill it out, including your bank details. When leaving the country, present the receipt for the purchase together with the completed form to a French customs official and have the goods in question at hand. If you're at an airport, look for the window labeled *douane de détaxe* and be sure to budget at least two hours for this exquisitely painful encounter with French bureaucracy. On a train, find an official (they won't find you) or get off at a station close to the border. Eventually the refunds will work their way into your account. Some shops will exempt you from paying the tax at the time of purchase; you must still complete the above process. Note that food products, tobacco, medicine, unmounted precious stones, cars, and "cultural goods" do not qualify for a refund.

GOING HOME. Upon returning home, you must declare all articles acquired abroad exceeding the allowance established by your country's customs service, and pay duty on them. There is normally a separate, smaller allowance for goods and gifts purchased at **duty-free** shops abroad; if you exceed this you must declare and pay duty and possibly sales tax on them as well. "Duty-free" merely means that you need not pay a tax in the country of purchase. Note that duty free has been abolished for trips starting and ending within the EU.

To speed up your return, make a list of any valuables brought from home, along with their serial numbers, and register them with customs before departure. Keep all receipts for goods acquired abroad. For more info, contact:

Australia: Australian Customs National Information Line (in Australia ☎1300 363 263, from elsewhere call +61 (2) 6275 6666; www.customs.gov.au).

Canada: Canadian Customs, 2265 St. Laurent Blvd., Ottawa, ON K1G 4K3 (☎800-461-9999 (24hr.), from elsewhere call 204-983-3500; www.revcan.ca).

Ireland: Customs Information Office, Irish Life Mall, Lower Abbey St., Dublin 1 (☎(01) 878 8811; taxes@revenue.iol.ie; www.revenue.ie).

New Zealand: New Zealand Customhouse, 17-21 Whitmore St., Box 2218, Wellington (☎(04) 473 6099; fax 473 7370; www.customs.govt.nz).

South Africa: Customs and Excise, P.O. Box 13802, Tramshed, Pretoria 0001 (☎(012) 334-6400; fax (012) 328 6478; www.gov.za).

United Kingdom: Her Majesty's Customs and Excise, Passenger Enquiry Team, Wayfarer House, Great South West Road, Feltham, Middlesex TW14 8NP (☎(020) 8910 3744; fax 8910 3933; www.hmce.gov.uk).

United States: US Customs Service, 1300 Pennsylvania Ave. NW, Washington, D.C. 20229 (☎202-927-1000; www.customs.gov).

MONEY

If you stay in hostels and prepare your own food, you'll spend from 100-140F/€15.25-21.35 per person per day. **Accommodations** start at about 130F/€19.82 per night for a double, while a basic sit-down meal with wine costs 65F/€9.91. Personal checks from home will meet with blank refusal, and traveler's checks are not widely accepted outside tourist-oriented businesses; moreover, many establishments will only accept franc- or euro-denominated traveler's checks.

CURRENCY AND EXCHANGE

The national currency of France is the **franc français** or French Franc (abbreviated to FF or F), though it has now been superseded by the **euro** (symbol €; see box, below). Each franc is divided into 100 **centimes.** The franc is available in brightly colored 20F, 50F, 100F, 200F and 500F notes, smart two-tone 10F and 20F coins, silvery 5F, 2F, and 1F coins and pale copper 5, 10, 20, and 50 *centimes* pieces.

THE EURO. Since January 2001, the official currency of 12 members of the European Union—Austria, Belgium, Finland, France, Germany, Greece, Ireland, Italy, Luxembourg, the Netherlands, Portugal, and Spain—has been the euro. Actual euro banknotes and coins will be available beginning on January 1, 2002; but you shouldn't throw out your francs just yet. The old national currencies remain legal tender through July 1, 2002, after which it's all euros all the time. *Let's Go: France* lists prices in both euros (€) and francs (F).

The currency has some important—and positive—consequences for travelers hitting more than one euro-zone country. For one thing, money-changers across the euro-zone are obliged to exchange money at the official, fixed rate (see below), and at no commission (though they may still charge a small service fee). So now you can change your guilders into escudos and your escudos into francs without losing fistfuls of money on every transaction. Second, euro-denominated traveler's checks allow you to pay for goods and services across the euro-zone, again at the official rate and commission-free.

The exchange rate between euro-zone currencies was permanently fixed on January 1, 1999 at 1 EUR = 40.3399 BEF (Belgian francs) = 1.95583 DM (German marks) = 166.386 ESP (Spanish *pesetas*) = 6.55957 FRF (French francs) = 0.787564 IRE (Irish pounds) = 1936.27 ITL (Italian *lire*) = 40.3399 LUF (Luxembourg francs) = 2.20371 NLG (Dutch guilders) = 13.7603 ATS (Austrian schillings) = 200.482 PTE (Portuguese *escudos*) = 5.94573 FIM (Finnish *markka*). For more info, see www.europa.eu.int.

The currency chart below is based on published exchange rates from August 2001, except for the euro rate which is fixed permanently at the value given. For a quick conversion, note that one euro is approximately equal to one US dollar.

CURRENCY

EURO€1 = 6.56F	1F = EURO€0.15
US$1 = 7.27	1F = US$0.14
CDN$1 = 4.73F	1F = CDN$0.21
UK£1 =10.39F	1F = UK£0.10
IRE£1 = 8.33F	1F = IRE£0.12
AUS$1 = 3.80F	1F = AUS$0.26
NZ$1 = 3.13F	1F = NZ$0.32
ZAR1=0.88F	1F = ZAR1.14

As a general rule, it's cheaper to convert money in France. Bring enough foreign currency to last for the first 24-72 hours of a trip to avoid being penniless after banking hours or on a holiday. Travelers living in the US can get foreign currency from the comfort of their homes; **International Currency Express** (☎888-278-6628) will deliver foreign currency (for over 120 countries) or traveler's checks overnight (US$15) or second-day (US$12) at competitive exchange rates.

Watch out for commission rates and check newspapers for the standard rate of exchange. Banks generally have the best rates. Look for a better deal elsewhere if the bank or *bureau de change* has more than a 5% margin between its buy and sell prices. Since you lose money on each transaction, convert in large sums (unless the currency is depreciating rapidly). If you use traveler's checks or bills, carry some in small denominations (US$50 or less), especially for times when you are forced to exchange money at disadvantageous rates, but bring a range of denominations since charges may be levied per check cashed. Store your money in a variety of forms; ideally, you will at any given time be carrying some cash, some traveler's checks, and an ATM and/or credit card.

TRAVELER'S CHECKS

Traveler's checks are one of the safest and least troublesome means of carrying funds, since they can be refunded if stolen. Several agencies and banks sell them, usually with a small percentage commission. A number of places in France only accept traveler's checks in francs or euros, so keep that in mind when buying checks. **American Express** and **Visa** are the most widely recognized. If you're ordering checks from a bank, do so well in advance, especially if requesting large sums. American Express offices often sell traveler's checks in major currencies over the counter. Each agency provides refunds if your checks are lost or stolen and many provide additional services, such as toll-free refund hotlines in the countries you're visiting, emergency message services, and stolen credit card assistance.

In order to collect a **refund** for lost or stolen checks, keep your check receipts separate from your checks and store them in a safe place or with a traveling companion. Record check numbers when you cash them, leave a list of check numbers with someone at home, and ask for a list of refund centers when you buy your checks. Never countersign your checks until you are ready to cash them and always bring your passport with you when you plan to use the checks.

American Express: Call 800 25 19 02 in Australia; in New Zealand 0800 441 068; in the UK 0800 521 313; in the US and Canada 800-221-7282. Elsewhere call US collect +1 801-964-6665; www.aexp.com. Traveler's checks are available in francs at 1-4% commission at AmEx offices and banks, commission-free at AAA offices. *Cheques for Two* can be signed by either of 2 people traveling together. For lost traveler's checks in France call 0800 90 86 00.

Citicorp: In the US and Canada call 800-645-6556; elsewhere call US collect +1 813-623-1709. Traveler's checks (available only in US dollars, British pounds, and German marks) at 1-2% commission. Call 24hr.

Thomas Cook MasterCard: In the US and Canada call 800-223-7373; in the UK call 0800 62 21 01; elsewhere call UK collect +44 1733 31 89 50. Checks available in 13 currencies at 2% commission. Thomas Cook offices cash checks commission-free.

Visa: In the US call 800-227-6811; in the UK call 0800 89 50 78; elsewhere call UK collect +44 20 7937 8091. Call for the location of their nearest office.

CREDIT CARDS

Credit cards are accepted in most businesses in France, though normally only for purchases of over 100F/€15.25. Major credit cards can be used to extract cash advances in francs from associated banks and cash machines throughout France. Credit card companies get the wholesale exchange rate, which is generally 5% better than the retail rate used by banks and other currency exchange establishments. The most commonly accepted cards, in both businesses and cash machines, are **Visa** (also known as Carte Bleue), and **Mastercard** (also called Eurocard). French-issued credit cards are fitted with a micro-chip (such cards are known as *cartes à puce*) rather than a magnetic strip *(cartes à piste magnétique);* in untouristed areas, cashiers may attempt (and fail) to scan the card with a microchip reader. In such circumstances you should ask for a more senior staff member who (hopefully) will know to swipe your card through the magnetic strip reader. Self-service and cash machines should have no problem scanning magnetic cards. **American Express** cards also work in some cash machines, as well as at AmEx offices and major airports. All such machines require a **Personal Identification Number (PIN).** You must ask your credit card company for a PIN before you leave; without it, you will be unable to withdraw cash with your credit card outside your home country. If you already have a PIN, check with the company to make sure it will work in France. Credit cards often offer an array of other services, from insurance to emergency assistance. Check with your company to find out what is covered.

CREDIT CARD COMPANIES. Visa (US ☎800-336-8472) and MasterCard (US ☎800-307-7309) are issued in cooperation with banks and other organizations. American Express (US ☎800-843-2273) has an annual fee of up to US$55. AmEx cardholders may cash personal checks at AmEx offices abroad, access an emergency medical and legal assistance hotline (24hr.; in North America call 800-554-2639, elsewhere call US collect +1 715-343-7977), and enjoy American Express Travel Service benefits (including plane, hotel, and car rental reservation changes; baggage loss and flight insurance; mailgram and international cable services; and held mail). The Discover Card (in US call 800-347-2683, elsewhere call US +1 801-902-3100) offers cashback bonuses on most purchases, but it may not be accepted in France.

CASH CARDS

24-hour **cash machines** (also called **ATMs**) are widespread in France; they can normally be found at post offices as well as banks. Depending on the system that your home bank uses, you can probably access your personal bank account whenever you need money. ATMs get the same wholesale exchange rate as credit cards. Despite these perks, do some research before relying too heavily on automation. There is normally a limit on the amount of money you can withdraw per day (usually from 800-3000F/€122-457), and computer networks sometimes fail. Your home bank may also charge a fee for using ATM facilities abroad.

The two major international money networks are **Cirrus** (US ☎800-424-7787) and **PLUS** (US ☎800-843-7587). To locate ATMs around the world, call the above numbers, or consult www.visa.com/pd/atm or www.mastercard.com/atm.

CASH CARD ALERT. To use a cash or credit card to withdraw money from a machine in France, you must have a four-digit **Personal Identification Number (PIN).** These are not usually automatically assigned to credit cards, so ask your card issuer to assign you one before you leave. If your PIN is longer than four digits, ask your bank whether the first four digits will work. There are no letters on the keypads of most French cash machines, so use the following chart to work out your PIN: 1=QZ; 2=ABC; 3=DEF; 4=GHI; 5=JKL; 6=MNO; 7=PRS; 8=TUV; and 9= WXY. If you mistakenly punch the wrong code into a French machine three times it will swallow your card for good. If you **lose your card** in France, call the following numbers, all of which have English-speaking operators: **AmEx** (☎01 47 77 72 00), **Mastercard** (☎08 00 90 13 87), and **Visa** (☎08 00 90 11 79).

Visa TravelMoney is a system allowing you to access money from any ATM that accepts Visa cards. (For local customer assistance in France, call 08 00 90 12 35.) You deposit an amount before you travel (plus a small administration fee), and you can withdraw up to that sum. The cards, which give you the same favorable exchange rate for withdrawals as a regular Visa, are especially useful if you plan to travel through many countries. Obtain a card by either visiting a nearby Thomas Cook or Citicorp office, by calling toll-free in the US 877-394-2247 or checking with your local bank or to see if it issues TravelMoney cards. **Road Cash** (US ☎877-762-3227; www.roadcash.com) issues cards in the US with a minimum US$300 deposit.

GETTING MONEY FROM HOME

American Express: Cardholders can withdraw cash from their checking or current accounts without fees at any of AmEx's major offices and many of its representatives' offices, up to US$1000 every 21 days. AmEx also offers Express Cash at their ATMs in France. Express Cash withdrawals are automatically debited from the Cardmember's checking account or line of credit. AmEx Green card holders may withdraw up to US$1000 in a seven day period. For more info or to enroll in Express Cash, in the US ☎(800) CASH-NOW (227-4669); in the UK ☎(01273) 696 933; in Canada ☎800-716-6661; in Australia ☎ 800 230 100; in New Zealand ☎ 0800 109 109. The AmEx national number in France is ☎01 47 77 70 00.

Western Union: Travelers from the US, Canada, and the UK can wire money abroad through Western Union's international money transfer services. ☎(800) 325-6000 in the US; ☎0800 83 38 33 in the UK; ☎800-235-0000 in Canada; ☎01 08 25 00 98 98 in France. Rates for sending cash are generally US$10-11 cheaper than with a credit card, and the money is usually available within an hour. Western Union has offices in many French post offices; consult www.westernunion.com for the nearest location.

US State Department (US Citizens only): In dire emergencies only, the US State Department will forward money within hours to the nearest consular office, which will then disburse it according to instructions for a US$15 fee. Contact the Overseas Citizens Service division of the US State Department (☎202-647-5225; nights, Sundays, and holidays 647-4000).

TIPPING

By law, service must be included at all **restaurants, bars,** and **cafés** in France. It is not unheard of to leave extra change at a café or bar, maybe a franc or two per drink; exceptionally good service may be rewarded with a 5-10% tip. Otherwise, tipping is only expected for **taxis** and **hairdressers;** 10-15% is the norm. People like concierges may also expect to be tipped for services beyond the call of duty; in such cases, never tip less than 10F/€1.53.

SAFETY AND SECURITY

EMERGENCY AND CRISIS TELEPHONE NUMBERS	
	Police: ☎17
	Ambulance and info on nearby medical care: ☎15
	Fire *(pompiers)*: ☎18
	English language crisis line: ☎01 47 23 80 80 (3-11pm)

France has a far lower rate of violent crime than the US, but tourists are the biggest targets for petty and less than petty crimes. Con artists work singly or in gangs, and are often groups of children who surround you and go through your pockets while you flail away helplessly. Be especially suspicious in unexpected situations; do not respond or make eye contact, walk quickly away, and keep a solid grip on your belongings. Contact the police if a hustler is insistent or aggressive. If you are driving, keep your doors locked at all times and keep bags away

TRAVEL ADVISORIES. The following government offices provide travel information and advisories by telephone, by fax, or via the web:

Australian Department of Foreign Affairs and Trade: ☎(2) 6261 1111; www.dfat.gov.au.

Canadian Department of Foreign Affairs and International Trade (DFAIT): In Canada call 800-267-6788, elsewhere call +1-613-944-6788; www.dfait-maeci.gc.ca. Call for their free booklet, *Bon Voyage...But.*

New Zealand Ministry of Foreign Affairs: ☎(04) 494 8500; fax 494 8511; www.mft.govt.nz/trav.html.

United Kingdom Foreign and Commonwealth Office: ☎(020) 7238 4503; fax 7238 4545; www.fco.gov.uk.

US Department of State: ☎202-647-5225, auto faxback 202-647-3000; http://travel.state.gov. For *A Safe Trip Abroad,* call 202-512-1800.

from the windows; scooter-borne thieves often snatch purses and bags from cars stopped at lights. In **Paris,** be especially careful on public transportation at rush hour and on the way to and from the airport. Theft is also common on Métro line #1 and at department stores, particularly on the escalators. Additionally, the RER B line to de Gaulle Airport in Paris is a known pickpocketer haunt. At all **airports and train stations,** be vigilant with your baggage, and also be sure to take a **licensed taxi,** as unlicensed drivers are often out to scam you. Outside Paris, tourist-related crime is most prevalent on the **Côte d'Azur,** as well as in **Marseille** and **Montpellier.**

BLENDING IN

What may look perfectly innocuous in Miami will mark you out instantly in Menton. The French are known for their conservative stylishness—it's unlikely you'll be able to compete with them. Go for restrained sneakers or closed shoes, solid-color pants or jeans, and plain T-shirts or button-down shirts, rather than Teva sandals, baggy pants, or torn jeans. French people rarely wear shorts, but if you choose to wear them, they shouldn't be too short. For women, skirts or dresses are more appropriate, especially in summer. Carrying a large bag with you everywhere is another giveaway, as well as a burden—leave it behind in the hostel.

Women and men should dress conservatively when going into churches. Women should wear long pants or a long skirt and cover their shoulders; men should remove their hats and cover their upper bodies. Beach wear is unacceptable and may preclude your entrance if guards are vigilant.

Familiarize yourself with your surroundings before setting out; if you must check a map on the street, duck into a café, shop, or doorway. Also, carry yourself with confidence. If you are traveling alone, be sure that someone at home knows your itinerary and **never admit that you're traveling alone.** If night falls and you're nervous, find a well-lit street with many cars and walk along it, no matter how much time this adds to your walk home.

DRIVING

The French have a deserved reputation for aggressive and dangerous driving. They regularly flout the speed limits on their albeit excellent roads and often flout them drunk. Corsican roads are some of the most lethal in Europe; think twice about driving here and don't be intimidated by drivers trying to overtake you on narrow, twisting coast roads. Always be on the look out for mopeds, especially in the south; they can speed out from narrow alleys or pedestrian zones. Wearing a seatbelt is required by law of all passengers. In cities, and especially on the Côte d'Azur, be sure to park your vehicle in a well-lit area. Sleeping in your car is one of the most dangerous (and often illegal) ways to get your rest; don't do it. If your car breaks down on an autoroute, wait for the police to assist you. *Let's Go* does not recommend hitchhiking under any circumstances, particularly for women—see **Getting Around,** p. 63, for more info on not doing this.

SELF DEFENSE

There is no sure-fire way to avoid being harassed, but a good self-defense course will give you ways to avoid attack and concrete ways to respond to it. **Impact, Prepare, and Model Mugging** can refer you to local self-defense courses in the US (☎800-345-5425) and Vancouver (☎604-878-3838). Workshops (2-3hr.) start at US$50; full courses run US$350-500.

FINANCIAL SECURITY

PROTECTING YOUR VALUABLES. Don't keep all your valuables and documents in one place, or they'll all get stolen at once. **Photocopies** of important documents help you to recover them in case they are lost or filched. Carry one copy separate from the documents and leave another copy at with a friend at home. Label every piece of luggage both inside and out. Don't put a wallet in your back pocket. Never count your money in public and carry as little as possible. If you carry a handbag, buy a sturdy one with a secure clasp and carry it crosswise on the side, away from the street with the clasp against you. Secure packs with small combination padlocks. A **money belt** combines convenience and security and is the best way to carry cash; you can buy one at most camping stores. A **neck pouch** is equally safe, although far less accessible; refrain from pulling it out in public. Keep some money separate from the rest to use in an emergency or in case of theft.

ACCOMMODATIONS AND TRANSPORTATION. Never leave your belongings unattended. If you feel unsafe, look for places with either a curfew or a night attendant. Lockers are available in many hostels and a few major train stations: *Let's Go* lists availability. You may need your own padlock for hostel lockers. Most hotels also provide lock boxes free or for a minimal fee.

Be particularly careful on **buses,** carry your backpack in front of you where you can see it, and don't trust anyone to "watch your bag for a second." Thieves thrive on **trains,** particularly on the Rome-to-Nice line running up the coast; professionals wait for tourists to fall asleep and then carry off everything they can. Keep important documents and other valuables on your person and try to sleep on top bunks with your luggage stored above you (if not in bed with you). If you travel by car, take any valuable possessions with you when you leave the car. Lock all bags out of sight in the trunk.

DRUGS, DRINKS, AND SMOKES

Possession of **illegal drugs** (including marijuana) in France can end your vacation abruptly; convicted offenders should expect a jail sentence and fines. Never bring any illegal drugs across a border. It is vital that **prescription drugs,** particularly insulin, syringes, or narcotics, be accompanied by the prescriptions themselves and a statement from a doctor and left in original, labeled containers. In France, police may stop and search anyone on the street—no reason is required. It is not unknown for pushers to boost their profits by selling drugs to a tourist and then turning him in to the authorities for a reward. If you are arrested, your home country's consulate can provide a list of attorneys and tell your family and friends, but it can't get you out of jail. For more info, write the Bureau of Consular Affairs, Public Affairs #6831, Department of State, Washington, D.C. 20520 (☎202-647-1488).

The French like to drink, but they do it carefully. Virtually no one drinks "to get drunk" and only winos and the youngest of teenagers drink on the street. Restaurants may serve alcohol to children as young as 14. Though smoking is officially banned in public places, and many restaurants designate non-smoking areas, the French light up just about anywhere. If you are a smoker, you will feel like you're in friendly territory; if not, you may have a difficult time either dealing with the ubiquitous smoke clouds or convincing anyone to put out his *clope*.

HEALTH

Common sense is the simplest prescription for good health. Travelers complain most often about their feet and their gut, so take precautionary measures; drink lots of fluids to prevent dehydration and constipation, wear sturdy, broken-in shoes and clean socks, and use talcum powder to keep your feet dry.

BEFORE YOU GO

Preparation, preparation, preparation. For minor health problems bring a compact **first-aid kit. Contact lens** wearers who use heat disinfection might consider switching to chemical cleansers. Moleskin or similar blister protection will come in handy. Additionally, women report being unable to find applicator **tampons** with in France, though other kinds are available at pharmacies and groceries.

In your **passport,** write the names of any people you want contacted in case of a medical emergency and list any **allergies** or medical conditions. Allergy sufferers might want to obtain a full supply of any necessary medication before the trip. Matching a prescription to its foreign equivalent is not always easy, safe, or possible. Carry up-to-date, legible prescriptions or a statement from your doctor giving the medication's trade name, manufacturer, chemical name, and dosage. While traveling, be sure to keep all medication with you in your carry-on luggage.

USEFUL ORGANIZATIONS AND PUBLICATIONS. The US **Centers for Disease Control and Prevention** (CDC; ☎877-FYI-TRIP; www.cdc.gov/travel), is an excellent source of info for travelers. The comprehensive booklet *Health Information for International Travelers*, an annual rundown of disease, immunization, and general health advice, is free on the website or US$22 via the Government Printing Office (☎202-512-1800). The **US State Department** (http://travel.state.gov) compiles Consular Info Sheets on health, entry requirements, and other issues for various countries. For quick info on health and other travel warnings, call the **Overseas Citizens' Services** (☎202-647-5225; after-hours 647-4000), contact a US passport agency or a US embassy or consulate abroad, or send a self-addressed, stamped envelope to the Overseas Citizens' Services, Bureau of Consular Affairs, #4811, US Department of State, Washington, D.C. 20520. For info on medical evacuation services and travel insurance firms, see http://travel.state.gov/medical.html. The **British Foreign and Commonwealth Office** also gives health warnings (www.fco.gov.uk). Or try the **International Travel Health Guide,** Stuart Rose, MD (Travel Medicine, US$20; www.travmed.com). For general health info: **American Red Cross** (☎800-564-1234).

MEDICAL ASSISTANCE ON THE ROAD. Medical care in France is as good (and as expensive) as anywhere in the world and all but the smallest towns have a hospital, listed under the Practical Information for towns covered by *Let's Go.* Every town has a **24-hour pharmacy** *(pharmacie de garde);* this burden rotates among the various pharmacies in town. The police will be able to tell you which one is open on any given night; on Sundays pharmacies must post a list on their door saying which is on duty.

EU citizens can get reciprocal health benefits, entitling them to immediate urgent care, by filling out an **E-111** form before departure; this is available at major post offices. EU citizens studying in France also qualify for long-term care. Other travelers should ensure they have adequate medical insurance before leaving; if your regular **insurance** policy does not cover travel abroad, you may wish to purchase additional coverage. With the exception of Medicare, most health insurance plans cover members' medical emergencies during trips abroad; check with your insurance carrier to be sure. For more info, see **Insurance,** p. 45.

If you need a doctor **(un médecin),** call the local hospital for a list of nearby practitioners, or stop in at a pharmacy. If you are receiving reciprocal health care, make sure you call an **honoraires opposables** doctor, who will be linked to the state health care system. They may not charge more than 110F/€16.77 for a consultation at their surgery. Doctors described as **honoraires libres** can charge whatever they like, and their fees will not be reimbursed under reciprocal health care agreements. Hospitals generally have English-speaking staff. Note that the same medicines may go under different names in France from your home country; check with your doctor before you leave. RxList (http://www.rxlist.com) lists generic names for most drugs, along with the brand names they carry in foreign countries.

If you are concerned about **medical support,** try one of the following special services. The *MedPass* from **Global Emergency Medical Services (GEMS),** 2001 Westside Dr., #120, Alpharetta, GA 30004, USA (☎800-860-1111; fax 770-475-0058; www.globalems.com), provides 24-hour international medical assistance, support, and medical evacuation resources. The **International Association for Medical Assistance to Travelers** (IAMAT; US ☎716-754-4883, Canada ☎416-652-0137, New Zealand ☎03 352 2053; www.sentex.net/~iamat) has free membership and lists English-speaking doctors worldwide. If your regular **insurance** policy does not cover travel abroad, you may wish to purchase additional coverage (see p. 45).

Those with medical conditions (diabetes, allergies to antibiotics, epilepsy, heart conditions) may want to obtain a stainless-steel **Medic Alert** ID tag (first year US$35, annually thereafter US$20), which identifies the condition and gives a 24hr. collect-call number. Contact the Medic Alert Foundation, 2323 Colorado Ave, Turlock, CA 95382, USA (☎888-633-4298; www.medicalert.org). Diabetics can contact the **American Diabetes Association,** 1701 N. Beauregard St., Alexandria, VA 22311 (☎800-342-2383; www.diabetes.org) and request travel info.

OUTDOOR HAZARDS

Those hiking or spending a lot of time outdoors should be careful with their health. The summer heat can lead to rapid dehydration and sunburn. If you go mountaineering or on long-distance hikes in the Alps, the Pyrenees, or Corsica, remember that storms can strike in any season; every year adds a few to France's total number of ill-prepared, dead outdoorsmen. When hiking, plan your route carefully and tell the local authorities where you're going; see **Wilderness Safety, p. 52,** for more info.

Heat exhaustion and dehydration: Avoid heat exhaustion, whose symptoms include fatigue, headaches, and nausea, by eating salty foods and imbibing enough clear drinks to keep your urine clear. Stay off alcoholic and caffeinated drinks, which are dehydrating. Wear a hat and a lightweight long-sleeved shirt in hot sun, and take time to acclimatize to a hot destination before seriously exerting yourself. Continuous heat stress can eventually lead to **heatstroke,** characterized by rising body temperature, severe headache, and cessation of sweating. Heatstroke is rare but serious and victims must be cooled off with wet towels and taken to a doctor as soon as possible.

Hypothermia and frostbite: A rapid drop in body temperature is the clearest warning sign of overexposure to cold. Victims may also shiver, feel exhausted, have poor coordination or slurred speech, hallucinate, or suffer amnesia. Seek medical help, and **do not let hypothermia victims fall asleep**—it may prove fatal. To avoid hypothermia, keep dry, wear layers, and stay out of the wind. In wet weather, wool and synthetics such as pile retain heat. Most other fabrics, especially cotton, will make you colder. When the temperature is below freezing, watch for **frostbite.** If a region of skin turns white, waxy, and cold, do not rub the area. Drink warm beverages, get dry, and slowly warm the area with dry fabric or steady body contact, until a doctor can be found.

High altitude: Travelers to high altitudes must allow their bodies a couple of days to adjust to lower oxygen levels in the air before exerting themselves. At high altitude, alcohol is more potent, and the risk of sunburn is greater, even in cold weather.

PREVENTING DISEASE

TICK- AND INSECT-BORNE DISEASES. Many diseases are transmitted by insects and ticks. **Mosquitoes** are most active from dusk to dawn. Use insect repellents, wear long pants and long sleeves, and buy a mosquito net. Wear closed shoes and socks and tuck long pants into socks. Soak or spray your gear with permethrin, which is licensed in the US for use on clothing. Calamine lotion or topical cortisones (like Cortaid) may stop insect bites from itching, as can a bath with a half-cup of baking soda or oatmeal. **Ticks**—responsible for Lyme and other diseases—can be particularly dangerous in rural and forested regions. Pause periodically while walking to brush off ticks using a fine-toothed comb on your neck and scalp. Do not try to remove ticks by burning them or coating them with nail polish remover or petroleum jelly.

FOOD- AND WATER-BORNE DISEASES. Prevention is the best cure: be sure that everything you eat is cooked properly and that the water you drink is clean. This is unlikely to be a problem in France, although most French people drink mineral water as a matter of taste and style; in rural areas you may wish to imitate them.

Traveler's diarrhea in France is usually nothing more than your body's temporary reaction to bacteria in unfamiliar food ingredients and tends to last 3-7 days. If the nasties hit you, eat quick-energy, non-sugary foods with protein and carbohydrates to keep your strength up. Over-the-counter remedies (such as Immodium) provide symptomatic relief, but they can complicate serious infections; only use them in conjunction with rehydration salts. These can be purchased, but are simple to make: mix one cup of clean water with half a teaspoon of sugar or honey and a pinch of salt. Soft drinks without caffeine and salted crackers are also good. If you develop a fever or symptoms persist longer than five days, consult a doctor. If children develop diarrhea, consult a doctor, since treatment is different.

INFECTIOUS DISEASES

Rabies is transmitted through the saliva of infected animals and is fatal if untreated. If you are bitten, wash the wound thoroughly and seek immediate medical care. Once you begin to show symptoms (thirst and muscle spasms), the disease is in its terminal stage. A rabies vaccine is available but is only semi-effective.

Hepatitis B is a viral infection of the liver transmitted through transfer of bodily fluids, by sharing of needles, or during unprotected sex. Its incubation period varies widely. A person may not begin to show symptoms until many years after infection. Vaccination is recommended for health-care workers, sexually active travelers, and anyone planning to seek medical treatment abroad. Vaccination consists of a 3-shot series given over a period of time, and should begin 6 months before traveling.

Hepatitis C is like Hepatitis B, but the modes of transmission are different. Intravenous drug users, those with occupational exposure to blood, hemodialysis patients, or recipients of blood transfusions are at the highest risk, but the disease can also be spread through sexual contact and sharing of items like razors and toothbrushes.

RECENT DEVELOPMENTS

Mad Cow Disease: Bovine spongiform encephalopathy (BSE), better known as Mad Cow Disease, is a chronic degenerative disease affecting the central nervous system of cattle that broke out in alarming numbers of cattle in 2001. The human variant is called Cruetzfeldt-Jakob disease (nvCJD), and both forms involve invariably fatal brain diseases. Info on nvCJD is not conclusive, but the disease is supposedly caused by consuming infected beef; however, the risk is very small (around 1 case per 10 billion servings). It is believed that consuming milk and milk products does not pose a risk.

Foot and Mouth Disease (FMD): Foot and Mouth Disease experienced one of its worst outbreaks in 2001, largely in the United Kingdom and other countries in Western Europe. FMD is easily transmissible between cloven-hoofed animals (cows, pigs, sheep, goats and deer), but does not pose a health threat to humans, causing few or mild symptoms. Western European countries have not, as of publication, restricted travel to infested countries, but do limit excursions to farms and other rural areas. FMD is believed to be killed by heat, making cooked meats apparently safe for consumption.

AIDS, HIV, STDS

Acquired Immune Deficiency Syndrome (**AIDS; SIDA** in French) is a major problem in France; Paris has the largest HIV-positive community in Europe. There are as many heterosexuals infected as homosexuals in France, and among infected heterosexuals, more women than men. The easiest mode of HIV transmission is through direct blood-to-blood contact; *never* share intravenous drug, tattooing, or other needles. The most common mode of transmission is sexual intercourse. You can greatly reduce the risk by using latex condoms. (See **Women's Health,** p. 45.)

For detailed info on **AIDS** in France, call the **US Centers for Disease Control's** 24-hour hotline at ☎800-342-2437, or contact the **Joint United Nations Programme on HIV/AIDS (UNAIDS),** 20 av. Appia 20, CH-1211 Geneva 27, Switzerland (☎+41 (22) 791 36 66; fax 791 41 87). France's AIDS hotline can be called at 01 44 93 16 16. The Council on International Educational Exchange's pamphlet, *Travel Safe: AIDS and International Travel*, is posted on their website (www.ciee.org/Isp/safety/travelsafe.htm), along with links to other online and phone resources.

Sexually transmitted diseases (STDs) such as gonorrhea, chlamydia, genital warts, syphilis, and herpes are easier to catch than HIV and can be just as deadly. **Hepatitis B** and **C** are also serious STDs (see **Infectious Diseases,** above). Though condoms may protect you from some STDs, oral or even tactile contact can lead to transmission. Warning signs include swelling, sores, bumps or blisters on sex organs, the rectum, or the mouth; burning and pain during urination and bowel movements; itching around sex organs; swelling or redness of the throat; and flu-like symptoms. If these symptoms develop, see a doctor immediately.

WOMEN'S HEALTH

Women traveling in parts of France might be susceptible to **vaginal yeast infections,** a treatable but uncomfortable illness likely to flare up in hot and humid climates. Wearing loosely fitting trousers or a skirt and cotton underwear will help. Yeast infections can be treated with an over-the-counter remedy like Monistat (generic name "miconazole") or Gynelotrimin (generic name "clotrimazole"). Bring supplies from home if you are prone to infection, as they may be difficult to find.

Contraception is readily available in most pharmacies and supermarkets. To obtain **condoms** in France, visit a pharmacy and tell the clerk, "*Je voudrais une boîte de préservatifs*" (zhuh-voo-DRAY oon BWAHT duh PREY-zehr-va-TEEF).

Abortions, both surgical and pharmaceutical, have been difficult to get in France, but recent changes have relaxed the requirements. The pregnancy has to be fewer than 12 weeks along. Minors no longer need the permission of a parent or guardian, but simply of any legal adult. Non-EU citizens should check with their home insurance provider to find out whether or not they are covered. EU citizens have a reciprocal health care agreement in which abortions are covered if deemed medically necessary. Contact the French branch of the International Planned Parenthood Federation, the **Mouvement Français pour le Planning Familial** (**MFPF;** ☎01 48 07 29 10), which can supply the names of French hospitals and OB/GYN clinics performing abortions (approximately 3600F if not covered by insurance). Contact info for family planning centers in other countries can be obtained through the **International Planned Parenthood Federation,** European Regional Office, Regent's College Inner Circle, Regent's Park, London NW1 4NS (☎020 7487 7900), who can give you help in English.

INSURANCE

Travel insurance generally covers four basic areas: medical/health problems, property loss, trip cancellation/interruption, and emergency evacuation. Be sure to check whether your regular insurance policies extend to travel-related accidents; even if they do, you may consider purchasing travel insurance if the cost of potential trip cancellation/interruption or emergency medical evacuation is greater than you can absorb.

ESSENTIALS

US residents' **medical insurance** (especially university policies) often covers costs incurred abroad; check with your provider. **US Medicare does not cover foreign travel.** Canadians are protected by their home province's health insurance plan for up to 90 days after leaving the country; check with the provincial Ministry of Health or Health Plan Headquarters for details. **Homeowners' insurance** (or your family's coverage) often covers theft during travel and loss of travel documents (passport, plane ticket, railpass, etc.) up to US$500.

ISIC and **ITIC** (see p. 33) provide basic insurance benefits, including US$100 per day of in-hospital sickness for up to 60 days, US$3000 of accident-related medical reimbursement, and US$25,000 for emergency medical transport. Cardholders have access to a toll-free 24hr. helpline (run by the insurance provider TravelGuard) for medical, legal, and financial emergencies overseas (US and Canada ☎877-370-4742, elsewhere call US collect +1 715-345-0505). **American Express** (US ☎800-528-4800) grants most cardholders automatic car rental insurance (collision and theft, but not liability) and ground travel accident coverage of US$100,000 on flight purchases made with the card.

INSURANCE PROVIDERS. **Council** and **STA** (see p. 57) offer a range of plans that can supplement your basic coverage. Other private insurance providers in the US and Canada include: **Access America** (☎800-284-8300); **Globalcare Travel Insurance** (☎800-821-2488; www.globalcare-cocco.com); and **Travel Assistance International** (☎800-821-2828; www.worldwide-assistance.com). Providers in the **UK** include **Campus Travel** (☎01865 25 80 00) and **Columbus Travel Insurance** (☎020 7375 0011). In **Australia,** try **CIC Insurance** (☎9202 8000).

PACKING

Pack lightly: lay out only what you absolutely need, then take half the clothes and twice the money. The less you have, the less you have to lose (or store, or carry on your back). If you plan to do a lot of hiking, see the **Camping & the Outdoors,** p. 50.

CLOTHING. No matter when you're traveling, it's always a good idea to bring a **warm jacket** or wool sweater, a **rain jacket** (Gore-Tex® is both waterproof and breathable), sturdy shoes or **hiking boots,** and **thick socks. Flip-flops** or waterproof sandals are must-haves for grubby hostel showers. If you plan to visit any religious or cultural sites, which you likely will in France, remember that you'll need something besides tank tops and shorts to be respectful and even just to enter.

SLEEPSACK. Some hostels require that you either provide your own linen or rent sheets from them. Save cash by making your own sleepsack: fold a full-size sheet in half the long way, then sew it closed along the long side and one of the short sides.

CONVERTERS & ADAPTERS. In France, electricity is 220 volts AC, enough to fry any 110V North American appliance. 220/240V electrical appliances don't like 110V current, either. **Americans** and **Canadians** should buy an **adapter** (which changes the shape of the plug) and a **converter** (which changes the voltage). Don't make the mistake of using only an adapter (unless appliance instructions explicitly state otherwise). **New Zealanders** and **South Africans** as well as **Australians** won't need a converter, but will need a set of adapters to use anything electrical.

OTHER USEFUL ITEMS. A **basic first-aid** kit including bandages, pain reliever, antibiotic cream, a thermometer, a Swiss Army knife etc. is a good idea. For safety purposes, you should bring a **money belt** and small **padlock.** Basic **outdoors equipment** (plastic water bottle, compass, waterproof matches, pocketknife, sunglasses, sunscreen, hat) may also prove useful. **Quick repairs** of torn garments can be done on the road with a needle and thread; also consider bringing electrical tape for patching tears. **Other things** you're liable to forget: an umbrella; sealable **plastic bags** (for damp clothes, soap, food, shampoo, and other spillables); an **alarm clock;** safety pins; rubber bands; a flashlight; earplugs; garbage bags; and a small **calculator.**

IMPORTANT DOCUMENTS. Don't forget your passport, traveler's checks, ATM and/or credit cards, and adequate ID (see p. 33). Check that you have any of the following that might apply to you: a hosteling membership card (see p. 47); driver's license (see p. 33); travel insurance forms; and/or rail or bus pass (see p. 63).

ACCOMMODATIONS

HOSTELS

A HOSTELER'S BILL OF RIGHTS. There are certain standard features that we do not include in our hostel listings. Unless we state otherwise, you can expect that every hostel has: no lockout, no curfew, a kitchen, free hot showers, secure luggage storage, and no key deposit.

Hostels generally offer dormitory accommodations in large single-sex or coed rooms with 4-10 beds, though some have as many as 60 and some offer private rooms at reasonable prices. They sometimes offer kitchens and utensils for your use, bike rental, storage areas, and laundry facilities, as well as internet access. There can be drawbacks: some hostels close during certain daytime "lock-out" hours, have a curfew, don't accept reservations, and/or impose a maximum stay. In France, a bed in a hostel will average around 50-100F/€7.62-15.25.

If you plan to do a lot of hosteling, it is definitely worth joining **Hostelling International (HI)** before you leave home. In France, Hostelling International's affiliate is called **FUAJ,** the **Fédération Unie des Auberges de Jeunesse,** and it operates 178 hostels within France. Officially, all HI hostels require that you purchase a **membership card;** alternatively, you can buy a 19F/€2.90 stamp with each night you stay at an HI hostel, until you have purchased six stamps and are entitled to full membership. This membership policy is not always enforced; those hostels that do enforce it are generally listed as **"Members only"** in our accommodations coverage. Some accept reservations via the **International Booking Network** (Australia ☎02 9261 1111; Canada ☎800-663-5777; England and Wales ☎1629 58 14 18; Northern Ireland ☎1232 32 47 33; Republic of Ireland ☎01 830 1766; NZ ☎03 379 9808; Scotland ☎8701 55 32 55; US ☎800-909-4776; www.hostelbooking.com). Other hosteling resources include www.hostels.com/fr.html, www.hostelplanet.com, and www.eurotrip.com/hostels, which includes travelers' reviews of individual French hostels.

Australian Youth Hostels Association (AYHA), Level 3, 10 Mallett St., Camperdown NSW 2050 (☎02 9565 1699; fax 9565 1325; www.yha.org.au). AUS$52, under 18 AUS$16.

Hostelling International-Canada (HI-C), 400-205 Catherine St., Ottawa, ON K2P 1C3 (☎800-663-5777; fax 237-7868; www.hostellingintl.ca). CDN$35, under 18 free.

An Óige (Irish Youth Hostel Association), 61 Mountjoy St., Dublin 7 (☎01 830 4555; fax 830 5808; anoige@iol.ie; www.irelandyha.org). IR£10, under 18 IR£4.

Youth Hostels Association of New Zealand (YHANZ), P.O. Box 436, 193 Cashel St., 3rd Floor Union House, Christchurch 1 (☎03 379 9970; fax 365 4476; info@yha.org.nz; www.yha.org.nz). NZ$40, under 17 free.

Hostels Association of South Africa, 3rd fl. 73 St. George's St. Mall, P.O. Box 4402, Cape Town 8000 (☎021 424 2511; fax 424 4119; www.hisa.org.za). ZAR45.

Scottish Youth Hostels Association (SYHA), 7 Glebe Crescent, Stirling FK8 2JA (☎01786 89 14 00; fax 89 13 33; www.syha.org.uk). UK£6.

Youth Hostels Association (England and Wales) Ltd., Trevelyan House, 8 St. Stephen's Hill, St. Albans, Hertfordshire AL1 2DY (☎0870 870 8808; fax 01727 84 41 26; www.yha.org.uk). UK£12.50, under 18 UK£6.25, families UK£25.

Hostelling International Northern Ireland (HINI), 22-32 Donegall Rd., Belfast BT12 5JN (☎02890 31 54 35; fax 43 96 99; www.hini.org.uk). UK£10, under 18 UK£6.

Hostelling International-American Youth Hostels (HI-AYH), 733 15th St. NW, #840, Washington, D.C. 20005 (☎202-783-6161; fax 783-6171; hiayhserv@hiayh.org; www.hiayh.org). US$25, under 18 free.

HOTELS

Two or more people traveling together can often save money by staying in cheap hotels rather than hostels. The French government grants hotels between zero and four stars, depending on the facilities they provide. *Let's Go* chooses and ranks hotels according to such qualities as charm, friendliness, convenience, and value for money; most have zero stars or one, with a smattering of two stars. Hotels in each town are listed in our order of preference; particularly outstanding ones are awarded the **Let's Go thumb** (☒). Prices are generally per room, although *demi-pension* (half-board: includes room, breakfast, and/or dinner) and *pension* (room and all meals) are always quoted per person. A room described in this guide as "with bath" has both its own toilet and its own shower or bathtub. If the room is not so described, it doesn't. TV, telephone, and so on—really anything other than the presence or absence of a bathroom—are not consistently noted and their absence from a listing does not necessarily mean that the hotel lacks them. Hotels without 24-hour reception generally give out keys to guests, so "Reception 7pm-midnight" probably doesn't mean you'll have to dash home at midnight—but ask first to avoid being left out in the cold.

Expect to pay, at the very least, 110F/€16.77 for a single room and 130F/€19.82 for a double. If you want a room with twin beds, make sure to ask for *une chambre avec deux lits* (oon chAMBR-avEK duh LEE; a room with two beds); otherwise you may find yourself in *une chambre avec un grand lit* (oon chAMBR avEK anh grANH LEE; a room with a double bed). You may have to pay a **taxe de séjour** (residency tax) of 5-10F/€0.76-1.53 per person per night, depending on the region. Breakfast in hotels normally runs 25-40F/€3.81-6.10, which should include coffee or hot chocolate and bread and/or croissants; check whether it's obligatory—it usually is—because you may be able to get a better deal at a local café. Rooms in cheap hotels normally have no en suite facilities and often not even a sink; normally facilities are to be found in the hallway. Occasionally you will have to pay extra for a hot shower (10-25F/€2.29-3.81), and some very cheap hotels have no washing facilities at all; *Let's Go* notes this if it is the case. Otherwise, rooms can come with a variety of add-ons: *avec WC* or *avec cabinet* means with sink and toilet, *avec douche* means with shower, and *avec salle de bain* is with a full bathroom. Most bathrooms also have a *bidet*, a low toilet-like apparatus which is intended for cleaning genitalia. "Turkish toilets"—porcelain-rimmed holes in the floor—are becoming less common but still exist in many parts of France; put your feet where it says to, don't fall over, and make sure the light timer doesn't run out on you. All French hotels must display on the back of each room's door a list showing the prices of rooms, breakfast, and any residency tax. It is illegal for them to charge you more than is shown, though you can try to bargain for a lower rate if you are staying longer than a few days.

The hotels listed by *Let's Go* are generally small, family-run establishments close to sights of interest, but France also has a number of hotel chains that cater to the budget traveler. Found on the outskirts of most major towns, and often accessible only by car, unrated chains like *Hôtels Formule 1*, *Etap Hôtel*, and *Hôtels Première Classe* charge about 175-200F/€26.68-30.49 for one to three person rooms. All rooms have a sink and TV, with hall showers, toilets, and telephones. When the reception is closed, you can rent a room with your credit card.

If you plan to visit a popular tourist area, especially during a festival, it is a good idea to write or fax ahead for reservations. Most hotel owners will require either a deposit or credit card number as a guarantee of your reservation: if you don't show up or stay less time than you booked for, they have the right to charge you for their loss of earnings. When in doubt, reserve for just one night.

OTHER OPTIONS

GITES D'ETAPE AND MOUNTAIN REFUGES. **Gîtes d'étape** are rural accommodations for cyclists, hikers, and other ramblers. They are located in less populated areas, normally on popular trails, and provide lodgings in farmhouses, cottages, and even campgrounds. Though they vary widely in price and quality, you can expect *gîtes* to provide beds, a kitchen facility, and a resident caretaker. Facilities range from single rooms and hot showers to bare beds and hole-in-the-ground toilets; as the scouts say, be prepared. During the high season, *gîtes* in resort towns fill up fast, so reserve in advance. Averaging 60F/€9.15 a night and spaced along hiking trails, *gîtes* allow you to pass through for a night or stay several days, and sometimes to take advantage of guided hikes led by caretakers. Don't confuse *gîtes d'étapes* with *gîtes ruraux*, country houses available for rent by the week, or *Gîtes de France*, an organization of small hotels.

Another type of French lodging used mostly by hikers and skiers on extended treks is a **refuge,** a rustic shelter usually guarded by a caretaker moonlighting as chief, fix-it person, and sage. *Refuges* dot the wilderness, ranging in price from 45-80F/€6.86-12.20. Expect to pay another 80F/€12.20 for a hot, home-cooked meal—while you savor it, remember that supplies often have to be carried up by hand or mule! *Refuges* are not always guarded year-round, but the doors generally remain open throughout the seasons to accommodate hikers and skiers on the road.

CHAMBRES D'HOTE (BED AND BREAKFASTS). Many French house-owners supplement their income by letting out rooms to travelers. These **chambres d'hôte,** or bed-and-breakfasts, range from acceptable rooms in modern townhouses to palatial accommodation in Baroque châteaux and are priced accordingly; most cost 200-300F/€30.49-45.74 per night, with a few slightly lower prices as well as many that exceed your pre-tax income. Those restricted to public transportation may find these hard to reach; but for drivers, hikers, and bikers, they're often a perfect rural home base. For a comprehensive listing of *chambres d'hôte* in France, buy **Selected Bed & Breakfasts in France 2001** in a bookstore or contact Thomas Cook Publishing at P.O. Box 227, Thorpe Wood. Peterborough PE3 6PU, UK (☎01733 50 35 71; www.thomascook.com/books). Catalogues cost UK£12, US$23, or CDN$30; for buyers abroad, the charge is UK£19. **Fleurs de Soleil** lists *chambres d'hôte* throughout France at www.fleurs-soleil.tm.fr, as does **B&B** at www.bedbreak.com. For more info on B&Bs around the world, including a number in France, contact **InnFinder,** 6200 Gisholt Dr. #105, Madison, WI 53713 (☎608-285-6600; www.inncrawler.com) or **InnSite** (www.innsite.com).

UNIVERSITY HOUSING. In many towns, out-of-session universities open their residence halls to travelers, and some do so even in term-time. These accommodations are usually very clean. Getting a room may take a couple of phone calls and require advance planning. Rates tend to be low. Look in the *Let's Go* accommodations listings for each town to see if university accommodation is available.

HOME EXCHANGE AND RENTALS. **Home exchange** offers the traveler various types of homes (houses, apartments, villas, even castles in some cases), plus the opportunity to live like a native and cut down dramatically on accommodation fees. On the other hand, you have to give up your own castle to someone else while you're away. Once you join or contact one of the exchange services listed below, it is up to you to decide with whom you want to exchange homes. If you're unwilling to hand your keys over to strangers, **home rentals** can still work out much cheaper than hotels for larger groups.

HomeExchange, P.O. Box 30085, Santa Barbara, CA 93130, USA. ☎805-898-9660; fax 805-898-9660; www.HomeExchange.com. US$30 for a one-year listing.

Intervac International Home Exchange, 230 bd. Voltaire, 75011 Paris. ☎01 43 70 21 22; fax 01 43 70 73 35; info@intervac.fr; www.intervac.org/france.

ESSENTIALS

The Invented City: International Home Exchange, 41 Sutter St., Suite 1090, San Francisco, CA 94104, USA. ☎800-788-2489/CITY in the US or (415) 252-1141 elsewhere; www.invented-city.com). For US$75, you get unlimited access to the club's database containing thousands of homes for exchange.

FURTHER READING. *The Complete Guide to Bed and Breakfasts, Inns and Guesthouses in the US, Canada, and Worldwide,* by Pamela Lanier (Ten Speed Press, US$17).

CAMPING AND THE OUTDOORS

After three thousand years of settled history, true wilderness in France is hard to find and almost nowhere is far from some human activity. The French are very keen campers, but it is not camping as you may know it. Forget setting up your tent in some forgotten spot and cooking freshly-fished trout on a wood fire. It's illegal to camp in most public spaces, including and especially national parks, and you wouldn't want to be caught lighting your own fire, either. Instead, look forward to organized *campings* (campsites), where you'll share your splendid isolation with vacationing families, bawling French babies, and all manner of vehicular recreation. Most campsites have toilets, showers, and electrical outlets, though you may have to pay extra for such luxuries (10-40F/€1.53-6.10); you'll often need to pay a 20-50F/€3.05-7.62 supplement for your car, too. Otherwise, expect to pay 50-90F/€7.62-13.72 per site.

PUBLICATIONS AND WEB RESOURCES

For info about camping, hiking, and biking, write or call the publishers listed below to receive a free catalogue. Campers heading to Europe should consider buying an International Camping Carnet. Similar to a hostel membership card, it's required at a few campgrounds and provides discounts at others. It is available in North America from the Family Campers and RVers Association and in the UK from The Caravan Club (see below). An excellent general resource for travelers planning on camping or spending time in the outdoors is the **Great Outdoor Recreation Pages** (www.gorp.com).

Automobile Association, A.A. Publishing. Orders and enquiries to TBS Frating Distribution Centre, Colchester, Essex, CO7 7DW, UK (☎01206 25 56 78; www.theaa.co.uk). Publishes *Camping and Caravanning: Europe* (UK£9), as well as *Big Road Atlases* for Europe, France, Spain, Germany, and Italy.

The Caravan Club, East Grinstead House, East Grinstead, West Sussex, RH19 1UA, UK (☎01342 32 69 44; www.caravanclub.co.uk). For UK£27.50, members receive equipment discounts, a 700pp directory and handbook, and a monthly magazine.

Family Campers and RVers/National Campers and Hikers Association, Inc., 4804 Transit Rd., Bldg. #2, Depew, NY 14043, USA (☎/fax 716-668-6242). Membership fee (US$25) includes their publication *Camping Today.*

Sierra Club Books, 85 Second St., 2nd fl., San Francisco, CA 94105, USA (☎415-977-5500; www.sierraclub.org/books). Publishes general resource books.

The Mountaineers Books, 1001 SW Klickitat Way, #201, Seattle, WA 98134, USA (☎800-553-4453 or 206-223-6303; www.mountaineersbooks.org). Over 400 titles on hiking, biking, mountaineering, natural history, and conservation.

The **Institut Géographique National (IGN)** publishes the acclaimed **Blue Series** of 1:25,000 scale maps for hikers, as well as a full range of road maps. They are sold throughout France; for more info contact their map superstore in Paris, **Éspace IGN** (☎01 43 98 80 00; espace-ign@ign.fr), 107 rue La Boétie, 75008 Paris, or use the clickable map on their website at www.ign.fr/GP/adresse/. You can buy IGN maps in **Australia** from **Hema maps,** P.O. Box 4365, Eight Mile Plains QLD 4113 Australia (☎07 334 00 00), in **Canada** from **Ulysse,** 4176 St Denis, Montreal, Québec H2W 2M5

(☎514-843-9447; www.ulysse.ca), in the **UK** from Travellers World Bookshop, Newmarket Court, Derby DE24 8NW (☎01332 57 37 37; www.map-world.co.uk), and in the **USA** from Map Link Inc., 30 S. La Patera Lane, Unit #5, Santa Barbara, CA 93117 (☎805-692-6777; fax 962-6787; www.maplink.com).

CAMPING AND HIKING EQUIPMENT

WHAT TO BUY...

Good camping equipment is both sturdy and light. Camping equipment is generally more expensive in Australia, New Zealand, and the UK than in North America.

Sleeping Bag: Most sleeping bags are rated by season ("summer" means 30-40°F at night; "four-season" or "winter" often means below 0°F). They are made either of **down** (warmer and lighter, but more expensive, and miserable when wet) or of **synthetic** material (heavier, more durable, and warmer when wet). Prices range from US$80-210 for a summer synthetic to US$250-300 for a good down winter bag. **Sleeping bag pads** include foam pads (US$10-20), air mattresses (US$15-50), and Therm-A-Rest self-inflating pads (US$45-80). Bring a **stuff sack** to store your bag and keep it dry.

Tent: The best tents are free-standing (with their own frames and suspension systems), set up quickly, and only require staking in high winds. Low-profile dome tents are the best all-around. Good 2-person tents start at US$90, 4-person at US$300. Seal the seams of your tent with waterproofer, and make sure it has a rain fly. Other tent accessories include a **battery-operated lantern,** a **plastic groundcloth,** and a **nylon tarp.**

Backpack: Internal-frame packs mold better to your back, keep a lower center of gravity, and flex adequately to allow you to hike difficult trails. **External-frame packs** are more comfortable for long hikes over even terrain, as they keep weight higher and distribute it more evenly. Make sure your pack has a strong, padded hip-belt to transfer weight to your legs. Any serious backpacking requires a pack of at least 4000 in^3 (16,000cc), plus 500 in^3 for sleeping bags in internal-frame packs. Sturdy backpacks cost anywhere from US$125-420—this is one area in which it doesn't pay to economize. Fill up any pack with something heavy and walk around the store with it to get a sense of how it distributes weight before buying it. Either buy a **waterproof backpack cover,** or store all of your belongings in plastic bags inside your pack.

Boots: Be sure to wear hiking boots with good **ankle support.** They should fit snugly and comfortably over 1-2 pairs of wool socks and thin liner socks. Break in boots over several weeks first in order to spare yourself painful and debilitating blisters.

Other Necessities: Synthetic layers, like those made of polypropylene, and a pile jacket will keep you warm even when wet. A "space blanket" will help you to retain your body heat and doubles as a groundcloth (US$5-15). Plastic water bottles are virtually shatter- and leak-proof. Bring water-purification tablets for when you can't boil water. Although most campgrounds provide campfire sites, you may want to bring a small metal grate or grill of your own. For those places that forbid fires or the gathering of firewood (this includes virtually every organized campground in Europe), you'll need a camp stove (the classic Coleman starts at US$40) and a propane-filled fuel bottle to operate it. Also don't forget a first-aid kit, pocketknife, insect repellent, calamine lotion, and waterproof matches or a lighter.

WHERE TO BUY CAMPING EQUIPMENT. The mail-order/online companies listed below offer lower prices than many retail stores, but a visit to a local camping or outdoors store will give you a good sense of the look and weight of certain items.

Campmor, 28 Parkway, P.O. Box 700, Upper Saddle River, NJ 07458, USA (US ☎888-226-7667; elsewhere US ☎+1 201-825-8300; www.campmor.com).

Discount Camping, 880 Main North Rd., Pooraka, South Australia 5095, Australia (☎08 8262 3399; www.discountcamping.com.au).

Eastern Mountain Sports (EMS), 327 Jaffrey Rd., Peterborough, NH 03458, USA (☎888-463-6367 or 603-924-7231; www.shopems.com)

ESSENTIALS

L.L. Bean, Freeport, ME 04033 (US and Canada ☎800-441-5713; UK ☎0800 891 297; elsewhere, call US +1 207-552-3028; www.llbean.com).

Mountain Designs, P.O. Box 1472, Fortitude Valley, Queensland 4006, Australia (☎07 3252 8894; www.mountaindesign.com.au).

Recreational Equipment, Inc. (REI), Sumner, WA 98352, USA (☎800-426-4840 or 253-891-2500; www.rei.com).

YHA Adventure Shop, 14 Southampton St., London, WC2E 7HA, UK (☎020 7836 8541). The main branch of one of Britain's largest outdoor equipment suppliers.

WILDERNESS SAFETY

Stay warm, stay dry, and stay hydrated. Most life-threatening wilderness situations can be avoided by following this simple advice. Prepare yourself for an emergency, however, by always packing raingear, a hat and mittens, a first-aid kit, a reflector, a whistle, high energy food, and extra water for any hike. Dress in wool or warm layers of synthetic materials designed for the outdoors.

Check **weather forecasts** and pay attention to the skies when hiking, since weather patterns can change suddenly; www.intellicast.com/LocalWeather/World/Europe and www.meteo.fr provide up-to-date meteorological info. Whenever possible, let someone know when and where you are going hiking, either a friend, your hostel, a park ranger, or a local hiking organization. Do not attempt a hike beyond your ability—you may be endangering your life. See **Health,** p. 42, for info about outdoor ailments and basic medical concerns.

KEEPING IN TOUCH

MAIL

SENDING MAIL TO FRANCE. Airmail letters from the US to France take 4 to 7 days and cost US$0.80 for mail up to one ounce. Letters from Canada cost CDN$1.05 for 20g. Allow at least 5 working days from Australia (postage AUS$1.50 for up to 50g) and 3 days from Britain (postage UK£0.30 for up to 20g). Envelopes should be marked *"par avion"* (airmail) to avoid having letters sent by sea. If regular airmail is too slow, **Federal Express** (US ☎for international operator 800-247-4747; UK ☎0800 123 800; Australia ☎13 26 10; Ireland ☎1800 535 800; South Africa ☎011 923 8000; New Zealand ☎0800 733 339) can get a letter from New York to Paris in two days for a whopping US$27.56; rates among non-US locations are prohibitively expensive (overnight from London to Paris, for example, costs upwards of UK£31). Using a **US Global Priority Mail** flat-rate envelope, a letter from New York would arrive within four days and would cost US$7.

RECEIVING MAIL IN FRANCE. Mail can be held for pick-up through **Poste Restante** (French for General Delivery) to almost any city or town with a post office. Address letters to: DOE, Jane; *Poste Restante: Recette Principale;* [5-digit postal code] TOWN; FRANCE; mark the envelope HOLD. *Let's Go* lists post offices and postal codes; we also note when the Poste Restante has a different postal code, or if mail is held at a different branch than the one listed. The mail will go to the central post office, unless you specify a branch office by address or postal code. As a rule, it's best to use the main post office in the area, and mail may be sent there regardless of what is written on the envelope. To pick it up, bring a passport and 3F/€0.46 to pay the charge, and have them check under your first name if they're not under your last. Note that post offices will not accept courier service deliveries (e.g. Federal Express) for Poste Restante, nor will they accept anything that requires a signature for delivery. Also, there is a 15 day hold limit.

SENDING MAIL HOME FROM FRANCE. Aerogrammes, printed sheets that fold into envelopes and travel via airmail, are available at post offices. Mark them **par avion** (airmail) if they are not already. Most post offices will charge exorbitant fees or simply refuse to send aerogrammes with enclosures.

Regular **airmail** (not aerogrammes) from France to Australia or the USA takes 5 to 8 days, and from France to South Africa 5-7 days; within Europe letters can arrive in as little as 2 days. Costs are 3F/€0.46 within the EU, 4.40F/€0.67 to North America, and 5.20F/€0.79 to Australia and New Zealand. You can buy stamps at any post office or at *tabacs*. **Surface mail** is by far the cheapest and slowest way to send mail. It takes one to three months to cross the Atlantic and two to four to cross the Pacific—appropriate for sending large quantities of items you won't need to see for a while.

TELEPHONES

CALLING FRANCE FROM HOME. To call France direct from home, dial:

1. The **international access code** of your home country, listed on the inside back cover.
2. 33 (France's country code).
3. The French number **without the first zero.**

Thus if a French number was listed as 01 23 45 67 89, you would dial the international access code followed by 33 1 23 45 67 89.

CALLING HOME FROM FRANCE. A **calling card** is the most convenient way to call home from abroad, but it's not always the cheapest. There are two basic types, billed and prepaid. In the first, the card is issued free or for a small charge and calls are charged either to your home account or to the person you are calling. Luckily, you won't see the bill until you get home, as calls with these cards can be ruinously expensive. Avoid using these for calls inside France or to countries other than the issuing one, since you'll probably be charged twice: for both a call back to your home country and out again to the person you're calling. Their advantage is convenience—the card doesn't need to be renewed half-way through your vacation. Prepaid cards are far cheaper, as they contain a limited number of calling credits. Since few public phones remain coin-operated, you may have to buy a *télécarte* (see below).

BILLED CARDS. Calls are billed either collect or to your account. **MCI WorldPhone** also provides access to MCI's Traveler's Assist, which gives legal and medical advice, exchange rate info, and translation services. Other phone companies provide similar services to travelers. **To obtain a calling card** before you leave home, contact the appropriate company for your country. The inside back cover of this book lists corresponding numbers to call from within France.

Australia: Telstra Australia Direct (☎1800 03 80 00; www.telstra.com)

Canada: Bell Canada **Canada Direct** (☎800-668-6878; www.bell.ca)

Ireland: Telecom Éireann **Ireland Direct** (☎1 850 337 337; www.eircom.ie)

New Zealand: Telecom New Zealand (☎0800 00 00 00; www.telecom.co.nz)

South Africa: Telkom South Africa (☎0800 012 255; www.telkom.co.za)

UK: British Telecom **BT Direct** (☎800 34 51 44; www.bt.com)

US: AT&T (☎800-222-0300; www.att.com); **Sprint** (☎888-217-4953; www.sprint.com); **MCI WorldCom** (☎800-955-0925; www.wcom.com).

PREPAID CARDS. You can buy prepaid cards at home or in France which can be used anywhere in the world; the number of varieties available is bewildering but beware that the cheaper the calls offered, the more likely you are to have trouble getting through. Most major telecommunications companies issue them too; these are generally widely available in kiosks and travel stores. Common prepaid cards you can buy at home include Telstra **PhoneAway** (Australia), Telecom

I'LL TRADE YOU MY '52 MANTLE FOR YOUR '88 GERARD LONGUET If you're going to be in France for any length of time, you'll eventually give up the futile search for coin-operated telephones and invest in a *télécarte*. These cards, of course, only last so long, so where is the *télécarte* graveyard? The answer is simple but surprising: collectors' albums. The ads and artwork on the cards turn some designs into valuable commodities—so valuable that an entire *télécarte* collection business has developed around the credit-card sized *chef d'oeuvres*. Common and uncommon cards may be sold in stores for 5-10F each, while rare specimens reside under protective covering in acrylic cases. The condition of a card, of course, drastically affects its value, while the number of call-enabling *unités* is irrelevant. A 1987-88 carte by Gerard Longuet is one of the gems in the *télécarte* collector's crown. Only 40 exist, and an unblemished one will net you 34,000F. For the real prize, seek out the November 1988 card "Les Boxeurs," with artwork by Gilles Chagny. There are 100 out there, but only one is signed by the artist. Maybe it's down at your feet right now as you make your call—it's worth checking; if it *is* there, you've just stumbled across a cool 60,000F.

Éireann **CallCard,** AT&T **PrePaid Phone Card** (USA), Telecom New Zealand **YABBA,** and Canada Direct **Calling Card.** You can also buy prepaid cards in France; the most popular is the **Carte Intercall Monde,** available in most *tabacs*. These are available in 50F/€7.62 and 100F/€15.25 denominations, and give up to 75% off standard French international call rates.

DIRECT DIAL. If you must use a pay phone, prepare yourself in advance with a fully charged **télécarte** (see **calling within France,** below), and be ready to watch the units drop. Calls with a 120-unit card are 50% cheaper after 7pm Monday to Friday, from noon to midnight Saturday, and all day Sunday. Expect to pay about 3F/€0.46 per minute to the UK, Ireland, and North America and about 10F/€1.53 per minute to Australia, New Zealand, and South Africa. Use only public **France Télécom** payphones, as private ones often charge more. Although convenient, in-room hotel calls invariably include an arbitrary and sky-high surcharge (as much as US$10).

If you do dial direct, you must first insert a *télécarte*, then dial 00 (the international access code for France), the country code, and then the number of your home. **Country codes** include: Australia 61, Ireland 353, New Zealand 64, South Africa 27, UK 44, US and Canada 1. Note that when calling the UK from abroad you should drop the first zero of the local area code.

CALLING COLLECT. The expensive alternative to dialing direct or using a calling card is using an international operator to place a **collect call,** *faire un appel en PCV*. An English-speaking operator from your home nation can be reached by dialing the appropriate service provider listed above.

CALLING WITHIN FRANCE. French public payphones only accept stylish microchip-toting phonecards called ***Télécartes;*** some payphones in Paris also take credit cards. *Télécartes* are available in 50-unit (49F/€7.47) and 120-unit (98F/€14.94) denominations; a unit lasts about a minute for a local call. A small digital screen on the phone will issue a series of simple commands; press the small button marked with a British flag to get instructions in English. If none exists, proceed with caution, since French payphones are as unforgiving as the bureaucracy they serve. *Décrochez* means pick up; you will then be asked to *patientez* (wait) before you can put your card in. Only when you are told *numérotez* or *composez* should you dial. *Raccrochez* means "hang up" and this generally means you've done something wrong. If you want to make another call, don't hang up at the end of the first one; just press the green button. French phone boxes also normally display a complicated wall chart showing phone rates depending on the time of day, the day of the week, and the place you are calling. In very remote rural areas, as well as in most bars, hotels, and cafés, you will still find coin-operated telephones; be warned that privately owned pay phones can be more expensive. Info: ☎ 12.

CELLULAR PHONES. To use a cell phone from outside Europe in France, you'll need to make sure you're registered at home for international service. You also have to switch the phone's band to 900/1800. Once you've switched bands, your phone will automatically register with one of the three French cell phone servers: Bouygue, Itineris, or France Télécom. Switch servers on the phone's menu if you're having trouble with reception.

EMAIL

Most major **post offices** and some branches now offer Internet access at special "cyberposte" terminals; 50F/€7.62 buys you about 50 minutes of access, stored on a little rechargeable card purchasable in the post office itself. Note that *Let's Go* **does not list** "cyberposte." Most large towns in France have a cybercafé; check the Practical Information section of town listings to see if there is one. Rates and speed of connection vary widely; occasionally there are free terminals in technologically-oriented museums or exhibition spaces. **Cybercafé Guide** (www.cyberiacafe.net/cyberia/guide/ccafe.htm#working_france) can help you find cybercafés.

To send and receive email you will need an email account. Free, web-based email providers include **Hotmail** (www.hotmail.com), **RocketMail** (www.rocketmail.com), and **Yahoo! Mail** (www.yahoo.com).

If you have a laptop you can use a **modem** to call your home internet service provider; beware that many hotel switchboards use the **PBX** system, which will fry most modems without a **converter** (about US$50). Long-distance phone cards specifically intended for such calls can defray high phone charges. Check with your long-distance phone provider to see if they offer this option.

GETTING TO FRANCE

BY PLANE

When it comes to airfare, a little effort can save you a bundle. If your plans can accommodate the restrictions, courier fares are the cheapest. Tickets bought from consolidators and standby seating are also good deals, but last-minute specials, airfare wars, and charter flights often beat these fares. The key is to hunt around, to be flexible, and to ask persistently about discounts. Students, seniors, and those under 26 should never pay full price for a ticket.

DETAILS AND TIPS

Timing: Airfares to France peak between June and September. Easter and Christmas are equally expensive travel periods. Most cheap fares require a Saturday night stay. Traveling with an "open return" ticket can be pricier than fixing a return date when buying the ticket. Most budget tickets, once bought, allow no date or route changes to be made; student tickets sometimes allow date changes for a price.

Route: Round-trip flights are by far the cheapest; "open-jaw" (arriving in and departing from different cities, e.g. London-Paris and Marseille-London) tickets tend to be pricier. Flights between capitals or regional hubs offer the cheapest fares; Paris is the most affordable point of entry from everywhere outside of Europe, while from Ireland and the UK, budget fares to certain smaller cities (see below) compete with Paris for cost.

Round-the-World (RTW): If France is only 1 stop on a more extensive globe-hop, consider a RTW ticket. Tickets usually include at least 3 stops and are sold by total mileage. They are usually valid for about a year; prices range US$3500-5000. Try **Northwest Airlines/KLM** (US ☎800-447-4747; www.nwa.com) or **Star Alliance,** a consortium of 13 airlines including United Airlines (US ☎800- 241-6522; www.star-alliance.com).

Average Fares: Round-trip fares to Paris from the US range from US$250-500 (during the off-season) to US$300-800 (during the summer). From Australia, count on paying between AUS$1600 and AUS$2500, depending on the season. From New Zealand, fares range from NZ$5000-9000. Flights from the UK to France are a comparative snip at UK£60-80 for London-Paris, while a return flight from Dublin to Paris can cost as little as IR£120 return.

Checking in: Whenever flying internationally, pick up tickets for international flights well in advance of the departure date and reconfirm by phone within 72 hours of departure. Most airlines require that passengers arrive at the airport at least two hours before departure. For scheduled flights departing from an EU country, you are entitled to full compensation if a flight is overbooked and you have a confirmed ticket (indicated by an 'OK' in the relevant box on the ticket), provided that you checked in on time. One carry-on item (max 5kg) and two pieces of checked baggage weighing up to 60kg total is the norm for non-courier intercontinental flights; for flights within Europe, the checked baggage allowance is normally 20-30kg, regardless of the number of pieces.

BUDGET AND STUDENT TRAVEL AGENCIES

While knowledgeable agents specializing in flights to France can make your life easy and help you save, they may not spend the time to find you the lowest possible fare—they do get paid on commission, after all. Students and those under age 26 holding **ISIC** and **IYTC cards** (see p. 33) respectively, qualify for big discounts from student travel agencies. Most flights from budget agencies are on major airlines, but in peak season some may sell seats on less reliable chartered aircraft.

Council Travel (www.counciltravel.com). Countless US offices, including branches in Atlanta, Boston, Chicago, L.A., New York, San Francisco, Seattle, and Washington, D.C. Check the website or call 800-2-COUNCIL (226-8624) for the office nearest you.

CTS Travel, 44 Goodge St., **London** W1T 2AD (☎0207 636 0031; fax 0207 637 5328; ctsinfo@ctstravel.co.uk).

STA Travel, 7890 S. Hardy Dr., suite 110, Tempe AZ 85284 (24hr. reservations and info ☎800-777-0112; www.statravel.com). A student and youth travel organization with countless offices worldwide (check their website for a listing of all offices). Ticket booking, travel insurance, railpasses, and more. In the UK, walk-in office 11 Goodge St., **London** W1T 2PF or call 0870-160-6070. In New Zealand, 10 High St., **Auckland** (☎09 309 0458). In Australia, 366 Lygon St., **Melbourne** Vic 3053 (☎03 9349 4344).

StudentUniverse, 545 Fifth Ave., Suite 640, New York, NY 10017 (☎800-272-9676, outside the US 212-986-8420; www.studentuniverse.com), is an online student travel service offering discount ticket booking, travel insurance, railpasses, destination guides, and more. Customer service line open M-F 9am-8pm and Sa noon-5pm EST.

Travel CUTS (Canadian Universities Travel Services Limited), 187 College St., **Toronto,** ON M5T 1P7 (☎416-979-2406; fax 979-8167; www.travelcuts.com). 60 offices across Canada. Also in the UK, 295-A Regent St., **London** W1R 7YA (☎0207-255-1944).

usit world (www.usitworld.com). Over 50 **usit campus** branches in the UK (www.usitcampus.co.uk), including **Edinburgh** (☎0131 668 3303); 52 Grosvenor Gardens, **London** SW1W 0AG (☎0870 240 10 10); and **Manchester** (☎0161 273 1880). Nearly 20 **usit NOW** offices in Ireland, including **Belfast** (☎02 890 327 111; www.usitnow.com); and 19-21 Aston Quay, O'Connell Bridge, **Dublin** 2 (☎01 602 1600; www.usitnow.ie). Offices also in Athens, Auckland, Brussels, Frankfurt, Johannesburg, Lisbon, Luxembourg, Madrid, Paris, Sofia, and Warsaw.

Wasteels, Skoubogade 6, 1158 Copenhagen K., Denmark (☎+45 3314 4633 fax 7630 0865; www.wasteels.dk/uk). A huge chain with 165 locations across Europe. Sells Wasteels BIJ tickets discounted 30-45% off regular fare, 2nd-class international point-to-point train tickets with unlimited stopovers for those under 26 (sold only in Europe).

COMMERCIAL AIRLINES

The commercial airlines' lowest regular offer is the **APEX** (Advance Purchase Excursion) fare, which provides confirmed reservations and allows "open-jaw" tickets. Generally, reservations must be made 7-21 days in advance, with 7- to 14-day minimum and up to 90-day maximum-stay limits, and hefty cancellation and change penalties (fees rise in summer). Book peak-season APEX fares early, since by May you will have a hard time getting the departure date you want.

Although APEX fares are probably not the cheapest possible fares, they will give you a sense of price from which to measure other bargains. Specials advertised in newspapers may be cheaper but have more restrictions and fewer available seats. Popular carriers include:

Icelandair (US ☎800-223-5500; www.icelandair.net) features stopovers in Iceland for no extra cost on most transatlantic flights. New York to Paris May-Sept. US$500-730; Oct.-May US$390-450. For last minute offers, subscribe to their email Lucky Fares.

Air France (☎0 802 802 802; www.airfrance.com) is France's national airline, connecting France to the world with 162 flights per week to the US alone.

United Airlines (US ☎800-538-2929 for international reservations; www.ual.com). Mammoth US carrier offers last-minute special e-fares deals available only online.

Cathay Pacific (in France ☎01 41 43 75 75; in Australia ☎13 17 47) features reasonable RTW fares and flights to Paris, connecting to Australia via Hong Kong.

BUYING TICKETS OVER THE INTERNET. The Web is a great place to look for travel bargains–it's fast, it's convenient, and you can spend as long as you like exploring options without driving your travel agent insane.

Many airline sites offer special last-minute deals on the Web. Virtually all of the airlines and agencies we list maintain a website; services range from flight quotes to full planning assistance. Many other sites can arrange deals for you–try www.bestfares.com, www.cheapflights.com, www.onetravel.com, www.lowestfare.com, and www.travelzoo.com. **Expedia** (msn.expedia.com) and **Travelocity** (www.travelocity.com) offer full travel services. **Priceline** (www.priceline.com) allows you to specify a price and forces you to buy any ticket that meets or beats it; be prepared for undesirable hours and odd routes. **Skyauction** (www.skyauction.com) allows you to bid on both last-minute and advance-purchase tickets.

One last note–to protect yourself, make sure that the site uses a secure server before handing over any credit card details. Happy hunting!

BUDGET FLIGHTS FROM BRITAIN & IRELAND

UK and Irish residents can take advantage of the growing number of no-frills carriers operating in Europe. In return for giving up free in-flight food and drink and a few inches of legroom, these offer flights to a number of regional destinations at prices that often beat rail. To keep costs down, they only accept direct booking by phone or Internet; you won't find them quoted by any travel agent. They also only rarely allow bookings more than four months ahead. The **Air Travel Advisory Bureau** in London (☎(020) 7636 5000; www.atab.co.uk) provides referrals to travel agencies and consolidators that offer discounted airfares out of the UK.

easyJet (UK ☎(0870) 600 0000; www.easyjet.co.uk) flies from London and Liverpool to Nice up to four times per day for as little as UK£27.50 one-way (excluding tax).

Ryanair (Ireland ☎(01) 821 12 12; UK (0870) 156 9569; www.ryanair.ie) From Dublin, London, and Glasgow to destinations in France and elsewhere. Deals from as low as UK£9 on limited weekend specials.

Virgin Express (UK ☎(020) 7744 0004; France ☎(0800) 528 528; www.virgin-express.com) connects London to Nice via Brussels from UK£39 one-way.

OTHER CHEAP ALTERNATIVES

AIR COURIER FLIGHTS. Those who travel light should consider courier flights. Couriers help transport cargo on international flights by using their checked luggage space for freight. Generally, couriers must travel with carry-ons only and must deal with complex flight restrictions. Most flights are round-trip only, with short fixed-length stays (usually one week) and a limit of a single ticket per issue. Most of these flights also operate only out of major gateway cities, mostly in North America. Generally, you must be over 21 (in some cases 18). In summer the most popular destinations usually require an advance reservation of about two weeks (you can usually book up to two months ahead). Super-discounted fares are common for "last-minute" flights (three to 14 days ahead).

Groups such as the **Air Courier Association** (☎800-282-1202; www.aircourier.org), **Global Courier Travel** (www.globalcouriertravel.com), the **International Association of Air Travel Couriers** (☎561-582-8320; iaatc@courier.org; www.courier.org), and the **Worldwide Courier Association** (☎800-780-4359, ext. 441; www.massiveweb.com) provide their members with lists of opportunities and courier brokers worldwide for an annual fee. For more info, consult *Air Courier Bargains* by Kelly Monaghan (The Intrepid Traveler, US$15) or the *Courier Air Travel Handbook* by Mark Field (Perpetual Press, US$13).

STANDBY FLIGHTS. Traveling standby requires considerable flexibility in arrival and departure dates and cities. Companies dealing in standby flights sell vouchers rather than tickets, along with the promise to get you to your destination (or near your destination) within a certain window of time (typically 1-5 days). You call in before your specific window of time to hear your flight options and the probability that you will be able to board each flight. You can then decide which flights you want to try to make, show up at the appropriate airport at the appropriate time,

present your voucher, and board if space is available. Vouchers can usually be bought for both one-way and round-trip travel. You may receive a monetary refund only if every available flight within your date range is full; if you opt not to take an available (but perhaps less convenient) flight, you can only get credit toward future travel. Carefully read agreements with any company offering standby flights as tricky fine print can leave you in the lurch. To check on a company's service record in the US, call the Better Business Bureau (☎212-533-6200). It is difficult to receive refunds and clients' vouchers will not be honored when an airline fails to receive payment in time. One established standby company in the US is Whole Earth Travel, 325 W. 38th St., New York, NY 10018 (☎800-326-2009; fax 212-864-5489; www.4standby.com) and Los Angeles, CA (☎888-247-4482), which offers one-way flights to Europe from the Northeast (US$169), West Coast and Northwest (US$249), Midwest (US$219), and Southeast (US$199). Intracontinental connecting flights within the US or Europe cost US$79-139.

CHARTER FLIGHTS. Charters are flights a tour operator contracts with an airline to fly extra loads of passengers during high season. They fly less frequently than major airlines, make refunds especially difficult, and are usually fully booked. Schedules and itineraries may also change or be canceled at the last minute (as late as 48 hours before the trip and without a full refund) and check-in, boarding, and baggage claim are often much slower. However, they can also be cheaper.

Discount clubs and **fare brokers** offer members savings on last-minute charter and tour deals. Study all contracts closely; you don't want to end up with an unwanted overnight layover. **Travelers Advantage,** Trumbull, CT, USA (☎203-365-2000; www.travelersadvantage.com; US$60 annual fee includes discounts, newsletters, and cheap flight directories), specializes in European travel and tour packages.

TICKET CONSOLIDATORS. Ticket consolidators, or **"bucket shops,"** buy unsold tickets in bulk from commercial airlines and sell them at discounted rates. The best place to look is in the Sunday travel section of any major newspaper, where many bucket shops place tiny ads. Call quickly, as availability is typically extremely limited. Not all bucket shops are reliable, so insist on a receipt that gives full details of restrictions, refunds, and tickets, and pay by credit card (in spite of the 2-5% fee) so you can stop payment if you never receive your tickets.

In fact, the web provides many resources for those seeking discounted rates. Start with www.travel-library.com/air-travel/consolidators.html. For particular consolidators, consider the following: Rebel (www.rebeltours.com); Cheap Tickets (www.cheaptickets.com); NOW Voyager (www.nowvoyagertravel.com); and Travac (www.travac.com). Also check out Travel Avenue (www.travelavenue.com), which rebates commercial flights and searches for cheap ones. Keep in mind that these are just suggestions to get you started in your research; *Let's Go* does not endorse any of these agencies. As always, be cautious and research companies before you hand over your credit card number.

FURTHER RESOURCES. *Air Traveler's Handbook* (www.cs.cmu.edu/afs/cs/user/mkant/Public/Travel/airfare.html); *TravelHUB* (www.travelhub.com), a directory of travel agents, including a fare database from over 500 consolidators. *The Worldwide Guide to Cheap Airfares*, by Michael McColl (Insider, US$15); *Discount Airfares: The Insider's Guide*, by George Hobart (Priceless, US$14).

BY BUS

For British travelers, buses are the cheapest way to get to France, with return fares starting around UK£50 including ferry/chunnel transport. On the downside, buses take far longer than trains and planes and are more susceptible to delays. Often cheaper than railpasses, **international bus passes** typically allow unlimited travel on a hop-on, hop-off basis between major European cities. These services in general tend to be more popular among non-American backpackers. Note that **Eurobus,** a onetime UK-based bus service, is no longer in operation.

Eurolines, 4 Cardiff Rd., Luton LU1 1PP, UK (☎(08705) 14 32 19; fax (01582) 40 06 94; in London, 52 Grosvenor Gardens, London SW1 (☎(01582) 404 511; welcome@eurolines.uk.com; www.eurolines.co.uk). Roundtrip fares between London and Paris start at UK£49.

Busabout, 258 Vauxhall Bridge Rd., London SW1V 1BS, UK (☎(020) 7950 1661; fax 7950 1662; www.busabout.com). Offers 5 interconnecting bus circuits covering 60 cities and towns in Europe. Consecutive Day Passes and Flexi Passes both available. Consecutive Day Standard/student passes are valid for 15 days (US$249/219), 21 days (US$359/329), 1 month (US$479/429), 2 months (US$739/659), 3 months (US$909/829), or for the season (US$1089/979).

BY BOAT

Ferries across the English Channel (*La Manche*) link France to England and Ireland. The shortest route, between Dover and Calais, is also the most popular, with departures every hour. In recent years, the journey time has actually increased from an hour to an hour and a half, as ferry companies try to tempt passengers into spending more money on board; their giant "super-ferries" are little more than floating malls with a passenger business on the side. Catering to claustrophobes in a hurry, the fastest non-tunnel crossings are provided by Hoverspeed, with hovercraft and catamaran services. Many people in England (and most in Ireland) who holiday in the west of France choose to take longer crossings to Brittany and Normandy, and Normandy's Le Havre has the fastest road connections to Paris. Take the longer crossings overnight and you can awake refreshed and ready to start your day in France. The ferries cater both to car and foot passengers and French ports all have excellent rail and autoroute connections to the national networks.

The following prices are low-end **one-way** trips; most operators have special fares for fixed-period (usually within five days) returns. Prices for cars usually allow for up to two passengers; additional passengers are usually around UK£1. Campers or large cars may be charged more. **Bikes** are usually free, although you may have to pay up to UK£10 in the high season.

P&O Stena Line: UK ☎(08706) 00 0600; outside UK ☎00 44 1304 864003; www.posl.com. **Dover-Calais:** 1½ hr., every 45min. 7am-1am and hourly through the night. Foot passengers UK£26; car UK£145.

SeaFrance: UK ☎(08705) 711 711; France ☎08 03 04 40 45; www.seafrance.co.uk. **Dover-Calais:** 1½ hr., 16 trips daily. Foot passengers UK£15; car UK£132.

Hoverspeed: Reservations and bookings UK ☎(08705) 240 241; France ☎08 20 00 35 55. High speed hovercraft and catamaran services. **Dover-Calais:** 45min., 10 per day. Foot passengers UK£28; car and driver UK£99-165; car and 2 passengers UK£99-165. Also runs **Newhaven-Dieppe.**

Brittany ferries: UK ☎(0870) 90 12 400; France ☎08 03 82 88 28; www.brittanyferries.co.uk. Routes are **Portsmouth-Caen, Portsmouth-St-Malo, Plymouth-Roscoff, Poole-Cherbourg,** and **Cork-Roscoff.** Each runs up to 3 ferries per day, but some do not run at all in the off-season. Foot passengers from 140F, cars from 410F (prices vary widely between lines).

Irish Ferries: ☎1890 31 31 31 or 0800 018 22 11 (Ireland); ☎01 44 94 20 40 (France); www.irishferries.ie. Overnight ferries from **Rosslare** to **Cherbourg** and **Roscoff;** in the summer, one boat leaves every other day. Foot passengers €57-107, students and seniors €45-86; car and two passengers €189-455; additional passengers €0-40. Cabins from €35.

BY CHUNNEL FROM THE UK

Traversing 27 mi. under the sea, the Chunnel is undoubtedly the fastest, most covenient, and least scenic route from England to France.

BY TRAIN. Eurostar, Eurostar House, Waterloo Station, **London** SE1 8SE (UK ☎0990 18 61 86; US ☎800-387-6782; elsewhere call UK +44 1233 61 75 75; www.eurostar.com; www.raileurope.com), runs a frequent train service between London and the continent. Ten to twenty-eight trains per day run to Paris Gare du Nord (3hr., US$75-159, 2nd class), Brussels (3hr., every 50min., US$75-159, 2nd class), and Eurodisney. Routes include stops at Ashford in England and Calais and Lille in France. Book at major rail stations in the UK, at the office above, by phone, or on the web.

BY CAR. If you're traveling by car, **Eurotunnel** (UK ☎08000 96 99 92; France 03 21 00 61 00; www.eurotunnel.co.uk) shuttles cars and passengers between Kent and Nord-Pas-de-Calais. Return fares for vehicle and all passengers range from UK£219-299 with car, UK£259-598 with campervan, and UK£119-299 for a trailer/caravan supplement. Same-day return costs UK£110-150, five-day return UK£139-195. Book online or via phone.

GETTING AROUND FRANCE

Most travelers take advantage of France's comprehensive rail system to get around, since its network of high-speed services and local trains connect all but the most minor towns. In some areas buses fill in gaps in service, but where the bus and train compete along the same route the bus is normally only marginally cheaper and somewhat slower—though over short distances buses can be faster than slow local trains. While France is also blessed with an extremely efficient and well-maintained network of roads, high *autoroute* tolls and gasoline costs can make driving more expensive than trains for one or two people, even without including the price of renting a car. However, a car will offer greater freedom to explore the countryside, and you will no longer be at the whim of timetables designed primarily for local needs.

To buy a one-way ticket for a train, bus, or plane in France, ask for **un billet aller-simple;** for a roundtrip ticket, request **un billet aller-retour.** Roundtrip fares are often cheaper than two one-ways.

HOW TO USE TRANSPORTATION LISTINGS: CENTER-OUT
Let's Go employs a center-out principle for transportation listings: from each town we give details only on how to get to towns of similar or greater importance. So if you're in a big city and we don't list a bus or train to nearby towns, don't despair–the information you're looking for will be in the transport sections of the towns themselves.

BY PLANE

Only real high-flyers get around France by plane. With most major cities linked by high-speed rail lines, flying really doesn't save any time once you've counted getting to out-of-the-way airports, checking in, taxiing around runways, waiting for luggage, and then getting from the arrival airport into the city. The one exception is getting to **Corsica** and back; frequent services from Nice, Marseille, and Paris to Ajaccio and Bastia offer serious competition to 10-hour ferry crossings. See **Corsica: Getting There,** p. 321, for details; expect to pay about US$100 round-trip from **Nice** to Corsica or US$150 from **Paris.**

BY BOAT

FERRIES. Aside from the many coastal islands dotted around the French seaboard, the only time you're likely to want to take a ferry within France is to get to Corsica and back. While far, far slower than flying (expect a 7- to 12-hour trip) and barely any cheaper, ferries offer a relaxing break from endless sights, and make a great place to meet people. By traveling overnight, you won't waste any time, either. Expect to pay about 600F/€91.48 roundtrip per person and 200-600F/€30.49-91.48 per car. There is also a high-speed hydrofoil service from Nice to Calvi and Bastia, which takes about 3 hours. For details see **Corsica: Getting There,** p. 321.

RIVERBOATS. France has over 5300 miles of navigable rivers and canals, and every year thousands take advantage of them for relaxing vacations spent meandering through the French countryside. It's possible to boat from the English channel right through to the Mediterranean, though this takes planning and experience. For details of regulations get the French Government Tourist Office to send you a copy of their English-language pamphlet *Boating on the Waterways*. For a list of companies renting out boats and organizing waterborne vacations, contact the **Fédération des Industries Nautiques** (☎01 44 37 04 00; fax 01 45 77 21 88), Port de Javel Haut, 75015 Paris, or check out the *Maison de la France* website at www.francetourism.com/activities/boatrent.htm.

BY TRAIN

SNCF HOTLINE	☎08 36 35 35 35 for timetable info and reservations.

The French national railway company, **SNCF,** operates one of the most efficient transportation systems around; their **TGVs** (*train à grande vitesse*, or high-speed train) are the fastest trains in the world. Many high speed and intercity services require a paid supplement in addition to the regular ticket price; railcard holders must generally pay these too. If you're not in a hurry, take the slower **Rapide** service; local trains are slowest of all and confusingly called **Express,** or sometimes **TER** (for Train Express Regional). Trains are not always safe; keep your valuables on your person. For long trips make sure you are on the correct carriage, as trains are sometimes split to two different destinations. Towns listed in parentheses on French train schedules require a change of train.

Even a ticket or railpass does not guarantee you a seat; during busy periods, it's advisable to buy a **reservation** for a small fee—these are required for TGV services. A limited number of **standby** tickets are sold for most TGVs, which guarantee travel on the train but not necessarily a seat. For overnight travel, you can purchase a reclining seat though you may prefer the affordable luxury of a tight, open-bunk **couchette.** These are mixed, with up to six people in triple-stacked bunks per compartment, so be prepared to sleep in your day clothes. Both seat and couchette reservations can be made by a travel agent or in person at the train station. TGV reservations can be made up to a few minutes before departure; for other services reserve before noon for departures after 5pm and before 8pm the previous day for departures before 5pm. Anyone with ID under 26 is entitled to a discount (*tarif réduit*) on train tickets, though tellers usually won't offer it unless you ask.

COMPOSTEZ! Before you board a train, you must validate your ticket by having it *composté* (stamped with the date and time) by one of the orange machines near the platforms. You must also re-validate your ticket at any connections in your trip.

RAILPASSES

Ideally, a railpass would allow you to jump on any train in the specified zone, go wherever you want whenever you want, and change your plans at will for a set length of time. In practice, it's not so simple; you must still wait to pay for supplements, seat reservations, and couchette reservations. More importantly, railpasses don't always pay off. France has a bevy of different discount fares (see **Discount Rail Tickets,** p. 68) and travelers (especially those under 26) should be able to get away without paying full-price. But if you are planning to spend extensive time on trains, hopping between big cities, a railpass would probably be worth it. For ball-

park estimates, consult the SNCF website for prices of point-to-point tickets, add them up, and compare with railpass prices. Prices listed below are for second-class travel; first-class passes can be bought at considerably higher prices.

FRANCE-ONLY RAILPASSES. SNCF offers a number of railpasses valid only in France, which can be bought through many European travel services. All railpasses also offer savings on Eurostar trains from Paris to London.

France Railpass: 3 days unlimited rail travel in any 30-day period. US$175 for 1 adult, $141 each for 2 or more traveling together. Add up to 6 extra days for $30 each.

France Rail'n'drive pass: 3 days rail travel and 2 days Avis car hire (excluding insurance) US$240 for 1 adult, US$170 each for 2 traveling together. Additional rail days (up to 7) $30 each, additional car days $49.

France Youthpass: For travelers under 26. 4 days of unlimited travel within a 2 month period for US$130; add up to 6 days for $20 each.

EURO DOMINO. Available to anyone who has lived in Europe for at least six months. These single-country passes are available for 29 European countries and Morocco. Reservations must still be paid for separately. The Euro Domino pass is available for first- and second-class travel (with a special rate for under age 26), for three to eight days of unlimited travel within a one-month period. Euro Domino is not valid on Eurostar. **Supplements** for many high-speed (e.g., French TGV) trains are included, though you must still pay for **reservations** where they are compulsory (about 20F/€3.05 on the TGV). The pass must be bought within your country of residence; each country has its own price for the pass. Inquire with your national rail company for more info.

Euro-Domino France pass: 3 days 1145F/€174.57, 4 days 1343F/€204.76, 5 days 1545F/€235.55, 6 days 1747F/€266.35, 7 days 1950F/€297.30, 8 days 2152F/€328.10.

Euro-Domino France Youth pass: Must be under 26. 3 days 839F/€127.92, 4 days 1003F/€152.92, 5 days 1162F/€177.16, 6 days 1326F/€202.17, 7 days 1485F/€226.41, 8 days 1648F/€251.26.

EURAIL PASSES FOR NON-EUROPEAN RESIDENTS. A **Eurailpass** remains the best option for non-European travelers who plan on hitting major cities in several countries. Eurail is valid in most of Western Europe: Austria, Belgium, Denmark, Finland, France, Germany, Greece, Hungary, Italy, Luxembourg, the Netherlands, Norway, Portugal, the Republic of Ireland, Spain, Sweden, and Switzerland. It is not valid in the UK. Standard **Eurailpasses,** valid for a consecutive given number of days, are most suitable for those planning on spending extensive time on trains every few days. **Flexipasses,** valid for any 10 or 15 (not necessarily consecutive) days in a two-month period, are more cost-effective for those traveling longer distances less frequently. **Saverpasses** provide first-class travel for travelers in groups of two to five (prices are per person). **Youthpasses** and **Youth Flexipasses** provide parallel second-class perks for those under 26.

EURAIL-PASSES	15 DAYS	21 DAYS	1 MONTH	2 MONTHS	3 MONTHS
1st class Eurailpass	US$554	US$718	US$890	US$1260	US$1558
Eurail Saverpass	US$470	US$610	US$756	US$1072	US$1324
Eurail Youthpass	US$388	US$499	US$623	US$882	US$1089

EURAIL FLEXIPASSES	10 DAYS IN 2 MONTHS	15 DAYS IN 2 MONTHS
1st class Eurail Flexipass	US$654	US$862
Eurail Saver Flexipass	US$556	US$732
Eurail Youth Flexipass	US$458	US$599

Passholders receive a timetable for major routes and a map with details on possible ferry, steamer, bus, car rental, hotel, and Eurostar discounts. Passholders often also receive reduced fares or free passage on many bus and boat lines. **Eurail freebies** (excepting surcharges such as reservation fees and port taxes) include ferries between **Ireland** (Rosslare/Cork) and **France** (Cherbourg/Le Havre).

EUROPASS. Allows travel throughout France, Germany, Italy, Spain, and Switzerland for 5-15 days within a window of 2 months. **First-Class Europasses** (for individuals) and **Saverpasses** (for people traveling in groups of 2-5) range from US$348/296 per person (5 days) to US$688/586 (15 days). **Second-Class Youthpasses** for those ages 12-25 cost US$244-482. For a fee, you can add **additional zones** (Austria/Hungary; Belgium/Luxembourg/Netherlands; Greece Plus, including the ADN/HML ferry between Italy and Greece; and/or Portugal): $60 for one associated country, $100 for two. You are entitled to the same **freebies** afforded by the Eurailpass, but only when they are within or between countries that you have purchased. Plan your itinerary before buying a Europass: it will save you money if your travels are confined to three to five adjacent Western European countries or if you only want to go to large cities, but would be a waste if you plan to make lots of side-trips. If you're tempted to add many rail days and associate countries, consider a Eurailpass.

SHOPPING AROUND FOR A EURAIL OR EUROPASS. Eurailpasses and Europasses are designed by the EU itself and are purchasable only by non-Europeans almost exclusively from non-European distributors. These passes must be sold at uniform prices determined by the EU. However, some travel agents tack on a US$10 handling fee and others offer certain bonuses with purchase, so shop around. Also, keep in mind that pass prices usually go up each year, so if you're planning to travel early in the year, you can save cash by purchasing before January 1 (you have three months from the purchase date to validate your pass in Europe). It is best to buy your Eurail or Europass before leaving; only a few places in major European cities sell them and at a marked-up price. Once in Europe, you'd probably have to use a credit card to buy over the phone from a railpass agent in a non-EU country (one on the North American East Coast would be closest) who could send the pass to you by express mail. Eurailpasses are non-refundable once validated; if your pass is completely unused and invalidated and you have the original purchase documents, you can get an 85% refund from the place of purchase. You can get a replacement for a lost pass only if you have purchased insurance on it under the Pass Protection Plan (US$10). Eurailpasses are available through travel agents, student travel agencies like STA and Council (see p. 57), and **Rail Europe,** 500 Mamaroneck Ave., Harrison, NY 10528 (US ☎888-382-7245, fax 800-432-1329; Canada ☎800-361-7245, fax 905-602-4198; UK ☎0990 84 88 48; www.raileurope.com) or **DER Travel Services**, 9501 W. Devon Ave. #301, Rosemont, IL 60018 (US ☎888-337-7350; fax 800-282-7474; www.dertravel.com).

INTERRAIL PASSES FOR EUROPEAN RESIDENTS. If you have lived for at least six months in one of the European countries where InterRail Passes are valid, they prove an economical option. There are eight **InterRail zones;** France is in Zone E (along with Belgium, the Netherlands, and Luxembourg). The **Under 26 InterRail Card** allows either 22 days or one month of unlimited travel within one, two, three or all of the eight zones; the cost is determined by the number of zones the pass covers (UK£129-229). If you buy a ticket including the zone in which you have claimed residence, you must still pay 50% fare for tickets inside your own country. The **Over 26 InterRail Card** provides the same services as the Under 26 InterRail Card, but at higher prices: UK£185-319.

Passholders receive **discounts** on rail travel, Eurostar journeys, and most ferries to Ireland, Scandinavia, and the rest of Europe. Most exclude **supplements** for high-speed trains. For info and ticket sales in Europe contact **Student Travel Center,** 24 Rupert St., 1st fl., London W1V 7FN (☎020 74 37 81 01; fax 77 34 38 36; www.student-travel-centre.com). Tickets are also available from travel agents or main train stations throughout Europe.

DISCOUNT RAIL TICKETS. SNCF offers a wide range of discounted roundtrip tickets for travelers in France which go under the name **tarifs Découvertes**—you should rarely have to pay full price. Get a calendar from a train station detailing **période bleue** (blue period), **période blanche** (white period), and **période rouge** (red period) times and days; blue gets the most discounts, while red gets none. The **Découverte à deux, Découverte Séjour,** and **Découverte 12-25** all give a 25% discount on tickets on a limited number of seats on all TGV services and on any other journey starting during a blue period. They differ in eligibility requirements. The *Découverte à deux* is only available to two adults traveling together on both legs of a roundtrip journey, the *Découverte Séjour* applies to roundtrip journeys of at least 200km and requires a stay over a Saturday night, and the *Découverte 12-25* (270F/€41.16) is only available to travelers between the ages of 12 and 25. The *Carte Senior* (290F/€44.21) and *Carte Enfants+* (350F/€53.36) offer similar discounts. SNCF discounts also earn you savings on Avis car rental from SNCF stations.

Those under the age of 25 can also take advantage of the **Carte 12-25.** This is available for 270F/€41.16 at SNCF stations and is valid for a year from the date of purchase; you'll need proof of age and a passport-sized photo to buy one. With it you get 25-50% off all TGV trains, 50% off all other trips which started during a blue period, and 25% off those starting in a white period. Those over the age of 21 can also take advantage of savings on Avis car rentals. The SNCF often has special offers for youth travelers—check their website for details (see below).

For travelers under 26, **BIJ** tickets (Billets Internationals de Jeunesse; a.k.a. **Wasteels, Eurotrain,** and **Route 26**) are a great alternative to railpasses. Available for both international trips within Europe and travel within France as well as most ferry services, they knock 20-40% off regular second-class fares. Tickets are good for 60 days after purchase and allow a number of stopovers along the normal direct route of the train journey. Issued for a specific international route between two points, they must be used in the direction and order of the designated route and must be bought in Europe. **BIGT** tickets, the over-26 equivalent, provide a 20-30% discount on 1st- and 2nd-class international tickets for business travelers, temporary residents of Europe, and their families. Both types of tickets are available from European travel agents or at Wasteels or Eurotrain offices. Wasteels agents are widespread in France, and *Let's Go* lists many in town write-ups.

FURTHER READING & RESOURCES ON TRAIN TRAVEL.

Point-to-point fares and schedules: www.raileurope.com/us/rail/fares_schedules/index.htm. Allows you to calculate whether buying a railpass would save you money. For a more convenient resource, see our **railplanner** at the front of this book.

SNCF: www.sncf.fr; www.sncf.fr/indexe.htm is in English.

Wasteels: www.voyages-wasteels.fr.

European Railway Servers: mercurio.iet.unipi.it/home.html. Links to rail servers throughout Europe.

Info on rail travel and railpasses: www.eurorail.com; www.raileuro.com.

Thomas Cook European Timetable, updated monthly, covers all major and most minor train routes in Europe. In the US, order it from Forsyth Travel Library (US$28; ☎800-367-7984; www.forsyth.com). In Europe, find it at any Thomas Cook Money Exchange Center. Alternatively, buy directly from Thomas Cook (www.thomascook.com).

Guide to European Railpasses, Rick Steves. Available online and by mail (US ☎425-771-8303; fax 425-671-0833; www.ricksteves.com). Free; delivery $8.

On the Rails Around Europe: A Comprehensive Guide to Travel by Train, Melissa Shales. Thomas Cook Ltd. (US$18.95).

Eurail and Train Travel Guide to Europe. Houghton Mifflin (US$15).

BY BUS

In France, long-distance buses are a secondary transportation choice and service is rare and infrequent compared to most other European countries. However, within a given region buses can be indispensable for reaching out-of-the-way towns and villages and in some areas they rival trains for speed. Many bus services are operated by the SNCF itself; these accept railpasses. Other services are operated by regional companies; prices and punctuality vary for these. *Let's Go* lists the local bus companies and relevant destinations for each town. Bus stations are usually adjacent to the train station. Bus schedules usually tell you whether the buses run during *"période scolaire"* (during the school year), *"période de vacances"* (vacations), or both. Sundays and holidays are *"jours feriés"*; there are few buses on these days.

BY CAR

Unless you are traveling in a group of three or more, you won't save money traveling long distance by car rather than train, thanks to highway tolls, high gasoline costs, and rental charges. If you can't decide between train and car travel, you may benefit from a combination of the two; RailEurope and other railpass vendors offer rail-and-drive packages both for both individual countries and for all of Europe. Fly-and-drive packages are also often available from travel agents or airline/rental agency partnerships.

The French drive on the right-hand side of the road. Speed limits on *autoroutes* are 130km/h (81 mph); smaller highways are 110km/h (68mph) and cities are usually 50-60km/h (about 35 mph). Since *autoroute* toll tickets are printed with the time you left the booth, the ticket-takers at the other end can calculate how fast you've been going (and the accompanying penalty). **Fines** range from 900F/€137 to 5000F/€762, though you can get a 30% reduction on speeding and other driving fines by paying at the time of the ticketing or within 24 hours. France has a **mandatory seatbelt law** and children under 10 may not ride in the front of the car.

One quirk of the French highway code is that cars entering a road from the right have priority, even when joining major roads; thus be prepared for people to turn onto the road in front of you with little or no warning. If you see inverted triangle road signs with exclamation marks proclaiming *"vous n'avez pas la priorité"* or *"cédez le passage,"* this rule does not apply and you will be expected to yield before turning right; this is normally the case on major roundabouts. Flashing of highbeams means "I AM going first, you incompetent slug," not "Go right ahead." An invaluable resource for those planning to drive is **iTinéraire** (www.iti.fr); you enter your starting and end points and it draws up various routes according to speed and budget, along with estimates of driving time and toll and gas costs. **Gas stations** in most towns won't accept cash after 7pm, but they will take the French *Carte Bleue* credit card; if you're in a pinch, ask someone who has one and then reimburse him. Gas generally costs around 5.50F-7.50/€0.84-1.14 per liter. If you **break down** or get in an accident, walk to the nearest phone and dial 17, the universal emergency number. They'll need to know what town you're near.

FINDING YOUR WHEELS

RENTALS. You can **rent** a car from an international firm (e.g. Avis, Budget, or Hertz) with European offices, from a European-based company with local representatives (e.g. Europcar), or from a tour operator (e.g. Auto Europe, Europe By Car, or Kemwel Holiday Autos), which will arrange a rental for you from a European company at its own rates. Multinationals offer greater flexibility, but tour operators often strike better deals. Expect to pay at least US$150 per week, plus 20.6% tax, for a small car; you'll probably have to purchase insurance as well (see below). Automatic gearboxes cost extra and are often unavailable on the cheaper cars; most Europeans prefer the performance and economy of stick-shifts. Diesel *(gazole)* fuel tends to be cheaper than unleaded *(essence sans plomb)*. Reserve well before leaving for France and pay in advance if at all possible.

Always check if prices quoted include tax, unlimited mileage, and collision insurance; some credit card companies cover this automatically. Ask about discounts and check the terms of insurance, particularly the size of the deductible. Non-Europeans should check with their national motoring organization (like AAA or CAA) for international coverage. Ask your airline about fly-and-drive packages; you may get up to a week of free or discounted rental. The minimum age for renting is usually 21, though some agencies won't rent to anyone under 23; those under 25 will often have to pay a surcharge. At most agencies, all that's needed to rent a car is a valid drivers' license and proof that you've had it for a year.

Car rental can now be done over the Internet, and many websites will search out deals from multiple companies for you. Check out **Travel Now** (www.travel.com/mall/2) and the **Internet Travel Network** (www.itn.net/cgi/get?itn/cb/traveldotcom/index). Rental agencies in France include:

Auto Europe: US ☎888-223-5555; UK ☎0800 89 9893; Australia ☎0011 800 223 5555 5; www.autoeurope.com.

Avis: US and Canada ☎800-230-4898; UK ☎(0870) 606-0100; Australia ☎136 333; New Zealand ☎(0800) 655 111; www.avis.com.

Budget: US and Canada ☎800-527-0700; www.budgetrentacar.com.

Europe by Car: US ☎800-223-1516 or 212-581-3040; www.europebycar.com.

Europcar: US ☎800-227-3876; Canada ☎877-940-6900; France ☎(33) 1 30 44 00 00; www.europcar.com. Europcar is one of the few international services which will rent to those age 21-24 at many sites.

Hertz: US ☎800-654-3001; Canada ☎800-263-0600; UK ☎(08708) 448844; Australia ☎61 (3) 9698 2555; www.hertz.com.

LEASING. An option only for non-EU residents, **leasing** can be cheaper than rental for periods longer than 17 days; it is often the only option for those aged 18-21. The cheapest leases are agreements to buy the car and then sell it back to the manufacturer at a prearranged price. As far as you're concerned it's a lease and doesn't entail enormous financial transactions. While the base price of a lease may not seem very different from a regular car rental, recall they include comprehensive insurance, unlimited mileage, and are tax-free—you just pay what's quoted, plus gas. Expect to pay at least US$1200 for 60 days. Contact **Auto Europe,** or **Europe by Car** (see above). There's a fair deal of paperwork to be done in advance—you should arrange the lease at least 30 days before your departure.

BUYING. If you're brave and know what you're doing, buying a used vehicle in France and reselling it before you leave can provide the cheapest wheels for long trips. Check with consulates for import-export laws concerning used vehicles, registration, and safety and emission standards. Camper-vans and motor homes give the advantages of a car without the hassle and expense of finding lodgings. Most of these vehicles are diesel-powered and deliver roughly 24-30 miles per gallon.

PERMITS AND CAR INSURANCE

INTERNATIONAL DRIVING PERMIT (IDP). Those in possession of a valid EU-issued driving license are entitled to drive in France with no further ado. While others may be legally able to drive in France on the strength of their national licenses for a few months, not all police know it; it's safest to get an International Driving Permit (IDP), which is essentially a translation of your regular license into 10 languages, including French. The IDP, valid for one year, must be issued in your own country before you depart. You must be 18 years old to receive the IDP. The IDP is an addition, not a replacement, for your home license and is not valid without it. An application for an IDP usually needs to include one or two photos, a current local license, an additional form of identification, and a fee.

Australia: Contact your local Royal Automobile Club (RAC) or the National Royal Motorist Association if in NSW or the ACT (☎08 9421 4444; www.rac.com.au/travel). AUS$15.

Canada: Contact any Canadian Automobile Association (CAA) branch office or write to CAA, 1145 Hunt Club Rd., #200, K1V 0Y3. (☎613-247-0117; www.caa.ca/CAAInternet/travelservices/internationaldocumentation/idptravel.htm). CDN$10.

Ireland: Contact the nearest Automobile Association (AA) office or write to the UK address below. The Irish Automobile Association, 23 Suffolk St., Rockhill, Blackrock, Co. Dublin (☎(01) 617 9999), honors most foreign automobile memberships (24hr. breakdown and road service ☎(800) 667 788; toll-free in Ireland). IR£4.

New Zealand: Contact your local Automobile Association (AA) or their main office at Auckland Central, 99 Albert St. (☎(09) 377 4660; www.nzaa.co.nz.). NZ$10.

South Africa: Contact the Travel Services Department of the Automobile Association of South Africa at P.O. Box 596, 2000 Johannesburg (☎(11) 799 1400; www.aasa.co.za). ZAR28.50.

UK: To visit your local AA Shop, contact the **AA General Information** (☎(0870) 600 0371), or write to: The Automobile Association, International Documents, Fanum House, Erskine, Renfrewshire PA8 6BW. For more info, see www.theaa.co.uk/motoringandtravel/idp/index.asp. UK£4.

US: Visit any American Automobile Association (AAA) office (call ☎800-564-6222 for the office nearest you) or write to AAA Florida, Travel Related Services, 1000 AAA Drive (mail stop 100), Heathrow, FL 32746 (☎407-444-7000. You do not have to be a member of AAA to purchase an IDP. US$10.

CAR INSURANCE. EU residents driving their own cars do not need any extra insurance coverage in France. For those renting, paying with a gold credit card (or a standard American Express) usually covers basic insurance; if your home car insurance covers you for liability, make sure you get a **green card** or **International Insurance Certificate** to prove it. If you have a collision abroad, the accident will show up on your domestic records if you report it to your insurance company. Otherwise, be prepared to shell out US$5-10 per day for insurance on a rental car. Leasing should include insurance and the green card in the price. Some travel agents offer the card; it may also be available at border crossings.

BY BICYCLE

Many airlines will count your bike as your second piece of luggage, but some charge about US$60-110 each way. Bikes must be packed in a cardboard box with the pedals and front wheel detached; buy a box at the airport (US$10). Most ferries let you take your bike for free or for a nominal fee. You can always ship your bike on trains, though the cost varies. Renting a bike beats bringing your own if your touring is confined to a few regions. Some hostels rent bicycles for low prices.

Riding a bike with a frame pack strapped on it or your back is not safe; a **basket** or a **panier** is essential. The first thing to buy is a suitable **bike helmet** (US$25-50). The most secure locks are U-shaped **Citadel** or **Kryptonite** locks (from US$30). Contact **Bike Nashbar,** 4111 Simon Rd., Youngstown, OH 44512 (☎800-627-4227; www.nashbar.com), which ships anywhere in the US or Canada.

If you are nervous about striking out on your own, **Blue Marble Travel** (☎519-624-2494 in Canada; ☎973-326-9533 in US; ☎01 42 36 02 34 in France; www.bluemarble.org) offers bike tours designed for adults aged 20 to 50. Pedal with or without your 10 to 15 companions through the Alps, Austria, France, Germany, Italy, Portugal, Scandinavia, and Spain. Full-time graduate and professional students may get discounts and "stand-by" rates may be obtained in Europe through the Paris office. **CBT Tours,** 2506 N. Clark St., #1003, Chicago, IL 60614 (US ☎800-736-2453; www.cbttours.com), offers full-package 7 to 12 day biking, mountain biking, and hiking tours (around US$200 per day). Tours run June to September, with departures every 7-10 days, and visit Belgium, the Czech Republic, France, Germany, Holland, Hungary, Ireland, Italy, Luxembourg, Switzerland, and the UK.

For further info, **Mountaineers Books,** 1001 S.W. Klickitat Way #201, Seattle, WA 98134 (☎800-553-4453; www.mountaineers.org), offers *Europe By Bike*, by Karen and Terry Whitehill (US$15), and country-specific biking guides.

BY MOPED AND MOTORCYCLE

Motorbikes don't use much gas and are a good compromise between the high cost of car travel and the limited range of bicycles. However, they're uncomfortable for long distances, dangerous in the rain, and unpredictable on rough roads and gravel. Always wear a helmet and never ride with a backpack. If you've never been on a moped before, a twisting Alpine road is not the place to start. Expect to pay about 100-150F/€15.25-22.90 per day; try auto repair shops and remember to bargain. Motorcycles are more expensive and require a license, but are better for long distances. **Bosenberg Motorcycle Excursions,** Mainzer Str. 54, 55545 Bad Kreuznach, Germany (☎(+49) 671 673 12; www.bosenberg.com), arranges tours in the Alps, Austria, France, Italy, and Switzerland; they also rent motorcycles April to October. Before renting, ask if the quoted price includes tax and insurance or you may be hit with an unexpected additional fee. Avoid handing your passport over as a deposit; if you have an accident or mechanical failure you may not get it back until you cover all repairs. Pay ahead of time instead. For **further info,** consult *Europe by Motorcycle*, by Gregory Frazier (Arrowstar Publishing, US$20).

BY FOOT

France's grandest scenery can often be seen only by foot. *Let's Go* describes many daytrips and short hikes for those who want to hoof it, but tourist offices, locals, hostel owners, and fellow travelers are the best source of tips. France is criss-crossed by over 30,000km of footpaths known as **sentiers de grandes randonnées** or just **GR**, signposted and dotted with campsites and *refuges*.The **Fédération française de randonnée pédestre (FFRP),** 14 rue Riquet, 75019 Paris (☎01 44 89 93 93; fax 01 40 35 85 67; www.ffrp.asso.fr) publishes the *Topoguide* series of guides for each GR route in French, with maps and details of accommodations on the way.

The route of the GR65, which runs from Le Puy-en-Velay in the Massif Central to St-Jean-Pied-de-Port on the way to Santiago de Compostella in Spain, was trod for centuries before hiking became a fashionable form of relaxation. Thousands of people still undertake **pilgrimages** on foot; Le Puy and Santiago are the oldest and best-known destinations and trails lead to them from all over Europe. Pilgrims can stay at monasteries and special pilgrim hostels along the way; to stay there you'll need a letter from your local priest stating that you are a bonafide pilgrim.

For more info, check out **France on Foot** (www.franceonfoot.com), and **Hiking in France** (www.hejoly.demon.nl/countries/france.html).

BY THUMB

No one should hitch (*"faire l'autostop"*) without careful consideration of the risks involved. Not everyone can be an airplane pilot, but any bozo can drive a car. Hitching means entrusting your life to a total stranger, risking theft, assault, sexual harassment, unsafe driving, and exposure to never-ending reminiscences about the Crimean War. Be warned that many consider France the hardest country in Europe to get a lift in. If you're a woman traveling alone, don't hitch—it's just too dangerous. A man and a woman are a safer combination, two men will have a hard time getting lifts, and three people will go nowhere.

THUMBS DOWN? *Let's Go* urges you to consider the risks before you choose to hitch-hike. We do not recommend hitching as a safe means of transportation and none of the information presented here is intended to do so.

Where you stand is very important. Experienced hitchers pick a spot outside built-up areas, where drivers can stop and return to the road safely and have time to look over potential passengers as they approach. Hitching (or even standing) on *autoroutes* is illegal; one can only thumb at rest stops, tollbooths, or highway entrance ramps. *Let's Go* occasionally lists reportedly strategic hitching spots.

Success also depends on what a hitcher looks like. Successful hitchers travel light and stack their belongings in a compact but visible cluster. Most Europeans signal with an open hand, rather than a thumb; many write their destination on a sign in large, bold letters and draw a smiley-face under it or write "S.V.P." (*"s'il vous plait,"* or "please"). Drivers prefer hitchers who are neat and wholesome. No one stops for anyone wearing sunglasses. It's a good idea to wait at places where drivers are forced to slow down, but can easily pull over to pick you up—off-ramps, roundabouts, and the like. One of the best methods is to approach people directly as they get into their cars in parking lots.

Safety issues are always foremost, even for those who are not hitching alone. Safety-minded hitchers avoid getting in the back of a two-door car and never let go of their backpacks. They will not get into a car that they can't get out of again in a hurry. If they ever feel threatened, they insist on being let off, regardless of where they are. Acting as if you're going to open the car door or vomit on the upholstery will usually get a driver to stop. Hitchhiking at night can be particularly dangerous; experienced hitchers stand in well-lit places and expect drivers to be leery of nocturnal thumbers (or open-handers). For the most thorough website on hitch-hiking (though it contains little on France specifically) check out **H's Guide to Everywhere** (www.suite101.com/welcome.cfm/hitch_hiking).

An often safer alternative is to contact a ride service, a cross between hitchhiking and the ride boards common at many universities, which pairs drivers with riders; the fee varies according to destination. **Eurostop International** (**Allostop** in France; www.ecritel.fr/allostop/) is one of the largest in Europe. Riders and drivers can enter their names on the Internet through the **Taxistop** (www.taxistop.be) website. Not all of these organizations screen drivers and riders; ask in advance.

SPECIFIC CONCERNS

WOMEN TRAVELERS

NATIONAL RAPE HOTLINE	**SOS Viol:** ☎0800 05 95 95 offers counseling and assistance in French. Open M-F 10am-6pm.

Women exploring on their own face additional safety concerns, but it's easy to be adventurous without taking undue risks. If you are concerned, consider staying in hostels which offer single rooms that lock from the inside. Communal showers in some hostels are safer than others; check before settling in. Stick to central accommodations and avoid solitary late-night walks or travel.

Women traveling alone or in small groups are inevitably going to get unwanted attention, especially in the south. French men often regard solo women travelers as soft targets; the best response to their advances is the one French women have developed: a withering, icy stare. Speaking to *dragueurs* (as the French call them), even to say "NO!", is only inviting a reply, but if you feel threatened don't hesitate to call out to others or to draw attention to yourself. A loud *"laissez-moi tranquille!"* (leh-SEH mwa tranhk-EEL; "leave me alone!") or *"au secours!"* (oh-S'KOOR; "help!") will embarrass them and hopefully send them on their way. Harassment can be minimized by making yourself as inconspicuous as possible (see **Blending In,** *p. 40*, for tips), though in some cities you might be harassed no matter how you're dressed. A conspicuous **wedding ring** may dissuade unwanted overtures. Even a mention of a husband waiting back at the hotel can be enough.

Hitching is never safe for lone women or even for two women traveling together. If traveling long-distance by train, choose coach-style carriages over compartments; if this is impossible, choose a compartment occupied by other women or couples. Always look as if you know where you're going and consider approaching older women or couples for directions if you're lost or feel uncomfortable.

ESSENTIALS

Don't hesitate to seek out a police officer or a passerby if you are being harassed. *Let's Go* lists crisis numbers in the Practical Information listings of most cities. **In an emergency, dial 17 for police assistance.** Carry a **whistle** or an airhorn on your keychain and don't hesitate to use it in an emergency. A **model mugging** self-defense course will not only prepare you for a potential attack, but will also raise your level of awareness of your surroundings and your confidence. Women also face some specific health concerns when traveling (see **Women's Health,** p. 45).

TRAVELING ALONE

Traveling alone has obvious benefits, but any solo traveler is also a good target for harassment and street theft. Lone travelers need to be well-organized and look confident at all times. Try not to stand out as a tourist and be especially careful in deserted or very crowded areas. If questioned, never admit that you are traveling alone. Maintain regular contact with someone at home who knows your itinerary.

A number of organizations supply info for solo travelers and others find travel companions for others. A few are listed here. For further info, consult *Traveling Solo*, by Eleanor Berman (Globe Pequot, US$17).

Connecting: Solo Travel Network, 689 Park Road, Unit 6, Gibsons, BC V0N 1V7, Canada (☎604-886-9099; www.cstn.org). Bi-monthly newsletter features solo tips and travel companion ads. Annual directory lists holiday suppliers that avoid single supplement charges. Advice and lodging exchanges between members. Membership US$28.

Travel Companion Exchange, P.O. Box 833, Amityville, NY 11701, USA (☎(631) 454-0880; www.whytravelalone.com). Publishes the pamphlet *Foiling Pickpockets & Bag Snatchers* (US$5) and *Travel Companions*, a newsletter (subscription US$48).

OLDER TRAVELERS

Almost all museums and sights in France offer discounts for senior citizens and many cities also offer special rates for public transportation. France is very popular with older travelers and major sights are well equipped to deal with their special needs. However, budget accommodations are not so accommodating; for example, they rarely have elevators and often have extremely steep stairs. Make sure to call ahead to check facilities if you have any special concerns.

Elderhostel, 75 Federal St., Boston, MA 02110-1941, USA (☎877-426-8056 M-F 9am-9pm; www.elderhostel.org; registration@elderhostel.org). Programs at colleges, universities, and other learning centers in Europe, including Paris, on varied subjects lasting 1-4 weeks. Must be 55 or over (spouse can be of any age).

Walking the World, P.O. Box 1186, Fort Collins, CO 80522, USA (☎800-340-9255; www.walkingtheworld.com), organizes trips for travelers over 50 to France.

FURTHER READING. *No Problem! Worldwise Tips for Mature Adventurers*, by Janice Kenyon (Orca Book Publishers, US$16); *A Senior's Guide to Healthy Travel*, by Donald L. Sullivan (Career Press, US$15).

BISEXUAL, GAY, AND LESBIAN TRAVELERS

France has been changing its ways alongside the rest of the modern world; gay communities, with help lines, bars, and meeting places have sprung up in all its major cities. The **Marais,** in Paris has a notably gay-friendly atmosphere, as do parts of Bordeaux and the French Riviera. **Montpellier** is regarded as the center of gay life in southern France. In general, however, the French countryside and many towns retain their traditional stereotypes. To avoid possibly offending or uncomfortable situations, use discretion when interacting with your significant other in public and don't assume that a stretchy shirt or a little flamboyance is a blip on your gay-dar. Listed below are contact organizations, mail-order bookstores and publishers which offer materials addressing some specific concerns.

Gay's the Word, 66 Marchmont St., London WC1N 1AB, UK (☎(020) 7278 7654; www.gaystheword.co.uk). The largest gay and lesbian bookshop in the UK, with both fiction and non-fiction titles. Mail-order service available.

Giovanni's Room, 1145 Pine St., Philadelphia, PA 19107, USA (☎215-923-2960; www.queerbooks.com). An international lesbian/feminist and gay bookstore with mail-order service (carries many of the publications listed below).

International Gay and Lesbian Travel Association, 52 W. Oakland Park Blvd. #237, Wilton Manors, FL 33311, USA (☎954-776-2626; fax 776-3303; www.iglta.com). An organization of over 1350 companies serving gay and lesbian travelers worldwide.

International Lesbian and Gay Association (ILGA), 81 rue Marché-au-Charbon, B-1000 Brussels, Belgium (☎+32 2 502 2471; www.ilga.org). Provides political info, such as homosexuality laws of individual countries.

FURTHER READING. *Spartacus International Gay Guide 2001-2002* (Bruno Gmunder Verlag, US$33); *Damron Men's Guide, Damron's Accommodations,* and *The Women's Traveller* (Damron Travel Guides, US$14-19; for more info, call 800-462-6654 or visit www.damron.com); *Ferrari Guides' Gay Travel A to Z, Ferrari Guides' Men's Travel in Your Pocket,* and *Ferrari Guides' Inn Places* (Ferrari Publications, US$16-20; purchase online at www.ferrariguides.com); *The Gay Vacation Guide: The Best Trips and How to Plan Them* (Mark Chesnut, Citadel Press, US$15).

TRAVELERS WITH DISABILITIES

Rail is probably the most convenient form of travel for disabled travelers in France. SNCF offers wheelchair compartments on all TGV services, while availability on other services is indicated by a wheelchair icon on train timetables. Ask for the *Guide du voyageur a mobilité réduit* at train stations for more details. Guide dog owners from Britain and Ireland will have trouble getting their pooches past quarantine on the return trip; contact the PETS helpline at (087) 0241 1710 or consult www.maff.gov.uk/animalh/quarantine for details. Others should inquire as to the specific quarantine policies of their own country, as well as regulations for entering France. In Paris and other major cities, public transport has seats which are earmarked for disabled or infirm passengers. Taxis are obliged to take wheelchair-bound passengers and to help you in and out of the car; they must also take guide-dogs. Hertz, Avis, and National car rental agencies have hand-controlled vehicles at some locations, but they must be reserved at least 48 hours in advance.

Unfortunately, budget hotels and restaurants are generally ill-equipped for handicapped visitors. Handicapped-accessible bathrooms are virtually non-existent in the one- to two-star range of hotels. The brochure *Paris-Ile-de-France for Everyone* (available in French and English for 60F/€9.15 at most Parisian tourist offices) lists accessible sites, hotels, and restaurants, as well as useful tips.

Many museums and sights are wheelchair-accessible and some provide guided tours in **sign language;** contact the museum in advance to assure availability. The following organizations provide info or publications that might be useful:

Comité National Français de Liaison pour la Réadaption des Handicapés (CNFLRH), 236bis, r. de Tolbiac, 13*ème* (☎01 53 80 66 66; fax 01 53 80 66 67; cnrh@worldnet.net; www.handitel.org). Publishes *Paris-Ile-de-France for Everyone,* an English-language guide to hotels and sights with wheelchair access (60F/€9.15 in France, 80F/€12.20 abroad).

Mobility International USA (MIUSA), P.O. Box 10767, Eugene, OR 97440, USA (☎(541) 343-1284 voice and TDD; info@miusa.org; www.miusa.org). Sells *A World of Options: A Guide to International Educational Exchange, Community Service, and Travel for Persons with Disabilities* (US$35).

Society for the Advancement of Travel for the Handicapped (SATH), 347 Fifth Ave., #610, New York, NY 10016, USA (☎212-447-7284; www.sath.org). An advocacy group that publishes free online travel info and the travel magazine *OPEN WORLD* (US$18, free for members). Annual membership US$45, students and seniors US$30.

Directions Unlimited, 123 Green Ln., Bedford Hills, NY 10507, USA (☎800-533-5343; www.travel-cruises.com). Specializes in arranging individual and group vacations, tours, and cruises for the physically disabled.

FURTHER READING. *Access in Paris*, by Gordon Couch (Quiller Press, US$12); *Resource Directory for the Disabled*, by Richard Neil Shrout (Facts on File, US$45); *Wheelchair Through Europe*, by Annie Mackin (Graphic Language Press, US$13); *Global Access* (www.geocities.com/Paris/1502/disabilitylinks.html) has links for disabled travelers in France.

MINORITY TRAVELERS

Like much of Europe, France has experienced a wave of reverse-colonization in the past few decades. The biggest group of immigrants are North Africans, who number over a million, followed by West Africans and Vietnamese. This influx has led to a surge in support for the far-right National Front party and many French people are sympathetic to its cry of *"la France pour les français"* (France for the French). Anyone who might be taken for **North African** can encounter verbal abuse and is more likely than other travelers to be stopped and questioned by the police. Racism is especially bad in the Southeast, and the police may not be entirely helpful if you get into trouble with racists. The following organizations can provide you both with advice about your travel and help in the event of a racist encounter:

S.O.S. Racisme, 28, rue des Petites Ecuries, 10*ème* (☎01 53 24 67 67; www.sos-racisme.org). Occupied primarily with helping illegal immigrants and people with irregular documentation. They provide legal services and are used to negotiating with police.

MRAP (Mouvement contre le racisme et pour l'amitié entre les peuples), 43, bd. Magenta, 10*ème* (☎01 53 38 99 99; fax 01 40 40 90 98; www.mrap.asso.fr/mrap.htm). Handles immigration issues, monitors racist publications and propaganda.

TRAVELERS WITH CHILDREN

Family vacations often require that you slow your pace and always require advance planning. If you're thinking of staying at a B&B, **call ahead** and make sure it's child-friendly. If you rent a car, make sure the rental company provides a car seat for younger children; French law mandates that children sit in the rear. Be sure that your child carries some sort of ID in case of an emergency, and arrange a reunion spot in case of separation when sight-seeing.

Parents of **fussy eaters** should make sure there's something acceptable before choosing a restaurant. Cheaper restaurants often have a children's menu. Most museums and tourist attractions also have a **children's rate,** usually included in each *Let's Go* listing. Children under two generally fly for 10% of the adult airfare on international flights (this does not necessarily include a seat). International fares are usually discounted 25% for children from age two to 11.

FURTHER READING. *Backpacking with Babies and Small Children*, by Goldie Silverman (Wilderness Press, US$10); *Take Your Kids to Europe*, by Cynthia W. Harriman (Globe Pequot, US$17); *How to take Great Trips with Your Kids*, by Sanford and Jane Portnoy (Harvard Common Press, US$10); *Have Kid, Will Travel: 101 Survival Strategies for Vacationing With Babies and Young Children*, by Claire and Lucille Tristram (Andrews and McMeel, US$9).

DIETARY CONCERNS

Those with special dietary requirements may feel left behind in France. **Vegetarians** will find dining out difficult (see **A French Food Primer, p. 24**) and **vegans** will find it near impossible. Both are most likely to find something at ethnic restaurants. Though the French are very fond of salads, be especially careful to make sure they understand that you don't want fish, chicken livers, or cheese with your greens.

For more info about vegetarian travel, contact the **North American Vegetarian Society** (P.O. Box 72, Dolgeville, NY 13329; US ☎518-568-7970; www.navs-online.org) for a copy of *Transformative Adventures*, a guide to vacations and retreats (US$15). Another valuable resource is the **International Vegetarian Union** (www.ivu.org), which publishes a biannual newsletter and maintains a comprehensive website including links to French vegetarian organizations.

Kosher food exists in France, which has one of Western Europe's largest Jewish populations, but tracking it down may prove difficult, especially in rural regions. Kosher travelers should contact synagogues in larger cities for info on restaurants; your home synagogue or college Hillel should have lists of Jewish institutions across the nation. If you observe strictly, you may have to prepare your own food. **The Jewish Travel Guide,** edited by Michael Zaidner, lists synagogues, kosher restaurants, and Jewish institutions in over 100 countries and is available in Europe from Vallentine Mitchell Publishers, Crown House, 47 Chase Side, Southgate, London N14 5BP, UK (☎(020) 8920 2100; fax 8447 8548) and in the US at 5824 NE Hassalo St., Portland, OR, 97213 (☎800-944-6190; fax 503-280-8832) for $16.95.

FURTHER READING. *The Vegetarian Traveller: Where to Stay if You're Vegetarian, Vegan, or Environmentally Sensitive*, by Jed and Susan Civic (US$16); *Europe on 10 Salads a Day*, by Greg and Mary Jane Edwards (Mustang Publishing, US$10); *The Jewish Travel Guide*, by Betsy Sheldon (Hunter, US$17).

ALTERNATIVES TO TOURISM

STUDY

France is one of the most popular international spots for academic study, and hundreds of institutions offer courses from a few weeks of French language immersion to advanced degrees in all fields. You don't even need to speak French to get a degree; in a 1999 bid to bolster the long-term standing of France (and earn a little foreign currency on the side), the French government announced a program to offer some degree courses in English to overseas students. Though **Paris** has the highest concentration and variety of programs, student options can be found in **Lille, Lyon,** and **Nice** as well as in almost any French city with a university.

All non-EU citizens need a study visa if they intend to spend more than three months studying in France, while all foreigners (both EU and non-) need a residency permit. As long as you have been accepted into a course and can show proof of financial independence, you should have no trouble getting a study visa. For details, see **Visas and Work Permits, p. 33**.

FRENCH UNIVERSITIES. Higher education is a government service in France and as such is extremely accessible. French universities are segmented into three degree levels. Programs at the first level (except the *Grandes Ecoles*, below) are two or three years long, generally focus on science, medicine, and the liberal arts, and must admit anyone holding a *baccalauréat* (French graduation certificate) or recognized equivalent. A certificate or diploma of secondary-school completion in most countries is enough, although French competency or other testing may be required (for Americans, two years of college French are expected). The more selective and more demanding **Grandes Ecoles** cover specializations from physics to photography to veterinary medicine. These have notoriously difficult entrance examinations which require a year of preparatory schooling.

French universities are far cheaper than their American equivalents; however, it can be hard to receive academic credit at home for a non-approved program. Expect to pay at least 3000F/€457 per month in living expenses. EU citizens studying in France can take advantage of the 3-12 month **SOCRATES** program, which offers grants to support inter-European educational exchanges. Most UK and Irish universities will have details of the grants available and the application procedure.

EU law dictates that educational qualifications be recognized across the Union (with the exception of some professional subjects). These organizations can supply further info on academic programs in France:

American Institute for Foreign Study, College Division, River Plaza, 9 West Broad St., Stamford, CT 06902, USA (☎800-727-2437, ext. 5163; www.aifsabroad.com). Organizes programs for high school and college study in universities in France.

Central College Abroad, Office of International Education, 812 University, Pella, IA 50219, USA (☎800-831-3629 or 641-628-5284; studyabroad.com/central). Offers semester- and year-long programs in France. US$25 application fee.

School for International Training, College Semester Abroad, Admissions, Kipling Rd., P.O. Box 676, Brattleboro, VT 05302, USA (☎800-336-1616 or 802-258-3267; www.sit.edu). Semester- and year-long programs in France run US$10,600-13,700. Also runs the **Experiment in International Living** (☎800-345-2929; fax 802-258-3428; eil@worldlearning.org), 3- to 5-week summer programs that offer high-school students cross-cultural homestays, community service, ecological adventure, and language training in France and cost US$1900-5000.

Agence EduFrance, 173 bd. Saint-Germain, 75006 Paris (☎01 53 63 35 00; www.edufrance.fr), is a one-stop resource for North Americans thinking about studying for a degree in France. Info on courses, costs, grant opportunities, and student life in France.

American University of Paris, 60 East 42nd St., Suite 1463, New York NY 10017 (☎(212) 983-1414; www.aup.fr); 31 Avenue Bosquet, 75343 Paris (☎01 40 62 07 20), offers US-accredited degrees and summer programs taught in English at its Paris campus. Tuition and living expenses total about US$28,000 per year.

Université Paris-Sorbonne, 1, rue Victor Cousin, 75230 Paris Cedex 05 (☎01 40 46 22 11; www.paris4.sorbonne.fr), the grand-daddy of French universities, was founded in 1253 and is still going strong. Inscription into degree courses costs about 2500F/ €381.16 per year. Also offers 3-9 month-long programs for American students.

Study Abroad, 1450 Edgmont Ave., Suite 140, Chester, PA 19013, USA (☎610-499-9200; www.studyabroad.com), maintains a compilation of countless international exchanges and study programs, including about 175 in France.

LANGUAGE SCHOOLS. Many French universities offer language courses during the summer, while independent organizations run throughout the year. The American University in Paris also runs a summer program (see above). For more info on language courses in France, contact your national **Institut Français,** official representatives of French culture attached to French embassies around the world (contact your nearest French embassy or consulate for details). The Canadian chapter has created a fantastic **clickable map** of language schools in France at www.ambafrance.org/COURS/index_eng.html. Other well-known schools include:

Alliance Française, Ecole Internationale de Langue et de Civilisation Françaises, 101 bd. Raspail, 75270 Paris Cedex 06 (☎01 42 84 90 00; www.alliancefr.org). Instruction at all levels, with specialized courses in legal and business French. Courses are 1-4 months in length, costing around 1500F/€228.69 for 2hr. per day and 3200F/€487.82 for 4hr. per day.

Cours de Civilisation Française de la Sorbonne, 47 rue des Écoles, 75005 Paris (☎01 40 46 22 11; www.fle.fr/sorbonne). Courses in the French language at all levels, along with a comprehensive lecture program of French cultural studies taught by Sorbonne professors. Must be at least 18 and at *baccalauréat* level. Semester- and year-long courses during the academic year and 4-, 6-, 8-, and 11-week summer programs.

Eurocentres, Head Office, Seestrasse 247, CH-8038 Zurich, Switzerland (☎+41 1 485 5040; www.eurocentres.com) and offices around the world. Language programs and homestays for US$1132 a month. 2-week to academic year programs for beginners to advanced. Schools in **Paris, Amboise, Tours, La Rochelle, Lausanne,** and **Neuchatel.**

WORK

Anyone hoping to come to France and slip easily into a job will face the tough reality that employers are still understandably more sympathetic toward French jobseekers than unqualified or very qualified foreigners.

OPTIONS FOR WORK. Non-EU citizens will find it almost impossible to get a work permit without a job offer; networking among your fellow country-men will prove your best bet for (illegal) employment. Full-time students at US universities can apply to work permit programs run by **Council on International Educational Exchange (Council)** and its member organizations. For a US$225 application fee, Council can procure three- to six-month work permits and a handbook to help you find work and housing. The **French-American Chamber of Commerce (FACC),** International Career Development Programs, 1350 Avenue of the Americas, 6th Floor, New York, NY 10019; ☎212-765-4598; fax 765-4650) has *Work In France* programs, internships, teaching and public works. Farm work is another option; the autumn *vendanges* (grape harvest) provides plentiful opportunities for backbreaking work in return for a small allowance and cheap wine. Check out **WWOOF** (Willing Workers on Organic Farms; WWOOF International, P.O. Box 2675, Lewes BN7 1RB, UK; www.phdcc.com/wwoof), which maintains an international list of farms seeking temporary workers in exchange for room and board.

Among other options for legal, gainful employment are **au pair** positions, which offer lodging, board, and a small stipend to young women (or, less commonly, young men) in return for childcare and household chores. You are unlikely to land a job **teaching English** in France unless you have a **TEFL** (Teaching of English as a Foreign Language) certificate or equivalent and a couple of years experience. If you are an experienced English teacher, though, you can try for an official position as a **Teaching Assistant** in a French school; contact your national French embassy for details. For more info on visas, see **Study and Work Permits, p. 32**.

EU citizens can work in France without a visa or work permit, though they will still need a **residency permit** (see p. 32). Those without an offer of employment have a grace period of three months in which to seek work; during this time they are eligible for social security benefits. To receive benefits, you must arrange in advance with your local social security office; be aware that EU bureaucracy often takes most of the three months just to process the paperwork. If you do not succeed in finding work during that time, you must return home unless you can prove your financial independence. By law, all EU citizens must be given equality of opportunity when applying for jobs not directly related to national security, so theoretically if you speak French you have as much chance of finding a job as an equivalently qualified French person. Theoretically.

AU PAIR

L'Accueil Familial des Jeunes Etrangers, 23 rue du Cherche-Midi, 75006 Paris (☎01 42 22 50 34; fax 01 45 44 60 48; afjeparis@aol.com). Arranges summer and 9-month or longer au pair jobs (placement fee 645F/€98.34 for Americans, Canadians, and EU citizens, 810F/€123.49 for others). Will help switch families if you are unhappy. Can also place you in paying guest (*hôte payant*) positions.

Accord Cultural Exchange, 750 La Playa, San Francisco, CA 94121, USA (☎415-386-6203; www.cognitext.com/accord), offers au pair jobs to people aged 18-29 in France. Au pairs work 5-6hr. per day, 30hr. per week, plus 2 evenings of babysitting. Program fees US$750 for the summer, US$1200 for the academic year. US$40 application fee.

Childcare International, Ltd., Trafalgar House, Grenville Place, London NW7 3SA (☎020 8906 3116; www.childint.co.uk) offers au pair positions in France. The organization prefers a long placement but does arrange summer work. UK£100 application fee.

TEACHING ENGLISH

International Schools Services, Educational Staffing Program, P.O. Box 5910, Princeton, NJ 08543, USA (☎609-452-0990; www.iss.edu). Recruits teachers and administrators (with at least a B.A. and 2 years of relevant experience) for instruction in English in American and English schools in France. Nonrefundable US$150 application fee. Publishes *The ISS Directory of Overseas Schools* (US$35).

Office of Overseas Schools, US Department of State, Room H328, SA-1, Washington, D.C. 20522, USA (☎202-261-8200; fax 261-8224; www.state.gov/www/about_state/schools/). Keeps a comprehensive list of schools abroad and agencies that arrange placement for Americans to teach abroad.

ARCHAEOLOGICAL DIGS

Archaeological Institute of America, 656 Beacon St., Boston, MA 02215, USA (☎617-353-9361; www.archaeological.org). The *Archaeological Fieldwork Opportunities Bulletin* (US$20 for non-members) lists field sites throughout Europe.

FINDING WORK ONCE THERE. Check help-wanted ads in French newspapers, especially *Le Monde*, *Le Figaro*, and the English-language *International Herald Tribune*, as well as *France-USA Contacts* (*FUSAC*), a free weekly circular filled with classifieds. Many of these jobs are "unofficial" and illegal (you risk deportation), but they often don't ask for a work permit. Be aware of your rights as an employee and always get written confirmation of your agreements. Youth hostels frequently provide room and board to those willing to help run the place.

In Paris, start your job search at the **American Church,** 65 quai d'Orsay, Paris 75007 (☎01 40 62 05 00) which posts a bulletin board (view daily 10am-10pm) full of job and housing opportunities for Americans abroad. Those with ambition and an up-to-date resume, in both French and English, should stop by the **American Chamber of Commerce in France,** 156 bd. Haussmann, 75008 Paris (☎01 56 43 45 67; fax 01 56 43 45 60; www.amchamfrance.org; open M-F 9am-5pm), an association of American businesses in France. Your resume will be kept on file for two months and placed at the disposal of French and American companies. Chamber of Commerce membership directories can be browsed in the Paris office, or you can have it send to you beforehand. (Library open Tu and Th 10am-12:30pm. Admission 50F/€7.62.) The **Agence Nationale Pour l'Emploi (ANPE),** 4 impasse d'Antin, *8ème* (☎01 43 59 62 63; fax 01 49 53 91 46; www.anpe.fr), has specific info on employment. (Open M-W and F 9am-5pm, Th 9am-noon.) Remember to bring your work permit and, if you have one, your *carte de séjour.* The **Centre d'Information et de Documentation Jeunesse (CIDJ),** 101 quai Branly, *15ème* (☎01 44 49 12 00; fax 01 40 65 02 61), an invaluable state-run youth center provides info on education, resumes, employment, and careers. English spoken. Jobs are posted at 9am on the bulletin boards outside. (Open M, W-Th 9:30am-6pm, Tu and F 9:30am-7pm, Sa 9:30am-1pm.) EU citizens can benefit from the **European Employment Services (EURES),** (☎+33 0800 90 9700) which facilitate employment between EU countries.

FURTHER READING. *Overseas Summer Jobs 2001, Work Your Way Around the World,* and *Directory of Jobs and Careers Abroad* (Peterson's, US$14-15 each); *International Jobs: Where they Are, How to Get Them,* by Eric Koocher (Perseus Books, US$16); *How to Get a Job in Europe,* by Robert Sanborn (Surrey Books, US$22); and *Work Abroad: The Complete Guide to Finding a Job Overseas,* by Clayton Hubbs (Transitions Abroad, US$16).

VOLUNTEERING

Volunteer jobs are readily available, and many provide room and board in exchange for labor. You can sometimes avoid high application fees by contacting individual workcamps directly. **Service Civil International Voluntary Service (SCI-IVS),** 814 NE 40th St., Seattle, WA 98105, USA (☎/fax 206-545-6585; www.sci-ivs.org). Arranges placement in work camps in Europe. (18+. Registration US$65-150, depending on location.) For **further information,** consult *The International Directory of Voluntary Work,* by Louise Whetter (Vacation Work Publications, US$16).

OTHER RESOURCES

USEFUL PUBLICATIONS

We've included these books because we like them and think you might. A good travel bookstore is the next place to start looking for more.

Fragile Glory: A Portrait of France and the French, Richard Bernstein. Plume, 1991 (US$14.95). A witty look at France by the former New York Times Paris bureau chief.

Portraits of France, Robert Daley. Little, Brown & Co., 1991 (US$23). An engaging, quietly knowledgeable collection of essays on France and the French, organized by region.

Culture Shock: A Guide To Customs and Etiquette, Sally Adamson Taylor. Graphic Arts Center Publishing Company, 1991 (US$13.95). Tips and warnings.

Merde! The Real French You Were Never Taught at School, Michael Heath Genevieve. Fireside, 1998 ($9). Lots of gutter slang and a collection of very dirty things to say.

French or Foe? Getting the Most Out of Visiting, Living and Working in France, Polly Platt. Distribooks Intl., 1998 (US$16.95). A popular guide to getting by in France.

A Traveller's Wine Guide to France, Christopher Fielden. Traveller's Wine Guides, 1999 (US$19.95). Exactly what it says it is, by a well-known oenophile.

Michelin Green Guides, Michelin. Around US$20. The little green books only cover sights and are pretty dry in tone, but they are the authoritative source.

THE WORLD WIDE WEB

Below are sites of purpose too general for any particular section above.

Maison de la France (www.francetourism.com) the French government's site for tourists. Tips on everything from accommodation to smoking laws. English version.

Youth Tourism (www.franceguide.com) Designed for youths planning extended stays in France. Page itself (thought not all links) in English.

France Diplomatie (www.france.diplomatie.fr/) is the site of the Department of Foreign Affairs. Info on **visas** and and current affairs. Most info available in English.

Secretariat for Tourism (www.tourisme.gouv.fr) has a number of government documents and about French tourism; links to all French tourist authorities. In French.

Tourism in France (www.tourisme.fr) has info in French and mildly amusing English.

Nomade (www.nomade.fr) is a popular French search engine.

TF1 (www.tf1.fr) is the home page of France's most popular TV station, with news, popular culture, and weather and traffic reports in French.

Météo-France (www.meteo.fr) has 2-day weather forecasts and maps. In French, but reasonably easy for anglophones to navigate.

THE ART OF BUDGET TRAVEL

How to See the World: www.artoftravel.com. A compendium of great travel tips, from cheap flights to self defense to interacting with local culture.

Rec. Travel Library: www.travel-library.com. Fantastic general info and travelogues.

Lycos: http://cityguide.lycos.com. Introductions to cities and regions throughout France.

Backpacker's Ultimate Guide: www.bugeurope.com.

Backpack Europe: www.backpackeurope.com. Helpful tips, a bulletin board, and links.

TravelPage: www.travelpage.com. Links to official tourist office sites throughout Europe.

INFORMATION ON FRANCE

CIA World Factbook: www.odci.gov/cia/publications/factbook/index.html. Vital stats.

Foreign Language for Travelers: www.travlang.com. Online translating dictionary.

Geographia: www.geographia.com. Highlights, culture, and people of France.

Atevo Travel: www.atevo.com/guides/destinations. Travel tips. Suggested itineraries.

World Travel Guide: www.travel-guides.com/navigate/world.asp. Helpful practical info.

AND OUR PERSONAL FAVORITE...

Let's Go: www.letsgo.com. Our constantly expanding website features photos and streaming video, online ordering of all our titles, info about our books, a travel forum, and links that will help you find everything you ever wanted to know about France.

PARIS

City of light, site of majestic panoramas and showy store windows; unsightly city, invisible city—Paris somehow manages to do it all. From alleys that shelter the world's best bistros to broad avenues flaunting the highest of haute couture, from the old stone of Notre Dame's gargoyles to the futuristic motions of the Parc de la Villette, from the relics of the first millennium to the celebration of the second, Paris presents itself as both a harbor of tradition and a place of impulse. You can't conquer Paris, old or new, in one week or in thirty years—you can get acquainted in a day, though, and in a week, you may find you're old friends.

HISTORY

Paris owes its name to its first inhabitants, the Gaulish Parisii tribe who settled in the Ile de la Cité in the 3rd century BC. In an early display of Parisian pride, the inhabitants chose to burn down their city rather than surrender it to Julius Cæsar in 52 BC. Though the Romans established Lutetia on its site, the town was just another provincial city until Clovis captured it for the Franks and made it his capital at the end of the 5th century AD. The area bounded by the Seine, the Marne, the Beuvronne, the Oise, and the Nonette rivers thus became known as Francia, and, as it became France, its water-bound heartland took the name Ile de France. When the Count of Paris, Hugh Capet, became king in 987, Paris became the definitive hub of the kingdom. The city prospered, and King Philippe-Auguste (1179-1223) formally recognized the three distinct quarters of medieval Paris: the academic left bank, the commercial right bank, and the cité on the island.

Philippe-Auguste was also responsible for extending the fractured royal domain from the Ile de France to encompass the rest of the country. But while France was more or less unified, trouble was brewing in the capital. The merchants viewed with a greedy eye the success of the free Flemish towns to the north, and coveted independence. In 1356, their leader Etienne Marcel had the royal administrators murdered and allied himself with the English invaders. While French control was soon reinstated, in 1415 an Anglo-Burgundian alliance occupied the city with little resistance, and Paris accepted the English Henry VI as its king. Only in 1437 did Charles VII make his triumphant entry into the city; perhaps unsure of its loyalty, he and his heirs chose to reside in the Loire Valley. During the Wars of Religion in the 16th century, Paris came down firmly on the Catholic side after the St. Bartholomew's Day Massacre in 1572. The city rose against the religiously moderate Henri III in 1588 and refused entry to the Protestant Henri IV in 1590. In 1594, Henri gave in, converted to Catholicism, and took up residence in the Louvre. Under his son Louis XIII, Paris sparkled. Squares and gardens were laid out, Richelieu built the Palais Royal, the aristocracy moved into mansions in the Marais, and two uninhabited Seine islands were joined together to make the Ile St-Louis.

Paris remained at the center of French cultural life even when Louis XIV moved the court to Versailles in the 17th century. The Sun King continued to expand the Louvre, which had been rebuilt under François Ier, and laid out the Champs-Elysées, while the centralization of government under his reign increased the power and wealth of the city. However, the discontent of Parisians boiled over in 1789 as the Revolution unfolded in the capital and then spread to the provinces. The dreaded Guillotine was set up in pl. de la Concorde, its blade falling on Louis XVI in 1793. Despite all the construction, Paris remained very much a medieval city; conditions were so bad that a cholera epidemic in 1832 killed almost 20,000 people, while the maze of streets allowed mobs to assemble and disperse with impunity. In 1852, Napoleon III ordered Baron Haussmann to remodel the city and, over the next 18 years, medieval buildings were razed, grand avenues were laid out, and modern Paris was created. Revitalized, Paris held out for three months when the Second Empire collapsed before the Prussian advance in 1870. After the peace was signed, the new Third Republic did not prove to the city's liking, and disenchantment boiled over into the left-wing Communard revolt of 1871, ruthlessly crushed by city authorities.

In the 19th century, the industrialized city was captured by Impressionists, from Toulouse-Lautrec's scenes of Parisian nightlife to Monet's smoke-filled *Gare St-Lazare*. The city's international preeminence was evident at the Universal Exhibition in 1889, crowned by the new Eiffel Tower. Paris remained the intellectual capital of the world until WWII, attracting artists from Sisley to Brancusi and writers from Wilde to Hemingway, but France's defeat in 1939 forced many into exile or hiding. While the city suffered little structural damage from the war, a new generation of thinkers could not disguise the fact that Paris had lost its cultural crown to an upstart across the Atlantic. Nevertheless, the city continues to hold its head high as it enters the new millennium. The Grande Arche, a 20th-century reply to the Arc de Triomphe, towers over high-tech La Défense; the Louvre has been revitalized by I.M. Pei's pyramid; and Paris demonstrated that its proud spirit is still alive after France's 1998 World Cup victory at the new Stade-de-France.

SUGGESTIONS

Paris is first and foremost an international city, and only second capital of France. Wandering down the grand **Champs-Elysées** (p. 129), the student-filled **Latin Quarter** (p. 123), the ex-aristocratic **Marais** (p. 120), and medieval **Montmartre** (p. 134) will give you a good feel for the city. No one can visit Paris without seeing the **Louvre** (p. 136), the **Eiffel Tower** (p. 127), and **Notre Dame** (p. 115), but don't neglect Paris' Latin past in the **Musée de Cluny** (p. 138), the other side of iron-age construction in the **Grand Palais** (p. 129), or Gothic architecture's finest jewel, **La Sainte-Chapelle** (p. 116). Near Paris, **Versailles** (p. 147) is the best-known château, and **Chartres** (p. 150) the best-known cathedral.

ORIENTATION

Flowing from east to west, the **Seine River** crosses the heart of Paris. The **Ile de la Cité** and neighboring **Ile St-Louis** sit at the geographical center of the city, while the Seine splits Paris into two large expanses—the Rive Gauche (Left Bank) to its south and the Rive Droite (Right Bank) to its north. In the time of Louis XIV, the city had grown to 20 *quartiers*. Modern Paris is divided into 20 *arrondissements* (districts) that spiral clockwise around the Louvre, each referred to by its number (e.g. the 3rd, 12th). The French equivalent of the English "th" as in 8th is *"ème."* The exception is the 1st, and the French abbreviation is 1*er (premier*, PREM-yay*)*.

SEINE ISLANDS

ILE DE LA CITE. If any place could be called the heart of Paris, it is this slip in the river, in the very center of the city. All distance points in France are measured from **kilomètre zéro,** a circular sundial in front of Notre Dame (see **Sights,** p. 115).

ILE ST-LOUIS. Somewhere between a small village and an exclusive neighborhood, this island retains a certain remoteness from the rest of Paris. Inhabitants even declared the island an independent republic in the 1930s.

RIVE GAUCHE (LEFT BANK)

LATIN QUARTER: 5EME AND 6EME ARRONDISSEMENTS. The **Latin Quarter,** which has an intellectual reputation, contains the **Sorbonne** and encompasses the **5ème arrondissement** and parts of the **6ème.** The boundary between the 5*ème* and the 6*ème*, **bd. St-Michel,** overflows with cafés, cinemas, boutiques, and bookstores. As you head southeast, hotel prices fall. Farther east, the neighborhood around **pl. de la Contrescarpe,** at the center of the 5*ème*, is more intimate and cheaper. A cornucopia of ethnic restaurants graces **rue Mouffetard,** the indisputable culinary heart of the *5ème*. Crossing bd. St-Michel and running east-west, **bd. St-Germain** in the *6ème* lends its name to the neighborhood **St-Germain-des-Prés,** which has turned the sidewalk café into an art form.

7EME ARRONDISSEMENT. Don't stay in the **7ème** for the view or for the party atmosphere. This area has museums like the **d'Orsay,** monuments like the **Eiffel Tower,** and excellent shopping, but it's not the best bet for a cheap room.

MONTPARNASSE: 13EME AND 14EME ARRONDISSEMENTS. A vast urban sprawl in the midst of an architectural face-lift, the **13ème** is in the fetal stages of a hip rebirth. **Montparnasse,** where the chic *6ème* meets the commercial **14ème** just south of the Latin Quarter, attracted expatriates in the 1920s. Picasso, Hemingway, and Gertrude Stein kicked up their heels here. Today, areas near the fashionable **bd. du Montparnasse** maintain their glamor, while nearby blocks are more residential. Sex shops and sleazy nightlife dominate the northern end of av. du Maine. East of the *14ème*, Paris' "Chinatown" overflows with East Asian cuisine.

15EME ARRONDISSEMENT. The most populous *arrondissement*, the **15ème** is middle-class Parisian life at its best. The expansive **Parc André Citroën** attracts families on weekends. Hotels scramble for guests in the summer, and tourists can sometimes bargain for rates.

RIVE DROITE (RIGHT BANK)

1ER ARRONDISSEMENT. Paris' royal past is conspicuous in much of the **1er,** home to the Louvre. Chanel and the Ritz hotel set the scene; the few budget hotels here are rarely accompanied by budget accoutrements (laundromats, grocery stores, etc.). Although above ground the *1er* is one of the safest areas in Paris, the métro stops Châtelet and Les Halles are best avoided at night.

2EME ARRONDISSEMENT. Devoid of its own sights, the **2ème** is within walking distance of the Marais, the Centre Pompidou, the Louvre, Notre Dame, and more. Many cheap little restaurants and hotels populate this mostly working-class area and make it an excellent place to stay. Although the eastern end of rue St-Denis is a center of prostitution and pornography, its seediness does not spread far.

MARAIS: 3EME AND 4EME ARRONDISSEMENTS. Absolutely *the* place to live in the 17th century, the **Marais,** in the **3ème** and **4ème,** has regained its glory, thanks to extensive renovations. Once-palatial mansions have become exquisite museums, and the tiny twisting streets have been adopted by fashionable boutiques and galleries. The area shelters some terrific accommodations at reasonable rates. Prices drop as you head north through the *4ème* into the *3ème*. **Rue des Rosiers,** in the heart of the *4ème*, is the focal point of the city's Jewish population. Superb kosher delicatessens neighbor Middle Eastern restaurants. The area is lively on Sundays, when other districts shut down. The Marais has also recently become the center of gay Paris.

8EME ARRONDISSEMENT. Full of expansive mansions, expensive shops and restaurants, grand boulevards, and grandiose monuments, the **8ème** is decidedly Paris' most glamorous *arrondissement*. Obscenely upscale *haute couture* boutiques line the Champs-Elysées, the Madeleine, and the rue du Faubourg St-Honoré. Euphoric mobs rush to the *8ème* when France succeeds—most recently whipping out the bands of red, white, and blue for the Euro Cup final, the end of the Tour de France, and boisterous Bastille Day celebrations. For the most part, budget travelers should visit the *8ème's* grand boulevards and dine elsewhere.

9EME ARRONDISSEMENT. The **9ème** links some of Paris' most affluent and touristed quarters with less popular and glitzy ones. There are plenty of hotels, but many to the north are used for the local flesh trade. Nicer but not-so-cheap hotels are available near the respectable and central bd. des Italiens and bd. Montmartre.

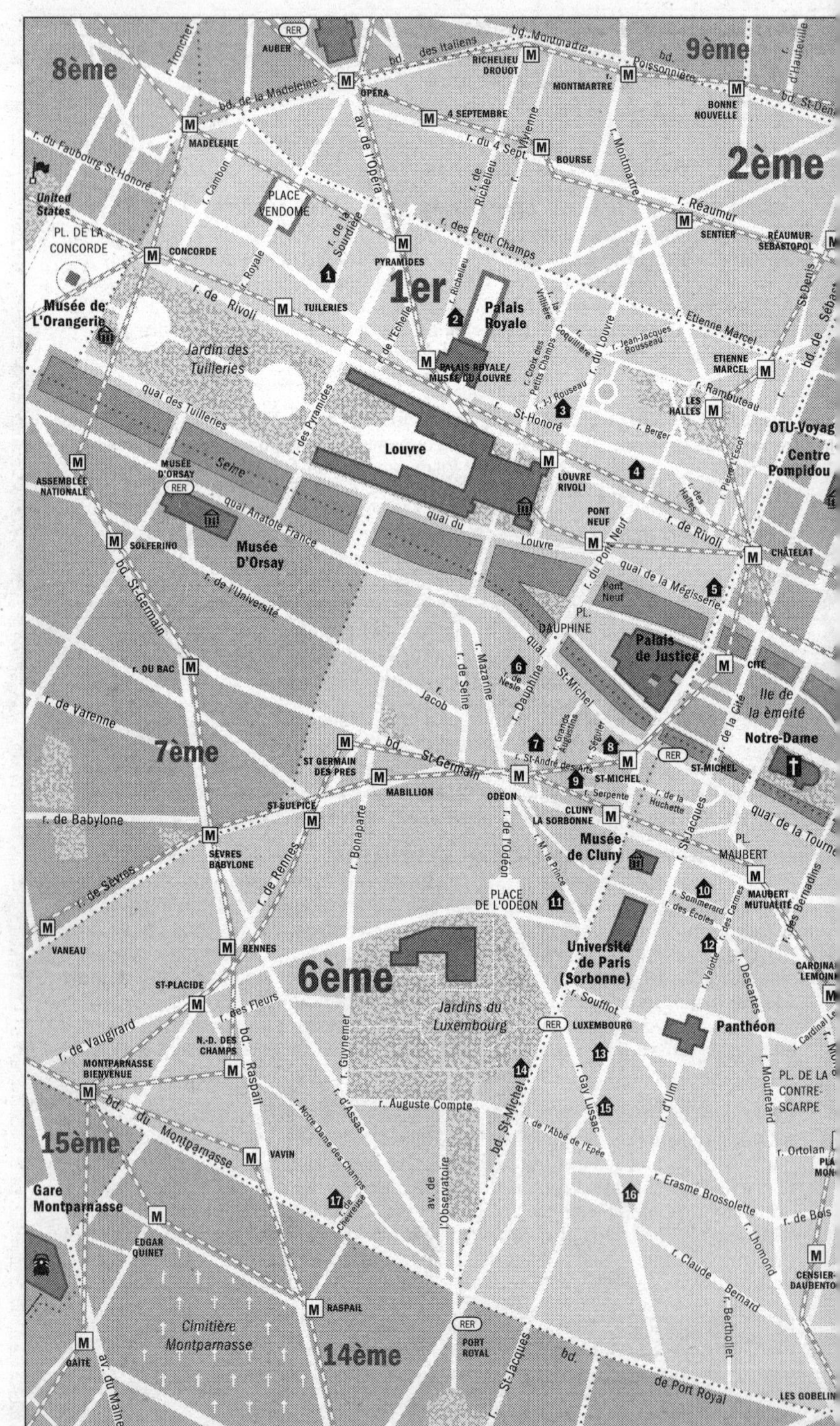
8ème
9ème
2ème
1er
7ème
6ème
15ème
14ème
Musée de L'Orangerie
Jardin des Tuilleries
Louvre
Palais Royale
Musée D'Orsay
Palais de Justice
Notre-Dame
Musée de Cluny
Université de Paris (Sorbonne)
Panthéon
Jardins du Luxembourg
Cimitière Montparnasse
Gare Montparnasse
Centre Pompidou
OTU-Voyag
United States
PL. DE LA CONCORDE
PLACE VENDOME
PLACE DE L'ODEON
PL. DAUPHINE
PL. MAUBERT
PL. DE LA CONTRE-SCARPE
Ile de la émeité
Seine
quai des Tuilleries
quai Anatole France
quai du Louvre
quai de la Mégisserie
quai St-Michel
quai de la Tourne
r. de Rivoli
r. St-Honoré
bd. de la Madeleine
bd. des Italiens
bd. Montmartre
bd. Poissonnière
r. du 4 Sept.
r. Réaumur
r. des Petit Champs
r. Etienne Marcel
r. Rambuteau
bd. St-Germain
bd. St-Michel
bd. du Montparnasse
bd. Raspail
r. de Rennes
r. de Vaugirard
r. de Sèvres
r. de Babylone
r. de Varenne
r. de l'Université
r. Jacob
r. Mazarine
r. de Seine
r. Dauphine
r. de l'Odéon
r. Soufflot
r. Gay Lussac
r. d'Ulm
r. Mouffetard
r. Descartes
r. St-Jacques
r. Claude Bernard
r. Erasme Brossolette
r. Auguste Compte
av. de l'Opéra
av. de l'Observatoire
av. du Maine
bd. de Port Royal
MADELEINE
CONCORDE
TUILERIES
PYRAMIDES
OPÉRA
AUBER
4 SEPTEMBRE
RICHELIEU DROUOT
MONTMARTRE
BONNE NOUVELLE
BOURSE
SENTIER
RÉAUMUR-SEBASTOPOL
PALAIS ROYALE/ MUSÉE DU LOUVRE
LOUVRE RIVOLI
PONT NEUF
ETIENNE MARCEL
LES HALLES
CHÂTELAT
CITE
ST-MICHEL
ODEON
CLUNY LA SORBONNE
MAUBERT MUTUALITÉ
ASSEMBLÉE NATIONALE
MUSÉE D'ORSAY
SOLFERINO
r. DU BAC
ST GERMAIN DES PRES
MABILLION
ST-SULPICE
SÈVRES BABYLONE
VANEAU
RENNES
ST-PLACIDE
N.-D. DES CHAMPS
MONTPARNASSE BIENVENUE
VAVIN
EDGAR QUINET
RASPAIL
GAITÉ
PORT ROYAL
LUXEMBOURG
CENSIER-DAUBENTO
LES GOBELIN
CARDINA LEMOIN
1
2
3
4
5
6
7
8
9
10
11
12
13
14
15
16
17

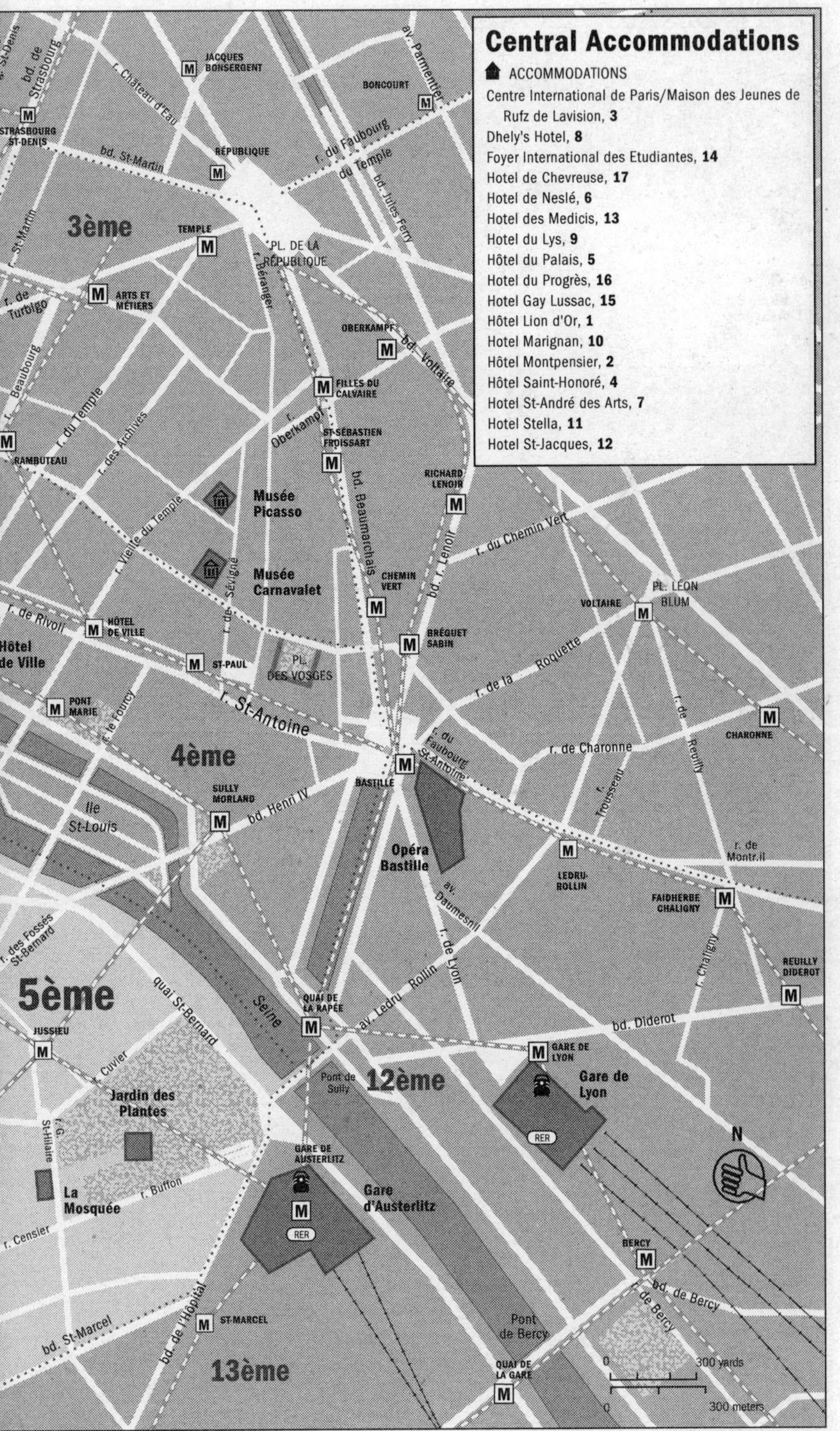
Central Accommodations
ACCOMMODATIONS
Centre International de Paris/Maison des Jeunes de Rufz de Lavision, 3
Dhely's Hotel, 8
Foyer International des Etudiantes, 14
Hotel de Chevreuse, 17
Hotel de Neslé, 6
Hotel des Medicis, 13
Hotel du Lys, 9
Hôtel du Palais, 5
Hotel du Progrès, 16
Hotel Gay Lussac, 15
Hôtel Lion d'Or, 1
Hotel Marignan, 10
Hôtel Montpensier, 2
Hôtel Saint-Honoré, 4
Hotel St-André des Arts, 7
Hotel Stella, 11
Hotel St-Jacques, 12
3ème
4ème
5ème
12ème
13ème
JACQUES BONSERGENT
BONCOURT
RÉPUBLIQUE
STRASBOURG ST-DENIS
TEMPLE
PL. DE LA RÉPUBLIQUE
ARTS ET MÉTIERS
OBERKAMPF
FILLES DU CALVAIRE
ST-SÉBASTIEN FROISSART
RAMBUTEAU
RICHARD LENOIR
Musée Picasso
Musée Carnavalet
CHEMIN VERT
VOLTAIRE
PL. LÉON BLUM
HÔTEL DE VILLE
Hôtel de Ville
BRÉGUET SABIN
ST-PAUL
PL. DES VOSGES
PONT MARIE
CHARONNE
BASTILLE
SULLY MORLAND
Ile St-Louis
Opéra Bastille
LEDRU-ROLLIN
FAIDHERBE CHALIGNY
REUILLY DIDEROT
QUAI DE LA RAPÉE
JUSSIEU
GARE DE LYON
Gare de Lyon
Pont de Sully
Jardin des Plantes
GARE DE AUSTERLITZ
Gare d'Austerlitz
La Mosquée
RER
BERCY
ST-MARCEL
Pont de Bercy
QUAI DE LA GARE
Seine
N
0 300 yards
0 300 meters
bd. de Strasbourg
r. St-Denis
r. Château d'Eau
av. Parmentier
r. du Faubourg du Temple
bd. St-Martin
bd. Jules Ferry
r. St-Martin
r. Béranger
r. de Turbigo
bd. Voltaire
r. Beaubourg
r. du Temple
r. des Archives
r. Oberkampf
bd. Beaumarchais
r. Vieille du Temple
r. de Sévigné
bd. r. Lenoir
r. du Chemin Vert
r. de Rivoli
r. de la Roquette
r. St-Antoine
r. du Faubourg St-Antoine
r. de Charonne
r. de Reuilly
r. Trousseau
r. de Montr.il
r. le Fourcy
bd. Henri IV
av. Daumesnil
r. de Lyon
av. Ledru Rollin
r. Chaligny
bd. Diderot
r. des Fossés St-Bernard
quai St-Bernard
r. Cuvier
r. G. St-Hilaire
r. Buffon
r. Censier
bd. de l'Hôpital
bd. St-Marcel
bd. de Bercy
r. de Bercy

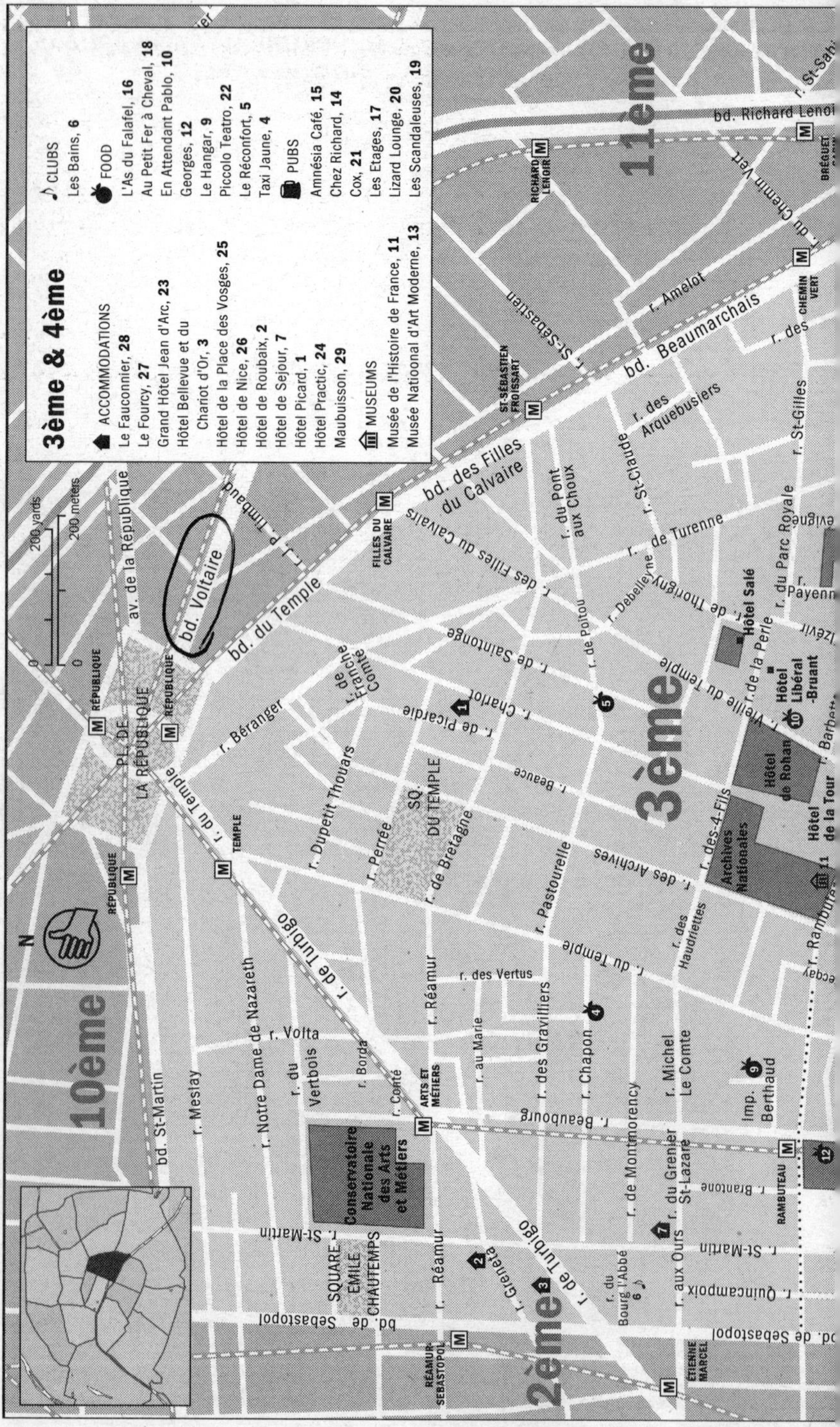

3ème & 4ème

ACCOMMODATIONS
- Le Fauconnier, **28**
- Le Fourcy, **27**
- Grand Hôtel Jean d'Arc, **23**
- Hôtel Bellevue et du Chariot d'Or, **3**
- Hôtel de la Place des Vosges, **25**
- Hôtel de Nice, **26**
- Hôtel de Roubaix, **2**
- Hôtel de Sejour, **7**
- Hôtel Picard, **1**
- Hôtel Practic, **24**
- Maubuisson, **29**

MUSEUMS
- Musée de l'Histoire de France, **11**
- Musée Natioonal d'Art Moderne, **13**

CLUBS
- Les Bains, **6**

FOOD
- L'As du Falafel, **16**
- Au Petit Fer à Cheval, **18**
- En Attendant Pablo, **10**
- Georges, **12**
- Le Hangar, **9**
- Piccolo Teatro, **22**
- Le Réconfort, **5**
- Taxi Jaune, **4**

PUBS
- Amnésia Café, **15**
- Chez Richard, **14**
- Cox, **21**
- Les Etages, **17**
- Lizard Lounge, **20**
- Les Scandaleuses, **19**

N
0 200 yards
0 200 meters
10ème
2ème
3ème
11ème
RÉPUBLIQUE
PL. DE LA RÉPUBLIQUE
av. de la République
bd. St-Martin
bd. Voltaire
bd. du Temple
r. du Temple
TEMPLE
r. Meslay
r. Béranger
r. J. P. Timbaud
r. Notre Dame de Nazareth
r. Volta
r. du Vertbois
r. de Turbigo
r. Dupetit Thouars
r. de Franche Comté
FILLES DU CALVAIRE
bd. des Filles du Calvaire
r. des Filles du Calvaire
SQUARE EMILE CHAUTEMPS
Conservatoire Nationale des Arts et Metiers
r. Borda
r. Conté
r. Perrée
SQ. DU TEMPLE
ARTS ET MÉTIERS
RÉAMUR-SEBASTOPOL
bd. de Sebastopol
r. St-Martin
r. Réaumur
r. de Bretagne
r. de Picardie
r. Charlot
r. de Saintonge
r. au Marie
r. des Vertus
r. Greneta
r. des Gravilliers
r. Pastourelle
r. Beauce
r. Beaubourg
r. Chapon
r. du Pont aux Choux
r. de Poitou
ST-SÉBASTIEN FROISSART
r. St-Sébastien
RICHARD LENOIR
r. du Bourg l'Abbé
r. de Montmorency
r. Debelleyme
r. St-Claude
r. des Arquebusiers
bd. Beaumarchais
r. Amelot
r. aux Ours
r. du Grenier St-Lazare
r. Michel Le Comte
r. des Haudriettes
r. des Archives
r. de Thorigny
r. de Turenne
ÉTIENNE MARCEL
r. Quincampoix
r. Brantone
Imp. Berthaud
r. des-4-Fils
Archives Nationales
r. Vieille du Temple
Hôtel Salé
r. de la Perle
Hôtel de Rohan
Hôtel Libéral-Bruant
r. du Parc Royale
r. St-Gilles
CHEMIN VERT
r. du Chemin Vert
bd. Richard Lenoir
RAMBUTEAU
r. Rambuteau
Hôtel de la Tour
r. Barbette
r. Payenne
BRÉGUET

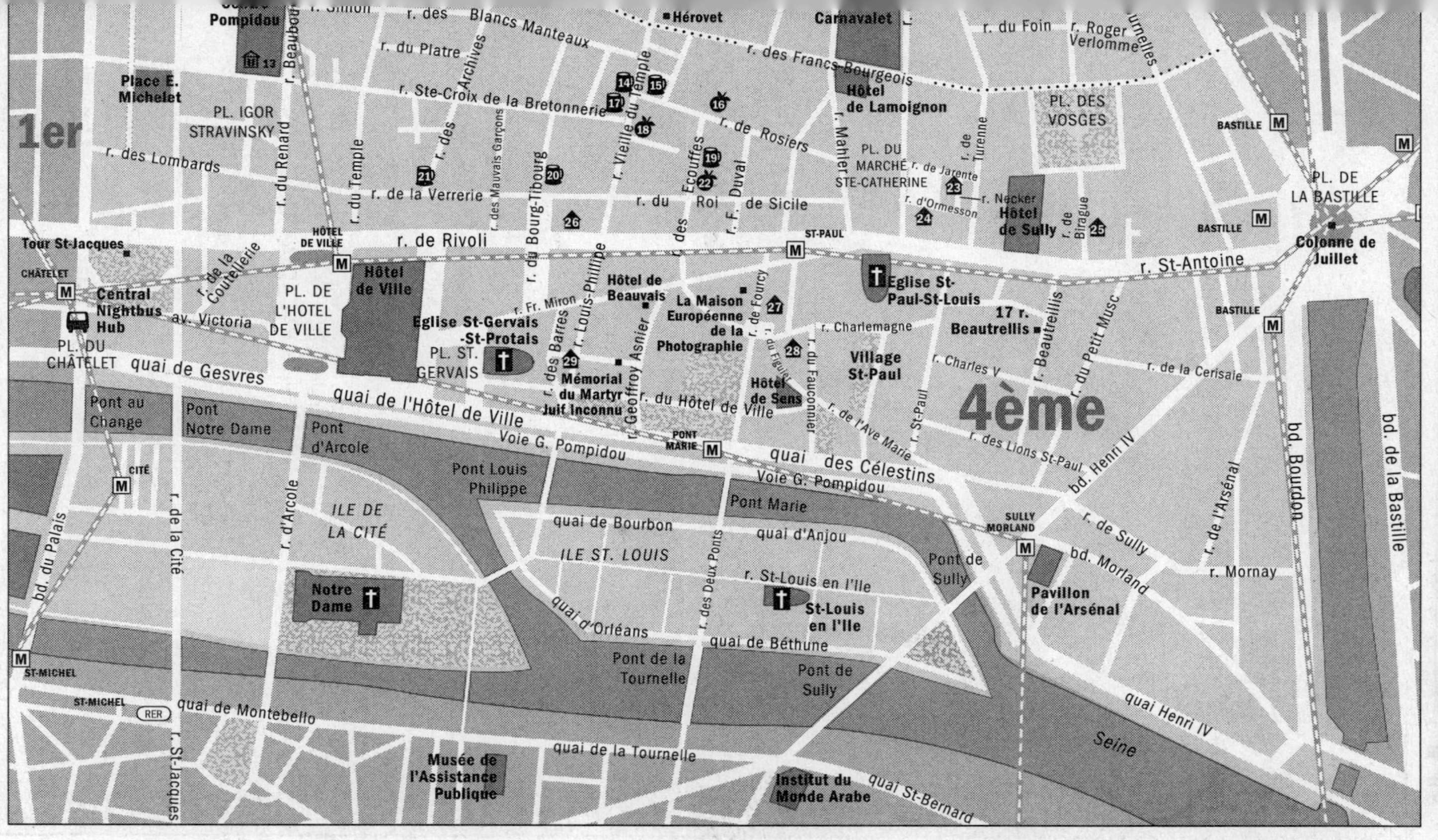
Pompidou
r. des Blancs Manteaux
Hérovet
Carnavalet
r. du Foin
r. Roger Verlomme
r. des Francs-Bourgeois
Place E. Michelet
r. Beaubourg
r. du Platre
r. des Archives
r. Ste-Croix de la Bretonnerie
Hôtel de Lamoignon
PL. DES VOSGES
1er
PL. IGOR STRAVINSKY
r. Vieille du Temple
r. de Rosiers
BASTILLE
r. des Lombards
r. du Renard
r. du Temple
r. des Mauvais Garçons
PL. DU MARCHÉ STE-CATHERINE
r. Mahler
r. de Jarente
r. de Turenne
PL. DE LA BASTILLE
r. de la Verrerie
r. du Bourg-Tibourg
r. des Ecouffes
r. F. Duval
r. du Roi de Sicile
r. d'Ormesson
r. Necker
Hôtel de Sully
r. de Birague
Tour St-Jacques
HÔTEL DE VILLE
r. de Rivoli
ST-PAUL
Colonne de Juillet
CHÂTELET
r. de la Coutellerie
Hôtel de Ville
r. Louis-Philippe
Hôtel de Beauvais
r. St-Antoine
Eglise St-Paul-St-Louis
Central Nightbus Hub
PL. DE L'HOTEL DE VILLE
r. Fr. Miron
La Maison Européenne de la Photographie
r. de Fourcy
av. Victoria
Eglise St-Gervais -St-Protais
r. Charlemagne
17 r. Beautreillis
PL. DU CHÂTELET
PL. ST. GERVAIS
r. Geoffroy Asnier
r. du Figuier
r. du Fauconnier
Village St-Paul
r. Charles V
r. Beautreillis
r. du Petit Musc
r. de la Cerisale
quai de Gesvres
r. des Barres
Mémorial du Martyr Juif Inconnu
r. du Hôtel de Ville
Hôtel de Sens
4ème
bd. de la Bastille
Pont au Change
Pont Notre Dame
Pont d'Arcole
quai de l'Hôtel de Ville
r. de l'Ave Maria
r. St-Paul
bd. Bourdon
Voie G. Pompidou
PONT MARIE
r. des Lions St-Paul
bd. Henri IV
quai des Célestins
Pont Louis Philippe
CITÉ
Voie G. Pompidou
Pont Marie
r. de l'Arsénal
r. d'Arcole
ILE DE LA CITÉ
quai de Bourbon
quai d'Anjou
SULLY MORLAND
r. de Sully
bd. du Palais
r. de la Cité
ILE ST. LOUIS
Pont de Sully
bd. Morland
r. Mornay
r. St-Louis en l'Ile
Notre Dame
r. des Deux Ponts
St-Louis en l'Ile
Pavillon de l'Arsénal
quai d'Orléans
quai de Béthune
Pont de la Tournelle
Pont de Sully
ST-MICHEL
quai de Montebello
RER
quai Henri IV
Seine
quai de la Tournelle
Musée de l'Assistance Publique
r. St-Jacques
Institut du Monde Arabe
quai St-Bernard

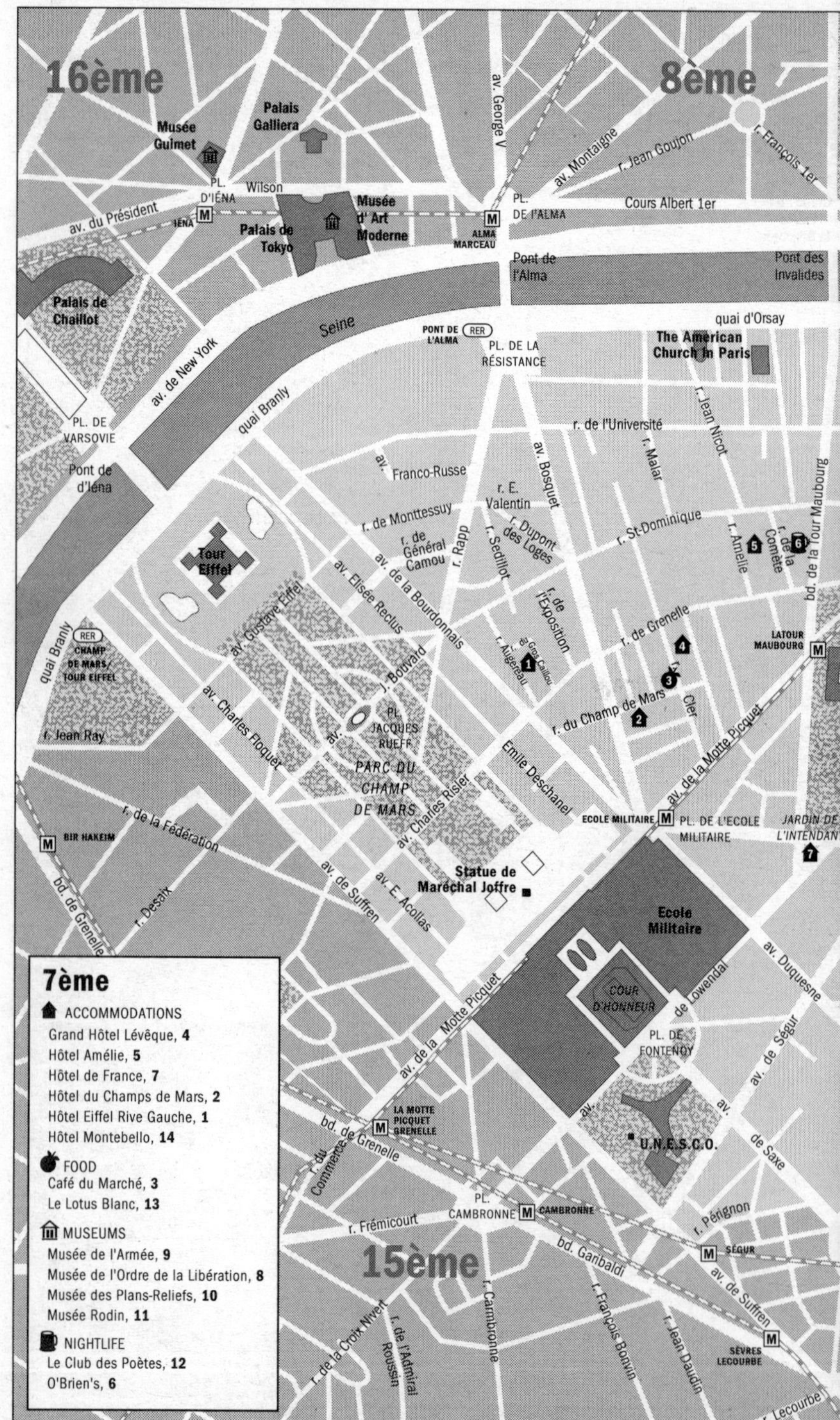
16ème
8ème
15ème
Palais Galliera
Musée Guimet
PL. D'IÉNA
Wilson
av. du Président
IÉNA
Palais de Tokyo
Musée d' Art Moderne
av. George V
PL. DE L'ALMA
ALMA MARCEAU
av. Montaigne
r. Jean Goujon
r. François 1er
Cours Albert 1er
Pont de l'Alma
Pont des Invalides
Palais de Chaillot
Seine
av. de New York
quai Branly
PONT DE L'ALMA
RER
PL. DE LA RÉSISTANCE
quai d'Orsay
The American Church in Paris
PL. DE VARSOVIE
Pont de d'Iéna
r. de l'Université
r. Jean Nicot
r. Malar
av. Bosquet
av. Franco-Russe
r. E. Valentin
r. de Monttessuy
r. Dupont des Loges
r. St-Dominique
r. Amélie
r. de la Comète
bd. de la Tour Maubourg
Tour Eiffel
r. de Général Camou
r. Rapp
r. Sedillot
av. Elisée Reclus
av. de la Bourdonnais
r. de l'Exposition
r. de Grenelle
LATOUR MAUBOURG
av. Gustave Eiffel
r. Augereau
r. du Gros Caillou
CHAMP DE MARS/ TOUR EIFFEL
J. Bouvard
r. du Champ de Mars
Cler
av. Charles Floquet
PL. JACQUES RUEFF
r. Jean Ray
PARC DU CHAMP DE MARS
Emile Deschanel
av. de la Motte Picquet
av. Charles Risler
ECOLE MILITAIRE
PL. DE L'ECOLE MILITAIRE
JARDIN DE L'INTENDANT
r. de la Fédération
BIR HAKEIM
Statue de Maréchal Joffre
av. de Suffren
av. E. Acollas
r. Desaix
bd. de Grenelle
Ecole Militaire
av. Duquesne
COUR D'HONNEUR
de Lowendal
PL. DE FONTENOY
av. de Ségur
av. de la Motte Picquet
LA MOTTE PICQUET GRENELLE
bd. de Grenelle
r. du Commerce
U.N.E.S.C.O.
av. de Saxe
PL. CAMBRONNE
CAMBRONNE
r. Frémicourt
r. Pérignon
SÉGUR
bd. Garibaldi
av. de Suffren
r. Cambronne
r. François Bonvin
r. Jean Daudin
r. de la Croix Nivert
r. de l'Admiral Roussin
SÈVRES LECOURBE
r. Lecourbe
7ème
ACCOMMODATIONS
Grand Hôtel Lévêque, 4
Hôtel Amélie, 5
Hôtel de France, 7
Hôtel du Champs de Mars, 2
Hôtel Eiffel Rive Gauche, 1
Hôtel Montebello, 14
FOOD
Café du Marché, 3
Le Lotus Blanc, 13
MUSEUMS
Musée de l'Armée, 9
Musée de l'Ordre de la Libération, 8
Musée des Plans-Reliefs, 10
Musée Rodin, 11
NIGHTLIFE
Le Club des Poètes, 12
O'Brien's, 6

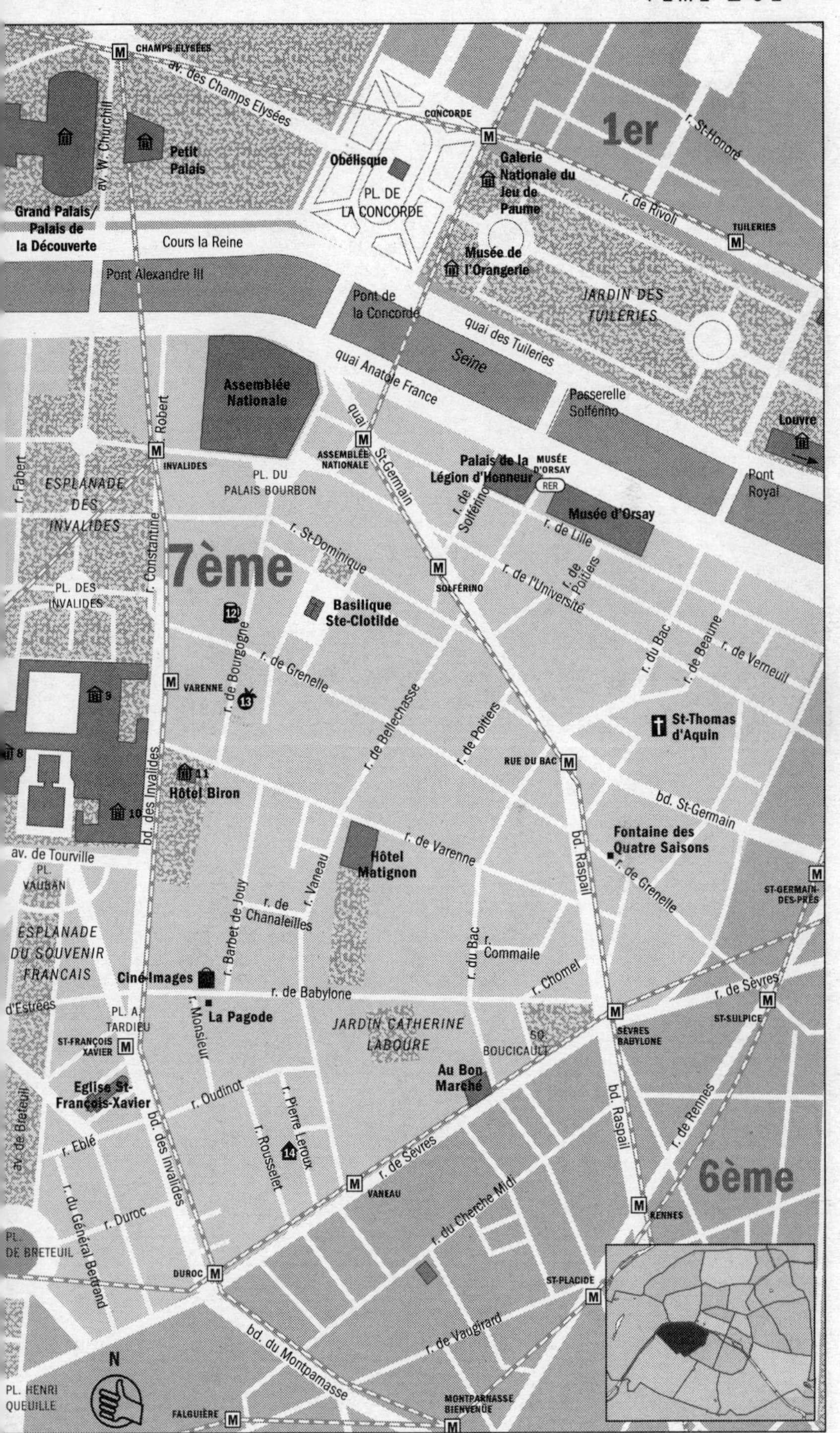

CHAMPS ELYSÉES
av. des Champs Elysées
CONCORDE
1er
r. St-Honoré
Petit Palais
av. W. Churchill
Obélisque
PL. DE LA CONCORDE
Galerie Nationale du Jeu de Paume
r. de Rivoli
TUILERIES
Grand Palais/ Palais de la Découverte
Cours la Reine
Musée de l'Orangerie
Pont Alexandre III
Pont de la Concorde
JARDIN DES TUILERIES
quai des Tuileries
Seine
quai Anatole France
Assemblée Nationale
Passerelle Solférino
Louvre
r. Robert
INVALIDES
ASSEMBLÉE NATIONALE
quai St-Germain
Palais de la Légion d'Honneur
MUSÉE D'ORSAY
RER
Pont Royal
r. Fabert
ESPLANADE DES INVALIDES
PL. DU PALAIS BOURBON
r. de Solférino
Musée d'Orsay
r. de Lille
r. Constantine
7ème
r. St-Dominique
SOLFÉRINO
r. de l'Université
r. de Poitiers
PL. DES INVALIDES
12
Basilique Ste-Clotilde
r. du Bac
r. de Beaune
r. de Verneuil
VARENNE
r. de Bourgogne
r. de Grenelle
13
r. de Bellechasse
r. de Poitiers
St-Thomas d'Aquin
9
8
RUE DU BAC
11
Hôtel Biron
10
bd. des Invalides
bd. St-Germain
Fontaine des Quatre Saisons
r. de Varenne
av. de Tourville
PL. VAUBAN
Hôtel Matignon
bd. Raspail
r. de Grenelle
ST-GERMAIN-DES-PRÉS
r. Vaneau
r. Barbet de Jouy
r. de Chanaleilles
ESPLANADE DU SOUVENIR FRANCAIS
r. du Bac
r. Commaile
r. Chomel
Ciné-Images
r. de Babylone
r. de Sèvres
d'Estrées
PL. A TARDIEU
La Pagode
r. Monsieur
JARDIN CATHERINE LABOURE
SÈVRES BABYLONE
ST-SULPICE
ST-FRANÇOIS XAVIER
SQ. BOUCICAULT
Au Bon Marché
Eglise St-François-Xavier
r. Oudinot
r. Pierre Leroux
bd. Raspail
r. de Rennes
av. de Breteuil
r. Eblé
r. Rousselet
14
bd. des Invalides
r. de Sèvres
6ème
VANEAU
r. du Cherche Midi
RENNES
r. du Général Bertrand
r. Duroc
PL. DE BRETEUIL
DUROC
ST-PLACIDE
r. de Vaugirard
bd. du Montparnasse
N
PL. HENRI QUEUILLE
FALGUIÈRE
MONTPARNASSE BIENVENÜE

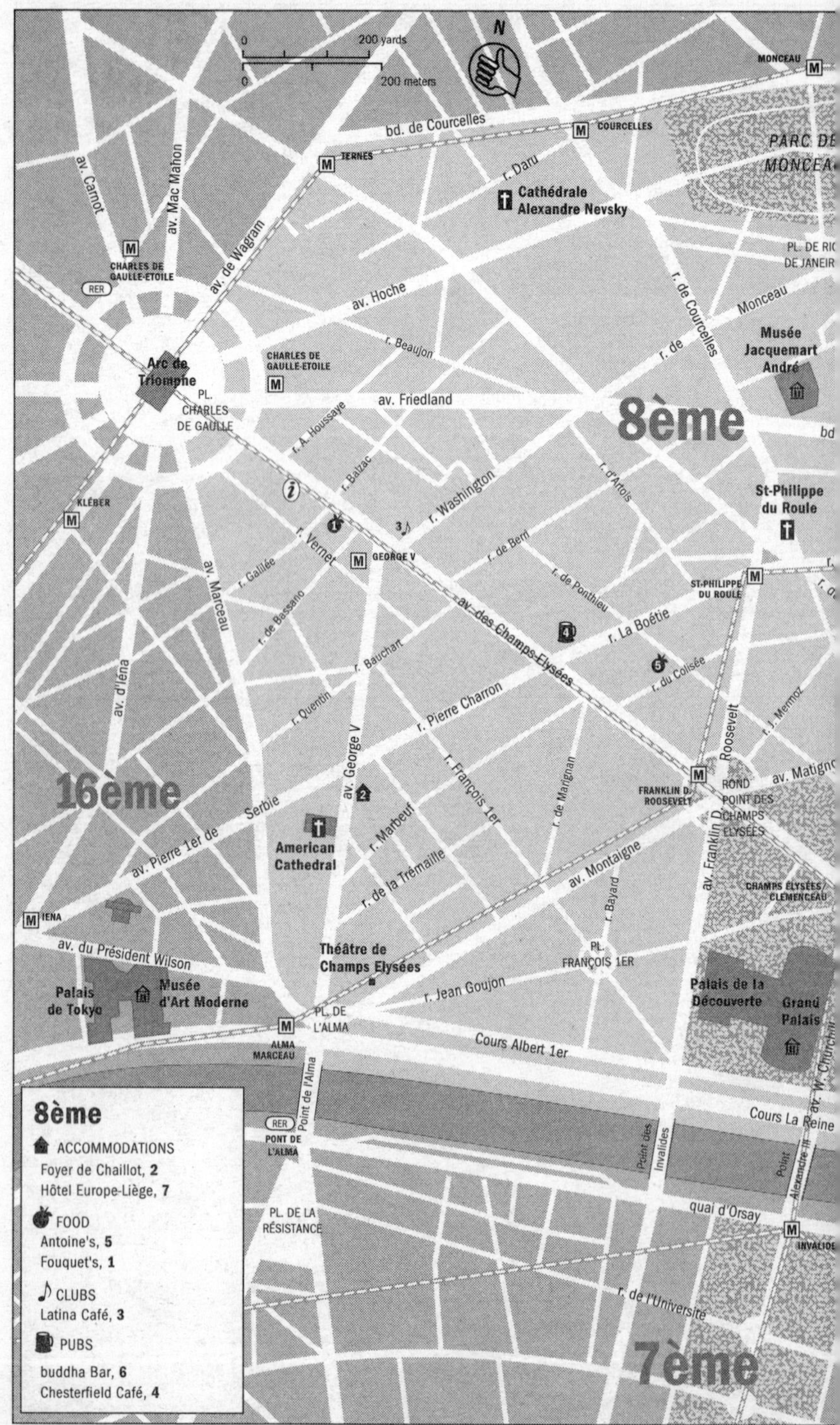

0 200 yards
0 200 meters
N
MONCEAU
bd. de Courcelles
COURCELLES
TERNES
r. Daru
Cathédrale
Alexandre Nevsky
av. Carnot
av. Mac Mahon
CHARLES DE
GAULLE-ETOILE
RER
av. de Wagram
av. Hoche
r. de Courcelles
PL. DE RIO
DE JANEIRO
Monceau
r. de
Musée
Jacquemart
André
r. Beaujon
CHARLES DE
GAULLE-ETOILE
Arc de
Triomphe
PL.
CHARLES
DE GAULLE
av. Friedland
8ème
r. A. Houssaye
r. Balzac
r. Washington
r. d'Artois
St-Philippe
du Roule
KLÉBER
3
1
r. Vernet
GEORGE V
r. de Berri
r. de Ponthieu
ST-PHILIPPE
DU ROULE
r. Galilée
r. de Bassano
av. Marceau
av. des Champs-Elysées
4
r. La Boétie
5
r. du Colisée
av. d'Iéna
r. Bauchart
r. Quentin
r. Pierre Charron
r. J. Mermoz
Roosevelt
r. François 1er
r. de Marignan
FRANKLIN D.
ROOSEVELT
ROND
POINT DES
CHAMPS
ELYSÉES
16ème
av. George V
2
Serbie
av. Pierre 1er de
American
Cathedral
r. Marbeuf
r. de la Trémaille
av. Montaigne
av. Franklin D.
CHAMPS ELYSÉES/
CLEMENCEAU
IENA
r. Bayard
av. du Président Wilson
Théâtre de
Champs Elysées
PL.
FRANÇOIS 1ER
Palais de la
Découverte
Grand
Palais
Palais
de Tokyo
Musée
d'Art Moderne
r. Jean Goujon
PL. DE
L'ALMA
ALMA
MARCEAU
Cours Albert 1er
Point de l'Alma
RER
PONT DE
L'ALMA
Cours La Reine
Pont des
Invalides
Pont
Alexandre III
av. W. Churchill
quai d'Orsay
PL. DE LA
RÉSISTANCE
r. de l'Université
7ème
8ème
ACCOMMODATIONS
Foyer de Chaillot, 2
Hôtel Europe-Liège, 7
FOOD
Antoine's, 5
Fouquet's, 1
CLUBS
Latina Café, 3
PUBS
buddha Bar, 6
Chesterfield Café, 4

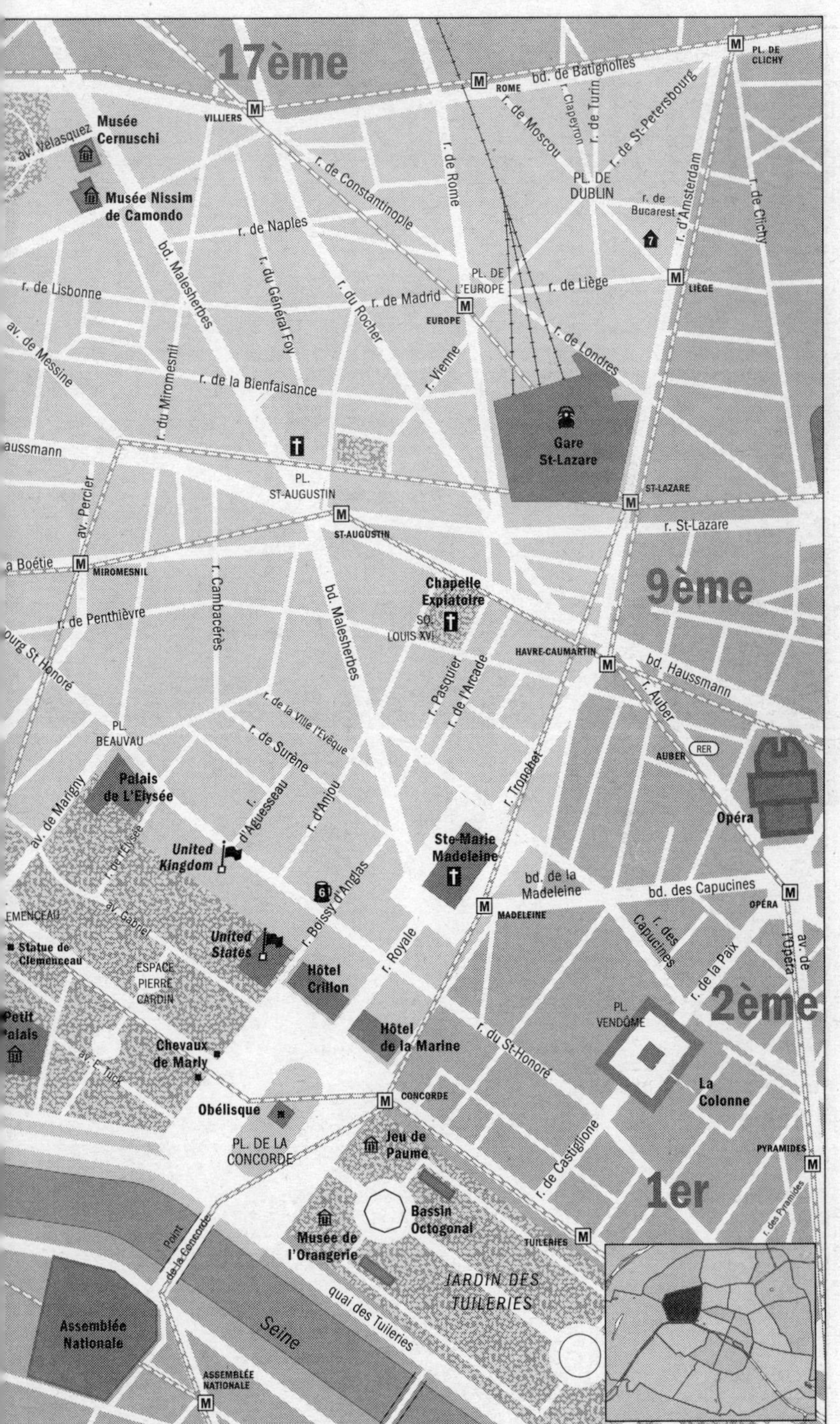
17ème
9ème
2ème
1er
bd. de Batignolles
ROME
VILLIERS
PL. DE CLICHY
Musée Cernuschi
av. Velasquez
Musée Nissim de Camondo
r. de Moscou
r. Clapeyron
r. de Turin
r. de St-Petersbourg
r. de Constantinople
r. de Rome
PL. DE DUBLIN
r. de Bucarest
r. d'Amsterdam
r. de Clichy
r. de Naples
bd. Malesherbes
r. du Général Foy
r. du Rocher
PL. DE L'EUROPE
r. de Liège
LIÈGE
r. de Lisbonne
r. de Madrid
EUROPE
av. de Messine
r. Vienne
r. de Londres
r. du Miromesnil
r. de la Bienfaisance
Gare St-Lazare
Haussmann
PL. ST-AUGUSTIN
ST-LAZARE
ST-AUGUSTIN
r. St-Lazare
av. Percier
La Boétie
MIROMESNIL
r. Cambacérès
Chapelle Expiatoire
SQ. LOUIS XVI
r. de Penthièvre
Faubourg St Honoré
HAVRE-CAUMARTIN
bd. Haussmann
r. Auber
r. Pasquier
r. de l'Arcade
r. de la Ville l'Evêque
r. de Surène
PL. BEAUVAU
AUBER
RER
Palais de L'Elysée
r. d'Aguesseau
r. d'Anjou
r. Tronchet
Opéra
av. de Marigny
r. de l'Elysée
United Kingdom
Ste-Marie Madeleine
bd. de la Madeleine
bd. des Capucines
OPÉRA
MADELEINE
CLEMENCEAU
av. Gabriel
r. Boissy d'Anglas
r. des Capucines
r. de la Paix
av. de l'Opéra
Statue de Clemenceau
United States
ESPACE PIERRE CARDIN
Hôtel Crillon
r. Royale
PL. VENDÔME
Petit Palais
Hôtel de la Marine
r. du St-Honoré
av. F. Tuck
Chevaux de Marly
La Colonne
Obélisque
CONCORDE
PL. DE LA CONCORDE
Jeu de Paume
r. de Castiglione
PYRAMIDES
r. des Pyramides
Pont de la Concorde
Musée de l'Orangerie
Bassin Octogonal
TUILERIES
JARDIN DES TUILERIES
quai des Tuileries
Seine
Assemblée Nationale
ASSEMBLÉE NATIONALE

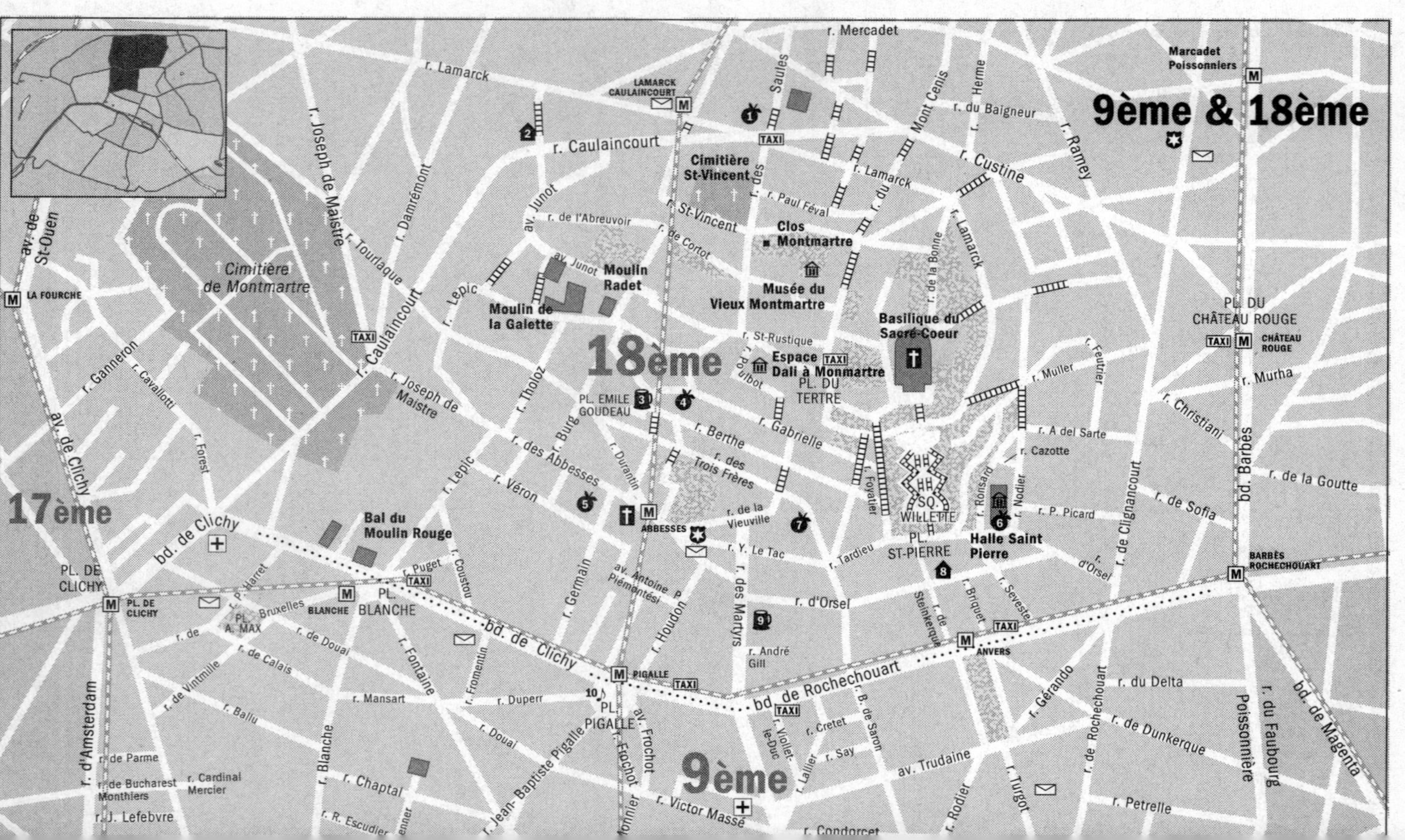

9ème & 18ème
18ème
9ème
17ème
Basilique du Sacré-Coeur
Musée du Vieux Montmartre
Clos Montmartre
Espace Dali à Monmartre
Cimitière St-Vincent
Moulin Radet
Moulin de la Galette
Halle Saint Pierre
Bal du Moulin Rouge
Cimitière de Montmartre
PL. DU TERTRE
PL. EMILE GOUDEAU
PL. ST-PIERRE
SQ. WILLETTE
PL. DU CHÂTEAU ROUGE
PL. PIGALLE
PL. BLANCHE
PL. DE CLICHY
PL. A. MAX
Marcadet Poissonniers
CHÂTEAU ROUGE
BARBÈS ROCHECHOUART
ANVERS
ABBESSES
PIGALLE
BLANCHE
LAMARCK CAULAINCOURT
LA FOURCHE
TAXI
bd. de Magenta
bd. Barbès
bd. de Rochechouart
bd. de Clichy
av. de Clichy
av. de St-Ouen
av. Junot
av. Trudaine
av. Frochot
av. Antoine Piémontési
r. du Faubourg Poissonnière
r. Mercadet
r. Lamarck
r. Caulaincourt
r. Joseph de Maistre
r. Damrémont
r. Tourlaque
r. Lepic
r. Ganneron
r. Cavallotti
r. Forest
r. de l'Abreuvoir
r. St-Vincent
r. de Cortot
r. des Saules
r. Paul Féval
r. du Mont Cenis
r. Herme
r. du Baigneur
r. Custine
r. Ramey
r. de la Bonne
r. St-Rustique
r. Poulbot
r. Gabrielle
r. Berthe
r. des Trois Frères
r. Tholoz
r. Burq
r. des Abbesses
r. Durantin
r. Véron
r. de la Vieuville
r. Y. Le Tac
r. Tardieu
r. Foyatier
r. Muller
r. Feutrier
r. A del Sarte
r. Cazotte
r. Ronsard
r. Nodier
r. P. Picard
r. d'Orsel
r. de Clignancourt
r. Christiani
r. Murha
r. de la Goutte
r. de Sofia
r. Puget
r. Coustou
r. Germain
r. Houdon
r. des Martyrs
r. André Gill
r. de Steinkerque
r. Briquet
r. Seveste
r. Harret
r. Bruxelles
r. de Douai
r. de Calais
r. de Vintmille
r. Ballu
r. Fontaine
r. Fromentin
r. Mansart
r. Duperr
r. Douai
r. Jean-Baptiste Pigalle
r. Frochot
r. Viollet-le-Duc
r. Cretet
r. B. de Saron
r. Lallier
r. Say
r. Gérando
r. de Rochechouart
r. du Delta
r. de Dunkerque
r. Turgot
r. Rodier
r. Petrelle
r. Condorcet
r. Victor Massé
r. Chaptal
r. R. Escudier
r. Blanche
r. d'Amsterdam
r. de Parme
r. de Bucharest
Monthiers
r. Cardinal Mercier
r. J. Lefebvre

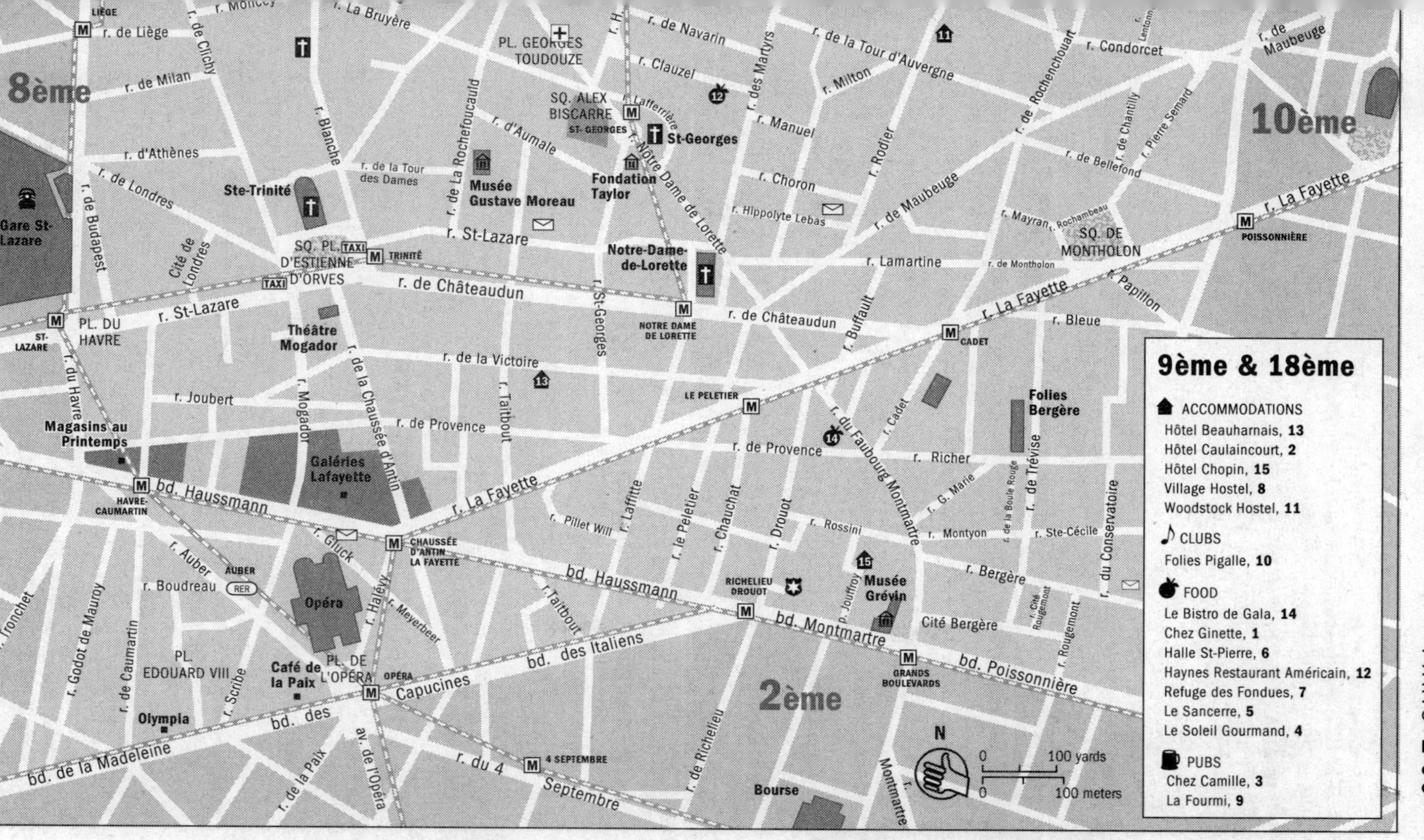
9ème & 18ème
ACCOMMODATIONS
Hôtel Beauharnais, 13
Hôtel Caulaincourt, 2
Hôtel Chopin, 15
Village Hostel, 8
Woodstock Hostel, 11
CLUBS
Folies Pigalle, 10
FOOD
Le Bistro de Gala, 14
Chez Ginette, 1
Halle St-Pierre, 6
Haynes Restaurant Américain, 12
Refuge des Fondues, 7
Le Sancerre, 5
Le Soleil Gourmand, 4
PUBS
Chez Camille, 3
La Fourmi, 9
N
0
100 yards
0
100 meters
10ème
2ème
8ème
Folies Bergère
Musée Grévin
Bourse
St-Georges
Fondation Taylor
Notre-Dame-de-Lorette
Musée Gustave Moreau
Ste-Trinité
Théâtre Mogador
Galeries Lafayette
Opéra
Café de la Paix
Olympia
Magasins au Printemps
Gare St-Lazare
SQ. DE MONTHOLON
SQ. ALEX BISCARRE
PL. GEORGES TOUDOUZE
SQ. PL. D'ESTIENNE D'ORVES
PL. DE L'OPÉRA
PL. EDOUARD VII
PL. DU HAVRE
POISSONNIÈRE
CADET
LE PELETIER
NOTRE DAME DE LORETTE
ST-GEORGES
RICHELIEU DROUOT
GRANDS BOULEVARDS
4 SEPTEMBRE
CHAUSSÉE D'ANTIN LA FAYETTE
TRINITÉ
OPÉRA
AUBER
HAVRE-CAUMARTIN
ST-LAZARE
LIÈGE
r. La Fayette
r. de Maubeuge
r. Condorcet
r. de Rochechouart
r. de la Tour d'Auvergne
r. des Martyrs
r. de Navarin
r. Clauzel
r. Milton
r. Manuel
r. Rodier
r. Choron
r. Hippolyte Lebas
r. Lamartine
r. de Châteaudun
r. Buffault
r. Cadet
r. du Faubourg Montmartre
r. Richer
r. de Provence
r. Bleue
r. de Trévise
r. Montyon
r. Rossini
r. Drouot
r. Chauchat
r. Le Peletier
r. Laffitte
r. Taitbout
r. St-Georges
r. Notre Dame de Lorette
r. de la Victoire
r. St-Lazare
r. de La Rochefoucauld
r. d'Aumale
r. Blanche
r. de la Chaussée d'Antin
r. Mogador
r. Joubert
r. de Clichy
r. de Milan
r. d'Athènes
r. de Londres
r. de Budapest
r. du Havre
r. de Liège
r. La Bruyère
r. Auber
r. Boudreau
r. Scribe
r. de Caumartin
r. Godot de Mauroy
r. Tronchet
r. Gluck
r. Halévy
r. Meyerbeer
r. du 4 Septembre
r. de la Paix
av. de l'Opéra
r. de Richelieu
r. Montmartre
r. Bergère
Cité Bergère
r. Rougemont
r. du Conservatoire
r. Ste-Cécile
r. Papillon
r. de Bellefond
r. de Chantilly
r. Pierre Semard
bd. Haussmann
bd. Montmartre
bd. Poissonnière
bd. des Italiens
bd. des Capucines
bd. de la Madeleine

10EME ARRONDISSEMENT. This area is home to the Gare de l'Est and Gare du Nord and a flock of inexpensive hotels roosts near the stations. It is far from sights and nightlife and is somewhat unsafe. Use special caution west of pl. de la République along rue du Château d'Eau.

11EME ARRONDISSEMENT. Five métro lines converge at M: République and three at M: Bastille, making the **11ème** a transport hub and mammoth center of action—the hangout of the young and fun. Budget accommodations line these streets and are likely to have space. The neighborhood is generally safe, but be wary in the pickpocket-strewn pl. de la République.

12EME ARRONDISSEMENT. The **12ème** is generally safe (although be careful around Gare de Lyon); the streets around the Bois de Vincennes offer some of the city's most pleasant places to stay, but are removed from the city center.

16EME ARRONDISSEMENT. Wealthy and residential, the museum-spattered **16ème** is a short walk from the Eiffel Tower but a 20-minute métro ride to the center. This quarter has over 60 embassies, about half of Paris' museums, the Trocadéro, and the rambling Bois de Boulogne. Métro stops are few and far between. Hotels here are relatively luxurious and apt to have vacancies.

17EME ARRONDISSEMENT. Hugging the northwestern edge of the city and sandwiched in between more luxurious and famous areas, the **17ème** suffers from a bit of multiple personality disorder. In between the aristocratic *8ème* and *16ème arrondissements* and the more tawdry *18ème* and Pigalle, the *17ème* is a working-class residential neighborhood. Some of its hotels cater to prostitutes, others to visiting businesspeople. Be careful near pl. de Clichy.

MONTMARTRE: 18EME ARRONDISSEMENT. This area owes its reputation to the fame of artists who once lived there. Hotel rates rise as you climb to the Basilique Sacré-Coeur. Food near the church and pl. du Tertre is pricey. Downhill and south at seedy pl. Pigalle, hotels tend to rent by the hour. At night avoid M: Anvers, M: Pigalle, and M: Barbès-Rochechouart; use M: Abbesses instead.

19EME AND 20EME ARRONDISSEMENTS. The **19ème** and **20ème** are by no means central; apart from the *19ème's* Parc de la Villette and the *20ème's* Père Lachaise, expect at least a 30-minute métro ride to the city's sights. The *19ème's* Parc des Buttes-Chaumont is great for picnics and jogs. Though cheap high-rises dot the hillsides, a few charming streets preserve the old-Paris feel. Two-star hotels are a good bet if you're stuck. Rue de Belleville can be dangerous at night.

GETTING INTO PARIS

TO AND FROM THE AIRPORTS

ROISSY-CHARLES DE GAULLE. Transatlantic flights. 24hr. English-speaking info center (☎01 48 62 22 80; www.parisairports.com).

RER: From Roissy-CDG to Paris, take the free shuttle bus (*Navette*) from Terminal 1 (every 10min.). From there, the RER B (one of the Parisian commuter rail lines) will transport you to central Paris. To transfer to the métro, get off at Gare du Nord, Châtelet-Les-Halles, or St-Michel. **To go to Roissy-CDG from Paris,** take the RER B to "Roissy," which is the end of the line. Then change to the free shuttle bus if you need to get to Terminal 1 (30-35min.; RER every 10min. 5am-12:30am, bus 10min.; 49F/€7.47).

Shuttle Buses: Roissybus (☎01 49 25 61 87) leaves from the corner of rue Scribe and rue Auber, near M: Opéra, and stops at Porte 11 of Terminals 2A and 2C, Porte 0.08 of Terminal 2F, Porte 9 of Terminals 2D and 2B; T9; and 1. Buy tickets on bus (45min.; to and from airport every 15min. 6am-8pm, every 20min. 8-11pm; 48F/€7.32). **Air France Buses** (recorded info available in English ☎01 41 56 89 00) run daily to 2 areas of the city. Buy tickets on bus. **Line 2** runs to and from the Arc de Triomphe (M:

Charles de Gaulle-Etoile) at 1 av. Carnot (35min., every 12min. 5:45am-11pm, one-way 65F/€9.91), and to and from pl. de la Porte de Maillot/Palais des Congrès (M: Porte de Maillot) on bd. Gouvion St-Cyr (same schedule and prices). **Line 4** runs to and from rue du Commandant Mouchette opposite the Méridien Hotel (M: Montparnasse-Bienvenüe; to airport every 30min. 7am-9:30pm; one-way 75F/€11.44, round-trip 130F/€19.83; 15% group discount); and to and from Gare de Lyon (M: Gare de Lyon), at 20b bd. Diderot (same schedule and prices). The shuttle stops at or between terminals 2A-2F, and at terminal 1 on the departures level.

ORLY. Charters and many continental flights. 18km south of the city. (☎01 49 75 15 15 for info, in English, 6am-11:45pm.)

RER: From Orly Sud gate H or gate I, platform 1, or Orly Ouest level 0, gate F, take the **Orly-Rail** shuttle bus (every 15min. 5:40am-11:15pm, 12F/€1.83) to the **Pont de Rungis/Aéroport d'Orly** train stop, where you can board the **RER C2** for a number of destinations in Paris. (Call RATP 08 36 68 41 14 for info in English; 25min., every 15min. 6am-11pm, 35F/€5.34.) The **Jetbus** (every 12min. 6am-10pm, 30F/€4.58), provides a quick connection between Orly Sud, gate H, platform 2, or Orly Ouest level 0, gate C and M: Villejuif-Louis Aragon on line 7 of the métro.

Bus: Another option is the RATP **Orlybus** (☎01 40 02 32 94), which runs to and from métro and RER stop Denfert-Rochereau, 14*ème*. Board at Orly Sud, gate H, platform 4 or Orly Ouest level 1 (30min., every 15-20min. 6am-11:30pm, 35F/€5.34). You can also board the Orlybus at Dareau-St-Jacques, Glacière-Tolbiac, and Porte de Gentilly; additional descent points at Jourdan-Tombe Issoire, Parc Montsouris, and Alésia-René Coty. **Air France Buses** run between Orly and **Gare Montparnasse,** near the Hôtel Méridien, 6*ème* (M: Montparnasse-Bienvenüe), and the Invalides Air France agency, pl. des Invalides (30min.; every 12 min. 6am-11pm; 50F/€7.63 one-way, 85F/€12.96 round-trip). Air France shuttles stop at Orly Ouest and then Orly Sud, at the departures levels.

Orlyval: RATP also runs **Orlyval** (☎08 36 68 41 14), a combination of métro, RER, and VAL rail shuttle. The VAL shuttle goes from Antony (a stop on the RER line B) to Orly Ouest and Sud. You can either get a ticket just for the VAL (Orly to Antony, 46F/€7.01), or combination VAL-RER tickets that include the VAL ticket and the RER ticket (56-68F/€8.69-10.37). Be careful when taking the RER B from Paris to Orly, because it splits into 2 lines right before the Antony stop. Buy tickets at any RATP booth, or from the Orlyval agencies. (35min. from Châtelet, 40min. from Charles de Gaulle-Etoile, 50min. from La Défense; every 7min. during peak hours from Antony to Orly M-Sa 6am-10:30pm, Su and holidays 7am-11pm.) From Orly, the VAL leaves from Orly-Sud at baggage claim in gate K, from Orly-Ouest Gate W - Level 1 or Gate J - Level 0. Trains arrive at Orly Ouest 2min. after reaching Orly Sud. (30min. from Châtelet; Antony-Orly M-Sa 6am-8:30pm, Su and holidays 7am-11pm; Orly-Antony every 7min. M-Sa 6am-10:30pm, Su 7am-10:57pm).

TRAINS

Each of Paris' six train stations is a veritable community of its own. Locate the ticket counters *(guichets)*, platforms *(quais)*, and tracks *(voies)*, and you will be ready to roll. Each terminal has two divisions: the *banlieue* (suburb) and the *grandes lignes* (big important trains). Some cities can be accessed by both regular trains and **trains à grande vitesse** (**TGV;** high speed trains), which are more expensive, much faster, and require reservations that cost a small fee. For **train info** or to make reservations, contact SNCF (☎08 36 35 35 35; www.sncf.fr; 3F/€0.46 per min.). Yellow **ticket machines** (*billetteries*) at every train station sell tickets to anyone who knows his PIN and has a MasterCard, Visa, or American Express (only MC/V at booths).

BUSES

International buses arrive in Paris at **Gare Routière Internationale du Paris-Gallieni** (M: Gallieni), just outside Paris at 28 av. du Général de Gaulle, Bagnolet 93170. **Eurolines** (☎08 36 69 52 52; www.eurolines.fr) sells tickets to most destinations in France and neighboring countries. Pick up schedules for departures from the station or the office at 55 rue St-Jacques, 5*ème* (M: Maubert-Mutualité).

GETTING AROUND PARIS

RATP helpline (☎08 36 68 77 14, daily 6am-9pm; www.ratp.fr; 2.21F/€0.34 per min.).

FARES AND PASSES

Individual tickets for the RATP cost 8.50F/€1.30 each, or can be bought in a *carnet* of 10 for 61F/€9.30. Each métro ride takes one ticket, and the bus takes at least one, sometimes more. For directions on using the tickets, see **Métro,** below. If you're staying in Paris for several days or weeks, a **Carte Orange** can be very economical. Bring an ID photo (taken by machines in most stations) to the ticket counter and ask for the weekly *carte orange hebdomaire* (87F/€13.27) or the monthly *carte orange mensuelle* (291F/€44.38). Prices quoted here are for passes in Zones 1 and 2 (the métro and RER in Paris and suburbs), and work on all métro, bus, and RER modes of transport. If you intend to travel to the suburbs, you'll need to buy RER passes for more zones (they go up to 5). If you're only in town for a day or two, a cheap option is the **Carte Mobilis** (33F/€5.03 for a one-day pass in Zones 1 and 2; ☎01 53 90 20 20), which provides unlimited métro, bus, and RER transportation within Paris. Always write the number of your *carte* on your coupon. **Paris Visite tickets** are valid for unlimited travel on bus, métro, and RER, as well as discounts on sightseeing trips, bike rentals, and stores; they can be purchased at the airport or at métro and RER stations. These passes are available for 1 day (55F/€8.38), 2 days (90F/€13.72), 3 days (120F/€18.29), or 5 days (175F/€26.60), but the discounts you receive do not necessarily outweigh the extra cost.

METRO

Métro stations are marked with an "M" or with the "*Métropolitain*" lettering designed by art nouveau legend Hector Guimard. The first trains start running around 5:30am, and the last ones leave the end-of-the-line stations (the "*portes de Paris*") for the center of the city at about 12:15am. Connections to other lines are indicated by orange *correspondance* signs, exits by blue *sortie* signs. Transfers are free if made within a station, but it is not always possible to reverse direction on the same line without exiting the station. To pass through the turnstiles, insert the ticket into the small slot in the metal divider just to your right as you approach the turnstile. It disappears for a moment, then pops out about a foot farther along, and a little green or white circle lights up, reminding you to retrieve the ticket. **Hold onto your ticket** until you exit the métro, and pass the point marked **Limite de Validité des Billets.** Do not count on buying a métro ticket home late at night. Some ticket windows close as early as 10pm. Stay away from the most dangerous stations at night (Barbès-Rochechouart, Pigalle, Anvers, Châtelet-Les-Halles, Gare du Nord, Gare de l'Est). When in doubt, take a taxi.

RER

The RER *(Réseau Express Régional)* is the RATP's suburban train system, which passes through central Paris. Within the city, the RER travels much faster than the métro. There are five RER lines, marked A-E, with different branches designated by a number, such as the C5 line to Versailles-Rive Gauche. The RER runs, as does the métro, from about 5:15am to midnight.

BUS

Although slower and often more costly than the métro, buses can be cheap sight-seeing tours and helpful introductions to the city's layout. Bus tickets are the same as those used in the métro, and can be purchased either in métro stations or on the bus from the driver. *Cartes oranges* and other transport passes (Paris Visite, Mobilis, etc.), are equally valid in buses and subways (see **Métro,** above). When you wish to leave the bus, just press the red button and the *arrêt demandé* sign will magically light up.

NIGHT BUSES. Most buses run daily 6:30am-8:30pm, although those marked **Autobus de nuit** continue until 1am. Still others, named **Noctambus,** run all night. Night buses (15F/€2.29, with or without transfers) start their runs to the *portes* (end-of-the-line stations) of the city from the "Châtelet" stop and leave daily every hour on the half hour 1:30-5:30am. Buses departing from the suburbs to Châtelet run every hour on the hour 1-6am. Noctambuses I through M, R, and S have routes along the Left Bank en route to the southern suburbs. Those marked A through H, P, T, or V have routes on the Right Bank going north. Look for bus stops marked with a bug-eyed moon sign. Ask at a major métro station for more info.

TOUR BUSES. **Balabus** (call the RATP 08 36 68 41 14 for info in English) stops at virtually every major sight in Paris (Bastille, St-Michel, Louvre, Musée d'Orsay, Concorde, Champs-Elysées, Charles-de-Gaulle-Etoile; whole loop takes 1¼hr.). The fare is the same as any standard bus (3 tickets, since it covers more than the 2-zone region). The loop starts at the Grande Arche de La Défense or Gare de Lyon.

PARIS

TAXIS

Taxis are expensive, and only take three passengers. **Alpha Taxis** ☎01 45 85 85 85. **Taxis 700** ☎01 42 70 00 42. **Taxis Bleus** ☎01 49 36 10 10. **Taxis G7** ☎01 47 39 47 39.

USEFUL SERVICES

For consulates and embassies, see **Essentials,** p. 30.

TOURIST OFFICES

Bureau d'Accueil Central, 127 av. des Champs-Elysées, *8ème.* (☎08 36 68 31 12; www.paris-touristoffice.com. M: Georges V. Open in summer daily 9am-8pm; off-season Su 11am-6pm.) **Bureau Gare de Lyon,** *12ème.* (☎01 43 43 33 24. M: Gare de Lyon. Open M-Sa 8am-8pm.) **Bureau Tour Eiffel,** Champs de Mars, *7ème.* (☎08 92 68 31 12. M: Champs de Mars. Open May-Sept. daily 11am-6pm.)

USEFUL PUBLICATIONS AND LISTINGS

The weeklies **Pariscope** (3F/€0.46; www.pariscope.fr) and **Officiel des Spectacles** (2F/€0.31) have the most comprehensive listings of movies, plays, exhibits, festivals, clubs, and bars. *Pariscope* also includes an English-language section called **Time Out Paris.** The tourist office's free monthly **Where: Paris** highlights exhibits, concerts, walking tours, and events. The Mairie de Paris, 29 rue de Rivoli, *4ème* (☎01 42 76 42 42; M: Hôtel-de-Ville), publishes the free monthly **Paris le Journal,** with articles about what's on around the city. On Wednesday, the newspaper *Le Figaro* includes **Figaroscope,** a supplement about what's happening in Paris. **Free Voice,** a monthly English-language newspaper published by the American Church, and the bi-weekly **France-USA Contacts (FUSAC)** list jobs, housing, and info for English speakers and are available for free from English-speaking bookstores, restaurants, and travel agencies throughout Paris.

CURRENCY EXCHANGE

Many, but not all, banks will exchange money 9am-noon and 2-4:30pm. Beware of *bureaux de change* at airports, train stations, and in touristy areas; banks are normally a better bet. There's also **American Express,** 11 rue Scribe, *9ème.* (☎01 47 14 50 00. M: Opéra or Auber. Open M-F 9am-6:30pm, Sa 10am-5:30pm; exchange counters open Su 10am-5pm.) Or try **Thomas Cook,** 73 av. des Champs-Elysées, *8ème.* (☎01 45 62 89 55. M: Georges V. Open daily 8:30am-10pm.)

HEALTH AND CRISES

Emergency numbers: Ambulance (SAMU) ☎15. **Fire** ☎18. **Poison** ☎01 40 05 48 48. In French, but some English assistance available. **Police** ☎17. **Emergencies only.**
Rape: SOS Viol (☎0 800 05 95 95). Open M-F 10am-7pm. **S.O.S Help!** (☎01 47 23 80 80). Anonymous, confidential English crisis hotline. Open daily 3-11pm.

Hospitals: Hôpital Américain de Paris, 84 bd. Saussaye, Neuilly (☎01 46 41 25 25). M: Port Maillot, then bus #82 to the end of the line. A private hospital. **Hôpital Franco-Britannique de Paris,** 3 rue Barbès, in the Parisian suburb of Levallois-Perret (☎01 46 39 22 22). M: Anatole-France. Some English spoken, but don't count on it. **Hôpital Bichat,** 46 rue Henri Buchard, 18*ème* (☎01 40 25 80 80). M: Port St-Ouen. Emergency services.

24hr. Pharmacies: Every arrondissement should have a **pharmacie de garde** which will open in case of emergencies. The locations change, but the name of the nearest one is posted on each pharmacy's door. **British & American Pharmacy,** 1 rue Auber, 9*ème* (☎01 42 65 88 29). M: Auber or Opéra. Open M-F 8:30am-8pm, Sa 10am-8pm.

Birth control: Mouvement Français pour le Planning Familial (MFPF), 10 rue Vivienne, 2*ème* (☎01 42 60 93 20). M: Bourse. Open for calls M-F 9:30am-5:30pm. On F, the clinic is held at 94 bd. Massanna, M: Porte Ivry, on the 1st fl. of the Tour Mantoue, door code 38145, 13*ème* (☎01 45 84 28 25); 10am-4pm, call ahead.

Emotional Health: SOS Crisis Help Line Friendship ☎01 47 23 80 80. English spoken. Daily 3-11pm. **International Counseling Service (ICS)** ☎01 45 50 26 49. Open M-F 8am-8pm, Sa 8am-4pm. Provides access to psychologists, psychiatrists, social workers, and a clerical counselor. Open M-F 9:30am-6pm, Sa 9:30am-1pm. Leave a message on its answering machine. Call for an appointment.

COMMUNICATIONS

Internet Access: Easy Everything, 37 bd. Sébastopol, 1*er* (☎01 40 41 09 10). M: Châtelet-les-Halles. Purchase a User ID for any amount, minimum 20F/€3.05 and recharge the ID with 10F/€1.53 or more. Number of minutes depends on the time of day and how busy the store is. Open 24hr. **Le Jardin de l'Internet,** 79 bd. St-Michel, 5*ème* (☎01 44 07 22 20). RER: Luxembourg. 15min. minimum. 1F/€0.15 per min., 40F/ €6.10 per hr., 190F/€28.98 for 5hr. Open daily 9am-11pm. **WebBar,** 32 rue de Picardie, 3*ème* (☎01 42 72 66 55). M: République. 20F/€3.05 per hr. Open daily 8:30am-2am.

Federal Express: ☎08 00 12 38 00. Call M-F before 5pm for pick up. Or, drop off at 2 rue du 29 Juillet, between Concorde and rue du Rivoli, 1*er*. Open M-Sa 9am-7pm; drop off by 4:45pm. **Also** at 63 bd. Haussmann, 8*ème*.

Poste du Louvre: 52 rue du Louvre, 1*er* (info ☎01 40 28 20 40). M: Louvre. Open 24hr.

ACCOMMODATIONS

ILE DE LA CITE

Henri IV, 25, pl. Dauphine (☎01 43 54 44 53). M: Pont Neuf. One of Paris' best located and least expensive hotels. Big windows and charming views of the tree-lined *place*. Showers 15F/€2.29. Reserve at least one month in advance, even earlier in the summer. Singles 140F/€21.35; doubles 165-215F/€25.16-32.78, with shower and toilet 350F/€53.36; triples 255F/€38.88, with shower 305F/€46.50; quads 300F/ €45.74.

FIRST ARRONDISSEMENT

Hôtel Montpensier, 12 rue de Richelieu (☎01 42 96 28 50; fax 01 42 86 02 70). M: Palais-Royal. Walk around left side of the Palais-Royal to rue de Richelieu. Clean rooms, lofty ceilings, bright decor, and English-speaking staff. Breakfast 40F/€6.10. Shower 25F/€3.81. Reserve a month ahead in high season. Singles with toilet 300F/€45.74; doubles with toilet 340F/€51.84. Rooms with toilet and shower 455F/€69.37; with toilet, bath, and sink 535F/€81.57. Extra bed 80F/€12.20. AmEx/MC/V.

Hôtel du Palais, 2 quai de la Mégisserie (☎01 42 36 98 25; fax 01 42 21 41 67). M: Châtelet-Les-Halles. Most rooms have exceptional views of the Seine and Left Bank, but are within earshot of traffic below. Breakfast 35F/€5.34. Reserve 3 weeks in advance. Singles with shower 293F/€44.67, with shower or bath and toilet 363F/€55.35; doubles 336F/€51.23, with shower and toilet 366F/€55.80, with bath and toilet 396F/

€60.38; triples 462F/€70.44; quad 562F/€85.68; quint with bathroom 662F/€100.93; 6-person room 772F/€117.70. Extra bed 70F/€10.67. AmEx/MC/V.

Centre International de Paris (BVJ)/Paris Louvre, 20 rue J.-J. Rousseau (☎01 53 00 90 90; fax 01 53 00 90 91). M: Louvre or Palais-Royal. From M: Louvre, take rue du Louvre away from the river, turn left on rue St-Honoré and right on rue J.-J. Rousseau. 200 beds. Bright, dorm-style rooms with 2-10 beds per room. Internet 1F/€0.15 per min. Breakfast and showers included. Lockers 10F/€1.53. Reception 24hr. Weekend reservations (by phone only) up to 1 week in advance. They hold your rooms for only 10min. after your given check-in time; call if you'll be late. 145F/€22.11 per person.

Hôtel Lion d'Or, 5 rue de la Sourdière (☎01 42 60 79 04; fax 01 42 60 09 14; www.hotelduliondor.com). M: Tuileries. Walk down rue du 29 Juillet away from the park and turn right on rue St-Honoré, then left on rue de la Sourdière. Clean and carpeted rooms, most with TV. Breakfast 35F/€5.34. Reserve 1 month ahead in high season. Singles with shower 380F/€57.94, with bath and toilet 480F/€73.18; doubles with shower 480-560F/€73.18-85.38; triples with shower 680F/€103.67, with bath and toilet 750F/€114.35. Extra bed 60F/€9.15. AmEx/MC/V.

Hôtel St-Honoré, 85 rue St-Honoré (☎01 42 36 20 38 or 01 42 21 46 96; fax 01 42 21 44 08; paris@hotelsainthonore.com). M: Louvre, Châtelet, or Les Halles. From M: Louvre, cross rue de Rivoli onto rue du Louvre and turn right on rue St-Honoré. Sizable, modern rooms with shower, toilet, and TV. Friendly, English-speaking staff, and young clientele. Breakfast 29F/€4.42. Reserve ahead and confirm the night before. Singles 320F/€48.79; doubles 440F/€67.08, with bathtub 490F/€74.71; triples and quads 540F/€82.33. AmEx/MC/V.

Maisons des Jeunes de Rufz de Lavison, 18 rue J.-J. Rousseau (☎01 45 08 02 10; fax 01 40 28 11 43). M: Louvre or Palais-Royal. Next door to BVJ Louvre. In winter, an all-male dorm. From mid-June to mid-Aug., it's co-ed and primarily for long-term stays. Quiet, spacious rooms. 5 night min. stay. Reception 9am-7pm. No curfew; entrance code given. Reservations starting June 15; night's payment required. Singles 165F/€25.16; doubles 145F/€22.11 per person. Monthly: singles 4600F/€701.33; doubles 3460F/€527.52 per person; 500F/€76.23 deposit.

SECOND ARRONDISSEMENT

Hôtel Tiquetonne, 6 rue Tiquetonne (☎01 42 36 94 58; fax 01 42 36 02 94). M: Etienne-Marcel. Walk against traffic on rue de Turbigo; turn left on rue Tiquetonne. Near Marché Montorgueil, rowdy English bars near Etienne-Marcel, and St-Denis' sex shops—what more could you want in a location? Elevator. Breakfast 30F/€4.58. Showers 30F/€4.58. Closed Aug. and 1 week at Christmas. Singles with shower 153-233F/€23.33-35.53; doubles with shower and toilet 266F/€40.57. AmEx/MC/V.

Hôtel Favart, 5 rue Marivaux (☎01 42 97 59 83; fax 01 40 15 95 58; FAVART.HOTEL@wanadoo.fr). M: Richelieu Drouot. Turn left down bd. des Italiens and left on rue Marivaux. Once home of painter Goya. Sizable rooms with cable TV, shower, and toilet. One wheelchair-accessible room. Breakfast included. Prices with *Let's Go:* singles 550F/€83.88; doubles 695F/€106; extra bed 100F/€15.25. AmEx/MC/V.

Hôtel Vivenne, 40 rue Vivienne (☎01 42 33 13 26; fax 01 40 41 98 19; paris@hotel-vivienne.com). M: Grands Boulevards. Follow the traffic on bd. Montmartre past the Théâtre des Variétés and turn left on rue Vivienne. Showers in all rooms. Elevator. Breakfast 40F/€6.10. Singles 310F/€47.28, with toilet 480F/€73.20; doubles 400F/€61, with toilet 480F/€73.20; extra person over 10 add 30%. MC/V.

Hôtel des Boulevards, 10 rue de la Ville Neuve (☎01 42 36 02 29; fax 01 42 36 15 39). M: Bonne Nouvelle. Walk against traffic on av. Poissonnière and go right on rue de la Ville Neuve. In a funky neighborhood that's become a little run-down. Simple rooms have TVs and new carpets. Breakfast included. Reserve 2 weeks ahead and confirm with credit card deposit. 10% *Let's Go* discount. Singles and doubles 256F/€39, with shower 327F/€49, with bath 348-360F/€53-55; extra bed 66F/€10. AmEx/MC/V.

PARIS

THIRD ARRONDISSEMENT

Hôtel du Séjour, 36 rue du Grenier St-Lazare (☎/fax 01 48 87 40 36). M: Etienne-Marcel. Follow the traffic on rue Etienne-Marcel, which becomes rue du Grenier St-Lazare. A block from Les Halles and the Centre Pompidou. Clean, bright rooms. Reserve a week ahead. Showers 20F/€3.05. Reception 7am-10:30pm. Singles 200F/€30.50; doubles 275F/€42, with shower and toilet 355F/€54, extra person 150F/€22.88.

Hôtel de Roubaix, 6 rue Greneta (☎01 42 72 89 91; fax 01 42 72 58 79). M: Réaumur-Sébastopol. Walk opposite traffic on bd. de Sébastopol and turn left on rue Greneta, or take bus #20 from Gare de Lyon to "St-Nicolas des Champs." Helpful staff; clean rooms with shower, toilet, and TV. Breakfast included. Reserve a week ahead. Singles 310-350F/€47.28-53.38; doubles 380-410F/€57.95-62.53; triples 450-500F/€68.63-76.25; quads 540F/€82.35; quints 570F/€86.93. MC/V.

Hôtel Picard, 26 rue de Picardie (☎01 48 87 53 82; fax 01 48 87 02 56). M: Temple. Walk against traffic down rue du Temple, take the first left on rue du Petit Thouars, and at the end of the street turn right. Not much English spoken. Simple pastel rooms. Breakfast 30F/€4.58. Hall showers 20F/€3.05. Apr.-Sept. reserve 2 weeks ahead. 5% *Let's Go* discount. Singles 210F/€32.03, with shower, toilet, and TV 260F/€39.65; doubles 250-270F/€38.13-41.18, 330F/€50.33; triples 520F/€79.30. MC/V.

Hôtel Bellevue et du Chariot d'Or, 39 rue de Turbigo (☎01 48 87 45 60; fax 01 48 87 95 04). M: Etienne-Marcel. Walk against traffic on rue de Turbigo. Belle Epoque lobby. 59 clean and modern rooms with TVs, toilets, and baths. Breakfast 35F/€5.34. Reserve about 2 weeks in advance. Singles 330F/€50.31; doubles 376F/€57.40; triples 480F/€73; quads 590F/€90. AmEx/MC/V.

Hôtel de Bretagne, 87 rue des Archives (☎01 48 87 83 14). M: Temple. Take rue du Temple against traffic and turn left onto rue de Bretagne; the hotel is on the right, at the corner with rue des Archives. Friendly reception and well-kept rooms. Breakfast 30F/€4.58. Reserve 1 week in advance. Singles with toilet 170F/€25.93, with full bath and telephone 350F/€53.38; doubles with toilet 210F/€32.03, with twin beds 230F/€35.08, with full bath and telephone 390F/€59.48; triples with toilet 300F/€45.75, with full bath and telephone 500F/€76.25.

FOURTH ARRONDISSEMENT

Hôtel des Jeunes (MIJE) (☎01 42 74 23 45; fax 01 40 27 81 64; www.mije.com). Books beds in Le Fourcy, Le Fauconnier, and Maubuisson (see below), 3 small hostels located on cobblestone streets in beautiful old Marais residences. No smoking. English spoken. The La Table d'Hôtes restaurant (at Le Fourcy) offers a main course with drink (50F/€7.63) and coffee and 3-course "hosteler special" (60F/€9.15). Internet 1F/€0.15 per minute. Breakfast, shower, and sheets included. Public phones and free lockers (with a 2F/€0.31 deposit). **Ages 18-30 only.** 7-day max. stay. Reception 7am-1am. Lockout noon-3pm. Curfew 1am. Quiet after 10pm. Arrive before noon the first day of reservation (call in advance if you'll be late). Groups may reserve 1 year in advance. Individuals should reserve at least 2-3 weeks in advance. 4- to 6-bed dorms 145F/€22.11; singles 240F/€36.60; doubles 175F/€26.69; triples 155F/€23.64.

Le Fourcy, 6 rue de Fourcy. M: St-Paul. Walk opposite the traffic for a few meters down rue François-Miron and turn left on rue de Fourcy. Hostel surrounds a social courtyard.

Le Fauconnier, 11 rue du Fauconnier. M: St-Paul. Take rue du Prevôt, turn left on rue Charlemagne, and turn right on rue du Fauconnier. Steps away from the Seine and Ile St-Louis.

Maubuisson, 12 rue des Barres. M: Pont Marie. Walk opposite traffic on rue de l'Hôtel de Ville and turn right on rue des Barres, a silent street by the St-Gervais monastery. Elevator.

Grand Hôtel Jeanne d'Arc, 3 rue de Jarente (☎01 48 87 62 11; fax 01 48 87 37 31; www.hoteljeannedarc.com). M: St-Paul. Walk opposite traffic on rue de Rivoli and turn left on rue de Sévigné, then right on rue de Jarente. Nicely renovated rooms with showers, toilets, and TVs. 2 rooms on the ground floor are wheelchair-accessible. Breakfast 38F/€5.80. Reserve 2 months in advance. Singles 347F/€53.00; doubles 420-479F/€64.00-73.00; triples 702F/€107; quads 800F/€122. Extra bed 75F/€11.44. MC/V.

Hôtel de la Place des Vosges, 12 rue de Birague (☎01 42 72 60 46; fax 01 42 72 02 64; hotel.place.des.vosges@gofornet.com). M: Bastille. Take rue St-Antoine; rue de Birague is the third right. By pl. des Vosges. Beautiful interior with exposed beams and stone walls. TVs and full baths in all rooms. Breakfast 40F/€6.10. Reserve by fax 2 months ahead with 1 night's deposit. Singles 495F/€75.49; doubles 600F/€91.50, with twin beds 690F/€105.23; quads 900F/€137.25. AmEx/MC/V.

Hôtel de Nice, 42bis rue de Rivoli (☎01 42 78 55 29; fax 01 42 78 36 07). M: Hôtel-de-Ville. Walk opposite traffic on rue de Rivoli for about 4 blocks. Wonderful, bright rooms with vintage illustrations, TVs, toilets, and showers, a few with balconies. Hot in the summer (fans provided). Elevator. Breakfast 40F/€6.10. Check-in 2pm, but you can leave your bags earlier. Check-out 11:30am. Reserve by fax or phone with 1 night's deposit 1 month ahead for summer. Singles 380F/€57.95; doubles 580F/€88.45; triples 710F/€108.28; quads 810F/€123.53. Extra bed 130F/€19.83. MC/V.

Hôtel Practic, 9 rue d'Ormesson (☎01 48 87 80 47; fax 01 48 87 40 04). M: St-Paul. Walk against traffic on rue de Rivoli, then turn left on rue de Sévigné and right on rue d'Ormesson. On a cobblestone square in the heart of the Marais. A/C expected by 2002. Rooms are modest but bright, and all have TVs. English spoken. Breakfast 25F/€3.81. Reserve by fax 1 month in advance. Singles with toilet 290F/€44.23, with shower 420F/€64.05, with both 520F/€79.30; doubles with toilet 409F/€62.37, with shower 460F/€70.15, with both 560F/€85.40; triples with both 635F/€96.84. Extra bed 80F/€12.20. Tax 3F/€0.46. MC/V.

PARIS

FIFTH ARRONDISSEMENT

Young and Happy (Y&H) Hostel, 80 rue Mouffetard (☎01 45 35 09 53; fax 01 47 07 22 24). M: Monge. Cross rue Gracieuse and take rue Ortolan to rue Mouffetard. A funky hostel on the emblematic street of the hopping student quarter. Laid-back staff, clean rooms, and commission-free currency exchange. Internet access. Breakfast included. Sheets 15F/€2.29. Towels 5F/€0.76. Laundry nearby. Lockout 11am-5pm. Curfew 2am. 25 rooms, a few with showers and toilets. Doubles 157F/€23.94 per person, triples and quads 137F/€20.89 per person; Jan.-Mar. prices 10F/€1.53 lower per night.

Hôtel St-Jacques, 35 rue des Ecoles (☎01 44 07 45 45; fax 01 43 25 65 50). M: Maubert-Mutualité. Turn left on rue des Carmes, then left on rue des Ecoles. Spacious, faux-elegant rooms at reasonable rates, with balconies, renovated bathrooms and TVs. Internet access. Breakfast 45F/€6.86. Singles 270F/€41.16, with toilet and shower 415F/€63.27; doubles 470F/€71.66, 630F/€96.05; triples 700F/€106.72. Daily tax 5F/€0.76. AmEx/MC/V.

Hôtel des Argonauts, 12 rue de la Huchette (☎01 43 54 09 82; fax 01 44 07 18 84). M: St-Michel. With your back to the Seine, take the first left off bd. St-Michel onto rue de la Huchette. Cheerful blue and yellow Mediterranean rooms. Breakfast 25F/€3.81. Reserve 3-4 weeks in advance in high season. Singles with shower 285F/€43.45, with toilet 405F/€61.75; doubles with shower 320F/€48.79, with bath and toilet 460F/€70.13; triples with shower and toilet 465F/€70.90 (request in advance). AmEx/MC/V.

Hôtel d'Esmeralda, 4 rue St-Julien-le-Pauvre (☎01 43 54 19 20; fax 01 40 51 00 68). M: St-Michel. Walk along the Seine on quai St-Michel toward Notre Dame, then turn right at Parc Viviani. Rooms have a professorial feel and views of the park and Seine. Breakfast 40F/€6.10. Singles 180F/€27.44, with shower and toilet 380F/€57.94; doubles 450-490F/€68.61-74.71; triples 580F/€88.43; quads 650F/€99.10.

Hôtel du Progrès, 50 rue Gay-Lussac (☎01 43 54 53 18). M: Luxembourg. Walk away from Jardin du Luxembourg on rue Gay-Lussac. Cheap rooms with no frills (bring your own soap!). Reservation with deposit; call 2-3 weeks in advance. Singles 170-250F/€25.92-38.12, with shower and toilet 350F/€53.36; doubles 270-295F/€41.16-44.98, with shower and toilet 360F/€54.89; triples 375F/€57.17. Cash or traveler's checks only.

Hôtel Gay-Lussac, 29 rue Gay-Lussac (☎01 43 54 23 96; fax 01 40 51 79 49). M: Luxembourg. Stately old rooms. Reserve by fax at least 2 weeks in advance (1 month in summer). Singles 200F/€30.49, with toilet 310F/€47.26, with shower and toilet 390F/€59.46; doubles 340F/€51.84, with toilet 420F/€64.03; triples 350F/€53.36, with toilet 370F/€56.41, with toilet and shower 480F/€73.18; quads 620F/€94.53.

Hôtel Marignan, 13 rue du Sommerard (☎01 43 54 63 81; fax 01 43 25 16 69). M: Maubert-Mutualité. Turn left on rue des Carmes, then right on rue du Sommerard. Decent, basic rooms with TV. Breakfast included. Shower until 9pm. Kitchen. Internet access. Free laundry. Reserve 2 months ahead with deposit. Singles 290F/€44.21; doubles 400F/€60.98, with toilet 460F/€70.13, with shower and toilet 590F/€89.95; triples 620-720F/€94.53-109.77; quads 650-790F/€99.10-120.45; quints 750-950F/€114.35-144.84.

Hôtel des Médicis, 214 rue St-Jacques (☎01 43 54 14 66). M: Luxembourg. Turn right on rue Gay-Lussac and then left on rue St-Jacques. Jim Morrison slummed here (room #4) for 3 weeks in 1971. Free shower (only one for the whole hotel). Reception 9am-11pm. No reservations in summer; arrive early in the morning and hope for a vacancy. Singles 100-200F/€15.25-30.49; doubles 200F/€30.49; triples 300F/€45.74.

Centre International de Paris (BVJ): Paris Quartier Latin, 44 rue des Bernardins (☎01 43 29 34 80; fax 01 53 00 90 91). M: Maubert-Mutualité. Walk with traffic on bd. St-Germain and turn right on rue des Bernardins. Boisterous, generic, and only slightly dingy hostel. Internet. Kitchen. Breakfast included. Showers in rooms. Lockers 10F/€1.53. Reception 24hr. Check-out 9am. Reserve at least a week in advance and confirm, or arrive at 9am to check for room. 138 beds. 5- and 6-person dorms 145F/€22.11; singles 175F/€26.68; doubles and triples 155F/€23.63 per person.

PARIS

SIXTH ARRONDISSEMENT

Hôtel de Nesle, 7 rue du Nesle (☎01 43 54 62 41). M: Odéon. Walk up rue Mazarine, take a right onto rue Dauphine and then take a left on rue du Nesle. Fantastic and absolutely sparkling. No reservations accepted; come in the morning around 10am. Singles 328F/€50, with shower and toilet 380-452F/€58-69; doubles 453F/€69, with shower and toilet 650F/€99; extra bed 79F/€12. AmEx/MC/V.

Hôtel du Lys, 23 rue Serpente (☎01 43 26 97 57; fax 01 44 07 34 90). M: Odéon or St-Michel. From either stop, take rue Danton; rue Serpente is a side street. This splurge is well worth it for the sublime French country feel. All rooms include bath or shower, TV, phone, and hair dryer. Reserve one month in advance in summer. Singles 430-580F/€65.58-88.45; doubles 630F/€96.08; triples 680F/€103.70. MC/V.

Dhely's Hôtel, 22 rue de l'Hirondelle (☎01 43 26 58 25; fax 01 43 26 51 06). M: St-Michel. TV with satellite dish and phone in rooms. Breakfast and tax included. Showers 25F/€3.81. Reserve 15-20 days in advance with deposit. Singles 258-378F/€39.35-57.65, with shower 428-478F/€65.27-72.90; doubles 376-416F/€57.34-63.44, with shower 466-516F/€71.07-78.69; triples 516-606F/€78.69-92.42, with shower 606-752F/€92.42-114.68; extra bed 100F/€15.25. MC/V.

Hôtel St-André des Arts, 66 rue St-André-des-Arts (☎01 43 26 96 16; fax 01 43 29 73 34; hsaintand@minitel.net). M: Odéon. Take rue de l'Ancienne Comédie, walk one block, and take a right on rue St-André-des-Arts. Stone walls and exposed beams; new bathrooms. Breakfast included. Reservations recommended. Singles 400F/€61.00; doubles 500-540F/€76.25-82.35; triples 610F/€93.03; quads 680F/€103.7. MC/V.

Hôtel Stella, 41 rue Monsieur-le-Prince (☎01 40 51 00 25 or 06 07 03 19 71; fax 01 43 54 97 28). M: Odéon. Walk against traffic on bd. St-Germain and make a left on rue Monsieur-le-Prince. Reserve in advance with deposit. Singles 262F/€40; doubles 328F/€50; triples 450F/€70; quads 525F/€80. No credit cards.

Hôtel de Chevreuse, 3 rue de Chevreuse (☎01 43 20 93 16; fax 01 43 21 43 72). M: Vavin. Walk up bd. du Montparnasse away from the Tour and turn left on rue de Chevreuse. Small, clean, quiet rooms with TVs. Breakfast 35F/€5.34. Reserve one month in advance; confirm by fax. Singles 235F/€35.84, with shower, TV, and toilet 385F/€58.71, with full bath 415F/€63.29; doubles 295F/€44.99, with shower, TV, and toilet 385F/€58.71, with full bath 415F/€63.29; triples with shower, TV, and toilet 535F/€81.59. Daily tax 3F/€0.46. MC/V.

Foyer International des Etudiantes, 93 bd. St-Michel (☎01 43 54 49 63). RER: Luxembourg. Library, TV lounge, kitchenettes, laundry, and spacious, elegant rooms. Breakfast and shower included. July-Sept. hotel is co-ed, open 24hr.; Oct.-June **women only.** Reserve in writing two months in advance, and as early as Jan. for the co-ed summer months. 200F/€30.50 deposit. Check-out 10am. Call ahead or arrive at 10am for no-shows. 2-bed dorms 122F/€18.61; singles 172F/€26.23.

SEVENTH ARRONDISSEMENT

Hôtel du Champs de Mars, 7 rue du Champ de Mars (☎01 45 51 52 30; fax 01 45 51 64 36). M: Ecole-Militaire. Just off av. Bosquet. Quality rooms with phone and satellite TV. Breakfast 39F/€5.95. Reserve 1 month ahead and confirm by fax or email with a credit card number. Small elevator. Singles with shower 400F/€61.00; doubles with shower 440F/€67.10; triples with bath 560F/€85.40. MC/V.

Hôtel Montebello, 18 rue Pierre Leroux (☎01 47 34 41 18; fax 01 47 34 46 71). Amazing prices for this upscale neighborhood; behind the unassuming facade are clean, cheery rooms with full baths. Reserve at least 2 weeks in advance. Breakfast served 7:30-9:30am, 22F/€3.36. Singles 240F/€36.60; doubles 260F/€39.65.

Hôtel Eiffel Rive Gauche, 6 rue du Gros Caillou (☎01 45 51 24 56; fax 01 45 51 11 77; eiffel@easynet.fr). M: Ecole-Militaire. Walk up av. de la Bourdonnais, turn right on rue de la Grenelle, then left on Gros-Caillou. This family-run hotel is a favorite of anglophones. Rooms have cable TV, phone, and full baths. Dogs allowed. Breakfast 45F/€6.86. Singles 345-445F/€52.61-67.86, with twin beds 505F/€77.01; doubles 385-495F/€58.71-75.49; triples 495-595F/€75.49-90.74. Extra bed 90F/€13.73. MC/V.

Hôtel de France, 102 bd. de la Tour Maubourg (☎01 47 05 40 49; fax 01 45 56 96 78). M: Ecole Militaire. Amazing views of the Hôtel des Invalides. Multilingual staff. Newly renovated rooms sparkle. 2 wheelchair-accessible rooms (500F/€76.25). All rooms with cable TV and full bath. Breakfast 45F/€6.86. Singles 420F/€64.05; doubles 530F/€80.83; connecting rooms for 4-5 people available. AmEx/MC/V.

Hôtel Amélie, 5 rue Amélie (☎01 45 51 74 75; fax 01 45 56 93 55; www.123france.com). M: Latour-Maubourg. Walk in the direction of traffic on bd. de la Tour Maubourg, make a left onto rue de Grenelle, and then a right onto rue Amélie. On a quaint back street, tiny yet charmingly decorated. Full baths in all rooms. Breakfast 40F/€6.10. Reserve 2 weeks in advance. Singles 460F/€70.15; doubles 580F/€88.45. AmEx/MC/V.

Grand Hôtel Lévêque, 29 rue Cler (☎01 47 05 49 15; fax 01 45 50 49 36; www.hotel-leveque.com). M: Ecole-Militaire. Take av. de la Motte-Picquet to the cobbled rue Cler. Cheery and clean. Satellite TV, safe (20F/€3.05), private telephone line. Breakfast 40F/€6.10. Reserve 1 month ahead. Singles 300F/€45.73; doubles with shower and toilet 400-500F/€60.98-76.22; triples with shower and toilet 600F/€91.47. AmEx/MC/V.

EIGHTH ARRONDISSEMENT

Hôtel Europe-Liège, 8 rue de Moscou (☎01 42 94 01 51; fax 01 43 87 42 18). M: Liège. Walk down rue d'Amsterdam and turn left on rue de Moscou. Quiet and reasonably priced hotel with newly painted rooms. All rooms have TV, shower, or bath. 2 wheelchair-accessible rooms on the ground floor. Breakfast 37F/€5.64. Reserve 15 days in advance. Singles 390F/€59.48; doubles 500F/€76.25. AmEx/MC/V.

Foyer de Chaillot, 28 av. George V (☎01 47 23 35 32; fax 01 47 23 77 16; www.ufjt.org). M: George V. Make a right down av. George V and walk about 3 blocks until you see a high-rise silver office building called Centre Chaillot Galliera. Take the elevator to the foyer on the 3rd floor. Cheerful, well-equipped, modern rooms, in an upscale dorm-like environment for **women ages 18-25 only.** Singles have sinks, doubles have showers, too. Kitchen. Internet access. Breakfast and dinner included M-F. Minimum 1-month stay. Doubles 3150F/€480.26 per month per person; after a stay of 2 months, you can request a single for 3600F/€548.86 per month.

NINTH ARRONDISSEMENT

Hôtel Chopin, 10 bd. Montmartre, or 46 passage Jouffroy (☎01 47 70 58 10; fax 01 42 47 00 70). M: Grands Boulevards. Walk west on bd. Montmartre and make a right onto passage Jouffroy. Very clean, new rooms. All rooms have TV, phone, and fans by request; most have shower and toilet. Elevator. Breakfast 40F/€6.10. Singles 355-455F/€54.14-69.39; doubles 450-520F/€68.63-79.30; triples 595F/€90.74. AmEx/MC/V.

Hôtel Beauharnais, 51 rue de la Victoire (☎01 48 74 71 13; fax 01 44 53 98 80). M: Le Peletier. Follow traffic on rue de la Victoire. This small hotel exudes warmth. Breakfast 30F/€4.58. All rooms have shower. Reservations recommended 2 weeks in advance. Special *Let's Go* rates: doubles without toilet 320F/€48.80; triples 600F/€91.50; quads 800F/€122; quints 1000F/€152.46. No credit cards.

Woodstock Hostel, 48 rue Rodier (☎01 48 78 87 76; fax 01 48 78 01 63; www.woodstock.fr). M: Anvers or Gare du Nord. From M: Anvers, walk against traffic on pl. Anvers, turn right on av. Trudaine, and then left on rue Rodier. From M: Gare du Nord, turn right on rue de Dunkerque (with the station at your back); at pl. de Roubaix, veer left on rue de Maubeuge, veer right on rue Condorcet, and turn left on rue Rodier (15min.). Incense, reggae music, and tie-dye paraphernalia. Kitchen, safe deposit box, Internet, and fax. Sheets 20F/€3.05, towels 10F/€1.53. Call ahead to reserve. Max. stay around 2 weeks. Singles 147F/€22.42; doubles 127F/€19.37; 3-4 person dorms 117F/€17.84; extra mattress 107F/€16.32; max. 7 people per room.

TENTH ARRONDISSEMENT

Cambrai Hôtel, 129bis bd. de Magenta (☎01 48 78 32 13; fax 01 48 78 43 55; www.hotel-cambrai.com). M: Gare du Nord. Follow traffic on rue de Dunkerque to pl. de Roubaix and turn right on bd. de Magenta. Clean rooms with high ceilings and TVs. Breakfast 35F/€5.34. Showers 20F/€3.05. Singles 200F/€30.50, with toilet 240F/€36.60, with shower 270F/€41.18, with full bath 300F/€45.75; doubles with toilet 270F/€41.18, with shower 300F/€45.75, with full bath 340F/€51.85, with twin beds and full bath 380F/€57.95; triples 500F/€76.25; family suite 550F/€83.88 is wheelchair-accessible. MC/V.

Hôtel Palace, 9 rue Bouchardon (☎01 40 40 09 46; fax 01 42 06 16 90). M: Strasbourg/St-Denis. Walk against traffic on bd. St-Denis until the small arch; follow rue René Boulanger on the left, then turn left on rue Bouchardon. Hotel privacy; hostel rates. Breakfast 22F/€3.36. Shower 20F/€3.05. Reserve 2 weeks ahead. Singles 133F/€20.28, with shower 203F/€30.96; doubles 160-170F/€24.40-25.93, with shower 236F/€35.99; triples 310F/€47.28; quads 380F/€57.95; quints 450F/€68.63. MC/V.

Hôtel Moderne du Temple, 3 rue d'Aix (☎01 42 08 09 04; fax 01 42 41 72 17). M: Goncourt. Walk with traffic on rue du Faubourg du Temple then turn right on rue d'Aix. Simple, immaculate rooms. Breakfast 23F/€3.51. Singles 140-160F/€21.35-24.40, with full bath 230F/€35.08; doubles 190F/€28.98, 260F/€39.65. AmEx/MC/V.

ELEVENTH ARRONDISSEMENT

Hôtel Moderne, 121 rue de Chemin-Vert (☎01 47 00 54 05; fax 01 47 00 08 31; www.modern-hotel.fr). M: Père Lachaise. A few blocks from the métro. Newly renovated. Rooms are on the 6th floor; no elevator. Breakfast 25F/€3.81. Singles 380F/€57.95; doubles 420F/€64.05; quads 510F/€77.78; extra bed 110F/€16.78. MC/V.

Hôtel Rhetia, 3 rue du Général Blaise (☎01 47 00 47 18; fax 01 48 06 01 73). M: Voltaire. Take av. Parmentier and turn right on rue Rochebrune, then left on rue du Général Blaise. Calm and clean. Breakfast 15F/€2.29. Hall showers 10F/€1.53. Reception 7:30am-10pm. Reserve ahead. Singles 180F/€27.45, with shower 223F/€34.01; doubles 206F/€31.42, 246F/€37.51; triples 309F/€47.12; quads 359F/€54.73.

Hôtel Beaumarchais, 3 rue Oberkampf (☎01 53 36 86 86; fax 01 43 38 32 86; www.hotelbeaumarchais.com). M: Oberkampf. Exit on rue de Malte and turn right on rue Oberkampf. More expensive, but newly renovated. Suites include TV room with desk and breakfast table. A/C. Breakfast 40F/€6.10. Reserve 2 weeks in advance. Singles 450-550F/€68.63-83.88; doubles 650F/€99.13; suites 850F/€129.63. AmEx/MC/V.

Plessis Hôtel, 25 rue du Grand Prieuré (☎01 47 00 13 38; fax 01 43 57 97 87; hotel.plessis@club_internet.fr). M: Oberkampf. From the métro, walk north on rue du Grand Prieuré. 5 floors of clean, bright rooms. Rooms with showers have hair dryers, fans, TVs, and balconies. Breakfast 38F/€5.80. Closed Aug. Singles 232F/€35.50, with shower and toilet 328F/€50, with bath 348F/€53; doubles 233-394F/€35.50-60; twin beds with shower 413F/€63. AmEx/MC/V.

Auberge de Jeunesse "Jules Ferry" (HI), 8 bd. Jules Ferry (☎01 43 57 55 60; fax 01 43 14 82 09; auberge@easynet.fr). M: République. Walk east on rue du Faubourg du Temple and turn right on the far side of bd. Jules Ferry. Clean rooms with 100 bunk beds and sinks; mirrors and tiled floors. Party atmosphere. Breakfast and rudimentary showers included. Lockers 10F/€1.53. Sheets included. Laundry 30F/€4.57. 1 week max. stay. Internet 1F/€0.15 per min. Reception and dining room 24hr. Lockout 10am-2pm. No reservations; arrive by 8am. If there are no vacancies, the hostel can book you in another one. Dorms 118F/€18.00; doubles 120F/€18.30 per person. MC/V.

TWELFTH ARRONDISSEMENT

Hôtel de l'Aveyron, 5 rue d'Austerlitz (☎01 43 07 86 86; fax 01 43 07 85 20). M: Gare de Lyon. Walk away from the train station on rue de Bercy and take a right on rue d'Austerlitz. Clean, unpretentious rooms. Breakfast 25F/€3.81. Reserve 1 month in advance. Singles and doubles 190F/€28.97, with shower 260F/€39.64; triples 250F/€38.12, with shower and toilet 315F/€48.03. MC/V.

Centre International du Séjour de Paris: CISP "Ravel," 6 av. Maurice Ravel (☎01 44 75 60 00; fax 01 43 44 45 30; cisp@csi.com). M: Porte de Vincennes. Walk east on cours de Vincennes, then take the first right on bd. Soult, left on rue Jules Lemaître, and right on av. Maurice Ravel (10min.). Large, clean rooms (most with less than 4 beds), outdoor public pool (25F/€3.81). Cafeteria and restaurant. Internet 10F/€1.53 per 10min. Breakfast, sheets, and towels included. Reception 6:30am-1:30am; you can arrange to have the night guard let you in after 1:30am. Reserve at least a few days ahead by phone. Dorms with shower 126F/€19.21; singles with shower, toilet 196F/€29.88; doubles with shower, toilet, 156F/€23.78. AmEx/MC/V.

PARIS

THIRTEENTH ARRONDISSEMENT

Centre International du Séjour de Paris: CISP "Kellerman," 17 bd. Kellerman (☎01 44 16 37 38; fax 01 44 16 37 39; www.cisp.asso.fr). M: Porte d'Italie. Cross the street and turn right on bd. Kellerman. This 396-bed hostel resembles a spaceship on stilts. TV room, laundry, and cafeteria. Breakfast included (7-9am). No reception 1:30-6:30am, but if you arrange in advance, the night guard will let you in during that time. Wheelchair-accessible. Reserve 2-3 weeks in advance. 101F/€15.40; 2- to 4-bed dorms 126F/€19.21, shower included; singles with shower and toilet 196F/€29.88; doubles with shower and toilet 156F/€23.78. AmEx/MC/V.

FOURTEENTH ARRONDISSEMENT

Ouest Hôtel, 27 rue de Gergovie (☎01 45 42 64 99; fax 01 45 42 46 65). M: Pernety. Walk against traffic on rue Raymond Losserand and turn right on rue de Gergovie. A clean hotel with modest furnishings, outstanding rates, and a library. Breakfast 20F/€3.05. Hall shower 20F/€3.05 (sometimes long waits). Singles with small bed 120F/€18.30; singles with larger bed and doubles with 1 bed 160F/€24.40, with shower 220F/€33.55; 2-bed doubles 200F/€30.50, with shower 230F/€35.08. MC/V.

Hôtel de Blois, 5 rue des Plantes (☎01 45 40 99 48; fax 01 45 40 45 62). M: Mouton-Duvernet. Turn left on rue Mouton Duvernet then left on rue des Plantes. A great deal. TVs, phones, hair dryers. Laundromat across the street, pool next door. Breakfast 30F/€4.57. Reserve 10 days ahead. Singles 250F/€38.12, with shower and toilet 290F/€44.21; doubles 260F/€39.64, with shower and toilet 300F/€45.74, with bath and toilet 320F/€48.79; triples 390F/€59.46; extra bed 50F/€7.62. AmEx/MC/V.

FIAP Jean-Monnet, 30 rue Cabanis (☎01 43 13 17 00, reservations 01 43 13 17 17; fax 01 45 81 63 91; www.fiap.asso.fr). M: Glacière. Walk straight down bd. Auguste-Blanqui, turn left on rue de la Santé and then right on rue Cabanis. 500-bed international student center; spotless rooms with phone, toilet, and shower. Concrete complex has a game room, TV rooms, laundry, sunlit piano bar, restaurant, terrace, and disco. Breakfast included, but add 10F/€1.53 for buffet. Curfew 2am. Reserve 2-4 weeks in advance. Specify if you want a dorm bed, or you will be booked for a single. 50F/€7.62 deposit per person per night in check or credit card. Wheelchair-accessible. 8-bed dorms 139-194F/€21.35-29.58; singles 310F/€47.26; doubles 200F/€30.49 per person; triples or quads 175F/€26.68; rooms with 5 or 6 beds 142F/€21.65. MC/V.

FIFTEENTH ARRONDISSEMENT

Hôtel Printemps, 31 rue du Commerce (☎01 45 79 83 36; fax 01 45 79 84 88; hotel.printemps.15e@wanadoo.fr). M: La Motte-Picquet-Grenelle. Pleasant, clean, and cheap. Breakfast 25F/€3.81. Hall showers 15F/€2.29. Reserve 3-4 weeks ahead. Singles and doubles with sink 176F/€26.83, with shower 216F/€32.93, with shower and toilet 236F/€35.98; twin with shower 256F/€39.03. MC/V.

La Mason Hostel, 67bis rue Dutot (☎01 42 73 10 10). M: Volontaires. Cross rue de Vaugirard on rue des Volontaires, take the second right, and go 2 blocks. Clean rooms in a quiet neighborhood. All rooms have shower and toilet. Internet happy hour 2-5pm. Kitchen. Breakfast included. Doubles come with sheets; otherwise, sheets 15F/€2.29 to rent, towels 5F/€0.76. Reception 8am-2am. Lockout 11am-5pm. Curfew 2am. Reserve 1 month in advance. In summer 2- and 3-bed dorms 137F/€20.89; doubles 157F/€23.94; off-season dorm (starts Nov.) 117F/€17.84; doubles 137F/€20.89.

Three Ducks Hostel, 6 pl. Etienne Pernet (☎01 48 42 04 05; fax 01 48 42 99 99; www.3ducks.fr). M: Félix Faure. Walk against traffic on the left side of the church; the hostel is on the left. Aimed at Anglo fun-seekers. Enjoy the in-house bar until the 2am curfew (residents only). Kitchen, lockers, and small 2- to 8-bed dorm rooms. Shower and breakfast included. Sheets 15F/€2.29; towels 5F/€0.76. Reception 8am-2am. Lockout 11am-5pm. 1 week max. stay. Reserve ahead with credit card. Dorms 137F/€20.89; doubles 157F/€23.94. 10F/€1.53 less Nov.-Mar. MC/V.

SIXTEENTH ARRONDISSEMENT

Villa d'Auteuil, 28 rue Poussin (☎01 42 88 30 37; fax 01 45 20 74 70). M: Michel-Ange-Auteuil. Walk up rue Girodet and turn left on rue Poussin. At the edge of the Bois de Boulogne. Classy rooms with shower, toilet, phone, TV, and faux velvet. Breakfast 30F/€4.57. 10% discount with *Let's Go.* Singles 320-340F/€48.79-51.84; doubles 370-390F/€56.41-59.46; triples 445F/€67.85. MC/V.

Hôtel Ribera, 66 rue La Fontaine (☎01 42 88 29 50; fax 01 42 24 91 33). M: Jasmin. Walk down rue Ribera to its intersection with rue La Fontaine. Cheerful rooms with TV. Breakfast 28F/€4.27. 10% discount July 15-Aug. Singles 250F/€38.12, with shower 280F/€42.69, with shower and toilet 320F/€48.79; doubles 280F/€42.69, with shower 310F/€47.26 (with two beds 330F/€50.31), with shower and toilet 360F/€54.89 (with two beds 380F/€57.94). AmEx/MC/V.

SEVENTEENTH TO TWENTIETH ARRONDISSEMENTS

Hôtel Caulaincourt, 2 sq. Caulaincourt, 18*ème* (☎01 46 06 46 06; fax 01 46 06 46 16; www.caulaincourt.com). M: Lamarck-Caulaincourt. Walk up the stairs to rue Caulaincourt and proceed to your right, between nos. 63 and 65. Former artists' studios, these simple rooms have wonderful views of Montmartre. Breakfast 28F/€4.27. Reserve up to one month ahead. Singles 175F/€26.68, with shower 235F/€35.83, with shower and toilet 285F/€43.45, with bath and toilet 320F/€48.78; doubles 230-250F/€35.06-38.11, 290-310F/€44.21-47.26, 340-360F/€51.83-54.88, 370-390F/€56.41-59.46; triples with shower 340-360F/€51.83-54.88, with shower and toilet 380-400F/€57.93-60.98. MC/V.

Hôtel Riviera, 55 rue des Acacias, 17*ème* (☎01 43 80 45 31; fax 01 40 54 84 08). M: Charles-de-Gaulle-Etoile. Walk north on av. MacMahon, then turn left on rue des Acacias. Close to the Arc de Triomphe. Modern rooms with TVs. Breakfast 35F/€5.34. Reserve 2-3 weeks ahead. Singles with shower 300F/€45.75, with toilet 380-430F/€57.95-65.58; doubles with toilet and bath or shower 410-460F/€62.53-70.15; triples with toilet and bath or shower 530F/€80.83; quads 600F/€91.50. Daily tax 5F/€0.76. AmEx/MC/V.

Hôtel Champerret Héliopolis, 13 rue d'Héliopolis, 17*ème* (☎01 47 64 92 56; fax 01 47 64 50 44). M: Porte de Champerret. Turn left off av. de Villiers. Brilliant and sparkling blue-and-white rooms, some with balconies. One wheelchair-accessible room. Breakfast 45F/€6.86. Reserve 2 weeks ahead. Singles 420F/€64.05; doubles 495F/€75.49, with bath 540F/€82.35; triples with bath 580F/€88.45. AmEx/MC/V.

Village Hostel, 20 rue d'Orsel, 18*ème* (☎01 42 64 22 02; fax 01 42 64 22 04; www.villagehostel.fr). M: Anvers. Go uphill on rue Steinkerque and turn right on rue d'Orsel. Right in the midst of the heavy Sacré-Coeur tourist traffic, but new, clean and cheap. Fitness room. Kitchen. TV, stereo, telephones, and Internet access in the lounge. Every room has toilet and shower. Breakfast included. Sheets 15F/€2.29. Towel 5F/€0.76. Lockout 11am-4pm. Curfew 2am. Reservations by fax or email. Same-day phone reservations accepted–call at 8am when reception opens. Dorms 137F/€20.89; 1-bed or 2-bed double with sheets 314F/€47.89; triples 441F/€67.25. No credit cards.

Rhin et Danube, 3 pl. Rhin et Danube, 19*ème* (☎01 42 45 10 13; fax 01 42 06 88 82). M: Danube; or bus #75 from M: Châtelet. Spacious, well-maintained rooms, most of which look onto a quaint little *place*. All rooms have kitchens with fridge, dishes, and coffee maker. Hair dryers, shower, toilet, and satellite TVs. Singles 302F/€46; doubles 400F/€61; triples 479F/€73; quads 541F/€82.50. MC/V.

Auberge de Jeunesse "Le D'Artagnan" (HI), 80 rue Vitruve, 20*ème* (☎01 40 32 34 56; fax 01 40 32 34 55; artahost@gofornet.com). M: Porte de Bagnolet. Walk south on bd. Davout and make a right on rue Vitruve. Neon lights and funky decorations in every color imaginable welcome legions of boisterous backpackers. Restaurant, bar, small cinema (free films nightly). Breakfast and sheets included. Lockers. Laundry 20F/€3.05. 6 nights max. stay. Reception 24hr. Lockout noon-3pm. Reservations by fax or email a must; hostel is packed Feb.-Oct. 3-, 4-, and 8-bed dorms 121F/€18.45 per person.

PARIS

FOOD

ILE DE LA CITE

Le Caveau de Palais, 19 pl. Dauphine (☎01 43 26 04 28). M: Cité. A chic, intimate restauran. Two *menus* (140F/€21.35 and 220F/€33.54) include appetizer, *plat*, and dessert. Some Basque specialties; great grilled monkfish. Reservations encouraged. MC/V.

Le Rouge et Blanc, 26 pl. Dauphine (☎01 43 29 52 34). M: Cité. Simple, *provençal* bar and bistro. *Menus* 105F/€16 and 180F/€27.44. Open M-Sa 11am-3pm and 7-10:30pm. Closed when it rains. MC/V.

ILE ST-LOUIS

Brasserie de l'Ile St-Louis, 55 quai de Bourbon (☎01 43 54 02 59). M: Pont Marie. Cross the Pont Marie and make a right on rue St-Louis-en-l'Ile and walk to the end of the island. Old-fashioned brasserie is known for Alsatian specialities like *choucroute garnie* (95F/€14.48). Open M-Tu and F-Su noon-1am, Th 6pm-1am. MC/V.

FIRST AND SECOND ARRONDISSEMENTS

Jules, 62 rue Jean-Jacques Rousseau (☎ 01 40 28 99 04). M: Les Halles. Take the rue Rambuteau exit from the métro, walk toward the church St-Eustache, then take a left onto rue Coquillère and a right on rue J.-J. Rousseau. Subtle blend of modern and traditional French cooking; award-winning chef. 4-course *menu* 130F/€19.82 includes terrific cheese course. Open M-F noon-2:30pm and 7-10:30pm. AmEx/MC/V.

Le Fumoir, 6 rue de l'Amiral Coligny (☎01 42 92 05 05). M: Louvre. On rue du Louvre, cross rue de Rivoli and rue du Louvre will become rue de l'Amiral Coligny. Decidedly untouristy types drink their chosen beverage in deep leather sofas. Part bar, part tea house in feel, Le Fumoir serves the **best brunch in Paris** (120F/€18.30). Coffee 15F/€2.29. Open daily 11am-2am. AmEx/MC/V.

Le Café Marly, 93 rue de Rivoli (☎01 49 26 06 60). M: Palais Royal. One of Paris' classiest cafés, Marly is in the Richelieu wing of the Louvre. Breakfast (includes pastry, toast, jam, juice, and coffee or hot chocolate; 80F/€12.20) served 8-11am. Main dishes from 100-130F/€15.25-19.83. Open daily 8am-2am. MC/V.

Les Noces de Jeannette, 14 rue Favart, and 9 rue d'Amboise (☎01 42 96 36 89). M: Richelieu Drouot. Exit onto bd. des Italiens, turn left, and go left onto rue Favart. *Menu du Bistro* (172F/€26.23) includes large salad entrees; roasted fish, duck, and grilled meat *plats*. Reservations recommended. Open daily noon-1:30pm and 7-9:30pm.

Le Dénicheur, 4 rue Tiquetonne (☎01 42 21 31 01). M: Etienne-Marcel. Walk against traffic on rue de Turbigo and go left on rue Tiquetonne. Diner turned disco/junkyard café, filled with lawn gnomes. Dinner *menu* 98F/€14.95. Su brunch 85F/€12.96. Reservations recommended. Open Tu-Su noon-3:30pm and 7:30pm-1am. MC/V.

Lamen Kintar, 24 rue St-Augustin (☎01 47 42 13 14). M: Quatre Septembre. From the métro, walk with traffic down rue Monsigny; turn right onto rue St-Augustin. In the heart of Paris' Japanese quarter. Noodle bowls 50F/€7.63; lunch *menu* with *entrée,* sushi, sashimi, and soup 90-135F/€13.73-20.59. Open M-Sa 11:30am-10pm. MC/V.

La Victoire Suprême du Coeur, 41 rue des Bourdonnais (☎01 40 41 93 95). M: Châtelet. From the métro take the rue des Halles exit. Follow traffic on rue des Halles and turn left on rue des Bourdonnais. Run by the devotees of guru Sri Chinmoy who have both body and soul in mind. It's all vegetarian, and very tasty. All-day 3-course *menu* 95F/€14.48. Open M-F noon-3:30pm and 6-10pm, Sa noon-10pm. MC/V.

THIRD AND FOURTH ARRONDISSEMENTS

Piccolo Teatro, 6 rue des Ecouffes (☎01 42 72 17 79). M: St-Paul. Walk with the traffic down rue de Rivoli and take a right on rue des Ecouffes. A romantic vegetarian hideout. Weekday lunch *menus at* 52-63F/€7.93-12.96. *Plats* 65-78F/€9.91-11.90. Open Tu-Sa noon-3pm and 7:15-11pm. AmEx/MC/V.

Au Petit Fer à Cheval, 30 rue Vieille-du-Temple (☎01 42 72 47 47). M: St-Paul. Go with the traffic on rue de Rivoli and turn right; the restaurant will be on your right. An oasis of *chèvre,* kir, and *Gauloises.* Open daily 10am-2am; food served noon-1:15am. MC/V. (If the outdoor seating is full—and it will be—try the neighboring **Les Philosophes** or **La Chaise au Plafond**, all owned by the same charming, lucky fellow.

Georges, on the 6th floor of the Centre Pompidou (☎01 44 78 47 99). Entrance through the center and also from a separate door just to the left of the Pompidou's main entrance on rue Beaubourg. M: Rambuteau. Ultra-sleek, zen-cool café, especially the terrace. Its minimalist design is even exhibited in the museum. Menu supposedly designed by Dior menswear creator Hedi Slimane. Open W-M noon-2am.

L'As du Falafel, 34 rue des Rosiers (☎01 48 87 63 60). M: St-Paul. This kosher falafel stand and restaurant displays pictures of Lenny Kravitz, who credited it with "the best falafel in the world, particularly the special eggplant falafel with hot sauce." Go his way. Falafel special 25F/€3.81. Open Su-Th 11:30am-11:30pm. MC/V.

Taxi Jaune, 13 rue Chapon (☎01 42 76 00 40). M: Arts et Métiers. Walk along rue Beaubourg and turn left onto rue Chapon. The eclectic taxi-themed art may make a tourist or two look askance. Lunch *menu* 78F/€11.90 or 84F/€12.81. Open M-F noon-2:30pm and 7:30pm-2am; food served until 10:15pm. MC/V.

Le Réconfort, 37 rue de Poitou (☎01 42 76 06 36). M: St-Sébastien-Froissart. Walk along rue du Pt-Aux-Choux to rue de Poitou. Hyper-eclectic, swank eating experience. French, Indian, and Middle Eastern tastes yield creations like the chicken with honey and spices (82F/€12.51). Lunch *menu* 72-92F/€10.98-14.03; main courses 82-105F/€12.51-16.01, but the lunchtime *plat du jour* is only 62F/€9.46. Open M-F noon-2pm and 8-11pm, Sa 8-11pm. MC/V.

Le Hangar, 12 impasse Berthaud (☎01 42 74 55 44). M: Rambuteau. Take impasse Berthaud from the métro. In an alley near the Centre Pompidou, Le Hangar is bright and intimate. Avocado gazpacho 52F/€7.93, fish and meat dishes 68-138F/€10.37-21.05. Open M 7:30pm-midnight, Tu-Sa noon-3pm and 7:30pm-midnight. Closed Aug.

En Attendant Pablo, 78 rue Vieille-du-Temple (☎01 42 74 34 65). M: Hôtel-de-Ville. From rue de Rivoli, turn left on rue Vieille-du-Temple. This intimate pâtisserie/lunch café serves enormous salads (58F/€8.79) and *tartines* (58F/€8.79). Large selection of fruit juices (26-28F/€3.97-4.27). Open W-Su noon-6pm. MC/V.

FIFTH AND SIXTH ARRONDISSEMENTS

Savannah Café, 27 rue Descartes (☎01 43 29 45 77). M: Cardinal Lemoine. Follow Cardinal Lemoine uphill, turn right on rue Clovis, and walk 1 block. Cheerfully yellow restaurant prides itself on its Lebanese food and international selections. *Menu gas-*

tronomique 142F/€21.65. Open M-Sa 7-11pm. MC/V. Around the corner is Savannah's little sister, **Comptoir Méditerranée,** 42 rue Cardinal Lemoine (☎01 43 25 29 08), with similar food, take out, and lower prices. Select from 20 dishes to make your own plate (4 items 35F/€5.34, 6 items 51F/€7.93). Open M-Sa 11am-10pm.

Le Bistro d'Henri, 16 rue Princesse. M: Mabillon. Walk down rue du Four and left onto rue Princesse. Classic Left Bank bistro–simple food, fresh ingredients–has *gigot d'agneau* and *gratin dauphinois* (layered potatoes and cheese), rumored to be the best in Paris. Dinner *menu* 160F/€24.40. Open daily noon-2:30pm and 7-11:30pm. MC/V. Also, around the corner is **Le Machon d'Henri,** 8 rue Guisarde (☎01 43 29 08 70), which serves the same *menus* in a slightly smaller, white-stone alcove. Also in the 5*ème*, the same restaurant done slightly more elegant: **Chez Henri,** 9 rue de la Montagne-Ste-Geneviève (☎01 43 29 12 12).

Le Petit Vatel, 5 rue Lobineau (☎01 43 54 28 49). M: Mabillon. Follow traffic on bd. St-Germain, turn right on rue de Seine, and then take the second right onto rue Lobineau. Charming little home-run bistro with sunny yellow walls serves Mediterranean French specialties like *catalan pamboli* (bread with pureed tomatoes, ham, and cheese) for 60F/€9.15. Open Tu-Sa noon-2:40pm and 7-10:30pm.

Aux Portes de l'Orient, 39 rue Geoffrey St-Hilaire (☎01 43 31 38 20). M: Censier Daubenton. In the Mosquée de Paris. An Islamic café with fountains, white marble floors and an exquisite terrace. Persian mint tea 10F/€1.53. Tea room open daily 9am-11:30pm; restaurant open daily noon-3pm and 7:30-10:30pm; *hammam* open for men Tu 2-9pm and Su 10am-9pm; women M, W-Th, Sa 10am-9pm and F 2-9pm. MC/V.

Le Sélect, 99 bd. du Montparnasse (☎01 45 48 38 24). M: Vavin. Walk west on bd. du Montparnasse; across the street from La Coupole. Trotsky, Satie, Breton, Cocteau, and Picasso all frequented this huge art deco café. Surprisingly local crowd. *Café* 7-12F/€1.07-1.83 at the counter depending on the time of day. Open daily 7am-3am. MC/V.

Café de Flore, 172 bd. St-Germain (☎01 45 48 55 26). M: St-Germain-des-Prés. Walk against traffic on bd. St-Germain. Sartre composed *Being and Nothingness* here; Apollinaire, Picasso, Breton, and Thurber sipped brew. Espresso 25F/€3.81, *salade Flore* 75F/€11.44, pastries 38-65F/€5.80-9.91. Open daily 7am-1:30am. AmEx/MC/V.

La Palette, 43 rue de Seine (☎01 43 26 68 15). Truly the most authentic of the Left Bank's gallery cafés. *Café* 14F/€2.14, beer 25F/€3.81, wine 22-25F/€3.36-3.81, sandwiches 22-30F/€3.36-4.58, and *guillotines* 35F/€5.34. Open M-Sa 8am-2am.

Au Jardin des Pâtés, 4 rue Lacépède (☎01 43 31 50 71). M: Jussieu. Walk up rue Linné and turn right on rue Lacépède. Organic gourmet pastas, including *pâtés de seigle* (ham, white wine, and sharp comté cheese; 58F/€8.84), fill the menu. Main dishes 47-77F/€7.17-11.74. Open daily noon-2:30pm and 7-11pm. MC/V.

La Crêpe Rit du Clown, 6 rue des Canettes (☎01 46 34 01 02). M: Mabillon. Walk down rue du Four and turn left on rue des Canettes. Do not be afraid of the clown statue at the door. Just try the tasty, inexpensive crêpes. Present *Let's Go* for a free *kir breton. Formule* 63F/€9.61, crêpes 35-42F/€5.34-6.41. Open M-Sa noon-11:30pm. MC/V.

Così, 54 rue de Seine (☎01 46 33 35 36). M: Mabillon. Walk down bd. St-Germain and make a left onto rue de Seine. Enormous, tasty, inexpensive sandwiches built on fresh, brick-oven bread. A "Stonker" combines tomato, mozzarella, and roquette (40F/€6.10). Sandwiches 32-48F/€4.88-7.32 depending on number of ingredients. Desserts 18-22F/€2.75-3.36. Open daily 11am-midnight.

SEVENTH ARRONDISSEMENT

Café du Marché, 38 rue Cler (☎01 47 05 51 27). M: Ecole Militaire. Walk up rue de la Motte Piquet and turn left onto rue Cler. Beautiful terrace on an adorable street. Good, American-style food like a Caesar salad (50F/€7.63) or pastrami club sandwich (50F/€7.63). Open M-Sa 7am-1am, food served until 11pm, and Su 7am-3pm. MC/V.

Le Lotus Blanc, 45 rue de Bourgogne (☎01 45 55 18 89). M: Varenne. Walk on bd. des Invalides, toward the Invalides; turn left onto rue de Varenne and then left again onto rue de Bourgogne. Vietnamese specialties. Lunch and all-day *menus* (59-146F/€9.10-22.30). Reservations encouraged, especially for lunch. Open M-Sa noon-2:30pm and 7-10:30pm. Closed Aug. 15-23. AmEx/MC/V.

EIGHTH ARRONDISSEMENT

Antoine's: Les Sandwiches des 5 Continents, 31 rue de Ponthieu (☎01 42 89 44 20). M: Franklin D. Roosevelt. Walk toward the Arc de Triomphe on the Champs-Elysées, then go right on av. Franklin D. Roosevelt and left on rue de Ponthieu. Bright, modern sandwich shop with intimate upstairs eating area and no-nonsense cafeteria bar. 40F/€6.10 meal includes panini, yogurt, and a drink. Open M-F 8am-6pm. V.

Bangkok Café, 28 rue de Moscou (☎01 43 87 62 56). M: Rome. Take a right onto rue Moscou. Talented Thai chef and her French husband serve inventive seafood salads and soups (54-68F/€8.24-10.37), and a range of meats (82-120F/€12.51-18.30). Open M-F noon-2:30pm and 7-11:30pm and Sa 7-11:30pm. AmEx/MC/V.

Fouquet's, 99 av. des Champs-Elysées (☎01 47 23 70 60). M: George V. Beneath its red awning reside stagey grandeur and snobbery so "French" that it seems like a Disney caricature of itself. Love that bank-breaking coffee (30F/€4.58)! Main dishes 60-145F/€9.15-22.11. Food served all day in the café, while the restaurant serves from noon-3pm and 7pm-midnight. Open daily 8am-2am. AmEx/MC/V.

NINTH AND TENTH ARRONDISSEMENTS

Le Bistro de Gala, 45 rue du Faubourg-Montmartre (☎01 40 22 90 50). M: Grands Boulevards. Walk north on rue du Faubourg-Montmartre. Spacious bistro, the reputed hangout of some of Paris' theater elite. Favorites like *foie gras* and *confit de canard. Menu* 170F/€25.93, and definitely worth it. Summer *menu* 140F/€21.35. Reservations recommended. Open M-F noon-2:30pm and 7-11:30pm, Sa 7-11:30pm. AmEx/MC/V.

Haynes Restaurant Américain, 3 rue Clauzel (☎01 48 78 40 63). M: St-Georges. Head uphill on rue Notre Dame de Lorette and turn right on rue H. Monnier, then right on rue Clauzel to the end of the block. The first African-American owned restaurant in Paris (1949), a center for expatriates, and a former hangout of Louis Armstrong, James Baldwin, and Richard Wright. "Original American Soul Food" and its down-home hospitality. Very generous portions under 100F/€15.25. Vocal jazz concerts F nights; funk and groove Sa nights. Open Tu-Sa 7pm-12:30am. AmEx/MC/V.

Cantine d'Antoine at Lili, 95 quai de Valmy (☎01 40 37 34 86). M: Gare de l'Est. Go down rue Faubourg St-Martin and make a left on rue Récollets; it'll be on the corner of quai de Valmy. On the Canal St-Martin and too cute for words. Choose from a variety of flavored lemonades (15F/€2.29). Nachos 25F/€3.81; salads 55F/€8.39; quiches 50F/€7.63. Open W-Sa 11am-1am, Su-Tu 11am-8pm. AmEx/MC/V.

Paris-Dakar, 95 rue du Faubourg St-Martin (☎01 42 08 16 64). M: Gare de l'Est. With your back to the *gare,* take rue du Faubourg St-Martin ahead of you. Senegalese cuisine, dance videos, and soap operas. Features include *tiébou dieune* (fish with rice and veggies) and the house drink *bissap,* made from African flowers and fresh mint. Lunch *menu* 59F/€9, dinner *menu* 149F/€22.72, African *menu* 199F/€30.35. Open Tu-Th and Sa-Su noon-3pm and 7pm-2am, F 7pm-2am. AmEx/MC/V.

ELEVENTH AND TWELFTH ARRONDISSEMENTS

Chez Paul, 13 rue de Charonne (☎01 47 00 34 57). M: Bastille. Take rue du Faubourg St-Antoine and turn left on rue de Charonne. Worn exterior hides a kicking bistro. Peppercorn steak 78F/€11.90. Reservations a must. Open daily noon-2:30pm and 7pm-2am; food served until 12:30am. Closed for lunch Aug.1-15. AmEx/MC/V.

Café de l'Industrie, 16 rue St-Sabin (☎01 47 00 13 53). M: Breguet-Sabin. Huge and happening café pays tribute to France's colonialist past with photos of natives, palm trees, and weapons on the walls. Coffee 10F/€1.53, salads 45-58F/€6.86-8.85. After 10pm, add 4F/€0.61. Open Su-F 10-2am; lunch served noon-1pm.

Pause Café, 41 rue de Charonne (☎01 48 06 80 33). M: Ledru-Rollin. Walk along av. Ledru-Rollin and turn left onto rue de Charonne. Pause is all the cooler for having starred in the film *Chacun Cherche Son Chat.* Salads 40-50F/€6.10-7.63; beer 18F/€2.75. Open M-Sa 8am-2am, Su 8:30am-8pm. MC/V.

Les Broches à l'Ancienne, 21 rue St-Nicolas (☎01 43 43 26 16). M: Ledru-Rollin. Walk along rue du Faubourg St-Antoine away from the Bastille column and turn right onto rue St-Nicolas. High-quality meats are slow-cooked over flames in a stone oven. Shoulder of lamb with fries 89F/€13.5. Jazz F nights; dinner and performance 150F/€22.90; reserve ahead. Open M-Sa noon-2:30pm; Tu-Sa 7:30-10:30 or 11pm. AmEx/MC/V.

THIRTEENTH AND FOURTEENTH ARRONDISSEMENTS

Café du Commerce, 39 rue des Cinq Diamants (☎01 53 62 91 04). M: Pl. d'Italie. Take bd. Auguste Blanqui and turn left onto rue des Cinq Diamants; it'll be on your left. A strictly word-of-mouth, local establishment. *Menus* 55-65F/€8.39-9.91, with options like *boudin antillais* (spiced bloodwurst) or steak with avocado and strawberries. Open daily noon-3pm and 7pm-2am. Reservations recommended for dinner. AmEx/MC/V.

Phinéas, 99 rue de l'Ouest (☎01 45 41 33 50). M: Pernety. Follow the traffic on rue Pernety and turn left on rue de l'Ouest. It's on your left. The restaurant also doubles as a comic book shrine: the menus are pasted into old comic books, and the patron is famous for her extravagant comic book cakes. Open Tu-Sa 9am-noon for takeout, noon-11:30pm for dine-in. AmEx/MC/V.

La Lune, 36 av. de Choisy (☎01 44 24 38 70). M: Port de Choisy. An enormous selection of Vietnamese, Thai, Cambodian, and Chinese food. *Banh coun* (a sort of slippery ravioli filled with spiced beef) 45F/€6.86. Classic soups 30-40F/€4.58-6.10; other dishes 24-75F/€3.66-11.44. Open Th-Tu 7:30am-10:30pm. MC/V.

La Coupole, 102 bd. du Montparnasse (☎01 43 20 14 20). M: Vavin. Half-café, half-restaurant, La Coupole's Art Deco chambers have hosted Lenin, Stravinsky, Hemingway, and Einstein. Though touristy and pricey, it's worth it for nostalgia. Coffee 11F/€1.68; *croque monsieur* 28F/€4.27. Dancing Tu, Th, and Sa (salsa, disco, R&B) 10pm-5am; cover 100F/€15.25. Open daily 7:30am-2am. AmEx/MC/V.

FIFTEENTH ARRONDISSEMENT

Chez Foong, 32 rue Frémicourt (☎01 45 67 36 99). M: Cambronne. Walk across pl. Cambronne; turn left onto Frémicourt. Superb Malaysian fare. Grilled fish in banana leaves with coconut 69F/€10.52; mango and shrimp salad 59F/€9.15. 3-course lunch and dinner *menus* 90F/€13.72 (M-F). Open M-Sa noon-2:30pm and 7-11pm. MC/V.

Thai Phetburi, 31 bd. de Grenelle (☎01 41 58 14 88;). M: Bir-Hakeim. From the métro, walk away from the river on bd. de Grenelle; the restaurant is on your left. Cheap, award-winning food. Try the *tom yam koung* (shrimp soup with lemongrass, 42F/€6.40) or the *keng khiao wan kai* (chicken in green curry sauce, 48F/€7.32). AmEx/MC/V.

Aux Artistes, 63 rue Falguière (☎01 43 22 05 39). M: Pasteur. Follow Pasteur away from the rails for 2 blocks and make a left onto rue Falguière. One of the 15*ème's* coolest spots. Lunch *menu* 58F/€8.84, dinner *menu* 80F/€12.20. Open M-F noon-12:30am, Sa noon-2pm.

SIXTEENTH ARRONDISSEMENT

La Rotunde de la Muette, 12 Chaussée de la Muette (☎01 45 24 45 45). M: La Muette. 2min. from the métro; head toward the Jardin de Ranelagh. Stylish red and yellow lamps, hip music, and plush Burgundy seats. Fabulous outdoor seating. Two philosophical debates a month. Open daily noon-11pm. AmEx/MC/V.

Restaurant GR5, 19 rue Gustave Courbet (☎01 47 27 09 84). M: Rue de la Pompe. Walk up rue de la Pompe and turn right on rue Gustave Courbet. *Raclette* (115F/€17.53), or *fondue savoyarde* for two (210F/€32.02) on checkered table cloths. Main dishes 70-90F/€10.67-13.72; *menu* 125F/€19.06. Open M-Sa 11am-11pm.

SEVENTEENTH AND EIGHTEENTH ARRONDISSEMENTS

Le Soleil Gourmand, 10 rue Ravignan (☎01 42 51 00 50). M: Abbesses. Facing the church in pl. des Abbesses, head right down rue des Abbesses and go right (uphill) on rue Ravignan. *Provençale* fare: specialty *bricks* (fried stuffed filo dough, 70F/€10.68), 5-cheese *tartes* with salad (62F/€9.46), and house-baked cakes (30-44F/€4.58-6.71). Evening reservations a must. Open daily 12:30-2:30pm and 8:30-11pm.

Refuge des Fondues, 17 rue des Trois Frères (☎01 42 55 22 65). M: Abbesses. Walk down rue Yvonne le Tac and take a left on rue des Trois Frères. Only two main dishes: *fondue bourgingnon* (meat fondue) and *fondue savoyarde* (cheese fondue). The wine is served in baby bottles with rubber nipples; leave your Freudian hang-ups at home and join the family-style party at one of two long tables. *Menu* 92F/€14.03. Reserve or show up early. Open W-M 5pm-2am. Closed for part of July and Aug. No credit cards.

Chez Ginette, 101 rue Caulaincourt (☎01 46 06 01 49). M: Lamarck-Caulaincourt. Upstairs from the métro. An unspoiled slice of Montmartre. Monkfish with prawn sauce 100F/€15.25; specialty omelettes 40-55F/€6.10-8.39. Open M-Sa noon-2:30pm and 7:30pm-2am. Closed Aug. MC/V.

Le Sancerre, 35 rue des Abbesses (☎01 42 58 08 20 or 01 42 58 47 05). M: Abbesses. Facing the church in pl. des Abbesses, head right on rue des Abbesses. Classic Montmartre café with an edgy, scruffy, and bohemian crowd and throbbing techno music. *Bruschettas* (50-55F/€7.63-8.39) and *chili con carne* (49-80F/€7.47-12.20). Beer 17-24F/€2.59-3.66, *apéritifs* 20-40F/€3.05-6.10, wines 17-30F/€2.59-4.58; Sa-Su brunch 65F/€9.91. Open daily 7am-2am. MC/V.

Halle St-Pierre, 2 rue Ronsard (☎01 42 58 72 89). M: Anvers. Walk up rue de Steinkerque, turn right at pl. St-Pierre, then left onto rue Ronsard. A quiet café in the gallery of the same name, with assorted coffee and tea (8-20F/€1.22-3.05), cookies, brownies, and cakes (15F/€2.29), salads, and the major French newspapers. A pleasant setting, relatively free from the tourists outside. Open Tu-Su 10am-6pm.

The James Joyce Pub, 71 bd. Gouvion St-Cyr (☎01 44 09 70 32). M: Porte Maillot (exit at Palais de Congrès). Take bd. Gouvion St-Cyr past Palais des Congrès. Upstairs is a restaurant with stained-glass windows depicting scenes from Joyce's novels. Spectacular Su brunch (noon-3pm) is a full Irish fry: eggs, bacon, sausage, black and white puddings, beans, chips, and coffee (65F/€9.91). An informal tourist office for middle-aged and younger Anglophone ex-pats. Pub open M-Th 7pm-1:30am, F-Su 11am-2am; restaurant M-Sa noon-3pm and 7:30-10:30pm, Su noon-5pm. AmEx/MC/V.

NINETEENTH AND TWENTIETH ARRONDISSEMENTS

Café Flèche d'Or, 102 rue de Bagnolet (☎01 43 72 04 23). M: Alexandre-Dumas. Follow rue de Bagnolet until it crosses rue des Pyrénées; the café is on the right. Near Porte de la Réunion at Père Lachaise. This bar/performance space/café is housed in a defunct train station. North African, French, Caribbean, and South American cuisine with nightly jazz, ska, folk, salsa, samba (cover 10-25F/€1.53-3.81). Su brunch *menu* 69F/€10.52, dinner *menus* 110-125F/€16.78-19.06. Open bar/café daily 10am-2am; dinner daily 8pm-1am. MC/V (100F/€15.25 minimum).

Lao-Thai, 34 rue de Belleville (☎01 43 58 41 84). M: Belleville. Thai and Laotian specialties on an all-you-can-eat buffet with 12 different dishes, rice, and dessert. Perfect for the poor and hungry traveler. At 15F/€2.29, a martini is only 3F/€0.46 more than a Coke. Lunch M-F 50F/€7.63, Sa-Su 56F/€8.54. Dinner Su-Th 74F/€11.29, F-Sa 80F/€12.20. Open Tu-Su noon-2:30pm and 7-11:15pm. MC/V.

SALONS DE THE

Parisian *salons de thé* (tea rooms) fall into three categories: those stately salons straight out of the last century piled high with macaroons, Seattle-inspired joints for pseudo-intellectuals, and cafés that simply want to signal they also serve tea.

Angelina's, 226 rue de Rivoli, 1*er* (☎01 42 60 82 00). M: Concorde or Tuileries. Where *grandmère* takes little Delphine after playing in the Tuileries. Audrey Hepburn's favorite. *Chocolat africain* (hot chocolate) 36F/€5.49; *Mont Blanc* (meringue with chestnut nougat) 37F/€5.64. Afternoon tea 33F/€5.03. Open daily 9am-7pm. AmEx/MC/V.

Mariage Frères, 30 rue du Bourg-Tibourg, 4*ème* (☎01 42 72 28 11). M: Hôtel-de-Ville. Started by 2 brothers who found British tea shoddy, this exquisite salon has 500 varieties of tea (40-80F/€6.10-12.20) poured in kid gloves under palm fronds in an attempt to bring back the Empire. Tea *menu* includes sandwich, pastry, and tea (115F/€17.54). Classic brunch *menu* 140F/€21.35; reserve ahead. Open daily 10:30am-

7:30pm; lunch M-Sa noon-3pm; afternoon tea 3-6:30pm; brunch Su 12:30-6:30pm. AmEx/MC/V. **Also** at 13 rue des Grands Augustins, 6*ème* (☎01 40 51 82 50), M: St-Michel; and at 260 rue du Faubourg St-Honoré, 8*ème* (☎01 46 22 18 54).

Ladurée, 16 rue Royale, 8*ème* (☎01 42 60 21 79). M: Concorde. Like dining inside a Fabergé egg, full of well-heeled shoppers. Scrumptious specialty tea *Ladurée mélange* 35F/€5.34. Open daily 8:30am-7pm; lunch served until 3pm. AmEx/MC/V. **Also** at 75 av. des Champs-Elysées, 8*ème* (☎01 40 75 08 75). M: FDR.

MARKETS

Marché rue Montorgueil, 2*ème*. M: Etienne Marcel. From the métro, walk along rue Etienne Marcel away from the river. Rue Montorgueil is the 2nd street on your right. A center of food commerce and gastronomy since the 13th century, the marble Mount Pride Market sells wine, cheese, meat, and produce. Open Tu-Su 8am-7:30pm.

Marché Port Royal, 5*ème*. M: Censier-Daubenton. Make a right on bd. du Port-Royal in front of the Hôpital. Toward the intersection of bd. du Port-Royal. Colorful, fun, and busy. Fresh produce, meat, fish, and cheese; other tables are loaded with shoes, cheap chic, and housewares. Open Tu, Th, and Sa 8am-1:30pm.

Marché Mouffetard, 5*ème*. M: Monge. Walk through pl. Monge and follow rue Ortolan to rue Mouffetard. Cheese, meat, fish, produce, and housewares sold here. Visit the well-regarded bakeries. Open Tu-Su 8am-1:30pm.

UNIVERSITY RESTAURANTS

Most of the following offer a cafeteria-style choice of sandwiches, regional and international dishes, grilled meats, and drinks: **Bullier,** 39 av. Georges Bernanos, 5*ème* (RER: Port-Royal; open 8am-4:30pm); **Cuvier-Jussieu,** 8bis rue Cuvier, 5*ème* (M: Cuvier-Jussieu; open 9am-4:15pm); **Censier,** 31 rue Geoffroy St-Hilaire, 5*ème* (M: Censier-Daubenton; open 11am-2:30pm); **Assas,** 92 rue d'Assas, 6*ème* (M: Notre-Dame-des-Champs; open 7:30am-6:30pm).

SIGHTS

ILE DE LA CITE

Ile de la Cité is the birthplace of France. It housed a Gallic tribe until the 5th century, then became the site of Clovis' palace and, eventually, the seat of the French monarchy.

NOTRE-DAME

> The Cathedral of Notre Dame does not budge an inch for all the idiocies of the world.
>
> —e.e. cummings

Notre Dame was once the site of a Roman temple to Jupiter, and its holy place housed three churches before Maurice de Sully began construction of the Catholic cathedral in 1163. Sully, the bishop of Paris, aimed to create an edifice filled with air and light, in a style that would later be dubbed **Gothic.** He died before his plan was completed, and it was up to later centuries to rework the cathedral into the composite masterpiece, finished in 1361, that stands today. Notre Dame has seen royal weddings, Joan of Arc's trial, and Napoleon's coronation. Revolutionary secularists renamed the cathedral Le Temple de la Raison (The Temple of Reason), hiding Gothic arches behind plaster facades of virtuous Neoclassical design. Although reconsecrated after the Revolution, the building fell into disrepair and was used to shelter livestock. Victor Hugo's 1831 novel *Notre Dame-de-Paris* (The Hunchback of Notre Dame) revived the cathedral's popularity and inspired Napoleon III and Haussmann to invest time and money in its restoration. The modifications by Eugène Viollet-le-Duc (including a new spire, gargoyles, and a statue of himself admiring his own work) restored and reinvigorated the cathedral. In 1870 and again in 1940 thousands of Parisians attended masses to pray for deliverance from invading Germany. On August 26, 1944, Charles de Gaulle braved Nazi sniper fire to come here and give thanks for the imminent liberation of Paris.

EXTERIOR. Begun in the 12th century, work on the facade continued into the 17th century when artists were still adding Baroque statues. The oldest work is found above the **Porte de Ste-Anne** (right), mostly dating from 1165-1175. The **Porte de la Vierge** (left), relating the life of the Virgin Mary, dates from the 13th century. The central **Porte du Jugement** (Door of Judgement) was almost entirely redone in the 19th century; the figure of Christ dates from 1885. Revolutionaries wreaked havoc on the facade during the 1790s. Not content with decapitating Louis XVI, they attacked the statues of the Kings of Judah above the doors, which they thought were his ancestors. The heads are now housed in the Musée de Cluny (see p. 138).

TOWERS. The two towers—home to the cathedral's most famous fictional resident, Quasimodo the Hunchback—were a mysterious, imposing shadow on the Paris skyline for years. The claustrophobia-inducing staircase emerges onto a spectacular perch, where rows of gargoyles survey the city, particularly the Latin Quarter and the Marais. In the south tower, a tiny door opens onto the 13-ton bell that even Quasimodo couldn't ring: it requires the force of eight people to move.

INTERIOR. From the inside, the cathedral seems to be constructed of soaring, weightless walls. This effect is achieved by the spidery **flying buttresses** that support the vaults of the ceiling from outside, allowing for delicate stained glass walls. The transept's **rose windows,** nearly 85% 13th-century glass, are the most spectacular feature of the interior. The cathedral's **treasury,** south of the choir, contains an assortment of gilded artifacts. The famous Crown of Thorns, which is supposed to have been worn by Christ, was moved to Notre Dame at the end of the 18th century. The relic is "not ordinarily exposed" and is only presented on Fridays during Lent, from 5 to 6pm. Far below the cathedral towers, the **Crypte Archéologique,** pl. du Parvis du Notre Dame, houses artifacts unearthed in the construction of a parking garage. *(M: Cité. ☎01 42 34 56 10.* ***Cathedral*** *open M-F 8am-6:45pm, Sa-Su 8am-7:45pm.* ***Towers*** *open daily 9:30am-6pm. 35F/€5.34, under 25 23F/€3.51. Free* ***Tours*** *begin at the booth to the right. In English W-Th noon, Sa 2:30pm; in French M-F noon, Sa 2:30pm.* ***Treasury*** *open M-Sa 9:30-11:30am and 1-6pm. 15F/€2.29, students and ages 12-17 10F/€1.53, 6-12 5F/€0.76. Roman Catholic* ***Mass*** *M-F 6:15pm;* ***Vespers*** *sung 5:45pm in the choir.* ***High Mass*** *with Gregorian chant Su 10am, with music at 11:30am, 12:30, and 6:30pm. After Vespers, free organ recital.* ***Crypt*** *open daily 10am-6pm. 22F/€3.35, under 27 or over 60 free.)*

PALAIS DE JUSTICE

The Palais de la Cité harbors the infamous Conciergerie, a Revolutionary prison, and Ste-Chapelle, the private chapel of St-Louis. Since the 13th century, the buildings between the Conciergerie and the Ste-Chapelle have housed the Palais de Justice (the district courts of Paris today). After WWII, Maréchal Pétain was convicted in Chambre I of the Cour d'Appel. All trials are open to the public, as long as you can navigate your way through the marble hallways. *(Within the structure called Palais de la Cité, 4 bd. du Palais, in the same courtyard as Ste-Chapelle. M: Cité. ☎01 44 32 51 51. Courtrooms open M-F 9am-noon and 1:30-6pm. Free.)*

STE-CHAPELLE. Ste-Chapelle remains the foremost example of flamboyant Gothic architecture and a tribute to the craft of medieval stained glass. Construction of the chapel began in 1241 to house the most precious of King Louis IX's possessions: the Crown of Thorns from Christ's Passion. Bought along with a section of the Cross by the Emperor of Constantinople in 1239 for the ungodly sum of 135,000 pounds, the crown required an equally princely home. Although the crown itself—minus a few thorns that St-Louis gave away in exchange for political favors—has been moved to Notre Dame, Ste-Chapelle is still a wonder to explore. No mastery of the lower Chapel's dim gilt can prepare the visitor for the **Upper Chapel,** where light pours through walls of stained glass and frescoes of saints and martyrs shine. *(4 bd. du Palais. M: Cité. Within the structure Palais de la Cité. ☎01 53 73 58 51. Open Apr.-Sept. daily 9:30am-6:30pm; Oct.-Mar. 10am-5pm. 36F/€5.49, twin ticket with Conciergerie 50F/€7.62, seniors and ages 18-25 23F/€3.51, under 18 free.)*

CONCIERGERIE. Around the corner from the Palais de Justice from the entrance to Ste-Chapelle, this dark but historically rich monument to the Revolution stands over the Seine. Originally an administrative building, it became a royal prison and was taken over by the Revolutionary Tribunal after 1793. You can see rows of cells complete with preserved props and plastic people in the clothing of their day. Plaques explain how, in a bit of opportunism on the part of the Revolutionary leaders, the rich and famous could buy themselves private cells with cots and tables for writing while the poor slept on straw in pestilential cells. Its most famous prisoners were Robespierre and Marie Antoinette, two of the 2700 people sentenced to death here between 1792 and 1794. *(1 quai de l'Horloge. M: Cité. ☎01 53 73 78 50. Open Apr.-Sept. daily 9:30am-6:30pm; Oct.-Mar. 10am-5pm. 36F/€5.49, students 23F/€3.51. Includes tour in French, 11am and 3pm. For English tours, call ahead.)*

OTHER ISLAND SIGHTS

MEMORIAL DE LA DEPORTATION. A simple but thought-provoking memorial erected for the French victims of Nazi concentration camps; 200,000 flickering lights represent the dead, and an eternal flame burns close to the tomb of an unknown deportee. The names of all the concentration camps glow in gold triangles, while a series of humanitarian quotations is engraved into the stone walls—most striking of which is the injunction, "*Pardonne. N'Oublie Pas*" ("Forgive. Do Not Forget"), over the exit. It's frequented on holidays by old men who chant the kaddish, the Jewish prayer for the dead. The memorial only takes a few minutes to see, but it takes the rest of the day to digest. *(M: Cité. At the very tip of the island on pl. de l'Ile de France, a 5min. walk from the back of the cathedral, and down a narrow flight of steps. Open Apr.-Sept. daily 10am-noon and 2-7pm; Oct.-Mar. 10am-noon and 2-5pm. Free.)*

PONT NEUF. Leave Ile de la Cité by the oldest bridge in Paris, named the Pont Neuf (New Bridge), located just behind pl. Dauphine. Completed in 1607, the bridge broke tradition since its sides were not lined by houses, and was, before the construction of the Champs-Elysées, Paris' most popular thoroughfare, attracting peddlers, performance artists, and thieves. More recently, Christo, the Bulgarian performance artist, wrapped the entire bridge in 44,000 square meters of nylon.

ILE ST-LOUIS

From Ile de la Cité, a short walk across the **Pont St-Louis** will take you to this elegant enclave. Originally two small islands, it was considered suitable for duels, cows, and little else throughout the Middle Ages. It became residential in the 17th century, and architect Louis Le Vau gave it architectural unity in the mid-17th century. Today the island looks much as it did then. Over time, its *hôtels particuliers* have attracted an elite crowd, including Voltaire, Ingres, Baudelaire, and Cézanne. Today the island is visited by tourists for its specialty food shops and art galleries.

QUAI DE BOURBON. Sculptor **Camille Claudel** lived and worked at **no. 19** from 1899 until 1913, when her brother, the poet Paul Claudel, had her incarcerated in an asylum. The protegé and lover of sculptor Auguste Rodin, Claudel's most striking work is displayed in the Musée Rodin (see **Museums**, p. 138). At the intersection of the quai and rue des Deux Ponts sits the café **Au Franc-Pinot,** whose wrought-iron facade is almost as old as the island itself. Closed in 1716 after authorities found a basement stash of anti-government tracts, the café-cabaret reemerged as a treasonous address during the Revolution. Cécile Renault, daughter of the proprietor, mounted an unsuccessful attempt on Robespierre's life in 1794 and was guillotined the following year. Today the Pinot houses a mediocre jazz club. *(Immediately to the left after crossing the Pont St-Louis, the quai wraps around the northwest edge of the island.)*

EGLISE ST-LOUIS-EN-L'ILE. This church is a Louis Le Vau creation, built between 1664 and 1726, with a blazing Rococo interior lit by more windows than would appear to exist from the outside. The third chapel houses a splendid gilded wood relief, *The Death of the Virgin*. *(19bis rue St-Louis-en-l'Ile. ☎01 46 34 11 60. Open Tu-Su 9am-noon and 3-7pm. Check with FNAC or call the church for details on concerts; tickets 80-150F/€12.20-22.90.)*

FIRST ARRONDISSEMENT

The 1*er* stretches her culture-flecked flanks under the shadow of the Louvre (see p. 136), former home to kings and queens. Today, the royal chambers house the world's finest art, and the Sun King's well-tended gardens are filled with sunbathers, cafés, and carnival rides (for more on Louis XIV, see **History,** p. 8). The Ritz stands in the regal **pl. Vendôme,** while less-ritzy souvenir shops crowd **rue du Louvre** and **Les Halles.** Elegant boutiques line the **rue St-Honoré,** the street that passes the Comédie Française where actors still pay tribute to Molière, the company's founder. Further west, smoky jazz clubs pulse on **rue des Lombards** while restaurants on **rue J-J Rousseau** serve up France's most divine culinary finery.

EAST OF THE LOUVRE

JARDIN DES TUILERIES. Sweeping down from the Louvre to the pl. de la Concorde, the Jardin des Tuileries celebrates the victory of geometry over nature. Missing the public promenades of her native Italy, Catherine de Médicis had the gardens built in 1564. In 1649, André Le Nôtre (gardener for Louis XIV and designer of the gardens at Versailles) imposed his preference for straight lines upon the Tuileries. Be sure to notice the **Arc de Triomphe du Carrousel** and the glass pyramid of the Louvre's Cour Napoléon. Sculptures by Rodin and others stand amid the gardens' cafés and courts. In the summer, the rue de Rivoli terrace becomes an amusement park with children's rides, food stands, and a huge Ferris wheel. Flanking the pathway at the Concorde end of the Tuileries are the Galerie Nationale du Jeu de Paume (see p. 140) and the Musée de l'Orangerie (see p. 140). *(M: Tuileries. ☎01 40 20 90 43. Open Apr.-Sept. daily 7am-9pm; Oct.-Mar. 7:30am-7:30pm.)*

PLACE VENDOME. Stately pl. Vendôme, three blocks north of the Tuileries, was begun in 1687 by Louis XIV. Designed by Jules Hardouin-Mansart, the square was built to house embassies, but bankers created lavish private homes for themselves within the elegant facades. Today, the smell of money is still in the air: bankers, perfumers, and jewelers, including Cartier (at no. 7), line the square. In the center, Napoleon stands atop a large **column** dressed as Caesar.

PALAIS-ROYAL AND SURROUNDINGS

PALAIS-ROYAL. One block north of the Louvre along rue St-Honoré lies the once regal and racy Palais-Royal. It was constructed between 1628 and 1642 by Jacques Lemercier as Cardinal Richelieu's Palais Cardinal. After the Cardinal's death in 1642, Queen Anne d'Autriche moved in, preferring the Cardinal's palace to the Louvre. She brought with her a young Louis XIV, and the palace became a royal one. It later served as a sort of 18th-century shopping mall and then a place of Revolutionary ferment. In the central courtyard, the **colonnes de Buren**—a set of black and white striped pillars—are as controversial today as they were when installed by artist Daniel Buren in 1986. *(Fountain open June-Aug. daily 7am-11pm; Sept. 7am-9:30pm; Oct.-Mar. 7am-8:30pm; Apr.-May 7am-10:15pm.)*

COMEDIE FRANÇAISE. On the southwestern corner of the Palais-Royal, facing the Louvre, the Comédie Française is home to France's leading dramatic troupe (see p. 141). Built in 1790 by architect Victor Louis, the theater became the first permanent home for the Comédie Française troupe, which was created by Louis XIV in 1680. The entrance displays busts of famous actors by celebrated sculptors, including Voltaire by Houdon. Ironically, Molière, the company's founder, took ill here on stage while playing the role of the Imaginary Invalid. The chair onto which he collapsed can still be seen. At the corner of rue Molière and rue Richelieu, Visconti's Fontaine de Molière is only a few steps from where Molière died at no. 40.

LES HALLES AND SURROUNDINGS

EGLISE DE ST-EUSTACHE. There is a reason why Richelieu, Molière, and Mme. de Pompadour were all baptized here—it's a magnificent blend of history, beauty, and harmony. Eustache (Eustatius) was a Roman general who adopted Christianity upon seeing the sign of a cross between the antlers of a deer. As punishment for converting, the Romans locked him and his family into a brass bull that was placed over a fire until it became white-hot. Construction of the church in his honor began in 1532 and dragged on for over a century. In 1754, the unfinished facade was demolished and replaced with the Romanesque one that stands today—incongruous with the rest of the Gothic building, but appropriate for its Roman namesake. The chapels contain paintings by Rubens, as well as the British artist Raymond Mason's bizarre relief *Departure of the Fruits and Vegetables from the Heart of Paris*. Summer concerts are played on the exquisite organ, commemorating St-Eustache's premieres of Berlioz's *Te Deum* and Liszt's *Messiah* in 1886. Parts of the church are under renovation. *(M: Les Halles. Above rue Rambuteau. ☎01 42 36 31 05. Open M-F 9am-8pm and Su 9am-12:45pm and 2:30-8pm. High Mass with choir and organ Su 11am and 6pm. Free organ recital Su 5:30pm-6pm.)*

LES HALLES. The métro station Les Halles exits directly into the underground mall. To see the gardens, use one of the four "portes" and ride the escalators up toward daylight. A sprawling market since 1135, Les Halles received a much-needed face-lift in the 1850s with the construction of large iron-and-glass pavilions to shelter the vendors' stalls. In 1970, when authorities moved the old market to a suburb, politicians and city planners debated next how to fill *"le trou des Halles"* ("the hole of Les Halles"), 106 acres that presented Paris with the largest urban redesign opportunity since Haussmannization (see p. 13). Planners destroyed the pavilions to build a subterranean transfer-point between the métro and the new commuter rail, the RER, and a subterranean shopping mall, the **Forum des Halles.** Now, you can descend on one of the four main entrances to discover over 200 boutiques and three movie theaters. Watch out for pickpockets.

FONTAINE DES INNOCENTS. From M: Châtelet, take the rue de la Ferronnerie exit and walk down this street until you reach pl. J. du Bellay. Built in 1548 and designed by Pierre Lescot, the Fontaine des Innocents is the last trace of the Eglise and Cimetière des Sts-Innocents, which once bordered and overlapped Les Halles. Until its demolition in the 1780s, the edges of the cemetery were crowded by tombstones, the smell of rotting corpses, and vegetable merchants selling their produce.

SECOND ARRONDISSEMENT

The *2ème* has a long history of trade and commerce, from 19th-century passageways full of goodies to the ancient Bourse where stocks and bonds were traded. The oldest and most enduring trade of the area, prostitution, has thrived on rue St-Denis since the Middle Ages. Abundant fabric shops and cheap women's clothing stores line rue du Sentier and rue St-Denis, while upscale boutiques keep to the streets in the *2ème's* western half.

TO THE WEST

GALLERIES AND PASSAGES. Behold the world's first shopping malls. In the early 19th century, speculators built **passageways** designed to attract window shoppers ("window lickers," in French), using sheets of glass held in place by lightweight iron rods. This startling new design allowed the daylight in, and gas lighting and electric heating attracted customers (of every sort) all night long.

For a tour, begin at the most beautiful of the remaining passages, the **Grand Cerf** (10 rue Dussoubs-145 rue St-Denis). Worth visiting for its stained-glass portal windows and the exquisite iron work—it has the highest glass and iron arches in Paris. Returning to rue Etienne Marcel, walk ten minutes until you reach rue Montmartre on your right. Follow rue Montmartre onto bd. Montmartre. Between bd. Montmartre and rue St-Marc is the oldest of Paris' remaining galleries, **Passage des Panoramas** (10 rue St-Marc and 11 bd. Montmartre). A chocolate shop (François Marquis), a printer (no. 8), and an engraver (no. 47), who have managed to stay open since the 1830s, are all worth a visit, as they have conserved much of their old machinery. Street theater adds to the area's liveliness. Across bd. Montmartre, mirroring the Passage des Panoramas, find **Passages Jouffry** and **Verdeau.**

From bd. Montmartre, make a left onto rue Vivienne. On your left, just before reaching the Palais Royal, you'll find the most fashionable *galeries* (posh passageways) of the 1820s. Inlaid marble mosaics swirl along the floor, and stucco friezes grace the **Galerie Vivienne** (4 rue des Petits Champs-6 rue Vivienne).

BIBLIOTHEQUE NATIONALE. With a 12 million volume collection that includes Gutenberg Bibles and first editions from the 15th century, the Bibliothèque Nationale is possibly the largest library in Continental Europe. Since 1642, every book published in France has been legally required to enter the national archives. At one point, books considered a little too titillating for public consumption descended into a room named "Hell," to which only the most qualified docents were granted access. In the late 1980s, the French government eschewed annexes as a short-term solution and resolved to build the mammoth **Bibliothèque de France** in the 13*ème*, where the collections from the 2*ème's* Richelieu branch were relocated between 1996 and 1998.

Today Richelieu still holds collections of stamps, money, photography, medals, and maps, as well as original manuscripts written on everything from papyrus to parchment. Scholars must pass through a strict screening process to gain access to the main reading room; plan to bring a letter from your university, research advisor, or editor stating the nature of your research and two pieces of photo ID. For the general public, the **Galerie Mazarin** and **Galerie Mansart** host excellent temporary exhibits of books, prints, and lithographs. Upstairs, the **Cabinet des Médailles** displays coins, medallions, and confiscated *objets d'art* from the Revolution. Across from the library's main entrance, **pl. Louvois'** sculpted fountain personifies the four great rivers of France—the Seine, the Saône, the Loire, and the Garonne—as heroic women. *(58 rue de Richelieu. M: Bourse. Just north of the Galeries Vivienne and Colbert, across rue Vivienne. Info ☎ 01 53 79 59 59; galleries ☎ 01 47 03 81 10; cabinet ☎ 01 47 03 83 30. Library open M-Sa 9am-5:30pm. Galleries open Tu-Su 10am-7pm only when there are exhibits. 35F/€5.34, students 24F/€3.66. Cabinet des Médailles open M-F 1-6pm, Sa 1-5pm; free.)*

THIRD ARRONDISSEMENT

The 3*ème* and 4*ème arrondissements* comprise the area known as the **Marais.** Drained by monks in the 13th century, the Marais ("swamp") was land-filled to provide building space for the Right Bank. With Henri IV's construction of the **Pl. des Vosges** (see **Sights,** p. 123) at the beginning of the 17th century, the area became the city's center of fashionable living. Leading architects and sculptors of the period designed elegant *hôtels particuliers* with large courtyards. During the Revolution, many *hôtels* fell into ruin or disrepair, but in the 1960s the Marais was declared a historic neighborhood and a 30-year period of gentrification attracted trendy boutiques, cafés, and museums. The area's narrow streets, now swarming with the newest of fashion and the hottest of the 21st century, nevertheless retain the stamp of a medieval village.

RUE VIEILLE-DU-TEMPLE. This street is lined with stately residences including the 18th-century Hôtel de la Tour du Pin (no. 75) and the more famous Hôtel de Rohan (no. 87). Built between 1705 and 1708 for Armand-Gaston de Rohan, Bishop of Strasbourg and alleged love-child of Louis XIV, the *hôtel* has housed many of his descendants. Frequent temporary exhibits allow access to the interior Cabinet des Singes and its original decorations. The Hôtel de Rohan, part of the National Archives, also boasts an impressive courtyard and rose garden. Across rue Vieille-du-Temple, the alleyway at 38 rue des Francs-Bourgeois, gives a sense of what Henri IV's dark and claustrophobic Paris felt like. At the corner of rue des Francs-Bourgeois and rue Vieille-du-Temple, the flamboyant Gothic Hôtel Hérouët and its turrets were built in 1528 for Louis XII's treasurer, Hérouët. *(M: Hôtel-de-Ville or St-Paul. Hôtel de Rohan: call 01 40 27 60 96 for info on temporary exhibits.)*

ARCHIVES NATIONALES. Housed in the 18th-century Hôtel de Soubise, the **Musée de l'Histoire de France** is the main exhibition space of the National Archives. The Treaty of Westphalia, the Edict of Nantes, the Declaration of the Rights of Man, Louis XVI's diary, letters between Benjamin Franklin and George Washington, and Napoleon's will are all preserved here, though few are displayed. Louis XVI's entry for July 14, 1789 (Bastille Day) reads simply "*Rien*" (Nothing). *(60 rue des Francs-Bourgeois. M: Rambuteau. ☎01 40 27 64 19. Open M-Sa 9am-5:45pm.)*

FOURTH ARRONDISSEMENT

The **Lower Marais** is a supremely fun neighborhood. It's accessible. It's red wine. It's just-barely-affordable, sort-of-designer shops. It's falafel and knishes. It's gay men out for brunch. It's family-run goodness. Let the festivities begin. (And nearly everything is open on Sunday.)

TO THE NORTH: BEAUBOURG

CENTRE POMPIDOU. One of the most visible examples of renovation in the *4ème* is the Centre Pompidou, the ultra-modern exhibition, performance, and research space considered alternately as an innovation or an eyesore (see **Museums**, p. 137). Its architects, Richard Rogers, Gianfranco Franchini, and Renzo Piano, designed a building whose color-coded electrical tubes (yellow), water pipes (green), and ventilation ducts (blue) highlight the exterior of the building. More people visit the Pompidou every year than visit the Louvre. Initially designed to accommodate 5000 visitors a day, the center and its **Musée National d'Art Moderne** attract more like 20,000. Head to the Pompidou to revel in its success or just to hang out in the cobblestone square out front, which gathers a mixture of artists, musicians, rebels, passersby, and pickpockets. *(M: Rambuteau or Hôtel-de-Ville.)*

RUE DES ROSIERS. At the heart of the Jewish community of the Marais, the rue des Rosiers has kosher shops, butchers, bakeries, and falafel counters galore. Until the 13th century, Paris' Jewish community was concentrated in front of Notre-Dame. When Philippe-Auguste expelled the Jewish population from the city limits, many families moved to the Marais, just outside the walls. Since then, this quarter has been Paris' Jewish center, witnessing the influx of Russian Jews in the 19th century and new waves of North African Sephardim fleeing Algeria in the 1960s. Assisted by French police, Nazi soldiers stormed the Marais during WWII and hauled Jewish families to the Vélodrome d'Hiver, an indoor cycling stadium, where they awaited deportation to work camps like Drancy, in a northeastern suburb of Paris, or to camps farther east in Poland and Germany. Today the Jewish community thrives in the Marais with two synagogues at 25 rue des Rosiers and 10 rue Pavée, designed by Art Nouveau architect Hector Guimard. *(Four blocks east of Beaubourg, parallel to rue des Francs-Bourgeois. M: St-Paul.)*

MEMORIAL DU MARTYR JUIF INCONNU. The Memorial to the Unknown Jewish Martyr commemorates European Jews who died at the hands of the Nazis and their French collaborators. The crypt and monument contain ashes brought back from concentration camps and from the Warsaw ghetto. Upstairs, the **Centre de Documentation Juive Contemporaine** (Jewish Contemporary Documentation Center) holds more than 50,000 documents and one million items relating to the Nazi era. *(17 rue Geoffroy de l'Asnier. M: St-Paul. ☎01 42 77 44 72. Memorial and Documentation Center open Su-Th 10am-1pm and 2-6pm, F 10am-1pm and 2-5pm. 15F/€2.29.)*

RUE VIEILLE-DU-TEMPLE AND RUE STE-CROIX DE LA BRETTONERIE. Like a scene from the movie *Grease*, hair-slicked men in muscle-tees and tight-pants-women in heels fill the shops and outdoor café-bars of this *super-hyper-chic* neighborhood, as their convertible-blessed fellow cool cats cruise between them. The only exception: Sandy falls for Rizzo and Danny has no problem giving Kenickie a hug. The heart of Paris' vibrant gay community, this is where the boys are. And although many establishments fly the rainbow flag, both gay and straight go together. *(M: St-Paul or Hôtel de Ville. One block north of rue de Rivoli runs the parallel rue du Roi de Sicile; rue Vieille-du-Temple meets it and then meets rue Ste-Croix de la Brettonerie.)*

HOTEL DE VILLE AND SURROUNDINGS

HOTEL DE VILLE. Paris' grandiose city hall dominates a large square with fountains and Belle Epoque lampposts. The present edifice is a 19th-century creation built to replace the original medieval structure, a meeting hall for the cartel that controlled traffic on the Seine. The building witnessed municipal executions on pl. Hôtel-de-Ville; in 1610, Henri IV's assassin Ravaillac was quartered here, and we're not referring to accommodations. On May 24, 1871, the *communards* doused the building with petrol and set it afire. Lasting a full eight days, the blaze spared nothing but the frame. The Third Republic built a virtually identical structure on the ruins. *(29 rue de Rivoli. M: Hôtel-de-Ville. ☎01 42 76 43 43. Open M-F 9am-6 or 6:30pm.)*

TOUR ST-JACQUES. The Tour St-Jacques stands alone in the center of its own park. This flamboyant Gothic tower is the only remnant of the 16th-century Eglise St-Jacques-la-Boucherie. Its meteorological station and the statue of Pascal at its base commemorate Pascal's experiments on the weight of air, performed here in 1648. The tower marks Haussmann's *grande croisée* of rue de Rivoli and bd. Sébastopol, the intersection of his east-west and north-south axes for the city, only meters from where the earliest Roman roads crossed 2000 years ago. *(39-41 rue de Rivoli. M: Hôtel-de-Ville. Two blocks west of the Hôtel-de-Ville.)*

SOUTH OF RUE ST-ANTOINE AND RUE DE RIVOLI

HOTEL DE BEAUVAIS. The Hôtel de Beauvais was built in 1655 for Pierre de Beauvais and his wife Catherine Bellier. Bellier, Anne d'Autriche's chambermaid, had an adolescent tryst with the Queen's son, 15-year-old Louis XIV. From the balcony of the *hôtel*, Anne d'Autriche and Cardinal Mazarin watched the entry of Louis XIV and his bride, Marie-Thérèse, into Paris. A century later, as a guest of the Bavarian ambassador, Mozart played his first piano recital here. Restored in 1967, the half-timbered 14th-century **Maison à l'Enseigne du Faucheur** and **Maison à l'Enseigne du Mouton** directly across the street illustrate what medieval Paris looked like. *(68 rue François-Miron. M: Hôtel-de-Ville.)*

HOTEL DE SENS. The Hôtel de Sens is one of the city's few surviving examples of medieval residential architecture. Built in 1474 for Tristan de Salazar, the Archbishop of Sens, its military features reflect the violence of the day. The former residence of Queen Margot, Henri IV's first wife, the Hôtel de Sens has witnessed some of Paris' most daring romantic escapades. In 1606, the 55-year-old queen drove up to the door, in front of which her two lovers were arguing. One opened the carriage door, and the other shot him dead. Unfazed, the queen demanded the execution of the other, which she watched the next day. The *hôtel* now houses the **Bibliothèque Forney** and a beautiful courtyard. *(1 rue du Figuier. M: Pont Marie. Courtyard open to the public. Library open Tu-F 1:30-8:30pm, Sa 10am-8:30pm; closed July 1-16.)*

EGLISE ST-PAUL-ST-LOUIS. The Eglise St-Paul-St-Louis dominates rue St-Antoine and dates from 1627 when Louis XIII placed its first stone. Its large dome—a trademark of Jesuit architecture—is visible from afar, but hidden by ornamentation on the facade. Paintings inside the dome depict four French kings: Clovis, Charlemagne, Robert the Pious, and St-Louis. The embalmed hearts of Louis XIII and Louis XIV were kept in vermeil boxes carried by silver angels before they were destroyed during the Revolution. The church's Baroque interior is graced with three 17th-century paintings of the life of St-Louis and Eugène Delacroix's dramatic *Christ in the Garden of Olives* (1826). The holy-water vessels were gifts from Victor Hugo. *(99 rue St-Antoine. M: St-Paul. ☎01 49 24 11 43. Open M-Sa 9am-8pm, Su 9am-8:30pm. Mass Sa 6pm, Su 9:30, 11:15am, and 7pm.)*

17 RUE BEAUTREILLIS. Jim Morrison died (allegedly of a heart attack) here in his bathtub on the third floor. His grave can be found at the Cimetière Père Lachaise (see **Sights,** p. 135).

PLACE DES VOSGES AND SURROUNDINGS

PLACE DES VOSGES. At the end of rue des Francs-Bourgeois sits the magnificent pl. des Vosges, Paris' oldest public square. The central park, lined with immaculately manicured trees centered around a splendid fountain, is surrounded by 17th-century Renaissance townhouses. Kings built several mansions on this site, including the Palais de Tournelles, which Catherine de Medici ordered destroyed after her husband Henri II died there in a jousting tournament in 1563.

Each of the 36 buildings has arcades on the street level, two stories of pink brick, and a slate-covered roof. The largest townhouse, forming the square's main entrance, was the king's pavilion; opposite, the pavilion of the queen is smaller. The marriage of Louis XIII's sister to the crown prince of Spain drew a crowd of 10,000 here in 1612. Originally intended for merchants, the square attracted the wealthy, including Mme. de Sévigné and Cardinal Richelieu. Molière, Racine, and Voltaire filled the grand parlors with their *bon mots*. Mozart played a concert here at the age of seven. Even when the city's nobility moved across the river to the Fbg. St-Germain, this remained among the most elegant spots in Paris. Leave pl. des Vosges through the corner door at the right of the south face (near no. 5), which leads into the garden of the Hôtel de Sully. *(M: Chemin Vert or St-Paul.)*

HOTEL DE SULLY. Built in 1624, the Hôtel de Sully was acquired by the Duc de Sully, minister to Henri IV. Often cuckolded by his young wife, Sully asked only that she keep her paramours off the staircase. The small inner courtyard offers the fatigued tourist stone benches and an elegant formal garden. *(62 rue St-Antoine. M: St-Paul. ☎01 44 61 20 00. Open M-Th 9am-12:45pm and 2-6pm, F 9am-12:45pm and 2-5pm.)*

PARIS

FIFTH ARRONDISSEMENT

TO THE WEST: THE LATIN QUARTER

Even as wave after wave of tourists breaks on the Rive Gauche, the *5ème* maintains its reputation as the nerve center of young Paris. The autumn influx of Parisian students to the *5ème*'s countless research institutions and universities (including the now-legendary **Sorbonne**) is undoubtedly the prime cultural preservative of the *Quartier Latin*, which takes its name from the old-time language used in its prestigious *lycées* and universities prior to 1798. Compared to the now opulent café scene of ex-literati haunts along **St-Germain-des-Prés,** the Latin Quarter is laid back and genuinely intellectual. Those more interested in Fendi than Foucault should look elsewhere.

PLACE ST-MICHEL

The busiest spot in the Latin Quarter, pl. St-Michel is a historically significant one: the Paris Commune began here in 1871, as did the student uprising of 1968. The majestic 1860 fountain features bronze dragons, an angelic St-Michel slaying the dragon, as well as a WWII memorial commemorating the citizens who fell here defending their *quartier* during the Liberation of Paris in August 1944.

Bibliophiles, rejoice! The *Quartier Latin* is home to scores of antiquarian booksellers and university presses ready to indulge even the most arcane of literary appetites. For the more gastronomically inclined, ice cream shops and crêpe stands line **rue St-Séverin,** while Greek *gyro* counters hawk snacks on the bustling corridors and bazaar-like alleyways of **rue de la Huchette.**

The nearby **Eglise St-Julien-le-Pauvre** (a right off bd. St-Michel and another right onto rue St-Julien le Pauvre) was begun in 1170 and is one of the oldest churches in Paris. Across bd. St-Jacques is another architectural behemoth, the bizarre and wonderful **Eglise St-Séverin.** Inside, spiraling columns and modern stained glass ornament this Gothic complex. At the intersection of bd. St-Germain and bd. St-Michel, the **Hôtel de Cluny,** 6 pl. Paul-Painlevé, was once a medieval monastery, built on the ruins of a first-century Roman bath house. Today, the building houses the **Musée de Cluny's** extraordinary collection of medieval art, tapestries, and illuminated manuscripts (see **Museums,** p. 138). As a major tourist thoroughfare, **bd. St-Michel** (or *boul' Mich'*) won't give you much of an impression of local life.

LA SORBONNE. Walk away from the Seine on bd. St-Michel and make a left on rue des Ecoles. **Pl. de la Sorbonne's** cafés and bookstores face out from the Sorbonne, one of Europe's oldest universities. Founded in 1253 by Robert de Sorbon as a dormitory for 16 poor theology students, it soon became the administrative base for the University of Paris. In 1469, Louis XI established France's first printing house here. As it grew in power and size, the Sorbonne often contradicted the authority of the French throne; it sided with England during the Hundred Years' War. Commissioned in 1642 by Cardinal Richelieu, the university's main building, **Ste-Ursule de la Sorbonne,** on rue des Ecoles, is closed to the public, but the **Cour d'Honneur,** with its statues of Hugo and Pasteur, impressive views of the chapel's Neoclassical facade, and murals by J. J. Weerts, is open for ambling visits and is excellent for student-watching. *(45-7 rue des Ecoles. M: Cluny-La Sorbonne or RER: Luxembourg. Entrance to main courtyard from pl. de la Sorbonne.* ***Open*** *M-F 9am-6pm.)*

COLLEGE DE FRANCE. Created by François Ier in 1530 to contest the university's authority, the Collège de France stands behind the Sorbonne. The outstanding courses at the Collège, given by such luminaries as Henri Bergson, Pierre Boulez, Paul Valéry, and Milan Kundera, are free and open to all. Check the schedules that appear by the door in September. (*11 pl. Marcelin-Berthelot. M: Maubert Mutualité. From the métro, walk against traffic on bd. St-Germain, turn left on rue Thenard; the entrance to the Collège is at the end of the road, up the stairs. Courses run Sept.-May. Info ☎01 44 27 12 11. Closed in Aug.)*

THE PANTHEON. Visible all the way from the Luxembourg gardens to St-Germain to the Ecole Normale Supérieure, the Panthéon is an extravagant landmark in a city known for its extravagance. Unreal airiness and fabulous geometric grandeur are the Panthéon's architectural claims to fame. Fans of *Le Petit Prince* can visit the memorial to Antoine de St-Exupéry in the main rotunda.

The inscription in stone across the front of the Panthéon dedicates the building "To great men from a grateful fatherland," but originally, the Panthéon was simply a man's dedication to his wife. In AD 507, King Clovis converted to Christianity and had a basilica designed to accommodate his tomb and that of his wife, Clotilde. In 512, the basilica became the resting place of **Ste-Geneviève,** who was believed to have protected Paris from the attacking Huns with her prayers. Louis XV was also feeling pretty darn grateful after surviving a grave illness in 1744, a miracle he ascribed to the powers of Ste-Geneviève. He vowed to build a prestigious monument to the saint and entrusted the design of the new basilica to the architect Soufflot in 1755. The Revolution converted the church into a mausoleum of heroes on April 4, 1791. In 1806, Napoleon reserved the crypt for the interment of those who had given "great service to the State." The Panthéon is full of some of France's most valuable citizens: in the **crypt** you will find writers Voltaire, Rousseau, Hugo, and Zola, scientists Marie and Pierre Curie, politician Jean Jaurès, and Louis Braille, inventor of the reading system for the blind. At Hugo's burial in 1885, two million mourners followed the coffin to its resting place.The Panthéon's other attraction is a giant fifth-grade experiment taken to new extremes: the plane of oscillation of **Foucault's Pendulum** stays fixed as the Earth rotates around it. *(Pl. du Panthéon. M: Cardinal Lemoine. From the métro, walk down rue Cardinal Lemoine and turn right on rue Clovis; walk around to the front of the building to enter. ☎01 44 32 18 00. Open in summer daily 9:30am-6:30pm; in winter 10am-6:15pm. 42F/€6.40, students 26F/€3.96, under 18 free. Tours in French leave from inside the main door daily at 2:30 and 4pm.)*

TO THE EAST: PLACE DE LA CONTRESCARPE

South on rue Descartes, past the prestigious Lycée Henri IV, **pl. de la Contrescarpe** is the geographical center of the *5ème*. Lovely outdoor restaurants and cafés cluster around a circular fountain. From Contrescarpe, it's only a five-minute walk to St-Germain, the Panthéon, or the Jardin des Plantes.

RUE MOUFFETARD. South of pl. de la Contrescarpe, **rue Mouffetard** plays host to one of the liveliest street markets in Paris (see **Markets,** p. 115). Today, rue Mouffetard and **rue Monge** bind much of the tourist and student social life. Hemingway lived down the Mouff' at 74 rue du Cardinal Lemoine, and poet Paul Verlaine died at 39 rue Descartes in 1844.

JARDIN DES PLANTES. In the eastern corner of the *5ème*, the Jardin des Plantes offers 45,000 square meters of carefully tended flowers and lush greenery. Opened in 1640 by Louis XIII's doctor, the gardens originally grew medicinal plants to promote His Majesty's health. Today, the Jardin, whose grounds attract Parisian families and sprawling sunbathers in the summer, is home to some of the most exquisite gardens in Paris. The **Ecole de Botanique** is a landscaped botanical garden tended by students, horticulturists, and amateur botanists; the **Roserie** is a luscious, fragrant display of roses from all over the world (in full bloom in mid-June); the two big, botanical boxes of the **Grandes Serres** (big greenhouses) span two climates. The gardens also include the tremendous **Musée d'Histoire Naturelle** (see **Museums,** p. 140) and the **Ménagerie Zoo.** Although no match for the Parc Zoologique in the Bois de Vincennes, the zoo will gladden anyone's day with its 240 mammals, 500 birds, and 130 reptiles. *(M: Gare d'Austerlitz, Jussieu, Censier-Daubenton. ☎01 40 79 37 94. Jardin des Plantes and Roserie open in summer daily 7:30am-8pm; in winter 7:30am-5:30pm. Free. Ménagerie Zoo, 3 quai Saint-Bernard and 57 rue Cuvier. Open daily 10am-5pm; until 5:30pm in winter; until 6pm in summer. 30F/€4.57, students 20F/€3.05.)*

PARIS

MOSQUEE DE PARIS. The Institut Musulman houses the beautiful Persian gardens, elaborate minaret, and shady porticoes of the mosque, constructed in 1920 by French architects to honor the role played by the countries of North Africa in WWI. The cedar doors open onto an oasis of blue and white where Muslims from around the world come to meet around the fountains and pray in the carpeted prayer rooms (visible from the courtyard but closed to the public). The Mosquée is also home to an exquisite *hammam* and gorgeous café, known for its mint tea, making this a perfect place to spend a sunny afternoon. *(Behind the Jardin des Plantes at pl. du Puits de l'Ermite. M: Jussieu. Walk down rue Linne, turn right on rue Lacépède, and left on rue de Quatrefages; entrance to the left. ☎01 48 35 78 17. Open June-Aug. Sa-Th 9am-noon and 2-6pm. Tour 15F/€2.29, students 10F/€1.53.)*

ARENES DE LUTECE. Once an outdoor theater, now a glorified sandpit, the Arènes de Lutèce were built by the Romans in the 1st century AD to accommodate 15,000 spectators. Similar to oval amphitheaters in Rome and southern France, these ruins were unearthed in 1869 and restored in 1910; all the seats are reconstructions. *(At the intersection of rue de Navarre and rue des Arènes.)*

ALONG THE SEINE

SHAKESPEARE & CO. BOOKSTORE. This bookstore is the absolute center of young anglophone Paris. While not the original Sylvia Beach incarnation (at 8 rue Dupuytren), this rag-tag bookstore has become a cultish landmark. Frequented by Allen Ginsberg and Lawrence Ferlinghetti, and run by the purported grandson of Walt Whitman, it hosts poetry readings and Sunday evening tea parties. *(37 rue de la Bucherie. M: St-Michel. Open daily noon-midnight.)*

INSTITUT DU MONDE ARABE. Housed in one of the city's most striking buildings and facing the Seine, the IMA resembles a ship, representing the boats on which Algerian, Moroccan, and Tunisian immigrants sailed to France. It houses permanent and rotating exhibitions on North African, Near Eastern, and Middle Eastern Arab cultures. *(1 rue des Fossés St-Bernard. M: Jussieu. Walk down rue Jussieu away from the Jardin des Plantes and make your first right onto rue des Fossés St-Bernard. ☎01 40 51 38 38. Open Tu-Su 10am-7pm. 25F/€3.81, ages 12-18 20F/€3.05, under 12 free.)*

SIXTH ARRONDISSEMENT

The sleek and stylish *6ème* gives the Sorbonne students a run for their intellectual money. Like the *5ème's* better-kempt older brother, the *6ème* is the home to two of Paris' still-vibrant cultural staples: literary cafés and innovative art galleries. The cafés of the now-legendary **bd. St-Germain-des-Prés** (see **Food,** p. 109) are the former stomping grounds of Hemingway, Sartre, Picasso, Camus, Baudelaire, and just about anyone else who was in Paris during the first half of the 20th century. The art exhibits of the Left Bank's prestigious gallery district continue to display some of the area's most exciting contemporary work. However, the Picassos and Picabias have moved to the outskirts, and the *haute bourgeois* have moved in—and brought their designer boutiques, sky-high prices, and shameless materialism.

JARDIN DU LUXEMBOURG AND ODEON

JARDIN DU LUXEMBOURG. Parisians flock to these formal gardens to sunbathe, write, stroll, read, and gaze at the rose gardens, central pool, and each other. A residential area in Roman Paris, the site of a medieval monastery, and later the home of naughty 17th-century French royalty, the gardens were liberated during the Revolution and are now free to all. *(M: Odéon; RER: Luxembourg. Open Apr.-Oct. daily 7:30am-9:30pm; Nov.-Mar. 8:15am-5pm. The main entrance is on bd. St-Michel. Tours in French first W of the month, Apr.-Oct. at 9:30am; depart from pl. André Honorat behind the observatory.)*

PALAIS DU LUXEMBOURG. The Palais du Luxembourg, located within the park and now serving as the home of the French Senate, was built in 1615 at Marie de Medici's request. The palace went on to house a number of France's most elite nobility, and in later years, became a prison for those nobles awaiting the guillotine and then for Revolutionary Jacobin perpetrators.

Imprisoned in the palace during the Revolution with her Republican husband, Beauharnais, the future Empress Josephine returned five years later to take up official residence with her second husband, the new Consul Napoleon Bonaparte. During World War II, the palace was occupied by the Nazis, who made it the headquarters of the *Luftwaffe*.

EGLISE ST-SULPICE. The balconied, Neoclassical facade of the huge Eglise St-Sulpice dominates the enormous square of the same name. Designed by Servadoni in 1733, the church remains unfinished. Inside, St-Sulpice's claims to fame are a set of fierce, gestural Delacroix frescoes in the first chapel on the right, a *Virgin and Child* by Jean-Baptiste Pigalle in a rear chapel, and an enormous organ. *(M: St-Sulpice or Mabillon. ☎01 46 33 21 78. Open daily 7:30am-7:30pm. Tour in French daily 3pm.)*

ST-GERMAIN-DES-PRES

Known as *le village de Saint-Germain-des-Prés*, the crowded area around **bd. St-Germain** between St-Sulpice and the Seine is packed with cafés, restaurants, galleries, cinemas, and expensive boutiques.

BD. ST-GERMAIN. Known by most as the ex-literati hangout of Existentialists (who frequented the Flore) and Surrealists like André Breton (who frequented the Deux Magots), the Boulevard is home to a host of cafés, both new and old. The long-standing rivalry between **Café de Flore** and **Aux Deux Magots** is still very much the *noblesse oblige* version of Family Feud. The café culture of post-intellectual St-Germain-des-Prés is implicated more in a sort of grand cultural nostalgia than in a preservation of literary greatness.

The boulevard and its many side-streets around rue de Rennes has become in recent years a shopping mecca, with designer boutiques from Louis Vuitton to Emporio Armani. But art isn't only behind glass. Public art is alive and well in the *village St-Germain:* sculptures of all sorts can be found throughout the area; one of the best is the earthquake-inspired fountain in pl. du Québec across from the Eglise St-Germain-des-Prés.

EGLISE DE ST-GERMAIN-DES-PRES. The Eglise St-Germain-des-Prés is the oldest standing church in Paris, and it shows: the only decorations on the exterior are the pink and white hollyhocks growing to the side. King Childebert I commissioned a church on this site to hold relics he had looted from the Holy Land. Completed in 558, it was consecrated by St-Germain, Bishop of Paris, on the very day of King Childebert's death—the king had to be buried inside the church's walls.

The rest of the church's history reads like an architectural Book of Job. Sacked by the Normans and rebuilt three times, the present-day church dates from the 11th century. On June 30, 1789, the Revolution seized the prison in a dress rehearsal for the storming of the Bastille. The church then did a brief stint as a saltpeter mill and in 1794, the 15 tons of gunpowder that had been stored in the abbey exploded. The ensuing fire devastated the church's artwork and treasures, including much of its monastic library. Baron Haussmann destroyed the last remains of the deteriorating abbey walls and gates when he extended rue de Rennes to the front of the church and created pl. St-Germain-des-Prés.

Completely redone in the 19th century, the magnificent interior is painted in shades of maroon, deep green, and gold with enough regal grandeur to counteract the building's modest exterior; pay close attention to the fabulous royal blue and gold-starred ceiling, frescoes depicting the life of Jesus (by a pupil of Ingres), and decorative mosaics along the archways. In the second chapel—on the right after the apse—you'll find a stone marking the interred heart of 17th-century philosopher René Descartes, who died of pneumonia at the frigid court of Queen Christina of Sweden, as well as an altar dedicated to the victims of the September 1793 massacre in which 186 Parisians were slaughtered in the courtyard. Pick up a free map of the church with info in English on St-Germain's history, artifacts, and frequent concerts; as in most medieval churches, built in an age without microphones, the acoustics are awesome. *(3 pl. St-Germain-des-Prés. M: St-Germain-des-Prés. ☎ 01 55 42 81 33. Open daily 8am-7:45pm. Info office open Tu-Sa 10:30am-noon and 2:30-7pm.)*

ODEON. **Cour du Commerce St-André,** branching off bd. St-Germain to the North, is one of the most picturesque walking areas in the *6ème*, with cobblestone streets, centuries-old cafés (including **Le Procope**), and outdoor seating in the summer. After the arch stands the **Relais Odéon,** a Belle Epoque bistro whose stylishly painted exterior, decked with floral mosaics and a hanging sign, is a fine example of Art Nouveau, as is the doorway of 7 rue Mazarine, several blocks north.

Just to the south of bd. St-Germain-des-Prés, the **Carrefour d'Odéon,** a favorite Parisian hangout, is a delightful, tree-lined square filled with bistros, cafés, and outdoor seating. The **Comptoir du Relais** still holds court here, while newcomer cafés strut their flashy selves across the street.

PONT DES ARTS. The wooden footbridge across from the Institut, appropriately called the Pont des Arts, is celebrated by poets and artists for its delicate ironwork, beautiful views of the Seine, and spiritual locus at the heart of France's prestigious Academy of Arts and Letters.

SEVENTH ARRONDISSEMENT

Since the 18th century, the *7ème* has stood its ground as the city's most elegant residential district. Home to the National Assembly, countless foreign embassies, the Invalides, the Musée d'Orsay (see **Museums,** p. 138), and the Eiffel Tower, this section of the Left Bank is a medley of France's diplomatic, architectural, and military achievements. Whether in the Musée Rodin's rose gardens or the public markets of the rue Cler, the *7ème* simultaneously offers some of the most touristic and most intimate sights in all of Paris.

TO THE WEST

THE EIFFEL TOWER. Gustave Eiffel, its designer, wrote: "France is the only country in the world with a 300m flagpole." Designed in 1889 as the tallest structure in the world, the Eiffel Tower was conceived as a monument to engineering that would

PARIS

surpass the Egyptian pyramids in size and notoriety. Yet before construction had even begun, shockwaves of dismay reverberated through the city. Critics dubbed it "metal asparagus" and a Parisian tower of Babel. After the building's completion, the writer Maupassant ate lunch every day at its ground-floor restaurant—the only place in Paris, he claimed, from which he couldn't see the offensive thing.

Nevertheless, when it was inaugurated in March 1889 as the centerpiece of the Universal Exposition, the tower earned the love of Paris; nearly 2,000,000 people ascended during the event. The radio-telegraphic center atop the tower worked during WWI to intercept enemy messages, including the one that led to the arrest and execution of Mata Hari, the Danish dancer accused of being a German spy. *(M: Bir Hakeim or Trocadéro. ☎01 44 11 23 23. Open June 22-Aug. daily 9am-midnight; Sept.-Dec. 9:30am-11pm (stairs 9:30am-6:30pm); Jan.-June 21 9:30am-11pm (stairs 9:30am-6:30pm). Elevator to 1st floor 24F/€3.66, under 12 14F/€2.13; 2nd floor 45F/€6.86, under 12 25F/€3.81; 3rd floor 65F/€9.91, under 12 35F/€5.34. Stairs to 1st and 2nd floors 20F/€3.05.)*

NEAR THE TOWER

CHAMPS DE MARS. Although close to the *7ème's* military monuments and museums, the Champs de Mars (Field of Mars) celebrates the God of War for other good reasons. It was here that Julius Caesar finally squelched the rebellious Parisii tribe in 53 BC. One hundred and forty years later, Viking ships were rolled over it. However, neither of these heroic encounters are the reason for the lawn's name. Champs de Mars comes from the days of Napoleon's Empire when it was used as a drill ground for the adjacent Ecole Militaire. In 1780, Charles Montgolfier launched the first hydrogen balloon from here. During the Revolution, the park witnessed civilian massacres and political demonstrations. At the Champs's 1793 Festival of the Supreme Being, Robespierre proclaimed Reason the new Revolutionary religion. Today the God of War would be ashamed to see his park turned into a series of daisy-strewn lawns stretching from the Ecole Militaire to the Eiffel Tower and littered with lounging tourists.

TO THE EAST

INVALIDES. The gold-leaf dome of the Hôtel des Invalides shines at the center of the *7ème.* The green, tree-lined **Esplanade des Invalides** runs from the *hôtel* to the **Pont Alexandre III,** a bridge with gilded lampposts from which you can catch a great view of the Invalides and the Seine. The **Musée de l'Armée, Musée des Plans-Reliefs,** and **Musée de l'Ordre de la Liberation** are housed within the Invalides museum complex, as is **Napoleon's tomb,** in the **Eglise St-Louis.** Enter from either pl. des Invalides or pl. Vauban and av. de Tourville. To the left of the Tourville entrance, the **Jardin de l'Intendant** offers shady benches for rest when you've had your fill of guns and emperors. Lined with foreign cannons, the ditch used to be a moat and still makes it impossible to leave by any but the two official entrances. *(127 rue de Grenelle (main entrance) or 2 av. de Tourville. M: Invalides.)*

ASSEMBLEE NATIONALE. The Palais Bourbon's original occupants probably could not recognize their former home, east of the Esplanade. Built in 1722 for the Duchesse de Bourbon, daughter of Louis XIV, today the palace is the well guarded home of the French parliament.

Free tours (in French, with pamphlet in English) include a visit to the **Salon Delacroix** and the library (both spectacularly painted by Eugène Delacroix). The tour continues in the Assembly chamber, the **Salle des Séances,** where the Président du Conseil presides. *(33 quai d'Orsay. M: Assemblée Nationale. Tours ☎01 40 63 64 08; M and F-Sa every 20min. 8:40-11:40am and 2-5pm. Arrive early, entrance is first come, first serve.)*

EIGHTH ARRONDISSEMENT

The showy elegance here has a tendency to make tourists feel schlumpy; just remember that the *8ème* has a historical inferiority complex of its own. Faubourg St-Honoré was once an extension of the Tuileries, home of *nouveau riche* wannabes, while the residential Faubourg St-Germain on the left bank was the stomping ground of true blue bloods. The neighborhood didn't really take off until the turn of the 19th century. While the main attraction today is the Champs-Elysées, the Parc Monceau is an elegant place to relax, and the streets around Gare St-Lazare provide upbeat, affordable shopping.

ALONG THE CHAMPS-ELYSEES

ARC DE TRIOMPHE. It is hard to believe that the Arc de Triomphe, looming gloriously above the Champs-Elysées at pl. Charles de Gaulle-Etoile, was first designed as a huge, bejeweled elephant. Oh, those crazy Empire architects. The world's largest triumphal arch crowns a flattened hill between the Louvre and pont de Neuilly—an ideal vantage point. Fortunately for France, construction of this international symbol of her military prowess was not started until 1805, when Napoleon envisioned a monument somewhat more appropriate for welcoming troops home. There was no consensus on what symbolic figures could cap the monument, and so it has retained its simple unfinished form.

Since Napoleon, the horseshoe-shaped colossus has been a magnet for various triumphal armies. The victorious Prussians marched through in 1871, inspiring the mortified Parisians to purify the ground with fire. On July 14, 1919, however, the Arc provided the backdrop for an Allied celebration parade headed by Maréchal Foch. His memory is now honored by the boulevard that bears his name and stretches out from the Arc into the 16*ème*. French sanctification of the Arc was frustrated once more during WWII; Frenchmen were reduced to tears as the Nazis goose-stepped through their beloved arch. After the torturous years of German occupation, a sympathetic Allied army made sure a French general would be the first to drive under the famous edifice.

The Tomb of the Unknown Soldier has been under the Arc since November 11, 1920. It bears the inscription, "Here lies a French soldier who died for his country, 1914-1918," but represents the 1,500,000 men who died during WWI. The eternal flame is rekindled every evening at 6:30pm, when veterans lay wreaths decorated with blue, white, and red. Inside the Arc, climb 205 steps up a winding staircase to the mezzanine between the Arc's two supports, and then 29 more to the museum. Or, tackle the lines at the elevator for a lift. Handicapped visitors should be aware that the elevator is often out of service; call in advance to check. *(M: Charles-de-Gaulle-Etoile. ☎ 01 55 37 73 77. Open Apr.-Sept. daily 9:30am-11pm; Oct.-Mar. 10am-10:30pm. 42F/€6.41, ages 12-25 26F/€3.97, under 12 free. Buy your ticket in the pedestrian underpasses before going up to the ground level. AmEx/MC/V for charges over 50F/€7.67.)*

AVENUE DES CHAMPS-ELYSEES. The av. des Champs-Elysées is the most famous of the 12 symmetrical avenues radiating from the huge rotary of pl. Charles de Gaulle-Etoile. Although it's been fashionable since the 17th century, it was still pretty unkempt until the early 19th century, when the city built sidewalks and installed gas lighting. Elegant houses, restaurants, and less subdued bars and panoramas sprung up and the *beau monde* was guaranteed to see and be seen. Balls, café-concerts, restaurants, and circuses drew enormous crowds. Today the avenue is an intriguing mixture of old and new, inviting tourists to tramp through the mini-mall, while managing to preserve pockets of greenery and timeless glamor. Six avenues radiate from the Rond Point des Champs-Elysées. Av. Montaigne runs southwest and shelters Paris' finest houses of haute couture.

GRAND AND PETIT PALAIS. At the foot of the Champs-Elysées, the Grand and Petit Palais face one another on av. Winston Churchill. Built for the 1900 World's Fair, they were widely received as a dazzling combination of "banking and dreaming," exemplifying the ornate Art Nouveau architecture. While the Petit Palais houses an eclectic mixture of artwork belonging to the city, its big brother has been turned into a space for temporary exhibitions on architecture, painting, sculpture, French history, and recently devoted its space to an overview of Paris at the millennium. The Grand Palais also houses the **Palais de la Découverte.** Most beautiful at night, the glass dome of the Grand Palais glows greenly from within, and its statues are backlit.

AROUND PLACE DE LA CONCORDE

Paris' largest and most infamous public square forms the eastern terminus of the Champs-Elysées. With your back to av. Gabriel, the Tuileries Gardens are to your left; across the river lie the gold-domed Invalides and the columns of the Assemblée Nationale. Behind you stands the Madeleine. Constructed between 1757 and 1777 to provide a home for a monument to Louis XV, it later became pl. de la Révolution, the site of the guillotine that severed 1343 necks from their blue-blooded bodies. On Sunday, January 21, 1793, Louis XVI was beheaded by guillotine on a site near where the Brest statue now stands. The celebrated heads of Marie-Antoinette, Lavoisier, Danton, Robespierre, and others rolled into baskets here and were held up to the cheering crowds that packed the pavement. After the Reign of Terror, the square was optimistically renamed **pl. de la Concorde** (place of Harmony), though the noise pollution of the cars zooming through this intersection today hardly makes for a harmonious visit.

In the center of the *place* is the monumental **Obélisque de Luxor.** Erected in 1836, Paris' oldest monument dates back to the 13th century BC and recalls the deeds of Ramses II. At night the obelisk, fountains, and cast-iron lamps are illuminated, creating a romantic glow, somewhat eclipsed by the hordes of cars rushing by.

Flanking the Champs-Elysées at pl. de la Concorde stand replicas of Guillaume Coustou's **Chevaux de Marly,** also known as *Africans Mastering the Numidian Horses*. The original sculptures are now in the Louvre to protect them from the effects of city pollution.

THE MADELEINE. Mirrored by the Assemblée Nationale across the Seine, the Madeleine was begun in 1764 by Louis XV and modeled after a Greek temple. Construction was halted during the Revolution, but was completed in 1842. The structure stands alone amongst a medley of Parisian churches, distinguished by its four ceiling domes that light the interior, 52 exterior Corinthian columns, and a curious altarpiece. An immense sculpture of the ascension of Mary Magdalene, the church's namesake, adorns the altar. A colorful flower market thrives alongside the church facing the Assemblée Nationale. *(Pl. de la Madeleine. M: Madeleine. ☎01 44 51 69 00. Open daily 7:30am-7pm. Regular organ and chamber concerts.)*

TO THE NORTH

CHAPELLE EXPIATOIRE. Pl. Louis XVI includes the improbably large Chapelle Expiatoire, its monuments to Marie-Antoinette and Louis XVI, and a lovely park. Although Louis XVIII had his brother and sister-in-law's remains removed to St-Denis in 1815, the Revolution's Most Wanted still lie here. Marat's assassin Charlotte Corday and Louis XVI's cousin Philippe-Egalité (who voted for the king's death only to be beheaded himself) are buried on either side of the staircase. *(29 rue Pasquier, just below bd. Haussmann. M: Madeleine. ☎01 44 32 18 00. Open Th-Sa 1-5pm. 16F/€2.44.)*

PARC MONCEAU. The Parc Monceau, an expansive urban oasis guarded by gold-tipped, wrought-iron gates, borders the elegant bd. de Courcelles. An array of architectural follies—a pyramid, a covered bridge, an East Asian pagoda, Dutch windmills, and Roman ruins—make this formal garden and kids' romping ground (complete with roller rink) a Kodak commercial waiting to happen. *(M: Monceau or Courcelles. Open Apr.-Oct. daily 7am-10pm; Nov.-Mar. 7am-8pm.)*

CATHEDRALE ALEXANDRE-NEVSKI. Thanks primarily to Catherine the Great, almost all young, upper-class Russians came to Paris to seek culture. Built in 1860, the onion-domed Eglise Russe, also known as Cathédrale Alexandre-Nevski, is a Russian Eastern Orthodox church. The golden domes, spectacular from the outside, are equally beautiful on the inside. *(12 rue Daru. M: Ternes. ☎01 42 27 37 34. Open Tu, F, Su 3-5pm. Services in French and Russian Su at 10am and Sa 6-8pm.)*

NINTH ARRONDISSEMENT

THE OPERA AND SURROUNDINGS

The area around the southernmost border of the *9ème* is known simply as **l'Opéra** after the area's distinguishing landmark, the **Opéra Garnier,** which is surrounded by Haussmann's grand boulevards. Just to the north of the Opéra is the most trafficked area in the *9ème:* the city's enormous shopping malls, **Galeries Lafayette** and **Au Printemps**, which offer some of the best large-scale shopping in Paris—especially during July, when the summer sale season begins.

OPERA GARNIER. The stunning facade of the Opéra Garnier—with its stately flamboyance, newly restored multi-colored marble facade, and sculpted golden goddesses that glitter in the sun—is one of the most breathtaking sights in all of Paris. Designed by Charles Garnier under Napoleon III, the Opéra is historically perhaps most famous as home to the legend of the Phantom of the Opera. But it remains one of the city's most extravagant architectural wonders. Having recently undergone massive renovation, the brilliant facade shimmers on bright days like alabaster and gold. *(M: Opéra. ☎ 08 36 69 78 68, tour info ☎ 01 40 01 22 63.* ***Tours*** *are available in several languages. Concert hall and museum open Sept.-mid July daily 10am-5pm, last entry 4:30pm; mid-July-end of Aug. 10am-6pm. 30F/€4.58; ages 10-16, students, or over 60 20F/€3.05. English tours daily at noon in the summer; 60F/€9.15; students, ages 10-16, or over 60 45F/€6.86; under 10 25F/€3.81.)*

NORTH OF THE OPERA

EGLISE NOTRE-DAME-DE-LORETTE. The Eglise Notre Dame de Lorette was built in 1836 to "the glory of the Virgin Mary." This Neoclassical church is filled with statues of saints and frescoes of scenes from the life of Mary. **Rue Notre Dame de Lorette,** however, is a whole other barrel of fish. Somewhat less saintly than its namesake, this street was the debauched hangout of Emile Zola's Nana and a thoroughfare of serious ill-repute in the late 1960s. Lorette even came to be a term used to refer to the quarter's young prostitutes. *(M: Notre-Dame-de-Lorette. Leave the métro and the church will be in front of you on pl. Kossuth.)*

PIGALLE. Farther north, at the border of the *18ème*, is the infamous area named Pigalle, the extravagant un-chastity belt of Paris. Stretching along the trash-covered bd. de Clichy from pl. Pigalle to pl. Blanche is a salacious, voracious, and generally pretty naughty neighborhood. The home of famous cabarets-*cum*-nightclubs (Folies Bergère, Moulin Rouge, Folies Pigalle) and well-endowed newcomers with names like "Le Coq Hardy" and "Dirty Dick," this dirty, neon neighborhood is raunchy enough to make even Jacques Chirac blush. Although Pigalle is supposedly undergoing a slow gentrification, the area has not yet shaken its sleazy reputation. The areas to the north of bd. Clichy and south of pl. Blanche are comparatively calmer, but visitors should **exercise caution at all times.** *(M: Pigalle.)*

TENTH ARRONDISSEMENT

Far from most tourist itineraries, the *10ème's* working-class neighborhoods offer a few hidden sights. The tree-lined **Canal St-Martin** is a refreshing break from the city, and the **Faubourg St-Denis** features North and West African markets, restaurants, and shops. Europe's train lines converge at the **Gare de l'Est** and the **Gare du Nord,** and the *3ème*, *10ème*, and *11ème* converge at pl. de la République. One word of caution: bd. Magenta and bd. Faubourg tend to be unsafe at night.

ELEVENTH ARRONDISSEMENT

The *11ème* is most famous for hosting the Revolutionary kick-off at the Bastille prison on July 14, 1789 (see **History,** p. 8). It was most recently reincarnated as a seedy working-class area, but the 1989 opening of the glassy Opéra Bastille on the bicentennial of the Revolution has breathed new life into the *11ème*. In the early 1990s, the neighborhood near the Opéra Bastille was touted as the city's latest Bohemia. But the Bastille's 15 minutes are over. In the scramble to find the next new "in" place, crowds have surged north toward **rues Oberkampf** and **Ménilmontant,** which burst with noise, restaurants, bars, and diversity—revel in their off-beat cafés, Art Nouveau galleries, and impressive international dining options.

THE BASTILLE PRISON. Originally commissioned by Charles V to safeguard the eastern entrance to Paris, and made into a state prison by Louis XIII, the Bastille was hardly the hell-hole that the Revolutionaries who tore it down imagined it to be. Titled inmates were allowed to furnish their suites, have fresh linen, bring their own servants, and receive guests.

Having sacked the Invalides for weapons, Revolutionary militants stormed the Bastille for munitions. Surrounded by an armed rabble, too short on food to entertain a siege, and unsure of the loyalty of the Swiss mercenaries who defended the prison, the Bastille's governor surrendered. Demolition of the prison began the day after its capture and concluded in October 1792. Despite the gruesome details, the storming of the Bastille has come to symbolize the triumph of liberty over despotism. Its first anniversary was the cause for great celebration in Revolutionary Paris. Since the late 19th century, July 14 has been the official state holiday of the French Republic and is usually a time of glorious firework displays and consumption of copious amounts of alcohol. *(M: Bastille.)*

THE JULY COLUMN. Yes, the column topped by the conspicuous gold cupid doing an arabesque at the center of pl. de la Bastille is in fact a statue of Liberty. In 1831, King Louis-Philippe laid the cornerstone for the July Column to commemorate Republicans who died in the Revolutions of 1789 and 1830. Emblazoned names commemorate the 504 martyrs of 1830 buried inside along with two mummified Egyptian pharaohs. *(M: Bastille.)*

TWELFTH ARRONDISSEMENT

OPERA BASTILLE. Once known as the "Red Belt" around Paris because of its participation in both the 1830 and 1848 Revolutions, the 12*ème* also saw its residents make up large sectors of the Parisian Resistance during WWII. But the only rebellions staged these days are over the Opéra Bastille, one of Mitterrand's *grands projets*. Presiding over the **pl. de la Bastille** and designed by Carlos Ott, a Canadian architect, the Opéra opened in 1989 to protests over its unattractive design. On the tour (expensive but interesting and extremely impressive) you'll see a different side of the largest theater in the world. Although the immense auditorium seats 2703 people, the rest of the building constitutes 95% of the theater's surface area, housing other exact replicas of the stage for rehearsal purposes and the workshops for both the Bastille and Garnier operas. *(130 rue de Lyon. Look for the words "Billetterie" on the building. M: Bastille. ☎01 40 01 19 70; www.opera-de-paris.fr. 1hr. tour almost every day, usually at 1 or 5pm; call ahead (tours in French, but groups can arrange for English). 60F/€9.15; students, under 25, and over 60 45F/€6.86.)*

VIADUC DES ARTS AND PROMENADE PLANTEE. The *ateliers* in the **Viaduc des Arts** house artisans who make everything from haute couture fabric to hand-painted porcelain, to space-age furniture. Restorers of all types fill the arches of the old railway viaduct (reopened as gallery space in 1995), and they can make your oil painting, 12th-century book, grandmother's linen, architectural model, or childhood dollhouse as good as new. Above the viaduct runs the **Promenade Plantée,** Paris' longest and skinniest park, perfect for a late-afternoon stroll. *(9-129 av. Daumesnil. M: Bastille. The viaduct extends from rue de Lyon to rue de Charenton. Entrances to the Promenade are at Ledru Rollin, Hector Malot, and bd. Diderot. Open M-F 8am, Sa-Su 9am; closing hours vary, around 5:30pm in winter and 9:30pm in summer.)*

FOURTEENTH ARRONDISSEMENT

The first of many generations of immigrants to make the 14*ème* home were Bretons who settled in the neighborhood in the 19th century. Breton crêperies, handicraft shops, and cultural associations line **rue du Montparnasse.**

Like Montmartre and the *Quartier Latin*, the 14*ème* has long been a haven for 20th-century artists and writers like Man Ray, Modigliani, and Henry Miller. While gentrification has forced struggling artists out of those *quartiers*, the 14*ème's* affordability and café culture still attract young artists and students, who debate at the **Cité Universitaire.** There is no single street that best characterizes the area, but restaurants (both cheap and Lost Generation *chic*), a few remaining galleries, cafés, and the **Montparnasse cemetery** make the 14*ème* worth a visit.

THE CATACOMBS. The **Catacombs,** a series of tunnels 20m below ground and 1.7km in length, were originally excavated to provide stone for building the city. By the 1770s, much of the Left Bank was in danger of caving in and digging promptly stopped. The former quarry was then used as a mass grave to relieve Paris' noisome and overcrowded cemeteries. During WWII, the Empire of Death was full of life when the Resistance set up headquarters among the departed. The catacombs are like an underground city, with street names on walls lined with femurs and craniums. The catacombs are not recommended for the faint of heart or leg; there are 85 steep steps to climb on the way out. Beware the low ceilings, and bring a sweater. *(1 pl. Denfert-Rochereau. M: Denfert-Rochereau. From the métro, take exit pl. Denfert-Rochereau, cross av. du Général Leclerc; the entrance is the dark green structure straight ahead. ☎01 43 22 47 63. Open Tu-F 2-4pm, Sa-Su 9-11am and 2-4pm. 33F/€5.03, under 25 22F/€3.35, under 7 free. Tour lasts 45min.)*

SIXTEENTH ARRONDISSEMENT

When Notre Dame was under construction, this now elegant suburb was little more than a couple of tiny villages in the woods. For the next few centuries, kings and nobles chased deer and boar through its forests. Finally, in 1859, at the height of Haussmannization, the area was transformed. The wealthy villages of Auteuil, Passy, and Chaillot banded together and joined Paris, forming what is now the 16*ème*. The area's original aristocratic families continue to hold their ground, making the 16*ème* a stronghold of upper-crust conservative politics, fashion, and culture. Over half of Paris' museums can be found here, and nearly every block is the site of a prime Art Nouveau or Art Deco architectural masterpiece.

TROCADERO AND SURROUNDINGS

The pl. d'Iéna positions you next to the rotunda of the **Conseil Economique** and in front of a sweep of popular museums, including the round facade of the **Musée Guimet,** the **Musée de la Mode et du Costume** (see **Museums,** p. 140), and the **Palais de Tokyo,** just down the street. Henri Bouchard's impressive facade for the **Eglise St-Pierre de Chaillot** (1937), is between rue de Chaillot and av. Pierre I de Serbie, five minutes away. *(M: Iéna. Open M-Sa 9:30am-12:30pm and 3-7pm, Su 9:30am-12:30pm.)*

PLACE DU TROCADERO. In the 1820s, the Duc d'Angoulême built a memorial to his Spanish victory at Trocadéro—hence the present name. Jacques Carlu's more modern design for the 1937 World Exposition (which beat out Le Corbusier's plan) for the **Palais de Chaillot** features two white stone wings cradling an austere, Art Deco courtyard that extends from the *place* over spectacular cannon-shaped fountains. Surveyed by the 7.5m tall bronze *Apollo* by Henri Bouchard and eight other figures, the terrace attracts tourists, vendors, skateboarders, and in-line skaters and offers brilliant panoramic **views** of the Eiffel Tower and Champs de Mars, particularly at night (bring your camera). Be aware of pickpockets and traffic as you gaze upward. As parts of the Jardins du Trocadéro are not well-lit at night, be careful, and don't go alone.

EIGHTEENTH ARRONDISSEMENT

Built on a steep hill high above the rest of Paris, **Montmartre** is one of the few Parisian neighborhoods Baron Haussmann left intact when he redesigned the city and its environs. A rural area outside the city limits until the 20th century, its picturesque beauty and low rents attracted bohemians like Toulouse-Lautrec and Erik Satie as well as performers and impresarios like Aristide Bruant. Toulouse-Lautrec, in particular, immortalized Montmartre with his paintings of life in disreputable nightspots like the Bal du Moulin Rouge (see below). Filled with bohemian cabarets like "Le Chat Noir," satirical journals, and proto-Dada artist groups like *Les Incohérents* and *Les Hydropathes*, the whole *butte* became the Parisian center of free-love, fun, and *fumisme* (the satiric jabbing of social and political norms). A generation later, just before WWI, the Lapin Agile cabaret welcomed Picasso, Modigliani, Utrillo, and Apollinaire. Nowadays Montmartre is a mix of upscale bohemia above rue des Abbesses and sleaze along bd. de Clichy—not to mention the legions of panting tourists near Sacré Coeur, the front of which provides a dramatic panorama of the city. *(Every Su at 2:30pm May-Oct. 15 the city organizes historic 2hr. walking tours in French, which allow a unique view into some of the less-touristed spots. Meet at funicular station; 38F/€5.80.)*

MOUNTING MONTMARTRE

One does not merely visit Montmartre; one climbs it. The standard approach is from the south, via M: Anvers or M: Abbesses, although other directions provide interesting, less-crowded climbs. For a less difficult ascent, use the glass-covered **funicular** from the base of rue Tardieu (from M: Anvers, walk up rue Steinkerque and take a left on rue Tardieu). *(Funicular open daily 6am-12:30am. 8.50F/€1.30.)*

BASILIQUE DU SACRE-COEUR. The Basilica of the Sacred Heart is like an exotic head-dress floating above Paris. In 1873, the Assemblée Nationale selected the birthplace of the Commune as the location for Sacré-Coeur, "in witness of repentance and as a symbol of hope," although politician Eugène Spuller called it "a monument to civil war." The Catholic establishment hoped that the Sacré-Coeur would "expiate the sins" of France after the bloody civil war in which thousands of communards (leftists who declared a new populist government, known as the Commune of Paris; see p. 135) were massacred by government troops. After a massive fund-raising effort, the basilica was completed in 1914 and consecrated in 1919. Its hybrid style of onion domes, arches, and white color set it apart from the smoky grunge of most Parisian buildings. Most striking inside the basilica are the mosaics, especially the depiction of Christ on the ceiling and the mural of the Passion at the back of the altar. The narrow climb up the dome offers the highest vantage point in Paris and a view that stretches as far as 50km on clear days. Farther down, the **crypt** contains a relic of what many believe to be a piece of the sacred heart of Christ. While the views up the grassy slopes to the Basilica are among the most beautiful in Paris, the streets beneath the winding pedestrian pathways leading up to the Basilica are hideously over-touristed; to circumvent the onslaught, walk up rue des Trois Frères instead. *(35 rue du Chevalier de la Barre. M: Anvers, Abbesses, or Château-Rouge. ☎01 42 51 17 02. Open daily 7am-11pm. Free. Dome and crypt open daily 9am-6pm. Admission to each 15F/€2.29, students 8F/€1.22.)*

DOWNHILL

CIMETIERE MONTMARTRE. Parallel to rue Lepic, rue Caulaincourt leads downhill to the secluded Cimetière Montmartre, where writers Alexandre Dumas and Stendhal, painter Edgar Degas, physicists André Ampère and Léon Foucault, composer Hector Berlioz, and filmmaker François Truffaut are buried. In 1871, this cemetery became the site of huge mass graves after the siege of the Commune. *(20 av. Rachel. M: Pl. de Clichy or Blanche. ☎01 43 87 64 24. Open daily 8am-5:30pm.)*

BAL DU MOULIN ROUGE. Along the bd. de Clichy and bd. de Rochechouart, you'll find many of the cabarets and nightclubs that were the definitive hangouts of the Belle Epoque, including the infamous cabaret Bal du Moulin Rouge immortalized by the paintings of Toulouse-Lautrec and the music of Offenbach. At the turn of the century, Paris' bourgeoisie came to the Moulin Rouge to play at being bohemian. After WWI, Parisian bohemians relocated to the Left Bank and the area around pl. Pigalle became a world-renowned seedy red-light district (see **Sights,** p. 131). Today, the crowd consists of tourists out for an evening of sequins, tassels, and skin. The revues are still risqué, but the admission is prohibitively expensive. *(M: Blanche. Directly across from the métro. ☎01 53 09 82 82. Shows at 7, 9, and 11pm.)*

NINETEENTH ARRONDISSEMENT

Like Paris' other periphery arrondissements, the 19*ème* is predominantly working-class. But near Parc des Buttes-Chaumont, wealthy Parisians pay handsomely for houses with views of one of Paris' finer parks. The 19*ème* is also home to a large part of Paris' Asian community and full of wonderful, inexpensive restaurants. At night, avoid rue David d'Angiers, bd. Indochine, and av. Corentin Cariou.

PARC DE LA VILLETTE. Cut in the middle by the **Canal de l'Ourcq** and the **Canal St-Denis,** the **Parc de la Villette** separates the Cité des Sciences from the Cité de la Musique. Rejecting the 19th-century notion of the park as natural oasis, Bernard Tschumi designed a 20th-century urban park which feels like a step into the future. Constructed in 1867 as the La Villette beef building, the steel-and-glass **Grande Halle** (☎01 40 03 75 03) features frequent plays, concerts, temporary exhibitions, and films. Unifying the park is a set of red cubical structures that form a grid of squares, known as **Folies.** The **Promenade des Jardins** links several thematic gardens, such as the **Mirror Garden,** which uses an array of mirrors to create optical illusions, the **Garden of Childhood Fears,** which winds through a wooded grove resonant with spooky sounds, and the roller coaster **Dragon Garden.** The promenade ends at Jardin des Dunes and the Jardins des Vents, a playground for kids 12 and under (with parental accompaniment, lest the fun get out of control). Join a gaggle of moppets leaping on trampolines and running on rolling hills in what may be the highlight of a child's trip to Paris. *(Promenade open 24hr. Free.)*

PARC DES BUTTES-CHAUMONT. To the south, Parc des Buttes-Chaumont is a mix of man-made topography and transplanted vegetation. Nostalgic for London's Hyde Park, where he spent much of his time in exile, Napoleon III built Parc des Buttes-Chaumont. Before the construction of the Buttes-Chaumont, the *quartier* was (since the 13th century) host to a *gibbet* (an iron cage filled with the rotting corpses of criminals), a dumping-ground for dead horses, a breeding-ground for worms, and a gypsum quarry (the source of "plaster of Paris"). Making a park out of this mess took four years and 1000 workers. Designer Adolphe Alphand had all of the soil replaced and the quarried remains built up with new rock to create enormous fake cliffs surrounding a lake. Today's visitors walk the winding paths surrounded by lush greenery, dynamic hills, and enjoy a great view of the *quartier* from the cave-filled cliffs topped with a Roman temple. *(M: Buttes-Chaumont. Open daily 7am-11pm. Gates close 15min. before.)*

TWENTIETH ARRONDISSEMENT

As Haussmannization expelled many of Paris' workers from the central city, thousands migrated east to **Belleville** (the northern part of the 20*ème*), **Ménilmontant** (the southern), and **Charonne** (the southeastern). By the late Second Republic, the 20*ème* had come to be known as a "red" *arrondissement*, characterized as both proletarian and radical. Some of the heaviest fighting during the suppression of the Commune took place in these streets, where the *communards* made desperate last stands on their home turf. Caught between the Versaillais troops to the west and the Prussian lines outside the city walls, the Commune fortified the Parc des Buttes-Chaumont and the **Cimetière du Père Lachaise** but soon ran out of ammunition. On May 28, 1871, the *communards* abandoned their last barricade and surrendered. After the Commune, the *20ème* kept on as the fairly isolated home of those workers who survived the retributive massacres following the government's takeover. Today the *arrondissement* has a similar feel, with busy residential areas and markets that cater not to visitors but to locals. The area is also home to sizable Greek, North African, Russian, and Asian communities.

PERE LACHAISE CEMETERY. With its winding paths and elaborate sarcophagi, Cimetière du Père Lachaise has become the final resting place of French and foreign giants. Balzac, Colette, David, Delacroix, La Fontaine, Haussmann, Molière, and Proust are buried here, as are Chopin, Jim Morrison, Gertrude Stein, and Oscar Wilde. With so many tourists, however, they're hardly resting in peace.

The cemetery is a bustling 19th-century neighborhood-of-the-dead laid out in streets. Many of the tombs in this landscaped grove strive to remind visitors of the dead's many worldly accomplishments: the tomb of French Romantic painter **Géricault** wears a reproduction of his *Raft of the Medusa;* on **Chopin's** tomb sits his muse Calliope. **Oscar Wilde's** grave is marked by a larger-than-life striking Egyptian figure. **Haussmann,** the man of the boulevards, wanted to destroy the cemetery as part of his urban-renewal project, but obviously relented; he now occupies a mausoleum in Père Lachaise. Remembered by plaques here are dancer **Isadora Duncan,** author **Richard Wright,** opera diva **Maria Callas,** and artist **Max Ernst.** The most visited grave is that of **Jim Morrison,** the former lead singer of The Doors. His graffiti-covered bust was removed from the tomb, leaving his fans to fill the rest of the cemetery with their messages. In summer, dozens of young people bring flowers, joints, beer, poetry, and Doors paraphernalia to his tomb; the sandbox in front of the stone is now the sanctioned site for the creative expression of such pensive mourners. At least one guard polices the spot at all times.

Perhaps the most moving sites in Père Lachaise are those that mark the deaths of collective groups. The **Mur des Fédérés** (Wall of the Federals) has become a site of pilgrimage for left-wing sympathizers. In May 1871, a group of *communards* murdered the Archbishop of Paris, who had been taken hostage at the beginning of the Commune. They dragged his mutilated corpse to their stronghold in Père Lachaise and tossed it in a ditch. Four days later, the victorious Versaillais found the body. In retaliation, they lined up 147 Fédérés against the eastern wall of the cemetery, shot them, and buried them on the spot. Near the wall, a number of moving monuments commemorate the Résistance fighters of WWII as well as Nazi concentration camp victims. *(16 rue du Repos. M: Père Lachaise. ☎01 55 25 82 10. Open Mar.-Oct. M-F 8am-6pm, Sa 8:30am-6pm, Su and holidays 9am-6pm; Nov.-Feb. M-F 8am-5:30pm, Sa 8:30am-5:30pm, Su and holidays 9am-5:30pm. Free. Free maps supposedly available at guard booths by main entrances, but they're usually out; it may be worth the 10F/€1.53 or so to buy a detailed map from a nearby tabac before entering. 2hr. tour in English June-Sept. Sa 3pm; in French Sa at 2:30pm, occasionally Tu at 2:30pm and Su at 3pm as well as numerous "theme" tours. 38F/€5.80, students 26F/€3.97. Tours meet at bd. de Ménilmontant entrance.)*

MUSEUMS

*The **Carte Musées et Monuments** offers admission to 70 museums in the Paris area. This card may save you money and will enable you to sail past all of the frustrated tourists standing in line. It's sold at major museums and in almost all métro stations. A pass for 1 day is 85F/€12.96; for 3 consecutive days 170F/€25.92; for 5 consecutive days 255F/€38.88. For more info, call **Association InterMusées,** 4 rue Brantôme, 3ème (☎01 44 61 96 60; www.intermusees.com).*

MUSEE DU LOUVRE. Construction of the Louvre began in 1190, and it still isn't finished. King Philippe-Auguste built the original structure as a fortress connected to a city wall to defend Paris while he was away on a crusade. In the 14th century, Charles V built a second city wall enclosing the first beyond what is now the Jardin des Tuileries (see **Sights,** p. 118), thus stripping the Louvre of its defensive utility. Not one to let a good castle go to waste, Charles converted the fortress into a residential château. In 1528, François Ier returned to the Louvre in an attempt to flatter the Parisian bourgeoisie, razing Charles' palace and commissioning Pierre Lescot to build a new royal palace in the open style of the Renaissance. The old foundations are displayed in an underground exhibit, **Medieval Louvre,** on the ground floor of the Sully wing. Henry II's widow, Catherine de Medici, had the Tuileries Palace built looking onto an Italian-style garden (it was later burned by the *communards* in 1871). Henri IV completed the Tuileries and embarked on what he called the Grand Design—a project to link the Louvre and the Tuileries with the two large wings you see today in a "royal city." He only built a fraction of the project before his death in 1610. Louis XIV moved back to Paris and into the Louvre in 1650, hiring a trio of architects—Le Vau, Le Brun, and Perrault—to transform it into the grandest palace in Europe, but he abandoned it in favor of Versailles.

In 1725, after years of relative abandonment, the Academy of Painting inaugurated annual salons in the halls to show the work of its members. In 1793, the exhibit was made permanent, creating the Musée du Louvre. Napoleon filled the Louvre with plundered art, most of which had to be returned. He happily continued Henri IV's Grand Design, extending the Louvre's two wings to the Tuileries palace and remodeling the facades of the older buildings. Mitterrand's *Grands Projets* campaign transformed the Louvre into an accessible, well-organized museum. Architect I.M. Pei came up with the idea of moving the museum's entrance to the center of the Cour Napoléon, on an underground level surmounted by his stunning and controversial **glass pyramid.**

Renaissance works include Leonardo da Vinci's *Mona Lisa (La Joconde)* and canvases by Raphael and Titian, while among the French paintings are David's *Oath of the Horatii*, Ingres' sensual *Odalisque*, Géricault's gruesome *Raft of the Medusa*, and Delacroix's patriotic *Liberty Leading the People.* Sculptures include Michelangelo's *Slaves*, as well as an incredible collection of antiquities; be sure to see the *Venus de Milo* and the *Winged Victory of Samothrace.* The underground complex beneath the Pyramid also houses **temporary exhibitions.** Visitors can either enter through the pyramid or directly from the métro into the new Carrousel du Louvre mall—follow the signs; if you have a *Carte Musée et Monuments*, you can enter directly from the Richelieu entrance, in the passage connecting the Cour Napoléon to the rue de Rivoli. Otherwise, you can buy full-price tickets from machines underneath the pyramid; reduced-rate tickets must be bought from ticket offices. The Louvre is less crowded on weekday afternoons and on Monday and Wednesday evenings, when it stays open until 9:45pm. The museum is enormous; you'll only be able to cover a fraction of it in any one visit. Pick up an updated **map** at the info desk below the pyramid, or take an English tour. *(M: Palais-Royal/Musée du Louvre. ☎01 40 20 51 51. Open M and W 9am-9:45pm, Th-Su 9am-6pm. Last entry 45min. before closing, but people are asked to leave 15-30min. before closing. 46F/€7.01 M and W-Sa 9am-3pm; 30F/€4.57 M and W-Sa 3pm-close and Su, under 18 and first Su of the month free. Temporary exhibits in the Cour Napoléon open at 9am. Sign up at the info desk for English tours (M and W-Sa at 11am, 2, 3:45pm 17F/€2.59).*

CENTRE POMPIDOU. Often called the Beaubourg, the **Centre National d'Art et de Culture Georges Pompidou** has inspired architectural controversy ever since its inauguration in 1977, as a cultural center for music, cinema, books, and the graphic arts. Richard Rogers and Renzo Piano's building-turned-inside-out bares its circulatory system to all. Piping and ventilation ducts in various colors run up, down, and sideways along the outside (blue for air, green for water, yellow for electricity, red for heating). It attracts more visitors per year than any other museum or monument in France—eight million annually compared to the Louvre's three million. The **Musée National d'Art Moderne,** the Pompidou's main attraction, houses a rich selection of 20th-century art, from the Fauvists and Cubists to Pop and Conceptual Art. *(Rue Beaubourg, 4ème. M: Rambuteau or Hôtel de Ville; RER: Châtelet-Les-Halles. ☎01 44 78 12 33, wheelchair info ☎01 44 78 49 54. Museum open W-M 11am-9pm. Permanent collection 30F/€4.58, students and over 60 20F/€3.05, under 13 free, 1st Su of month free. Permanent collection, current exposition, and the Atelier Brancusi: 60F/€9.15, students and seniors 50F/€7.63. Audio guides 30F/€4.58.)*

PARIS

MUSEE D'ORSAY. If only the old cronies who turned the Impressionists away from the Louvre could see the Musée d'Orsay today! Hundreds come daily to see these famous rejects. Paintings, sculpture, decorative arts, architecture, photography, and cinema are presented in this former railway station, with works spanning the period from 1848 until WWI. An escalator at the far end of the building ascends directly to the Impressionist level. If it's your first visit, start from the right-hand side of the first floor as you enter, and follow the signs—it's organized very well.

The order in which to visit the museum is (counterintuitively) the ground floor, the top floor, and then the mezzanine. This is clearly indicated both by signs and maps. The central atrium is dedicated to **sculpture** and highlights the likes of Jean-Baptiste Carpeaux. Galleries around the atrium display 19th-century works of the **Neoclassical, Romantic, Barbizon,** and **Realist** schools; important canvases include Manet's *Olympia*, Ingres' *La Source*, Delacroix's *La Chasse aux Lions*, and Courbet's *Un Enterrement à Ornans*. The top floor is dedicated to the **Impressionists,** with important works by virtually all of the school of light's movers and shakers; famous works include Monet's *Gare St-Lazare* and Manet's *Déjeuner sur l'Herbe*. The **Post-Impressionist** collection includes van Gogh's *Portrait of the Artist* (1889) and still lifes and landscapes by Cézanne. The small mezzanine, meanwhile, is dedicated to **Rodin,** and is dominated by his huge *La Porte de l'Enfer*. The museum is least crowded on Sunday mornings and Thursday evenings; avoid Tuesdays, when the Louvre is closed. *(62 rue de Lille. 7ème. M: Solférino; RER: Musée d'Orsay. ☎01 40 49 48 48. Open June 20-Sept. 20 Tu-W and F-Su 9am-6pm, Th 9am-9:30pm; Sept. 21-June 19 Tu-W and F-Su 10am-5:45pm, Th 10am-9:45pm. Last tickets 45min. before closing. 45F/€6.86, ages 18-25 and Su 33F/€5.03, under 18 free. Tours in English Tu-Sa 11:30am and 2:30pm, 90min., 36F/€5.49. MC/V.)*

MUSEE RODIN. The elegant 18th-century **Hôtel Biron,** where Auguste Rodin lived and worked at the end of his life. He was among the country's most controversial artists, classified by many as Impressionism's sculptor. Today, almost all acknowledge him as the father of modern sculpture. This is one of Paris' best museums, housing many of Rodin's better known sculptures *(La Main de Dieu* and *Le Baiser)*. Many of the sculptures rest on beautiful antiques that are labeled for their own merits, and the walls are adorned with paintings and photographs by artists like Renoir, Van Gogh, Meunier, and Steichen. In addition, the museum has several works by **Camille Claudel,** Rodin's muse, collaborator, and lover. The *hôtel*'s expansive garden displays Rodin's work amongst rose trees and fountains, including the collection's star: *Le Penseur (The Thinker)*. On the other side of the garden stands one version of Rodin's largest and most intricate sculpture, the unfinished *La Porte de l'Enfer* (*The Gates of Hell*, 1880-1917). *(77 rue de Varenne, 7ème. M: Varenne. ☎01 44 18 61 10. Open Apr.-Sept. Tu-Su 9:30am-5:45pm; Oct.-Mar. 9:30am-4:45pm. 28F/€4.27; seniors, ages 18-25, and all on Su 18F/€2.75. Park open Apr.-Sept. Tu-Su 9:30am-6:45pm; Oct.-Mar. 9:30am-5pm. 5F/€0.76. Audio tour 25F/€3.81. MC/V.)*

MUSEE DE CLUNY. The **Musée National du Moyen Age** is one of the world's finest collections of medieval art, jewelry, sculpture, and tapestries. In the 15th century, this *hôtel* was the home of the monastic Order of Cluny, led by the powerful Amboise family. In 1843, the state converted the *hôtel* into the medieval museum; excavations after WWII unearthed Roman baths below. The museum's collection includes art from Paris' most important medieval structures: Ste-Chapelle, Notre Dame, and St-Denis. The museum's unequivocal star is the exquisite series of allegorical tapestries, *La Dame et la Licorne (The Lady and the Unicorn)*. *(6 pl. Paul Painlevé, 5ème. M: Cluny-Sorbonne. ☎01 53 73 78 00. Open W-M 9:15am-5:45pm. 36F/€5.49; students, under 25, over 60, and Su 26F/€3.96; under 18 free. Tours in English Sa-Su 3:45pm. 36F/€5.49, under 18 25F/€3.81. Concerts ☎01 53 73 78 16. F 12:30pm, Sa 5pm, and summer evenings. 66F/€10.06, students and seniors 56F/€8.54, under 18 20F/€3.05.)*

CITE DES SCIENCES ET DE L'INDUSTRIE. Dedicated to bringing science to young people, the **Explora science museum** is La Villette's star attraction. The architecture of the buildings rocks on its own, but the exhibits can only be described as absolutely fabulous; kids will love them. The museum also features a **planetarium,** a **3-D cinema,** and a modest **aquarium.** The Explora's Cité des Enfants offers one set of programs for kids ages 3-5 and another for ages 5-12. Both require adult accompaniment. (*M: Porte de la Villette. ☎01 40 05 70 00 in French. Museum open M-Sa 10am-6pm, Su 10am-7pm. A 1-day Cité-Pass covers entrance to Explora, the planetarium, and 3-D cinema; 50F/€7.62, under 7 free. Cité des Enfants programs about every 2hr. Tu-Su; 1½hr. long; 25F/€3.81.)*

CITE DE LA MUSIQUE. At the opposite end of La Villette from the Cité des Sciences is the Cité de la Musique. Designed by Franck Hammoutène and completed in 1990, the complex of buildings is visually stunning, full of curves and glass ceilings. The highlight is the **Musée de la Musique,** a collection of paintings, sculptures, and 900 instruments. Visitors don a pair of headphones that tune in to musical excerpts and explanations of each instrument. The Cité de la Musique's two performance spaces—the enormous 1200-seat **Salle des Concerts** and the 230-seat **Amphithéâtre**—host an eclectic range of shows and concerts year-round. The Cité de la Musique also contains a **music information center** and the **Médiathèque Pédagogique.** (*M: Porte de Pantin. ☎01 44 84 44 84. Open Tu-Th and Sa noon-6pm, F noon-9:30pm, Su 10am-6pm; last admission 45min. before closing. 40F/€6.10, children 6-18 15F/€2.29, under 6 free; 15F/€2.29 more for temporary exhibits. Tours in French; 66F/€10, reduced 50F/€7.60, under 18 30F/€4.60. Médiathèque open Tu-Su noon-6pm. Free.)*

PARIS

GRAND AND PETIT PALAIS

Designed for the 1900 Universal Exposition, most of the building houses the Palais de la Découverte, but the *palais* also hosts temporary exhibits.

PALAIS DE LA DECOUVERTE. Kids tear around the Palais' interactive science exhibits, pressing buttons that start comets on celestial trajectories, spinning on seats to investigate angular motion, and glaring at all kinds of creepy-crawlies. The **planetarium** has four shows per day. (*In the Grand Palais, entrance on av. Franklin D. Roosevelt. ☎01 56 43 20 20, planetarium ☎01 40 74 81 73. M: FDR or Champs-Elysées-Clemenceau. Open Tu-Sa 10am-6pm, Su 9am-7pm. 37F/€5.64, students, seniors, and under 18 24F/€3.66. Planetarium 20F/€3.05. Family entrance 80F/€12.20.)*

PETIT PALAIS. Also called the Palais des Beaux-Arts de la Ville de Paris. Built for the 1900 Universal Exposition, the palais houses 17th- to 20th-century Flemish, French, and Dutch painting and sculpture, but will be **closed for renovations** until spring 2002. (*3 av. du Général Eisenhower. ☎01 44 13 17 30 or 01 44 13 17 17. M: Champs-Elysées-Clemenceau. Follow av. W. Churchill toward the river; the museum is on your right. Open Th-M 10am-8pm, W 10am-10pm; last entry 45min. before closing. Admission varies by exhibit; around 60F/€9.15, students 35F/€5.39, under 13 free.)*

OTHER MAJOR COLLECTIONS

MUSEE PICASSO. When Picasso died in 1973, his family paid the French inheritance tax in artwork. The French government put this collection on display in 1985 in the 17th-century **Hôtel Salé.** The museum leads the viewer through Pablo Picasso's early work in Spain to his Cubist and Surrealist years and his Neoclassical work in France. (*5 rue de Thorigny, 3ème. M: Chemin-Vert. ☎01 42 71 63 15. Open Apr.-Sept. W-M 9:30am-6pm; Oct.-Mar. 9:30am-5:30pm; last entrance 30min. before closing. 30F/€4.58, ages 18-25 and Su 20F/€3.05, under 18 free.)*

MUSEE D'ART MODERNE DE LA VILLE DE PARIS. Housed in the magnificent Palais de Tokyo, this museum contains one of the world's foremost collections of 20th-century art, on a small scale. Two stand out: Matisse's *La Danse Inachevée* and Dufy's fauvist epic of electricity, *La Fée Electricité.* (*11 av. du Président Wilson. M: Iéna. From Iéna, follow av. du Président Wilson. ☎01 53 67 40 00. Open Tu-F 10am-5:30pm, Sa-Su 10am-6:45pm. 30F/€4.57, students 20F/€3.05, free Su morning; special exhibits 30-45F/€4.57-6.86, students 20-35F/€3.05-5.34.)*

MUSEE CARNAVALET. Housed in Mme. de Sévigné's 16th-century hôtel particulier, this museum traces Paris' history, with exhibits on the city from prehistory and the Roman conquest to 18th-century splendor and Revolution, 19th-century Haussmannization, and Mitterrand's *grands projets*. *(23 rue de Sévigné. M: Chemin-Vert. Take rue St-Gilles as it turns into rue de Parc Royal, and turn left onto rue de Sévigné. ☎01 44 59 58 58. Open Tu-Su 10am-5:40pm; last entrance at 5:15pm. 35F/€5.34, 25F/€3.81 for temporary exhibits, the permanent exhibit is free for under 27; free for all Su 10am-1pm.)*

MUSEE GREVIN. In the lavish, mirrored, and disorienting garish halls of Paris' surreal wax museum, visitors can lose all sense of reality while peering quizzically at the lifelike figures of Madonna and Molière. Some gruesome scenarios with Black Plague victims and a pre-execution Joan of Arc are also on display. *(0 bd. Montmartre. ☎01 47 70 85 05. M: Grands Boulevards. Open Apr.-Aug. daily 1-7pm; Sept.-Mar. 1-6:30pm, last entry 6pm. 99F/€15.10; ages 6-14 60F/€9.15.)*

PARIS

MUSEE D'HISTOIRE NATURELLE. Three museums in one. The new-fangled **Grande Galerie de l'Evolution** has naturalistic stuffed animals telling the story of evolution via a Genesis-like parade. Next door, the **Musée de Minéralogie** contains some lovely jewels. The **Gallery of Comparative Anatomy and Paleontology,** at the other end of the garden, whose exterior looks like a Victorian house of horrors, is filled with a ghastly cavalcade of fibias, rib-cages, and vertebrae formed into historic and pre-historic animals. *(57 rue Cuvier, in the Jardin des Plantes. ☎01 40 79 30 00. M: Gare d'Austerlitz. Grande Galerie de l'Evolution: open W-M 10am-6pm, open Th until 10pm. 40F/€6.10, students 30F/€4.57. Musée de Minéralogie and Galeries d'Anatomie open Apr.-Oct. W-M 10am-5pm, Sa-Su 10am-6pm. Each 30F/€4.57, students 20F/€3.05.)*

MUSEE DE LA MODE ET DU COSTUME (FASHION AND CLOTHING MUSEUM). With 30,000 outfits and 70,000 accessories, the museum has no choice but to rotate temporary exhibitions showcasing fashions of the past three centuries. A fabulous place to visit to see the history of Parisian fashion, society, and *haute couture*. *(In the Palais Galleria, 10 av. Pierre I-de-Serbie. M: Iéna. ☎01 47 20 85 23. Open Tu-Su 10am-6pm; last entry 5:30pm. 45F/€6.86, students and seniors 35F/€5.34.)*

MUSEE DE L'ORANGERIE. The museum is home to works by Renoir, Cézanne, Rousseau, Matisse, and Picasso, but is unfortunately **closed until December 2003** for renovations. *(Southwest corner of the Jardin des Tuileries. M: Concorde. ☎01 42 97 48 16.)*

GALERIE NATIONALE DU JEU DE PAUME. Connoisseurs and tourists alike come to appreciate the changing contemporary art exhibitions. Scheduled upcoming exhibitions for 2002 include Oscar Niemeyer. *(M: Concorde. ☎01 47 03 12 50; recorded info ☎01 42 60 69 69. Open Tu noon-9:30pm, W-F noon-7pm, Sa-Su 10am-7pm. 38F/€5.80, students under 26, seniors, and ages 13-18 28F/€4.27. Tours in French W and Sa 3pm, Su 11am.)*

MUSEE MARMOTTAN MONET. Owing to generous donations by the family of Monet and others, the Empire-style house has been transformed into a lucrative shrine to Impressionism. The top floor is dedicated to paintings by Berthe Morisot, the First Lady of Impressionism. *(2 rue Louis-Boilly. M: La Muette. ☎01 44 96 50 33. Open Tu-Su 10am-5:30pm. 40F/€6.10, students and seniors 20F/€3.05, under 8 free.)*

MUSEE D'ART ET D'HISTOIRE DU JUDAISME. Newly renovated and housed in the grand **Hôtel de St-Aignan,** once a tenement for Jews fleeing Eastern Europe, this museum displays a history of Jews in Europe, France, and North Africa. An ornate 15th-century Italian ark, letters written to wrongly accused French general Dreyfus, a small collection of Chagall and Modigliani paintings, and modern art collections looted from Jewish homes by the Nazis reside here. (*71 rue du Temple. M: Hôtel de Ville. ☎01 53 01 86 53. Open M-F 11am-6pm, Su 10am-6pm; last entrance at 5:15pm. 40F/€6.10, students and 18-26 25F/€3.81, under 18 free; includes an excellent English audioguide.)*

MUSEE DE LA MARINE (MUSEUM OF THE NAVY). A dream come true for kids of all ages, with model ships of astounding detail. A few real boats from the 17th-19th centuries are anchored here, including the lavishly golden dinghy built for Napoleon in 1810. *(17 pl. du Trocadéro. M: Trocadéro. In the Palais de Chaillot. ☎01 53 65 69 69. Open W-M 10am-6pm. 45F/€6.86, students and seniors 35F/€5.34, under 18 25F/€3.81.)*

ENTERTAINMENT

The primary pastimes of Parisians, as they would have it, are fomenting revolution and burning buildings. Actually, their nighttime pleasures tend more toward drinking, relaxing, and people-watching. Those looking for live music, especially jazz, are in for a heavenly time.

OPERA

Opéra de la Bastille, pl. de la Bastille, *12ème* (☎08 92 69 78 68; www.opera-de-paris.fr). M: Bastille. Opera and ballet with a modern spin. Because of acoustical problems, it's not the place to splurge for front row seats. Subtitles in French. Tickets 46-690F/€7.02-105.23. Call, write, or stop by for a free brochure of the season's events. Tickets can be purchased by Internet, mail, fax, phone (M-Sa 9am-7pm), or in person (M-Sa 11am-6pm). Rush tickets for students under 25 and anyone over 65 15min. before show. Wheelchair accessible, but call ahead. MC/V.

Opéra Comique, 5 rue Favart, *2ème* (☎01 42 44 45 46). M: Richelieu-Drouot. Operas on a lighter scale–from Rossini to Offenbach. Box office open M-Sa 11am-7pm. Tickets 50-610F/€7.63-93.03. Student rush tickets available 15min. before show starts.

Opéra Garnier, pl. de l'Opéra, *9ème* (☎08 92 69 78 68; www.opera-de-paris.fr). M: Opéra. Hosts the Ballet de l'Opéra de Paris, operas, symphonies, and chamber music. Tickets available 2 weeks before shows. Box office open M-Sa 11am-6pm. Ballet tickets 33-420F/€5.03-64.05; opera tickets up to 690F/€105.23. Last-minute, discount tickets available 1hr. before showtime. MC/V.

CABARET

Au Lapin Agile, 22 rue des Saules, *18ème* (☎01 46 06 85 87). M: Lamarck-Coulaincourt. Turn right on rue Lamarck, then right up rue des Saules. Picasso, Verlaine, Renoir, and Apollinaire hung out here during the heyday of Montmartre; now a mainly tourist audience crowds in for comical poems and songs. Shows Tu-Su 9pm-2am. Admission and first drink 130F/€19.83, students 90F/€13.73. Subsequent drinks 35F/€5.34.

THEATER

La Comédie Française, 2 rue de Richelieu, *1er* (☎01 44 58 15 15; www.comedie-francaise.fr). M: Palais-Royal. Founded by Molière, now the granddaddy of all French theaters. Expect wildly gesticulated slapstick farce; you don't need to speak French to understand the jokes. Performances take place in the 896-seat Salle Richelieu. Expect canonized plays by French greats Molière, Racine, and Corneille in the coming season. Box office open daily 11am-6pm. Tickets 30-190F/€4.57-28.97, under 27 30-50F/€4.57-7.62. Rush tickets for students (66F/€9.99) available 1hr. before show.

Odéon Théâtre de l'Europe, 1 pl. Odéon, *6ème* (☎01 44 41 36 36; www.theatre-odeon.fr). M: Odéon. Programs in this elegant Neoclassical building range from classics to avant-garde, but the Odéon specializes in foreign plays in their original language. 1042 seats. Also **Petit Odéon,** an affiliate with 82 seats. Box office open daily 11am-6pm. Tickets 30-180F/€4.57-27.44 for most shows; under 27 rush tickets 50F/€7.63, available 90min. before performance; cheaper rates available Th and Su, call ahead. Petit Odéon 70F/€10.67, students 50F/€7.62. Call ahead for wheelchair access. MC/V; no credit card purchases over the phone.

JAZZ

Au Duc des Lombards, 42 rue des Lombards, *1er* (☎01 42 33 22 88). M: Châtelet. From rue des Halles, walk down rue de la Ferronnerie and make a right on rue St-Denis and another right on rue des Lombards. Murals of Ellington and Coltrane cover the exterior of this premier jazz joint. Still the best in French jazz, with occasional American soloists, and hot items in world music. Beer 28-48F/€4.27-7.32, cocktails 55F/€8.39. Cover 80-120F/€12.20-18.30, music students 50-90F/€7.63-13.73. Music starts at 9:30pm in summer and 9pm in winter and wails on until 2am (3am on weekends). Open daily 7:30pm-3am. MC/V.

Le Baiser Salé, 58 rue des Lombards, 1*er* (☎01 42 33 37 71). M: Châtelet. From rue des Halles, walk down rue de la Ferronnerie and make a right on rue St-Denis and another right on rue des Lombards. Cuban, African, Antillean music featured together with modern jazz and funk. Open daily 4pm-dawn. AmEx/MC/V.

Le Petit Opportun, 15 rue des Lavandières-Ste-Opportune, 1*er* (☎01 42 36 01 36). M: Châtelet. From the métro, walk to rue des Halles and make a right onto rue des Lavandières-Ste-Opportune. Some of the best modern jazz around, including American. Drinks 30-60F/€4.58-9.15. Cover 80-100F/€12.20-15.25. Open Sept.-July Tu-Sa 9pm-5am; music begins between 9:30 and 10:30pm.

CINEMA

Musée du Louvre, 1*er* (info ☎01 40 20 53 17, schedules ☎01 40 20 52 99; www.louvre.fr). M: Louvre. Art films, films on art, and silent movies. Open Sept.-June. Free.

Les Trois Luxembourg, 67 rue Monsieur-le-Prince, 6*ème* (☎01 46 33 97 77). M: Cluny. Turn left on bd. St-Michel, right on rue Racine, and left on rue M-le-Prince. High-quality independent, classic, and foreign films, all in original language. Tickets 40F/€6.10, students and seniors 30F/€4.57.

Cinémathèque Française, pl. du Trocadéro, 16*ème* (☎01 45 53 21 86, schedule ☎01 47 04 24 24). M: Trocadéro. At the Musée du Cinéma in the Palais de Chaillot; enter through the Jardins du Trocadéro. **Branch:** 18 rue du Faubourg-du-Temple, 11*ème*. M: République. A must for film buffs. Two to three classics, near-classics, or soon-to-be classics per day. Foreign films usually in original language. 28F/€4.27, students 17F/€2.60. Open W-Su 5-9:45pm.

PARIS

NIGHTLIFE

Those on the prowl for dancing may be at first frustrated by Paris' rather closed (and sometimes downright nasty) club scene, but *Let's Go* tries to list places that are tolerant of non-models. If you'd rather just drink and watch the world go by, Parisian bars and the cafés that blend into bars at sundown won't disappoint. For gay and lesbian nightlife, Paris is tops (but also check out Montpellier, p. 727).

PLACE DE LA REPUBLIQUE: 3EME, 4EME, 11EME

L'Apparemment Café, 18 rue des Coutures St-Gervais. M: St-Paul. Beautiful wood-and-red lounge complete with games and a calm, young crowd. Late-night meals 68-82F/€10.37-12.51, served until closing.

Chez Richard, 37 rue Vieille-du-Temple (☎01 42 74 31 65). M: Hôtel-de-Ville. Inside a courtyard off rue Vieille-du-Temple, and reminiscent of Casablanca. Beer 23-36F/€3.51-5.49, cocktails 52-60F/€7.93-9.15. Open daily 6pm-2am. MC/V.

Lizard Lounge, 18 rue du Bourg-Tibourg (☎01 42 72 81 34). M: Hôtel-de-Ville. A happening, split-level space for Anglo/Franco late 20-somethings. The cellar has DJs every night. Happy Hour upstairs 6-8pm (cocktails 30F/€4.58), everywhere 8-10pm (cocktails 28F/€4.27). Pint of lager 33F/€5.03. Open daily noon-2am. Food served noon-3pm and 7-10:30pm, weekend brunch noon-4pm. MC/V.

Café Charbon, 109 rue Oberkampf (☎01 43 57 55 13). M: Parmentier or Ménilmontant. A spacious bar that proudly wears traces of its *fin-de-siècle* dance hall days but still manages to pack in a crowd of young locals and artists. Beer 15-20F/€2.29-3.05. Happy Hour 5-9pm. Open daily 9am-2am. MC/V.

Le Bar Sans Nom, 49 rue de Lappe (☎01 48 05 59 36). M: Bastille. Walk down rue de la Roquette and make a right onto rue de Lappe. Facing the Mix Café, a blank red front is all that distinguishes the bar from others along the packed rue de Lappe. Dim, jazzy lounge famous for its inventive cocktails, some *flambé*. Free tarot-card reading Tu 7-9pm. Beer 30-40F/€4.58-6.10, cocktails 60F/€9.15. Open M-Sa 7pm-2am. MC/V.

Les Bains, 7 rue du Bourg l'Abbé (☎01 48 87 01 80). M: Etienne-Marcel or Réaumur-Sébastopol. From Etienne-Marcel, take rue Etienne Marcel east, turn left onto bd. Sébastopol, and take the next right. Ultra-selective, super-crowded, and expensive.

Used to be a public bath, more recently visited by Madonna and Mick Jagger. Funky house and garage grunge, W is hip-hop. Cover and 1st drink Su-Th 100F/€15.25; F-Sa 120F/€18.30. Clubbing daily 11pm-6am; open for dinner from 9pm—if you want it that bad (and for that much money); reservations a must. AmEx/MC/V.

Les Etages, 35 rue Vieille-du-Temple (☎01 42 78 72 00). M: St-Paul. Set in an 18th-century hotel-turned-bar, and filled strictly with chill kids basking in dim orange-red lighting. Sangria 25F/€3.81. Open daily 3:30pm-2am (earlier for Su brunch). MC/V.

Amnésia Café, 42 rue Vieille-du-Temple (☎01 42 72 16 94). M: Hôtel-de-Ville. Amnésia's wood interior and plush sofas attract a largely gay crowd and is one of the top see-and-be-seen spots in the Marais, especially on Sa nights. Espresso 12F/€1.83; kir 22F/€3.36. Open daily noon-2am. MC/V.

Cox, 15 rue des Archives (☎01 42 72 08 00). M: Hôtel-de-Ville. Buns-to-the-wall men's bar with bulging and beautiful boys. So crowded that the boys who gather here block traffic on the street. Very cruisy; not the place for a quiet weekend cocktail. Happy Hour (beer half-off) daily 6-9pm. Beer 19F/€2.90. Open daily noon-2am.

Les Scandaleuses, 8 rue des Ecouffes (☎01 48 87 39 26). M: St-Paul. Walk along rue de Rivoli in the direction of traffic and turn right onto rue des Ecouffes. The best-known, hip lesbian bar set to techno beats. Men welcome if accompanied by women. Beer 23F/€3.51. Happy Hour 6-8pm. Open daily 6pm-2am. AmEx/MC/V.

PARIS

LEFT BANK: 5EME, 6EME, 7EME, 13EME

Le Reflet, 6 rue Champollion (☎01 43 29 97 27). M: Cluny-La Sorbonne. Walk away from the river on bd. St-Michel, then make a left on rue des Ecoles. Take the 1st right. Small, crowded with students and younger Frenchies. Beer 11-16F/€1.68-2.44, cocktails 12-32F/€1.83-4.88 at bar. Open M-Sa 10am-2am, Su noon-2am. MC/V.

Le Caveau des Oubliettes, 52 rue Galande (☎01 46 34 23 09). Three entertainments in one: the bar upstairs has a real-live guillotine; downstairs, there's an outstanding jazz club; and beneath the club, a prison where criminals were locked up and forgotten. Attracts a (mostly local) set of mellow folk. Jazz concerts every night; free *soirée boeuf* (jam session) on M-W and Su; other nights, concerts 50F/€7.63. Beers 25-45F/€3.81-6.86. Rum 25F/€3.81. Happy Hour 5-9pm. Open daily 5pm-2am.

Le Piano Vache, 8 rue Laplace (☎01 46 33 75 03). M: Cardinal Lemoine or Maubert-Mutualité. Walk up rue de la Montagne Ste-Geneviève and make a right on rue Laplace. Once a butcher-shop, now a dark, poster-plastered bar hidden behind the Panthéon and full of cow paraphernalia. 2nd drink free with *Let's Go.* Happy Hour 6-9pm. Open July-Aug. daily 6pm-2am, Sa-Su 9pm-2am; Sept.-June noon-2am, Sa-Su 9pm-2am.

Le Bar Dix, 10 rue de l'Odéon (☎01 43 26 66 83). M: Odéon. Walk against traffic on bd. St-Germain and make a left on rue de l'Odéon. A classic student hangout. Sangria (19F/€2.90). Open daily 5:30pm-2am.

Chez Georges, 11 rue des Cannettes (☎01 43 26 79 15). M: Mabillon. Walk down rue du Four and make a left on rue des Cannettes. This former cabaret lives a double life: upstairs it's a wine bar full of old men playing chess; downstairs it's a candle-lit cellar rampant with bebopping Anglo students. Beer 23-30F/€3.51-4.58, wine 10-22F/€1.53-3.36, sandwiches 18-28F/€2.75-4.27. Open Tu-Sa noon-2am (upstairs), 10pm-2am (cellar). Closed Aug.

Le Club des Poètes, 30 rue de Bourgogne (☎01 47 05 06 03). M: Varenne. Walk up bd. des Invalides with the Invalides behind you and to your left; go right on rue de Grenelle and left onto rue de Bourgogne. For 40 years, Jean-Pierre Rosnay has been making "poetry contagious and inevitable." A restaurant by day, at 10pm, a troupe of readers, including Rosnay's family, transform the place into a poetry salon. If you arrive after 10pm, wait to enter until you hear clapping or a break in the performance. The food's not cheap, but come for a drink after 10pm to be part of the fun. Drinks 60F/€9.15, for students 45F/€6.86. Open M-Sa noon-2:30pm and 8pm-1am. AmEx/MC/V.

O'Brien's, 77 rue St-Dominique (☎01 45 51 75 87). M. Latour-Maubourg. Follow traffic along bd. de La Tour Maubourg. A lively Irish pub. Gather before their big screen TV for soccer matches. Sept.-July, you can win yourself a bottle of Champagne on quiz night, Su 9pm. Happy Hour M-F from opening time until 8pm, pints 29F/€4.42. Open M-Th 6pm-2am, F-Su 4pm-2am. MC/V.

La Folie en Tête, 33 rue de la Butte-aux-Cailles (☎01 45 80 65 99). M: Corvisart. *The* artsy axis mundi of the 13*ème*. World music and exotic instruments line the walls. Crowded concerts on Sa nights, usually Afro-Caribbean music (50F/€7.63); no concerts July-Aug. Beer 10F/€1.53 before 8pm, 15F/€2.29 after; cocktails 35-40F/€5.34-6.10. Open M-Sa 5pm-2am; usually opens at 6pm during the summer. MC/V.

Batofar, facing 11 quai François-Mauriac (☎01 56 29 10 33). M: Quai de la Gare. You'll see the river; facing it, walk right along the quai–Batofar has red lights. On a light-boat, this barge/bar/club has made it big with the electronic music crowd. Friendly, industrial environment. During June, a trailer parked outside provides free music for the many who get down right on the quai. Open daily 9pm-3am, F-Sa until 4am; hours may change for film and DJ events. Cover up to 60F/€9.15; usually includes 1st drink. MC/V.

RIGHT BANK: 1ER, 2EME, AND 8EME

Le Fumoir, 6 rue de l'Amiral Coligny (☎01 42 92 05 05). M: Louvre. As cool by night as it is by day. Extra dry martini 68F/€10.37. Happy Hour 6-8pm with 35F/€5.34 cocktails and 45F/€6.86 champagne.

Banana Café, 13-15 rue de la Ferronnerie (☎01 42 33 35 31). M: Châtelet. From the Porte du Pont Neuf of Les Halles, go straight, left on rue St-Honoré; rue de la Ferronnerie is ahead past the Châtelet métro stop. This *très branché* (way cool) evening arena is the most popular gay bar in the 1*er*. Legendary theme nights. The "Go-Go Boys" W-Sa midnight-dawn. From 4 to 10pm, drinks are two for one, except cocktails. Beer 34F/€5.18 weekdays, 44F/€6.71 weekends. Open daily 4pm-dawn. AmEx/MC/V.

Le Champmeslé, 4 rue Chabanais (☎01 42 96 85 20). M: Pyramides or Quatre Septembre. Walk down av. de l'Opéra and make a right on rue des Petits Champs. Make another right onto rue Cabanais. This comfy lesbian bar is Paris' oldest and most famous. Mixed crowd in the front, women-only in back. Drinks 30-45F/€4.58-6.86. Popular cabaret show Th 10pm. Free drink during the month of your birthday. Open M-Th 2pm-2am, F and Sa 2pm-5am. MC/V.

buddha-bar, 8 rue Boissy d'Anglas (☎01 53 05 90 00). M: Madeleine or Concorde. Step off your private jet, slip on your stilettos, and don't forget to be seen (as late as possible) at the buddha-bar. The giant buddha keeps watch over those *really* important people eating on the ground floor, but try and find a table upstairs. Mixed drinks and martinis 69F/€10.52, the mysterious Pure Delight 80F/€12.20. Open daily 6pm-2am.

Chesterfied Café, 124 rue La Boétie (☎01 42 25 18 06). M: Franklin D. Roosevelt. Walk toward the Arc on the Champs-Elysées, and rue La Boétie will be the second street on your right. Friendly and happening American bar with first-class live music. Americans and Frenchies mix happily with the attractive waitstaff. Snack bar has good ol' yankee fare. Cocktails 49F/€7.47, beer 23-48F/€3.51-7.32, coffee 12F/€1.83. No cover Su-Th. Open daily 10am-5am. AmEx/MC/V.

Latina Café, 114 av. des Champs-Elysées (☎01 42 89 98 89). M: George V. Drawing one of the largest nightclub crowds on the glitzy Champs-Elysées, Latina Café plays an energetic world music mix. Drinks 56F/€8.54. Cover 100F/€15.25. Live concerts Th. Open daily 7:30pm-2am, club open daily 11:30am-6:30am.

Rex Club, 5 bd. Poissonnière (☎01 42 36 10 96). M: Bonne-Nouvelle. A non-selective club which presents the most selective of DJ line-ups. Young break-dancers and veteran clubbers fill this casual, subterranean venue to hear cutting-edge techno, jungle, and house fusion. Shots 25-30F/€3.81-4.58, beer 30-45F/€4.58-6.86. Cover varies 50-80F/€7.63-12.20. Open Th-Sa 11:30pm-6am.

PLACE PIGALLE: 9EME, 18EME

Chez Camille, 8 rue Ravignan (☎01 46 06 05 78). M: Abbesses. From the métro, walk down rue de la Veuville and make a left on rue Drevet and another left on rue Gabrielle which becomes rue Ravignan. Small, trendy, bright yellow bar on the safe upper slopes of Montmartre with pictures of Serge Gainsbourg, funky charm, and a pretty terrace looking down the *butte* to the Invalides dome (especially dramatic at night). Cheap coffee (6-8F/€092-1.22) and tea (14F/€2.14). Beer 15-20F/€2.29-3.05, wine from 15F/€2.29, and cocktails 30-50F/€4.58-7.63. Open Tu-Sa 9am-2am, Su 9am-8pm.

La Fourmi, 74 rue des Martyrs (☎01 42 64 70 35). M: Pigalle. Walk east on bd. Rochechouart and make a left on rue des Martyrs. Popular stop-off before clubbing; this bar has an artsy atmosphere and a hyper-hip, energetic, and scrappy young crowd. Beer 15-21F/€2.29-3.20, wine 16-19F/€2.44-2.90, cocktails 45-60F/€6.86-9.15. Open M-Th 8:30am-2am, F-Sa 8:30am-4am, Su 10:30am-2am. MC/V.

Folies Pigalle, 11 pl. Pigalle (☎01 48 78 55 25). M: Pigalle. This club is the largest and wildest of the sleazy Pigalle *quartier.* A former strip joint, the Folies Pigalle is popular among gay and straight clubbers. Mostly house and techno. Su gay and transsexual night. Very crowded, even at 4am. Cover 100F/€15.25 with drink. Drinks 50F/€7.63. AmEx/MC/V. Open Tu-Th 11pm-6am, F-Sa 11pm-noon, Su 5pm-6am.

SHOPPING

Paris is an endless parade of all that is extravagant, form-fitting, and flattering, and stylish clothes and accessories are spread democratically through a variety of price ranges. In the more exclusive boutiques, assistants have perfected the art of disapproval—ignore them and waltz on in. The two great *soldes* (sales) of the year start right after New Year's and at the very end of June. If you don't mind slimmer pickings, the best prices are at the beginning of February and the end of July. And at any time of the year, if you see the word *braderie* (clearance sale) on a store window, march on in! Non-EU residents who have made purchases worth over 1200F in one store should ask about getting a refund on the 20.6% value-added tax (see **Reclaiming Value-added Tax,** p. 33).

BY ARRONDISSEMENT

ETIENNE-MARCEL AND LES HALLES (1ER AND 2EME). Fabrics here are a little cheaper, and the style younger. At the **Agnès b.** empire on rue du Jour, you'll find classy, casual fashion. The stores on rue Etienne Marcel and rue Tiquetonne are best for outrageous club wear. **Forum Les Halles,** a subterranean shopping mall, just south of the Etienne-Marcel area, and the streets that surround it contain a large range for a full urban warrior aesthetic. *(M: Etienne-Marcel.)*

MARAIS (4EME AND THE LOWER 3EME). The Marais has a line-up of affordable, trendy boutiques, mostly mid-priced clothing chains, independent designer shops, and vintage stores that line **rue Vieille-du-Temple, rue de Sévigné, rue Roi de Sicile** and **rue des Rosiers.** Lifestyle shops line **rue de Bourg-Tibourg** and **rue des Francs-Bourgeois.** The best selection of affordable-chic menswear in Paris can be found along **rue Ste-Croix-de-la-Bretonnerie.** *(M: St-Paul or Hôtel de Ville.)*

ST-GERMAIN-DES-PRES (6EME AND EASTERN BORDER OF 7EME). St-Germain-des-Prés, particularly the triangle bordered by **bd. St-Germain, rue St-Sulpice,** and **rue des Sts-Pères,** is saturated with high-budget names. **Rue du Four** (M: St-Germain-des-Prés) boasts fun and affordable designers such as **Paul and Joe** (no. 40, ☎01 45 44 97 70; open daily 11am-7:30pm) and **Sinéquanone** (no. 16, ☎01 56 24 27 74; open M-Sa 10am-7:30pm). The sleek **Nauninani** (☎01 42 89 14 70) on rue St-Sulpice (M: Mabillon) across from the church sells distinctive handbags and outfits. Near Luxembourg, calm rue de Fleurus hosts **A.P.C.** as well as **t***** at no. 7 (M: St-Placide). In the 7*ème*, visit rue de Pré-aux-Clercs and rue de Grenelle; though generally expensive, there are some impressive little boutiques around the Bon Marché department store on rue de Sèvres, and rue du Cherche Midi. *(M: Vaneau, Duroc, Sèvres-Babylone, Rue du Bac.)*

PARIS

DEPARTMENT STORES

Paris is the birthplace of the *grand magasin*, those meccas of one-stop shopping. The old stores are as noteworthy for their Belle Epoque architecture and Art Nouveau details as for their acres of accessories. You can see where it all started: **Au Bon Marché,** 22 rue de Sèvres, *7ème*, Paris' oldest department store. Across the street is **La Grande Epicerie de Paris,** Bon Marché's celebrated gourmet food annex. (☎01 44 39 80 00. M: Sèvres-Babylone. Open M-W and F 9:30am-7pm, Th 10am-9pm, Sa 9:30am-8pm. AmEx/MC/V.) **Samaritaine,** 67 rue de Rivoli, on the quai du Louvre, *1er* is not as chic as the others, as it dares to sell souvenirs, and merchandise at down-to-earth prices (the horror!). The rooftop observation deck provides one of the best views of the city; take the elevator to the 9th floor and climb the short, spiral staircase. Most hotels have 10% discount coupons for the store. (☎01 40 41 20 20. M: Pont-Neuf, Châtelet-Les-Halles, or Louvre-Rivoli. Open M-W and F-Sa 9:30am-7pm, Th 9:30am-10pm.) Two heavyweights duke it out on bd. Haussmann in the *9ème*: the first is **Au Printemps,** at no. 64, which caters more to women's fashion than men's. Most hotels have 10% discounts for use in the store. (☎01 42 82 50 00. M: Chaussée d'Antin-Lafayette or Havre-Caumartin; and other locations throughout the city. Haussmann location open M-W and F-Sa 9:30am-7pm, Th 9:30am-10pm.) Right by it is the more chaotic, more spectacular **Galeries Lafayette,** at no. 40. The equivalent of Paris' entire population visits here each month. It carries it all, including mini-boutiques of Kookaï, Agnès B., Gap, and Benetton. (☎01 42 82 34 56. M: Chaussée d'Antin. Also at other locations throughout Paris. Open M-W and F-Sa 9:30am-7pm, Th 9:30-9pm.)

PARIS

CLOTHES

OUTLET STORES

Stock is French for outlet store, with big names for less—often because they have small imperfections or are from last season. Many are on rue d'Alésia in the *14ème* (M: Alésia), including **Cacharel Stock,** no. 114 (☎01 45 42 53 04; open M-Sa 10am-7pm); **Stock Chevignon,** no. 122 (☎01 45 43 40 25; open M-Sa 10am-7pm); **Stock Daniel Hechter,** no. 92 (☎01 47 07 88 44; open M-Sa 10am-7:30pm); and a great **Sonia Rykiel Store** at no. 64 (☎01 43 95 06 13; open Tu 11am-7pm, W-Sa 10am-7pm). **Stock Kookaï** bustles at 82 rue Réamur, *2ème* (☎01 45 08 93 69; open M-Sa 10:30am-7:30pm); and **Haut-de-Gomme Stock,** with names like Armani and Dolce & Gabbana has two locations: 9 rue Scribe, *9ème* (☎01 40 07 10 20; open M-Sa 10am–7pm; M: Opéra) and 190 rue de Rivoli, *1er* (☎01 42 96 97 47; open daily 11am-7pm; M: Louvre-Rivoli).

SECOND-HAND AND VINTAGE

La Clef des Marques, 20 pl. du Marché St-Honoré, *1er*, is two stories of designer merchandise; you could find Prada pumps for less than your hotel room. (☎01 47 03 90 40. M: Pyramides. Open M 12:30-7pm, Tu-F 10am-2:30pm and 3:30-7pm, Sa 10am-1pm and 2-7pm. MC/V.) Similar is **Mouton à Cinq Pattes,** 8-10-18 rue St-Placide, *6ème*. (☎01 45 48 86 26. M: Sèvres-Babylone. Open M-Sa 10am-7pm. Also at 19 rue Grégoire de Tours, *6ème* (☎01 43 29 73 56), M: Odéon. AmEx/MC/V.) Although a bit on the beat tip, **Antiquités New-Puces,** 43 rue Mouffetard, *5ème*, goes from campy to classy. (☎01 43 36 70 78. M: Monge. Usually open Tu-Su 11am-7pm, summer noon-6pm. AmEx/MC/V.) **Guerrisold,** 9, 21, and 21bis bd. Barbès, *18ème*, has silk shirts, leather coats, jeans, and more. (☎01 42 80 66 18. M: Barbès-Rochechouart; 17bis bd. Rochechouart, *9ème*, M: Cadet; and 22 bd. Poissonière, *9ème* (☎01 47 70 35 02), M: Bonne Nouvelle. Most branches open M-Sa 10am-7pm.)

WOMEN'S AND MEN'S

MKDM, 24 rue de Sévigné, *4ème* (☎01 42 77 00 74). M: St-Paul. Japanese designers; the latest in trendy casual wear. Open M 2:30-7:30pm, Tu-Su 11:30am-7:30pm. MC/V.

Le Shop, 3 rue d'Argout, *2ème* (☎01 40 28 95 94). M: Etienne-Marcel. Two levels, 1200 sq. m, and 24 corners of original, sleek, Asian-inspired club wear. Prices range from reasonable to ludicrous. Open M 1-7pm, Tu-Sa 11am-7pm. AmEx/MC/V.

Zadig & Voltaire, 15 rue du Jour, *1er* (☎01 42 21 88 70). M: Etienne-Marcel. Also at 1 rue des Vieux Colombiers, *6ème* (☎01 43 29 18 29), M: Odéon, and 12 rue Ste-Croix-de-la-Bretonnerie (☎01 42 72 15 20), M: St-Paul. Men's and women's designs by DKNY, T. Gillier, Helmut Lang, etc. Their own label is soft and feminine. Great selection of handbags. Main branch open M 1-7:30pm, Tu-Sa 10:30am-7:30pm. AmEx/MC/V.

Petit Bateau, 26 rue Vavin, *6ème,* and many other locations (☎01 55 42 02 53). M: Vavin or Notre-Dame-des-Champs. T-shirts, tanks, undies, and pyjamas in the softest of cottons. It's a children's store, but the PB size for age 16 is about an American 6, and they go up to age 18. Tanks 32F/€4.88; a bottle of their fresh signature scent 130F/€19.83. Open M-Sa 10am-7pm; opens at 2pm M during Aug. AmEx/MC/V.

SPECIALTY SHOPS

Muji, 27 rue St-Sulpice, *6ème* (☎01 46 34 01 10). M: Odéon. Made in Japan: this bric-à-brac is affordable, modern, and minimalist. Open M-Sa 10am-8pm. AmEx/MC/V.

Espace Colette, 213 rue St-Honoré, *1er* (☎01 55 35 33 90). M: Concorde. An "anti-department store" whose bare display tables feature an eclectic selection of scuba watches, Japanese vases, and mineral water. Everything from Dior sunglasses to scotch tape. Open M-Sa 10:30am-7:30pm. AmEx/MC/V.

Robin des Bois, 15 rue Ferdinand Duval, *4ème* (☎01 48 04 09 36). M: St-Paul. Environmentally safe alternatives to the usual wares. Beautiful, handmade recycled stock stationary (30-75F/€4.57-11.44); whale-saving jojoba bath products (45-450F/€6.86-68.63); and jewelry (necklace 200F/€30.50—made from Amazonian palm fruits). Open M-Sa 10:30am-7:30pm, Su 2:30-7:30pm. AmEx/MC/V.

PARIS

BOOKS

Paris overflows with high-quality bookstores. The *5ème* and *6ème* are particularly bookish: interesting shops line every large street in the Latin Quarter, not to mention the endless stalls *(bouquinistes)* along the quais of the Seine. Some specialty bookshops serve as community centers, too. English bookshops like **Shakespeare & Co.** (below) and **The Village Voice,** 6 rue Princesse, *6ème,* have bulletin boards where you can post and read events and housing notices. (Village Voice ☎01 46 33 36 47. M: Mabillon. Open M 2-8pm, Tu-Sa 10am-8pm, Su 2-7pm; closed Su in Aug.) **Les Mots à la Bouche,** 6 rue Ste-Croix de la Bretonnerie, *4ème,* offers gay, bisexual, and lesbian info. (☎01 42 78 88 30; www.motalabouche.com. M: Hôtel-de-Ville. Open M-Sa 11am-11pm and Su 2-8pm.) **L'Harmattan,** 21bis rue des Ecoles, *5ème,* can direct you to Caribbean, Maghrébin, and West African resources. (☎01 46 34 13 71. M: Cluny la Sorbonne. Open M-Sa 10am-12:30pm and 1:30-7pm. MC/V.)

The large, English-language **W.H. Smith,** 248 rue de Rivoli, *1er,* has many scholarly works and magazines. Sunday *New York Times* available Monday after 2pm. (☎01 44 77 88 99. M: Concorde. Open M-Sa 9am-7:30pm, Su 1-7:30pm. AmEx/MC/V.) **Brentano's,** 37 av. de l'Opéra, *2ème,* is an American and French bookstore with an extensive selection of English literature. (☎01 42 61 52 50. M: Opéra. Open M-Sa 10am-7:30pm. AmEx/MC/V.) **Shakespeare & Co.,** 37 rue de la Bûcherie, *5ème,* across the Seine from Notre-Dame is run by *bon vivant* George Whitman. This shop sells a quirky and wide selection of new and used books. Bargain bins outside have books for 30F/€4.58. (M: St-Michel. Open daily noon-midnight.)

NEAR PARIS

VERSAILLES

By sheer force of ego, the Sun King converted a simple hunting lodge into the world's most famous palace. The sprawling château and bombastic gardens stand as a testament to the despotic playboy-king, Louis XIV, who lived, entertained, and governed here on the grandest of scales. A century later, while Louis XVI and Marie-Antoinette entertained in lavish style, the peasants of Paris starved.

A child during the aristocratic insurgency called the Fronde, Louis XIV is said to have entered his father's bedchamber one night only to find (and frighten away) an assassin. Fearing conspiracy the rest of his life, Louis chose to move the center of royal power out of Paris and away from potential aristocratic insubordination. In 1661, the Sun King renovated the small hunting lodge in Versailles, enlisting the help of architect Le Vau, painter Le Brun, and landscape architect Le Nôtre. The court at Versailles became the nucleus of noble life, where France's aristocrats vied for the king's favor.

No one knows just how much it cost to build Versailles; Louis XIV burned the accounts to keep the price a mystery. At the same time, life there was less luxurious than one might imagine: courtiers wore rented swords and urinated behind statues in the parlors, wine froze in the drafty dining rooms, and dressmakers invented the color *puce* (literally, "flea") to camouflage the insects crawling on the noblewomen. Louis XIV died in 1715 and was succeeded by his great-grandson Louis XV in 1722. He commissioned the Opéra, in the North Wing, for the marriage of Marie-Antoinette and Louis XVI. The newlyweds inherited the throne and Versailles when Louis XV died of smallpox at the château in 1774. The Dauphin and Marie-Antoinette changed little of the exterior, redecorating inside to create Marie-Antoinette's personal pretend playland, the Hamlet. On October 5, 1789, 15,000 Parisian fishwives and National Guardsmen marched out to the palace and brought the royal family back to Paris, where they were guillotined in 1793.

During the 19th century, King Louis-Philippe established a museum to preserve the château, against the wishes of most French people, who wanted Versailles demolished just as the Bastille had been. In 1871, the château took the limelight once again, when Wilhelm of Prussia became Kaiser Wilhelm I of Germany in the Hall of Mirrors. That same year, as headquarters of the Thiers regime, Versailles sent an army against the Parisian Commune. The *Versaillais* pierced the city walls and crushed the *communards*. On June 28, 1919 at the end of WWI, France forced Germany to sign the ruinous Treaty of Versailles in the Hall of Mirrors, the very room of modern Germany's birth.

PRACTICAL INFORMATION

Trains: The **RER** runs from M: Invalides or any stop on RER Line C5 to the Versailles Rive Gauche station (30-40min., departs every 15min., round-trip 31F/€4.73). From Invalides or other RER Line C stop, take trains with labels beginning with "V."

Tourist Office: Office de Tourisme de Versailles, 2bis av. de Paris (☎01 39 24 88 88; fax 01 39 24 88 89; www.versailles-tourisme.fr). On av. de Paris before you reach the courtyard of the château. Open in summer daily 9am-7pm; in winter 9am-6pm.

Tours: ☎01 30 83 76 79; www.chateauversailles.com. Open May-Sept. Tu-Su 9am-6:30pm; Oct.-Apr. 9am-5:30pm. Admission and **self-guided tour, entrance A:** 49F/€7.47; ages 18-25, over 60, and after 3:30pm 35F/€5.34. Supplement for **audio tour, entrance C:** 1hr., 26F/€3.96, under 7 free. Supplement for **guided tour, entrance D:** 1hr. tour of Chambres du Roi, 26F/€3.96, ages 7-17 17F/€2.59; 1½hr. tour of the apartments of Louis XV and the opéra 37F/€5.64, ages 7-17 26F/€3.96; **full-day tour** (two 1½hr. segments, one in the morning, the other in the afternoon) 117F/€17.84. Sign-language tours available; call ahead at 01 30 83 77 88.

SIGHTS

Arrive early in the morning to avoid the crowds, which are worse on Sundays from May to September, and in late June. Pick up a map at one of the entrances or the info desk in the center of the courtyard. Figuring out how to get into the château is the hardest part; there are half a dozen entrances, many of which offer different sights. Most visitors enter at **Entrance A,** on the right-hand side in the north wing, or **Entrance C,** in the archway to the left (either ticket allows free entrance to the other; native speakers of Russian, Chinese, Japanese, Spanish, or Italian should start at C). **Entrance B** is for groups, **Entrance D** is where tours with a living, breathing guide begin, and

Entrance H is for those in wheelchairs. **General admission** allows entrance to the following rooms: the *grands appartements;* the War and Peace Drawing Rooms; the *Galerie des Glaces* (Hall of Mirrors); and Marie-Antoinette's public apartment. Head for Entrance C to purchase an **audioguide.** From Entrance D, at the left-hand corner as you approach the palace, you can choose between four excellent, scholarly **tours** of different parts of the château (the best is the 1½hr. tour of the Louis XV apartments and opéra). To avoid the excessive wait for tours, arrive before 11am.

SELF-GUIDED TOUR. Begin at **Entrance A.** Start in the **Musée de l'Histoire de France,** created in 1837 by Louis-Philippe. Along its walls are portraits of those who shaped the course of French history. The 21 rooms (arranged in chronological order) seek to construct a historical context for the château.

Up the staircase to the right is the dual-level **royal chapel** by architect Hardouin-Mansart from 1699 to 1710. Back toward the staircase and to the left is a series of gilded **drawing rooms** in the **State Apartments** that are dedicated to Hercules, Mars, and the ever-present Apollo (the Sun King identified with the sun god). The ornate **Salon d'Apollo** was Louis XIV's throne room. Framed by the **War and Peace Drawing Rooms** is the **Hall of Mirrors,** which was originally a terrace until Mansart added a series of mirrored panels and windows to double the light in the room and reflect the gardens outside. These mirrors stretched the limits of 17th-century technology, an unthinkable extravagance. Le Brun's ceiling paintings (1679-1686) tell the story of Louis XIV, culminating with *The King Governs Alone.*

The **Queen's Bedchamber,** where royal births were public events, is now furnished as it was on October 6, 1789, when Marie-Antoinette left the palace for the last time. A version of the David painting of Napoleon's self-coronation dominates the **Salle du Sacré** (also known as the Coronation Room). The **Hall of Battles** installed by Louis-Philippe is a monument to 14 centuries of France's military.

THE GARDENS

***Open** daily sunrise-sundown. **Free. Fountains** turned on for special displays, such as the **Grandes Eaux Musicales,** Apr.-Oct. Sa-Su 11am-noon and 3:30-5:30pm. 33F/€5.03. **Discovering Groves Tour:** call 01 30 83 77 88; 1½hr.; 20F/€3.05. The most convenient place for **bike rentals** is across from the base of the canal (☎01 39 66 97 66). 32F/€4.88 per hr., 20F/€3.05 per 30min. Open Feb.-Nov. M-F 1pm-closing, Sa-Su 10am-closing. Rent **boats** for 4 at the boathouse to the right side of the base of the canal (☎01 39 66 97 66). 72F/€10.98 per hr., 52F/€7.93 per 30min.; 50F/€7.63 refundable deposit. Open Tu-F noon-5:30pm, Sa-Su 11am-6pm. **Horse-drawn carriages** run Tu-Su, departing from just right of the main terrace (☎01 30 97 04 40).*

Numerous artists—Le Brun, Mansart, Coysevox—executed statues and fountains, but master gardener André Le Nôtre provided the overall plan for Versailles' gardens. Louis XIV wrote the first guide to the gardens himself, entitled the *Manner of Presenting the Gardens at Versailles.* Tours should begin, as the Sun King commanded, on the terrace.

To the left of the terrace, the **Parterre Sud** graces the area in front of Mansart's **Orangerie,** once home to 2000 orange trees; the temperature inside still never drops below 6°C (43°F). In the center of the terrace lies the **Parterre d'Eau,** while the **Bassin de Latone** fountain below features Latona, mother of Diana and Apollo, shielding her children as Jupiter turns villains into frogs. Past the fountain and to the left is one of the garden's undisputed gems: the flower-lined, exotic sanctuary of the **Jardin du Roi,** accessible only from the easternmost side facing the **Bassin du Miroir.** Near the south gate of the grove is the magnificent **Bassin de Bacchus,** one of four seasonal fountains depicting the God of wine crowned in vine branches reclining on a bunch of grapes. Working your way north toward the center of the garden you can see where the king used to take light meals amid the exquisite **Bosquet de la Colonnade's** 32 violet and blue marble columns, sculptures, and white marble basins, just east of the Jardin du Roi. The north gate to the Colonnade exits onto the 330m-long **Tapis Vert** (Green Carpet), the central mall linking the château to the garden's conspicuously central fountain, the **Bassin d'Apollon,** whose charioted Apollo rises, youthful and god-like, out of the water to enlighten the world.

On the north side of the garden is Marsy's incredible **Bosquet de l'Encelade.** When the fountains are turned on, a 25m high jet bursts from Titan's enormous mouth, which is plated with shimmering gold, and half buried under a pile of rocks. Flora reclines on a bed of flowers in the **Bassin de Flore,** while a gilded Ceres luxuriates in sheaves of wheat in the **Bassin de Cérès.** The **Parterre Nord,** full of flowers, lawns, and trees, overlooks some of the garden's most spectacular fountains. The **Allée d'Eau,** a fountain-lined walkway, provides the best view of the **Bassin des Nymphes de Diane.** The path slopes toward the sculpted **Bassin du Dragon,** where a dying beast slain by Apollo spurts water 27m high into the air. Ninety-nine jets of water attached to urns and seahorns surround Neptune in the **Bassin de Neptune,** the gardens' largest fountain. Beyond the classical gardens stretch wilder woods, meadows, and farmland perfect for a picnic away from the manicured perfection of Versailles. Stroll along the **Grand Canal,** a rectangular pond beyond the Bassin d'Apollon measuring 1535m long.

THE TRIANONS AND MARIE-ANTOINETTE'S HAMLET

Shuttle trams from the palace to the Trianons and the Hameau leave from behind the palace facing the canals; head right. Round-trip 33F/€5.03, ages 3-12 20F/€3.05. The walk takes 25min. Both Trianons: Open Tu-Sa noon-5:30pm; Apr.-Oct. noon-6pm. 30F/€4.58.

The Trianons and Hameau provide a racier counterpoint to the château: here kings trysted with lovers, and Marie-Antoinette lived like the peasant she wasn't.

PETIT TRIANON. On the right down the wooded path from the château is the **Petit Trianon,** built between 1762 and 1768 for Louis XV and his mistress Madame de Pompadour. Marie-Antoinette took control of the Petit Trianon in 1774, and it soon earned the nickname "Little Vienna." In 1867, the Empress Eugénie, who worshipped Marie-Antoinette, turned it into a museum.

Exit the Petit Trianon, turn left, and follow the marked path to the libidinous **Temple of Love,** a domed rotunda with 12 white marble columns and swans. Marie-Antoinette held many intimate nighttime parties in the small space, during which thousands of torches would be illuminated in the surrounding ditch. The Queen was perhaps at her happiest and most ludicrous when at the **Hameau,** her own pseudo-peasant "hamlet" down the path from the Temple of Love. Inspired by Rousseau's theories on the goodness of nature and the hameau at **Chantilly,** the queen aspired fashionably for a more simple life. She commissioned Richard Mique to build a compound of 12 buildings (including a mill, dairy, and gardener's house, all surrounding a quaint artificial lake) in which she could play at country life, though the result is something of a cross between English Romanticism and Euro-Disney. At the center is the **Queen's Cottage;** any illusions of country-style slumming disappear after crossing the doors. The rooms contained ornate furniture, marble fireplaces, and walk-in closets for linens, silverware, and footmen.

GRAND TRIANON. The single-story, stone-and-pink-marble Grand Trianon was intended as a château-away-from-château for Louis XIV. Here the king could be reached only by boat along the **Grand Canal.** The palace, which consists of two wings joined together by a central porch, was designed by Mansart. **Formal gardens** are located behind the colonnaded porch. The mini-château was stripped of its furniture during the Revolution but was later restored and inhabited by Napoleon and his second wife.

CHARTRES

Were it not for a piece of fabric, the cathedral of Chartres and the town that surrounds it might be only a sleepy hamlet. Because of this sacred relic—the cloth that the Virgin Mary supposedly wore when she gave birth to Jesus—Chartres became a major medieval pilgrimage center. The spectacular cathedral that towers above the surrounding rooftops is not the only reason to take the train ride here: the *vieille ville* (old town) is also a masterpiece of medieval architecture.

PRACTICAL INFORMATION

Trains: Chartres is accessible by frequent trains from **Gare Montparnasse, Grandes Lignes** (☎08 36 35 35 35). At least 1 per hr. in summer; call ahead for winter schedule. 1hr.+; round-trip 148F/€22.57, under 26 and groups of 2-4 112F/€17.08, over 60 74F/€11.29. To reach the cathedral from the train station, walk straight along rue Jehan de Beauce to pl. de Châtelet and turn left into the *place*, right onto rue Ste-Même, and left onto rue Jean Moulin, or just head toward the massive spires.

Tourist Office: (☎02 37 18 26 26; fax 02 37 21 51 91). In front of the cathedral's main entrance at pl. de la Cathédrale. Open Apr.-Sept. M-Sa 9am-7pm, Su and holidays 9:30am-5:30pm; Oct.-Mar. M-Sa 10am-6pm, Su and holidays 10am-1pm and 2:30-4:30pm; closed some holidays. For those with difficulty walking or who want a relaxed tour, *Le petit train Chart'train* (☎02 37 21 87 60), runs Apr.-Oct. with 30min. narrated tours (in French) of the old city. **Tours** begin in front of the tourist office, check board outside for daily departure times. 32F/€4.88, under age 12 18F/€2.75.

PARIS

SIGHTS

☎02 37 21 75 02. Open daily 8am-8pm. No visits during mass, M, W-Th, and Sa at 11:45am and 6pm; Tu and F at 9, 11:45am, and 6pm; Su 9:15am (Latin), 11am, and 6pm (in the crypt). Treasury closed indefinitely at press time. North Tower open May-Aug. M-Sa 9am-6pm, Su 2-6pm; Sept.-Oct. and Mar.-Apr. M-Sa 9:30-11:30am and 2-5pm, Su 2-5pm; Nov.-Feb. M-Sa 10-11:30am and 2-4pm, Su 2-4pm. 26F/€3.97, ages 18-25 16F/€2.44, under 18 free. English tours begin outside the gift shop and last 1¼hr. Easter to early Nov. M-Sa noon and 2:45pm, call 02 37 28 15 58 for winter schedule; 52F/€8, students 33F/€5. French tours of the crypt leave from inside (☎02 37 21 56 33). Tours 30min.; Apr.-Oct. M-Sa 11am, 2:15, 3:30, and 4:30pm; Nov.-Mar. 11am and 4:15pm; additional 5:15pm tour June 22-Sept. 21; no 11am tours anytime during the year on Su. 15F/€2.29, students 10F/€1.53, under 7 free.

The Cathédrale de Chartres is the best-preserved medieval church in Europe, escaping major damage during the Revolution and WWII. A patchwork masterpiece of Romanesque and Gothic design, the cathedral was constructed by generations of unknown masons, architects, and artisans who labored for centuries.

SANCTA CAMISIA. The year after he became emperor in 875, Charlemagne's grandson, Charles the Bald, donated to Chartres the Sancta Camisia, the cloth believed to have been worn by the Virgin Mary when she gave birth to Christ. However, it cannot be seen until the Treasury reopens. Although a church had existed on the site as early as the mid-700s, the emperor's bequest required a new cathedral to accommodate the growing number of pilgrims. The sick were nursed in the crypt below the sanctuary. The powers of the relic were heralded in AD 911 for saving the city; under attack from invading Goths and Vikings, the Viking leader Rollon converted to Christianity, and he became the first duke of Normandy.

STAINED GLASS. At a time when most people were illiterate, the cathedral served as an educational tool. Most of the stained glass dates from the 13th century and was preserved through WWI and II by heroic town authorities, who dismantled and stored the windows in the Dordogne. The famous Blue Virgin, Tree of Jesse, and Passion and Resurrection of Christ windows are among the surviving 13th-century stained glass. The center window shows the story of Christ from the Annunciation to the ride into Jerusalem. Bring binoculars if you have them.

LABYRINTH. A winding labyrinth is carved into the floor in the rear of the nave. Designed in the 13th century, the labyrinth was laid out for pilgrims as a substitute for a journey to the Holy Land. By following this symbolic journey on their hands and knees, the devout would act out a voyage to heavenly Jerusalem.

TOUR JEHAN-DE-BEAUCE. The adventurous can climb the cathedral's north tower for a stellar view of the cathedral roof, the flying buttresses, and the city below. The tower, a wonderful example of flamboyant Gothic style, provides a striking counterpart to its more sedate partner, the Romanesque **octagonal steeple** (the tallest in its style still standing), built just before the 1194 fire.

CRYPT. Parts of Chartres' crypt, such as a well down which Vikings tossed the bodies of their victims during raids, date back to the 9th century. You can enter the 110m long subterranean crypt only as part of a tour that leaves from La Crypte, the store opposite the cathedral's south entrance. The tour is in French, but info sheets are available in English.

DISNEYLAND PARIS

It's a small, small world and Disney is hell-bent on making it even smaller. When Euro-Disney opened on April 12, 1992, Mickey Mouse, Cinderella, and Snow White were met by the jeers of French intellectuals and the popular press, who called the Disney theme park a "cultural Chernobyl." Resistance seems to have subsided since Walt & Co. renamed it Disneyland Paris and started serving wine. Despite its dimensions, this Disney park is the most technologically advanced yet, and the special effects on some rides will knock your socks off.

PRACTICAL INFORMATION

The detailed *Park Guide Book* (free at Disney City Hall to the left of the entrance) has a map. The *Guests' Special Services Guide* has info on wheelchair accessibility. For more info on Disneyland Paris, call 01 60 30 60 81 (from the US) or 01 60 30 63 53 from all other countries, or visit www.disneylandparis.com.

Trains: RER A4 from M: Gare de Lyon or Châtelet-Les-Halles, and take the train (dir: "Marne-la-Vallée") to the last stop, Marne-la-Vallée/Chessy." Before boarding the train, check the boards hanging above the platform to make sure there's a light next to the Marne-la-Vallée stop; otherwise the train won't end up there (45min., 2 per hr., round-trip 78F/€11.90). The last train to Paris leaves Disney at 12:22am, but you may have trouble getting the métro once you get back–it closes at midnight. **TGV** service from de Gaulle reaches the park in a mere 15min.

Car: Take the A4 highway from Paris and take Exit 14, marked "Parc Disneyland Paris," (30min. total). Park for 40F/€6.10 per day in 1 of the 11,000 spaces available.

Bus: Disneyland Paris buses travel between the terminals at Orly and de Gaulle airports and the bus station near the Marne-la-Vallée RER (40min.; departs every 45-60min. 8:30am-7:45pm, 8:30am-10pm at de Gaulle on weekends; round-trip 85F/€12.96).

Tickets: Disneyland Paris issues **passeports,** available at the ground floor of the Disneyland Hotel. You can also buy *passeports* at the Paris tourist office at the Champs-Elysées, FNAC, Virgin Megastores, Galeries Lafayette, or at any of the major stations on RER line A. Buy ahead if you plan on coming on a weekend.

Admission: Apr.-Oct. 220F/€33.55, ages 3-11 170F/€25.93; Jan. 2-Mar. and Nov.-Dec. 22 170F/€25.93, ages 3-11 140F/€21.35; Dec. 23-Jan. 1 225F/€34.31, ages 3-11 175F/€26.69. 2- and 3-day *passeports* also available.

Hours: Open July 8-Sept. 3 daily 9am-11pm; Sept. 4-Oct. 20 and Nov. 6-Dec. 22 M-F 10am-8pm, Sa-Su 9am-8pm; Oct. 21-Nov. 5 and Dec. 23-Jan. 1 daily 9am-8pm; Dec. 31 9am-1am. Hours subject to change in winter.

GIVERNY

Drawn to the verdant hills, haystacks, and lily pads on the Epte river, Impressionist painter Claude Monet and his eight children settled in Giverny in 1883. By 1887, John Singer Sargent, Paul Cézanne, and Mary Cassatt had placed their easels beside Monet's and turned the village into an artists' colony.

PRACTICAL INFORMATION

Trains: SNCF runs sporadically from Paris **Gare St-Lazare** to **Vernon,** the nearest station to Giverny. To get to the Gare St-Lazare, take the métro (M: St-Lazare), and take the rue d'Amsterdam exit, then walk straight into the right-hand entrance of the Gare. From there, go to the Grandes Lignes reservation room. To schedule a trip, ask for a schedule of timetables at the Grandes Lignes reservation room; contact the SNCF (☎08 36 35 35 35; www.sncf.fr). 136F/€20.73 round-trip, 102F/€15.55 special for two. From Vernon to Giverny, take a **bus** (☎02 32 71 06 39; 10min.; Tu-Su 4 per day; 15min. after the train arrives in Vernon; 3 from Giverny to Vernon; look for the schedule inside the info office in the train station; 12F/€1.83, round-trip 24F/€3.66). Coordinate train and bus schedules before you start your trip to avoid 3hr. delays.

SIGHTS

FONDATION CLAUDE MONET. Monet's house and gardens are maintained by the Fondation Claude Monet. From April to July, Giverny overflows with wild roses, hollyhocks, poppies, and the scent of honeysuckle. The water lilies, the Japanese bridge, and the weeping willows of the Orientalist Water Gardens look like—well, like Monets. The serenity is broken only by the crowds of tourists and school children. The only way to avoid the rush is to go early in the morning and, if possible, early in the season. Monet's thatched-roof home houses his collection of 18th- and 19th-century Japanese prints. *(84 rue Claude Monet. ☎02 32 51 28 21. Open Apr.-Oct. Tu-Su 10am-6pm. 35F/€5.34, students 25F/€3.81, ages 7-12 20F/€3.05. Gardens 25F/€3.81.)*

MUSEE D'ART AMERICAIN. The incongruously modern but respectfully hidden Musée d'Art Américain is the sister institution to the Museum of American Art in Chicago and houses a small number of works by American expatriates like Mary Cassatt. *(99 rue Claude Monet. ☎02 32 51 94 65; www.maag.org. Open Apr.-Oct. Tu-Su 10am-6pm. 35F/€5.34; students, seniors, teachers 20F/€3.05; under 12 15F/€2.29.)*

SAINT-DENIS

Surrounded by modern buildings, markets, and non-Christian communities, the Basilique de St-Denis stands as an odd, archaic symbol of the long-dead French monarchy. Buried in the transept, *crevet*, and crypt are the remains of three royal families, 41 kings, 32 queens, 63 princes and princesses, 10 dignitaries, and the relics of three saints. During the height of the French monarchy, the basilica was, in effect, the national church of France; it became synonymous with the crown as the protector of the country's most valuable political artifacts: the *Oriflamme* (the royal banner) and coronation paraphernalia.

PRACTICAL INFORMATION

The most direct route to the tourist office and the basilica is by métro (M: St-Denis-Basilique, line 13); visitors headed to the Stade should take the RER (RER: Stade de France, line B, or RER: St-Denis, line D). The **tourist office,** 1 rue de la République, has English-speaking guides and info on the basilica and the town. From the métro, turn left down rue Jean Jaurès, following the signs to the tourist office, and turn right on rue de la République. (☎01 55 87 08 70; www.ville-saint-denis.fr. Open M-Sa 9:30am-1pm and 2-6pm, Su and bank holidays 10am-1pm and 2-6pm.)

BASILIQUE DE ST-DENIS

1 rue de la Légion d'Honneur and 2 rue de Strasbourg. From the métro, head toward the town square down rue Jean Jaurès and turn left at the tourist office on rue de la République. ☎01 48 09 83 54. ***Open*** *Apr.-Sept. M-Sa 10am-6:30pm, Su noon-6:30pm; Oct.-Mar. M-Sa 10am-4:30pm, Su noon-4:30pm. Admission to nave, side aisles and chapels free. Admission to transept, ambulatory, and crypt 36F/€5.49, seniors and students 12-25 23F/€3.51, under 18 free.* ***Audioguide*** *in various languages 25F/€3.81.* ***Tours*** *in French daily at 11:15am and 3pm.*

The first church on this site was built on top of an existing Gallo-Roman cemetery, in honor of Paris' first bishop, St-Denis, whose story is told in stained glass on the northern side of the nave. Of the more famous monarchs, Clovis, François Ier, Anne d'Autriche, Louis XIV, Louis XVI, and Marie-Antoinette lie here. The most elaborate **Renaissance tombs** generally have two sets of sculptures: the marble corpses inside the catafalque symbolize the inevitability of death (even for semi-divine monarchs), while the effigies on top, usually decked in full regalia, symbolize the spiritual power of the crown. The single most spectacular monument is the Renaissance-era **mausoleum of Louis XII and Anne de Bretagne.** Located on the left side of the transept, this extravagant structure features a pair of grotesquely grinning, naked marble corpses. The basilica's 12th-century **ambulatory** was the first instance of Gothic architecture in Europe (the scornful term "Gothic" was coined by Italian critics to describe St-Denis' extravagant style). Nicknamed "Lucerna" (Latin for "lantern") for its luminosity, the basilica features enormous stained-glass windows, high vaults, and exceptionally wide, airy transepts. These and other innovations were ordered by St-Denis' great patron, **Abbot Suger** (1122-1151), who had grown dissatisfied with the dark interiors of Romanesque churches and began rebuilding the basilica to open it to the "uninterrupted light of the divine."

Suger's celebrated, color-flooded **crevet** was originally built to displace the crowds of pilgrims who flooded into the crypt. The crowds got so immense at times that women, rumor has it, would faint and even suffocate to death in the tiny, air-deprived vault. The terrified monks worried that the reliquaries would be stolen and had taken to jumping out the windows with the remains in their arms.

Sadly, almost all of the original stained glass was replaced in the 19th century after the originals were shattered during the Revolution. Some of the 12th-century windows can still be seen, however, in the center of the ambulatory. Look closely at those on the left-hand side and you can discern something other than biblical tales: Abbot Suger ensured his immortality by having his likeness—a small monk prostrate before the Virgin Mother—added to the design.

Suger died in 1151, having firmly established the unfinished basilica as France's seat of theological power. Several queens were crowned here, and in 1593, underneath the nave, Henri IV converted to Catholicism. With such a royalist pedigree, St-Denis was a prime target for the wrath of the Revolution. Most of the tombs were destroyed, windows were shattered, and the remains of the Bourbon family were thrown into a ditch. With the restoration of the monarchy in 1815, Louis XVIII ordered that the necropolis be reestablished, and Louis XVI and Marie-Antoinette were buried here with great pomp in 1819. The remains of the Bourbons were dug out of their ditch and placed in a small **ossuary** inside the crypt, and tombs and funerary monuments were relocated and replaced.

BEAUVAIS

In 1664, as part of his effort to restore France's exhausted treasury, Louis XIV's finance minister Colbert established a national tapestry factory in Beauvais; the city's tapestries and carpets soon became world-renowned. Today, the town is worth visiting for its museum and magnificent 13th-century Gothic cathedral.

PRACTICAL INFORMATION

Trains: run from the Gare du Nord in Paris, to pl. de la Gare in Beauvais (1hr., up to 10 per day via Creil, 74F/€11.28).

Tourist Office: 1 rue Beauregard (☎03 44 15 30 30; fax 03 44 15 30 31). To get there from the station, walk straight ahead for just over a block and turn left onto rue de la Madeleine. At pl. Jeanne Hachette, turn right, and then make left at the fountain; the office will be on the corner on the left. Free map of the town center. Open M 10am-1pm and 2-6pm, Tu-Sa 9:30am-6:30pm, Su 10am-5pm.

SIGHTS

Visitors expecting yet another faded Renaissance scene will be pleasantly surprised by the **Galerie Nationale de la Tapisserie,** 22 rue St-Pierre, next to the cathedral. Many of the extraordinary tapestries—from the unicorn classics of the 16th century to those produced when Napoleon restored the weavers to the state payroll in 1804—could pass for paintings; they're that detailed and rich. (Open Apr.-Sept. W-M 9:30-11:30am and 2-6pm; Oct.-Mar. 10-11:30am and 2:30-4:30pm. 15F/€2.29, under age 25 5F/€0.76; free first Su of the month Oct.-May.) The **Cathédrale St-Pierre,** built between 1225 and 1573, is a gem of flamboyant Gothic style. Money ran out for the nave, but the choir, at 48½m, is the tallest in the world. Inside, the light-drenched cathedral features few surviving panels of stained glass dating from the 13th to 16th centuries, and some exceptional paintings of the Crucifixion and Ascension on the back of the choir. Designed in 1865, the **astronomical clock** compresses Christian theology into a matter of moving cogs. A 25-minute audio-visual tour of the clock's functions presents 68 biblical characters in stiff-jointed action. Look for the virgin and the sinner parading out to get their souls weighed on a scale. (Shows in English and French at 10:40 and 11:40am and 2:40, 3:40, and 4:40pm, except Su mornings and religious holidays. Cathedral open May-Oct. daily 9am-12:15pm and 2-6:15pm; Nov.-Apr. 9am-12:15pm and 2-5:30pm. Free.)

LYON AND THE AUVERGNE

France's visitors crowd Paris to the north and descend to Provence and the Riviera in the south. Wine lovers linger in Bordeaux or Beaune, and outdoor enthusiasts scale and ski the Alps or Pyrenees. Few, however, penetrate the Auvergne, the country's interior. The lucky adventurer who does will find rugged beauty without mobs of tourists. Giant lava needles, extinct volcanic craters, and verdant pine forests rise out of the Massif Central. The mineral waters of Vichy, Le Mont Dore, and Volvic attract both *curistes* and bottling entrepreneurs. During World War II the region achieved eternal infamy as the empty hotels of Vichy became the headquarters for the collaborationist French government headed by Maréchal Pétain.

TRANSPORTATION

Trains run to major cities and a few small villages along the way; more remote areas are served only by private bus companies with schedules timed for workers and local students. Really the only way to visit the lost, enchanted hamlets of the Massif Central is by car. Bikers be warned: the Auvergne's steep, winding roads are best used by the *Tour de France*, not those looking for a leisurely pedal. The locals tend to be friendly, which bodes well for those inclined to hitch.

1 **Lyon:** France's 2nd city; friendlier, more relaxed than Paris, with less to see and do **(p. 156)**
2 **Pérouges:** Tiny village, cobblestone streets, preserved 15th-century houses **(p. 167)**
3 **The Beaujolais:** Best known for cool, fruity wine; terraced hills and sleepy villages **(p. 167)**
4 **Clermont-Ferrand:** Sinister dark stone and smoke-spitting factories **(p. 168)**
5 **Puy de Dôme:** Why visit C-F? Massive, flat-top volcanic dome, astounding views **(p. 173)**
6 **Le Mont Dore:** Ski resort and spa near a green, cratered string of dormant volcanoes **(p. 173)**
7 **Le Puy-en-Velay:** Pilgrimage site with immense overhung cathedral **(p. 176)**
8 **Vichy:** Famous healing springwater; nostalgic city crawling with the aged and sickly **(p. 180)**

LYON

France's second-largest city is second in little else. Lyon (pop. 1.5 million) is friendlier and more relaxed than Paris, with a few centuries' more history. Augustus ordered roads connecting this provincial capital of Gaul to Italy and the Atlantic, permanently establishing Lyon's status as a major crossroads and cultural capital. During the Renaissance, the city's tax-free permanent markets encouraged foreign merchants and bankers to set up shop here, and in the 15th century, Lyon became Europe's printing house. Silkworms imported from China in the 16th century also contributed to the city's rise to economic power. The ornate facades and elegant courtyards of 16th-century townhouses in Vieux Lyon attest to this period of wealth. Today Lyon is the stomping ground of world-renowned chefs Paul Bocuse, Georges Blanc, and Jean-Paul Lacombe, as well as the breeding ground for new culinary genius. There's no doubt you can eat *really* well at one of the masters' spin-off restaurants. This modern city has every urban comfort imaginable, with skyscrapers and cafés, nifty transport systems and flowering parks, concert halls and *discothèques*. King of the culinary jungle and UNESCO World Heritage site, this is not a city to be taken lyon down.

INTERCITY TRANSPORTATION

Flights: Aéroport Lyon-Saint-Exupéry (☎04 72 22 72 21). Flights within France and around Europe, North Africa, and the Middle East. Daily service to New York City. The TGV, which stops at the airport, is cheaper and more convenient than the 50 daily flights to Paris. **Satobuses/Navette Aéroport** (☎04 72 68 72 17) shuttle to **Gare de la Part-Dieu, Gare de Perrache** and subway stops **Grange-Blanche, Jean Mace,** and **Mermoz Pinel** (every 20min., daily until 9pm, 52.50F/€8). **Air France,** 17 rue Victor Hugo, 2*ème* (☎0 820 820 820).

Trains: To: **Dijon** (2hr., 13 per day, 137F/€20.89); **Geneva,** Switzerland (2hr., 6 per day, 118F/€18.00); **Grenoble** (1¼hr., 15 per day, 99F/€15.10); **Marseille** (3hr., 13 per day, 221F/€33.70); **Nice** (6hr., 15 per day, 299F/€45.60); **Paris** (2hr., 20 TGVs per day, 324-410F/€49.41-62.53); and **Strasbourg** (5½hr., 9 per day, 248F/€37.82). Trains passing through Lyon stop only at **Gare de la Part-Dieu,** bd. Marius Vivier-Merle (M: Part-Dieu), in the business district on the east bank of the Rhône. SNCF info desk open M-F 9am-7pm, Sa 9am-6:30pm. Those terminating in Lyon make a further stop at **Gare de Perrache,** pl. Carnot (M: Perrache). SNCF info and reservation desk open M-F 9am-7pm, Sa 9am-6:30pm. At Part-Dieu, there is **baggage storage,** in addition to lockers. Open daily 6am-midnight. 30F/€4.57.

Buses: On the lowest level of the Gare de Perrache (☎04 72 77 63 03) and at the Gare de Part-Dieu (**Allô Transports,** ☎04 72 61 72 61). Third station at "Gorge de Loup" in the 9*ème* (☎04 78 43 40 74). Domestic companies include **Philibert** (☎04 78 98 56 00) and **Transport Verney** (☎04 78 70 21 01), but it's almost always cheaper, faster, and simpler to take the train. **Eurolines** (☎04 72 56 95 30; fax 04 72 41 72 43) travels out from France. Ask about student prices. Station open M-Sa 8am-8:30pm.

ORIENTATION

Lyon is divided into nine *arrondissements;* the 1*er*, 2*ème*, and 4*ème* lie on the **presqu'île** (peninsula), a narrow strip of land jutting south toward the confluence of the Saône and Rhône rivers. Starting in the south, the **2ème** (the city center) includes the Perrache train station and **pl. Bellecour,** as well as most of the city's boutiques, hotels, and fast-food joints. The **1er** is home to the nocturnal Terreaux neighborhood, with its sidewalk cafés and student-packed bars. Farther north, the *presqu'île* widens into the **4ème** and the Croix-Rousse, a residential neighborhood that once housed Lyon's silk industry. The main pedestrian arteries of the *presqu'île* are **rue de la République,** affectionately known as "la Ré," to the northeast of pl. Bellecour, and **rue Victor Hugo,** to the south of Bellecour.

To the west is the oldest part of the city: Vieux Lyon, with narrow streets and traditional restaurants, and the **Fourvière** hill, with a Roman theater, a basilica, and fabulous views. Most people live east of the Rhône (3*ème* and 6-8*ème*), along with the **Part-Dieu** train station and modern commercial complex. Orient yourself with Fourvière and its **Tour Metallique,** a mini-Eiffel Tower, in the west and the **Tour du Crédit Lyonnais,** a reddish-brown crayon towering over Part-Dieu, in the east.

Most trains terminating in Lyon stop at both the **Gare de Perrache** and the **Gare de la Part-Dieu.** Perrache is more central and considered safer at night, but both are connected to Lyon's **métro,** which is the fastest way to the tourist office in the **tourist pavilion** on pl. Bellecour. To walk from Perrache, head straight onto rue Victor Hugo and follow it until it ends at pl. Bellecour; the tourist office is on the right (15min.). From Part-Dieu, leave the station by the fountains and turn right, walk right for three blocks and turn left onto cours Lafayette, cross the Rhône on pont Lafayette and continue as the street changes to pl. des Cordeliers, then turn left on rue de la République and follow it to pl. Bellecour (30min.). Lyon is a reasonably safe city. Watch out for pickpockets inside Perrache, at pl. des Terreaux, and in pl. Bellecour's crowds.

LOCAL TRANSPORTATION

TCL (☎04 78 71 70 00) has info offices at both stations and major metro stops. *Plan de Poche* (pocket map) available from the tourist office or any TCL branch. Tickets are valid for all methods of mass transport, including the **métro, buses, funiculars,** and **trams.** Tickets 8.50F/€1.30; *carnet* of 10 68.50F/€10.44, student discount includes 10 passes valid for one month 58.50F/€8.92. One pass is valid 1hr. in 1 direction, connections included. *Ticket Liberté* day pass (24F/€3.74) is a great deal for short-term visitors. The fast, frequent, and efficient **métro** runs 5am-midnight. **Buses** run 5am-9pm (a few until midnight). **Funiculars (cable cars)** swing between the Vieux Lyon métro Stop and pl. St-Jean, the top of Fourvière and St-Just until midnight. **Trams** have 2 different lines; T1 connects Part-Dieu to Perrache directly.

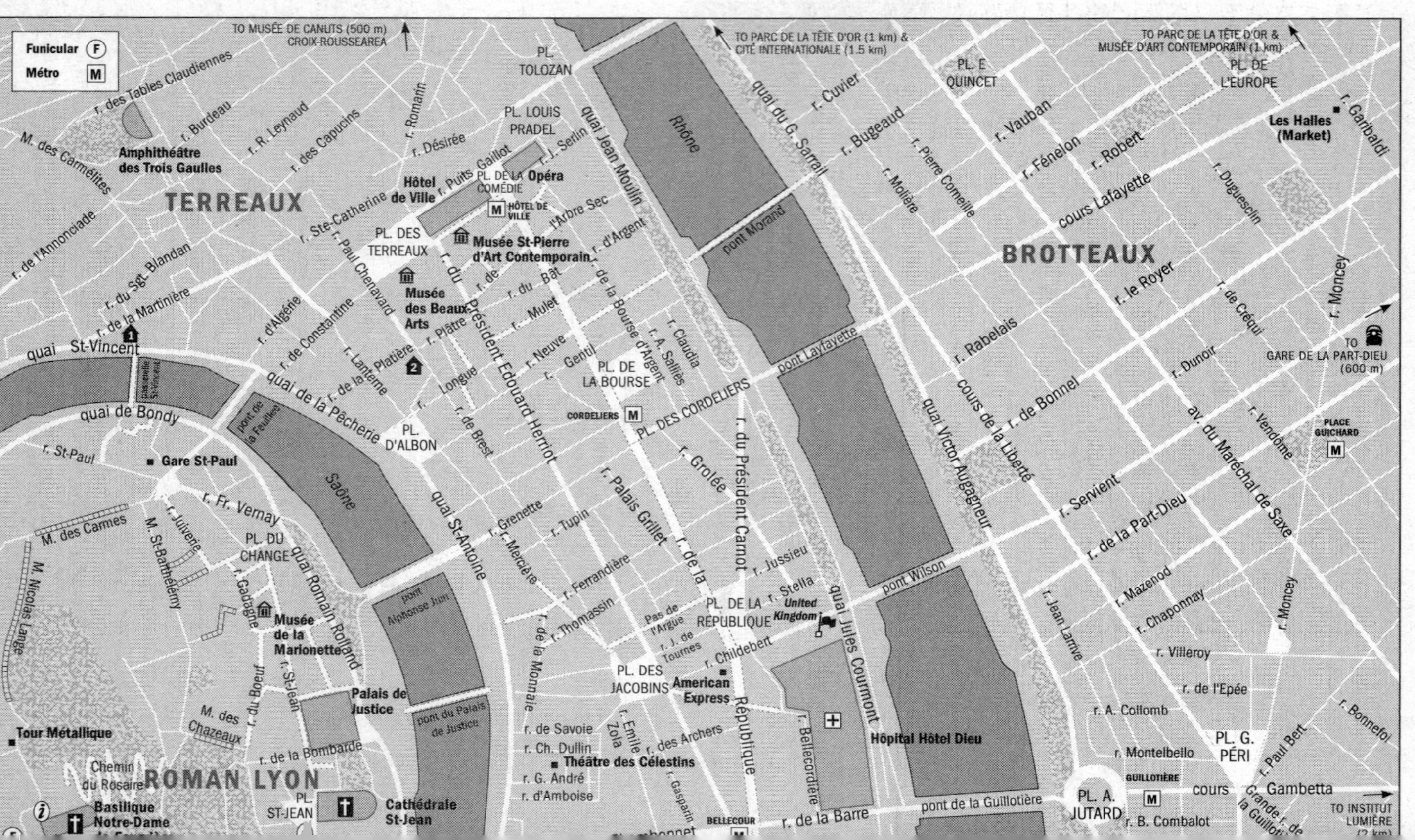
Funicular
Métro
TO MUSÉE DE CANUTS (500 m) CROIX-ROUSSEAREA
TO PARC DE LA TÊTE D'OR (1 km) & CITÉ INTERNATIONALE (1.5 km)
TO PARC DE LA TÊTE D'OR & MUSÉE D'ART CONTEMPORAIN (1 km)
TO GARE DE LA PART-DIEU (600 m)
TERREAUX
BROTTEAUX
ROMAN LYON
Rhône
Saône
Amphithéâtre des Trois Gaulles
Hôtel de Ville
Opéra
Musée St-Pierre d'Art Contemporain
Musée des Beaux Arts
Les Halles (Market)
Gare St-Paul
Musée de la Marionette
Palais de Justice
Cathédrale St-Jean
Tour Métallique
Basilique Notre-Dame
Théâtre des Célestins
American Express
United Kingdom
Hôpital Hôtel Dieu
PL. TOLOZAN
PL. LOUIS PRADEL
PL. DE LA COMÉDIE
HÔTEL DE VILLE
PL. DES TERREAUX
PL. DE LA BOURSE
CORDELIERS
PL. DES CORDELIERS
PL. D'ALBON
PL. DU CHANGE
PL. DE LA RÉPUBLIQUE
PL. DES JACOBINS
PL. ST-JEAN
PL. E QUINCET
PL. DE L'EUROPE
PLACE GUICHARD
PL. G. PÉRI
PL. A. JUTARD
GUILLOTIÈRE
BELLECOUR
quai St-Vincent
quai de Bondy
quai de la Pêcherie
quai St-Antoine
quai Romain Rolland
quai Jean Moulin
quai du G. Sarrail
quai Victor Augagneur
quai Jules Courmont
pont Morand
pont Lafayette
pont Wilson
pont de la Guillotière
pont Alphonse Juin
pont du Palais de Justice
pont de la Feuillée
passerelle St-Vincent
cours Lafayette
cours de la Liberté
av. du Maréchal de Saxe
cours Gambetta
r. du Président Edouard Herriot
r. du Président Carnot
r. de la République
r. de la Bourse
r. Palais Grillet
r. Grolée
r. de la Monnaie
r. de la Barre
TO INSTITUT LUMIÈRE

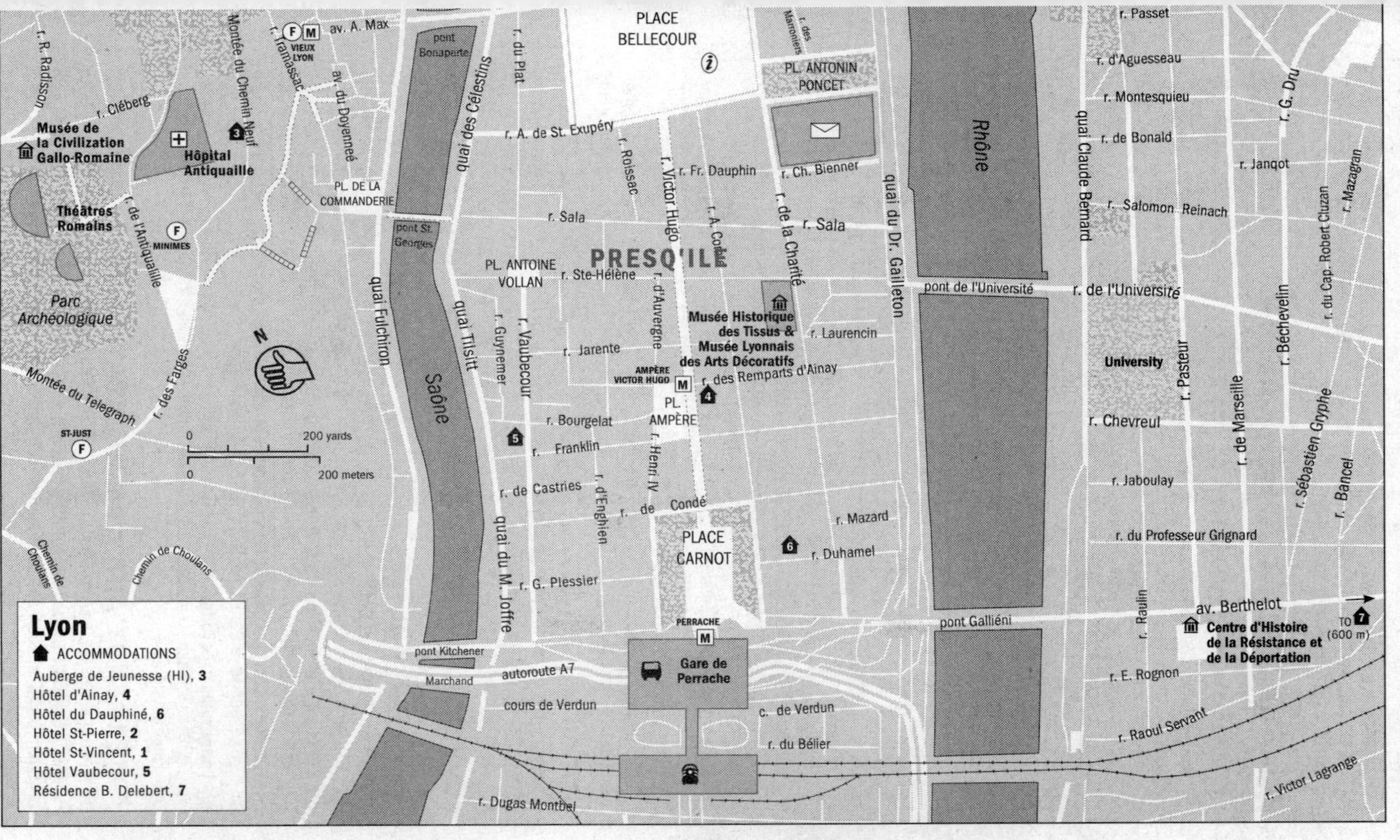
Lyon
ACCOMMODATIONS
Auberge de Jeunesse (HI), 3
Hôtel d'Ainay, 4
Hôtel du Dauphiné, 6
Hôtel St-Pierre, 2
Hôtel St-Vincent, 1
Hôtel Vaubecour, 5
Résidence B. Delebert, 7
0
200 yards
0
200 meters
N
Rhône
Saône
PRESQU'ILE
PLACE BELLECOUR
PLACE CARNOT
PL. ANTONIN PONCET
PL. ANTOINE VOLLAN
PL. AMPÈRE
PL. DE LA COMMANDERIE
Gare de Perrache
PERRACHE
AMPÈRE VICTOR HUGO
VIEUX LYON
MINIMES
ST-JUST
University
Musée Historique des Tissus & Musée Lyonnais des Arts Décoratifs
Centre d'Histoire de la Résistance et de la Déportation
TO 7 (600 m)
Hôpital Antiquaille
Musée de la Civilization Gallo-Romaine
Théâtres Romains
Parc Archéologique
quai Claude Bernard
quai du Dr. Gailleton
quai du M. Joffre
quai Tilsitt
quai des Célestins
quai Fulchiron
pont de l'Université
pont Galliéni
pont Bonaparte
pont St. Georges
pont Kitchener
Marchand
autoroute A7
cours de Verdun
c. de Verdun
av. Berthelot
av. A. Max
av. du Doyenneé
r. Victor Hugo
r. de la Charité
r. Vaubecour
r. Guynemer
r. de l'Université
r. Pasteur
r. de Marseille
r. Béchevelin
r. Sébastien Gryphe
r. Bancel
r. du Cap. Robert Cluzan
r. Mazagran
r. G. Dru
r. Janqot
r. Chevreul
r. Jaboulay
r. du Professeur Grignard
r. Raulin
r. E. Rognon
r. Raoul Servant
r. Victor Lagrange
r. Passet
r. d'Aguesseau
r. Montesquieu
r. de Bonald
r. Salomon Reinach
r. des Marroniers
r. A. de St. Exupéry
r. Fr. Dauphin
r. Ch. Bienner
r. Roissac
r. Sala
r. Ste-Hélène
r. d'Auvergne
r. Jarente
r. Laurencin
r. des Remparts d'Ainay
r. Bourgelat
r. Franklin
r. Henri IV
r. de Castries
r. d'Enghien
r. de Condé
r. Mazard
r. Duhamel
r. G. Plessier
r. du Plat
r. du Bélier
r. Dugas Montbel
r. Cléberg
r. R. Radisson
r. Tramassac
Montée du Chemin Neuf
r. de l'Antiquaille
r. des Farges
Montée du Telegraph
Chemin de Choulans

Taxis: Taxi Radio de Lyon (☎04 72 10 86 86). To airport from Perrache and Part-Dieu 220F-240F/€33.54-36.59 from 7am-7pm, 300F/€45.74 afterward. 24hr. Also **Allô Taxi** (☎04 78 28 23 23).

PRACTICAL INFORMATION

TOURIST AND FINANCIAL SERVICES

Tourist Office: In the Pavilion, at pl. Bellecour, *2ème* (☎04 72 77 69 69; fax 04 78 42 04 32). M: Bellecour. Incredibly efficient, and hungry for your tourism. Brochures and info on rooms and restaurants. Hotel reservation office. Indispensable **"Map & Guide"** in 7 languages has museum listings, a subway map, and a blow-up of the city center (5F/€0.76). Ask about the wide range of excellent **city tours** in French (and English during the summer). Tours 50-60F/€7.62-9.15, students 25-35F/€3.81-5.34. 3hr. audio-tours through are available in 4 languages (40F/€6.10). Also available is an insightful, anecdotal book that describes walking tours through the five quarters included in the UNESCO World Heritage list (35F/€5.34), which humbles the best of guidebook writers (that's us). Equally invaluable is the **Lyon City Card,** which authorizes unlimited public transportation along with admission to the 14 biggest museums, tours, audio-tours, and boat tours. Valid for 1, 2, or 3 days. 90F/€13.72, 160F/€24.39, and 200F/€30.49, respectively. **SNCF desk** for tickets and info. **Internet access** available but expensive. Office open May-Oct. M-Sa 9am-6pm; Nov.-Apr. daily 10am-6pm. For info on entertainment and cinema, try the weekly *Lyon Poche* (7F/€1.07) or seasonal *Lyon Libertin* (10F/€1.53) and *Guides de l'été de Lyon: Restaurant Nuits* (10F/€1.53), all available in *tabacs*. For longer stays starting in October, get the free gold mine of all goings-on, *Le Petit Pomme*.

Bus Tours: Philibert (☎04 78 98 56 00; fax 04 78 23 11 07; webescapes@philibert.fr). 1½hr. tour of Lyon, with audio-guides in 6 languages. You can get on or off at any point and reconnect later on. Tour starts at Perrache. Apr.-Nov. daily. 110F/€16.77.

Budget Travel: Wasteels (☎08 03 88 70 44), in Perrache's Galerie Marchande. International youth tickets available for those under 25. Open M-F 9am-12:30pm and 2-6pm, Sa 9:30am-12:30pm. MC/V.

Consulates: Canada, 21 rue Bourgelat, *2ème* (☎04 72 77 64 07), 1 block west of the Ampère-Victor Hugo métro. Open M-F 9am-noon. **Ireland,** 58 rue Victor Lagrange, *7ème* (☎06 85 23 12 03). Open M-F 9am-noon. **UK,** 24 rue Childebert, *2ème* (☎04 72 77 81 70). M: Bellecour. Open M-F 9am-12:30pm and 2-5:30pm. **US,** in the World Trade Center, 16 rue de la République, *2ème* (☎04 78 38 33 03). Open 9am-noon and 2-6pm.

Money: Currency exchange in the tourist office, or for poor rates at **Thomas Cook** in train stations. Part-Dieu (☎04 72 33 48 55) open M-Sa 8am-8pm, Su 9:30am-7pm. Perrache (☎04 78 38 38 84) open M-Sa 8:30am-1pm and 2-6:45pm, Su 10am-1pm and 2-6:45pm.

LOCAL SERVICES

English Bookstore: Decitre, 6 pl. Bellecour, *2ème* (☎04 26 68 00 12). Fantastic selection and English-speaking salespeople to advise. Open M-Sa 9:30am-9pm. MC/V.

Bureau d'Informations de Jeunesse (BIJ), 9 quai des Célestins (☎04 72 77 00 66), lists jobs and more. Open M noon-6pm, Tu-F 10am-6pm, Sa 10am-2pm and 2-5pm.

Women's Center: Centre d'Information Féminine, 18 pl. Tolozan, *1er* (☎04 78 39 32 25). Open M-Th 9am-1pm and 1:30-5pm, F 9am-1pm.

Laundromat: Lavadou, 19 rue Ste-Hélène, north of pl. Ampère, *2ème*. Open daily 7:30am-8:30pm. **Lav 123,** 123 rue Jean Jaurès. Open Mar.-Oct. daily 7am-8pm, Nov.-Feb 8am-8pm.

EMERGENCY AND COMMUNICATIONS

Police: 47 rue de la Charité (☎04 78 42 26 56). **Emergency:** ☎17.

Crisis Lines: SOS Amitié (☎04 78 29 88 88). **SOS Racisme** (☎04 78 39 24 44). Tu 6-8pm. **AIDS** info service, 2 rue Montebello, *3ème* (toll-free ☎0800 840 800).

LYON & AUVERGNE

Hospitals: All hospitals should have English-speaking doctors on call. **Hôpital Edouard Herriot,** 5 pl. Arsonval (☎04 72 11 73 11). M: Grange Blanche. Best equipped for serious emergencies, but far from the center of town. More central is **Hôpital Hôtel-Dieu,** 1 pl. de l'Hôpital, 2*ème* (☎04 72 41 30 00), near quai du Rhône. **SOS Médecins,** 10 pl. Dumas de Loire (☎04 78 83 51 51), arranges home visits.

Internet Access: Station-Internet, 4 rue du President Carnot, 2*ème* (☎08 00 69 20 01). 40F/€6.10 per hr., students 30F/€4.57. Open M-Sa 10am-7pm. **Connectix Café,** 19 quai St-Antoine, 2*ème* (☎04 72 77 98 85). 50F/€7.62 per hr. Open M-Sa 11am-7pm.

Post Office: pl. Antonin Poncet, 2*ème* (☎04 72 40 65 22), next to pl. Bellecour. **Currency exchange.** Open M-F 8am-5pm, Sa 8am-12:30pm. **Poste Restante:** 69002. **Postal Codes:** 69001-69009; last digit indicates *arrondissement.*

ACCOMMODATIONS AND CAMPING

France's second financial center fills its central hotels weekday nights with businessmen who leave by the weekend. Fall is the busiest season; it's easier and cheaper to find a place in the summer, but is still prudent to get reservations or you may find yourself sleeping under the stars. Budget hotels cluster east of pl. Carnot. Prices rise as you approach pl. Bellecour, but there are some inexpensive options north of pl. des Terreaux. Vieux Lyon tends to break budgets.

HOSTELS AND CAMPING

Auberge de Jeunesse (HI), 41-45 montée du Chemin Neuf (☎04 78 15 05 50; fax 04 78 15 05 51). M: Vieux Lyon. From pl. Bellecour, walk west toward the old city and cross the Saône at pont Bonaparte. Turn right through pl. St-Jean and then left onto rue de la Bombarde. Follow the hairpin turn left onto montée du Chemin Neuf and prepare for a good climb. The hostel is 10min. up on the left (15min. from Bellecour, 25min. from Perrache). Or take the funicular from Vieux Lyon to Minimes, walk down the stairs and go left down the hill for 5min. Stunning views, but rooms can be hot in summer. Bar, laundry, **Internet access** 1F/€0.15 per min., kitchen. Modern, split-level 4- to 8- bunk rooms with showers. Breakfast included. Sheets 17F/€2.59. Reception 24hr. Reservations recommended. Bunks 75F/€11.44. **Members only.** V.

Résidence Benjamin Delessert, 145 av. Jean Jaurès, 7*ème* (☎04 78 61 41 41; fax 04 78 61 40 24). M: Jean Macé. From Perrache, take bus #11 or 39 to "Jean Macé," walk under the railroad tracks, and look left after 3 blocks. From Part-Dieu, take the métro to Jean Macé. Reserve in advance. Full of student lodgers during the academic year; feels like a dorm year-round. TV room. **Internet access** 40F/€6.10 first hr., 30F/€4.57 extra hr. Laundry. Reception 24hr. Singles 91F/€13.88, with shower 95F/€14.48.

Camping Dardilly, 10km from Lyon in a dull suburb (☎04 78 35 64 55). From the Hôtel de Ville, take bus #19 (dir: "Ecully-Dardilly") to "Parc d'Affaires." Pool, TV, and restaurant. Reception 8am-10:30pm. 20F/€3.05 per person; tent 40F/€6.10, caravan 50F/€7.62, car free. Electricity 20F/€3.05 in summer, 30F/€4.57 in winter. MC/V.

HOTELS

Hôtel St. Vincent, 9 rue Pareille, 1*er* (☎04 78 27 22 56; fax 04 78 30 92 87), just off quai Saint-Vincent. Simple, elegant rooms, within stumbling distance of much nightlife. Breakfast 30F/€4.57. Reception 24hr. Reserve ahead. Singles with shower 180F/€27.44, with bath 230F/€35.07; doubles 230F/€35.07, 270F/€41.16. MC/V.

Hotel Vaubecour, 28 rue Vaubecour, 2*ème* (☎04 78 37 44 91; fax 04 78 42 90 17). In an antique building, with has gorgeous, high ceilings. Breakfast 25F/€3.81. Reception 7am-midnight. Reserve in summer. Singles from 150F/€22.90; doubles from 170F/€25.92; triples and quads from 355F/€54.14. Extra bed 80F/€12.20. MC/V.

Hôtel d'Ainay, 14 rue des Remparts d'Ainay, 2*ème* (☎04 78 42 43 42; fax 04 72 77 51 90). M: Ampère-Victor Hugo. Basic, cheap, and sunny rooms. Breakfast 26F/€3.97. Shower 15F/€2.29. Reception 7am-10pm. Singles from 145F/€24, with shower from 210F/€35; doubles 180F/€27.44, 220F/€33.54. MC/V.

Hôtel du Dauphiné, 3 rue Duhamel, *2ème* (☎04 78 37 24 19; fax 04 78 92 81 52). Plain, comfortable rooms with showers. Rooms over 205F/€31.26 have TV. Breakfast 27F/€4.12. Reception 24hr. Check-out 11:30am. Singles from 130F/€19.82; doubles from 210F/€32.02; triples from 250F/€38.12; quads 320F/€48.80. MC/V.

Hôtel St-Pierre des Terreaux, 8 rue Paul Chenavard (☎04 78 28 24 61; fax 04 72 00 21 07). M: Hôtel de Ville. While it emits a certain 1970s vibe, this cheery hotel is well situated. All rooms have baths or showers. Breakfast 35F/€5.34. Reception 6:30am-midnight. Reserve well ahead. Singles 190-250F/€28.97-38.12; doubles 230-270F/€35.07-41.16. MC/V.

FOOD

The galaxy of Michelin stars adorning the city's restaurants confirms what the locals proudly declare—this is the gastronomic capital of the Western world. *Lyonnais* food is as bizarre as it is elegant and as creative as it is delicious. A typical delicacy consists of a flagrantly unacceptable cow part prepared in a subtle, creamy sauce. For dessert, finish off with *tarte tatin*, an apple tart baked upside-down and then turned over. Luckily, the tradition is an intrinsic part of the city's fabric; you can sample fine food even in inexpensive restaurants.

THE PRIDE OF LYON

The pinnacle of the *lyonnais* food scene is *chez* **Paul Bocuse,** 50 rue de la Plage in Collonges-au-Mont-d'Or (☎04 72 42 90 90), 9km out of town, where meals cost approximately the equivalent of Andorra's GNP. You need not sell your inner organs to enjoy Bocusian cuisine, however. The master has two spots in Lyon with scrumptious yet affordable food. At **Le Nord,** 18 rue Neuve, *2ème*, Bocuse's traditional food graces the 110F/€16.77 *menu*. (☎04 72 10 69 69; fax 04 72 10 69 68. Open daily noon-2:30pm and 7pm-midnight. AmEx/MC/V.) Bocuse's kitchens serve up more Mediterranean fare at the appropriately named (and beautifully situated) **Le Sud,** 11 pl. Antonin Poncet, *2ème*, which also has a 125F/€19.06 *menu*, plus pizzas and pastas from around 70F/€10.67. (☎04 72 77 80 00. Open noon-2:30pm and 7pm-midnight. AmEx/MC/V.) Whether you're heading north or south, you'll need to reserve two to three days ahead.

Locals take pride in their *cocons* (chocolates wrapped in marzipan), made in Lyon's grandest pâtisserie, **Bernachon,** 42 cours F. Roosevelt, *6ème*. Their chocolate is made entirely from scratch, starting with the very bean. The showcases sparkle with pastries and the ambrosial *palets d'or*, which are recognized as the best chocolates in France—and not only because they're made with gold dust. (☎04 78 24 37 98. Open M-F 9am-7pm, Sa 8:30am-7pm and Su in the winter.)

OTHER FLEURS-DE-LYON

If *haute cuisine* doesn't suit your wallet and university canteens don't suit your palate, try one of Lyon's many **bouchons,** descendants of the inns where travelers would stop to dine and have their horses *bouchonné* (rubbed down). These cozy restaurants serving local fare can be found along **rue Mercière** and **rue des Marronniers** in the *2ème*. Most places in Vieux Lyon are sure to feed you very well; try the *bouchons* along rue St-Jean, which have *menus* from 75F/€11.43. Also consider the cheaper ethnic restaurants on the wide streets off **rue de la République** (*2ème*) or the kebab joints around the Hôtel de Ville.

Chez Mounier, 3 rue des Marronniers, *2ème* (☎04 78 37 79 26). Delicious and generous traditional specialties. Scared of the unrecognizable? Consult the *patron*, who'll be happy to talk over your choice of *menu*. 4-course *menus* 61F/€9.30, 86F/€13.12, and 96F/€14.64. Open Tu-Sa noon-2pm and 7-10:30pm, Su noon-2pm.

Chabert et Fils, 11 rue des Marronniers, *2ème* (☎04 78 37 01 94). One of the best-known *bouchons*. *Museau de bœuf* (snout of cattle) makes it to the 99F/€15.10 *menu*.

For dessert, try the indescribable *Guignol*, but arrange to take a long nap after. Lunch *menus* from 50F/€7.62. Open daily noon-2pm and 7-11pm. MC/V.

Mister Patate, pl. St. Jean, 5*ème* (☎04 78 38 18 79). A fantastic option for vegetarians. All potatoes, all the time, with plates from 35-50F/€5.34-7.62. Open M-Sa 11:30am-3pm and 6-11:30pm, Su 11:30am-3pm and 6:30-10pm.

La Crêpe d'Or, 2 pl. St. Paul, 5*ème* (☎04 78 27 94 85). Whipped up in the house where the creator of Guignol the puppet lived, these enormous crêpes are sure to satisfy. *Menus* 58-85F/€8.85-12.96. Open daily noon-midnight.

L'Etoile de l'Orient, 31 rue des Remparts d'Ainay, 2*ème* (☎04 72 41 07 87). M: Ampère-Victor Hugo. Food and decor is straight out of *Casablanca*. Salads 25-40F/€3.81-6.10, *menu* 120F/€18.30. Open M noon-2pm, Tu-Su noon-2pm and 7-11pm.

SUPERMARKETS

Supermarkets include a **Monoprix** on rue de la République at pl. des Cordeliers, 2*ème* (open daily until 9:30pm). If you're craving a more gourmet experience, shop at **Maréchal Centre,** rue de la Platière at rue Lanterne, 1*er*. (☎04 72 98 24 00. Open M-Sa 8:30am-8:30pm.) You won't find any culinary masterpieces in Lyon's many university restaurants, but they're sure to please your wallet. One is **Résidence la Madeleine,** 4 rue Sauveur, 7*ème*. (☎04 78 72 80 62. Open Nov.-July 13.)

SIGHTS

VIEUX LYON

Stacked up against the Saône at the bottom of the Fourvière hill, the narrow streets of Vieux Lyon wind between lively cafés, tree-lined squares, and magnificent Medieval and Renaissance houses. The colorful *hôtels particuliers*, with their delicate carvings, shaded courtyards, and ornate turrets, sprang up between the 15th and 18th centuries when Lyon controlled Europe's silk and publishing industries. The regal homes around rue St-Jean, rue du Bœuf, and rue Juiverie have housed Lyon's elite for 400 years—and still do.

TRABOULES. The distinguishing feature of Vieux Lyon townhouses is the *traboules*, tunnels leading from the street through a maze of courtyards, often with vaulted ceilings and statuary niches. Although their original purpose is still debated, later *traboules* were constructed to transport silk safely from looms to storage rooms. During WWII, the passageways proved invaluable as info-gathering and escape routes for the Resistance. Many are open to the public at specific hours; get a list of addresses from the tourist office or, better yet, take one of their tours. *(Tours everyday at 2pm in summer, irregular hours during rest of year, consult tourist office. 60F/€9.15, students 30F/€4.57.)*

CATHEDRALE ST-JEAN. The southern end of Vieux Lyon is dominated by the Cathédrale St-Jean, whose soaring columns and stained glass windows look too fragile to have withstood eight centuries of religious turmoil. Paris might have been worth a mass, but Lyon got the wedding cake; it was here that Henri IV met and married Maria de Medici in 1600. Inside, every hour between noon and 4pm, automatons pop out of the 14th-century astronomical clock in a charming reenactment of the Annunciation. The clock can calculate Church feast days until 2019. *(Cathedral open M-F 8am-noon and 2-7:30pm, Sa-Su 2-5pm.)*

MUSEUMS. Down rue St-Jean, turn left at pl. du Change for the **Hôtel de Gadagne,** a typical 16th-century Vieux Lyon building, and its relatively minor museums. The best is the **Musée de la Marionette,** which displays puppets from around the world, including models of **Guignol,** the famed local cynic, and his inebriated friend, Gnafron. *(Pl. du Petit College, 5ème. M: Vieux Lyon. ☎04 78 42 03 61. 1hr. tours on request. Open W-M 10:45am-8pm. 25F/€3.81, students 13F/€1.98, 18 and under free.)*

FOURVIERE AND ROMAN LYON

From the corner of rue du Bœuf and rue de la Bombarde in Vieux Lyon, climb the stairs heading straight up to reach **Fourvière Hill,** the nucleus of **Roman Lyon.** From the top of the stairs, continue up via the rose-lined **Chemin de la Rosaire,** a series of switchbacks that leads through a garden to the **Esplanade Fourvière,** where a model of the city points out local landmarks. Most prefer to take the less strenuous **funicular** (known as "*la ficelle*") to the top of the hill. It leaves from the head of av. A. Max in Vieux Lyon, off pl. St-Jean. The **Tour de l'Observatoire** offers a more acute angle on the city. On a clear day, scan for Mont Blanc, about 200km to the east. *(Jardin de la Rosaire: Open daily 6:30am-9:30pm. Tower: Open W-Su 10am-noon and 2-6:30pm.)*

BASILIQUE NOTRE-DAME DE FOURVIERE. Lyon's archbishop vowed to build a church if the city was spared attack during the Franco-Prussian War. His bargain was met, and the bishop followed through. The basilica's white, merengue-like exterior is delectable from a distance. The low, heavy crypt, used for mass, was conceived by the architect Pierre Bossan to contrast with the high thunderstorm of gold that blazes above in the Byzantine basilica. Here, the walls are decked with gorgeous, gilded, gigantic mosaics depicting religious scenes, Joan of Arc at Orléans, and the naval battle of Lepante. *(Behind the Esplanade at very top of the hill. Chapel open daily 7am-7pm; basilica open 8am-7pm.)*

MUSEE GALLO-ROMAIN. Almost invisible from the outside, circling deep into the historic hillside of Fourvière, this brilliant museum holds a collection of arms, pottery, statues, and jewelry. Artifacts are well-labeled in English and French. Highlights include six large, luminous mosaics and a bronze tablet inscribed with a speech by Lyon's favorite son, Emperor Claudius. *(Open Mar.-Oct. Tu-Su 10am-6pm; Nov.-Feb. 10am-5pm. 25F/€3.80, students 15F/€2.30. Free for everyone on Thursday.)*

PARC ARCHEOLOGIQUE. Just next to the Minimes/Théâtre Romain funicular stop, the Parc holds the almost too well-restored 2000-year-old **Théâtre Romain** and the smaller **Odéon,** discovered when modern developers dug into the hill. Both still function as venues for shows during the *Nuits de Fourvière* (see **Festivals,** p. 167). *(Open July-Aug. daily 7am-6pm; Sept.-June 9am-8pm. Free.)*

LA PRESQU'ILE AND LES TERREAUX

Monumental squares, statues, and fountains are the trademarks of Presqu'île, the lively area between the Rhône and the Saône. At its heart is **pl. Bellecour,** from which pedestrian **rue Victor Hugo** quietly strolls south, lined with boutiques and bladers. To the north, crowded **rue de la République,** or "la Ré," is the urban aorta of Lyon. It runs through **pl. de la République** and ends at **pl. Louis Pradel** in the 1*er*, at the tip of the Terreaux district. Once a marshy wasteland, the area was filled with soil, creating dry terraces *(terreaux)* and establishing the neighborhood as the place to be for chic locals. Now bars, clubs, and sidewalk cafés fill up after 8pm and keep this area hopping late into the night. Across the square at **pl. Louis Pradel** is the spectacular 17th-century facade of the **Hôtel de Ville,** framed by an illuminated cement field of miniature geysers. The **Opéra,** pl. Louis Pradel, is a 19th-century Neoclassical edifice supporting what looks like an airplane hangar.

MUSEE DES BEAUX-ARTS. Second only to the Louvre, the museum includes a comprehensive archaeological wing, a distinguished collection of French paintings, works by Spanish and Dutch masters, a wing devoted to the Italian Renaissance, and a lovely sculpture garden. Even the more esoteric works mixed into all-star pre-, post-, and just-plain-Impressionist collections are delightful. Be sure to visit Maillol's bronze *Venus*, whose classic composure is disrupted by a single displaced lock of hair. *(20 pl. des Terreaux. ☎04 72 10 17 40. Open W-M 10:30am-6pm. Sculptures closed noon-2pm; paintings closed 1-2pm. 25F/€3.81, students with ID 13F/€1.98.)*

LA CROIX-ROUSSE AND THE SILK INDUSTRY

Lyon is proud of its historical dominance of European silk manufacture. The 1801 invention of the power loom by *lyonnais* Joseph Jacquard intensified the sweatshop conditions endured by the *canuts* (silk workers). Unrest came to a head in the 1834 riot in which hundreds were killed. Mass silk manufacturing is based elsewhere today, and Lyon's few remaining silk workers perform delicate handiwork, reconstructing and replicating rare patterns for museum and château displays.

MUSEE HISTORIQUE DES TISSUS. It's not in the Croix-Rousse quarter, but textile and fashion fans—along with anyone else who's ever worn clothes—will have a field day here. This world-class collection includes examples of 18th-century elite garb, scraps of luxurious Byzantine textiles and silk wall-hangings that look like stained glass windows. Included with admission is the neighboring **Musée des Arts Décoratifs,** housed in an 18th-century *hôtel. (34 rue de la Charité, 2ème. ☎04 78 38 42 00. Tissus: Open Tu-Su 10am-5:30pm. Arts Décoratifs: Open Tu-Su 10am-noon and 2-5:30pm. Maps in English. Tour in French Su 3pm. 30F/€4.57, students with ID 15F/€2.29.)*

LA MAISON DES CANUTS. Some old silk looms in a tiny back room are all that remains of the weaving techniques of the *canuts*. The Maison's shop sells silk made by its own *canuts*. Though a scarf costs 130F/€19.82 and up, you can take home a silkworm cocoon for a few francs. or a handkerchief for 30F/€4.57. *(10-12 rue d'Ivry, 4ème. ☎04 78 28 62 04; fax 04 78 28 16 93. Tours by arrangement. Open M-F 8:30am-noon and 2-6:30pm, Sa 9am-noon and 2-6pm. 25F/€3.81, 15F/€2.29 students.)*

EAST OF THE RHONE AND MODERN LYON

Lyon's newest train station and monstrous space-age mall form the core of the ultra-modern Part-Dieu district. Locals call the commercial **Tour du Crédit Lyonnais** *"le Crayon"* for its unwitting resemblance to a giant pencil standing on end. Next to it, the shell-shaped **Auditorium Maurice Ravel** hosts major cultural events.

CENTRE D'HISTOIRE DE LA RESISTANCE ET DE LA DEPORTATION. The center is housed in a building in which Nazis tortured detainees during the Occupation. Here you'll find an impressive collection of assembled documents, photos, and films of the Resistance, whose national headquarters were based in Lyon. *(14 av. Bertholet, 7ème. M: Jean Macé. ☎04 78 72 23 11. Open W-Su 9am-5:30pm. 25F/€3.81, students 13F/€1.98. Admission includes an audio-guide in French, English, and German.)*

MUSEE D'ART CONTEMPORAIN. In the futuristic **Cité International de Lyon,** a super-modern complex with offices, shops, theaters, and Interpol's world headquarters, you'll find this extensive, wholly entertaining mecca of modern art. All the museum's exhibits are temporary; the walls themselves are built anew for each installation. *(Quai Charles de Gaulle, next to Parc de la Tête d'Or, 6ème. Bus #4 from M: Foch. ☎04 72 69 17 18. Open Tu-Su noon-7pm, W until 10pm. 25F/€3.81, students 13F/€1.98.)*

PARC DE LA TETE D'OR. This massive and completely free park, one of the biggest in Europe, owes its name to a legend that a golden head of Jesus lies buried somewhere within its grounds. The park sprawls over 259 acres; you can rent paddle boats to explore its artificial lake and island. Reindeer, elephants, and a thousand other animals fill the zoo; giant greenhouses encase the botanical garden. The 60,000-bush rose gardens are stunning. *(M: Charpennes or Tram T1 from Perrache, dir: "IUT-Feyssine." ☎04 78 89 02 03. Open in summer daily 11am-7pm; in winter 6am-9pm.)*

NIGHTLIFE

Nightlife in Lyon is fast and furious; the city is crawling with nightclubs. There's a row of semi-exclusive joints off the Saône, on quais Romain Rolland, de Bondy, and Pierre Scize in Vieux Lyon (5*ème*), but the city's best and most accessible late-night spots are a strip of riverboat dance clubs by the east bank of the Rhône. Students congregate in a series of bars on **rue Ste-Catherine** (1*er*) until 1am before heading to the clubs. More suggestions can be found in *Lyon Libertin* and *Guides de l'Eté de Lyon: Restaurant/Nuits*, each 10F/€1.53 at *tabacs*.

Le Fish, across from 21 quai Augagneur (☎04 72 87 98 98), plays salsa, jungle, hip-hop, and disco in a swank boat with a packed dance floor. Students only. 60-80F/€9.15-12.20 cover includes 1st drink, free before 11pm F-Sa. Open W-Sa 10pm-5am.

Le Chantier, 20 rue Ste-Catherine (☎04 78 39 05 56), has 12 tequila shots for 100F/€15.25. You have to slip down a spiral slide to reach the dance floor downstairs, which is filled with a crowd of students and locals. Open Tu-Sa 9pm-3am, sometimes later.

Tavern of the Drunken Parrot, next door to Le Chantier, serves homemade, extremely potent rum drinks (10F/€1.53). Open daily 6pm-3am.

Ayers Rock Café, 2 rue Desirée (☎04 78 29 13 45), and the **Cosmopolitan,** (☎04 72 07 09 80) right next door. If you can still see, be sure to stumble over, as both places are usually packed with students. Both have shooters for 20F/€3.05. Ayers has fabulous bartenders who put on as much of a show as those scandalous people in the corner. Ayers open M-Sa 6pm-3am; Cosmo open M-W 8pm-2am, Th-Sa 8pm-3am.

Le Voxx, 1 rue d'Algérie (☎04 78 28 33 87), packed with stylish French and almost-stylish exchange students, is the latest in a series of quai hotspots radiating off pl. des Terreaux. Open M-Sa 8pm-2am, Su 10pm-2am.

La Marquise (☎04 78 71 78 71), next door to Le Fish, spends less on the boat but more on big-name jungle and house DJs. Cover 50F/€7.62. Open W-Sa 10pm-dawn.

GAY AND LESBIAN NIGHTLIFE

The tourist office's city guide lists spots catering to Lyon's active gay community, and *Le Petit Pomme* offers superb tips. The most popular gay spots are in the *1er*.

L'United Café, impasse de la Pêcherie (☎04 78 29 93 18), in an alley off quai de la Pêcherie. The weekend club circuit normally starts here around midnight, with American and Latino dance hits. Theme nights throughout the week range from the post office to beach party–and there are lip-shaped urinals to boot. No cover; drinks from 35F/€5.34. Open daily 10pm-5am.

Le Village Club, 6 rue Violi (☎04 72 07 72 62), off rue Royale, north of pl. Louis Pradel. Drag queens nightly, and is the place to be on Su nights. A mostly male, mid-20s to mid-30s crowd. Drinks 20-35F/€3.05-5.34. Open W-Th 9pm-3am, F-Sa 10pm-4am.

L'Echiquier, 38 rue de l'Arbre-Sec (☎04 78 29 18 19). Mixed gay/lesbian crowd. Karaoke steals the show on Tu and W nights. Cover 50F/€7.62. Open W-M 10pm-dawn.

Le Verre à Soi, 25 rue des Capucins, *1er* (☎04 78 28 92 44). A little, local lesbian bar with a post-20s crowd. Drinks half-price 2-8pm. Open M-Sa 6am-3am.

Le Village, 8 rue St-George (☎04 78 42 02 19), off pl. de la Commanderie in the 5*ème*. Lesbians flock to this all-female *pub dansant*. Drinks 20-45F/€3.05-6.86. No cover. Open W-Th, Su 9pm-1am; F-Sa 9pm-4am.

ENTERTAINMENT

LIVE PERFORMANCE AND CINEMA

Lyon's major theater is the **Théâtre des Célestins,** pl. des Celestins, *2ème* (☎04 72 77 40 00; tickets 65-250F/€9.91-38.12, discounts for under 26 and over 65). The **Opéra,** pl. de la Comédie, *1er* (☎04 72 00 45 45), has pricey tickets (70-400F/€10.67-60.98), but 50F/€7.62 tickets for those under 26 and over 65 go on sale 15 minutes before the show. (Reservations office open M-Sa noon-7pm.) The acclaimed **Orchestre National de Lyon** plays a full season (Oct.-June; ☎04 78 95 95 95). The **Théâtre National Populaire** is at 8 pl. Lazare-Goujon, in the suburb of Villeurbanne (☎04 78 03 30 40). The **Maison de la Danse** (☎04 72 78 18 00) keeps pace with the dance scene. Lyon, the birthplace of cinema, is a superb place to see quality film. The **Cinéma Opéra,** 6 rue J. Serlin (☎04 78 28 80 08), and **Le Cinéma,** 18 impasse St-Polycarpe (☎04 78 39 09 72), specialize in black and white undubbed classics (34-40F/€5.19-6.10).

FESTIVALS

In summer, Lyon has a festival or special event nearly every week. The **Fête de la Musique** (June 21) and **Bastille Day** (July 14) engender major partying. The end of June sets off the two-week **Festival du Jazz à Vienne,** welcoming jazz masters to Vienne, a medieval town south of Lyon, accessible by bus or train. (☎04 74 85 00 05 or Vienne's tourist office, 11 cours Brillier, ☎04 74 53 80 30. Tickets 160F/€24.39, students 150F/€22.90, children 12-16 years 110F/€16.77, under 12 free.) The *Pavillon de Tourisme* may provide special festival buses, as parking in Vienne is difficult. **Les Nuits de Fourvière,** is a two-month summer festival held in the ancient Théâtre Romain and Odéon, beginning in mid-June. Popular artists are interspersed with classical concerts, movies, dance, and plays. (☎04 72 32 00 00. Tickets and info at the Théâtre Romain or the FNAC shop on rue de la République.)

The biennial **Festival de Musique du Vieux Lyon,** 5 pl. du Petit Collège, *5ème*, brings artists from around the world to perform in Lyon's old town from mid-November to mid-December. (☎04 78 42 39 04. Tickets 90-230F/€13.72-35.06.) Every December 8, locals place candles in their windows and ascend with tapers to the basilica for the **Fête des Lumières.** The celebration (which turns into a city-wide block party) honors the Virgin Mary for protecting Lyon from the Black Plague.

DAYTRIP FROM LYON: PEROUGES

This tiny hamlet is such a source of history and pride for Europe that it was the site for the G-7 summit in 1996. Pérouges' streets, affectionately called *"galets,"* made with rounded stones collected from nearby rivers, and their shape and color blend into the structure of the homes. While legend has it that Pérouges was built by a tribe of Gauls coming from Italy, the town has changed nationalities many times due to its location between feuding dukes and kings. Most of the buildings in the town date to the 15th century, a period of prosperity during which weaving was preeminent. Exquisitely preserved, the castles, caves, and plentiful, draping flora invoke romantic associations of royalty. The town's culinary specialty is *galette de Pérouges*, which is served with *cerdon*, a magnificent wine/champagne.

A superb way to see the evolution of the area's history is to stop in at the **Musée de Vieux Pérouges,** in the Maison des Princes, to which citizens have donated ancient wares. (Open daily 10am-noon and 2-6pm. 20F/€3.05.) The **tourist office** can help with getting around. (☎04 74 61 01 14. Open M-F 10am-noon and 2-6pm.)

Pérouges is only 35km outside of Lyon. **Trains** run from **Lyon** (30min., M-F 12 per day, 32F/€4.88). From the train station, make a left onto rue de Verdun. At the fountain, make another left and then take your second right onto rue Pérouges. After 10 minutes, make a right onto a steep road which brings you uphill to town. Or take a **Philibert Tour** from Lyon with commentaries in English. (Tours leave Apr.-Oct. Sa from Part-Dieu at 1:15pm, Bellecour at 1:30pm, and Perrache at 1:45pm, returning by 6pm. 210F/€32.02.)

NEAR LYON: BEAUJOLAIS

The very mention of Beaujolais provokes a thirst for the cool, fruity wine that is one of this region's main exports. Beaujolais lies roughly between the Loire and the Saône, with Lyon at its foot and Mâcon at its head, and is home to an important textile and lumber industry, especially in the more mountainous regions to the west. The tourist offices dotting the countryside can give you suggested bike or car routes that wind through endless vineyards, sleepy villages, and medieval châteaux, with a couple of *dégustations* (tastings) thrown in for good measure.

The most beautiful areas in Beaujolais are difficult to access by public transportation; trains run between Mâcon and Lyon, but stop mostly in uninteresting industrial towns like Villefranche. The best option is to rent a car in Lyon or Mâcon or venture in by bike, though bike rental is tough to find. **Bus tours** from Lyon in English are available through the tourist office with **Philibert,** which has a tour of the Beaujolais culminating in a *dégustation* in Le Hameau. (☎04 78 98 56 98. Apr.-Oct. Th-F and Su around 1:15pm; return to Lyon at 7pm. 210F/€32.02.)

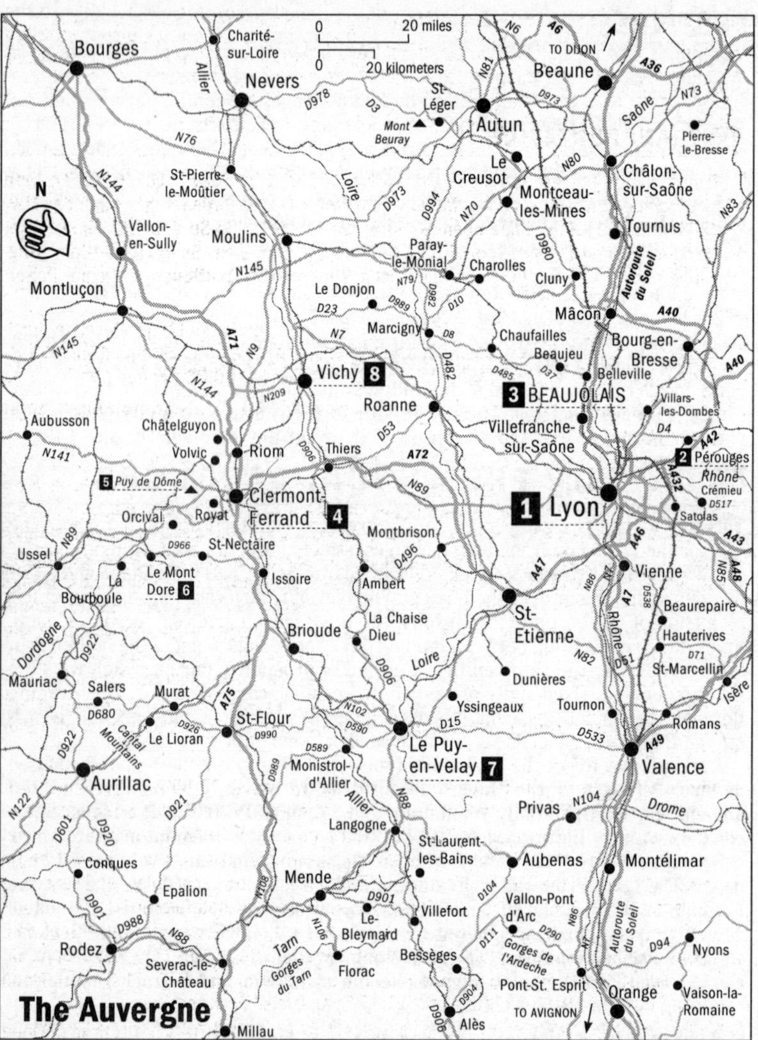

CLERMONT-FERRAND

During the Middle Ages, Clermont-Ferrand was two distinct cities, Clermont and Montferrand. It was in the former that Urban II preached the First Crusade, beginning the first in a long series of religious (and not so religious) wars that lasted until the 15th century. Back in France, a long-standing economic and political rivalry raged between Clermont and Montferrand until Louis XIII ordered their merger in 1630. Clermont got the better end of the deal; the city built walls to exclude Montferrand, and the latter, a 40-minute walk away, is now often forgotten. Many locals simply call their city Clermont.

For most of this century, Clermont (pop. 140,000) was synonymous with Michelin tires. Mme. Daubrée, niece of the Scottish scientist Macintosh (whose experiments with rubber and benzene led to the invention of a damn good rainproof coat), made some rubber balls to keep her children busy. The balls caught on, and in 1886 her Michelin relatives used the rubber to make bicycle tires, kicking off the town's major industry. Recently, the city has poured its resources into upgrading its universities. Clermont may serve better as a stopover on a mountain trip rather than a destination in itself.

TRANSPORTATION

Trains: av. de l'Union Soviétique. To: **Le Puy** (2½hr., 2 per day, 110F/€16.77); **Lyon** (3hr.; 9 per day, some indirect M-Sa; 141F/€21.50); and **Paris** (3½hr., 4 per day M-F, 244F/€37.21). Info office open M-F 4:45am-11:15pm, Sa-Su 7am-11:15pm; ticket window open M-Th 5am-9pm, F 5:20am-8pm, Sa 6am-8pm, Su 7:10am-10pm. **Baggage check** 20F/€3.05. Open M-F 7am-7:30pm. **SNCF Boutique:** av. Nestor Perret. Open M 11:50am-7pm, Tu-Sa 10am-7pm.

Buses: 69 bd. F. Mitterrand (☎04 73 93 13 61), near the Jardin Lecoq. Buses to destinations throughout the Auvergne, including **Vichy** (110min., 2 per day, 55F/€8.39). Office open M-Sa 8:30am-6:30pm. **Luggage storage:** 5F/€0.76 per day.

Local Transportation: 15-17 bd. Robert Schumann (☎04 73 28 56 56). Buses cover the city. Ticket 7.50F/€1.14, day pass 25F/€3.81. Service 5:30am-9pm.

Taxis: Taxi Radio Clermontois (☎04 73 19 53 53) or **Allô Taxi** (☎04 73 90 75 75).

ORIENTATION AND PRACTICAL INFORMATION

Buses #2, 4, and 14 go from the station downtown to the lively **pl. de Jaude.** Bounded on either end by statues of local hero Général Desaix and the valiant Vercingetorix, the *place* is lined with cafés, a theater, and the modern **Centre Jaude,** a vast shopping center. If you'd rather make the 25-minute walk, go left from the station onto av. de l'Union Soviétique, left again onto bd. Fleury, and take a quick right onto av. Carnot. The street bends to the left and turns into rue Maréchal Joffre for two blocks, then curves back right, turning into rue Maréchal Juin and then bd. Desaix before it dumps you onto pl. de Jaude. Get a map at the tourist office in the train station before you go.

Tourist Office: pl. de la Victoire (☎04 73 98 65 00; fax 04 73 90 04 11; www.ot-clermont-ferrand.fr). From the train station, make a left onto av. de l'Union Soviétique. Take a left at pl. de L'Esplanade and a quick right onto av. Carnot (changes names several times) walk about 10min. and make a right onto rue St. Genès. The office will be on your right, before the cathedral (20min.). Excellent map, bus schedules, and very competent staff. In its basement, **L'Espace Massif Central** has further info on natural spaces in the Auvergne. **Walking tours** June to Sept. 15. Office open June-Sept. M-F 9am-7pm, Sa-Su 10am-6pm; Oct.-May M-F 9am-6pm, Sa 10am-1pm and 2-6pm, Su 9:30am-12:30pm and 2-6pm. **Annex** at the train station (☎04 73 91 87 89). Open June-Sept. M-Sa 9:15-11:30am and 12:15-5pm; Oct.-May closed Sa.

Budget Travel: Wasteels, 11 av. des Etats Unis (☎08 03 88 70 34). BIJ tickets. Open M-F 9:30am-noon and 2-6pm, Sa 9:30am-noon.

Youth Centers: Espace Info Jeunes, 5 av. St-Genès (☎04 73 92 30 50). Open M-F 10am-6pm, Sa 10am-1:45pm. Closed Sa July 15-Aug. 12.

Laundromat: 6 pl. Hippolyte Renoux (☎06 75 02 88 81). Open daily 7am-8pm.

Police: 2 rue Pélissier (☎04 73 98 42 42, emergency ☎17).

Hospital: Centre Hospitalier Universitaire, 30 pl. Henri Dunant (☎04 73 75 07 50). **SOS Médecins,** 28 av. Léon Blum (☎04 73 42 22 22).

24-Hour Pharmacy: Pharmacie Ducher, 1 pl. Delille (☎04 73 91 31 77).

Internet Access: Virtua Network, 5 bd. Trudaine (☎04 73 91 65 53). 20F/€3.05 per hr. noon-2pm, 25F/€3.81 per hr. 2-5pm and 30F/€4.57 per hr. 5pm-midnight. **France Télécom,** 67 bd. Mitterand. Use up those last units of your *télécarte* to pay; no cash accepted. Open M, W-Th 9am-12:30pm and 2-6:30pm, Tu 9:30am-12:30pm and 2-6:30, F 9am-12:30pm and 2-4:30pm.

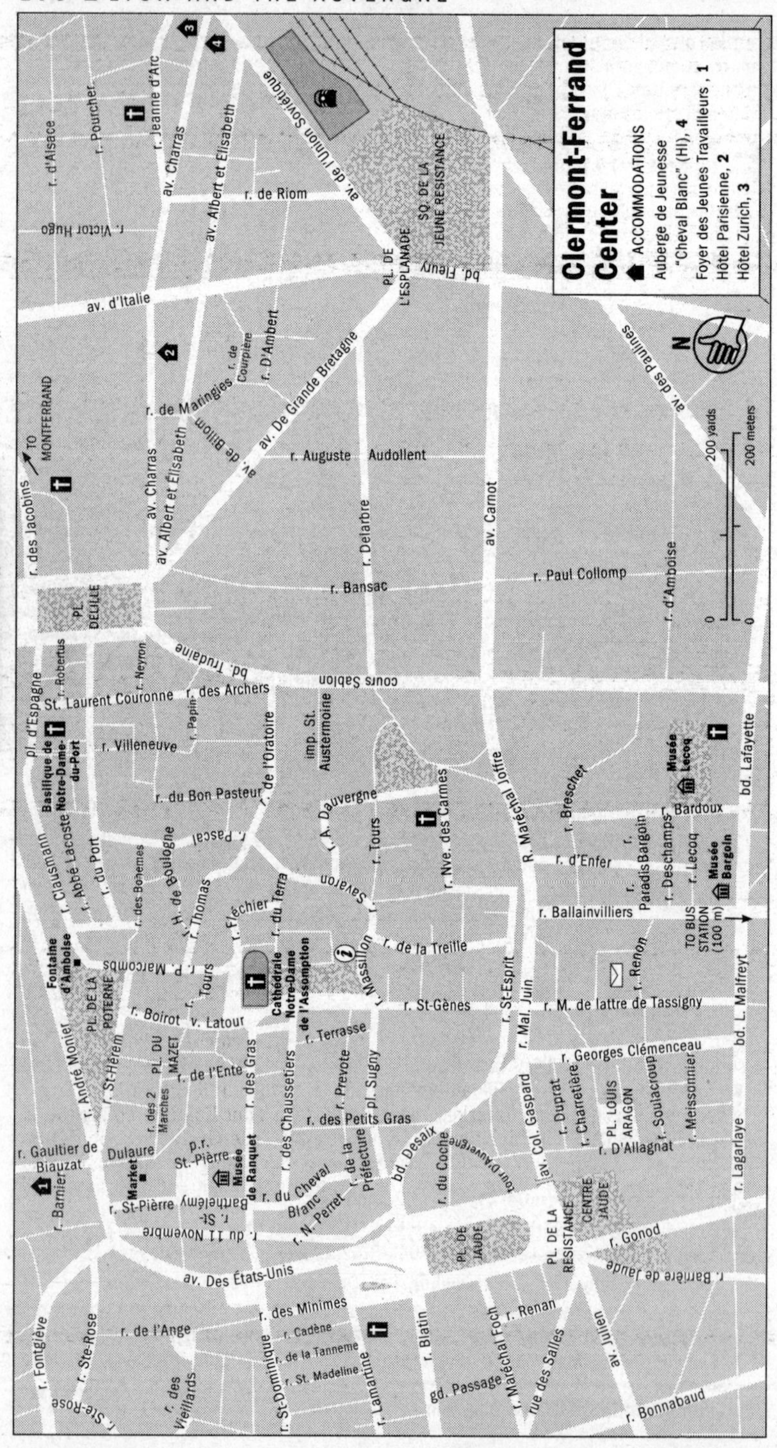

Clermont-Ferrand Center
ACCOMMODATIONS
Auberge de Jeunesse "Cheval Blanc" (HI), 4
Foyer des Jeunes Travailleurs, 1
Hôtel Parisienne, 2
Hôtel Zurich, 3
N
200 yards
200 meters
TO MONTFERRAND
TO BUS STATION (100 m)
r. d'Alsace
r. Pourcher
r. Jeanne d'Arc
av. Charras
av. Albert et Elisabeth
av. de l'Union Soviétique
SQ. DE LA JEUNE RESISTANCE
r. de Riom
r. Victor Hugo
av. d'Italie
PL. DE L'ESPLANADE
bd. Fleury
av. des Paulines
r. de Courpière
r. D'Ambert
r. de Maringues
av. de Billom
av. De Grande Bretagne
r. Auguste Audollent
r. des Jacobins
r. Delarbre
av. Carnot
r. Paul Collomp
r. d'Amboise
r. Bansac
PL. DELILLE
bd. Trudaine
cours Sabion
r. Robertus
r. Neyron
St. Laurent Couronne
r. des Archers
pl. d'Espagne
Basilique de Notre-Dame-du-Port
r. Villeneuve
r. Papin
imp. St. Austermoine
r. de l'Oratoire
r. du Bon Pasteur
r. A. Dauvergne
r. Nve. des Carmes
R. Maréchal Joffre
r. Brescher
Musée Lecoq
bd. Lafayette
r. Bardoux
r. Clausmann
r. Abbé Lacoste
r. du Port
r. des Bohemes
r. H. de Boulogne
r. Pascal
r. Tours
r. Savaron
r. d'Enfer
r. Paradis
r. Bargoin
r. Deschamps
r. Lecoq
Musée Bargoin
r. Ballainvilliers
Fontaine d'Amboise
r. P. Marcombs
r. Thomas
r. Fléchier
r. du Terra
Cathédrale Notre-Dame de l'Assomption
r. Massillon
r. de la Treille
r. Renon
r. St-Esprit
PL. DE LA POTERNE
r. Boirot
v. Latour
r. St-Gènes
r. M. de lattre de Tassigny
bd. L. Malfreyt
r. André Moinier
r. St-Hérem
PL. DU MAZET
r. de l'Ente
r. des Gras
r. des Chaussetiers
r. Terrasse
r. Prevote
pl. Sugny
r. Mal. Juin
r. Georges Clémenceau
r. des 2 Marches
r. des Petits Gras
av. Col. Gaspard
r. Duprat
r. Charretière
PL. LOUIS ARAGON
r. Soulacroup
r. Meissonnier
r. D'Allagnat
r. Gaultier de Biauzat
Dulaure
p.r. St-Pierre
Market
Musée de Ranquet
r. de la Préfecture
bd. Desaix
r. du Coche
tour d'Auvergne
r. Lagarlaye
r. Barnier
r. St-Pierre
r. St-Barthélemy
r. du Cheval Blanc
r. N. Perret
PL. DE LA RESISTANCE
CENTRE JAUDE
r. du 11 Novembre
PL. DE JAUDE
r. Gonod
av. Des États-Unis
r. Barrière de Jaude
r. des Minimes
r. Cadène
r. de la Tannerie
r. St. Madeline
r. de l'Ange
r. Fontgiève
r. Ste-Rose
r. des Vieillards
r. St-Dominique
r. Lamartine
r. Blatin
gd. Passage
r. Maréchal Foch
r. Renan
rue des Salles
av. Julien
r. Bonnabaud

Post Office: 1 rue Maurice Busset (☎04 73 30 65 00). **Currency exchange** and **Cyberposte.** Open M-F 8am-7pm, Sa 8am-noon. **Branch** at 2 pl. Galliard (☎04 73 31 70 00). Open M-F 9am-7pm, Sa 8:30am-12:30pm. **Postal code:** 63000.

ACCOMMODATIONS AND CAMPING

There are a couple of inexpensive hotels conveniently clustered near the train station. Finding a cheap room in the center of town can be more difficult.

Foyer des Jeunes Travailleurs (Corum Saint Jean), 17 rue Gauthier de Biauzat (☎04 73 31 57 00; fax 04 73 31 59 99), off pl. Gaillard. From the station, take bus #2 or 4 to "Gaillard." Modern complex holds well-furnished rooms (some with private bath), a bar, and laundry facilities. Great location near the *vieille ville.* Breakfast included. Meals 38-44F/€5.80-6.71. Reception 9am-7pm. Often full during the school year; call ahead. Singles or doubles 100-120F/€15.25-18.30 per person.

Auberge de Jeunesse "Cheval Blanc" (HI), 55 av. de l'Union Soviétique (☎04 73 92 26 39; fax 04 73 92 99 96). Across from and to the right of the station. Windows in characterless rooms look onto concrete. Squat toilets only. Kitchen. Breakfast included. Sheets 17F/€2.59. Reception 7-9:30am and 5-11pm. Lockout 9:30am-5pm. Curfew 11pm. Open Apr.-Oct. 1- to 8-bunk rooms 69F/€10.52 per person. **Members only.**

Hôtel Parisienne, 78 rue Charras (☎04 73 91 52 62), about 50m directly in front of train station. This calm hotel, with flowered wallpaper and squeaky floors, is a spectacular bargain. No reservations. Reception about 7am-11pm. Singles and doubles 95-110F/€14.48-16.77, with bath 130F/€19.82; triples 120F/€18.30.

Hôtel Zurich, 65 av. de l'Union Soviétique (☎04 73 91 97 98), right of the train station past the hostel. Homey rooms, and a grandmotherly *patronne.* Call ahead for reception. Singles and doubles 100-140F/€15.25-21.35, with shower 150-160F/€22.90-24.39; twins with bath 180-220F/€27.44-33.54; triples/quads 180F/€27.44.

Camping: Le Chancet, av. Jean-Baptiste Marrou (☎04 73 61 30 73). 6km outside Clermont, on the Nationale 89 (dir: "Bordeaux"). From the station, take bus #4C (dir: "Ceyrat") to "Préguille." 3-star site has sports, activities, and biking and hiking excursions in summer. Laundry. Reception 8am-10pm in summer. Open year-round. 16F/€2.44 per adult, ages 4-10 9F/€1.37; 30F/€4.57 per tent; 9F/€1.37 per car. Caravan site with electricity 54F/€8.23.

FOOD

Clermont-Ferrand is not known for its food. While tasty restaurants are rare, cheap, ethnic ones abound, especially around **rue St-Dominique,** off av. des Etats-Unis. There are a number of fast food joints on **av. des Etats-Unis,** and some brasseries near the tourist office and cathedral. **Av. Charras,** right near the train station, has many ethnic eateries. The freshest lunch place is **Le Marché de Nathalie,** 6 rue des Petits Gras, near the cathedral. (☎04 73 19 12 12. 75F/€11.43 *menu* and 30F/€4.57 cheeses. Open M-Sa 11:30am-4pm and Th, F and Sa until 7pm. MC/V.)

There is a **Champion** supermarket, rue Giscard de la Tour Fondue. To get there, make a left at pl. de la Résistance and a right onto rue Giscard. (Open M-Sa 8:20am-8pm, Su 9am-12:20pm.) For local fruits, veggies, and cheese, the **Marché Couvert/Espace St-Pierre,** off pl. Gaillard, is a huge covered market with hundreds of regional specialties (M-Sa 6am-7:30pm).

SIGHTS

The ***Passe découverte*** *(60F/€9.15) is accepted at the city's five major museums.*

The *vieille ville* of Clermont, called the *Ville Noire* (Black City), is one of the best-known districts in France; the buildings are made of black volvic stone, contrasting with their bright red roofs. The Roman ruins on nearby **Puy de Dôme** (p. 173) and the relics in the city's museums are significant and well-preserved.

CATHEDRALE NOTRE-DAME DE L'ASSOMPTION. First built in 450, the church was completely reconstructed in the Gothic style between 1248 and 1295 and now commands attention from miles away. The strength of the lava-based material allowed the architects to elongate the graceful, jet-black spires to a height of 100m; you can ascend the tower for a panoramic view. Seen from the surrounding squares, three massive black rose windows seem to wither in the cathedral walls, but in the dark, airy interior their glass blooms brilliantly. *(Pl. de la Victoire. Open June-Sept. 15 daily 8am-6pm; Sept. 16-May 20 8am-noon and 2-6pm. 13F/€1.98 for tower.)*

BASILIQUE DE NOTRE-DAME-DU-PORT. Less magnificent but more intriguing than the cathedral is this 11th- to 12th-century church built in the local Auvergnat Romanesque style. The basilica has a particularly beautiful choir, surrounded by an ambulatory and radiating chapels. It was probably here that Urban II first preached the First Crusade. On the Sunday after May 14, pilgrims stream in to see the icon of the Black Virgin; the ex-voto plaques in the crypt attest to recent miracles. *(Pl. Notre-Dame-du-Port. ☎04 73 91 32 94. For info about tours call M-F 10am-noon and 2:30-7pm. Open daily 8am-7pm.)*

MUSEE BARGOIN AND MUSEE DES TAPIS ET DES ARTS TEXTILES. Undoubtedly the most interesting museum in Clermont, the Musée Bargoin is devoted to prehistoric and Gallo-Roman archaeology. It displays artifacts recovered from the Temple of Mercury on the Puy de Dôme, as well as Pompeiian wall paintings, 2000-year-old hair braids, and mummified infants. Most striking are the 3500 Gallo-Roman votive offerings, mostly wooden carvings of limbs, found near a local spring in 1968. The **Musée des Tapis et des Arts Textiles** lays out a beautiful collection of rugs from around the world. Panels in French and English help decode the symbolism of the rugs—you'll be able to tell whether you're treading on the female sex organ or the tree of life. *(45 rue Ballainvilliers. Bargoin ☎04 73 91 37 31; Tapis ☎04 73 90 57 48. Both open Tu-Su 10am-6pm. Each museum 26F/€3.96, students 13F/€1.98.)*

MONTFERRAND. Most of Montferrand's best sights are inconspicuous *hôtels particuliers*, private mansions which date from the Middle Ages and the Renaissance. The best way to visit the town, which rises above an unattractive commercial district 40 minutes away up av. de la République, is on a two-hour **walking tour** given by the tourist office. (Tours depart Tu, Th, and Sa from pl. Louis Deteix at 3pm; 32F/€4.88, students 16F/€2.44.) Take bus #17 (dir: "Blanzat" or "Cébazat") or 10M (dir: "Aulnat") from the train station. Like Clermont, Montferrand is dominated by a (less magnificent) volcanic stone church. **Notre-Dame-de-Prospérité** stands on the site of the long-demolished château of the *auvergnat* counts. Having served as everything from a nunnery to police headquarters, the 18th-century convent on rue du Seminaire is now the **Musée d'Art Roger-Quillot,** pl. Louis Deteix, containing 14 centuries of art. *(Musée ☎04 73 16 11 30. Open Tu-Su 10am-6pm. 25F/€3.81, students 13F/€1.98, free the first Su of each month.)*

ENTERTAINMENT AND FESTIVALS

Clermont's students complain that the city's nightlife is sluggish, but they struggle valiantly to start it up at a few popular nightspots. Check *Le Guide de l'Etudiant Clermont-Ferrand* (available at the tourist office) for complete listings. All types play pool and drink cheap beer in the many bars across from the train station. **Le Palais de la Bière,** 3 rue de la Michodière, on the corner of pl. Galliard and av. des Etats-Unis, lacks a little in ambience, but compensates with exotic beers and late-night brasserie fare. (☎04 73 37 15 51. Open Tu-Sa 7pm-1:30am.) Or imbibe with students and townies at **The John Barleycorn Pub,** 9 rue du Terrail. The bearded bartender is sure to entertain. (☎04 73 92 31 67. Open daily 5pm-2am.)

From Feb. 1 to 9, 2002, filmmakers from all over Europe will gather for Clermont-Ferrand's annual **Festival International du Court Métrage** (International Festival of Short Films), considered the "Cannes du Court." For info, contact La Jetée, 6 pl. Michel de l'Hospital, 63058 Clermont-Ferrand Cedex 1 (☎04 73 91 65 73).

NEAR CLERMONT-FERRAND: PUY DE DOME

Clermont-Ferrand's greatest attraction is its proximity to an extinct volcanic hinterland filled with crystalline lakes and pristine mountains. Puy de Dôme is the mountain in the middle, and is part of the **Parc Naturel Régional des Volcans d'Auvergne,** which is west of Clermont-Ferrand (☎04 73 65 64 00; fax 04 73 65 66 78). Hikers, bikers, and skiers enjoy unspoiled terrain in France's largest national park. A booklet available at the Clermont-Ferrand tourist office marks and catalogues hiking paths. The protected area includes three main sections: the **Mont-Dore,** the **Monts du Cantal,** and the **Monts Dômes**—the last of which is the best base for exploring the mountains.

From the top of the massive, flat-topped **Puy de Dôme** (1465m), you can see across the teacup-shaped **Chaîne des Puys,** a green ridge of extinct volcanos which runs north-south from Clermont-Ferrand. If you scale the Dôme in late autumn, you may behold the wondrous *mer de nuages* (sea of clouds), a blanket of clouds that obscures the plains below, from which only isolated peaks protrude into the clear blue sky. (Puy-de-Dôme open Mar.-Oct. daily.) If you want to join the paragliders in the air, contact **Volcan Action** (☎04 73 62 26 00; fax 04 73 62 16 41). A 15-minute flight with an instructor will cost you 400F/€60.98 (all gear provided). At the peak, the **Centre d'Accueil de Puy de Dôme** has regional info, maps, informative displays on volcanoes, and free tours (every hr.) of the summit. (☎04 73 62 21 46. Open July-Aug. daily 9am-7pm; Oct. daily 10am-6pm; May-June and Sept. M-F 10am-6pm, Sa-Su 10am-7pm.) The **Comité Départemental de Tourisme du Puy de Dôme,** pl. de la Bourse in Clermont-Ferrand, has reams of pamphlets on the area and sells a guide (50F/€7.62) with historical info on the area. (☎04 73 42 22 50. Open M-Th 8:30am-12:15pm and 1:45-5:30pm, F 8:30am-12:15pm and 1:45-5pm.)

Although Puy-de-Dôme is only 12km from Clermont-Ferrand, reaching it takes planning. The Clermont tourist office's **Espace Massif Central** desk has info on how to get there. **Voyage Maisonneuve,** 24 rue Clemenceau, organizes infrequent **bus excursions** to the summit and other parts of the Auvergne. (5hr. July-Sept.; see tourist office for details. 70F/€10.67 to Puy de Dôme. Office ☎04 73 93 16 72. Open M-F 8:30am-noon and 2-6:30pm, Sa 9am-noon.) Your best bet, though, is to hike, drive, or hitch (not recommended by *Let's Go*). Hikers take the regular bus line to Royat (#14); from there it's about a three-hour hike along the PR Chamina to the summit. Hitchers head out of town on av. du Puy de Dôme and follow the signs for about 8km to the base of the mountain. It's illegal to walk up the road that cars take, and the rule is heavily enforced. Stand at the toll for an easy hitch, or follow the D941 a few kilometers west to the Col de Ceyssat, where you can grab the **sentier des muletiers,** a Roman footpath that leads to the top in an hour. Buy a good map (such as the IGN Chaîne des Puys), and listen to the weather forecast for the day, as conditions change rapidly—hailstorms on the summit are not uncommon, even in June. Bring warm clothes and rain gear. From 10am to 6pm in July and August, and Sundays and holidays in May, June, September, and October, drivers must leave their cars at the base and take a bus (13F/€1.98 one-way, 22F/€3.36 round-trip; free parking at base and summit); otherwise, the toll is 30F/€2.29.

LE MONT-DORE

Ski resort and hiking mecca Le Mont-Dore (pop. 1700) lies at the highest point of an isolated valley, right at the foot of the biggest of a range of dormant volcanoes. The odd rock phenomena, deep craters, craggy peaks and ridges, and varying shades of green give the place a primordial feel; elephants, rhinoceri, and tigers once roamed through bamboo forests here, and their fossils remain encrusted in volcanic rock. Pine trees and meadows now cover the slopes, populated with *curistes* seeking relief in the warm waters that seep up through cracks in the lava. In the winter, skiers flock to Puy de Sancy, the highest peak in the Auvergne.

PRACTICAL INFORMATION. **Trains** run from pl. de la Gare to **Clermont-Ferrand** (1½hr., 5-6 per day, 66F/€10.07). (☎04 73 65 00 02. Info desk open daily 6am-12:30pm and 2-6pm.) **Taxis** are run by **Claude Taxi** (☎04 73 65 01 05) and **Taxi Sepchat** (☎04 73 65 09 38). Rent **bikes** and **skis** at **Bessac Sports,** rue de Maréchal Juin. (☎04 73 65 02 25. Bikes 60-130F/€9.15-19.82 per half-day, 90-200F/€13.72-30.49 per day. Passport or 600F/€91.48 deposit. Skis 45-135F/€6.86-20.58 per day. Snowboards and hiking equipment also available. Open in summer daily 9am-noon and 2-7pm; in winter 8:30am-7pm. MC/V.)

From the train station, head up av. Michel Bertrand and follow the signs to the **tourist office,** av. de la Libération, behind the ice-skating rink on the other side of the Dordogne. It distributes a practical guide to the city, helps you find accommodations (for stays over 3 days) and organizes hikes and bike circuits in the summer. **Internet access** is also available here; inquire at the desk. (☎04 73 65 20 21; fax 04 73 65 05 71. Open July-Aug. and Feb. M-Sa 9am-7pm, Su 10am-noon and 2-6pm; May-June and Sept. M-Sa 9am-7pm, Su 10am-noon and 2-5pm; Oct.-Jan. and Mar.-Apr. M-Sa 9am-7pm. Circuits half-day 35F/€5.34, full day 60F/€9.15.) **Voyages Maisonneuve** runs **bus excursions** (5hr.) to the region's lakes, volcanoes, and châteaux. (☎04 73 69 96 96. June-Sept. almost daily. 92-148F/€14.03-22.57; book at the tourist office.) The **police station** (☎04 73 65 01 70, or 17) is on av. M. Bertrand, and the **hospital** is at 2 rue du Capitaine-Chazotte (☎04 73 65 33 33), off pl. Charles de Gaulle. The **post office,** pl. Charles de Gaulle, **exchanges currency.** (☎04 73 65 02 47. Open M-F 8:30am-noon and 2-5pm, Sa 8:30am-noon.) **Postal code:** 63240.

ACCOMMODATIONS AND CAMPING. The **Auberge de Jeunesse "Le Grand Volcan" (HI),** rte. du Sancy, is 3km from town. From the station, climb av. Guyot-Dessaigne, which becomes av. des Belges. Continue on D983 (which changes names several times) into the countryside. When you see ski lifts, the hostel will be on your right. The train station has info on local buses which go by the hostel. The slope-side chalet at the foot of Puy de Sancy has 1- to 6-bed rooms; avoid the cramped loft singles. Kitchen, bar, and laundry facilities. Reception 8am-noon and 2-10:30pm. (☎04 73 65 03 53; fax 04 73 65 26 39. Breakfast 19F/€2.90. Lunch and dinner 50F/€7.62. Bunks 51F/€7.78. **Members only.**) Le Mont-Dore is blessed with over a dozen hotels with rooms around 150F/€22.90, so finding a cheap one, even if you have to reserve ahead, isn't a problem. Turn off your engines at **Hôtel Le Parking,** 19 av. de la Libération, right behind the tourist office. Complete with turret, this sparkling, partially pink interiored hotel has sizable, comfortable rooms, many with spectacular view. (☎04 73 65 03 43. Breakfast 25F/€3.81. Reception 7am-9pm. Closed Nov. Singles and doubles 120F/€18.30, with shower 160F/€24.39, with bath 200F/€30.49; triples with bath 280F/€42.69. MC/V.) Or chill with supposed Italian nobles at **Castel Medicis,** 5 rue Duchatel, right at the top of the main part of town. Modern wood paneling gives this hotel a clean, bright feel. Helpful proprietress speaks some English. (☎04 73 65 30 50. Breakfast included. Reception summer 8am-9pm, winter 8am-8pm. Singles and doubles 130F/€19.82, with shower 170F/€25.92, with bath 190F/€28.97. Extra bed 50F/€7.62. MC/V.)

There are four **campsites** in and around town. The most convenient is **Des Crouzets,** av. des Crouzets, across from the station in a pleasant, crowded hollow along the Dordogne. You can set up first and pay later. (☎/fax 04 73 65 21 60. Office open M-F 9am-noon and 4-6pm, Sa-Su 9:30am-noon. Open mid-Dec. to Oct. No reservations. 16F/€2.44 per person, 14.50F/€2.21 per site; car included. Electricity 11.50-33F/€1.75-5.03.) One kilometer behind the station is **L'Esquiladou,** rte. des Cascades. The gravelly sites are better suited to caravans, but it feels less crowded than Des Crouzets. (☎/fax 04 73 65 23 74. Reception July-Aug. 8am-noon and 3-8pm; May-June, Sept.-Oct. 9am-noon and 3-6pm. 18.60F/€2.84 per person, 15.50F/€2.36 per tent. Electricity 11.50-33F/€1.75-5.03.)

FOOD. It's difficult to find a restaurant in Le Mont-Dore that isn't attached to a hotel; such *pensions* serve everyone, but usually give discounts to guests. Most *menus* in town begin at 65F/€9.91, and a good one is usually 70-90F/€10.67-13.72. For a tasty pizzeria, try **Le Tremplin,** 3 av. Foch. Although selection is somewhat sparse, this family owned joint makes you feel welcome and the prices can't be beat. (☎04 73 65 25 90. Pizzas 40-56F/€6.10-8.54. MC/V.) The cheapest and most scenic meals are mountaintop picnics. The streets are full of boutiques hawking delicious regional specialties—wedges of soft, sweet St-Nectaire cheese and lengths of sausage. **Eco Service supermarket** is on rue du Cap-Chazzotte. (Open July-Aug. daily 7am-1:30pm and 3-8pm; Sept.-June M-Sa 7am-12:30pm and 3-7:30pm.)

SIGHTS. There's not a whole lot to do in the town, but you can introduce yourself to the *curiste* tradition at the **Etablissement Thermal,** pl. du Panthéon. Five of the springs used today were first channeled by the Romans, who found that the water did wonders for their horses' sinuses. The curious can visit the *thermes* via French tours; the visit ends with a dose of the *thermes'* celebrated *douche nasale gazeuse*, a tiny blast of carbon and helium that evacuates those sinuses like no sneeze ever could. (☎04 73 65 05 10. Tours M-F 2:30-5:30pm. 20F/€3.05.) Down the hill on av. Michel Bertrand, the **Musée Joseph Forêt** honors the celebrated art editor, a Mont-Dore native who left much of his collection to the town in 1985. For his grand finale, Forêt recruited seven painters and seven writers to collaborate in the publication of the largest book in the world. *Le Livre de l'Apocalypse*, weighing a quarter-ton, includes works by Dalí and Cocteau. The original was sold in bits to pay for itself, but a facsimile sits in the back. (☎04 73 65 00 91. Call 12:30-3pm to set up a time to come in. 15F/€2.29, students 10F/€1.53.)

HIKING AND BIKING. Trails through these volcanic mountains cover dense forests, crystal-clear waterfalls and cascades, and bizarre, moon-like rock outcroppings. Scaling the peaks is relatively easy—the summit of Puy de Sancy (1775m) is a six-hour hike—but as always, if you plan on taking an extended hike, go over your route with the tourist office, which has fantastic maps and will help you plan. Leave an itinerary with the **peloton de montagne** (mountain police; ☎04 73 65 04 06), on rue des Chaussers at the base of Puy de Sancy, for any multi-day route. All hikers should get maps and weather reports—mist in the valley can mean hail or snow in the peaks. The tourist office sells the pocket-sized *Massif du Sancy* (45F/€6.86), with hiking and biking circuits, complemented by a detailed map (35F/€5.34) with topographical info and routes. You may also want their *Massif du Sancy et Artense* guide (94F/€14.34), which covers 38 hikes originating in all areas of Le Sancy. An IGN map (either Massif du Sancy or the larger Chaîne des Puys) is necessary for any serious trek (58F/€8.85).

To get all the views without all that exertion, make use of the **téléphérique,** which whisks people up from the base station by the hostel to the Puy de Sancy. (☎04 73 65 02 73. July-Aug. every 15-20min. 9am-5:30pm; Dec.-Apr. 9am-5pm; May-June and Sept. 9am-12:30pm and 1:30-5pm. 31F/€4.73 one-way, 38F/€5.80 round-trip.) A **funicular** runs from near the tourist office up to the Salon des Capucins (1245m). (July-Aug. every 20min. 10am-6:40pm; May and Sept. 10:10am-12:10pm and 2-6:40pm; 21F/€3.20 one-way, 27F/€4.12 round-trip.)

If you have a car or a bike, don't miss the chance to visit one of the many volcanic lakes, like **Lac Servière** (20km northeast), which fill in the craters of the Mont-Dore region and are suitable for windsurfing, sailing, fishing, and swimming. **Lac d'Aydat,** to the northeast, offers pedal-boats and other amusements, as does **Lac Chambon,** 20km east of Le Mont-Dore via D996E, near Murol, where actors fill a château with 13th-century repartee. (Lac Chambon ☎04 73 88 67 11. Call for seasonal hours. 45F/€6.86, ages 5-16 35F/€5.34.)

For an **easy hike** (3½km round-trip, 1½hr.), try the **Grande Cascade** waterfall. From the *thermes*, follow rue des Desportes a few meters to the right and climb the stairs on your left to join the chemin de Melki Rose, which then leads into the rte. de Bresse and the chemin de la Grande Cascade. After crossing a road, the trail continues through birch woods and then winds up a narrow, pine-covered gorge. From there it's a quick climb on the metal stairway to the top of the waterfall. Another easy option is the **Salon du Capucin** (4½km round-trip, 1½hr.). From the tourist office, take av. Jules Ferry and follow the signs.

A great **intermediate hike** (8km round-trip, 3-4hr.) begins at the base of the Puy de Sancy, near the hostel. Ascend the mountain via the Val de Courre, clearly labeled with yellow markers. At **Puy Redon,** you join the GR30, and the trail climbs to the summit of Puy de Sancy. Summer snow patches are not uncommon, and on clear days the Alps are visible to the east. On the south side of the peak, wildflowers and other rare vegetation carpet the immense **Vallée de la Fontaine Salée.** Smart hikers who don't want to follow the GR4 all the way back (see below) retrace their steps along the Val de Courre instead of suffering through the marked ski trails of the GR4e. Another **half-day hike** (5-6hr. round-trip) starts just off the D996, a few hundred meters west of **le Marais.** Follow the yellow-marked PR as it curves right and ascends through a thick wood. At the juncture of the GR30 you can turn left and follow a 2km detour to climb the Puy Gros. Otherwise, continue right for several kilometers, passing by another yellow-marked PR, and on to the Lac de Guerey.

The most ambitious, **advanced full-day hike** (6hr.) follows a series of trails that make a complete loop around the town and hit all of the major natural attractions along the way. Start from the tourist office and follow the signs to the Salon du Capucin, a towering mass of rocks overlooking town. Another vertical 200m takes you to the **Pic du Capucin,** where the trail hooks up with the GR30, marked with parallel red and white lines. The GR30 follows a narrow ridge, then skirts the summit of **Puy Redon,** hovering over the spectacular Val de Courre, and ascends another 100m to the summit of **Puy de Sancy,** the highest peak in the Massif Central. From there, follow the GR4 as it loops back north and descends a series of ski trails before climbing back into the trees. The weary should take the GR4e, which descends straight to the base of the ski mountain.

LE PUY-EN-VELAY

Jutting crags of volcanic rock pierce the sky at Le Puy (pop. 21,000), sharing the horizon with gentle green hills. A pilgrimage site since the first churches were built atop these natural skyscrapers, Le Puy has always thrived on its visitors. Perhaps for this reason, most of its residents are accommodating and friendly.

TRANSPORTATION

Trains: pl. Maréchal Leclerc. To: **Clermont-Ferrand** (some via Brioude; 2½hr., M-F 5 per day, 110F/€16.77); **Lyon** (2½hr., M-F 4 per day, 110F/€16.77); and **St-Etienne** via Châteaucreux (1¼hr.; M-F 10 per day, 7 on Sa; 74F/€11.29). Ticket counters open M 4:45am-7:10pm, Tu-Sa 5:40am-7:10pm, Su 10:05am-8:10pm. Info M-Sa 9:25am-5:50pm, Su 10:05am-8:10pm.

Buses: pl. Maréchal Leclerc, next to the train station (☎04 71 09 25 60). **Chavanelle** goes to **St-Etienne** (2¼hr., 4 per day, 42F/€6.41). Those traveling into the *midi* should bus to **Langogne** (2hr., 3 per day, 46F/€7.01) to catch a train. Open M-F 7:30am-12:30pm and 2-6pm, Sa 7:30am-12:30pm. Buy tickets on bus.

Local Transportation: S.A.E.M. TUDIP, pl. du Breuil. Info at the tourist office. Timetables in *Horaire Hiver* or *Horaire Eté*. Tickets bought individually on the bus 6F/€0.92. *Carnet* of 10 at the tourist office 44F/€6.71.

Taxis: Radio-Taxis, pl. du Breuil (☎04 71 05 42 43). 24hr.

ORIENTATION AND PRACTICAL INFORMATION

Most trains arriving from the south or Clermont-Ferrand require a change at Brioude, while trains from Lyon or Paris change at St-Etienne (Châteaucreux). From the station, walk left along av. Charles Dupuy, cross sq. H. Coiffier, and turn left onto bd. Maréchal Fayolle. After five minutes you'll reach two adjacent squares, **pl. Michelet** and **pl. du Breuil.** The tourist office and most hotels are here and on nearby bd. St-Louis; the cathedral, hostels, and *vieille ville* are way uphill to the right.

Tourist Office: pl. du Breuil (☎04 71 09 38 41; fax 04 71 05 22 62). Free accommodations service. Free, well-marked map with 3 different walking tours. Open July-Aug. M-Sa 8:30am-7:30pm, Su 9am-noon and 2-6pm; Sept.-June M-Sa 8:30am-noon and 1:30-6:15pm, Su 9am-noon and 2-6pm; Oct.-Mar. Su 10am-noon only.

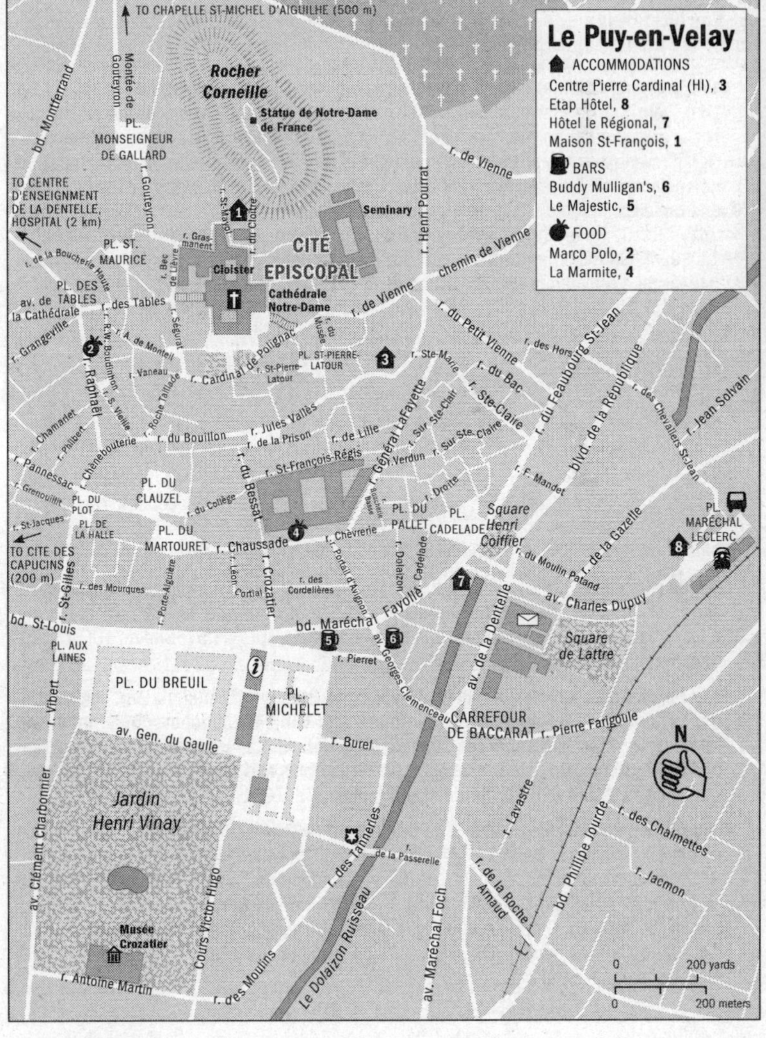

Laundromat: 12 rue Chèvrerie (☎04 71 09 32 60). Open M-Sa 7:30am-noon and 1-7pm. **Lav'Flash,** 24 rue d'Avignon. Open M-Sa 8am-8pm, Su 9:15am-6:30pm.

Police: rue de la Passerelle (☎04 71 04 04 22).

Medical Assistance: Centre Hospitalier Emile Roux, bd. Dr. Chantemesse (☎04 71 04 32 10). **Clinique Bon Secours,** 67bis av. M. Foch (☎04 71 09 87 00).

Internet Access: Forum Café, 5 rue Général Lafayette (☎04 71 04 04 98), is dirt cheap (10F/€1.53 per hr.) but you need to sign up in advance. Open Tu-Sa 1-7pm.

Post Office: 8 av. de la Dentelle (☎04 71 07 02 05). **Currency exchange.** Open M-F 8am-7pm, Sa 8am-noon. **Branch office:** 49 bd. St-Louis (☎04 71 09 77 61). Open M-F 9am-noon and 2-5:30pm, Sa 9am-noon. **Postal code:** 43000.

ACCOMMODATIONS AND CAMPING

Le Puy has few hotels and even fewer cheap ones. Reserve ahead in summer, especially for the mid-June pilgrimage.

Centre Pierre Cardinal (HI), 9 rue Jules Vallès (☎04 71 05 52 40; fax 04 71 05 61 24). From the station, head left down av. Dupuy. Cross the square at the end of the street and turn left on rue Chèvrerie. Turn right on rue Général Lafayette, and, after the zigzag, swing left; the hostel is on your right in a beautiful former barracks (15min.). If no one's in, use the phone at the entrance to call the staff (dial 20). 72 beds in numerous quads and one 18-bed dorm. Excellent kitchen. Breakfast 11.50F/€1.75. Sheets 21F/€3.20. Reception July-Aug. daily 2-11:30pm; Apr.-June and Sept. M-Sa 2-11:30pm, Su 8-10pm. Curfew 11:30pm. Closed holidays, Christmas vacation and in July for the Festival des Musicales. Bunks 42F/€6.41. **Members only.**

Maison St-François, rue St-Mayol (☎04 71 05 98 86; fax 04 71 05 98 87). Walk up rue Raphael and make a left onto rue des Tables, then go left on rue Bec de Lièvre, right up rue Gasmanent, and pass through the portal and around a bend; rue St-Mayol will be on your left. Practically *in* the cathedral. Kitchen and convent garden. Caters primarily to pilgrims in summer, but there is often room in winter. Breakfast included. Meals 60F/€9.15. No sheets available. Reception 2-6pm. Call ahead. Beds 70F/€10.67.

Hôtel le Régional, 36 bd. Maréchal Fayolle (☎04 71 09 37 74), near pl. Michelet. In a noisy area with sound-proofed windows. Breakfast 29F/€4.42. Reception 7am-11pm. Singles and doubles 140F-180F/€21.35-27.44, with shower from 170F/€25.92; triples from 220F/€33.54; quads 310F/€47.26. AmEx/MC/V.

Gîte des Capucins, 29 rue des Capucins (☎04 71 04 28 74), off bd. St. Louis. Small, extremely friendly place with immaculate 4-6 bed dorms, each with private bath. Kitchen facilities and quaint garden in back. Breakfast 30F/€4.57. Sheets 10F/€1.53. Reception 4-8pm. Beds 82F/€12.51.

Etap Hôtel, 25 av. Charles Dupuy (☎04 71 02 46 22; fax 04 71 02 14 28), across from the train station. An ultra-clean chain hotel with compact, modern rooms. Breakfast 24F/€3.66. 24hr. computerized credit-card reception; staff on hand M-Sa 6:30-11am and 5-10pm. Apr.-Oct. singles 215F/€32.79, doubles and triples 240F/€36.59; Nov.-Mar. singles 185F/€28.21; doubles and triples 205F/€31.25 for 2-3. AmEx/MC/V.

Camping du Puy-en-Velay, chemin de Bouthezard (☎04 71 09 55 09), in the northwest corner of town, under the stone spike of St-Michel D'Aiguilhe, near the river. Walk up bd. St-Louis, continue on bd. Carnot, turn right at the dead end onto av. d'Aiguille, and look to your left (10-15min.). Or take bus #6 (dir: "Mondon") from pl. Michelet (10min., 1 per hr., 5F/€0.76). Grassy, but not very private. Reception 8am-9pm. Open Easter-Oct. 14.30F/€2.18 per person; 15.30F/€2.33 per tent, 10.20F/€1.55 per car; 50F/€7.62 for 2 people, site, and car.

FOOD

In 1860, Rumillet Charnetier created **Verveine,** an alcoholic *digestif* of local herbs and honey with a sweet mint flavor (65-149F/€9.91-22.72 per bottle). Speaking of things green, Le Puy is known for its **lentils,** which you'll find everywhere in local food. Inexpensive restaurants are on the side streets off **pl. du Breuil.** There is a **Casino supermarket** on the corner of av. de la Dentelle and rue Farigoule (open M-Sa 8:30am-8pm), with a **cafeteria** above (meals 29-50F/€4.42-7.62; open daily 11:30am-9:30pm). On Saturdays, there's a vast **market** in practically every square as farmers bring in fresh produce (6am-12:30pm). The market in pl. du Plot throws in a few live chickens, rabbits, and puppies; the adjacent pl. du Clauzel hosts an antique market (Sa 7:30am-1pm). At pl. du Breuil, the biggest spread of all includes clothing, hardware, toiletries, and shoes.

Marco Polo, 46 rue Raphael, serves massive 3-course *formules* (89-139F/€13.57-21.20). Specialties include an *osso bucco* that could slay an ox (72F/€10.98). (☎04 71 02 83 11. Open Tu-Sa noon-2pm and 7pm-1am. Reserve for Sa. MC/V.) If you have conquered Marco Polo and are ready for more, try **La Marmite,** 59 rue Chaussade, where they serve up 1kg of mussels for 68-74F/€10.37-11.29. (☎04 71 04 15 15. *Menus* 78-118F/€11.90-18. Open Tu-Sa noon-2pm and 5:30-midnight.)

SIGHTS

*The **billet jumelé** (sold Feb.-Oct., 45F/€6.86) includes admission to all the sights in the Cité Episcopale, as well as the Musée Crozatier, Chapelle St-Michel, and Rocher Corneille. Sold at tourist office or at the first site. Pick up the English-language **guide pratique.***

CATHEDRALE NOTRE-DAME. Towering over the lower city, the **Cité Episcopale** has attracted pilgrims and tourists for over 1000 years. Built on a rock, known as "le puy," where the Virgin appeared and healed a woman in the 5th century, it has a long and varied past. While built as a Christian cathedral, many of its workers were Muslim, and their influence can be noticed on the doors on either side of the entrance, where "There is only one true God" is written in Arabic. At the altar, a copy of Le Puy's mysterious **Vierge Noir** (Black Virgin) smiles enigmatically. A side chapel houses the celebrated Renaissance mural **Les Arts Libéraux.** It is thought to be unfinished—of the seven liberal arts, only Grammar, Logic, Rhetoric, and Music are represented. *(☎04 71 05 98 74. Open daily 7am-8pm. July-Aug. free tours.)*

CLOISTER. The most remarkable of the sights near the cathedral, its black, white, and peach stone arcades reflect an Islamic influence brought from Spain. Beneath flame-red tiling and black volcanic rock is an intricate frieze of grinning faces and mythical beasts. Amid the Byzantine arches of the *salle capitulaire*, a vivid and well-preserved 13th-century fresco depicts the Crucifixion. The same ticket allows a look at the **Trésor d'Art Religieux,** containing walnut statues and jeweled capes. *(☎04 71 05 45 52. Both open daily July-Sept. 9:30am-6:30pm; Apr.-June 9:30am-12:30pm and 2-6pm; Oct.-Mar. 9:30am-noon and 2-4:30pm. 26F/€3.96, ages 12-25 with ID 16F/€2.44.)*

NOTRE-DAME DE FRANCE. At the edge of the *vieille ville* is the **Rocher Corneille,** the eroded core of a volcano. The summit looks out over a dreamscape of jagged crags and manicured gardens. Thrill-seekers can climb the cramped 16m **Notre-Dame de France,** a statue cast from cannons captured during the Crimean war. Notre-Dame earned national fame in 1942, when 20,000 young people came here to pray for the liberation of France. *(Open July-Aug. daily 9am-7:30pm; Mar. 16-Apr. 9am-6pm; May-June and Sept. 9am-7pm; Oct.-Mar. 15 10am-7pm. 20F/€3.05, students 10F/€1.53.)*

CHAPELLE ST-MICHEL D'AIGUILHE. Just outside the old city, this primitive chapel crowns an 80m spike of volcanic rock like a holy tentpeg securing one end of the sky. Its rustic stained glass barely illuminates a fading 12th-century fresco and the 10th-century woodcut crucifix discovered during excavations here. The chapel was built in AD 950 by the first pilgrim to complete the Chemin de St-Jacques, a trail from Le Puy to Spain still traveled by the pious. *(☎04 71 09 50 03. Open June 15-Sept. 15 daily 9am-7pm; Feb.-Mar. 14 2-4pm; Mar. 15-31 10am-noon and 2-5pm; Apr.-May 10am-noon and 2-6pm; June 1-14 9am-noon and 2-7pm; Sept. 16-Nov. 12 9:30am-noon and 2-5pm. 15F/€2.29, under age 14 8F/€1.22.)*

NIGHTLIFE AND FESTIVALS

Bars here are filled with locals, ready to welcome the tourist into their revelry. Most memorable is **The King's Head,** 17 rue Grenouillit, an English pub, which serves beers and fish and chips. The English owner gives it clout as a legitimate pub. (☎04 71 02 50 35. Open M 5pm-1am, Tu-Sa 11am-1am, Su 8pm-1am; Sept.-June closed Su.) Equally Anglo is **Buddy Mulligan's,** 13 av. Georges Clemenceau, packed with a young crowd and home to wild Halloween and St. Patrick's Day celebrations. Pints from 20F/€3.05. (☎04 71 02 52 17. Open daily noon-1am.) **Le Majestic,** 8 bd. Maréchal Fayolle, a brasserie by day, spills out onto a terrace at night. (☎04 71 09 06 30. Piano bar Th, techno F-Sa. Open M-Sa 7am-1am, Su 10am-1am.)

Le Puy likes to party, and hosts seven other festivals, ranging from music to theater, beginning in early July. There's a different one each week until they culminate in mid-September with the **Fête Renaissance du Roi de L'Oiseau** (☎04 71 02 84 84). Locals dress in costume, jugglers and minstrels ramble the streets, and food and drink are bought with specially minted festival currency. A tunnel system carved centuries ago into the rock below the *vieille ville* is opened up and turned into one great party hall, where beer and wine flow freely. *(From 20F/€3.05, depending on activity. Free to those in costume. For costume rentals call 04 71 09 16 53.)*

VICHY

Vichy moors itself in the days when its history recorded little other than the comings and goings of Napoleon III because more recent events are too painful to recall. From 1940 to 1944, sedate Vichy was the capital of France. Forced by the occupying German troops to leave Paris, the French administration, a Nazi puppet government, set up shop in this central spa town. Maréchal Philippe Pétain, a WWI hero, was elected as the leader of the new state (see **History,** p. 10). Understandably, today's Vichy has chosen to preserve its memories of the Belle Epoque, rather than recall its part in the darkest days of 20th-century France. Still, the lack of a single monument, museum, or plaque acknowledging Vichy's role in WWII creates an eerie historical gap.

PRACTICAL INFORMATION. The station on pl. de la Gare has service to **Clermont-Ferrand** (35min., 14 per day, 51F/€7.78); **Nevers** (1hr., 5 per day, 88F/€13.42); and **Paris** (3hr., 2 per day, 219F/€33.40). (Ticket counters open M-Th 5:45am-8:50pm, F 5:40am-9:50pm, Sa 6:30am-8:50pm, Su 6:45am-9:50pm. **Baggage check** 15F/€2.29. Open M-Sa 9am-noon and 2-5pm.) The **bus station** is in a brick building next to the train station (office open M-F 8am-noon and 2-6pm). **Public buses** run around town from 3am to 6pm (6.40F/€0.98). Schedules are available at the tourist office and at Bus Inter (☎04 70 97 81 29), on pl. Charles de Gaulle near the post office. Rent **bikes** at **Vichy Velo,** Chalet des Suppliques, at the end of Pont de Bellerive. (☎06 80 76 05 08. 100F/€15.25 per day, 500F/€76.23 per week. Passport or credit card deposit. Open June-Aug. daily 9am-7pm.)

Vichy's sleek and well-managed **tourist office,** 19 rue du Parc, as well as the most popular *sources*, lies in the **Parc des Sources,** 10 minutes from the train station. Leaving the station, walk straight on rue de Paris; at the fork turn left onto rue Clemenceau and then right onto rue Sornin. The tourist office is straight ahead

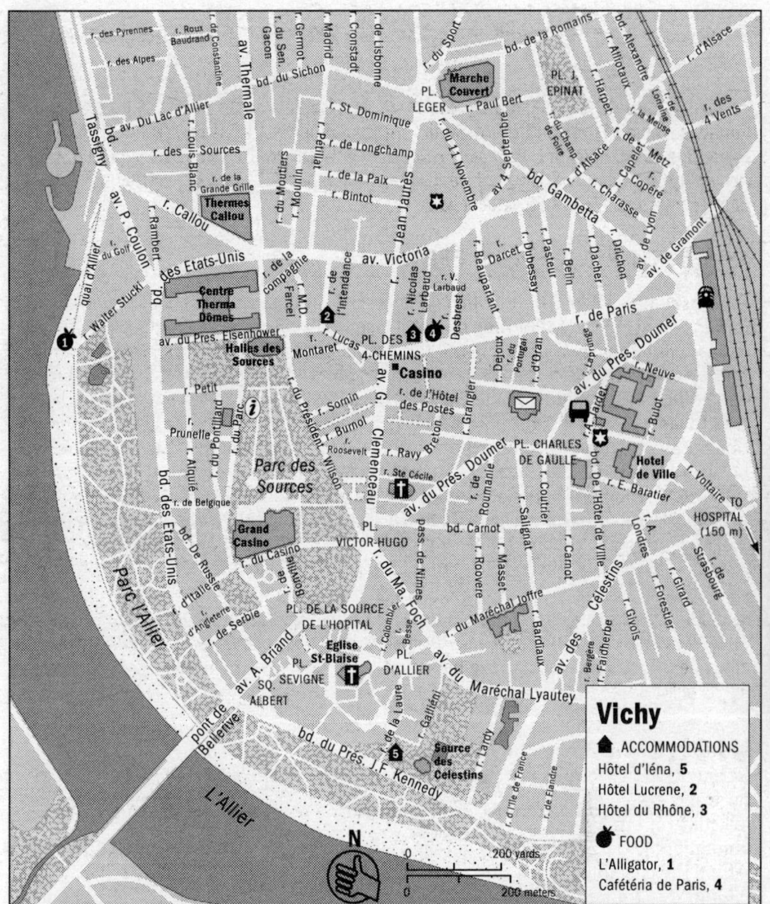

across the park, in the former Hôtel du Parc that housed the Pétain leadership. The staff gives away a good map, a list of hotels and restaurants, and has a free **accommodations service.** Ask for the booklet of suggested tours in Vichy and the region, or book a **bus tour** with them. Find out about operas, concerts, and other events in town from the free, French-language *Vichy Quinzaine*, or the free *Vichy Guide*, in English. (☎04 70 98 71 94; fax 04 70 31 06 00; www.ville-vichy.fr. Office open July-Aug. M-Sa 9am-7:30pm, Su 9:30am-12:30pm and 5-7pm; Apr.-June and Sept. M-Sa 9am-12:30pm and 1:30-7pm, Su 9:30am-noon and 3-7pm; Oct.-Mar. M-F 9am-noon and 1:30-6pm, Sa 9am-noon and 2-6pm, Su 2:30-5:30pm.) The **police** are at 35 av. Victoria (☎04 70 98 60 03, emergency ☎17). The **Centre Hospitalier** (☎04 70 97 33 33) is on bd. Denière. Be sure to bring 2F coins if you want to take advantage of the **Wash'n Dry** at 3 bd. Gambetta. (☎06 78 78 08 92. Open daily 7am-9pm.) The **post office,** pl. Charles de Gaulle, offers **currency exchange** at competitive rates. (☎04 70 30 10 75. Open M-F 8am-7pm, Sa 8am-noon.) **Postal code:** 03200.

ACCOMMODATIONS AND FOOD. In keeping with Vichy's mission to pamper, even its budget hostels are deluxe. On **rue de Paris,** hotels jostle for business, with rooms starting around 130F/€19.82. The **Hôtel du Rhône,** 8 rue de Paris, between the train station and the *thermes*, offers delightful doubles and triples and an air-conditioned salon, managed by the friendly multilingual owner. In the spacious courtyard a single koi nudges the rim of its pond. The restaurant downstairs offers regional specialties. (☎04 70 97 73 00; fax 04 70 97 48 25. Breakfast 19-29F/€2.90-4.42, buffet 39F/€5.95. *Menus* 69-250F/€10.52-38.12. Reception 24hr. Singles and doubles with shower 150-250F/€22.90-38.12; deluxe rooms with bath 220F-450F/€33.54-68.61. Extra bed 40F/€6.10. AmEx/MC/V.) **Hôtel Lucrene,** 8 rue de l'Intendance, is centrally located, with well-maintained rooms. (☎04 70 98 24 46; fax 04 70 31 71 61. Breakfast 28F/€4.27. Reception 6:30am-10pm. Open Apr.-Oct. 15. Singles 130-140F/€19.82-21.35, with shower 150-180F/€22.90-27.44; doubles 380-480F/€57.95-73.20. MC/V.) **Hôtel d'Iéna,** 56 bd. John Kennedy, right across the Parc d'Allier. From the train station, bear left onto av. des Célestins and follow it all the way to bd. Kennedy. Turn right, and the hotel will be past the Source des Célestins to the right (25min.). Friendly hotel with small, comfy rooms. (☎04 70 32 01 20. Breakfast 24F/€3.66. Showers 10F/€1.53. Singles 125F/€19.06; doubles 140F/€21.35, with bath 165F/€25.16; triples 185F/€28.21; quads 215F/€32.79. MC/V.) The riverside four-star **Camping Les Acacias** has a grocery store, private pool, and laundry. Take bus #7 from the train station (dir: "La Tour") to "Charles de Gaulle" and transfer to bus #3 to "Les Acacias"; otherwise it's 3½km by foot. (☎04 70 32 36 22. Open Apr. to mid-Oct. Reception May-Aug. 7:45am-11pm; Apr. and Oct. 8am-9pm. 28F/€4.42 per person, 30F/€4.57 per tent. Electricity 15F/€2.29.)

For a picnic in Vichy's superb parks, head to **Casino supermarket,** pl. Charles de Gaulle and l'Hôtel des Postes. (Open M-Sa 8:30am-12:30pm and 2:30-7:30pm, Su 9am-noon.) There's a covered **morning market** on pl. Léger at the intersection of rue Jean Jaurès and bd. Gambetta (Tu-Sa). Restaurants in Vichy are usually expensive, and most are connected to hotels. There are bars, pubs, and cheap pizzerias on **rue de Paris. Cafétéria de Paris,** 13 rue de Paris, has hot dishes for 22-78F/€3.36-11.90, full meals for 50-60F/€7.62-9.15. (☎04 70 97 81 26. Open daily 11am-9:30pm.) Stroll along the river and snap up a tasty treat at **L'Alligator,** 1 quai d'Allier. (☎04 70 98 30 47. *Menus* 68-103F/€10.37-15.71. Open Mar.-Oct. noon-2pm and 7-10:30pm.)

SIGHTS AND ENTERTAINMENT. The only way to see Pétain's Vichy is to take a French **tour** from the tourist office—significant buildings of the World War II era are not marked, so you won't notice anything otherwise. (Tours July-Aug. Tu-W and F-Sa at 3:30pm; June and Sept. Tu-W and F. 25F/€3.81.)

Take a sip of Vichy's nectar, and you'll wonder how the town ever made it big—the water tastes disgusting. The *sources* bubble free of charge at the **Sources des Célestins** on bd. Kennedy, a **cold spring.** (Open Apr.-Sept. M-Sa 7:45am-8:30pm, Su 8am-8:30pm; Oct.-Mar. daily 8am-6pm). In the rotunda of the **Source d'Hôpital,** behind the casino, you can slurp from a nauseating **hot spring.** (Open M-Sa 6:30am-8:30pm, Su 7:45am-8:30pm.) The heart of the action, though, is the **Halle des Sources** at the edge of the **Parc des Sources.** Anyone can drink for 10F/€1.53. (☎04 70 97 39 59. Open daily 7:30am-7pm.) If you go, take small swigs—it looks like plain water, but it's powerful stuff. **Célestins** is easiest to digest and was proven to relieve arthritis in a 1992 study by the Hôpital Cochimin in Paris. **Parc** is tougher on the stomach, and **Lucas** is chock-full of sulphur, hence the rotten-egg smell. Still thirsty? The hot springs are even more vile. **Chomel** is the most popular; **Grand Grille** is the hardest-hitting. Recover in the beautiful Parc des Sources. Surrounded by a wrought-iron Art Nouveau gallery and Opéra, it's Vichy elegance at its height.

A wide array of flora and fauna fall within the confines of the English-style gardens in the elegant riverside **Parc de l'Allier,** commissioned by Napoleon III. Across the river and a brisk 20- to 25-minute walk along the promenade to the right of Pont de Bellerive, lies Vichy's ultimate recreational facility. The sprawling **Centre Omnisports** offers sailing, wind-surfing, archery, canoeing, kayaking, rafting, tennis, swimming, and mountain biking. (☎04 70 59 51 00. Open daily 8am-10pm. Half-day activities pass 36F/€5.47, full day 58F/€8.85, week 205F/€31.26.)

The tourist office posts a daily list of upcoming events in Vichy. There are cheap thrills at the **Grand Casino** in the Parc des Sources. (Open daily noon-4am.) **Operas** and **concerts** take place during the summer in the beautiful **Opéra,** 1 rue du Casino. (☎04 70 30 50 30. Open M-Sa 1:30-6:30pm. Operas 150-390F/€22.90-59.46, under 25 90-310F/€13.72-47.28; concerts 100-200F/€15.25-30.49.)

BURGUNDY (BOURGOGNE)

Encompassing the Côte d'Or, the Plateau de Langres, and the wild, forested Morvan, Burgundy is best known for its Romanesque architecture and the 40 million bottles of wine it produces annually. Battleground of Gallic border wars in the first century BC, the region was a major player in the Roman conquest; Autun, in fact, was founded as a Roman capital. In the 5th century, the Burgundians, one of many Germanic tribes to pour across the Empire's borders during its final years, settled on the plains of the Saône and modestly named the region after themselves.

What the Loire is to châteaux, Burgundy is to churches. During the Middle Ages, the duchy was at the heart of the religious fever sweeping Europe; abbeys burgeoned in size and wealth, and towns eager for pilgrim traffic built magnificent cathedrals. Most powerful of all was Cluny, whose abbot governed over 10,000 monks in the 12th century and was second only to the Pope in power and influence. While the Wars of Religion and the Revolution ended the pre-eminence of religious institutions in Burgundian life, the 19th century saw a revival, with new pilgrimages beginning to Paray-le-Monial and Nevers.

TRANSPORTATION

Burgundy is crisscrossed by **train** lines which intersect at Dijon, but these manage to miss many of the finest destinations. Towns which lack train stations are served by combinations of trains and **SNCF** or **TRANSCO buses** (☎03 80 42 11 00 in Dijon). Burgundy is primarily an agricultural region, so timetables favor early morning departures and early evening returns, and it's not uncommon to be stranded for a night due to cryptic bus schedules. The terrain is perfect for hiking and biking, but winter weather in Burgundy can be harsh. Many parts of the Morvan and some small towns and châteaux can only be reached by bike, car, or foot.

1. **Dijon:** Smart, modern Burgundian capital renowned for its snobbery and mustard (p. 183)
2. **Gevrey-Chambertin:** Château surrounded by France's arguably best vineyards (p. 193)
3. **Clos de Vougeot:** Gothic frat-castle owned by an association of alcoholic knights (p. 194)
4. **Beaune:** Wine. Wine? Wine. Come here if you like wine (p. 190)
5. **Château de Rochepot:** Fairy-tale pointed turrets, slate roof, wooden drawbridge (p. 194)
6. **Mâcon:** Quiet town, once populous, with carved houses and strange medieval bits (p. 194)
7. **Cluny:** Once the most powerful abbey in Europe, now ruined and dismantled (p. 196)
8. **Val Lamartinien:** Valley peppered with châteaux and Romantic poetry (p. 198)
9. **Paray-le-Monial:** Huge pilgrimage site, architecturally a sort of mini-Cluny (p. 198)
10. **Autun:** Quiet town with cathedral, medieval ruins, serpentine streets (p. 200)
11. **Nevers:** Leafy provincial city at the confluence of two rivers; known for fine porcelain (p. 202)
12. **Auxerre:** Mid-sized, skippable city which retains some of its medieval charm (p. 204)
13. **Avallon:** Sensible base from which to approach the forest of the Morvan; little more (p. 206)
14. **Vézelay:** One of the most beautiful villages in France; its cathedral is legendary (p. 208)
15. **Semur-en-Auxois:** Lovely, typical Burgundian town: ramparts, mossy gargoyles (p. 209)

DIJON

Dijon (pop. 160,000) is about more than just mustard. The capital of Burgundy is an appealing city with the usual Burgundian attractions, such as gardens, fine wines, a couple of good museums, an old half-timbered *vieille ville*. It is also full of students and young travelers, a combination which, when mixed properly, can create sparks until the wee hours of the morning.

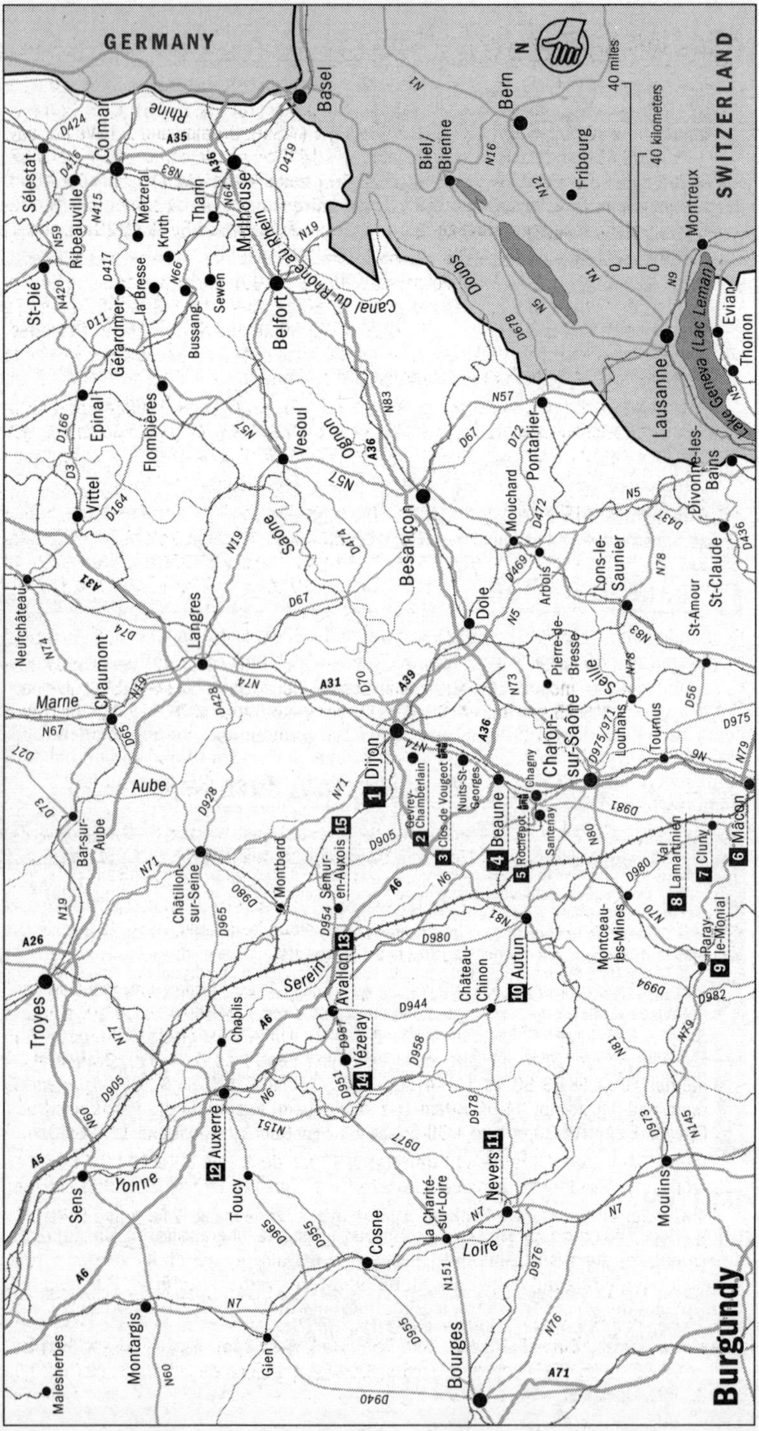

BURGUNDY

Burgundy

1 Dijon
2 Gevrey-Chambertain
3 Clos de Vougeot
4 Beaune
5 Rochepot
6 Mâcon
7 Cluny
8 Val Lamartinien
9 Paray-le-Monial
10 Autun
11 Nevers
12 Auxerre
13 Avallon
14 Vézelay
15 Semur-en-Auxois

GERMANY

SWITZERLAND

0 – 40 miles
0 – 40 kilometers

TRANSPORTATION

Trains: cours de la Gare, at the end of av. Maréchal Foch. To: **Beaune** (30min., 21 per day, 38F/€5.79); **Clermont-Ferrand** (4hr., 1 per day, 191F/€29.12); **Lyon** (2hr., 11 trains and 5 TGVs per day, 137F/€20.89); **Nice** (7-8hr., 9 trains and 2 TGVs per day, 386F/€58.85); and **Paris** (1½hr.; 2 trains and 14 TGVs per day; trains 196F/€29.88, TGVs 213F/€32.47). 24hr. ticket counters. Reservations and info office M-F 9am-7pm, Sa 9am-6pm. **SOS Voyageurs** (☎03 80 43 16 34) open M-F 8:30am-7pm and Sa 8:30am-5pm. **Baggage storage** open M-F 8am-7:45pm, Sa-Su 9-11:20am and 2-5:45pm. 15F/€2.29 for one bag, 25F/€3.81 for two.

Buses: TRANSCO, av. Maréchal Foch (☎03 80 42 11 00), connected to the train station, to the left as you exit. Ticket and info office open M-F 5:30am-8:30pm, Sa 6:30am-12:30pm and 4-8:30pm, Su 9:30am-12:30pm and 4:40-8:30pm. Otherwise, buy tickets on the bus or at the *chef de gare's* office near the bus terminal. Service to the **Beaune, Côte d'Or, Chalon-sur-Saône,** and **Autun.**

Local Transportation: STRD (☎03 80 30 60 90), pl. Grangier. Office open M-Sa 6:30am-7:15pm. Map at the tourist office. Tickets 5.20F/€0.79, available on bus. 12-trip pass 46F/€7.01; 1-day pass 17.40F/€2.65; 1-week pass 46F/€7.01. Buses run 6am-8pm, with limited evening service until 12:15am and on Su morning.

Taxis: Taxi Dijon (☎03 80 41 41 12). 24hr.

Car Rental: Avis, 5 av. Maréchal Foch (☎03 80 43 60 76) or at 7bis cours de la Gare (☎03 80 42 05 99). Cars from 515F/€78.51 for 24hr. with 250km, 560F/€85.38 with insurance; 1710F/€260.71 per week with 1750km and insurance included. Av. Foch branch: Open M-F 8am-12:30pm and 2-6pm. Train station branch: M-F 8am-12:30pm, 2-8pm, and 8:30-9:30pm, Sa 8am-12:30pm and 2-6pm, Su 5:15-9:15pm.

Bike Rental: Euro-bike, 4 rue du Faubourg Raines (☎03 80 45 32 32), rents bikes, tandems, scooters, motorcycles, and in-line skates. Mountain bikes 60F/€9.15 per half-day, 100F/€15.25 per day, 430F/€65.56 per week. Open M-Th 8am-12:30pm and 1:30-6:30pm, F 8am-12:30pm and 2-7pm, Sa 9am-noon and 3-6:30pm. MC/V.

ORIENTATION AND PRACTICAL INFORMATION

Despite its size, Dijon is easy to navigate. Its main east-west axis, the pedestrian **rue de la Liberté,** runs roughly from **pl. Darcy** and the tourist office to **pl. St-Michel.** From the train station, follow av. Maréchal Foch straight to pl. Darcy (5min.). The *vieille ville* and most of Dijon's sights are on the small streets radiating north and south from rue de la Liberté. The **pl. de la République,** northeast of pl. Darcy, is the central roundabout for roads leading out of the city.

Tourist Office: pl. Darcy (☎03 80 44 11 44). Sells 5F/€0.76 map with museums and organizes daily themed **city tours** July-Sept., some in English (40F/€6.10, students 30F/€4.57). Reserve. **Accommodations service** 15F/€2.29 plus 10% deposit. **Currency exchange.** Open July-Aug. daily 9am-8pm; Sept.-June 9am-7pm. **Branch** at 34 rue des Forges(☎03 80 44 11 44). Open May to mid-Oct. M-Sa 9:30am-1pm and 2-6pm; mid-Oct. to Apr. M-F 9:30am-1pm and 2-6pm. **Accueil** in the Palais des Ducs. Open M-F 8am-12:30pm and 1:30-6:30pm, Sa-Su 9am-12:30pm and 1:30-6:30pm.

English Bookstore: Librairie de l'Université, 17 rue de la Liberté (☎03 80 44 95 44). Erotic novels and thriller paperbacks on 2nd floor. Open M 1-7pm, Tu-Sa 9:30am-7pm.

Youth Information: Centre Régional d'Information Jeunesse de Bourgogne (CRIJ), 18 rue Audra (☎03 80 44 18 44). Info on lodging, classes, grape-picking jobs, and travel. Open M-Tu and Th-F 10am-1pm and 2-6pm, W 10am-6pm.

Budget Travel: Wasteels, 16 av. Foch (☎03 80 41 81 94). Open M-Sa 9am-noon and 2-6pm. MC/V.

Laundromats: 36 rue Guillaume Tell. Open daily 6am-9pm. Also at 55 rue Berbisey (☎06 80 02 85 49). Open daily 7am-8:30pm. Also at 8 pl. de la Banque (☎06 80 02 85 49). Open daily 7am-8:30pm.

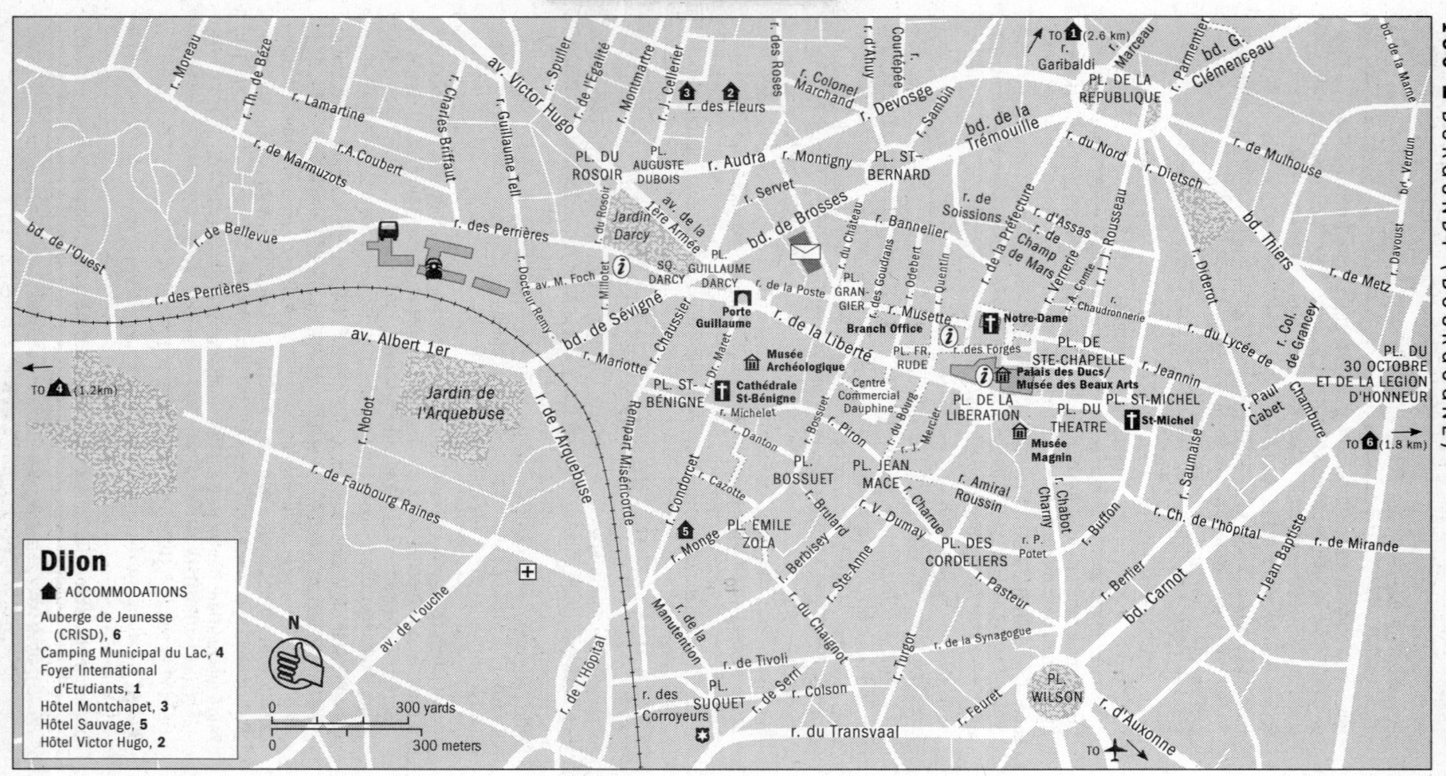
Dijon
ACCOMMODATIONS
Auberge de Jeunesse (CRISD), 6
Camping Municipal du Lac, 4
Foyer International d'Etudiants, 1
Hôtel Montchapet, 3
Hôtel Sauvage, 5
Hôtel Victor Hugo, 2
N
0 300 yards
0 300 meters
TO 4 (1.2km)
TO 1 (2.6 km)
TO 6 (1.8 km)
TO
PL. DE LA REPUBLIQUE
PL. DU 30 OCTOBRE ET DE LA LEGION D'HONNEUR
PL. WILSON
PL. DE STE-CHAPELLE
PL. DU THEATRE
PL. ST-MICHEL
PL. DE LA LIBERATION
PL. DES CORDELIERS
PL. JEAN MACE
PL. BOSSUET
PL. EMILE ZOLA
PL. SUQUET
PL. ST-BÉNIGNE
PL. DARCY
PL. GRANGIER
PL. FR. RUDE
PL. ST-BERNARD
PL. DU ROSOIR
PL. AUGUSTE DUBOIS
SQ. DARCY
PL. GUILLAUME
Jardin Darcy
Jardin de l'Arquebuse
Notre-Dame
Palais des Ducs/ Musée des Beaux Arts
St-Michel
Musée Magnin
Branch Office
Centre Commercial Dauphine
Musée Archéologique
Cathédrale St-Bénigne
Porte Guillaume
bd. de la Marne
bd. Verdun
r. Davout
r. de Metz
r. de Mulhouse
bd. Thiers
r. Col. de Grancey
r. du Lycée de
Chambure
r. Paul Cabet
r. de Mirande
r. Jean Baptiste
r. Diderot
r. Dietsch
bd. G. Clémenceau
r. Parmentier
r. Marceau
r. Garibaldi
r. du Nord
r. J.-J. Rousseau
r. Jeannin
r. Saumaise
r. Ch. de l'hôpital
bd. Carnot
r. Berlier
r. d'Auxonne
r. Buffon
r. Chabot Charny
r. Chaudronnerie
r. A. Comte
r. d'Assas
r. de la Verrerie
r. Champ de Mars
r. de la Préfecture
bd. de la Trémouille
r. de Soissons
r. Quentin
r. Musette
r. des Forges
r. Amiral Roussin
r. P. Potet
r. Pasteur
r. de la Synagogue
r. Feuret
r. Turgot
r. Sambin
r. Courtépée
r. Devosge
r. d'Ahuy
r. Colonel Marchand
r. Bannelier
r. Odebert
r. des Goudrans
r. du Château
r. de la Liberté
r. du Bourg
r. J. Mercier
r. Charrue
r. V. Dumay
r. Ste-Anne
r. du Transvaal
r. Montigny
r. de la Poste
bd. de Brosses
r. Piron
r. Bossuet
r. Brulard
r. Berbisey
r. du Chaignot
r. Colson
r. de Tivoli
r. de Serri
r. des Roses
r. des Fleurs
r. Audra
r. Servet
av. de la 1ère Armée
r. Dr. Maret
r. Michelet
r. Danton
r. Cazotte
r. Monge
r. Condorcet
r. de la Manutention
r. des Corroyeurs
r. J. Cellerier
r. Montmartre
r. de l'Egalité
r. du Rosoir
r. Millotet
r. Chaussier
bd. de Sévigné
Rempart Miséricorde
r. Spuller
av. Victor Hugo
av. M. Foch
r. Mariotte
r. de l'Arquebuse
r. de L'Hôpital
r. Guillaume Tell
r. Docteur Remy
r. des Perrières
r. Charles Briffaut
av. Albert 1er
av. de L'Ouche
r. Lamartine
r. A.Coubert
r. de Marmuzots
r. Nodot
r. de Faubourg Raines
r. Th. de Bèze
r. de Bellevue
r. Moreau
bd. de l'Ouest

Internet: Multi Rezo, cours de la Gare (☎03 80 42 13 89). Open M-Sa 10am-midnight, Su 2-10pm. 15F/€2.29 for 30min., students 30F/€4.57 per hr. **Reveil Informatique,** 38 rue Planchettes (☎03 80 63 89 71). Open M-F 9:30am-12:30pm and 2-7pm. 60F/€9.15 per hr. **Dicolor,** 57 av. du Drapeau (☎03 80 74 19 19). Open M-F 8am-midnight, Sa 8am-6pm. 80F/€12.20 per hr.

Police: 2 pl. Suquet (☎03 80 44 55 00).

Medical Assistance: Centre Hospitalier Regional de Dijon, 3 rue fbg. Raines (☎03 80 29 37 53). **SOS Médecins** (☎03 80 73 55 55) has doctors on call.

Post Office: pl. Grangier (☎03 80 50 62 19), near pl. Darcy. **Currency exchange.** Open M-F 8am-7pm, Sa 8am-noon. **Poste Restante:** 21031. **Postal code:** 21000.

ACCOMMODATIONS AND CAMPING

Hôtel Montchapet, 26-28 rue Jacques Cellerier (☎03 80 53 95 00; fax 03 80 58 26 87; www.Hotel-Montchapet.com). In a quiet neighborhood 10min. from the station, north of av. de la Première Armée Française off pl. Darcy. Kind proprietors let bright, comfortable rooms, many to students. Breakfast 33F/€5.03. Reception 7am-10:30pm. Check-out 11am. Singles 155F/€23.63, with toilet 194F/€29.58, with bath 250F/€38.12; doubles with toilet 230F/€35.06, with bath 296F/€45.13; triples and quads with bath 347-378F/€52.90-57.63. Extra bed 30F/€4.57. AmEx/MC/V.

Hôtel Victor Hugo, 23 rue des Fleurs (☎03 80 43 63 45; fax 03 80 42 13 01). From pl. Darcy, take av. Victor Hugo, make right onto rue Audra, left on rue de Roses and right onto rue des Fleurs. Quiet but convenient. Immaculate, spacious rooms with shower or bath and toilets make it worth every penny. Breakfast 30F/€4.57. Singles 180F-230F/€27.44-35.06; doubles 230F-280F/€35.06-42.69. 24hr. reception. MC/V.

Foyer International d'Etudiants, 6 rue Maréchal Leclerc (☎03 80 71 70 00; fax 03 80 71 60 48). Since it is a very long walk (30-40min.), take bus #4 from pl. Darcy (dir: "St-Apollinaire") to "Parc des Sports." From av. Paul Doumer, turn right onto rue du Stade, then take the first left. A very international crowd. TV rooms, tennis court, laundry, kitchen, and a lawn for sunbathing. Cafeteria open M-F. Reception 24hr. Huge singles 90F/€13.72, with credit card 100F/€15.25. AmEx/MC/V.

Auberge de Jeunesse (HI), Centre de Rencontres Internationales, 1 av. Champollion (☎03 80 72 95 20; fax 03 80 70 00 61), 4km from the station. Take bus #5 (or night bus A) from pl. Grangier to "Epirey," right in front of the concrete megahostel. Laundry. Internet access (1F/€0.15 per min). Breakfast included. Lockers 10-20F/€1.53-3.05. Reception 24hr. No keys before midday, no lockout. Reservations advised June-Sept. Lunch or dinner 35-65F/€5.34-9.91. Dorms 72-78F/€10.98-11.89. Singles with shower 180F/€27.44; doubles and triples with bath 90-155F/€13.72-23.63. MC/V.

Hôtel du Sauvage, 64 rue Monge (☎03 80 41 31 21; fax 03 80 42 06 07). In a former 15th-century post office. Half-timbered facade opens onto a flower-strewn courtyard. Breakfast 33F/€5.03. Reception 7am-11pm. Reserve 1-2 weeks in advance during the summer. Flawless singles with bath 220-280F/€33.54-42.69; doubles 240-300F/€36.59-45.74. Huge 5-person loft 520F/€79.28. Extra bed 60F/€9.15. MC/V.

Camping Municipal du Lac, 3 bd. Kir (☎03 80 43 54 72). Exit the back of the station and turn right on av. Albert 1er. After 1km, turn left on bd. Kir and follow the signs; if you cross a bridge, you've gone too far. Or take bus #12 from pl. Darcy (dir: "Fontaine d'Ouche") to "Hôpital des Chartreux." A park and canal are nearby. Grassy and calm, but crowded in summer. Open Apr.-Oct. 15. Reception Apr.-May and Oct. 8:30am-noon and 2:30-7pm; June and Sept. 8:30am-noon and 1:30-5pm, July-Aug. 8:30am-8pm. 17F/€2.59 per person, 9F/€1.37 per child under 7; 9F/€1.37 per car; 13F/€1.98 per site. Electricity 16.50F/€2.52.

FOOD

Dijon's reputation for high cuisine is well-deserved—and restaurant prices reflect it. Still, charcuteries provide an economical way to sample local specialities such as the popular *tarte bourguignonne* (creamy meat and mushroom pie), mushroom quiche, and *jambon persillé* (ham with parsley).

Rue Berbisey, rue Monge, and **pl. Emile Zola** host a wide variety of reasonably-priced restaurants. There's a **supermarket** in the basement of Galeries Lafayette, 41 rue de la Liberté (open M-Sa 9am-7pm), and within **Prisunic,** 11 rue Piron, off pl. Jean Macé (open M-Sa 9am-9pm). There is a colorful **market** in the pedestrian area around Les Halles (M and Th-F mornings; all day Sa).

The light green decor, the aquarium underfoot, and the display cases full of frog paraphernalia are all symptomatic of a full-fledged croaker fetish at **Le Germinal,** 44 rue Monge. (☎03 80 44 97 16. Reserve ahead. Lunch *menu* 60F/€9.15; dinner *plats* from 62F/€9.45. Open Tu-Th noon-2pm and 7-11pm, F noon-2:30pm and 7-11pm, Sa 7-11pm, Su 7-10:30pm. MC/V.) **L'Eglefin,** 8 ruelle Quentin, slipped into an alley off rue Quentin across from Les Halles, serves simple but delicious Burgundian cuisine. (☎03 80 30 31 63. *Menus* 69-142F/€10.52-21.65. Open M-W and F 7-9:30pm, Th and Sa-Su noon-2pm and 7-9:30pm. MC/V.)

SIGHTS

PALAIS DES DUCS DE BOURGOGNE (MUSEE DES BEAUX-ARTS). The Dukes of Burgundy (1364-1477) were the best sort of rulers: fearless (Jean sans Peur), good (Philippe le Bon), and bold (Philippe le Hardi and Charles le Téméraire). At the center of the *vieille ville*, the 52m **Tour Philippe le Bon** is the most conspicuous vestige of ducal power. The palace and its semicircular arcade were designed in the late 17th century by the royal architect, Jules Hardouin-Mansart. *(Tours run in summer daily every 45min., first tour 9am, last tour 5:30pm. In winter, call 03 80 74 52 71. 15F/€2.29, students 8F/€1.22.)* Most of the buildings currently house administrative offices, but the elegant **Musée des Beaux-Arts,** pl. de la Ste-Chapelle, occupies the palace's east wing. In its courtyard is the 15th-century kitchen, whose six gigantic hearths feed into one behemoth flue. The highlight of the museum is the section dedicated to "modern" art, that includes a Monet, a Sisley, modern abstract painters, and, perhaps most alluring, 20th-century paintings by Lapicque. *(Pl. de la Libération. ☎03 80 74 52 70. Open W-M 10am-6pm. Modern art wing closed 11:30am-1:45pm. 22F/€3.35; groups and seniors 10F/€1.53; students with ID free; free Su.)*

BURGUNDY

EGLISE NOTRE-DAME. The one 11th-century cult statue of the Black Virgin here is credited with the liberation of the city on two desperate occasions: first in 1513 from a Swiss siege and secondly from the German occupation in 1944. Both liberations occurred on September 11; two sumptuous tapestries depicting the miracles were commissioned for the Virgin in gratitude. The **Horloge à Jacquemart** clock, ticks above the church's tower, hauled off as plunder by Philippe le Hardi after his 1382 victory over the Flemish. After leaving the church, touch the rubbed-down *chouette* (owl) on the left side of the exterior in the rue de la Chouette to ensure extra good luck. *(Pl. Notre Dame. ☎03 80 74 35 76. English pamphlet 3F/€0.46.)*

MUSEE ARCHEOLOGIQUE. Next door to the cathedral, the cave-like Musée Archéologique, which is partially underground, unearths the history of the Côte d'Or. Housed in the former cloisters of St. Bénigne's abbey, it includes Gallo-Roman sculpture, medieval statuary and arms, and prehistoric jewelry. *(5 rue Dr. Maret. ☎03 80 30 88 54. Open June-Sept. Tu-Su 9am-6pm; Oct.-May 9am-noon and 2-6pm. 14F/€2.13, students free. Free Su.)*

EGLISE ST-MICHEL. Begun at the end of the 15th century, this church changed in style from Flamboyant to Renaissance during its construction, resulting in a Gothic interior and colonnaded exterior. Like the Eglise Notre-Dame, it suffered severe damage during the Revolution, but was lovingly restored by Abbé Deschamps, who put his heart into the job—he's buried in one of the chapels. The Renaissance facade has been revamped and now sparkles above the buildings in the old city. *(Pl. St-Michel. ☎03 80 63 17 84.)*

CATHEDRALE ST-BENIGNE. Undergoing a three-year renovation, this Gothic cathedral commemorates a 2nd-century missionary whose remains were unearthed nearby in the 6th century. Its brightly-tiled roof makes it one of Dijon's most prominent landmarks. Don't miss the 18th-century organ designed by Charles Joseph Riepp and the unusual (and somewhat spooky) circular crypt, originally the rotunda of an early 11th-century Romanesque church. *(Pl. St-Bénigne. ☎03 80 30 14 90. Open daily 9am-6:30pm. Crypt 7F/€1.07.)*

MUSEE MAGNIN. The elegant 17th-century Hôtel Lantin now houses this extensive collection of 16th- to 19th-century paintings. Though most of the art is obscure, the ensemble is well worth a visit. With period furnishings, rich wallpapers, and works clustered in intimate groups, it's like being invited to an art collector's home for a private showing. *(4 rue des Bons Enfants. ☎03 80 67 11 10. Open Tu-Su 10am-noon and 2-6pm. 20F/€3.05, students 15F/€2.29.)*

OTHER SIGHTS. The **Jardin de l'Arquebuse** provides a welcome retreat from Dijon's churches and monuments, with reflecting pools, an arboretum, and 3500 species in the meticulously laid-out botanical garden. A weeping willow trailing over the little canal was grown from a cutting taken from a tree on the tomb of Napoleon at St. Helena. *(1 av. Albert 1er. ☎03 80 76 82 84. Open July-Sept. daily 7:30am-8pm; Oct.-Feb. 7:30am-5:30pm; Mar.-June 7:30am-7pm.)* No trip to Dijon could be complete without a stop at the source of **Grey Poupon,** the Maille Boutique, 32 rue de la Liberté, where *moutarde au vin* became chic. It sells twenty different mustards, from 12F/€1.83. *(☎03 80 30 41 02. Open M-Sa 9am-7pm. MC/V.)*

ENTERTAINMENT AND FESTIVALS

The city's best nightspot is **Le Privé,** 20 av. Garibaldi, just north of pl. de la République. Students and 20-somethings hang out in leopard-skin booths or dance to techno, house, and hip-hop under golden palm trees and in steel cages Don't show up before midnight, or you will be dancing with yourself. (☎03 80 73 39 57. F-Sa 50F/€7.62 cover includes one drink, 60F/€9.15 cover includes 2 beers. Su-Th cover 30F/€4.57, 50F/€7.62 with one drink. Open Tu-Sa 10pm-5am, Su-M 11pm-5am.) Next to Le Privé is **Coco Loco**, 18 av. Garibaldi, a bar/cantina full of 20-somethings. (☎03 80 73 29 44. Open Tu-Sa 8pm-2am.) **Rue Berbisey** is lined with bars and cafés. At blue-shuttered **Cappuccino,** 132 rue Berbisey, the boisterous clientele mingles to rock, jazz, and hip-hop. (☎03 80 41 06 35. Open M-Sa 3pm-2am.) Stop across the street at **Pub McCarthy's,** 93 rue Berbisey, for more rowdy fun (☎03 80 44 96 54). At **Atmosphère Internationale,** 7 rue Audra, students grind during the week and local youth hang on weekends in the bar/pool hall/nightclub. Again, the party starts late. Thursday nights are *soirées internationales.* (☎03 80 30 52 03. Open daily 8pm-5am. No cover for international students, Su-W free for everyone, Th-Sa 14F/€2.13 includes a drink. MC/V.) **L'Univers',** 47 rue Berbisey, attracts a worldly bunch. (☎03 80 30 98 29. Open M-Sa 11am-2am, Su 5pm-2am; live music Sa.)

Opera is performed from mid-October to late April at the beautiful 18th-century **Théâtre de Dijon,** pl. du Théâtre. (☎03 80 68 46 40. Tickets 140-280F/€21.35-42.69, students 60F/€9.15 1hr. before curtain. Office open M-F 1-7pm and Sa 4-7pm during production months.) Check out the shows (both classic and contemporary) at the **Nouveau Théâtre de Bourgogne,** Théâtre du Parvis St-Jean, rue Danton, in a former church. (☎03 80 30 12 12. Open Oct.-June M-F 1-7pm, Sa 4-7pm; performances M, F, Sa 8:20pm and W 7:30pm. Bar open 1hr. prior to performance.)

Dijon's **Estivade** brings cheap dance, music, and theater to the streets and indoor venues from late June to late July. Pick up a program at the tourist office. (☎03 80 30 31 00. Tickets free-50F/€7.62.) The city devotes a week in late summer to the **Fêtes de la Vigne** and the **Folkloriades Internationales,** a well-attended grape celebration, accompanied by over 20 foreign dance and music troupes. (☎/fax 03 80 30 37 95. Tickets 56-250F/€8.54-38.12, discounts for those under 25.)

BEAUNE

The puns are easy enough to make: *le vin de Beaune, c'est du bon vin.* But the throngs of dapper 40-somethings and red-faced septuagenarians who come to this viticultural hotspot (pop. 24,000) often don't speak enough French to get them. While Beaune is hardly French—yen, dollars, and deutschmarks drip from hallowed wine-presses—the bunches of visitors unite with the locals in their deep love of the liquid that Louis Pasteur called "the healthiest and most hygienic drink." Nestled along the Côte d'Or, 40km south of Dijon, the town serves as a base for shippers and wineries. Meandering along the maze of Beaune's short cobblestone streets with the recent memory of a (free!) fine vintage on the palate, you'll never want to leave.

TRANSPORTATION

Trains: av. du 8 Septembre (☎03 80 22 13 13). To: **Chalon-sur-Saône** (25min., 21 per day, 57F/€8.69); **Dijon** (25min.; 28 per day, including 3 TGVS, 17 on Su; 38F/€5.80); **Lyon** (1½hr., 10 per day, 117F/€17.84); and **Paris** (2hr., 18 per day, 243-300F/€37.08-45.74). Buy tickets M-F 5:30am-8:30pm, Sa 5:45am-8pm and Su 6:15am-8:30pm. Information and reservations open M-F 10am-noon and 2-7pm.

Buses: TRANSCO (☎03 80 42 11 00 in Dijon). To: **Autun** (80min.; 1 per day; 47.20F/€7.20); **Châlon-sur-Saône** (1hr., 2 per day, 41F/€6.25); and **Dijon** (1hr., 9 per day, 39.20F/€5.98). Stops along the **Côte d'Or.** Schedule available at the tourist office. Buses depart from rues Jules Ferry, Buttes, Clemenceau, and Pasteur.

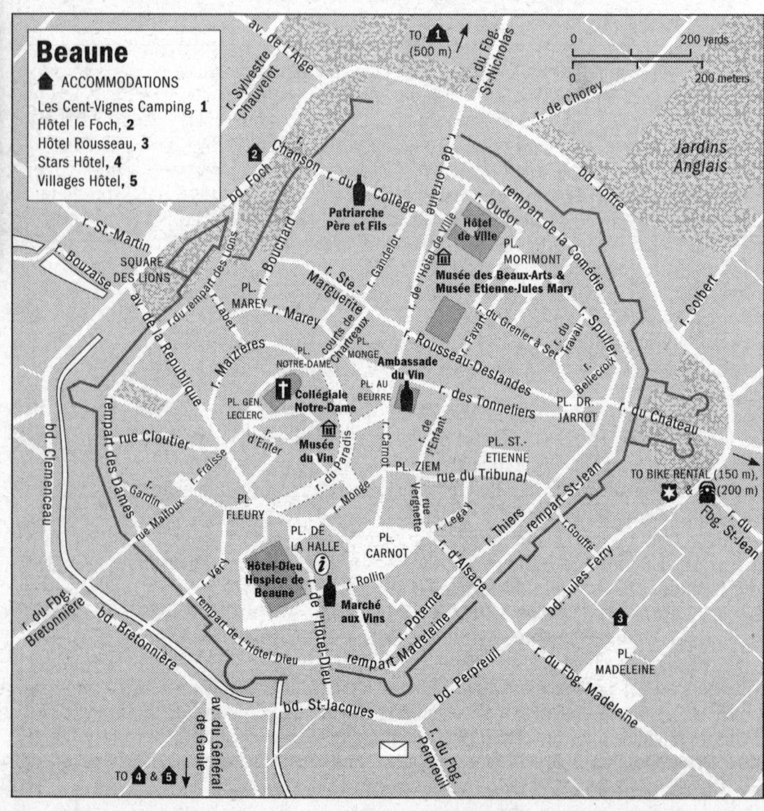

Car Rental: ADA, 26 av. du 8 Septembre (☎03 80 22 72 90; fax 03 80 22 72 92), across from the train station. From 209F/€31.87 for 24hr., 1499F/€228.54 per week (1250km included). Open M-Sa 8:10am-noon and 2-6pm. MC/V.

Bike Rental: Bourgogne Randonnées, 7 av. du 8 Septembre (☎03 80 22 06 03), near the station. Gives free maps with routes and itineraries. 20F/€3.05 per hr., 90F/€13.72 per day; 170F/€25.92 for 2 days; 400F/€60.98 per week. Credit card deposit. Open M-Sa 9am-noon and 1:30-7pm, Su 10am-noon and 2-6pm. MC/V.

ORIENTATION AND PRACTICAL INFORMATION

Almost everything there is to see lies within the circular ramparts (*remparts*) enclosing Beaune's *vieille ville.* To get to the town center from the station, head straight on av. du 8 Septembre, which becomes rue du Château. Once through the city walls, turn left onto rempart St-Jean, following it up and down the stairs as it crosses rue d'Alsace and mutates into rempart Madeleine. The fourth right is **rue de l'Hôtel-Dieu,** which leads to the Hôtel-Dieu and the **tourist office** (15min.). The streets of the town center run in concentric rings around the **Basilique Notre-Dame.**

Tourist Office: 1 rue de l'Hôtel-Dieu (☎03 80 26 21 30; fax 03 80 26 21 39). Free maps and lists of *caves.* **Hotel reservations** with 10% down payment. Daily *vieille ville* **tours** in English depart at noon. (July-Sept. 17 40F/€6.10 per person, 65F/€9.91 per couple). 85F/€12.96 *passeporte* to 3 sights of choice. **Currency exchange** Sa-Su and bank holidays. Open Jan.-Mar. M-F 10am-6pm, Su 10am-1pm and 2-5pm; Apr.-June 14 M-Sa 9:30am-7pm, Su 10am-5pm; June 15-Sept. 22 M-Sa 9:30am-8pm, Su 9:30am-6pm; Sept. 23-Nov. 15 M-Sa 9:30am-8pm, Su 9:30am-6pm; Nov. 16-18 9am-8pm; Nov. 19-Dec. M-F 10am-1pm and 2-5pm.

Laundromat: 19 rue fbg. St-Jean (☎03 80 24 09 78). Open daily 6:30am-9pm.

Police: 5 av. du Général de Gaulle (☎03 80 25 09 25).

Hospital: Centre Hospitalier, av. Guigone de Salins, northeast of the town center (☎03 80 24 44 44). **Ambulance:** ☎03 80 20 20 09.

Internet Access: Diz, 28 rue de Lorraine (☎03 80 26 36 01). Open M-Sa 10am-9pm, Su 2-7pm. 40F/€6.10 per hr. Minimum 15min.

Post Office: bd. St-Jacques (☎03 80 26 29 50). **Currency exchange.** Open M-F 8am-7pm, Sa 8am-noon. **Postal code:** 21200.

BURGUNDY

ACCOMMODATIONS AND CAMPING

Visitors swarm to Beaune from April to November; make reservations at least a week in advance. For cheaper accommodations, base yourself in Dijon.

Hôtel Rousseau, 11 pl. Madeleine (☎03 80 22 13 59). From the station, head straight down av. du 8 Septembre, taking a left on bd. Jules Ferry and another on ruelle Madeleine. Just a couple of minutes from the town center, at the end of a little gravel walk in the corner of the *place.* Acceptable rooms that open onto a secluded courtyard, where flora and fauna abound. Breakfast included. Shower 20F/€1.53. Curfew 11:30pm. Singles from 145F/€22.11; doubles from 190F/€28.98, with shower 300F/€45.74; triples and quads from 300F/€45.74.

Hôtel le Foch, 24 bd. Foch (☎03 80 24 05 65; fax 03 80 24 75 59). Take av. de la République from the tourist office and turn right on bd. Foch. Pleasant rooms. Breakfast 35F/€5.34. Reception 7am-9pm. Singles and doubles 165F/€25.16, with shower 200-250F/€30.49-38.12; quad 250F/€38.12. Extra bed 60F/€9.15. MC/V.

Stars Hotel, rue Ampère (☎03 80 22 53 17; fax 03 80 24 10 14). From train station, walk up rue Château and make a left onto rue Jules Ferry. Make a left onto rue Charles de Gaulle, and the hotel is 10min. down on the left. Prim and proper rooms, each with shower and toilet. Breakfast 35F/€5.34. Reception 24hr. Rooms 169F/€25.77 M-F, 185F/€28.21 Sa-Su. MC/V

Villages Hotel, rue Burglat (☎03 80 24 15 80; fax 03 80 24 14 15). Right next to Stars, this large hotel is quite similar. Each tiny room has a double bed, a bunk, toilet, and shower. Breakfast 25F/€3.81. Reception M-F 6:30am-10pm, Sa-Su 7am-10pm. Singles through triples 175F/€26.69. MC/V.

Les Cent-Vignes, 10 rue Dubois (☎03 80 22 03 91), 500m from the town center off rue du fbg. St-Nicolas. Head north on rue Lorraine from pl. Monge. Arrive early in summer. Gravelled or grassy sites made pleasant and private by hedges. Laundry, restaurant, and grocery store. Open Mar. 15-Oct. Reception 8am-10pm. 18F/€2.74 per person. Site 25F/€3.81. Car included. Electricity 20F/€3.05. MC/V.

FOOD

Food is expensive here. The restaurants around **pl. Madeleine** and **pl. Carnot** serve the least exorbitant *menus*, but even here prices for the local wine are uniformly high. The streets just east of **pl. Monge** hawk sandwiches and cheap North African food. There are three **Casino supermarkets,** at 28 rue du fbg. Madeleine (open M-Sa 8:30am-7:30pm), rue Carnot (open M 3-7pm, Tu-Sa 7:30am-12:30pm and 3-7pm, Su 7am-12:30pm), and 15 rue Maufoux (open M-Sa 7am-12:30pm and 3-7pm). A large **market** on pl. Carnot livens up Wednesday and Saturday mornings. If you're willing to dispense with formality, you can eat a good full meal for under 60F/€9.15 at the locally popular cafeteria **Crescendo,** Stoc Centre Commercial, av. Charles de Gaulle. (Open daily 11:30am-2:30pm and 6:30-9:30pm; tea 11:30am-10pm.)

Monsieur Neaux, chef of **Relais de la Madeleine,** 44 pl. Madeleine, wants you to try everything he cooks—your only regret will be that your belly isn't large enough. House specialties like duck pâté, *boeuf bourguignon*, and peppered trout are *haute cuisine*. (☎03 80 22 07 47. *Menus* 72F/€10.98, 94F/€14.33, and 147F/€22.41. Open Th-Tu noon-2pm and 7-10pm. AmEx/MC/V.)

SIGHTS AND SIPS

Though Beaune's hospital might have cured any outward ills, it is wine that has always kept the city, if not its inhabitants, in good health. This tradition continues today, with visitors milling about the central squares and boulevards before descending into one of Beaune's many *caves*. If you want to plan your attack on the caves before entering, you may decide on the **visiotrain,** which leaves from the tourist office (☎03 80 24 04 96; every 1½hr. June-Aug.; M-F starting at 10:30am, 4 per day on Su; 30F/€4.57). Head to the tourist office for a list of *caves*.

HOTEL-DIEU. In 1443, Nicolas Rolin, chancellor to the Duke of Burgundy, built this hospital to help the city recover from the ravages of war, poverty, and famine. Patients were treated here until 1971; the building is now the town's biggest non-potable tourist attraction, and by far its best. The hospital has held on to Rolin's bequest of 143 acres of the area's finest vineyards, and each year, on the third Sunday of November, the most recent vintages are whipped out for a charity auction. The courtyard is an excellent point from which to admire the magnificent tiled roofs that make this building one of France's architectural icons. The Hôtel's great treasure, however, is the polyptych *Last Judgment* by Roger van der Weyden, whose exquisite detail can be viewed with a giant magnifying glass. *(Open daily 9am-6:30pm. 33F/€5.03, students 26F/€3.96. Tour 10F/€1.53.)*

PATRIARCHE PERE ET FILS. The largest *cave* in Beaune is reached via the altar of an 18th-century chapel. Over 4 million bottles currently mature in these 5km of dark corridors. In the final *caves*, a *dégustation* of 13 different wines is led by expert sommeliers. *(5-7 rue du Collège. ☎03 80 24 53 78. Open daily 9:30-11:30am and 2-5:30pm; arrive at least 1hr. before closing. 50F/€7.62; all proceeds to charity.)*

MUSEE DU VIN. If you can still walk, stagger to this museum, housed inside the 15th- to 16th-century Hôtel des Ducs de Bourgogne. You can see its wine cellar, vats, and immense presses for free. Other exhibits trace the evolution of wine bottles, wine glasses, and carafes from ancient Rome to today. *(Rue d'Enfer, off pl. Général Leclerc. ☎03 80 22 08 19. Open daily 9:30am-5:30pm; closed Tu Dec.-Mar. 25F/€3.81, students 15F/€2.29. Includes Musée de Beaux-Arts, below, and the Musée Etienne-Jules Marey.)*

OTHER SIGHTS. The **Musée des Beaux-Arts** has a small collection of Gallo-Roman sculpture and a cache of paintings by 15th- and 16th-century Dutch and Flemish artists and 18th- to 19th-century French artists. *(Rue de l'Hôtel de Ville. ☎03 80 24 56 92. Open Apr.-Nov. daily2-6pm. For admission, see Musée du Vin, above.)* No visit to Beaune is complete without a peep at the Burgundian-Romanesque church **Collégiale Notre-Dame** and the priceless set of late 15th-century tapestries behind its altar, which illustrate the life of the Virgin. *(Open daily 8:30am-6:45pm. Tapestries open M-Sa 9:30am-12:30pm and 2-7pm. 15F/€2.29, students and groups 10F/€1.53. Tours upon request.)*

THE COTE D'OR

The nectar fastidiously stored in Beaune's dark cellars began its life basking on the sunny acres of the Golden Slopes to the north and south. The Côte d'Or—a 60km strip of land from Dijon to the village of Santenay, 20km south of Beaune—has nurtured grapes since around 500 BC. Traces of limestone in the soil, the right amount of rainfall, and perfect exposure and drainage make it a godsend for viticulturists, and therefore among the most valuable real estate in the world.

The Côte d'Or is divided into two regions. The **Côte de Nuits,** stretching south from Dijon through **Nuits-St-Georges** to the village of **Corgoloin,** produces red wines made from the Pinot Noir grape. Running from Corgoloin south to **Santenay,** the **Côte de Beaune** produces great white wines from Chardonnay grapes. The aptly-named **Route des Grands Crus** ("great wine route") winds through the region, passing through famous vineyards and wine-producing villages. Without a car and plentiful funds, the villages are hard to get to and stay in. Tastings are free, but remember that most wine-makers will expect you to buy something.

While the region's wines are superlative, the methods of transportation around the vineyards can't claim the same. If you're up for adventure, the best way to get to the vineyards near either **Beaune** or **Dijon,** is to rent a mountain bike and pedal down the **Route de Grands Crus.** Bike rental shops in both cities arrange tours of differing lengths that can get you where you want to go. If you have a little more cash, renting a car in **Dijon** or **Beaune** (around 400F/€60.98 per day includes tax, insurance, and gas) is the easiest way to the grapes, but if you are planning on taking part in your fair share of wine tasting, this might not be the best option. **TRANSCO** buses (☎03 80 42 11 00) will also get you to **Beaune** (1hr.; 14 per day, 2 on Su; 41F/€6.25), **Gevrey-Chambertin,** leaving from Dijon (30min.; 20 per day, 5 on Su; 15.60F/€2.38), and **Nuits-St-Georges** (45min.; 13 per day, 2 on Su; 26F/€3.96). TRANSCO will also bring you from Beaune to **Château de Rochepot** (6 per day, 15.60F/€2.38).

Lodging on the Côte is expensive; some reasonable options are given below, but your best bet is to reserve a room days in advance at one of the many *chambres d'hôte* dotting the villages. The tourist office in Beaune or Gevrey-Chambertin will supply you with a copy of *Chambres et Tables d'hôte,* a comprehensive list of bed and breakfasts along the Côte d'Or and throughout France.

BURGUNDY

GEVREY-CHAMBERTIN

Perhaps the finest vineyards in all of France are 10km south of Dijon around Gevrey-Chambertin. Nine of the Côte's 29 *grands crus* are grown here, all with "Chambertin" in their name. Perched atop the vineyards, the **Château de Gevrey-Chambertin** provides a perfect way to unwind, especially after a long bike ride. The gracious proprietress will take you through her 10th-century château, built to protect the wine and the villagers (in that order). The tour ends with a taste of the prized vintages, which cost 90F/€13.72 a bottle and up. (☎03 80 34 36 13. Open Apr. 16-Nov. 18 daily 10am-noon and 2-6pm; Jan.-Apr. 15 and Nov. 19-Dec. 22 10am-noon and 2-5pm. 20min.-1hr. tour 20F/€3.05.)

The Gevrey-Chambertin **tourist office** is small, but very helpful. (☎03 80 34 38 40. Open M and Sa 9:30am-12:30pm and 1:30-5:30pm, Tu-F 9am-12:30pm and 1:30-6pm, Su 10am-12:30pm and 1:30-5:30pm.) Bunk down at the **Marchands,** 1 pl. du Monument aux Morts. (☎03 80 34 38 13; fax 03 80 34 39 65. Closed on M until 7pm. Singles 150F/€22.90; doubles 200-250F/€30.49-38.12. MC/V.) Or call ahead to the tourist office for names of other bed and breakfasts, and reserve early in summer.

CHATEAU DE CLOS DE VOUGEOT

The D122 turns back southward from Gevrey-Chambertin, passing just to the east of minor châteaux in Morey-St-Denis and Chambolle-Musigny before arriving at the **Château du Clos de Vougeot,** a few kilometers north of Nuits-St-Georges. Built in 1098, it was renovated to its present state in the 15th century by Louis XI, who regarded it as one of his greatest conquests. Today, this magnificent castle stands sentinel over a 125-acre vineyard, which its owners lease to several different *vignerons* (vintners). It is these owners who give the château its spark: the **Confrérie des Chevaliers du Tastevin** (Brotherhood of the Knights of the Tastevin) was founded in 1934 to promote the sale of Burgundian *crus* during a slump in sales brought on by Prohibition and the Depression in the US. The 12,000 members hold frequent parties at the château as part of their strict duty to spread the gospel of Burgundian wine: "*Jamais en vain, toujours en vin*" ("Never in vain, always in wine"). They may have their fun here, but there's no wine tasting or buying at the château for the plebeians. (☎03 80 62 86 09. Open Apr.-Sept. Su-F 9am-6:30pm, Sa 9am-5pm; Oct.-Mar. Su-F 9-11:30am and 2-5:30pm, Sa 9-11:30am and 2-5pm; closes at nightfall during the winter. 1hr. tours depart every 30min. 20F/€3.05, students and children 15F/€2.29, under 8 free. AmEx/MC/V.)

BURGUNDY

CHATEAU DE ROCHEPOT

The **Château de Rochepot,** 15km southwest of Beaune, springs straight out of a fairy tale, with its wooden drawbridge, slate roof, and pointed turrets. "To enter, knock three times," declares the ancient sign. The 45-minute tour includes a peek at the Guard Room, the ingenious kitchens, the dining room, the old chapel, and the "Chinese" room, a gift of the last empress of China. (☎03 80 21 71 37. Open Apr.-June W-M 10:30-11:30am and 2-5:30pm; July-Aug. 10am-6pm; Sept. 10:30-11am and 2-5:30pm; Oct. 10:30-11:30am and 2-4:30pm. 37F/€5.64.)

While lodging is scarce in this tiny town, **Le Relais du Château,** rte. de Nolay, has a friendly, English-speaking proprietor, and the bright, clean rooms are a fantastic deal. (☎03 80 21 71 32. Breakfast 34F/€5.19. Doubles with shower 180F/€27.44, with shower and toilet 260F/€39.64. Extra bed 50F/€7.62. MC/V.)

MACON

Balanced between Burgundy and the Beaujolais, Mâcon (pop. 36,000) is a crossroads between the north and south. Laid against the right bank of the Saône, "Matisco" was an important Roman colony and later became a frontier city between French lands and the Holy Roman Empire. Romantic poet, politician, and ladies' man Alphonse de Lamartine (1790-1869) was *mâconnais*, but his fame and fervor far outstripped his quiet birthplace. For those with transportation, Mâcon is an ideal base for exploring the Beaujolais vineyards, as well as for daytrips to Cluny and Paray-le-Monial.

ORIENTATION AND PRACTICAL INFORMATION

The town center is a fairly compact area framed by rue Gambetta, rue Victor Hugo, cours Moreau, and the Saône. To reach the **tourist office,** pl. St-Pierre, from the rue Bigonnet station, go straight down rue Gambetta and take a left onto rue Carnot.

Trains and Buses: rue Bigonnet. To: **Dijon** (1¼hr., 17 per day, 96F/€14.64); **Lyon** (1hr., 28 per day, 63F/€9.61); and **Paris** (2hr., 6 TGVs per day, 292-362F/€44.53-55.21). Ticket booth open M-F 4:55am-9:55pm, Sa 4:55am-7:40pm, Su 6:05am-10:50pm. Info desk open M-F 9am-12:45pm and 1:45-5:40pm, Sa 9am-12:45pm and 1:45-5:40pm. **TGVs** stop at **Mâcon-Loche,** 6km away. SNCF **buses** shuttle occasionally between the two stations (7 per day).

Taxis: ☎03 85 38 05 95. 24hr. About 110F/€16.77 from Mâcon-Loche to Mâcon.

Tourist Office: 1 pl. St-Pierre (☎03 85 21 07 07; fax 03 85 40 96 00). Accommodations service 15F/€2.29; requires a 10% down payment. The office offers 5 different themed visits in French (July-Sept. Sa 2:30pm, 30F/€4.57, under age 12 free. Ask for a schedule. Open June-Sept. M-Sa 10am-7pm, Su 3-7pm; Oct.-May M-Sa 10am-6pm. Nov.-Mar. closed 10am-12:30pm and 1:30-6pm.

Laundromat: 22 rue Gambetta. Open daily 7am-10pm.

Police: 36 rue Lyon (☎03 85 32 63 63).

Internet Access: Le Victor Hugo Café, 37 rue Victor Hugo (☎03 85 39 26 16). 15F/€2.29 per 30min., 40F/€6.10 per hr. Open M-Sa 8am-1am, Su 3pm-1am.

Post Office: 3 rue Victor Hugo (☎03 85 21 05 50). **Currency exchange.** Open M-F 8:30am-7pm, Sa 8:30am-noon. **Postal code:** 71000.

ACCOMMODATIONS

Reasonably priced rooms are common in Mâcon, though you should reserve in July and August. **Hôtel Escatel,** 4 rue de la Liberté, is a bit out of the way but extremely well-priced. From the station turn left onto rue V. Hugo and follow it past pl. de la Barre as it flows into rue de l'Héritan. The hotel is to the right across from the intersection of rue de l'Héritan and rue de Flace (15min.). The hum of traffic from the intersection fills its long college-dorm hallways and modern, cheerful rooms. (☎03 85 29 02 50; fax 03 85 34 19 97. Breakfast 38F/€5.80. Reception 24hr. Check-out noon. Singles 99-145F/€15.10, with shower 170F/€25.92; doubles 185F/€28.21, with shower 200F/€30.49. Rooms with bathtubs more expensive. Extra bed 50F/€7.62. AmEx/MC/V.) If you want something a little closer to the action, stay at **Le Promenade,** 266 quai Lamartine. From the station, walk straight down rue Gambetta and make a left onto quai Lamartine. A neat, accommodating, sometimes quite crowded hotel provides more than sufficient budget travel rooms, all with toilet and shower. (☎03 85 38 10 98; fax 03 85 38 94 01. Breakfast 25F/€3.81. Reception 10am-3:30pm and 6:30-midnight. Singles and doubles 120-190F/€18.30-28.97, triples 200F/€30.49. V.)

FOOD

Situated between Burgundy and Beaujolais, Mâcon enjoys the best of both wine worlds, and it also produces its own Chardonnays, *Pouilly Fuissé* and *Mâcon Clessé*, which go well with *quenelles* (smooth, creamy fish dumplings) and *coq au vin*. A small **market** is held daily on pl. aux Herbes; a larger one is held on esplanade Lamartine (Sa 7am-1pm). There's also a **Marché Plus** on 18 rue Lacretelle off rue V. Hugo. (Open M-Sa 7am-9pm, Su 9am-1pm. MC/V.)

It's not difficult to find reasonably-priced restaurants in Mâcon, but much of the budget eating is located on the *quais* in busy brasseries next to the noisy highway. For a night on the town, start off with an *apéritif* at **La Maison de Bois,** 13 pl. aux Herbes, a friendly bar specializing in champagne, located in a 15th-century monastic house with grotesque carvings. (☎03 85 38 03 51. Beer 30-35F/€4.57-5.39. Open M 4pm-1am, Tu-Sa 8am-1am.) **Restaurant Paradis,** 51 rue Gambetta, serves up Chinese and Thai food. With lunch menus on weekdays at 57F/€8.69 and 72F/€10.98, and dinner *plats* for 82F/€12.51 and 97F/€14.79, it is one of the cheapest eats in town. (☎03 85 39 48 10. Open W-M noon-2:30pm and 7-11pm, MC/V.)

SIGHTS

Students and those under 26 have free entry to the museums and monuments listed below.

RESIDENCE SOUFFLOT. This hospital, designed in 1752 by Soufflot, architect of the Panthéon in Paris (see p. 124), continues to serve. Its centerpiece is an oval multi-level Italianate chapel, which let the sick participate in mass without having to descend to the ground floor, and a *tonneau tournant* (revolving cupboard), which allowed mothers to orphan children anonymously. *(249 rue Carnot. Ask for the chapel key at the tourist office. Open M-F 10am-7pm.)*

MAISON DE BOIS. Rue Carnot and rue Dombey have a number of late medieval houses, the most famous being the Maison de Bois (see **Food,** above), on the corner of rue Dombey and pl. aux Herbes. Built between 1490 and 1510, the facade has a marvelous array of carvings, with naughty monkeys and other animals, and the house is one of only four of its kind left in France. At rue du Pont, turn right and walk across the **Pont St-Laurent** for a good view of the city. Though the bridge itself is unremarkable, the view highlights how Mâcon—originally a border town—was built up almost exclusively on the west bank.

VIEUX ST-VINCENT. Back in town stands this sad ruin, which got its name in 543, when King Childebert donated a piece of St. Vincent's tunic on his journey back from Spain. Only the 12th-century narthex and a pair of octagonal 11th- to 13th-century towers remain, but wonderful, apocalyptic carvings line an arch inside. The figures' features are worn away, but their posture and narrative remain clear. *(Rue de Strasbourg. Narthex open June-Sept. Tu-Sa 10am-6pm; Oct.-May Tu-Sa 10am-5:30pm, Su noon-5:30pm. South tower open June-Sept. M and W-Sa 10am-noon and 2-6pm, Su 2-6pm; Oct.-May call ahead. 10F/€1.53, students with ID and under 16 free.)*

MUSEE DES URSULINES. Two blocks behind Vieux St-Vincent is one of the best small museums in Burgundy. Its archaeological exhibits include the occupied stone coffin of a Frankish warrior, opened to reveal the bones and possessions of the original tenant. The second floor is devoted to the ethnology and traditions of the *mâconnais.* The third floor has some choice furniture, including a chair in which the servants of Louis XIV would carry him. *(Rue des Ursulines. ☎03 85 39 90 38. Open Tu-Sa 10am-noon and 2-6pm, Su 2-6pm. 15F/€2.29.)*

ENTERTAINMENT AND FESTIVALS

Cafés on the *quais* are full all day long and well into the evening. Just behind quai Jean Jaurès are lively concert-bars, including **Bar L'Insolite,** 65 rue Franche, which specializes in karaoke. (☎03 85 38 07 63. Open M-Sa 10am-2am.) The big summer event is the four-week **L'Eté Frappé,** a festival that features a variety of free shows at indoor and outdoor venues around Mâcon, with films, jazz, classical music, comedians, and dancing, from early July to mid-August. For goings-on in the region, ask the tourist office for the free annual *Les Rendez-vous* or *L'Eté Bleu.*

CLUNY

Cluny's population of 5000 has not grown since the 11th century, when those few controlled 10,000 monks, 1200 monasteries, and more than a few kings. Its once enormous abbey, which produced almost a dozen popes, faded into obscurity following the Wars of Religion and was sold and largely destroyed during the Revolution. Cluny now exports mustard jars and top-notch engineers from ENSAM *(Ecole Nationale Supérieure d'Arts et Métiers)*, but it is the town's rich medieval heritage that draws pilgrims from all over Europe.

ORIENTATION AND PRACTICAL INFORMATION

Cluny has no train station; buses are torturously routed and treacherously infrequent. To get from the bus stop to the **tourist office,** walk against the traffic on rue Porte de Paris, turn right at pl. du Commerce, and continue for five minutes.

Buses: SNCF goes to **Châlon-sur-Saône** (80min., 4 per day, 47F/€7.17); **Mâcon** (40min., 6 per day, 19F/€2.90); and **Paray-le-Monial** (2½hr., 1 per day, 56F/€8.54). The **Boutique SNCF,** 9 rue de la République (☎03 85 59 07 72), can help you through the connection maze. Open M-F 9am-noon and 1:30-5:30pm, Sa 9am-12:30pm.

Taxis: ☎03 85 59 04 87.

Bike Rental: at the **campground** (☎06 73 20 13 51 or 03 85 59 03 97). 50F/€7.62 per day, 75F/€11.44 Sa-M morning. 200F/€30.49 deposit. Open May-Oct. M-W 9am-noon and 1-6pm, Th 9am-5pm, F 9am-noon and 1-6pm.

Tourist Office: 6 rue Mercière (☎03 85 59 05 34; fax 03 85 59 06 95), in the Tour des Fromages. Here you'll find a helpful map, a free *guide pratique,* and **currency exchange** on weekends. Open July-Aug. daily 10am-7pm; Apr.-June and Sept. 10am-12:30pm and 2:30-7pm; Oct. M-Sa 10am-12:30pm and 2:30-6pm; Nov.-Mar. until 5pm. **Tours** are available from mid-July to August–inquire at the Cluny Abbey info desk.

Laundromat: 2 rue de Merle. Open daily 7am-10:30pm.

Police: rue Porte de Paris (☎17).

Internet Access: Point Accueil Jeune (☎03 85 59 25 36). 5F/€0.76 per hr. Open M-F 10am-noon and 2-7pm, Sa 10am-7pm.

Post Office: (☎03 85 59 86 00) off chemin du Prado, near pont de la Levée. Open M-F 8am-noon and 2-6pm, Sa 8am-noon. **Postal code:** 71250.

ACCOMMODATIONS AND CAMPING

Budget lodgings fill quickly in summer; reserve early or daytrip-it from Mâcon.

Cluny Séjour (☎03 85 59 08 83; fax 03 85 59 26 27), rue Porte de Paris, behind the bus stop. This converted 18th-century chandlery was once inhabited by Cluny's monks; the bright, clean rooms could be seen as either unfurnished or austere. Breakfast included. Reception Jan. M-Sa 9am-noon and 3-7:30pm; Feb.-Mar. 9am-noon and 3-7:30pm; Apr.-May and Oct. 9am-noon and 3-9pm; July-Aug. 7am-10pm; Nov.-Dec. 9am-noon and 3-7pm. 2- to 4-bed dorms 80F/€12.29. MC/V.

Hôtel du Commerce, 8 pl. du Commerce (☎03 85 59 03 09). The essence of the non-descript, passable hotel. The plain rooms (some with TV) have decent everything: beds, showers, owners, and noise level. Breakfast 29F/€4.42. Reception 6:30am-noon and 4:30-10:30pm. Singles 115-140F/€17.54-21.35; doubles 145-160F/€22.11-24.39, with shower 205F/€31.26. Extra bed 40F/€6.10. AmEx/MC/V.

St-Vital, rue de Griottons (☎/fax 03 85 59 08 34). A grassy, open three-star site next to the municipal swimming pool. Reception July-Aug. 7am-10pm; May and Sept. 9am-noon and 3-9pm. Reservations recommended. Open May-Sept. 20F/€3.05 per person, 10F/€1.53 per child under 7; 12F/€1.98 per tent or car; electricity 16F/€2.44.

FOOD

La Renaissance, 47 rue Merciera, offers large portions, 50-80F/€7.62-12.20 *menus*, and pizzas ranging from 20-50F/€3.05-7.62. (☎03 85 59 01 58. Open M-Sa noon-2pm and 7pm-nightfall. MC/V.) There is a **Casino supermarket** at 29 rue Lamartine. (Open M 9am-noon and 3-7pm, Tu-Sa 8am-12:30pm and 3-7:30pm, Su 8am-12:30pm.) The **local market** is held every Saturday morning near the abbey.

SIGHTS AND FESTIVALS

Begin your tour with a great view from atop the 120 steps of the **Tour des Fromages,** right next to the tourist office. The tower was part of the abbey until the Revolution, when it was bought by a woman who used it to dry her cheeses (6F/€0.92, students 4F/0.61). Then follow rue Mercière one block and turn right onto rue de la République. This area, particularly rue d'Avril and rue Lamartine, is home to the best of the well-preserved **Maisons Romanes** (medieval houses) that dot the city. The path leads straight through the **Porte d'Honneur,** which frames the remaining abbey spires. The Romanesque **abbey church,** dedicated to St. Peter and St. Paul, is the third church on the site and goes under the imaginative name of **Cluny III.** The order of the Cluniacs was founded in the 10th century in an effort to reform monastic life. They quickly traded in their credo for influence, prestige, and wealth, attracting some of the brightest minds of the 11th and 12th centuries. At the height of its power, Cluny controlled a vast network of daughter abbeys and, by virtue of its unique charter, escaped the control of every ruler except the pope. Cluny III was the largest church in the world until the construction of St. Peter's in Rome, and the abbot's sway and swag rivaled that of the Holy See. During the Wars of Religion, the Revolution, and its aftermath, the abbey was looted, sold, and used as a quarry. A mental reconstruction of the abbey's scale requires some effort, but its wealth can still be glimpsed in the ornamentation of the Gothic **Pope Gelasius** facade. What remains is now home to the **Ecole Nationale Supérieure d'Arts et Métiers,** with a central cloister surrounded by students' rooms.

Buy your tickets to the abbey as well as to the **Musée d'Art et d'Archéologie** in the building on the left. The museum houses a reconstruction of the abbey and some religious art which escaped destruction. (☎03 85 59 12 79. Abbey and museum open July-Aug. 9am-7pm; Sept. 9am-6pm; Apr.-June 9:30am-noon and 2-6pm; Oct. 9:30am-noon and 2-5pm; Nov.-Feb. 15 10am-noon and 2-4pm; Feb. 16-Mar. 10am-noon and 2-5pm. 8 tours per day July-Aug; museum and abbey tour in French 32F/€4.88, under 25 21F/€3.20. Ask about night tours, 2 per week July-Aug.)

The yearly festival **Les Grandes Heures de Cluny** in July and August mixes classical music with bacchic encounters. Concerts in various venues throughout Cluny are followed by local *dégustations* and viticultural luncheons in the Val Lamartinien. (Contact the tourist office for tickets. Concerts 120F/€18.30, students 100F/€15.25; *programme oenologique* 55F/€8.39.)

NEAR CLUNY: VAL LAMARTINIEN

The sights and roadsides of the area around Cluny are splashed with signs bearing verses by Romantic poet Alphonse de Lamartine (1790-1869).

Twelve kilometers north of Cluny is the **Château de Cormatin,** complete with moat, formal gardens, aviary, and maze. The monumental open-well staircase in the north wing was the height of sophisticated engineering at the time of its building (1605-1616). The Italian-style rooms, though unrestored, are well-preserved. You can **bike** by taking the car-free **la Voie Verte,** a 44km stretch of road devoted to bikers and bladers, which covers a good deal of the countryside near Cluny in a fairly flat stretch of land. You can also get to the château by taking an **SNCF bus** from **Cluny** (25min., 7 per day, 12F/€1.83) or **Mâcon** (65min., 6 per day, 36F/€5.49). (☎03 85 50 16 55; fax 03 85 50 72 06. Open Apr.-Nov. 11 daily 10am-noon and 2-5:30pm. Tours in French with written translation every 30min. 40F/€6.10, students with ID ages 17-26 32F/€4.88, ages 10-16 25F/€3.81. Park only 23F/€3.51.)

PARAY-LE-MONIAL

Paray-le-Monial (pop. 10,000) owes its fame to a 25-year-old nun. It was here, in 1673, that Christ began to appear before Sister Marguerite-Marie Alacoque, revealing his heart with the words, "Here is the heart that so loved mankind." The adoration of the Sacred Heart caught on in the late 19th century, and Paray quickly gained fame throughout the Christian world. The growing cult rated a visit by

Pope Pius IX, who elevated the town's simple cathedral to the status of a basilica in the 1850s. Sister M-M was canonized in 1920. Since then Paray has become a pilgrimage site second only to Lourdes in France.

PRACTICAL INFORMATION. **Trains** are infrequent; check times or risk getting stuck. (☎03 85 81 13 25. Ticket counter open M 4:45am-noon and 12:30-8pm; Tu-F 5:30am-noon and 12:30-8pm; Sa 7:30am-noon and 2:30-5:30pm, Su 10:10am-noon and 2:30pm-8pm.) They go to **Dijon** (1 per day, 100F/€15.25); **Lyon** (13 per day, 95F/€14.48); **Moulins** (4 per day, 59F/€9.00); and indirectly to **Paris** (6 per day, 247F/€37.67). **SNCF buses** go to **Cluny** (2½hr., 1 per day, 56F/€8.54), where you can change for **Mâcon** (72F/€10.98), and to local hubs **Le Creusot,** which has a TGV terminal (5 per day, 52F/€7.93) and **Roannes** (5 per day, 45F/€6.86). For a **taxi,** call 03 85 88 85 01. To get to the **tourist office,** 25 av. Jean-Paul II, leave the station to the left and turn right on av. de la Gare. Cross the canal bridge and veer right onto av. de Gaulle. At the end of the street, turn left on rue des Deux Ponts, continue straight until you cross the bridge over the Bourbince, and then turn right on av. Jean Paul II. When the road forks, you'll be in front of the office, next to the basilica (15min.). (☎03 85 81 10 92; fax 03 85 81 36 61. Open July-Aug. daily 9am-7pm; Sept.-June M-Sa 9am-noon and 1:30-6:30pm, Su 10am-12:30pm and 2:30-6:30pm. The **post office** is on rue du Marché. (Open M-F 8am-12:15pm and 1:15-6pm, Sa 8am-noon.) **Postal code:** 71600.

ACCOMMODATIONS AND CAMPING. Paray draws pilgrims year-round, and rooms are difficult to find during religious sessions (mostly in July and August); two months' advance reservation is strongly recommended. Cheap, comfortable rooms can be found in the Christian *foyers* near the basilica. The **Foyer du Sacré-Cœur,** 14 rue de la Visitation, is a charming, quiet place in the center of town. Rooms are tastefully decorated, some with crucifixes hovering protectively over the bed. Pilgrims predominate, but pagans and tourists are welcome. (☎03 85 81 11 01; fax 03 85 81 26 83. Breakfast 25F/€3.81, lunch 75F/€11.43, dinner 70F/€10.67. Reception noon-10pm. Singles from 115F/€17.54; doubles 205-215F/€31.26-32.79; triples 275-295F/€41.93-44.98.) The **Hôtel du Nord,** 1 av. de la Gare, has simple rooms and a comfortable sitting room with TV. (☎03 85 81 05 12. Breakfast 30F/€4.57. Showers 15F/€2.29. Reception 6:30am-11pm. Singles 145F/€22.11, with shower 170F/€25.92; doubles with bath 240F/€36.59; quads 225F/€34.31. MC/V.) In town is **Hôtel du Champ de Foire,** 2 rue Desrichard, with clean, simple rooms, with showers, and a friendly proprietor. (☎03 85 81 01 68; fax 03 85 88 86 30. Breakfast 25F/€3.81. Singles 140F/€21.35; doubles 180-200F/€27.44-30.49; triples 220F/€33.54; quads 260F/€39.64. MC/V.) **Camping de Mambré** is on route du Gué-Léger. From the end of av. de la Gare, turn left and walk for 25 minutes. This bustling campsite has a pool and laundry. (☎03 85 88 89 20; fax 03 85 88 87 81. Reception 8am-11pm. Open for camping June 6-Sept.; for bungalows June 16-Sept 1. Camping June 6-30: site 34F/€5.19, 14F/€2.14 per person, electricity 15F/€2.29; June 30-Aug. 25: site 40F/€6.10, 14F/€2.135 per person, electricity 18F/€2.75. Bungalows June 16-June 30 200F/€30.49; June 30-July 7 260F/€39.64; July 7-Aug. 25 340F/€51.84; Aug. 25-Sept. 1 260F/€39.64.

FOOD. **Markets** are held on bd. du Collège (F 7:30am-1pm). A string of cheap eateries unravels on **rue Victor Hugo** off pl. Guignault, but a prettier place for lunch is in one of the cheap brasseries on the south side of the Bourbince, with views of the basilica. There's a **8-Huit** grocery store on the corner of rue Victor Hugo and rue du Marché. (Open M-Sa 8am-12:30pm and 2:30-8pm, Su 8:30am-12:30pm.) There is also the extremely affordable **Le Saxo** cafeteria, 44 av. Charles de Gaulle, with a 29F/€4.42 menu for students under 28 with ID. (☎03 85 81 42 57. Open M-Th 9am-4pm, F-Su 9am-3pm and 6-10pm.) Or try the tasty **La Taïga,** 9 rue Victor Hugo, with *menus* from 46-78F/€7.02-11.90, and cheap salads under 40F/€6.10. (☎03 85 81 21 66. Open July-Aug. daily 9am-10pm: Sept.-June 9am-midnight.)

THE WICKED SAMARITAN As you enter Autun's Cathédrale St-Lazare, look for the second and third capitals to the right. These tell the tale of Simon Magus, a Samaritan sorcerer who could reputedly change shape, fly, and take his head off at will. When Jesus upstaged him on the miracle front, Simon lost his head and bribed the Apostles to sell him the Holy Ghost. The arrogant magician was soon brought down to earth—literally. His rise and fall are illustrated in the carvings; one shows Simon flying to demonstrate his power, while on the other he crashes to the ground as a result of the Apostles' prayers.

SIGHTS. The spire of **Basilique du Sacré-Cœur** is visible throughout the town. Although Paray didn't emerge as a religious center until the first pilgrimage was organized in 1873, the basilica dates from the 11th century. This production of the Cluny architectural workshop is brought to you by the number three (symbolizing the Trinity), with a tripartite elevation and division on the facade, three major towers, and three radiating chapels. (Open daily 9am-7pm.)

Rue de la Visitation leads from the basilica to the other religious sights. The **Parc des Chapelains,** behind the church, is a peaceful spot for reflection in the outdoor chapel, whose nave is formed by plane trees. The **Accueil Pélerinage de Paray** next door welcomes the curious with a multilingual video and info on religious sessions. (Pilgrimage Center ☎03 85 81 62 22. Open daily 9:30am-noon and 2-6pm.) Continue along rue de la Visitation to the **Monastère de la Visitation,** sometimes referred to as *la Chapelle des Apparitions,* where Jesus is said to have revealed himself to Marguerite-Marie and where her relics are now kept. At the end of rue de la Visitation, turn left to get back to the town center. On **pl. Guignault,** the sand-colored facade of the early 16th-century **Maison Jayet** (now the **Hôtel de Ville**) is adorned with portraits of French royalty. The **Tour St-Nicholas,** also 16th-century, stands guard over pl. Guignault. Once the belfry of the long-gone St-Nicholas church, it is now just another pretty facade adorned by a beautiful staircase. Art exhibits are held inside regularly, mostly during the summer (hours and prices vary with exhibitions; contact the tourist office).

BURGUNDY

AUTUN

Around 15 BC, Emperor Augustus founded Augustodunum to create a "sister and rival of Rome." The name was later shortened to Autun. The only remaining evidence of Autun's former status is an impressive collection of rubble. Stirred by civic jealousy of nearby Vézélay's success, the town erected the Cathédrale St-Lazare (1120-1146) and made a successful push for the lucrative medieval pilgrimage business. Despite the ravages of eight none-too-kind centuries, the cathedral still boasts some of the finest Romanesque sculpture in the world. Though a recent lack of pilgrims has pushed Autun (pop. 20,000) off the beaten path, its serpentine streets, cathedral, and Roman ruins make it a compelling stop.

ORIENTATION AND PRACTICAL INFORMATION. The main street, **av. Charles de Gaulle,** connects the station to the central **pl. du Champ de Mars.** To get to the *vieille ville* from the *place*, follow the signs leading to the cathedral from rue aux Cordeliers or rue Saint-Saulge. The **tourist office** is off pl. du Champ du Mars.

Trains do run from pl. de la Gare on av. de la République, but Autun is far from any major railway line and thus difficult to get to. Most journeys to and from Autun require a change at **Châlon-sur-Saône** or **Etang,** and many involve tortuous connections. The quickest way to get to **Lyon** is to catch a bus to **Gare Le Creusot** (45min., 3 per day, 49F/€7.47) and take the TGV from there (50min., 4 per day, 144F/€21.96). **TGVs** leave Gare Le Creusot for **Paris** as well (1½hr., 5 per day, 356F/€54.29). It is possible to get to Dijon almost directly by train, by connecting in Etang (2hr., 3 per day to Dijon, price). The **SNCF buses** leave from outside the Autun station for **Chalon-sur-Saône** (2hr., 4 per day, 57F/€8.69). Helpful station office open M-F 7:05am-7:10pm, closed M-F 11:50am-12:10pm. Sa 9:05am-12:30pm and 2:30-6:30pm, Su 12:05-7:30pm. **TRANSCO buses** (☎03 80 42 11 00) leave from pl. de la Gare for **Dijon** daily at 5:10pm (2½hr., 79F/€12.05). For a **taxi,** call 03 85 52 04 83.

The **tourist office,** 2 av. Charles de Gaulle, offers various themed city **tours,** most as well as nocturnal tours in summer that mix music and historical sketches in the *vieille ville.* (☎03 85 86 80 38; fax 03 85 86 80 49. City tours 35F/€5.39, children 17.50F/€2.67. Night tours (July-Aug. 10pm) 50F/€7.62, under age 12 free. Office open May-Oct. daily 9am-7pm; Nov.-Apr. M-Sa 9am-noon and 2-7pm.) There's an **annex** at 5 pl. du Terreau, next to the cathedral. (☎03 85 52 56 03. Open May-Oct. 9am-7pm.) The **hospital** is at 9 bd. Fr. Latouche (☎03 85 52 09 06). The **police** (☎03 85 52 14 22) are at 29 av. Charles de Gaulle. The **Cybercafé Explorateur,** 17 rue Guerin, caters to email addicts. (☎03 85 86 68 84. 40F/€6.10 per hr.) There is a **laundromat**, 14 rue des Fusilliers, to air your dirty laundry. (Open 7am-10pm.) You can **exchange currency** at the **post office,** 8 rue Pernette. (☎03 85 86 58 10. Open M-F 8:30am-6:30pm, Sa 8:30am-noon). **Postal code:** 71400.

ACCOMMODATIONS, CAMPING AND FOOD. Most cheap hotels are across from the train station. Make reservations a couple of weeks in advance during the summer. **Hôtel de France,** 18 av. de la République. Comfy, modern hotel across from the train station and over a quiet bar and restaurant. The little rooms under the slope of the roof are charming but warm in summer. (☎03 85 52 14 00; fax 03 85 86 14 52. Breakfast 30F/€4.57. Reception daily 8am-11pm. Singles and doubles 130F/€19.82, with toilet 150F/€22.89, with shower 165F/€25.16; triples 185-230F/€28.21-35.06, with shower 200F/€30.49; quads 240-300F/€36.59-45.74. MC/V.) Right next door is the **Hotel of Commerce and Touring**, 20 av. de la Republique. With extremely pleasant and inviting rooms, it is a good bang for your buck. (☎03 85 52 17 90; fax 03 85 52 37 63. Breakfast 32F/€4.88. Reception 6:30am-11pm. Closed Jan. Singles and doubles 145F/€22.11, with shower 185F/€28.21, with shower and toilet 195F/€29.73. Extra bed 50F/€7.62. MC/V.) The **Camping Municipal de la Porte d'Arroux,** an easy 20min. walk from town, rides the soft banks of a river in the fields. From the train station, turn left on av. de la République, left on rue de Paris, and go under the Porte d'Arroux. Cross the bridge and veer right on rte. de Saulien; the campground is on your left. There is a restaurant and a grocery store; fishing and swimming are a few feet away. (☎03 85 52 10 82; fax 03 15 52 88 56. Open Apr.-Oct. Office open daily 8:30-10am and 5-7pm. Check out at noon. 16F/€2.44 per person; 14F/€2.14 per tent, 8.50F/€1.30 per car. Electricity 16.50F/€2.52. July-Aug. 15F/€2.29 fee for campground security.)

Autun's ruins are prime picnicking territory. Prepare your feast at **Intermarché,** pl. du Champs de Mars (open M-Th 8:30am-12:45pm and 2:30-7:30pm, F-Sa 8:30am-7:30pm). Champs de Mars is the *place* for **markets** (W and F). Bright little restaurants line the cobblestone streets of the upper city.

SIGHTS AND EXCURSIONS. At the top of the upper city, the **Cathédrale St-Lazare** rises above the Morvan countryside. In the course of 900 years of clerical quarrels, one group objected to the marvelous tympanum above the church doors and covered it in plaster, unwittingly protecting the masterpiece from the ravages of the Revolution. Today, Jesus still presides over the Last Judgment while Satan tinkers with the weighing of the souls. The artist's name, Gislebertus, is visible below Jesus' feet. In the dimly lit nave, intricately carved capitals illustrate biblical scenes; to see them at eye level, climb up to the *salle capitulaire* above the sacristy. Beware the basilisk, an imaginary serpent whose gaze reputedly turns humans into stone. (Open daily 8am-7pm.)

The **Musée Rolin,** 3 rue des Bancs, next to the cathedral, houses a diverse historical collection in the 15th-century mansion of Burgundian chancellor Nicolas Rolin. It includes a Roman helmet shaped like a leafy human face, Gislebertus' poignant sculpture of Eve at the Fall, the noseless man of Nazareth, and a magnificent collection of Gothic tableaux. (☎03 85 52 09 76; fax 03 85 52 47 41. Open Apr.-Sept. W-M 9:30am-noon and 1:30-6pm; Oct.-Mar. M, W-Sa 10am-noon and 2-5pm, Su 10am-noon and 2:30-5pm. 20F/€3.05, students 10F/€2.29.) Finally, if you are a dino lover, stop into the **Natural History Museum**, 14 rue Saint Antoine. With excavations and birds from the nearby environs, it fills in Autun's time line. (Open W-Su 2-5:30pm; in winter Sa-Su 2-5pm. 20F/€3.05, students with ID 10F/€1.53.)

There aren't many signs that Autun was the largest city in Roman Gaul, but enough remains to more than merit a visit. The cushy way is to sit back on **le Petit Train,** which leaves from pl. du Champs de Mars and from the tourist office annex near the cathedral (45min.; June-Aug. 7 French tours per day; 30F/€4.57, children 20F/€3.05). If you plan to do the ruins solo, be sure to arm yourself with a free map from the tourist office. Standing in the fields behind the train station, across the river Arroux, is the huge brick **Temple de Janus.** Once 24m high and 16m wide, this 1st-century temple was dedicated to an unknown Roman deity, not the double-headed Janus of mythology. The two extant walls tower over the fields, white clouds drifting through their eroded, gaping windows. To reach them from the train station, walk northeast along av. de la République and take a left onto rue du fbg. d'Arroux, passing under one of the city's two remaining Roman gates, the **Porte d'Arroux.** These two large arches for vehicles and two smaller ones for pedestrians led to the Via Agrippa, the main trade road between Lyon and Boulogne. The other gate, **Porte St-André,** at the intersection of rue de la Croix Blanche and rue de Gaillon, is better preserved.

The **Théâtre Romain,** near the lake to the northeast of the *vieille ville*, is delightfully unrestored. Its stones, vivid and fresh, emerge from a grassy hillside, and picnickers relax where 12,000 enthralled spectators once sat. The ampitheater whimpers back to life during the first three weekends in August, when 600 locals bring chariot races and Roman games to life in the *Augustodunum* show. (☎03 85 86 80 13 for info. 80F/€12.20, children under 12 50F/€7.62. Tickets sold at tourist office.) From the rear of the amphitheater, you can see the 30m pile of bricks which is the **Pierre de Couhard.** The purpose of this heap remained unknown until excavations unearthed a 1900-year-old plaque that cursed anyone who dared to disturb the eternal slumber of the man buried inside. *Let's Go* does not recommend incurring dormant wrath. To reach the site, leave the *vieille ville* through the Porte de Breuil southeast of the cathedral and climb into the hills.

Autun's ramparts and towers are best seen from the hills above; to get there, take the path from near the cathedral to the Pierre de Couhard. Or rent a **bike** from the **Service Du Sports** on the far side of the lake. (☎03 85 86 95 80. 55F/€8.39 per half-day, 95F/€14.48 per day; open Apr.-Oct. 8:30am-noon and 2-5pm.)

NEVERS

Although this city (pop. 55,000) in western Burgundy was the setting for Marguerite Duras' novel and screenplay *Hiroshima Mon Amour*, its original claim to fame is its status as the final resting place of St. Bernadette de Lourdes. Bernadette Soubirous, a young girl who reported conversing with the Virgin Mary in Lourdes (see p. 682), came to Nevers in July of 1866 to enter the Couvent St-Gil-dard. Beyond the bustle of a modern industrial city, Nevers is a town of carefully tended parks, modest squares, cobblestone streets, exquisite medieval and Renaissance architecture, and a long tradition of decorative arts: glass, enamel, and most of all, porcelain. If at first you aren't impressed by this shy city, remember Duras' admonition: "Saying that Nevers is a tiny town is an error of both the heart and the mind."

TRANSPORTATION AND PRACTICAL INFORMATION. **Trains** go through Nevers to: **Bourges** (38-55min., 16 per day, 61F/€9.30); **Clermont-Ferrand** (1½hr., 13 per day, 120F/€18.30); **Dijon** (2¾hr., 5 per day, 147F/€22.41); **Moulins** (32-60min., 16 per day, 54F/€8.23); and **Paris** (2½hr., 7 per day, 167F/€25.46). (Ticket windows open daily 6am-9pm.) **Local buses** leave from rue de Charleville, left of the train station as you exit (☎03 86 57 16 39; 5.50F/€0.84 to city center). For a **taxi,** call 03 86 57 19 19 (7am-11pm) or 03 86 59 58 00. **Rent bikes** at **Belair,** 31bis rue de la Préfecture. (☎03 86 61 24 45. 100F/€15.2 per day, 450F/€68.61 per week. 2000F/€304.92 deposit. Open M-Sa 8:30am-12:30pm and 1:30-7pm.) The town center is an easy eight-minute walk away. From the station, head four blocks up av. Général de Gaulle to Nevers' main square, **pl. Carnot.** Diagonally across the square from av. de Gaulle is rue Sabatier, where the multilingual **tourist office** is housed in the Palais

Ducal, 4 rue Sabatier. The office offers free maps of the city and a self-guided walking tour in several languages. (☎03 86 68 46 00; fax 03 86 68 45 98; www.ville-nevers.fr. Office open May-Oct. 1 M-Sa 9am-7pm, Su 10am-7pm; Oct. 2-Apr. M-Sa 9am-6pm, Su 10am-6pm.) The **police** are at 6bis av. Marceau (☎03 86 60 53 00); the **Centre Hospitalier** at 1 av. Colbert (☎03 86 68 30 30). Across the street from the post office is **France Télécom,** which will let you check **email** on its showroom computers if you ask politely. (Open M 10am-7pm, Tu-F 8:30am-7pm, Sa 9am-noon and 2:30-7pm.) There's more **Internet access** at **Pain et Friandaises,** 5 rue de la Pelleterie. (☎03 86 59 26 69. 1F/€0.15 first 3min., 0.50F/€0.08 per extra minute. Open M-Sa 8am-7:30pm.) There's **currency exchange** with a 15F/€2.29 charge at **Crédit Municipal,** on pl. Carnot (M-F 8:15-11:45am and 1:15-5:15pm, Sa 8:15-11:45am), and at the **post office,** 25bis av. Pierre Bérégovoy, where the fee for changing money depends on the currency; there is no charge for American dollars. (☎03 86 21 50 21; open M-F 8am-6:30pm, Sa 8am-noon). **Poste Restante:** 58000. **Postal code:** 58019.

ACCOMMODATIONS AND CAMPING. Rooms near the station and the city center start around 130F/€19.82. Several blocks left of the train station and opposite the convent, **Hôtel Beauséjour,** 5bis rue St-Gildard, has a lovely garden and rooms that can hold up to 2 people, but are available for one. (☎03 86 61 20 84; fax 03 86 59 15 37. Breakfast 32F/€4.88. Reception 7am-10pm. Singles 145F/€22.11; doubles with shower 180-230F/€27.44-35.06. Extra bed 50F/€7.62. MC/V.) To reach the friendly **Foyer Clairjoie,** 2 rue du Cloître St-Cyr, walk up av. Général de Gaulle to the pl. Carnot, and cross the *place* to the right to the rue de Doyenné. Turn right onto rue du Cloître St-Cyr. The foyer caters mostly to long-term residents under the age of 30; it feels like a college dormitory and has laundry facilities. Inside its stone wall is a large central garden where residents chat and play ping-pong at night. Even when other hotels are booked solid, there are usually rooms available here. (☎03 86 59 86 00. Singles only 150F/€22.90. MC/V.) **Hôtel de Verdun,** 4 rue de Lourdes, has newly renovated rooms, English-speaking owners, and a terrace. (☎03 86 61 30 07; fax 03 86 57 75 61; hotel.de.verdun@wanadoo.fr. Breakfast 30F/€2.3. Reception M-Sa 7am-9pm, Su 7am-noon. Singles and doubles 130F/€19.82, with shower 170F/€25.92, with shower and toilet 200F/€30.49, with bath and toilet 230F/€35.06. Extra bed 50F/€7.62. MC/V.) **Camping Municipal** surveys the *vieille ville* from across the Loire. Along with the view come showers and toilets. To get to there, follow rue de la Cathédrale down to the river, cross the bridge, and turn left; it's five minutes by car from the city center. (☎03 86 37 56 52. Reception 7am-10pm. Open May-late Sept. 20F/€3.05 per person, 20F/€3.05 per tent, 10F/€1.53 per car.)

FOOD. Nevers' *vieille ville* is studded with pricey brasseries, but there are less expensive spots in all directions from pl. Carnot. **Rue du 14 juillet,** between pl. Carnot and the cathedral, has many decent, inexpensive restaurants. They are mostly grills and patisseries, although there are a few ethnic choices. **Marché Carnot** hosts a covered **market** with fresh fruits, cheeses, and meats. Enter on av. du Général de Gaulle and on rue St-Didier. (Open M-F 7am-12:40pm and 3-6:55pm, Sa 6:30am-7pm.) A **Champion supermarket,** 12 av. du Général de Gaulle, is half a block from pl. Carnot. (Open M-F 9am-7:30pm, Sa 8:30am-7:30pm, Su 9am-noon.) **Restaurant L'Univers,** 5bis rue du 14 juillet, specializes in eat-in and takeout Greek and Turkish dishes. Choices include salads, sandwiches, and main dishes (mostly steak and kabobs), plus an array of wines from France, Greece, and Turkey. (☎03 86 61 44 07. Open in summer Su-F 10am-2am; in winter Su-F 10am-1am.) **Le Goemon Crêperie,** 9 rue du 14 juillet, boasts handmade omelettes and crêpes of all flavors (15-36F/€2.29-5.49) in a wooden interior. (☎03 86 59 54 99. Open daily noon-2pm and 7-10pm.) **Pizzeria San Rémo,** 12 rue du 14 juillet, indulges those Italian cravings with large portions and lively music. (☎03 86 36 74 55. Pizzas, pastas, salads, and meat dishes 34-75F/€5.18-11.43. Open daily noon-2:30pm and 7-11:30pm. MC/V.) **Restaurant La Tour,** 2 pl. du Palais, has a public cafeteria connected to the inner courtyard of the foyer Clairjoie. There's not much choice, but you'll get a full meal for 50F/€7.62. (☎03 86 59 86 07. Open M-F 11:30am-2pm and 7-8:30pm.)

SIGHTS. The most visible structure in Nevers is the Renaissance **Cathédrale St-Cyr et Ste-Juliette,** off pl. Carnot and up rue du Doyenné. St-Cyr's charm is in its unusual double-heeled arrangement—to the west is an enormous Romanesque apse with a fresco of Christ Pantokrator, while to the east is the 14th-century Gothic response. Be sure to notice the modern stained glass, created by five different artists between 1977 and 1983. (☎03 86 59 06 54. Open June-Sept. Tu-Sa 10am-noon and 2-7pm. Free tours 11am, 3, and 6pm.) Opposite the cathedral, fairy-tale turrets cap the 15th-century **Palais Ducal,** once the seat of regional government. (☎03 86 68 46 00. Enter from tourist office. Free.) The beautiful **Couvent St-Gildard,** on the corner of rue Jeanne d'Arc and rue St-Gildard, houses the Sisters of Charity of Nevers and the body of St. Bernadette (1844-1879). Thousands of pilgrims come each year to visit this spiritual center, in which St. Bernadette spent her last 13 years in seclusion at the Virgin Mary's personal urging. (☎03 86 57 79 99. Open Apr.-Oct. daily 7am-12:30pm and 1:30-7:30pm; Nov.-Mar. 7:30am-noon and 2-7pm. Free. Mass M-F 8 and 11:30am, Su 10am.)

A walk in the gardens lining the **Promenade des Remparts,** from the Loire to av. Général de Gaulle, follows the crumbled remains of 12th-century Nevers. Along the Promenade is the **Musée Municipal Frédéric Blandin.** Installed in the 7th-century Abbaye Notre-Dame, the museum houses a collection of the ceramics, glasswork, and earthenware for which Nevers is famous. (☎03 86 71 67 90. Open Oct.-Apr. M and W-Sa 1-5:30pm, Su 10am-noon and 2-5:30pm; May-Sept. W-M 10am-6:30pm. 15F/€2.29, reduced 8F/€1.22, under 18 and students free.) Just outside the museum gardens, the imposing 14th-century **Porte du Croux** now houses an archaeology museum. Meander through the crowds on the pedestrian rue François Mitterrand, lined with classy stores, and venture out toward rue St-Etienne to see a neighborhood that flourished with the 11th century's monastic boom. Before leaving Nevers, cross over the **Pont de Loire** for a last view of the gentle green slopes and blue water of the Loire river and its banks. In the center of town is the peaceful **Parc Roger Salengro,** across from pl. Carnot. For two weeks every June, the park hosts a carnival replete with bumper cars, cotton candy, and pinball machines.

AUXERRE

Auxerre began its days as Autessiodrum, a Roman hub along the via Agrippa. Converted early, Auxerre's monastic community blossomed in the 5th century under the learned bishop Germain (AD 378-448) and his successors. The many monasteries surrounding Auxerre were referred to as the city's "sacred walls." Though the ravages of wars humbled or destroyed these defenses, Auxerre was saved from obscurity by its Chablis wine, which was supplied en masse to an insatiable Parisian market. Today Auxerre (pop. 40,000), a bustling village with scores of businesses, is unobscured by tourists.

ORIENTATION AND PRACTICAL INFORMATION

Trains: Gare Auxerre-St-Gervais, rue Paul Doumer, east of the Yonne. To: **Avallon** (1hr.; M-Sa 6 per day, Su 3 per day; 51F/€7.78); **Dijon** (2½hr., 7 per day, 124F/€18.91); **Lyon** (3-5hr., 3 per day, 220F/€33.54); and **Paris** (2hr.; M-Sa 9 per day, Su 6 per day; 123F/€18.75). Ticket counter open M-F 5:15am-8:30pm, Sa 6:15am-8:30pm, Su 6:30am-9:30pm.

Buses: Les Rapides de Bourgogne, at the train station. To **Avallon** (1 per day, 3:30pm, 48F/€7.32). Not the best means of transport: stick to the trains.

Local Transportation: Le Bus has service around town, and there are plenty of stops. M-Sa 7am-7:30pm. Tickets 6.50F/€0.99. Schedules at tourist office.

Taxis: ☎03 86 46 78 78 or 03 86 52 30 51.

Tourist Office: 12 quai de la République (☎03 86 52 06 19; fax 03 86 51 23 27). From the station, veer left and cross onto rue Jules Ferry. Turn right onto av. Gambetta, and cross the river on pont Bert. Take a right–the office is 2 blocks down quai de la

République (12min.). Accommodations service (15F/€2.29), **currency exchange** when banks are closed, biking and walking **tours,** and **bike rental** (50F/€7.62 per half-day, 80F/€12.20 per day; 1000F/€152.46 and ID deposit; electric bikes at same prices). Open mid-June to mid-Sept. M-Sa 9am-1pm and 2-7pm, Su 9:30am-1pm and 3-6:30pm; mid-Sept. to mid-June M-Sa 9am-12:30pm and 2-6:30pm, Su 10am-1pm.

Hospital: 2 bd. de Verdun (☎03 86 48 48 48).

Police: 32 bd. Vaulabelle (03 86 51 85 00).

Laundromat: Lav-o-claire, 138 rue le Paris.

Internet Access: 13 rue Cochois. 30F/€4.57 per hr. Open M-F 9:30am-12:30pm and 2-7pm.

Post Office: pl. Charles-Surugue (☎03 86 72 68 60). **Currency exchange.** Open M-F 8:30am-7pm, Sa 8:30am-noon. **Postal code:** 89000.

ACCOMMODATIONS AND CAMPING

Hôtel le Seignelay, rue du Pont (☎03 86 52 03 48; fax 03 86 52 32 39). Rooms in this 18th-century inn are well-lit, tidy, and uniquely designed. Breakfast 38F/€5.79. Reception 7am-10pm. Closed Feb. Reserve during the summer. Singles from 150F/€22.90, with bath 220F/€33.54; doubles from 180F/€27.44, with bath 280F/€42.69. Triples and quads with bath 320-370F/€48.79-56.41. AmEx/MC/V.

Foyer des Jeunes Travailleurs (HI), 16 bd. Vaulabelle (☎03 86 52 45 38). Follow the signs from the train station to the *centre ville,* cross pont Bert, and turn left on quai de la République; the first right is rue Vaulabelle. The *foyer* is in an apartment building back from the street, immediately past a gas station. Clean hallways and neat rooms. Breakfast included. Meals 43F/€6.56. Reception 2-8pm. Singles 80F/€12.20.

Hôtel Saint Martin, 9 rue Germain Benard (☎03 86 52 04 16). Sober, clean, dirt-cheap rooms with hall bathrooms, above a *bar-tabac* off bd. Davout. Breakfast 24F/€3.66. Reception 6:30am-9pm; Sept.-July M-Sa 6:30am-9pm. Singles 100F/€15.25; doubles 110-170F/€16.77-25.92. A 2-room, 5-person suite 250F/€38.12. **Cash only.**

Camping: 8 rte. de Vaux (☎03 86 52 11 15), south of town on D163. Reception Apr. 7am-8pm; May and Sept. 7am-9pm; June-Aug. 7am-10pm. Open Apr.-Sept. 14F/€2.13 per site, 16F/€2.44 per person. Car included. Electricity 13F/€1.98.

FOOD

The **Monoprix supermarket,** 10 pl. Charles Surugue in the heart of the old town, also has a cheap cafeteria, with *plats* from 25-50F/€3.81-7.62. (Supermarket open M-Sa 8:30am-6:30pm. Cafeteria open M-Sa 11:30am-2pm; *salon de thé* open M-Sa 2:30-6pm.) **Markets** are held on pl. de l'Arquebuse (Tu and W morning, F until 6pm) and on pl. Degas, on the outskirts (Su morning). There are numerous pizza joints to be found all over the city. For slightly better fare, **La Marmite Napolitaine,** 34 rue du Pont, serves a mixture of local and Italian recipes under the time-blackened timbers of an ancient house. The three-course *menu* that includes *escargot* (82F/€12.50). (☎03 86 51 08 83. Open M 7-10:30pm, Tu-Sa noon-2pm and 7-10:30pm. Closed July 16-31. Reserve on Saturdays. MC/V.)

SIGHTS

From Pont Paul-Bert, there's a lovely view of the city and its churches. The **Quartier de la Marine,** around pl. St-Nicolas, is lined with the old wooden houses formerly occupied by rivermen. From the Yonne, wander up to the **Cathédrale St-Etienne,** begun in 1215, whose wounded facade still displays statuettes decapitated by Huguenots when they occupied the city in 1567. The iconoclasts also smashed much of the stained glass, but didn't get to the 13th-century windows in the ambulatory. The Gothic structure sits on top of an 11th-century Romanesque **crypt,** which preserves an ochre fresco of *Christ on Horseback.* The **treasury** on the south wall guards relics, illuminated manuscripts, and St-Germain's 5th-century tunic. (Cathedral open daily 9am-6pm. Crypt 15F/€2.29; treasury 10F/€1.53. *Son-et-lumière*, translated into English, nightly at 10pm in June-Aug. 30F/€4.57.)

The Gothic **Abbaye St-Germain,** 2 pl. St-Germain, attracted pilgrims to the tomb of the former bishop of Auxerre and medieval scholars to the attached ecclesiastic college. Part Carolingian, the underground chapel preserves the oldest frescoes in France. Only monks were allowed in this privileged space; pilgrims had to be content to hand bits of cloth down into the tomb of St. Germain from the upper church. (Open May-Sept. W-M 10am-6:30pm; Oct.-Apr. 10am-noon and 2-6pm. Crypt tours. 36F/€5.49 including Musée Leblanc, students under 26 free.)

Toward pl. de l'Hôtel de Ville, the **Tour de l'Horloge,** a turreted 15th-century clock tower in white and gold, is the gateway to the *vieille ville.* The **Musée Leblanc-Duvernoy,** 9bis rue d'Egleny, between rue Gaillard and rue de l'Egalité, contains painting, pottery, and elegant 18th-century Beauvais tapestries. (☎03 86 51 09 74. Open W-M 2-6pm. 13F/€1.98, free for students under 26.) Shroomers get their jollies with the **Société Mycologique Auxerroise,** 5 bd. Vauban, which organizes mushroom-hunting expeditions in spring and autumn (☎03 86 72 76 40).

AVALLON

The tiny *vieille ville* of Avallon (pop. 8560) peeks over medieval walls high on a granite hill. Its ramparts were designed by the prolific military architect Sébastien "The Fortifier" Vauban. Although the outskirts of town haven't quite held off waves of urban development, the center still reflects small-town charm. Though poor on museums and monuments, it does have one of the region's few train stations and can be used as a base for exploring the Morvan or nearby Vézelay.

PRACTICAL INFORMATION

Trains: ☎03 86 34 01 01. **SNCF trains** are slow and cryptically scheduled. To: **Autun** (1¾hr.; 3 per day, Sun 2 per day; 73F/€11.13); **Auxerre** (1½hr., M-Sa 8 per day, 50F/€7.62); **Dijon** (2-3hr., M-Sa 3 per day, 102F/€15.55); and **Paris** (2½-3hr.; M-Sa 4 per day, Su 1 per day; 155F/€23.63). Station open M-F 5:30am-12:15pm and 1:15-8pm, Sa 5:30am-7:30pm, Su 8:30am-8pm.

Buses: SNCF (03 86 94 95 00) leaves from the train station for: **Dijon** (1¾hr.; M-Sa 3 per day, Su 2 per day; 102F/€15.55); **Paris** (M-Sa 3 per day, Su 3 per day; 152F/€23.17). **TRANSCO** (☎03 80 42 11 00) roll from the train station to **Dijon** (2½hr.; M-Sa 3 per day, Su 1 per day; 90F/€13.72) via **Semur-en-Auxois** (45min.). The tourist office has schedules.

Taxis: ☎03 86 31 60 00.

Bike Rental: Touvélo, 26 rue de Paris (☎03 86 34 28 11). 100F/€15.25 per day. Open Tu-Sa 8am-noon and 2-7pm.

Tourist Office: 6 rue Bocquillot (☎03 86 34 14 19). Next to the Eglise St-Lazare. Head straight on av. du Président Doumer and turn right onto rue Carnot. At the large intersection, turn left onto rue de Paris, which passes a large parking lot, becomes the pedestrian Grande Rue A. Briand, passes through the Tour de l'Horloge, and lands you at the office (15min.). Free map in English. **Accommodations service** (15F/€2.29). **Internet** access 20F/€3.05 per 15min. Open July-Aug. daily 9:30am-7:30pm; Sept.-June 10am-noon and 2-6pm; Nov.-Mar. closed Su.

Laundromat: Hallwash, 8 rue du Marché, off pl. de Gaulle. Open daily 7am-9pm.

Hospital: 1 rue de l'Hôpital (☎03 86 34 66 00), down the street from the post office.

Police: 2 av. Victor Hugo (☎03 86 34 17 17), near the Foyer des Jeunes Travailleurs. Smaller office at 37 Grande Rue. Open M-F 9am-noon, 2-5pm, Sa 9am-noon.

Post Office: 9 rue des Odebert (☎03 86 34 91 08). Open M-F 8am-noon and 1:30-6pm, Sa 8am-noon. **Postal code:** 89200.

It's Your World...

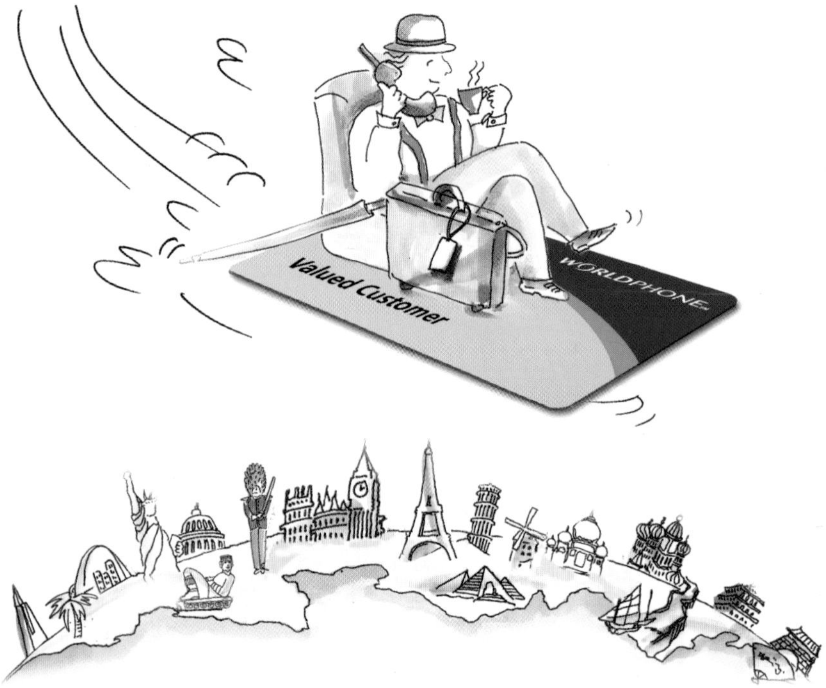

MCI®

www.mci.com/worldphone

ACCOMMODATIONS AND CAMPING

Foyer des Jeunes Travailleurs, 10 av. Victor Hugo (☎03 86 34 01 88; fax 03 86 34 10 95). 20min. from the station and 15min. from the *vieille ville*. From the station, walk straight ahead on av. du Président Doumer, turn right onto rue Carnot, which becomes rte. de Paris after the intersection. Take your second left onto chemin de Thory, and then make your first right onto rue du Stade. Make a left onto rue John Kennedy and then a left onto av. Victor Hugo. Sober, 70s-style singles in a depressingly modern high-rise. Breakfast 17F/€2.59. Meals 42F/€6.40. Reception 24hr. Singles 85F/€12.96.

Hôtel du Parc, across from the station (☎03 86 34 17 00). Well-maintained rooms in a 17th-century hotel with a nice terrace bar. There are no hall showers, so if you want to be squeaky clean, opt for a room with a shower. Breakfast 25F/€3.81. Reception 7am-11pm. Closed late Dec. to mid-Jan. Singles and doubles 115-130F/€17.53-19.82, with shower 149-210F/€22.72-32.02. Extra bed 55-75F/€8.39-11.43. MC/V.

Camping Municipal de Sous-Roche, 3km away (☎03 86 34 10 39). Walk straight from the train station onto av. du Président Doumer, left onto rue Carnot, then straight through the big intersection. Head straight along rte. de Lourmes, make a left onto rte. de Lourmes and then veer left on rue de Sous Roche. Climb to the quiet riverside campground. Reception 8am-10pm. Open Apr.-Sept. 18F/€2.74 per person; 13F/€1.98 per site; 13F/€1.98 per tent or car. Electricity 18F/€2.74.

FOOD

At the top of town, **La Tour,** 84 Grande Rue A. Briand, cooks up scrumptious Italian and regional food in a warm, half-timbered 15th-century house behind the Tour de l'Horloge. Big salads go for 22-46F/€3.35-7.01; pizzas for 35-56F/€5.95-8.54; and pastas range 46-54F/€7.01-8.23. (☎03 86 34 24 84. Open daily 11:45am-2:30pm and 6:45-11pm. AmEx/MC/V.) There's also **Restaurant Indochine,** 8 rue de Odebert, off rue d'Hôpital. (☎03 86 34 51 24. Generous portions of Chinese and Vietnamese entrees; *plat du jour* 70F/€10.67, beef, pork, and chicken meals 40-52F/€6.10-7.93, and fish dishes for 46F/€7.01. Open M 7-9:30pm, Tu and Th-Su noon-1:30pm and 7-9:30pm, W 7-9:30pm. **Cash only.**) For do-it-yourselfers, the **Petit Casino supermarket,** rue de Paris, is a block or two past the intersection with rue Carnot toward town (open M-Sa 9am-5:30pm). Morning **markets** are held on pl. Vauban (Sa) and in the pl. du Général de Gaulle, a small square (Th).

BURGUNDY

SIGHTS

The countryside around Avallon is undeniably beautiful, and more compelling than anything within the town itself. A walk along the narrow paths of the western and southern ramparts reveals an excellent view of the dense forests, verdant pastures, and crumbling châteaux of the Vallée du Cousin. The tourist office can give you a free map of an 8km walk that covers the area's highlights.

The charming **Musée du Costume,** 6 rue Belgrand, off Grande Rue A. Briand, fills the rooms of the prince of Condé's 17th-century house with bustles and *bijoux* each summer as mannequins don period dress for the different pieces exhibited annually. Superb for fashion or history lovers. (☎03 86 34 19 95. Open Easter-Oct. daily 10:30am-12:30pm and 1:30-5:30pm. Tours in French. 25F/€3.81, students 15F/€2.29.)

Two prominent remnants of days gone by stand side by side at the southern end of the *vieille ville*. The 15th-century slate **Tour de l'Horloge** straddles Grande Rue A. Briand. Down the street, the **Eglise Collégiale St-Lazare** gained its present name in AD 1000 when Henri Le Grand, Duke of Burgundy, donated a part of St. Lazare's skull to the church. The main Romanesque portal is ornamented with a series of recessed arches, adorned by carvings depicting cherubim, the Zodiac, and the Elders of the Apocalypse carrying musical instruments. Note the spiraling colonnettes on either side of the doors. (Church open daily 9am-noon and 2-6pm; closed in winter.) Behind the tourist office, the slightly neglected **Musée de l'Avallonais** contains an interesting collection of artifacts from prehistory to the Middle Ages. The results of regional archaeological digs are particularly fascinating. (☎03 86 34 03 19. Open May-Oct. W-M 2-6pm. 20F/€3.05, students 15F/€2.29.)

VEZELAY

High up a hillside 15km from Avallon, the village of Vézelay (pop. 497) watches over dense forest, golden wheat, and the white flecks of cattle in distant pastures. Vézelay is considered one of the most beautiful villages in France, and so it is; most people, however, have visited the town for its famous basilica, which, since the 11th century, has contained the relics of Mary Magdalene.

ORIENTATION AND PRACTICAL INFORMATION. There's no train station in Vézelay; **trains** run from **Paris** via **Auxerre** to **Sermicelles** (2½hr., 4 per day, 144F/€21.95); from here you can wait for the shuttle bus that runs between Vézelay and Avallon on Saturdays at 11:48am (call Cars de la Madéleine at 03 86 33 35 95) or **Taxi Vezelay** (☎03 86 32 31 88; 24hr.). A **SNCF bus** leaves the train station at Avallon for Vézelay at 9:36am (M-F through Aug.), 7:58pm (M-Sa), 10:46am (Su through Sept. 1), and returns at 5:29pm daily during the summer (22min., 23F/€3.5). You might prefer to bike or take a taxi (from Avallon 120F/€18.30). Vézelay's tiny **tourist office,** rue St-Pierre, just down the street from the church, has free maps and a *guide pratique* with accommodations listings. (☎03 86 33 23 69; fax 03 86 33 34 00. Office open June-Oct. daily 10am-1pm and 2-6pm; Nov.-May closed Th.) The **post office,** rue St-Etienne, has an **ATM.** (☎03 86 33 26 35. Open M-F 8:30am-12:30pm and 1:30-5pm, Sa 8:30am-noon.) **Postal code:** 89450.

ACCOMMODATIONS. An option used primarily by pilgrims is the *maisons* run by the Fraternité Monastique de Jerusalem. Contact the tourist office for info. Fifteen minutes from the bus stop, the rural **Auberge de Jeunesse (HI),** rte. de l'Etang, offers simple 4- to 6-bed rooms and a 12-bed dorm. Follow the signs to the *gendarmerie;* the hostel is 400m past it on your left. (☎03 86 33 24 18. Kitchen. Bring sheets. Reception 5-7pm. Lockout 10am-5:30pm. Open Feb.-Dec., but from Nov.-Mar. only for groups. Reservations essential. Beds 45F/€6.86, non-members 56F/€8.54.) There's a grassy, intimate **campsite** attached to the hostel with exquisitely clean bathroom facilities. (18F/€2.74 per person; 5F/€0.76 per tent; 5F/€0.76 per car; 10F/€1.53 per caravan. Electricity 10F/€1.53.) Right by the bus stop, the **Hotel du Cheval** has nine quaint rooms. (☎03 86 33 22 12. Breakfast 38F/€5.79. There is no hall shower. Reservations a must. Closed Dec.-Jan. Singles and doubles with toilet 120F/€18.30; with shower and toilet 160F-260F.) Attached to the hotel is a restaurant which serves up salads (50-52F/€7.62-7.93) and three *plats* (85F/€12.96, 100F/€15.25, and 130F/€19.82). In Saint-Père, a short hike away, the *bar-tabac-hôtel* **A la Renommée,** has large, well-decorated rooms in tranquil blues, yellows, and mauves. (☎03 86 33 21 34; fax 03 86 33 34 17. Breakfast 37F/€5.64. Shower 10F/€1.53 for those staying only one night. Open Mar.-Dec. Doubles with toilet 180-330F/€27.44; quads 420F/€64.03. Extra bed 60F/€9.15.)

FOOD. With its ruddy tile floor and smoky fireplace, the rustic **Auberge de la Coquille,** 81 rue Saint-Perre, perfectly suits the local specialties it serves—spicy *escargots* and crumbling rounds of *fromage epoisses*, among others. (☎03 86 33 35 57. 3- and 4-course *menus* from 65-145F/€9.91-22.11. Open June-Aug. daily noon-10pm; Feb. 16 to May and Sept. to Nov. 15 noon-3pm and 6:30-9:30pm. Open weekends and holidays during the winter. Reservations in summer.) Buy your own food at Vival **supermarket,** near the bottom of rue St. Etienne. (Open June M-Sa 8:15am-1pm and 3:30-7:30pm; July-Aug. M-Sa 8am-8pm, Su 9am-8pm; Oct.-June Tu and Th-Sa 8am-12:30pm and 3:30-7:30pm, M and W 8am-1pm, Su 9am-1pm.)

SIGHTS. St. Bernard of Clairvaux, one of medieval France's greatest theologians, launched the Second Crusade with an impassioned speech here in 1146. The **basilica** he spoke in—and the one that still stands today—was rebuilt after a fire in 1120 destroyed the Carolingian original. The real star here is the array of grotesque and lyrical carved column capitals, depicting Biblical monsters and various hellbound unfortunates. The second column on the right features a fire-fed demon impaled on his own sword and a waifish woman whose insides are devoured by a serpent. **Mary Magdalene's relics** have been somewhat less visited since the 13th century, when another set was discovered near where she reputedly landed in AD 40. They're still sanctified by the Church, though, and you can visit them in the rough crypt below. Above ground, a little bit of saintly bone wrapped in pearls and gold has been embedded in a column. (☎03 86 33 39 50. Open daily 8am-7:30pm. Tours in English with reservation; pamphlets in English. Suggested donation 30F/€4.57.)

SEMUR-EN-AUXOIS

Although legend attributes Semur-en-Auxois' founding to Hercules, the earliest written record of the town (pop. 5100) dates from 606. In that year, monks of the Abbaye de Flavigny signed their charter in a village they called *Sene Muros*—the "old walls." The *vieille ville*'s towers and ramparts now crown an unspoiled provincial town of cobblestones and archways that overlook a bend in the Armençon river. Venture under the Sauvigny Gate (built in 1417) and the arch that bears the city's motto in old French: *Les Semurois se plaisent fort en l'acointance des Estrangers* ("The people of Semur take great pleasure in welcoming strangers").

PRACTICAL INFORMATION. Trains run only to **Montbard,** 18km away; a bus completes the journey to Semur (see below). It's best to go direct; **TRANSCO** (☎03 80 42 11 00) runs **buses** to: **Avallon** (45min.; M-Sa 3 per day, Su 1 per day; 42F/€6.40); **Dijon** (1½hr.; M-Sa 3 per day, Su 1 per day; 60F/€9.15); and **Montbard** (25min.; M-Sa 3 per day, Su 2 per day; 15F/€2.29). For a **taxi,** call 03 80 97 09 71.

The **tourist office,** pl. Gaveau, where rue de la Liberté meets the gates of the *vieille ville*, has bus schedules, free maps, and a list of hotels. The staff runs **tours** in English during the summer (by reservation; 18-25F/€2.74-3.81) and tours for students, in French, 15F/€2.29). (☎03 80 97 05 96. Open mid-June to mid-Sept. M-Sa 9am-7pm, Su 10am-noon and 3-6pm; rest of year M-Sa 8:30am-noon and 2-6:30pm.) Internet available by 2002. Rent **bikes** (for use in town only) here for 60F/€9.15 per day, 300F/€45.74 per week with a 500F/€76.23 or ID deposit. You can also find bikes for use in the countryside at **Robert Bonvalot's Bike Shop,** at 10 Rue de L'Ancienne Comédie. (☎03 80 97 01 91. 35F/€5.34 per half-day, 60F/€9.15 per day.) The tourist office also has a **SNCF info and reservation office.** (Open Tu-F 9am-noon and 2-6pm, Sa 9am-noon and 2-5pm.) Most businesses in Semur are closed on Monday. The **police** (☎03 80 97 11 17) and the **hospital** (☎03 80 89 64 64) are on av. Pasteur, east of the center. **Laundromat La Buanderie** is at the Centre Commercial Champlon. (☎03 80 97 08 91. Open daily 9am-8pm.) The **post office,** pl. de l'Ancienne Comédie, has **currency exchange.** (☎03 80 89 93 06. Open M-F 8:30am-noon and 1:30-5:30pm, Sa 8am-noon.) **Postal code:** 21140.

ACCOMMODATIONS AND CAMPING. The **Foyer des Jeunes Travailleurs,** 1 rue du Champ de Foire, off rue de la Liberté and about 300m from the tourist office, has tattered but functional singles. While occupied mostly by long-term youngsters, there might be room for wandering tourists, but check by phone first. (☎03 80 97 10 22; fax 03 80 97 36 97. Breakfast 10F/€1.53, meals 48F/€7.32. Reception M-Th 9am-9pm, F 9am-8pm, Sa-Su 11am-2pm and 6-8pm; call ahead if arriving at a different time. Bunks 100F/€15.25.) The **Hôtel des Gourmets,** 4 rue Varenne, offers large, beautifully furnished rooms in an old house in the heart of the *vieille ville*. (☎03 80 97 09 41; fax 03 80 97 17 95. Breakfast 35F. Free parking. Closed M evening and Tu. Closed Dec. Singles and doubles 160-250F/€24.39-38.12, with bath 230F/

€35.06; triples and quads 200F/€35.06; 6-person room 260F/€39.04. Extra bed 30F/€4.57. AmEx/MC/V.) **Hôtel le Bory,** 19 rue de la Liberté, is also right in the middle of the action, as it were, and lets spotless, spacious rooms. (☎03 80 96 64 40; fax 03 80 97 00 18. Breakfast 30F/€4.57, in bed 35F/€5.34. Reception 24hr. Singles and doubles 160F/€24.39, with shower 190F/€28.97; doubles and quads with bath or shower, 230-320F/€35.06-48.79. Extra bed 50F/€7.62. AmEx/MC/V.) **Camping Municipal du Lac de Pont** offers a spot in the sun 3km south of Semur on a scenic lake with a beach, tennis courts, and bike rental, laundry, and a mini-mart. (☎03 80 97 01 26. Reception 9am-noon and 4-8pm. Open May-Sept. 15. 20F/€3.05 per person, 11F/€1.68 per site, 10F/€1.53 per car. Electricity 15F/€2.29.)

FOOD. For groceries, stop at **Intermarché,** av. du Général Maziller (open M-Th 9am-12:15pm and 2:30-7:15pm, F 9am-7:45pm, Sa 9am-7:15pm). **Markets** take place at pl. Charles de Gaulle on Th morning, and on pl. Notre Dame on Su mornings. **Le Sagittaire,** 15 rue de la Liberté, has inexpensive, tasty dishes and a three-course weekday lunch *menu*, including wine and coffee, for 59F/€9. (☎03 80 97 23 91. Open daily noon-2:30pm and 7-11pm. MC.) Check out the **crêperie** which complements the Hôtel le Bory, 19 rue de la Liberté. 60F/€9.15 *menu*, crêpes from 35-60F/€5.34-9.15. (☎03 80 86 64 40. Open M-Sa noon-2:30pm, 7-10pm. Closed Dec.)

SIGHTS. The tourist office schedules walking tours, offers free brochures with self-guided itineraries, and runs a 45-minute **petit train** in summer. (July-Aug. 3 per day, Sept.-June schedules vary and reservations needed; ask tourist office for schedules. 25F/€3.81, children 15F/€2.29.) Make sure to walk around the ramparts and the orchard-lined river Armençon. The *vieille ville* is illuminated nightly from 10pm-midnight (mid-June to Sept.).

In the medieval town, down rue Buffon, lean, mossy gargoyles menace the *place* from the 15th-century facade of the **Collégiale Notre-Dame.** The 13th-century tympanum on the **porte des Bleds** faces rue Notre-Dame, while on the skinny left pillar, two sculpted snails slime their way to St. Thomas' feet—no doubt seeking divine intervention from their likely fate in a tasty butter-and-garlic sauce. The church offers up a full three-course meal; after the snail entree, gluttons can meditate in the Chapels of the Butchers and then that of the Bakers, donated by their respective guilds in the 15th century. (Open daily 9am-noon and 2-6:30pm; closes 5pm in winter. English pamphlet available.) Check out the light show in summer. (F-Sa nights at 10:30pm. By reservation during the rest of the year.)

The *beaux-arts* wing of the **Musée Municipal,** rue Jean-Jacques Collenot, off pl. de l'Ancienne Comédie, houses medieval statues and carvings, and painting and sculpture from the 17th to the 19th centuries—including three Corot canvases and plaster models by Augustin Dumont. The zoology section includes the frail skeleton of an infant, hanging in a case over the mummified limbs of a young girl. Those without a cast-iron stomach should stick to the stuffed owls and ferrets. (☎03 80 97 24 25. Open W-M 2-6pm. 20F/€3.05, students 10F/€1.53, under age 12 free.)

BERRY-LIMOUSIN

All too often passed over for beaches and bigger cities, Berry-Limousin offers peaceful countryside, tiny villages, and striking cities. Its landlocked position and lack of world-famous attractions have made it very much the poorer sister of its neighbors when it comes to attracting tourist dollars—so much the better for the intrepid few who do venture here! Nourished by the waters of the Cher, Indre, Creuse, and Vienne rivers, the countryside is rippled by hills, forests, yawning valleys, and Limousin cattle. The wrap-around *limousine* capes worn by the local herdsmen somehow gave their name to the first luxury motor-cars.

In the 12th century, the region was absorbed into the empire of the Anglo-French king-dukes, until Philippe-Auguste wrested it from John Lackland in 1200. In the 14th century, Limousin gave three popes to Avignon, the last of whom, Gre-

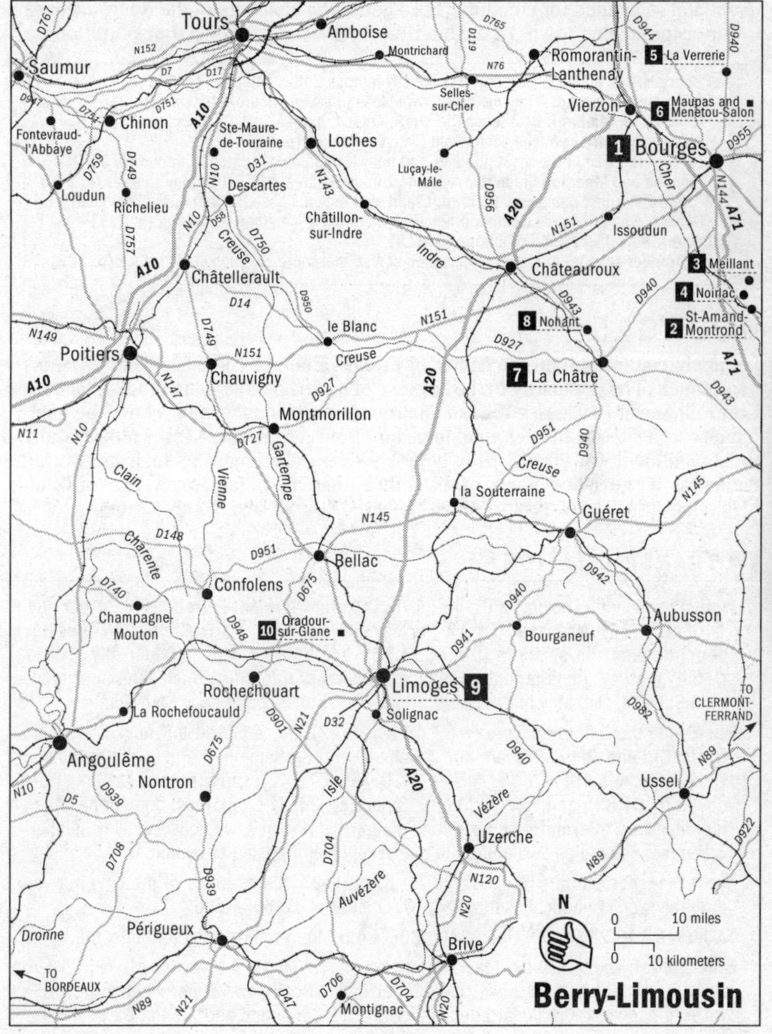

gory XI, returned the papacy to Rome. During the same period, Berry was in the hands of Jean de Berry, third son of King Jean le Bon. Though his greed and treachery resulted in a siege by the Royal Army in 1412, the duke is most famous for commissioning an exquisite book of medieval miniatures, *Les Très Riches Heures du Duc de Berry*. Upon Jean's death, Berry passed to the dauphin Charles VII—and just in time, for the English then possessed Paris. Bourges served as the capital of France and benefited from the lavish attention of the king's financier, Jacques Cœur, who built a lavish string of châteaux, now known as the Route Jacques Cœur. Later on, Berry-Limousin became an artistic and literary breeding ground, home to Georges Sand, Auguste Renoir, and Jean Giraudoux.

TRANSPORTATION

You may want to consider renting a car or bike to explore the region: while most towns have train and bus connections to Bourges and Limoges, service is infrequent and scheduled for commuters. To get to the châteaux of the Route Jacques Cœur or the smaller towns of the interior, you'll need your own transportation.

1 **Bourges:** The area's largest city; has a justly famous Gothic cathedral **(p. 212)**
2 **St-Amand-Montrond:** A tiny medieval town close to several nearby châteaux **(p. 216)**
3 **Château de Meillant:** Best reached from St-Amand, a huge Gothic fortress **(p. 217)**
4 **Abbaye de Noirlac:** A nine-century-old Cistercian abbey **(p. 217)**
5 **La Verrerie:** One of the most popular—and heavily decorated—châteaux around **(p. 217)**
6 **Maupas and Menetou-Salon**: Two eccentric, in-use châteaux bikeable from Bourges **(p. 218)**
7 **La Châtre:** A quiet, peaceful little town, useful as a regional base; Chopin festival **(p. 218)**
8 **Nohant:** George Sand's childhood home, and Chopin's sometime hometown **(p. 219)**
9 **Limoges:** Porcelain capital of Europe **(p. 219)**
10 **Oradour-sur-Glane:** Site of France's worst Nazi massacre; untouched ever since **(p. 222)**

BOURGES

Lounging comfortably in the center of France, Bourges (pop. 80,000 *bourgeois*) owes much of its popularity to the largesse of a corrupt politician. In 1433, Jacques Cœur, financier of Charles VII and all-around commercial genius, chose the humble city as a site for his personal mansion. Bourges now possesses a beautifully preserved medieval *vieille ville*, lying under the shadow of its majestic Gothic cathedral. Within a few blocks of the station, there lies a fairy-tale village of winding cobblestone streets, colorful half-timbered houses, and Gothic turrets.

TRANSPORTATION

Trains: pl. Général Leclerc (☎02 48 51 00 00). To: **Clermont-Ferrand** (2hr., 4 per day, 146F/€22.26); **Nevers** (1hr., 12 per day, 61F/€9.30); **Paris** (2½hr., 5-8 per day depending on the season, 156F/€23.78); and **Tours** (1½hr., 10 per day, 108F/€16.47). Many trains require a change at **Vierzon.** Info office open June-Sept. daily 9am-6:30pm; Oct.-May M-Sa 9am-6:30pm. Ticket office open daily 6am-9pm.

Buses: rue du Champ de Fiore (☎02 48 24 36 42). Office closed July-Aug.; Sept.-June open M-Tu and Th-F 8-9:30am and 4-6pm, W and Sa 8am-noon. Buses run to: nearby villages (tickets 10F/€1.35, *carnet* of 10 75F/€11.43); **Châteauroux** (1¾hr., 2 per day, 32F/€4.88); and **Vierzon** (1¼hr., 3 per day, 24F/€3.66). Most popular neighboring village is **St-Germain** (bus #4, from station "La Nation"), with bowling alley and several pubs. Schedules available from tourist office and posted at station.

Local Transportation: CTB (☎02 48 50 82 82) services all areas of the city, but you probably won't need it. Tickets 7F/€1.07, *carnet* of 10 50F/€7.62.

Taxis: ☎02 48 24 50 00. Open 24hr. 30F/€4.57 from train station to tourist office.

Bike Rental: Narcy, 39 av. Marx-Dormoy (☎02 48 70 15 84; fax 02 48 70 02 61). 40F/€6.10 per half-day, 50F/€7.62 per day, 100F/€15.25 per weekend, 300F/€45.74 per week. Credit card deposit. Open Tu-F 9am-noon and 2-7pm, Sa until 6pm.

Car Rentals: Hertz 4 av. Henri Laudier (02 48 70 22 92), near train station. Cars from 435F/€66.32 per 24hr. 21+; 143F/€21.80 fee per day for anyone under 25. AmEx/MC/V. Continue up av. Henri Laudier to its continuation, av. Jean Jaurès, to **Autop,** 21 av. Jean Jaurès (☎02 48 70 63 63). Small cars from 387F/€59 for 24hr. Open M-F 8am-noon and 2-6:30pm, Sa 8am-noon and 2-5pm. **Eurorent,** 31 bd. Juranville (☎02 48 65 46 46), and **Général Automobile de Bourges** (☎02 48 23 44 40), on rte. de la Charité. Both from 400F/€60.98. Both open M-Sa 8am-noon and 2-6:30pm; Général Automobile until 7:30pm.

ORIENTATION AND PRACTICAL INFORMATION

Bourges is remarkably easy to navigate. Head first to the tourist office to pick up its invaluable and detailed map.

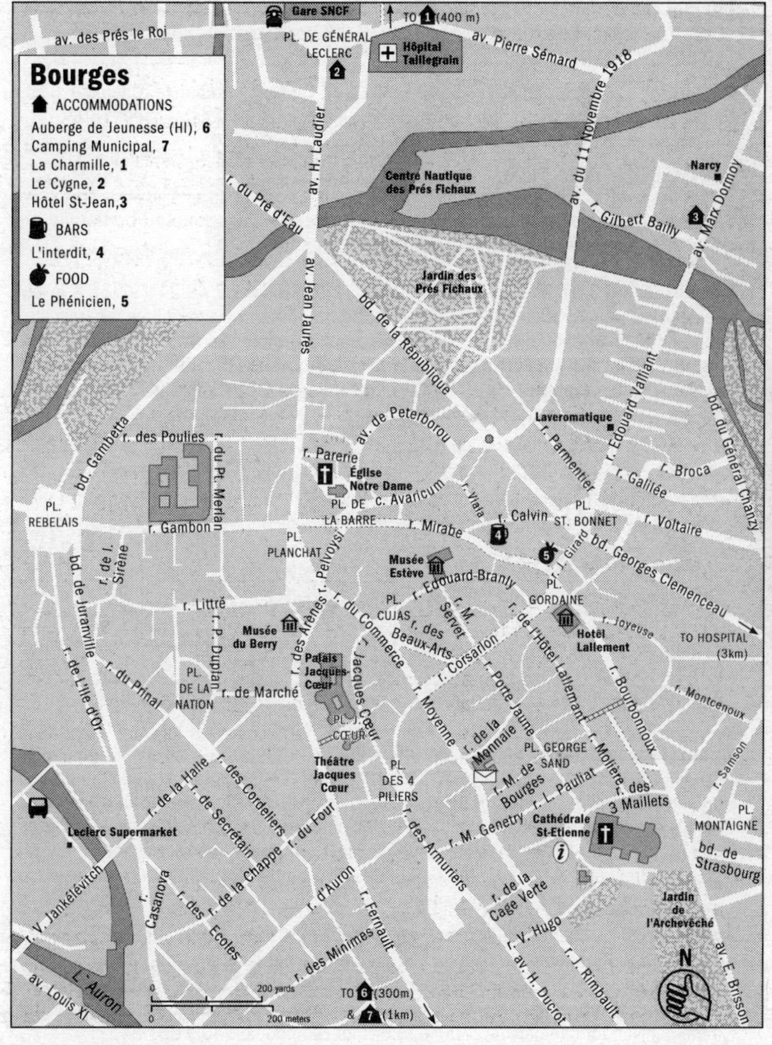

Tourist Office: 21 rue Victor Hugo (☎02 48 23 02 60; fax 02 48 23 02 69; www.ville-bourges.fr), facing rue Moyenne near the cathedral. Cross the street in front of station and follow av. Henri Laudier and its continuation, av. Jean Jaurès, into the *vieille ville*. From there, bear left onto rue du Commerce. Continue straight onto rue Moyenne, which leads to office (15min.). Or catch bus #1 (dir: "Val d'Auron," 7F/€1.07) to "Victor Hugo." Hotel reservations 5F/€0.76. **Walking tours** July-Sept. daily, 2pm in English, 3pm in French. 1½hr. 30F/€4.57, students 20F/€3.05. Free night tours in English, July 15-Aug. 15 Th-Sa 8pm. Free English tours of *vieille ville* every day at 10:30am and of cathedral July 15-Aug. 15 daily 3pm. Open M-Sa 9am-7pm, Su 10am-7pm.

Laundromat: Laveromatique, 117 rue Edouard Valliant and 15 bd. Juranville. Open daily 7am-8pm.

Police: rue Mayet Genetry (☎02 48 75 55 20). For **emergencies** dial 17.

Hospital: 145 rue François Mitterrand (☎02 48 48 48 48).

Internet Access: Médiathèque, bd. Lamarck/Parc St-Paul (☎02 48 23 22 50). Free, by God! You'll wait. Open July-Aug. Tu-F 12:30-6:30pm, Sa 9am-noon; Sept.-June M-W 12:30-6:30pm, Th 12:30-8pm, F 12:30-6:30pm, Sa 10am-5pm.

Post Office: 29 rue Moyenne (☎02 48 68 82 82). **Currency exchange.** Open M-F 8am-7pm, Sa 8am-noon. **Poste Restante:** 18012 Bourges Cedex. **Postal code:** 18000.

ACCOMMODATIONS AND CAMPING

Bourges's cheaper hotels are outside the city center. Unoccupied beds may be hard to find during festivals and in the height of summer.

Hôtel St-Jean, 23 av. Marx-Dormoy (☎02 48 24 13 48; fax 02 48 24 79 98). A lovely hostess lets generic, clean, carpeted rooms, only a 10min. walk from both the train station and the center of town. The owners will treat you more like family than like boarders. Breakfast 23-31F/€3.51-4.73. Singles 140F/€21.35, with bath 150-170F/€22.90-25.92; doubles 170F/€25.92, with shower 170-210F/€25.92-32.02. V.

Auberge de Jeunesse (HI), 22 rue Henri Sellier (☎02 48 24 58 09; fax 02 48 65 51 46), 10min. from town center, far from train station. From station, take av. Henri Laudier onto av. Jean Jaurès to pl. Planchat. Follow rue des Arènes, which becomes rue Fernault. At busy intersection, cross to rue René Ménard, which curves around a pink wall to the right. Turn left at rue Henri Sellier, and walk about another block. Hostel on the right, set back from the street behind a brown and white building (25min.). Or take bus #1 (dir: "Val d'Auron") to "Conde." From bus stop, cross parking lot to your right, take paved footpath to the left that crosses the park patch in front of you. Continue straight ahead down rue Vieil Castel. Hostel across street, 30m down a driveway slightly to right. Bar, laundry, kitchen, parking, and bare but clean 3- to 8-bunk rooms, some with showers. Breakfast 19F/€2.90. Sheets 17F/€2.59. Ask for door code to avoid 11pm curfew and noon-2pm lockout. Reception M-F 8am-noon and 2pm-1am, Sa-Su 8am-noon and 5-10pm; closed Dec. 17, 2001-Jan. 6, 2002. Beds 50F/€7.62.

Centre International de Séjour, "La Charmille," 17 rue Félix-Chédin (☎02 48 23 07 40; fax 02 48 69 01 21). Cross the footbridge over the tracks at the station and head up rue Félix-Chédin (5min.). La Charmille—half hostel, half *foyer*—is the skateboard mecca of Europe, with bowls, ramps, and half-pipes to prove it. Skating classes in summer. Social atmosphere—many teenage guests. Super-clean rooms, each with its own shower. Breakfast included. Meals 55F/€8.39. Laundry. Call ahead for larger group accommodations. Singles 98F/€14.94; 72F/€10.98 apiece for two or more. MC/V.

Le Cygne, 10 pl. du Général Leclerc (☎02 48 70 52 05; fax 02 48 69 09 91). Across from the train station with an attached restaurant, but a 20min. walk from center of town. Rooms are cozy and very well kept. Breakfast 30F/€4.57. Parking 20F/€3.05. Singles and doubles with shower 180F/€27.44, with shower and toilet 210F/€32.02; demi-pension for one person 260F/€39.64; for two people 340F/€51.84.

Camping Municipal, 26 bd. de l'Industrie (☎02 48 20 16 85; fax 02 48 50 32 39). Follow directions to the *auberge* (see above) but continue on rue Henri Sellier and turn right on bd. de l'Industrie. Landscaped 3-star campgrounds in a pleasant residential neighborhood, far from the city center. Free access to swimming pool. Reception 7am-9pm; June-Aug. 7am-10pm. Open Mar. 15-Nov. 15 8am-9pm. 19F/€2.90 per person; 19F/€2.90 per tent and car; 27F/€4.12 per caravan. Electricity 16-26F/€2.44-3.96.

FOOD

The outdoor tables on **pl. Gordaine** and **rue des Beaux-Arts** fill with locals in spring and summer. For a touch of elegance, try regional cuisine at one of the restaurants on **rue Bourbonnoux** or **rue Girard.** Look for specialties such as *poulet en barbouille* (chicken roasted in aromatic red wine) and *oeufs en meurette* (eggs in red wine). The largest **market** is held on pl. de la Nation (Sa morning), another livens up pl. des Marronniers (Th until 1pm), and there is a smaller **covered market** at pl. St-Bonnet (Tu-Sa 7:30am-1pm and 3-7:30pm, Su 7:30am-1pm). Cheap sandwich shops line **rue Moyenne** and **rue Mirabeau,** while the huge **Leclerc supermarket,** on rue Prado off bd. Juranville, can provide the fixings for your own culinary experiments. (Open M-F 9:15am-7:20pm, Sa 8:30am-7:20pm.)

Cake-Thé, 74 promenade des Remparts (☎02 48 24 94 60). Beautiful little tearoom down a lavender-lined passage. Full of music, flowers, lace—for those secure in their masculinity. Tea 12-20F/€1.83-3.05; coffee 20F/€3.05. Open Sept.-July Tu-Sa 3-7pm.

Le Phénicien, 13 rue Jean Girard, off pl. Gordaine (☎02 48 65 01 37). This Middle Eastern eatery offers the penniless pita made on the premises. Vegetarian options available. Sandwiches 22F/€3.35. Lunch menu with 4 appetizers and main course 44F/€6.71, with dessert and coffee 55F/€8.39. Open M-Sa 11am-11pm.

SIGHTS

CATHEDRALE ST-ETIENNE. Built in the 13th century, St-Etienne is one of France's most magnificent cathedrals, comparable to Notre Dame in Paris. A stunning set of 13th-century stained glass in dark reds and blues runs along its straight walls; visit between 10 and 11am for the best light. You can visit the "underground church" by buying a ticket to the cathedral crypt; the same ticket allows you to climb St-Etienne's northern tower. *(**Cathedral** open Apr.-June daily 9am-noon and 2-6pm; July-Aug. 9am-7pm; Sept.-Oct. 9am-noon and 2-6pm; Nov.-Mar. 9am-noon and 2-5pm. Closed Su morning. **Crypt and towers** July-Aug. daily 9am-6pm. 36F/€5.49, students 23F/€3.51. Mass June-Aug. M-F 6:30pm; Sept.-May M 6:30pm, F 9am. Grand Mass year-round Su 11am.)*

PALAIS JACQUES-CŒUR. This mansion, commissioned in 1443 by Jacques, was intended primarily to be a place to entertain high society guests and flaunt his personal fortune. The palace is unfurnished, but exquisite carved mantelpieces, gargoyles, ceilings built in the shape of ship galleys, and a heavily decorated chapel still remain. Jacques saw little of the palace; he was imprisoned for embezzlement in 1451, years before its completion. *(10bis rue Jacques-Cœur. ☎02 48 24 06 87. Tours offered every hr. July-Aug. 9am-6pm; Apr.-June and Sept.-Oct. 9am-noon and 2-6pm; Nov.-Mar. 9am-noon and 2-5pm. English text available. 36F/€5.49, ages 18-24 23F/€3.51, under 18 free.)*

MUSEUMS. Bourges also houses several small, free museums, all with explanations in only French. The **Musée du Berry** has locally excavated prehistoric, Gallo-Roman, and medieval artifacts. *(4 rue des Arènes. ☎02 48 57 81 15. Open M, W-Sa 10am-noon and 2-6pm, Su 10am-noon.)* A 15th-century merchant built the Neo-Renaissance **Hôtel Lallemant,** which houses furniture, tapestries, and decorative works from the 16-18th centuries. *(6 rue Bourbonnoux. ☎02 48 57 81 17. Open Tu-Sa 10am-noon and 2-6pm, Su 2-6pm.)* The **Musée Estève** displays oil paintings by the local contemporary artist of the same name.*(13 rue Edouard Branly. ☎02 48 24 75 38. Open M, W-Sa 10am-noon and 2-6pm, Su 2-6pm.)* The **Musée des Meilleurs Ouvriers de France,** in the Hôtel de Ville, charts the work of artists and workers in the region. A small fashion museum with historical and modern dress is on the first floor. *(Pl. Etienne Dolet. ☎02 48 57 82 45. Open July-Aug. 10am-6pm., Tu-Sa 10am-noon and 2-6pm.)*

OUTDOORS. The **Jardin de l'Archevêché,** behind the cathedral, has rows of perfectly manicured flowers and cone-shaped trees. *(Open June-July daily 8am-10pm; May and Aug. 8am-9pm; Mar. 8am-7pm; Apr. and Sept. 8am-8pm; Oct.-Feb. 8am-6pm.)* The **Jardin des Près-Fichaux,** off bd. de la République, adds a beautiful river to the scene. Stroll past Roman ramparts and back gardens on the **Promenade des Remparts,** between rue Bourbonnoux and rue Molière. The dirt pathway along the Marais is supremely tranquil, and lets you peek at some of the more rural homes in Bourges.

ENTERTAINMENT AND FESTIVALS

Bars and cafés pepper the *vieille ville.* The late-night crowd gathers at **Pub Dublin,** 108 rue d'Auron, for pool and meters of beer, from 70F/€10.67. (☎02 48 26 38 33.) Electronic music sets the pulse of **L'interdit,** 5 rue Calvin, a small, social bar frequented by gay men (but not exclusively). Knock or buzz to be let in through the locked door. (☎02 48 65 90 57. Open Th-Su 5pm-2am.) **Le Wake Up,** 147 chemin de Villeneuve, is a house of techno filled with teens and early twenty-somethings dancing the night away to a live DJ. There's also laser tag in the 500-meter labyrinth of ramps and walls. (☎02 48 67 90 46. Open daily 4pm-1am.)

End an evening stroll with **Les Nuits Lumière de Bourges,** a lovely nighttime tour of Bourges during which selected streets in the city center are highlighted with blue lampposts. This self-guided tour begins with music and a slide-show presentation of local history, then directs you to several stops along a mapped-out route. The route officially begins at the Jardin de l'Archevêché. (June-Oct. 2hr. Free.)

Over 200,000 ears perk up in April for the **Festival Printemps de Bourges.** Most tickets cost 50-180F/€7.62-27.44, but some informal folk, jazz, classical, and rock concerts are free. (Contact the Association Printemps de Bourges, on rue Henri Sellier, ☎02 48 70 61 11.) From June 21 until September 21, there is free culture every night during **Un Eté à Bourges,** a conflagration of classical and rock concerts and theater. (Tickets 50-90F/€7.62-13.72, some events free.)

ROUTE JACQUES CŒUR

Jacques may have left his *cœur* in Bourges, but his ego spilled far into the surrounding countryside. The Route Jacques Cœur is the name of a string of 17 châteaux (plus one 12th-century abbey for good measure) that stretches from La Buissière in the north to Culan in the south. Less ostentatious than those of the Loire, these castles see much less tourism, and many are still inhabited by the families that made them famous. Châteaux make relaxing daytrips, but are not serviced by public transportation; you will need a car or bike to reach them. Fortunately, the routes are very well marked. Arrange lodging in advance. The tourist offices in Bourges (p. 212) and St-Amand-Montrond (see below) have free maps of the route in English, and have info on excursions.

SOUTH OF BOURGES

ST-AMAND-MONTROND

Forty-five kilometers south of Bourges, St-Amand-Montrond (pop. 12,000) is a good base for exploring the southern part of the Route. Though the neighboring châteaux and hectares of hikeable forest have made it famous, the town itself deserves a few hours of your attention. A pedestrian tour organized by the tourist office walks you past the city's two medieval churches, **Paroisse de St-Amand** and **Eglise St-Roche** You can also see the ruins of the ancient **Forteresse de Montrond.** (☎02 48 96 79 64; call ahead to schedule a visit.)The **tourist office,** pl. de la République, has maps indicating sights within the city and environs. To get there from the train station, follow av. de la Gare, directly in front of the station, and its continuation, av. Jean Jaurès, to the town center. You will run right into pl. de la République; the tourist office is on your left (20min.). (☎02 48 96 16 86; fax 02 48 96 46 64. Open M-Sa 9am-noon and 2-6:45pm.) To get to St-Amand, take the **train** from **Bourges.** (45min.-1¾hr.; M-Sa 6 per day, Su 3 per day; 56F/€8.54.) While several châteaux are within biking distance of St-Amand, there is no place to rent bikes.

CHATEAU DE MEILLANT

A beautiful 8km bike ride from St-Amand through the **Grand Bois de Meillant** forest ends at the foot of the imposing, heavily spired 15th- to 16th-century building. In the 15th century, it was bought by the Amboise family, who imported Italian architects, sculptors, and decorators. Its curious mixture of styles is especially visible in the **Tour du Lion,** the upper part of which was designed by none other than Leonardo da Vinci. Pay tribute to Matel by visiting the second floor collection of over a hundred Barbie and Ken dolls fashioned after historical and Hollywood stars, including Marilyn Monroe, Madonna, Clark Gable, Frank Sinatra, and Wonder Woman. To get to Meillant from **St-Amand,** take rue Nationale north out to the D10. (☎02 48 63 32 05. Open Feb.-Nov. daily for tours; Apr.-Oct. 9-11:45am and 2-6:45pm; Feb.-Mar. and Nov. 9-11:45am and 2-5:30pm. Closed Dec.-Jan. Château and gardens 45F/€6.86, students 25F/€3.81, ages 7-15 20F/€3.05.)

ABBAYE DE NOIRLAC

Just 4km west of St-Amand-Montrond, the **Abbaye de Noirlac** sits peacefully. The abbey is typically Cistercian, with spacious rooms, undecorated arches, and geometric stained glass windows. Most of the monks' **chapter house** dates from the original 12th-century construction. Within the complex, the **Centre de l'Enluminure et de l'Image Médiévale** holds a collection of medieval art. In summer, the popular **L'Eté de Noirlac** fills the space with jazz and classical music. From St-Amand, take rue Henri Barbusse out to the D925 west (direction "Bourges") and follow the signs. (☎02 48 62 01 01. Open July-Aug. daily 9:45am-6:30pm; Apr.-June and Sept. 9:45am-noon and 1:45-6:30pm; Oct.-Mar. 9:45am-noon and 1:45-5pm; Oct.-Jan. closed Tu. Ticket office shuts 1hr. before closing. French tours offered every hr. from 10am. English explanations available; July-Aug. no tours noon-1:45pm. Call ahead for a tour in English. 35F/€5.34, students 25F/€3.81, under 16 20F/€3.05.)

NORTH OF BOURGES

LA VERRERIE

The 15th-century La Verrerie, set on a gorgeous lake in the Ivoy forest 45km north of Bourges, is one of the most popular châteaux on the Route. Like many of its Loire cousins, it has a long history of British control, but a pleasantly non-violent one. Inside are 18th-century Beauvais tapestries and hand-carved tables from the 16th and 17th centuries. To get to La Verrerie from Bourges, take N940 (direction "Montargis"). At La Chapelle, turn right toward Auxerre on rte. 926. After 10km, signs for La Verrerie will appear. (☎02 48 81 51 60. Open Apr.-Nov. 15 daily 10am-6pm. Accessible only through tour; English follow-along texts are available. Tours leave to meet demand. 40F/€6.10, students 30F/€4.57, under age 7 free.)

THE ORIGINAL BOY GEORGE While most girls called Amandine-Aurore-Lucile might like to give themselves a snappier title, a boy's name wouldn't normally top the list–especially in the 19th century. But George Sand (1804-1876) never worried about convention. Prolific novelist, proto-feminist, and passionate lover, she achieved fame and notoriety that could scarcely be expected from a provincial *mademoiselle* from Nohant. After leaving her home and husband for the excitement of the capital in 1831, she embarked on a series of amorous adventures–her conquests included Alfred de Musset, Prosper Mérimée (the author of *Carmen),* and, most famously, Frédéric Chopin. Sand adopted male clothing as part of her protest against the social strictures of the day. She returned to Nohant in 1839 with the consumptive Chopin; while he composed some of his best-loved works, she celebrated the beauty of her homeland with novels such as *La Mare au Diable* and *La Petite Fadette.*

MENETOU-SALON AND MAUPAS

A bit closer to Bourges and easy to reach by bike, Maupas and Menetou-Salon make a perfect daytrip. **Menetou-Salon** lies 20km north of Bourges. Jacques bought the estate in 1448, but his imprisonment and the Revolution left the castle in ruins until the 19th century, when the Prince of Arenburg decided to complete it. Though the current prince resides in New York and only visits his hunting lodge four times a year, his personal touches make Menetou a treat. From Bourges, take D940 north to D11 and follow the signs to Menetou-Salon. (☎02 48 64 08 61. Open July 14-Aug. daily 10am-6:30pm.)

To continue to **Maupas,** follow the signs to Parassy and Moroques. The château is on your left, about 1km before Moroques. Keep your eyes open for the white iron gates tucked away on the curbside. This 13th-century castle is decorated with antique furniture collected by Antoine Agard, whose family has lived there since 1686. The gardens are perfectly manicured in the shape of the *fleur de lys.* The 45-minute tour leads you through bedrooms, playrooms, the dining salon, and kitchen of the Comte de Chambord, the last legitimate Bourbon pretender to the French throne. (☎02 48 64 41 71. Open July-Sept. 15 10am-noon and 2-7pm; Easter-June and Sept. 16-Oct. 15 M-Sa 2-7pm, Su and holidays 10am-noon and 2-7pm; Oct. 15-Nov. 15 Su 2-6pm. Tours leave to meet demand; follow-along texts available in English. 40F/€6.10, students 30F/€4.57, ages 7-15 25F/€3.81.)

LA CHATRE

La Châtre (pop. 5500) is an exceptionally pretty base from which to visit the sights of Berry. The city hosts a lively Saturday market, and a well-attended Chopin festival at the end of July. The tourist office's guide maps out a pedestrian tour of La Châtre; the walk takes visitors past 15th-century houses, the 12th- to 14th-century **Eglise St-Germain,** and the **Musée George Sand et de la Vallée Noire,** 71 rue Venose, housed in a square, 15th-century keep. The museum has plenty of Sand's souvenirs and drawings to pick over, as well as a large ornithological collection. (☎02 54 48 36 79. Open July-Aug. daily 9am-7pm; Sept.-Dec. and Feb.-Mar. 9am-noon and 2-7pm; Apr.-Sept. 9am-5pm. 25F/€3.81; students and children 20F/€3.05.) July 21-28, 2002 will see the huge **Rencontre Internationale Frédéric Chopin,** with seminars and nightly recitals in the town and nearby Nohant (tickets 30-220F/€4.57-33.54).

If you call at least two days in advance, you can stay at the romantic, 52-bed **Auberge de Jeunesse (HI),** rue Moulin Borgnon (leave a message if no one picks up). To get to the hostel from the tourist office, continue down av. George Sand across pl. du Marché, then veer left on rue de Saint-Roche. Turn right and follow the road downhill. The hostel is on your right, behind a park overlooking a valley. (☎02 54 06 00 55; fax 02 54 48 48 10. Sheets 20F/€3.05. Bunks 57F/€8.69. 19F/€2.90 extra for **non-members.**) A large **STOC supermarket,** pl. du Général de Gaulle (☎02 54 48 05 24), sells the basics. The **market** is on pl. du Marché (Sa 8am-noon).

The **tourist office,** is in the park on av. George Sand. From the train station, leave the parking lot and head straight out on av. Aristide Briand. About four blocks past pl. Jules Neraud, turn left on av. George Sand; the office is ahead on your right, set back from the street. (☎02 54 48 22 64; fax 02 54 06 09 15. Open July-Aug. M-Sa 9am-12:30pm and 2:30-7pm, Su 10am-noon and 2-6pm; Apr.-June and Sept. M-Sa 9:30am-12:30pm and 2:30-7pm, Su until 6pm; Oct.-Mar. M-Sa 9:30am-12:30pm and 2-6:30pm, Sa until 5:30pm.)

La Châtre no longer has a working train station; the town is only accessible by **bus** from **Châteauroux** (40min., 5 per day, 35.50F/€5.41) or **Montlucon** (1hr., 5 per day, 56F/€8.54). The **SNCF Info Boutique,** 142 rue Nationale, in the center of town, can help organize outbound journeys that connect the bus with trains at Châteauroux. (☎02 54 48 00 06. Open Tu-Sa 9am-noon and 2-6pm.)

NEAR LA CHATRE: NOHANT

Tiny **Nohant** (pop. 481), 8km from La Châtre, consists of one unpaved square housing an ancient church beside George Sand's childhood home. It was here that Sand wrote her first novel, *Indiana* and here that many great literary and artistic figures came to dine, among them Balzac, Delacroix, Flaubert, and Liszt. Chopin stayed 10 years here with Sand; the puppet theater downstairs, which he built with Sand's son, is still in perfect condition, as is the study upstairs where the composer wrote over 15 of his pieces. (☎02 54 31 06 04. Open July-Aug. daily 9am-1pm and 2-7:30pm; Apr.-June and Sept.-Oct. 15 9am-noon and 2-6pm; Oct. 16-Mar. 9am-noon and 2-6pm. Last tour 30min. before closing. 36F/€5.49, students 23F/€3.51.)

To get to Nohant, take the **bus** (direction "Châteauroux," 10min., 3 per day, 8F/€1.22) from **La Châtre.** The square will be to your right when you get off. A good time to visit is the last weekend in July, when **La Fête au Village** puts a little more sparkle into the tiny town square, with outdoor dining, music, and market vendors selling traditional wares and culinary specialties.

LIMOGES

Limoges (pop. 150,000) is famous for its traditions of porcelain and enamel manufacture, and has for centuries been the chief supplier of crockery to the French upper classes. That trade enriched the town and gave it many of the assets that now make Limoges worth visiting: a beautiful old town, an exquisite Gothic cathedral, and countless workshops and galleries full of *émaux d'art* (enamelled art) and *faïenceries* (glazed earthenware).

TRANSPORTATION

Trains: Gare des Bénédictins, pl. Maison-Dieu (☎05 55 11 11 88), off av. de Gaulle, restored to its 1920s Art Deco splendor. To: **Bordeaux** (3hr., 7 per day, 158F/€24.09); **Brive** (1hr., 5 per day, 82F/€12.50); **Lyon** (5-7hr., 6 per day, 245F/€37.35); **Paris** (3-4hr., 12 per day, 240F/€36.59); **Poitiers** (2hr., 3 per day, 108F/€16.47); and **Toulouse** (3½hr., 8 per day, 199F/€30.34).

Buses: pl. des Bénédictins (☎05 55 04 91 95). The bus station is in the same terminal as the train station. **Jet Tours,** 3 rue Jean Jaurès (☎05 55 32 47 48), and **Bernis Tourisme,** 24 rue de la République (☎05 55 34 30 50), also run buses to locations outside the city. Call for more info.

Taxis: Taxis Limoges (☎05 55 37 81 81 or 05 55 38 38 38). Open 24hr.

ORIENTATION AND PRACTICAL INFORMATION

To get to the tourist office from the train station, keep left by the train tracks down av. du Général de Gaulle and follow the path, which cuts diagonally across pl. Jourdan to bd. de Fleurus. It's at the end of bd. de Fleurus on the left.

Tourist Office: 12 bd. de Fleurus (☎05 55 34 46 87; fax 05 55 34 19 12; ot.limoges.haute-vienne@en-france.com), near pl. Wilson. English-speaking staff has maps and lists *chambres d'hôte*. **Currency exchange** with 4% commission. Themed **walking tours** of the city July-Aug., available in English on request. Office open June 15-Sept. 15 M-Sa 9am-7pm, Su 10am-6pm; Sept. 16-June 14 M-Sa 9am-noon and 2-7pm.

Money: Banque de France, 8 bd. Carnot (☎05 55 11 53 00), has commission-free counters and good rates. Exchange desk open M-F 8:45am-noon.

Laundromat: Le forum des lavendières, 14 rue des Charseix (☎05 55 32 62 89). Open M-Su 8am-9pm. **Laverie,** 31 rue de Drancois Chinieux. Open daily 7am-9pm.

Police: 84 av. Emile Labussière (☎05 55 14 30 00).

Hospital: 2 av. Martin Luther King (☎05 55 05 61 23).

Internet Access: Free access in 14-computer multimedia room at the brand new **Bibliothèque Francophone Multimédia de Limoges,** 2 rue Louis Longequeue (☎05 55 45 96 00), just beyond the Hôtel de Ville. Open W 10am-7pm, Sa 10am-6pm.

Post Office: av. Garibaldi near av. de la Libération. **Currency exchange** with no commission. Open M 2-7pm, Tu-Sa 10am-7pm. **Postal code:** 87000.

ACCOMMODATIONS AND FOOD

The **Foyer d'Accueil,** 20 rue Encombe Vineuse, rents clean, simple singles and doubles with sinks; long-term residents gather in the TV room every evening and love company. With your back to the train station, descend the stairs to the right. At the bottom, cut across the grass to the street, curving slightly to your right. Rue Théodore Bac is across the street on your left. Take this to pl. Carnot, turn left onto av. Adrien Tarrade, and take the first left onto rue Encombe Vineuse (15min.). (☎05 55 77 63 97. Breakfast included. Reception 24hr. Singles 85F/€12.96; doubles 130F/€19.82.) There are several inexpensive hotels closer to the train station. **Hôtel de Paris,** 5 cours Vergnaud. With your back to the train station, walk up av. du Général de Gaulle for about 200ft., then veer right onto cours Bugeaud. Walk past the gardens on your right, and turn right onto cours Vergnaud. Most of the spacious rooms look out over the champs de Juillet. (☎05 55 77 56 96. Breakfast 25F/€3.81. Singles 150-300F/€22.90-45.74; doubles 170-300F/€25.92-45.74. MC/V.) The rooms of **Mon Logis,** 16 rue du Général du Bessol, are lined with nature posters of Limoges and its surrounding areas. Descend the stairs to the right of the train station, leading to cours Gay Lussac. Turn left onto Gay Lussac and make your first right onto rue du Général du Bessol. (☎05 55 77 41 43. Breakfast 30-32F/€4.57-4.88. Singles with shower 135F/€20.58, with bath 198F/€30.19; doubles 165-190F/€25.16-28.97.) The musty but perfectly adequate **Hôtel St-Exupéry,** 3 imp. St-Exupéry, often has room. From the train station, follow cours Gay Lussac and turn right at the second block. (☎05 55 77 50 14. Breakfast 22F/€3.35. Reception 7am-noon and 2pm-closing. Singles 110F/€16.77, with shower 130F/€19.82; doubles with shower 140F/€21.35.)

Camping Municipal D'Uzurat, 5km north of Limoges, is the only campground near town, right on the shore of lake Uzurat. Grounds have tennis courts, minigolf, and lead to hiking trails. Take bus #20 (M-Sa 6am-8:30pm, 6.50F/€0.99); if walking, take av. Général Leclerc from pl. Carnot and follow signs to Uzurat. (☎05 55 38 49 43. 59F/€9 for 2 people and tent, 74F/€11.28 with caravan; off-season 50F/€7.62, 65F/€9.91. Extra person 16-18F/€2.44-2.74. Electricity 21-25F/€3.20-3.81.)

The central Les Halles **indoor market** faces pl. de la Motte (daily); a larger market brightens pl. Carnot on Saturday mornings. There's also a **Monoprix supermarket** at 11 pl. de la République (open M-Sa 8:30am-8pm), and a huge **STOC** in the Saint Martial shopping mall on the north side of town (av. Garibaldi; open M-F 8am-8pm; Sa 9am-8pm). Restaurants in the old quarter provide a more chic (and expensive) dining experience than the restaurant-bars of the far less beautiful pl. de la République. For a younger, more relaxed crowd, try pl. Denis Dussoubs.

SIGHTS

CATHEDRALE ST-ETIENNE. This is one of the few great Gothic constructions south of the Loire. The cathedral, which took 600 years to complete, was built on the remains of a 1013 Roman temple, of which the original crypt and bell tower porch remain. The Gothic reworking took place from the 13th to 16th centuries. *(Pl. St-Etienne. Ask at the tourist office for directions. Open to visitors M-Sa 10am-noon and 2-6pm, Su 2:30-6:30pm. Free tours in French M-Sa 11am.)*

MUSEE NATIONAL ADRIEN DUBOUCHE. This museum houses the largest porcelain collection in Europe, spanning centuries. The large, blue-and-white Chinese plate (dating from 1345) with a dragon in its center on the second floor is one of the most valuable pieces of china in the world. *(8bis pl. Winston Churchill. ☎05 55 33 08 50. Open July-Aug. W-M 10am-5:45pm; Sept.-June 10am-12:30pm and 2-5:45pm. 25F/€3.81, ages 18-25 and Su 17F/€2.59. First Su of the month and under 18 free.)*

CRYPTE ST-MARTIAL. This crypt is all that remains of the medieval Benedictine Abbaye St-Martial, demolished after the Revolution. The saint who evangelized Augustoritum (the Roman name for Limoges) in the 3rd century was also its first bishop. The abbey was run by monks of the Cluniac order; now wholly underground, the ruins of the abbatial city, the surrounding Roman necropolis from the first century, and the tombs of St-Valérie and St-Martial can be seen by tour. *(Entrance on pl. de la République. Open July-Sept. 9:30am-noon and 2:30-7pm. Free.)*

MAISON DE LA BOUCHERIE. Unique to Limoges, this district of narrow streets and medieval houses in the town center is where the town's butchers have lived since the 10th century. For a slice of their life, visit the **Maison Traditionelle de la Boucherie,** 36 rue de la Boucherie. Guides lead tours of a butcher's house. *(Open July-Sept. daily 2:30-7pm; Free.)*

OTHER SIGHTS. Surrounding the cathedral, the **Evêché Botanical Gardens** are a gorgeous and relaxing place to enjoy the view from the banks of the Vienne. The Garden doubles as a botanical museum, with an explanation of each type of flower. In the far left corner of the garden lies the **Pavillon de L'Orangerie,** which hosts temporary exhibits of French art and culture. *(☎05 55 45 62 67. Garden tours by appointment.)* Follow up by walking along the tree-lined promenade which runs between the 12th- and 13th-century **Pont St-Martial** (built on first-century Roman foundations) and the **Pont St-Etienne** on the far side of the Vienne river. The path meanders beside flowering gardens and an outdoor climbing wall. **St-Pierre-du-Queyroix,** whose Limousin-Romanesque bell tower was the model both for the Eglise St-Michel and the cathedral, lies in the city center on pl. St-Pierre. The **Musée Municipal de l'Evêché,** also known as the **Musée de l'Email,** fill the 18th-century bishop's palace with their impressive collections of Egyptian art, Merovingian capitals, masonry, sarcophagi, local Roman artifacts, and, of course, the inescapable enamels and porcelain. There are also five paintings by Auguste Renoir, born in Limoges in 1841. *(Next to the cathedral. ☎05 55 34 44 09 or 05 55 45 61 75. Open June W-M 10-11:45am and 2-6pm; July-Sept. daily 10-11:45am and 2-6pm; Oct.-May W-M 10-11:45am and 2-5pm. Free.)* The **Eglise St-Michel des Lions,** built between the 14th and 16th centuries, contains an exquisite carved stone chapel with altars to Limoges natives St-Martial, St-Valérie, and St-Loup. *(On pl. St-Michel, next to pl. de la Motte. Open M-Sa 7:45am-noon and 2-6pm, Su 8:15am-12:30pm and 4-7pm.)* Of the 48 distilleries which speckled Limoges prior to 1900, only one remains: the **Musée des Distilleries Limougeaudes,** 54 rue de Belfort, offers 30-minute tours (including tastings) of their still-functioning liquor works. Interesting *and* tasty! *(☎05 55 77 23 57. No English translations available.)* **Atelier Mosaïque,** 17 rue Montmailler, is one of the hidden treasures of Limoges. In his small shop, Mr. Soubeyrand de Saint Prix offers delicately designed mosaics all done by hand on the premises. Half-finished mosaics lie around his work area, and the finished products adorn the walls in the form of mirrors, portraits, jewelry boxes, clocks, and more. *(☎05 55 77 73 05. Open M-Sa 9:30am-10:30pm. 2-week seminars offered continuously.)*

ENTERTAINMENT AND FESTIVALS

The nightlife in Limoges is nothing to get revved up about, but a smattering of small bars and clubs line **rue Charles-Michels** in the center of town. These include **Cheyenne Café,** 4 rue Charles-Michels, which is usually the loudest and most crowded. (☎05 55 32 32 62. Open daily 10am-2am.) An unusually diverse crowd frequents **Café des Anciennes Majorettes de la Baule,** 27 rue Haute-Vienne; older people drink and chat outside, while young locals pack the vintage-library interior to socialize over French music. (Open Tu-Sa 10am-2am.) **Café Traxx,** 12 rue des Filles de Notre Dame/pl. Fontaine des Barre, is a fairly small, social house-techno gay bar. (☎05 55 32 07 55. Open daily 6pm-2am.) Around 2am, Limoges's late-night crowd comes out; like the bar-hoppers of earlier hours, these crowds jump between clubs, but the gay bar, **Le Boy,** 137 av. du Maréchal de Lattre-de-Tassigny, is social all night long. (☎05 55 31 19 41. Cover 30F/€4.57. Open Su-Th 10pm-5am,

F-Sa until 6am.) **La Bibliothèque,** 7 rue Turgot, is a cool and informal bar. Mahogany stools, red carpeting, chandeliers in the shape of candelabras, and walls lined with shelves of leather-bound books help give the feeling of being in a private library, but the books are just for show. (☎05 55 11 00 47. Open daily 11am-2am.)

For those with earlier bedtimes, the **Grand Théâtre,** 48 rue Jean Jaurès, presents 60 ballet, orchestral, operatic, and choral productions from September to the end of May/early June. (☎05 55 34 12 12 for reservations; 30-200F/€4.57-30.49.) The **Théâtre de l'Union,** 20 rue des Coopérateurs (☎05 55 79 90 00), also has a season from September to May. On weekdays, the five **Centres Culturels Municipaux** put on a vast array of concerts, theater productions, and films to meet every taste; contact the **Centre Culturel Jean-Moulin,** 76 rue des Sagnes (☎05 55 35 04 10), or **Centre Culturel Jean Gagnant,** 7 av. Jean Gagnant (☎05 55 34 45 49), for more info.

The **Fête de la St-Jean** takes place at the end of June and includes diving, fireworks, water shows, dancing, and musical performances. The popular **Fête des Arts de la Rue,** URBAKA (☎05 55 45 63 85), takes over the last three days in June with nightly fire shows and concerts spread throughout the city. The **Festival International des Théâtres Francophones** brings in over 15,000 French Canadians, French-speaking Africans, and francophones from all over the world at the end of September. The third Friday in October brings the mother of all Limousin meals with **La Frairie des Petits Ventres** (Festival of Small Stomachs), a street banquet where residents consume meat in mass quantities. Additionally, one of the most glorified events in Limoges is the **Ostensions,** which takes place once every seven years, when all regional butchers parade into the Chapelle St-Aurélien to retrieve the relics of St-Aurélien, their patron saint; they then proceed through the streets and eat more meat. The next feast is in 2002.

NEAR LIMOGES: ORADOUR-SUR-GLANE

On June 10, 1944, Nazi SS troops massacred all the inhabitants of the farming village **Oradour-sur-Glane** without warning or provocation, then set the entire town ablaze. Perhaps France's most vivid testimony to WWII, the town remains in ruins; train wires dangle from slanting poles, and 50-year-old cars rust next to crumbling walls. You can walk freely along the main thoroughfare and peer into the remnants of each home. Signs indicate the name and profession of each person who lived there. No one knows the precise reason for the Nazis' decision, although one theory holds that they mistook this town for Oradour-sur-Vayres, an important center of the Resistance. The Nazis entered at two in the afternoon; by three-thirty the women and children had been corralled into the church and the men into six barns. At four, a shot was fired to start the massacre. Those in the church were burned alive; the men were tortured, shot, and then burned. By seven o'clock, 642 people, including 205 children, had been slaughtered. Most of the SS troops participating in the attack were tried in 1953, found guilty, and then immediately freed as the result of a general amnesty decreed by the French government; Heinz Barth, commander of the unit, is currently serving a life sentence in a German jail. Plaques with heartbreaking messages and pictures mark two glass tombs containing the bones and ashes of the dead. A small memorial between the cemetery and town displays bicycles, toys, and many watches, all stopped at the same moment by the heat of the fire. A museum, **Le Centre de la Mémoire,** recounts the events leading up to the massacre in vivid detail. (☎05 55 43 04 30. Museum and town open July-Aug. daily 9am-8pm; Sept-Oct. and Mar.-Apr. 9am-6pm; Nov.-Dec. 16 and Feb. 9am-5pm; May-June 9am-7pm; closed Dec. 16-Feb. 1. 30F/€4.57, students and children 25F/€3.81. Free entry into town—access via museum.) After some hesitation, a new Oradour (pop. 2000) was built next to the obliterated village.

Transportation to Oradour is limited. One **bus** per day, which leaves at 6:30am from the central bus station, returns from Oradour at approximately 6pm. Oradour can be easily reached by car (45min.). Ask for a map at the info booth.

PROVENCE

Carpets of olive groves and vineyards unroll along hills dusted with lavender, sunflowers, and mimosa, while the fierce winds of the *mistral* carry the scent of sage, rosemary, and thyme. Provence inspired artists from the medieval troubadours to Cézanne, Gauguin, and Picasso. Van Gogh also ventured to Provence, searching for "another light...a more limpid sky." Since Roman times, writers have rhapsodized about Provence's fragrant and varied landscape—undulating mountains to the east, flat marshlands in the Camargue, and rocky cliffs in the Vaucluse.

Marseille, with 2600 years of history, is the second most populous city in France and serves as the linchpin for the area, linking Provence to the glitz and glamor of the Riviera. With their Roman remnants and cobblestone grace, Orange and Arles meet the Rhône as it flows to the Mediterranean. Briefly home to the medieval papacy, Avignon still holds the formidable Palais des Papes. The region is perhaps most popular today for its festivals; in the summer, even the smallest hamlets whirl with music, dance, theater, and antique markets.

TRANSPORTATION

Rail and bus service between the larger cities in the region is excellent, with direct connections to most of France as well as Italy and Spain. Buses connecting smaller towns are frustratingly infrequent; be sure to check bus schedules carefully. The best way to see the region, especially the Lubéron, is to rent a car and take the smaller roads; or, alternatively, bike or walk.

1 **Marseille:** Hot, pungent; one of Provence's most real and gritty cities **(p. 223)**
2 **Calanques:** Freshwater inlets just off Marseille, surrounded by blinding white cliffs **(p. 233)**
3 **Cassis:** A jewel-green port surrounded by villas, gardens, and rock stairways **(p. 233)**
4 **Aix-en-Provence:** a twisty, elegant, fountain-filled little city with many festivals **(p. 234)**
5 **Avignon:** regional heavyweight has the Popes' Palace and a huge theater festival **(p. 241)**
6 **Villeneuve:** Just across the river and worlds away; green, quiet, monument-strewn **(p. 246)**
7 **L'Isle-sur-la-Sorgue:** First, wateriest village of the Vaucluse; entangled in canals **(p. 248)**
8 **Fontaine de Vaucluse:** A romantic little village with an impossibly deep spring **(p. 248)**
9 **Oppède-le-Vieux:** A ghost village with an exquisitely ruined castle **(p. 249)**
10 **Ménerbes:** Peter Mayle's village, beautiful as every other Vaucluse hamlet **(p. 250)**
11 **Lacoste:** Indistinguishably pretty; home to the Marquis de Sade's ruined castle **(p. 250)**
12 **Bonnieux:** The flower-filled capital of the Vaucluse
13 **Roussillon:** Most famous of the entirely red "ochre villages" **(p. 251)**
14 **Gordes:** One of the odder villages around, known for its prehistoric mound-huts **(p. 251)**
15 **Arles:** A provençal favorite, guardian of the region's traditions; great Roman arena **(p. 254)**
16 **Abbaye de Montmajour:** Huge abbey with magnificent Romanesque stonework **(p. 260)**
17 **Les Baux-de-Provence:** Possessed of the most splendidly ruined castle on earth **(p. 251)**
18 **Tarascon:** Not much to see in this little city; great fallback housing, though **(p. 252)**
19 **St-Rémy:** A pretty little city with Roman ruins and traces of Van Gogh **(p. 253)**
20 **Stes-Maries-de-la-Mer:** Capital of the marshy Camargue; dear to tourists, gypsies **(p. 261)**
21 **Aigues-Mortes:** A Camarguais city with fantastically preserved ramparts **(p. 263)**
22 **Nîmes:** Known for its Roman structures—an arena and a perfect nearby aqueduct **(p. 264)**
23 **Uzès:** Stony old town with a huge castle and an oft-destroyed cathedral **(p. 269)**
24 **Orange:** Well-preserved Roman theater; good museum; little else **(p. 270)**
25 **Vaison-la-Romaine:** Easy daytrip from Orange; good ruins **(p. 272)**

MARSEILLE

France's third-largest city, Marseille (pop. 900,000), is like the *bouillabaisse* soup for which it is famous: steamy and pungently spiced, with a little bit of everything mixed in. Unlike Provence and the Riviera, Marseille doesn't care if you visit. Even so, the city Dumas called "the meeting place of the entire world" remains strangely alluring, a jumble of color and commotion. Whatever Marseille lacks in architectural unity or social sophistication is more than made up for by its vibrancy.

Its beginnings date back to 600 BC, when Phoenician Greeks sought shelter in Marseille's port. The well-located city quickly grew into a trading center and an independent ally of Rome. In the first century BC, an imprudent policy of neutrality during the Roman civil war vexed Julius Caesar, and so he came, he saw, and he conquered Marseille. Marseille has since found neutrality elusive—through centuries of warfare, trade, plague, and immigration it has developed a reputation for roughness and danger. As a gateway to Europe, Marseille sees many immigrants from North and sub-Saharan African, making it a thriving stew of cultures which has sadly fueled ethnic tensions. Unfortunately, this Mediterranean hot spot can also be problematic for women, as the men can be quite aggressive. A mix of wild nightclubs, beaches, islands, gardens, and big-city adventure, Marseille flips the bird to Monaco, Nice, and Paris, and gets on with the business of living.

ORIENTATION

The city is divided into 16 *arrondissements*, but they are referred to as neighborhoods instead, with the names of major streets as dividing lines. **La Canebière,** a street affectionately known to English sailors as the "can o' beer," divides the city into north and south, funneling into the **vieux port** (old port) to the west and becoming bland urban sprawl to the east. North of the *vieux port* and west of bd. République, working-class residents of many ethnicities pile into the hilltop neighborhood of **Le Panier.** East of Le Panier, between cours Belsunce and bd. Athènes, and between cours St-Louis and bd. Garibaldi, the foreign-feeling **Quartier Belsunce's** dilapidated buildings house the city's Arab and African communities.

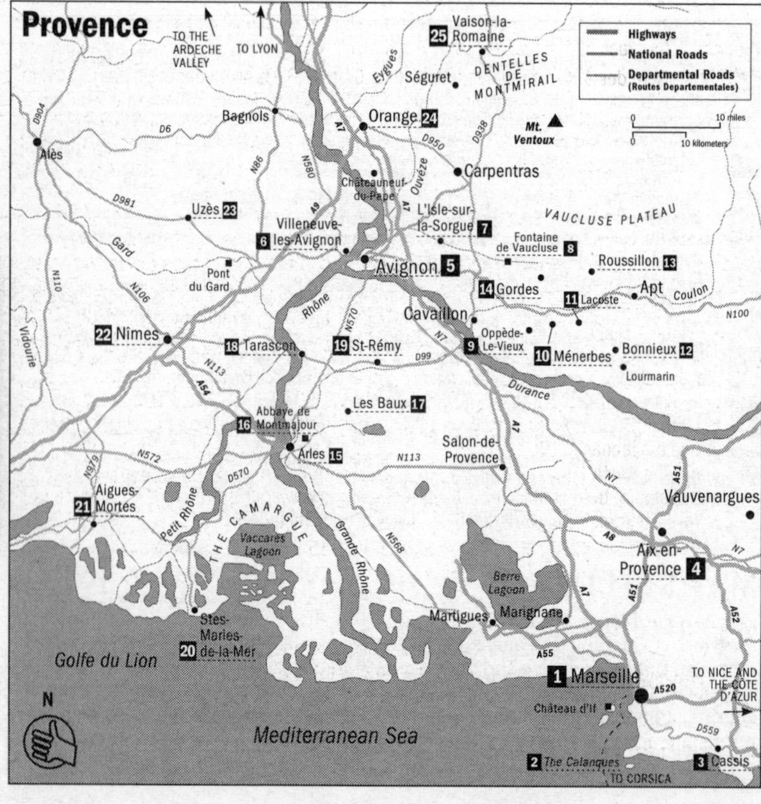

Use caution in this neighborhood at night. While both the bus and train stations lie at the top of bd. Athènes, near this troublesome quarter, staying on major streets can reduce problems. Upscale restaurants and nightlife cluster around the *vieux port*, on quai de Rive Neuve, cours Estienne d'Orves, and pl. Thiers. East of the *vieux port*, La Canebière, rue St-Ferreol, and rue Paradis contain the city's largest stores and fashion boutiques. The narrow streets past rue de Rome (near La Canebière) are full of colorful African markets. The areas in front of the Opéra (near the port) and around rue Curiol (near rue Sénac) are meeting grounds for prostitutes and their clients; be particularly cautious here after dark. A few blocks southeast, **cours Julien,** with funky shops and tiny concert spaces, has a countercultural feel. Marseille's two metro lines ("M" in this text) are clean and simple. The bus system is thorough, if complex—a route map helps enormously. Use the buses to access the beach, which stretches along the coast southwest of the *vieux port*.

TRANSPORTATION

Flights: Aéroport Marseille-Provence (☎04 42 14 14 14). Flights to **Corsica, Lyon,** and **Paris.** Shuttle buses connect airport to Gare St-Charles from 5:30am (from train to plane) and 6:15am (from plane to train) to 9:50pm (3 per hr., 50F/€7.62).

Trains: Gare St-Charles, pl. Victor Hugo. M: Gare St-Charles. To: **Lyon** (3½hr.; M-F 3 per day, Sa-Su 2 per day; 213F/€32.47; 4 TGVs per day, 277F/€42.23); **Nice** (2¾hr., M-Sa 13 per day, 152F/€23.17; 7 TGVs per day, 162F/€24.70); and **Paris** (4¾hr., 17 TGVs per day, 406-496F/€61.90-75.62). Info and ticket counters open daily 4:30am-1am. **Baggage service** open daily 7:15am-midnight. 15-30F/€2.29-4.57 per bag. **SOS Voyageurs** (☎04 91 62 12 80), in the station, helps tourists find lodgings. Open July-Aug. daily 10am-6pm; Sept.-June 9am-7pm. **Note:** While listed on train schedules, many trains to nearby cities, like Aix-en-Provence, may actually be buses. Make sure to check the track info; if it says "car," and doesn't list a number, inquire at the help desk.

Buses: Gare des Autocars, pl. Victor Hugo (☎04 91 08 16 40), near the train station. M: Gare St-Charles. Ticket counters open M-Sa 6:15am-7pm, Su 6-9am and 3-5:50pm. Info and baggage service open M-Sa 7am-4:30pm, Su 9am-noon and 2-4pm. 10F/€1.53 per bag. **Cartreize** (☎04 42 96 59 00) is an organization of local operators. Buy tickets on the bus (except to Nice) with exact change. To: **Aix-en-Provence** (every 20min., 26F/€3.96); **Arles** (2-3hr., 5 per day, 88F/€13.42); **Avignon** (2hr., 4 per day, 92F/€14.03); **Cannes** (2¼-3hr., 4 per day, 100F/€15.25); and **Nice** (2¾hr., 1 per day, 140F/€21.35). **Eurolines** also makes international trips. Open M-Sa 9am-6pm.

Ferries: SNCM, 61 bd. des Dames (☎08 91 70 18 01 for Corsica, Italy, and Sardinia, ☎08 91 70 28 02 for Algeria and Tunisia). To: **Algeria** (3180F/€484.82); **Corsica** (640-720F/€97.57 round-trip, students 12% less); **Sardinia** (750-850F/€114.35-129.59); and **Tunisia** (1620F/€246.99). Prices vary according to season and port of arrival. Open M-F 8am-6:30pm, Sa 8:30am-noon and 2-6pm.

Local Transportation: RTM, 6-8 rue des Fabres (☎04 91 91 92 10). Office open M-F 6:10am-6:30pm, Sa 9am-noon and 2-5:30pm. **Tickets** sold at bus and metro stations, or use exact change (9F). Day pass (25F/€3.81) sold at tourist office, bus or metro stations. The **Carte Liberté** costs 50-100F/€7.62-15.25 for 7-14 voyages. Metro lines #1 and 2 stop at train station. Line #1 (blue) goes to *vieux port* (dir: "Timone"). **Metro** runs M-Th 5am-9pm, F-Su 5am-12:30am. Tourist office has map.

Taxis: (☎04 91 02 20 20). 24hr. 100-150F/€15.25-22.90 to hostels from Gare St-Charles.

PROVENCE

PRACTICAL INFORMATION

Tourist Office: 4 La Canebière (☎04 91 13 89 00; fax 04 91 13 89 20). Has brochures of walking tours, free maps, and accommodations service. Bus and metro day pass 25F/€3.81. Open July-Aug. M-Sa 9am-8pm, Su 10am-6pm; Oct.-June M-Sa 9am-7pm, Su and holidays 10am-5pm. **Annex** (☎04 91 50 59 18) at train station. Open daily 10am-6pm, weekends closed from 3-4pm.

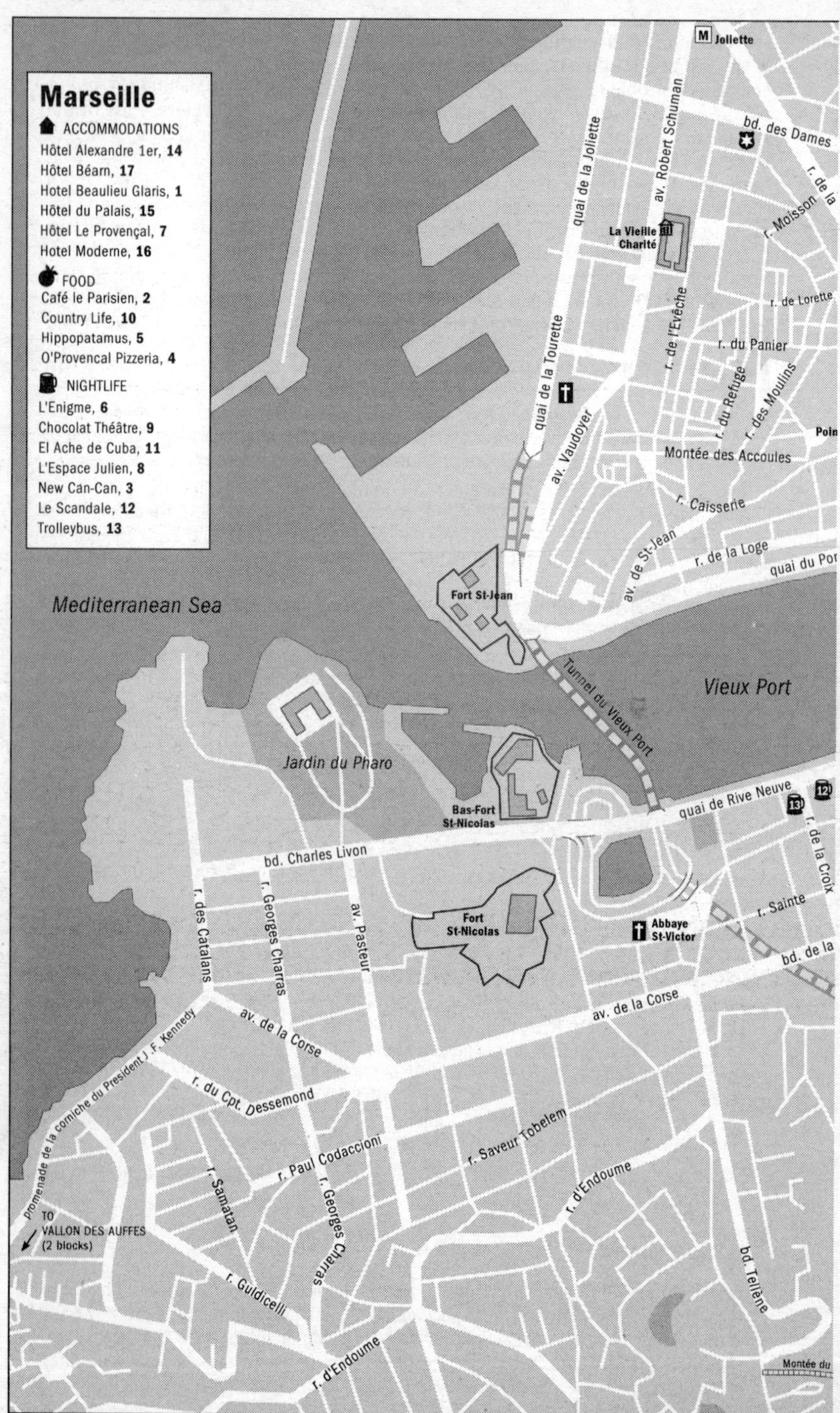
Marseille
ACCOMMODATIONS
Hôtel Alexandre 1er, 14
Hôtel Béarn, 17
Hotel Beaulieu Glaris, 1
Hôtel du Palais, 15
Hôtel Le Provençal, 7
Hotel Moderne, 16
FOOD
Café le Parisien, 2
Country Life, 10
Hippopatamus, 5
O'Provencal Pizzeria, 4
NIGHTLIFE
L'Enigme, 6
Chocolat Théâtre, 9
El Ache de Cuba, 11
L'Espace Julien, 8
New Can-Can, 3
Le Scandale, 12
Trolleybus, 13
Mediterranean Sea
Joliette
bd. des Dames
quai de la Joliette
av. Robert Schuman
r. de la
r. Moisson
La Vieille Charité
r. de Lorette
r. de l'Evêche
quai de la Tourette
r. du Panier
r. du Refuge
r. des Moulins
av. Vaudoyer
Montée des Accoules
r. Caisserie
av. de St-Jean
r. de la Loge
quai du Por
Fort St-Jean
Vieux Port
Tunnel du Vieux Port
Jardin du Pharo
Bas-Fort St-Nicolas
quai de Rive Neuve
r. de la Croix
bd. Charles Livon
r. des Catalans
r. Georges Charras
av. Pasteur
Fort St-Nicolas
Abbaye St-Victor
r. Sainte
bd. de la
av. de la Corse
Promenade de la Corniche du President J. F. Kennedy
r. du Cpt. Dessemond
r. Saveur Tobelem
r. Paul Codaccioni
r. Samatan
r. d'Endoume
TO VALLON DES AUFFES (2 blocks)
r. Guidicelli
bd. Tellène
Montée du

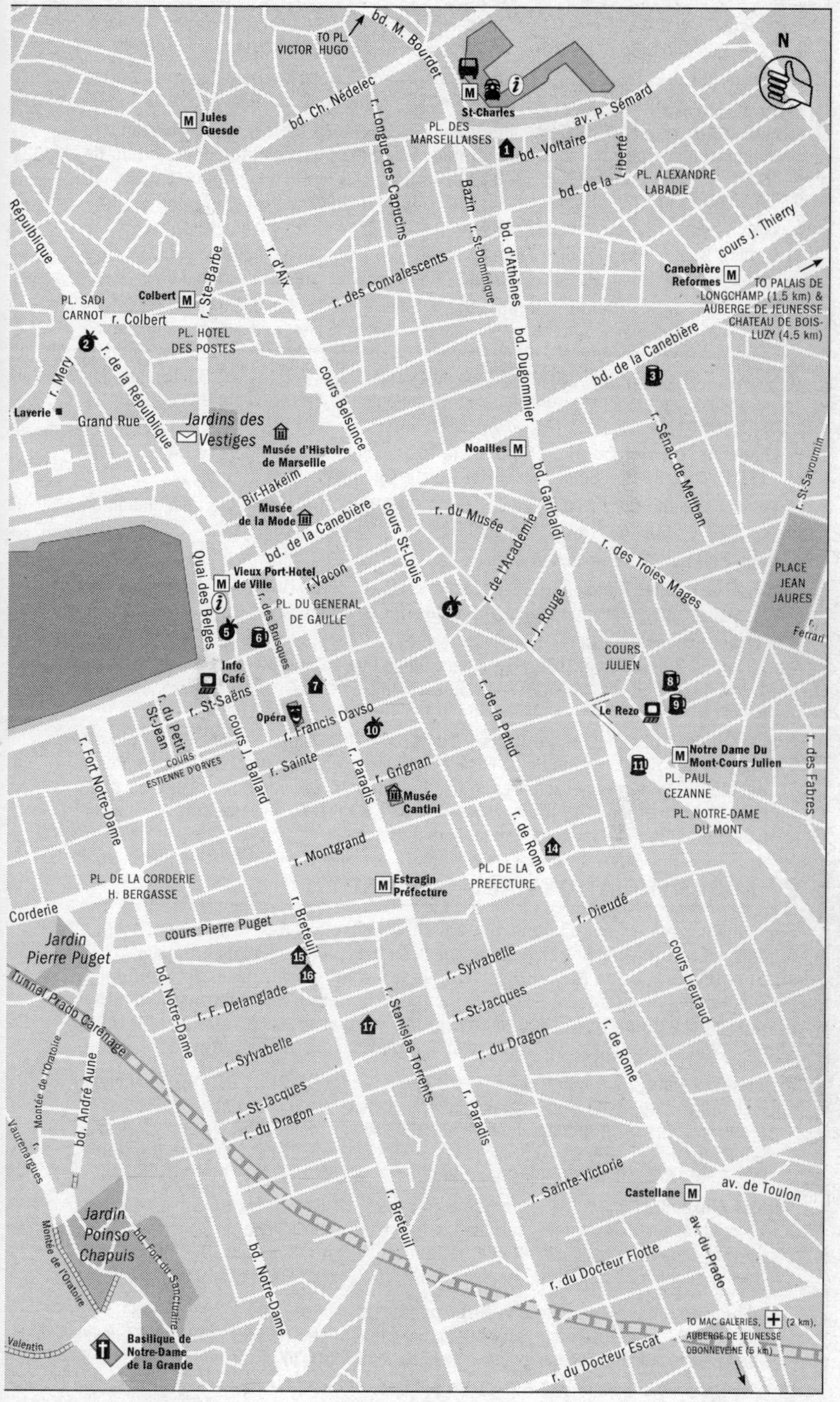
N
TO PL. VICTOR HUGO
bd. M. Bourdet
St-Charles
av. P. Sémard
PL. DES MARSEILLAISES
bd. Voltaire
bd. Ch. Nédelec
Jules Guesde
r. Longue des Capucins
Bazin
r. St-Dominique
bd. d'Athènes
bd. de la Liberté
PL. ALEXANDRE LABADIE
cours J. Thierry
Canebrière Reformes
TO PALAIS DE LONGCHAMP (1.5 km) & AUBERGE DE JEUNESSE CHATEAU DE BOIS-LUZY (4.5 km)
République
r. d'Aix
r. des Convalescents
r. Ste-Barbe
Colbert
PL. SADI CARNOT
r. Colbert
PL. HOTEL DES POSTES
bd. Dugommier
bd. de la Canebière
r. Mery
r. de la République
Laverie
Grand Rue
Jardins des Vestiges
Musée d'Histoire de Marseille
cours Belsunce
Noailles
r. Sénac de Meilhan
r. St-Savournin
bd. Garibaldi
Bir-Hakeim
Musée de la Mode
bd. de la Canebière
cours St-Louis
r. du Musée
r. de l'Academie
r. des Troies Mages
PLACE JEAN JAURES
Quai des Belges
Vieux Port-Hotel de Ville
r. Vacon
r. des Brisques
PL. DU GENERAL DE GAULLE
r. J. Rouge
r. Ferrari
COURS JULIEN
Info Café
r. St-Saëns
r. du Petit St-Jean
cours J. Ballard
Opéra
r. Francis Davso
r. de la Palud
Le Rezo
Notre Dame Du Mont-Cours Julien
PL. PAUL CEZANNE
PL. NOTRE-DAME DU MONT
r. des Fabres
r. Fort Notre-Dame
COURS ESTIENNE D'ORVES
r. Sainte
r. Paradis
r. Grignan
Musée Cantini
r. de Rome
r. Montgrand
Estragin Préfecture
PL. DE LA PREFECTURE
PL. DE LA CORDERIE H. BERGASSE
Corderie
cours Pierre Puget
r. Breteuil
r. Dieudé
Jardin Pierre Puget
cours Lieutaud
bd. Notre-Dame
r. Sylvabelle
r. F. Delanglade
r. St-Jacques
Tunnel Prado Carénage
r. Stanislas Torrents
r. du Dragon
r. Sylvabelle
r. de Rome
Montée de l'Oratoire
bd. André Aune
r. St-Jacques
r. du Dragon
r. Paradis
Vauvenargues
r. Sainte-Victorie
Castellane
av. de Toulon
r. Breteuil
Jardin Poinso Chapuis
bd. Fort du Sanctuaire
Montée de l'Oratoire
av. du Prado
bd. Notre-Dame
r. du Docteur Flotte
Valentin
Basilique de Notre-Dame de la Grande
TO MAC GALERIES, (2 km), AUBERGE DE JEUNESSE OBONNEVEINE (5 km)
r. du Docteur Escat

Budget Travel: Wasteels, 67 La Canebière (☎08 03 88 70 46). Open M-F 9:15am-12:15pm and 2-6pm, Sa 9:30am-12:30pm.

Consulates: UK, 24 av. du Prado (☎04 91 15 72 10). Open M-F 9am-noon and 2-5pm. **US,** 12 bd. Paul Peytral (☎04 91 54 92 00). Open by appt. M-F 9am-noon and 2-4pm.

Money: La Bourse, 3 pl. Général de Gaulle (☎04 91 13 09 00). Good rates and no commission. Open M-F 8:30am-6:30pm, Sa 9am-5pm. **Comptoir Marseillais de Bourse,** 22 La Canebière (☎04 91 54 93 94). Excellent rates and no commission. Open M-Sa 9am-7pm. **American Express,** 39 La Canebière, located in Afat Voyages (☎04 91 13 71 21). Open M-F 9am-6pm, Sa 9am-noon and 2-5pm.

English Bookstore: Librairie Fueri-Lamy, 21 rue Paradis (☎04 91 33 57 03). Slim paperback selection. Open M 2:15-7pm, Tu-Sa 9:30am-1pm and 2-7pm. MC/V.

Youth Information: Centre d'Information Jeunesse, 96 La Canebière (☎04 91 24 33 50). Info on sports, short-term employment, leisure activities, and services for disabled persons. Open July-Aug. M-F 9am-1pm; Sept.-June 8am-8:30pm, closed Tu morning. Closed July 30-Aug. 17. **CROUS,** 42 rue du 141*ème* R.I.A. (☎04 91 62 83 60), has info on housing, work, and travel. Open M-F 9am-noon and 1:30-4:30pm; May 30-July 27 10am-1pm.

Laundromat: Point Laverie, 56 bd. de la Libération, and 6 rue Mery (☎04 91 25 37 18). Open daily 7am-8pm. Also on rue Bruetil. Open M-Sa 8am-7pm.

Police: 2 rue du Commissaire Becker (☎04 91 39 80 00). Also in the train station on esplanade St-Charles (☎04 91 14 29 97).

Rape Hotline: SOS Femmes Violées (☎04 91 56 04 10). 24hr.

Hospital: Hôpital Timone, bd. Jean Moulin (☎04 91 38 60 00). Take metro line #1 to "Castéllane," then take bus #91. **SOS Médecins** (☎04 91 52 91 52), on-call doctors.

Internet Access: Info Café, 1 quai Rive Neuve (☎04 91 33 53 05). Open M-Sa 9am-10pm, Su 2:30-7:30pm. 13F/€1.98 per 30min. **Bug's Cafe,** 80 cours Julien (☎04 96 12 53 43). Open M-Sa 10am-11pm, Su 2-7pm. 30F/€4.57 per hr. **Le Rezo,** 68 cours Julien (☎04 91 42 70 02). Open M-Sa 10am-10pm. 30F/€4.57 per hr.

Post Office: 1 pl. Hôtel des Postes (☎04 91 15 47 20). Follow La Canebière toward the sea and turn right onto rue Reine Elisabeth as it becomes pl. Hôtel des Postes. **Poste Restante** and **currency exchange** at this branch only. Open M-F 8am-7pm, Sa 8am-noon. **Branch office** at 11 rue Honnorat (☎04 91 62 80 80), near the station. Open M-F 8am-6:45pm, Sa 8am-noon. **Postal code:** 13001.

PROVENCE

ACCOMMODATIONS AND CAMPING

Marseille has many cheap hotels, but few reputable ones. Resist the cheap accommodations in the Quartier Belsunce; the area may be dangerous after dark, and some hotels are fronts for brothels. Hotels listed here prioritize safety and location. Both hostels are far from the city center and offer an escape from the hubbub of the center without losing access to the city, but bus access is infrequent in summer, so plan ahead. They usually have space year-round, but call a few days ahead.

Hôtel du Palais, 26 rue Breteuil (☎04 91 37 78 86; fax 04 91 37 91 19). Competent, kind owner runs a tight ship and rents large, well-maintained rooms at a great value. A/C and soundproofing shut out the busy street below. All rooms have TVs and showers or baths. Breakfast 30F/€4.57. Singles 195F/€29.73; doubles 230F/€35.06; triples 280-300F/€42.69-45.74. Extra bed 50F/€7.62. MC/V.

Hôtel Alexandre 1er, 111 rue de Rome (☎04 91 48 67 13; fax 04 91 42 11 14). Located right across from pl. Préfecture, this hotel is a quality choice. Spacious rooms, all with showers. Breakfast 30F/€4.57. Reception 24hr. Singles 180-230F/€27.44-35.06; doubles 230F/€35.06; triples 300F/€45.73; quads 400F/€60.98. MC/V.

Auberge de Jeunesse Bonneveine (HI), impasse Bonfils (☎04 91 17 63 30; fax 04 91 73 97 23), off av. J. Vidal. From the station, take metro line #2 to "Rond-Point du Prado," and transfer (keeping your ticket) onto bus #44 to pl. Bonnefon. At the bus stop, walk back toward the traffic circle and turn left at J. Vidal. After #47, turn onto impasse Bonfils; the hostel is on the left. Swimming and sunbathing are just 200m away. A well-organized hostel full of young people. Bonneveine's cement-block building houses a bar, restaurant, Internet access, pool table, video games, vending machines, and 150 beds. Breakfast included. Dinner 50F/€7.62. Lockers 10F/€1.53. Laundry. Maximum stay 6 days (3 in summer). Reception 7am-1am. No lockout. Curfew 1am. Reserve ahead in summer. Closed Dec. 22-Feb. Dorms Apr.-Aug. 83F/€12.65 first night, 72F/€10.98 thereafter; doubles 103F/€15.70 first night, 93F/€14.18 thereafter. Feb.-Mar. and Sept.-Dec. dorms 78F/€11.89 first night, 67F/€10.21 thereafter; doubles 98F/€14.94 first night, 93F/€14.18 thereafter. **Members only.** MC/V.

Auberge de Jeunesse Château de Bois-Luzy (HI), allée des Primevères (☎/fax 04 91 49 06 18). Take bus #6 from cours J. Thierry at the top of La Canebière to "Marius Richard." 10m up the hill from the bus stop, take a right onto bd. de l'Amandière and walk to the soccer fields. Follow the road down to the right and around the fields to reach the hostel. Or take bus #8 (dir: "Saint-Julien") from "La Canebière" to "Felibres Laurient", walk up hill and make the first left, hostel will be on your left. Night bus T also leaves "La Canebière" for "Marius Richard." The big yellow tower-topped hostel used to house a count and countess, or so they say; those days are long gone now. Mostly 3- to 6-bed dorms and a few doubles. Breakfast 18F/€2.74. Dinner 48F/€7.32. Luggage storage 5F/€0.76 per day. Sheets 10F/€1.53. Laundry. Reception 7:30am-noon and 5-10:30pm. Lockout noon-5pm. Strict curfew May-Oct. 11pm; Nov.-Apr. 10:30pm. Dorms 48F/€7.32; singles 70F/€10.67; doubles 55F/€8.39. **Members only.**

Hôtel Béarn, 63 rue Sylvabelle (☎04 91 37 75 83; fax 04 91 81 54 98). On a quiet side street near the port, between rue Paradis and rue Breteuil. Large, perfectly adequate rooms with high, airy ceilings. Breakfast (with homemade jam) 25F/€3.81, 30F/€4.57 in bed. Singles and doubles with shower 110-140F/€16.77-21.35, with bath 210F/€32.02; triples with bath 260F/€39.64. MC/V.

Hôtel Beaulieu Glaris, 1 pl. des Marseillaises (☎04 91 90 70 59; fax 04 91 56 14 04). Right at the foot of the staircases of Gare St-Charles, this comfortable hotel is perfect for late-night arrivals or early morning departures. Rooms are cramped but clean. Though the surrounding neighborhood has a reputation for late-night unsavoriness, the hotel is quite safe; rooms lock and keys must be left with desk attendant. The cheapest rooms are often booked, but last minute cancellations may provide a saving grace. Breakfast 25F/€3.81. Reception 7am-midnight. Singles 130-150F/€19.82-22.90; singles and doubles 160-200F/€24.39-30.49, with shower 230F/€35.06, with bath 250F/€38.12; doubles and triples 250F/€38.12, with shower 320F/€48.79. MC/V.

Hôtel Le Provençal, 32 rue Paradis (☎04 91 33 11 15; fax 04 91 33 47 08). Provençal's small, newly refurbished rooms are bare and clean; they overlook a bustling street around the corner from L'Opéra and are 2min. from the *vieux port.* Breakfast 25F/€3.81. 24hr. reception. Singles 145F/€22.11; doubles 165F/€25.16, with shower 195F/€29.73; triples 220F/€33.54, with shower 250F/38.12. AmEx/MC/V.

Hôtel Moderne, 30 rue Breteuil (☎04 91 53 29 93). Low prices and a great location near the *vieux port* might make this hotel worth it, despite the gloom and street noise. If you don't have a shower in the room, you won't shower. Breakfast 25F/€3.81. Singles 100F/€15.25, with shower 125F/€19.06, with bath 150F/€22.90; doubles 150F/€22.90, with bath 160-175F/€24.39-26.69. MC/V.

FOOD

Marseille has a good number of ethnic restaurants, among which the North African places just above and below the Canebière stand out as a budget traveler's dream—they make excellent and filling dishes for under 40F/€6.10. The city's restaurant density soars around the *vieux port*, peaking on **pl. Thiers** and the **cours Estienne d'Orves,** where you can eat outside for as little as 60F/€9.15. Once the staple of penniless fishermen, the city's trademark **bouillabaisse** (a full meal comprising various Mediterranean fish, fish broth, and a spicy sauce called "*rouille*" or "rust") has become high cuisine and is priced to match. Still, you can find a reasonable bouillabaisse in any number of restaurants near the *vieux port* and on rue Fortia and rue St-Saens. For a more artsy crowd and cheaper fare, head up to **cours Julien** and take your pick from the restaurants lining the pedestrian mall. Locals stock up at the **fish market,** where ingredients for homemade bouillabaisse are sold inches from the fishing boats on quai des Belges (daily 9am-noon). There is a **vegetable market** on cours Julien (M-Sa 8am-1pm) and an **open-air market** on cours Pierre Puget, beginning at rue Breteuil (M-Sa, starts at 8am). Before you head for the hostels, stock up on the second floor of **Monoprix supermarket,** on La Canebière, across from the AmEx office (open M-Sa 8:30am-8:30pm).

O'Provençal Pizzeria, 7 rue de la Palud (☎04 91 54 03 10), off rue de Rome. Perfect portions, fast service, and A/C on hot days make the best pizza in town better. Open M-Sa noon-2pm and 7:30pm-midnight. MC/V.

Hippopotamus, 33 quai des Belges (☎04 91 59 91 40). This small French chain aims to please, with the biggest hamburgers east of the Atlantic. *Menus* from 76F/€11.59. 30% reduction in grill prices M-F 2:30-7:30pm. Open daily 8am-midnight. AmEx/MC/V.

Country Life, 14 rue Venture (☎04 96 11 28 00), off rue Paradis. All-you-can-eat vegan food under a huge skylight and amid a forest of foliage. *Menus* 62F/€9.45; students and children 38F/€5.80. Open M-F 11:30am-2:30pm; health-food store open M-Th 9am-6:30pm, F 9am-3pm. AmEx/MC/V.

Café le Parisien, 1 pl. Sadi Carnot (☎04 91 90 05 77). Moneyed hipsters, local socialites, and card- and dice-playing old men sup at the city's most famous café. The stunning *trompe l'œil* interior recalls 1901, when the café first opened its doors. Decadent lunches are pricey, but coffee in all its incarnations costs much the same as elsewhere. Open Sa-W 4am-9pm. Open until midnight or 1am Th-F for tapas nights.

SIGHTS

A walk through the city's streets is more rewarding than any other sights-oriented itinerary, and trips are well-marked with maps from the tourist office. There's always the cheesy Petit Train, which departs from quai Belges for two different circuits. (☎04 91 40 17 75. 30F/€4.57, children 15F/€2.29.)

BASILIQUE DE NOTRE DAME DE LA GARDE. A clear, stunning view of the city, surrounding mountains, and stone-studded bay made this church's hilltop site strategically important for centuries. In WWII, during the liberation of Marseille, a fierce battle raged for days before FFI forces took back the basilica; the east face of the church remains pocked with bullet holes and shrapnel scars. Towering nearly 230m above the city, its golden statue of Madonna bearing the infant Christ, known affectionately as *"la bonne mère,"* is regarded by many as the symbol of Marseille. *(Take bus #60 (dir. "Notre Dame"); or, from the tourist office, walk up rue Breteuil and make left onto rue Grignon. It will become bd. de la Corderie. Make a left onto bd. André Aune and you will see huge staircase. ☎04 91 13 40 80. Open in summer daily 7am-8pm; in winter 7am-7pm. Free.)*

ABBAYE ST-VICTOR. St-Victor, an abbey fortified against pirates and Saracen invaders, is one of the oldest Christian sites in Europe. The eerie 5th-century catacombs and basilica contain pagan and Christian relics, including the remains of two third-century martyrs. Sarcophagi are piled up along the walls; some, partially excavated remain half-embedded in the building's foundations. The abbey hosts concerts all year. *(Perched on rue Sainte at the end of quai de Rive Neuve. Follow the signs from the quai. ☎04 96 11 22 60. Open daily 8:30am-6:30pm. 10F/€1.53 for crypt entrance.)*

LE JARDIN DES VESTIGES. The remains of the original port of Marseille rest peacefully in this quiet garden. The grassy harbor, full of limestone stacked like giant Legos, makes a good picnic stop. Your ticket to the garden also admits you to the **Musée d'Histoire de Marseille,** whose intriguing millennia-old artifacts are poorly displayed. *(Enter through the Centre Bourse mall. Museum ☎04 91 90 42 22. Gardens open Mar.-Nov. M-Sa noon-7pm; Dec.-Feb. noon-6pm. 12F/€1.83, students 6F/€0.91, ages 10-16 6F/€0.91, over 65 and under 10 free.)*

LA VIEILLE CHARITE. The crowning achievement of the famous 17th-century local architect Pierre Puget, La Charité sheltered orphans, the elderly, and other undesirables. It broke new ground in the field of child abandonment; parents could leave their unwanted children in front, where a wooden turnstile near the gate kept the nuns inside from ever seeing their faces. Now home to many of Marseille's cultural organizations, it is part of the city's network of museums, including Egyptian, prehistoric, and classical collections as well as temporary exhibits. The building exhibits both grace and balance with high, blank, exterior walls facing the *Panier* district and a contrasting sunny interior with colonnades. The building culminates in a stunning Baroque chapel. *(2 rue de la Charité. ☎04 91 14 58 80. Open June-Sept. W-M 11am-6pm, Oct.-May Tu-Su 10am-5pm. Temporary exhibits 18F/ €2.90, permanent 12F/€1.83, students with ID half-price.)*

HARBOR ISLANDS. The **Château d'If,** sun-blasted, blunt, and bright, guards the city from its golden rock outside the harbor. Its dungeon, immortalized in Dumas' *Count of Monte Cristo*, once held a number of hapless Huguenots. While their cells were sightly drafty and underdecorated, the view from their barred windows would have made a life sentence near-bearable. Graffiti by visitors and prisoners covers the walls. Nearby, the windswept **Ile Frioul** quarantined suspected plague victims for two centuries, starting in the 1600s. It was only marginally successful as an outbreak in 1720 killed half the city's 80,000 citizens. The hospital is now a public monument and holds occasional raves. The ride out to the islands takes you between the batteries of the **Fort St-Jean,** whose original tower guarded a giant chain that closed off the harbor in times of trouble. *(Reserve in advance in the high season. Boats depart from quai des Belges at M: quai des Belges for both islands. Call the Groupement des Armateurs Côtiers, ☎04 91 55 50 09, after 8pm 06 09 95 89 26. 20min., round-trip 50F/€7.62 for each island, 80F/€12.20 for both. Château ☎04 91 59 02 30. Open Apr.-Sept. daily 9:30am-6:30pm; Oct.-Mar. Tu-Su 9:30am-5:30pm. 26F/€3.96, under age 25 16F/€2.44.)*

LA CORNICHE AND THE VALLON DES AUFFES. From the Palais du Pharo to the Avenue du Prado, the **promenade de la Corniche** takes you along Marseille's most beautiful stretch of beaches and inlets. Though traffic is almost always heavy, you won't mind winding slowly past the luminous Mediterranean. Be sure to stop, however, at the **Vallon des Auffes.** This hidden fishing port looks today much as it did 50 years ago, with rows of brightly painted, traditional fishing boats dipping and tucking at their moorings. *(Pedestrians take bus #83 from the Vieux Port (dir: "Rond-Point du Prado") to "Vallon des Auffes.")*

PALAIS LONGCHAMP. Inaugurated in 1869, the palace was built to honor the completion of a canal which brought fresh water to alleviate Marseille's cholera outbreak. Endowed with towering columns and, shockingly, flowing water, the monument itself is only the center of the complex, which includes two museums, a park, and an observatory. The **Musée de l'Histoire Naturelle** includes a ridiculous assortment of stuffed animals, and through 2002, an exhibit on the history of milk. *(☎04 91 14 59 50. Open Tu-Su 10am-5pm. 12F/€1.83, students and children 6F/€0.91.)* The **Musée des Beaux-Arts** includes your basic beautiful paintings. *(To get there, take metro #1 to Cinq Avenues Longchamps. ☎04 91 14 59 30. Open June-Sept. Tu-Su 11am-6pm, Oct.-May Tu-Su 10am-7pm. 12F/€1.83, students 6F/€0.91.)*

OTHER SIGHTS. The memorable **Musée Cantini** chronicles the region's artistic successes of the last century. *(19 rue Grignan. ☎04 91 54 77 75. Open Tu-Su 11am-6pm. 16F/€2.44, students 8F/€1.22, over 65 and under 10 free.)* The **Musée de la Mode** (Fashion Museum) carries ever-changing, eccentric exhibits of contemporary fashion. *(Espace Mode Méditerranée, 11 La Canebière. ☎04 91 56 59 57. Free tours in French Sa-Su 4pm. Open Tu-Su noon-7pm. 12-18F/€1.83-2.44; students and ages 10-16 half-price, over 65 free.)* The **MAC, Galeries Contemporaines des Musées de Marseille,** features art from the 1960s to today, including works by César and Wegman. *(69 av. d'Haifa. ☎04 91 25 01 07. Open Tu-Su 11am-7pm. 18F/€2.74, students and children 10-169F/€1.37.)*

BEACHES

Bus #83 (dir: "Ront-Point du Prado") takes you from the *vieux port* to Marseille's public beaches. Catch it on the waterfront side of the street and get off just after it rounds the statue of David (20-30min.). Or take #19 (dir: "Madrague") from M: Castellane or M: Rond-Point du Prado. Both **plage du Prado** and **plage de la Corniche** offer wide beaches, clear water, grass for impromptu soccer matches, good views of the cliffs surrounding Marseille, and less-than-ideal sand. **Supermarché Casino et Cafeteria,** across from the statue, will serve your every need. (Open M-Sa 8:30am-8:30pm. Cafeteria open daily 8:30am-10pm.)

ENTERTAINMENT AND FESTIVALS

Don't let Marseille's reputation for seediness keep you inside, but make sure to exercise caution. Try not to end up in far-flung areas of the city late at night, since night buses are scarce, taxis expensive, and the metro closed after 9pm. After dark, don't venture far from the busy streets near the *vieux port;* after 10pm, everyone should avoid the North African quarter, cours Belsunce, and bd. d'Athènes. People-watching and nightlife center around **cours Julien,** east of the harbor, and **pl. Thiers,** near the *vieux port.*

Theater buffs can check out the program at the **Théâtre National de Marseille,** 30 quai de Rive Neuve. (☎04 96 17 80 80. Tickets 59-164F/€9-25. Box office open by telephone Tu-Sa 10am-7pm, in person 1-7pm.) There's also **Théâtre Gymnase,** 4 rue du Théâtre Français. (☎04 91 24 35 35; call from 11am-6pm. Tickets 131.20-183.70F/€20-28; students 78.70F/€12. Box office open Oct.-June M-Sa noon-6pm.) Unwind with the latest French and American films at **Le César,** 4 pl. Castellane. (☎04 91 37 12 80. 38F/€5.80, students and seniors 36F/€5.49.)

BARS AND CLUBS

Trolleybus, 24 quai de Rive Neuve (☎04 91 54 30 45; info 06 16 13 13 56). Has to be seen to be believed. This mega-club, occupying an 18th-century warehouse, has a room each for house-garage, rock, pop-rock, and soul-funk-salsa as well as a new discothèque built around 2 regulation-size *boule* courts. Local and international DJs have been playing here for 12 years. Beer from 30F/€4.57, drinks 40F/€6.10. Sa cover 60F/€9.15 (includes 1 drink). Open in summer W-Sa 11pm-7am, in winter Th-Sa.

Le Scandale, 16 quai de Rive Neuve (☎04 91 54 46 85). Young locals crowd this vibrant joint right on the *vieux port*. People drink and groove into the wee hours to nightly DJs. Pints from 30F/€4.57. Happy Hour 6-10:30pm. Open daily 1pm-5am.

El Ache de Cuba, 9 pl. Paul Cézanne (☎04 91 42 99 79 or 06 88 21 19 52). A slice of Havana, with music blaring out of speakers and onto the sidewalk of this friendly café. Weekly Latin dance and Spanish lessons (Oct.-June only). Must be a member to order something (10F/€1.53), but it's a ticket into the community. After that, drinks are under 20F/€3.05. "House Punch" 15F/€2.29. Open W-Sa 5pm-2am.

L'Enigme, 22 rue Beauvau (☎04 91 33 79 20), parallel to rue Paradis and pl. de Gaulle. This friendly spot is one of the only gay/lesbian places around. Frequented mostly by men, but women show up occasionally. Drinks 10F/€1.53 7:30-10pm; from 10pm on, they start at 30F/€4.57. Open daily 7:30pm-2am or later.

New Can-Can, 3 rue Sénac (☎04 91 48 59 76). A perpetual weekend party for the city's gay/lesbian community. M-W no cover; Th 70F/€10.67; F free before midnight then 80F/€12.20, Sa 50F/€7.62 before midnight, 90F/€13.72 after, Su free before midnight; 70F/€10.67 after. Open 11pm-dawn; show at 2am.

LIVE PERFORMANCE

For more info on performance or cultural activities, call the **Office de la Culture de Marseille,** 42 La Canebière. (☎04 91 11 04 60. Open M-Sa 10am-6:45pm.)

L'Espace Julien, 39 cours Julien (☎04 91 24 34 10). Nightly concerts (8:30pm) range from jazz to funk and reggae. Closed July-Aug. 30-60F/€4.57-9.15 for café; concerts from 65F/€9.91. For info, call M-F 9am-noon and 2-6pm.

Chocolat Théâtre, 59 cours Julien (☎04 91 42 19 29). Comic pieces and stand-up at 9pm. Tickets Tu-Th 82F/€12.51, F 92F/€14.03, Sa 112F/€17.08. Dinner and show 200F/€30.49, students 170F/€25.92.

Le Poste à Galene, 103 rue Ferrari (☎04 91 47 57 99), features both local groups and the cutting-edge famous. Techno and everything else. Open M-F from 8:30pm, shows at 9:30pm. Tickets 30-110F/€4.57-16.77.

FESTIVALS

Expect the **International Documentary Film Festival** in June and the **Lesbian and Gay Pride March** in late June and early July. The **Festival de Marseille Méditerranée** keeps Marseille full of music, dance, and theater in July. December brings the **Festival de Musique,** a week-long jubilee of jazz, classical, and pop music at l'Abbaye de St-Victor. Call the tourist office or the Culture Office (☎04 96 11 04 60) for info.

DAYTRIP FROM MARSEILLE: LES CALANQUES

The Calanques (and *calanques* in general) are inlets of clear water surrounded by walls of jagged, blinding white rock. Stretching from Marseille to Toulon, their precipices and seas shelter a rare and fragile balance of terrestrial and marine plants and wildlife—pine, juniper, and wild asparagus, foxes, bats, owls, and peregrine falcons. Bleached white houses skirt the hills, looking down on swarms of scuba divers, mountain climbers, cliff divers, and nudists.

The **Société des Excursionistes Marseillais,** 16 rue de la Rotonde (☎04 91 84 75 52; call M-F 5:30-7:30pm) conducts walking tours of the Calanques. After paying the 140F/€21.35 membership fee, you can participate in their hiking expeditions. A far cheaper option is to take bus #21 to "Luminy" (9F/€1.37); this leaves you near the *calanques* **Morgiou** and **Sormiou.** The first of the inlets, **Callelongue,** also lies at the farthest reaches of Marseille bus line S. Take #19 from the *vieux port* to "Samena," then catch #20 and follow the coastal roads until its terminus. Service is sporadic, but you can kill time by exploring trails in the nearby hills. Line #20 sometimes ends prematurely at **Goudes** (the town before Callelongue), which offers trails leading to secluded inlets.

NEAR MARSEILLE: CASSIS

PROVENCE

Twenty-three kilometers from Marseille, the charming resort town of Cassis clings to a hillside overlooking the Mediterranean. Immaculate white villas clump around the slopes above, and the town itself—a network of winding staircases, slender alleyways, and thick gardens—leads down to a jewel-green port. During the summer, unfortunately, there is often a line of honking cars between you and this delicate beauty. Parking is a competitive sport, and all the harbor bars are filled with tourists. Luckily, the relative peace and unquestionable beauty of the *calanques* are nearby; follow the signs to the **Calanque de Port-Pin,** about an hour east of town. From there, it's a half-hour hike to the popular **En Vau** *calanque* and beach.

TRANSPORTATION AND PRACTICAL INFORMATION. Since the train station is 3km outside town, it's easiest to take a **bus** from **Marseille** (30min.-1hr.; in summer 3 per day, inquire at bus station for winter; 20F/€3.05). From the bus stop, go two blocks down the hill, pass the casino, and turn right into the Jardin Public. The **tourist office** is on your left as you leave the park. Their maps are especially helpful when trekking to the hostel. (☎04 42 01 71 17; fax 04 42 01 28 31. Open July-Aug. daily 9am-7pm; Sept.-June M-F 9am-5:30pm, Sa 10am-12:30pm and 1:30-5pm, Su 10am-12:30pm. **Beach annex** opens in 2002.) If the town's too steep, call a **taxi** at 04 42 01 78 96 or 06 81 60 48 51. The **police** can be reached at ☎04 42 01 15 30. Send your naked sunbathing pictures back home at the **post office,** in the public garden. (☎04 42 01 98 30. Open M and W-F 8:30am-noon and 2-7pm, Tu 9am-noon and 2:30-5pm, Sa 8:30am-noon.)

ACCOMMODATIONS AND FOOD. Cassis makes a terrific daytrip from Marseille, since hotel prices in the town itself can be steep. If you can't stand leaving, try the **Auberge de Jeunesse de la Fontasse (HI),** 20km from Marseille off D559, near En Vau. The hostel is a sweaty 4km climb from the Cassis tourist office (1hr.), but the gorgeous view makes it worthwhile. Flop onto one of 66 beds in 6- to 10-person dorms, powered by solar energy and irrigated with filtered rain water (from taps). There are no showers, and light chores are required of all guests. To get there, start from Cassis' port and follow signs for the Calanques. When the road ends at two paths, take the steep right path and then watch closely for the signs printed on rocks. (☎04 42 01 02 72. Reception 8-10am and 5-10pm. Closed Jan.-Feb. Reserve ahead. Bunks 52F/€7.93. **Members only.**) Or if you have planned your trip in advance, stay at **Le Provençal,** 7 rue Victor Hugo. The A/C, TVs, and location make the stay worthwhile. (☎04 42 01 72 13. Breakfast 35F/€5.34. Reception 7:30am-10pm. May-Sept. doubles with shower 280F/€42.69, with bath 350-360F/€53.34-54.89, triples with shower 390F/€59.48, with bath 430F/€65.56; Jan.-Apr. and Oct. doubles with shower 220-250F/€33.54-38.12, with bath 300-310F/€45.74-47.28; triples with shower 320F/€48.79, with bath 390F/€59.47. Extra bed 70F/€10.67.) To find the crowded **Camping Les Cigales,** take av. Agostina to av. Colbert, then turn right onto av. de la Marne (20min.). (☎04 42 01 07 34; fax 04 42 01 34 18. Bring your own toilet paper. Open Mar. 15-Nov. 15. Reception 7:30am-8pm. 32F/€4.88 per person, 16F/€2.44 per child, 30F/€4.57 per site, 63F/€9.61 for 1 person with tent, 96F/€14.64 for 2 people with tent. Cars and campers extra.)

The roads right next to the beach are lined reasonably priced crêperies. There is also a **Petit Casino,** rue Victor Hugo (open M-Sa 8am-12:30pm and 3:30-7:30pm, Su 8am-12:30pm and 4-7pm). Cheap pizzas and monstrous plates of mussels and fries can be had at **Le Petit Cassis,** 19 rue Michel Blanc. (☎04 42 01 17 32. Open daily noon-2pm and 7-10:30pm. Closed Nov.-Jan.)

SIGHTS AND ACTIVITIES. You can explore the crystalline water with a kayak at **Kayak de Mer,** pl. Montmorin, on the beach. (☎04 42 01 80 01. Single kayak 150F/€22.90 per half-day, 250F/€38.12 per day; double 150F/€22.90 per half-day, 400F/€60.98 per day. Or see the cliffs on a **boat tour** (☎04 42 01 90 83. 45-90min., different tours bring you to various *calanques*. Boats leave from port Feb.-Nov. 15. 60-95F/€9.15-14.48.)

AIX-EN-PROVENCE

Aix (pronounced "X," pop. 150,000) is one of those rare cities that caters to tourists without being spoiled by them. This is the city of Paul Cézanne, Victor Vasarely, and Emile Zola, and every golden facade or dusty café has had its brush with greatness. Aix is endowed with several art collections ; tourists come for these and for the peculiar feel of the place—the intimacy of its tiny squares, twisty streets, and flowing fountains. Aix's large student population keeps it far in the cultural forefront of Provence. In end of June through early August, dance, opera, jazz, and classical music take over the city.

TRANSPORTATION

Trains: at the end of av. Victor Hugo, off rue Gustave Desplace. Almost every train goes through Marseille. To: **Cannes** (3½hr., 8 per day, 155F/€23.63); **Marseille** (35min., about 21 trains per day, 38F/€5.80); and **Nice** (3-4hr., 8 per day 171F/€26.07). Ticket window open daily 5am-10pm. Reservations and info open daily 9am-7pm. (**Note:** Some trains to and from Marseille are actually buses; check the departure info before leaving. If it says "car", your "train" is actually a bus.)

Buses: av. de l'Europe (☎04 42 91 26 80), off av. des Belges. Companies compete for the heavy commuter traffic to **Marseille,** with buses almost every 10min. **SATAP** (☎04 42 99 20 80) serves **Avignon** (2hr.; M-Sa 5 per day, 1 on Su; 86F/€13.11). **Phocéens**

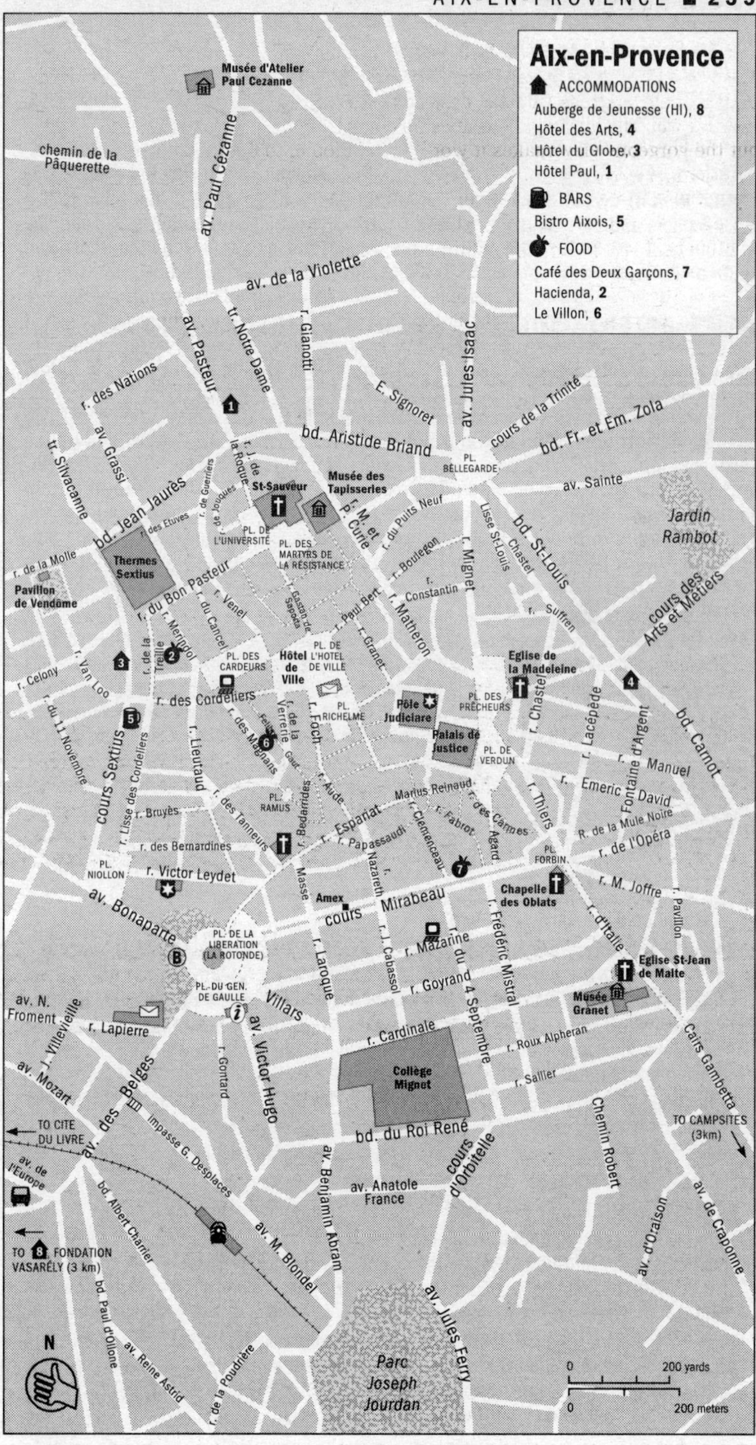
Aix-en-Provence
ACCOMMODATIONS
Auberge de Jeunesse (HI), 8
Hôtel des Arts, 4
Hôtel du Globe, 3
Hôtel Paul, 1
BARS
Bistro Aixois, 5
FOOD
Café des Deux Garçons, 7
Hacienda, 2
Le Villon, 6
Musée d'Atelier Paul Cezanne
chemin de la Pâquerette
av. Paul Cézanne
av. de la Violette
av. Pasteur
tr. Notre Dame
r. Gianotti
av. Jules Isaac
E. Signoret
cours de la Trinité
bd. Fr. et Em. Zola
bd. Aristide Briand
PL. BELLEGARDE
av. Sainte
Jardin Rambot
r. des Nations
av. Grassi
tr. Silvacanne
bd. Jean Jaurès
Musée des Tapisseries
St-Sauveur
PL. DE L'UNIVERSITÉ
PL. DES MARTYRS DE LA RÉSISTANCE
r. du Puits Neuf
r. Boulegon
r. Constantin
r. Mignet
Lisse St-Louis
bd. St-Louis
cours des Arts et Métiers
r. de la Molle
Pavillon de Vendôme
Thermes Sextius
r. du Bon Pasteur
r. Venel
r. du Cancel
r. Paul Bert
r. Matheron
r. Granet
r. Suffren
Eglise de la Madeleine
r. Celony
r. Van Loo
r. des Cordeliers
PL. DES CARDEURS
Hôtel de Ville
PL. DE L'HOTEL DE VILLE
PL. RICHELME
r. Foch
Pôle Judiciare
Palais de Justice
PL. DES PRÊCHEURS
PL. DE VERDUN
r. Chastel
r. Lacépède
Fontaine d'Argent
bd. Carnot
r. Manuel
r. Emeric David
r. du 11 Novembre
cours Sextius
r. Lisse des Cordeliers
r. Lieutaud
r. des Magnans
r. Bruyès
PL. RAMUS
r. Aude
r. Espariat
Marius Reinaud
r. Fabrot
r. des Carmes
r. Thiers
R. de la Mule Noire
r. de l'Opéra
r. des Tanneurs
r. des Bernardines
r. Papassaudi
r. Clemenceau
PL. FORBIN
PL. NIOLLON
r. Victor Leydet
Masse
Nazareth
Amex
cours Mirabeau
Chapelle des Oblats
r. M. Joffre
r. Pavillon
r. d'Italie
av. Bonaparte
PL. DE LA LIBERATION (LA ROTONDE)
PL. DU GEN. DE GAULLE
r. Laroque
r. J. Cabassol
r. Mazarine
r. du 4 Septembre
r. Frédéric Mistral
r. Goyrand
Eglise St-Jean de Malte
Musée Granet
av. N. Froment
r. Lapierre
Villars
av. Victor Hugo
r. Gontard
r. Cardinale
r. Roux Alpheran
r. Sallier
Collège Mignet
Cours Gambetta
J. Villevieille
av. Mozart
av. des Belges
impasse G. Desplaces
Chemin Robert
TO CITÉ DU LIVRE
bd. du Roi René
cours d'Orbitelle
TO CAMPSITES (3km)
av. de l'Europe
av. Benjamin Abram
av. Anatole France
av. d'Oraison
av. de Craponne
bd. Albert Charrier
av. M. Blondel
TO 8 FONDATION VASARÉLY (3 km)
bd. Paul d'Ollone
av. Reine Astrid
r. de la Poudrière
av. Jules Ferry
Parc Joseph Jourdan
N
0 200 yards
0 200 meters

PROVENCE

Cars (☎04 93 85 66 61) goes to **Cannes** (2½hr., 2 per day, 133F/€20.28) and **Nice** (4hr., 2 per day, 140F/€21.35). **Ceyte** (☎04 90 93 74 90) runs to **Arles** (1¾hr.; M-Sa 5 per day, 1 on Su; 70F/€10.67). Ask for under-26 student discounts for Nice or Cannes (ISIC required). Baggage service open M-Sa 7:20am-5:30pm, 10F/€1.53 per bag. Info desk open daily 7:30am-6:30pm; tickets 6:45am-6pm.

Taxis: ☎04 42 27 71 11. 24hr. 50-60F/€7.62-9.15 from train station to hostel.

Bike Rental: Cycles Zammit, 27 rue Mignet (☎04 42 23 19 53), between pl. des Prêcheurs and pl. Bellegarde. Bikes 50F/€7.62 per half-day, 80F/€12.20 per day, 200F/€30.49 Sa-Tu, 400F/€60.98 per week. Passport or driver's license deposit. Open Tu-Sa 9am-12:30pm and 3-7:30pm. AmEx/MC/V.

ORIENTATION AND PRACTICAL INFORMATION

The **cours Mirabeau** sweeps through the center of town, linking **La Rotonde** (a.k.a. **pl. du Général de Gaulle**) to the west with **pl. Forbin** to the east. Fountain-dodging traffic along the *cours* separates cafés on one side from banks on the other. The mostly pedestrian *vieille ville* snuggles inside the *périphérique*—a ring of boulevards including bd. Carnot and cours Sextius. The **tourist office** and the central terminus for city buses are on **pl. du Général de Gaulle.** To reach them from the train station, go straight onto av. Victor Hugo and bear left at the fork, staying on av. Victor Hugo (5min.) until it feeds into **La Rotonde.** The tourist office is on the left, between av. des Belges and av. Victor Hugo. To get there from the bus station, go up av. de l'Europe, take a left onto av. des Belges and follow it to La Rotonde. The tourist office will be on the right.

Tourist Office: 2 pl. du Général de Gaulle (☎04 42 16 11 61; fax 04 42 16 11 62). Provides tours by foot, dinky little train, and bus, some in English. Hotel reservations service July-Aug. daily 9am-8pm. Free Internet 8-10pm. Sells city museum pass for 40-60F/€6.10-9.15 and "Visa for Aix" card (10F/€1.53) with reduced rate to museums. Open July-Aug. daily 8:30am-10pm; Sept.-June M-Sa 8:30am-10pm, Su 10am-6pm.

Budget Travel: Wasteels, 7 cours Sextius (☎08 03 88 70 28). Open M-F 9:30am-12:30pm and 2-6pm, Sa 9:30am-12:30pm.

Money: Change Nazareth, 7 rue Nazareth (☎04 42 38 28 28), off cours Mirabeau, behind Monoprix. Open July-Aug. M-Sa 9am-7pm; Sept.-June M-Sa 9am-6:30pm.

American Express: in Afat Voyages, 15 cours Mirabeau (☎04 42 26 93 93; fax 04 42 26 79 03). Open July-Aug. M-Sa 9am-7:30pm, Su 10am-2pm; Sept.-June M-F 9am-6:30pm, Sa 9am-1pm and 2-5pm.

English Bookstore: Paradox Bookstore, 15 rue du 4 Septembre (☎04 42 26 47 99). New and used books. Also videos, CD-ROMs, and job listings. Open M-Sa 9am-12:30pm and 2-6:30pm. Also, check out the **Cité du Livre** (see **Sights,** below).

Laundromat: Lavomatique, 15 rue Jacques de la Iroquois (☎06 08 01 02 13). Open daily 7am-8pm. Also at 3 rue Fonderie (open daily 7am-8pm), and 3 rue Fernand Dol (open daily 7am-8pm).

Help Lines: SIDA Info Service (☎08 00 84 08 00) is an AIDS hotline. **SOS Viol** (☎04 91 56 04 10) is a rape hotline. Call **SOS Médecins** (☎04 42 26 24 00) for medical advice (24hr.). **Service des Etrangers** (☎04 42 96 89 48) helps out foreigners.

Hospital: av. des Tamaris (☎04 42 33 50 00).

Police: 10 av. de l'Europe (☎04 42 25 99 11), near the Cité du Livre.

Internet Access: Millennium, 6 rue Mazarine (☎04 42 27 39 11), off cours Mirabeau. 20F/€3.05 per hr. Open daily 10am-2am. Also **Virtu@us,** 40 rue Cordeliers (☎04 42 26 02 30). 15F/€2.29 per 30min., 25F/€3.81 per hr. Open M-Sa 10am-1am, Su 2pm-1am.

Post Office: 2 rue Lapierre (☎04 42 16 01 50), just off La Rotonde. Open M-F 8:30am-6:45pm, Sa 8:30am-noon. **Currency exchange.** The **annex,** 1 pl. de l'Hôtel de Ville (☎04 42 63 04 66), has the same services. Open M-F 8am-6:30pm, W-Th 8:30am-6:30pm, Sa 8am-noon. **Postal code:** 13100.

ACCOMMODATIONS AND CAMPING

There are few inexpensive hotels near the city center, and during the festival they may be booked in advance. Reserve early or hope for cancellations.

Hôtel du Globe, 74 cours Sextius (☎04 42 26 03 58; fax 04 42 26 13 68). 5min. from town. Spacious rooms with pristine bathrooms and TVs; some have balconies. Breakfast 49F/€7.97. Reception 24hr. Singles 180F/€27.44, with shower 200F/€30.49; singles and doubles with shower 298F/€45.54, with bath 335F/€51.07; 2 small beds with shower 335F/€51.07, with bath 360F/€54.88; triples with shower 389F/€59.30, with bath 399F/€60.83; quads with bath 448F/€68.30. Extra bed 55F/€8.39.

Hôtel Paul, 10 av. Pasteur (☎04 42 43 23 89; fax 04 42 63 17 80; hotel.paul@wanadoo.fr), past the Cathédrale St-Sauveur. Spacious, simple, immaculate rooms in a bright and modern hotel; some with gratuitously sized bathrooms. Breakfast 28F/€4.30. Reception 7am-10pm, closed Su noon-6pm. Singles with shower 203F/€31; doubles with shower 206F/€31.40; triples 309F/€47.10, quads (2 adults and 2 kids) 362F/€55.20; rooms facing garden about 60F/€9.15 more. MC/V.

Hôtel des Arts, 69 bd. Carnot at rue Portalis (☎04 42 38 11 77; fax 04 42 26 77 31). Identical, compact, modern rooms. All rooms have shower, toilet, phone, and TV. Breakfast 28F/€4.27. Reception 24hr. Singles and doubles 149-205F/€22.72-31.25, depending on whether you face noisy bd. Carnot or the quiet rue de la Fonderie. MC/V.

Campsites: Two campgrounds lie outside of town, accessible by bus #3 from La Rotonde at the "Trois Sautets" and "Val St-André" stops, respectively. **Arc-en-Ciel,** rte. de Nice, is 2km from the city center (☎04 42 26 14 28). Small, comfortable campsite is divided by the Arc–several sites have a view of Cézanne's Pont des Trois Sautets. Pool and hot showers, multilingual management. 36F/€5.80 per person, 32F/€4.88 per site, parking included. **Chantecler,** av. St-André, by rte. de Nice, is 2km from the city center (☎04 42 26 12 98; fax 04 42 27 33 53). Sites have views of Mont Ste-Victoire on a quiet, wooded hill. Pool, impeccable hot showers and restrooms, restaurant, and bar. Open year-round. Reception 8am-11pm. June-Aug. 32F/€4.88 per person, 37F/€5.64 per site; Sept.-May 31F/€4.73 and 36F/€5.49.

FOOD

Aix's culinary reputation stands on its sweets. The city's *bonbon* is the *calisson d'Aix*, a small iced marzipan-and-melon treat created in 1473. Other specialties include soft nougat and hard praline candies. Check out the pâtisseries on rue Espariat or rue d'Italie; rue d'Italie also has bakeries, charcuteries, and fruit stands. The roads north of cours Mirabeau are packed with restaurants, as is **rue de la Verrerie,** off rue des Cordeliers. For orgasmic fruit and the freshest vegetables, try the markets on pl. de la Madeleine (Tu, Th, and Sa 7am-1pm) and pl. Richelme (daily, same times). Supermarket aficionados can choose from three **Petit Casinos,** at 3 cours d'Orbitelle (☎04 42 27 61 43; open M-Sa 8am-1pm and 4-8pm), 16 rue Italie (open M-Sa 8am-1pm and 4:30-8pm, Su 8:30am-12:45pm), and 5 rue Sapora (open M and W-Sa 8:30am-7:30pm). The cheapest meal in town, if they'll let you in, has to be at the university **Cafétéria Les Gazelles,** where local students get traditional Provençal cuisine every day for 15F-25F/€2.29-3.81. Take av. Victor Hugo from La Rotonde, turn left on bd. du Roi René, and then right on cours d'Orbitelle, which turns into av. J. Ferry. Pass Parc Jourdan and it's up the incline to the left (15min. from city center). (Open M-F 11:45am-1:30pm and 6:45-8pm, Sa-Su 11:45am-1pm and 6:45-8pm. Closed July.)

The Aixois like nothing better than to watch each other preen, and their cafés along **cours Mirabeau** encourage a polite voyeurism. Though eating on Mirabeau is generally more expensive, an espresso at the ancient gilt-and-mirrored **Café des Deux Garçons** won't kill you. The former watering hole of Cézanne and Zola, affectionately known as the "Deux Gs," charges a mere 9F/€1.37 for a coffee (12F/€1.83 after 10pm). (☎04 42 26 00 51. Open daily 6am-2am.)

At lunch and dinner-time, little restaurants spill their colorful tables into the squares of Aix. One mouth-waterer is **Hacienda,** 7 rue Mérindol, on pl. des Fontêtes off pl. des Cardeurs. (☎04 42 27 00 35. Lunch *menus* 55-65F/€8.39-9.91. Dinner *menu* 90F/€13.72. Reserve in advance, but if you show up, you may be lucky and get a seat. Closed Aug. Open M-Th noon-2pm, F-Sa noon-10pm.) Or try **Le Villon,** 14 rue Félibre Gaut, off rue des Cordeliers. There's outside seating, but inside there's candlelight and jazz, even at lunchtime. (☎04 42 27 35 27. Lunch *menu* 63F/€9.61; dinner *menu* 75-118F/€11.43-17.99. Open M-Sa noon-2pm and 6-11pm. MC/V.)

SIGHTS

Every corner of Aix has some remarkable edifice and every *place* has its own museum. individual discovery is best—those who hike from exhibit to exhibit are likely to miss Aix's languorous charm. All museums but the Fondation Vasarely are included on a **pass** (60F/€9.15, students 40F/€6.10; available at the tourist office or any museum). Or purchase the "Visa for Aix," sold at tourist office or Cézanne's house, which gives you reduced price at museums, a free tour of Thermes Sextius, and half-price on a town tour of your choice (Visa 10F/€1.53).

THE CHEMIN DE CEZANNE. A self-guided walking tour (2hr.) moves through the landmarks of Aix's most famous son. An English brochure (free at the tourist office) and sidewalk bronze markers lead you around the artist's birthplace and hangouts. In his studio, the **Atelier Paul Cézanne,** the artist's beret still hangs in the corner of a room filled with paint-smeared palettes and the props he used for still-lifes, as though he might step inside from the overgrown garden at any moment and pick them up. *(9 av. Paul Cézanne. Take bus #21 north of Aix. Or just walk up av. Paul Cézanne (10min.). ☎04 42 21 06 53. Open July-Aug. daily 10am-6:30pm; Apr.-May. and Sept. 10am-noon and 2:30-6pm; Oct.-Mar. 10am-noon and 2-5pm. 35F/€5.34 in summer; 25F/€3.81 in winter; students, children, and seniors 10F/€1.53.)*

FONDATION VASARELY. This funky black-and-white museum is an absolute must-see for modern art fans. Designed in the 1970s by the Hungarian-born artist Victor Vasarely, famed for his eye-boggling geometrics and the development of "kineticism," this building contains some of the old man's most monumental and original work in eight huge hexagonal spaces. *(Av. Marcel-Pagnol, Jas-de-Bouffan, next to the youth hostel. ☎04 42 20 01 09. Open July-Sept. daily 10am-7pm; Oct.-May 10am-1pm and 2-6pm. 40F/€6.10, students and ages 7-18 25F/€3.81.)*

CATHEDRALE ST-SAVEUR. A dramatic mix of Romanesque, Gothic, and Baroque naves built on (and with) stones from a preexisting Roman site, this church is pure architectural whimsy. The 16th-century carved panels of the main portal remain in mint condition. During the Revolution, the bas-relief representing a "transfiguration" was completely destroyed, leaving a blank space above the doors, and all the statues in the great front were decapitated. They were recapitated in the 19th century with disappointing new heads—the originals are lost. *(Rue Gaston de Saporta, on pl. de l'Université. ☎04 42 23 45 65. Open daily 8am-noon and 2-6pm, except during services.)*

PAVILLON DE VENDOME. In the winter, this 17th-century building houses paintings and furniture from the turn of the 18th century, while in summer there are a variety of temporary exhibits. The glorious gardens are pure Aix, with soothing smells of boxwood and roses, a fountain, and shrubs cutting into swirling green merengues. *(32 rue Célony. ☎04 42 21 05 78. Museum open July-Aug. daily 10am-6pm, Sept.-May 9:45am-noon and 2-5pm. 20F/€3.05, students 10F/€1.53, in winter 10F/€1.53. Gardens open daily 9am to at least 5:30pm. Free.)*

CITE DU LIVRE. This former match factory has been turned into cultural center, with three major components. The **Bibliothèque Méjanes** contains the largest library in the region and a gallery of contemporary art. Bookended by giant, rusty steel replicas of French classics, this bright library stocks current *Newsweeks* and a good collection of British and American literature. The **Discothèque** loans a wide selection of music from around the world. The air-conditioned **Videothèque d'Art Lyrique** affords the opportunity to view operas, ballets, and concerts of past *Festivals d'Aix* for free. *(8-10 rue des Allumettes, southeast of La Rotonde. Bibliothèque and Discothèque ☎04 42 25 98 88. Both open Tu-Th noon-6pm; W and Sa 10am-6pm. Videothèque ☎04 42 37 70 89. Open Tu-F 1-6pm, Sa 10am-noon and 1-6pm. While it's all open to the public, borrowing from the Cité requires a 95F/€14.48 membership.)*

OTHER SIGHTS. The **Musée Granet** contains several lesser-known Cézannes, a smattering of works by David, Ingres, and Delacroix, as well as an archaeological section. Only part of the full collection is accessible—it's undergoing extensive renovations until 2006. *(Pl. St-Jean-Marie-de-Malte. ☎04 42 38 14 70. Open July-Aug. daily 10am-6pm; Sept.-May W-M 10am-noon and 2-6pm. 30F/€4.57, ages 18-25 15F/€2.29, under 18 free.)* A fine collection of 17th- and 18th-century tapestries hangs in the **Musée des Tapisseries.** The highlight is the series depicting the story of Don Quixote. *(Palais Archiépiscopal, 2nd fl., 28 pl. des Martyrs de la Résistance. ☎04 42 23 09 91. Open July-Aug. daily 10am-5:45pm; Sept.-June W-M 8am-noon and 2-5:45pm. In summer 20F/€3.05, students 10F/€1.53; in winter 10F/€1.53, students free. Free tours in French July-Aug. F 2pm.)*

NIGHTLIFE

Partying is a year-round pastime in Aix. Most clubs open at 11:30pm but don't get going until 2am. Pubs and bars have earlier hours. **Rue de la Verrerie** has the highest concentration of bars and clubs; candlelit cafés line the **Forum des Cardeurs,** behind the Hôtel de Ville. House and club music prevails at **Le Richelm,** 24 rue de la Verrerie, literally an underground club, connected to a swanky bar. (☎04 42 23 49 29. Cover includes 1 drink: Tu-Th 60F/€9.15, F 80F/€12.20, Sa 100F/€15.25. Women free Tu-Th. Open Tu-Sa 11:30pm-dawn.) **Bistro Aixois,** 37 cours Sextius, off la Rotonde, packs loads of students and alcohol into a cramped space. (☎04 42 27 50 10. Open daily 6:30pm-3 or 4am. MC/V.) Techno, dance, R&B, house and all bodies surge at **Le Mistral,** 3 rue F. Mistral; don't show up here in shorts, jeans, or sandals. (☎04 42 38 16 49. Tu ladies night, free with one drink, men cover 100F/€15.25; W-F 70F/€10.67 cover includes one drink, Sa 100F/€15.25 cover includes one drink. Open Tu-Sa 11:30pm-5am.) **Le Scat,** 11 rue Verrerie, is a happening jazz, rock, and dance club. (☎04 42 23 00 23. Concerts nightly 1am; free M-Th, F-Sa 80F/€12.20 cover includes one drink. Open M-Sa 11pm-whenever.) **Ciné Mazarin,** 6 rue Laroque (☎08 36 68 72 70), off cours Mirabeau, and **Renoir,** 24 cours Mirabeau (☎08 36 68 72 70), project French films and several foreign films at a time, some in English (48F/€7.32, students 38F/€5.80, under 13 30F/€4.57).

FESTIVALS

Aix's overwhelming festival season kicks off in the beginning of June with **Cinestival,** a week-long film festival. If you pick up the free *"billet scoop"* from the tourist office, it's 20F/€3.05 per film. Aix's **International Music Festival,** a famous series of operas and orchestral concerts, is held from June to July. (Ticket office at 11 rue Gaston de Sapora. ☎04 42 17 34 34; www.aix-en-provence.com/festartlyrique. A 100F/€15.25 ticket bought in April lets you sit in on master classes and rehearsals.) For two weeks at the end of July and the beginning of August, Aix holds a **Dance Festival** with ballet, modern, and jazz performances. (☎04 42 96 05 01, reservations 04 42 23 41 24; call M-F 10am-noon and 2-5pm. 90-250F/€13.72-38.12, students 50-160F/€7.62-24.39.) Tickets can be bought at the tourist office or at 1 pl. John Rewald (before June 29 M-F 2-5pm, from July 2-July 15 M-F 10am-1pm and 2-5pm and from July 16 M-Sa 10am-1pm and 2-5pm). For two weeks in early July, the city puts on a two-week **Jazz Festival,** with concerts also including salsa and big band (30-120F/€4.57-18.30). The **Office des Fêtes et de la Culture,** Espace Forbin, 1 pl. John Rewald (☎04 42 63 06 75), can fill you in on all the festivals. **Aix en Musique,** 3 pl. John Rewald (☎04 42 21 69 69), sponsors concerts all year.

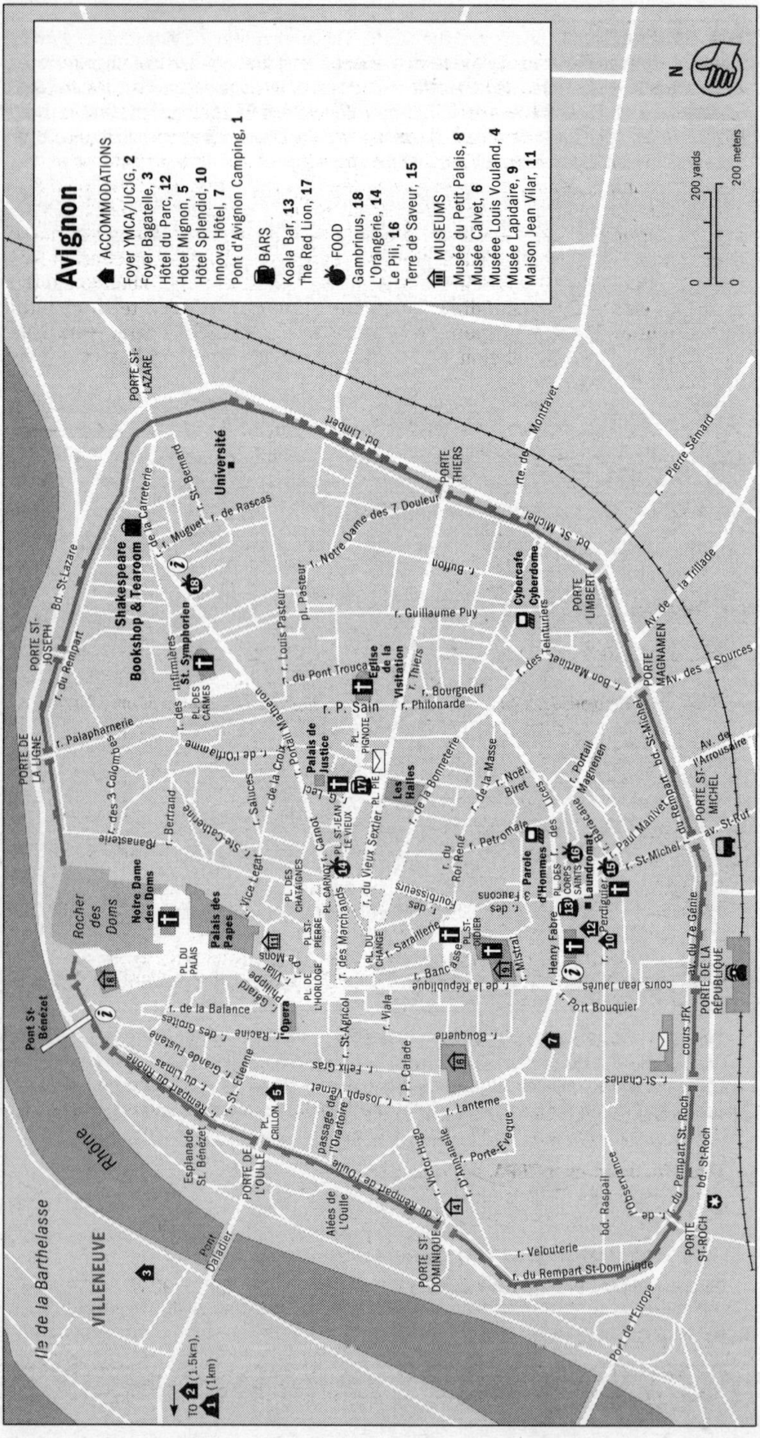

Avignon

ACCOMMODATIONS
- Foyer YMCA/UCJG, **2**
- Foyer Bagatelle, **3**
- Hôtel du Parc, **12**
- Hôtel Mignon, **5**
- Hôtel Splendid, **10**
- Innova Hôtel, **7**
- Pont d'Avignon Camping, **1**

BARS
- Koala Bar, **13**
- The Red Lion, **17**

FOOD
- Gambrinus, **18**
- L'Orangerie, **14**
- Le Pili, **16**
- Terre de Saveur, **15**

MUSEUMS
- Musée du Petit Palais, **8**
- Musée Calvet, **6**
- Musée Louis Vouland, **4**
- Musée Lapidaire, **9**
- Maison Jean Vilar, **11**

0 — 200 yards
0 — 200 meters

N

TO 2 (1.5km), 1 (1km)

AVIGNON

The crooked rabbit-run of Avignon's streets is crowned by the unparalleled Palais des Papes, a sprawling Gothic fortress known in its time as "the biggest and strongest house in the world." Some 700 years ago, political dissent in Italy led the homesick French pontiff Clement V to shift the papacy to Avignon. During this "Second Babylonian Captivity of the Church," as it was dubbed by the stunned Romans (see p. 7), seven popes erected and expanded Avignon's Palais, making the city a "Rome away from Rome." Gregory XI returned the papacy to Rome in 1377, but his reform-minded Italian successor so infuriated the cardinals that they elected an alternate pope, who again set up court in Avignon, beginning the Great Schism. In 1403 the last "anti-pope" abandoned the luxurious ecclesiastical buildings, but the town remained Papal territory until the Revolution. Though the popes have gone, the city seems to carry on its role as a capital of worldly religion, and the rough energy of the papal courts spills out of history into modern Avignon.

Avignon (pop. 100,000) is chiefly known for the famous Festival d'Avignon, a hugely popular theatrical celebration. From early July to early August, performers, singers, and con men roam the streets, entertaining hordes of French tourists. Prices soar, accommodations become scarce, and authorities crack down on festival-induced vagrancy. Avignon quiets down after the festival, but its sights and street life still make the city a good base for trips to some of Provence's most beautiful villages: the hamlets of the Alpilles (p. 251) and of the Lubéron (p. 247).

TRANSPORTATION

Trains: porte de la République (☎04 90 27 81 89). To: **Arles** (30min., 10 per day, 36F/€5.49); **Lyon** (2hr., 7 per day, 155F/€23.63); **Marseille** (70min., 6 per day, 94F/€14.33); **Montpellier** (1hr., M-F 12 per day, 80F/€12.20); **Nice** (3½hr., 4 per day, 210F/€32.02); **Nîmes** (30min., M-F 14 per day, 47F/€7.17); and **Toulouse** (3½hr., 6 per day, 210F/€32.02). Info desk and ticket counters open daily 4am-1am. **TGV station and trains:** Get there by taking a shuttle bus (6.50F/€0.99). Shuttle buses run every 10min. 6:15am-11:10pm from stop right near porte de la République, inside city walls. TGV ticket counters open daily 5:40am-10pm. To: **Dijon** (2¾hr., 247F/€37.66, TGV 317F/€48.33); **Lyon** (1hr., 11 per day, TGV 218F/€33.24); and **Paris** (3½hr., 21 per day, 377-425F/€57.48-64.80).

Buses: bd. St-Roch, right of the train station. Info desk (☎04 90 82 07 35) open M-F 8am-6pm, Sa 8am-noon. Buy tickets on bus. Various carriers go to: **Arles** (45min., M-Sa 5 per day, 49F/€7.47); **Les Baux** (1hr., July-Aug. 2 per day, 51F/€7.78); **Marseille** (2hr., 4 per day, 97F/€14.80); **Nîmes** (1-1½hr., 5+ per day, 45F/€6.86); and **St-Rémy** (45min., July-Aug. 2 per day, 34F/€5.18).

Bus Tours: Autocars Lieutaud (☎04 90 86 36 75) runs excursions to **Les Baux, La Camargue, Gordes, Nîmes, Roussillon,** and **Vaison-la-Romaine** for 100-150F/€15.25-22.90 (Apr.-Nov.). **Les Provençals** (Avignon ☎04 32 74 32 74, Villeneuve☎04 90 25 61 33) goes to many nearby locales. June-Oct. W-F half-day 150F/€22.90, full day 250F/€38.12. Pass (see **Sights**) gets you 20-30F/€3.05-4.57 off.

Local Transportation: TCRA, av. de Lattre de Tassigny (☎04 32 74 18 32), near porte de la République. Tickets 6.50F/€0.99, *carnet* of 10 or unlimited weekly pass 50F/€7.62. Office open M-F 8:30am-12:30pm and 1:30-6:30pm, Sa 9am-noon.

Taxis: Radio Taxi, porte de la République (☎04 90 82 20 20). 24hr.

Bike Rental: Aymard Cycles Peugeot, 80 rue Guillaume Puy (☎04 90 86 32 49). 60F/€9.15 per day, 240F/€36.59 per week. 800F/€121.97 deposit. Open Tu-Sa 8am-noon and 2-7pm. MC/V.

Bus tours: Autocars Lieutaud (☎04 90 85 57 07) offers excursions to **Les Baux, La Camargue,** and **Vaison-la-Romaine** (Apr.-Oct. 100-150F/€15.25-22.90).

ORIENTATION AND PRACTICAL INFORMATION

Avignon's 14th-century ramparts enclose a labyrinth of alleyways, squares, and cramped little streets. To reach the tourist office from the train station, walk straight through porte de la République onto cours Jean Jaurès. The tourist office is about 200m up on the right. Cours Jean Jaurès becomes rue de la République and leads directly to **pl. de l'Horloge,** Avignon's central square. Just southeast of l'Horloge, little pedestrian streets glitter with boutiques. At night, lone travelers should avoid the area around rue Thiers and rue Philonarde and stay on well-lit paths. Avignon also supports many car thieves and pickpockets, especially during the festival.

Tourist Office: 41 cours Jean Jaurès (☎04 32 74 32 74; fax 04 90 82 95 03). Open July M-Sa 10am-8pm and Su 10am-5pm; Apr.-June and Aug.-Sept. M-Sa 9am-6pm; Oct.-Mar. M-F 9am-6pm, Sa 9am-1pm and 2-5pm, Su 10am-noon. **Annex** at pont St-Bénezet open Apr.-Oct. daily 10am-7pm. **Bureau du Festival,** 8 bis rue de Mons (☎04 90 27 66 50), has festival info. Reservations start mid-June (☎04 90 14 14 14).

City Tours: Les Trains Touristiques (☎04 90 82 64 44). Groups to Palais des Papes from the tourist office. 35min. city tours; longer ones include garden tours of the Rocher des Doms. Mar. 15-Oct. 15 daily 10am-7pm. City tours every 35min., 35F/€5.34; with garden tour 45F/€6.86.

English Bookstore: Shakespeare Bookshop and Tearoom, 155 rue Carreterie (☎04 90 27 38 50), down rue Carnot toward the ramparts. Paperbacks and English cream teas. Open Tu-Sa 9:30am-12:30pm and 2-6:30pm.

Youth Information: Espace Info-Jeunes, 102 rue Carreterie (☎04 90 14 04 05). Info on jobs, study, health care, housing, and work. Open M-F 9am-noon and 2-5:30pm.

Laundromat: 66 pl. des Corps Saints (☎04 90 27 16 85). Also at 48 rue Carreterie. Both open daily 7am-8pm.

Police: bd. St-Roch (☎04 90 16 81 00), left of the train station.

Hospital: 305 rue Raoul Follereau (☎04 32 75 33 33), south of the town center.

Internet Access: Parole d'Hommes, 46 rue des Lices (☎04 90 86 98 08). Lots of computers, rarely crowded. 25F/€3.81 per 30min.; 35F/€4.57 per hr. Open M-Sa 10am-9:30pm. **Cyberdrome,** 68 rue Guillaume Puy (☎04 90 16 05 15). Hip café with 15 stations and games. 20F/€3.05 per 30min.; 30F/€4.57 per hr. Open daily 8am-1am.

Post Office: cours Président Kennedy, near porte de la République (☎04 90 27 54 00). **Currency exchange.** For Poste Restante specify **Poste Restante-Avignon.** Open M-F 8am-7pm, Sa 8am-noon. **Branch office** on pl. Pie (☎04 90 14 70 70). Open M-F 8:30am-12:30pm and 1:30-6:30pm, Sa 8:30am-noon. **Postal code:** 84000.

ACCOMMODATIONS AND CAMPING

Avignon's hotels and *foyers* usually have room outside of festival season, but unreserved beds vanish once the theater troupes hit town. Also note that these prices all go up 50-100F/€7.62-15.25 during festival season in July. The tourist office has a list of organizations that set up cheap housing during the festival; you might also consider staying in Arles, Nîmes, Orange, and Tarascon, and commuting by train (36F/€5.49, 47F/€7.17, 29F/€4.42, and 24F/€3.66, respectively). Note that all hotels and campsites sell reduced-price tickets to the Palais.

Foyer YMCA/UCJG, 7bis chemin de la Justice, Villeneuve (☎04 90 25 46 20; fax 04 90 25 30 64; info@ymca-avignon.com). From the train station, turn left and follow the city wall; cross the second bridge (pont Daladier) and the Ile Barthelasse and go straight ahead. After 200m take a left onto chemin de la Justice; the foyer will be up the hill on your left (30min.). From the post office, take bus #10 (dir: "Les Angles-Grand Angles") to "Général Leclerc" or #11 (dir: "Villeneuve-Grand Terme") to "Pont d'Avignon." Clean, modern, and cheerfully decorated rooms with terraces; great views of the Palais or pool.

Breakfast 25F/€3.81. Reception 9:30am-noon and 1:30-6pm. On summer weekends, reception is held at on-site restaurant, but somebody's always around. Reserve ahead. *Demi-pension* obligatory in July. Apr.-Oct. 20 170F/€25.92 per person, 110F/€16.77 per person for 2 people, 100F/€15.25 per person for 3 people; rates drop after 3 nights and 30% in other months. AmEx/MC/V.

Foyer Bagatelle, Ile de la Barthelasse (☎04 90 86 30 39 or 04 90 85 78 45; fax 04 90 27 16 23). Follow directions for the YMCA to pont Daladier; Bagatelle is just across it on the right (10min. from the town center). Or take bus #10 or 11 to "La Barthelasse." Incomparable view of the city; this hostel is right on the banks of the Rhône. Simple 4-, 6-, or 8-bed rooms, plus some doubles. Internet access 1F/€0.15 per min. Supermarket, 2 cafeterias, and bike rental (100F/€15.25 per day with 1000F/€152.46 deposit). Breakfast priced à la carte. Reception 11am-10pm. Lockout 2-5pm. Beds 65F/€9.91; doubles 140F/€21.35. Excellent **camping** facilities available in the dense shade of plane trees. Reception 8am-10pm. 1 person and tent 44F/€6.71, 2 people and tent 71F/€10.82. Electricity 16F/€2.44. MC/V.

Hôtel Mignon, 12 rue Joseph Vernet (☎04 90 82 17 30; fax 04 90 85 78 46; hotelmignon@wanadoo.fr). Fashion-conscious hotel on a chic street near great shopping; different color scheme in each comfortable, well-equipped room. Breakfast included. Parking 38F/€5.80. Singles with bath 269.40F/€41.07; doubles with bath 298.80F/€45.56; triples with bath 358.20F/€54.61, quads 467.20F/€71.23. MC/V.

Hôtel Splendid, 17 rue Perdiguier (☎04 90 86 14 46; fax 04 90 85 38 55), near the tourist office. Charming rooms on a quiet street in a busy area; some quite small. Breakfast 28F/€4.27. Reception 7am-10:30pm. Singles with shower 170-240F/€25.92-36.59; doubles with shower 240-300F/€36.59-45.74. Extra bed 30F/€4.57. MC/V.

Hôtel du Parc, 18 rue Agricol Perdiguier (☎04 90 82 71 55; fax 04 90 85 64 86), right off cours Jean Jaurès, near the tourist office. Sweet-smelling, modern rooms with a rustic feel. Right across from the Hôtel Splendid, and just as good. Breakfast 30F/€4.57. Reserve well ahead. Reception noon-10pm. Singles 185F/€28.21, with shower 245F/€37.35; doubles with bath 280F/€42.69; triples with bath 300F/€45.74. MC/V.

Innova Hôtel, 100 rue Joseph Vernet (☎04 90 82 54 10; fax 04 90 82 52 39). Clean, spare, perfectly adequate rooms within moments of everything. Breakfast 30F/€4.57. Bike storage available. Singles 150F/€22.90; doubles with shower 230F/€35.06, with bath 250F/€38.12. MC/V.

Camping: Pont d'Avignon, 300 Ile de la Barthelasse, 10min. past Foyer Bagatelle (☎04 90 80 63 50; fax 04 90 85 22 12). Hot showers, laundry, restaurant, supermarket, pool, and sports courts. Reception 8:30am-8:30pm; July-Aug. until 10:45pm. Open Mar. 27-Oct.28. June-early Sept. 1 person and tent 67-87.50F/€10.21-13.34; 2 people and tent 95-125F/€14.48-19.06; electricity 15F/€2.29; extra person 20-25F/€3.05-3.81. Late Mar.-May and early Sept.-Oct. 1 person and tent 43-46.50F/€6.56-7.09; 2 people and tent 60-65F/€9.15-9.91; electricity 15-17F/€2.29-2.59; extra person 18-19F/€2.74-2.90. MC/V.

FOOD

There's a smattering of lively restaurants in crooked **rue des Teinturiers.** The cafés of **pl. de l'Horloge** are good for a drink after dinner, when clowns, mimes, and street musicians milk the crowds for smiles and centimes. The Vietnamese restaurants that are scattered throughout the city, usually found on small impasses or in alleys off major thoroughfares, are often great budget options. For those with midnight-snacking tendencies and few dietary scruples, **snack bars** line the boulevards and places of Avignon, serving up all manner of hot, greasy sandwiches as well the occasional vegetarian option. **Parc de Rocher des Doms,** overlooking the Rhône, provides good picnic spots and has an outdoor café near the pond. **Les Halles,** the large indoor **market** on pl. Pie (Tu-Su 7am-1pm) promises no end of regional produce. The same fare may be less expensive at the **open-air markets** outside the city walls near porte St-Michel (Sa-Su 7am-noon) and on pl. Crillon (F 7am-noon). Go down to the basement for **Shopi** super market, rue de la République, about 100m from the tourist office (open M-Sa 8:30am-8pm, Su 8am-2pm). Or try the reliable **Petit Casino** on rue Saint Agricol (open M-F 8:30am-1pm and 3-8pm, Sa 9am-1pm and 3-8pm) and at 3 rue Corps Saints (open M-Sa 8am-noon and 2:30-6:30pm).

Terre de Saveur, 1 rue St-Michel (☎04 90 86 68 72), just off pl. des Corps Saints. Homey provençal restaurant makes hearty dishes with organic vegetables and rye bread on the side. Vegetarian *menu* 85F/€12.96; omnivore one 98F/€14.98. *Plats* 38-68F/€5.79-10.37. Open M-Sa 11:30am-2:30pm, during festival also 7-9:30pm. MC/V.

L'Orangerie, 3 pl. Jérusalem (☎04 90 86 86 87), near pl. Carnot. In an expensive city, this restaurant is a real find, offering fresh provincial specialities from tagliatelles to daily market selections. *Menus* 80F/€12.20 and 95F/€14.48. Open M-Sa noon-3pm and 7pm-midnight. Oct-Feb. closed M, Tu, and W nights. MC/V.

Le Pili, 34 pl. des Corps Saints (☎04 90 27 39 53). Serves up sumptuous Mediterranean fare, including pizzas at unbeatable prices. 52F/€7.93 lunch *menu* includes wine. Dinner *menus* 78F/€11.89, 120F/€18.30. Open M-Sa 11:30am-2pm and 6:30-11pm. Closed M night and Sa lunch. MC/V.

Gambrinus, 62 rue Carreterie (☎04 90 86 12 32), 200m down the street from porte St-Lazare. Specializes in huge portions of mussels. Traditional *moules marinières* with fries (45F/€6.86); *moules à la bière* (50F/€7.62). Beer, you say? The bar has 6 on tap and 60 in bottles (drafts 14F/€2.13). Billiards 10F/€1.53. Open M-Sa 7am-1:30am. Closed Aug. 1-17 and Jan. 1-15. MC/V.

SIGHTS

Avignon has set up a ***Pass*** *system for its sights. At the first monument or museum you visit, you'll pay full admission (regardless of age or status); afterwards you pay only the reduced price. The pass is good for all sights listed here, and can be used for 15 days.*

PALAIS DES PAPES. This golden Gothic palace, the largest in Europe, launches gargoyles out over the city and the Rhône. Its sheer, battlemented walls are oddly cut with the tall, ecclesiastical windows of the Grande Chapelle and the dark cross of the arrow-loops. Begun in 1335 by the third pope of Avignon Benoît XII, and finished less than twenty years later by his successor Clément VI, the papal palace is neatly divided into two styles: the strict, spare grandeur of Benoît's former order (Cistercian), versus the astonishing scale and ostentation of the portion built by the aristocratic Clément.

Although Revolutionary looting stripped the interior of its lavish furnishings, the giant rooms and their frescoed walls are still spectacular. In the Grand Tinel, a long banquet hall, blue canvas flecked with gold stars decks the ceiling, simulating an endless sky. But what dazzles the viewer most in the Palais is the way after it unrolls almost endlessly chamber after chamber. It's almost impossible to come to grips with this place as a whole. An amazingly comprehensive and detailed audio-guide in seven languages is included. The Palais houses exhibitions in the most beautiful rooms every year (May-Sept.), which have recently included Picasso and Rodin; call for details of the 2002 exhibition. *(☎04 90 27 50 74. Open July-Sept. daily 9am-8pm; Apr.-June and Oct. 9am-7pm; Nov. 2-Mar. 14 9:30am-5:45pm; Mar. 15-31 9:30am-6:30pm. Last ticket 1hr. before closing. Palace and exhibition each 46F/€7.01, pass 36F/€5.49; together 56F/€8.54, pass 46F/€7.01.)*

PONT ST-BENEZET. This 12th-century bridge is known to all French children as the "Pont d'Avignon," immortalized in a famous nursery rhyme. In 1177 Bénézet, a shepherd boy, was commanded by angels to build a bridge across the Rhône. He announced his intentions to the population of Avignon, but the people laughed at him, and the Archbishop, derisively pointing to a gigantic boulder in front of the cathedral, told Bénézet that he would have to place the first stone himself. Miraculously, the shepherd heaved up the rock and tossed it into the river. This holy shotput convinced the townspeople, and Bénézet turned to equally miraculous fundraising to finish the bridge by 1190. Despite the divinely chosen location, the bridge has suffered a number of destructive setbacks thanks to warfare and the unruly Rhône. Today it steps into the river and stops only partway across, as if it had made its point with four arches and the rest was understood. Housed on the second arch is the **St-Nicolas Chapel,** dedicated to the patron saint of mariners. You can enjoy the bridge from the riverbanks; it costs 20F/€3.05 (pass 16F/€2.44) to dance on it. *(☎04 90 85 60 16. Includes a detailed audio-guide in 7 languages. Open daily Apr.-Nov. 9am-7pm; July-Sept. open until 8pm; Nov.-Mar. 9:30am-5:45pm.)* Farther down the river, **Pont Daladier** makes it all the way across the river to the campgrounds and offers free views of the broken bridge and the Palais.

MUSEE DU PETIT PALAIS. The big "little" cardinal's palace on the pl. du Palais des Papes is crowded with local art, much of it religious, within view of the shores of Villeneuve. *(☎04 90 86 44 58. Open July-Aug. W-M 10am-1pm and 2-6pm; Sept.-June 9:30am-1pm and 2-5:30pm. 30F/€4.57, pass 15F/€2.29. Oct.-Feb. Su free.)*

MUSEE CALVET. This elegant 18th-century *hôtel particulier* houses a number of paintings by French artists, its most famous work being *Sainte Face* by Bernard Buffet. It also boasts a hall's worth of memorable marble sculptures. *(65 rue Joseph Vernet. ☎04 90 86 33 84. Open W-M 10am-1pm and 2-6pm. 30F/€4.57, pass 15F/€2.29.)*

OTHER SIGHTS. For those with a penchant for the finer things, a 19th-century *hôtel* houses the small but intriguing decorative arts collection of the **Musée Louis Vouland.** *(17 rue Victor Hugo. ☎04 90 86 03 79. Visits available in English with reservation. Open May-Oct. Tu-Sa 10am-noon and 2-6pm, Su 2-6pm; Nov.-Apr. Tu-Sa 2-6pm. 25F/€3.81, pass 10F/€1.53.)* You can inspect all that is chipped, unlimbed, inscribed, and antique in the **Musée Lapidaire.** The collection housed in this small Baroque chapel includes Gallo-Roman statuary and some surprising Egyptian artifacts. *(27 rue de la République. ☎04 90 85 75 38. Open W-M 10am-1pm and 2-6pm. 10F/€1.53, pass 5F/€0.76.)* For those budding paleontologists, the **Musée Requien** may hold some interest. With impressive fossils and the full skeleton of a 35 million-year-old horse, it is worth passing through. *(67 rue Joseph-Vernet. ☎04 90 14 68 56. Open Tu-Sa 9am-noon and 2-6pm. Free.)* Next to the Palais sits the 12th-century **Cathédrale Notre-Dame-des-Doms,** which contains the Flamboyant Gothic tomb of Pope John XXII. *(Open daily 10am-7pm.)* On the hill above the cathedral, the beautifully sculpted **Rocher des Doms park** has vistas of Mont Ventoux, St-Bénézet, and the fortifications of Villeneuve. The **Maison Jean Vilar,** dedicated to the founder of the festival, celebrates the performing arts with recordings, workshops, lectures, exhibits, and free movies. *(8 rue de Mons. ☎04 90 86 59 64. Open Tu-F 9am-noon and 1:30-5:30pm, Sa 10am-5pm. Most exhibits free; otherwise 25F/€3.81, students and those with pass 15F/€2.29.)*

ENTERTAINMENT AND FESTIVALS

Regular performances of opera, drama, and classical music take place in the **Opéra d'Avignon,** pl. de l'Horloge (☎04 90 82 81 40). **Rue des Teinturiers** is lined with theaters holding performances from the early afternoon through the wee hours of the morning, including the **Théâtre du Chien qui Fume** at no. 75 (☎04 90 85 25 87). The **Théâtre du Balcon,** 38 rue Guillaume Puy (☎04 90 85 00 80), and the **Théâtre du Chêne Noir,** 8bis rue Ste-Catherine (☎04 90 82 40 57), are two other busy theaters. The **Utopia Cinéma,** behind the Palais des Papes on 4 rue Escalier Ste-Anne, screens a wide variety of movies in *v.o.* (☎04 90 82 65 36. 32F/€4.88, 10 showings 250F/€38.12.) The **Maison Jean Vilar** (see **Other Sights,** above) shows free videos.

Avignon has surprisingly little nightlife for a city of its size. Brasseries on **cours Jean Jaurès** and **rue de la République** are open late with quiet crowds on their terraces. A few lively bars color **pl. des Corps Saints.** Cheap suds and a major sound system draw boisterous Australians and backpackers to the **Koala Bar,** 2 pl. des Corps Saints. (☎04 90 86 80 87. Beer from 12F/€1.83, drinks from 20F/€3.05. Happy hour W and F-Sa 9-10pm. Open 8:30pm-1:30am, until 1am in winter; 9am-3am during festival.) Avignon university students and world travelers pack **The Red Lion,** 21-23 rue St-Jean Le Vieux, right in pl. Pie. Live music four nights a week, Thursday theme nights and beer from 15F/€2.29. (☎04 90 86 40 25. Open daily 8am-1:30am; happy hour daily 5-8pm.)

The riotous **Festival d'Avignon** is on from early July to early August, as Gregorian chanters rub shoulders with all-night *Odyssey* readers and African dancers. The official festival, also known as the **IN,** is the most prestigious theatrical gathering in Europe and offers at least 30 different venues from factories to cloisters to palaces. (Info and tickets ☎04 90 14 14 14. Festival office ☎04 90 27 66 50; fax 04 90 27 66 83. Tickets free-200F/€30.49 per event. Reservations accepted from mid-June. Tickets also on sale at venue 45min. before the show; students and those under 25 get about a 50% discount.) The cheaper and more experimental **Festival OFF** presents over 400 plays, some in English, from mid-July to early August. (OFFice on pl. du Palais. ☎01 48 05 01 19; www.avignon-off.org. You must go to the venue or the OFFice to get tickets; you cannot call and purchase them in advance. Tickets 50-80F/€7.62-12.20.) You don't always need to buy a ticket to get in on the act—fun, free theater overflows into the streets during the day and particularly at night. The Centre Franco-Américain de Provence sponsors the **French-American Film Workshop** in late June at the Cinéma Vox. The festival showcases feature-length and short films directed by young French and American aspirants, with an occasional attention-grabbing name. Meals, parties, and lectures allow for hobnobbing and name dropping. Films are in *v.o.* with French or English subtitles. (☎04 90 25 93 23. Films 40F/€6.10, morning films 10F/€1.53, day pass 350F/€53.36.)

DAYTRIP FROM AVIGNON: VILLENEUVE-LES-AVIGNON

*The **Bateau Bus** boat, allées de l'Oulle near the Pont Daladier, cruises past Pont St-Bénézet and docks at Villeneuve. From there, a free Petit Train will take you to the town center. (☎04 90 85 62 25. July-Aug. 6 per day 10:30am-6:30pm. Round-trip 40F/€6.10, children 20F/€3.05; 20% off with pass. Get tickets on board or at tourist office in Avignon.) Note: The very last boat to arrive in Villeneuve does not have a free train.*

Villeneuve-lès-Avignon ("new town by Avignon") sits on a hill overlooking Avignon. Founded by the 13th-century French to intimidate their provençal neighbors, it became the home of many of the dignitaries who attended the papal court, earning it the nickname "City of Cardinals." When you need some respite from the street performers during the festival in Avignon, take a short walk across the river to the much calmer Villeneuve, and picnic in the shade of Fort St-André.

La Chartreuse du Val de Bénédiction, rue de la République, is one of the largest Cartusian monasteries in France. The six centuries or so since its construction have only improved it; the back wall of the church has collapsed, making the focus of the nave a glorious and unobstructed view of Fort St-André. (☎04 90 15 24 24. Open Apr.-Sept. daily 9am-6:30pm; Oct.-Mar. 9:30am-5:30pm. 36F/€5.49, students and pass 23F/€3.51.) Crowning Mont Andaon is the Gothic **Fort Saint-André.** Built by King Philip the Fair in the 14th century, its 750m fortified walls and double towers contained an abbey and a little town, while commanding the French side of the Rhône. The shady hill, with its wide views, is perhaps the best picnic spot in all of France. The towers served as prisons after losing their strategic value; you can still see, on the stone floors and walls inside, carvings that the prisoners made to pass their time, with designs such as a dinner plate surrounded by cutlery, Christ, and a ship. (☎04 90 25 45 35. Open Apr.-Sept. daily 10am-1pm and 2-6pm; Oct.-Mar. 10am-noon and 2-5pm. "Twin towers" 26F/€3.96, students and pass 16F/€2.44, 18 and under free.) Equally idyllic is the 11th-century Benedictine **Abbaye Saint-André,** the first major construction on Mont Andaon, located within the confines of the fort. The original buildings were mostly destroyed during the Revolution, but they have been replaced with one of the most beautiful gardens in France. The hidden fountains and arcades of cypresses have views of the Rhône valley and Avignon. The foundations of the first churches on the Mont have been turned into gravel walks in the garden, with olive branch arches and keystones of sky. (☎04 90 25 55 95. Open Apr.-Sept. Tu-Su 10am-12:30pm and 2-6pm; Oct-Mar. Tu-Su 10am-noon and 2-5pm. 20F/€3.05, pass 15F/€2.29.)

Down the hill is the **Musée Municipal Pierre de Luxembourg,** on rue de la République, which features a small collection of both 14th- and 15th-century religious works and 17th- and 18th-century provençal paintings; but its claim to fame is the *Coronation of the Virgin* by Enguran Quarton, which garners a whole room for itself. (☎04 90 27 49 66. Open June 15-Sept. 15 daily 10am-12:30pm and 3-7pm; Sept. 16-June 14 Tu-Su 10am-noon and 2-5:30pm. 20F/€3.05, pass 12F/€1.83.) The most prominent monument visible from Avignon is the Gothic **Tour Philippe Le Bel,** at the intersection of av. Gabriel Péri and Montée de la Tour. It once guarded the end of the Pont St-Bénézet on the French side of the river. A climb of 125 steps takes you to a wind-whipped stone platform with a dizzying view. (☎04 32 70 08 57. Tower open Apr.-Sept. daily 10am-12:30pm and 3-7pm; Oct.-Mar. 10am-noon and 2-5:30pm. 10F/€1.53, students and pass 6F/€0.91.) The **tourist office** is at 1 pl. Charles David. (☎04 90 25 61 33; fax 04 90 27 91. Open July-Aug. M-F 10am-7pm, Sa-Su 10am-1pm and 2:30-7pm; Sept.-June M-Sa 9am-12:30pm and 2-6pm.)

THE LUBERON AND THE VAUCLUSE

"No nature is more beautiful."

—Petrarch

Just when you thought that nothing could possibly be more picturesque than Arles or Avignon, you find a region of such stunning beauty that it leaves you gasping for breath. The Vaucluse, and the neighboring national park of the Lubéron, is where all those perfect postcards of Provence come from. Tiny medieval villages perched on rocky escarpments, fields of lavender as far as the eye can see, and ochre hills that seem to burn in the sunset are a backdrop to the village squares filled with elderly men drinking *pastis* and playing *pétanque*. For centuries, this mini-Eden has been a home and inspiration to writers, from Petrarch to the Marquis de Sade to Samuel Beckett. So when the Avignon festival crowds get too oppressive, head east. Note that although we list a few famous beauties here, you can only find these regions at their untainted best on your own—the happiest visitors are those who wander into the areas left out of guidebooks.

TRANSPORTATION. These regions, of course, are easiest to access by car—but by combining the occasional bus with walking or biking between towns (usually 7-15km), those in no hurry will be rewarded with all the intimacies of Provence's varied landscapes. Locals often choose to hitch, since rides are reportedly easy to come by; but *Let's Go* does not recommend hitchhiking. **Voyages Arnaud** (☎04 90 38 15 58) runs buses from **Avignon** to **Isle-sur-la-Sorgue** (40min.; M-Sa 10 per day, 5 on Su; 14F/€2.13) and on to **Fontaine de Vaucluse** (55min., 3 per day, 26F/€3.96). More buses (☎04 90 82 07 35) scoot from **Avignon** to **Apt,** stopping at **Isle-sur-la-Sorgue** and **Bonnieux** (70min., 3 daily, 17F/€2.59 to each town). **Les Express de la Durance** (☎04 90 71 03 00) buses travel to **Cavaillon** (40min.; M-Sa 12 per day, 2 per day leaving in morning in summer; 19F/€2.90), from which less regular buses (Autocars Barlatier ☎04 90 73 23 59), for which you must have a **reservation** in summer, run to **Bonnieux,** stopping at **Lacoste** (21F/€3.20), **Ménerbes** (17.50F/€2.67), and **Oppède-le-Vieux** (14F/€2.13). (1hr.; 1 daily in summer, 2 daily during school year.) Confused? Ask the extremely helpful woman at the bus station for advice on constructing your trip. A good chunk of the Lubéron could easily be covered in two days by **car,** by far the easiest way to go. Pick one up in Avignon, which is chock-full of rental companies. N100 blows right through the middle of the Lubéron park and branches off to the smaller towns, but the twisting, narrow roads from one town to the next are often more picturesque. Expect to pay 10-15F/€1.53-2.29 for parking in most villages. The regional **tourist office** is in **Bonnieux** (see p. 250). However you travel, good walking **shoes** are a must as most of the villages are hilly and not always well paved. Bring enough **cash** to tide you over, since many restaurants and some hotels do not take credit cards, and banks are scarce.

PROVENCE

QUIT HOGGING THE TRUFFLES! If you see a group of diners in a French restaurant with their napkins over their heads, don't be alarmed. They're merely savoring the delicate aroma of the most sought-out mushroom in the world—the *truffe noir,* or black truffle. Not to be confused with the Belgian chocolate blobs that bear a minimal visual resemblance to them, the real, honest-to-goodness truffle is found growing in the roots of oak and hazelnut trees. Picked fresh, a truffle is worth its weight in gold to the gastronomically obsessed. Why so dear? The truffle hides underground and defies systematic cultivation. Fortunately, nature has provided the French with the truffle-hunter *par excellence.* Pigs, which are attracted to the sexy odor emitted by the truffle, can snuffle out these delicacies in no time, and a good truffle-hunter is worth far more than his bacon. The biggest problem is making off with the treasured *truffe* with a greedy pig in hot pursuit.

L'ISLE-SUR-LA-SORGUE

L'Isle-sur-la-Sorgue is the first step away from Avignon and into the true Vaucluse countryside. Entangled in the green ribbon of its river, this quiet town (pop. 18,000) surrenders itself to the rush of water. The clear, shallow waters of the Sorgue are split into numerous channels to the east of the city, surrounding and running beneath the town center, aptly nicknamed "Venice." These waters are the heart of the city; their harvest of crayfish and trout once fed a hundred families. The mossy spokes of waterwheels turn everywhere you look, while children splash in the rushing water, and you might see a traditional low fishing boat (called "*Nego-Chin*" or "Drowning Dog"), formed of only three planks. The river provides an excellent lunch vista, but not much else.

The town's main attraction is its **open-air market** (Th and Su 7:30am-1pm). August 6 sees a **water market** in which the Sorgue is decked with boats and *Nego-Chins* full of hawkers' wares. In July, the city and its neighbors host the **Festival de la Sorgue,** celebrating the river with water jousting and concerts.

The easiest way to L'Isle-sur-la-Sorgue is by **train** from Avignon (20min.; 12 per day, first one leaves Avignon 5:58am, last one leaves l'Isle-sur-la-Sorgue 8:26pm; 24F/€3.66). Camping at **La Sorguette,** on rte. d'Apt (RN100) along the river 2km north of the town center, is a great base from which to explore the Vaucluse. (☎04 90 38 05 71; fax 04 90 20 84 61; www.camping-sorguette.com. July-Aug. kayaks 40F/€6.10 per hr., 90F/€13.72 per half-day. Reception 7:30am-10:30pm. Open Mar. 15-Oct. 24. July-Aug. 18 2 people with car 90.20F/€13.75; Mar.-June and Aug. 19-Oct. 15 85.20F/€12.99. Extra person 29-31.10F/€4.44-4.74, child under 7 15-16F/€2.29-2.44. Electricity 20F-22/€3.05-3.35.) **Isle 2 Roues (Cycles Peugeot),** on av. de la Gare right outside the train station, rents **bikes.** (☎04 90 38 19 12. Open Tu-Sa 8am-noon and 2-7pm. 85F/€12.20 per day; 5 bikes or more 70F/€10.67 each. Passport deposit.) If biking isn't your thing, you can always take a **taxi** (☎06 08 09 19 49). The **tourist office,** in the church on pl. de l'Eglise, supplies info on festivals, markets, and hiking in the Vaucluse. (☎04 90 38 04 78; fax 04 90 38 35 43. Open July-Aug. M-Sa 9am-1pm and 2:30-6:30pm, Su 9am-1pm; Sept.-June M-Sa 9am-12:30pm and 2-6pm, Su 9am-noon.)

FONTAINE DE VAUCLUSE

Both hope and chilly water spring eternal in spectacular Fontaine de Vaucluse (pop. 500). The Sorgue rushes full-grown here from **Le Gouffre,** one of the largest river sources in the world. At its spring peak, Le Gouffre pours 90 cubic meters of water per second into the Sorgue. This pool at the base of a stone cliff defies understanding; its depth is unmeasurable and its wetness incomprehensible, even to Jacques Cousteau, who probed the Gouffre but never hit bottom. Equally fruitless were the quests of Petrarch, who pined after his "Laura," the lovely young wife of an early Marquis de Sade. After spotting Laura in an Avignon church on April 6, 1327, Petrarch spent two decades composing sonnets in Fontaine; his *De Vita Sol-*

itaria recounts the time he spent here. Sitting high on the hill above town is a ruined château from the 13th century; while it's possible to climb to it with the right equipment, locals will chuckle at your daring desire. During July and August, tourists swarm into Fontaine; consider yourself warned.

The 10m **Colonne** in the center of town commemorates Petrarch's life and labor, as does the small **Musée Petrarque** across the bridge. (☎04 90 20 37 20. Open Apr.-Oct. W-M 10am-noon and 2-6pm; Oct.1-15 Sa-Su 10-noon and 2-6pm; Oct. 16-31 Sa-Su 10am-noon and 2-5pm; Nov.-Mar. closed except to groups. 20F/€3.05, students 10F/€1.53.) This side of the river houses several small museums, including the **Musée d'histoire 1939-1945,** which reconstructs daily life under the Occupation. (☎04 90 20 24 00. Open July-Aug. W-M 10am-7pm; Apr. 15-June and Sept.-Oct. 15 W-M 10am-noon and 2-6pm; Oct. 16-Dec. Sa-Su 10am-noon and 1-5pm; Mar.-Apr. 14 Sa-Su 10am-noon and 2-6pm. 20F/€3.05, students 10F/€1.53, under 12 free.) There's also **Le Monde Souterrain,** which offers underground tours through reconstructed caverns. (☎04 90 20 34 13. Open June-Sept. daily 9:30am-7:30pm; Feb.-May and Oct.-Nov. 9:30am-noon and 2-6pm. Tours 32F/€4.88, under age 18 22F/€3.35.) If you need more info, stop at the **tourist office,** about 100m to the left of the Colonne. (☎04 90 20 32 22; fax 04 90 20 21 37. Open daily M-Sa 10am-7pm.)

Surprisingly inexpensive lodgings can be found at the **Hôtel Font de Lauro,** 1½km from Fontaine de Vaucluse, right off the road to l'Isle-sur-la-Sorgue. Rooms have a rustic feel and views of vineyards. A pool puts a bow on this bargain package. The sign is small, so be on the lookout. (☎/fax 04 90 20 31 49. Breakfast 37F/€5.64. Reserve in summer. Gate closes at midnight. 8 doubles with shower 177F/€27; 8 with bath 245F/€37; one triple with bath 325F/€49.50. MC/V.) The rural **Auberge de Jeunesse (HI),** chemin de la Vignasse, is 1km from town. Follow signs from the Colonne, or ask the bus driver to let you off near the *auberge.* Wake to a chorus of roosters in this idyllic stone country house. (☎04 90 20 31 65; fax 04 90 20 26 20. Kitchen access. Laundry. Breakfast 19F/€2.90. Sheets 17F/€2.59. Reception 8-10am and 5:30-10pm. Curfew 11:30pm. Open Feb.-Nov. 15. Bunks 52F/€7.93, camping 30F/€4.57. **Members only.**) The hostel can also offer suggestions for **hiking** in the Lubéron, especially on the nearby national hiking trails, GR6 and GR91.

Kayak Vert, about 500m from Fontaine on the road to l'Isle-sur-la-Sorgue, rents kayaks for an 8km trip down to L'Isle-sur-la-Sorgue. A friendly mandatory guide will escort you, and they'll minibus you back to Fontaine. The Sorgue is a class 1 river, meaning it's easy and safe for people of all ages. (☎04 90 20 35 44; fax 04 40 20 20 28; www.canoefrance.com. 2-person kayak 220F/€33.54; 1-person kayak 110F/€16.77; university students with ID 90F/€13.72; children under 10 free. Open Apr.-Nov., weather permitting. Reserve ahead.) There is a **post office** with a rare **ATM** up the street from the Colonne, away from the river (open M-F 9am-noon and 2-5pm, Sa 8:30-11:30am). Across from it you'll find a **mini-market.** (Open in summer Tu-Su and holidays 7am-8pm; in winter 7:15am-12:30pm and 3:30-6:30pm.)

OPPEDE-LE-VIEUX

The ghost town of Oppède-le-Vieux clings to the mountainside below an exquisitely ruined château and above gardened terraces of lavender and olive groves. This medieval village was slowly deserted in the 16th century and definitively abandoned in the early 20th century for the *hameau* (hamlet) in the plain. Only the sun-baked stone buildings are left, along with a couple of artists' studios and a tiny square. This town is so deserted that tourists' cars are not allowed, and must be parked below the hills. Signs will direct you to the square (5-10min.); from there, wander up to the 11th- to 13th-century **Eglise Notre-Dame d'Alidon,** which complements the **château.** Private property signs around the ruined castle are largely ignored, but the warning signs shouldn't be, as precarious arches and cliff-top towers are always ready to drop a loose stone on your head. Nevertheless, the sight of the valley from this vantage point is superb, and the entire experience, including the hill prior to the town, is breathtaking. To drive there, follow signs to Oppède; the road to the ruins is well marked.

MENERBES

This is the town made famous in Peter Mayle's *A Year in Provence.* Apparently, the popular author had to leave after he kept finding fans swimming in his pool—rumor has it that he's on his way back, though, and it seems as though tourists may have discovered this, as there are more there than in other towns its size in the area. A magnificent view of the valley and neighboring stone quarries awaits from the church at the top of the village. Just outside town, about 1km in the direction of Cavaillon, on the road leading to Menerbes, is the **Domaine de la Citadelle,** a vineyard which harbors the **Musée du Tire-Bouchon.** The tour of this collection of over 1000 corkscrews, in every shape and size, includes those shaped like men in which the screw is found in an intriguing place. The tour is appropriately topped off with a *dégustation.* (☎04 90 72 41 58. Open Apr.-Oct. M-F 9am-noon and 2-7pm, Sa-Su 10am-noon and 3-7pm; Nov.-Mar. M-Sa 9am-noon and 2-6pm. 24F/€3.66, students 19F/€2.90, children under 15 free.) **Taxis** can be reached at 04 90 72 31 41 or 06 07 86 23 88. The town is even big enough to have a **post office.** (Open July-Sept. M-F 9am-noon and 2-5pm, Sa 9am-noon; Oct.-June M-F 9:30am-noon and 2:30-5pm, Sa 9am-noon.) Or maybe it's just to handle fan Mayle. **Postal code:** 84560.

LACOSTE

You'd expect Lacoste to be haunted by the demons of its past—the picturesquely ruined château perched above the village was home from 1774 to 1778 to the **Marquis de Sade,** who abducted local peasants to satisfy his sexual needs until his arrest and imprisonment. But this sleepy town is as restrained as the notorious château—modestly boarded up, the estate resists all but the most persistent assaults by curious sightseers. The raciest thing left in the village (pop. 440) is a group of American art students who rush around capturing the beauty of the site.

Lacoste is home to one of the few affordable accommodations in the valley. The **Café de Sade,** a giant, camp-style dormitory, has unbelievable views, and the picturesque hotel rooms are as welcoming as the countryside. (☎04 90 75 82 29; fax 04 90 75 95 68. Breakfast 32F/€4.88. Sheets 20F/€3.05. Closed Jan.-Feb. Bunks 75F/€11.43, *demi-pension* 185F/€28.21; doubles 240-270F/€36.59-41.16, with bath 300F/€45.74.) A **market** is held on Tuesday mornings in the tiny square next to the post office. Lacoste has a **post office** (open June 15-Sept. 15 M-F 9am-noon and 2:30-4:30pm, Sa 9-11am; Sept. 16-June 14 M-F 9-11am and 2:30-4:30pm, Sa 9-11am, closed W afternoon). **Postal code:** 84480.

BONNIEUX

Flowers burst from the balconies and windows of well-restored houses that clutter the hillside of Bonnieux (pop. 1420). This *village perché* is the capital of the Lubéron, linking its postcard lavender fields with the real world. The **market** on pl. du Terrail sells regional specialties, including crusty cheese and barbarous *saucisson* (F mornings). Atop the town, on a windswept cedared ledge, the Templar knights' 12th-century **Eglise Haute** offers a panorama that redeems the hard climb up. Baguette-lovers mustn't miss the **Musée de la Boulangerie,** 12 rue de la République, which traces the history of French bread-making in a 17th-century bakery. (☎04 90 75 88 34. Open July-Aug. W-M 10am-1pm and 2-6:30pm; Apr.-June and Sept. W-M 10am-12:30pm and 2:30-6pm; Oct. Sa-Su 10am-12:30pm and 2:30-6pm. 20F/€3.05, students 10F/€1.53.) The **tourist office** is responsible for all the villages in the Lubéron, and has piles of pamphlets and other info. (☎04 90 75 91 90; fax 04 90 75 92 94. Open M-Sa 9:30am-12:30pm and 2-6:30pm.) Stock up at the **Relais des Mousquetaires,** off pl. Carnot (open M-Sa 8:30am-12:30pm and 3:45-7:15pm, Su 8:30am-12:30pm, closed W afternoon). Rent **bikes** at Location de Vélos, rue Marceau, which has free delivery within 15km of Bonnieux (including Lacoste). (☎04 90 75 89 96, mobile 06 83 25 48 07. 50F/€7.60 per half day; 90F/€13.70 per day; week 490F/€74.70. Open Mar.-Nov. 8:30am-noon and 1-6:30pm.) Call a **taxi** at 06 81 75 87 13. You can camp at **Le Vallon,** 1km from town toward Ménerbes. (☎/fax 04 90 75 86 14. Open mid-Mar. to mid-Nov. 14F/€2.13 per person, 9F/€1.37 per car; 16F/€2.44 per tent; electricity 16F/€2.44; camping car, 2 people, and electricity 89F/€13.57.)

ROUSSILLON

The most famous of the ochre villages is a must-see town even in this must-see region. The site itself can be seen from as far away as Gordes—a wild, red-orange incision in the lush, green countryside. The village (pop. 1200), built on and of the world's biggest vein of natural ochre, is a wonderland of reds—every doorway, windowsill, and wall tinted with every warm and vibrant shade the earth can produce. Be sure to check out the *Sentier des Ochres*, where you can walk through the vast, dusty ochre deposit between stunning wind-sculpted cliffs. White shoes and clothing are a bad idea. (Open July-Aug. daily 9am-7:30pm; Mar.-Nov. 10am-5:30pm. 10F/€1.53; mid-Nov.-Mar. free. Closed on rainy days for safety's sake.) To feed your appetite for a hike, stop at the **bakery,** av. de la Burlière (open 7am-1pm and 3:30-7pm). The **tourist office,** on pl. de la Poste, has hotel listings. (☎04 90 05 60 25; fax 04 90 05 63 31. Open Apr.-Oct. M-Sa 9:30am-noon and 1:30-6:30pm, Su 2-6:30pm; Nov.-Apr. M-Sa 1:30-5:30pm.) There's **currency exchange** and a 24-hour **ATM** at the **post office** next door (open M-F 9am-noon and 2-5pm, Sa 9am-noon).

GORDES

Perhaps the most picturesque of the hillside towns, Gordes (pop. 2050) is famous for its *bories*, drystone huts and dwellings built through the skillful placement of stone upon stone without the use of mortar. Often seen in the middle of fields or lost in the tangled undergrowth of the hills, they predate the Romans but were built and used until quite recently. The **Village des Bories** outside town is a unique hamlet of *bories*, inhabited until the mid-19th century. These giant mounds of local stone serve as complete and self-sustaining dwellings, with their own chimneys, wine cellars, bread ovens, and space for livestock. (☎04 90 72 03 48. Open daily 9am-sunset. 35F/€5.34, ages 10-17 20F/€3.05.) The **château** in the middle of town was originally a 12th-century fortress but was renovated in the 16th century. It houses the Hôtel de Ville and a collection of 200 vibrantly sexy paintings in the **Musée Pol Mara.** (Open daily 10am-noon and 2-6pm. 25F/€3.81, ages 10-17 20F/€3.05.) An enormous **market** surrounds the château on Tuesday mornings, selling everything from pottery to paintings, sausage to socks. **Sénanque Abbey,** an active Cistercian community famous for the exquisite fields of lavender which surround it, is 4km away from Gordes. The site was occupied by monks from 1148 until the Revolution, then re-populated and restored in the mid-19th century; today you can buy honey, lavender products, and *sénacole*, a liqueur produced by the monks here. (☎04 90 72 05 72. Abbey open Mar.-Oct. M-Sa 10am-noon and 2-6pm, Su 2-6pm; Nov.-Feb. M-F 2-5pm, Sa-Su 2-6pm. 30F/€4.57, under 18 12F/€1.83.)

Even though hordes of tourists inflate the prices in this town, try **Cannelle,** rue Baptistin Pica, a small place with shockingly reasonable fare. (☎04 90 72 07 86. Open M-F 9am-7pm. Salads from 30F/€4.57; pizzas from 40F/€6.10; sandwiches 20F/€3.05. Closed Th Feb.-June and Sept.-Dec.; closed Jan.) The **tourist office** is also in the château. (☎04 90 72 02 75. Open June-Sept. M-Sa 9am-noon and 2-6:30pm, Su 10am-12:30pm and 2-6pm; Oct.-May M-Sa 9am-noon and 2-6pm, Su 10am-noon and 2-6pm.) There's even a 24-hour **ATM** in the *place* in front of it. The **post office,** is in the center of town (open M-F 9am-noon and 4-7pm, Su 9am-noon).

THE ALPILLES

Provence is at its best in small towns. The quiet hills of the Alpilles, north of Arles and s[illegible] of Avignon, shelter some of the area's finest: it is castle-strewn, ruin-dotted, [illegible]

ROVENCE

LES [illegible]

ble and savage bel[illegible]

“T[illegible] found in the annals [illegible] onging to feudal history of which an e[illegible] ton Symonds [illegible] of Les Baux.”

Les Baux-de-Provence is known for its medieval ruins, demolished castle, and gracefully restored Renaissance homes. The village sits 245m up on a rocky spur of the Alpilles—easy to defend and very, very difficult to take. The Baux lords plundered medieval Provence from this eagle's nest of a town, managing at one point to hold 72 individual towns in the region. Even Dante came to their court—it's thought that he found inspiration for his *Inferno* in the twisted, tortured Val de l'Enfer ("Valley of Hell") below the castle. The Baux line died out in the 14th century, and Louis XIII humiliated the town by destroying its castle and ramparts in 1632. You can still see the spectacular ruined château and poke around a few of the town's medieval streets. The only down side to a visit here is the phenomenal number of tourists; over a million come to Les Baux annually, and the tiny town center that Louis XIII demolished has been rebuilt with souvenir shops and cafés.

The ruined halls and towers of the mountaintop **Château des Baux** (☎04 90 54 55 56) cover an area five times that of the village below. Private apartments, once the seats of courtly love, are cracked open to the wind, their windows gaping over empty air. Slim limestone stairs climb into the blue sky. Those who arrive early will enjoy the eerie treat of having the mountaintop, valley, and distant Mediterranean all to themselves. Hold on to children and lighter possessions, as they could easily fly off the windy cliff. Housed in a cool Romanesque chapel inside the château's gates, the tiny **Chapelle St-Blaise** has a delightful slideshow of van Gogh and Cézanne's paintings of olive trees. (Open in summer daily 9am-8:30pm; in autumn and spring 9am-6:30pm; in winter 9am-5pm. Thorough audio guide in 5 languages. 40F/€6.10, students with ID 30F/€4.57, under 18 20F/€3.05.) Walk down the hill to the **Fondation Louis Jou,** rue Frédéric Mistral, which commemorates Les Baux's favorite son with major works by the printmaker as well as engravings by Dürer and Goya. If it seems shut down, continue 50m and inquire at the small shop; it's not really closed. (☎04 90 54 34 17. Open Tu and Th-Su 8am-10pm. 20F/€3.05, students 10F/€2.29.) Les Baux is known for its limestone quarries, one of which has been converted into the fantastic, surprising **Cathédrale d'Images.** From the bus stop, continue down the hill, turn right at the crossroads, and follow the sign (7min.). Dozens of projectors splash images from above into gigantic man-made subterranean galleries to the accompaniment of mysterious and booming music. 2002 will see a display of scenes from East Asia. (☎04 90 54 38 65. Open Mar.-Sept. daily 10am-7pm; Oct.-Feb. 10am-6pm. 45F/€6.86, ages 8-18 27F/€4.12.)

Mas de la Fontaine, at the foot of the village in the Val d'Enfer, offers seven elegant and fashionably decorated rooms in a traditional *mas* (provençal farm) with a garden and pool. This place is worth the splurge, and travelers know it so make reservations. Follow signs to the Gendarmerie, and the hotel is two minutes downhill on your right. (☎04 90 54 34 13. Breakfast 37F/€5.64. Open Mar. 15-Oct. Doubles with shower 260F/€39.64, with bath 360F/€54.89; triples 425F/€64.80. Extra bed 65F/€9.91.) Most backpackers bring picnics to the Cité Morte, but you can buy supplies at the small **bakery** in the parking lot. (Open Mar.-Sept. daily 8:30am-6:30pm; Nov.-Feb. Tu-Su 8am-2pm.) Sandwich stands and crêperies abound.

The **tourist office** in the Hôtel de Ville, about halfway up the hill between the parking lot and the Cité Morte, gives out a free map. (☎04 90 54 34 39. Open Apr.-Sept. daily 9am-7pm; Oct.-Mar. 9:30am-noon and 1:30-6:30pm.) **CTM buses** from Les Baux run to **Arles** (30min., M-Sa 4 per day, 30.50F/€4.65). **Taxis** also run up and down the hills (☎06 80 27 60 92).

TARASCON

The small city of Tarascon (pop. 12,000) is intimately linked to provençal folklore. In the first century AD the Tarasque, a monster bred in the pathless swamps of the Rhône, began to visit and devour local livestock and children by night. Legend has it that St. Martha, armed only with a wooden cross and her rope belt, finally domesticated the beast. For four days over the last we[illegible] a replica of the monster is paraded through the town, ac[illegible] **Fête de l**[illegible], bullfights, horse shows, and folkloric events during the [illegible] Nîmes (2[illegible] [illegible]con's proximity to Arles (17km), Avignon (23km), and N[illegible] [illegible]er cities' [illegible] easy daytrip or a good fallback if festivals clog the bigg[illegible] [illegible]vise, there isn't enough here to keep you more than a few [illegible] hours.

Whatever Tarascon lacks in activity, it makes up for in accommodations. To reach the **Auberge de Jeunesse (HI),** 31 bd. Gambetta, from the train station, turn right and follow the tracks until you reach bd. Victor Hugo. Cross the street and follow the path between the tracks and the wall for 20m, turning left on the next major road. The hostel is another five minutes farther, on your left near a phone booth. It has comfortable beds in 8- to 12-bed dorms, kitchen facilities, a secure bike area, and free parking. Reservations are accepted by email (tarascon@fuaj.org), but this gem of a hostel is rarely full. (☎04 90 91 04 08. 19F/€2.90 breakfast obligatory first morning. Lockout 10am-6pm. Reception 7:30am-noon and 6-11pm. Sheets 18F/€2.74. Beds 50F/€7.62.) **Hôtel du Viaduc,** 9 rue du Viaduc, has clean, cozy rooms. From train station, head directly left; the hotel is a five-minute walk on your right. Popular with cyclists, it offers a locked bike area and free parking, and boasts jovial, partially English-speaking proprietors. (☎04 90 91 16 67. Abnormally large French breakfast 30F/€4.57. Shower 10F/€1.53. Rooms June-Sept. 150F/€22.90, with bath 190F/€28.97; Oct.-May 130F/€19.82, with bath 160F/€24.39. Rooms sleep 1-2 people; some triples available for same prices or 200-230F/€30.49-35.06.) **Camp** at **Tartarin,** bd. du Roy René behind the château on the Rhône, a simple campsite with bar, snack stand, free showers, and lots of shade. The ground, unfortunately, is hard with spotty grass. (☎04 90 91 01 46; fax 04 90 91 10 70. Reception 9am-noon and 3-5pm. Open Apr.-Oct. 20F/€3.05 per person, 18F/€2.74 per tent, 10F/€1.52 per car. Electricity 16F/€2.44.)

The prize of Tarascon is the imposing 15th-century **Château de Tarascon,** built above a wedge of the Rhône. This luxurious fortress, built by Louis II of Anjou, saw few years of warfare and was maintained as a prison for centuries; it is, therefore, in unbelievable condition. Surrounded by a swampy moat, it boasts a lovely provençal garden, medieval graffiti, an apothecary, and stunning tapestries. The climb to the roof is well worth it; there is a picture-perfect view from here of Tarascon's rival château, the ruined Château de Beaucaire, across the river. (☎04 90 91 01 93. Open Apr.-Sept. daily 9am-7pm; Oct.-Mar. 9am-noon and 2-5pm. 36F/€5.49, ages 18-25 23F/€3.51, under 18 free.)

You can get to Tarascon by **train** from **Arles** (10min., at least 8 per day, 17F/€2.59) or **Avignon** (10min., at least 12 per day, 24F/€3.66). Ticket windows open M-Sa 6am-6:30pm, Su 6am-noon and 2-6pm. **Cevennes Cars** (☎04 66 29 27 29) sends **buses** from the train station to **Avignon** (35min.; M-Sa 4-5 per day, 2 on Su; 24F/€3.66) and **St-Rémy** (25min.; 4 per day, 2 on Sa, summer M-Sa 2 per day; 18F/€2.74). If you're stuck, call **Taxi Accord** (☎06 11 65 64 63 or 04 90 91 34 50). The wonderful women of the **tourist office,** 59 rue des Halles, can give you a free guide and map. From the train station, walk across the courtyard and turn left on cours A. Briand; walk for two minutes, and rue des Halles will be on your right. (☎04 90 91 03 52. Open Apr.-Sept. M-Sa 10am-7pm, Su 10am-noon; Oct.-Mar. M-F 9am-12:30pm and 2-6pm. The **post office** is to the left of the train station. (☎04 90 91 52 00. Open M-F 8:30am-5:30pm, Sa 8:30am-noon.) **Postal code:** 13150.

ST-REMY

A little city approached through luminous arcades of plane trees, St-Rémy has a smattering of Roman remnants. The ruins of ancient Glanum were Vincent van Gogh's favorite daytrip when the asylum let him out for good behavior.

The sights of St-Rémy are concentrated in two areas. The town center has several worthy museums, including the **Centre d'Art Présence van Gogh** in the 252-year-old Hôtel Estrine, 8 rue Estrine. Although it lacks original paintings, the museum has rotating exhibits on the master's work. (☎04 90 92 34 72; fax 04 90 92 04 84. Open Tu-Su 10:30am-12:30pm and 2:30-6:30pm. 20F/€3.05, students 15F/€2.29.) The 15th-century **Hôtel de Sade,** rue de Parage, houses all the best finds from nearby Glanum, including amazingly well-preserved glasswork. (☎04 90 92 64 04; fax 04 90 92 64 02. Open July-Aug. daily 10am-noon and 2-7pm; Apr.-June and Sept. 10am-noon and 2-6pm; Jan.-Mar. 10am-noon and 2-5pm. 15F/€2.29.)

Glanum, a settlement from the 7th century BC, lies nearly 1km south of the town center, past the tourist office on av. Vincent Van Gogh (15min.). It takes a critical eye to call this ancient city ruined; though unroofed and excavated, the houses, temples, springs, and sacred wells seem like they were in use more recently than 2000 years ago. Dedicated to Cybele, the Mother Goddess, the town once prospered as a stop on the main road linking Spain to Italy (the *Via Domitia*); it now provides a fascinating insight into the hybrid Gallo-Roman culture that emerged in Provence. (☎04 90 92 23 79. Open Apr.-Sept. daily 9am-7pm; Oct.-Mar. 9am-noon and 2-5pm. 36F/€5.49, ages 12-25 23F/€3.51.) Standing in solitary splendor across the street are the well-preserved **Antiques,** a commemorative arch and mausoleum built during the reign of Augustus. You can check out or into the nearby monastery and invalids' home of **Saint-Paul de Mausole,** chemin des Carrières. Van Gogh interned himself here and spent the last year of his life above the flowered cloister, which now shows exhibits by current patients. (☎04 90 92 77 00. Open Apr.-Oct. Tu-Su 9:30am-7pm; Nov.-Mar. Tu-F 10:30am-1pm and 1:30-5pm. 17F/€2.59, students with ID 12F/€1.83.) The Monday after Pentecost brings a veritable stampede of farm animals—mostly sheep—through the town center during the *Fête de la Transhumance*, a celebration of provençal migration traditions in which the flocks leave the plains for Alpine pastures. The **Carreto Ramado,** a pagan festival dedicated to field work, in which 50 horses draw an enormous cart of fruits and vegetables, and the big **Féria Provençale,** where bulls are teased but not killed, take place around August 15th. The tourist office gives out the *Patrimoine* handbook of St-Rémy, with tons of cultural info (free).

Restaurants are almost all pricey, but you can eat a cheap lunch at the simple **Le Saint-Remy-de-Provence,** 48 av. Durand Maillane, to the left of the parking lot in front of the tourist office. (☎04 90 92 36 58. *Menus* from 50F/€7.62. Open daily noon-2:30pm and 6:30pm-midnight, Apr.-Oct. closed Th. MC/V.) Near the statue of Nostradamus are a smattering of good brasseries and a **Petit Casino** supermarket across the road on rue de la Résistance. (Open M-Sa 7:30am-12:30pm and 3:30-7:30pm.) To take in the vistas that Vincent did, get the pamphlet that includes the *Promenade sur les lieux peints par Van Gogh* from the **tourist office,** pl. Jean Jaurès. From the bus stop, walk up av. Durand Maillane; the office will be on the left, in a parking lot, next to the police station. Ask about group tours in English from Apr. 15 to Sept. 10. (☎04 90 92 05 22; fax 04 90 92 38 52. Free map. Tours 35F/€5.34, 10F/€1.53 more for the visit to St-Paul. Open June-Sept. M-Sa 9am-9pm, Su 9am-2pm; Oct.-May M-Sa 9am-6pm, Su 9am-2pm.) **Buses** (☎04 90 14 59 00) come from **Avignon** (45min.; M-Sa at least 9 per day, summer 7 per day; 32F/€4.88) and **Tarascon** (25min.; 3 per day, 2 in summer; 16.50F/€2.52).

ARLES

Each street in Arles (pop. 35,000) seems to run into or out of the great Roman arena, which binds together the distant past and bustling present. The city's historical wealth and relative intimacy have always made it a favorite among visitors to Provence; Van Gogh lost two years and an ear here, and Picasso loved Arles' bullfights enough to donate 70 of his drawings to the city. Today, the international photography festival attracts both amateurs and professionals, and transforms each hall, museum, nook, and cranny into an exhibit. As a plus, the hills of the Alpilles and the Camargue marshlands are an easy daytrip away.

ORIENTATION AND PRACTICAL INFORMATION

Northwestern Arles touches the Rhône. The train station is in the north, the tourist office in the south, and the heart of the old city in between.

Trains: av. P. Talabot. To: **Avignon** (30min.; M-Sa 19 per day, Su 15 per day; 36F/€5.49); **Marseille** (1hr., 8 per day, 76F/€11.59); **Montpellier** (1hr.; M-Sa 7 per day, Su 6 per day; 76F/€11.59); and **Nîmes** (30min.; M-Sa 5 per day, Su 7 per day; 42F/€6.40). Ticket counters open M-Sa 5:50am-8:50pm, Su 5:50am-8:40pm.

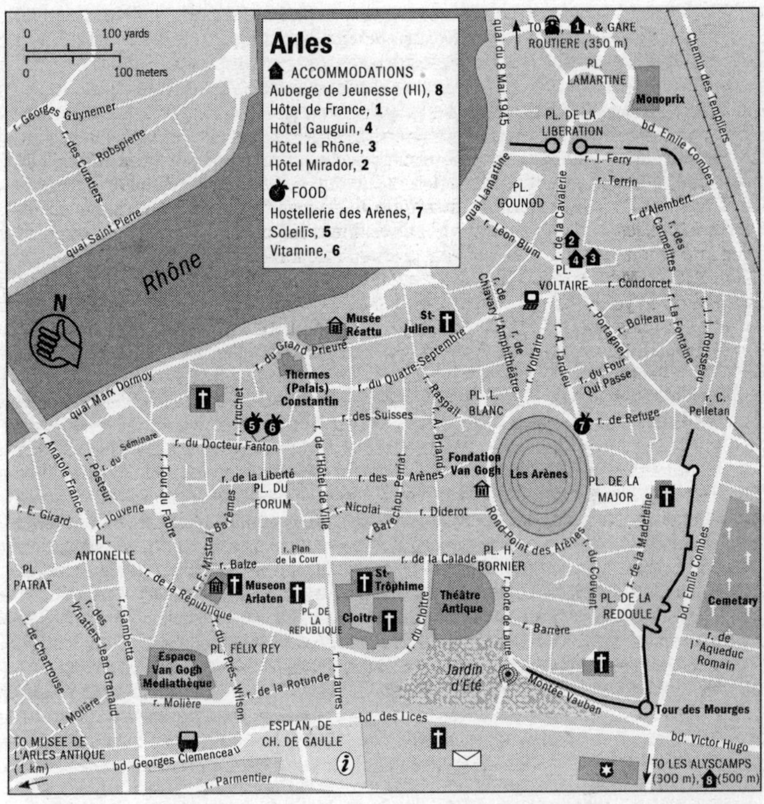

Buses: av. P. Talabot, just outside the train station (☎04 90 49 38 01). Info desk open M-F 9am-4pm. **Les Cars de Camargue,** 24 rue Clemenceau (☎04 90 96 36 25). Info desk open M-Th 8:15am-noon and 2-5:30pm, F 8:15am-noon and 2-4:30pm. To **Nîmes** (50min., M-Sa 5 per day, 34F/€5.18). **Cars Ceyte et Fils** and **CTM,** 21 chemin du Temple (☎04 90 93 74 90), go to **Avignon** (45min., M-Sa 5 per day, 46F/€7.01).

Taxis: A.A.A. Arles Taxis (☎04 90 93 31 16); **Arles Taxis Radio** (☎04 90 96 90 03).

Bike Rental: at the **hostel** (see below).

Tourist Office: Esplanade Charles de Gaulle, bd. des Lices (☎04 90 18 41 20; fax 04 90 18 41 29). Turn left outside the station and walk to pl. Lamartine; after the Monoprix turn left down bd. Emile Courbes. Continue to the big intersection by the southeast old city tower; turn right onto bd. des Lices. Accommodations service 5F/€0.76 plus down payment. Open Apr.-Sept. daily 9am-6:45pm; Oct.-Mar. M-Sa 9am-5:45pm, Su 10:30am-2:30pm. **Branch** in the station (☎04 90 18 41 20) open M-Sa 9am-1pm.

Money: Arène Change, 22bis rond-point des Arènes (☎04 90 93 34 66). No commission on US dollars. Open W-M 9am-12:30pm and 2:30-6:45pm; Apr.-Sept. closed Su afternoon.

Laundromat: Lincoln Laverie, 6 rue de la Cavalerie. Open daily 7am-9pm.

Police: on the corner of bd. des Lices and av. des Alyscamps (☎04 90 18 45 00).

Hospital: Centre Hospitalier J. Imbert, quartier Fourchon (☎04 90 49 29 29).

Internet Access: Point Web, 10 rue du 4 Septembre (☎04 90 18 91 54). Only 2 computers, but the only one in town open year-round. Open M-Sa 8:30am-12:30pm and 1:30-7:30pm. 10F/€1.53 for 15min.

Post Office: 5 bd. des Lices, between the tourist office and the police station (☎04 90 18 41 10). **Currency exchange.** Open M-F 8:30am-6:30pm, Sa 8:30am-12:30pm. **Postal code:** 13200.

ACCOMMODATIONS AND CAMPING

Arles has plenty of inexpensive hotels, especially around **rue de l'Hôtel de Ville** and **pl. Voltaire.** Note that hotel prices do not include a municipal residency tax of 5F/€0.76 per person per night. Reservations are crucial during the photography festival in July and should be made a month or two in advance.

Hôtel Gauguin, 5 pl. Voltaire (☎04 90 96 14 35; fax 04 90 18 98 87). Cheerful saffron yellows and smells of lavender bring the warmth of Provence into every elegant room; some with balcony. Breakfast 30F/€4.57. Reception 7am-8pm. Doubles with shower 180-210F/€27.44-32.02, 2 beds with bath 220F/€33.54; triples 260F/€39.64. Extra bed 50F/€7.62. MC/V.

Hôtel Mirador, 3 rue Voltaire (☎04 90 96 28 05; fax 04 90 96 59 89). Unusually well-located hotel. Sleep cozily in salmon-colored modern rooms, all with TV. Breakfast 28F/€4.27, in winter 30F/€4.57. Reception 7am-10pm. July-Aug. singles and doubles with shower 190F/€28.97, with bath 265F/€40.40. Sept.-June singles and doubles 190F/€28.97, with bath 245F/€37.35. Extra bed 60F/€9.15. AmEx/MC/V.

Auberge de Jeunesse (HI), 20 av. Maréchal Foch (☎04 90 96 18 25; fax 04 90 96 31 26), 10min. from the town center and 20min. from the station. From the station, take the "Starlette" bus to "Clemenceau," and then take the #4 bus (dir: "L'Aurelienne") to "Foch" (5.20F/€0.79). There are no Starlette buses on Su, and the last bus from the station that connects at Clemenceau is in the late afternoon. To walk from the station, follow directions to the tourist office, but instead of turning on bd. des Lices, cross it and continue down av. des Alyscamps; follow the signs. Modern, with a quiet garden and ramshackle toilets. Near the municipal pool and cinema. Personal lockers. **Bike rental** 80F/€12.20 per day (500F/€76.23 deposit). Breakfast and sheets included. Dinner 52F/€7.93 on nights when there are groups eating. Bar open until midnight. Reception 7-10am and 5-11pm. Lockout 10am-5pm. Curfew 11pm in winter, midnight in summer. Reservation (by letter or fax) recommended Apr.-June. Bunks 82F/€12.50; 70F/€10.98 after first night. MC/V.

Hôtel le Rhône, 11 pl. Voltaire (☎04 90 96 43 70; fax 04 90 93 87 03). Eager owners and an adorable breakfast room. Smaller than average, these pink rooms with modern bathrooms have great prices for the premium location. The *place* can be loud; ask for a room facing a quiet sidestreet. Breakfast 28F/€4.27. Singles and doubles 150F/€22.90, with shower 180F/€27.44, with bath 230F/€35.06; doubles and triples with shower 200-220F/€30.49-33.54, with toilet 230-250F/€35.06-38.12. MC/V.

Hôtel de France, 1-3 pl. Lamartine (☎04 90 96 01 24). 2min. from the train station and another 2 from the center of town, this has the cheapest rooms in Arles, but the cheap single is *sans* shower access. Comforting rooms are spic-and-span, with quality beds. Breakfast 30F/€4.57. Reception 7am-1am; Oct-Apr. closed Su. Singles 110F/€16.77, with shower 180F/€27.44; doubles with bath 200-220F/€30.49-33.54; triples with shower 300F/€45.74; quads 350F/€53.36. Extra bed 50F/€7.62. MC/V.

CORRIDA OR COCARDE? In the Camargue and the south of France, there are two major types of bullfight: the Spanish **corrida** and the *camarguais* **cocarde.** The *corridas* are the gory spectacles everyone associates with bullfighting: Spanish bull, French *matador*, up to 500F/€76.23 for a chance at watching the one kill the other. The *cocardes*, on the other hand, hurt only the bull's ego and use free-range bulls raised in the swampy Camargue. Twenty to thirty *rasateurs*, usually dressed in white, wear a brightly colored mitt in one hand and a razor-edged glove on the other; the bull has multi-colored pom-poms strung between his horns. The *rasateur* distracts the bull with his mitted hand while attempting to swipe the pom-poms from the bull's head with the other.

Camping-City, 67 rte. de Crau (☎04 90 93 08 86), is the closest site to town. 2-star site, with pool, snack bar, and laundry. Take bus #2 from station ("Starlette" bus to "Clemenceau"). Then take bus #2 (dir: "Pont de Crau") to "Hermite" (5.20F/€0.79). Reception 8am-8pm. Open Apr.-Sept. 25F/€3.81 per person, 18F/€2.74 per child under 7; 25F/€3.81 per site, 18F/€2.74 per car.

FOOD

Bargains still exist here, though locals are rapidly discovering what foreigners will pay for their food. The cheapest bites are found in the many cafés and brasseries in the small squares. Local specialties are seasoned with thyme, rosemary, and garlic, all of which grow in the region. Other regional produce fills the **open-air markets** on bd. Emile Combes (W 7am-1pm) and bd. des Lices (Sa 7am-1pm). There are two **supermarkets** in town: **Monoprix** on pl. Lamartine, close to the train station and the city gates (open M-Th 8:30am-7:30pm, F-Sa 8:30am-8pm), and **Casino,** 26 rue Président Wilson, off bd. des Lices toward the center of town. (Open M-Sa 7:30am-12:30pm and 3:30-7:30pm, Su 8:30am-12:30pm.) The cafés on **pl. Voltaire** are strung with colored lights and animated by a jovial international crowd. On summer evenings, the **pl. du Forum** bustles as much as it ever did in Roman days.

Hostellerie des Arènes, 62 rue Refuge (☎04 90 96 13 05). While a few francs more than the places next door, the mouth-watering home-made plates are worth more than that, including to-die-for lasagna. 85F/€12.96 *menu*; veggie *menu* 95F/€14.48. Open M-Sa noon-2pm and 7-11pm. MC/V.

Vitamine, 16 rue du Docteur Fanton (☎04 90 93 77 36). Heaven-sent for vegetarians. Pasta and 38 different salads (20-50F/€3.05-7.62). Try the 30F/€4.57 *nougat glacé.* Open M-Sa noon-3pm and 7-10:30pm or midnight. Closed Nov.-Mar. Reserve for terrace seating. MC/V.

Soleilis, 9 rue Doctor Fanton (☎04 90 93 30 76). After dinner, find room for the best ice cream in Arles, and possibly in Provence, made with freshly-picked fruits. 10F/€1.53 for one scoop and home-made waffle cone, 6F/€0.91 for regular cone. Mountainous sundaes 30F/€4.57. Open July-Aug. daily 2-7pm and 8:30-10:30pm or later; Mar.-May and Sept.-Oct. 3-6:30pm.

SIGHTS

*There are two different types of **passes:** one for **"Monuments,"** which is more inclusive than the other, **"Circuit Arles Antique."** Monuments: 65F/€9.91, students and under age 18 50F/€7.62. Circuit Arles Antique: 55F/€8.39, students and under age 18 40F/€6.10. Those sights included on either pass are noted with an asterisk (*) below. Note that most sights are actually open 30min. later than we list; the times here are the last time to purchase tickets. For info on monuments, call the **Régie des Monuments** at 04 90 49 36 74.*

Every snack bar and café in Arles has a Roman ruin beneath it. Get an English copy of *Arles et Vincent* (5F/€0.76 from the tourist office), which explains four sets of ground markers that crisscross the city in an attempt to organize its monuments. A less strenuous way to get a glimpse of the historical city is the **Petit Train,** a 35-minute tour. (☎04 93 41 31 09. Leaves from the arena entrance and tourist office Apr.-Oct. daily 10am-7pm. 35F/€5.34, ages 3-10 20F/€3.05.)

LES ARENES*. It's always a surprise to emerge from the medieval network of streets here and meet the high, layered arches of a Roman amphitheater. Built in the first century AD, this structure—the largest of its kind surviving in France—was so cleverly designed that it could evacuate all 25,000 spectators in five minutes. In the 8th century, homes were built on and in the original structure, converting it into a fortified village, and two towers built during that era still remain. The high wall is original; it separated the seating area from the field of combat. The highest tower bears witness to a thousand years of vandalism, including names scratched in by WWII American GIs. *Corridas* (see box below) staged here from

Easter through September are as bloody as anything the Romans watched. *(Arenas ☎04 90 49 36 86. Open May-Sept. daily 9am-6:30pm; Mar.-Apr. and Oct. 9am-5:30pm; Nov.-Feb. 10am-4:30pm. Included on Monument Pass and Circuit Arles Antique, otherwise 20F/€3.05, children and students 15F/€2.29. Corridas and cocardes ☎04 90 96 03 70. Bullfights from 90F/€13.72, children 40F/€6.10.)*

THEATRE ANTIQUE*. Squeezed between the amphitheater and the gardens, this partially ruined theater is a reminder of the refined side of Roman culture. Capitols lie around the flower-filled backstage, and only two columns of the stage wall stand, but enough remains for modern productions to take advantage of the theater's magnificent acoustics. *(Rue de la Calade. For reservations call the Théâtre de la Calade at 04 90 93 05 23 or the tourist office. Open May-Sept. daily 9am-6:30pm; Mar.-Apr. and Oct. 9-11:30am and 2-5:30pm; Nov.-Feb. 10am-1:30am and 2-4:30pm. Included on Monument pass, otherwise 20F/€3.05, students and children 15F/€2.29.)* Just behind the theater, the shady **Jardin d'Eté** is a great place to picnic and eavesdrop on concerts. Wander through to notice the bizarrely morbid head of Van Gogh mounted on a large stone. *(Open May-Sept. daily 7am-8:30pm; Oct.-Apr. 7am-5:30pm.)*

MUSEE D'ARLES ANTIQUE*. This museum is almost as well-designed as its collection is well-assembled: the ultramodern blue structure sets off the Roman tools, mosaics, sarcophagi, and other local artifacts that it contains. While pondering how much wine can fill one of the immense jugs, walk a few feet to see the tombs where those who drank it went. Also includes spectacular, almost complete, mosaics dating from the 2nd century, and large, to scale models of Roman architecture, including the ingenious pontoon bridge that was once the symbol of Arles. *(Av. de la 1ère D.F.L., 10min. from the center of town. With your back to the tourist office, turn left, walk along bd. G. Clemenceau to its end, and follow the signs. ☎04 90 18 88 88. Open Mar.-Oct. daily 9am-7pm; Nov.-Feb. 10am-5pm. Part of Monument pass and Circuit Arles Antique, otherwise 35F/€5.34, students 25F/€3.81, children 5F/€0.76. Tours in French by reservation.)*

LES ALYSCAMPS*. This cemetery was one of the most famous burial grounds of the ancient world; its name is a twist on Champs-Elysées, or "Elysian Fields." Consecrated by St-Trôphime, first bishop of Arles, it kept its function during the Christian era and now holds 80 generations of locals. Les Alyscamps even rated a mention in Dante's *Inferno*. The most elaborate sarcophagi have been destroyed or removed, but the atmosphere here is intact; a sense of overpowering quiet and unbreakable peace hangs heavily in the poplared avenues and the 12th-century abbey at their end. *(10min. from the center of town. From the tourist office, head east on bd. des Lices to its intersection with bd. Emile Courbes. Turn right onto av. des Alyscamps, follow the canal, and cross the tracks. ☎04 90 49 36 87. Open May-Sept. daily 9am-6:30pm; Mar.-Apr. and Oct. 9am-11:30am and 2-5:30pm; Nov. 11-Feb. 10-11:30am and 2-4:30pm. Included on Monument pass, otherwise 20F/€3.05, students and children under 18 15F/€2.29.)*

CLOITRE ST-TROPHIME*. The city's famous medieval cloister is an oasis of calm and shade. Each carved column in its arcades is topped by lions in brushwood, saints in stone leaves, and strange flora. Adjoining the cloister is the Eglise St-Trôphime, built between the 11th and 15th centuries. Its elaborate facade deserves a place in art-history books: in a chapel inside are the reliquaries and remnants of some 30 saints—you can observe the sturdy shinbones of St-Roch, and ogle the skulls of Saints Genes and Innocent. *(Pl. de la République. ☎04 90 49 33 53. Open May-Sept. daily 9am-6:30pm; Mar.-Apr. and Oct. 9am-5:30pm; Nov.-Feb. 10am-4:30pm. Part of Monument pass, otherwise cloisters 20F/€3.05, students 15F/€2.29. Church free.)*

FONDATION VAN GOGH. You'll find no van Goghs here—only tributes to him by other artists. Though the museum houses big names like Lichtenstein and Jasper Johns, some of the best work here is by relative unknowns: a painting by Doutreleau, for example, capturing what it would be like to pass van Gogh on the street. *(26 rond-point des Arènes. ☎04 90 49 94 04. Open Apr.-Oct. 15 daily 10am-7pm; Oct. 16-Mar. Tu-Su 9:30am-noon and 2-5:30pm. 30F/€4.57, students and children 20F/€3.05.)*

MUSEON ARLATEN*. Various provençal artifacts attempting to recreate a vision of 19th-century daily life are brought together in a superb folk museum founded by poet Frédéric Mistral, who dedicated his life to reviving local traditions, using the money from his 1904 Nobel Prize to buy this striking 16th-century building, built around the ruins of a small Roman forum. Staffers are even clothed in traditional garb. Items range from parasols and hairpieces to drawings and instruments. *(29 rue de la République. ☎04 90 93 58 11. Open June-Aug. daily 9:30am-1pm and 2-6:30pm; Apr.-May and Sept. Tu-Su 9:30am-12:30pm and 2-6pm; Oct.-Mar. Tu-Su 9:30am-12:30pm and 2-5pm. Part of Monument pass, otherwise 20F/€3.05, students 15F/€2.29.)*

MUSEE REATTU*. Once a stronghold of the knights of St. John, this spacious museum now houses a collection of contemporary art, watercolors, oils of the Camargue by Henri Rousseau, and two rooms of canvases by the Neoclassical artist Réattu. Its pride and joy are the 57 drawings with which Picasso honored Arles in 1971; most attempt to capture the many "faces" (literally) of the town. One of the great pleasures here is the building itself, with gargoyled rooftops, courtyards, and a view of the broad Rhône. *(Rue du Grand Prieuré. ☎04 90 49 37 58. Open Apr.-Sept. daily 10am-noon and 2-6:30pm; Oct. 10am-12:30pm and 2-5pm; Nov. 10am-noon and 2-6pm; Dec.-Jan. 10-11:30am and 2-4pm; Feb. 10am -11:30am and 2-4:30pm. Part of Monument pass, otherwise 30F/€4.57, students 25F/€3.81.)*

OTHER SIGHTS. A visit to the **Cryptoportiques du Forum*,** inside a former Jesuit chapel, is an unforgettable experience. Dating from the first century BC, these gloomy underground galleries provided the foundations for the Roman forum. Hold your breath and walk into the darkness. *(Rue Balze. Open May-Sept. daily 9am-6:30pm; Mar.-Apr. and Oct. 9-11:30am and 2-5:30pm; Nov. 11-Feb. 10-11:30am and 2-4:30pm. Part of Monument pass and Circuit Arles Antique, otherwise 20F/€3.05, students and under age 18 15F/€2.29.)* The ruins of the **Thermes de Constantin*,** rue D. Maïsto, barely evoke what was once the largest Roman bath complex in Provence. *(Open May-Sept. daily 9am-6:30pm; Mar.-Apr. and Oct. 9am-11:30am and 2-5:30pm; Nov.-Feb. 10-11:30am and 2-4:30pm. Part of Monument pass and Circuit Arles Antique, otherwise 20F/€3.05, students and under age 18 15F/€2.29.)* The forgettable **Espace Van Gogh,** pl. Félix Rey, houses a book and video library, a small theater showing free films, and art exhibitions within the original walls of the hospital where Van Gogh lopped off his ear. *(For info about exhibits ☎04 90 49 38 34. Open July-Aug. daily 9am-8pm; Sept.-June 10:30am-8pm. Library ☎04 90 49 39 39. Open Tu-F 1-6:30pm, Sa 10am-noon and 1-5pm.)*

FESTIVALS

The major cultural event of the year in Arles is the **Rencontres Internationales de la Photographie,** held in the first week of July. Undiscovered photographers from around the world court agents by roaming around town with portfolios under their arms. More established photographers present their work in 15 locations (including the Abbaye de Montmajour), conduct nightly slide shows (40-50F/€6.10-7.62), participate in debates, and offer colloquia with artists, some free. When the festival crowd departs, the remarkable exhibits are left behind. (20-30F/€3.05-4.57 per exhibit, 70F/€18.29 for 4 exhibits, all exhibits 120F/€18.29, with catalogue 250F/€38.12; under 25 free.) For more info, visit the tourist office or contact **Rencontres,** 10 Rondpoint des Arènes (☎04 90 96 76 06). During the festival, tickets can be bought in the Espace Van Gogh.

Of more interest to the casual tourist are Arles' many colorful provençal festivals. On May 1, the ancient Confrèrie des Gardians ("brotherhood of herders" of the Camargue's wild horses) parades through town and gathers in the arena for the **Fête des Gardians.** On the last weekend in June and the first in July, bonfires blaze in the streets and locals wear traditional costume for the beautiful **Fêtes d'Arles.** Halfway through the festival, bareback riders race through the bd. des Lices on white *camarguais* horses for the **course de Satin,** while every three years, at its end, the city crowns the *Reine d'Arles* (Queen of Arles), a young woman chosen to represent the region's language, customs, and history. Traditional ceremonies, dance performances, and fireworks occur in the arena at midnight (free). The next day brings the **Cocarde d'or,** when the new queen crowns the winning *rasateur* (see box, p. 256); bulls are then run through the streets between the horses of the shepherds. **Bullfights** are more common, occurring in April, around Easter, July and September. (Cheapest tickets around 76-340F/€11.58-51.84. For more info, call the Bureau des Arènes at 04 90 96 03 70; fax 04 90 96 64 31.)

DAYTRIP FROM ARLES: ABBAYE DE MONTMAJOUR

From M-Sa, 8 buses per day run from Arles, 2 on Su (10F/€1.53). Abbey (☎/fax 04 90 54 64 17) open Apr.-Sept. daily 9am-7pm; Oct.-Mar. W-M 10am-1pm and 2-5pm. 35F/€5.34, ages 18-25 23F/€3.51, children free.

Grim, stony Montmajour Abbey dominates the fields just 7km from Arles. Though the monastery never had more than 60 monks, it was old (founded 948) and rich enough to possess a huge architectural complex, including a 26m fortified tower and the 10th- and 11th-century **Chapelle St-Pierre.** The empty nave of the abbey church is stunningly large. The stonework conserves a human touch in its details: the light, arched ceilings in the crypt's rotunda and five radiating chapels are laced with distinctive worker's marks that ensured the builders' pay. The west wall of the cloister bears markings of a less official nature: detailed graffiti of medieval galleons, scratched into the stone in the 12th or 13th centuries. The abbey's appeal is accentuated by its rotating, extensive photo exhibits, which are accompanied by written commentary in English.

THE CAMARGUE

In stark contrast to the provençal hills to the north, the Camargue is a vast delta lined with tall grasses and prowled by all manner of wildlife. Pink flamingos, black bulls, and the famous local white horses roam freely across the flat expanse of wild marshland, protected by the confines of the national park. The human inhabitants include *gardians*, rugged herders from a 2000-year-old line of cowboys, and the gypsies who have made the area one of their stopping-points for 500 years. The Camargue is anchored in the north by Arles and in the south by Stes-Maries-de-la-Mer and Aigues-Mortes.

Aspiring botanists and zoologists should stop at the **Centre d'Information de Ginès,** which distributes info on the region's unusual flora and fauna. (☎04 90 97 86 32. Open Apr.-Sept. daily 10am-5:30pm; Oct.-Mar. Sa-Th 9:30am-5pm.) Next door, the **Parc Ornithologique de Pont de Gau,** on the bus line between Stes-Maries and Arles, provides several kilometers of paths through the marshes and offers views of birds and grazing bulls. (☎04 90 97 82 62. Park open Apr.-Sept. daily 9am-sunset; Oct.-Mar. 10am-sunset. 36F/€5.49, under age 18 18F/€2.74.)

The best way to see the Camargue is on **horseback,** and the region is dotted with stables offering tours throughout the park on horses. The beautiful beasts can go far into the marshes, wading through deep water into the range of birds and bulls inaccessible by any other means. Most rides are oriented toward novices, so don't be afraid if you've never saddled up before. Do, however, wear tennis shoes or boots and long pants. The stables are all united under a single association, the **Association Camarguaise de Tourisme Equestre** (☎04 90 97 86 32; fax 04 90 97 70 82), and their prices remain within a few francs of one another. Other options include **jeep safaris** and **boat trips;** most leave from Stes-Maries, but some are offered in Arles and Aigues-Mortes as well. Although most of the trails are open only to horseback riders, **bicycle touring** is a great way to see much of the area. Keep in mind that bike trails may be sandy and difficult to ride. Trail maps indicating length, level of difficulty, and danger spots are available from the tourist office. Bring an ample supply of fresh water—it gets hotter than Hades. A two-hour pedal will reveal some of the area, but you'll need a whole day if you plan to stop along the wide, deserted white-sand beaches that line the trail.

STES-MARIES-DE-LA-MER

According to legend, in AD 40 Mary Magdalene, Mary Salomé (mother of the Apostles John and James), Mary Jacobé (Jesus' aunt), and their servant Sara were put to sea to die. Their ship washed ashore here; Stes-Maries' dark, fortified church, its only real sight, was built to house their relics. The tourist traffic it occasions has made Stes-Maries into a sort of monster, a honky-tonk collection of overpriced snack trailers and stores willing to cast anything provençal in plastic. The place is still worth a visit, though; besides possessing the aforementioned church, Stes-Maries is the unofficial capital of the Camargue, and most expeditions into that strange wilderness start from here. The town is also dear to gypsies, who come here as pilgrims every May.

ORIENTATION AND PRACTICAL INFORMATION. The town is wedged between untouched conservation land to the north, sea to the south, and marshes to the east. **Buses** leave from **Arles** (1hr.; M-Sa 6 per day, Su 4 per day; 39F/€5.95); contact **Les Cars de Camargue** (☎04 90 96 36 25) for info. The bus stop in Stes-Maries-de-la-Mer lies just north of pl. Mireille. Once here, **rent bikes** at **Le Vélociste,** 6 rue de la République. (☎04 90 97 83 26. 40F/€6.10 per 2hr., 50F/€7.62 per half-day, 90F/€13.72 per day, passport deposit. Open July-Aug. daily 8:30am-8pm; Sept.-June 9am-6:30pm.) Or try **Location de Vélos,** rue de la République (☎04 90 97 74 56. Same prices as Vélociste. Open daily 8:30am-7pm.) If you get really stuck in the Camargue's mud, call **Allô Taxi** at 04 90 97 83 83 or 06 20 73 87 06.

To get to the **tourist office,** 5 av. Van Gogh, walk toward the ocean down rue de la République from the bus station or down rue Victor Hugo from the church. They give out the free *Camargue Naturellement*, which lists all the biking, hiking, boating, and horseback tours in the area, and provides a very helpful list of the area lodgings. (☎04 90 97 82 55. Open July-Aug. daily 9am-8pm; Apr.-June and Sept. 9am-7pm; Oct.-Feb. 9am-5pm.) Access the **Internet** at **Cyber Planète,** pl. des Impériaux. (☎04 90 97 89 37. Open daily 2:30pm-1am, until 2am in summer. 50F/€7.62 per hr.) **Crédit Agricole,** on pl. Mireille, **exchanges currency** for a 25F/€3.81 commission and has an ATM outside the tourist office. (☎04 90 97 81 17. Open July-Aug. Tu-W and F 9am-4:30pm, Th 10am-4:30pm, Sa 9am-noon; Sept.-May closed daily between 12:30-2pm. The **police** are on av. Van Gogh, right next to Les Arènes (☎04 90 97 89 50). The **post office** is on 6 av. Gambetta. (Open July-Aug. M-F 9am-12:30pm and 1:30-4:30pm, Sa 8:30am-1:30pm; Sept.-May M-F 9am-noon and 1:30-4:30pm, Sa 8:30am-1:30pm.) **Postal code:** 13460.

ACCOMMODATIONS AND CAMPING. Hotels fill quickly in summer, and rooms under 200F/€30.49 are scarce. You can base yourself in Arles and make the town a daytrip; many choose instead to sleep illegally on the beach. North of Stes-Maries in the heart of the Camargue is the **Auberge de Jeunesse (HI) hameau de Pioch Badet.** To get there, take the bus that runs between Stes-Maries and Arles to "Pioch Badet" (15min., 5 per day, 12F/€1.83 from Stes-Maries; 40min., 29F/€4.42 from Arles). The quiet, camp-style hostel fills early in summer, so take the first bus you can. (☎04 90 97 51 72. Kitchen. Bike rental 60F/€9.15 per day, passport deposit. Horse tours 70F/€10.63 per hr., 350F/€53.36 per day. Picnic lunch 45F/€6.86. Sheets 18F/€2.75. Reception 7:30-10:30am and 5-11pm; call ahead if you plan to arrive later. Lockout 10:30am-5pm. July-Aug. curfew midnight; extended during festivals. Closed Jan. except to groups. Obligatory *demi-pension* 133F/€20.28.)

The **Hôtel Méditerranée,** 4 bd. Frédéric Mistral, off rue Victor Hugo, is a pretty hotel exploding with flowers; some of the beautiful rooms have little terraces. (☎04 90 97 82 09; fax 04 90 97 76 31. Breakfast 38F/€5.80. Reception 8am-8pm. Reserve ahead in summer. Occasionally closed in Jan. Doubles 250-280F/€38.11-42.69; triples 380F/€57.93; quads 400F/€60.78. About 20F/€3.05 cheaper off-season. MC/V.) But stars like these beg to be slept under; **camp** at **La Brise,** a large site crossed by watery ditches and stands of reeds. It's five minutes east of the city center (take the bus from Arles to "La Brise") and has a pool and laundry. (☎04 90

97 84 67. Reception 9am-9:30pm. July-Aug. 1 person with tent 60F/€9.10, 2 people with car 110F/€16.80, 40F/€6.10 per person; Apr.-June 1 person with tent 50F/€7.60, 2 people with car 90F/€13.72, 30F/€4.60 per person; Jan.-Mar. and Oct.-Dec. 1 person with tent 36F/€5.50, 2 people with car 70F/€10.67, 25F/€3.80 per person. Electricity 26F/€4. Be warned: the Camargue breeds mosquitoes.)

FOOD. The Camargue's main crop is a sweet, fat-grained rice; you will find it in gelatinous cakes sold at pâtisseries, at local restaurants, and on the shelves of **supermarkets** like the **Petit Casino** on av. Victor Hugo. (☎04 90 97 90 60. Open in summer daily 8am-8pm; in winter 8am-noon and 4-8pm) A **market** fills pl. des Gitanes on Mondays and Fridays (7am-noon). Restaurants cluster away from the waterfront around **rue Victor Hugo,** especially on **pl. Esprit Pioch,** where they serve seafood, the ubiquitous paella, *pavé de taureau*, and refreshing sangria. Most *menus* start around 65-70F/€9.91-10.67, but 55F/€8.39 is reasonable for lunch.

SIGHTS. The only major sight in town, and the focus of Stes-Maries, is the gray 12th-century **fortified church** looming high above the town's menagerie of snack bars. These grim parapets guard a startling view of sea, sunset, and Camargue; the dark Romanesque interior offers a cool respite from the shadeless town, as well as gaudy, bizarre artifacts. In the crypt, the relics of the saints are visible year-round, and a statue of St-Sara glimmers in the corner, almost obscured in her layers of gilt and brocaded cloaks. The saints' power supposedly has cured the blind, healed the lame, and halted the *mistral* winds of 1833. (☎04 90 97 87 60. Church open daily 8am-12:30pm and 2-7pm. Free. Roof and tower open in summer daily 10am-8pm; in winter 10am-12:30pm and 2-6:30pm. 10F/€1.53.)

FESTIVALS. According to legend, the family chief of the region's native gypsies, Sara, welcomed the Stes-Maries and asked that she and her people be baptized into Christianity. The **Pèlerinage des Gitans** is a yearly event uniting gypsy pilgrims from all over Europe (May 24-25). A costumed procession from the church to the sea bears statues of the saints and reenacts their landing. A **festival** on the weekend around October 22 honors the Maries, with similar ceremonies but minus the gypsy element. In the second week of July, the **Féria du Cheval** brings horses from around the world for shows, competitions, and rodeos at the Stes-Maries and Méjanes arenas. (Call the Arènes de Méjanes at 04 90 97 10 60 for details. 100-420F/€15.25-64.03.) During July, August, and September, **bullfights** and horse shows occur regularly at the modern arenas. (Call the Arènes at 04 90 97 85 86. Tickets from 90F/€13.72.)

EXCURSIONS. Stes-Maries is undoubtedly the capital of the Camargue, and most organized visits to the region leave from here. While we list some tours here, the tourist office is teeming with brochures with more info. The exception are horseback tours, which are run by the many stables lining the road from Arles to Stes-Maries. Contact the **Association Camarguaise de Tourisme Equestre** or pick up their list of members from the tourist office. Organized rides are geared mostly toward equestrian novices and follow somewhat limited routes; rates are the same from one establishment to another. (☎04 90 97 86 32; fax 04 90 97 70 82. 70-100F/€10.67-15.25 per hr., 140-180F/€21.35-27.44 per 2hr., 450F/€68.61 per day; picnic usually included on day trips.) For **jeep safaris,** contact **Le Gitan,** 13 av. de la Plage. Safaris explore the banks of the Grand and Petit Rhône. The jeeps hold 7-8 people. (☎04 66 70 09 65; fax 04 66 70 22 47. 2hr. trips at 200F/€30.49 per person depart continually from 9am-6pm; 4hr. trips 220F/€33.54 (depart from *Safari Nature Camargue*, 6 rue Alliés); day-long voyage with lunch 500F/€76.23. Sunrise tour (350F/€53.36) departs at 5am and returns at noon. Open year-round daily 9am-8pm.) **Camargue,** 5 rue des Launes, sends **boats** from Port Gardian deep into the Petit Rhône for up-close bird- and bull-watching. (☎04 90 97 84 72; fax 04 90 97 73 50. Open Mar.-Nov. 1½hr., 3-4 per day; first departure at 10:30am, last departure 4:10pm. 60F/€9.15, children 40F/€6.10.)

THE COLOR OF THE WATER The reddish water that surrounds Aigues-Mortes is the result of the salt production that creates the specialty sea salt "*fleur du sel de Camargue.*" The red vegetable plankton called *Dunaliella salina* is in all sea water, but most of the algae is usually eaten by its counterpart animal plankton *Artemia salina*. When the salt level is too high–as in Aigues-Mortes where the water is trapped and evaporated to produce salt–the *Artemia* die and the reddish carotene-filled plankton proliferate. The waters of Aigues-Mortes become progressively more colorful as the water evaporates over the summer months until finally only salt is left and, in September, the salt is collected and the process begins anew.

AIGUES-MORTES

Aigues-Mortes' landscape hasn't changed much in its 800-year history. This curiously inland port city, whose name means "Dead Waters," is home to salt marshes spotted with herons, egrets, and flamingos, surrounded the thick defensive wall of the city. In summer, the water surrounding Aigues-Mortes takes on a purplish hue as it evaporates to create the famous *fleur du sel de Camargue*. Inside the walls, boutiques and restaurants sell the specialty foods of the Camargue while tourists stroll along the towered battlements.

TRANSPORTATION AND PRACTICAL INFORMATION. SNCF **trains** and **buses** run to **Nîmes** (1hr., 4 per day, 39F/€5.95; open M-F 6:40am-7:30pm, Sa-Su 8am-7:30pm), as do STDG buses (1hr., 5 per day, 37F/€5.64). **Les Courriers du Midi** run **buses** to **Montpellier** (1½hr., M-Sa 2 per day, 38F/€5.79). The **tourist office,** porte de la Gardette, is in the dark tower on the inside of the main gate to the left. (☎04 66 53 73 00; fax 04 66 53 65 94. Open July-Sept. M-F 9am-8pm, Sa-Su 10am-8pm; Oct.-June M-F 9am-6pm, Sa-Su 10am-noon and 2-6pm.)

ACCOMMODATIONS AND FOOD. The cheapest option in town is the **Hôtel L'Escale,** 3 av. Tour de Constance, directly across the street from the tower, which has many rooms with A/C. (☎04 66 53 71 14; fax 04 66 53 76 74. Reception 6:30am-11pm. Reservations usually required July 15-Aug. 15. Singles and doubles with sink and shower 160F/€24.39, with toilet 190F/€28.97; triples with sink and shower 190F/€28.97, with toilet 250F/€38.12; one quint 360F/€54.89. MC/V.) The **Hôtel Tour de Constance,** 1 bd. Diderot, is slightly more expensive with sparkling tile floors. (☎04 66 53 83 50. Breakfast 30F/€4.57. Reception until 10pm. Doubles with shower 190F/€28.97, with TV 210-230F/€32.02-35.06; triples with shower 280F/€42.69; quads with shower 310F/€47.26. AmEx/MC/V.)

Fast food and small **boutiques** can be found on **rue Jean Jaurès,** while lively, well-priced eateries fill the central **pl. St-Louis.** A **market** often spans the length of the wall just outside the city's fortifications (W-Su 6am-12:30pm). **Le Moulin de Pauline,** 22 rue Emile Zola, sells a huge selection of Camargue specialties including fleur de sel, jams, dry bull sausage, wines, and *apéritifs*. Customers are invited to taste one of the apéritifs. (☎04 66 51 97 67. Open July-Aug. daily 10am-9:30pm, Sept. and Apr.-June 10am-7:30pm; Oct.-Mar. 10:30am-12:30pm and 2:30-6:30pm.

SIGHTS AND ENTERTAINMENT. Louis IX (St-Louis) built this *bastide* as a springboard from which to reconquer the Holy Land; he launched the Seventh and Eighth Crusades from here in 1248 and 1270. Though the crusades were fatal for St-Louis—he was captured on the first and died on the second—the town has succeeded marvelously, its planned grid still enclosed by 13th-century walls. The **Tour de Constance,** keystone of the city's defensive fortifications, has been perfectly preserved, probably as a result of its impenetrable 6m-thick walls. An optional tour in French (every 45min.) takes you to the top of the tower and through the vaulted prison on the way down. Built to wage war on infidels abroad, the tower ultimately proved more effective in silencing those at home. Forty-five Templar Knights were imprisoned and tortured here when their order fell out of favor in the 14th century, and for almost half of the 18th century Marie Durand sat here along with other Protestant women who refused to renounce their faith. (☎04 66 53 61 55. Tower and ramparts open June-Aug. daily 9:30am-8pm; May and Sept. 9:30am-7pm; Mar.-Apr. and Oct. 10am-6pm; Nov.-Feb. 10am-5pm. 36F/€5.49, under 26 23F/€3.51. 10-11 daily tours in French.) **Place St-Louis** honors the town's founder with a statue. On the corner of the *place* is the 13th-century **Notre Dame des Sablons,** St-Louis' final stop in France before his first crusade. The church now features modern painted-glass windows. (Open daily 8:30am-noon and 2-7pm.)

L'Aventure runs daily **boat tours** into the Camargue. (☎06 03 91 44 63. 40F/€6.10 for 1½hr., 50F/€7.62 for 2hr.) If time is short or the sun too hot, let the images of the Camargue drift by without the mosquito bites in the **3-D Cinéma** across the canal. (Open Feb. 15-Nov. 15. Shows every hr.; July-Aug. 3-10pm, Sept.-June 3-7pm. 37F/€5.64, children 12 and under 22F/€3.35.) During the second weekend of October, *raseteurs* participate in the **Fête Votive's** *Course Camarguaise*. In this Camarguaise tradition, a bull is released into an arena with a tassel attached to his horns. A prize is awarded to the *raseteur* who can detach the tassel. The first week in August brings Mediterranean singers to the town for the **Festival des Nuits d'Encens.** (Info ☎04 66 73 91 23. Concert tickets 130F/€19.82, students 110F/€16.77). On the last weekend in August, the **Fête de St-Louis** recreates the past with historical pageants, jousting, and a medieval market.

NIMES

It is the Spanish feel of Nîmes (pop. 132,000) that draws the vacationing French; they flock here for the *férias*, celebrations featuring bull runs, bullfights, flamenco dancing, and all manner of hot-blooded fanfare. Nîmes isn't a place to linger; the city has passable nightlife and the amenities of a metropolis, but it sprawls too much for comfort and lacks the intimacy of other provençal cities or the glitz of the Côte d'Azur. Nîmes' status as an all-star tourist destination is for one reason only: its incredible Roman structures. The arena, the Maison Carré, and especially the nearby Pont du Gard aqueduct are simply too exceptional to miss.

TRANSPORTATION

Trains: bd. Talabot. To: **Arles** (30min., 10 per day, 48F/€7.32); **Bordeaux** (6hr., 6 per day, 300F/€45.74); **Marseille** (1¼hr., 6 per day, 98F/€14.95); **Montpellier** (30min., 10 per day, most in the afternoon, 47F/€7.17); **Orange** (1½hr., 3 per day, 66F/€10.07); **Paris** (4½hr., 7 per day, TGV 508F/€77.47); and **Toulouse** (3hr., 10 per day, 187F/€28.52). Info office open M-F 5:45am-9:30pm, Sa 6:45am-9:45pm, Su 6:45am-10pm.

Buses: at the bus station, rue Ste-Félicité (☎04 66 29 52 00), behind the train station. Info office open M-F 8am-noon and 2-6pm. **Société des Transports Départementaux du Gard (STDG)** (☎04 66 29 27 29) runs to **Avignon** (1½hr.; M-F 8 per day, 6 on Sa, 2 on Su; 44F/€6.71); **Cars de Camargue** (☎04 90 96 36 25) serves **Arles** (M-F 5 per day, 3 on Sa; 35F/€5.34) and **Montpellier** (M-Sa 2 per day; 55F/€8.39).

Local Transportation: T.C.N. (☎04 66 38 15 40). Tickets good for 1hr. Buses stop running at 7:30pm. Ticket 6F/€0.92, *carnet* of 5 24.50F/€3.74.

Taxis: TRAN office (☎04 66 29 40 11) in train station. 24hr.

ORIENTATION AND PRACTICAL INFORMATION

Nîmes' shops, museums, and cafés cluster in the *vieille ville* between bd. Victor Hugo and bd. Admiral Courbet. From the train station, follow av. Feuchères, veer left around the park, and scoot clockwise around the arena. This is the start of the *vieille ville*. To get to the tourist office, go straight on bd. Victor Hugo for five blocks until you reach the Maison Carré, a Roman temple in the middle of pl. Comédie, whose facade faces rue Auguste and the tourist office.

Tourist Office: 6 rue Auguste (☎04 66 67 29 11; fax 04 66 21 81 04). Free accommodations service. Info on bus and train excursions to Pont du Gard, the Camargue, and nearby towns. Free detailed map and festival info. The free *Nîmescope* lists events. Open July-Aug. M-F 8am-8pm, Sa 9am-7pm, Su 10am-6pm; May and Sept. M-F 8am-7pm, Sa 9am-7pm, Su 10am-6pm. **Branch office** (☎04 66 84 18 13) in the train station. Open July-Sept. M-Sa 9:30am-12:30pm and 2-6pm, Su 9:30am-12:30pm and 1:30-3:30pm; Oct.-June M-F 9:30am-12:30pm and 2-6pm.

City tours: Le Petit Train (☎04 66 70 26 92). Leaves almost every hr. from the Esplanade Charles de Gaulle in front of the Palais de Justice. July-Aug. daily 9:30am-7:30pm; Apr.-June and Sept.-Oct. 9:30-11:30am and 2:30-5:30pm. 30F/€4.57, ages 3-12 10F/€1.53.

Budget Travel: Nouvelles Frontières, 1 bd. de Prague (☎04 66 67 38 94; fax 04 66 78 38 62). Open M-Sa 9am-7pm.

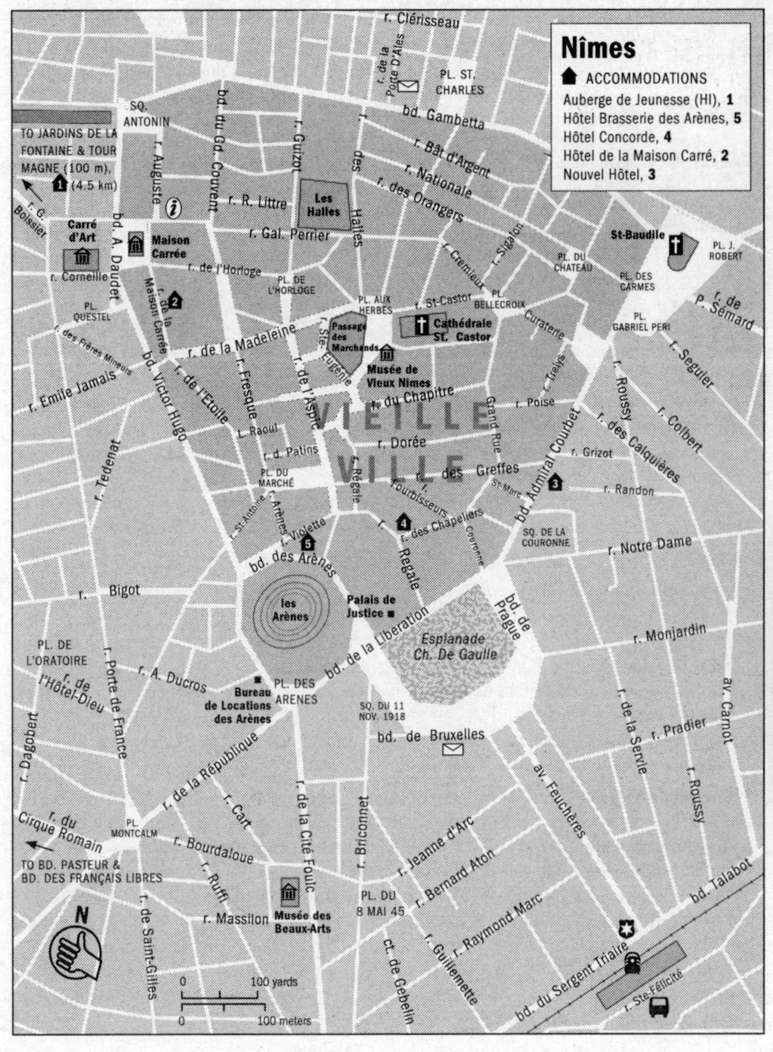

Money: Banque de France, 2 sq. du 11 Novembre (☎04 66 76 82 00), offers **currency exchange** with no commission. Exchange desk open M-F 8:30am-12:15pm.

Laundromat: Lavomatique, 5 rue des Halles. Open daily 7am-8pm.

Internet access: Netgames, 25 rue de l'Horloge, pl. de la Maison Carré (☎04 66 36 36 16). 25F/€3.81 per hr. Open daily 10am-midnight.

Hospital: Hôpital Caremeau, rue Professeur Robert Debré (☎04 66 68 68 68).

Police: 16 av. Feuchères (☎04 66 62 82 82).

Post Office: 1 bd. de Bruxelles (☎04 66 76 69 50), across from the park at the end of av. Feuchères. **Currency exchange** with no commission. Open M-F 8am-7pm, Sa 8am-noon. **Branch offices:** 19 bd. Gambetta (☎04 66 36 32 60) and 11 pl. Belle Croix. **Poste Restante:** 30006. **Postal codes:** 30000 and 30900.

ACCOMMODATIONS AND CAMPING

The *vieille ville* is dotted with hotels, most of which have relatively high prices. If you're prepared for a long walk or bus ride into town, the hostel is unquestionably the way to go. For hotels, it's best to reserve a couple of weeks ahead during the festival in early June and during the biggest summer concerts.

Auberge de Jeunesse (HI), 257 chemin de l'Auberge de la Jeunesse (☎04 66 68 03 20; fax 04 66 68 03 21), off chemin de la Cigale, 4½km from quai de la Fontaine. Take bus #2 (dir: "Alès" or "Villeverte") to "Stade, Route d'Alès;" follow the signs bearing left and up the hill. After buses stop running at 8pm, the hostel minibus (call ahead to arrange) will pick you up at the station for free, and take you back in the morning for 8F/€1.22. To walk, pass the Maison Carré on bd. Victor Hugo and continue straight on bd. A. Daudet. Go left at sq. Antonin onto quai de la Fontaine. The Jardins de la Fontaine will be on your right–continue alongside the garden straight on av. Roosevelt. Signs for the Auberge will lead you right onto rte. d'Alès and left onto chemin de la Cigale. Follow the signs (40min.). This wonderfully modern and hospitable hostel is worth the walk. 4- to 6-bed dorms with bath are accessed by magnetic key-cards. Individual, locking cupboards for luggage. Ping-pong, pétanque, foosball, laundry, kitchen, and bar until 1am. **Bikes** €8 per day. **Scooter** €20 per day. May-Oct. bike/kayak combo to Pont du Gard €20. Breakfast €3.20. Dinner €8.50. Sheets €2.70 per week. Reception Mar.-Sept. 24hr. (night guard). No lockout or curfew. Some family rooms available. Reservations advised. Bunks €8.65. **Camping** €4.95. MC/V. **Members only.**

Hôtel Brasserie des Arènes, 4 bd. des Arènes (☎04 66 67 23 05; fax 04 66 67 76 93; hotel@brasserie-arenes.com). In a perfect location, facing the arena, with big, well-kept rooms. Breakfast 25F/€3.81. Singles 120-140F/€18.30-21.35; doubles 155-160F/€23.64-24.39; triples 205F/€31.26; quads 290F/€44.21. MC/V.

Hôtel Concorde, 3 rue des Chapeliers (☎/fax 04 66 67 91 03), off rue Regale. The cramped rooms in this small hotel are clean and the staff is friendly. If you get a room with a toilet, don't expect privacy–a small and ineffective barrier separates the toilet from the bedchamber. Breakfast 25F/€3.81. Singles and doubles 120F/€18.30, with shower and toilet 200F/€30.49; triples 250F/€38.12. MC/V.

Hôtel de la Maison Carré, 14 rue de la Maison Carré (☎04 66 67 32 89; fax 04 66 76 22 57). Dirty carpets notwithstanding, the rooms in this hotel are cheerful and brightly lit, with showers and TVs in all but the smallest single. Breakfast 35F/€5.34. Reservations recommended. Singles 170F/€25.92, with shower 245F/€37.35; doubles 230-290F/€35.07-44.21; triples 345F/€52.61; quad with bath 370F/€56.43. MC/V.

Nouvel Hôtel, 6 bd. Amiral Courbet (☎04 66 67 62 48), along the major boulevard that leads from the amphiteater; all rooms have TVs. A big hotel with an institutional feel. Breakfast 30F/€4.57. Shower 20F/€3.05. Singles and doubles 155F/€23.64, with shower and toilet 230F/€35.07; triples with shower and toilet 270F/€41.16; quads with shower but no toilet 255F/€38.88. AmEx/MC/V.

Campsite: Domaine de La Bastide (☎/fax 04 66 38 09 21), rte. de Générac, 5km south of the train station. Take bus D (dir: "La Bastide", last bus 7:30pm) to the terminus. By car, leave Nîmes heading to Montpellier, then take rte. de Générac. 3-star site with grocery store, laundry, and recreational facilities. Open year-round. 48F/€7.32 per person, 76F/€11.59 for 2 people. Caravan with electricity 68F/€10.37 per person, 96F/€14.64 for 2 people.

FOOD

Local cooking is often seasoned with *herbes de Provence* (a mixture of local herbs) and *aïoli* (a thick sauce made with garlic and olive oil). The specialty is *la brandade de morue*, dried cod crushed with olive oil and served as a turnover, pastry, or soufflé. Sadly though, the restaurants are unspectacular in Nîmes—most aren't worth paying for. Especially if you're staying in the hostel, it's probably a good idea to pick up supplies and cook your own meal. *Caladons*, honey cookies sprinkled with almonds, are Nîmes' favorite sweet. Cafés and bakeries line the squares in the center of town, while there are brasseries along **bd. Victor Hugo, bd. Amiral Courbet,** and the Arena. Terraced **Pl. du Marché,** with its crocodile fountain, is full of chatter until late at night. To get off the trampled path, cross bd. Victor Hugo and choose a Vietnamese restaurant or bistro along **impasse Porte-de-France** or **rue Bigot.** The terraced herb gardens and ponds on the back slopes of the **Jardins de la Fontaine** make for unforgettable picnicking. Hostelers can stock up at the **open-air market** on bd. Jean-Jaurès (F 7am-1pm), the **market** in Les Halles (daily 6am-1pm), or the large **Marché U,** 19 rue d'Alès, just down the hill from the hostel (open M-Sa 8am-12:45pm and 3:30-8pm). The boulangerie and pâtisserie, **La Maison Villaret,** 13 rue de la Madeleine, has guarded the secret of its *"croquants Villaret"* since 1775—dry biscuits made of crushed almonds and baked in the same wood-burning ovens since their invention. (☎04 66 67 41 79. Open M-Sa 7am-7:30pm.)

SIGHTS

*A three-day **pass** to all sights is on sale at each sight (60F/€9.15, students 30F/€4.57).*

LES ARENES. This huge Roman amphitheater, the city's pride and joy, is the best-preserved in France. Impressive even when empty, the amphitheater is glorious when filled with screaming crowds for the concerts and bullfights that are still held within its stone bleachers. The elliptical arena, built in AD 50, holds approximately 23,000 people. *(☎04 66 76 72 77. For the ticket office, call 04 66 02 80 80. Open in summer daily 9am-6:30pm; in winter 9am-5:30pm. 28F/€4.27, students 20F/€3.05.)*

MAISON CARRE AND CARRE D'ART. The long, rectangular temple known as the **Maison Carré** was dedicated to Caius and Lucius Caesar, the grandson and adopted son of the emperor Augustus. It's sturdy stone pillars are a constant reminder of the Roman presence in Nîmes. The temple's purity of form and its exquisite carvings have always arrested the eye; Louis XIV took such a liking to it, in fact, that the Maison almost became a lawn ornament at Versailles. *(☎04 66 36 26 76. Open in summer daily 9am-noon and 2:30-7pm; in winter 9am-12:30pm and 2-6pm. Free.)* The Maison Carré is gracefully reflected in Norman Foster's ultra-modern **Carré d'Art** across the square, which houses a good collection of contemporary art displayed beautifully on huge, white walls. *(☎04 66 76 35 70. Library and museum open Tu-Su 10am-6pm. Library free; museum 28F/€4.27, students 20F/€3.05.)*

JARDINS DE LA FONTAINE. Wander up the quai de la Fontaine to while away the afternoon amid lush floral and marble sculptures in the evocatively ruined **Temple de Diane.** This formal garden, built by an 18th-century military engineer after the 17th-century designs of Le Nôtre, uses water from the Nemausus spring in its fabulous fountains and reflecting pools. The sound of running water mingles with the murmur of old men playing *boule* on the shaded sands. *(Off pl. Foch to the left along the canals from the Maison. Garden open Apr.-Sept. 15 daily 7:30am-10pm; Sept. 16-Nov. 7:30am-*

6:30pm; Nov.-Mar. 8am-7pm. Free.) Climb the staircases up the park to reach the **Tour Magne.** Built in the Iron Age and renovated by Augustus in 15 BC for use in the city's ramparts, this massive tower pinned down a corner of Rome with its blunt stone spike. Now the eroded ruins offer a God's-eye-view of Nîmes and the surrounding countryside from the top of its 140 steps. *(☎04 66 67 65 56. Open July-Aug. daily 9am-7pm; Sept.-June 9am-5pm. 15F/€2.29, students 12F/€1.83.)*

MUSEE DE BEAUX ARTS AND MUSEE DU VIEUX NIMES. Both of Nîmes' major museums can be skipped if you're pressed for time. The **Musée de Beaux-Arts,** housed in a Neoclassical building accented with marble pillars and Roman mosaic floors, contains paintings of the French, Italian, Flemish, and Dutch schools from the 15th to 19th centuries as well as temporary exhibits. The **Musée du Vieux Nîmes,** in a 17th-century palace, displays mostly 17th-century clothing in meticulously reconstructed period rooms. *(Beaux-Arts: rue de la cité Foule. ☎04 66 67 38 21. Vieux Nîmes: pl. aux Herbes, next to the cathedral. ☎04 66 36 00 64. Both open in summer Tu-Su 10am-6pm; in winter 11am-6pm. 28F/€4.27, students 20F/€3.05.)*

ENTERTAINMENT AND FESTIVALS

During the *férias* (see below), many bars stay open late, but the night ends fairly early during the rest of the year. The best option is to sit in one of the cafés in the pl. du Marché. Bustling **O'Flaherty's,** 21 bd. Amiral Courbet, has 24-34F/€3.66-5.19 pints of beer and live music on Thursday nights in winter. The dart-filled, Guinness-sloppy bar is a favorite of anglophones, anglophiles, and just plain Englishmen. (☎04 66 67 22 63. Open M-Th 11am-2am, F 11am-3am, Sa 5pm-3am, Su 5pm-2am.) The area around **impasse Porte-de-France** is home to many hopping bars. **Lulu Club,** 10 impasse de la Curaterie, off rue de la Curaterie, is a gay dance bar. (☎04 66 36 28 20. Sa, 50F/€7.62 cover includes 1 drink. Open Tu-Sa 11pm onward.) **Cinéma Le Sémaphore,** 25 rue Porte de France, plays non-French films in their original languages. (☎04 66 67 88 04. 32F/€4.88, noon shows 24F/€3.66. Closed July-Aug.)

Concerts, movies, plays, and operas take place at the *arènes* throughout the year (60-300F/€9.15-45.74). Summer acts have included Ray Charles, and Ben Harper. For info and reservations, contact the **Bureau de Location des Arènes,** 1 rue Alexandre Ducros. (☎04 66 02 80 80. Open M-F 9am-noon and 2-6pm.)

It is worth changing travel plans to see one of the famous *férias* of Nîmes. In all, Nîmes holds three important *férias:* the **Féria de Primavera** in mid-February, the **Féria des Vendages** in mid-September, and the most boisterous, the **Féria de Pentecôte.** For five days, the streets here resound with the clattering of hooves as bulls are herded to the *arènes* for combat. Nights are spent dancing, singing, and boozing. The **courses camarguaises,** held at varying dates through June, July, and August, offer more humane entertainment: fighters strip decorations from the bulls' horns, narrowly avoiding the lethal points and vaulting over the barriers to safety. (Tickets 70-350F/€10.67-53.36. Cheap seats usually available on the day of the event.) South American culture is everywhere in mid-July during the three-day **Horas Latinas** festival, which features extravagant music and dance shows (☎04 66 67 29 11). During **les marchés du soir** (a.k.a. **Jeudis de Nîmes**), the city center fills with local painters, artists, and musicians entertaining crowds late into the night (July-Aug. Th 7-11pm).

DAYTRIP FROM NIMES: PONT DU GARD

The centerpiece of the Roman aqueduct that supplied Nîmes with water through the first century is the Pont du Gard, bridging the gorge of the Gardon River. It is not to be missed: three dizzying, diminishing levels of arches rise 50m above the water and span 275m from bank to bank. Visitors can walk through the huge water channels of the bridge and swim in the cool river below. The bridge was the work of Agrippa, a close friend of Emperor Augustus. He built the aqueduct in 19 BC to bring water from the Eure springs near Uzès to the baths and fountains of Nîmes. His achievement is impressive as much from an engineer's standpoint as from a spectator's; the covered canal carried water 50km with only 17m total fall in altitude. The entire aqueduct averages a gradient of only 0.34 degrees, requiring a near-perfect precision in its construction.

If you have a whole day to spend, the best way to see the Pont du Gard is to start from **Collias,** 6km toward Uzès. Here **Kayak Vert** rents two-person **canoes, kayaks,** and **bikes.** The pleasant two- to three-hour paddle down the river takes you past the Château de St-Privat (where a treaty was signed to end the religious wars), and on to the Pont du Gard. From here a bus shuttles passengers back to Collias. (☎04 66 22 84 83. Trip to Pont du Gard 95F/€14.48; bikes 80F/€12.20 per half-day. Canoes and kayaks 35F/€5.34 per hr. 15% discount for students or residents at the hostel in Nîmes.) The **Société des Transports Départementaux du Gard (STDG** ☎04 66 29 27 29) runs daily buses from the bus station to the Pont du Gard (30min.; M-Sa 5 per day, 2 on Su; 31F/€4.73). Buses also leave for the Pont du Gard from **Avignon** (45min., 7 per day, 33F/€5.03). The bus will drop you off and pick you up at the roundabout by the Hôtel L'Auberge Blanche in what seems to be the middle of nowhere. Follow signs to the parking lot (10min.). **Camping le Barralet,** rue des Aires in Collias, offers a pool and hot showers in addition to river bathing. A grocery store is 200m away. (☎04 66 22 84 52; fax 04 66 22 89 17. Open Mar.-Sept. Person with car 38-48F/€5.80-7.32; 2 people 70-85F/€10.68-12.96; 3 people 85-105F/€12.96-16.01. Lower prices Apr.-June and Sept. MC/V.)

UZES

26km north of Nîmes, in lush, rolling countryside, lies the small city of Uzès. The boulevards are alive with bakeries and brasseries that reflect the sunlight filtered through giant plane trees. In the pl. aux Herbes of this miniature town, with its ancient stone fountain surrounded by arching buildings, the filming was done for *Cyrano de Bergerac* and the film *Le Jour de Gloire*.

TRANSPORTATION AND PRACTICAL INFORMATION. STDG (☎04 66 29 27 29) runs buses to Uzès from **Avignon** (1hr., 3 per day, 48F/€7.32) and **Nîmes** (1hr.; M-Sa 9 per day, Su 2 per day; 33F/€5.03). During the week, about six buses from **Uzès** to the **Pont du Gard** (20min., 20F/€3.05) and back make the combination a good daytrip if all is timed correctly. There are fewer buses on weekends and holidays. At the **tourist office,** pl. Albert 1er, northeast of the bus station on the bd. Gambetta, you can pick up a free booklet on Uzès that includes a tourist-friendly map. (☎04 66 22 68 88; fax 04 66 22 95 19. Open June-Sept. M-F 9am-6pm, Sa-Su 10am-1pm and 2-5pm; Oct.-May M-F 9am-noon and 1:30-6pm, Sa 10am-1pm.)

ACCOMMODATIONS AND FOOD. Most accommodations are expensive, but a pool and sturdy bare-mattressed bunks in rooms for 2 to 14 people can be found at **Le Prieuré du Christ Roi,** av. de la Gare. This ancient converted farm is used mostly by religious groups but is happy to accommodate backpackers as well. To get there from the bus station, walk down av. de la Libération and cross the rotary road. Take the Anduze direction. The *prieuré* is just past the Peugeot garage on the right (10min.). (☎04 66 22 68 67; fax 04 66 03 35 42. Dinner 60F/€9.15 for groups. Pool 15F/€2.29. Sheets 20F/€3.05. Beds 80F/€12.20.) Another option is the three-star **Camping La Paillote** north of town, with wooded, well-managed sites, hot showers, a pool, a bar, and laundry. From the tourist office, take rue Cigalon north to rue Masbourguet, which becomes rue St-Firmin. Take a left in front of the cemetery, then on the far side take a right onto the little road marked "Chemin de Grezac." La Paillote is 200m down on the right. (☎04 66 22 38 55; fax 04 66 22 26 66; dr.nicolae@freesbee.fr. 2 people with car 100F/€15.25. Extra person 30F/€4.57.)

The boulevards surrounding the *vieille ville* are lined with bakeries and cafés, and there are restaurants in pl. aux Herbes. Wednesday and Saturday mornings see a **market** in pl. aux Herbes and on the surrounding boulevards. A **Petit Casino** supermarket lies on the corner of bd. Gambetta and av. Général Vincent. (Open Tu-Sa 7:30am-12:30pm and 3:30-7:30pm, Su 8am-12:30pm.)

SIGHTS AND ENTERTAINMENT. Dominating the city with its gigantic medieval tower is **Le Duché,** pl. du Marché. Built in the 11th century and never challenged, the fortress has been continuously renovated for seven centuries. The resulting structure is an intriguing blend of period styles, with a gothic chapel and delicately carved and columned Renaissance facades. The palace remains home to the family of Crussol d'Uzès, descendants of the first duke and duchess of France. The spirit evident in their family motto, *"ferro non auro"* ("by iron, not gold") was embodied in the late Duchesse Anne, the first French woman to get her driver's license in 1898 and a fine for speeding soon after. Admission to the entire palace includes a tour in French with a written English translation. For a lower price you can climb the tower and survey the town of Uzès. (☎04 66 22 18 96. Open July-Sept. 15 daily 10am-1pm and 2-6:30pm; Sept. 16-June 10am-noon and 2-6pm. Tour 60F/€9.15, students 40F/€6.10, ages 7-11 20F/€3.05. Tower only 30F/€4.57.)

The **Cathédrale St-Théodorit,** pl. de l'Evêché, was burned, rebuilt, and restored many times during its turbulent history and is now a mishmash of Renaissance, Baroque, and neo-medieval styles. The cathedral's remarkable 17th-century, 2772-pipe organ includes delicately carved shutters trimmed with gold. (Open daily 9am-6:30pm. Free organ concerts in Oct. and spring.) Next to the cathedral is the 12th-century **Tour Fenestrelle,** the belltower of a cathedral destroyed in the 16th century. The tower isn't open for climbing, but its magnificent arched windows and tiled roof are Uzès' most beautiful sight. To the cathedral's left, a stone balcony provides a magnificent view of the countryside.

Bulls stampede through the streets and cascades of *pastis* flow freely during the week-long **Fête Votive** starting on the first Friday of August. Truffle buffs hit cloud nine on the third Sunday of January during **la Journée de la Truffe,** when fresh truffles are trafficked en masse and truffling tips disclosed to the faithful. Restaurants across Uzès produce special truffle-inflected menus. (Info ☎04 66 22 58 36.) The second half of July sees the **Nuits Musicales d'Uzès.** Ancient chants, religious music, and even opera are performed in Uzès' historical landmarks. Tickets (70-220F/€10.67-33.54 per performance) are available at the tourist office.

ORANGE

Despite its name, this northern provençal town hasn't hosted a single citrus grove in its two millennia; "Orange" is a perversion of the name of the Roman city "Arausio." Orange's juice comes from its renowned vineyards, producers of the Côtes du Rhône vintage. *Caves* scattered throughout the region offer *dégustations* to those willing to buy. The immense theater and elaborate triumphal arch, astonishingly well-preserved, are the chief reasons for visiting Orange. After you've seen those, unless there is a festival, there's nothing much to keep you here.

ORIENTATION AND PRACTICAL INFORMATION

Orange centers around **pl. Clemenceau, pl. République,** and **pl. aux Herbes.** To reach the main tourist office from the train station at the eastern edge of town, follow the signs to the *centre ville,* walking away from the station along **av. Frédéric Mistral,** and keep left as it becomes rue de la République; continue through pl. République, go around the right side of the building at the far end, and go straight on rue St-Martin, which becomes av. Charles de Gaulle. The tourist office is across cours Aristide Briand, and to your right (15min.).

Trains: av. Frédéric Mistral. To: **Avignon** (20min.; M-Sa 19 per day, Su 13 per day; 30F/€4.57); **Marseille** (1¼hr., 5 per day, 111F/€16.92); **Lyon** (2½hr.; M-Sa 7 per day, Su 4 per day; 140F/€21.35); and **Paris** (3½hr., 2 TGVs per day, 405F/€61.75). Info desk open daily 7:30am-7:45pm.

Buses: (☎04 90 34 15 59), on cours Pourtoules. To **Avignon** (55min.; M-Sa about every hr., Su 5 per day; 30.50F/€4.65). Office open M-F 8-11:50am and 2-4:50pm.

Taxi: Taxi Monge (☎04 90 51 00 00).

Tourist Office: 5 cours Aristide Briand (☎04 90 34 70 88; fax 04 90 34 99 62), near the *autoroute*. Spirited staff will help you in English and make last-minute reservations for 100F/€15.25 deposit. Free lists of daytrips. Free tours of Théâtre Antique in English, July-Aug. 1 per day. **Currency exchange.** Open Apr.-Sept. M-Sa 9am-7pm, Su 10am-6pm; Oct.-Mar. M-Sa 10am-1pm and 2-5pm. **Branch office,** pl. des Frères Mounet, opposite Théâtre Antique. Open July-Aug. M-Sa 10am-1pm and 2-7pm, Su 10am-6pm; Apr.-June and Sept. M-F 10am-1pm and 2-7pm.

Laundromat: 5 rue St-Florent, off bd. E. Daladier. Open daily 7am-8pm.

Police: 427 bd. E. Daladier (☎04 90 51 55 55).

Hospital: Louis Giorgi, chemin de l'Abrian (☎04 90 11 22 22), on av. H. Fabré.

Internet Access: Bar Victor Hugo, 1 rue Victor Hugo (☎04 90 34 12 63), within sight of the Arch. 1 computer. 10F/€1.53 for 15min., 35F/€5.34 per hr. Open M-Sa 8am-9pm.

Post Office: 679 bd. E. Daladier (☎04 90 11 11 00), on cours Pourtoules. **Currency exchange.** Open M-F 8am-6:30pm, Sa 8am-noon. **Postal code:** 84100.

ACCOMMODATIONS AND CAMPING

Decent, cheap rooms should not be hard to find in Orange. However, as in the rest of Provence, book ahead in late July and early August.

Hôtel St-Florent, 4 rue du Mazeau, near pl. aux Herbes (☎04 90 34 18 53; fax 04 90 51 17 25). Jovial family has painted frescoes on every wall of their lovely small hotel. While some rooms are small, the antique wooden bed frames compensate. Breakfast €6. Closed Dec.-Feb. Singles €20, with shower €25; doubles with shower €32, with bath (some with TV) €40-48; triples with bath and TV €50; quads with bath €55-65. Prices a little higher July-Aug. Extra bed €8. MC/V.

Arcôtel, 8 pl. aux Herbes (☎04 90 34 09 23; fax 04 90 51 61 12). Simple, cheery rooms. Some triples and quads are huge. Overlooks a quiet plaza just a stone's throw from the Roman theater. Buffet breakfast 36F/€5.49. Reception 7:15am-11pm. Singles 110F/€16.77; doubles 150-180F/€22.90-27.44, with bath 210-230F/€32.02-35.06; triples with bath 260F/€39.64; quads with bath 310F/€47.26. AmEx/MC/V.

Camping: Le Jonquier (☎04 90 34 49 48; fax 04 90 51 16 97), on rue A. Carrel. From the tourist office, walk toward the *autoroute* and turn right after the big school onto av. du 18 Juin 1940. Take a left onto rue H. Noguères, and after 5min. go right on rue A. Carrel; the site will be up on your left (15min.). 3-star site with pool, free tennis and mini-golf, hot showers, mini-mart, and horseback riding. High bushes offer some privacy in grassy sites. Reception 8am-8pm. Open Apr.-Sept. 1 or 2 people, car and tent 125F/€19.06, 20F/€3.05 per additional person. Electricity 5F/€0.76. V.

FOOD

During the nights of the *Chorégies* (see **Entertainment,** below), the cafés on pl. aux Herbes and pl. de la République raise prices and keep concert-goers up until 3am. Many restaurants serve *pan bagna*, the traditional salad-filled sandwich of the south. For groceries, head to the **Petit Casino,** 16 rue de la République. (Open M-Sa 7:30am-12:30pm and 3:30-7:30pm, Su 7:30am-12:30pm.) Every Thursday the town erupts with an **open-air market** centered on pl. République, pl. Clemenceau, and cours A. Briand, with everything from produce to handmade jewelry (7am-1pm). On Saturday afternoon, there is also a provençal market in the same square.

Be prepared to spend all night, love every minute, and roll home after a meal at **Le Yaca,** 24 pl. Silvain. Be entertained by the gruffly good-natured *patron* and enjoy a view of the Roman theater. Search as you may, you will never find such a copious *menu* at these prices. Never ever. (☎04 90 34 70 03. Lunch *menus* from 60F/€9.15, dinner *menus* from 70F/€10.67. Open Th-Tu noon-2pm and 7-10pm; Sept.-June closed Tu evenings. MC/V.)

SIGHTS AND ENTERTAINMENT

Built around the first century, Orange's striking **Théâtre Antique** is the best-preserved Roman theater in Europe. Its 3811 sq. ft. stage wall is one of only three left in the world; Louis XIV is said to have called it the most beautiful wall in his kingdom. The theater originally held 10,000 spectators and adjoined a gymnasium complete with running tracks, combat platform, sauna, and temple. After the fall of Rome, this house of pagan entertainment fell into disrepair and became a house of peasant containment, as local homes sprung up in and around its walls. In the mid-19th century, engineers rediscovered its fantastic acoustics and used the three remaining rows as a template for rebuilding the seating area, which can now accommodate 9000. A 3½m headless statue, discovered in the orchestra pit and reconstructed in 1931 to resemble the city's founder, Augustus, presides over the scene from above the portal. Free, interesting history lessons disguised as one-hour tours in French are offered three times daily in July and August; call the tourist office for schedules. (☎04 90 51 17 60. Open Apr.-Sept. daily 9am-6:30pm; Oct.-Mar. 9am-noon and 1:30-7pm.) Across the street is the mildly interesting **Musée Municipal,** which includes many antique objects found in excavations around Orange, as well as rooms dedicated to the more recent history of the Orange family and to the fabrication of provençal cloth. (☎04 90 51 18 24. Open Apr.-Sept. daily 9:30am-7pm; Oct.-Mar. 9:30am-noon and 1:30-5:30pm. Theater and museum 30F/€4.57, students 25F/€3.81.)

Above the theater, the overgrown park **Colline St-Eutrope** features a panoramic view and free, though acoustically poor, concert standing room amid the few ragged remnants of the Prince of Orange's castle. Orange's other major monument, the **Arc de Triomphe,** stands on the ancient via Agrippa, which once connected Arles to Lyon. Built during Augustus' time, the arch, dedicated to Tiberius in AD 25, is now slightly bedraggled. Eight Corinthian columns adorn this three-arched monument, whose facades depict Roman victories over the Gauls on land and sea. During the Middle Ages, it was filled in to create a defensive tower, the Tour de l'Arc. An embarrassing **Petit Train** visits these sites from June-Sept., leaving from the tourist office in front of the Théâtre Antique. (☎04 90 37 28 28. 30min. 25F/€3.81, under age 12 10F/€1.53.)

From July 6 to August 3, the Théâtre Antique returns to its original function with the **Chorégies,** a series of grand opera and choral productions. (Info available from the Maison des Chorégies, 18 pl. Sylvain, next to the theater. ☎04 90 34 24 24; fax 04 90 11 04 04. Open June M-Sa 9am-noon and 2-6pm; July daily 9am-7pm; Feb.-May M-F 9am-noon and 2-5pm. Tickets run 30-990F/€4.57-150.94; from 100F/€15.25 for operas. Students under age 28 can buy tickets for as little as 15F/€2.29, 50F/€7.62 for operas, and get up to 50% off on all other seats.) In August, more laid-back rock concerts, films, and variety shows take the stage (tickets free-250F/€38.12). For info, call the Service Culturel, located next door to Maison des Chorégies, where you can also inquire about other performances. (☎04 90 51 57 57. Open M-Th 8:30am-noon and 1:30-5:30pm, F 8:30am-noon and 1:30-4:30pm.)

NEAR ORANGE: VAISON-LA-ROMAINE

A drive through seemingly endless vineyards and past cozy hamlets brings you to Vaison-la-Romaine (pop. 6000). This once-wealthy Roman town still charms, even if it requires a touch of imagination to conjure up lavish villas and luxurious baths amid the sprawling rubble. The dream houses of wealthy Romans were followed by a 12th-century defensive fortress and its accompanying medieval village; the Ouvèze river now conveniently divides the cobblestoned, ivy-covered *haute ville* from the Roman excavations and the modern town. Every Tuesday the new quarter is overrun by vendors' carts piled with Provençal crafts, honey, lavender, olives, cheese, and wine.

FRENCH KISSIN' Wondering how to get a little closer? Don't be shy! The *bise* (a small peck on the cheek) is *de rigueur* for those meeting and greeting friends and family—even new acquaintances—in a social setting. Though males shake hands between themselves, everyone is expected to extend a cheek in mixed or all-women settings. Protocol varies by region, from two (one on each side; mind your nose during the switch) to three, which is most common in the south, to just one, a trend gaining popularity among Parisian teenagers. When in doubt of the magic number, pull back when they do. While lip-to-cheek contact is expected (a loud "mwaah" while kissing the air will not suffice), a *bise* should be no more than a crisp, methodical peck—not surprisingly, however, such an intimate opportunity isn't always thrown away lightly. Beware of (or indulge in) the soft, lingering *bise*; such tongue-on-cheek business bespeaks an interest beyond mere friendship.

PRACTICAL INFORMATION. **Buses** run to **Avignon** (1½hr., M-Sa 2 per day, 42.50F/€6.48) and **Orange** (50min., M-Sa 2-3 per day, 25.50F/€3.89). Call **Voyages Lieutard** for details (Avignon ☎04 90 86 36 75; Vaison ☎04 90 36 05 22). To reach the **tourist office,** pl. du Chanoine Sautel, from the bus station (stop at "Bx Lieutard"), cross the parking lot of the gas station and turn right on av. Victor Hugo to pl. Monfort. Continue past the *place* for a block and turn right onto Grande Rue. The tourist office is two blocks down on the right (10min.). The office offers **currency exchange** when the banks are closed. (☎04 90 36 02 11; fax 04 90 28 76 04. Open July-Aug. daily 9am-12:30pm and 2-6:45pm; Sept.-June M-Sa 9am-noon and 2-5:45pm, Su 9am-noon.) Rent a **bike** at **Peugeot Motos Cycles,** 17 av. Jules Ferry. (☎04 90 36 03 29. 50-80F/€7.62-12.20 per day, passport deposit. Open M-Sa 9am-noon and 2-7pm.) The Internet-dependent will be pleased that **Carte Cyber Café** is at 30 ZA de L'Ouvèze. (☎04 90 28 97 41. 25F/€3.81 per 30min., 40F/€6.10 per hr. Open M-F 9am-noon and 1:30-6pm.) Do **laundry** at 48 cours Tauligan (open M-Sa 8am-10pm). The **police** can be reached at 04 90 36 04 17; call a **taxi** or **ambulance** at 04 90 36 00 04. The **post office** is at pl. du 11 Novembre and has no-commission **currency exchange.** (☎04 90 36 06 40. Open M-W and F 8:30am-noon and 1:30-5:15pm, Th 8:30am-noon and 1:45-5:15pm, Sa 8:30am-noon.) **Postal code:** 84110.

ACCOMMODATIONS AND FOOD. Most hotels are pricey. **Hotel Burrhus,** 1 pl. Montfort, has the cheapest rooms in town, and feels like a country home, with wrought-iron bed frames and a breezy breakfast patio. (Breakfast 35F/€5.34. Reception 9am-8pm. Closed Dec.-Jan. Single with shower 190F/€28.97; in summer doubles with shower 250-310F/€38.11-47.26, with bath 290-330F/€44.21-50.31; in winter doubles with shower 240-300F/€36.59-45.73, with bath 280-320F/€42.69-48.78. AmEx/MC/V.) The best budget lodgings here belong to the 4-star **Camping Théâtre Romain,** chemin du Brusquet, ten minutes from the town center. From the tourist office, take the road between office and Puyamin. At the traffic circle, follow signs for "camping" and walk down chemin du Brusquet. Lots of shade under colorful, leafy trees. (☎04 90 28 78 66; fax 04 90 28 78 76. Bar, pool, laundry, and bike rental (100F/€15.25 per day). Reception 8am-12:30pm and 2-8pm. Open Mar. 15-Nov. 15. July-Aug. 44F/€6.71 per tent or car, 25F/€3.81 per additional person, electricity 16F/€2.44; Mar. 15-June and Sept.-Oct. 27F/€4.12 per tent or car, 23F/€3.51 per additional person. Electricity 16F/€2.44.)

The best sources of inexpensive food are the **markets** in the town center (Tu and Sa 8am-1pm). **Super U supermarket,** is at the intersection of av. Choralies and av. Victor Hugo, right after the bus stop. (☎04 90 10 06 00. Open M-Sa 8:30am-7:30pm.) Most cafés and brasseries in Vaison have *menus* starting at 65F/€9.91. A beacon in this expensive town shines from **Le Vieux Port,** 43 cours Tauligan, off Grande Rue. Ironically, their specialty is seafood, which they manage to serve you cheaply. (☎04 90 28 76 36. 59F/€8.99 for mussels and fries, *menus* 79F-128F/€14.48-19.06. Open Tu-Sa noon-2pm and 7:30-9:30pm, Su noon-2pm. MC/V.)

SIGHTS AND FESTIVALS. A **passport,** good for the duration of your stay, allows access to all the sites (41F/€6.25, students under age 25 22F/€3.35, ages 12-18 14F/€2.13). The passport also includes tours in French (daily in summer) and English (2-3 per week to the Puymin site). Ask at tourist office for times. The tourist office divides the Roman city into the **Quartier de Puymin** and the **Quartier de la Villasse,** where ruins of houses, baths, and mosaics stretch over hills carpeted with pines and cypress trees. Although few traces are left of the ancients, the excellent city guides will conjure up the Roman way of life. The Puymin excavation includes a reconstruction of the **Roman theater,** which regularly hosts events in the summer and offers a beautiful view of the surrounding vineyards. Also in Puymin is small **Musée Theo Desplans,** which houses the best-preserved sculptures, mosaics, and ceramics from the excavations. (Puymin open July-Sept. daily 9:30am-6pm; Nov.-Feb. 10am-noon and 2-4:30pm; Mar.-May and Oct. 10am-12:30pm and 2-6pm. Museum open July-Aug. daily 9:30am-6:45pm; June and Sept. 9:30am-6:30pm; Nov.-Feb. 10am-noon and 2-4pm; Mar.-May and Oct. 10am-1pm and 2:30-6pm. Villasse has same schedule, except June-Sept. closed 12:30-2:30pm.)

Included in the passport is the 12th-century **cloister** near the Quartier de la Villasse. With its columns and stylized capitals perfectly intact, the gallery has become a display case for remnants of the 6th-century Merovingian church. Connected to the cloister, the 11th- to 13th-century **Cathédrale de Notre-Dame** sits on a foundation of recycled Roman columns. Architecture buffs and George de Brigard will notice the lack of gothic vaulting. (Both open July-Sept. daily 9:30am-12:30pm and 2-6pm; Mar.-May and Oct. 10am-noon and 2-6pm; Nov.-Feb. 10am-noon and 2-4:30pm. Cloister 8F/€1.22 without pass.)

Across the well-preserved **Pont Romain** and up the hill is the medieval *haute ville*, where lush, flowery gardens spill over walks and wooden gates. The 12th-century **fortress** (known locally as the "château"), built under Count Raymond V of Toulouse, still fends off invaders—including you. The only way to visit is by taking one of the tourist office's tours (Apr.-Sept. only), but this may not help as the ones to the old village are only in French. Even with the pass, they are 10F/€1.53 extra. The stronghold is locked up for safety reasons, but the climb will give you a great view of the town below, the wine-covered Ouvèze valley, and **Mont Ventoux's** fabled peak (1912m). The tourist office in nearby **Malaucène** (☎04 90 65 22 59) organizes **night hikes** for the intrepid up to the Mont at 8:30pm on Fridays in July and August. (50F/€7.62, ages 12-16 30F/€4.57. Call ahead for reservations.)

In July the city puts on an impressive **festival d'été,** which brings ballet, opera, drama, and classical music to the Roman theater almost nightly. (For reservations and info, call the Service Culturel at 04 90 28 74 74. Tickets 120-250F/€18.30-38.12; student rates available.) Also in July and August is the **Festival des Choeurs Lauréats,** in which professional choral groups come and perform in Vaison. (Tickets 100F/€15.25. For info and reservations, call the tourist office or Centre A Cœur-Joie at 04 90 36 00 78.) **Les Journées Gourmandes,** a celebration of the food of Provence, takes place at the end of October.

THE COTE D'AZUR

A sunny place for shady people.
—Somerset Maugham

Between Marseille and the Italian border, the sun-drenched beaches and warm waters of the Mediterranean form the backdrop for this fabled playground of the rich and famous: professional sunbathers bronze *au naturel* here on pebbly beaches; high rollers drop their millions in the casinos; cultural types finger Gallo-Roman fragments or wander in abandoned coastal fortifications; and Europe's trendiest youth swing until dawn in the continent's most exclusive nightclubs.

One of the most touristed parts of France, the Côte d'Azur began as a Greco-Roman commercial base. Forts, ports, and prosperous villages sprang up here around 600 BC, only to be razed by barbarian invaders toward the middle of the first millennium. Throughout the Dark Ages, local powers struggled for possession of the coast; the region didn't see any prolonged stability until the 16th century, when the French monarchy managed to assimilate it for good. The Riviera's resort status is a comparatively recent phenomenon. English and Russian aristocrats of the late 18th century started it all, wintering here to avoid their native countries' abominable weather. Soon Nice was drawing a steady crowd of the idle rich. In the 1920s, Coco Chanel popularized the provençal farmer's healthy tan among her society customers; parasols went down, hemlines went up, and the upper class' ritual sun-worship began.

Some of the past century's greatest artists came to the Côte for restoration and inspiration, from F. Scott Fitzgerald and Cole Porter at Cap d'Antibes to Picasso, Renoir, and Dufy in Nice. Like a beautiful and unscrupulous woman, the Riviera has been the passion, the death, and, finally, the chief beneficiary of many a famous painter; most towns along the eastern stretch of the Côte now lay claim to a chapel, room, or wall decorated by Matisse or Chagall.

Today this choice stretch of sun and sand is a curious combination of high-handed millionaires and low-budget tourists. Modern celebrities sport the ultimate accessory—a vacation home in St-Tropez while high society steps out yearly for the Cannes Film Festival and the Monte-Carlo Grand Prix, both in May. Less exclusive are Nice's raucous *Carnaval* (early February) and various summer jazz festivals. Penny-pinching travelers can soak up the spectacle as well plenty of sun, sea, and, albeit crowded, sand.

TRANSPORTATION

The coast from Marseille to Italy is served by frequent, inexpensive trains and buses. Most attractions lie along the stretch from St-Raphaël to Menton. **Trains** for the Côte leave Paris' Gare de Lyon hourly in summer; the TGV trip to Marseille takes five hours, to Nice anywhere from five and a half to eight.

BEACHES

In summer, the best time to swim is from 7pm to 9pm, just before sunset. Bring a beach mat (20F/€3.05 at supermarkets); even the sand beaches are a bit rocky. Since almost all the towns on the Côte lie along one local rail line, just hop off and on to see what you can find. The largest cities have the worst beaches: Marseille's are artificial, Nice's rocky, Cannes' private, and St-Tropez's remote. Smaller beaches between towns, like Cap Martin (between Monaco and Menton), St-Jean-Cap-Ferrat (between Monaco and Nice), and St-Raphaël-Fréjus (between Cannes and St-Tropez), are better options. Nearly all beaches are topless or top-optional, and it's seldom hard to find a private little spot if you want to go bottomless, too. Nudity is the norm at the astounding Héliopolis on the Ile du Levant (see p. 320), and in the *calanques* between Eze-sur-Mer (see p. 290) and Cap d'Ail (see p. 291). Don't neglect less-frequented islands: Porquerolles, the Ile du Levant, and the Iles des Lérins off Cannes all have fine rock ledges and secluded coves.

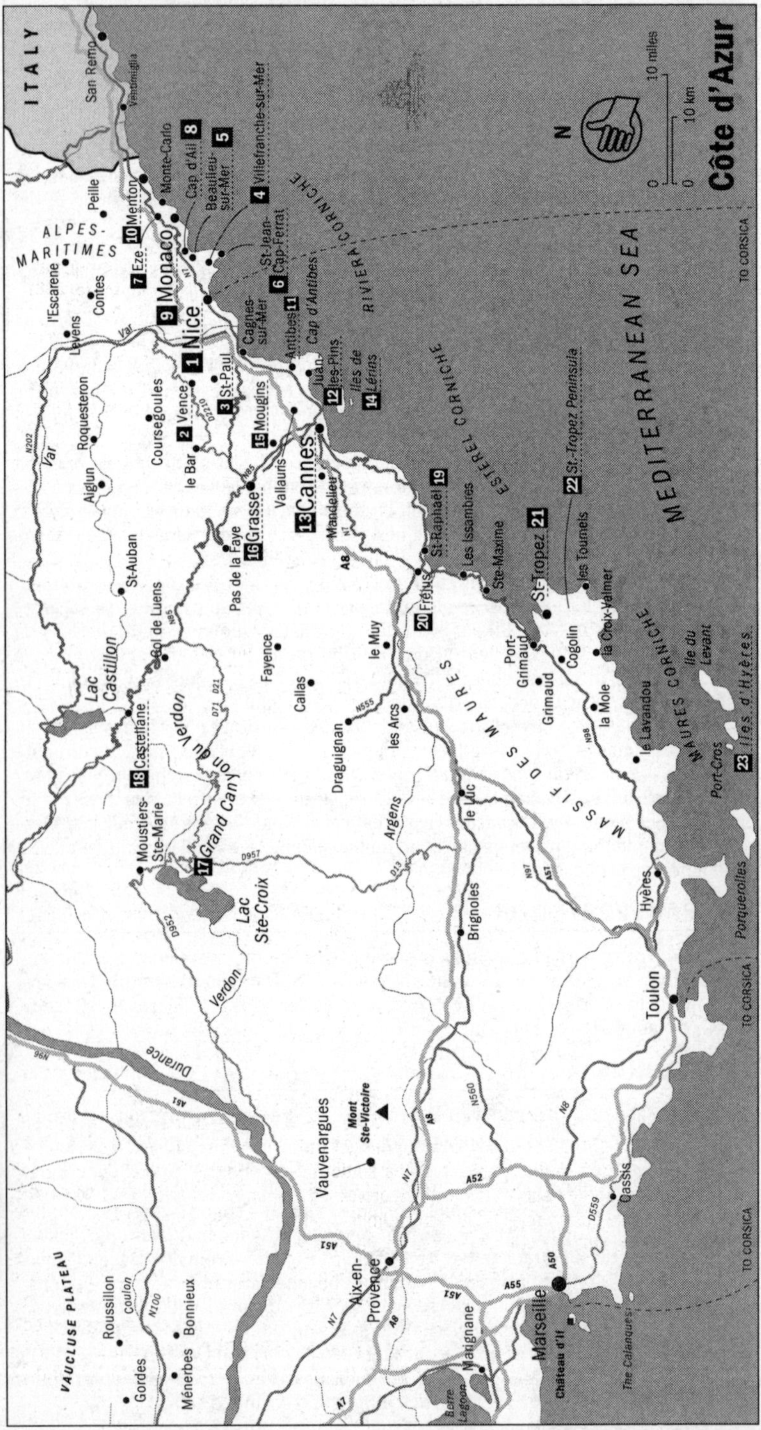

Côte d'Azur
ITALY
San Remo
Ventimiglia
Monte-Carlo
8 Cap d'Ail
5 Beaulieu-sur-Mer
4 Villefranche-sur-Mer
10 Menton
Peille
ALPES-MARITIMES
7 Eze
9 Monaco
6 St-Jean-Cap-Ferrat
1 Nice
Contes
l'Escarene
Levens
Var
Cagnes-sur-Mer
11 Antibes
Cap d'Antibes
RIVIERA CORNICHE
Juan-12 les-Pins
14 Iles de Lérins
3 St-Paul
2 Vence
Coursegoules
Roquesteron
Aiglun
le Bar
15 Mougins
Vallauris
13 Cannes
Mandelieu
16 Grasse
Pas de la Faye
St-Auban
Col de Luens
Lac Castillon
18 Castellane
Grand Canyon du Verdon
Moustiers-Ste-Marie
17
Lac Ste-Croix
Verdon
Fayence
Callas
Draguignan
les Arcs
le Muy
Argens
19 St-Raphael
20 Fréjus
ESTEREL CORNICHE
Les Issambres
Ste-Maxime
21 St-Tropez
22 St-Tropez Peninsula
les Tournels
la Croix-Valmer
Cogolin
Port-Grimaud
Grimaud
la Mole
MASSIF DES MAURES
MAURES CORNICHE
le Lavandou
Ile du Levant
Port-Cros
23 Iles d'Hyères
Porquerolles
le Luc
Brignoles
Hyères
Toulon
MEDITERRANEAN SEA
TO CORSICA
Durance
Vauvenargues
Mont Ste-Victoire
Aix-en-Provence
Marignane
Berre Lagoon
Marseille
Château d'If
The Calanques
Cassis
VAUCLUSE PLATEAU
Roussillon
Gordes
Ménerbes
Bonnieux
Coulon
N100
N96
A51
A8
A7
N7
A52
N560
N8
D559
A50
A55
D952
D957
N85
D71
D21
N555
N97
A57
N98
D2210
N202
0 10 km
0 10 miles
N

COTE D'AZUR

Many travelers used to sleep on the beaches here, but the practice seems to be dying out. Nice's beach is notoriously unsafe—don't take the risk. In some of the classier towns (Cannes, Cap d'Ail), beaches are a nighttime hangout for local drug dealers and riffraff; many respectable-looking kids earn their summer salaries in tourists' jewelry, mopeds, and cash. If you decide to bed down on the beach, choose populated, well-used beaches that attract neither thugs nor cops—St-Raphaël-Fréjus is one of the better options. In the daytime, a number of beaches provide showers, toilets, and towels for a small fee (10-15F/€1.53-2.29).

NICE

Sun-drenched and spicy, Nice (pop. 345,892) is the unofficial capital of the Riviera. This former stomping ground of dukes and czarinas continues to draw tourists to its non-stop nightlife, superlative shopping, and first-rate museums. With excellent transportation and budget lodgings galore, the fifth-largest city in France makes a cheap base for sampling the Côte D'Azur's pricier delights. Year-round, the old town's maze of pedestrian streets abounds with colorful markets by day and lively bars by night. Prepare to make new friends, to hear more English than French, and to have more fun than you'll be able to remember.

TRANSPORTATION

Flights: Aéroport Nice-Côte d'Azur (☎04 93 21 30 30). Open 24hr. **Air France,** 10 av. Félix-Faure (☎08 20 82 08 20), serves **Bastia** in **Corsica** (569F/€86.75, under 25 411F/€62.66) and **Paris** (1427F/€217.56, 424F/€64.64 under 25). Open M-Sa 9am-6pm. **EasyJet** flies to **London** (see **Budget Airlines,** p. 58). Sunbus #23 (☎04 93 13 53 13) goes to the airport from the station (every 30min. 6am-8:30pm; 8.50F/€1.30). Ask for the Sunbus stop. The more expensive airport bus (☎04 93 21 30 83) runs from the bus station (M-Sa every 20min., Su every 30min.; 23F/€3.51).

Trains: Gare SNCF Nice-Ville, av. Thiers (☎04 92 14 81 62). To: **Cannes** (35min., every 15-45min., 32F/€4.88); **Marseille** (2¾hr., every 30-90min., 152F/€23.17); **Monaco** (25min., every 10-30min., 20F/€3.05); and **Paris** (7hr.; June-Sept. about 3 per day, Oct.-May 2 per day; 484F/€73.79). Open daily 5am-1:15am. **Luggage storage** in lockers open daily 7am-10:30pm (30F/€4.57 large, 20F/€3.05 medium, 15F/€2.29 small). **Gare du Sud,** 4bis rue Alfred Binet (☎04 97 03 80 80 or 04 93 82 10 17), 800m from Nice-Ville.

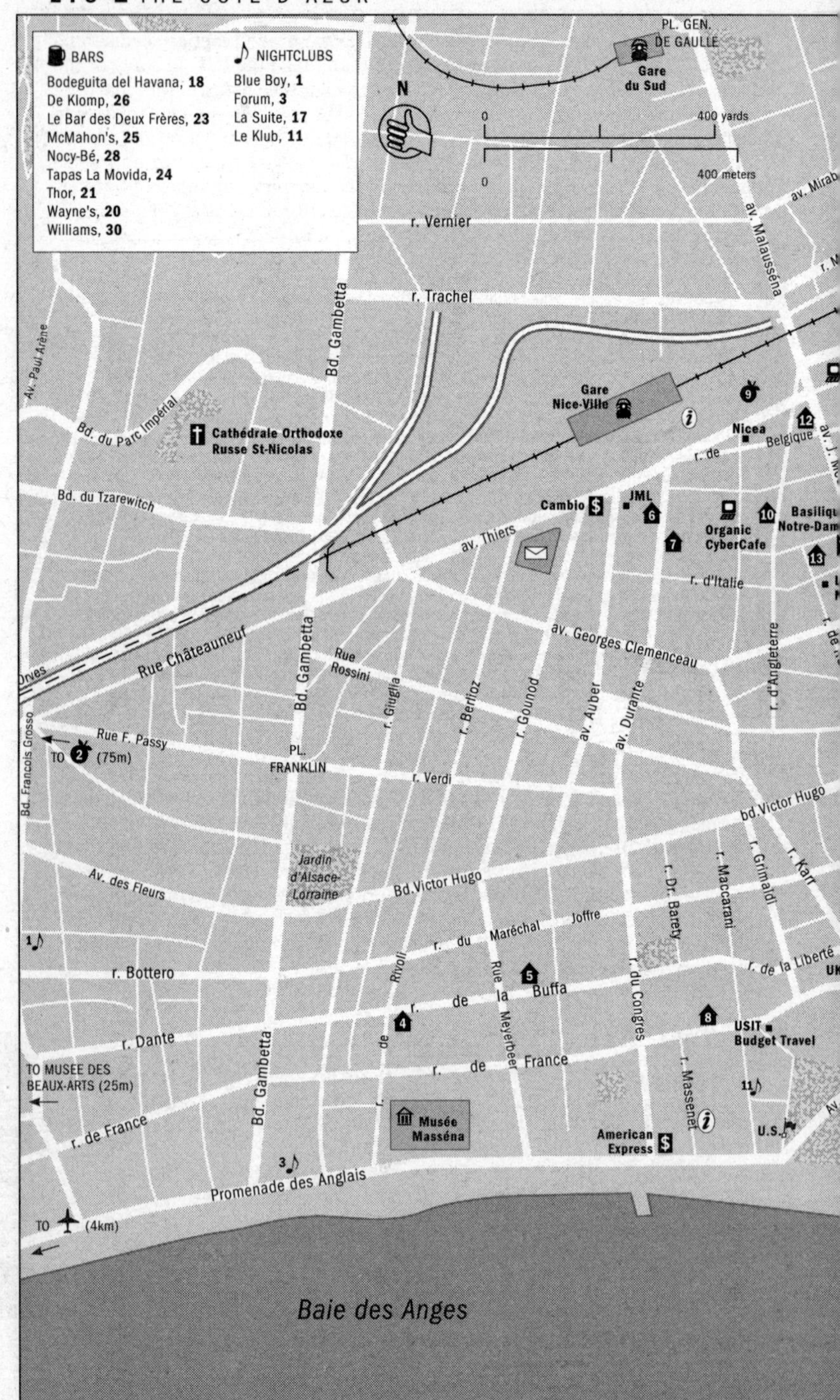

BARS
Bodeguita del Havana, 18
De Klomp, 26
Le Bar des Deux Frères, 23
McMahon's, 25
Nocy-Bé, 28
Tapas La Movida, 24
Thor, 21
Wayne's, 20
Williams, 30
NIGHTCLUBS
Blue Boy, 1
Forum, 3
La Suite, 17
Le Klub, 11
N
0
400 yards
0
400 meters
PL. GEN. DE GAULLE
Gare du Sud
r. Vernier
r. Trachel
av. Malausséna
av. Mirab
Bd. Gambetta
Av. Paul Arène
Bd. du Parc Impérial
Cathédrale Orthodoxe Russe St-Nicolas
Gare Nice-Ville
Nicea
r. de Belgique
Bd. du Tzarewitch
Cambio
JML
Organic CyberCafe
Basiliqu
Notre-Dam
av. Thiers
r. d'Italie
av. Georges Clemenceau
Rue Châteauneuf
Rue Rossini
r. Giuglia
r. Berlioz
r. Gounod
av. Auber
av. Durante
r. d'Angleterre
Rue F. Passy
TO (75m)
Bd. Francois Grosso
PL. FRANKLIN
r. Verdi
bd.Victor Hugo
Jardin d'Alsace-Lorraine
Av. des Fleurs
Bd.Victor Hugo
r. Dr. Barety
r. Maccarani
r. Grimaldi
r. Karr
r. du Maréchal Joffre
r. Bottero
Rue Meyerbeer
r. de la Buffa
r. du Congres
r. de la Liberté
r. de Rivoli
r. Dante
r. de France
USIT Budget Travel
TO MUSEE DES BEAUX-ARTS (25m)
r. Massenet
r. de France
Musée Masséna
American Express
U.S.
Promenade des Anglais
TO (4km)
Baie des Anges

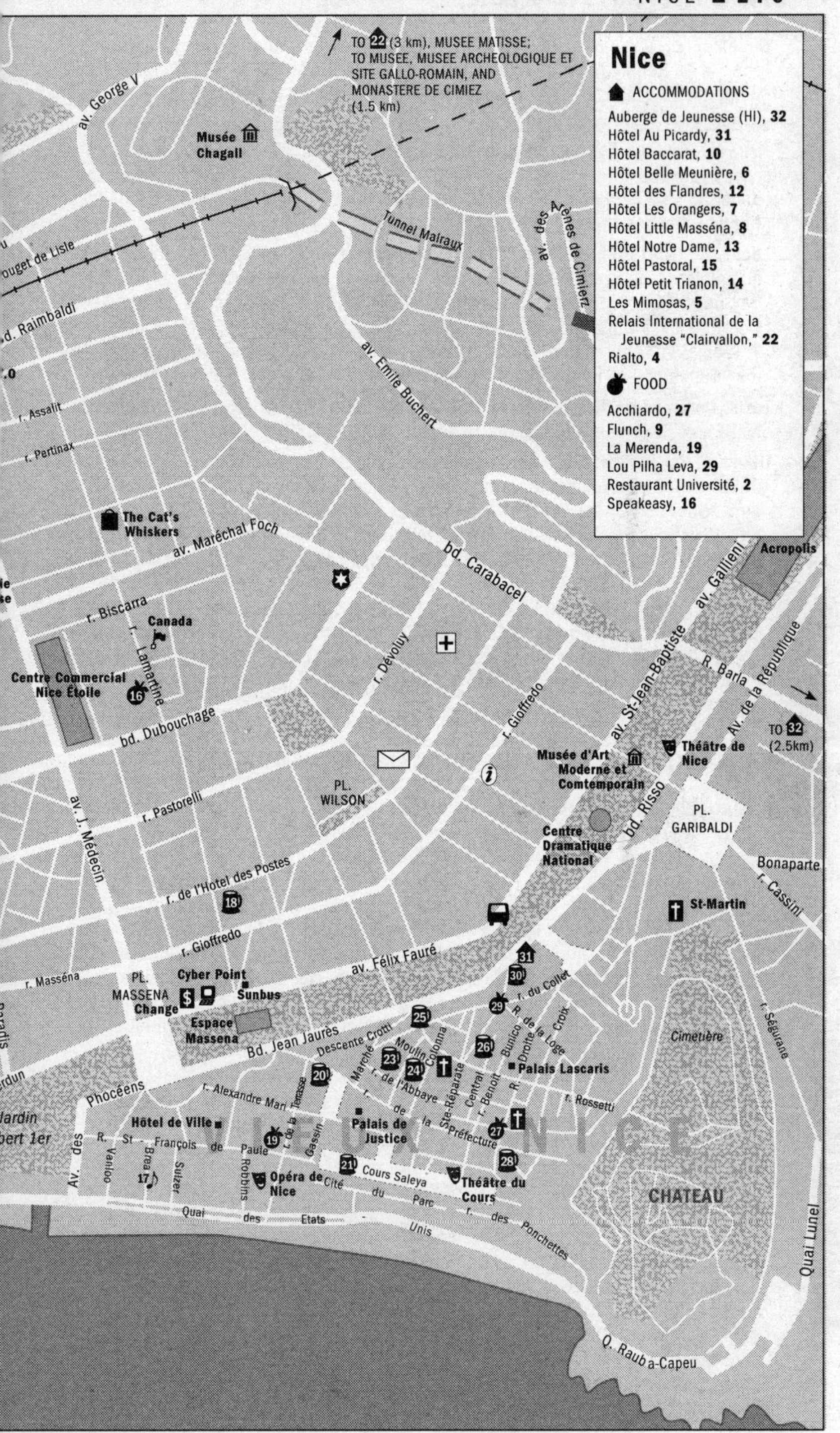
Nice
ACCOMMODATIONS
Auberge de Jeunesse (HI), 32
Hôtel Au Picardy, 31
Hôtel Baccarat, 10
Hôtel Belle Meunière, 6
Hôtel des Flandres, 12
Hôtel Les Orangers, 7
Hôtel Little Masséna, 8
Hôtel Notre Dame, 13
Hôtel Pastoral, 15
Hôtel Petit Trianon, 14
Les Mimosas, 5
Relais International de la Jeunesse "Clairvallon," 22
Rialto, 4
FOOD
Acchiardo, 27
Flunch, 9
La Merenda, 19
Lou Pilha Leva, 29
Restaurant Université, 2
Speakeasy, 16
TO 22 (3 km), MUSEE MATISSE; TO MUSEE, MUSEE ARCHEOLOGIQUE ET SITE GALLO-ROMAIN, AND MONASTERE DE CIMIEZ (1.5 km)
Musée Chagall
av. George V
Tunnel Malraux
av. des Arènes de Cimiez
av. Emile Buchert
bd. Raimbaldi
r. Assalit
r. Pertinax
The Cat's Whiskers
av. Maréchal Foch
bd. Carabacel
Acropolis
r. Biscarra
Canada
r. Lamartine
Centre Commercial Nice Étoile
bd. Dubouchage
r. Dévoluy
r. Gioffredo
av. St-Jean-Baptiste
av. Gallieni
R. Barla
Av. de la République
TO 32 (2.5km)
Musée d'Art Moderne et Comtemporain
Théâtre de Nice
PL. WILSON
r. Pastorelli
av. J. Médecin
bd. Risso
PL. GARIBALDI
Centre Dramatique National
Bonaparte
r. Cassini
r. de l'Hotel des Postes
St-Martin
r. Gioffredo
av. Félix Faure
r. Masséna
PL. MASSENA
Cyber Point
Sunbus
Change
Espace Massena
r. du Collet
Bd. Jean Jaurès
Descente Crotti
Cimetière
r. Ségurana
Palais Lascaris
r. Rossetti
Phocéens
r. Alexandre Mari
Hôtel de Ville
Palais de Justice
Jardin Albert 1er
Opéra de Nice
Cours Saleya
Théâtre du Cours
CHATEAU
Quai des Etats Unis
r. des Ponchettes
Quai Lunel
Q. Rauba-Capeu
VIEUX NICE

Buses: 5 bd. Jean Jaurès (☎04 93 85 61 81), left at the end of av. Jean Médecin. Info open M-Sa 8am-6:30pm. If booth is closed, buy tickets on the bus. To **Cannes** (1½hr., 3 per hr., 37.50F/€5.72) and **Monaco** (40min., 4 per hr., 20F/€3.05).

Ferries: SNCM (☎04 93 13 66 66; fax 04 93 13 66 89; reservations ☎04 93 13 66 99) and **Corsica Ferries** (☎04 92 00 43 76; fax 04 92 00 43 77), both at the port. Take bus #1 or 2 (dir: "Port"). Service to **Corsica** (225-255F/€34.30-38.88 one-way, under 25 195-225F/€29.73-34.30; bikes 91F/€13.87, small cars 300F/€45.74; see **Corsica: Getting there,** p. 321, for more info.

Local Transportation: Sunbus, 10 av. Félix Faure (☎04 93 16 52 10), near pl. Leclerc and pl. Masséna. Long treks to museums, the beach, and hostels make the 25F/€3.81 day pass, 55F/€8.39 10-ticket *carnet,* 85F/€12.96 5-day pass, or 110F/€16.77 weeklong pass worth the cost. Buy passes at the agency (open M-F 7:15am-7pm, Sa 7:15am-6pm) or on board. Individual tickets 8.50F/€1.30. Ask at the tourist office for the **"Sunplan"** bus map and the **"Guide Infobus,"** which lists schedules and routes.

Taxis: Central Taxi Riviera (☎04 93 13 78 78). Get a price range before boarding, and make sure the meter is turned on. To airport 160F/€24.39.

Bike and Car Rental: Nicea Location Rent, 12 rue de Belgique (☎04 93 82 42 71; fax 04 93 87 76 36), around the corner from the station. Scooter from 325F/€49.55 per day, 350F/€53.36 for 24hr., 1650F/€251.56 per week, deposit 9000F/€1372.16. Also rents bikes, in-line skates, and motorcycles. 5-10% discount for students. Open daily 9am-6pm. Closed Oct.-Nov. **JML Location,** 34 av. Auber (☎04 93 16 07 00; fax 04 92 93 02 10), opposite the station. Bikes 70F/€10.67 per day, 301F/€45.89 per week. Scooters 240F/€36.59 for 24hr., 1302F/€198.51 per week. 1500F/€228.69 credit card deposit for bikes, 6000F/€914.77 for scooters. Cars 297F/€45.28 per day with 200km free, 0.79F/€0.12 each additional km. Minimum age 23 for car rental. Open June-Sept. daily 8am-6:30pm; Oct.-May M-Sa 8am-1pm and 2-6:30pm, Sa 8am-1pm, Su 9am-1pm and 4-6:30pm.

ORIENTATION AND PRACTICAL INFORMATION

The train station, **Nice-Ville,** is next to the tourist office on av. Thiers in the north of the city. The area around the station is packed with cheap restaurants, budget hotels, and triple-X video stores. To the left as you come out of the station is **av. Jean Médecin,** an artery street that runs toward the water to **pl. Masséna** (10min.). Heading right, you'll run into **bd. Gambetta,** the other main water-bound street. Sweeping along the coast, the **promenade des Anglais** (which becomes quai des Etats-Unis east of av. Jean Médecin) is a people-watching paradise, as are the cafés, boutiques, and overpriced restaurants of the rue Masséna pedestrian zone west of bd. Jean Médecin. Below and to the left of Jean Médecin, **Vieux Nice** pulsates in the southeast. Even farther in this direction, on the opposite side of Le Château, is **Port Lympia,** a warren of alleyways, brasseries, and tabacs.

Unfortunately, Nice's big-city appeal is coupled with big-city crime. At night, women should avoid walking alone, and everyone should **exercise caution** around the train station, in Vieux Nice, and on the Promenade des Anglais.

Tourist Office: av. Thiers (☎04 93 87 07 07; fax 04 93 16 85 16; www.nice-coteazur.org and www.nicetourism.com), beside the train station. Makes same-day reservations for hotels in Nice; your chances of nabbing a room are best 9-11am. Ask for the English-language *Nice: A Practical Guide* and *Museums and Churches of Nice* plus a map (essential in Vieux Nice). To find out what's happening, pick up the *Semaine des Spectacles* (5-8F/€0.76-1.22 at tabacs), published every W, which lists entertainment for the entire Côte. Open June-Sept. M-Sa 8am-8pm, Su 9am-7pm; Oct.-May M-Sa 8am-7pm. From June-Sept., there's also a hotel reservation service (☎04 92 14 48 12). **Branches:** 5 promenade des Anglais (☎04 92 14 48 00; fax 04 92 14 48 03); same hours as above). Also at airport terminal 1 (☎04 93 21 44 11; fax 04 93 21 44 50); open June-Sept. daily 8am-10pm; Oct.-May closed Su.

Budget Travel Offices: USIT, 15 rue de la France (☎04 93 87 34 96; fax 04 93 87 10 91), near pl. Masséna. Open M-Sa 9:30am-6:30pm. Books cheap international flights and bus and train trips within France (also arranges excursions and camping trips).

Consulates: Canada, 10 rue Lamartine (☎04 93 92 93 22). Open M-F 9am-noon. **UK,** Le Palace, 8 rue Alphonse Karr (☎04 93 82 32 04). Open M, W, and F 9:30-11:30am. **US,** 7 av. Gustave V (☎04 93 88 89 55; fax 04 93 87 07 38). Open M-F 9-11:30am and 1:30-4:30pm.

Currency Exchange: Cambio, 17 av. Thiers (☎04 93 88 56 80), opposite the train station. No commission except for 5% on French traveler's checks. Open daily 7am-10pm. **Change,** 10 av. Félix Faure (☎04 93 80 36 67). AmEx Traveler's Checks, no commission. Open M-Sa 9:30am-12:30pm and 2-5:30pm. **American Express,** 11 prom. des Anglais (☎04 93 16 53 53; fax 04 93 16 51 67), at the corner of rue des Congrès. Open daily 9am-8:30pm.

English Bookstore: The Cat's Whiskers, 30 rue Lamartine (☎04 93 80 02 66). Great selection of everything from best-sellers to cookbooks. Open July-Aug. M-Sa 10:30am-12:30pm and 3:30-7pm; Sept.-June M-F 9:30am-noon and 2-6:45pm, Sa 9:30am-noon and 3-6:30pm.

Youth Center: Centre d'Information Jeunesse, 19 rue Gioffredo (☎04 93 80 93 93; fax 04 92 47 86 79; www.crij.org/nice), near the Museum of Contemporary Art. Helps with long-term stays, job hunts, excursions, culture, and nightlife. Posts student summer jobs. Most useful if you speak some French. Open M-F 10am-7pm, Sa 10am-5pm.

Laundromat: Laverie Niçoise, 7 rue d'Italie (☎04 93 87 56 50), beside the Basilique Notre-Dame. Open M-Sa 8:30am-12:30pm and 2:30-7:30pm.

Police: ☎04 92 17 22 22. At the opposite end of bd. M. Foch from bd. Jean Médecin.

Hospital: St-Roch, 5 rue Pierre Devoluy (☎04 92 03 33 75).

Post Office: 21 av. Thiers (☎04 93 82 65 22; fax 04 93 88 78 46), near the station. Open M-F 8am-7pm, Sa 8am-noon. **Postal code:** 06033 Nice Cedex 1.

Internet Access: Organic CyberCafé, 16 rue Paganini (☎04 93 16 97 82); the sign on the door says "CyberCafé Bio." Drink organic coffees while you type. 9F/€1.37 per 15min., 16F/€2.44 per 30min., 34F/€5.18 for 1hr. Open daily 9am-10pm. Mention *Let's Go* for these prices. Nearby **3.W.O.,** 32 rue Assalit (☎04 93 80 51 12), features American keyboards. 10F/€1.53 per 15min., 20F/€3.05 per 30min., 30F/€4.57 per hr. Open M-Sa 9am-9am, Su 9am-6pm.

ACCOMMODATIONS

Nice's hostels are out of the way and often full, so call three to five days in advance. The city has two clusters of budget hotels. Those by the station are new but badly located; those nearer to Vieux Nice and the beach are well situated but tend to be less modern. Reserve at least two to three weeks ahead in the summer. In the morning, the tourist office may be able to help with accommodations.

HOSTELS

Relais International de la Jeunesse "Clairvallon," 26 av. Scudéri (☎04 93 81 27 63; fax 04 93 53 35 88; clajpaca@cote-dazur.com), in Cimiez, 4km out of town. Take bus #15 to "Scudéri" (dir: "Rimiez," 20min., every 10min.) from the train station or pl. Masséna; after 9pm, take the N2 bus from pl. Masséna only. Get off the bus, turn right, and head uphill. Take the first left. To walk from the station, turn left and left again on av. Jean Médecin, then right before the overpass on bd. Raimbaldi. Go 6 blocks and turn right on av. Comboul, then left on bd. Carabacel. Follow it up the hill as it becomes bd. de Cimiez. Turn right before the hospital onto av. de Flirey, and keep trudging uphill until you reach av. Scudéri. Turn left and follow the signs. It's you and 150 new friends in the luxurious villa of a deceased marquis. Tennis courts, a lovely TV and dining room, a fountained garden, and a swimming pool (open 5-7pm). In a pretty, residential neighborhood. Laundry. 4- to 10-bed rooms. Breakfast included. 5-course dinner 55F/€8.39. Check-in 5pm. Lockout 9:30am-5pm. Curfew 11pm. Dorms 82F/€12.50.

Auberge de Jeunesse (HI), rte. Forestière du Mont-Alban (☎04 93 89 23 64; fax 04 92 04 03 10), 4km away from it all. From the bus station, take #14 (dir: "Mont Boron") to "l'Auberge" (M-F every 15min., Sa-Su every 30min.; last bus 7:30pm). From the train station, take #17 and tell the driver you need to switch to the #14. Otherwise, it's a 50min. walk: from the train station, turn left and then right on av. Jean Médecin. Follow it through pl. Masséna and turn left on bd. Jaurès. Turn right on rue Barla, following the signs up the hill. Far from the action, this ultra-clean hostel draws a cool, friendly crowd. 56 beds in 8- to 10-bed dorms. Lockers in dorms. Kitchen. Sheets 17F/€2.59. Laundry 40F/€6.10. Breakfast included. Lockout 10am-5pm. Curfew 12:30am. Dorms 71F/€10.82. **Cash only.**

NEAR THE TRAIN STATION

Hôtel Belle Meunière, 21 av. Durante (☎04 93 88 66 15; fax 04 93 82 51 76), directly across from the train station. Birds chirp in the courtyard of this converted mansion and backpackers become friends over free breakfast and nighttime imbibing. Some rooms bear Belle Epoque ornamentation. Reception until midnight; access code for the wee hours. Showers 10F/€1.53. Laundry. Luggage storage free, 10F/€1.53 after check-out. 4- to 5-bed co-ed dorms 80F/€12.20 per person, with shower 115F/€17.53; doubles with shower 290F/€44.21; triples 255F/€38.88, with shower 345F/€52.60.

Hôtel Baccarat, 39 rue d'Angleterre (☎04 93 88 35 73; fax 04 93 16 14 25; www.hotel-baccarat.com), second right off rue de Belgique. Large, well-kept rooms with floral bedspreads, pastel trimmings, and carefully chosen furniture. Homey, secure atmosphere, plus baths in all rooms. Delicious morning crêpes 12F/€1.83, coffee and croissant 10F/€1.53. Reception 24hr.; no luggage storage. Free beach mat loan. Remember your reservation code! 3- to 5-person dorms 95F/€14.48 per person; singles 187F/€28.51; doubles 230F/€35.06; triples 284F/€43.30. AmEx/MC/V.

Hôtel Les Orangers, 10bis av. Durante (☎04 93 87 51 41; fax 04 93 82 57 82), across from the station. Bright and airy coed dorms, with closely packed beds, all with showers and fridges (hotplate on request). English-speaking owner loans beach mats and stores luggage for free, and may direct you elsewhere if he's full. Breakfast 20F/€3.05. Dorms 85F/€12.96; singles 95-100F/€14.48-15.25; doubles 210-230F/€32.02-35.06; triples 270-300F/€41.16-45.74; quads 360F/€54.89. Closed Nov. MC/V.

Hôtel des Flandres, 6 rue de Belgique (☎04 93 88 78 94; fax 04 93 88 74 90), across from the train station on a downward-sloping street. With an imposing entrance, large rooms with bath, and high ceilings, this hotel feels far more expensive than it is. Breakfast 30F/€4.57. Reception 24hr. Largest rooms accommodate 5-6 people, 110F/€16.77 per person; singles 230F/€35.06; doubles 290-310F/€44.21; triples 370F/€56.41; quads 390-410F/€59.46-62.51. Extra bed 70F/€10.67. MC/V.

Hôtel Pastoral, 27 rue Assalit (☎04 93 85 17 22), on the far side of av. Jean Médecin near the train station. Big hardwood rooms with elegant furniture in a secure atmosphere; caring owner is friendly to backpackers. Breakfast 20F/€3.05. Free luggage storage. Singles 120F/€18.30; doubles 160F/€24.39, with shower 170F/€25.92, with bath 190F/€28.97; triples or quads 80F/€12.20 per person.

Hôtel Notre Dame, 22 rue de Russie (☎04 93 88 70 44; fax 04 93 82 20 38; jyung@caramail.com), at the corner of rue d'Italie, 1 block west of av. Jean Médecin. Friendly owners let fresh-scented rooms with Grecian white and blue colors. Reception 24hr.; free luggage storage. Breakfast 25-30F/€3.81-4.57. Singles 200F/€30.49; doubles 250F/€38.12; triples 350F/€53.36; quads 400F/€60.98. Extra bed 60F/€9.15. AmEx/MC/V.

NEAR VIEUX NICE AND THE BEACH

Hôtel Little Masséna, 22 rue Masséna (☎/fax 04 93 87 72 34). Small but clean and comfortable rooms with TV and kitchenette in a boisterous and touristy part of town. Owners are young and friendly. Singles and doubles 170F/€25.92, with shower 220F/€33.54, with bath 270F/€41.16. Extra person 30F/€4.57. Oct.-May prices 10-30F/€1.53-4.57 lower. MC/V.

Les Mimosas, 26 rue de la Buffa (☎04 93 88 05 59; fax 04 93 87 15 65). A monumental staircase leads to ten small but newly renovated rooms filled mostly with backpackers. Bows on doors and soap on beds add a touch of home. Close to the beach and lively rue Masséna. Free coffee, beach towel loan, and luggage storage until 9pm. Singles 170F/€25.92; doubles 200F/€30.49; triples 240F/€36.59; quads 310F/€47.26. Oct.-Apr. prices 30F/€4.57 lower. Cash only.

Hôtel Au Picardy, 10 bd. Jean Jaurès (☎/fax 04 93 85 75 51), across from the bus station. Ideally located next to Vieux Nice; rooms are decorated in every shade of brown. Streetside chambers can be noisy; prepare to sleep with the window shut. Breakfast 17.50F/€2.67. Showers 10F/€1.53. Singles 125F/€19.06, with shower 179F/€27.29; doubles 179F/€27.29, with bath 209F/€31.86; triples 220-260F/€33.54-39.64; and quads 260-299F/€39.64-45.59. Extra bed 45F/€6.86. Cash only.

Hôtel Petit Trianon, 11 rue Paradis (☎04 93 87 50 46), a left off the pedestrian rue Masséna. Humble rooms with elegant chandeliers and tasteful wallpaper. The new owner is friendly and helpful. Free beach mat loan. Singles 100F/€15.25; doubles 200F/€30.49; triples 300F/€45.74. Extra bed 50F/€7.62.

Rialto, 55 rue de la Buffa (☎/fax 04 93 88 15 04). A little farther from the main event. More apartment building than hotel. Eight bright and spacious hardwood rooms all have bath and sizeable kitchen. Doubles 360F/€54.89; triples 386F/€58.85; quads 480F/€73.18; studios of 6-8 people 90F/€13.72 per person.

FOOD

Nice is, above all, a city of restaurants, from little outdoor terraces to tiny pungent holes-in-the-wall. Inexpensive local specialties, flavored with North African spices, local herbs, or olives, are sold at pâtisseries and bakeries. Try *pan bagnat*, a round, crusty bread with tuna, sardines, and vegetables; *pissaladière*, a pizza topped with onions, anchovies, and olives; *socca*, a thin, olive oil-flavored chickpea bread; and *bouillabaisse*, a hearty stew of mussels, potatoes, and fish. *Salade niçoise* is made with tuna, potatoes, tomatoes, and a spicy mustard dressing.

Cafés and food stands along the beach are expensive, so shop for lunch before you hit the waves. The fruit, fish, and flower **market** at cours Saleya is the best place to pick up fresh olives, cheeses, and melons (Su-M 6am-noon, Tu-Sa 6am-5:30pm). A **fruit and vegetable market** also materializes daily on av. Malaussena (known as av. Jean Médecin south of the train station), toward pl. Général de Gaulle. If you want to eat out, dozens of cheap Chinese and Indian joints congregate around the train station. Expensive gourmet fare lines rue Masséna, where your best bet is a 60F/€9.15 pizza; av. Jean Médecin hosts reasonable brasseries and *panini* vendors; and Vieux Nice is a mix of hidden gems and tourist dross. A tip: any restaurant fronted by a menu-toting hostess is sure to be an expensive disappointment. Backpackers and geriatrics alike fill the generic but cheap **Flunch,** av. Thiers, next to the train station, where 25F/€3.81 all-you-can-eat buffets cater to tight budgets and easy-to-please tastebuds. (☎04 93 88 41 35. Open daily 7:30am-9:30pm.) For more scholarly fare, head to **Restaurant Université,** 3 av. Robert Schumann, which serves students filling meals. (☎04 93 97 10 20. Meals 30F/€4.57, with student ID 15F/€2.29. Open Sept.-June daily 11:30am-1:30pm.)

Lou Pilha Leva, 13 rue du Collet (☎04 93 13 99 08), in Vieux Nice. Tourists and locals pack the outdoor wooden benches of this Vieux Nice favorite. Munch on lots of local food for a little money; 10F/€1.53 pizza slices, 12F/€1.83 *socca,* 12F/€1.83 *pissaladière,* and 37F/€5.64 *moules* (mussels) are hard to resist. Open daily 8am-11pm.

Speakeasy, 7 rue Lamartine (☎04 93 85 59 50). No mad cows here; just delectable and affordable vegetarian and vegan lunch options lovingly prepared by the American chef/animal-rights activist. Organic bean patties, couscous, and daily specialties will convert even the staunchest carnivore. Open M-Sa 11:45am-2pm.

Acchiardo, 38 rue Droite (☎04 93 85 51 16), in Vieux Nice. Simple but tasty Italian-French dishes in a farm-like interior, complete with hanging corn husks and bronze pans. Reasonable pastas (from 35F/€5.34) are popular with a loyal local clientele. Open M-F noon-1:30pm and 7-9:30pm, Sa noon-1:30pm.

Nocy-Bé, 4-6 rue Jules Gilly (☎04 93 85 52 25). Take a time-out at this mellow tearoom, adorned with low-hanging lamps and comfortable floor rugs. Dozens of teas to choose from (15-25F/€2.29-3.81). Open W-M 4pm-12:30am.

La Merenda, 4 rue de la Terrasse. Doesn't cater to tourists; outsiders may even feel unwelcome. Those brave enough to pass the beaded entrance can savor the work of a culinary master who abandoned a 4-star hotel to open this local legend. Amazing value for the area (40-75F/€6.10-11.43). Open M-F noon-1:30pm and 7-9:30pm.

SIGHTS

Many visitors head straight for the beaches and don't retreat from the sun until the day is done. However, contrary to popular opinion, there are activities in Nice aside from naked sunbathing. Strategically or inconveniently placed on all corners of the city, Nice's impressive museums are worth a visit.

MUSEE NATIONAL MESSAGE BIBLIQUE MARC CHAGALL. Chagall founded this extraordinary concrete and glass museum in 1966 to showcase his 17 *Message Biblique* paintings. In addition to these huge, colorful canvases, the museum has a cursory photobiography of Chagall, a wonderful garden, and a small stained-glass-filled auditorium that the artist decorated himself. *(Av. du Dr. Ménard. 15min. walk north of the station. Or take bus #15 (dir: "Rimiez") to "Musée Chagall." ☎04 93 53 87 20. Open July-Sept. W-M 10am-6pm; Oct.-June 10am-5pm. Last tickets sold 30min. before closing. 36F/€5.49, under age 26 and Su 26F/€3.96, under 18 free.)*

MUSEE MATISSE. No one contributed more to the fame of Nice than Henri Matisse, who, after first visiting the city in 1916, immediately decided to live and work there until he died: "When I realized that this light would return every day," the artist explained, "I couldn't believe my good fortune." Housed in a 17th-century Genoese villa, the museum's collection of paintings is disappointingly small, but the three-dimensional work, including bronze reliefs and dozens of cut-and-paste tableaux, is dazzling. *(164 av. des Arènes de Cimiez. Take bus #15, 17, 20, or 22 to "Arènes." ☎04 93 81 08 08. Open Apr.-Sept. W-M 10am-6pm; Oct.-Mar. 10am-5pm. 25F/€3.81, students 20F/€3.05. Call for info on lectures, free with admission.)*

MUSEE D'ART MODERNE ET D'ART CONTEMPORAIN. Housed in a large concrete, glass, steel, and marble complex, the minimalist galleries feature European and American avant-garde pieces dating from 1960 to the present. Emphasizes French New Realists and American Pop Art, including works by such greats as Lichtenstein, Warhol, and Klein. *(Promenade des Arts, at the intersection of av. St-Jean Baptiste and traverse Garibaldi. Take bus #5 (dir: "St-Charles") to "Promenade des Arts." The museum is behind the bus station. ☎04 93 62 61 62. Open W-M 10am-6pm. 25F/€3.81, students 15F/€2.29.)* Across from the museum sits another epic piece of modern architecture, the conspicuous gold eyesore that is the **Acropolis.** Though both exterior and interior resemble a sci-fi film set, it actually functions as a conference center, office space, and auditorium.

VIEUX NICE. Sprawling southeast from bd. Jean Jaurès, this neighborhood is the center of Nice's nightlife and one of the most colorful quarters on the Côte. Tiny balconies overflowing with pansies, fountained public squares, hand-painted awnings, and an assortment of exceptional churches crowd Vieux Nice's labyrinthine streets. In the morning, the charming area is host to a number of lively **markets,** including a fish frenzy at **pl. St-François** (Tu-Su 6am-1pm) and a flower market on **cours Salaya** (Su-M 6am-noon, Tu-Sa 6am-5:30pm); in the evening there are knick-knack stands, cafés, and restaurants.

CATHEDRALE ORTHODOXE RUSSE ST-NICOLAS. Also known as the **Eglise Russe,** this cathedral—the first to be so christened outside of Russia—was commissioned by Empress Marie Feodorovna, widow of Tsar Nicholas I, who died in Nice. Modeled after St. Basil's cathedral in Moscow, the onion-domed structure quickly became popular with exiled Russian nobles looking for a place to worship. The altar, rather than occupying center stage as in a French cathedral, is hidden behind a gilded screen, decorated with paintings of Christ, the Virgin, and the saints. There's one dead giveaway, however, that the Cathedral stands on local soil: traditionally dark and somber colors have been replaced by the light blues and yellows of the Mediterranean village and sky. *(17 bd. du Tsarevitch, off bd. Gambetta. ☎ 04 93 96 88 02. Open June-Aug. daily 9am-noon and 2:30-6pm; Sept.-May 9:30am-noon and 2:30-5pm. 15F/€2.29, students 12F/€1.83.)*

LE CHATEAU. At the eastern end of the promenade, Le Château is a flowery green hillside park crowned with an artificial waterfall and the remains of an 11th-century cathedral. Despite its name, there's no château—it was demolished in a battle during the 8th century. Jog up more than 400 steps for a spectacular view of the rooftops of Nice and the sparkling blue Baie des Anges, or ascend via elevator at the Tour Bellanda. *(Park open daily 7am-8pm. Elevator runs 9am-7:30pm; 7F/€1.07.)*

MUSEE DES BEAUX-ARTS. Housed in the former villa of Ukraine's Princess Kotschoubey, this museum's collection of French academic painting is overshadowed by rooms devoted to Van Dongen and Raoul Dufy. Dufy, Nice's second greatest painter, celebrated the spontaneity of his city with explosive pictures of the town at rest and play. *(33 av. Baumettes. Take bus #38 to "Chéret" or #12 to "Grosso." ☎ 04 92 15 28 28. Open Tu-Su 10am-noon and 2-6pm. 25F/€3.81, students 15F/€2.29.)*

MONASTERE DE CIMIEZ. This monastery has housed Nice's Franciscans since the 13th century, and a few still call Cimiez home. In their former living quarters is the **Musée Franciscain,** filled with illuminated manuscripts, medieval crosses, and a Giotto painting of St. Francis. The complex also features a church, lovely surrounding gardens, and a crowded cemetery where Matisse and Dufy are given pride of place. *(Pl. du Monastère. Take bus #15 (dir: "Rimiez") or #17 (dir: "Cimiez") to "Monastère" from the station, or follow the signs and walk from the Musée Matisse. ☎ 04 93 81 55 41. Museum open M-Sa 10am-noon and 3-6pm. Church open daily 8am-12:30pm and 2-6:30pm. Gardens open daily 8am-7pm, winter 8am-6pm. Cemetery open daily 8am-6pm. Free.)*

MUSEE ARCHEOLOGIQUE ET SITE GALLO-ROMAIN. Built next to the site of ancient Gallo-Roman baths, this museum contains relics found in the area from the Bronze through the Middle Ages, including excavated coins, jewelry, and sarcophagi. *(160 av. des Arènes de Cimiez. ☎ 04 93 81 59 57. Take bus #15, 17, 20, or 22 to "Arènes." Next to Musée Matisse. Open Apr.-Sept. Tu-Su 10am-noon and 2-6pm; Oct.-Mar. 10am-1pm and 2-5pm. 25F/€3.81, students 15F/€2.29.)*

JARDIN ALBERT IER AND ESPACE MASSENA. Jardin Albert 1er, the most central of the city's parks, provides a temporary refuge from Nice. Along with benches and fountains, it contains the Théâtre de Verdun, a small amphitheater that hosts jazz and outdoor theater in summer. *(Between av. Verdun and bd. Jaurès, off promenade des Anglais and quai des Etats-Unis. Box office open daily 10:30am-noon and 3:30-6:30pm.)*

OTHER SIGHTS. Named for the rich English community that commissioned it, the **Promenade des Anglais,** a rich palm-lined seaside boulevard, is Nice's response to the great pedestrian thoroughfares of Paris, London, and New York. Today the promenade is full of luxury hotels like the stately **Négresco,** toward the west end, where the staff still don top hats and 19th-century uniforms. Just east of the Négresco, the **Espace Masséna** is a picnic-perfect, creative public space with a large fountain and plenty of shady benches. Standing guard over the palm trees is the **Musée Masséna,** 35 promenade des Anglais, which is temporarily closed for renovation. **Private beaches** crowd the water between bd. Gambetta and the Opéra, but lots of public spaces compensate, especially west of bd. Gambetta. Whatever dreams you've had of Nice's beaches, the hard reality is a stretch of rocks somewhat smoothed by the sea—so bring a beach mat.

ENTERTAINMENT AND FESTIVALS

BARS

Nice guys really do finish last—the party crowd here swings long after the folks in St-Tropez and Antibes have called it a night. The bars and nightclubs around rue Masséna and Vieux Nice move with constant dance, jazz, and rock. For info on events pick up *l'Excés* (www.exces.com), a free brochure available at the tourist office and in some bars. To enjoy Nice's nightlife without spending a centime, head down to the **promenade des Anglais,** where street performers, musicians, and hundreds of pedestrians wander the beach and boardwalk into the night. Local men have a reputation for hassling people on the promenade; lone women and even those in groups should decide carefully where to walk at night.

The dress code at all bars and clubs is simple: look good. Though some places (pubs) let patrons dress messy, most will turn you away if they catch you in shorts, sandals, or a baseball cap. Sneakers are rarely acceptable for nightclubs. For men, grays and blacks are in, and for women, the tighter the better. But remember: the French are known for dressing *classe* ("in good taste"). Don't go over the top, or you'll stick out like a sore *Let's Go* thumb.

Thor, 32 cours Saleya (☎04 93 62 49 90). Svelte blonde bartenders pour pints for a youthful crowd in this raucous Scandinavian pub. Backpackers and locals alike let loose to live music (10pm nightly) in the Nordic-inspired interior. Open daily 6pm-2am.

Wayne's, 15 rue de la Préfecture (☎04 93 13 46 99). The common denominators in this wild, crowded bar: young, anglo, and on the prowl. Live, loud music M-Sa in the summer. Happy Hour daily 6-9pm with 25F/€3.81 pints and 30F/€4.57 cocktails. Open Su-Th 11am-1am, F-Sa 11am-1:30am.

Bodeguita del Havana, rue Chauvain (☎04 93 92 67 24), just above rue Gioffredo. A recreation of 1940s Havana, where Castro may be coming but Guantanamera is king. Late-20s crowd. Cuban cocktails 55F/€8.39. Live salsa daily. Cover 50F/€7.62 F-Sa. Open June-Aug. daily 8pm-2:30am; Sept.-May 8pm-12:30am.

De Klomp, 6 rue Mascoinat (☎04 93 92 42 85). Anything goes in this friendly Dutch pub, where a diverse crowd dances to live salsa and jazz nightly. Sample one of their 40 whiskeys (from 40F/€6.10) or 18 beers on tap (pint 45F/€6.86). Happy Hour 5:30-9:30pm with 25F/€3.81 pints. Open M-Sa 5:30pm-2:30am, Su 8:30pm-2:30am.

Le Bar Des Deux Frères, 1 rue du Moulin (☎04 93 80 77 61). Hidden behind the facade of an old restaurant, this hip local favorite is guaranteed to show everyone a good time. A young, funky crowd throws back tequila (20F/€3.05) and beer (15F/€2.29) amid red curtains and smoky tables. Open daily 9pm-3:30am; winter closed M.

McMahon's, 50 bd. Jean Jaurès (☎04 93 71 16 23). Join the locals and (many) expats who lap up Guinness at this low-key Irish pub. Happy Hour daily 6-9pm, karaoke on Tu, drink promos on Th, and dancing barmaids nightly. Open daily 6pm-2:30am.

Tapas la Movida, 2 bis rue de l'Abbaye (☎04 93 62 27 46), resembles a revolutionary secret meeting spot, but the only plotting you'll do is how to get home after braving the bar-o-mètre (100F/€15.25), a meter-long wooden box of shots. Live reggae and rock concerts M-Th (10F/€1.53). Open M-Sa 7pm-12:30am.

Williams, 4 rue Centrale (☎04 93 62 99 63). When the other bars have called it a night, Williams keeps the kegs flowing for an Anglo crowd. Make a spectacle of yourself with karaoke nights M-Th. Live music F and Sa. Open M-Sa 11am-6am.

NIGHTCLUBS

Nice's nightclubs can quickly drain your funds. Going on Thursdays, Sundays, before midnight, or being female are all good ways to reduce the cover. Cover usually includes the first drink. The scene in Nice is in constant flux, with new clubs replacing old ones almost daily and the *it* spot shifting rapidly.

Forum, 45-47 promenade des Anglais (☎04 93 96 67 00). Nice's hottest club, where Hawaiian-shirted bartenders pour exotic drinks, showgirls play with fire, and "little people" dance on platforms. Cover 100F/€15.25. Open F-Sa 11pm-6am.

La Suite, 2 rue Bréa (☎04 93 92 92 91). This small club attracts a funky, well-dressed, moneyed crowd. Velvet theater curtains drape the walls and go-go dancers show some skin on weekends. Cover 80F/€12.20, free W. Open W-Su 11:30pm-2:30am.

Blue Boy, 9 rue Jean-Baptiste Spinetta (☎04 93 44 68 24), in west Nice. Though far from town, Blue Boy remains Nice's most popular gay club. Men free, women pay 200F/€30.49 cover. Open daily 11pm-5am.

Le Klub, 6 rue Halévy (☎06 60 55 26 61). This popular gay club caters to a fabulous, well-tanned crowd, with a cocktail lounge and video projections on the dance floor. Cover 70F/€10.67 on Sa. Open July-Aug. daily 11:30pm-6am; Sept.-June closed M.

CULTURE

The **Théâtre du Cours,** 5 rue Poissonnerie in Vieux Nice, stages traditional drama. (☎04 93 80 12 67. 80F/€12.20, students 60F/€9.15.) The grand **Théâtre de Nice,** on the promenade des Arts, hosts theatrical performances (☎04 93 13 90 90; 45-180F/€6.86-27.44; student discounts), while the **Opéra de Nice,** 4 rue St-François de Paule, has an annual performance series of visiting symphony orchestras and soloists (☎04 93 13 98 53 or 04 92 17 40 40; 50-250F/€7.62-38.12). The **FNAC** (☎04 92 17 77 77) in the Nice Etoile shopping center at 24 av. Jean Médecin sells tickets for virtually every musical or theatrical event in town.

FESTIVALS

In mid-July, the **Nice Jazz Festival** attracts world-famous jazz and non-jazz musicians from around the world. The 2001 lineup included Van Morrison and B.B. King. (Arènes et Jardins de Cimiez. ☎08 20 80 04 00; www.nicejazzfest.com. Tickets 50-250F/€7.62-38.12.) During the **Carnaval** in Lent, Nice gives Rio a run for its money with three weeks of parades, fireworks, and outlandish costumes.

NEAR NICE

Just inland from Nice, the small towns of St-Paul and Vence hide their art treasures far away from the mania of the coast.

TRANSPORTATION. SAP Buses (☎04 93 58 37 60) sends buses #400-410 to Vence and St-Paul from **Nice** (40min.; 19 per day; 26.50F/€4.04 to St-Paul, 29.50F/€4.50 to Vence). To get to St-Paul from **Cannes,** take the train to Cagnes-sur-Mer and change to bus #400-410 (10F/€1.53). The trip from Vence to St-Paul costs 8F/€1.22. The last #400-410 leaves St-Paul for Nice and Cagnes-sur-Mer at 6:40pm from the stop just outside the town entrance.

VENCE

The former Roman market town of Vence (pop. 17,000) snoozes in the green hills above Nice. The medieval village and modern surrounding town make a picturesque break from the coastal crowds, with plenty of marketplaces and fountains. Sights abound in the old town (pick up a walking tour map at the tourist office). Stroll through the **Château de Villeneuve,** a grand 17th-century villa filled with religious works by Matisse and others (☎04 93 58 15 78). The central **cathedral** features a paintbox-bright mosaic of *Moses in the Bulrushes* by Chagall. Vence's architectural masterpiece, the **Chapelle du Rosaire,** was designed and overseen by Henri Matisse, from the green, blue, and yellow stained-glass windows down to the sacerdotal robes. From the bus stop, facing the tourist office, turn left and walk up av. de la Résistance. Take a right on rue Elise and a left on av. des Poilus; at the roundabout go right onto av. de Matisse, cross the bridge, and follow the little brown sign, keeping on av. de Matisse (1½km). (☎04 93 58 03 26. Open Tu and Th 10-11:30am and 2-5:30pm, M, W, and F 2-5:30pm. 5F/€0.76.)

A few kilometers from Vence is a dazzling art gallery, the **Galerie Beaubourg.** Housed in a 19th-century château, this place displays—and will sell—all of the biggest modern names, from Picasso to Miró to Arman. Prices range from a budget-friendly 2000F/€304.92 to 4,000,000F/€604,849.06. (☎ 04 93 24 52 00; fax 04 93 24 52 19. Open Apr.-Sept. M-Sa 11am-7pm; Oct.-Mar. Tu-Sa 12:30pm-5:30pm. 30F/€4.57, students 15F/€2.29.) From in front of the tourist office, take bus #14 (dir: "Tourettes") to "Notre Dame des Fleurs" (9 per day, 5F/€0.76). A **taxi** from Vence to the gallery costs about 50F/€7.62.

You'll sleep like a cherub at **La Closerie des Genets,** 4 impasse Marcellin Maurel, just off av. Maurel outside the *vieille ville.* Lovingly-decorated rooms have blue shutters and new beds, as well as private baths. A lucky few have views of the sea. (☎ 04 93 58 33 25; fax 04 93 58 97 01; lacloserie@free.fr. Breakfast 32F/€4.88. Singles 150-200F/€22.90-30.49; doubles 230-350F/€35.06-53.36; triples 350-500F/€53.36-76.23; quads or quints 550F/€83.85. Extra bed 50F/€7.62. AmEx/MC/V.) **La Victoire,** pl. du Grand Jardin, offers less in the way of rooms, but is well-located by the bus stop. (☎ 04 93 58 61 30; fax 04 93 58 74 68. Breakfast 33F/€5.03. Singles with bath 160-190F/€24.39-28.97; doubles with bath 190-220F/€28.97-33.54. Extra person half the cost of the entire room. MC/V.)

The **tourist office** lies at pl. du Grand Jardin, across from the bus stop. (☎ 04 93 58 06 38; fax 04 93 58 91 81; www.ville-vence.fr. Open July-Sept. M-Sa 9am-7pm, Su 9am-1pm and 2-7pm; Oct.-June M-Sa 9am-1pm and 2-6pm.)

ST-PAUL

If you visit one medieval village on the Côte D'Azur, make it St-Paul. Ever since Chagall discovered St-Paul's colors and light and made it his home, the clifftop village has become an art lover's paradise, packed with over 80 galleries selling local paintings, pottery, and handcrafts, not to mention works by the likes of Léger and Ernst. As you stroll through the well-trampled village, make sure to see Chagall's gravestone and the exquisite cathedral, home to the mounted skull of St. Etienne.

Much of St-Paul's art is in the nearby **Fondation Maeght,** 1km from the town center. Get off at the "St-Paul" bus stop and follow the signs first down and then up the chemin des Gardettes. Designed by Joseph Sert, the foundation is part museum and part park, with shrubs and fountains mixed in among works by Miró, Calder, Arp, and Léger. Maeght, an art dealer, was inconsolable after the death of his eldest son. Encouraged by his artist friends, he commissioned a small, somber chapel with stained glass by Braque and Ubac, now part of the museum. (☎ 04 93 32 81 63. Open July-Sept. daily 10am-7pm; Oct.-June 10am-12:30pm and 2:30-6pm. 50F/€7.62, students 40F/€6.10. Photography permit 15F/€2.29.)

The **tourist office,** 2 rue Grande, just inside the walls of St-Paul, dispenses free maps and info on galleries and exhibitions. They even give personal one-hour tours (10am-5:30pm) of the medieval city on request in English for 50F/€7.62 per person. (☎ 04 93 32 86 95; fax 04 93 32 60 27; artdevivre@wanadoo.fr. Open June-Sept. daily 10am-7pm; Oct.-May 10am-6pm.)

THE CORNICHES

Rocky shores, pebble beaches, and luxurious villas glow along the coast between hectic Nice and high-rolling Monaco. More relaxing and less touristed than their glam-fab neighbors, these tiny towns glisten with interesting museums, architectural finds, and breathtaking countryside. The train offers an exceptional glimpse of the coast up close, while buses maneuvering along the high roads of the *corniches* provide a bird's-eye view of the steep cliffs and crashing sea below. Take one mode of transport out and the other back—you won't be disappointed.

TRANSPORTATION. Trains and buses between Nice and Monaco serve most of the Corniche towns. With a departure about every hour, **trains** from **Nice** to **Monaco** stop at **Villefranche-sur-Mer** (7min., 13F/€1.98), **Beaulieu-sur-Mer** (10min., 16F/€2.44), **Eze-sur-Mer** (16min., 18F/€2.74), and **Cap d'Ail** (20min., 21F/€3.20).

Numerous numbered **RCA buses** (☎04 93 85 64 44; www.rca.tm.fr) run between Nice and Monaco, making different stops along the way. **#111** leaves Nice, stopping in **Villefranche-sur-Mer** (10 per day). Two buses continue on to **St-Jean-Cap-Ferrat** (M-Sa). **#117** runs between Nice and **Villefranche-sur-Mer** 11 times daily. **#112** runs 7 times per day (3 on Su) between Nice and Monte-Carlo, stopping in **Eze-le-Village. RCA** and **Broch** (☎04 93 31 10 52 or 04 93 07 63 28; daily every hr.) run between Nice and **Villefranche-sur-Mer** (15min., 9F/€1.37), **Beaulieu-sur-Mer** (20min., 14F/€2.14), **Eze-le-Village** (25min., 15F/€2.29), **Cap d'Ail** (30min., 17F/€2.59), **Monaco-Ville** (40min., 20F/€3.05), and **Monte-Carlo** (45min., 20F/€3.05). Most tickets include free same-day return; inquire.

VILLEFRANCHE-SUR-MER

The stairwayed streets and pastel houses of Villefranche-sur-Mer have earned the town a reputation as one of the Riviera's most photogenic gems. The backdrop for dozens of films (from a James Bond installation to *Dirty Rotten Scoundrels*), the town has enchanted artists and writers from Aldous Huxley to Katherine Mansfield to Tina Turner, who makes an annual pilgrimage to her hillside villa here. Despite the celebrity attention, Villefranche remains a true provençal town, with one of the area's better beaches and some interesting sights.

As you walk from the station along quai Courbet, a sign for the *vieille ville* points the way along the 13th-century **rue Obscure,** the oldest street in Villefranche. A right at the end of rue Obscure takes you to the **Church of Saint Michel,** which contains an impressive wooden statue of a martyred Christ, sculpted by an anonymous slave. At the end of the *quai* stands the pink and yellow 14th-century **Chapelle St-Pierre,** decorated from floor to ceiling by Jean Cocteau, former resident, film-maker, and jack-of-all-arts. (☎04 93 76 90 70. Hours fluctuate—call ahead. 12F/€1.83.) The rather dull 16th-century **Citadelle** houses three small museums, the most interesting of which is the rustic **Musée Volti** (☎04 93 76 33 27), dedicated to Antoniucci Volti, who experimented with bronze, clay, canvas, and copper, to create curvaceous female forms. (☎04 93 76 33 33. Open July-Aug. W-Sa and M 10am-noon and 3-7pm, Su 3-5pm; June and Sept. W-Sa and M 9am-noon and 3-6pm, Su 3-6pm; Oct.-May W-Sa 10am-noon and 2-5pm, Su 2-5pm. Free.)

If you're dead-set on spending a night in the Corniches rather than nearby, budget-friendly Nice, Villefranche has some pleasant but pricey hotels. At **La Régence,** 2 av. Maréchal Foch, boxy carpeted rooms sit atop an all-night bar on the main drag. (☎04 93 01 70 91. **Internet access.** Singles 246F/€37.51; doubles 246-286F/€37.51-43.60; triples 349F/€53.21.) For a quieter, more private stay, settle in at **Le Home,** av. de Grande-Bretagne, which offers furnished rooms overlooking an exquisite garden, each with fridge and sink. (☎04 93 76 79 88. 2 night minimum. July-Aug. 250F/€38.12; June and Sept. 240F/€36.59; Oct.-May 230F/€35.06.)

To find the **tourist office** from the train station, exit on quai 1 and head inland on av. G. Clemenceau. Continue straight when it becomes av. Sadi Carnot. The office is at the end of the street in the Jardin François. It gives out a walking tour of the town and can suggest excursions to nearby villages. (☎04 93 01 73 68; fax 04 93 76 63 65; ot-villefranchesurmer@rom.fr; www.villefranche-sur-mer.com. Open July-Aug. daily 9am-noon and 2-6:30pm; mid-Sept.-June M-Sa 9am-noon and 2-6pm.)

BEAULIEU-SUR-MER

Reportedly named by Napoleon, who called it a "*beaulieu*" (beautiful place) upon his arrival, Beaulieu-sur-Mer is a seaside resort with a ritzy past. Belle Epoque villas, a classy casino, and ornate four-star hotels along the waterfront attest to the town's past as *the* place to winter for Europe's elite, who had no need of its small, prickly beach when they could take in the sun by the pool. While many of the moneyed have moved on to quieter mansions in nearby St-Jean-Cap-Ferrat, Beaulieu still attracts its share of stars. For those of lesser means, however, the spectacular villa is all that justifies a visit to this relatively uninteresting town.

On a plateau overlooking the sea, Renaissance man Theodore Reinach built his dream villa **Kérylos,** proof that money can buy happiness. This ode to antiquity is a perfect imitation of an ancient Greek dwelling: columns, mosaics, and marble sculptures are all copied from original masterpieces, while the frescoes in the foyer have been artificially aged. Even the piano was made to order in the Grecian "style." The villa is surrounded by gardens with statues of the Olympian gods, and an expensive café serves *moussaka* (70F/€10.67) on one of the coast's prettiest terraces. (☎04 93 01 01 44; www.villa-kerylos.com. Open July-Aug. daily 10:30am-7pm; Feb. 15-June and Sept.-Nov. 11 daily 10:30am-6pm; Dec. 15-Feb. 14 M-F 2-6pm, Sa-Su 10:30am-6pm; closed Nov. 12-Dec. 15. 45F/€6.86, students 33F/€5.03.)

A promenade along the waterfront passes by the major hotels. If you'd rather walk than gawk, the **tourist office,** pl. Georges Clemenceau, suggests scenic routes to nearby towns. (☎04 93 01 02 21; fax 04 93 01 44 04; www.ot-beaulieu-sur-mer.fr. Open July-Sept. M-Sa 9am-12:15pm and 2-7pm; Oct.-June M-F 9am-12:15pm and 2-6pm, Sa 9am-12:15pm and 2-5pm.)

ST-JEAN-CAP-FERRAT

As if the *Riviera* needed a trump card! St-Jean-Cap-Ferrat is a haven for the upper-class—the King of Belgium still makes a yearly appearance. The town is serviced by **bus #111,** but nothing compares to the 25-minute seaside walk from Beaulieu. Passing lavish villas, rocky beaches, and once-beautiful docks, it could take up to an hour with all the photo-ops.

The **Fondation Ephrussi de Rothschild** is just off av. D. Semeria, in between the tourist office and the Nice-Monaco road. Housing the furniture and art collections of the eccentric Baroness de Rothschild and her famous father, the interior features Monet canvases, Gobelins tapestries, Chinese vases, and a stunning tea room. Outside, each of seven lush gardens reflects a different part of the world, from Spain to Japan and, *bien sûr*, France. The villa can be accessed directly from Beaulieu. Follow the shore path toward St-Jean, turning right after the three-pronged tree and before the pink villa that separates the path from the Mediterranean; from the top of this walled shore access, turn left and follow the road uphill, turning right at the sign to the Fondation. (☎04 93 01 33 99. Open July-Aug. daily 10am-7pm; Sept.-Oct. and Feb. 15-June daily 10am-6pm; Nov.-Feb. 14 M-F 2-6pm, Sa-Su 10am-6pm. 50F/€7.62, students 38F/€5.79.)

St-Jean's **beaches** have earned the area the nickname "*presqu'île des rêves*" ("peninsula of dreams"). Attracting mainly locals, who descend from their villas to bask in the sun, the beaches here have a secluded, peaceful feel. With so many to choose from, you'll want to pass on the aptly named **plage Passable,** just down the hill from the tourist office; instead, continue on to the Cap's best beach, the wide **plage Paloma,** just past the port on av. Jean Mermoz. For a more solitary sunbath, make a right off av. Mermoz at the junction of pl. Paloma and try **Les Faussettes,** and farther on, **Les Fausses.** These beautiful rocky stretches look on to a quiet and unpopulated bay. The tiny **tourist office,** 59 av. Denis Séméria, is half-way along the winding street that runs from Nice and Monaco to the port. It has free maps of the region and *St-Jean-Cap-Ferrat à Petits Pas*, free walking tour maps of the peninsula's 11km of trails, and directions to more hidden beaches. (☎04 93 76 08 90; fax 04 93 76 16 67. Open July-Aug. M-Sa 8:30am-12:30pm and 1-5:30pm, Su 1-5:30pm; Sept.-June M-Sa 8:30am-noon and 1-5:30pm, Su 1-5:30pm.)

EZE

Three-tiered Eze owes its fame to the pristine medieval village that perches precariously on the cliffside. The seaside town, **Eze Bord-de-Mer** (also called **Eze-sur-Mer**) houses the train station and a stretch of pebble beach popular with windsurfers, kayakers, and sailors, but not much else. The upper tier, **Col d'Eze,** is mostly residential. It is the middle tier, **Eze-le-Village,** that has attracted international attention. This Roman-village-turned-medieval citadel has been occupied by everyone from Moors to Piedmontese, but has been finally overwhelmed by its most recent visitors—the thousands of tourists who flood it every year.

Photo-snapping tourists aside, Eze-le-Village is a remarkable museum of the Riviera's past. The **Porte des Maures,** erected in remembrance of a fatally successful surprise attack by the Moors, dates to the tumultuous 10th century when they controlled much of the Côte. The **Eglise Paroissial** contains sleek Phoenician crosses mixed in with old-fashioned Catholic gilt (open daily 9am-noon and 2-6pm). The **Jardin Exotique,** which provides fabulous views of the sea and the Cap d'Antibes, is planted around a Savoy fortress destroyed in 1706 by an invading Louis XIV. (Open daily 9am-7:30pm. 15F/€2.29, students 10F/€1.53.) Eze-le-Village offers more than narrow streets and nice views—the **Fragonard Parfumerie,** has its second-largest factory here, open for free tours explaining the process of making perfume, and the opportunity to buy at warehouse prices. (☎04 93 41 05 05. Open daily 8:15am-6:45pm.) The more intimate **Parfumerie Galimard** has a free **museum.** (☎04 93 41 10 70. Open Apr.-Oct. daily 8:30am-6:30pm; Nov.-Mar. 9am-noon and 2-6pm.)

The best views go to those who venture 40 minutes up or down the **Sentier Friedrich Nietzsche,** a winding trail where its namesake found inspiration to compose the third part of *Thus Spake Zarathustra.* The trail begins in Eze Bord-de-Mer, 100m east of the train station and tourist office, and ends near the base of the medieval city, by the Fragonard parfumerie. Be warned—unless you're a superman, the hike up may be too much for your lungs.

The **tourist office,** pl. de Gaulle, has free maps and info. To find it, take the Navette mini-bus from the train station. (☎04 93 41 26 00; fax 04 93 41 04 84; www.eze-riviera.com. Open Apr.-Oct. daily 9am-7pm; Nov.-Mar. 9am-6:30pm.)

To get to Eze, take the train from **Nice** (16min., 18F/€2.74). From May 1-Oct. 15, a **Navette** mini-bus connects Eze's three tiers, stopping in **Eze Bord-de-Mer** in front of the tourist office and in **Eze-le-Village** where the main road meets the path to the medieval city (7 per day 9:30am-6:30pm, 25F/€3.81). If you miss the bus, a **taxi** up costs about 130F/€19.82.

CAP D'AIL

Villa-strewn Cap d'Ail (pop. 5000) isn't a place to visit for provincial flavor. Three kilometers of cliff-framed, foamy seashore, a hostel that's actually a waterfront villa, and numerous airy footpaths make it a great place to sunbathe, though—especially without any clothes on. Dozens of illegal naturists make sure there's always a full moon over the Cap at **Les Pissarelles.** To join them, or to seek the sun on the more modest **plage Mala,** turn left from the train station and make another left into a stone tunnel leading down to the mansion-lined av. R. Gramaglia. From here, go straight down to the sea and jump onto the **sentier du bord de mer,** a winding, stairwayed path that curves along the cliffs and takes you to Mala. You'll recognize the path by its ultramarine guardrail. To get to Les Pissarelles beach, you'll have to walk 15 minutes along av. du 3 Septembre, the town's main thoroughfare.

The **Relais International de la Jeunesse "Thalassa,"** on bd. F. de May, can be reached by following the signs from the train station (7min.). It has the sort of waterfront location that plutocrats would kill for, and draws a friendly, fun-loving crowd, housed in single-sex dorms. (☎04 93 78 18 58; fax 04 93 53 35 88; clajpaca@cote-dazur.com. Breakfast included. Dinner 55F/€8.39. Free luggage storage. Lockout 9:30am-5:30pm. Curfew midnight. Open Apr.-Oct. Dorms 80F/€12.20.) Hostelers who miss the curfew sometimes take their chances illegally bedding down on plage Mala, as few of Cap d'Ail's police are interested in walking down 152 steps just to oust sleeping backpackers. However, as with most Riviera beaches, pickpockets and drug addicts may be likely to make the sand their nighttime haunt; *Let's Go* recommends a legal bed and a roof above your head.

The **tourist office,** 87bis av. du 3 Septembre, has free maps and info on daytrips. Walk uphill, keeping left until you leave the residential area. Turn right at the village, continuing on av. de la Gare. Turn left on rue du 4 Septembre, and the office will be on your right (20min.). (☎04 93 78 02 33; fax 04 92 10 74 36; www.montecarlo.mc/cap-d'ail. Open July-Aug. M-Sa 9am-12:30pm and 2:30-6:30pm, Su 9am-12:30pm; Sept.-June M-F 9am-12:30pm and 2-6pm, Sa 9am-12:30pm.)

MONACO AND MONTE-CARLO

This tiny principality (native pop. 5000; 30,000 with hangers-on) is, square inch for square inch, one of the wealthiest places in the world. The rest of the Côte may be glamorous, but Monaco doesn't have to bother with glamor; it has money, lots of it, invested in its ubiquitous surveillance cameras, high-speed luxury cars, and sleek multimillion dollar yachts. At Monaco's spiritual heart, if that's not giving it too much credit, is its famous casino, located in the capital city, Monte-Carlo, a magnet for the wealthy and dissolute since 1885. The sheer spectacle of it all, along with exceptional tourist attractions thanks to Monaco's royal family, is definitely worth the daytrip from Nice.

TRANSPORTATION

Trains: Connections approximately every 30min. to: **Antibes** (62min., 38F/€5.80); **Cannes** (60min., 46F/€7.02); **Menton** (10min., 12F/€1.83); and **Nice** (25min., 20F/€3.05). Station open 5:30am-1am. Info desk open M-F 8:05-11:55am and 2-5:35pm. No luggage storage.

Buses: Buses to **Menton** (1¼hr., every 15min., 28F/€4.27) and **Nice** (45min., every 15 min., 20F/€3.05) leave from pl. d'Armes or pl. du Casino. For info on buses, call 04 93 85 61 81 in Nice, **E. Broch** (☎04 93 31 10 52), or **RCA** (☎04 93 85 64 44).

Public Transportation: Five routes (☎97 70 22 22) connect the entire hilly town every 11min. 7am-8:30pm (Su and holidays every 20min. 7:30am-8:30pm), though schedules vary. Bus #4 links the train station to the casino in Monte-Carlo; bus #2 connects the *vieille ville* and *jardin exotique* via pl. d'Armes. Tickets 8.50F/€1.30, *carnet* of 4 21.50F/€3.28, *carnet* of 8 34F/€5.19. Buy tickets on board.

Taxis: ☎93 15 01 01. Around 50F/€7.62 from pl. du Casino to the hostel, 80-100F/€12.20-15.25 to the Relais de Jeunesse in Cap d'Ail.

Scooter Rental: Auto-Moto Garage, 7 rue de Millo (☎93 50 10 80). 150F/€22.90 from 9am-7pm, 170F/€25.92 for 24hr., 952F/€145.14 per week. Credit card deposit. Open M-F 8am-noon and 2-7pm, Sa 8am-noon.

ORIENTATION AND PRACTICAL INFORMATION

Though small, this jam-packed principality is surprisingly difficult to navigate. Matters were complicated in 2000 when Monaco built a mammoth new train station in the center of town, which shoots up over four stories and lacks a principal entrance. The site of the former station, referred to by locals as *"l'ancienne gare,"* is now the **av. Prince Pierre** entrance, connected to the train quays by a marble tunnel with moving walkways. Follow the signs for "Le Rocher" and "Fontvieille" to this exit; it's close to pl. d'Armes and the **La Condamine** quarter, Monaco's port and the hub of its restaurants and nightlife. To the right of La Condamine, the old city (**Monaco Ville** or "The Rock") rises fortress-like over the harbor, while the museum-laden **av. de Fontvieille** stretches out below and behind it. Leaving the station in the opposite direction (bd. Princesse Charlotte) or below (pl. St-Dévote), you'll end up on the other side of the port, closer to **Monte-Carlo** and its fabled tables. Up the hill from the casino and across an imperceptible border is less ritzy **Beausoleil,** France. Walking from one end of town to the other is no problem, but climbing the winding streets and stairwells can be tiring; look for strategically placed public elevators.

Tourist Office: 2a bd. des Moulins (☎92 16 61 16; fax 92 16 60 00; www.monaco-congres.com), near the casino. Maps, guides, and hotel reservations. **Annexes** are set up in the train station at the av. Prince Pierre exit and in the port June 15-Sept. Main office open M-Sa 9am-7pm, Su 10am-noon.

Money: Compagnie Monégasque de Change, parking du chemin des Pêcheurs (☎93 25 02 50), near Fort Antoine at the end of the port, has reasonable rates and no commission. Open Su-F 9:30am-5:30pm. Closed Nov.-Dec. 25. **American Express,** 35 bd. Princesse Charlotte (☎97 70 77 59). Open M-F 9:30am-noon and 2-6:30pm.

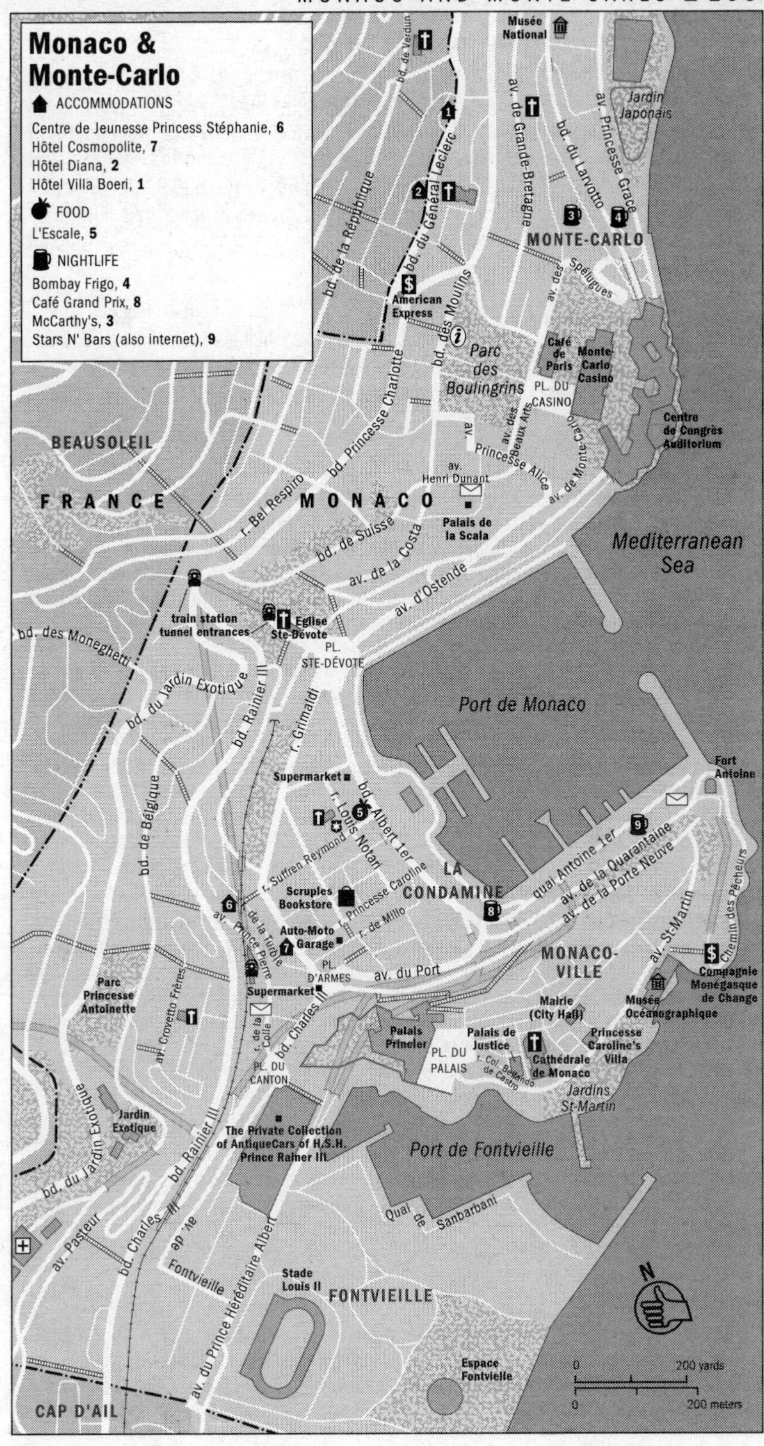
Monaco & Monte-Carlo
ACCOMMODATIONS
Centre de Jeunesse Princess Stéphanie, 6
Hôtel Cosmopolite, 7
Hôtel Diana, 2
Hôtel Villa Boeri, 1
FOOD
L'Escale, 5
NIGHTLIFE
Bombay Frigo, 4
Café Grand Prix, 8
McCarthy's, 3
Stars N' Bars (also internet), 9
Musée National
Jardin Japonais
MONTE-CARLO
American Express
Parc des Boulingrins
Café de Paris
Monte-Carlo Casino
PL. DU CASINO
Centre de Congrès Auditorium
BEAUSOLEIL
FRANCE
MONACO
Palais de la Scala
Mediterranean Sea
train station tunnel entrances
Eglise Ste-Dévote
PL. STE-DÉVOTE
Port de Monaco
Supermarket
Fort Antoine
LA CONDAMINE
Scruples Bookstore
Auto-Moto Garage
PL. D'ARMES
MONACO-VILLE
Compagnie Monégasque de Change
Musée Océanographique
Mairie (City Hall)
Palais de Justice
Princesse Caroline's Villa
Palais Princier
PL. DU PALAIS
Cathédrale de Monaco
Jardins St-Martin
Parc Princesse Antoinette
PL. DU CANTON
Jardin Exotique
The Private Collection of AntiqueCars of H.S.H. Prince Rainier III
Port de Fontvieille
Quai de Sanbarbani
Stade Louis II
FONTVIEILLE
Espace Fontvielle
CAP D'AIL
200 yards
200 meters

Police: 3 rue Louis Notari (☎93 15 30 15).

Hospital: Centre Hospitalier Princesse Grace, av. Pasteur (☎97 98 99 00 or emergency 97 98 97 95), off bd. Rainier III, which runs along the train tracks.

Internet Access: Stars 'N' Bars, 6 quai Antoine 1er (☎97 97 95 95). 40F/€6.10 for 30min. Open daily 10am-midnight.

Post Office: Palais de la Scala, Monte-Carlo (☎97 97 25 25). Monaco issues its own stamps; French stamps cannot be used in Monaco. **Branch office** across from Hôtel Terminus at the av. Prince Pierre train station exit. Both offices open M-F 8am-7pm, Sa 8am-noon. **Postal code:** MC 98000 Monaco.

PHONING TO AND FROM MONACO	Monaco's country code is 377. To telephone Monaco from France, dial 00377, then the 8-digit Monaco number. To call France from Monaco, dial 0033, and drop the first zero of the French number.

ACCOMMODATIONS

Commoners can't afford to stay within a stone's throw of the casino. Unless you're James Bond, the action is in **La Condamine,** where bargains are near the old train station. Alternatively, cross the street to **Beausoleil,** France, and watch prices drop by hundreds of francs. Consider staying at the lovely hostel in Cap d'Ail, one train stop away or a good walk along the beach. Access to Monaco is quick and cheap from any of the coastal towns between Menton and Nice.

Centre de Jeunesse Princesse Stéphanie, 24 av. Prince Pierre (☎93 50 83 20; fax 93 25 29 82; info@youthhostel.asso.mc). In the train station, follow the signs for "Le Rocher/Fontvieille" and board the moving walkways to the av. Prince Pierre exit. Turn left up the hill and walk 100m to the hostel, a pink building straight ahead. A bit sterile but excellent location, only four guests per room, and a small backyard. Binders with as much info as the tourist office has. Breakfast included. Lockers in rooms (30F/€4.57 deposit). Sheets free with ID deposit. Laundry 30F/€4.57. **Must be aged 16-31.** 7-day max. stay, 5 days July-Aug. Reception July-Aug. 7am-1am; Sept.-June 7am-midnight. Check-out 9:30am. Curfew strictly enforced. Reservations. Closed mid-Nov. to mid-Dec. Beds 100F/€15.25 (July-Aug. 10- and 12-bed dorms 90F/€13.72). Cash only.

Hôtel Cosmopolite, 4 rue de la Turbie (☎93 30 16 95; fax 93 30 23 05), near the center of town. Follow the signs for "Le Rocher/Fontvieille" and leave the train station at av. Prince Pierre. Cross the street, go down the small stairway between Bar de la Gare and the Monasouca Shop, and make a left. Clean rooms feature firm beds, elegant furniture, and classic views of the city. Breakfast 36F/€5.49. Free luggage storage. Singles 216F/€32.94, with shower 298F/€45.45; doubles 258F/€39.35, 338F/€51.55; triples 368-479F/€56.12-73.05; quads 410F/€62.53. Cash only.

Hôtel Villa Boeri, 29 bd. du Général Leclerc (☎04 93 78 38 10; fax 04 93 41 90 95), in Beausoleil, France, closer to the casino. Leave the train station at bd. Princesse Charlotte and keep to the left. Walk about 15min. Bd. du Général Leclerc is called bd. de France on the Monaco side. Fragrant flowers guard this friendly hotel, where mirrored hallways and plastic furniture recall the days of disco. All rooms have A/C and telephone. Breakfast 30F/€4.57. Singles with bath 210-290F/€32.02-44.21; doubles with bath 270-360F/€41.16-54.89; triples with bath 335-420F/€51.09-64.05; quads with bath 500F/€76.23. Prices rise 10-25% July-Aug. AmEx/MC/V.

Hôtel Diana, 17 bd. du Général Leclerc (☎04 93 78 47 58; fax 04 93 41 88 94), in Beausoleil, France. A marble staircase leads to functional rooms with 1970s flare. Unless you have a shower in your room, you won't shower. Breakfast 38F/€5.80. Singles 190-310F/€28.97-47.26; doubles 190-370F/€28.97-56.43; triples 375-400F/€57.19-60.98. AmEx/MC/V.

FOOD

Not surprisingly, Monaco has little budget grub. Picnics are a good bet; stop by the fruit and flower **market** on pl. d'Armes (open daily 6am-1pm) at the end of av. Prince Pierre, or the huge **Carrefour** in Fontvieille's shopping plaza (☎92 05 57 00; open M-Sa 8:30am-10pm). A **Casino** supermarket sits on bd. Albert 1er. (☎93 30 56 78. Open M-Sa 8:30am-8pm.) If you crave a sit-down meal, **L'Escale,** 17 bd. Albert 1er, lets you dine in first-class with coach prices. (☎93 39 13 44. Pizzas and pastas from 50F/€7.62; seafood risotto for 55F/€8.39.Open daily noon-3pm and 6-11pm.)

SIGHTS

MONTE-CARLO CASINO. Monte-Carlo's wealth and allure revolve around the famous gambling house where Richard Burton wooed Liz Taylor and Mata Hari shot a Russian spy. This sumptuous 1878 building was designed by Charles Garnier, and it resembles his Paris opera house; its position over the rocky coast is perfect for suicide, an end once sought by as many as four bankrupts per week. Even if you're not a gambler, the extravagant, red-curtained, gilt-ceilinged interior is worth a look. For those who'd like to press their luck, **slot machines** (M-F from 2pm, Sa-Su from noon) and **blackjack** and **roulette** (daily from noon) await. While all casinos have **dress codes** (no shorts, sneakers, sandals, or jeans), the exclusive *salons privés*, where such French games as *chemin de fer* and *trente et quarante* begin at noon, require coat and ties as well as an extra 50F/€7.62 cover. A bit more relaxed, the **Café de Paris** next door opens for gambling at 10am and has no cover charge. The 21+ rule is well enforced—bring a passport. The Monte-Carlo casino also houses the ornate Atrium du Casino theater, which is closed for renovation until 2003. *(☎92 16 20 00; www.casino-monte-carlo.com. Admission 50F/€7.62.)*

PALAIS PRINCIER. High above the casino, this cliffside palace is the sometime home of Prince Rainier and his tabloid-darling family. The Grimaldis have ruled their small but doggedly independent state since 1297, when François Grimaldi escaped Genoa and captured Monaco with a few men-at-arms dressed as monks. Hence the Grimaldi coat of arms you'll see at the palace: a pair of armed monks. Ever-vigilant for renegade monks, Monaco's soldiery performs the changing of the guard outside the palace daily at 11:55am and 5pm. In their summer uniforms, complete with dainty white gun holders (they change to black after Labor Day, in accordance with the laws of fashion), the soldiers look as functional as the palace cannon, strategically positioned to bombard the shopping district. When the flag is down, the prince is away and the doors open to tourists. Take a tour of the small but lavishly decorated palace, with its frescoes and marble inlay. Also on display are a hall of mirrors, Princess Grace's official state portrait, Prince Rainier's throne, and the chamber where England's King George III died. *(☎93 25 18 31. Open June-Sept. 9:30am-6pm; Oct. 10am-5pm. 30F/€4.57, students 15F/€2.29 before 5pm.)*

MUSEE OCEANOGRAPHIQUE. An educational break from Monaco's excesses, the oceanographic museum is the aquatic endeavor of founder prince-cum-marine biologist Albert I and former director Jacques Cousteau. The main attraction is a 90-tank aquarium, filled with seawater pumped directly from the Mediterranean. Biology buffs will enjoy the shark lagoon and 1.9m green moray eel, thought to be the largest on display in the world. *(Av. St-Martin. ☎93 15 36 00. Open July-Aug. daily 9am-8pm; Apr.-June and Sept. 9am-7pm; Oct. and Mar. 9:30am-7pm; Nov.-Feb. 10am-6pm. 70F/€10.67, students and ages 6-18 35F/€5.34. Aquarium audioguide 20F/€3.05.)*

CATHEDRALE DE MONACO. This white neo-Romanesque-Byzantine church is the burial site of the Grimaldi family as well as the location of Prince Rainier and Grace Kelly's 1956 wedding. The victim of a 1982 car accident, Princess Grace lies in a tomb behind the altar marked with her latinized name, "Patritia Gracia." Her younger daughter, Princess Stéphanie, chose a local judge's chambers for her marriage to her former bodyguard six years ago, but stopped by the cathedral on her wedding day to place flowers on her mother's grave. To the right of Grace's tomb, encased in glass, is a newly restored and much-ballyhooed painting of Monaco's patron saint, Nicolas, by *niçois* painter Louis Brea. A full choir sings mass every Sunday from September to June at 10:30am and on Saturdays at 6pm. *(Pl. St-Martin, near the Palais. ☎93 30 87 70. Open Mar.-Oct. daily 7am-7pm; Nov.-Feb. 7am-6pm. Free.)*

JARDIN EXOTIQUE. Designed as a photo-op, this meticulously-constructed garden offers sweeping views of the old city amidst an extensive cactus collection. Free tours (on the hour) descend to the park's dungeon-like grottoes, complete with stalagmites and stalactites. To get there, take the #2 bus (dir: "Jardin Exotique"), or ride the public elevator on bd. de Belgique. *(52 bd. du Jardin Exotique. ☎95 15 29 80. Open May 15-Sept. 15 daily 9am-7pm; Sept. 16-May 14 9am-6pm or until sundown. 41F/€6.25, students 20F/€3.05, under 6 free.)*

CAR COLLECTION. The mouthful **The Private Collection of Antique Cars of H.S.H. Prince Rainier III** is the best of an assemblage of small museums on the Terrasses de Fontvieille. All 105 of the sexiest cars ever made are part of Prince Rainier's personal collection. It includes the toy race cars of the fun-loving Prince Albert and the 1956 Rolls Royce Silver Cloud that carried Prince Rainier and his movie-star bride on their wedding day. The museum also displays the car that won the first Grand Prix de Monaco in 1929. *(Terrasses de Fontvieille. ☎92 05 28 56. Open daily 10am-6pm. 30F/€4.57, students 15F/€2.29.)*

OTHER SIGHTS. Napoleonophiles and war enthusiasts will appreciate the **Collections des Souvenirs Napoléonais et des Archives Historiques du Palais,** just to the left of the palace entrance. The small museum houses Napoleon paraphernalia and attempts to explain the history of Monaco through coins, documents, and paintings. *(Next to the Palais Princier entrance. ☎93 25 18 31. Open June-Sept. daily 9:30am-6:30pm; Oct. 10am-5pm; Dec.-May Tu-Su 10:30am-12:30pm and 2-5pm. 20F/€3.05, students 10F/€1.53.)* While you're on the Rock, it's worth your while to stroll in the seaside **Jardin St-Martin,** off the avenue of the same name, which has a dramatic statue of Albert I and good views of the coast. *(Open Apr.-Sept. daily 7am-10pm; Oct.-Mar. 7am-6pm.)* Keep your eyes peeled for **Princess Caroline's villa,** occupying a choice spot just outside the gardens between the cathedral and the oceanography museum. Though guards are forbidden to disclose its location, you can spot this unassuming pink palace by the armed monk emblem on its gates. If you've come to Monaco for enlightenment, drink tea among cherry trees and tiny brooks in the **Jardin Japonais,** designed by Japanese architect Yasua Beppu. *(Open daily 9am-sunset. Free.)*

NIGHTLIFE AND FESTIVALS

Though a few people still frequent Monte-Carlo's old-school clubs—a handful of Vegas-style discos on the **av. des Spélugues**—most now head to the port in **La Condamine,** where bar-cum-restaurants make up most of the Monaco nightlife.

Despite the name, **Stars 'N' Bars,** 6 quai Antoine 1er, in La Condamine, is trafficked mostly by locals and European tourists. A restaurant by day, its dance floor is filled by night with tight clothes and slick hair. (☎97 97 95 95. Restaurant open daily 10am-midnight. Disco open Sept.-June F-Sa midnight-5am; July-Aug. daily midnight-5am. 21+. Cover for disco 50F/€7.62.) Those too cool for Stars 'N' Bars head up the port to **Café Grand Prix,** 1 quai Antoine 1er. The place to be at night. A mixed crowd dances to live music in the streamlined interior. (☎93 25 56 90. Open daily 10am-5am; live music starts around midnight.) **McCarthy's,** 7 rue du Portier, in Monte-Carlo, may have a ritzy address, but the mahogany, Guinness-adorned interior lets you kick back, leprechaun-style. (☎93 25 87 67. Open daily 6pm-dawn. Live music Th-Sa.) Do as the *monégasques* do and splurge at **Bombay Frigo,** 3 av. Princesse Grace, on the waterfront, west of the Jardin Japonais. A trendy mélange of Mediterranean and Indian influences, this *resto* attracts the upwardly mobile or the already there. Top DJs spin on weekends. Sharp dress is required, unearthly beauty a plus. (☎93 25 57 00. Open daily 6pm-3am.)

On May 31, Ascension Day, when most towns shut down for holy observance, Monaco explodes with activity. The best racecar drivers in the world descend upon the principality to compete for the prestigious **Formula One-Grand Prix.** Unless you like the pandemonium of mass sporting events, this is not the time to visit: most tourist attractions are closed, and access to the waterfront is barred so that only paying spectators can see the action. However, the Grand Prix is also a magnet for the most glamorous of the international jet-set, and for a week you can goggle at an endless parade of Jaguars and yachts. Other events include the **Festival International du Cirque,** Jan. 17-24, featuring the world's top circuses (☎92 05 26 00). The middle of May sees Monaco's **Flower-Arranging Competition** (☎93 30 02 04). Festival details: contact tourist office or Service Municipal des Fêtes (☎93 10 12 10).

MENTON

Often called the "Secret Riviera," Menton (pop. 30,000) feels far from the noise, flash, and glitter of nearby tourist traps. More than just a gateway to Italy, this is a place to wander through medieval alleys and lush gardens or relax on picturesque white-sand beaches. Mellow-minded travelers should visit Menton and experience more genuine Riviera charm than most cities can claim.

TRANSPORTATION

Trains: pl. de la Gare (☎08 36 35 35 35). Trains leave about every 30min. for: **Cannes** (1-1¼hr., 50F/€7.62); **Monaco** (10min., 12F/€1.83); and **Nice** (35min., 25F/€3.81). They also run to **Ventimiglia** (12min., 13F/€1.98), the first stop in Italy, where you can connect to **Genoa** (3hr., 8-12 per day, 110F/€16.77). Open 5am-11:45pm. Reservations 5am-noon and 12:45-7:35pm.

Buses: promenade Maréchal Leclerc (☎04 93 35 93 60), straight and to the left of the train station. Buses leave every 15min. 7am-8pm for **Monaco** (12.50F/€1.91) and **Nice** (28F/€4.27), served by **Autocars Broch** (☎04 93 31 10 52) or **Rapides Côte d'Azur** (☎04 97 00 07 00); it's the same price for one-way and return trips. Open M-F 8am-noon and 1-5pm, Sa 9-11am.

Taxis: (☎04 92 10 47 02). Taxi to the hostel from the train station costs 45F/€6.86.

Bike Rental: L'escale du 2 Roues, 105 av. de Sospel (☎04 93 28 86 05). 80F/€12.20 per day.

ORIENTATION AND PRACTICAL INFORMATION

Like so many other towns on the Riviera, Menton is divided into the *vieille ville*, the new town, and the beach. **Av. du Verdun** or **av. Boyer** (depending on the side of the street) is the new town's main thoroughfare, ending at a small casino. A left turn at the casino takes you to the crowded pedestrian **rue St-Michel** and the heart of the *vieille ville*, an untouristed tangle of serpentine streets and stairwells well worth getting lost in. By far the most lively beach is **plage des Sablettes,** a wide stretch of chalky pebbles below the Basilique St-Michel.

Tourist Office: 8 av. Boyer (☎04 92 41 76 76; fax 04 92 41 76 78; www.villedementon.com). From the station, walk straight out onto av. de la Gare. After a block, you'll hit a boulevard; cross to the far side and turn right onto av. Boyer. Free maps. Open July-Aug. M-Sa 9am-7pm, Su 10am-noon; Sept.-June M-F 8:30am-12:30pm and 1:30-6pm, Sa 9am-noon and 2-6pm.

Garden Tours: Service du Patrimoine, 5 rue Ciapetti (☎04 92 10 33 66). Call ahead for English tours. Open M-Sa 10:30am-12:30pm and 2-6pm.

Internet Access: Le Café des Arts, 16 rue de la République (☎04 93 35 78 67). 40F/€6.10 per hr.

Currency Exchange: Crédit Lyonnais, 4 av. Boyer (☎04 92 41 81 11). Open M-F 8:30am-noon and 1:30-5pm.

Post Office: Across from the tourist office at cours George V (☎04 93 28 64 84), offers **currency exchange.** Open M-W and F 8am-6:30pm, Th 8am-6pm, Sa 8am-noon. **Postal code:** 06500.

ACCOMMODATIONS AND CAMPING

Although there are a number of affordable hotels around the train station, budget travelers will want to head straight to the hostel.

Auberge de Jeunesse (HI), plateau St-Michel (☎04 93 35 93 14; fax 04 93 35 93 07). Though quite an uphill trek from the center of town, this hostel compensates for its inaccessibility with a friendly atmosphere and fabulous views of the sea. To get there, head dead straight from the train station along av. de la Gare (which becomes rue Henri Greville) and turn left at the second bridge, go under the train tracks, make a left and climb the stairs onto chemin des Rigauds. At the end of the stairs, take the right road past a restaurant. The hostel is beyond the campsite. If reading these directions has tired you out, take bus #6 from the bus station (8:40, 11:10am, 2, and 5pm; 7F/€1.07). The multilingual owner of this super-clean hostel has been hosteling for 30 years and serves free breakfast on a terrace overlooking the bay. Dinner 53F/€8.08. Sleepsack 18F/€2.74. Laundry 40F/€6.10. Reception 7am-noon and 5pm-midnight. Curfew Oct.-Apr. 11pm. Open Feb.-Nov. Beds 73.50F/€11.21.

Hôtel Beauregard, 10 rue Albert 1er (☎04 93 28 63 63; fax 04 93 28 63 79; beauregard.menton@wanadoo.fr). Take the steps behind Le Chou Chou brasserie and turn right. A friendly staff lets airy rooms in crimson, blue, and off-white. Breakfast 30F/€4.57. Singles and doubles 190F/€28.97, with toilet 210F/€32.02, with bath 240F/€36.59; triples with toilet and bath 320F/€48.80. Extra bed 60F/€9.15.

Hôtel de Belgique, 1 av. de la Gare (☎04 93 35 72 66; fax 04 93 41 44 77; hotel.de.belgique@wanadoo.fr), offers attractive rooms with wallpapered doors. Singles 160F/€24.39; doubles 200-210F/€30.49-32.02, with bath 280-290F/€42.69-44.21; triples 340F/€51.84. Extra bed 60F/€9.15. MC/V.

Hôtel Richelieu, 26 av. Partouneux (☎04 93 35 74 71; fax 04 93 57 69 61; hotelrichelieu.menton@wanadoo.fr), is a left turn off av. Boyer just before the tourist office. Marble staircase and upholstered walls give this hotel a downtown feel. Singles with bath 250F/€38.12; doubles with bath 300F/€45.74. Prices 50F/€7.62 higher in Aug.

Camping Municipal du Plateau St-Michel, 50 steps shy of the hostel on rte. des Ciappes de Castellar (☎04 93 35 81 23; fax 04 93 57 12 35). Tents and the cars that brought them park on this noisy, tiered hillside. Free hot showers, an affordable restaurant-bar, and a panoramic view of the sea. Reception M-Sa 8:30am-noon and 3-6:30pm, Su 8:30am-noon and 3:30-6:30pm. No reservations. 19F/€2.90 per person, 21F/€3.20 per small tent, 26F/€3.97 per large tent, 21F/€3.20 per car. Electricity 14F/€2.14. Prices 1-2F/€0.15-0.31 higher June 15-Sept. 15.

FOOD

Get fresh food at the small **Marché Carëi,** on av. Sospel at the end of av. Boyer (open daily 7am-12:30pm), or at the **Shopi** supermarket, 35 av. Félix Faure (☎04 93 57 56 56; open July-Sept. M-Sa 8:30am-8pm; Oct.-June 8:30am-7pm). Restaurants abound along the waterfront and the pedestrian **rue St-Michel** in the *vieille ville* including some good Italian places in bustling **pl. du Cap.** Street vendors in this most Italian of Riviera towns sell *panini* (Italian-style sandwiches) and *glace italienne.* **Le Café des Arts,** 16 rue de la République, features a gallery, Internet access, and delicious food in its airy interior. Large salads are 45F/€6.86, daily specials 60F/€9.15. (☎04 93 35 78 67. Open M-Sa 7:30am-7:30pm.)

SIGHTS

Menton's main attraction is the **Musée Jean Cocteau,** quai Napoléon III, on promenade du Soleil. Best known for his work in film and drama, Cocteau also experimented in the studio arts. This 17th-century building houses the multi-faceted artist's paintings, mosaics, and 3-D doodads, as well as photographs of Cocteau and Picasso. (☎04 93 57 72 30. Open M-Sa 10am-noon and 2-6pm. 20F/€3.05, students under 25 15F/€2.29, 18 and under free.) Another place of pilgrimage for Cocteau fans is the **Salle des Mariages** in the Hôtel de Ville. Cocteau decorated this wonderfully odd, windowless room, the only state-recognized place in town to get married, as a Greek temple, and then added Vegas-esque touches like leopard rugs and red velvet chairs. (☎04 92 10 50 29. Open M-F 8:30am-12:30pm and 1:30-5pm. 10F/€1.53, students 7.50F/€1.14, under 18 free.)

Rising above rue St-Michel is the bell-tower of the **Basilique St-Michel** in the *vieille ville.* Go to rue Général Gallieri and walk up the promenade du Val du Menton. Although the building has been repeatedly tinkered with since the first stones were laid in 1619, this church's Italianate facade is still a wonderful piece of Baroque eye candy. The 12 side-chapels contain crimson tapestries donated by the princes of nearby Monaco. (Open Su-F 10am-noon and 3-5:15pm, Su mass at 11am.) Next door is the charming **Chapelle des Pénitents Blancs;** instead of conventional flowers, the chapel is decorated with shellfish. The sea-stone mosaic of **pl. St-Michel,** between the two churches, is the base for the best vista in Menton—the plage des Sablettes below and the coastline of the Italian Riviera.

The **Monastère Annonciade,** site of the original Menton, sits on a mountain overlooking the town. To get there, take the **Chemin de Rosaire** (just west of the bus station, before the police station), a chapel-lined path built by a *monégasque* princess to thank God she hadn't caught the plague. The half-hour walk up the hill may seem tough on your legs, but think of the pilgrims who did it on their knees. The small monastery that awaits on top is eerie and beautiful, furnished with a set of femurs and other bony miscellanea. (☎04 93 35 76 92. Open daily 8-11:15am and 2:15-6:30pm.)

ANTIBES

While other Riviera towns flaunt their sun and sand like cheap costume jewelry, Antibes (pop. 73,000) sits demurely as the prize gem of the coast. Blessed with beautiful beaches, a charming *vieille ville*, and the renowned Picasso museum, the city remains less touristy than Nice and more relaxed than St-Tropez. Come summer, nearby **Juan-les-Pins** (see p. 302) is synonymous with debaucherous nightlife. While Antibes has been drawing crowds for years, the city has recently been inundated with thousands of young Anglophones looking for work on the yachts that float in the harbor. These globe-trotting "yachtees," along with theater, music festivals, and a seaside youth hostel, have turned Antibes into one of the best beach towns around.

ORIENTATION AND PRACTICAL INFORMATION

Av. Robert Soleau connects the train station with **pl. de Gaulle,** center of the new town and home to the tourist office. From here, a short walk along rue de la République runs past the bus station into **Vieux Antibes.** Continuing down tree-lined bd. Albert 1er from pl. de Gaulle and turning right at the water brings you to a long stretch of beach and the beginning of **Cap d'Antibes** (15min.), although the hostel and the tip of the peninsula are 30 minutes farther along.

Trains: av. Robert Soleau (☎08 36 67 68 69). To: **Cannes** (15min., every 30min., 14F/€2.13); **Nice** (30min., every 30min., 22F/€3.35); and **Marseille** (2½hr., 15 per day, 139F/€21.19). Open daily 8am-11:30pm.

Buses: Pl. de Gaulle (☎04 93 34 37 60). To **Cannes** (25min., every 30min., 15F/€2.29) and **Nice** (40min., every 20min., 26.50F/€4.04). Open M-F 8am-noon and 2-6pm, Sa 9am-12:30pm and 2-5pm.

Bike and Car Rental: French Riviera Location, 43 bd. Wilson (☎04 93 67 62 75). Bikes from 75F/€11.43 per day, 3000F/€457.39 deposit. Scooters from 130F/€19.82 per day, deposit 5000F/€762.31. Cars from 250F/€38.12 per day. Open June-Sept. daily 9am-noon and 2-7pm; Oct.-May M-Sa 9am-noon and 2-7pm. V.

Tourist Office: 11 pl. de Gaulle (☎04 92 90 53 00; fax 04 92 90 53 01; accueil@antibes-juanlespins.com; www.antibes-juanlespins.com). Free maps and info on accommodations, camping, and festivals. The staff helps with reservations. Open July-Aug. M-Sa 8:45am-7:30pm, Su 9:30am-12:30pm; Sept.-June M-F 9am-12:30pm and 2-6:30pm, Sa 9am-noon and 2-6pm. There is a **branch** at the train station. Open July-Aug. M-F 9am-12:30pm and 2-6:30pm, Sa 9am-noon and 2-6pm.

Currency Exchange: Delta Change, 17 bd. Albert 1er (☎04 93 34 12 76). Open M-Tu and Th-Sa 9:30am-noon and 2-6pm. June-Sept. also open W 9:30am-noon and 2-6pm.

Laundromat: Pressing Wilson, 103 bd. Wilson (☎04 93 61 22 16). Open Tu-Sa 8:15am-noon and 2:30-7pm.

Internet: Xtreme Cyber, Galérie du Port, 8 bd. d'Aguillon (☎04 93 34 09 96). 1F/€0.15 per min. Open M-F 9am-7pm, Sa 9am-1pm.

Taxi: Allô Taxi Antibes (☎04 93 67 67 67).

Police: 1 rue des Frères Oliviers (☎04 92 90 78 00).

Hospital: Rue de la Fontaine (☎04 92 91 77 77).

Post office: Pl. des Martyrs de la Résistance (☎04 92 90 61 00), between the park and parking lot. Open M-F 8am-7pm, Sa 8am-noon. **Postal code:** 06600.

ACCOMMODATIONS

Antibes doesn't have the budget hotels of Nice and Cannes, but there are a few hostels that will please your wallet. Accommodations in the *vieille ville* are good for sight-seekers, but if you're here just for the beach and nightlife, Juan-les-Pins' hotels might suit you better. Make sure to reserve one to two weeks in advance in summer.

Relais International de la Jeunesse (Caravelle 60), at the intersection of bd. de la Garoupe and av. l'Antiquité (☎/fax 04 93 61 34 40; www.riviera-on-line.com/caravelle), is a 40min. walk along the shore. From Juan-les-Pins, walk south on bd. Edouard Baudoin, which becomes bd. du M. Juin, and cross the peninsula on chemin des Ondes. Turn right on bd. Francis Meillard, then left on bd. de la Garoupe, following signs for Juan-les-Pins Bord de Mer. Or take bus #2A from the bus station at pl. Guynemer in Antibes (every 40min. 7:05am-7:45pm, 7.5F/€1.14). High-ceilinged dorms, spectacular views of the sea, and a party-inducing backyard make this hostel a backpacker's favorite. Breakfast included. Dinner 40F/€6.10. Sheets 10F/€1.53. Reception 8-10am and 6-11pm; luggage drop-off all day. Lockout 10am-5:30pm. No curfew. Dorms 75F/€11.44. **Camping** 35F/€5.34 per person.

The Crew House, 1 av. Saint Roch (☎04 92 90 49 39; fax 04 92 90 49 38; crewhouse_fr@yahoo.com). A yachtee's paradise, this centrally-located hostel attracts a fun Anglo crowd in between boat jobs. All backpackers are welcome in the clean dorms and lively central courtyard. From the train station, walk down av. de la Libération until it turns into av. de Verdun, then make a right onto av. Saint Roch. Internet 1F/€0.15 per min. Reception 7:30am-9pm. Laundry. Dorms June-Sept. 125F/€19.10, Oct.-May 100F/€15.25. Ask about weekly rates. AmEx/MC/V.

Hôtel Jabotte, 13 av. Max Maurey at the base of Cap D'Antibes (☎04 93 61 45 89; fax 04 93 61 07 04), is 2min. from the sea in a happening beach area. Helpful managers preside over cabana-style, all-white rooms. Central courtyard provides a respite from sun and sand. From pl. de Gaulle, follow bd. Albert 1er to its end, turn right on av. Maréchal Leclerc, and follow the beach for 10min.; av. Max Maurey is a right turn off the beach. Or take the free *navette* bus, which leaves from the train and bus stations every hr. M-Sa 7am-7pm. Breakfast 30F/€4.57. Check-in M-Sa before 7pm, Su before 1pm or after 6pm. Reception 8am-7:30pm. Singles and doubles 220-420F/€33.54-64.03; triples 430-570F/€65.56-86.90; quads 640-840F/€97.58-128.07. AmEx/MC/V.

Stella's, 5 av. Paul Arène (☎04 93 34 12 14). From the station, cross the street and take av. de la Libération toward the port. Av. Paul Arène is the third right after the roundabout. 15 beds on the top floor of Stella's beautiful, well-located Mediterranean home. Breakfast 35F/€5.34. Dorms 125F/€19.06, weekly 750F/€114.35.

FOOD

Vieil Antibes is loaded with restaurants frequented by locals and tourists alike. The narrow streets behind **rue de la République** have particularly tasty options. You can dine and shop at **Le Broc en Bouche,** 8 rue des Palmiers, off of rue Aubernon, where everything, from the inventive dishes (around 60F/€9.15) to the eclectic furniture (tables 2000F/€304.92), is for sale. While you wait, feast on delectable bread and ice-filled water! (☎04 93 34 75 60. Open July-Aug. daily 7-11pm; Sept.-June Tu-Sa noon-2pm and 7-11pm.) The **Marché Provençal,** on cours Masséna near the Picasso museum, is considered one of the best on the Côte d'Azur, with plenty to sample even if you're not going to buy (open daily 6:30am-12:30pm). Supermarket options include **Intermarché,** across pl. de Gaulle from the tourist office. (☎04 93 34 19 10. Open M-Sa 8am-8pm, Su 8:30am-12:30pm.)

SIGHTS

Once home to Pablo Picasso, Graham Greene, and Max Ernst, Antibes takes great pride in its resident artists. **Musée Picasso,** pl. Mariejol, in the Château Grimaldi, housed Picasso for a productive five months in 1946, and now features an excellent collection of his paintings and sculpture. (☎04 92 90 54 20. Open June-Sept. Tu-Th and Sa-Su 10am-6pm, F 10am-10pm; Oct.-May 10am-noon and 2-6pm. 30F/€4.57, students 15F/€2.29.) **Musée Peynet,** pl. Nationale, known as the "Museum of Love," displays over 300 colorful drawings and cartoons by local artist Raymond Peynet, who has something of a cult following among the cuteness-obsessed. (☎04 92 90 54 30. Open June-Sept. daily 10am-6pm; Oct.-May 10am-noon and 2-6pm. 20F/€3.05, students 10F/€1.53.) The **Musée Archéologique,** on the waterfront in the Bastion St-André-sur-les-Remparts, displays archaeological finds from the area as well as exhibits on the history of Antipolis (the ancient name for Antibes). (☎04 92 90 54 35. Open June-Sept. Tu-Th and Sa-Su 10am-6pm, F 10am-10pm; Oct.-May Tu-Su 10am-noon and 2-6pm. 20F/€3.05, students 10F/€1.53.) The attractive **Musée Napoléonien,** av. Kennedy in Cap d'Antibes, contains Bonapartist paraphernalia such as Canova's bust of the Emperor. (☎04 93 61 45 32. Open M-F 9:30am-noon and 2:15-6pm, Sa 9:30am-noon. Closed Oct. 20F/€3.05, students 10F/€1.53.) Next door, the renowned **Hôtel du Cap-Eden-Roc** is worth a walk through the lobby and grounds, although spending the night will cost you a pretty centime (☎04 93 61 39 01. Singles 1500-2700F/€228.69-411.65—and it just goes up from there! Cash only.)

As the largest private marina on the Mediterranean, **Port Vauban** hosts some spectacular sleek white yachts. The 16th-century **Fort Carré** stands guard over the waters of the port. (☎06 14 89 17 45. Open June-Sept. Tu-Su 10am-6pm; Oct.-May 10am-noon and 2-6:30pm. Last entrance 1hr. before closing. Tours cost 20F/€3.05 and begin every half-hour Tu-Su 10:15am-5:30pm.)

ENTERTAINMENT AND FESTIVALS

At night, your best bet for action is a trip to Juan-les-Pins; but before the clubs open, Antibes' bars draw a cool and cosmopolitan crowd. Boulevard d'Aguillon, near the port, is lined with bars and pubs that get going early (6pm) for happy hours favored by the Commonwealth yachtees that run this town. **La Gaffe,** 6 bd. d'Aguillon, is where the cool Anglo kids go. There's a great selection of fruity "alco-pops" for 36F/€5.49. (☎04 93 34 04 06. Live rock bands W and F-Sa. Happy hour daily 6-7pm and 11pm-midnight with half-price drinks. Open daily 11:30am-2:30am.) Across the street, **Le Blue Lady,** rue Lacan, is a low-key, Anglo bar with pool tables and a popular outdoor terrace. (☎04 93 34 41 00. Open M-Sa 7:30am-midnight.) A little more sedate, **The Hop Store,** 39 bd. d'Aguillon (☎04 93 34 15 33), has all the trimmings of an Irish pub. (Happy hour noon-1pm and 7-8pm with 20F/€3.05 pints. Live music on weekends. Open daily 8:30am-1:30am.) The classy **Xtreme Café,** 6 rue Aubernon, is a wine bar with a funky purple and stone interior. (☎ 04 93 34 03 90. Open July-Aug. daily 9:30am-2:30am, Sept.-June 9:30am-2:30am.)

In mid-July, Antibes holds the annual **Eté Musicale** in front of the château. Tickets (100-360F/€15.25-54.89) for jazz and classical concerts as well as operas are available at the Antibes and Juan-les-Pins tourist offices. The **Festival d'Art Lyrique** (☎04 92 90 54 60), during the first two weeks of July, brings world-class soloists to the *vieux port* (80-380F/€12.20-57.94).

NEAR ANTIBES: JUAN-LES-PINS

Although officially joined as one city, Antibes and Juan-les-Pins are 2km apart and have separate train stations, post offices, and tourist offices. They also move to different tempos—Juan-les-Pins is younger and more hedonistic, its streets packed with seekers of sun, sea, and sex (not necessarily in that order). In the summer, boutiques stay open until midnight, cafés until 2am, and nightclubs until the dancers head back to the beach.

PRACTICAL INFORMATION. The **train station** is on av. l'Estérel, where it joins av. du Maréchal Joffre. Trains leave roughly every 20 minutes for **Antibes** (5min., until 12:50am, 7F/€1.04), **Cannes** (10min., 13F/€1.98), and **Nice** (30min., 24F/€3.66). To **walk from Antibes,** follow bd. Wilson from pl. du Général de Gaulle for 1½km and turn left onto av. Dautheville. To get to the **tourist office,** 51 bd. Guillaumont, from the station, walk straight on av. du Maréchal Joffre and turn right onto av. Guy de Maupassant; the office is two minutes away on the right, at the intersection of av. Amiral Courbet and av. Guillaumont. (☎04 92 90 53 05. Same email and website as Antibes tourist office. Open June and Sept.-May M-F 9am-noon and 2-6pm, Sa 9am-noon; July-Aug. M-Su 9am-7pm.)

ACCOMMODATIONS AND FOOD. Juan-les-Pins has little in the way of budget lodgings, but the friendly manager at **Hôtel Trianon,** 14 av. de l'Estérel, caters to backpackers with free Internet access and nicely-furnished rooms. (☎/fax 04 93 61 18 11. Breakfast 25F/€3.81; included in off-season with a two-night stay. Singles 180F/€27.44; doubles 215-260F/€32.78-39.64; triples 260-280F/€39.64-42.69.) Next door, **Hôtel Parisiana,** 16 av. de L'Estérel, has more expensive but better-looking rooms, containing rich carpets, tablecloths, and little vase-and-flower combos. (☎04 93 61 27 03; fax 04 93 67 97 21. Breakfast 30F/€4.57. All rooms with fridge. Singles with bath 220F/€33.54; doubles with bath 305F/€46.50; triples with bath 377F/€57.48; quads with bath 420F/€64.03. Prices 50F/€7.62 lower outside of June-Sept. Stay more than four nights and the price goes down. AmEx/MC/V.) Although it's illegal, dangerous, and certainly not recommended by *Let's Go*, many serious carousers seem to fancy the beach's soft sand as a mattress.

Juan-les-Pins' restaurants are virtually indistinguishable, although **La Bamba,** 18 av. Dautheville, seems to be more popular than the others. (☎04 93 61 32 64. Open daily noon-2pm and 7-11:30pm.) **Casino supermarket,** on av. Admiral Courbet, is across from the tourist office and the beach. (☎04 93 61 00 56. Open M-W and F-Sa 7:30am-12:30pm and 3:30-7:30pm, Su 7:30am-12:30pm.)

ENTERTAINMENT AND FESTIVALS. Juan-les-Pins' nightlife centers on the Casino area, and cruising the strip can be entertainment in itself. Discothèques all open around 11pm and close around 5am, with cover charges around 100F/€15.25 (including one drink). The flavor of the moment is **Pulp,** av. Gallice, where a hip crowd fills the dance floor and plush red sofas. (☎04 93 67 22 74. Cover 100F/€15.25. F ladies free. Open July-Sept. daily midnight-5am; Oct.-June F-Sa midnight-5am.) **Le Village,** 1 bd. de la Pinède, features a Mexican-themed interior, with pueblo facades and life-size burros. (☎04 92 93 90 00. M disco, Tu ladies night, Th latino, Su house. 100F/€15.25, F ladies free. Open daily July-Aug. midnight-5am, Sept.-June Th-Sa midnight-5am.) **La Fourmi Rouge,** 5 bd. de la Pinède, is a mini club that spins techno for raver types. (☎04 93 61 71 74. Cover 40F/€6.10. Open June 15-Aug. daily 11pm-5am; Sept.-June 14 Th-Sa 11pm-5am.) In psychedelic **Whisky à Gogo,** 5 ave. Jacques Leonetti, a young crowd dances the night away to house, hiphop, and Latino beats amid water-filled columns. (☎04 93 61 26 40. Cover 100F/€15.25. Open July-Aug. daily 12:30am-6am; Sept.-June F-Sa 12:30am-6am.)

Most discothèques are only open on weekends in the off-season. Fortunately, there are bars. **Pam Pam Rhumerie,** 137 bd. Wilson, has a decidedly tropical feel, with bikinied showgirls vibrating to drumbeats and flaming drinks with names like *Waikiki*. (☎04 93 61 11 05. Open daily 3pm-5am.) Sharing the same owner, **Ché Café,** 1 bd. de la Pinède, and **La Réserve,** across the street, pack pre-clubbing crowds onto their large patios. (☎04 93 61 20 06. Open daily 3pm-5am.) Across from Ché, **Zapata** features lassos, sombreros, and jalapeno pepper lights in its Mexican-themed interior. (☎04 93 61 08 08. Open daily 5pm-2:30am.) If you have any money left after clubbing, lose it at the cave-like **Eden Casino,** bd. Baudoin. (☎04 92 93 71 71. Open daily 10am-5am. 18+. No shorts or sneakers. Free.)

In mid-July, Juan-Les-Pins hosts the **Festival International de Jazz (Jazz à Juan),** one of the Riviera's biggest festivals, which has welcomed the likes of B.B. King and Ray Charles. (Tickets 160-360F/€24.39-54.89, available at tourist offices in Juan-les-Pins and Antibes.)

CANNES

The name Cannes conjures up classic Riviera images: Catherine Deneuve sipping champagne by a celebrity-speckled pool, Marilyn posing red-lipped on the beach. With its renowned annual film festival, Cannes has more star associations than any other place on the coast. But the festival only happens once a year, and Cannes has to do *something* with itself in the meantime. That's when it becomes one of the most accessible of the Riviera's glam-towns, neither as rich as Monte-Carlo nor as exclusive as St-Tropez. A palm-lined boardwalk, a gorgeous sandy beach, and innumerable boutiques ensure that anyone can sport the famous Cannes style. If your legs are bronze, your sunglasses big, and your shopping bags full, you belong.

TRANSPORTATION

Trains: 1 rue Jean-Jaurès. Connections approximately every 30min. 5:20am-12:40am to: **Antibes** (15min., 14F/€2.13); **Monaco** (1hr., 46F/€7.01); **Nice** (35min., 32F/€4.88); and other coastal stops. Hourly trains to **Marseille** (2hr., 6:30am-11:05pm, 100F/€15.25) and **St-Raphaël** (25min., 34F/€5.18). TGV to **Paris** via Marseille 450-540F/€68.61-82.33. Station open daily 5:20am-1am; info desk and ticket sales 7am-11pm. **Luggage storage** 20F/€3.05 per piece, open daily 9am-1pm and 2:15-5pm, July until 8:30pm.

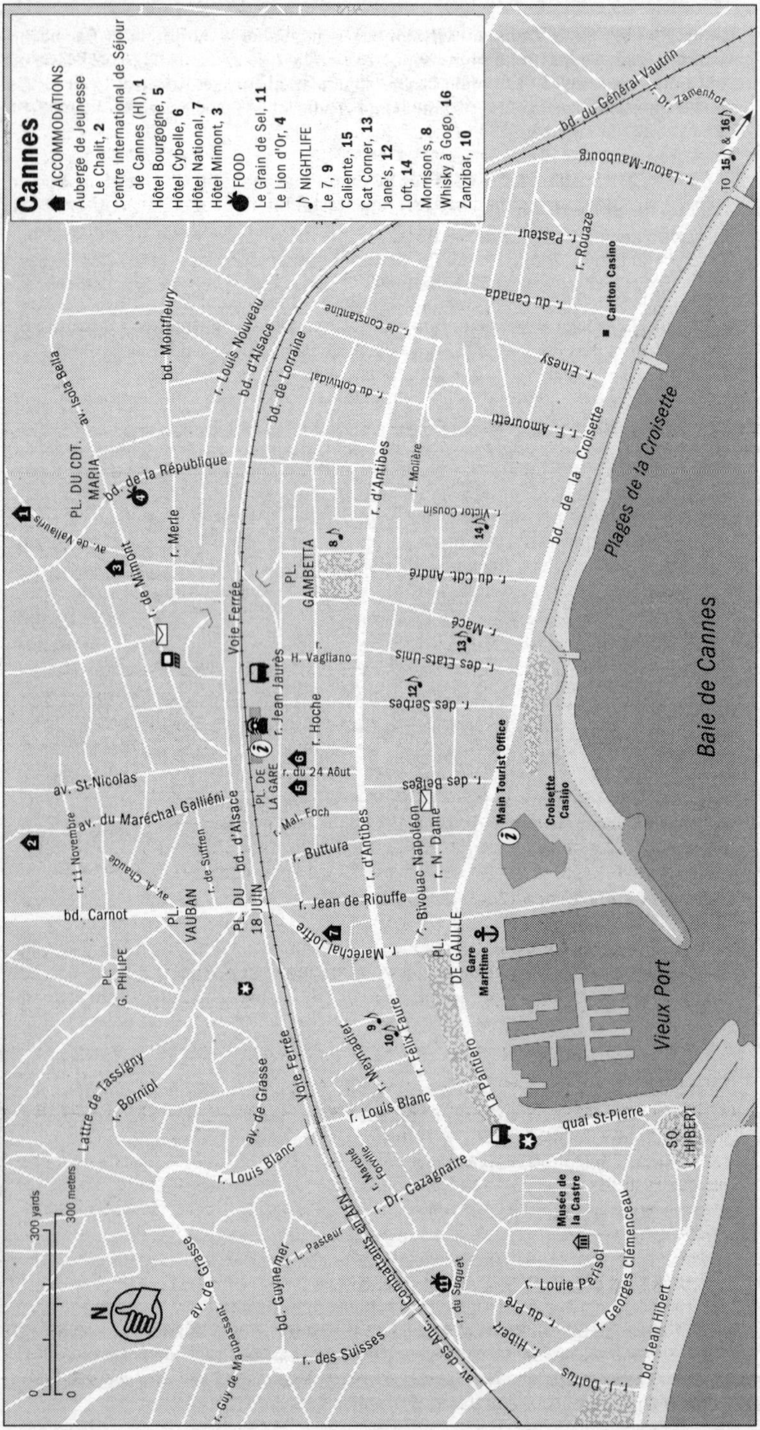

Cannes

ACCOMMODATIONS
Auberge de Jeunesse Le Chalit, **2**
Centre International de Séjour de Cannes (HI), **1**
Hôtel Bourgogne, **5**
Hôtel Cybelle, **6**
Hôtel National, **7**
Hôtel Mimont, **3**

FOOD
Le Grain de Sel, **11**
Le Lion d'Or, **4**

NIGHTLIFE
Le 7, **9**
Caliente, **15**
Cat Corner, **13**
Jane's, **12**
Loft, **14**
Morrison's, **8**
Whisky à Gogo, **16**
Zanzibar, **10**

Buses: Rapide Côte D'Azur, pl. de l'Hôtel de Ville (☎04 93 39 11 39). Open M-F 6am-6:30pm, Sa 6am-2pm. To: **Nice** (1½hr., every 20min., 37.50F/€5.72) and **Nice airport** (50min.; every 30min. M-Sa 5:50am-8pm, Su 8:30am-7:40pm; 80F/€12.20, under 25 60F/€9.15). Buses for **Grasse** (50min., every 30min., 24F/€3.66) leave from the train station.

Local Transportation: Bus Azur (☎04 93 45 20 08), at pl. de l'Hôtel de Ville. Bus tickets 8F/€1.22; *carnet* of 10 53F/€8.08, weekly pass 59F/€9.00.

Taxis: Allô Taxis Cannes (☎04 92 99 27 27).

Bike and Scooter Rental: Holiday Bikes, 16 rue du 14 Juillet (☎04 97 06 30 30). Bikes 75F/€11.43 per day, 350F/€53.36 per week; scooters from 190F/€28.97 per day, 950F/€114.84 per week. 3000F/€457.39 deposit or credit card. Open M-Sa 9am-7pm, Su 9am-noon and 5-7pm. AmEx/MC/V. **Alliance Location,** 19 rue des Frères Pradignac (☎04 93 38 62 62; fax 04 93 39 93 03). Inline skates 50F/€7.62 per day, 400F/€60.98 per week; scooters 170F/€25.92 per day, 1200F/€182.95 per week. 6000F/€914.77 deposit. Open Apr.-Oct. daily 9am-7pm.

ORIENTATION AND PRACTICAL INFORMATION

The *centre ville*, between the station and the sea, is the city's shopping hub, with **rue d'Antibes** running through its center. If you head right from the station on rue Jean-Jaurès, you'll end up in the old city, known as **le Suquet.** Here, there's flea-market-style shopping on **rue Meynadier** by day, and upscale dining on tiny **rue St-Antoine** by night. Star-gazers and those seeking the glamorous **tourist office** should follow rue des Serbes (across from the station) to **bd. de la Croisette,** Cannes' long and lavish coastal promenade. The tourist office is on the right in the huge Palais des Festivals, which is encircled by celebrity handprints. Cannes' beautiful **beach** begins here and stretches along the peninsular clubland known as **Palm Beach.**

Tourist Office: 1 bd. de la Croisette (☎04 93 39 24 53; fax 04 92 99 84 23; www.cannes-on-line.com). Open July-Aug. daily 9am-8pm; Sept.-June M-F 9am-6:30pm, Sa 9am-6:30pm, Su 10am-6pm. Longer hours during festivals. **Branch** office at train station (☎04 93 99 19 77). Open M-F 9am-noon and 2-6pm. For hotel reservations, call town's **centrale de reservation** (☎04 97 06 53 07). Open daily 9am-7pm.

Currency Exchange: Office Provençal, 17 rue Maréchal-Foch (☎04 93 39 34 37), across from train station. Open daily 8am-8pm. **American Express,** 1bis rue Notre Dame (☎04 93 99 05 45). Open M-F 9am-5:30pm; May-Sept. open Sa 9am-noon.

English Bookstore: Cannes English Bookshop, 11 rue Bivouac Napoléon (☎04 93 99 40 08; fax 04 93 66 39 72). Open M-Sa 10am-1pm and 2-7pm. AmEx/MC/V.

Youth Center: Cannes Information Jeunesse, 5 quai St-Pierre (☎04 93 06 31 31). Info on housing, jobs, and more. Open M-F 8:30am-12:30pm and 2-5pm.

Laundromat: Laverie Club Libre Service, 36 bd. Georges Clemenceau (☎04 92 98 78 00). Open M-F 8:30am-6:30pm, Sa 8:30am-noon.

Police: 1 av. de Grasse (☎04 93 06 22 22); 2 quai St-Pierre (☎08 00 11 71 18).

Hospital: Hôpital des Broussailles, 13 av. des Broussailles (☎04 93 69 70 00).

Internet Access: CyberCafé Institut Riviera Langue, 26 rue de Mimont (☎04 93 99 14 77). 10F/€1.53 for 15min., 35F/€5.34 per hr. Open daily 9am-10pm.

Post Office: 22 rue Bivouac Napoléon (☎04 93 06 26 50), off allée de Liberté near Palais des Festivals. Open M-F 8am-7pm, Sa 8:30am-noon. **Branch office** at 37 rue de Mimont (☎04 93 06 27 00). Open M-F 8:30am-noon and 1:30-5pm, Sa 8:30am-noon. **Postal code:** 06400.

ACCOMMODATIONS AND CAMPING

Though Cannes' restaurants may force you to stretch your budget, you can get a good night's sleep at reasonable prices. Hotel rates during the film festival triple, and rooms should be reserved at least a year in advance for those few weeks. Plan early for high season, too—August is particularly busy.

Centre International de Séjour de Cannes (HI), 35 av. de Vallauris (☎/fax 04 93 99 26 79). Take stairs that lead to a passageway under the station; follow signs at right to the hostel (10min.), past the unfortunately named Pizza Dick on your left. At the pl. du Commandant Maria, veer left. Travelers may want to avoid the underground passage at night; instead, leave the station and turn left on bd. Jean Jaurès, then left again on bd. de la République. Av. de Vallauris will be on your right. 6-bunk dorms in a sunny mansion with 3 fully equipped kitchens, an outdoor patio, and a friendly staff. First breakfast included, then 10F/€1.53. Laundry 25F/€3.81. Reception 8am-12:30pm and 2:30-10:30pm. Curfew 2am. May-Aug. bunks 80F/€12.20; Sept.-Apr. 70F/€10.67.

Auberge de Jeunesse—Le Chalit, 27 av. du Maréchal Gallieni (☎/fax 04 93 99 22 11 or 06 03 40 70 86). Take the stairs leading to a passage under the train station; signs will point you to the hostel (5min.). In the evening, travelers may want to avoid the dark tunnel—instead, turn right on bd. Carnot as you exit the station and follow it straight until av. 11 November. Take a right on 11 Nov. and a left onto av. Gallieni. Smaller than the other hostel. Movie posters adorn the light-filled rooms. Sheets 17F/€2.59. Reception June-Sept. 8:30am-1pm and 5-8pm, Oct.-May 9am-noon and 1-8pm. Lockout 10:30am-5pm. 24hr. access with door code, though the hall lights turn off after midnight. 4- to 8-bed dorms 90F/€13.72.

Hôtel Mimont, 39 rue de Mimont (☎04 93 39 51 64; fax 04 93 99 65 35). Rue de Mimont is two streets behind the train station. Either take the infamous underground passage (see hostel directions above) and walk straight for two blocks, or leave the train station to your left, turn left on bd. de la République, and then make another left on rue de Mimont. The best budget hotel in Cannes. Clean, spacious rooms have new beds with thick duvets and TVs. Breakfast 33F/€5.03. Reception 8am-11pm. Singles 170F/€25.92, with toilet 190F/€28.97; doubles 230F/€35.07, with toilet 260F/€39.64; triples with toilet 325F/€49.55—a real steal. Extra person 65F/€9.91. Prices 10% higher July and Aug. AmEx/MC/V.

Hôtel de Bourgogne, 11 rue du 24 août (☎04 93 38 36 73; fax 04 92 99 28 41), off rue Jean-Jaurès. Well-maintained rooms in muted shades of red. Not bursting with charm, but well-located right in the heart of things. Breakfast 30F/€4.57. Singles 180-250F/€27.44-38.12, with shower 240-290F/€36.59-44.21, with bath 280-380F/€42.69-57.94; doubles 240-300F/€36.59-45.74, with shower 240-340F/€36.59-51.84, with bath 320-415F/€48.79-63.27; triple 330-515F/€50.31-78.52. MC/V.

Hôtel National, 8 rue Maréchal Joffre (☎04 93 39 91 92; fax 04 92 98 44 06). Bland white rooms (all with TV) just steps away from the lively rue Meynadier and the *vieille ville*. Breakfast 30F/€4.57. Singles 150-200F/€22.90-30.49, with bath 200-275F/€30.49-41.93; doubles 200-280F/€30.49-42.69, with bath 250-350F/€38.12-53.36; triples 300-450F/€45.74-68.61. AmEx/MC/V.

Hôtel Cybelle, 14 rue du 24 Août (☎04 93 38 31 33; fax 04 93 38 43 47). Rooms in need of renovation contain simple, narrow beds. Well-located between the train station and the beach. Breakfast 25F/€3.81 (pre-order it). Singles 140F/€21.35, with bath 190-200F/€28.97-30.49; doubles 150F/€22.90, with bath 200-260F/€30.49-39.64. AmEx/MC/V.

Camping: Le Grand Saule, 24 bd. Jean Moulin (☎04 93 90 55 10; fax 04 93 47 24 55; le.grand.saule@wanadoo.fr; www.legrandsaule.com), in nearby Ranguin. Take bus #9 from pl. de l'Hôtel de Ville toward Ranguin or "La Boissière" (20min., 8F/€1.22). 3-star site with swimming pool, snack bar, billiards, and pinball machine feels more like a resort than the great outdoors. Sauna 35F/€5.34; laundry 20F/€3.05; tennis 50F/€7.62. Open May-Sept. July-Aug. 1 person 95F/€14.48, 2 people 135F/€20.59; Apr.-June and Sept. 1 person 65F/€9.91, 2 people 93F/€14.18. Car 20F/€3.05. MC/V. **Parc Bellevue,** 67 av. M. Chevalier (☎04 93 47 28 97; fax 04 93 48 66 25), in La Bocca, an enormous and daunting suburb. Take the #9 bus to "La Boissière" (30min.) and walk straight for 100m; site is on the right. Large (211-spot) campground with beautiful views and pine-scented trails. As many mobile homes as tents. July-Aug. 1 person with tent 60F/€9.15, 2 people with tent 90F/€13.72; Apr.-June and Sept. 1 person with tent 60F/€9.15, 2 people with tent 80F/€12.20. Car 10F/€1.53.

FOOD

You'll simply have to splurge here or settle for simple fare. There are **markets** on pl. Gambetta and on pl. du Commandant Maria. (Both open daily 7am-1pm.) You can also try **Champion supermarket,** 6 rue Meynadier. (Open May-Sept. M-Sa 8:45am-7:30pm; Oct.-Apr. M-Sa 9am-7:30pm.)

There are tasty and reasonably priced restaurants throughout the pedestrian zone, especially **rue Meynadier.** Farther along, the narrow streets of **le Suquet** beckon but the extra ambience will cost you. You will have to splurge here but **Le Grain de Sel,** 28 rue du Suquet, has the best deal with its 98F/€14.94 *menu*. Enjoy beautifully-presented provençal dishes in the warm yellow interior or on the romantic outdoor terraces. (☎04 93 39 21 24. Open Th-Tu 6-11:30pm.) A backpacker staple is **Le Lion d'Or,** 45 bd. de la République. Close to the hostels but not the tourists, it serves excellent provençal cuisine in a simple interior. Enjoy massive salads (50F/€7.62) or the delicious three-course *menu* for only 70F/€10.67. (☎04 93 38 56 57. Open Su-F noon-2pm and 7-10pm. MC/V.) The friendly chef at **Le Bourgogne,** concocts delicious French-Italian dishes in a rustic interior. (☎04 93 38 33 27. 75F/€11.43 *menu*. Open daily 11am-2:30pm and 6-11pm.)

SIGHTS AND SHOPPING

Situated at the top of the Suquet, **L'Eglise de la Castre** and its shady courtyard provide an excellent view of the bustling city below. Inside, the **Musée de la Castre** displays weapons, masks, and instruments from Ghana, the Congo and Nigeria. (☎04 93 38 55 26. Open July-Sept. W-M 10am-12:15pm and 3-7pm; Oct.-Mar. 10am-noon and 2-5pm; Apr.-June 10am-noon and 2-6pm. 10F/€1.53, students free.)

Blessed with streets upon streets of designer boutiques, Cannes has the best window shopping on the Riviera. **Boulevard de la Croisette,** along the waterfront, is lined with the luxury palaces of Cartier, Chanel, Dior, and the like. The more moderately priced **rue d'Antibes** and the surrounding neighborhood abound with high-end brand names and funky independent boutiques. **Rue Meynadier,** a carnivalesque street market, is strictly for dirt-cheap duds.

ENTERTAINMENT AND FESTIVALS

The world of cinema comes to Cannes for the **Festival International du Film** from May 15-26. Formally known as a "professional congress," the festival is closed to the public except by personal invitation—but the sidewalk show is free. Adult video stars, annoyed afresh every year at not getting invited, compete for their own *palme d'or* in a parallel festival, the **Hot d'or.** July 4 and 14, **Fête Américaine** and **Fête Nationale** respectively, are even more boisterous here than elsewhere.

Cannes' three casinos give you multiple options to blow your money. The least exclusive, **Le Casino Croisette,** 1 jetée Albert Edouard, next to the Palais des Festivals, has mostly slot machines, but also offers blackjack and roulette. (☎04 92 98 78 00. Gambling daily 8pm-4am, open for slots at 10am. No jeans, shorts, or T-shirts. 18+.)

NIGHTLIFE

If you're trying to get into one of Cannes' elite nightspots, dress to kill. Just as fun and half the price, cafés and bars near the waterfront stay open all night. Nightlife of every sort thrives around **rue Dr. G. Monod.**

Morrison's, 10 rue Teisseire (☎04 92 98 16 17). Guinness posters, mahogany walls, and a massive Irish flag cater to the pub-lovin'. Beer from 18F/€2.74. Music from 10pm W-Th. Open daily 5pm-2:30am. Happy hour July-Aug. 7-9pm; Sept.-June 5-8pm.

Jane's, 38 rue des Serbes (☎04 92 99 79 59). Cannes' favorite discothèque, located in the Hôtel Gray d'Albion, features go-go dancers, a reliably active dance floor, and a massive lounge area. Cover Th 60F/€9.15, F-Su 100F/€15.25 (all include first drink). F and Su before 1am ladies free. Open Th-Su 11pm-dawn.

Loft, 13 rue du Dr. G. Monod (☎04 93 39 40 39). A mellow crowd fills this dimly-lit lounge sipping cocktails to the beats of the live DJ. Downstairs, the Asian-French restaurant **Tantra** morphs into a club on weekends, with patrons dancing on the tables. No cover. Open daily 10pm-2:30am.

Cat Corner, 22 rue Macé (☎04 93 39 31 31). Plush velour sofas, funky lighting, and a central location make Cat Corner the home of Cannes' coolest. DJs spin house, R&B, and funk. Cover 100F/€15.25 (includes 1 drink). Open daily 11:30pm-5am.

Caliente, 83 bd. de la Croisette (☎04 93 94 49 59.) With its blaring neon sign and loud Latin beats, you can't miss this sizzling nightspot. A raucous crowd packs in for live salsa music and an unpretentious atmosphere. No cover. Open daily 10pm-5am.

Whisky à Go Go, 115 av. de Lérins (☎04 93 43 20 63), by Palm Beach. Torches lead the way to this flaming nightspot, packed with men on the prowl and the ladies who love them. Cover 100F/€15.25 (includes 1 free drink). F ladies free, men's cover includes 4 free drinks. Open F-Sa 11pm-dawn; July-Aug. daily.

Le 7, 7 rue Rougières (☎04 93 39 10 36). A guaranteed night of fun, Le 7 features nightly drag shows in its catwalk-like interior. When the queens leave, make your own spectacle on the dance floor. Cover 100F/€15.25 (includes one drink). Drag shows start at 1:30am. Open daily 11:30pm-dawn.

Zanzibar, 85 rue Félix Faure (☎04 93 39 30 75). Europe's oldest gay bar, serving drinks since 1885. Intimate patio and candle-lit cavern, both marine-themed: silver Poseidons, boat parts, the works. Open daily 6pm-dawn.

DAYTRIPS FROM CANNES

ILES DE LERINS

Société Planaria, *across from the Palais des Festivals on the port, sends boats to St-Honorat every hr. (☎/fax 04 92 98 71 38. May-Sept. daily 8am-5:30pm; Oct.-Apr. 8am-4:30pm. 50F/€7.62 round-trip.)* ***Compagnie Esterel Chanteclair,*** *around the corner, is cheapest for Ste-Marguerite. 15F/€2.29 discount with a brochure from Le Chalit hostel. (☎04 93 39 11 82; fax 04 92 98 80 32. Around every 30min. from 7:30am-6:15pm. Round trip 55F/€8.39.) No ferry service between the islands.*

Just a 15-minute ferry ride from Cannes, the Iles de Lérins provide a welcome respite from the city. If you're pressed for time, just visit the smaller island, **St-Honorat.** The island is home to pine forests and an active monastery **(Abbaye de Lérins).** Saint Honorat settled there in the 5th century and was gradually joined by other famous early Christians. Together they founded Lérins, one of Europe's most celebrated monasteries. Today, the order shares the land with the tourists who flock to their gift shop for homemade honey and wine. When less crowded, the islet is an isolated paradise, scattered with ancient chapels and serenaded by chattering birds. On the southeast corner of the island, the **original monastery** stands broken and deserted, full of rooms to be explored. (☎04 92 99 54 00. Open June-Sept. daily 9:40am-4:40pm; Oct.-May 10:40am-3:30pm. Free.)

Four times the size of its neighbor, the park island **Ste-Marguerite** is a densely forested place, dark with eucalyptus and parasol pines. Once home to St. Honorat's equally holy sister Margaret, its main attraction is **Fort Ste-Marguerite,** a fearsome, star-shaped, thankfully inactive prison that once held the Man in the Iron Mask (see below). **Le Musée de la Mer** features the masked man's cell, a bare rectangle with a small hole in the corner for a toilet. For more eye candy, head to the museum's collection of ceramic vessels culled from ancient shipwrecks and housed in a Roman cistern. (☎04 93 43 18 17. Open July-Sept. W-M 10:30am-12:15pm and 2:15-6:30pm; Apr.-June 10:30am-12:15pm and 2:15-5:30pm; Oct.-Mar. 10:30am-12:15pm and 2:15-4:30pm. 10F/€1.53, students free.)

THE MAN IN THE IRON MASK No one knows the identity of the man mythologized in Alexandre Dumas' novel, *Dix Ans plus tard ou le Vicomte de Bragelonne (The Man in the Iron Mask).* The only hard information available about this shadowy figure is that he was in the Pignerol prison before 1681, and died in the Bastille on Nov. 19, 1703. The name "Marchioly" and "aged about 45" were the only inscriptions on his tombstone. Voltaire proposed (and Dumas agreed) that he was the twin of Louis XIV, imprisoned by his brother and forced to wear the mask lest he attempt to claim the throne. Others thought he was the king's bastard elder half-brother or illegitimate son. A less romantic, if more credible, theory holds that the masked prisoner was Eustache Dauger, arrested in July 1669, for reasons unknown. In prison, Dauger became the valet for former finance minister Nicolas Fouquet. Upon Fouquet's death, Dauger's identity was hidden for fear that he might divulge state secrets—and the iron mask was actually a veil of black velvet.

MOUGINS

You can reach Mougins by bus #600 from Cannes' train station (direction "Grasse" or "Val du Mougins," 17min., every 30min., 10.5F/€1.60). From there, walk 25m back down the road and take a left, following signs and magnificent estates to Mougins (25min.).

Mougins is a village 8km from Cannes, elevated to affluent suburbia. The narrow stone streets, art galleries, and charming (though pricey) cafés are definitely worth a visit. The **Musée de la Photographie,** Porte Sarrazine, off rue Maréchal Foch, includes a collection of old cameras as well as photos of a trendy, stripe-shirted Picasso at work and play. The museum has access to the **clock tower,** from which you have a 360° view of the countryside, including nearby St-Paul and Vence. (☎ 04 93 75 85 67. Open W-Sa 10am-noon and 2-6pm, Su 2-6pm. 5F/€0.76.) The **tourist office,** 15 av. Jean-Charles Mallet, provides plenty of info on the area, including the enormous **Parc de la Valmasque.** (☎04 93 75 87 67; www.mougins-coteazur.org. Open July-Aug. daily 10am-8pm; Sept.-June M-Sa 10am-5:30pm.)

GRASSE

You'll know you're in Grasse when the smell of sea foam turns into citronella and tanning oil into tea rose. Capital of the world's perfume industry for 200 years, Grasse is home to France's three largest, oldest, and most distinguished *parfumeries.* The town is also near the GR4 trail, and an excellent springboard for exploration of the Grand Canyon du Verdon (see p. 311). However, if you're not a fan of *eau de toilette* or cologne, then stick to the sunny beaches of the coast.

ORIENTATION AND PRACTICAL INFORMATION. Grasse's proximity to Cannes makes it a pleasant afternoon excursion. Although the town spreads into the valley below, most tourist destinations are concentrated in the *vieille ville* and on the south-facing hillside. As you face the sea, the **bus station** is to the immediate left of the old city; **bd. de Jeu de Ballon** is the thoroughfare just above the station, home to the **tourist office annex** and, farther down, to the casino. A few steps more and you'll reach **pl. du Cours,** a large plateau overlooking the valley and within easy reach of the Fragonard perfumery and several museums.

The **bus station,** pl. de la Buanderie, has service daily to **Cannes** (40min.; every 30min., Su every hr.; 24F/€3.66) and **Nice** (1¼hr., every 40min., 38F/€5.79), thanks to **RCA** (☎04 93 36 08 43) and **SOMA** (☎04 93 36 49 61), respectively. No trains stop at Grasse, but there's an **SNCF info office** (☎04 93 36 06 13) across the *place* (open M-Tu and Th-F 7:30am-noon and 1:30-5:30pm, W 7:30-11:30am and 2-5pm). The **tourist office** is near the casino on cours Honoré Cresp in the Palais des Congrés. Pick up a map with an (1½hr.) annotated walking tour of the city. (☎04 93 36 66 66; fax 04 93 36 86 36. Open July-Sept. daily 9am-7pm; Oct.-June M-Sa 9am-12:30pm and 1:30-6pm.) Cash in at **Change du Casino,** 6 cours Honoré Cresp, near the casino. (☎04 93 36 48 48. Open M-Sa 9am-noon and 2-6:30pm.) The **post office** is in the parking garage under the bus station. (☎04 93 36 24 19. Open M-F 8:30am-noon and 2-5pm, Sa 8:30am-noon.) **Postal code:** 06130.

ACCOMMODATIONS AND FOOD. Grasse has several low-cost, no-frills hotels. To get to **Hôtel Ste-Thérèse,** 39 bd. Y.E. Baudoin, climb the street behind the tourist office annex, keeping left and continuing uphill on bd. Y.E. Baudoin (15min.). It looks and feels like the church it once was—religious images fill the bedrooms. (☎04 93 36 10 29; fax 04 93 36 11 73. Breakfast 30F/€4.57. Singles 165F/€25.16, with bath 225F/€34.30; doubles 220-265F/€33.54-40.40. Extra bed 50F/€7.62.) **Hôtel Les Palmiers,** 17 bd. Y.E Baudoin, on the way to Hôtel Ste-Thérèse, has colorful rooms in a large house overlooking a fragrant garden. (☎/fax 04 93 36 07 24. Breakfast 31F/€4.73. Showers 10F/€1.53. Singles 150-195F/€22.90-29.73, with bath 185-255F/€28.21-38.88; doubles 195-255F/€29.73-38.88; triples 255-295F/€38.88-44.98; quads 350F/€53.36. AmEx/MC/V 2+ nights.) **L'Oasis,** at the bus station, lacks charm, but is well-located. Lower-level chambers are dark and small. (☎04 93 36 02 72; fax 04 93 36 03 16. Breakfast 28F/€4.27. Singles with shower 175F/€26.68; doubles with shower 195F/€29.73, with bath 245F/€37.35; quads 315F/€48.03. AmEx/MC/V.)

There are dozens of specialty food stores, crêperies, and little cafés in the *vieille ville.* Stock up on groceries at the **Monoprix supermarket,** rue Paul Goby, under the bus station on the *vieille ville* border. (☎04 93 36 40 56. Open M-Sa 8:45am-7:30pm.) Or visit the morning **markets** on pl. aux Aires (M-Sa 7am-noon) and pl. aux Herbes. Grasse's most affordable restaurants also have the best ambience, centering around the cobblestone **pl. aux Aires.**

SIGHTS AND SMELLS. Follow the aromas of musky cologne and flowery eau de toilette to Grasse's three largest *parfumeries.* The best of the bunch, **Fragonard,** 20 bd. Fragonard, gives free tours of its original 1782 factory, still in use today; on display upstairs is the world's largest collection of perfume bottles dating from Ancient Egypt to the Age of Klein. (☎04 93 36 44 65. Free 20min. Tours in English. Open July-Sept. daily 9am-6:30pm; Nov.-Jan. 9am-12:30pm and 2-6pm; Feb.-Apr. 9am-6pm; May-June 9am-6:15pm.) **Molinard,** 60 bd. Victor Hugo, five minutes down av. Victor Hugo, has a newer factory and a small museum dedicated to provençal furniture. Concoct your own *eau de parfum* at the 1½-hour "Sniffer Workshop" for 250F/€38.12. (☎04 93 36 01 62; www.molinard-parfums.com. Free tours in English. Open July-Aug. daily 9am-7:30pm; Oct.-Mar. M-Sa 9am-12:30pm and 2-6pm; Apr.-June daily 9am-6:30pm.) **Galimard,** 73 rte. de Cannes, though well out of town, also offers two-hour sessions with one of their professional "noses," who'll help you create a personal fragrance for 220F/€33.54. (☎04 93 09 20 00; www.galimard.com. Open in June-Sept. daily 9am-6:30pm, Oct.-May 9am-12:30pm and 2-6pm; free tours daily.) To make sense of all these scents, head to the superb **Musée International de la Parfumerie,** 8 pl. du Cours, Grasse's most instructive and interesting museum. The second floor displays a 3000-year-old mummy's scented hand and foot, and you can sniff the basic components of perfume in the fourth floor greenhouse. (☎04 93 36 80 20. Open June-Sept. daily 10am-7pm; Oct. and Dec.-May W-M 10am-12:30pm and 2-5:30pm. 25F/€3.81, students 12.50F/€1.91.)

In Grasse's *vieille ville*, the Romanesque **Cathédrale Notre-Dame-du-Puy,** houses three works by Rubens, as well as Fragonard's only religious painting, *Lavement des Pieds*, commissioned especially for the lavish Baroque chapel inside. (☎04 93 39 11 03. Open M-Tu and Th-F 8:30am-noon and 3-6pm, W and Sa 9:30am-noon and 3-6pm, Su 8-11:30am.) Housed in his 17th-century villa, the **Musée Jean-Honoré Fragonard,** 23 bd. Fragonard, features originals and reproductions of the libertine painter's work. The extremely knowledgeable guard can point out a startling number of sexual acts and organs concealed in the paintings. (☎04 93 36 01 61. Open June-Sept. daily 10am-7pm; Oct.-May W-M 10am-noon and 2-5:30pm. 25F/€3.81, students 12.50F/€1.91.)

FESTIVALS. In early May, **Expo-Rose** attracts rose growers from around the world for the largest exhibition of its kind (50F/€7.62). The *Grassois* put down their eyedroppers again in the beginning of August for the musical **Les Nuits de la Terrasse,** and the fragrant **Fête du Jasmin** takes place in early August.

A NOSE BY ANY OTHER NAME What does it take to make it in the perfume world? A good nose, but also a good "nose"—the latter being the trade name for the master olfactors who produce haute couture's most famous fragrances. The best noses train for 15 years before ever extracting an essence; by the time they're ready to mix a scent, which itself can take up to two years, the snuffling students have memorized around 2000 smells. Noses are hot commodities (there's only a handful in the world) and are required by contract to protect their precious snouts. Alcohol, cigarettes, and spicy food are strictly forbidden—in France, the ultimate sacrifice.

GRAND CANYON DU VERDON

Sixty kilometers off the coast in Provence's rocky interior is the Grand Canyon du Verdon, Europe's widest and deepest gorge. Its plunging cliffs and topaz streams are especially worth a visit if you like water sports; the nearby town of Castellane is home to a micro-industry of adventure outfits. The canyon is also a memorable (if slow) way to move between the Riviera and the Alps; Napoleon himself did it in 1816. **Castellane,** 17km east of the canyon and the largest village in the area, is, unfortunately, a bit of a pain to reach from the coast. The canyon itself can be nearly inaccessible from Castellane outside of July and August.

CASTELLANE

The sleepy little town of Castellane is the best place from which to visit the canyon. **Autocars Sumian** (☎04 42 67 60 34) sends buses to **Marseille** (3½hr.; July-Sept. 15 M, W, and Sa; Sept. 16-June Sa only; 123F/€18.75). Also from **Aix-en-Provence** (3hr., same frequency, 101F/€15.40). **VFD** (☎08 20 83 38 33) runs from **Grasse** (70min., 1 per day, 72F/€10.98), **Nice** (2¼hr., 1 per day, 107F/€16.31), and **Digne** (70min., 1 per day, 67F/€10.22) and gives a 20% discount to students. More convenient is the timing of the **Chemins de Fer de Provence** (☎04 97 03 80 80 in Nice, ☎04 92 31 00 67 in Digne): take the little train from **Nice** (2¼hr., 1 per day M-Sa, 85F/€12.96) or **Digne** (50min., 4 per day, 42F/€6.41) to St-André les Alpes, then continue by bus to Castellane (bus departures matched with train arrivals, 21F/€3.20).

The **tourist office,** straight on rue Nationale from the bus stop, gives out hotel and campsite listings as well as 12F/€1.83 maps of the canyon. (☎04 92 83 61 14; fax 04 92 83 76 89; office@castellane.org; www.castellane.org. Open July-Aug. M-Sa 9am-12:30pm and 2-7pm, Su 10am-12:30pm; May, June, and Sept. M-F 9am-noon and 2-6pm, Sa 10am-noon and 3-6pm; Oct.-Apr. M-F 9am-noon and 2-6pm.) There's **Internet** at **Le Web du Verdon,** rue du 11 Novembre (☎04 92 83 66 24). The **police** (☎04 92 83 60 08) are at the end of town on the road to the Canyon. For the **hospital,** call ☎04 92 83 98 00. The **post office** is on pl. Eglise. (☎04 92 83 99 80. Open M-F 9am-noon and 2-5pm, Sa 9am-noon.) **Postal code:** 04120.

Rooms fill quickly in summer. The following accommodations are in Castellane itself, not in or near the canyon; if none of these pans out, try the tourist office's list of dorm-style *gîtes d'étape* closer to town. The cheapest beds are at the **Gîtes d'Etape L'Oustaou,** a backpacker-friendly hostel with light-filled 4- to 6-bed dorms off a twisty hallway. The area feels rural yet is conveniently close to town. To get there, take chemin des Listes next to pl. M. Sauvaire behind the Credit Agricole, turn right and follow the road along the river (3min.). (☎04 92 83 77 27; fax 04 92 83 78 02. Sheets 15F/€2.29. Lockout 10:30am-4:30pm. Curfew 11pm. Bed and breakfast 110F/€16.77, with dinner 175F/€26.68. MC/V.) **Le Verdon,** bd. de la République on pl. M. Sauvaire, has brown-orange rooms, some overlooking a garden. (☎04 92 83 62 02; fax 04 92 83 73 80. Breakfast 35F/€5.34. Singles 170F/€25.92, with shower 190F/€28.97, with bath 240F/€36.59; doubles 190-260F/€28.97-39.64. MC/V.)

There are a number of campsites and hostels closer to the canyon. Near the canyon entrance, actually within the gorge, is **Chalet C.A.F. Refuge de la Maline,** the last canyon bus stop. By car, follow D952 toward the canyon to La Palud-sur-Verdon. Then continue on D23 and follow signs for the chalet. The large dorms here are quite cramped but the view of the gorge is mind-boggling, and the restaurant downstairs is a popular stopping point for people heading in and out of the canyon. (☎04 92 77 38 05. Breakfast 25F/€3.81. Dinner 85F/€12.96. Sleepsack 10F/€1.53. No curfew or lockout. Open Apr.-Nov. Beds 74F/€11.28. **Camping** 25F/€3.81.) The strip between Castellane and the Canyon is dotted with campsites. The small, unexceptional **Camping Frédéric Mistral** is usually overcrowded, but has the advantage of being a two-minute walk down D952 from pl. M. Sauvaire toward the canyon (☎04 92 83 62 27. Tent 16F/€2.44, each person 25F/€3.81. Electricity 19F/€2.90.) About half a kilometer farther is **Nôtre-Dame,** a greener and more spacious campsite. (☎/fax 04 92 83 63 02. Open Apr.-Oct. 15. 2 people with tent and car 58F/€8.84. Electricity 18F/€2.74.)

Getting to the **canyon** from Castellane is difficult without a car. The **Navette Gorges du Verdon** sends free buses in to **Point Sublime, La Palud,** and **La Maline,** the entrance to the gorge (July-Aug. 2 per day; Apr.-June and Sept. 2 per day on weekends and holidays). Outside of these times, your best bet is the kindness of strangers (this is not recommended by *Let's Go*) or a taxi (☎04 92 83 68 06; 310F/€47.26 from Castellane to La Maline; consider carpooling). Some dynamos even **cycle** the mountainous 30km to the gorge. To give it a try, rent a **bike** at **Aboard Rafting,** 8 pl. de l'Eglise. (☎04 92 83 76 11. 70F/€10.67 per half-day, 120F/€18.30 per day.)

THE CANYON

Although the tree-speckled, chalky canyon is itself appealing, most people come here for the Verdon river and the immense Lac de Ste-Croix into which it flows. The canyon's most beaten track is **Sentier Martel,** a.k.a. the **GR4** trail. The six- to eight-hour hike traces the river from La Maline east to Point Sublime as the gorge widens and narrows, passing through tunnels and caves rumored to have once hidden fugitives. Flashlights are useful for the tunnels. Most people, upon arriving at Point Sublime, take a taxi back to La Maline (150F/€22.90) or hitch a ride. You can take the trail back, too—it's as well marked backward as forward, and has better views—but the uphills are punishing.

The Verdon river's water ends up in **Lac de Ste-Croix,** a mellow emerald lake at the mouth of the gorge that's perfect for canoeing and kayaking. The GR4 trail past La Palud-sur-Verdon will eventually take you there by foot. By car, take D952 past La Palud to Moustiers and then follow signs to Ste-Croix-de-Verdon, or take D957 before Moustiers to Les Salles-sur-Verdon.

Before venturing into the canyon, stock up on hiking gear at **L'Echoppe,** rue Nationale, Castellane's only outdoor outfitter. (☎/fax 04 92 83 60 06. Open Apr.-May M-Sa 9:30am-noon and 3-7pm; June and Sept. M-Sa 9am-12:30pm and 2:30-7:30pm, July-Aug. daily 8:30am-8pm. Closed Oct.-Mar.)

A number of **water sport** outfits run trips through the canyon. **Aboard Rafting,** 8 pl. de l'Eglise (☎/fax 04 92 83 76 11; www.aboard-rafting.com), offers all types of trips with an anglophone staff; **Acti-Raft,** rte.des Gorges du Verdon (☎04 92 83 76 64; fax 04 92 83 76 74; www.actiraft.com), **Aqua Viva Est,** 12 bd. de la République (☎/fax 04 92 83 75 74; www.guideprovence.com/activ/aquavivaest), and **Aqua Verdon,** 9 rue Nationale (☎04 92 83 72 75; www.aquaverdon.com), all run comparable outfits. Though **rafting** is the most conventional way to go down the river, summer water levels are only high enough about twice a week. (Usually Tu and F; 1½hr. trip 190-200F/€28.97-30.49; half-day trip 300-350F/€45.74-53.36; day trip 400-500F/€60.98-76.23. Reserve ahead.) The adventurous can try a number of other water sports, including **aqua-rando, canyoning, hydrospeeding,** and **water rambling** (call companies for descriptions and rates). Equestrian types can trot their way through the canyon on **horseback** with **Les Pionniers** in La Palud-sur-Verdon. (☎/fax 04 92 77 38 30; 160F/€24.39 for 2hr.; 220F/€33.54 per half-day; 400F/€60.98 per day.)

ST-RAPHAEL AND FREJUS

Situated along the Estérel Hills, the tightly linked cities of St-Raphaël and Fréjus provide an excellent base for a visit to St-Tropez. Package tourists flock to the beach town of St-Raphaël for its inexpensive accommodations, rollicking nightlife, and proximity to the sea. More independent tourists also find it invaluable for its train and bus stations, which provide convenient springboards for exploring the area. For those more keen on charm and history than golden sand, the nearby city of Fréjus is riddled with a Roman and Episcopal past, and is home to what is perhaps the Riviera's best hostel. Though both towns may play second fiddle to St-Tropez, they are far more friendly to budget travelers.

ST-RAPHAEL

St-Raphaël is basically defined by its beach. The boardwalk turns into a carnival midway on summer evenings, packed with vendors, gaming booths, and flirting teenagers. Though St-Raph certainly isn't the place to go for a quiet time, it isn't artificial, either, and the tourists here are real people looking for a good time. Cheap beds mean that you may end up staying in St-Raphaël if you're visiting St-Tropez or Fréjus. If so, stick to the beach and avoid the town itself, which is devoid of charm or interest.

ORIENTATION AND PRACTICAL INFORMATION. St-Raphaël is a major stop on the coastal train line, separated from Cannes by the Massif de l'Estérel, 40km of red volcanic rock and dry vegetation. There are hotels and restaurants in between the train station and the waterfront, a few blocks straight out of the rue Waldeck Rousseau exit.

Trains run from pl. de la Gare to: **Cannes** (25min., every 30min., 34F/€5.18); **Marseille** (1¾hr., every hr., 117F/€17.84); and **Nice** (50min., every 30min., 57F/€8.69). (Station open daily 5:45am-12:15am. Info office open daily 8:30am-5:30pm. **Luggage storage** ☎04 98 11 99 83; M-F 8:30-11:45am and 2-6pm; 20F/€3.05 per piece.) Buses leave from their own station behind the train station. **Estérel Bus** (☎04 94 53 78 46) serves **Forum Fréjus** (30min., every 30min., 7F/ €1.07). **Sodetrav** (☎04 94 95 24 82) goes to **St-Tropez** (1½hr., 10 per day, 55F/€8.39). **Beltrame** (☎04 94 83 87 63) goes to **Cannes** (70min., 8 per day, 34.50F/€5.26), and **Phocéens** (☎04 93 85 66 61) to **Nice** (1¼hr., 1 per day, 55F/€8.39). **Taxis** (☎04 94 83 24 24) wait outside the train station. **Les Bateaux de St-Raphaël** ferries at the old port go to **St-Tropez.** (☎04 94 95 17 46; fax 04 94 83 88 55. 1hr.; July-Aug. 5 per day, otherwise 2 per day; 60F/€9.15 one-way, 110F/€16.77 round-trip. If you're staying at the hostel in Fréjus, ask about fare reductions.) The **tourist office,** opposite the train station on rue Waldeck Rousseau, books accommodations. (☎04 94 19 52 52; fax 04 94 83 85 40; www.saint-raphael.com. Open July-Aug. daily 9am-8pm; Sept.-June M-Sa 9am-12:30pm and 2-6:30pm.) The **police** are on rue de Châteaudun (☎04 94 95 24 24). Get info about jobs and cheap travel at **Information Jeunesse,** 21 pl. Gallieni (☎04 94 19 47 38), on the main thoroughfare between the train station and the beach. There's **Internet access** at the overpriced **Cyber Bureau,** 123 rue Waldeck Rousseau, beside the train station. (☎04 94 95 29 36. Open M-F 7:30am-12:30pm and 1:30-6:30pm; Sept.-June also Sa 7:30-11am and 2-4pm. 20F/€3.05 for 15min., 50F/€7.62 per hr.) The **post office** is on av. Victor Hugo, behind the station. (☎04 94 19 52 00. Open M-F 8:30am-6:30pm, Sa 8am-noon.) **Postal code:** 83700.

ACCOMMODATIONS AND CAMPING. St-Raphaël's intense package tourism can make you feel like the only person in the world traveling independently, but accommodations are more plentiful here than in Fréjus, and cheaper than in St-Tropez. Be sure to book ahead in July and August. Fréjus' fun hostel is a short ride away (see p. 314). If you like sleeping under the stars, St-Raph is the place to do it—discreet beach-bivouacking is relatively safe and usually ignored by authorities. The best deal in town is **Hôtel les Pyramides,** 77 av. Paul Doumer. You can relax in the large green-and-white-rooms (all with TV, toilet, and shower) or the spacious lounge and outdoor patio. To get there, leave the station to the left, make a right onto av. Henri Vadon, and take the first left onto av. Paul Doumer. (☎04 98 11 10 10; fax 04 98 11 10 20; www.saint-raphael.com/pyramides. Breakfast 35F/€5.34. Open Mar. 15-Nov. 15. Four singles 150F/€22.90 each; doubles 220-350F/€33.54-53.36; triples 360F/€54.89; quads 400F/€60.98. Extra bed 80F/€12.20. MC/V.) Right on the waterfront, **Le Touring,** 1 quai Albert 1er, has cushioned furniture, welcoming rooms in every shade of brown, and its own bar and brasserie. Exit the station on the right; Albert 1er is your third left at the water. (☎04 94 95 01 72; fax 04 94 95 86 09; letouring@wanadoo.fr. Breakfast 30F/€4.57. Closed Nov. 15-Dec. 15. Singles and doubles with one bed and shower 210F/€32.02, with toilet 260F/€39.64 or 350F/€53.36 in summer; triples 450F/€68.61. AmEx/MC/V.) Near the train tracks, **La Bonne Auberge,** 54 rue de la Garonne, has rooms of varying quality, as well as a restaurant. (☎04 94 95 69 72. Breakfast 30F/€4.57. Open Feb.-Nov. Singles 120-160F/€18.30-24.39; doubles 140-160F/€21.35-24.39, with bath 170-220F/€25.92-33.54; triples and quads 70F/€10.67 per person, July-Aug. 80F/€12.20. MC/V.) **Royal Camping** includes perks like hot showers, a supermarket, and a restaurant. A bus leaves every hour from the St-Raphaël station to the "Camp-Long" stop. (☎/fax 04 94 82 00 20. Open mid-Mar. to Oct. 90-125F/€13.72-19.06 for 2 people.)

FOOD AND NIGHTLIFE. It's hard to come by interesting dining spots in a town where most people's meals are packaged with their rooms. The most lively and affordable restaurants are near the **old port,** bd. de la Libération. For a cheap and satisfying meal, **Le Mille Pâtes,** 138 rue J. Barbier off quai Albert 1er, serves pizzas and pastas (from 45F/€6.86) on a bright floral tablecloth, plus a 75F/€11.43 *menu*. (☎04 94 83 94 10. Open daily 9:30am-3pm and 5:30pm-midnight. MC/V.) The **Monoprix supermarket** is at 14 bd. de Félix Martin, off av. Alphonse Karr near the train station. (☎04 94 19 82 82. Open M-Sa 8:30am-8pm.) **Morning markets** color pl. Victor Hugo, down the hill from the bus station, pl. de la République, and the old port (daily 7am-12:30pm.) At night, the sunbathed head to **La Réserve,** promenade René Coty. (☎04 94 95 02 20. Open Th-Sa 11pm-5am. Cover 80F/€12.20.)

BEACHES AND FESTIVALS. Endless kilometers of golden sand run all along the coast from St-Raphaël west through Fréjus and east through Boulouris, which is more isolated and consequently less crowded. Most of it is public and dotted with snack stands. The first weekend in July is the free **Competition Internationale de Jazz New Orleans** in St-Raphaël. Hundreds of musicians face off in the streets and around the port. Call the cultural center (☎04 98 11 89 00) for details.

FREJUS

The charming town of Fréjus will inject any sun-soaked traveler with a welcome dose of culture. Founded by Julius Caesar in the first century BC, the town's many Roman ruins have given it the nickname "Pompei of Provence." Although Fréjus is far from the beach and surrounded by an oppressive sprawl of high-rises, its varied sights, adorable center, and superb hostel make it well worth a visit.

TRANSPORTATION AND PRACTICAL INFORMATION

Fréjus' five-kilometer beach, a 20-minute walk from the town center, is closer physically and spiritually to St-Raphaël than to Fréjus; visitors should stick to the *vieille ville* here and its surrounding sights. Fréjus is connected to St-Raphaël by regular **buses** until around 7pm. Fréjus' **train** station on rue Martin Bidoure (☎08 36 35 35 35) is little used—St-Raphaël processes most of the town's traffic. There's limited service to **St-Raphaël** (5min., 8 per day, 8F/€1.22), **Cannes** (45min., 8 per day, 37F/€5.64), **Nice** (1½hr., 8 per day, 59F/€9), and **Marseille** (2hr., 2 per day, 116F/€17.67). **Local buses** (7F/€1.07) connect the *vieille ville* with the beach, outlying sights, and **St-Raphaël.** The **bus station,** pl. Paul Vernet (☎04 94 53 78 46), is next to the tourist office. For **taxis,** call 04 94 51 51 12.

To get to the **tourist office,** 325 rue Jean Jaurès, from St-Raphaël, take bus #6 to pl. Paul Vernet. (☎04 94 51 83 83; fax 04 94 51 00 26; www.ville-frejus.fr. Open July-Aug. daily 9am-7pm; Sept.-June M-Sa 9am-noon and 2-6pm.) The **Hôpital Inter-communal** (☎04 94 40 21 21) is on the corner of av. André Léotard and av. de St-Lambert. The **police** are on av. Einaudi (☎04 94 51 90 00). The **post office,** av. Aristide Briand, is just down the hill from the tourist office. (☎04 94 17 60 80. Open M-F 8am-6:30pm, Sa 8am-12:30pm.) **Postal code:** 83600.

ACCOMMODATIONS AND FOOD

One of the best hostels on the Côte is the **Auberge de Jeunesse de St-Raphaël-Fréjus (HI),** chemin du Counillier. From the Fréjus tourist office, take av. du 15ème Corps d'Armée, then turn left on chemin de Counillier after the next roundabout (20min.). From St-Raphaël, a shuttle bus (7F/€1.07) leaves quai #7 of the bus station for the hostel at 6pm; return buses leave the hostel at 8:50am and 6:30pm. Local buses run every hour from 7:20am to 7pm; get off at "Les Chênes" (or "Paul Vernet," a farther but more frequent stop), and walk up av. Jean Calliès to chemin du Counillier. It's at the top of the unpaved road. Charles and Chantal will make you feel right at home at this peaceful, secluded hostel (1km off the freeway), complete with wooden dining rooms and a lovely 170-acre spread of tree-shaded parkland. Four- to eight-person single-sex dorms have a view of the inland valley. Ask about discounts on bike rentals and St-Tropez ferry tickets. (☎04 94 52 93 93 or 04 94 53 18 75; fax 04 94 53 25 86; youth.hostel.frejus.st.raphael@wanadoo.fr. Breakfast included, hearty dinner 60F/€9.15. Sheets 18F/€2.74. Reception 8-10am and 6-8pm. Lockout 10am-6pm. Curfew midnight July-Aug., 10:30pm Sept.-June. Closed Dec.-Jan. **Camping** 40F/€6.10 per person with tent. Dorms 75F/€11.43.)

In the center of town, **La Riviera,** 90 rue Grisolle, has cheerful, flamingo-pink rooms. To get there from pl. Paul Vernet, walk straight down rue Jean Jaurès past pl. de la Liberté, and turn left on rue Grisolle. (☎04 94 51 31 46; fax 04 94 17 18 34. Breakfast 30F/€4.57. Singles and doubles 190F/€28.97, with shower 220F/€33.54; triple 300F/€45.74. Prices 20F/€3.05 lower Nov.-June. MC/V.)

Budget restaurants cluster around **pl. de la Liberté.** Nearby, the unassuming **Faubourg de Saigon,** 126 rue St-François de Paule, off rue Jean Jaurès, serves excellent Vietnamese dishes (around 45F/€6.86) in its fan-and-lantern-filled interior. (☎04 94 53 65 80. Open daily noon-2pm and 7-10pm. AmEx/V.) The **Marché Provençal** fills **rue de Fleury** and **pl. Formigé** on Wednesday and Saturday mornings. If you're coming from the hostel, ask the bus driver to drop you off directly. There's a **Casino supermarket,** 168 av. André Léotard, at the bottom of the hill near the hostel. (☎04 94 44 51 00. Open M-Sa 8:30am-7:30pm, July -Aug. also Su 9am-12:30pm.)

SIGHTS

ROMAN RUINS. Built in the first and second centuries as entertainment for rowdy, homesick soldiers, the **Roman Amphitheater** lacks the embellishments of those in Nîmes or Arles, which were designed for more discerning patrician eyes. The former wrestling ground for gladiators and lions now hosts rock concerts and two bullfights a year, on July 14 and August 15. *(☎04 94 51 34 31. Rue Henri Vadon. From the tourist office, take rue Jean Jaurès to pl. de la Liberté, then turn right on rue de Gaulle. Open M and W-Sa Apr.-Oct. 10am-1pm and 2:30-6:30pm; Nov.-Mar. M and W-F 10am-noon and 1:30-5:30pm, Sa 9:30am-12:30pm and 1:30-5:30pm. Bullfights 140-400F/€21.35-60.98.)* The original wall of Fréjus' other ancient forum, the **Roman Theater,** remains intact, but much of the rest has been replaced to accommodate concerts and plays. *(From the roundabout at the tourist office, go about 250m on rue G. Bret. Open Apr.-Oct. M and W-Sa 7am-1pm and 2:30-7pm, Su all day; Nov.-Mar. M and W-Sa 8am-noon and 1:30-5pm, Su all day.)* Pillars and a few arches are all that's left of the 40km **aqueduct,** past the theater along av. du 15ème Corps d'Armée, but with a little imagination you can get a sense of its epic length. The one-room display at the **Musée Archéologique Municipal,** on pl. Calvini behind the Cathédrale St-Léonce, includes a Roman funeral stone, a decorative mosaic, and the double-headed sculpture that Fréjus adopted as a municipal emblem in 1970. *(☎04 94 52 15 78. Open Apr.-Oct. M and W-Sa 10am-1pm and 2:30-6:30pm; Nov.-Mar. 10am-noon and 1:30-5:30pm. Free.)*

THE FREJUS EPISCOPAL BUILDINGS. In the middle of the *vieille ville* is the remarkable product of 2000 years of building and rebuilding. Visible from a side entrance on pl. Formigé, the octagonal **baptistry,** dating back to the 5th century, is one of France's oldest buildings. At the two corners next to the iron grille, you can find the doors used during baptism, a low one to enter before the ceremony (it forced adult entrants to bow their heads), and a higher one leading to the cathedral, where the newly baptized would attend their first masses. The spectacular 12th- to 14th-century **cloisters** feature marble columns culled from Roman ruins and wooden-beamed ceilings decorated with over 1200 miniature paintings depicting an amazing assortment of subjects: fantastical beasts, human-animal hybrids, and bawdy medieval scenes. Look carefully for a woman lifting her skirt, a man riding a pig, and a backflipping village acrobat. Far less riotous (and less interesting) is the austere Gothic **cathedral,** with its walnut doors sculpted in 1530. *(Pl. Formigé. ☎04 94 51 26 30. Cloister open Apr.-Sept. daily 9am-7pm; Oct.-Mar. Tu-Su 9am-noon and 2-5pm. 26F/€3.96, students 16F/€2.44. Doors and baptistry accessible only by guided tour. Cathedral open daily 8am-noon and 2:30-7pm. Free.)*

OTHER SIGHTS. Fréjus has an assortment of sights neither medieval nor ancient, which you can probably do without visiting if you're pressed for time. **Villa Aurélienne,** on the hill next to the hostel, is an elegant 19th-century private home featuring art exhibitions and surrounded by an immense park. *(Av. du Général d'Aimée Calliès. ☎04 94 51 83 83. Open during exhibitions only; daily 10am-noon and 4-7pm.)* **The Pagode Hong-Hiên** was built in part by Vietnamese soldiers who fought for France during WWI and settled in Fréjus. Surrounded on both sides by noisy freeways, this is the closest Buddhism gets to kitsch: a weird assemblage of large plaster figures recounting the life of Buddha. *(13 rue H. Giraud, 10min. up av. Jean Calliès from the hostel. ☎04 94 53 25 29. Open daily 9am-noon and 2–7pm. 5F/€ 0.76.)* Two minutes farther up av. Jean Calliès is the **Memorial des Guerres en Indochine,** a stone monument to the French who were killed in the Indo-Chinese war as well as a one-room photographic history display. *(☎04 94 44 42 90. Open daily 10am-5:30pm. Museum closed Tu. Free.)* Diehard fans of the film director, artist, and "prince des poètes" can visit the circular **Cocteau Chapel,** which he designed and built, although it was left unfinished upon his death in 1963. *(Av. Nicola on the RN7 to Cannes. Bus #3 from "pl. Paul Vernet," 3 per day. ☎04 94 53 27 06. Open Apr.-Oct. M and W-F 2:30-6:30pm, Sa 10am-1pm and 2:30-6:30pm; Nov.-Mar. M and W-F 1:30-5:30pm, Sa 9:30am-12:30pm and 1:30-5:30pm. Free.)*

ST-TROPEZ

Nowhere is the glitz and glamour of the Riviera more apparent than in St-Tropez (pop. 6402). The town is named after Torpes, the highest steward of the Roman emperor Nero. In AD 68, Torpes' profession of Christianity angered Nero sufficiently that he decapitated the steward. However, its modern devotion is to sun, sand, and big boats. Originally a small fishing hamlet, St-Tropez first came into public view in 1892 with the arrival of Paul Signac and other Post-Impressionist artists. Sixty-four years later, Brigitte Bardot's nude bathing scene in *Et Dieu Créa la Femme* (*And God Created Woman*) sealed the town's celebrity status. Today, the former village's sleek yachts, exclusive clubs, and nude beaches continue to attract Hollywood stars, corporate giants, and daytripping backpackers, all trying to get a piece of the action.

ORIENTATION AND PRACTICAL INFORMATION. Reaching the "Jewel of the Riviera" requires some effort, as it lies well off the rail line. Once you get here, it's another hassle altogether to leave town for the outlying beaches and villages. Hitchers say that thumbing for lifts won't get you far, but you can get motorists' attention and trust by approaching them as they leave campsites or parking lots. That said, *Let's Go* does not suggest or recommend hitchhiking, which is a dangerous and foolhardy thing to do. The town itself is condensed and walking-friendly, with constant activity between the **port** and **pl. des Lices.**

The fastest, cheapest, and best way to get here is by **boat. Les Bateaux de St-Raphaël** (☎04 94 95 17 46; fax 04 94 83 88 55), at the old port, sail in from **St-Raphaël** (1hr.; July-Aug. 5 per day, otherwise 2 per day; 60F/€9.15 one-way, 110F/€16.77 round-trip). Otherwise, **Sodetrav buses** (☎04 94 97 88 51) leave from av. Général Leclerc, across from the ferry dock and public parking, for **St-Raphaël** (1½-2¼hr.; June-Aug. 14 per day, off-season 8 per day; 55F/€8.39) and **Toulon** (2¼hr., 8 per day, 106F/€16.16). You can rent a **bike or moped** at **Louis Mas,** 3-5 rue Quarenta. (☎04 94 97 00 60. Bikes 50F/€7.62 per day; deposit 1000F/€152.46. Mopeds 110F/€16.77 per day; deposit 2500F/€381.16. Open Easter-Oct. 15 M-Sa 9am-7pm, Su 1-5pm.) For **taxis**, call 04 94 97 05 27, or wait in front of the Musée de L'Annonciade.

The **tourist office** is on quai Jean Jaurès. After arriving by bus or ferry, walk into town along the waterfront for about 10 minutes until you hit a series of cafés. The tourist office is the one without outdoor seating. The tan and well-dressed staff gives out schedules for the municipal system of *navette* (shuttle) transport, and also the *Manifestations* event guide. (☎04 94 97 45 21; fax 04 94 97 82 66; www.saint-tropez.st. Open July-Aug. daily 9:30am-1:30pm and 3:30-10pm; May-June and Sept. 9:30am-1pm and 2-7pm; Oct.-Apr. 9am-noon and 2-6pm.) You can exchange currency and pleasantries at **Société Tropézienne de Change,** on av. Général Leclerc across from the bus station. (☎ 04 94 97 75 50. Open daily 8am-9pm. No commission.) **Master Change,** 18 rue Allard, is at the old port. (☎04 94 97 80 17. Open Mar.-Oct. daily 9am-8pm. 13F/€1.98 commission.) There's **Internet** access for a hefty sum at **FCDCI,** 2 ave. Paul Roussel. (☎04 94 54 84 81. Open July-Aug. daily 9am-9pm; Sept.-June M-Sa 9:30am-1pm and 2:30-7:30pm. 35F/€5.34 for 30min.; 60F/€9.15 per hr.) The **police** are on rue François Sibilli (☎04 94 56 60 30), near the church, and on av. Général Leclerc by the new port. The **hospital** is on av. Foch, off pl. des Lices (☎04 94 79 47 30). There is a **post office** on pl. A. Celli between the new and old ports. (☎04 94 55 96 50. Open M-Tu and Th-F 9am-noon and 2-5pm, W 9:30am-noon and 2-5pm, Sa 9am-noon.) **Postal Code:** 83990.

ACCOMMODATIONS AND CAMPING. Hotels are scarce and expensive in St-Tropez, and it's not rare to get here and find no accommodations available at all. A stay in St-Raphaël or Hyères is easier on the wallet but forces you to limit your time here—though staying up all night in St-Tropez and heading out the next day may be an option. The closest **hostel** is in Fréjus. **Camping** is the best and cheapest option. Though no sites are within walking distance of the town, a frequent ferry connects the large campsite at Port Grimaud with the peninsula (see below). The campgrounds flanking St-Tropez's famous beaches are smaller and often full; they should be booked months in advance. If you haven't reserved, the tourist office can tell you which ones have space. Camping on the beach is actively prohibited.

One (albeit not super-budget) solution to the accommodations dilemma may be the stately **La Méditerranée,** 21 bd. Louis Blanc, which provides guests with 13 spacious, light-filled rooms (some overlooking a garden) in a central location. From the ferry dock or bus station, walk inland to av. Général Leclerc and turn left. After a four-minute walk, bd. Louis Blanc and the hotel will be on your right. (☎04 94 97 00 44; fax 04 94 97 47 83. Breakfast 40F/€6.10. Open Mar. 21-Nov. 16. Singles and doubles with shower 250-320F/€38.12-48.79; doubles with bath 350-450F/€53.36-68.61; triples and quads 500-620F/€76.23-94.53. AmEx/MC/V.) The cheapest hotel in town, lacking convenience and comforts, is **Les Chimères,** port du Pilon. From the ferry dock or bus station, walk inland to av. Général Leclerc and turn right. The hotel is a six-minute walk ahead on the left, across from the gas station. Small rooms badly in need of a fix-up lack charm but get the job done. Roadside rooms are noisy but cheaper. (☎04 94 97 02 90; fax 04 94 97 63 57. Closed mid-Nov. to mid-Dec. Breakfast included. One single (book in advance) 200F/€30.49 June-Sept., otherwise 150F/€22.90; doubles 200-330F/€30.49-50.31, with shower 360F/€54.89; triples 300-540F/€45.74-82.33. MC/V.)

Campazur runs three campsites close to St-Tropez. Campers have it lucky at **Les Prairies de la Mer,** Port Grimaud. The huge, very social site is near a white beach and the canals of Port Grimaud, "France's Venice." Amenities include hot showers, tennis, and water sports. (☎04 94 79 09 09; fax 04 94 79 09 10; prairies@campazur.com; www.campazur.com. Open Apr.-Oct. July-Aug. one person and tent 82F/€12.50, two people 84F/€12.81, with car 204F/€ 31.10. Prices 50-70F/€7.62-10.67 off-season.) The **MMJ ferry** leaves the *capitainerie* three minutes away for St-Tropez once an hour (☎04 94 96 51 00; 30F, 58F/€8.84 round-trip). The smaller **Kon Tiki** has a choice location near the northern stretch of Pampelonne beach. Campers can soak up sun by day and the beach's wild nightlife (including Kon Tiki's own bar) by night. (☎04 94 55 96 96; fax 04 94 55 96 95; kontiki@campazur.com. Same dates and prices as above.) Next door is **Toison d'Or,** the smallest of the three sites. (☎04 94 79 83 54; fax 04 94 79 85 70; toison@campazur.com. Same dates and prices as above.) In July and August, Sodetrav sends a bus from the St-Tropez station to both sites Tu and Sa at 11:35am (12F/€1.83). Otherwise, take the free municipal shuttle (four a day) from pl. des Lices to "Capon-Pinet" and walk along the beach until you reach the site (30-40min.).

FOOD. St-Tropez's vibrant restaurant and café scene lies along the old port and the narrow streets behind the waterfront. Of course, like everything else, eating is a glamorous and costly affair. Budget travelers will do best to forgo the swanky restaurants and grab paninis from the snack shops. For a slice of Americana, head to **Basilic Burger,** pl. des Remparts, where fresh salads and juicy hamburgers (38-48F/€5.79-7.32) complement Coca-Cola memorabilia. (☎04 94 97 29 09. Open July-Aug. daily 9am-11:30pm, Sept.-June 9am-9pm. Cash only.) The popular **Delice des Lices,** pl. des Lices, is *the* place to go for a late-night snack. Hot and cold sandwiches 20-30F/€3.05-4.57. (☎04 94 54 89 84. Open 24hr.) If you prefer to create your own ambience, check out the fabulous **grand marché** on **pl. des Lices** (Tu and Sa 7:30am-1pm), or the **morning market** on **pl. aux Herbes,** behind the tourist office. There's also the **Prisunic supermarket,** 7 av. du Général Leclerc. (☎04 94 97 07 94. Open M-Sa 9am-8pm, Su 9am-1pm.)

SIGHTS. Though most travelers wouldn't come to St-Tropez on the merits of its museum scene, you can take a break from the sun at **Le Musée de l'Annonciade**, pl. Grammont. This converted chapel houses some of the Fauvist and neo-Impressionist paintings that first made St-Tropez famous. (☎04 94 97 04 01. Open June-Sept. W-M 10am-noon and 3-7pm; Oct.-May W-M 10am-noon and 2-6pm; closed Nov. 30F/€4.57, students 15F/€2.29.) **The Citadel** above the port contains the **Musée Naval.** The reasonably interesting collection follows St-Tropez's military history through WWII. Perhaps the best part of the museum is its troop of screaming peacocks. (☎04 94 97 59 43. Open in summer daily 10am-6pm; in winter 10am-noon and 1-5pm; closed Nov. 25F/€3.81, students 15F/€2.29.)

BEACHES. St-Tropez's pride and joy is its white, sandy, endless coastline. Unfortunately, the beaches are not convenient to get to; *"la navette"* (the municipal shuttle) is pretty much the only cheap way of getting there. It leaves from pl. des Lices four times a day (ask the tourist office for the often-changing schedule) for **Les Salins,** a rather secluded and uncrowded sunspot. Another line stops near **plage Tahiti** (stop: "Capon-Pinet"), the first stretch of the famous Pampelonne beachline, where exclusive beach clubs alternate with public stretches of sand. To find a beach that suits your style, try taking the *navette* to Les Salins and exploring the beaches to the left; you can follow the beautiful, rocky **sentier littoral** (coastal path) along the coast to the right until it melds with the Pampelonne beachline, passing a handful of unpopulated swimming spots and celebrity villas on the way (1hr.). Fifteen kilometers along the peninsula, great swimming and good rock climbing await at **plage de L'Escalet,** but you can only get there by foot or private car. If you don't have the time or inclination to seek out a better beach, there's a decent spot only 10 minutes from the old port. Follow chemin des Graniers, which curves around the citadel and the water, to the small, uncrowded **plage des Graniers.** Most spots allow or expect you to sun *au naturel*—in St-Tropez, tan lines mean you just got here.

ENTERTAINMENT AND FESTIVALS. At the height of St-Tropez's excess and exclusivity is its wild nightlife. When the sun sets, the port and the streets behind the waterfront become a playground for the tanned and glam. Even those relegated to the sidelines will enjoy the show. Unfortunately, one nighttime locus is the beachfront, which is not so convenient for travelers without cars or coastal villas of their own. Restaurant-bar **Bodega de Papagayo** (☎04 94 97 76 70), on the old port, and its accompanying nightclub **Le Papagayo** (☎04 94 97 07 56), are a magnet for moneyed youth and soccer stars. (Open Sept.-May F-Su 11:30pm-5am; June-Aug. daily. Club cover 130F/€19.82. No cover if you "look good.") Actual V.I.P.s frequent the plush Moroccan sofabeds of **V.I.P. Room,** a smaller club in the Résidence du Port that charges no cover if you're lucky enough to get in. (☎04 94 97 14 70. Open F-Su midnight-5am; daily July-Aug.) Below is **La Madrague,** a restaurant-lounge filled with leopard print couches, massive chandeliers, and paper roses. (☎04 94 97 44 84. Open daily 7pm-3am.) One of the hippest bars in St-Tropez, and the least frequented by tourists, is **Le Loft,** 9 rue des Remparts. The small candlelit space is adorned with carpets, cushions, and plush chairs. (☎04 94 97 60 50. Open daily 9:30pm-3am.) A down-to-earth Anglo crowd frequents **Kelly's Irish Pub,** a pretension-free joint toward the end of the old port. You can order a beer (20F/€3.05) or listen to live music here even if you're not wearing designer duds. (☎04 94 54 89 11. Open daily 10:30am-3am.) The epitome of sedentary style is the **Café de Paris,** a gold, velvet, and crystal-chandeliered café with an enormous patio in the center of the port. (☎04 94 97 00 56; www.cafedeparis.fr. Open daily 7am-3am. Beer and wine from 22F/€3.35.) **Le Pigeonnier,** 13 rue de la Ponche, is a casual nightclub catering to both gays and straights; George Michael is a regular. (☎04 94 97 84 26. Open daily 11:30pm-5am. No cover, but drinks cost 80F/€12.20.) **L'Esquinade,** 2 rue de Four, is self-proclaimedly "70% gay." Descend three stairwells off a tiny alley and groove to house techno in the small, cave-like space. (☎04 94 97 87 45; www.club-esquinade.com. Drinks 70F/€10.67. Open daily midnight-5pm.)

St-Tropez celebrates its historic ties to the idle rich with a yearly string of golf tournaments and yacht regattas. Every May 16-18, during **Les Bravades,** three intense days of costumed processions, locals pay homage to their military past and patron saint. June 27 brings **St. Peter's Day** and a torch-lit procession honoring the patron saint of fishermen.

DAYTRIPS FROM ST-TROPEZ

Sodetrav *(☎04 94 97 88 51) sends seven* ***buses,*** *M-Sa, from* ***St-Tropez*** *(20min., 20.50F/€3.13). Or take the* ***ferry*** *to Port Grimaud (see* ***St-Tropez Accommodations****), and catch the* ***petit train*** *at the top of the Prairies de la Mer campsite (every hr.).*

Less ritzy than the city but more endearing, the inland villages of the St-Tropez peninsula make excellent daytrips. These hilltop villages, with their picture-perfect settings and memorable views, are becoming highly desirable real estate. As tour groups start wanting a piece of the charm, they are beginning to lose their status as "secret gems"; come quickly, before the bottled water prices double.

The best of the peninsula is adorable **Grimaud.** One gets the sense that any adjustment here would be a deterioration. Remarkable stone houses line the meandering, fountain-filled streets of a town with a church in the middle and a castle on top. The narrow streets by pl. Neuve are home to boutiques and some expensive restaurants. Above pl. Neuve, signs point to the simple, Romanesque **Eglise St-Michel**. (Open daily 9am-6pm.)

Grimaud has to be a daytrip unless you're camping; it has no budget hotels. The **tourist office** is at 1 bd. des Aliziers, a few doors down from the museum. (☎04 94 43 26 98; fax 04 94 43 32 40; www.grimaud-provence.com. Open July-Aug. M-Sa 9am-12:30pm and 3-7pm; Sept.-June M-Sa 9am-12:30pm and 2:30-6:30pm.)

ILES D'HYERES

Ferries to the island run from the town of ***Hyères,*** *to the east of Toulon. Get there by* ***train*** *from* ***Toulon*** *(9 per day, 48F) or* ***Marseille*** *(6 per day, 72F), or by* ***bus. Sodetrav*** *(☎04 94 12 55 00) runs to* ***Toulon*** *(1hr., every 20min., 36F/€ 5.5) and* ***St-Tropez*** *(1½-2hr., 8 per day, 87F/€13.26), while* ***Phocéens-Cars*** *(☎04 93 85 66 61) go to* ***Cannes*** *(1½hr., 2 per day, 120F/€18.30) and* ***Nice*** *(2hr., 2 per day, 130F/€19.82). To get to the ferry ports, catch* ***Sodetrav local bus #67*** *to* ***Port La Gavine*** *(13.50F/€2.06) or* ***La Tour Fondue*** *(19F/€2.90).* ***TVM Ferries*** *run to* ***Porquerolles*** *from* ***Tour Fondue.*** *(☎04 94 58 95 14; www.tlv-tvm.com. 20min. July-Aug. 21 per day, off-season 6-14 per day; round-trip 87F/€13.26.) Ferries also run to* ***Port-Cros*** *(1hr.) and* ***Ile du Levant*** *(1¼hr.) from* ***Port La Gavine*** *(☎04 94 57 44 07; July-Aug. 5 per day, Sept.-June 2 per day; round-trip 125F/€19.06). In July and Aug., a boat from Hyères connects* ***Port-Cros*** *with* ***Ile du Levant*** *(145F/€22.11 gets you to both and back to the mainland). If you'd like to see both islands off season,* ***Le Lavandou*** *(☎04 94 71 01 02) shuttles between the two for 25F/€3.81 one-way.*

These exotic, underpopulated islands lie off the coast somewhere between St-Tropez and the grimy metropolis of Toulon. Nicknamed the "Iles d'Or" or "Golden Islands" by Henry II, the islands possess three main draws for tourists: nature, *natation* (swimming), and, of course, nudity.

The largest of the three islands and the one most easily accessed from the coast, **Porquerolles** (pop. 350) also has the most colorful history. It was home to a religious order until François I, in a stroke of genius, declared it an asylum for criminals who had agreed to defend the mainland against pirates. Not surprisingly, the convicts promptly transformed the island into a base for their own piratical activities. A century later, Louis XIV, fixer of all things, finally put a stop to their raiding. Today, mainlanders and tourists seek respite from the hectic Riviera in the island's rugged cliffs and small, hidden coves.

The **Ile du Levant** was also originally settled by monks, but its former inhabitants would be shocked if they could see it today, covered with naked people. Home to **Héliopolis,** Europe's oldest nudist colony, the entire island goes *au naturel* on the beaches and wears only the bare minimum (which is required) in the port and village. Walking straight uphill from the port, you'll eventually reach what passes for a town square, with restaurants, hotels, and a nightclub. Hotels tend to be expensive, but **camping** at **Colombero,** straight uphill from the ferry, is a good bet. (☎04 94 05 90 29. 40F/€6.10 per person.) Daytrippers are welcome here. There is **no bank.**

The smallest and most rugged of the three islands, **Port-Cros,** is a national park. Its mountainous terrain is home to 114 species of migratory birds, dozens of indigenous plants, and 241 non-indigenous human beings. The well-trodden **sentier des plantes** (plant trail) passes by several forts and the beautiful but crowded **Plage de la Palud.** To find a more solitary swimming hole, continue on the **sentier de Port Man,** a four-hour hike that circles the north end of the island and penetrates its jungly, unpopulated interior. There's good **scuba diving** in the clear water off Port-Cros; you can visit the area's many wrecks and look for the 40-lb. brown *mérou*, a massive grouper once thought to be extinct. **Sun Plongée** (☎04 94 05 90 16), beside the Sun Bistro, runs open-water dives for 240F/€36.59.

The Hyères **tourist office,** 3 av. Ambroise Thomas, below the Casino, supplies free maps and ferry schedules. (☎04 94 01 84 50; fax 04 94 01 84 51; www.ot-hyeres.fr. Open July-Aug. daily 8:30am-8pm; Sept.-June M-Sa 9am-6pm.)

If you need an island-hopping base, **Hôtel du Portalet,** 4 rue de Limans, lets tasteful pastel rooms with TV in a nice part of the *vieille ville*. The friendly owners are experts on the town. (☎04 94 65 39 40; fax 04 94 35 86 33; chbenit@oreka.com. Breakfast 30F/€4.57. Singles 155-170F/€23.63-25.92, with bath 190-210F/€28.97-32.02; doubles 165-180F/€25.16-27.44, 200-260F/€30.49-39.64; triples with bath 280-350F/€42.6-53.36. Rooms with bathtubs cost around 40F/€6.10 more.)

CORSICA (LA CORSE)

Plunging out of the turquoise waters of the Mediterranean is the island paradise of Corsica (pop. under 250,000), dubbed *Kallysté* (the most beautiful) by the Greeks. In the north, deep-green scrub is fringed with rocky outposts and fishing hamlets; the white cliffs of the south dive into a pristine sea; to the west, towering red mountains are shingled with pines; and the interior is a palate of glacial lakes, gorges, and disintegrating stone farms, attracting outdoorsmen and ethnologists.

The snootiness for which the mainland French are famed is nowhere to be seen on Corsica; you'd never guess that this little island has spent the past thousand years being exploited by ruthless foreign powers. By the ninth century Corsica was under Pisan control, from which Genoa spent five centuries trying intermittently to wrest it. The most obvious legacy of this tumultuous past is a ring of over 300 rounded Genoese watchtowers, built to protect the coastal cities—Bastia, Bonifacio, Calvi—from pillaging Saracens.

The Corsican War of Independence, also known as the Forty Years' War, began as a series of rebellions in 1729. By 1755, the revered general Pasquale Paoli had declared the island autonomous, created a university, and drafted the island's (and the world's) first modern constitution. Genoa was ultimately broken by debt. Among the Corsican officers who quickly swore allegiance to France was a certain Carlo Buonaparte. On August 15, 1769, his son Napoleone was born in Ajaccio. Napoleon (as he rechristened himself in France) did not support Corsican independence. In the past, the French government has prohibited Corsicans from using their language, or even implementing Corsican place names; Corsicans fought back by refusing to pay taxes. Today, the *Front de Libération National de la Corse* (FLNC) continues to try bombing its way to independence. Most Corsicans deplore this sort of extremism and question the wisdom of independence—France directly provides 70% of Corsica's GNP.

Corsica's main industry is tourism and, from mid-June to August, flocks of mainland French retreat to the island's renowned beaches and pricey resorts. The summer climaxes in a double-barrelled blast on August 15, when France celebrates the Fête de l'Assomption, and Corsicans observe **Napoleon's birthday.** Tourists depart by September, when the weather is at its best and the waters their warmest. Winter visitors can visit sleepy coastal towns or head inland to ski.

Corsican tourist offices have free guides to all of Corsica's accommodations, published by Agence du Tourisme de la Corse, 17 bd. du Roi Jérôme, Ajaccio (☎04 95 51 00 00; fax 04 95 51 14 40; www.visit-corsica.com). There are very few budget hotels, and they often fill weeks ahead in summer. Campsites lie close to most cities; a ban on unofficial camping is strictly enforced. Inland, *refuges* provide little more than a roof over your head; they don't take reservations, but you can usually pitch a tent outside. *Gîtes d'étape* allow you to reserve ahead, offering more comfortable surroundings that include electricity and homemade cuisine.

GETTING THERE

BY PLANE. Air France and its subsidiary **Compagnie Corse Méditerranée (CCM)** fly to **Bastia** and **Ajaccio** from **Paris** (without tax: from 1395F/€213, students 1094F/€167), **Nice** (912F/€139, students 839F/€128), **Marseille** (912F/€139, students 839F/€128), and **Lyon** (without tax: from 1114F/€170, students 924F/€141). There's also a direct link from **Lille** to **Bastia** (without tax: from 1485F/€226.41, students 1360F/€). Call Air France (☎08 20 82 08 20). **Air Liberté** services **Calvi** and **Porto Vecchio (Figari)** from **Nice** and **Marseille.** Air France/CCM offices are at the airports in Ajaccio (p. 324) and Bastia (p. 340). In Ajaccio, the Air France/CCM office is at 3 bd. du Roi Jérôme (☎08 20 82 08 20). As with all airfares, you can get significant reductions if you hunt around; ask a budget travel agency in France. **All fares listed here are round-trip.**

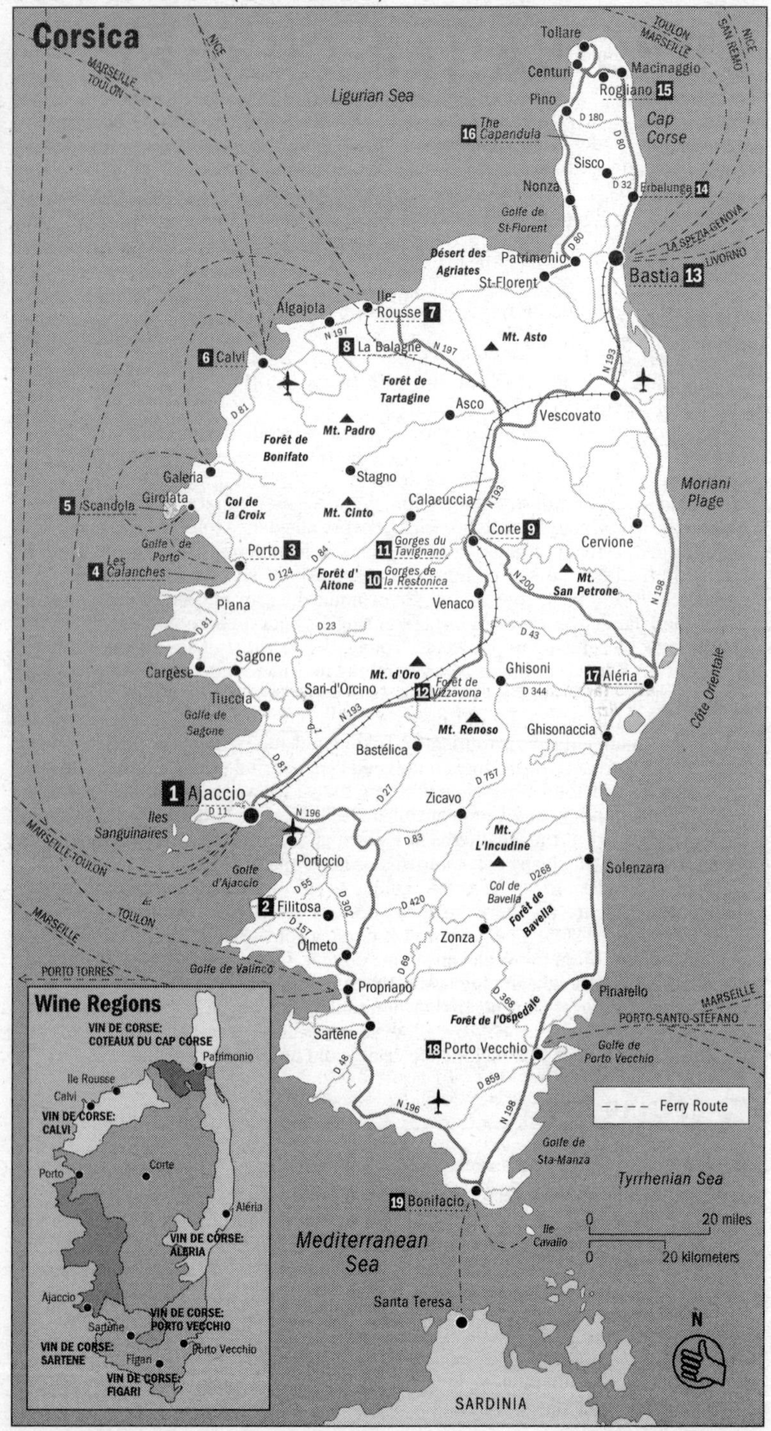

Corsica
Ligurian Sea
Tollare
Centuri
Macinaggio
Rogliano 15
Pino
16 The Capandula
Cap Corse
Sisco
Nonza
Erbalunga 14
Golfe de St-Florent
Désert des Agriates
Patrimonio
St-Florent
Bastia 13
Ile-Rousse 7
Algajola
8 La Balagne
6 Calvi
Mt. Asto
Forêt de Tartagine
Asco
Vescovato
Mt. Padro
Forêt de Bonifato
Stagno
Galeria
5 Scandola
Girolata
Col de la Croix
Mt. Cinto
Calacuccia
Moriani Plage
Corte 9
Cervione
Golfe de Porto
Porto 3
11 Gorges du Tavignano
4 Les Calanches
Forêt d' Aitone
10 Gorges de la Restonica
Mt. San Petrone
Piana
Venaco
Cargèse
Sagone
Mt. d'Oro
Ghisoni
17 Aléria
Tiuccia
Sari-d'Orcino
12 Forêt de Vizzavona
Golfe de Sagone
Mt. Renoso
Ghisonaccia
Côte Orientale
Bastélica
1 Ajaccio
Zicavo
Iles Sanguinaires
Mt. L'Incudine
Porticcio
Golfe d'Ajaccio
Solenzara
Col de Bavella
Forêt de Bavella
2 Filitosa
Zonza
Olmeto
Golfe de Valinco
Propriano
Pinarello
Forêt de l'Ospedale
Sartène
18 Porto Vecchio
Golfe de Porto Vecchio
Golfe de Sta-Manza
Tyrrhenian Sea
19 Bonifacio
Ile Cavallo
Mediterranean Sea
Santa Teresa
SARDINIA
Ferry Route
0 20 miles
0 20 kilometers
N
MARSEILLE TOULON
NICE
TOULON MARSEILLE
SAN REMO
LA SPEZIA-GENOVA
LIVORNO
MARSEILLE-TOULON
PORTO TORRES
MARSEILLE
PORTO-SANTO-STEFANO
D 180
D 80
D 32
N 197
N 193
D 81
D 84
D 124
N 200
N 198
D 23
D 43
D 344
N 196
D 11
D 27
D 757
D 83
D 268
D 55
D 302
D 420
D 157
D 69
D 368
D 48
D 859
Wine Regions
VIN DE CORSE: COTEAUX DU CAP CORSE
Patrimonio
Ile Rousse
Calvi
VIN DE CORSE: CALVI
Corte
Porto
Aléria
VIN DE CORSE: ALERIA
Ajaccio
VIN DE CORSE: PORTO VECCHIO
Sartene
Porto Vecchio
VIN DE CORSE: SARTENE
Figari
VIN DE CORSE: FIGARI

BY BOAT. Ferry travel between the mainland and Corsica can be a rough trip and, in some circumstances, not much cheaper than a plane. High-speed ferries run between Nice and Corsica and take about 3½hr. Overnight ferries from Toulon and Marseille take upwards of 10 hours. The **Société National Maritime Corse Méditerranée (SNCM)** (☎08 91 70 18 01; fax 04 91 56 35 86; www.sncm.fr) sends ferries from **Marseille** and (265-300F/€40-46, under 25 230-265F/€35-40), **Nice** (225-255F/€34-39, under 25 195-225F/€30-34) and **Toulon** (265-300F/40-46, under 25 230-265F/€35-40) to **Bastia, Calvi, Ile Rousse, Ajaccio, Porto Vecchio,** and **Propriano.** It costs 170-3030F/€26-462 to take a car, depending on the day and the car. In summer, up to nine boats float daily between Corsica and the mainland, dropping to three out of season. SNCM schedules and fees are listed in a booklet available at travel agencies and ports. **Corsica Ferries** (see below) has similar destinations and prices.

SAREMAR (☎04 95 73 00 96; fax 04 95 73 13 37) and **Moby Lines** (☎04 95 73 00 29; fax 04 95 73 05 50; www.mobylines.de) run from **Santa Teresa** in Sardinia to **Bonifacio.** (4-10 per day depending on the season, 50-75F/€7.62-11.43 per person and 140-280F/€21.35-42.69 per car one way.) **Corsica Ferries** (☎08 03 09 50 95; fax 04 95 32 14 71; www.corsicaferries.com) crosses from **Livorno** and **Savona** in Italy to **Bastia** (119-180F/€18.14-27.44).

1 **Ajaccio:** Swankiest town on the island; kicked-up nightlife; all things Napoleon **(p. 324)**
2 **Filitosa:** Mysterious 3000-year-old statues in the middle of the wilderness **(p. 328)**
3 **Porto:** Hikers' paradise between steep mountain slopes; town cheapened by tourism **(p. 329)**
4 **Les Calanches:** Wild geological formations–the work of the devil? **(p. 330)**
5 **Scandola:** Nature reserve accessible only by boat; caves, grottoes, rough terrain **(p. 331)**
6 **Calvi:** Small, sunny ferry port; crowded with tourists in summer, accordingly expensive **(p. 331)**
7 **Ile Rousse:** Powdery sand and opalescent waters, with fewer yacht-types around **(p. 335)**
8 **La Balagne:** Pristine thousand-year-old mountain villages **(p. 336)**
9 **Corte:** Corsica's only university; patriotic hotspot; precarious physical/emotional perch **(p. 336)**
10 **Gorges de la Restonica:** High-altitude canyon fed by glacial lakes; superior hikes **(p. 339)**
11 **Gorges du Tavignano:** Less rugged hiking; granite, waterfalls, and suspension bridge **(p. 339)**
12 **Forêt de Vizzavona:** Most popular walking area in Corsica; no vehicle required **(p. 340)**
13 **Bastia:** Refreshingly unpretentious city; only base for a visit to the cape **(p. 340))**
14 **Erbalunga:** Friendly fishing hamlet; perfect sunbathing on flat, secluded rocks **(p. 344)**
15 **Rogliano:** Shrunken little town with architecture worthy of a larger, richer place **(p. 345)**
16 **The Capandula:** Northern extremity of Corsica; great seaside hikes **(p. 345)**
17 **Aléria:** Greek and Roman ruins more worthwhile than the modern town **(p. 345)**
18 **Porto Vecchio:** Memorable beaches, nude or not; forgettable city; so expensive **(p. 345)**
19 **Bonifacio:** Wave-battered, isolated clifftop city close to Italy in geography and mood **(p. 348)**

GETTING AROUND

ON WHEELS. Rumor has it that Machiavelli and the Marquis de Sade collaborated on the design for Corsica's transportation system. **Train** service in Corsica is slow and limited to the half of the island north of Ajaccio—and it doesn't accept rail passes. Not for the faint of stomach, the antiquated trains are terrifying (or exciting) to travel on in windy mountainous areas. More comprehensive than trains are **buses,** which serve the greater part of the island. Call **Eurocorse Voyages** (☎04 95 21 06 30) for further info. Though *Let's Go* doesn't recommend it, **hitchhiking** on the island is possible for patient travelers, who often carry a sign displaying both their destination and their willingness to pay for gas: *"Je vous offre l'essence."* Ten liters of gas (about 60F/€9.15) usually covers 100km on flat roads, but buses are safer and about as cheap, though they're not always on time.

Corsica allegedly has the most dangerous roads in Europe, but if you're foolhardy enough to rent a **car,** expect to pay at least 300-500F/€45.74-152.46 per day or 1500-1705F/€228.69-259.95 per week. The unlimited mileage deals are best; otherwise you'll be coughing up 2-4F/€0.30-0.61 per km. Gas stations are scarce; the police will sometimes help if you run out. **Bicycle** rental can be pricey (about 80-150F/€12.20-22.90 per day with 1500F/€228.69 deposit). Puttering **mopeds** *(mobilettes)* or scooters run about 150-300F/€22.90-45.74 per day, with a 2000F/€305 deposit. Narrow mountain roads and high winds make cycling difficult and risky; drivers should be careful and honk before rounding mountain curves.

Hiking may be the best way to explore the island's mountainous interior. The longest marked route, the **GR20,** is an extremely difficult 200km, 14- to 15-day trail that takes hikers across the island from Calenzana (southeast of Calvi) to Conca (northeast of Porto-Vecchio), requiring a maximum of physical fitness and endurance. Do *not* tackle this trail alone, and be prepared for cold, snowy weather, even in early summer. For shorter and somewhat less challenging routes, try the popular **Mare e Monti,** a 10-day trail from Calenzana to Cargèse, and the easier **Da Mare a Mare Sud,** which crosses the southern part of the island between Porto-Vecchio and Propriano (4-6 days). All major trails are administrated by the **Parc Naturel Régional de la Corse,** 2 Sargent Casalonga, in Ajaccio (☎04 95 51 79 00; fax 04 95 21 88 17; www.parc-naturel-corse.com), whose jurisdiction encompasses most of the Corsican heartland. From June to September, the Parc runs regional offices in relevant cities, but only the head bureau in Ajaccio stays open all year round. For any route, a *topo-guide* (90F/€13.72; 100F/€15.25 with shipping), available for purchase at a Parc Naturel office in person, by fax, or over the phone, is essential. The guide includes detailed trail maps, listings of *gîtes* and *refuges*, and other important practical information. Prospective GR20 trekkers will want to consider buying *Le Grand Chemin* (98F/€14.94), a more complete guide that includes elevations and sources of potable water. For more info, contact the Parc Naturel.

AJACCIO (AIACCIU)

As the most French town in Corsica, Ajaccio (pop. 60,000) has often eschewed Corsican nationalism in favor of the mainland's side of life. It swings like nowhere else on the island, and with all the swank, you might think you're a few hundred kilometers north on the Riviera. If Ajaccio seems like a year-round celebration of Napoleon, wait until his birthday (August 15). Although beaches here don't match those elsewhere on the island, Ajaccio is one of the few Corsican towns with significant museums and considerable urban energy. Rich in history, nightlife, and high culture, the dynamic city is worth a stop.

TRANSPORTATION

Flights: Aéroport Campo dell'Oro (☎04 95 23 56 56), 5km away. To **Nice, Marseille,** and **Paris.** For info call **Air France,** 3 bd. du Roi Jérôme, or **Compagnie Corse Mediterranée** (☎08 20 82 08 20 for both). Office open M-F 8:30am-12:30pm and 2-6pm, Sa 8:30am-noon. TCA bus #8 shuttles to and from the bus station (26F/€3.96).

Ferries: *Gare maritime* (☎04 95 51 55 45). Open June-Aug. daily 6:30am-8pm; Sept.-June M-Sa 6:30am-8pm and for departures and arrivals. **SNCM,** quai l'Herminier (☎04 95 29 66 99; fax 04 95 29 66 77), across from the bus station, goes to **Marseille** (8½hr., 6 per week), **Nice** (4hr. by day, 10hr. overnight; 1-2 per day), and **Toulon** (7hr., 1 per week). 225-300F/€34.31-45.74, ages 12-25 195-265F/€29.73-40.40.

Trains: pl. de la Gare, (☎04 95 23 11 03), off bd. Sampiero, 400m from the *gare maritime* (toward the airport, away from the city center). Open daily 6:20am-8:20pm. To: **Bastia** (4hr., 4 per day, 143F/€21.81); **Calvi** via Ponte Leccia (4½hr., 2 per day, 166F/€25.32); and **Corte** (2hr., 4 per day, 76F/€11.59). **Luggage storage** 18F/€2.74 per day, 23F/€3.51 overnight.

Buses: quai l'Herminier (☎04 95 51 55 45), at the *gare maritime.* Services and companies change seasonally; info kiosk has the latest. Open June-Aug. daily 6:30am-8pm; Sept.-May M-Sa 6:30am-8pm. **Luggage storage** 10F/€1.53 per day. **Eurocorse Voyages** (☎04 95 21 06 30) goes to **Bastia** (3hr., M-Sa 2 per day, 110F/€16.77) via **Corte** (1½hr., 65F/€9.91). Also to **Bonifacio** (3½hr.; M-Sa 2 per day, daily July-Sept. 14; 125F/€19.06) via **Porto Vecchio** (3hr.; M-Sa 3 per day, daily July-Sept. 14; 125F/€19.06). **Autocars SAIB** (☎04 95 22 41 99) go to **Porto** (2hr.; July-Sept. M-Sa 3 per day, Su 2 per day, Oct.-June M-Sa 1 per day; 70F/€10.67). **Autocars Les Beaux Voyages** (☎04 95 65 15 02) go to **Calvi** (3½hr., M-Sa 1 per day, 135F/€20.59).

Local Transportation: TCA, Diamant III, pl. de Gaulle (☎04 95 51 43 23; fax 04 95 50 15 06). Buses run every 30min. M-Sa 6:30am-8pm, Su less often. Tickets 7.50F/€1.14, *carnet* of 10 59F/€9; available at *tabacs*. Extra fare on some trips. Buses #1, 2, and 3 go from pl. de Gaulle to the train station or down cours Napoléon. Bus #5 from av. Dr. Ramaroni and bd. Lantivy stops at Marinella and the beaches on the way to the **Iles Sanguinaires** (11.50F/€1.75).

Taxis: Accord Ajaccio Taxis, pl. de Gaulle (☎04 95 21 00 87) or **Jean-Marc Poli** (☎06 07 25 21 46). 130F/€19.82 to airport.

Car Rental: Ada (☎04 95 23 56 57), at the airport. 384F/€58.55 per day, 1594F/€243.02 per week, unlimited mileage. Deposit 2000F/€304.92. Open daily 8am-11:30pm. **Rent-a-Car,** 51 cours Napoléon (☎04 95 51 34 45), in the Hôtel Kallisté, and at the airport (☎04 95 23 56 36). 370F/€56.41 per day, 1540F/€234.80 per week. Deposit 2000F/€304.92. 23+. Open daily 8am-8pm. AmEx/MC/V.

Scooter Rental: Corsica Moto Rent, 51 cours Napoléon (☎04 95 51 34 45), in the Hôtel Kallisté. Motorbikes from 195F/€29.73 per day, 986F/€150.33 per week. 3000F/€457.39 credit card deposit required. 18+. Open daily 8am-8pm. AmEx/MC/V.

ORIENTATION AND PRACTICAL INFORMATION

Cours Napoléon, which runs from pl. de Gaulle past the train station, is the city's main thoroughfare. The pedestrian **rue Cardinal Fesch** starts at pl. Maréchal Foch and runs roughly parallel to cours Napoléon. Both are thick with cafés and boutiques. **Pl. de Gaulle, pl. Foch** with its Napoleonic fountain, and the **citadel** (still an active military base) enclose the *vieille ville.*

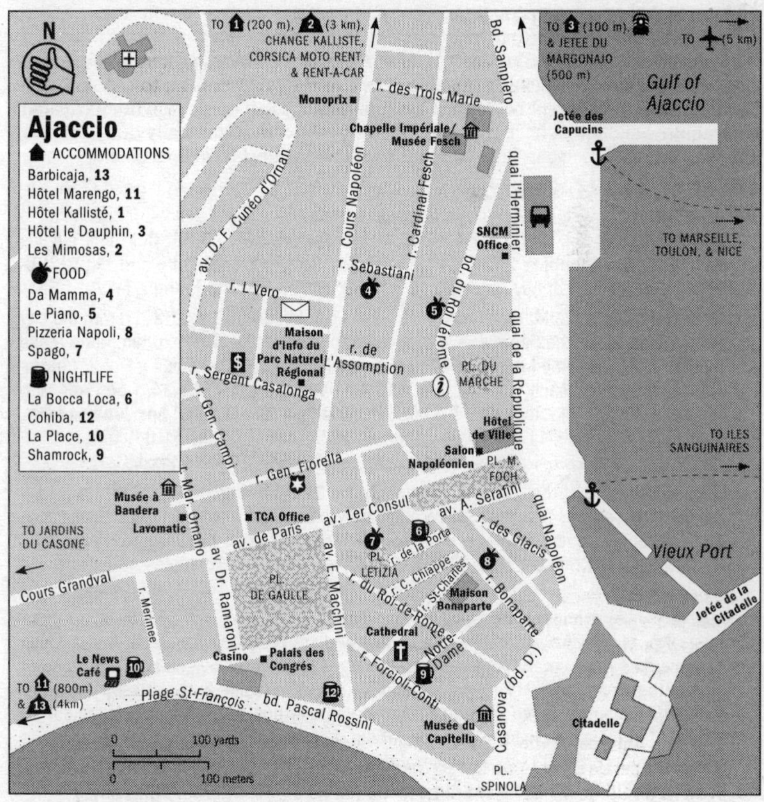

Tourist Office: 3 bd. du Roi Jérôme (☎04 95 51 53 03; www.tourisme.fr/ajaccio), pl. du Marché. Free maps and bus schedules. In summer, theme tours (30-60F/€4.57-9.15). Open July-Sept. M-Sa 8am-8:30pm, Su 9am-1pm; Nov.-Feb. M-F 8am-6pm, Sa 8am-noon and 2-5pm; Mar.-June M-Sa 8am-7pm, Su 9am-1pm. **Agence du Tourisme de la Corse,** 17 bd. du Roi Jérôme (☎04 95 51 00 00; fax 04 95 51 14 40; www.visit-corsica.com). Open 8:30am-12:30pm and 1:30-6pm.

Hiking: Maison d'Info du Parc Naturel Régional, 2 rue Sergent Casalonga (☎04 95 51 79 00, afternoons 04 95 51 79 10; fax 04 95 21 88 17; www.parc-naturel-corse.com), across from the *préfecture*. Has *topo-guides* for sale and multilingual pamphlets (free). Open July-Aug. M-F 8am-7pm, Sa 8am-noon and 2-7pm; Sept.-June M-F 8am-noon.

Money: Banque de France, 8 rue Sergent Casalonga (☎04 95 51 72 40), has the best exchange rates. Open M-F 8:45am-noon. **Change Kallisté,** 51 cours Napoléon (☎04 95 51 34 45), in the Hôtel Kallisté, changes at 7% below the fixed rate. Open daily 8am-8pm. It's also possible at the airport and in banks along cours Napoléon.

Laundromat: Lavomatic, 1 rue Maréchal Ornano (☎06 09 06 49 09), behind the *préfecture.* Open daily 7am-9pm.

Police: rue Général Fiorella (☎04 95 11 17 17), near the *préfecture.*

Hospital: 27 av. Impératrice Eugénie (☎04 95 29 90 90).

Internet Access: Le News Café, bd. Lantivy, Diamant II (☎04 95 21 81 91), charges 40F/€6.10 per hr. Open daily 9am-2am.

Post Office: 13 cours Napoléon (☎04 95 51 84 65). Open M-F 8am-6:45pm, Sa 8am-noon. **Postal code:** 20000.

ACCOMMODATIONS AND CAMPING

Ajaccio has many hotels, but brace yourself for prices that rival those of Paris. Call ahead from June to August, when rates soar and vacancies plummet. Ask hotels for the absolute cheapest room they have, and then ask if there's anything cheaper than that; some hotels have a couple of older rooms they generally don't offer or list. The tourist office can help you find a hotel or a short-term apartment.

Hôtel Kallisté, 51 cours Napoléon (☎04 95 51 34 45; fax 04 95 21 79 00; www.cyrnos.com); follow the signs from quai l'Herminier. Well-designed rooms all have bath, cable TV, fan, and A/C (40F/€6.10). Breakfast 38F/€5.79. Oct.-June singles 260F/€39.64, doubles 290F/€44.21, triples 380F/€57.94; July and Sept. 290-460F/€44.21-70.12; Aug. price range 350-560F/€53.36-54.89. AmEx/MC/V.

Hôtel Marengo, 2 rue Marengo (☎04 95 21 43 66; fax 04 95 21 51 26). From the city center, walk along the boardwalk with the sea to your left for about 20min., then make a right on bd. Madame Mère, and a left onto rue Marengo. Or, take bus #1 or 2. Charming rooms by the beach, all with bath and A/C. Breakfast 35F/€5.34. Open Apr.-Oct. July-Sept. singles and doubles 370F/€56.41, triples 420F/€64.03; Apr.-June and Oct. singles 275-315F/€41.93-48.03, doubles 295-335F/€44.98-51.07, triples 340-360F/€51.84-54.89. 4 rooms without bath 260-295F/€39.64-44.98. MC/V.

Hôtel le Dauphin, 11 bd. Sampiero (☎04 95 21 12 94 or 04 95 51 29 96; fax 04 95 21 88 69), between the train station and ferry port. Light, modern rooms have baths and TVs; some have sea views. Breakfast included (35F/€5.34); haggle if you don't want it. July-Sept. singles 280F/€42.69, doubles 350F/€53.36, triples 430F/€65.59; Oct.-June rooms 250-360F/€38.12-54.89. Extra bed 50F/€7.62. AmEx/MC/V.

Campsites: Les Mimosas, rte. d'Alata (☎04 95 20 99 85; fax 04 95 10 01 77). Follow cours Napoléon away from the city center and turn left on montée St-Jean, which becomes rue Biancamaria and then rte. d'Alata. Continue walking straight on the other side of the roundabout, taking an immediate left onto chemin de la Carrossacia; follow the signs 600m inland to the site (10min.). Or take bus #4 from cours Napoléon to "Brasilia" and walk straight to the roundabout, following the directions above. Close to town. Laundry 25F/€3.81. Reserve ahead. July-Aug. 30F/€4.57 per person; 12F/€1.83 per tent or car. Electricity 18F/€2.74. Prices 10% lower Apr.-June and Sept.-Oct.

15. **Barbicaja** (☎04 95 52 01 17; fax 04 95 52 01 17), 4km away. Take bus #5 from av. Dr. Ramaroni just past pl. de Gaulle to "Barbicaja" and walk straight ahead (last bus 7:30pm). Very close to beaches. Laundry 40F/€6.10. Open May-Sept. 40F/€6.10 per person, 12F/€1.83 per tent, 14F/€2.13 per car. Electricity 16F/€2.44.

FOOD

The **morning market** on pl. du Marché sells Corsican specialties like chestnut biscuits and sheep's cheese. A smaller market operates near the train station at pl. Abbatucci, on cours Napoléon (both Tu-Su 8am-noon). There's a **Monoprix supermarket** at 31 cours Napoléon. (☎04 95 51 76 50. Open July-Sept. M-Sa 8:30am-7:30pm; Oct.-June M-Sa 8:30am-7:15pm.) Head to the pedestrian streets off **pl. Foch** towards the citadel for dozens of restaurants serving local dishes. Pizzerias, bakeries, and one-stop panini shops are mostly on **rue Cardinal Fesch;** at night, patios on the festive quai offer affordable seafood and pizza. Midnight rumblings can be appeased at **Pizzeria Napoli,** rue Bonaparte. (☎04 95 21 32 79. Open July-Aug. daily 6:45pm-6am; Sept.-June Su-Th 6:45pm-4am, F-Sa 6:45pm-6am.)

Da Mamma, passage Guinguetta (☎04 95 21 39 44), off cours Napoléon. Heaping portions of hearty food for growing girls and boys. *Menus* from 65F/€9.91. Open Tu-Sa noon-2pm and 7:30-10:30pm, Su-M 7:30-10:30pm. AmEx/MC/V.

Le Piano, 13 bd. du Roi Jérôme (☎04 95 51 23 81). Touristy, but for good reason. The large patio, complete with mini-gazebos and a red carpet, fills with travelers enjoying delicious 70F/€10.67 *menus.* Open M-Sa noon-2pm and 7:30-11pm.

Spago, rue Emmanuel Arène (☎04 95 21 15 71), off av. du 1er Consul. Smooth young crowd; highly sexualized menu. Pastas 50-92F/€7.62-14.03. Open Su-F noon-2pm and 7:30-11pm, Sa 7:30-11pm. MC/V.

SIGHTS AND EXCURSIONS

If you're a Napoleonophile, you'll find Ajaccio's sights better than another 100 days. Even for tall anti-imperialists, this capital of Corsican museums is a good place to learn about the island's culture and history.

No one goes to Ajaccio without visiting the first home of the ubiquitous megalomaniac, the **Musée National de la Maison Bonaparte,** rue St-Charles, between rue Bonaparte and rue Roi-de-Rome. Napoleon's father rose to power as Paoli's right-hand man; his second son was to snub the nationalist cause for a somewhat larger aim. His original house, modestly tucked away in the *vieille ville*, has become a veritable warehouse of Bonaparte memorabilia, with relics like the smaller-than-average bed that the future emperor slept in on his way back from Egypt—the last time he would touch Corsican soil. (☎04 95 21 43 89. Open Apr.-Sept. M 2-6pm, Tu-Su 9am-noon and 2-6pm; Oct.-Mar. M 2-4:45pm, Tu-Su 10am-noon and 2-4:45pm. 25F/€3.81, ages 18-25 17F/€2.59, under 18 free.) In the glittering **Salon Napoléonien,** pl. Foch, in the Hôtel de Ville, Napoleon's portraits, sculptures, medals, and death mask are displayed. (☎04 95 51 52 53. Open June 15-Sept. 15 M-Sa 9-11:45am and 2-5:45pm; Sept. 16-June 14 M-F 9-11:45am and 2-4:45pm. 15F/€2.29).

Napoleon's uncle Fesch piled up a stash of money as a merchant during the Revolution, before leaving commerce for the cloth. His worldly wealth went into the **Musée Fesch,** 50-52 rue Cardinal Fesch, a truly impressive collection of 14th- to 19th-century Italian paintings. Also within the complex is the **Chapelle Impériale,** the final resting place of most of the Bonaparte family—though Napoleon himself is buried in a modest Parisian tomb (p. 128). (☎04 95 21 48 17. Open July-Aug. M 1:30-6pm, Tu-Th 9am-6:30pm, F 9am-6:30pm and 9pm-midnight, Sa-Su 10:30am-6pm; Apr.-June and Sept. M 1-5:15pm, Tu-Su 9:15am-12:15pm and 2:15-5:15pm; Oct.-Mar. Tu-Sa 9:15am-12:15pm and 2:15-5:15pm. Museum 35F/€5.34, students 25F/€3.81; chapel 10F/€1.53, students 5F/€0.76, under 15 free. Tours mid-July to Aug. F at 9:15pm; 60F/€9.15, students 50F/€7.62; museum included.)

The **Musée à Bandera,** 1 rue Général Levie, provides a comprehensive digest of Corsican history, covering all the major figures, from Corsu to Paoli to Resistance hero Scamaroni. It's incomprehensible without fluency in French. (☎04 95 51 07 34. Open June-Sept. daily 9am-7pm; Oct.-May M-F 9am-noon and 2-7pm, Sa 9am-noon and 2-6pm. 25F/€3.81, students 15F/€2.29.)

The vertiginous **Iles Sanguinaires,** southwest of Ajaccio at the mouth of the gulf, bare their black cliffs to the sea. **Nave Va,** at a kiosk on the port, runs excursions to the largest of the islands (☎04 95 51 31 31; Apr.-Oct. daily, 120F/€18.30). On the island is the **Tour Mezza Mare,** immortalized in the love letters of Alphonse Daudet. Visible from this tower is the corresponding **Tour de la Parata** on the mainland. Bus #5, which leaves from av. Dr. Ramaroni (1 per hr. 7am-7pm, 11.50F/€1.75), stops at Parata and numerous beaches, of which the most popular are the golden **Marinella** and the more remote **Capo di Feno.**

NIGHTLIFE AND FESTIVALS

Unlike most Corsican cities, Ajaccio can provide a wild night. To know what's happening, check out *RDV (Le Rendez-Vous)* and *Sortir*, both available at the tourist office. The hottest *avant boîte* is **Cohiba,** Résidence Diamant II, bd. Lantivy, where a well-dressed crowd fills a sumptuous interior. (☎04 95 51 47 05. DJ plays house F and Sa. Open daily 7am-2am.) At **La Bocca Locca,** 4 rue de la Porta, a fun-loving bunch goes wild for live salsa and tasty tapas. (☎06 07 08 68 69. Open Tu-Sa 7pm-2am.) A Corsican-Irish pub, **Shamrock,** 3 rue Forcioli Conti, off pl. de Gaulle, is ideal for some low-key lounging. (☎06 09 97 24 82. Open daily 2pm-2am; karaoke night W.) Ajaccio's major clubs are out of the city and require a car or motorbike. **La Cinquième Avenue** is 5km away on rte. des Sanguinares. (☎04 95 52 09 77. Open daily midnight-5am.) **Le Blue Moon** is farther away in Porticcio. (☎04 95 25 07 70. Open July-Sept. W-Sa midnight-5am.) In town, **La Place,** Résidence Diamant II, bd. Lantivy, caters to an older crowd. (☎04 95 51 09 10. Open F-Sa 11pm-5am.) Clubs tend to have no cover but a one-drink minimum. If you've still got some cash, head to the **Casino,** bd. Pascal Rossini. (☎04 95 50 40 60. Open daily 1pm-4am.)

Ajaccio often hosts a summer theater or music festival (call the tourist office for details). August 15 brings the three-day **Fêtes Napoléon,** commemorating the emperor's birth with Napoleonic plays, a parade, ceremonies, and a huge final *pyrosymphonie* (firework display) in the bay. But Ajaccio's real mania is apparent in the July and August **Shopping de Nuit,** when stores stay open and packed and musicians liven the streets until midnight on Friday nights.

DAYTRIP FROM AJACCIO: FILITOSA

***Eurocorse Voyages** (☎04 95 21 96 30) sends buses from Ajaccio to **Propriano** (1½hr., 2 per day, July-Sept. 15 4 per day, 65F/€9.91), where **Autocars Casablanca** (☎04 95 74 05 58) head to Porto-Pollo (July-Sept. 15 2 per day; call ahead). Ask to be dropped off at the juncture ("embranchement") between D157 and D57; it's a 6km walk inland on D57, easily hitched in high season, though* Let's Go *still does not endorse hitchhiking. Closes at sunset. For information on Filitosa, call 04 95 74 00 91.*

Forty kilometers south of Ajaccio are the mysterious monuments and dwellings of prehistoric Filitosa, untouched in the fertile Taravo Valley for over 3000 years. The site, unearthed in 1954, reveals little about its inhabitants but provides much fodder for the imagination. Filitosans suddenly graduated from prehistoric **megalithism**—the big-stone fad of circa 3000 BC, which gave us such hits as Stonehenge—to the construction of **statue-menhirs,** carved blocks of granite representing human beings. Some, like Filitosa V (the first you'll come to) are fitted with dagger and armor; the colossal **central monument** has the best faces, clearly expressing anger or surprise. They are thought to represent dead chieftains or the defeated Torréens, an invading people from Asia Minor. The Torréens finally conquered Filitosa in 1100 BC and built the **western monuments,** artfully rounded structures hiding cavernous nooks and crannies. Downhill from the Western monuments, you'll come across five more colossal statue-menhirs, each menacingly armed, and behind them the granite quarry that started it all. A 1200-year-old olive tree, perhaps the oldest living thing on the island, presides over the scene.

PORTO

A hiking paradise, the gulf of Porto combines all of the natural spectacles that make Corsica unique. Jagged volcanic mountains tower above a crystalline sea; lush pine groves nuzzle bridges as waterfalls pour into pools, and, to the north, a marine reserve conceals grottoes and rare species of plants and birds. Porto itself (pop. 432), devoted as it is to tourism, is no more than an extended souvenir shop, but lodgings are cheap and transportation convenient by Corsican standards.

ORIENTATION AND PRACTICAL INFORMATION

Porto is split into an upper town, **Haut Porto** or **Quartier Vaita,** and a coastal area, **Porto Marina,** where some 15 hotels and restaurants jostle for space. D81 connects Haut Porto to Calvi in the north and leads to Ajaccio in the south; the unnamed main road leads from D81 to the port.

Buses: Autocars SAIB (☎04 95 22 41 99), in Ajaccio. To **Ajaccio** (2hr.; M-Sa 2 per day, July-Sept. M-Sa 3 per day, Su 1 per day; 70F/€10.67) and **Calvi** (3hr.; M-Sa 1 per day, daily July-Aug.; 100F/€15.25). **Autocars Mordiconi** (☎04 95 48 00 04) to **Corte** (July-Sept. 15 M-Sa 1 per day, 110F/€16.77).

Taxis: Taxis Chez Félix (☎04 95 26 12 92).

Car, Bike, and Scooter Rental: Porto Locations (☎/fax 04 95 26 10 13), opposite the supermarkets in Haut Porto. **Cars** 390F/€59.46 per day, 2000F/€304.92 per week. 20+. **Scooters** 300F/€45.74 per day, 1500F/€228.69 per week. **Bikes** 100F/€15.25 per day, 450F/€68.61 per week. Credit card deposit. Open Apr.-Oct. daily 8:30am-7:30pm. AmEx/MC/V.

Tourist Office: (☎04 95 26 10 55; www.porto-tourisme.com), near marina on main road. Bus schedules; info on water sports, boat trips, lodging. *Topo-guide* for local hikes (15F/€2.29). Open July-Aug. daily 9am-8pm; Apr.-June and Sept.-Oct. M-Sa 9am-12:30pm and 2:30-7pm; Nov.-Mar. M-F 9am-noon and 2-6pm, Sa 9am-noon.

Currency Exchange: At **SPAR** supermarket, in Haut Porto. Open July-Aug. M-Sa 8am-8pm, Su 8am-noon and 5-8pm; Sept.-June M-Sa 8:30am-noon and 1-7pm.

Laundromat: Lavo 2000 (☎04 95 26 10 33), on the main road. Open daily 8am-9pm.

Post Office: (☎04 95 26 10 26), midway between marina and Haut Porto. Open July-Aug. M-F 9am-5pm, Sa 9-11:30am; Sept.-June M-F 9am-12:30pm and 2-4pm, Sa 9-11am. **Postal code:** 20150.

ACCOMMODATIONS

Porto's abundance of hotels makes the town more affordable than most of the island, although prices rise dramatically in July and peak in August.

Le Panorama (☎04 95 26 11 05), on the main road near the port, is the best value in town. Functional rooms with huge terraces overlooking marina and beach. Breakfast 30F/€4.57. Singles and doubles July-Aug. 150-180F/€22.90-27.44; Apr.-June and Sept. 130-150F/€19.82-22.90. Extra bed 30F/€4.57.

Bon Accueil (☎/fax 04 95 26 19 50; jesaispas@net-up.com), on the main road. Colorful rooms surround a central deck and garden. Breakfast 35F/€5.34. Singles and doubles July 15-Aug. 282F/€42.99, Sept.-July 14 180-220F/€27.44-33.54; triples 230-280F/€35.06-42.69; quads 320-370F/€48.79-56.41. Extra bed 50F/€7.62. MC/V.

Camping: Le Sole e Vista (☎04 95 26 15 71; fax 04 95 26 10 79), on your right before the supermarkets as you enter Porto, has shady hillside plots and a rockin' bar. Open Apr.-Oct. 30-34F/€4.57-5.18 per person; 12-14F/€1.83-2.13 per tent; 12F/€1.83

per car. Electricity 17F/€2.59. AmEx/MC/V. Similar arrangement at **Les Oliviers** (☎04 95 26 14 49; fax 04 95 26 12 49; guy.lannoy@wanadoo.fr), 200m toward Ajaccio on D81. Open Apr.-Oct. Reception open 8am-9pm. 30-37F/€4.57-5.64 per person; 15F/€2.29 per tent or car. Electricity 15F/€2.29. 2- to 3-room bungalows 230-700F/€35.06-106.72. AmEx/MC/V. **Camping Municipal** (☎04 95 26 17 76), straddling D84 in lower Porto, resembles a poorly planted parking lot, but always has vacancies. Open June 15-Sept. 30. Reception 8am-9:30pm. 30F/€4.57 per person; 11F/€1.68 per tent, 10F/€1.53 per car. Electricity 17F/€2.59. AmEx/MC/V.

Gîtes in Ota: Some of the cheapest accommodations in Corsica are available in the pleasant village of Ota, 5km inland and upwards, a starting point for many hikes. The bus from Ajaccio to Porto goes to Ota (10min., 20F/€3.05), and returns to Ajaccio via Porto twice a day. To walk from Porto, veer right and head uphill at the fork after the supermarkets; follow the signs to D124 and Ota. **Chez Felix** (☎/fax 04 95 26 12 92), just inside Ota, has pleasant 4- to 8-bed dorms. Kitchen access. Breakfast 35F/€5.34. Sheets 20F/€3.05. 65F/€9.91 per person, doubles with bath 200-250F/€30.49-38.12. AmEx/MC/V. **Chez Marie** (☎/fax 04 95 26 11 37) has more modern, spartan dorms with 4- to 6-beds. Kitchen access. Beds 70F/€10.67, demi-pension 170F/€25.92. Doubles 142F/€21.65. MC/V.

FOOD

Rule of thumb: avoid hotel restaurants, where prices are high and food mediocre. **La Marine,** on the main road near the marina, is one of the better eateries in town. Enjoy tasty pizzas (from 35F/€5.34) and affordable *menus* (from 60F/€9.15). (☎04 95 26 10 19. Open Apr.-Oct. daily 11:30am-2:30pm and 6:30-10:30pm.) The *gîtes* in Ota (above) have delicious Corsican specialties; the hike and the *menu* are worth the 110F/€16.77. The two supermarkets are next to each other in Haut Porto on the D81: **SPAR** (☎04 95 26 11 25; open July-Aug. M-Sa 8am-8pm, Su 8am-noon and 5-8pm; Sept.-June M-Sa 8:30am-noon and 1-7pm, Su 8:30am-noon) and **Supermarché Banco** (☎04 95 26 10 92; open July-Aug. daily 8am-8pm; Apr.-June and Sept.-Oct. M-Sa 8am-noon and 1-7pm, Su 8am-2pm).

HIKES AND SIGHTS

GORGES, POOLS, AND PINES. The old Genoese mail route from Ota to Evisa is a must for hikers of all levels. Rugged yet accessible, this trail (3hr.) winds its way through the deep **Gorges de la Spelunca,** passing by 15th-century bridges and plenty of spots to picnic or swim. The trail begins on the stairway just after the Mairie on the main road in Ota (see **Gîtes in Ota,** above, for buses); follow the painted orange rectangles. The most spectacular scenery lies near the beginning of the trail, from the first two Genoese bridges to the **Pont de Zaglia** (45min.). To do this shorter section, follow the main road from Ota to the first Genoese bridge (25min.), where you can pick up the orange-rectangle trail. There are no afternoon return buses from Ota or Evisa, but hitching is reportedly easy during high season. As always, *Let's Go* does not recommend hitchhiking.

Chestnut trees and 50m pines fill the mountainous **Fôret d'Aitone** between Evisa and Corte. This trail, part of the **Tra Mare e Monti,** is famous for its **piscines naturelles,** impromptu swimming holes formed by pooling waterfalls. The pools are an hour or so from Evisa; beyond them is a more difficult and secluded trail to Col. de Vergio (6-7hr.), where a *gîte d'etape* marks its intersection with the **GR20.**

LES CALANCHES. The most astounding scenery on the entire island may be south of Porto, where the geological formations of the Calanches resemble, in the words of Guy de Maupassant, a "menagerie of nightmares petrified by the whim of some extravagant god." Hikes here range from easy-as-pie to do-or-die. The **Château Fort,** in the former category, begins 6km south of Porto on D81; ask the Ajaccio-Ota bus driver to let you off at **Tête de Chien** (30min.). A more masochistic alternative awaits 2km farther south off D81; the marked trail, which begins near the stadium, climbs 900m to spectacular 1294m **Le Capo d'Orto** (3hr. one-way). From the top of the summit, you can join a trail heading back to Porto.

HOME ON THE RANGE The last thing you'd expect on a hike through a pine forest is a brood of squealing pigs—but around Porto, roaming snouts are everywhere. Corsican farmers take free-range herding to an extreme; their porkers fend for themselves for years, leading a semi-nomadic existence in the wild. And their absentee owners never forget a face—the animals are recognized and claimed on personal appearance alone. When it comes time for the slaughter, their meat is tender enough to earn Corsican charcuterie a reputation as the best in France.

SCANDOLA. Totally off-limits to hikers and divers, the caves, grottoes, and wild terrain of the **Reserve Naturelle de Scandola** can only be explored by **boat tours** from Porto. The reserve's most celebrated inhabitants are falcon-like buzzards, whose wailing call is immediately recognizable. **Porto Linea,** by Hôtel Monte Rosso, sends a 12-person boat into hard-to-reach caves and coves. *(☎04 95 26 11 50; Apr.-Oct. 3hr., 220F/€33.54; reserve ahead.)* Less intimate but equally spectacular, **Nave Va,** by Hôtel Le Cyrnée, tours Scandola with 50- to 180-person boats. *(☎04 95 26 15 16; Apr.-Oct. 3hr., 200F/€30.49; reserve ahead.)*

SIGHTS IN PORTO. Guarding over Porto's strip of hotels and postcard shops is one of Corsica's oldest Genoese towers, the 1549 **Tour Génoise.** After a 15-minute climb, enjoy spectacular views of the surrounding cliffs dropping majestically to the sea. *(Open Apr.-Oct. daily 9am-9pm. 15F/€2.29.)* See what's for dinner at the one-room **Aquarium de la Poudrière,** on the marina. The cave-like space features a giant stingray and other aquatic creatures from the Gulf of Porto. *(☎04 95 26 19 24. Open M-Sa 10am-10pm, Su 11am-7pm. 35F/€5.34.)*

CALVI

Calvi (pop. 5700) is sometimes called Corsica's Côte d'Azur, and it shares some of that coastline's best and worst traits. It's similarly yacht-bound and café-ridden, full of souvenir shops and the idle rich; it's also stunningly beautiful topographically, with a star-shaped citadel above town and a long, sandy beach below it, with a backdrop of snow-capped mountains. While Calvi may not be the most typically Corsican port, its two hostels and accessible beach make it the most backpacker-friendly town on the island.

TRANSPORTATION

Flights: Aéroport de Calvi Ste-Catherine, 7km southeast of town; a taxi ride in costs 110F/€16.77. **Air France** and subsidiaries **Air Littoral** and **Air Liberté** (☎08 20 82 08 20) fly to **Lille, Lyon, Marseille, Nice,** and **Paris** (see p. 321).

Ferries: For info and tickets call **Agence TRAMAR** (☎04 95 65 01 38), quai Landry, in the Port de Plaisance. Open M-F 8:30am-noon and 2-5:30pm, Sa 8:30am-noon. Both **SNCM** (☎04 95 65 17 77) and **Corsica Ferries** (☎04 95 65 43 21) send high-speed boats to **Nice** and have offices near the Capitainerie du Port de Commerce (open 2hr. before boat arrivals).

Trains: pl. de la Gare (☎04 95 65 00 61), on av. de la République near the Port de Plaisance. To: **Bastia** (3hr., 2 per day, 108F/€16.47); **Corte** (2½hr., 2 per day, 90F/€13.72); and **Ile Rousse** (45min., 2 per day, 29F/€4.42). **Tramways de la Balagne** is a supplementary service sending more frequent trains to **Ile Rousse** (50min.; June-Sept. 10 per day, Apr.-May and Oct. 4 per day; 25F/€3.81). Open daily 6am-9pm. **Luggage storage** 18F/€2.74 per day, 24F/€3.66 for 24hr.

Buses: Autocar SAIB buses (☎04 95 22 41 99) leave from Super U and head to **Porto** (3hr.; M-Sa 1 per day, daily July-Aug.; 100F/€15.25). **Les Beaux Voyages** (☎04 95 65 15 02), on av. Wilson, runs buses to **Ajaccio** (4¾hr., 1 per day, 135F/€20.58); **Bastia** (2¼hr., M-Sa 1 per day, 80F/€12.20) via **Ile Rousse** (25min., 20F/€3.05); and **Calenzana** (July-Aug. M-Sa 2 per day, Sept.-June M-Tu and Th-Sa 1 per day; 35F/€5.34), where the **GR20** begins. They stop in front of the agency at pl. Porteuse d'Eau, by the taxi stand; buy tickets on board. Open M-Sa 9am-noon and 2-7pm.

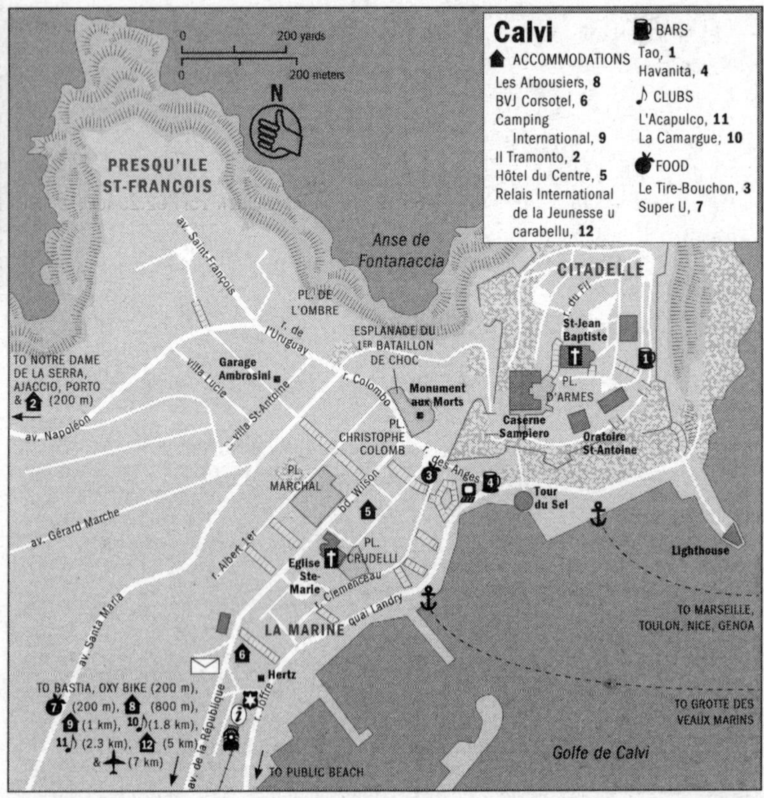

Car Rental: Europcar, av. de la République (Calvi ☎04 95 65 10 35, airport ☎04 95 65 10 19). 510F/€77.76 per day, 1734F/€264.37 per week. 21+. MC/V. Open M-Sa 8am-1pm and 2:30-7:30pm. **Hertz,** 2 rue Maréchal Joffre (May-Sept. Calvi ☎04 95 65 06 64; airport ☎04 95 65 02 96). 490F/€74.71 per day, 1700F/€259.19 per week. 21+. AmEx/MC/V. Open M-Sa 8am-noon and 3-8pm.

Bike Rental: Garage Ambrosini, pl. Christophe Colomb (☎04 95 65 02 13). 100F/€15.25 per day. Deposit 1500F/€228.69. Open June-Sept. daily 8am-noon and 2-6pm, Oct.-May closed Su. **Oxy Bike** (☎06 86 48 28 96), in a field across from Super U on av. Christophe Colomb. 65F/€9.91 per half-day, 100F/€15.25 per day. Deposit 1500F/€228.69. Open Apr.-Oct. daily 8:30am-7pm. **Scooter rental: Locat'loisirs** (☎04 95 60 29 11), 38 rue Clemenceau. 150F/€22.90 per 3hr., 250F/€38.12 per day. 14+. No driver's license required. Open Apr. to mid-Oct. daily 8:30am-midnight.

Taxi: ☎04 95 65 03 10. 24hr.

ORIENTATION AND PRACTICAL INFORMATION

The city is manageable in size and easy to walk, threaded by one main road following the curve of the coast, called **bd. Wilson** between the citadel and the post office, then **av. de la République,** and finally **av. Christophe Colomb** as you leave the city. The lovely pedestrian **rue Clemenceau** runs below bd. Wilson, parallel to the port.

Tourist Office: Port de Plaisance (☎04 95 65 16 67; fax 04 95 65 14 09; omt.calvi@wanadoo.fr). On 2nd floor of glass building at southern end of **Port de Plaisance.** Exit from back of train station, facing the beach, turn left, and follow the signs.

Makes on-the-spot hotel reservations. Ask for guides with info on the area. Open June-Sept. 15 daily 9am-7pm; May M-Sa 9am-6:30pm; Sept. 16-Apr. M-F 9am-5pm.

Currency exchange: Use one of the banks on bd. Wilson.

Police: ☎04 95 65 44 77. On Port de Plaisance, to the right of the tourist office.

Laundromat: Laverie, in Super U Plaza, av. Christophe Colomb. Open daily 8am-10pm.

Internet Access: Café de L'Orient (☎04 95 65 00 16), on the port near the Tour de Sel. 10F/€1.53 flat fee, plus 0.70F/€0.11 per min. Open Apr.-Oct. daily 8am-2am. Also **A Casa Di Cristofanu** (☎04 95 65 19 25), in the citadel. 15F/€2.29 for the first 15min., then 0.50F/€0.08 per min. Open Mar.-Oct. daily 10am-midnight.

Post office: (☎04 95 65 90 90), on bd. Wilson. Open M-F 8:30am-5:30pm, Sa 8:30am-noon. **Postal code:** 20260.

ACCOMMODATIONS AND CAMPING

With two of the only hostels in Corsica, Calvi caters to backpackers. There are also plenty of hotels, which get cheaper the farther you are from the center of town. Reserve ahead in the summer months, especially in July. Weekly rentals are often cheaper; ask about *tarifs dégressifs* at the tourist office.

Relais International de la Jeunesse U Carabellu (☎04 95 65 14 16). Leave the station, turn left on av. de la République, pass the Super U, turn right at rte. de Pietramaggiore (indicated by a billboard pointing to various hotels and campsites), and follow signs 5km into the hills. Continue past Bella Vista camping until road forks at a stop sign; veer right and continue. The route gets lonely at the top—women may not want to go alone. On a beautiful, isolated spot 5km from town. Spacious rooms with private baths, some marble. Incredible views of Calvi. No campsite, but staff lets you if you ask. Families get their own room; otherwise, single-sex dorms hold 3-12 beds. Ask about discounts for bike and car rentals, restaurants, and private beaches. Breakfast included. Sheets 20F/€3.05. Lockout 10am-5pm; drop off luggage any time. Open Mar.-Sept. Bunks 100F/€15.25. Demi-pension 160F/€24.39.

BVJ Corsotel "Hôtel de Jeunes," av. de la République (☎04 95 65 14 15; fax 04 95 65 33 72), across from train station parking lot. 2- to 8-bed dorms with blankets, shower, and sink are well-sized with high ceilings. Breakfast 20F/€3.05. Reception 7:30am-1pm and 5-10pm. Check-out 10am. Open Apr.-Oct. Bunks 115F/€17.53; 2-bed doubles July 125F/€19.06, Aug. 130F/€19.82, Apr.-June and Sept.-Oct. 115F/€17.53.

Il Tramonto, rte. d'Ajaccio R.N. 199 (☎04 95 65 04 17; fax 04 95 65 02 40; www.hotel-iltramonto.com), 800m from town, past the citadel. Fabulous sea views from art-deco rooms. Breakfast 30F/€4.57. Open Apr.-Oct. Aug. doubles 320F/€48.79; July 280F/€42.69; June and Sept. 260F/€39.64; May and Oct. 200F/€30.49; Apr. 180F/€27.44. Balcony 20F/€3.05 extra. Extra bed 80-100F/€12.20-15.25. MC/V.

Les Arbousiers, rte. de Pietramaggiore (☎04 95 65 04 47; fax 04 95 65 26 14), is 800m from town, after Super U. Eclectic rooms, all with bath and balcony. By the beach. Breakfast 30F/€4.57. Open May-Sept. July-Aug. singles 270F/€41.16, doubles 310F/€47.26; June and Sept. singles 225F/€34.30, doubles 235F/€35.83; May singles 200F/€30.49, doubles 215F/€32.78. AmEx/MC/V.

Hôtel du Centre, 14 rue Alsace Lorraine (☎04 95 65 02 01), behind rue Clemenceau. Smack in heart of Calvi. Simple, but slightly tired rooms. Breakfast 28F/€4.27. Open June-Oct. Aug. singles 230F/€35.06, with shower 270F/€41.16; doubles 240F/€36,54, with shower 280F/€42.69; triples 300F/€45.74, with shower 320F/€48.79. Prices 20-30F/€3.05-4.57 lower in July; 50-80F/€7.62-12.20 lower in June and Sept.; 70-100F/€10.67-15.25 lower Oct.

Camping International, RN 197 (☎04 95 65 01 75; fax 04 95 65 36 11), 1km from town. Walk past Super U, Hôtel L'Onda; immediately past the minigolf sign. Young people flock here for the nearby beach and on-site bar with bands three nights a week July-Aug. Open Apr.-Oct. July-Aug. 33F/€5.03 per person, children under 7 half-price, 19F/€2.90 per tent, 10F/€1.53 per car; Apr.-June and Sept.-Oct. 22F/€3.35 per person, children under 7 half-price; 15F/€2.29 per tent; 8F/€1.22 per car.

FOOD

Pickings are slim for cheap food in Calvi; try the **Super U Supermarché,** av. Christophe Colomb. (☎04 95 65 04 32. Open mid-June to mid-Sept. M-Sa 8am-8pm, Su 8am-1pm; otherwise M-F 8:30am-12:20pm and 3-7pm, Sa 8:30am-7pm.) Narrow rue Clemenceau abounds with specialty food shops and groceries and hosts a **covered market** beside the Eglise Ste-Marie (daily 7am-1pm). Cheap pizzerias line rue de la République, and stylish port restaurants offer a great view, but you'll want to stick to the pedestrian alleys for better food and local ambience. Spoil yourself at **Le Tire-Bouchon,** 15 rue Clemenceau, with authentic Corsican specialties. Portions, starting at 35F/€5.34, lie somewhere between an entree and a main course. (☎04 95 65 25 41. Open Apr.-Nov. M-Sa noon-3pm and 7-11pm, Su 7-11pm. MC/V.)

SIGHTS AND BEACHES

Driven to desperation by invasions from the south, 13th-century Calvi asked the protection of nearby Genoa—and for five centuries remained Corsica's most unshakable Italian stronghold. In recognition of Calvi's long-term loyalty, the Genoese crowned the entrance to the **citadel** with an inscription reading *civitas Calvi semper fidelis* (the city of Calvi is always faithful). Just beyond the entry portal, a welcome center distributes a useful free map and hawks a self-guided audio-tour of the citadel (1hr.; 35F/€5.34), which covers some of the lesser monuments. (☎04 95 65 36 74. Open W-M 10am-12:30pm and 4-7:30pm.) Round the first corner and climb the stairs to reach the citadel's center, dominated by the austere **Palais des Gouverneurs** (now—and not without irony—the messhall of France's foreign legion) and the 16th-century **Cathédrale St-Jean Baptiste.** Despite the church's Baroque domes, its interior is unusually sparse for the period; the 15th-century Madonna to the left of the choir, brought back from Peru by a wealthy emigré, is the pride and joy of all the town's religious processions. (Open daily 9am-noon and 2-7pm.) The **Oratoire St-Antoine,** tucked into the citadel's port-side wall, is largely abandoned, but a decaying 1530 fresco in the lower left corner, showing Christ accompanied by St-Sebastian, is worth a look.

Like several other Mediterranean towns, Calvi claims to be the birthplace of **Christopher Columbus.** The theory here is that a certain Calvi expatriate, Antonio Calvo, returned to his hometown sometime in the 15th century to enlist new recruits for the Genoese navy. The talents of his nephew caught his eye, so Calvo adopted the young Christophe and returned with him to Genoa. The scenario has its share of sceptics—but, if challenged, the tourist office claims it can produce the necessary evidence. In any case, a **plaque** in the north end of the citadel marks the ruins of the house where Columbus may have been born. The citadel's other famous house tells a more likely story: Napoleon and his family sojourned here in 1793 when fleeing political opponents in Ajaccio. Visit at the end of the day, since it's something of a tradition to watch the sunset at the far end of the citadel.

Calvi and the surrounding area abound with gorgeous sandy beaches and clear turquoise sea. With shallow waters throughout the coast, you can tiptoe many meters into the ocean, and the strong winds make for great windsurfing. If the 6km stretch of expansive **public beach** gets too windy, the rocks surrounding the citadel offer secluded and sun-drenched shelter. The **Tramways de la Balagne** (see **Transportation,** above) can take you to more remote coves further out of town.

ENTERTAINMENT AND FESTIVALS

The bars on the **Port de Plaisance** glitter brightly in the summer. Signs posted all over town advertise party nights in different spots along the northern coast. Locals come from far and wide to the two open-air nightclubs on the way to Ile Rousse. At **La Camargue,** 25 minutes up N197 by foot, scantily-clad youth bump 'n' grind in one of several discos or around outdoor pools, while an over-30 crowd swings in the piano bar. **L'Acapulco,** on D151 (rte. de Calenzana), a right-turn ten minutes after La Camargue, is a near-twin that enhances the tropical mood with flaming torches and waterfalls. (La Camargue ☎04 95 65 08 70. L'Acapulco ☎04 95 65 08 03. Both open July-Aug. daily 10:30pm-6am; June and Sept. weekends only; piano bars open all year. 60F/€9.15 cover. Free shuttles for La Camargue leave from the port parking lot near the tourist office, and L'Acapulco shuttles pick up at the Tour de Sel.) For a more mellow atmosphere and an older crowd, try the **Tao** piano bar and French/Asian restaurant in the citadel, overlooking the sea. (☎04 95 65 00 73. Open May-Sept. daily 11pm-dawn.) The funkiest bar on the port is **Havanita.** Loudly dressed bartenders serve Cuban cocktails amid straw huts and palm trees. (☎04 95 65 00 37. Open May-Sept. daily 6pm-2am.)

Calvi hosts several festivals, including the **Festival du Jazz** in the last week of June, when over 150 musicians give impromptu performances. (☎04 95 65 00 50. M-F 70F/€10.67, Sa 100F/€15.25.) In mid-September, the **Rencontres Polyphoniques** (☎04 95 65 23 57) draw international singers.

ILE ROUSSE

Stretching east from Calvi to the town of Ile Rousse (pop. 3000), Corsica's northern coast is lined with unblemished beaches and out-of-the-way coves. The scenery is at its best in Ile Rousse itself, which Pascal Paoli, the leader of independent Corsica, founded in 1759 in an effort to divert trade from Genoese-dominated Calvi. Today, Ile Rousse remains a favored spot for its powdery beach and clear, opalescent waters; the scenic train ride from Calvi alone justifies the trip.

SNCM sends **ferries** to **Nice** (3-10hr. depending on the boat; 2-7 per week; 225-255F/€34.30-38.88, students 195-225F/€29.73-34.30). Call **Agence CCR** on av. J. Calizi, below the tourist office, for more info. (☎04 95 60 09 56; fax 04 95 60 02 56. Open mid-June to Sept. M-Sa 9am-noon and 2-6pm; Oct. to mid-June M-F 8:30am-noon and 2-5:30pm, Sa 8:30am-noon.) The **train station** will **store luggage** for 18F/€2.74 per day. (☎04 95 60 00 50. Open July-Sept. daily 6am-8pm; otherwise 6am-noon and 2-7pm.) Tramways de la Balagne **trains** hug the coast on the way to **Calvi** (50min.; June-Sept. 10 per day, Apr.-May and Oct. 4 per day; 25F/€3.81). The line is divided into three sections, each of which costs 10F/€1.53; it's cheaper to buy tickets for Calvi in the train station. Several beaches and campsites lie along the route—just ask the ticket collector in your carriage to let you off when you see one that looks particularly enticing. Few can resist the charms of **Aregno Plage** and its accompanying campsite, three stops from Ile Rousse.

No more than 2km across, Ile Rousse is easy to navigate. The town center lies to the right of the train station, while the *gare maritime* and tower-topped peninsula are to the left. To get to the **tourist office** from the train station or ferry depot, walk right for about five minutes; it's in a small office on the opposite side of pl. Paoli. The staff will give you a practical guide and information on nearby villages. (☎04 95 60 04 35; fax 04 95 60 24 74; info@ot-ile-rousse.fr; www.ot-ile-rousse.fr. Open July-Aug. M-Sa 9am-8pm, Su 10am-noon and 5-7pm; Sept.-June M-F 9am-noon and 2-6pm.) **Leader's Sport,** av. Paul Doumer, rents **bikes.** (☎04 95 60 15 76. Open July-Aug. daily 7am-8:30pm; June 9am-noon and 2:30-7pm; Sept.-May M-Sa 9am-noon and 2:30-7pm. 100F/€15.25 per day, 500F/€76.23 per week; 1500F/€228.69 deposit. MC/V.) The **post office** on rte. de Monticello offers **Internet access.** (☎04 95 63 05 50. 50F/€7.62 per hr. Open M-F 8:30am-6pm, Sa 8:30am-noon.)

The city's signature **covered market** off pl. Paoli is filled with local fruits, the tentacled and finned catch of the day, and 10 different types of honey (open daily 7am-1pm). The local **Casino supermarket** on allée Charles de Gaulle takes up where the market leaves off. (☎04 95 60 24 23. Open July-Aug. M-Sa 8:30am-8pm, Su 8:30am-1pm; Sept.-June M-F 8:30am-12:30pm and 3-7pm, Sa 8:30am-7pm.) Inexpensive pizza and sandwiches await in the brasseries along pl. Paoli. **Restaurant des Voyageurs,** on rue Général Graziani, has prizeworthy Corsican *bruschetta* for 36-42F/€5.49-6.40. (☎04 95 60 00 39. Open Apr.-Oct. daily 9am-10pm. MC/V.)

As Ile Rousse tends to attract moneyed Frenchmen, there's only one budget hotel in town. To find **Hôtel le Grillon,** 10 av. Paul Doumer, go straight on av. Piccioni, beside the tourist office, and take a left. It has older, well-sized rooms with firm mattresses, sunny bedspreads, and baths. (☎ 04 95 60 00 49; fax 04 95 60 43 69. Breakfast 32F/€4.88. Open Mar.-Oct. Singles 190-220F/€28.97-33.54; doubles 200-260F/€30.49-39.64; triples 240-300F/€36.59-45.74. In Aug., obligatory demi-pension for singles 410F/€62.51, doubles 560F/€85.38, triples 720F/€109.77. MC/V.) You'll have more luck camping; campsites appear fairly regularly all along the Balagne coast, so just hop off the train when you see one that you like. In Ile Rousse, **Les Oliviers** is 800m from the town center on av. Paul Doumer, the road to Bastia. The congenial, coastal site offers excellent views of Ile Rousse and has tiny wooden chalets for two. (☎ 04 95 60 19 92 or 04 95 60 25 64; fax 04 95 60 30 91. Laundry. July-Aug. closed to cars after 11pm. Open Apr.-Oct. 30F/€4.57 per person, 17F/€2.59 per tent, 11F/€1.68 per car. Chalet doubles 170F/€25.92. MC/V.)

NEAR ILE ROUSSE: LA BALAGNE

La Balagne, the inland stretch between Calvi and Ile Rousse, is dotted with olive trees and pristine mountain villages, many of which are accessible by foot. **Lumio** is 15 minutes by train from Calvi or 30 minutes from Ile Rousse. Here, on the mountain that the Romans called *Ortus Solis* (where the sun rises), the modern village lies meters away from its ancient counterpart Occi, mysteriously abandoned one morning in 1852. Not far off is the **Site archéologique du Monte Ortu,** where neolithic artifacts have recently been discovered. Farther south, accessible by bus from Calvi and on the famous **GR20** trail, lies **Calenzana,** known as "the garden of the Balagne," with a 17th-century Baroque church that overlooks the peaceful **Cimetière des Allemands.** Every May 21, local Catholics make a pilgrimage to the **Sanctuaire de Ste-Restitude,** 1½km out of town, named for the regional patron saint.

Sant'Antonino, with its stone roofs, is to the east toward Ile Rousse. The highest village in the Balagne, it was built on a peak by the Moors in the 9th century, and its narrow streets remain accessible only by foot. Home to the renowned music school **Bartimore,** the village plays host to many musical concerts throughout the year, and local craftsmen make traditional Corsican instruments (call 04 95 61 77 31 for concert info). **Autocars Mariani,** bd. Wilson in Calvi, can take you to these sleepy old villages in a comfy tour bus. Buy tickets for their once-a-week excursion in the bureau beside the Ile Rousse tourist office. (☎ 04 95 65 00 47. Half-day tour 80F/€12.20. Open M-Sa 9am-noon and 2-7pm.) If your boots were made for walking, you can hike to Sant'Antonino in less than two hours on a trail that starts immediately after Pub's Discothèque. From the Casino supermarket, head inland on the rte. de Calvi for about ten minutes until you see the discothèque on your left. At Sant'Antonino, the trail doubles back and passes by the peaceful village of Corbara, the home of a Franciscan monastery dating from 1456.

CORTE (CORTI)

The most dynamic of Corsica's inland towns, Corte combines breathtaking natural scenery with an intellectual flair. Sheer cliffs, snow-capped peaks, and magical gorges create a dramatic backdrop for the island's only university, whose students (2600 of its 6000 residents) keep prices surprisingly low. Known to natives as "the heart of Corsica," the town gave birth to Pasquale Paoli's national constitution in 1731, and nowhere is the Corsican struggle felt more strongly today. Out of solidarity, most town natives speak the island's dialect, *Corse*, along with French, and mainland French visitors may be icily received. Those not flying a *fleur-de-lys* will be delighted by Corte's friendly people, authentic cuisine, and singular hikes.

SHOUTING FIRE ON A CROWDED CITADEL

In 1749, a band of patriots followed Jean-Pierre Gaffori, a local physician and eventual leader of the free Corsican nation, up the mountainside to besiege the city and retake it. As the Corsicans reached the top, the Genoese soldiers played their trump card: they held Gaffori's young son by the ankle from the citadel's eagle's-nest lookout. The bewildered Corsicans stopped dead, not daring to fire their cannons and risk hurting their leader's child. Suddenly, a woman leapt in front of the Corsican patriots, crying "Fire! Fire!" She was Faustine Gaffori, wife of their general and mother of the dangling child. "Don't think of my son!" she shouted, "Think of the homeland!" Reinvigorated, the Corsicans continued their assault and conquered the citadel, where they found the boy safe and sound.

TRANSPORTATION

Trains: (☎04 95 46 00 97), at the rotary where av. Jean Nicoli and the N193 meet. To: **Ajaccio** (2hr., 4 per day, 76F/€11.59); **Bastia** (1½hr., 4 per day, 67F/€10.22); and **Calvi** via **Ponte-Leccia** (2½hr., 2 per day, 90F/€13.72). **Luggage storage** 18F/€2.74 (open daily 6am-8pm).

Buses: Eurocorse Voyages (☎04 95 71 24 64). To: **Ajaccio** (1¾hr., M-Sa 2 per day, 65F/€9.91) and **Bastia** (1¼hr., M-Sa 2 per day, 60F/€9.15). **Autocars Mordiconi** (☎04 95 48 00 04), from the Tuffelli parking lot, just below pl. Paoli off av. Xavier Luciani. To: **Porto** (2½hr., July-Sept. M-Sa 1 per day, 110F/€16.77).

Taxis: Taxis Salviani (☎04 95 46 04 88), at the train station.

Car Rental: Europcar, 2 pl. Paoli (☎04 95 46 06 02). 21+. 510F/€77.76 per day, 1734F/€264.37 per week. Open M-Sa 9am-noon and 3-7:30pm. MC/V.

Bike Rental: Corte V.T.T. (☎06 12 42 09 45), next to train station. 65F/€9.91 per half-day, 100F/€15.25 per day. Open June-Oct. daily 9am-noon and 2-7pm.

ORIENTATION AND PRACTICAL INFORMATION

To reach the center of Corte from the station, turn right on D14 (alias av. Jean Nicoli), cross two bridges, and follow the road until it ends at **cours Paoli,** Corte's main drag. A left turn here leads to **pl. Paoli,** the town center; at the top-right corner, climb the stairwayed **rue Scolisca** to reach the citadel and the **tourist office.**

Tourist office: (☎04 95 46 26 70; fax 04 95 46 34 05; www.corte-tourisme.com). Useful bus schedule; bilingual brochure with popular hikes. **Parc Naturel Régional** expert available June-Sept. M-F 9am-noon and 2-6pm. Office open July-Aug. daily 9am-8pm; May-June and Sept. M-Sa 9am-1pm and 2-7pm; Oct.-Apr. M-F 9am-noon and 2-6pm.

Youth Center: Bureau Information Jeunesse de Corte (☎04 95 46 12 48), rampe Ste-Croix. Open M-Th 9am-noon and 2-6pm, F 9am-noon and 2-5pm.

Police: (☎04 95 46 04 81), southeast of town on N200.

Hospital: (☎04 95 45 05 00), allée du 9 Septembre.

Internet Access: Grand Café du Cours, 22 cours Paoli (☎04 95 46 00 33). 50F/€7.62 per hr. Open daily 7am-2am.

Post office: av. du Baron Mariani (☎04 95 46 08 20). Open M-F 8am-noon and 2-5pm, Sa 8am-noon. **Postal code:** 20250.

ACCOMMODATIONS

Hôtel-Residence Porette (H-R), 6 allée du 9 Septembre (☎04 95 45 11 11; fax 04 95 61 02 85). Bear left from station to stadium and follow it for 100m. Sterile cells, but fun young students. Sauna, weight room, and restaurant. Breakfast 34F/€5.18. Reception 24hr. Singles 135F/€20.98, with bath 199F/€30.34; doubles 145F/€22.11, with bath 279-289F/€42.54; triples 329F/€50.16; quads 350F/€53.36.

Hôtel de la Poste, 2 pl. du Duc de Padoue (☎04 95 46 01 37), off cours Paoli near post office. Well-located in town center, slightly worn rooms feature hardwood furniture and showers. Breakfast 30F/€4.57. Singles and doubles 190-275F/€28.97-41.93; triples 215-275F/€32.78-41.93; quads 275F/€41.93.

Camping: Restonica (☎04 95 46 11 59; fax 04 95 46 24 40; vero.camp@worldonline.fr). Follow directions from station to H-R Porette and continue until a sign points downhill to campsite. Restaurant. Reception 7:30am-10pm. Open Apr. 15-Oct. 15. 32F/€4.88 per person, 15F/€2.29 per tent, 14F/€2.13 per car. Electricity 21F/€3.20. AmEx/MC/V. **U Sognu,** on D623 (☎04 95 46 09 07; fax 04 95 61 00 76). From behind top of pl. Paoli, follow rue Prof. Santiaggi around the bend and turn right to cross the bridge; at the fork, turn right again. From train station, follow directions to *gîte* above, until a blue-and-white sign indicates an earlier turn-off. Limited shade but easy access to the nearby stream. Closed to cars after 11pm. Open Mar. 28-Oct. 15. 29F/€4.42 per person, 16F/€2.44 per tent or car. Electricity 18F/€2.74.

Gîte d'Etape: U Tavignanu, chemin de Balari (☎04 95 46 16 85; fax 04 95 61 14 01), turn left out of station and right when the road forks, first following allée du 9 Septembre and then signs at the base of the Citadel (20min.); last 5min. climb a steep dirt trail. *Gîte d'étape* with salt-of-the-earth owners. Converted hilltop farmhouse and shaded campsite. Inaccessible to cars. *Gîte*: Breakfast included. 85F/€12.96, July-Aug. obligatory demi-pension 170F/€25.92. Camping: 22F/€3.35 per person, 12F/€1.83 per tent; breakfast 22F/€3.35; dinner 85F/€12.96.

FOOD

Place Paoli is the spot to find sandwiches and pizza; **rue Scolisca** and the surrounding citadel streets abound with inexpensive local cuisine, with most *menus* around 60-70F/€9.15-10.67. **SPAR,** 5 av. Xavier Luciani, is in the town center. (☎04 95 46 08 59. Open July-Aug. M-Sa 7:30am-8pm, Su 9am-noon and 5-7:30pm; Sept.-June M-Sa 8am-12:30pm and 3-8pm, Su 9:30am-noon; Jan.-Feb. closed Su.) The mammoth **Casino** is near the train station on allée du 9 Septembre. (☎04 95 45 22 45. Open June 15-Aug. daily 8:30am-7:30pm; Sept.-June 14 M-F 8:30am-12:30pm and 3-8pm, Sa 8:30am-7:30pm.) **A Scudella,** 2 place Paoli, cooks up unbeatable regional cuisine, with meaty standouts. The 58F/€8.84 *menu* includes double portions and dessert. (☎04 95 46 25 31. Open M-Sa for lunch and dinner.)

SIGHTS AND EXCURSIONS

The *vieille ville* of Corte, with its steep, barely accessible streets and stone **citadel** peering over the Tavignano and Restonica valleys, has always been a bastion of Corsican patriotism. The route up is dedicated to the town's two heroes: **Pascal Paoli,** who drafted Corsica's famous constitution, proclaimed Corte the island's capital, and led the free state until Corsica lost the war with France in 1768; and Jean Pierre **Gaffori,** who preceded Paoli as governor (see box below) until his assassination by Genoese agents in 1753. In a plain-looking dwelling across from pl. Gaffori, a plaque honors the apartments where Charles Bonaparte, Napoleon I's father, lived for two years in the 1760s while serving the Paolian cause.

Rather than focusing on political ups and downs, the **Musée de la Corse,** at the top of rue Scolisca, provides an exclusively ethnographic history of Corsica. The thoughtful museum moves beyond regional costumes and handicrafts to contemplate issues such as the role of tourism on the island; the exhibits are only labeled in French and Italian, so the 10F/€1.53 English audio-guide is essential. Entrance includes a visit to the only inland **citadel** in Corsica, built in 1419. Visitors can wander through the dungeon, kitchens, and bathrooms (the latter a hole in the ground) as sheep graze nearby. (☎04 95 45 25 45; fax 04 95 45 25 36. Museum open June 20-Sept. 20 daily 10am-8pm; Sept. 21-Nov. Tu-Su 10am-6pm; Dec.-Mar. Tu-Sa 10am-6pm; Apr.-June 19 Tu-Su 10am-6pm. Citadel closes 1hr. earlier than museum. Tours of both in English July-Aug. M-Sa at 10:30am and 2:45pm, 10F/€1.53.

Museum and citadel 35F/€5.34, students 20F/€3.05.) Trek uphill from pl. Paoli and take a left at the Eglise de l'Annonciation to find a 360° **Belvedere** (viewpoint) on the oldest portion of the 15th-century city walls.

Corte's surrounding mountains and valleys feature countless trails. There's **hiking** (call the tourist office for maps and trail info; ☎08 92 68 02 20 for weather conditions); **biking** (see practical information); and **horseback riding** (at the Ferme Equestre Albadu, 1½km out of town on N193 toward Ajaccio; ☎04 95 46 24 55; 90F/€13.72 per hr., 200F/€30.49 per half-day, 400F/€60.98 per day with picnic).

DAYTRIPS FROM CORTE

GORGES DE LA RESTONICA

Southwest of Corte, the tiny D623 trail stretches 16km through the Gorges de la Restonica, a high-altitude canyon fed by glacial lakes lying in the shadow of icy peaks. The hot-blooded can swim in the gorge's chilly rivers and tributaries. To get to the gorge, descend rue Prof. Santiaggi at the back of pl. Paoli and cross the bridge at the right; head right again on D623 at the ensuing fork. Walk 2km following the signs for Restonica until you get to the Parc Naturel Régional information office, where, in an effort to limit traffic on the nerve-wrackingly narrow road, a free shuttle *(navette)* whisks hikers to the gorge's summit 13km uphill (July-Aug. daily 8am-2:30pm, return 3-5:30pm.)

If you have time for only one hike, make sure you tour the **glacial lakes** at the top of the gorge, one of the island's loveliest and least-populated areas, where hikers of all levels will enjoy the magnificent scenery. Take the *navette* to the Grotelle parking lot. To the right, a trail clearly marked in orange leads to a sheep-pen-turned-snackbar, then crosses the river and steadily mounts to the "most visited lake in Corsica," circular **Lac de Melo** (1hr.). This snow-fed beauty lies at 1711m, near the foot of Mont Rotondo (2622m), and is ringed by peaks including Corsica's highest—Mont Cinto (2700m). The trail may be marked *facile* (easy), but the climb is steep, rocky, and slippery when wet. Moreover, temperatures at the top can reach well below zero even when it's 25°C in town, so bring a sweater or windbreaker. From Melo, the trail continues, marked in yellow, to one of Corsica's largest and deepest lakes, the austere **Lac de Capitellu** (1930m; 45min.). From here, the trail meets the red-and-white marked **GR20,** Corsica's island-long path.

To turn your mountain promenade into a full-day adventure, you can follow the GR20 to the left until it intersects with a trail that leads to the **Refuge de Petra Piana** (3hr.), where you can spend the night or continue to the Lac de Rotondo (1½hr.). Less trodden but equally spectacular is the hike to **Lac de l'Oriente.** Take the free *navette* to **Pont de Tragone** and then follow the marked trail passing shepherd's houses until you reach the photogenic lake (3hr.) For more information on Restonica's offerings, consult the Tavignano-Restonica *topo-guide* (only in French; available in bookstores for 75F/€11.43) or the tourist office hiking expert.

GORGES DU TAVIGNANO

Less rugged than Restonica, the Tavignano gorges abound with waterfalls, natural pools, and picturesque hiking trails. With no road access, Tavignano is also likely to be less crowded than its better-known counterpart. A west-bound trail leaves directly from town at the base of the backside of the citadel, indicated by signs and marked in orange. The first two and a half hours of hiking along the Tavignano river lead to the **Passerelle du Russulinu** (902m), a suspension bridge surrounded by a picnic-friendly plain. Another three hours along the same trail leads to the **Refuge de la Sega** (1166m), where you can either spend the night or join two possible itineraries. To the right, a trail travels to the heartland village of **Calacuccia** (4hr.), on D84 about 45 minutes by car from Corte. To the left, a deservedly popular trail passes by centuries-old *bergeries* (sheep-pens) and abandoned shepherd huts as it crosses the **Plateau d'Alzo,** ending at the **Pont de la Frasseta,** 8km up on D623 in the heart of the Restonica (5hr.).

FORET DE VIZZAVONA

There's easily accessible hiking in the forests surrounding the town of Vizzavona, reached by one of the most beautiful train rides in Corsica (50min.; 4 per day, 5 per day July 10-Aug. 25; 35F/€5.34). Right outside the station, a billboard lists possible routes. The plunging falls and clear lagoons of the **Cascades des Anglais** provide the most inspiring scenery, about 45 minutes southwest of town along the red-and-white GR20. You can picnic on the cascade's flat rocks and shaded coves.

BASTIA

Bastia (pop. 40,000), Corsica's second largest city, doesn't really care whether you stay or leave. The island is neither cosmopolitan nor over-touristed and its well-serviced harbor and airport provide an obvious starting point for a tour. But Bastia's laid-back attitude, crumbling *vieille ville*, and exquisite Baroque churches often keep travelers here longer than expected. The city is also the only good base for a visit to the must-see Cap Corse (p. 343).

TRANSPORTATION

Flights: Bastia-Poretta, 23km away (☎04 95 54 54 54). An airport bus (☎04 95 31 06 65) scheduled to coincide with flights leaves from pl. de la Gare, by the préfecture (30min., 50F/€7.62). **Compagnie Corse Méditerranée** (☎08 02 80 28 02) flies to **Marseille, Nice,** and **Paris.**

Trains: pl. de la Gare (☎04 95 32 80 61), to the left of the roundabout at the top of av. Maréchal Sebastiani. To: **Ajaccio** (4hr., 4 per day, 143F/€21.81); **Calvi** (3hr.; 2 per day, 108F/€16.47); **Corte** (1½hr., 4 per day, 67F/€10.22); and **Ile Rousse** (2¼hr., 2 per day, 90F/€13.72). Luggage storage 18F/€2.74 per bag per day. Station and storage open daily 6am-8pm.

Buses: Eurocorse, rue du Nouveau Port (☎04 95 21 06 30). To **Ajaccio** (3hr., M-Sa 2 per day, 110F/€16.77). **Rapides Bleus,** 1 av. Maréchal Sebastiani (☎04 95 31 03 79), sends buses to **Porto Vecchio** (3hr.; M-Sa 2 per day, June 15-Sept. 15 daily; 120F/€18.30) via **Aléria** (1½hr., 70F/€10.67), from across from the post office.

Ferries: quai de Fango, next to pl. St-Nicolas; turn left from av. Maréchal Sebastiani just past pl. St-Nicolas. **SNCM** (☎04 95 54 66 99; fax 04 95 54 66 64), by the quai de Fango, sails to **Marseille, Nice,** and **Toulon. Corsica Ferries,** 5bis rue Chanoine Leschi (☎04 95 32 95 95), float to **Nice** and **Toulon,** and to **Livorno** and **Savona** in Italy. **Moby Lines,** 4 rue Commandant Luce de Casablanca (☎04 95 34 84 94; fax 04 95 32 17 94; mobylines.colonna@libertysurf.fr), services **Genoa** and **Livorno** in Italy. For details on air and ferry connections to mainland France, see **Getting There,** p. 321.

Car Rental: ADA, 35 rue César Campinchi (☎04 95 31 48 95; fax 04 95 34 46 95), with a second location at the airport (☎04 95 54 55 44). 290F/€44.21 per day, 1499F/€228.54 per week, unlimited mileage. Open M-F 8am-noon and 2-7pm, Sa 8am-noon.

Scooter Rental: Toga Location Nautique, port de Plaisance de Toga (☎04 95 34 14 14), near the north quai. Scooters 370F/€56.43 per day, 2300F/€350.66 per week; 5000F/€762.31 deposit. Open July-Aug. daily 8am-noon and 2-6pm, Sept.-June closed Su.

Taxis: (☎04 95 36 04 65 or 04 95 32 70 70). 210-220F/€32.02-33.54 to airport. 24hr.

ORIENTATION AND PRACTICAL INFORMATION

Find your bearings and the tourist office on rectangular **pl. St-Nicolas.** The main thoroughfares are **bd. du Général de Gaulle,** which runs along the inland length of the *place*, and the parallel **bd. Paoli** and **rue César Campinchi.** As you face the mountains, the old port and citadel are to the left and the ferry docks are to the right.

Tourist Office: pl. St-Nicolas (☎04 95 54 20 40; fax 04 95 31 81 34; ot-bastia@wanadoo.fr), has numerous maps of the city and Cap Corse. Ask for a copy of their indispensable bus schedule. Open July-Sept. daily 8am-8pm; Oct.-June M-Sa 8:30am-6pm.

Currency Exchange: Banque de France, 2 cours H. Pierangeli (☎04 95 32 82 00), at the opposite end of pl. St-Nicholas. Exchange desks open M-F 8:45am-noon. The **Change** (☎04 95 31 09 41) in the south ferry quai. Open daily 9am-7:30pm.

Centre Information Jeunesse: 9 rue César Campinchi (☎04 95 32 12 13). Open M-F 8am-noon and 2-6pm, Sa 8am-noon. Closed July 28-Aug. 15.

Hospital: rte. Impériale (☎04 95 59 11 11).

Police: rue Commandant Luce de Casablanca (☎04 95 55 22 22).

Internet Access: Cybercafé, 2 rue Castagno (☎04 95 34 30 34), in the old city. 25F/€3.81 per 30min. Open July-Aug. M-Sa 11am-1am; Sept.-June noon-1am.

Post Office: (☎04 95 32 80 70). At the intersection of av. Maréchal Sebastiani and bd. Général Graziani. Open M-F 8am-7pm, Sa 8am-noon. **Postal code:** 20200.

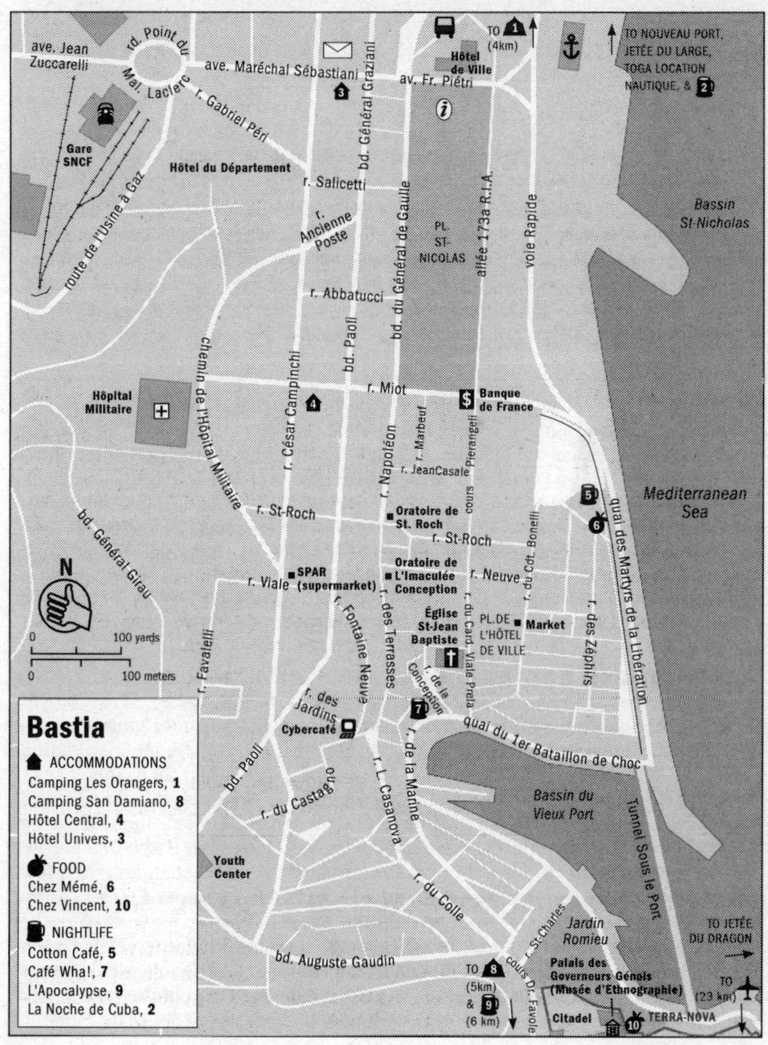

ACCOMMODATIONS AND CAMPING

Bastia's hotels are cheaper than those in Corsica's more popular resort towns. Off-season discounts and vacancies are common, but from June to September, call ahead. Campsites are far from town but well-serviced by local buses.

Hôtel Central, 3 rue Miot (☎04 95 31 71 12; fax 04 95 31 82 40; infos@centralhotel.fr). The motherly owner will make you feel welcome. The hotel *is* central; besides, it's got large and well-kept rooms with renovated bathrooms. Breakfast Apr.-Oct. 35F/€5.34, Nov.-Mar. 30F/€4.57. Singles with shower 230-260F/€35.07-39.64, with bath 280-300F/€42.69-45.74; doubles with shower 250-280F/€38.12-42.69, with bath 280-350F/€42.69-53.36, with bath, balcony, and kitchenette 400F/€60.98; triples 350-430F/€53.36-65.56; quads 490F/€74.71. Extra bed 80F/€12.20. AmEx/MC/V.

Hôtel Univers, 3 av. Maréchal Sebastiani (☎04 95 31 03 38; fax 04 95 31 19 91). Clean and modern rooms with colorful bedspreads. Breakfast 35F/€5.34. Singles 200F/€30.49, with bath 350F/€53.36; doubles 200F/€30.49, 400F/€60.98; triples 250F/€38.12, 450F/€68.61; quads 300F/€45.74, 600F/€91.50. Prices 50F/€7.62 higher in Aug. and 50-100F/€7.62-15.25 lower Sept.-June. AmEx/V.

Les Orangers, (☎04 95 33 24 09). To get there, take bus #4 from the tourist office to "Mioma Liciola" (every hr., 7.50F/€1.14), or follow bd. de Toga, parallel to the sea. A small, bare-minimum site 30 seconds from a popular pebble beach. Open Apr.-Oct. 15. 25F/€3.81 per person, 13F/€1.98 per tent, 10F/€1.53 per car. Electricity 20F/€3.05.

Camping San Damiano, Lido de la Marana (☎04 95 33 68 02; fax 04 95 30 84 10), is 5km south of Bastia. **S.T.I.B.** (☎04 95 31 06 65) sends buses from the bus station near pl. St-Nicolas. June-Aug. M-F 8 per day, Sa-Su 3 per day. 40F/€6.10. Camping open Apr.-Oct. 32F/€4.88 per person, 35F/€5.34 in July, 38F/€5.80 in Aug.; 12F/€1.83 per tent; 12F/€1.83 per car. Electricity 18F/€2.75.

FOOD

Inexpensive cafés crowd **pl. St-Nicolas.** The best food and most scenic views can be found at the **citadel,** along the **Vieux Port,** and on the broad terraces of the **quai des Martyrs de la Libération** along the boardwalk. Early birds hit the **market** on pl. de l'Hôtel de Ville (Tu-Su 6am-1pm). **SPAR supermarket** is at 14 rue César Campinchi. (☎04 95 35 45 65. Open M-Sa 8:30am-12:30pm and 2:30-7:30pm.) Just inside the citadel, **Chez Vincent,** 12 rue St-Michel, provides delectable pizzas (38-50F/€5.80-7.62) on a lovely terrace overlooking the sea. (☎04 95 31 62 50. Open daily 9:30am-3pm and 6:30pm-midnight. MC/V.) The seaside **Chez Mémé,** at the north end of quai des Martyrs de la Libération, has an unbeatable Corsican *menu* for 90F/€13.72. (☎04 95 31 44 12. Open daily noon-2:30pm and 7-11:30pm. AmEx/MC/V.)

SIGHTS AND BEACHES

A walk through Bastia's *vieille ville* reveals the town's former glory days as queen of Genoese-ruled Corsica. To the north, the 1380 **citadel,** also called Terra Nova, was the spot from which the Genoese projected their power over the island. Inside the fortified walls, the massive 1530 **Palais des Gouverneurs Génois** was the town's first building—now closed for renovations. Walking toward the citadel from pl. St-Nicolas on rue Napoléon, you'll stumble across the **Oratoire de St. Roch,** a jewel-box of a church with crystal chandeliers. A few blocks down, the 18th-century **Oratoire de L'Imaculée Conception,** features an organ that once spent two years thumping out "God Save the Queen" daily: during Corsica's brief stint as a joint Anglo-Corsican kingdom (1794-6) the British puppet parliament was housed in the oratory. The neoclassical towers of the **Eglise St-Jean Baptiste,** pl. de l'Hôtel de Ville, cover an immense interior with gilded domes and *trompe l'œil* ceilings.

Beach time in Bastia is reserved for hard-core sun-worshipers. If you don't feel like sharing a beach with the masses, head north to the pebbly turf of **Miomo,** and, farther on, the beautiful sands of the **Cap Corse.** Bus #4 leaves every hour from pl. St-Nicolas, sometimes going as far as Macinaggio; the closest sandy beach lies between **Erbalunga** (12F/€1.83) and **Sisco** (14F/€2.14). One and a half kilometers in the opposite direction, at Montesoro, is **L'Arinella**—two kilometers of smooth, gray sand marred by freeway noise and barbed wire. Get there by following the road that leaves Bastia just beyond the citadel, or take bus #1, which leaves every 15 minutes from pl. St-Nicolas and the citadel's entrance (7.50F/€1.14).

ENTERTAINMENT

Bastia is quiet come sunset, with its nightlife concentrated in the *vieux port.* Large and airy, **Cotton Café,** 22 quai des Martyrs de la Libération, serves tropical cocktails (35F/€5.34) among plush sofas and palm trees. (☎04 95 32 36 18. Live music July-Aug. daily, Sept.-June Sa-Su. Open daily 10am-2am.) **La Noche de Cuba,** 5 rue Chanoine Leschi, near the north quai, is a laid-back Latin bar with one of Bastia's few dance floors. (☎04 95 31 02 83. Open M-Tu 6am-9pm, W-Su 6am-2am.) At the old port, **Café Wha!,** rue de la Marine, stands out with its bright neon sign and memorable name. A hip, young crowd drinks 30F/€4.57 margaritas on the outdoor patio. (☎04 95 34 25 79. Open daily 11am-1am.) Other nightlife options await in the faraway **La Marana** area, which has Bastia's real night action—beachside bars and open-air dance clubs like trendy **L'Apocalypse.** (☎04 95 33 36 83. Cover 50F/€7.62. Open F-Sa 11:30pm-5am, July-Aug. also M.)

DAYTRIP FROM BASTIA: ALERIA

***Autocars Rapides-Bleus** (☎04 95 31 03 79) run from **Bastia** (1½hr.; M-Sa 2 per day, daily July-Sept. 15; 75F/€11.43) and **Porto Vecchio** (1½hr.; M-Sa 2 per day, daily July-Sept. 15; 75F/€11.43) to Aléria's post office. Farther down the road is the **tourist office.** (☎/fax 04 95 57 01 51. Open June 15-Sept. 15 M-F 8am-1pm and 2-7:30pm, Sa 10am-1pm and 4-7:30pm, Su 9am-noon; Sept. 16-June 14 M-F 9:30am-noon and 2-6pm.)*

Present-day Aléria (pop. 2500), halfway down Corsica's uninspiring eastern coastline, pales in comparison to the city's previous incarnations. This choice spot—parallel to Carthage and opposite Rome—has seen five major civilizations: the Phoenicians, Etruscans, Greeks, Carthaginians, and Romans. The ancient site of Aléria is a mound about 1km south of the city. The summit has exceptionally long views in both directions, a fact which induced the Greeks to build a settlement there. Now the fort holds the **Musée Jérôme Carcopino** (☎04 95 57 00 92). The exhibit of Etruscan pottery, Roman artifacts—including a cosmetic kit that rivals Marie Antoinette's—and an extensive Greek collection are all worth seeing. Just past the museum is the **Roman city** itself. After passing the ruins of the Greek acropolis, enter the middle of the Roman forum; to the left is a temple to Jupiter, to the right, the extensive baths. Under Augustus, the population of the city swelled to 20,000—almost ten times that of present-day Aléria. A walk around its perimeter helps you grasp these ancient dimensions. Archaeologists are only beginning to uncover the city's network of bedrooms and shops. (Museum open May 16-Sept. daily 8am-noon and 2-7pm; Oct.-May 15 M-F 8am-noon and 2-5pm; Roman city closes 30min. earlier. 10F/€1.53 for both, students 5F/€0.76.)

CAP CORSE

Stretching north from Bastia, the Cap Corse peninsula is a string of former fishing villages connected by a narrow road of perilous curves and breathtaking views. The 18 multi-village *communes* of Corsica's wildest frontier have largely resisted overdevelopment; the Cap is also a hiker's dream, with every jungly forest and *maquis*-covered cliff laying claim to some decaying Genoese tower or hilltop chapel. Get to a town, ask where the trails are, and you're off. Unfortunately, there are few budget hotels, and most require you to pay for dinner with your room. Camping is a better option; a handful of sites sit around the Cap.

TRANSPORTATION. A driving tour of the entire Cap is the best way to visit and takes at least half a day; consider renting a car in Bastia (see p. 340) or Calvi (see p. 331). Be alert and cautious; roads are narrow and winding, and Corsican drivers fear nothing. It's best to drive on a weekend, when traffic on the D80 thins out; you might consider starting the trip from the St-Florentine area (the west side of the peninsula), where your vehicle hugs the mountainside rather than the sea below. To start from Bastia on the west side, take bd. Paoli, then bd. Auguste Gaudin past the citadel onto N199 (dir: "St-Florentine"). For the east-to-west route, simply follow the coastal bd. north from pl. St-Nicolas, following signs for the Cap.

Cheaper than a car but far less flexible is a **bus tour. Transports Micheli,** in Ersa at the top of the peninsula, offers full-day tours of the Cap leaving from Bastia, stopping at villages and for lunch (not included) at the glorious blue slate beach at Albo. (☎04 95 35 64 02. Departs 1 rue de Nouveau Port, July-Aug. Tu, Th, and Sa 9am, returns at 6pm; 150F/€22.90.) From Calvi, **Autocars Mariani** runs similar excursions once a week (usually F), leaving at 7:30am and returning around 6:30pm. (☎04 95 65 04 72. Apr. 15-Sept. 16, 160F/€24.39.) Individual destinations such as **Centuri, Rogliano,** and **St-Florent** are serviced by several companies. Updated schedules and phone numbers for buses can be found in *Découverte Cap Corse*, an indispensable guide free at tourist offices. The cheapest and most convenient way to see the eastern side of Cap Corse is to take public **bus #4** from pl. St-Nicolas in Bastia. The bus leaves for **Erbalunga** (20min.; M-F every 30min., Sa-Su every hr.; 12F/€1.83) and **Marina di Siscu** (30min., every hr., 14F/€2.14); it also goes all the way to **Macinaggio** (50min., M-Sa 2 per day, 40F/€6.10). Ask nicely and the driver will drop you off wherever you feel the urge to explore. But keep in mind that most buses serve only the coast; you'll have to hike to get to the inland villages. (☎04 95 31 06 65. Service generally daily 6:30am-7:30pm.) You can also see the Cap by boat with **Compagnie Saint Jean,** Old Port. A fun-loving staff gives 1½-hour tours of the coast from April to October. (☎04 95 54 20 40 or 06 09 53 55 03. 100F/€15.25.) For updates on Cap tourism, contact the **Communauté de la Commune du Cap Corse,** Maison du Cap Corse, 20200 Ville di Pietra Bugno (☎04 95 31 02 32).

ERBALUNGA

The most accessible of Cap Corse's villages, **Erbalunga** makes a relaxing afternoon excursion from nearby Bastia. However, once you reach this tiny fishing hamlet, where fishermen drop lines from their sea-hugging houses, you'll never want to leave. Along the crystal blue waters, white pebble beaches and flat, secluded rocks invite sunbathers. In the hills above, Benedictine monks observe a vow of silence at the **Monastère du St-Sacrement,** which you can pass by on a short hike that begins to the right of a restaurant, **La Petite Auberge.** M. and Mme. Morganti serve Corsican specialties including seafood (75-100F/€11.43-15.25) and pastas (50-60F/€7.62-9.15); to get there, follow the main road three minutes north of the bus station. (☎04 95 33 20 78. Open daily 9am-3pm and 6pm-whenever. MC/V.) A supermarket, **SPAR,** is across from the bus station. (☎04 95 33 24 24. Open M-Sa 8am-12:30pm and 4-5:30pm, Su 8am-noon.) Two and a half kilometers south, in **Lavasina,** is the famous **Eglise de Notre-Dame des Graces,** where thousands make a candlelit pilgrimage on Sept. 8 to celebrate the miracle that gave the church its name. A disabled nun from Bonifacio, so the story goes, was miraculously granted the use of her legs after praying to an image of the Virgin that hangs in this church.

HIKE: SISCO

The *Découverte Cap Corse* guide, free at tourist offices, comes with a map listing 21 possible itineraries; hike #9, from **Sisco** (2hr.), is one of the best. Take bus #4 from pl. St-Nicolas to Marina di Sisco (30min., every hr., 14F/€2.14) and walk straight on route D32. Follow the painted orange rectangles as you begin to penetrate dense forests and expansive valleys, passing through miniature villages. The path ultimately leads to **Petrapiana,** where it intersects with other routes, but make sure you take a break at **Barriggioni** to admire the grandiose elegance of the **Eglise**

St-Martin, which houses the eerie, bronzed remains of St. John Chrysostomos. From here, you can also make a short detour by following the signs behind the church to visit the 11th-century **Chapelle St-Michel,** perched precariously on a hilltop promontory; when you get to the grove of ferns, turn right. Though you can't enter the chapel, the striking, panoramic view of the bowl-shaped valley below, sprinkled with Renaissance belltowers, is definitely worth the climb.

ROGLIANO

To get to this architecturally superb little town, take bus #4 to Macinaggio and walk or drive inland on route D353, which starts in front of the church, for about 5km. (Buses M-Sa 2 per day, 40F/€6.10.) This hilltop village's crumbling monuments seem to defy both gravity and time. At the heart of the village is the 16th- to 17th-century **Eglise St-Agnellu,** with its three-story belltower and Carrara marble altar, the latter a gift from emigrants who made their fortunes in Puerto Rico. Around the bend to the right of the church, turn left on chemin du Couvent to climb up to the impressive ruins of the **Château de la Mare,** a monumental Genoese fort that remains remarkably intact. If these buildings seem unduly large for a town of Rogliano's size, there's a reason: at 300 residents, the town has only a tenth of its sometime population. Before heading back to Macinaggio, treat yourself to an ice cream and breathtaking panoramic views at **Le Brasier.**

MACINAGGIO TO CENTURI: THE CAPANDULA

Crystal-clear waters, white sandy beaches, and deep-green escarpments characterize the "cap of the cap," an arid and windy extreme at the tip of Cap Corse. Inaccessible to cars, the Capandula—as this area is called—is a protected national reserve, being the last stop for African migratory birds heading north. That means that camping is forbidden, but hikers and bikers are blessed by the *sentier de Douaniers*, an extraordinary coastal trail named after the customs officials who first walked it. Beginning in **Macinaggio** or **Centuri,** the 8hr. hike passes by Genoese towers, secluded beaches, dramatic cliffs, and two villages. There are no amenities en route; bring lots of water, durable shoes, and sunscreen.

From the east coast, the trail takes off from **Macinaggio,** Rogliano's beachside sister, the spot to which Corsican leader Paolo Paoli returned in 1790 after 20 years of exile from his beloved island. Forty kilometers from Bastia, it's one of the few port towns where you can find supplies and services. The **tourist office,** above the *Capitainerie,* has small maps of the trail. (☎04 95 35 40 34. Open July-Aug. daily 9am-noon and 4-8pm; June and Sept. 1-15 daily 9am-noon and 2-7pm; Sept. 16-May M-F 9am-noon and 2-5pm.) Camping is a good bet here at **U Stazzu,** just steps away from the beach. Get there by following the signs on the road by the church. (☎04 95 35 43 76. Open Apr.-Sept. 30F/€4.57 per person, 15F/€2.29 per tent.) Enjoy Cap Corse cuisine at **Ostéria di u Portu,** right on the waterfront. Hearty 80F/€12.20 *menu.* (☎04 95 35 40 49. Open daily noon-2:30pm and 7-10:30pm.)

The miniature port of **Centuri** at the other end of the trail is one of the Cap's most picturesque spots, a place to sit at sunset and watch the boats bring in their daily haul of lobsters, mussels, and fish. On calm days, you can swim out from the rocky shores to a small nearby island. **Camping Caravaning L'isulotto,** just south of the town, has lots of amenities 150m from the sea. (☎04 95 35 62 81; fax 04 95 35 63 63. Adult 28F/€4.27, tent 15F/€2.29, car 10F/€1.53. Electricity 20F/€3.05.)

PORTO VECCHIO

Porto Vecchio (pop. 9000) features some of the best beaches in Corsica—turquoise waters alongside stretches of golden sand, all seven to twenty-five kilometers from town. The town itself, with its little hilltop citadel, is charming in a touristy way, but unreasonably expensive. Outside of high season, car-less travelers should steer clear of Porto Vecchio; its beaches, the only reason to come here, are only served by public transport during July and August.

TRANSPORTATION

Buses: Eurocorse Voyages (☎04 95 70 13 83) stops in front of Trinitours on rue Pasteur, behind the tourist office. To: **Ajaccio** (3hr.; M-Sa 3 per day, daily July-Sept. 15; 125F/€19.06) and **Bonifacio** (30min.; 1 per day, July-Sept. 15 4 per day; 40F/€6.10). **Autocars Rapides-Bleus** (☎04 95 31 03 79) stop outside the citadel walls in front of Corsicatours, 7 rue Jean Jaurès. To **Aléria** (1½hr., 75F/€11.43) and **Bastia** (3hr.; M-Sa 2 per day, July-Sept. 15 daily; 115F/€17.53).

Ferries: Intersud Voyages (☎04 95 70 06 03) has info. **SNCM** sails to **Marseille** (10hr.; 3 per week; 265-300F/€40.40-45.74, under 25 230-265F/€35.06-40.40).

Bike Rental: Les Années Jeunes, av. Georges Pompidou (☎04 95 70 36 50). To get there, turn left onto rue du Casavina from rue Pasteur and walk down to the roundabout. Bike 80F/€12.20 per day; scooters from 230F/€35.06 per day. No rentals for first-time scooter drivers. Open M-Sa 9am-noon and 2:30-7pm.

Taxi: ☎04 95 70 08 49.

ORIENTATION AND PRACTICAL INFORMATION

The **citadel,** centered on pl. de la République and the Eglise St-Jean-Baptiste, is bisected by cours Napoléon. Two blocks down, **Porte Génoise,** off rue Borgo along the citadel wall, leads from to the port. In the opposite direction from pl. de la République is **rue du Général Leclerc,** with the town's banks and post office. The tourist office is around the corner from pl. de la République. From rue Napoléon, walk through pl. de la République and turn right.

Tourist Office: (☎04 95 70 09 58; fax 04 95 70 03 72; www.accueil-portovecchio.com). Maps and hiking info. Open June-Sept. M-Sa 9am-7:30pm, Su 9am-1pm; Oct.-May M-F 9am-12:30pm and 2-6pm, Sa 9am-12:30pm.)

Money: Credit Lyonnais, at the corner of rue Fred Scamaroni and rue du Général Leclerc (☎04 95 70 94 81). Competitive rates of exchange. 25F/€3.81 commission on US dollars. Open M-F 8:30am-noon and 1:30-5pm.

Laundromat: in the *capitainerie* on the port.

Hospital: just north of town on rte. de Bastia (☎04 95 73 80 00).

Internet Access: Tabac Terrazzoni, 6 rue de Camille de Rocca Serra (☎04 95 70 01 39), a convenience store with one computer, next to the tourist office. 20F/€3.05 per 15min., 60F/€9.15 per hr. Open July-Aug. daily 8am-midnight; Sept.-June 8am-12:30pm and 2-8pm.

Post Office: rue du Général Leclerc (☎04 95 70 95 00), just behind the citadel. Open M-F 8:30am-6pm, Sa 8:30am-noon. **Postal code:** 20137.

ACCOMMODATIONS AND CAMPING

Corsica's trendiest town costs a small fortune in summer; travelers with wheels should avoid July and August. Otherwise, call ahead and pray there are vacancies at the following recommendations.

Le Modern, 10 cours Napoléon (☎04 95 70 06 36; www.modernhotel.ifrance.com). Minimalist whitewashed rooms in a prime location. Rooms on the top floor share a balcony with ocean views. Open Apr.-Sept. Doubles with shower: Apr. 250F/€38.12, June 300F/€45.74, July 400F/€60.98, Aug. 480F/€73.18; with bath 20-70F/€3.05-10.67 more. Triples: Apr. 350F/€53.36, July 450F/€68.61, Aug. 650F/€99.10.

U Palmu, on the port (☎04 95 70 33 26; fax 04 95 70 37 59). Large suites include a kitchen, living room, bathroom, and balcony; lower-floor rooms can be noisy in summer. Breakfast 40F/€6.10. Doubles Apr.-June and Sept. 350F/€53.36; July 400F/€60.98; Aug. 500F/€76.23; Oct.-Mar. 250F/€38.12. Extra bed 100F/€15.25. MC/V.

Hôtel da Mama, rte. de Bonifacio (☎04 95 70 56 64; fax 04 95 70 27 69). Walk south for 10min. along rue du Général Leclerc until it turns into rue Jean Jaurès, then into av. du Maréchal Juin, and then into rte. de Bonifacio. Simple rooms at more affordable prices. Breakfast 30F/€4.57. Doubles Apr.-June 14 220F/€33.54, with bath 280F/€42.69; June 15-July 14 and Sept. 280F/€42.69, with bath 360F/€54.89; July 15-Aug. 340F/€51.84, with bath 520F/€79.28. Extra bed 120F/€18.30. AmEx/MC/V.

Camping: La Matonara, Les Quatres Chemins (☎/fax 04 95 70 37 05), is a large, tree-shaded clearing 4min. from town. Take rue du Général Leclerc to the roundabout; buses from Bastia stop at the site. 30F/€4.57 per person, children under 7 10F/€1.53; 14F/€2.13 per tent; 12F/€1.83 per car. Electricity 15F/€2.29.

FOOD

The lively, crowded citadel is full of restaurants, all catering to tourists, and most quite expensive; crêpes and generic Italian food are the cheapest things to eat. You can get fresh Corsican specialties at the **market** on place de la Mairie (Su 8:30am-1pm). **Chez Mimi,** 5 rue du Général Abbatucci, makes delicious, filling meals on a little street behind the church. Vegetarian options, affordable seafood, and the 85F/€12.96 *menu* are best enjoyed on the patio—there's not much atmosphere within. (☎04 95 70 28 54. Open daily noon-2:30pm and 7pm-about midnight. MC/V.)

BEACHES

Porto Vecchio's daytime itinerary is simple and easy to follow: hit the sand. On an island full of memorable beaches, those on the Golfe de Porto Vecchio are truly special. Reaching them takes work: public buses only run during July and August. During high season, **Trinitours** (☎04 95 70 13 83) leaves from Camping Matonara and rue Pasteur for **Palombaggia,** with early-morning departures and early-evening returns (1 per day, 25F/€3.81). **Autocars Bradesi** (☎04 95 71 40 09) leaves from the church for **San Cipriano** and **Pinarello** (M-Sa 2 per day, 15-20F/€2.29). **Corsicatours** (☎04 95 70 10 36) leaves from Camping Matonara and the port for **Santa Giulia** (M-Sa 4 per day, 15F/€2.29). Schedules can be found at the tourist office.

Mile-long **Palombaggia** is one of Corsica's most famous beaches. Vacationers fill the sandy stretch in summer, but crowds thin out farther from the parking lot. The longer and more scenic way to Palombaggia winds around the peninsula, past a few small beaches and a large nudist colony. Head south from Porto Vecchio on N198, until the first turn-off, a giant boating billboard. You can get there faster by following N198 a little farther south and hanging a left at the "Ladu" billboard. A taxi costs about 150F/€22.90 on weekdays and 210F/€32.02 on weekends. **Santa Giulia,** farther south, is the most beautiful of Porto Vecchio's spots, a perfect circle of sand ringing a giant bay. From N198, turn left at the "Moby Dick/Castelli Verde" billboard. Though slightly removed from the spotlight, the beaches north of Porto Vecchio are also worthwhile. **Punta di Benedettu** is the first you'll hit, but it's worth continuing onward to the laid-back little paradise of **San Cipriano,** 20km to the north. Another 2km north is picturesque, remote **Pinarellu,** which looks out to the Ile de Pinarellu and the remains of a medieval castle.

ENTERTAINMENT

Cafés and ice cream shops on **pl. de la République** are the main evening hangouts, especially for the families visiting Porto Vecchio; bars in the port and old town cater to older, more staid crowds. On pl. de la République, two side-by-side bars are mainstays: **Shankabar** attracts a trendy bunch to its red-cushioned interior and outdoor patio with a DJ. (☎04 95 70 06 53. Open Apr.-Dec. daily 7am-2am.) Next door, at the classy **Le Tempo,** an older crowd lounges amid leather couches and hardwood tables. (☎04 95 70 16 28. Open July-Aug. daily 7am-2am; Sept.-June 7am-midnight.) For an unpretentious night of fun, **Pub Le Bastion,** 11 rue de la Citadelle, features a wide assortment of beers in its cave-like interior. (☎04 95 70 69 70. Local rock bands F-Sa. Open daily 9:30pm-5am.) **Via Notte,** a disco between Porto Vecchio and Bonifacio, is famous throughout Corsica, and for good reason; the elaborate outdoor club features cabana bars around luxurious swimming pools. To get there, follow the road to Bonifacio about 4km until a large blue and white sign tells you to turn left; after 500m, a second sign has you turn right. Walking takes about 45 minutes, while a taxi costs around 80F/€12.20. (☎04 95 72 02 12. Cover 70F/€10.67. Women free W. Open July-Aug. daily 10pm-5am; June 15-30 Sa 11pm-5am.)

BONIFACIO (BONIFAZIU)

The fortified city of Bonifacio (pop. 3000) rises like a Genoese sandcastle atop limestone cliffs tumbling straight into the sea. Both the landscape and the settlement here seem to have been carved by a master sculptor, from the sheltered port to the crescent-moon beaches to the magical *haute ville* hovering above it all. Although these spectacular vistas come with astronomical price tags and hordes of photo-snapping tourists, Bonifacio is not to be missed.

TRANSPORTATION

Buses: Eurocorse Voyages (☎04 95 21 06 30 in Ajaccio, ☎04 95 70 13 83 in Porto Vecchio) stops by the small ticket and info office in the port parking lot. To **Ajaccio** (3½hr.; M-Sa 2 per day, daily July-Sept. 15; 125F/€19.06) with stops at **Sartène** (1½hr., 60F/€9.15) and **Propriano** (2hr., 65F/€9.91). Also to **Porto Vecchio** (30min.; 1 per day, 4 per day July-Sept. 15; 40F/€6.10).

Ferries: leave from the *gare maritime* at the far end of the port. To: **Santa Teresa,** Sardinia (1hr.). **SAREMAR** (☎04 95 73 00 96; fax 04 95 73 13 37; July-Aug. 4 per day, Apr.-June and Sept. 3-Oct. 14 3 per day, Oct. 15-Mar. 2 per day; 45-56F/€6.86-8.54, cars 129-183F/€19.67-27.91). **Moby** is more expensive but has later departure times in summer (☎04 85 73 00 29; fax 04 95 73 05 50; July-Aug. 10 per day, Apr.-June and Sept.-Oct. 4 per day; 50-75F/€7.62-11.43, cars 140-280F/€21.35-42.69).

Taxis: at the port (☎04 95 73 19 08).

Bike and Scooter Rental: Corse Moto Services, quai Nord, on the port (☎04 95 73 15 16). Scooters 250F/€38.12 per day, 1600F/€243.94 per week, 2000F/€304.92 deposit. Open July-Aug. daily 10am-noon and 3-7pm. MC/V. **Tam Tam** (☎04 95 73 11 59). A windsurfing shop 200m from the port on D58, the road veering away from the citadel. Bikes 75F/€11.43 per 24hr., 450F/€68.61 per week. Open July-Aug. M-Sa 9am-1pm and 3:30-8pm; June and Sept. 9:30am-12:30pm and 3:30-7:30pm.

ORIENTATION AND PRACTICAL INFORMATION

Bonifacio is divided into the **port** and the **haute ville,** with a steep climb in between. The major highway is N198, which becomes av. Sylvère Bohn near the entrance to the town; when you hit Bonifacio, you'll see the port on your right, with the *haute ville* looming above it. Above the parking lot, the main road quickly veers left to become D58, a road to the nearby beaches. The most direct route to the tourist office is a walk along the port and up the stairs before the *gare maritime.*

Tourist Office: corner of av. de Gaulle and rue F. Scamaroni (☎04 95 73 11 88; fax 04 95 73 14 97; www.bonifacio.com). Open May-Oct. 15 daily 9am-8pm; Oct. 16-Apr. M-F 9am-noon and 2-6pm, Sa 9am-noon. **Annex** by the port open July-Aug. daily 9am-8pm.

Money: If you can, **exchange currency** in another city. **Change,** inside an art gallery on the port (☎04 95 73 56 16), charges a hefty 4% and 40F/€6.10 commission. Open July-Aug. daily 8am-midnight; Apr.-June and Sept. 8am-10pm; Oct. 10am-6pm.

Laundromat: on the port.

Police: on the port (☎04 95 73 00 17).

Hospital: toward the beaches on D58 (☎04 95 73 95 73).

Internet Access: Cybercafé, on the port (☎04 95 73 55 45). 15F/€2.29 for 15min., 50F/€7.62 per hr. Open daily 8am-2am.

Post Office: rue Simon Varsi (☎04 95 73 73 73), uphill from pl. Bonaparte near the citadel. Open M-F 8:30am-7:15pm, Sa 8:30am-noon. **Postal Code:** 20169.

ACCOMMODATIONS AND CAMPING

Finding a room in the summer is virtually impossible. Camping is by far the cheapest option, and many sites offer affordable lodging in bungalows or chalets. Porto Vecchio also has some cheaper hotels, making daytrips an economic option.

Hôtel des Etrangers, av. Sylvère Bohn (☎04 95 73 01 09; fax 04 95 73 16 97), on the road to Bonifacio. Spare, white rooms with bath, A/C, and TV. Breakfast included. Closed Oct. 30-Mar. 25. June-Sept. singles 290F/€44.21, doubles 360-390F/€54.89-59.46, triples 340-390F/€51.84-59.46, quads 390-490F/€59.46-74.71; Mar. 26-May and Oct. singles and doubles 250-290F/€38.12-44.21, triples 340-390F/€51.84, quads 390-490F/€59.46-74.74. Extra bed 60F/€9.15. MC/V.

Hôtel Le Royal, pl. Bonaparte (☎04 95 73 00 51; fax 04 95 73 04 68), in the *haute ville*. Modern blue-and-white rooms, all with bath, A/C, TV, and some with sweeping views of the sea. Singles Apr. 250F/€38.12, June and Oct. 290F/€44.21, July and Sept. 400F/€60.98, Aug. 600F/€91.48, Nov.-Mar. 200F/€30.49; doubles Apr. 290F/€44.21, June and Oct. 320F/€48.79, July and Sept. 450F/€68.61, Aug. 600F/€91.48, Nov.-Mar. 250F/€38.12. 30-50F/€4.57-7.62 more for rooms facing the port.

L'Araguina, av. Sylvère Bohn (☎04 95 73 02 96; fax 04 95 73 57 04; www.corse.sud/camping.araguina), at the beginning of town between Hôtel des Etrangers and the port. Makes up for an unceremonious, crowded setup by its proximity to the beaches and town. Open Mar. 15-Oct. 33-37F/€5.03-5.64 per person; 11F/€1.68 per tent or car. Electricity 16F/€2.44. 5-person bungalows also available for weekly rental.

Campo di Liccia, 4km from the beach and town (☎04 95 73 03 09; fax 04 95 73 19 94). The cheapest in a cluster of campsites on the road to Porto Vecchio. Pool. Open Apr.-Oct. 29-37F/€4.42-5.64 per person, 12F/€1.83 per tent, 19F/€2.90 per car. Electricity 16F/€2.44.

FOOD

Bonifacio's port is packed with repetitive, tourist-trapping restaurants. Make the climb to the *haute ville* for more authentic Corsican cuisine. For an excellent, filling meal, **Cantina Doria,** 27 rue Doria, in the *haute ville*, serves hearty regional specialties on wooden picnic tables. Sample their best bites with the hearty 85F/€12.96 *menu*. (☎04 95 73 50 49. Open Apr.-Oct. daily noon-3pm and 7-11pm. MC/V.) Alternatively, a couple of **supermarkets** line the port, and there's a popular **market** on place Loggia de l'Arsenal in the *haute ville* (W 8am-5pm).

SIGHTS

With 3km of fortifications above curvy white cliffs, Bonifacio is a marvel of man-made and natural architecture. Make sure to take a **boat tour** from one of the many companies on the port. The friendly staff at **Marina Croisières** gives tours of coves and limestone grottoes with optional add-ons to the **Iles Lavezzi** (see **Beaches,** below). (☎04 95 73 09 77 or 06 82 66 35 02. 70-140F/€10.67-21.35.) There's also a small **aquarium** on the port, where you'll learn that some crabs can fly and some lobsters are blue. (☎04 95 73 03 69. Open July-Aug. daily 10am-midnight; Apr.-June and Sept. 10am-9pm; Oct. 10am-5pm. 22F/€3.36, students 16F/€2.44.)

To explore the *haute ville* from the inside, head up montée Rastello, the steep, wide staircase halfway down the port, which offers excellent views of the harsh cliffs stretching east from Bonifacio. Continue up montée St-Roch to the lookout at **Porte de Gênes.** This drawbridge, constructed in 1588 to be the town's only entrance, is emphatically *not* Genoese. Eager to overthrow the imperial Italians, Corsican nationals joined forces with King Henri II to besiege the town. After successfully destroying the Genoese fortress with 6000 bullets, the triumphant rebels immediately began rebuilding a bigger and better one on the original ruins. Both the Porte de Gênes and the **Bastion de L'Etendard** next door are actually built in French military style—ironically, the first presence of Corsica's future encroachers. Though once a dungeon for prisoners, the Bastion is now a trap for tourists; the hokey historical displays inside the fortress are not worth your 10F/€1.53.

After soaking up all this history, stick to the left and head over to pl. du Marché for the best views of Bonifacio's famous cliffs and limestone formation, **Grain de Sable.** The little mound just out of reach is Sardinia, 12km away. Turn right on rue Cardinal to visit the **Eglise Ste-Mairie-Majeure,** Bonifacio's oldest building. This 12th-century church houses one of the town's most important objects: a morsel of the **true cross,** stripped from a shipwreck. Continue through Bonifacio's tiny, winding streets to reach the **cemetery** at the southern tip of the *haute ville.* This cemetery—like all burial grounds in Corsica—marks the dead with elaborate miniature mausolea instead of stones. On Corsica, they say, even death is beautiful.

 BEACHES

Bonifacio's beaches are hard to get to and harder to leave. The only ones within walking distance of town are intimate but uninspiring; a path leads from Camping l'Araguina to **plage de la Catena** (30min.) and the cleaner and prettier **plage de l'Arinella** (45min.). The peninsula east of Bonifacio is filled with good beaches, but you'll a car to get there. From the port, take D58 towards the water; virtually every road stemming from it leads to a beach. Isolated **Cala Longa** is 8km away; 6km farther is **plage Maora,** a large beach in a calm natural harbor. The turn- off for camping Rondinara, 10km north, leads to **plage de Rondinara,** one of Corsica's most famous beaches. You'll recognize its dunes and lagoons from postcards.

Even more impressive than the mainland beaches are the pristine sands of the **Iles Lavezzi.** All of the companies by the port run frequent ferries (30min.) to this nature reserve, where rock formations and expansive fields set a picturesque backdrop for calm turquoise waters. Just off the island, there are beautiful reefs, perfect for **scuba diving. Atoll,** on the port, offers dives for beginners or advanced divers. (☎04 95 73 53 83; fax 04 95 73 17 72; atoll@sitec.fr. Open Apr.-Nov. daily 8am-7:30pm. Dives 235-365F/€35.84-55.66.)

THE ALPS (LES ALPES)

Natural architecture is the Alps' real attraction. The curves of the Chartreuse Valley rise to rugged crags in the Vercors range and ultimately crescendo into Europe's highest peak, Mont Blanc. Skiers enjoy some of the most challenging slopes in the world; in the summer hikers take over the same mountains for their endless vistas and clean air. With two high seasons a year, you'll have to choose between the dependable crowds, dependable prices, and dependable weather of summer and winter, and the quieter but less predictable months between them.

The Alps are split between two historical provinces, Savoy and Dauphiné. The Dauphiné includes the Chartreuse Valley, Vercors regional park, Ecrins national park, the Belledonne and Oisans mountains, and Grenoble, its largest city. The region first became independent in the 11th century, under Guiges I. His great-grandson Guiges IV, evidently tiring of his family's favorite name, took the surname "Dauphin" (dolphin); in time the name acquired the status of a title. In the 14th century, when the last independent Dauphin sold his lands to France, the French monarchs adopted the practice of ceding the province to the heir to the throne, the Dauphin. In the 15th century, Louis XI established a permanent *parlement* (court) in Grenoble, which has since been the region's cultural and intellectual capital. Savoy, which includes the peaks of Haute Savoie, Olympic resorts in the expansive Tarentaise valley, and the awe-inspiring Vanoise park, bears the name of the oldest royal house in Europe.

Once you get to the Alps, head in the most logical direction—up. After the spring thaw, flowery meadows, icy lakes, and staggering views reward experienced and amateur hikers alike. Trails are clearly marked, but serious climbers should invest in a *Topo-Guide* (hiking map). Talk with local hiking info offices for advice on trail and weather conditions and itineraries. Skiing arrangements should be made a couple of months in advance; Chamonix and Val d'Isère are the easiest bases.

TRANSPORTATION

TGV **trains** will whisk you from Paris to Grenoble and Annecy; from there Alpine towns are serviced by scenic trains and slower **buses.** The farther into the mountains you want to go, the harder it is to get there, both in terms of travel time and frequency. Service is at least twice as frequent, especially on buses, during ski season (Dec.-Apr.). **Biking** is, needless to say, an option only for the most serious cyclist. **Hikes** range from simple strolls through mountain meadows to some of the most difficult climbing in the world. *Always* check with local hiking bureaus before starting *any* hike; there are snowstorms and avalanches even in summer.

1. **Grenoble:** Dynamic university city near snow-capped peaks and ice-blue lakes **(p. 351)**
2. **Hautrives:** Surreal, arabesque fortress made from pebbles by a local postman **(p. 359)**
3. **Chambéry:** Adorable gateway to the high Alps; Rousseau's happiest home **(p. 361)**
4. **Aix-Les-Bains and Lac du Bourget:** France's largest natural lake, plus sulfur springs **(p. 362)**
5. **Annecy:** Flower-filled, fairy-tale city on a crystalline lake; near dozens of alpine hikes **(p. 364)**
6. **Chamonix:** Famous mountain-sports town within ski range of Italy and Switzerland **(p. 369)**
7. **Val d'Isère:** Small, pricey ski town with great off-trail skiing **(p. 376)**

GRENOBLE

Every September, 55,000 students descend on Grenoble (pop. 156,203) making it one of the most dynamic cities in France. It's easy to see why so many students choose to live in the unofficial capital of the Alps. The city has the eccentric cafés, dusty bookshops, shaggy radicals, and earnest politics you'll find in any university town, but it's also near the snow-capped peaks and sapphire-blue lakes cherished by hikers, skiers, bikers, aesthetes, and set designers alike. The immigrant influx to France in the 60s gave Grenoble a sizable North and West African population, which combines with the university to accentuate the city's cosmopolitan feel.

The Alps
Pontarlier
Andelot
Frasne
Vallorbe
TO PARIS
Champagnole
SWITZERLAND
Lons-le-Saunier
FRANCHE-COMTÉ
BOURGOGNE
Lausanne
Lac Léman
Montreux
St-Amour
Evian
Thonon-Les-Bains
HAUTE-SAVOIE
Geneva
Annemasse
Martigny
Bourg-en-Bresse
Montréal la Cluse
Fort-l'Ecluse-Collonges
Bellegarde
Bonneville
Vallorcine
La-Roche-sur-Foron
SAVOIE
6 Chamonix
Tunnel de Mont Blanc
Ambérieu
5 Annecy
la Clusaz
St Gervais
Menthon
Talloires
Duingt
Megève
Mont Blanc (4807 m)
Rhône
Lac du Bourget 4
Lac d'Annecy
PENNINE ALPS
Abbaye d'Hautecombe
Mont Revard
Aix-les-Bains 4
Albertville
Isère
Bourg-St-Maurice
les Arcs
TO LYON
Chambéry 3
Tignes
LA CHARTREUSE
7 Val d'Isère
La Vanoise National Park
St-Laurent-du-Pont
Voiron
St-Pierre-de-Chartreuse
Lanslebourg
Arc
Modane
TO 2 HAUTE-RIVES
1 Grenoble
Chamrousse
l'Alpe-d'Huez
GRAIAN ALPS
DAUPHINÉ
Varces
Vizille
le Bourg d'Oisans
Pont-en-Royans
Villard-de-Lans
les Deux-Alpes
ITALY
Gresse-en-Vercours
Briançon
la Mure
Vassieux
Drac
St-Firmin
Guisane
COTTIAN ALPS
Saillans
Châtillon-en-Diois
N
Gap
Lac de Serre-Ponçon
Durance
Ubaye
Serres
MARITIME ALPS
Sisteron
0 20 miles
0 20 kilometers
TO AIX AND NICE
Ain
Isère

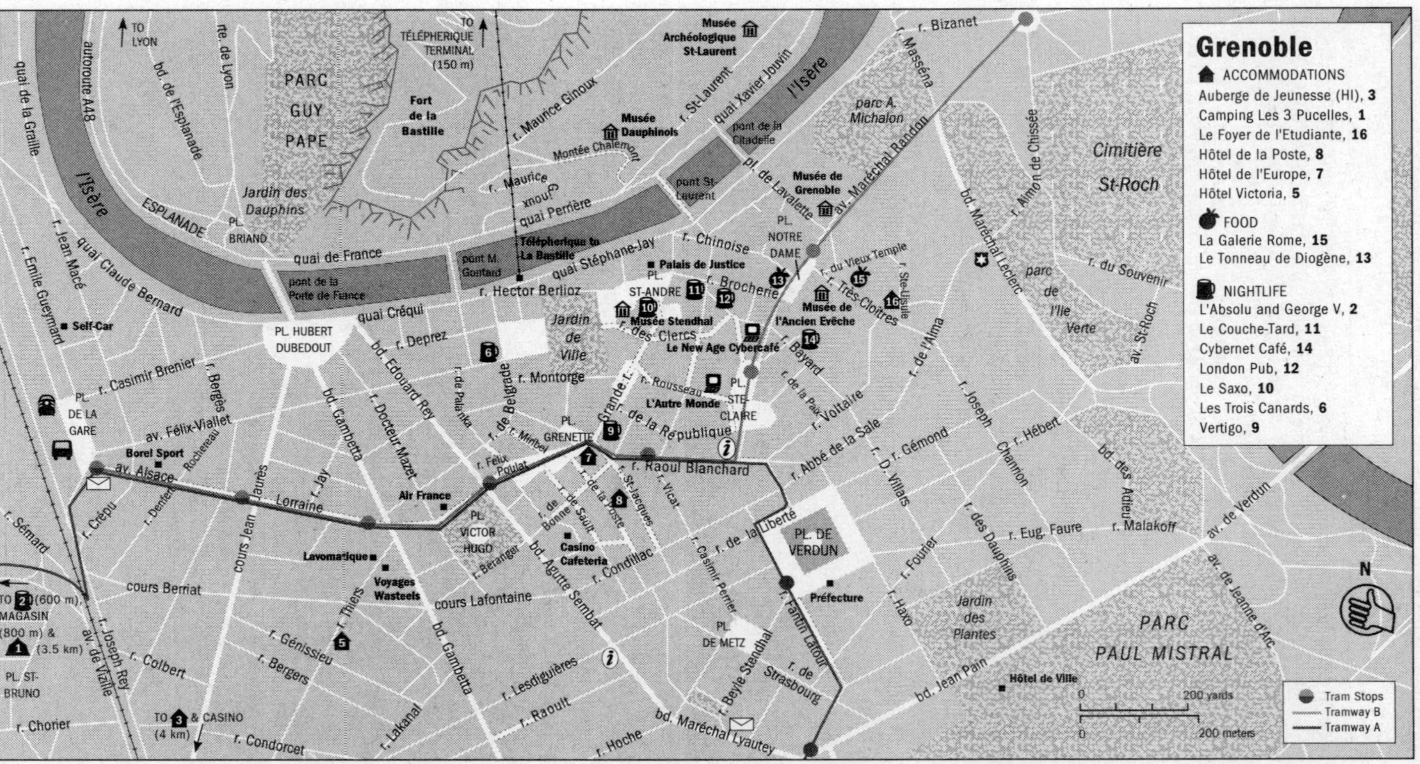
Grenoble
ACCOMMODATIONS
Auberge de Jeunesse (HI), 3
Camping Les 3 Pucelles, 1
Le Foyer de l'Etudiante, 16
Hôtel de la Poste, 8
Hôtel de l'Europe, 7
Hôtel Victoria, 5
FOOD
La Galerie Rome, 15
Le Tonneau de Diogène, 13
NIGHTLIFE
L'Absolu and George V, 2
Le Couche-Tard, 11
Cybernet Café, 14
London Pub, 12
Le Saxo, 10
Les Trois Canards, 6
Vertigo, 9
Tram Stops
Tramway B
Tramway A
0 200 yards
0 200 meters
N
PARC GUY PAPE
Fort de la Bastille
TO TÉLÉPHERIQUE TERMINAL (150 m)
Musée Archéologique St-Laurent
Musée Dauphinois
Musée de Grenoble
Palais de Justice
Musée Stendhal
Le New Age Cybercafé
Musée de l'Ancien Evêche
L'Autre Monde
Téléphérique to La Bastille
Jardin des Dauphins
Jardin de Ville
Cimitière St-Roch
parc A. Michalon
parc de l'Ile Verte
Jardin des Plantes
PARC PAUL MISTRAL
Hôtel de Ville
Préfecture
Casino Cafeteria
Air France
Lavomatique
Voyages Wasteels
Borel Sport
Self-Car
l'Isère
PL. HUBERT DUBEDOUT
PL. DE LA GARE
PL. VICTOR HUGO
PL. GRENETTE
PL. ST-ANDRE
PL. NOTRE DAME
PL. STE-CLAIRE
PL. DE VERDUN
PL. DE METZ
PL. BRIAND
PL. ST-BRUNO
ESPLANADE
pont de la Porte de France
pont M. Gontard
pont St-Laurent
pont de la Citadelle
TO LYON
TO 3 & CASINO (4 km)
TO 2 (600 m), MAGASIN (800 m) & 1 (3.5 km)

ALPS

TRANSPORTATION

Flights: Aéroport de Grenoble St-Geoirs, St-Etienne de St-Geoirs (☎04 76 65 48 48), 41km away. Buses leave 1¼hr. before each flight from bus station (☎04 76 93 40 00. 99F/€15.10). Domestic flights only. **Air France,** pl. Victor Hugo (☎08 20 82 08 20). Open M-F 8:30-6pm, Sa 9am-12:15pm.

Trains: Gare Europole, pl. de la Gare. To: **Annecy** (2hr., 12 per day, 91F/€13.88); **Chambéry** (1hr., 20 per day, 57F/€8.69); **Lyon** (1½hr., 18 per day, 99F/€15.10); **Marseille** (2½-4½hr., 15 per day, 196-242F/€29.89-36.91); **Nice** (5-6½hr., 5 per day, 301F/€45.90); and **Paris** (3hr., 6 per day, 378-474F/€57.65-72.29). Ticket booths open daily 7am-9pm. **Luggage storage** M-F 8:15am-7:30pm, Sa-Su 9:25am-7:30pm. 20F/€3.05 for first piece, 10F/€1.53 for additional bags.

Buses: Left of the train station. Open M-Sa 6:15am-7pm, Su 7:15am-7pm. **VFD** (☎08 20 83 38 33; www.vfd.fr) runs to: **Chamonix** (3hr., F-M 1 per day, 168F/€25.62); **Geneva** (3hr., 1 per day, 158F/€24.10); and **Nice** (10hr., 1 per day, 324F/€49.41). Frequent service to ski resorts and outdoor areas.

Local Transportation: Transports Agglomeration Grenobloise (TAG) (☎04 76 20 66 66). Info desk in the tourist office open M-F 8:30am-6:30pm, Sa 9am-6pm. Ticket 7.50F/€1.14, *carnet* of 10 58.50F/€8.92. Day pass 20F/€3.05; week pass 70F/€10.67. Two tram lines run roughly every 10min., 5am-midnight; buses run 6am-8pm.

Taxis: (☎04 76 54 42 54). 24hr. To airport (gulp) 430F/€65.58.

Car Rental: Self Car, 24 rue Emile Gueymard (☎04 76 50 96 96), near the train station. One day from 299F/€45.60, 100km included. Weekend 570F/€86.93, 600km included. Week 1299F/€198.05, 1000km included. Each additional km 1.20F/€0.18. 21+. Open M-F 8am-noon and 2-6pm, Sa 8am-noon. AmEx/MC/V.

ORIENTATION AND PRACTICAL INFORMATION

To get to the tourist office and the center of town from the station, turn right onto pl. de la Gare and take the third left onto av. Alsace-Lorraine, following the tram tracks. Continue along the tracks on rue Félix Poulat and rue Blanchard; the tourist complex will be on your left, just before the tracks fork (15min.).

Tourist Office: 14 rue de la République (☎04 76 42 41 41; fax 04 76 00 18 98; www.grenoble-isere-tourisme.com). From the train station, tram lines A and B (dir: "Echirolles" or "Domaine Universitaire") run to "Maison du Tourisme" before forking. The complex is the center of a visitor's universe, complete with a **bank, SNCF** counter, **local bus** office, and **post office.** Good map, hotel info, and train and bus schedules. Free copies of every local tourist publication. **Tours** of the old city (ask about prices). Office open M-Sa 9am-6:30pm, Su 10am-1pm and 2-5pm.

Hiking Information: Bureau Information Montagne, 3 rue Raoul Blanchard (☎04 76 42 45 90; fax 04 76 44 67 03; infos.montagne@grande-traversee-alpes.com), across from the tourist office. An indispensable source for info on hiking, mountaineering, biking, and cross-country skiing trails. Free brochures and expert advice. Detailed guides and maps for sale. Open M-F 9am-noon and 2-6pm, Sa 10am-noon and 2-6pm. **Weather:** ☎08 36 68 02 38. **Snow info:** ☎08 36 68 04 04.

Ski and Climbing Equipment Rental: Borel Sport, 42 rue Alsace-Lorraine (☎04 76 46 47 46). Skis, boots, and poles package 65-100F/€9.91-15.25 per day. Cross-country skis 130F/€19.82 per day. Via Ferrata climbing ensemble (harness, cord, helmet) 70F/€10.67 per day. Snowshoes 30F/€4.57 per day. Open M 9am-noon and 2-7pm, Tu-Sa 9am-noon and 2-7pm, Su 8-11am; May-Oct. closed Su-M. MC/V.

Budget Travel: Voyages Wasteels, 17 rue Thiers (☎0 803 88 70 39). Cheap travel packages. Open M-F 9am-noon and 2-6pm, Sa 9am-1pm. MC/V.

Laundromat: Lavomatique, 14 rue Thiers (☎04 76 96 28 03). Open daily 7am-10pm. **Très-Cloîtres,** 5 rue Très-Cloîtres (☎04 76 96 28 03). Open daily 7am-8pm.

Police: 36 bd. Maréchal Leclerc (☎04 76 60 40 40). Take bus #31 (dir: "Malpertuis") to "Hôtel de Police." In **emergencies,** dial 17.

Hospital: Centre Hospitalier Régional de Grenoble, La Tronche (☎04 76 76 75 75).

Internet Access: L'Autre Monde, 4 rue Jean-Jacques Rousseau (☎04 76 01 00 20). 25F/€3.81 per 30min.; 40F/€6.10 per hr. Open M-F 10am-1am, Sa 1pm-1am, Su 1-10pm. **Le New Age Cybercafé,** 1 rue Barnave (☎04 76 51 94 43), by pl. Notre Dame. 25F/€3.81 per 30min. Half-price noon-2pm and 7-9pm. Open daily 8am-10pm.

Post Office: 7 bd. Maréchal Lyautey (☎04 76 43 51 39). Open M-F 8am-7pm, Sa 8am-noon. **Branch office,** 11 rue Beyle-Stendhal (☎04 76 43 51 31). Open Sept. to mid-July M-F 8am-6pm, Sa 8am-noon; mid-July to Aug. M-F 9:15am-noon and 2-5:30pm, Sa 9:15am-noon. Both have **currency exchange** with good rates and no commission. **Postal code:** 38000.

ALPS

ACCOMMODATIONS AND CAMPING

A smattering of budget hotels dot downtown Grenoble, but most do good business year-round, so it's wise to call ahead. The student guide *Carnet de route*, free at the tourist office, has info on long-term stays. The tourist office has rental info.

Le Foyer de l'Etudiante, 4 rue Ste-Ursule (☎04 76 42 00 84; fax 04 76 42 96 67; stud.feg@wanadoo.fr). From the tourist office, follow pl. Ste-Claire to pl. Notre-Dame and take rue du Vieux Temple on the far right. Stately old building encloses a frieze-lined courtyard where backpackers and students mix. Kitchen, piano, free Internet access. Sheets 20F/€3.05. Laundry. 2-night minimum. Reception 24hr. **Oct.-Apr. women only.** Dorms 60F/€9.15; singles 90F/€13.72; doubles 140F/€21.35.

Auberge de Jeunesse (HI), 10 av. du Grésivaudan (☎04 76 09 33 52; fax 04 76 09 38 99; grenoble-echirolles@fuaj.org), about 4km from Grenoble in Echirolles. From the station, follow tram tracks down av. Alsace-Lorraine to cours Jean Jaurès; turn right and the bus stop is 25m to your right. Take bus #1 (dir: "Pont Rouge") to "La Quinzaine." The hostel is one block behind the Casino supermarket. Walking, follow cours Jean Jaurès and turn right just before Casino (1hr.). A bit too far, this hostel feels like a high school, but with more British backpackers. Breakfast included. Dinner 50F/€7.62. Sheets 18F/€2.75. Laundry. Reception M-Sa 7:30am-11pm, Su 7:30-10am and 5:30-11pm. Lockout 10am-7pm. No curfew. Small 4- to 6-bed rooms 72F/€10.98 per person, over 26 102F/€15.56. Singles with bath 110F/€16.77; doubles 170F/€25.92. MC/V.

Hôtel de la Poste, 25 rue de la Poste (☎/fax 04 76 46 67 25), in the heart of the pedestrian zone. Amazingly-priced rooms with antiquated charm and TV at this homey refuge for budget travelers. Get friendly with the staff–the only shower is four feet from the reception desk. Breakfast 28F/€4.27. Singles 100F/€15.25, with shower 130F/€19.82; doubles 160-170F/€24.39-25.92, with shower 220F/€33.54; triples 190F/€28.97; quads 220F/€33.54. MC/V.

Hôtel de L'Europe, 22 pl. Grenette (☎/fax 04 76 46 16 94; hotel.europe.gre@wanadoo.fr). Across from Grenoble's most beautiful square, this hotel's facade is a landmark. Well-renovated rooms. Small gym. Breakfast 36F/€5.49. Reception 24hr. Singles 157F/€23.94, with shower 210F/€32.02, with bath 265F/€40.40; doubles 170F/€25.92, with shower 230F/€35.07, with bath 289F/€44.07; triples with bath 321F/€48.95; quads with bath 400F/€60.98. Extra bed 52F/€7.93. AmEx/MC/V.

Hôtel Victoria, 17 rue Thiers (☎04 76 46 06 36; fax 04 76 43 00 14). This quiet hotel has large, dark rooms and a retro-lounge. Breakfast 33F/€5.03. Reception 7am-11:30pm. Curfew 11:30pm. Singles with shower 183F/€27.91, with bath 216F/€32.94; doubles with shower 216/€32.94F, with bath 256F/€39.04. AmEx/MC/V.

Camping Les 3 Pucelles, 58 rue des Allobroges (☎04 76 96 45 73; fax 04 76 21 43 73), in Seyssins, just on the southwest corner of Grenoble. Take tram A (dir: "Fontaine-La Poya") to "Louis Maisonnat", then take bus #51 (dir: "Les Nalettes") to "Mas des Iles"; turn left and the site is a couple of blocks down. Small and suburban, this is the closest campsite to town and the only one open all year. 30 sites and a swimming pool. Laundry. Call ahead in the summer. 48F/€7.32 per person, tent, and car. Extra person 18F/€2.75. Electricity 14F/€2.14.

FOOD

Grenoble has many affordable restaurants, and some have discounts or student *menus*. Given the number of students, cafeteria food is almost a local specialty. **University Restaurants** (URs) open during the school year, and meal tickets are sold in *carnets* of 10 during lunch to those with a student ID. (☎04 76 57 44 00. Single ticket 15.30F/€2.33.) The two URs in Grenoble *ville* are **Restaurant d'Arsonval,** 5 rue d'Arsonval (open M-F 11:30am-1:30pm and 6:30-7:45pm); and **Restaurant du Rabot,** rue Maurice Gignoux (open daily noon-1:15pm and 6:30-7:50pm). **Monoprix,** across from the tourist office (☎04 76 96 20 09; open M-Sa 8:30am-8pm), or **Casino,** near the youth hostel (☎04 76 23 43 01. Open M-Sa 8:30am-8pm), will supply your *al fresco* feasts. There's also a **Casino Cafeteria** on rue Guetal for cheap, fast service. (☎04 76 87 62 95. Salads 14-29F/€2.14-4.42, entrees 6-24F/€0.92-3.66, hot dishes 23-42F/€3.51-6.41. Open daily 11am-9:30pm.) Grenoble hosts 17 **markets;** the most lively are on pl. St-André, pl. St-Bruno, pl. Ste-Claire, and pl. aux Herbes (all Tu-Su 6am-1pm; pl. St-Bruno also all day F; pl. Ste-Claire also open F 3-8pm).

Regional restaurants cater to locals around **pl. de Gordes,** between pl. St-André and the Jardin de Ville. There are Asian eateries between pl. Notre-Dame and the river, and they virtually own **rue Condorcet.** Pâtisseries and North African joints congregate around **rue Chenoise** and **rue St-Laurent,** between the pedestrian area and the river. Cafés and restaurants cluster around **pl. Notre-Dame** and **pl. St-André,** both in the heart of the *vieille ville.* Crusts are tossed in dozens of lively, cheap pizzerias across the river on quai Perrière, below the *téléphérique.*

La Galerie Rome, 1 rue Très-Cloîtres (☎04 76 42 82 01). A *gourmand* owner presides over flawless French cuisine including the artery-clogging *gratin dauphinois* (55F/€8.39). He takes his art as seriously as his food—the restaurant is also a gallery. Patrons can strive for wall space with brown paper and crayons on tables. Open M noon-2:30pm, Tu-Su noon-2:30pm and 7-10pm. AmEx/MC/V.

Le Tonneau de Diogène, 6 pl. Notre-Dame (☎04 76 42 38 40). Nothing compares to Th nights (Sept.-May), when local intellectuals discuss the week's philosophical question. Anyone is welcome to join in; the topic's posted out front. Open daily 9am-1am. A set of back stairs leads to **Le Sphinx** (☎04 76 44 55 08), Grenoble's finest philosophy library/bookstore. Open M noon-7pm, Tu and F-Sa 9:30am-7pm, W-Th 9:30am-10pm.

SIGHTS

THE VIEILLE VILLE. Built over 17 centuries, Grenoble's *vieille ville* is a motley but charming collection of squares, fountains, and parks. Vestiges of the Roman ramparts are most visible near the town's historic center, **pl. St-André,** now Grenoble's most popular student hangout. The 13th-century **Collegiale Saint-André** was the traditional burial place for Dauphins before the French crown acquired both land and title in 1349; directly across, you can't miss the flamboyant Gothic **Palais de Justice,** first built by Dauphin prince and future king of France Louis XI in 1453 to house the Dauphiné's parliament. *(Tours depart from pl. St-André at 10am on first Sa of each month. 30F/€4.57.)* The **Café de la Table Ronde,** built in 1739, is the second-oldest coffee-spot in France. *(summer tours: ☎04 76 42 96 01.)*

TELEPHERIQUE GRENOBLE-BASTILLE. An icon of Grenoble, these gondolas pop out of the city every 10 minutes and head for the **Bastille,** a 16th-century fort hovering ominously 800 ft. above. From the top, you can look north toward the Lyon valley and its two converging rivers; the real peaks lie to the south, over the ridge of snow-capped mountains on the other side of Grenoble. Sporty types can continue up to **Mont-Jalla** (1hr.) but the views don't improve much. Back at the cable station, practice your alpine skills on the **via ferrata,** the first urban climbing site in the world, or descend via the **Parc Guy Pape,** which criss-crosses through the other ends of the fortress and deposits you at pl. Aristide Briand, just across the river from the train station (1¼hr.). *(**Téléphérique:** quai Stéphane-Jay. ☎04 76 44 33 65. Open July-Aug. M 11am-12:15am, Tu-Su 9:15am-12:15am; Nov.-Feb. M 11am-6:30pm, Tu-Su 10:45am-6:30pm; Mar.-May and Oct. M 11am-7:25pm, Tu-Sa 9:15am-11:45pm, Su 9:15am-7:25pm; June and Sept. M 11am-11:45pm, Tu-Sa 9:15am-11:45pm, Su 9:15am-7:25pm. Closed Jan. 8-19. 24F/€3.66, students 19F/€2.90; round-trip 35F/€5.34, 28F/€4.27.)*

MUSEE DAUPHINOIS. Situated on the north bank of the Isère in a beautiful 17th-century convent, this regional museum boasts multimedia extravagance, with futuristic exhibits and sound effects. The museum's highlight is "La Grande Histoire du Ski" (The Great History of Skiing). *(30 rue Maurice Gignoux. Cross the Pont St-Laurent and go up Montée Chalemont. ☎04 76 85 19 01. Open June-Sept. W-M 10am-7pm; Oct.-May 10am-6pm. 21F/€3.20, under 25 free.)*

MUSEE DE GRENOBLE. The sleek Musée de Grenoble houses one of France's most prestigious collections of fine art. Its masterpieces include larger-than-life canvases by Rubens, de la Tour, and Zubararan, as well as a top-notch 20th-century collection with an entire room devoted to Matisse. *(5 pl. de Lavalette. ☎04 76 63 44 44. Open July-Sept. Th-M 10am-6pm, W 10am-9pm; Oct.-June Th-M 11am-7pm, W 11am-10pm. 25F/€3.81, students 15F/€2.29. Guided visits in French Sa-Su at 3pm, 15F/€2.29.)*

OTHER MUSEUMS. In a former warehouse built by Gustave Eiffel, **MAGASIN (Centre National d'Art Contemporain)** is an exhibition center for cutting-edge contemporary art. Find out what's showing in *Le Petit Bulletin*. *(155 cours Berriat. Take tram A (dir: "Fontaine-La Poya") to "Berriat-Le MAGASIN." ☎04 76 21 95 84. Open Tu-Su noon-7pm. 20F/€3.05, students 10F/€1.53.)* On the north bank of the river and below Eglise St-Laurent, the **Musée Archéologique Saint-Laurent** contains the remaining Roman vestiges of Grenoble. *(Pl. St-Laurent. ☎04 76 44 78 68. Open W-M 9am-6pm. 21F/€3.20, students 10.50F/€1.60, under 25 free.)* Flanking pl. Notre-Dame, the **Musée de l'Ancien Evêche,** is built around Grenoble's 5th-century baptistry, but the museum's beautiful retrospective of the region through art and artifacts is more interesting. A Roman mosaic and 20th-century time capsule are worth your attention. *(2 rue Très-Cloîtres. ☎04 76 03 5 25. Open Th-M 10am-7pm, W 10am-9pm. 21F/€3.20, students 10.50F/€1.60. Free English audioguide.)* Next to the Jardin de Ville, the old Hôtel de Ville is now home to the elegant **Musée Stendhal,** which investigates Grenoble's most reluctant 19th-century citizen through a small collection of portraits, documents, and an informative video. *(1 rue Hector Berlioz. ☎04 76 54 44 14. Open July 15-Sept. 15 Tu-Su 9am-noon and 2-6pm; Sept. 16-July 14 2-6pm. Free.)*

ENTERTAINMENT AND FESTIVALS

Grenoble has all the funky cafés and raucous bars of a true college town. Most lie between **pl. St-André** and **pl. Notre-Dame.** Bars are cheaper than clubs, where covers are about 50-100F/€7.62-15.25 and drinks nearly as much. Hours listed here are for the school year; most places have more limited hours in summer.

The **Maison de la Culture** in the tourist office is so hip it calls itself **Le CARGO.** (☎04 76 01 21 21. Open Sept.-June Tu-Sa 9am-6:30pm.) Drunken scholars mix it up at **Le Couche-Tard,** 1 rue du Palais, a small bar with graffiti-covered walls. (☎04 76 44 18 79. Happy hour M-Sa 7-10:30pm with 15F/€2.29 cocktails. Open M-Sa 8pm-2am.) **Les Trois Canards,** 2 av. Felix Viallet, by the Jardin de Ville, has 10F/€1.53 shooters and a mind-boggling selection of flavored vodka to keep students happy. (☎04 76 46 74 74. Open daily 7am-1am; July-Aug. closed Su.) **Le Saxo,** 5 pl. Agier, is practically a Grenoble institution; a well-dressed crowd fills its spacious terrace and two small dance floors. (☎04 76 51 06 01. Open daily 7pm-2am.) They may have Internet access, but **Cybernet Café,** 3 rue Bayard, is not the place for email addicts. A funky crowd comes to this mellow, bric-a-brac-filled spot. (☎04 76 51 73 18. Happy hour 6-8:30pm. Internet 40F/€6.10 per hr. Open M-Sa 10am-1am.) Expat English fill the **London Pub,** 11 rue Brocherie, a hole-in-the-wall where watching the game is almost as important as getting smashed. (☎04 76 44 41 90. Happy hour M-Th 8-10pm. Open M-Sa 6pm-1am.) Grenoble has few gay clubs for a large city, but a good time is guaranteed at **L'Absolu and George V,** 124 cours Berriat, a friendly two-floorer with drag shows twice a month. (☎04 76 84 16 20. 60F/€9.15 cover includes one drink. Open Th-Su midnight-5:30am.) After the bars wind down, head to the centrally-located **Vertigo,** 18 Grande Rue, where local DJs spin. (☎04 76 15 27 95. Open Tu-Sa 1-5:30am. Cover Th-Sa 50F/€7.62, includes first drink.)

Grenoble is ablaze July 14 with fireworks over its very own (and still standing) Bastille. The **Festival du Court Métrage** (short films) takes place in early July. Contact the **Cinémathèque,** 4 rue Hector Berlioz (☎04 76 54 43 51). The **Festival de Théâtre Européen** hams it up in July. (☎04 76 44 60 92 for info. Shows free to 90F/€13.72. Open Su-Tu 9am-5pm.) In late November, the two-week **Festival 38*ème* Rugissants** brings contemporary music to Grenoble. (☎04 76 51 12 92) The weekly *Le Petit Bulletin*, free in cinemas and some restaurants, has movie schedules.

THE OUTDOORS

The four slopes around Grenoble aren't the only source of daytrips in the area. Dauphiné is proud of its "*Huit Merveilles*" (Eight Wonders), which include elaborate natural caves. The tourist office carries information on excursions to towns such as **Pont-en-Royans** and other natural beauties.

That said, you'd be nuts not to go **skiing** here. Rent equipment in Grenoble to avoid high prices at the resorts. The biggest ski areas are to the east in **Oisans.** The **Alpe d'Huez,** rising above one of the most challenging legs of the Tour de France, boasts an enormous 3330m vertical drop and sunny south-facing slopes; 220km of trails cover all difficulty levels. (Tourist office ☎04 76 11 44 44; fax 04 76 80 69 54; ski area ☎04 76 80 30 30. 213F/€32.48 per day, 1102F/€168.01 per week.) Popular with advanced skiers, **Les Deux Alpes** has the biggest skiable glacier in Europe, limited summer skiing, and a slope-side youth hostel. Its lift system includes two gondolas to whisk you up the 2000m vertical. (Tourist office ☎04 76 79 22 00; fax 04 76 79 01 38. Ski area ☎04 76 79 75 00. Youth hostel ☎04 76 79 22 80; fax 04 76 79 26 15. Lift tickets 203F/€30.96 per day, 1128F/€171.98 per week.)

The **Belledonne** region, northeast of Grenoble, lacks the towering heights of the Oisans but compensates with lower prices. **Chamrousse** is its biggest and most popular ski area. It offers a lively atmosphere and a youth hostel, but the skiing pales in comparison to that at Oisans. Nonetheless, if conditions are right, there's plenty of good skiing at great value, especially for beginners. (Tourist office ☎04 76 89 92 65; fax 04 76 89 98 06. Youth hostel ☎04 76 89 91 31; fax 04 76 89 96 66. Lift tickets 144F/€22 per day, 564F/€86 per week.) Only half an hour from Grenoble, the resort makes an ideal daytrip in the summer (50F/€7.62 bus ride). Chamrousse maintains four **mountain bike** routes of varying difficulty and has a 230km network of **hiking** trails. In January, the town hosts a renowned comedy film festival.

The neighborly slopes and affordable prices of **Vercors,** south of Grenoble, are popular with locals. In traditional villages with small ski resorts, such as **Gresse-en-Vercors,** vertical drops hover at 1000m, and the drive from Grenoble takes about 40 minutes. Rock-bottom prices make the area a stress-free option for beginners or anyone looking to escape the hassles of the major resorts. (Tourist office ☎04 76 34 33 40; fax 04 76 34 31 26. Tickets about 80F/€12.20 per day, 473F/€73.13 per week.) Infested by ibex and saturated with quaintness, Vercors and its regional park have plenty of great **hikes,** as well as **mountain bike** circuits in and around the villages of **Autrans** and **Meaudre,** just outside of Grenoble. Contact **Bureau Info Montagne** (see p. 354) for maps and details. **Mountain climbers** should ask specifically for the free, comprehensive guide "*Escalade en Dauphiné.*"

If you want to stay near town, a number of popular hikes are just a short bus ride away. In Vercors, views from the top of **Le Moucherotte** (1901m) are unparalleled. Take VFD bus #510 (dir: "Plateau du Vercors") to "St-Nizier du Moucherotte" (35min., 6 per day, 47F/€7.17) and head to the center of town. In front of the church, an easy trail starts to the right of the orientation table and quickly joins the **GR91,** which passes the remains of an old *téléphérique* before reaching the mountain's summit via a former ski trail. Descend along the same route (round-trip 4hr.). A steeper trail reaches the summit of the **Chamechaude** (2082m) in the heart of the Chartreuse natural park. Take VFD bus #714 to "Col de Porte." Then follow the dirt trail that leads from behind Hôtel Garin to the right until you reach the middle of a field; to the left, a second trail leads into the forest where it joins the main path, a zig-zag ascent up to the **source des Bachassons.** From here you can admire the view or continue to the top of the mountain. Descend the way you came up (4hr.). Before you go, you may want to pick up a free trail map called *La Carte des Sentiers des Franges Vertes* at the Bureau Info Montagne (see p. 354).

HAUTERIVES

The village of Hauterives has put itself on the map with a whimsical palace and an intriguing story behind it. In 1879, the local postman, Ferdinand Cheval, tripped over an oddly shaped rock as he was making his 32km of daily rounds. One pebble led to another, and soon he was taking a wheelbarrow into the fields every evening to collect piles of odd little rocks. Over the next 32 years, he shaped his stones into a fantasy palace just outside the village. Rock by rock, it grew into an unbelievably detailed world of grimacing giants, frozen palms, and swirling staircases. When the postman finally laid down his trowel, the **Palais Idéal** (Ideal Palace) was almost 80m long and over two stories high. The palace, an indescribable mix of Middle Eastern architecture and hallucinatory images, has become a national monument. You can climb all over it and explore its caves and crevices, mottoes and mysteries sculpted by two hands and the postman's unshakable faith. It is without a doubt the funkiest thing in all of France. (☎04 75 68 81 19. Open Apr. 15-Sept. 15 daily 9am-7pm; Sept. 16-Nov. and Feb.-Apr. 14 9:30am-5:30pm; Dec.-Jan. 10am-4:30pm. 30F/€4.57, students 24F/€3.66, under 16 20F/€3.05.)

Driving from Grenoble, take A48 north; at Voreppe, switch to A49 toward Romans. At Romans, take D538 north to Hauterives (about 1hr.; from Lyon, head south on A7 and change to D538 at Vienne). You can take the **train** from Grenoble to **Romans** (1hr., 11 per day, 63F/€9.61), and there find a **La Régie Drôme** (☎04 75 02 30 42) **bus** to Hauterives (40min.; M-Sa mornings, during school vacations W and F only, evening return; 26F/€3.97). **Hauterives's tourist office,** rue du Palais Idéal, has schedules. (☎04 75 68 86 82; fax 04 75 68 92 96. Open Apr.-Sept. daily 9:30am-noon and 1:30-6pm; Oct.-Nov. Tu-Su 9:30am-noon and 1:30-5:30pm; Dec.-Jan. Tu-Su 10am-noon and 1:30-4:30pm; Feb.-Mar. M-Sa 10am-noon and 1:30-6pm.)

CHAMBERY

Chambéry's main attraction is its magnificent château, settled by the savvy counts of Savoy in 1232. Because all traffic through the Alps passed beneath their windows, the counts' control of Chambéry brought them great influence and wealth. Today the château is run by the no-less-fearsome French bureaucracy, and its towers dominate streets of the pedestrian *vieille ville.* Slightly off the beaten track, Chambéry (pop. 57,000) is a good base from which to explore the Lac du Bourget.

TRANSPORTATION

Trains: pl. de la Gare. To: **Annecy** (45min., 27 per day, 49F/€7.47); **Geneva** (1¼hr., 7 per day, 82F/€12.51); **Grenoble** (1 hr., 20 per day, 57F/€8.69); **Lyon** (1½hr., 11 per day, 85F/€12.96); and **Paris** (3hr., 9 per day, 354-455F/€53.99-69.39). Open daily 5:30am-10pm. **Luggage storage:** 30F/€4.57. Open M-F 8:30am-noon and 2-6pm.

Buses: Several companies run from the bus station (☎04 79 69 11 88), across from the train station. Slow option for visiting Alpine villages. To **Annecy** (1hr., 7 per day, 37-54F/€5.64-8.24) and **Grenoble** (1¾hr., 5 per day, 53F/€8.08). Office open M-F 6:15am-7:15pm; Sa 6:30am-12:30pm and 2:30-5:30pm. Shorter hours in winter.

Local Transportation: STAC, bd. de la Colonne (☎04 79 68 67 00). Runs daily 7:30am-7:30pm. Nearly all buses leave from the ticket and info kiosk at bd. de la Colonne, at bus stop "Eléphants." From July-Aug. there's a bus that leaves from the train station for **Aix-les-Bains** and the lakes (5 per day, 6.60F/€1.01). Open M-F 7:15am-7:10pm, Sa 8:30am-12:15pm and 2:30-5:30pm. Ticket 6.60F/€1.01; *carnet* of 10 38.40F/€5.85, students 28.30F/€4.31.

Taxi: Taxi Allô (☎04 79 69 11 12). 24hr.

ORIENTATION AND PRACTICAL INFORMATION

Chambéry's *vieille ville* lies below and to the left of the train station, with the château in its bottom right corner. To reach the tourist office from the station, walk left on rue Sommeiller for one long block and cross busy pl. du Centenaire to bd. de la Colonne (5min.).

Tourist Office: 24 bd. de la Colonne (☎04 79 33 42 47; fax 04 79 85 71 39; www.chambery-tourisme.com). Wheelchair access from 19 av. des Ducs de Savoie. Maps and a brochure of numerous guided tours offered year-round (25-30F/€3.81-4.57, students 15-20F/€2.29-3.05). *La Savoie* booklets detail hiking, biking, mountain climbing, fishing, and skiing itineraries for the entire region. Open June 15-Sept. 15 M-Sa 9am-12:30pm and 1:30-6:30pm, Su 10am-12:30pm; Sept. 16-June 14 M-Sa 9am-noon and 1:30-6pm. In the same building, the **Association Départementale de Tourisme de la Savoie** (☎04 79 85 12 45) has practical information on regional tourism.

Laundromat: Laverie Automatique, 1 rue Doppet. Open daily 7:30am-8pm.

Police: 585 av. de la Boisse (☎04 79 62 84 00).

Hospital: Centre Hospitalier, pl. François-Chiron (☎04 79 96 50 50).

Internet Access: Ludotec, 9 Faubourg Montmelian (☎04 79 33 55 36). 30F/€4.57 per hr. Open M-Sa 10am-7pm.

Post Office: sq. Paul Vidal (☎04 79 96 69 15). **Currency exchange** with no commission on small sums; 2 days advance notice required for 100 dollar bills. Open M-F 8am-7pm, Sa 8am-noon. **Poste Restante:** 73010 Chambéry. **Postal Code:** 73000.

ACCOMMODATIONS AND CAMPING

The town center is packed with budget hotels, most in varying states of decay. Consider staying at the hostel in Aix-les-Bains, only 10 minutes away by train.

Hôtel du Château, 37 rue Jean-Pierre Veyrat (☎04 79 69 48 78). From the train station, cross the street and walk straight down rue de la Gare, passing the Musée des Beaux Arts, and continue straight down rue J.P. Veyrat. Homey rooms with curiously low beds and dim lighting. Excellent location. Breakfast 23F/€3.51. Reception 7am-8pm. Singles 90-130F/€13.72-19.82; doubles 130-180F/€19.82-27.44.

Hôtel du Lion d'Or, av. de la Boisse (☎04 79 69 04 96; fax 04 79 96 93 20), across from the station. Impersonal feel, but rooms have modern amenities. Breakfast 37F/€5.64. Singles 140F/€21.35, with bath 200F/€30.49; doubles 165F/€25.16, 260F/€39.64. Extra bed 70F/€10.67. AmEx/MC/V.

Hôtel le Mauriennais, 2 rue Ste-Barbe (☎04 79 69 42 78; fax 04 79 69 46 86). Follow directions to Hôtel du Château and then hang a right near the bottom of rue J.P. Veyrat. Dilapidated rooms feature fun-house mirrors and green floors. Only one shower for the entire hotel. Breakfast 25F/€3.81. Reception 10am-10pm. Singles 90-110F/€13.72-16.77; doubles 120F/€18.30; triples 170F/€25.92; quads 180F/€27.44.

Hôtel des Voyageurs, 3 rue Doppet (☎04 79 33 57 00). Hardwood floors and mushy mattresses. Breakfast 30F/€4.57. Reception 7:30am-9:30pm. Singles 130F/€19.82, with shower 150F/€22.90; doubles 160F/€24.39, with shower 180F/€27.44; quads 240F/€36.59, with shower 280F/€42.69; quints 280F/€42.69.

Camping Le Savoy, Parc des Loisirs (☎04 79 72 97 31; fax 04 79 72 58 50), in Challes-Les-Eaux, 6km away. From the station, take bus #8 (dir: "Chignin") to "Aviation". Turn right; the site is 6min. up the road on your left. By a park and lake. Laundry. Reception 9am-noon and 2-8pm. Reserve ahead. Open May-Sept. 20F/€3.05 per person, 15F/€2.29 per tent, 8F/€1.22 per car. Electricity 16F/€2.44. AmEx/MC/V.

FOOD

Budget meals are easy to find around the once-rich **rue Croix d'Or** in the *vieille ville.* The town's market is held in **Les Halles,** pl. de Genève (Sa 7am-noon). A **Prisunic supermarket** is on pl. du 8 Mai, but there's better food at the specialty stores in the *vieille ville* (☎04 79 35 22 15; open M-Sa 8:15am-7pm). **Le Bistrot,** 6 rue du Théâtre, offers well-priced Savoyard specialties beneath antique mirrors and chandeliers. Try their signature *rebluchonade des alpages* (84F/€12.81), a fondue served with a heaping salad of smoked ham and bacon. (☎04 79 75 10 78. Open Tu-Sa noon-2pm and 7-10pm.) The cheapest meals in town are at the **Casino Cafeteria,** 1 rue Claude Martin, where entrees go for 8-29F/€1.22-4.42 and hot plates from 21-44F/€3.20-6.71. (☎04 79 33 46 98. Open daily 11:30am-9:30pm.) **Flunch,** 16 av. Ducs de Savoie, is also a well-priced option; gorge on a 25F/€3.81 all-you-can-eat vegetarian buffet. (☎04 79 85 42 72. Open daily 11am-2:30pm and 6-10pm.)

SIGHTS

CHATEAU DES DUCS DE SAVOIE. For three centuries, Savoy's power emanated from this 13th-century château. At the height of their power, the dukes commanded a realm that stretched from Neufchâtel to Nice and from Turin to Lyon. Enter through the intimidating 15th-century **Porte de l'Eglise St-Dominique.** The Ste-Chapelle presents a two-faced exterior, the result of an 18th-century fire and its subsequent rebuilding and repainting (in the 19th century) in a *trompe l'œil* style. Invasions by French kings eventually convinced the dukes to transfer their capital, and Jesus' alleged burial cloth (kept in the chapel in the 16th century), to Turin, Italy, where the shroud has remained ever since. In the absence of the famous relic, Ste-Chapelle's largest attraction is its set of 70 bells, the largest and loveliest in all of Europe. The interior of the chapel, the underground rooms, and the Prefecture can only be visited on a guided tour. *(Concerts every Sa 10:30am and 5:30pm. 1hr. tours in French July-Aug. M-Sa 10:30am and 2:30-4:30pm; May-June and Sept. daily 2:30pm. 25F/€3.81, students 15F/€2.29. Oct.-Apr. 2hr. tours include a visit of the* vieille ville, *Sa-Su 2:30pm. 30F/€4.57, students 20F/€3.05. Call ahead for tours in English.)*

MUSEE DES CHARMETTES. This museum is the summer house in which Jean-Jacques Rousseau sojourned from 1736 to 1742 in semi-debauchery with the older and wiser Mme. de Warens, the divorcée entrusted with young Jacques's conversion to Catholicism. In his *Confessions,* Rousseau recounts the episode as the high point of his life. The little house, surrounded by reconstructions of 18th-century gardens, later became a place of pilgrimage for 19th-century writers. The scenic route up makes getting there half the fun—though not nearly as much fun as Rousseau must have had. *(From pl. de la République, follow rue de la République, which becomes rue Jean-Jacques Rousseau and eventually chemin des Charmettes. From there, it's a 15min. walk uphill along a bubbling brook. Turn right after the museum sign. ☎04 79 33 39 44. Shows W and F July at 9pm, Aug. at 8:30pm; 2hr.; 100F/€15.25. Reservations recommended. Musée open Apr.-Sept. W-M 10am-noon and 2-6pm; Oct.-Mar. W-M 10am-noon and 2-4:30pm. 20F/€3.05, students 10F/€1.53.)*

MUSEE SAVOISIEN. Housed in a 13th-century Franciscan monastery, this museum provides an ethnography of the Savoy region with crafts, maps, ecclesiastical paraphernalia, and the like. The exhibits move chronologically from prehistoric pottery to the present, with château life and the pivotal role of the Savoy during WWII as particular highlights. *(Sq. de Lannoy de Bissy. Leave the tourist office by the back door, turn left on bd. de la Colonne and walk past the Fontaine des Eléphants. ☎04 79 33 44 48. Open W-M 10am-noon and 2-6pm. 20F/€3.05, students 10F/€1.53.)*

MUSEE DES BEAUX ARTS. This small museum houses a representative collection of Italian and other European paintings from the 17th-19th centuries. *(Pl. du Palais de Justice. ☎04 79 33 75 03. Open W-M 10am-noon and 2-6pm. 20F/€3.05, students 10F/€1.53.)*

LA FONTAINE DES ELEPHANTS. The best-known monument in Chambéry was erected in 1838 to honor the Comte de Boigne. After leading military exploits in India, the Count returned with the spoils to his beloved Chambéry and spent most of it on public works for the city. True to his own history, the fountain fuses East and West with elephants standing in the traditional form of the Savoy cross, spouting showers of water under the weight of de Boigne himself. Locals call them *"les quatre sans culs"*—the "buttless four."

THE VIEILLE VILLE. Chambéry's *vieille ville*—with its sober facades, arcades, and courtyard porticos—has a distinctly Italian flavor; it's painted in the colors of Sardinia, once a Savoy holding. A number of trans-alpine *hôtels particuliers* line rue Croix-d'Or, pl. St-Léger, and rue Basse du Chateau, a tiny 11th-century alley overhung by a modest bridge. Take a look at the courtyard of **#70 rue Croix d'Or;** built in the early 16th century, the hybrid dwelling features Gothic windows, Renaissance door-frames, and a spiral staircase overlooking a lodge. Enter through the grill and climb the staircase to the right to see the original blue and red floor. Stately residences once home to dignitaries and ambassadors also line the **rue de la Juiverie,** but their elegance conceals a gruesome past. Accused of poisoning the town's water fountains when the Black Death broke out in 1349, Chambéry's Jewish population was confined to this street while awaiting trial. Angry townspeople massacred the community before they ever got to court; the few survivors were ultimately blamed and burned.

AIX-LES-BAINS AND LAC DU BOURGET

Colonized by the Romans for its sulphurous hotsprings, the thermal station and spa extraordinaire of Aix-les-Bains (pop. 26,000) is like a voyage in time—forward about forty years or so, to your own Golden Years. Virtually the only tourists are aching arthritics undergoing treatment at the largest medicinal baths in France. These *curistes,* as they're called, keep prices happily low, and make Aix-les-Bains a pleasant base for visiting France's other largest bath, the Lac de Bourget, a château-lined lake just 2km away and favored by sunbathers and windsurfers.

PRACTICAL INFORMATION. **Trains** from pl. de la Gare go to: **Annecy** (40min., 23 per day, 40F/€6.10); **Grenoble** (1hr., 11 per day, 66F/€10.07); **Lyon** (1½hr., 14 per day, 96F/€14.64); and **Paris** (3½hr., 9 per day, 354-455F/€53.99-69.39). Office open daily 5am-10pm; information and reservations open M-F 9am-8pm, Sa 9am-noon and 1:30-6pm. **Buses** (☎04 79 69 11 88) leave from in front of the train station for **Annecy** (5 per day, 49F/€7.47) and **Chambéry** (5 per day, 20F/€3.05). There's a **taxi** stand at the train station (☎04 79 88 99 08).

Aix's center is five minutes east of the station; the lake is a 25-minute walk in the opposite direction. To get to the **tourist office,** pl. Maurice Mollard, cross bd. Wilson, head down av. de Gaulle, cross pl. Moulin, and walk along the park's edge for one block. (☎04 79 88 68 00; fax 04 79 88 68 01; www.aixlesbains.com. Open June-Aug. daily 9am-6:30pm; Apr.-May and Sept. daily 9am-12:15pm and 2-6pm; Oct.-Nov. and Mar. M-Sa 9am-noon and 2-6pm; Dec.-Feb. closes at 5:30pm.) There's an **annex** at Grand Port, pl. Herriot. (☎04 79 34 15 80. Open June-Sept. daily 10am-12:30pm and 2-6:30pm; May Sa-Su 10am-12:30pm and 2-6pm.) Access the **Internet** at **Brasserie le Pavillon,** 35 bd. Wilson. (☎04 79 61 66 10. 50F/€7.62 per hr.Open M-Sa 6am-10pm or 1:30am, Su 8:30am-1pm.) The **post office,** av. Victoria, **exchanges currency.** (☎04 79 35 15 10. Open M-F 8am-7pm, Sa 8am-noon.) **Postal code:** 73100.

ACCOMMODATIONS AND FOOD. The **Auberge de Jeunesse (HI),** promenade de Sierroz, is by the lake. Take bus #2 from the station (dir: "Plage d'Aix"; 6.60F/€1.01; last bus 7pm) to "Camping," and walk three minutes along the stream away from the lake. A taxi from the station costs 60F/€9.15. The hostel often has groups in its 3- to 6-bed dorms and huge backyard. (☎04 79 88 32 88; fax 04 79 61 14 05; aix-les-bains@fuaj.org. Breakfast included. Dinner 50F/€7.62. Sheets 19F/€2.90. Laundry 40F/€6.10. Kitchen and Internet access. Reception 7-10am and 6-10pm. Call ahead to leave baggage earlier. Lockout 10am-6pm. Closed Nov.-Feb. Bunks 76F/€11.59. AmEx/MC/V.) **Hôtel Broisin,** 10 ruelle du Revet, in a quiet courtyard off rue des Bains, charms guests with its ideal location and friendly owner. (☎04 79 35 06 15; fax 04 79 88 10 10. Breakfast 25F/€3.81. Reception 6:30am-8pm. Reservations recommended. Open Mar.-Nov. Singles 137F/€20.89, with toilet 147F/€22.42, with bath 178F/€27.15; doubles 157F/€23.94, with toilet 167F/€25.47, with bath 198F/€30.20; twins 77-208F/€11.74-31.72. MC/V.) **Hôtel Central Clementine,** 6 rue Henri Murger, has large rooms with TVs. (☎04 79 88 14 10; fax 04 79 88 55 25. Breakfast 28F/€4.27. Reception 7:30am-2:30pm and 6:30-9:30pm. Singles and doubles 130F/€19.82, with bath 150F/€22.90. Extra bed 30F/€4.57. AmEx/MC/V.) **Camping Municipal Sierroz** is a large site by the lake, next to the hostel. (☎/fax 04 79 61 21 43. Reception M-Sa 8am-noon and 2:30-6:30pm, Su 8am-noon and 3:30-6:30pm. Open Mar. 15-Nov. 15. 17-19F/€2.59-2.90 per person; 31-41F/€4.73-6.25 per tent, 18F/€2.75 per car. Electricity 9-12F/€1.37-1.83. MC/V.)

Prisunic supermarket is at 15 rue de Genève (open M-Sa 8:30am-12:30pm and 2-7:30pm, Su 8:30am-12:30pm), and morning **markets** are held on pl. Clemenceau (W 8am-5pm, Sa 8am-1pm). **Grand Port** is dotted with restaurants with lake views and servings of the lake's scaly residents.

SIGHTS. In its heyday, Aix's **Thermes Nationaux** (☎04 79 35 38 50) was a luxury spa known the world over; its guests included Queen Victoria and Lamartine. Nowadays, just about any invalid (with necessary medical forms) can take a dip in the *piscine thermale* (thermal pool). Non-senior citizens can only experience the baths with a rather dry tour (1½hr.), in French, of the facilities that concludes with an excessively graphic video detailing potential treatments (Tu-Sa 3pm, buy tickets on the 3rd floor by 2:30pm; 26F/€3.97). Much more appealing is the **Musée Faure,** 10 bd. des Côtes, devoted to impressionist art. This 19th-century Genoese villa includes ballerinas sketched by Degas and a large room devoted to Rodin. (☎04 76 61 06 57. Open M and W-F 10am-noon and 1:30-6pm, Sa-Su 10am-noon and 2-6pm. 20F/€3.05, students 10F/€1.53, under 16 free.)

Though the *thermes* may be inaccessible to travelers, the **Lac du Bourget** welcomes all. Though France's largest natural lake may be twice as cold as the thermal baths, its mountainous scenery is far preferable to their wrinkled vistas. To get there from town, follow av. de Genève as it turns into av. du Grand Port, or take bus #2 from the baths or the train station (dir: "Plage d'Aix"; 6.60F/€1.01). There are two beaches at opposite ends of the Grand Port, **plage Municipale** and **plage de Mémars.** The **Centre Nautique,** pl. Daniel-Rops, has a heated pool on its private beach. (☎04 79 61 48 80. 28F/€4.27, under 18 21F/€3.20. Open daily 9:30am-7:30pm.) **Nautis-Aix,** in Grand Port, rents **motorboats.** (☎04 79 88 24 34. 300-450F/€45.74-68.61 per hr. Open daily 9am-7pm.) Though it has fewer spots for swimming, the opposite side of the lake is much more scenic, and makes for great **biking.** Rent wheels from **Sports Aix-treme,** 60 av. Franklin Roosevelt, off av. de Grand Port near the town center. (☎04 79 88 38 82. 70F/€10.67 per half-day, 100F/€15.25 per day. Open Tu-Sa 9am-noon and 2-7pm.) At the tip of the lake, a natural canal, replete with fish and waterfowl, points the way to **Chanaz,** a lively medieval village where you can visit a working oil mill and dairy (20km from Aix; Chanaz tourist office ☎04 79 54 59 59). The Aix-les-Bains tourist office has rough maps of the lake.

EXCURSION FROM AIX-LES-BAINS: ABBAYE D'HAUTECOMBE. The entire House of Savoy, give or take a few counts, is entombed in the Abbaye d'Hautecombe. The only part of this former Benedictine abbey accessible to visitors is its flamboyant Gothic **church,** the lavish result of eight centuries of necropolistic excess. Poor, exiled Umberto II, the last Savoy king, was the most recent occupant; he was stuffed inside in 1983, among 200 statues and 40 other tombs. One masterpiece is a marble statue of Marie Christine de Bourbon, who oversaw the church's restoration from Turin; the intricate sculpture took eight years to make and was carved from a single block of stone. A marble *pietà*, the church's prized possession, is given pride of place in the chapel to the left of the choir. The exuberant interior can only be visited with an audioguide. (☎04 79 54 26 12; www.chemin-neuf.org/hautecombe. Open M and W-Sa 10-11:30am and 2-5pm, Su 10:30am-noon and 2-5pm. English by request. Free.) The abbey is an ideal biking daytrip; follow the Tour du Lac signs north to Groisin, where you'll see signs for the abbey (3hr. round-trip). There's also a **boat** from Grand Port. (☎04 79 88 92 09; www.gwel.com. 2½hr. round-trip; July-Aug. 4 per day, Sept.-June 1-2 per day; 64F/€9.76.)

ANNECY

You may forget Annecy is a real town when you walk through its *vieille ville.* With its narrow cobblestone streets, winding canals, turreted castle, and overstuffed flower boxes, Annecy looks more like a fiberglass fairy-tale fabrication than a modern city with a metropolitan population of 50,262. Bordering these man-made charms are massive mountains and the purest lake in Europe, which together provide a stunning sight for both windsurfers below and paragliders above.

TRANSPORTATION

Trains: pl. de la Gare. To: **Chambéry** (45min., 27 per day, 49F/€7.47); **Chamonix** (2½hr., 7 per day, 106F/€16.16); **Grenoble** (2hr., 12 per day, 91F/€13.87); **Lyon** (2hr., 7 per day, 117F/€17.84); **Nice** (6hr., 2 per day, 352F/€53.66); and **Paris** (4hr., 9 per day, 370-465F/€56.41-70.89). Open M 4:45am-9:20pm, Tu-Sa 6am-9pm, Su 6am-10:30pm. **Luggage storage:** 30F/€4.57. Open July-Aug. daily 7:30am-8pm, otherwise M-Sa 8am-noon and 2-5pm.

Buses: adjacent to the train station. **Autocars Frossard** (☎04 50 45 73 90) runs to **Chambéry** (1¼hr., 6 per day, 54F/€8.23); **Geneva** (1¼hr., 6 per day, 57F/€8.69); and **Lyon** (3½hr., 2 per day, 102F/€15.55). Office open M-F 7:45-11am and 2-7:15pm, Sa 7:45-11am.

Local Transportation: SIBRA (☎04 50 10 04 04). Tickets 6.50F/€0.99, *carnet* of 8 42F/€6.40. Schedule at booth in Bonlieu, across from the tourist office beside the library. Open M-Sa 8:30am-7pm. Extensive service, but only the *ligne d'été* (summer line) runs on Su; fortunately, it goes to the hostel.

Bike, Ski, and In-line Skate Rental: Annecy Sports Passion, 3 av. de Parmelan (☎04 50 51 46 28). Bike 70F/€10.67 per half-day, 100F/€15.25 per day. Skis 85F/€12.96 per day, boots 40F/€6.10. Passport or credit card deposit. Open Tu-Sa 8:30am-noon and 2-7pm. MC/V. **Golf Miniature de l'Imperial,** 2 av. du Petit Port (☎04 50 66 04 99), beside plage de Paquier. In-line skates 30F/€4.57 per hr., 60F/€9.15 per half-day, 80F/€12.20 per day. Bicycles 70F/€10.67 per half-day, 100F/€15.25 per day. Open daily 9am-7pm, but rentals can be returned as late as 11pm at the mini-golf course next door (June-Sept. only).

Taxis: at the station (☎04 50 45 05 67). 24hr.

ORIENTATION AND PRACTICAL INFORMATION

Most activity centers around the lake, southeast of the train station. The canal runs east-west through the old town; the elevated château is on one side and the main shopping area, closer to the center of Annecy, on the other. To reach the

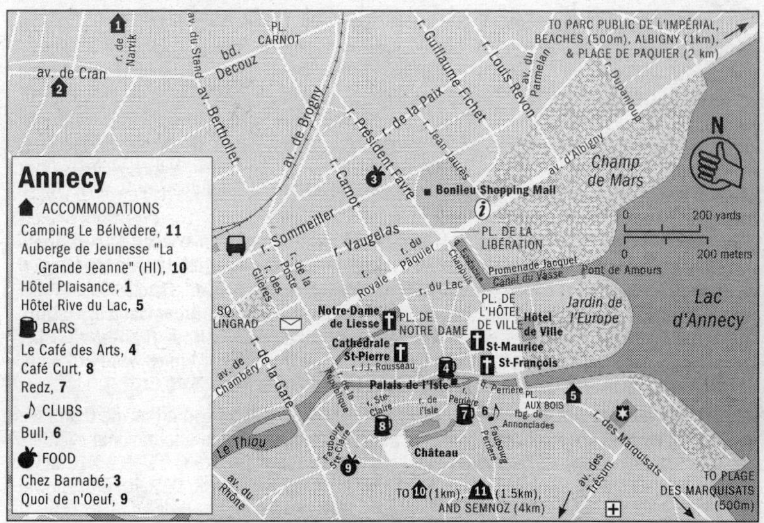

tourist office from the train station, take the underground passage to rue Sommeiller. Walk straight to rue Vaugelas, turn left, and follow rue Vaugelas for four blocks. The tourist office is straight ahead, in the large Bonlieu shopping mall.

Tourist Office: 1 rue Jean Jaurès (☎04 50 45 00 33 or 04 50 45 56 66; fax 04 50 51 87 20; ancytour@noos.fr), at pl. de la Libération. Detailed maps and info on hiking, hotels, campgrounds, rural lodgings, excursions, and climbing. Ask for the bilingual *Annecy Guide,* which has info about sights in and out of town. For hikes, the *Sentiers Forestiers guide* (20F/€3.05) details paths in the Semnoz forest; *Randonnées Pédestres* (25F/€3.81) describes jaunts around the entire lake and is available in English. 2hr. **tours** of the *vieille ville* (32F/€4.88) July-Aug. M-Sa at 3:30pm, English tours July-Aug. F at 4pm. *Topo-guides* 63F/€9.61. Open July-Aug. M-Sa 9am-6:30pm, Su 9am-12:30pm and 1:45-6:30pm; Sept.-June daily 9am-12:30pm and 1:45-6pm.

Laundromat: Lav'Presse, 13bis rue Revon (☎04 50 45 09 30). Open Su-F 7:45am-6:30pm.

Internet: Syndrome Cyber-café, 3bis av. de Chevenes (☎04 50 45 39 75), near the train station. 10F/€1.53 per 15min., 40F/€6.10 per hr. Open M-Sa noon-10pm, Su 2-10pm. **L'Emailerie,** fbg. des Annonciades (☎04 50 10 16 91), downtown, has American keyboards. 10F/€1.53 per 15min., 40F/€6.10 per hr. Open M-Sa 2-8pm.

Hospital: 1 av. de Trésum (☎04 50 88 33 33).

Police: 17 rue des Marquisats (☎04 50 52 32 00).

Post Office: 4bis rue des Glières (☎04 50 33 68 20), off rue de la Poste, down the street from the train station. **Currency exchange** at good rates, no commission. Open M-F 8:30am-6:30pm, Sa 8am-noon. **Poste Restante:** 74011. **Postal code:** 74000.

ACCOMMODATIONS AND CAMPING

Annecy's priciest accommodations lie in the charming *vieille ville* and by the lake. Budget travelers should ascend to the top-notch, hillside hostel. A couple of budget hotels behind the train station offer excellent value but nothing in the way of scenery. Reservations are recommended, especially in high season.

Auberge de Jeunesse "La Grande Jeanne" (HI), rte. de Semnoz (☎04 50 45 33 19; fax 04 50 52 77 52; annecy@fuaj.org). The *ligne d'été* (dir: "Semnoz") leaves the station and drops you off at the hostel (last bus 6:15pm; July-Aug. daily 6 per day; June and

Sept. Sa-Su only 6 per day; 6.50F/€0.99). At other times, take bus #1 (dir: "Marquisats") from the station to "Hôpital," in front of the police station. Turn right on av. de Tresum and follow the signs pointing to Semnoz. After a 10min. hike uphill, the hostel will be on your right. Beautiful modern building perched between the forest and the lake fosters a fun-loving atmosphere. 4- to 5-bed dorms are tiny but all have shower. Tell them if you want a single-sex room. Game room, kitchen, TV room, and laundry. Breakfast included. Dinner 50F/€7.62. Sheets 17F/€2.59. Reception 8am-10pm. No lockout or curfew. Reservations are advisable in summer, but require you to pay half in advance. Closed Dec. Bunks 74F/€11.28. AmEx/MC/V.

Hôtel Savoyard, 41 av. de Cran (☎04 50 57 08 08), in a pretty Savoyard mansion with courtyard. From the train station, exit left, walk around the station to av. Berthollet, and turn left again on av. de Cran. Caring managers let rustic, spacious rooms with grandmotherly floral wallpaper and wooden floors. Open June-Sept. Breakfast 20F/€3.05. Singles and doubles 124F/€18.91, with toilet 154F/€23.48, with shower 174F/€26.53, with bath 184F/€28.05, with bathtub 224F/€34.15; triples 156F/€23.78, with bath 226F/€34.45; quads 200F/€30.49, with bath 266F/€40.55.

Hôtel Plaisance, 17 rue de Narvik (☎/fax 04 50 57 30 42), a right off av. de Cran (see directions to Hôtel Savoyard, above). Charming owner caters to international clientele with intimate rooms and a woodsy breakfast and TV salon. Breakfast 25F/€3.81. Showers 13F/€1.98. Singles 140-150F/€21.35-22.90; doubles 150F/€22.90, with shower 198F/€30.19; triples 245F/€37.35; quads 298F/€45.44. MC/V.

Hôtel Rive du Lac, 6 rue des Marquisats (☎04 50 51 32 85; fax 04 50 45 77 40). Dark rooms and sinking beds yearn for renovations, but the location's ideal—right across from the lake and *vieille ville.* Breakfast 24F/€3.66. Showers 6F/€0.91, free for longer stays. Singles and doubles 142F/€21.65; triples and quads 207F/€31.56. MC/V.

Camping le Bélvèdere, 8 rte. de Semnoz (☎04 50 45 48 30; fax 04 50 51 81 62; camping@ville-annecy.fr), just above the youth hostel. Pretty site by the woods, with lots of things to do—TV, ping-pong, *pétanque*, and trails in the nearby forest. Open Apr. 15-Oct. 15. Reception July.-Aug. 8am-9pm; Apr. 15-June and Sept.-Oct. 15 8am-8pm. 1 person and tent 45F/€6.86 (July-Aug. 50F/€7.62), 2 people and tent 65F/€9.91 (July-Aug. 85F/€12.96). 17F/€2.59 per car. AmEx/MC/V.

FOOD

Annecy's *vieille ville* is lined with affordable restaurants, each one more charming than the next. Fill your picnic basket with the soft local *reblochon* cheese at the morning **markets** on pl. Ste-Claire (Tu, F, and Su 8am-noon) and on bd. Taine (Sa 8am-noon). Grocery stores line av. de Parmelan, and a **Monoprix supermarket** fills the better part of pl. de Notre-Dame. (☎04 50 45 23 60. Open M-Sa 8:30am-7:30pm.) The cleverly-named **Quoi de n'Oeuf,** 19 fbg. Ste-Claire, features plentiful portions on an adorable terrace in the *vieille ville.* Eggheads jump at the 60F/€9.15 *tartiflette*, salad, and dessert. (☎04 50 45 75 42. Open M-Sa noon-2pm and 7-9:45pm. MC/V.) With so many lovely gardens, it makes sense to nosh outdoors in Annecy. Paper-bag it at **Chez Barnabé,** 29 rue Sommeiller, with a wallet-friendly salad bar for 16-26F/€2.44-3.96. (☎04 50 45 90 62. Open M-Sa 10am-7:15pm.)

SIGHTS

VIEILLE VILLE. A stroll through the *vieille ville* may cost you several rolls of film and a hundred sighs. **The Palais de l'Isle** is a 13th-century château first occupied by the counts of Geneva after their hometown came under episcopal control. The tiny turreted building, on a skinny island in the middle of the canal, served as a prison last used to jail Resistance fighters during the war—you can still read their impassioned carvings on the walls. *(☎04 50 33 87 31. Open June-Sept. daily 10am-6pm; Oct.-May W-M 10am-noon and 2-6pm. 20F/€3.05, students 5F/€0.76.)* Straddling the town's narrowest canal, the large and bare **Eglise St-Maurice,** consecrated in 1445, has a rare 15th-century painting on the left-hand wall of the choir marking the tomb of Philibert de Monthoux, a noble who lived here. This macabre mural of a decomposing corpse—finished two years before its patron even died—is thought to have reflected anxiety over the Hundred Years' War. Beneath the towers of the castle on the opposite side of the canal, Annecy's abundant charm is displayed in the arcade-lined passages of **quai Perrière, rue de L'Isle,** and **rue Ste-Claire.**

GARDENS. Graced by manicured hedges, fountains, and the occasional long-necked swan, the shaded **Jardins de l'Europe** are Annecy's pride and joy. On the north side, the **Pont des Amours** (Bridge of Love)—one of the few such in France that earns its cheesy name—connects the European gardens to the **Champ de Mars,** a grand esplanade favored by picnickers, sunbathers, and frisbee-throwers. Annecy isn't one to gloat, but gardens like these helped it win the national *Ville Fleurie* (Flower City) contest three times in the last decade.

THE LAKE. After a stroll through the bustling streets, you may want to swim in Annecy's cold, crystalline lake. In summer, **Plage de Pâquier,** two to three kilometers up av. d'Albigny, is packed with tourists and locals who come for windsurf, sailboat, or kayak rentals (though no swimming), and trendy coastal restaurants. Also free, **Plage des Marquisats,** south of the city down rue des Marquisats, has swimming but is half the size and crowded. The Club de Voile Française there rents a limited selection of watercraft. There's nothing more peaceful than a **pedal boat** ride; there are plenty of rental companies along the port, but the best deals are on the south side of the Champ de Mars. *(50F/€7.62 per 30min., 75F/€11.43 per hr.; tours of the lake 35-90F/€5.34-13.72.)* It costs 21F/€3.20 to swim at the **Parc Public de l'Impérial,** an aquatic wonderland with waterslides, sailing, tennis, swimming, and, improbably, a casino. *(20min. up av. d'Albigny beside plage de Pâquier. ☎04 50 23 11 82. Open May-Sept. daily 11am-7:30pm.)* An unforgettable way to see the lake is from above. Purportedly one of the best places in the world for **paragliding** *(parapenting)*, Annecy has a variety of companies who offer comparable prices. **Takamaka** (see below) lets the adventurous run off a majestic cliff and fly above the crystal-blue lake waters. (Tandem 480F/€73.18; 5-day course 2800F/€426.89.)

CHATEAU. The 12th-century château towers over Annecy, a short but steep climb from the *vieille ville.* Once a stronghold of the counts of Geneva, the castle and its imposing parapets now house slightly dull archaeological and artistic exhibits. Inside the main building, the museum welcome desk occupies an enormous hearth that once fed a lively court—sneak back and take a look at its massive proportions. The 15th-century wooden statuary in the next room is worth a visit, as is the original ceiling of the banquet hall upstairs, the only survivor of a 1952 fire. The **Observatoire Régional des Lacs Alpins,** in the rear of the castle, has displays on lake ecosystems as well as an aquarium—if the exhibits don't impress you, the view will. *(☎04 50 33 87 30. Open June-Sept. daily 10am-6pm; Oct.-May W-M 10am-noon and 2-6pm. Château 30F/€4.57, students 10F/€1.53; entrance to grounds free.)*

HIKING

Although it may be hard to tear yourself away from Annecy's man-made charms, local Alpine forests have excellent hiking and biking trails. Dozens of breathtaking hikes begin on the **Semnoz,** a limestone mountain south of the city. The **Office National des Forêts** (☎04 50 23 84 10) distributes a color map, *Sentiers Forestiers,* with several routes (20F/€3.05 at the tourist office or hostel). One of the best begins at the **Basilique de la Visitation,** right near the hostel. If you're staying in town, take bus A to its terminus, "Visitation." Then, from the basilica, continue along the road until you reach a small parking lot. From there, follow the signs for "la Forêt du Crêt du Maure." Follow the Ste-Catherine trail in a meandering circle, with breathtaking views, around the Semnoz forest (2hr.). After about an hour, the trail intersects with the red-and-yellow-marked **GR96,** on which long-haulers can do a 40km circuit of the lake. There's an exquisite, 16km scenic *piste cyclable* (bike route) that hugs the lake shore for the entire eastern coast. After that, you can complete the entire loop (32km) on the main road, but watch out for traffic. The tourist office has a free lake map that includes the bike route and some departure points for hikes. The **Bureau des Guides** and **Takamaka,** 17 fbg. Ste-Claire, run excursions for all mountaineering activities, including hiking, biking, rock-climbing, ice-climbing, paragliding, and canyoning. (☎04 50 45 60 61; www.takamaka.fr. Open M-Sa 9am-noon and 2-7pm, Su 9am-1pm. Hikes 120F/€18.30 per half-day, 200F/€30.49 per day. Canyoning 360-450F/€54.89-68.61. Sign up the night before. AmEx/MC/V.) The *Guide Pratique* has information on outdoor recreation.

ENTERTAINMENT AND FESTIVALS

After a hard day shooting the rapids or gliding through the sky, you can relax at the bars lining the canal in the *vieille ville* or situated around the lake. **Le Café des Arts,** 4 passage de l'Isle, is an artsy bar with a choice spot opposite the illuminated island castle. (☎04 50 51 56 40. Open daily 9am-2am; live music Th nights.) Students and backpackers crowd the plant-filled bar **Café Curt,** 35 rue Ste-Claire, which maintains an easy-going atmosphere with 10F/€1.53 wine and 13F/€1.98 Kronenbourg. (☎04 50 51 74 75. Open daily 8am-1am.) **Redz,** 14 rue Perrière, is a flashy sports car of a bar that draws an older clientele with various theme nights. (☎04 50 45 17 13. Open daily 11am-3am.) For late-night dancing, **Bull,** 8 fbg. des Annonciades, is one of the more centrally-located nightclubs. (☎04 50 45 32 89. Cover F-Sa 50F/€7.62, includes one drink. Open Tu-Sa 10:30pm-5am.)

Performing arts and films are at the **Théâtre d'Annecy,** in the Bonlieu Mall across from the tourist office. (☎04 50 33 44 11. Tickets about 95F/€14.48, students 40F/€6.10.) *Fête* fetishists can pick up schedules at the Comité des Fêtes kiosk across from the tourist office. The grandpappy of them all is the **Fête du Lac,** the first Saturday in August, with fireworks and water shows (35-270F/€5.34-41.16).

AROUND LAC D'ANNECY

The smaller villages on the Lac d'Annecy make excellent daytrips. All are within 20km of Annecy and accessible by bus. ***Voyages Crolard*** *sends buses that circle the entire lake from the train station (about 10 per day, fewer on Su); you can also get on board at the bus stop in front of the tourist office and near plage de Pâquier. (☎04 50 45 00 56. Office open M-F 9am-noon and 1:45-7:30pm, Sa 9am-noon and 1:45-6pm. 15-46.50F/€2.29-7.09.) Driving, take D909 along the eastern shore, which intersects with N508 at Doussard on the southern point of the lake, and return to Annecy along the western shore.*

St. Bernard de Menthon, famous for the breed of dogs bearing his name, was born just across the lake, in a sumptuous 11th-century **château.** His enormously wealthy descendants still live in the castle, but the lower floors—with a walnut library, music salon, and 14th-century bedroom—are open to the public. (☎04 50 60 12 05. Open July-Aug. daily noon-6pm; May-June and Sept. Th and Sa-Su 2-6pm. Tours every 20-45min. 30F/€4.57. On weekends, tours (in period dress) are 35F/€5.34.)

Ten kilometers west of Annecy is the **Gorge du Fier,** a canyon formed by water erosion. (☎04 50 46 23 07 for info. Open June 15-Sept. 10 daily 9am-7pm; Mar. 15-June 14 and Sept. 11-Oct. 15 9am-noon and 2-6pm. 27F/€4.12.) Though the gorge itself is only 256m long and the visit half an hour, the trip's worth your while if you check out the **Château de Montrottier,** five minutes from the entrance to the canyon. The castle, formerly owned by the region's foremost collectors of *objets d'art*, contains centuries-old Asian costumes, armor, and pottery. (☎04 50 46 23 02. Open June-Aug. daily 10am-noon and 2-7pm; Mar. 15-May and Sept.-Oct. 15 W-M 10am-noon and 2-6pm; also closed mornings in Oct. 35F/€5.34, students 30F/€4.57.) To get there, take the coach to **Lovagny** (10min., 3-4 per day at odd hours, 12F/€1.83) and walk the 800m to the gorges. Alternatively, **Voyages Crolard** sends a bus tour that includes admission to the gorges and the château (W at 2pm, 110F/€16.77).

Talloires, 13km from Annecy, makes a good starting point for the one-hour hike to the waterfalls at **La Cascade d'Angon** and to the beautiful gardens of the **Ermitage de St-Germain** (also 1hr.). To reach the waterfalls, follow the Closettaz path out of the village and follow the signs. The trail passes under the raging 100m-high torrent and then climbs the rocks up to the top. Ask the tourist office in Annecy or Talloires about boat rides from Annecy to Talloires. (Tourist office ☎04 50 60 70 64; fax 04 50 60 76 59.) **Doussard,** south of the lake and surrounded by nature preserves, is known as "the source of the lake" because its rivers fill Lac d'Annecy. (Tourist office ☎04 50 44 30 45; fax 04 50 44 81 75.) Nearby **St-Jorioz** has great views of the mountains. (Tourist office ☎04 50 68 61 82; fax 04 50 68 96 11.)

The nearest **skiing resort** is **La Clusaz,** 32km away, with 130km of trails and 56 lifts. Contact the **tourist office** in La Clusaz for info. (☎04 50 32 65 00; fax 04 50 32 65 01; infos@laclusaz.com; www.laclusaz.com.) There is a **youth hostel** outside La Clusaz on rte. du Col de la Croix Fry (☎04 50 02 41 73; fax 04 50 02 65 85).

ALPS

CHAMONIX

The site of the first Winter Olympics in 1924, Chamonix (pop. 10,000) is the quintessential ski town. Its slopes are among the toughest in the world and its mountains supremely challenging to scale; some 62 *téléphériques* serve the various ridges and peaks, bringing up skiers in winter, hikers and cyclists in summer, and climbers in all seasons. The town itself combines the natural majesty of nearby Mont Blanc, the tallest mountain in Europe, with a lighthearted spirit, thanks to the hordes of Anglos who came for the season and never left. Be prepared to spend your days in the great outdoors and nights at raucous *après-ski* spots.

TRANSPORTATION

Trains: av. de la Gare (☎04 50 53 12 98). Chamonix is served by a special train running from **St-Gervais** to **Martigny;** all other destinations require a change of train. To: **Annecy** (2½hr., 7 per day, 106F/€16.16); **Geneva** (2½hr., 6 per day, 135F/€20.58); **Grenoble** (4hr., 4 per day, 170F/€25.92); **Lyon** (4-5hr., 6 per day, 190F/€28.97); and **Paris** (6hr., 6 per day, 400-504F/€60.98-76.84). Ticket sales daily 6:10am-8:10pm; info kiosk July-Aug. daily 9am-noon and 1:15-6:10pm. **Luggage storage:** 30F/€4.57 for 24hr. Open daily 6:10am-8:10pm.

Buses: Société Alpes Transports, at the train station (☎04 50 53 01 15). To: **Annecy** (2¼hr., M-F 1 per day, 95F/€14.48); **Courmayeur,** Italy (3½hr., M-Sa 1 per day, 100F/€15.25); **Geneva** (1½hr.; 2 per day; 170F/€25.92 to town, 195F/€29.73 to airport); and **Grenoble** (3hr., Su-M 1 per day, 161F/€24.55). Ticket office open M-F 7:45am-noon and 1:20-6:30pm, Sa 7:45am-noon and 3-5pm, Su 9am-noon and 3-5pm.

Local Transportation: Chamonix Bus (☎04 50 53 05 55). To get to the main bus stop, follow signs from pl. de l'Eglise. The area is divided into sections; you pay by the number of sections you go through. Tickets 7.50F/€1.14 per section; *carnet* of 6 38F/€5.80, of 10 59F/€9. Buses connect easily with ski slopes and hiking trails.

Taxis: at the station (☎04 50 53 13 94). **Alp Taxi Rochaix,** ☎04 50 54 00 48. 24hr.

ORIENTATION AND PRACTICAL INFORMATION

The center of town is the intersection of av. Michel Croz, rue du Docteur Paccard, and rue Joseph Vallot, each named for a past conqueror of Mont Blanc's summit. From the station, follow av. Michel Croz through town, turn left onto rue du Dr. Paccard, and take the first right to the pl. de l'Eglise and the tourist office (5min.).

Tourist Office: 85 pl. du Triangle de l'Amitié (☎04 50 53 00 24; fax 04 50 53 58 90; www.chamonix.com). Lists of hotels and dorms and campgrounds map. Hiking map *Carte des Sentiers d'Eté* (25F/€3.81) and free *Chamonix Magazine.* Info on area cable cars. Weather conditions in English. Internet access. Open July-Aug. daily 8:30am-7:30pm; Mar.-June and Sept.-Nov. 9am-noon and 2-6pm; Dec.-Feb. 8:30am-7pm. **Centrale de Reservation** (☎04 59 53 23 33; fax 04 50 53 58 90) books apartments or hotels in advance for a whopping 50F/€7.62.

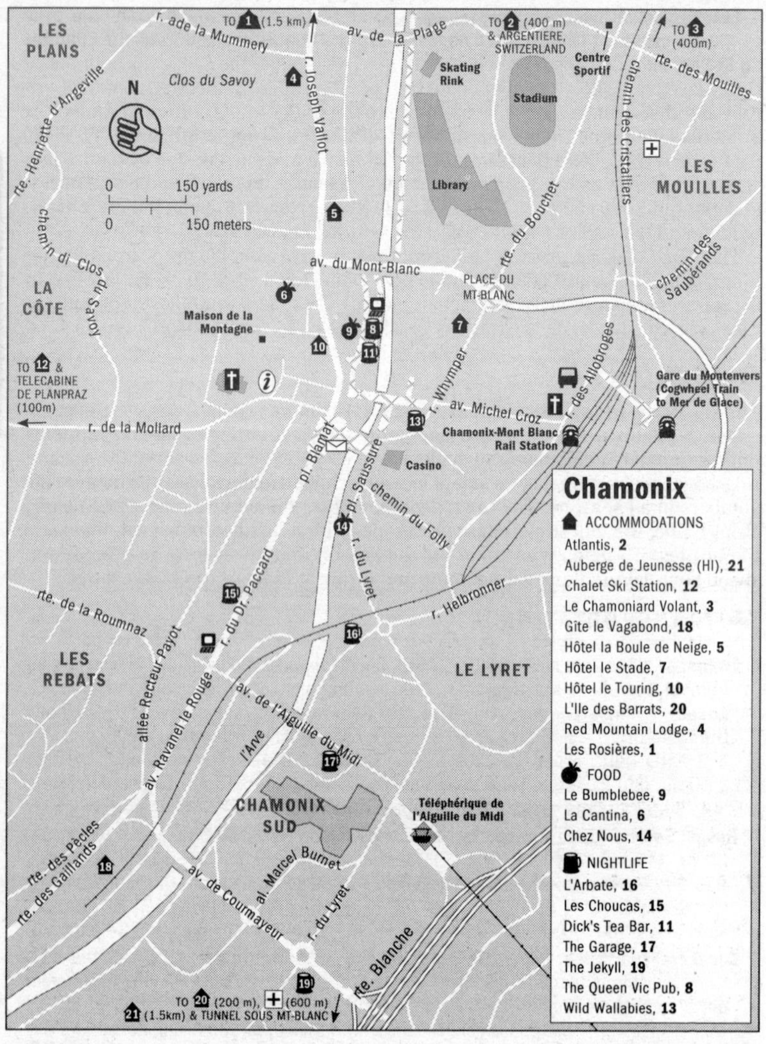

Currency Exchange: Comptoir de Change, 21 pl. Balmat (☎04 50 55 88 40), has the most competitive rates and a 24hr. exchange machine. Also changes AmEx traveler's checks. Commission 25F/€3.81. Open daily 8am-8pm.

Laundromat: Lav'matic, 40 impasse Primevère. Open daily 8am-8pm.

Hospital: Centre Hospitalier, 509 rte. des Pèlerins (☎04 50 53 84 00).

Police: 48 rue de l'Hôtel de Ville (☎04 50 53 75 02).

Internet Access: Plenty of downtown bars offer web access for about 1F/€0.15 per min. The best deal is at **Cybar,** 80 rue des Moulins (☎04 50 53 69 70). 0.50F/€0.08 per min. Open June-Nov. daily noon-midnight; Dec.-May 10am-1am. **Cyber Espace** (☎04 50 55 98 58), in the Galerie Blanc Neige, off rue du Dr. Paccard, is cheaper for longer periods: 50F/€7.62 per hr., 135F/€20.58 for 3½hr., using a divisible card. Open July-Aug. daily 9am-9pm; Sept.-June 10am-1pm and 3-9pm.

Post Office: pl. Jacques-Balmat (☎04 50 53 15 90), below the tourist office. **Currency exchange** at good rates, no commission. Open M-F 8:30am-noon and 2-6pm, Sa 8:30am-noon. **Postal code:** 74400.

SKIING, BIKING, AND HIKING RESOURCES

Hiking Information: Office de Haute-Montagne (☎04 50 53 22 08; fax 04 50 53 27 74; www.ohm-chamonix.com), on the 3rd floor of the Maison de la Montagne, across from the tourist office. The ultimate resource; an expert staff helps plan your adventures, gives info on weather conditions, and sells detailed maps (25-59F/€3.81-9). Open July-Aug. daily 9am-noon and 3-6pm; closed Su Sept.-June, closed Sa Oct.-Nov.

Club Alpin Français, 136 av. Michel Croz (☎04 50 53 16 03; fax 04 50 53 82 47; infos@clubalpin-chamonix.com). Best source for info on mountain *refuges* and road conditions. Register with guides 6-7:30pm the day before hikes. Bulletin board matches drivers, riders, and hiking partners; every F at 7pm, hikers from far and wide convene in the office to plan the weekend's trips and excursions. Open July-Aug. M-Sa 9:30am-noon and 3:30-7:30pm; Sept.-June M-Tu and Th-F 3:30-7pm, Sa 9am-noon.

Skiing and Hiking Information: Ecole du Ski (☎04 50 53 22 57), on the 2nd floor of the Maison de la Montagne. Open Nov.-Apr. daily 9am-noon and 2-7pm. On the main floor, the **Compagnie des Guides** (☎04 50 53 00 88) organizes skiing and climbing lessons and leads guided summer hikes and winter ski trips. Register at 6pm the evening before. Open Jan.-Mar. and July-Aug. daily 8:30am-noon and 3:30-7:30pm; Sept.-Dec. and Apr.-June Tu-Sa 10am-noon and 5-7pm.

Cycling Information: Pick up the free, invaluable map/guide *Itinéraires Autorisés aux Vélos Tout Terrain*, at the tourist office or at mountain biking rental shops.

Weather Conditions: at Maison de la Montagne, Club Alpin Français, and the tourist office. Call 08 92 68 02 74 for a French recording of weather and road conditions.

Mountain Rescue: PGHM Secours en Montagne, 69 rte. de la Mollard (☎04 50 53 16 89). 24hr. emergency service.

Hiking Equipment: Sanglard Sports, 31 rue Michel Croz (☎04 50 53 24 70). Boots 47F/€7.17 per day, 270F/€41.16 per week. Open July-Aug. daily 9am-7:30pm; Sept.-June 9am-12:30pm and 2:30-7:30pm. AmEx/MC/V.

Bike and Ski Rental: Dozens of places rent skis, bikes, and climbing equipment; don't pay over 80F/€12.20 per day or 350F/€53.36 per week for skis.

ACCOMMODATIONS AND CAMPING

Chamonix's hotels are expensive, but the more basic *gîtes* and dormitories are quite cheap. During summer weekends, call the tourist office for availability; there are many more accommodation options than *Let's Go* can list, they fill up fast, and it's possible to wander from one full *gîte* to another all day. Both hotels and *gîtes* are packed during the winter (reserve up to six weeks in advance), but they ease up in autumn and spring, and fill up again in the summer. The hardest time to get a room is early February, when a car race overruns the city. Mountain *refuges* tend to be remote, have few facilities, and are sometimes unattended. For information on nearby mountain *refuges*, see **Hiking,** below.

GITES AND HOSTELS

Red Mountain Lodge, 435 rue Joseph Vallot (☎04 50 53 94 97; fax 04 50 53 82 64; www.redmountainlodge.co.uk). One of the best lodges in France, this is more of a home than a hostel. The fun-loving Aussie owner and friendly Anglo staff keep guests beaming with plush furnishings, views of Mont Blanc, and prizeworthy barbecues (2-3 per week; 60-80F/€9.15-12.20). Breakfast and sheets included. Beautiful dorms 100F/€15.25; doubles and triples 140F/€21.35 per person, with shower 160F/€24.39. The owner's second Chamonix gem is **Atlantis,** 788 rte. du Bouchet (☎04 50 53 74 31), 15min. out of town in a more natural setting, with small bar, jacuzzi, sauna, tanning bed, and top-quality **mountain bike** rental (70F/€10.67 per half-day, 90F/€13.72 per day). To get to Atlantis, follow directions for Chamoniard Volant, below, and take a left on the train track by rte. de la Frasse. Breakfast and sheets included. In winter, all-inclusive ski packages offered. At Atlantis, 200F/€30.49 per person gets you luxurious accommodations plus breakfast (week packages only). Reserve ahead for both.

Auberge de Jeunesse (HI), 127 montée Jacques Balmat (☎04 50 53 14 52; fax 04 50 55 92 34; www.aj-chamonix.fr.st), in Les Pèlerins, at the foot of the Glacier de Bossons. Take the bus from the train station or pl. de l'Eglise (dir: "Les Houches") to "Pèlerins E Ecole" (4F/€0.61), and follow the signs uphill to the hostel. By train, get off at "Les Pèlerins" and follow the signs. You can also walk down rte. des Pèlerins (25min.). A beautiful modern chalet where the glacier looks close enough to touch. Many groups fill 2- to 6- person bunks in a separate building. Reductions on practically everything in town. All-inclusive winter ski packages 1550-3650F/€236.32-556.49 per week. Breakfast included. Dinner 55F/€8.39. Sheets 19F/€2.90. Reception 8am-noon and 5-10pm; drop bags off any time. Dorms 85F/€12.96; singles and doubles 100F/€15.25 per person, with shower 105F/€16.01. Camping 51F/€7.78. MC/V.

Gite le Vagabond, 365 av. Ravanel le Rouge (☎04 50 53 15 43; fax 04 50 53 68 21). An easygoing Anglo staff runs this sparkling-new *gîte* near the center of town. Popular bar. Internet access. Breakfast 33F/€5.03. Dinner 69F/€10/52. Reception 8-10:30am and 4:30pm-1am. 4- to 8-bunk dorms 80F/€12.20; 100F/€15.25 deposit.

Le Chamoniard Volant, 45 rte. de la Frasse (☎04 50 53 14 09; fax 04 50 53 23 25), 15min. from the center of town. From the station, turn right, go under the bridge, and turn right across the tracks, left on chemin des Cristalliers, and right on rte. de la Frasse. Popular *gîte* has a decidedly rustic flavor. Internet access. Breakfast 29F/€4.42. Dinner 66F/€10.06. Sheets 25F/€3.81. Reception 10am-10pm. Dorms 70F/€10.67.

Chalet Ski Station, 6 rte. des Moussoux (☎04 50 53 20 25), near *télécabine* Brevent. Straight up the steep hill from the tourist office (follow signs to Les Moussoux). Friendly wooden *gîte* provides a mix of town and country. Shower 5F/€0.76 for 5min. Sheets 15-30F/€2.29-4.57. Reception 9am-11pm. Open Dec. 20-May 10 and June 25-Sept. 20. 4- to 9-bunk dorms 65F/€9.91.

HOTELS

Hôtel le Touring, 95 rue Joseph Vallot (☎04 50 53 59 18; fax 04 50 53 67 25; ngulliford@aol.com). Large English-run hotel with charming alpine decor and spacious rooms. In winter it's almost always packed with groups, hence unavailable. Breakfast 35F/€5.34. Reception 8am-10pm. Singles with shower 225F/€34.30; doubles with shower 300F/€45.74, with bath 380F/€57.94. Third bed 60F/€9.15, fourth bed 40F/€6.10. Prices drop 50-80F/€7.62-12.20 outside of July 13-Aug. 27. MC/V.

Hôtel le Stade, 79 rue Whymper (☎04 50 53 05 44; fax 04 50 53 96 39). From the train station, exit straight and take the first right. Downtown hotel offers good value with large and simple rooms. A little farther from the action. Breakfast 32F/€4.88. Singles 140F/€21.35; doubles 220F/€33.54, with bath 300F/€30.49; triples 315F/€48.03, with bath 435F/€66.32.

Hôtel la Boule de Neige, 362 rue Joseph Vallot (☎04 50 53 04 48; fax 04 50 55 91 09; laboule@claranet.fr). Cute Alpine chalet with small but spotless rooms, above a bar in a busy part of town. Breakfast 35F/€5.34. Reception 7am-noon and 5-7pm. Aug. singles 236F/€31.40, with bath 255F/33.93; doubles 282F/€37.52, with bath 327F/€43.51; triples 393F/€52.29, with bath 432F/€57.48; quads with bath 485F/€64.53. Prices 30-40F/€4.57-6.10 lower Mar. and July; 60-100F/€9.15-15.25 lower June, Sept.-Oct., and Dec.-Apr. Closed Nov. MC/V.

Camping: Several sites lie near the foot of the Aiguille du Midi cable car. It's illegal to pitch tents in the Bois du Bouchet. **L'Ile des Barrats,** 185 chemin de l'Ile des Barrats (☎/fax 04 50 53 51 44), off rte. des Pèlerins, has great views and crowds. With your back to the cable car, turn left, pass the busy roundabout, continue 5min., and look right. Open May-Sept. Reception July-Aug. 8am-10:30pm; May-June and Sept. 8am-noon and 4-7pm. 32F/€4.88 per person, 24F/€3.66 per tent, 13F/€1.98 per car. Electricity 18F/€2.74. **Les Rosières,** 121 clos des Rosières (☎04 50 53 10 42; fax 04

50 53 29 55; www.campinglesrosieres.com), off rte. de Praz, is the close to the other side of Chamonix and often has room. Follow rue Vallot for 2km or take a bus to "Les Nants." Reception July-Aug. 8am-9pm; otherwise 8am-noon and 2-9pm. Open Feb.-Oct. 15. 30-35F/€4.5-5.2 per person, 14-17F/€2.1-2.5 per tent, 7-14F/€1.1-2.1 per car.

FOOD

The Chamonix tourist machine produces better restaurants than most. Regional fare like fondue and *raclette* shares menu space with international ski staples in restaurants; many bars serve good meals, too. The **Super U,** 117 rue Joseph Vallot, is the cheapest place for groceries. (☎04 50 53 12 50. Open M-Sa 8:15am-7:30pm, Su 8:30am-noon.) Morning **markets** are held on pl. du Mont Blanc (Sa) and Chamonix Sud (Tu; July-Aug. only), near the foot of the Aiguille du Midi *téléphérique* (both 8am-12:30pm). The **Jekyll** (see **Nightlife,** below) is a popular bar that also serves excellent food.

Chez Nous, 76 rue Lyret (☎04 50 33 91 29). *Savoyarde* specialties at this river-side spot will satiate any palate. Dip your bread into the assorted, highly-praised fondues (from 75F/€11.43). Open daily noon-2:30pm and 7-11:30pm.

Le Bumblebee, 65 rue des Moulins (☎04 50 53 50 03), features a creative menu with creations like thai fishcakes (42F/€5.59) and lots of vegetarian goodies. Sky-blue walls and soft tunes keep patrons mellow. Open daily 7pm-2am, summer also noon-3pm.

La Cantina, 37 impasse des Rhododendrons (☎04 50 53 83 80), off rue Joseph Vallot, is a funky Mexican restaurant popular with French natives. Open daily 7:30-11pm, until 2am weekends. Bar open daily 6pm-2am, summer W-Sa.

NIGHTLIFE

Chamonix's nightclubs are popular in the winter, when people shake what's left of their ski-weary bodies after the bars close down; during the summer, however, they can be painfully empty. On the other hand, Chamonix is a serious bar town all year long. You won't have to crawl far between drinks on bar-filled **rue des Moulins.**

The Jekyll, 71 rte. des Pèlerins (☎04 50 55 99 70). Straight out of Dublin, this intimate nightspot and local landmark is run (and overrun) by friendly foreigners. Huge portions of food. Open daily 6pm-2am; in summer W-Su. Closed May-June and Oct.-Nov.

Wild Wallabies, rue de la Tour (☎04 50 53 01 31). Complete with an outdoor pool and indoor games, this Aussie bar is like a mini-resort. In winter, exercise your talents with burping and wet T-shirt contests. Open daily 4pm-2am; in summer 11am-2am.

Dick's Tea Bar, 80 rue des Moulins (☎04 50 53 19 10), is the flagship of a bar-saturated street. London DJs keep the dance floor pumping at this hotspot, one of three *Dick's* in the Alps. Open in winter daily 10pm-4am; in summer F-Sa midnight-4am. Winter cover 70F/€10.67, includes one drink.

Les Choucas, 206 rue du Dr. Paccard (☎04 50 53 03 23). Alpine swank in a revamped chalet named after a little black local bird. Giant TV screen with extreeeeme skiing. Beer 20F/€3.05 before 10pm. Open daily 4pm-4am; Oct.-Nov. only F-Sa. Closed May-June.

The Queen Vic Pub, 74 rue des Moulins (☎04 50 53 91 98). Energetic English pub draws a young, mixed, easygoing crowd. Pool tables and mellow music. Open daily 6pm-2am, in summer 6pm-2am.

L'Arbate, 80 chemin du Sapi (☎04 50 53 44 43), draws live music acts and an older, French-er crowd into its two-floor bar. Happy hour 8-9pm. Open daily 5pm-4am. Music daily 11:30pm in winter; Th-Sa May-June and Sept.-Nov. Cover 50F/€7.62 for bands.

Le Garage, 200 av. de l'Aiguille (☎04 50 53 64 49), is generally considered the best of the Chamonix discos, catering to Anglos and Scandinavians with big-truck decor and lots of booze. Things get rolling after 1am. No cover, but one drink required (from 30F/€4.57). Open in winter and summer daily 10pm-4am; fall and spring Th-Sa 10pm-4am.

OUTDOOR PURSUITS

Whether you've come to climb up these mountains or to ski down them, you're in for a challenge, and basic precautions are in order. Steep grades, potential avalanches, and unique terrain mean that this is not the place to do things you haven't done before. A classic starter trip is France's largest glacier, **La Mer de Glace,** in Montenvers, a must for those who have never swum through a sea of ice. The 7km claw is accessible by special trains running from a small station next to the main one. (☎04 50 53 12 54. July-Aug. daily 8am-6pm every 20min.; May-June and Sept. 1-15 daily 8am-5pm every 30min.; Sept.16-Apr. daily 10am-4pm, reduced service. 62F/€8.25, round-trip 82F/€10.91.) From the Mer, a cable-car runs to an **ice cave** that is carved afresh every year—the glacier slides 30m per year, so look for last year's cave farther down the wall of ice (car descent 14F/€2.13; cave entrance 18F/€2.74). Consider taking the train up and then hiking back. It's downhill, and just as you run out of breath, the **Luge d'Eté,** a concrete chute, whisks you to the bottom. You can also ride the luge without the hike. (☎04 50 53 08 97. Open Apr.-Nov. 11. Open July-Aug. daily 10am-7:30pm, also M and Th 8:30-10:30pm; Sept. and June daily 1:30-5:30pm; Oct.-Nov. Sa-Su 1:30-5:30pm. 33F/€5.03.)

TELEPHERIQUES. Whether you're hiking in summer or skiing in winter, chances are you'll need to take a *téléphérique* (cable car) part of the way. Even if you're not the outdoorsy type, the ride and awe-inspiring views of Mont Blanc are not to be missed. A board on pl. de l'Eglise lists which lifts are currently open.

The **Aiguille du Midi** runs all year (☎04 50 53 30 80, 24hr. reservations ☎08 92 68 00 67). Those with acrophobia (fear of heights) or argentophobia (fear of expenditure) might avoid the pricey and often frightening ride, which rises above towering forests and rocky, snow-covered cliffs to the needlepoint peak at the top. Among the brave and well-to-do, however, few are disappointed. Go early, as clouds and crowds usually gather by mid-morning. The first stop, **Plan de l'Aiguille** (66F/€8.78, round-trip 89F/€11.84), is a starting point for hikes (see **Hiking,** below) but otherwise not worth stopping at; those with views in mind should continue to **l'Aiguille du Midi** ("Needle of the South"), which is twice as high. At the Aiguille, the panorama is breathtaking, as is the head-lightening 3842m oxygen. Bring warm clothes and take it easy up top. The brochure advises visitors to walk and talk at the same time. For an additional 14F/€2.13, an elevator goes right to the summit, where there's a glorious 360-degree view (round-trip 210F/€32.02).

High-altitude escapades don't end with a view of Europe's tallest peak; from the Aiguille du Midi summit, an extra 105F/€16.01 (and worth every centime) pays for a round-trip ticket to **Helbronner,** where you can stand on the French-Italian border (May-Sept. only). Four-person gondolas take you into the heart of the glacial beast and let you rest in Italy for great views of three countries, and the Matterhorn and Mont Blanc peaks; you can pack a picnic and eat on the "Glacier Géant" here. From Helbronner, a final *téléphérique* descends into Italy to **La Palud,** near the resort town of **Courmayeur.** Bring a passport and cash—the Italian side doesn't accept credit cards for the cable car. Check that the entire *téléphérique* route is in operation before setting out for this trip. (*Téléphérique* open Sept.-June daily 8am-4:45pm; July-Aug. 6am-5pm.)

For views of Mont Blanc, the Aiguille du Midi can't be beat, but several other *téléphériques* run year-round on the opposite side of the valley to whisk you to popular hiking trails or panoramic restaurants. **Le Brévent** (2525m) leaves from the corner of rte. Henriette and La Mollard up the street from the tourist office. (☎04 50 53 13 18. Open July-Aug. 8am-6pm; Sept.-June 9am-5pm. One-way 69F/€9.18, round-trip 88F/€11.71.) East of the city in Les Praz, **La Flégère,** on rue Joseph Vallot, makes an intermediary stop at an eponymous plateau before continuing to **l'Index** (2385m; one-way 69F/€9.18, round-trip 88F/€11.71), a starting point for the hike to Lac Blanc. (☎04 50 53 18 58. Open July-Aug. daily 8am-5pm; June and Sept. 8am-12:30pm and 1:30-4:45pm.)

SKIING. If you're in town for a few days, buy daily lift tickets at individual areas—one area is more than enough per day. If you plan to ski for a week, buy a **Cham'Ski** pass, available at the tourist office or major *téléphériques* (Brevent, Flégère, Aiguille du Midi). The 1100F/€168 ticket (which requires a passport photo) gives unlimited access to the Chamonix Valley—excluding the small Les Houches area—and includes a day in Courmayeur-Val-Veny in Italy.

Chamonix is surrounded by skiable mountains. The **southern side** of the valley opposite Mont Blanc is drenched in sunlight during the morning and offers easy to challenging terrain; in the afternoon, both the sun and extreme skiers head over to the death-defying **north face,** which abounds in advanced, off-*piste*, and glacial terrain. Public buses, free to Cham'Ski holders, and the trains of the Mont Blanc tramway connect the valley's string of resort villages from Les Bossons to La Tour.

At the bottom of the valley, **Le Tour-Col de Balme** (☎ 04 50 54 00 58), above the village of **Le Tour,** is the first of Chamonix's ski areas. Near the Swiss border, it provides a wide variety of sunny trails and is ideal for beginner to intermediate skiiers (day-pass 153F/€20.36). More dramatic runs for the non-expert skier congregate around the **Brévent** and **Flégère** *téléphériques*, closer to town. Connected by a cablecar, Brévent and Flégère together constitute Chamonix's largest ski area and offer good views of the Mont Blanc range; located steps from the tourist office, the Brévent *téléphérique* is particularly convenient. Note, however, that from the top of the Brévent gondola it's all advanced terrain; less confident skiers should get off at the intermediate stop **Planpraz,** from where they can access a variety of easier trails. (Brévent and Flégère day pass 160F/€24.39.)

Extreme skiers will have plenty of opportunities for near-death experiences on the opposite side of the Chamonix valley, starting with **Les Grands Montets** (3275m; ☎ 04 50 54 00 71), in Argentière. The *grande dame* of Chamonix's ski spots, it's virtually all advanced terrain, and skiers should test their mettle elsewhere before ascending. Les Grands Montets is also geared toward **snowboarding,** with a remodeled half-pipe and loads of off-*piste* powder (day pass 200F/€30.49). Directly above Chamonix, the infamous **Vallée Blanche** requires a healthy dose of courage and insanity. From the top of the Aiguille du Midi *téléphérique* (210F/€32.02), the ungroomed, unmarked, unpatrolled 20km trail cascades down a glacier to Chamonix town. Check the conditions before you go. Going with a guide who understands the terrain is highly recommended; going alone is simply stupid. Reserve a spot on the *téléphérique* in high season (☎ 08 92 68 00 67). Despite how they may look from down below, glaciers are not snowfields. Always stay within sight of trail markers, or you may end up at the bottom of a crevice. For any off-*piste* skiing, check your route with the **ski patrol** or the **Office de Haut Montagne.** The only really safe way to ski on a glacier or off-*piste*, especially if you're new to Chamonix, is with a guide hired from the **Compagnie des Guides** (see p. 371; about 350F/€53.36 per person). English-speaking guides not only tailor the itinerary to your desires and ability, but they'll make all the necessary arrangements, from equipment rental to lift reservations. If they don't want to ski on a glacier, beginners can ski beside one at the **Glacier du Mont Blanc** in Les Bossons, which also offers night skiing. (☎ 04 50 53 12 39. Night skiing W-Th.)

HIKING. Chamonix has hundreds of kilometers of hikes through terrain ranging from forests to glaciers. A web of trails, each marked by signs, wraps around the town. The 25F/€3.81 map, available at the tourist office, lists all the mountain *refuges* and gives departure points and estimated lengths for all the trails. Climbers should buy the **IGN topographic map** (see p. 50), available at the **Office de Haute Montagne** and local bookstores (59F/€9). Many trails begin in the far reaches of the Chamonix valley, but a handful of excellent ones are easily accessible from town.

If you're experienced in mountain climbing, you can ascend **Mont Blanc** (4807m), a two- or three-day climb—but don't try it solo. You can be caught in a vicious blizzard even in August; in 1996, the top had more snow in summer than at the height of winter. The Maison de la Montagne, the Compagnie des Guides, and the Club Alpin Français all have info (see **Skiing, Biking, and Hiking Resources,** p. 371).

Amateur hikers will enjoy the two ridges along the valley wall, called *balcons* or "balconies." The trails heading up here start at medium to high altitudes and are accessible either by *teléphérique* or via steep climbs out of Chamonix town. On the south side of the valley, the **Grand Balcon Sud** is a picturesque, wildflower-studded trail connecting the Brévent and Flégère *téléphériques;* from the Flégère cable car station, descend slightly and join the path that heads right toward a chimney. After two hours, the trail meets the Planpraz cable car station (1999m; the middle station of Brévent), from where you can hike (or ride) back to town, or embark on a difficult, scenic ascent to the **Col de Brévent** (2368m), at the top of the Brévent ski lift (1¾hr.). At the Flégère end of the Balcon Sud, another classic hike embarks for **Lac Blanc.** From the station, take the path that starts to the left near the stables and snakes its way up the hill. After passing by the Lac de la Flégère (2027m), the trail flattens out and continues to the Lac Blanc (1¾hr.), a beautiful glacial lake with the expensive **Refuge du Lac Blanc** nearby. (☎04 50 53 49 14. Breakfast and dinner included. By reservation only. 280F/€42.69 per person.) Intermediate hikers can spare themselves the cable-car fees by taking the steep trail originating at the bottom of the Flégère *téléphérique* in **les Praz** and ascending 800m to reach the middle station—and the treeline (3hr.). The Chalet de la Flégère **refuge** waits up top to welcome you. (☎04 50 53 06 13. July-Aug. 180F/€27.44, including dinner and breakfast. June and Sept., night only, 90F/€13.72.)

The **Grand Balcon Nord,** on the opposite side of the valley, is at a much higher altitude and offers the dramatic scenery of jagged ice cascades and peaks. Take the Aiguille du Midi cable car to the first stop, Plan de l'Aiguille, and descend to the Refuge du Plan de l'Aiguille. Don't take one of the paths going down to Chamonix, but keep to the trail that heads off horizontally to the right across la Tapia. After about two unforgettable hours, you'll hit the **Hôtel Montenvers,** at the foot of the Mer de Glace glacier. Mountaineers use the refuge as a base for ice climbing. (☎04 50 53 87 70. Breakfast and dinner included. Open June 15-Sept. 15. 227F/€30.20.) The two refuges are also accessible by foot from town; it's a middle-difficulty hike 900m up to the Hôtel Montenvers from the Montenvers train station, where signs mark the way (2½hr.), and a hard one 1300m to the Refuge Plan de l'Aiguille via any one of the steep trails (all 3½hr.) that begin at the Aiguille cable-car parking lot. (Refuge ☎06 65 64 27 53. 65F/€9.91; with breakfast and dinner 185F/€28.21.)

VAL D'ISERE

Val d'Isère (pop. 1750; 1850m) is named after the river that flows through the town, but it makes its livelihood from the peaks above. This world-class ski resort's sole purpose is to worship the mountains, the snow, and native son Jean-Claude Killy, who won gold in *all* the men's downhill events in the 1968 Grenoble Winter Olympics. But that's not the only reason he's a hero here; Killy is the dynamo who brought Olympic events to Val d'Isère in 1992, just after he helped turn its main street into a tourist-laden strip of expensive hotels, restaurants, and ski boutiques. In summer, snow and prices melt, bikers and climbers fill the open hotels, and skiers retreat to the Glaciers du Pissaillas, where slushy white stuff persists until mid-August. A particularly crazy time to come, is Dec. 8-12, when the Criterium de la Première Neige, the first international competition of the season, comes to Val.

TRANSPORTATION

Trains: pl. de la Gare in **Bourg St-Maurice.** To: **Annecy** (3hr., 6 per day, 138F/€21.05); **Grenoble** (3hr., 6 per day, 121F/€18.45); and **Lyon** (3-4hr., 8 per day, 144F/€21.96). Open daily 5am-10:30pm. **Luggage storage** 30F/€4.57 per piece. Open July-Aug. and Dec. 15-Apr. daily 8am-8:30pm.

Buses: Autocars Martin (☎04 79 06 00 42 for reservations), by the roundabout 150m below the tourist office. Open July-Aug. M 1:30-8:15pm, Tu-F 9-10am and 1:30-8:15pm, Sa 7-9:30am and 1-8pm; Dec.-Apr. M-F 9-11:30am and 1:30-7:45pm, Sa 6:30am-noon and 1-8:30pm, Su 7:30-11:30am and 1:30-7:45pm. **Main office** at pl.

de la Gare in Bourg St-Maurice (☎04 79 07 04 49). Open daily 8am-noon and 2-6pm. Dec.-Apr., buses go to **Geneva,** Switzerland (airport 4hr., Geneva proper 4½hr.; M-F 3 per day, Sa-Su 5 per day; 290F/€44.21) via **Annecy** (3½hr., 240F/€36.59); and **Lyon airport** (3½hr.; M-F and Su 2 per day, Sa 4 per day; 300F/€45.74). Year-round, buses go to the **hostel** in **Les Boisses** (10min.; Dec. 19-Apr. M-F 4 per day, Sa 1 per day, Su 2 per day; May-Dec. 18 M-F 3 per day, Sa-Su 3 per day; 18F/€2.75). **SNCF** info and reservation desks (☎04 79 06 03 55) are in the same building. Open July-Aug. Tu-Sa 9am-noon and 2-6pm; Dec.-Apr. M-Sa 9am-noon and 3-7pm.

Local Transportation: Val d'Isère runs **free shuttles** *(navettes)* about town. **Train Rouge** runs between La Daille and Le Fornet, while **Train Vert** runs only in summer from the tourist office and the bus station up to le Manchet Sports complex and the entrance to the Vanoise national park. Both are useful for shaving time off treks to the *refuges*. In winter, the *Train Rouge* runs every 10-15min. until between midnight and 2am. In summer, both shuttles run every 30min. until about 7:30pm.

Bike and Ski Rental: About 30 spots in town offer rental; ask at the tourist office.

Taxis: ABC (☎04 79 06 19 92); **Altitude Espace Taxi** (☎04 79 41 14 15).

Hitchhiking: Bad transport and sympathetic locals make hitching a popular mode of transport, although *Let's Go* does not recommend it under any circumstances. Those going from the hostel to Val d'Isère cross the dam and wait by the highway. No one hitches after dark. Not even you.

ALPS

ORIENTATION AND PRACTICAL INFORMATION

Val d'Isère has no train station—getting here takes time and money. The nearest station is in **Bourg-St-Maurice,** 30km to the north; a bus leaves for Val d'Isère (M-F 3 per day, 7 on Sa; 68F/€10.37). If you're going to the hostel, get off at **Tignes-Les Boisses,** 7km short of Val d'Isère (68F/€10.37). In summer, the last bus leaves at 6:30pm; service is more frequent in winter. The Val d'Isère mega-resort comprises three villages, all in a line: **Le Fornet** is at the top, **La Daille** is down below at the entrance to the valley, and **Val Village,** home to most accommodations and the **tourist office,** is right in the middle. Unless otherwise stated, most everything discussed below is in Val Village, the most substantial of the three. Although Val d'Isère's street names are neither used nor clearly indicated, the town is navigable with the map at the back of the tourist office's *Practical Guide*.

Tourist Office: (☎04 79 06 06 60; fax 04 79 06 04 56; www.valdisere.com), in Val Village. Distributes practical guides, available in 6 languages. Supplementary summer and winter guides detail prices and schedules. Open May-June and Sept.-Nov. daily 9am-noon and 2-6pm; July-Aug. daily 8:30am-7:30pm; Dec.-Apr. Su-F 8:30am-7:30pm, Sa 8:30am-8pm. **Annex** at the entrance to town, a small wooden hut on the right as you make your way up from La Daille (☎04 79 06 19 67). Open June-Aug. 7 daily 9am-noon and 3-6pm; Dec.-Apr. Sa-Su 9am-noon and 2-7pm.

Laundromat: Laverie Automatique, across from the bus station. Open daily 8:30am-9:30pm.

Weather, Ski, and Road Info: Call tourist office or listen to **Radio Val** (96.1FM; ☎04 79 06 18 66). **Weather forecast:** ☎08 36 68 02 73. **Ski Info:** ☎04 79 06 25 55. **Ski Lifts:** ☎04 79 06 00 35. **Ski Patrol:** ☎04 79 06 02 10.

Police: ☎04 79 06 03 41, above the tourist office and across from Casino supermarket.

Hospital: in Bourg St-Maurice (☎04 79 41 79 79).

Internet Access: Lodge Bar (☎04 79 06 19 31). Turn right at the roundabout above the bus station. Intimate lounge with low ceilings and mood lighting. Internet 60F/€9.15 per hr. Open in winter daily 4:30pm-1:30am; in summer 7pm-1:30am. Closed May-June. Also at **Dick's Tea Bar** (see below).

Post Office: Across from the tourist office (☎04 79 06 06 99) in "Vieux Val." **Currency exchange** with good rates and no commission. Open July-Aug. M-F 9am-noon and 2-5pm, Sa 9:30am-noon; in ski season M-F 8:30am-6:30pm, Sa 8:30am-noon; rest of year M-F 9am-noon and 2-5pm, Sa 9am-noon. **Postal code:** 73150.

ACCOMMODATIONS AND CAMPING

World-class slopes only feet away make it very tough to find a room here in winter. During the off-season many hotels close, but prices at open lodgings dip to unbelievable rates. The cheapest beds are at the two *refuges*, **Le Prariond** and **Le Fond Des Fours,** each at least a two-hour hike from downtown (see **Hiking,** p. 379, for directions and prices). Cheaper **gîtes** in Le Fornet offer a homey alternative to downtown hotels; the tourist office has a complete list. In July and August **Moris Pub,** 75m up from the tourist office, rents bright rooms upstairs for super-cheap prices. (☎04 79 06 22 11. 150F/€22.90 per person, includes breakfast. MC/V.)

Auberge de Jeunesse "Les Clarines" (HI) (☎04 79 06 35 07; reservations ☎04 79 41 01 93; fax 04 79 41 03 36; tignes@fuaj.org), in the village of **Les Boisses** at the junction of the routes to Val d'Isère (7km south) and Tignes (5km west). From Val d'Isère, a pleasant, well-marked trail begins at La Daille. Follow the river down to the lake and bear left along the shore until you ford a cascading creek. Turn right, cross the bridge, and take the small, unmarked path ascending to the right until it meets the road. To the right is Les Boisses and the hostel (1½hr.). Or take the "Tignes/Val Claret" bus to "Les Boisses" from Bourg-St-Maurice (68F/€10.37) or Val d'Isère (18F/€2.75). A free shuttle runs between Tignes and Les Boisses 2-3 times per day, more in winter. Wooden rooms for 4-6 people, all but 3 with toilet, overlooking the Lac du Chevril. The hostel arranges **skiing, hiking, biking,** and **water sports** packages (from 38F/€5.80 per day), as well as **paragliding** excursions and **horse riding, biking,** and **rock-climbing** trips led by experts. Discounts on ski and snowboard rental all year. Code to get in after 10pm. Reception 5-10pm; drop off bags any time. Reserve in Sept. for Dec. or Feb., 6 weeks ahead for Jan., Mar., or Apr. Closed May-June 25 and Sept.-Nov. Bunks 75F/€11.43 includes breakfast; 126F/€19.22 includes dinner; 183F/€27.91 includes a cross-country day pass, 240F/€36.59 an alpine day pass. Weekly skiing packages from 1790F/€272.91 in summer, 1920F/€292.73 in winter. MC/V.

Gîtes Bonnevie (☎04 79 06 06 26; fax 04 79 06 16 65), in Le Fornet. Cross the bridge and it's the first building on the right. Gorgeous wooden chalet-style studios for 2 to 10 people, all with bathrooms, kitchen, and splendid views. About as cheap as it gets. 100F/€15.25 per person in summer; in winter, weekly rentals only: doubles 1800F/€274.43; quads 2500-3200F/€381.16-487.88; 10-man 9500F/€1448.39. Winter prices fluctuate, so call to verify.

Hôtel Sakura/Les Crêtes Blanches (☎04 79 06 04 08; fax 04 79 41 10 65; sakura7@club-internet.fr). Turn right at the roundabout above the bus station. Spacious, wood-paneled rooms, some with balcony and TV. Plenty of rainy day fun in the cozy lounge area and adjacent terrace. 2- to 5-person studios have kitchen and breakfast table. Breakfast 40F/€6.10. Open July-Aug. for short stays; Dec.-Apr. 1-week minimum stay. Closed Sept.-Nov. and May-June. July-Aug. singles 205F/€31.26; doubles 250F/€38.12. In winter, studios 2175-7200F/€331.61-1097.73 per week. MC/V.

Le Relais du Ski (☎04 79 06 02 06; fax 04 79 41 10 64; lerelaisduski@valdisere.com), 300m up from the tourist office. Small, wood-panelled rooms with hall showers. Breakfast 60F/€9.15; speak up beforehand if you don't want it. Singles 250-330F/€38.12-50.33; doubles 300-450F/€45.74-68.61; triples 410-520F/€62.53-79.30; quads 465-620F/€70.91-94.55. Prices 80-170F/€12.20-25.92 lower July-Aug. AmEx/MC/V.

Camping les Richardes (☎/fax 04 79 06 26 60), 500m up from the tourist office. The free *Train Rouge* shuttle stops here. Plain campground in a beautiful valley, close to town. Crowded mid-Aug., when 4x4 competitions come around. Reception June 15-July 14 7:30am-12:30pm and 2-8pm; July 15-Sept. 15 9am-noon and 5-8pm. Open June 15-Sept. 15. 15F/€2.29 per person, 9F/€1.37 per tent, 8.50F/€1.30 per car. Electricity 12F/€1.83. Showers 6.50F/€1. AmEx/MC/V with a 100F/€15.25 minimum.

FOOD AND ENTERTAINMENT

Perhaps someday Jean-Claude Killy will bring affordable dining to Val d'Isère, just as Prometheus descended with fire to primitive man. Until then, the supermarkets will have to suffice. Pack for the slopes at **Marché U,** 130m below the tourist office. (☎04 79 06 01 98. Open July-Aug. daily 8:30am-1pm and 3:30-7:45pm; Dec.-Apr. 8am-8pm; May-June and Sept.-Nov. 9am-12:30pm and 4:30-7:30pm.) Many restaurants and virtually all nightlife close immediately after ski season. **Le Bananas** is on a side street by the bus station roundabout, near the base of the *téléphériques.* Ski instructors and dread-head boarders pack this rockin' chalet for bites and beers just inches from the slopes. Delicious dishes that riff off tex-mex cuisine include *quesadillas à la française* (90F/€13.72) and assorted salads (28-60F/€4.27-9.15). (☎04 79 06 04 23. Open daily noon-1:30am. Dec.-Apr. happy hour 7-8pm. MC/V.)

The roundabout above the bus station is Val d'Isère's unofficial nightlife strip. Start your drinking at **Lodge Bar** (see **Internet Access,** above). Then stumble up the block to **Café Face,** where DJs and sax players fill this lodge-like spot. (☎04 79 06 29 80. Open Dec.-May daily 4pm-2am; July-Aug. 10pm-2am.) Across the street, **Dick's Tea Bar** is the best late-night option. An Anglo crowd packs into this Val mainstay, complete with a large dance floor and Internet access. (☎04 79 06 14 87. Open in winter Tu-Su 4:30pm-4am; in summer from 7:30pm. Closed Sept.-Nov.)

OUTDOOR ACTIVITIES

SKIING. Skiing is king in Val d'Isère, with over 100 lifts providing access to 300km of trails. You can ski for a week without repeating a run. Lift tickets are cheaper over longer periods. They're valid on the entire **Espace Killy,** which includes every lift and run from **Val d'Isère** to **Tignes,** a ski station 7km away. The mountains are generally skiable from December through the beginning of May, with optimum conditions in mid-winter. (Lift tickets 164F/€25.01 per half-day, 233F/€35.53 per day, 1246F/€189.97 per week.)

Most good beginner runs are at higher altitudes, around the Marmottes and Borsat lifts on the south side of Bellevarde (that's the back side; take the Bellevarde lift up) and in the super-scenic Pissaillas area (take the Solaise cable car, then the Glacier and Leissier lifts). Intermediate and advanced skiers like the slopes surrounding Tignes, while the north side of Bellevarde is known for expert runs. There's a giant **snow park** between Val and Tignes; a classic boarder run starts at the top of the Mont Blanc lift and whirls its way through the park to La Daille, where a Funival car whisks boarders back to the Bellevarde summit for an encore.

Val d'Isère is proudest of its glorious off-*piste* opportunities. Skiers of the **col Pers** region, accessible from the Pissaillas glacier, speed past ibex and *chamois* through the Gorges de Malpassaet. Never ski off-*piste* alone, check weather conditions before you go, and let the ski patrol know your itinerary. Non-experts and those unfamiliar with the area might consider going with a **guide** (☎04 79 06 02 34).

From July to mid-August, Pissaillas also offers **summer skiing.** Lift tickets are available at the Le Fornet cable car, and from there a free bus takes you to the top. Conditions deteriorate and prices drop after 11am and there's no skiing after 1:30pm. (108F/€16.5 per half-day, 138F/€21 per day; after 11am, 98F/€14.95 per half-day, 114F/€17.39 per day. Lifts open at 7:30am.)

HIKING. Before hiking around Val d'Isère, be sure to check the weather report and to bring warm clothing; snowstorms and winter weather are possible even in summer. Some intermediate trails, when snow-covered, are passable only for those with the proper equipment and experience. Even though the trails around the Val are well-marked with blazes and signs, hikers should buy both the detailed *Val d'Isère—Balades et Sentiers* (25F/€3.81) and a **hiking map** (45F/€6.86) in English at the tourist office. These include over 40 routes spanning 100km.

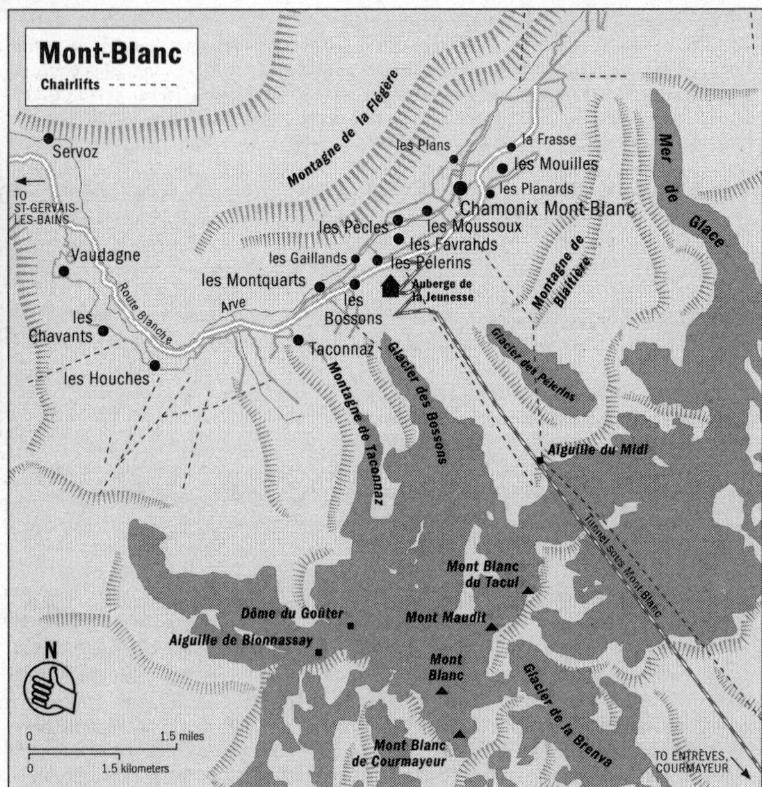

Until the construction of modern ski areas in the 60s, **Le Fornet** (1950m) was the highest year-round inhabited village in the French Alps. It can be reached by an easy 4km hike (1½hr.). Starting from the church in Val Village, follow the sign for Le Fornet. The trail leads through the Vieux Val to a small pedestrian road and then briefly joins up with the GR5 before forking again toward Le Fornet. Just before the village, the trail offers the option of doubling back via the beautiful 45-minute **sentier écologique** to meet up with the GR5 once again and return to town.

Val d'Isère's classic **intermediate** hikes lead through the Vanoise National Park, France's premiere wildlife reserve, to the two closest *refuges*. The trail to the **Refuge de Prariond** (one-way 3km; 1¾hr.; 300m vertical) begins in Le Fornet and is a must for animal lovers—acrobatic *bouquetin* (ibex), *chamois* (the antelope's little cousin), and furry marmots are plentiful. From the center of Le Fornet, cross the bridge and follow the signs to **pont St-Charles.** After the bridge, the marked trail switchbacks several times out of the far end of the parking lot before beginning a steep ascent up the **Gorges du Malpasset.** The trail then gains a plateau and continues gently to the *refuge*. (*Refuge* ☎ 04 79 06 06 02. Staffed Mar. 31-May 10 and June 15-Sept. 15. Otherwise, there is wood, gas, utensils, covers, and a tin box for your money. Hot showers 12F/€1.83, animal-skin sleeping sacks 14F/€2.14. Breakfast 35F/€5.34, *à la carte* lunch 90F/€13.72, dinner 90F/€13.72. Reserve ahead at the tourist office and get a map. 73F/€11.13 per person, students 54F/€8.24.) From Prariond, you can climb for another two hours and 600 vertical meters to the **Col de la Galise** pass (2987m) and the source of the Isère river, which affords one of the most stunning panoramas in the region. Coming out of the *refuge*, take the trail to the right. At the **Roche des Coses** (2750m), you can branch right for a 45-minute excursion into Italy and similarly stupendous vistas. Take care, since this trail is usually snow-covered year-round.

The second hike leads through alpine meadows to the **Refuge des Fours,** in the Vanoise National Park. Take the free shuttle to **le Manchet** (see **Local Transportation,** p. 377), and continue up the road to the trailhead near a cluster of old stone farmhouses. Take the trail on your right marked *"refuge des fours."* From there it's a steady climb to the hut in a high valley across from the Méan Martin glacier and alpine lakes. (One-way hike from le Manchet: 1¾hr., 560m vertical. *Refuge* ☎04 79 06 16 90; same prices and staffing months as Fornet.) There are numerous ways to return to Val without retracing your steps. One option is to cross the **Col des Fours** pass and head back to town via the **GR5.** Continue along the trail that took you to the *refuge*, and turn left onto the path that ascends the neckline between the Pelou Blanc (3135m) and the 3072m Pointe des Fours. (1¼hr.; 450m vertical). Where the trail ends, hang a left on the red-and-white marked **GR5** for a gloriously scenic descent to town via the **Col d'Iseran,** a favorite leg of the Tour de France (6km; 1½-2hr.; 900m descent).

An **advanced full-day trek** heads from le Fornet to the **Lac de la Sassière;** from the *téléphérique*, descend slightly and turn right at the trail marker for the Balcon des Barmettes. At the Balcon, head right on Trail #36, the **Bailletta,** which climbs steeply for 800m to the small **Lac de la Bailletta** (2½hr.), where it reaches a pass and descends gradually to the larger **Lac de la Sassière.** This man-made lake is crammed with trout and surrounded by *chamois*, ibex, and marmots. To return, retrace your steps for several hundred meters until the sign for **Picheru,** a steeper path than the Balletta route. Picheru passes over several very exposed knife-edge ridges before crossing just to the right of **Le Dome** and descending gradually into town. (Round-trip to Lac de la Sassière: 12.2km, 7hr., 940m vertical.) Another advanced trek heads from the campground; grab the man-killing **GR5** (marked with red and white; see above for an easy descent of the same trail) and hold on tight for a harrowing ascent to the **Col de l'Iseran** (2770m). About half-way up, you'll cross the RD902. From the top there's a different glacier in every direction. (One-way to Col 6km; 3hr.; 914m vertical.)

OTHER OUTDOOR ACTIVITIES. Mountain Guides (☎04 79 06 06 60) has **ice climbing** (morning session 500F/€76.23) and **rock climbing** schools (afternoon session 180F/€27.44) and full-day **canyoning trips** (420F/€64.05). They also lead nature expeditions for all levels.

For a relaxing trip to Val d'Isère's summit, take a *téléphérique* (cable car), which will whisk you up the peaks as glaciers and valleys unfold before you. Cable cars run to **Solaise** (Dec.-Apr. ascents every 10min. 8:45-6:45pm; July-Aug. every hr. 9am-noon and 2-4:50pm), a small summit surrounded by a lake and easy hiking trails, and the much higher **Bellevarde,** site of the 1992 Olympic downhill (Dec.-Apr. ascents every 10min. 9am-5:30pm; July-Aug. ascents every hr. 9:30am-4:30pm; last descent 4:40pm). From the top, you can descend a steep trail on the front of the mountain back to Val d'Isère or one on the back that heads to La Daille. The rest of the terrain has been sliced and ground by **mountain bikers,** for whom Bellevarde is a favorite playground. Both cable cars cost 55F/€8.39 (round-trip 70F/€10.67); you can bring a bike or parasail on board for free.

Though Val d'Isère has plenty of uncharted mountains perfect for advanced **climbers** (call the Bureau des Guides at 04 79 06 06 60), beginners will appreciate the **Via Ferrata** in La Daille. The two- to three-hour climb (360m vertical) via metal footholds and ropes hugs the side of the mountain facing the valley. Signs point from the La Daille chapel to the climbing site.

ALSACE, LORRAINE, AND FRANCHE-COMTE

As first prize in the endless Franco-German border wars, France's northeastern frontier has had a long and bloody history. The area has been trampled by invaders since the 3rd century, when barbarian tribes first swept westward through these regions into Roman Europe. Alsace-Lorraine was ravaged during the Franco-Prussian War of 1870-1871, when it was ceded to Germany, then devastated during the French reoccupation in WWI and blitzed once again when the Germans retook it in WWII. Franche-Comté, long a pawn of its more powerful neighbors, snuggles up to the Jura mountains in the south. Though the inhabitants had violently opposed France's final 1674 conquest of their land, their defense against the invading Prussians 193 years later earned them the right to stay French in 1871.

Alsace and Lorraine are far less similar than their hyphenated twinship leads most people to believe. In Alsace's Vosges, wooded hills slope down to sunlit valleys and deep blue lakes perfect for hiking, camping, and cross-country skiing. On the eastern foothills lie the striped, shiny vineyards of the Route du Vin, and Alsace's well-preserved towns offer geranium-draped, half-timbered Bavarian houses flanking tiny crooked streets and canals. In contrast, Lorraine unfolds to the west among wheat fields and gently undulating plains. The serenely elegant cities feature broad, tree-lined boulevards and stately Baroque architecture. Often overlooked by visitors to northeastern France, Franche-Comté is beginning to burst into the spotlight. Known for their lush, seemingly endless forests, the Jura mountains are an escape from the tourist-oriented kitsch to the north. Blanketed in snow in the winter, the Jura is home to some of France's finest cross-country skiing, including the Grand Traversée de Jura, a 400km network of trails.

1 **Nancy:** A planned city of fountains and wrought iron; the region's intellectual capital **(p. 384)**
2 **Metz:** A calm city good for strollers, with gardens and Chagall stained glass **(p. 388)**
3 **Verdun:** Ground zero for WWI's worst battle; memorials fill the surrounding countryside **(p. 392)**
4 **Strasbourg:** Capital of Alsace, financial and intellectual powerhouse; unmissable **(p. 395)**
5 **Saverne:** A calm mountain town; beautiful nearby hikes and France's best garden **(p. 401)**
6 **Kaysersberg:** Our favorite town along the Route du Vin; lovely and unspoiled **(p. 403)**
7 **Riquewihr:** Most visited wine route village, and deservedly so; but heavily touristed **(p. 404)**
8 **Barr:** One of the smallest, least kitschy, most picturesque of the wine villages **(p. 405)**
9 **Obernai:** A picturesque medieval town with a fine set of ramparts **(p. 405)**
10 **Sélestat:** Often mistakenly overlooked; calm, friendly, ancient, and a perfect base **(p. 405)**
11 **Château du Haut Koenigsbourg:** the legend-permeated castle of a half-blind duke **(p. 407)**
12 **Colmar:** Major base for the region's wine towns; a typical alsatian *bourg* in its own right **(p. 407)**
13 **Mulhouse:** A grim industrial town with excellent technical museums **(p. 410)**
14 **Belfort:** An old city, much invaded, near good hiking; worth it for Ronchamp **(p. 417)**
15 **Ronchamp:** a tiny hill town, home to a Corbusier masterwork cathedral **(p. 420)**
16 **Besançon:** Largest, busiest town in its area; good museums, lots of club-happy kids **(p. 412)**
17 **Lons:** A lively, mountain-sandwiched town with fewer excursions than Pontarlier **(p. 420)**
18 **Dole:** Tranquil transportation hub; perfect for a stopover **(p. 422)**
19 **Arbois:** A lusciously green wine-tasting town that hasn't lost its regional flavor **(p. 424)**
20 **Pontarlier:** A commercialized mountain town with amazing views and excursions **(p. 426)**

TRANSPORTATION

Metz, Nancy, Besançon, and Strasbourg are major train hubs. Between smaller towns, notably Verdun and the Route du Vin, buses are more practical. Biking is a good option within Lorraine and Alsace, although they're very hilly—the Vosges, the small mountain range dividing the two, will seem a lot larger when you're huffing and puffing your way up it. For hikers, hundreds of kilometers of trails dotted with *fermes auberges* (overnight farm refuges) are marked on maps and guides. Renting a car or bike, or taking a tour bus, are practical ways to see the battlefields at Verdun and many of the villages on the Route du Vin.

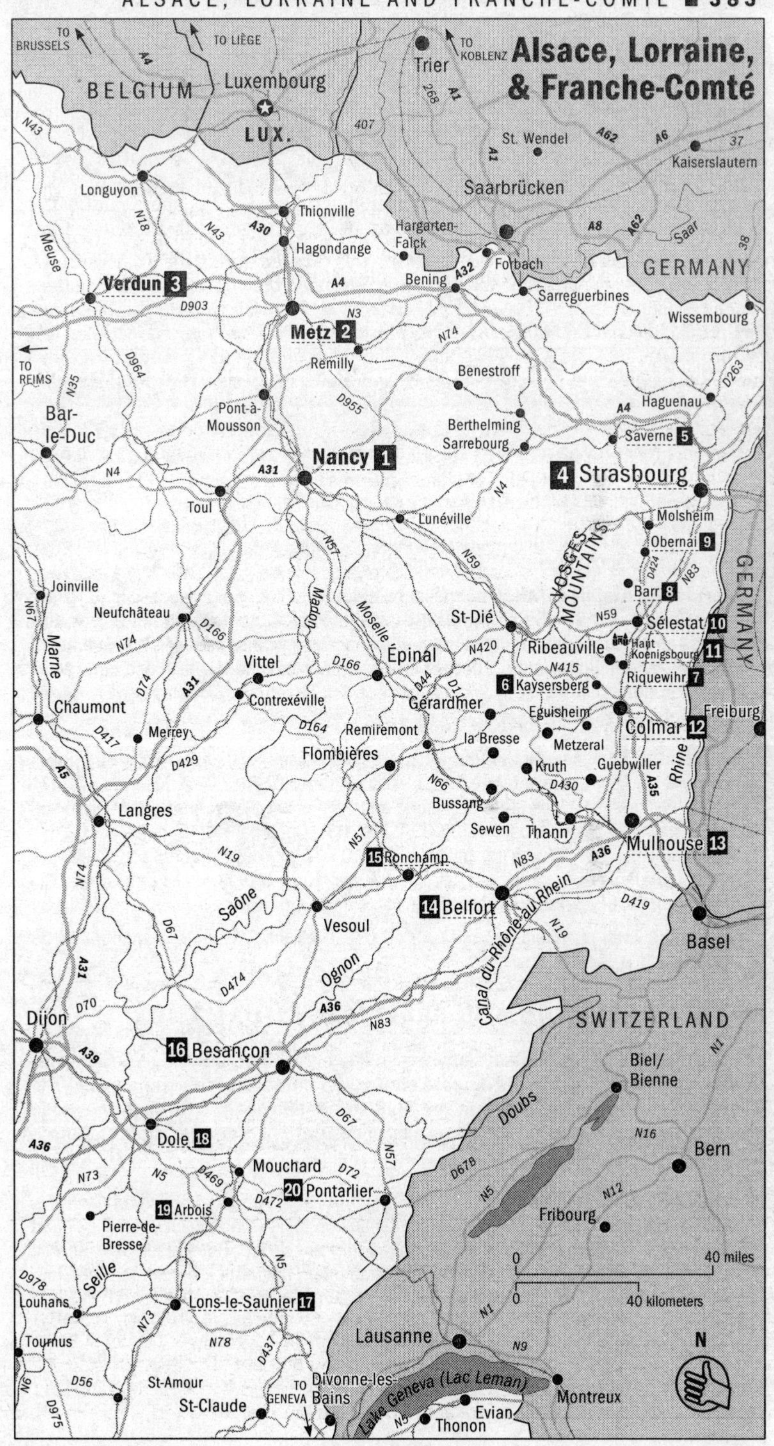
Alsace, Lorraine, & Franche-Comté
BELGIUM
LUX.
GERMANY
SWITZERLAND
Luxembourg
Trier
St. Wendel
Kaiserslautern
Saarbrücken
Longuyon
Thionville
Hagondange
Hargarten-Falck
Forbach
Bening
Sarreguerbines
Wissembourg
Verdun 3
Metz 2
Remilly
Benestroff
Haguenau
Bar-le-Duc
Pont-à-Mousson
Berthelming
Sarrebourg
Saverne 5
Nancy 1
4 Strasbourg
Toul
Lunéville
Molsheim
Obernai 9
Barr 8
VOSGES MOUNTAINS
Joinville
Neufchâteau
St-Dié
Sélestat 10
Haut Koenigsbourg 11
Ribeauville
Épinal
Vittel
Contrexéville
6 Kaysersberg
Riquewihr 7
Gérardmer
Eguisheim
Colmar 12
Freiburg
Chaumont
Merrey
Remiremont
la Bresse
Metzeral
Flombières
Kruth
Guebwiller
Bussang
Sewen
Thann
Mulhouse 13
Langres
15 Ronchamp
14 Belfort
Basel
Vesoul
Canal du Rhône au Rhein
Dijon
16 Besançon
Biel/Bienne
Bern
Dole 18
Mouchard
20 Pontarlier
19 Arbois
Fribourg
Pierre-de-Bresse
Louhans
Lons-le-Saunier 17
Tournus
Lausanne
St-Amour
St-Claude
TO GENEVA
Divonne-les-Bains
Lake Geneva (Lac Leman)
Montreux
Evian
Thonon
TO BRUSSELS
TO LIÈGE
TO KOBLENZ
TO REIMS
Meuse
Marne
Saône
Ognon
Doubs
Seille
Rhine
Moselle
Madon
Saar
40 miles
40 kilometers
N
ALSACE

NANCY

Nancy (pop. 100,000) owes its gilded beauty to the good Duke Stanislas, whose passion for urban planning transformed the city into a model of 18th-century classicism, with broad plazas, wrought-iron grillwork, and cascading fountains. Nancy has always been a city interested in beauty; it spawned a slew of art-nouveau sculptors and designers—the Nancy school—a century ago, and is today the artistic and intellectual heart of modern Lorraine, with symphony, opera, and ballet companies as well as a growing jazz and avant-garde art scene. Even if it weren't so lovely to walk around, Nancy's outgoing natives and nighttime *joie-de-vivre* would still make it one of the most enjoyable cities in northeastern France.

TRANSPORTATION

Flights: Aéroport de Metz-Nancy Lorraine (☎03 87 56 70 00). To: **Lyon, Marseille, Nice, Paris,** and **Toulouse.** Shuttle to the train station (30-40min.; 7 per day; 40F/€6.10, students 30F/€4.57).

Trains: pl. Thiers (☎03 83 22 12 46). To: **Metz** (40min., 24 per day, 52F/€7.93); **Paris** (3hr., 14 per day, 213F/€32.48); and **Strasbourg** (1hr., 19 per day, 112F/€17.08). **Ticket office** open M-Sa 5:40am-10pm, Su 6:30am-10pm.

Buses: Rapides de Lorraine, 52 bd. d'Austrasie (☎03 83 32 34 20), leave from in front of the train station. Open M-F 9am-noon and 2-6pm.

Local Transportation: STAN. Free bus maps at tourist office or at **Agence Bus,** 3 rue Dr. Schmitt (☎03 83 30 08 08). Most buses stop at Point Central on rue St-Georges. Buy tickets on board, at the train station, or from machines. Tickets 7.50F/€1.14, *carnet* of 10 51F/€7.78. Buses run 5:30am-8pm; some lines until midnight. Office open M-Sa 7am-7:30pm.

Taxis: Taxi Nancy, 2 bd. Joffre (☎03 83 37 65 37).

Bike Rental: Immense **Michenon,** 91 rue des 4 Eglises (☎03 83 17 59 59). Bikes 110F/€16.78 per day. Moped and scooter rental 210F/€32.03 with 8000F/€1219.70 deposit. Open M-Sa 9am-noon and 2-7pm. MC/V. **Cyclotop,** in the train station near the baggage deposit (☎03 83 22 11 63). Open daily 6:45am-9:30pm. 10F/€1.53 per hr., 25F/€3.81 per half-day, 35F/€5.34 per day. Motorbikes 30F/€4.57 per hr., tandems 50F/€7.62 per day. Identification and 300F/€45.74 deposit for bike or tandem, 500F/€76.23 for motorbike.

Car Rental: Avis, pl. Thiers (☎03 83 35 40 61). **Loca Vu,** 32 rue des Fabriques (☎03 83 35 15 05).

ORIENTATION AND PRACTICAL INFORMATION

The heart of the city is **pl. Stanislas.** As you leave the station to the left, take your first right on rue Raymond Poincaré (not to be confused with the parallel rue Henri Poincaré), which turns into rue Stanislas once you pass through the stone archway. Several blocks down, the street opens onto pl. Stanislas and the tourist office. Be careful around the train station at night.

Tourist Office: pl. Stanislas (☎03 83 35 22 41; fax 03 83 35 90 10; www.ot-nancy.fr). Ask for a map and *Le Fil d'Ariane*, a comprehensive guide written each year by a squad of students. **Currency exchange** only when banks are closed. Hotel reservation service 15F/€2.29, plus a 50-100F/€7.62-15.25 guarantee. Open Apr.-Sept. M-Sa 9am-7pm, Su 10am-5pm; Oct.-May M-Sa 9am-6pm, Su 10am-1pm.

City tour: Tourist office leads 1½hr. tours. July-Aug. Sa 4pm and Su 10:30am; Sept.-Nov. and Mar.-June Sa 4pm. 35F/€5.34. Call ahead for English tour, or rent an audioguide (35F/€5.34).

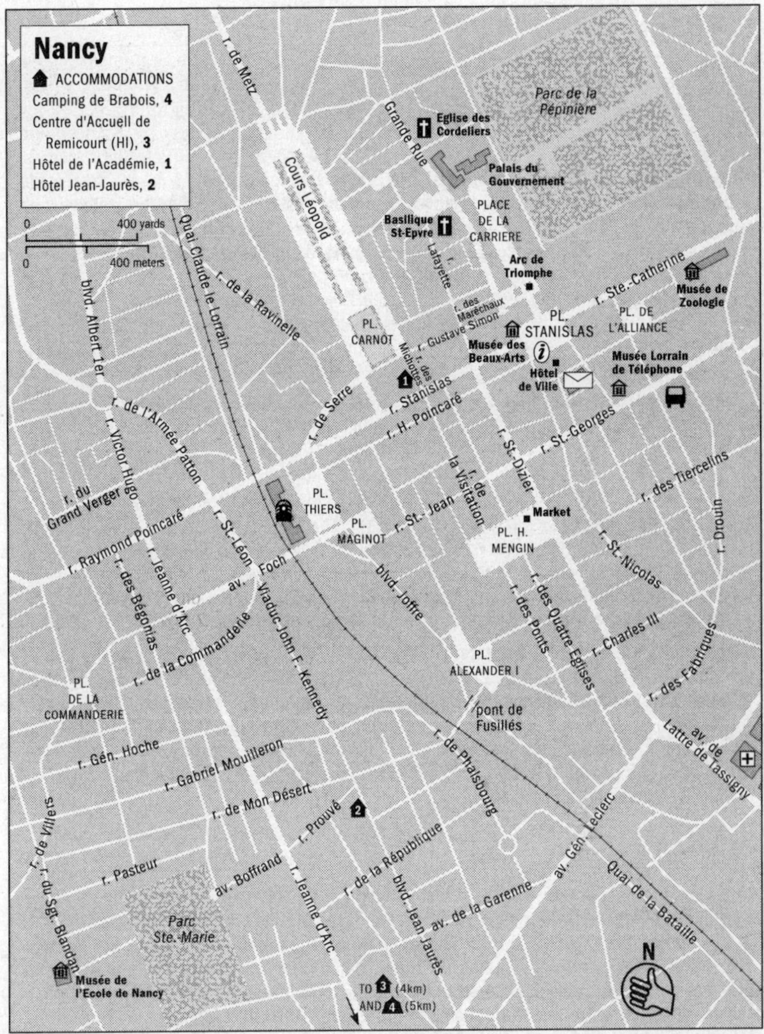

Budget Travel: Wasteels, 1bis pl. Thiers (☎08 03 88 70 52). Specializes in student passes and discount rates. Open M-F 9am-noon and 1-6pm, Sa 9am-noon.

Laundromat: Self Lav-o-matic, 107 rue Gabriel Mouilleron. Open daily 8am-8pm. **Le Bateau Lavoir,** 125 rue St-Dizier (☎03 83 35 47 47). Open daily 7:45am-9:30pm.

Police: 38 bd. Lobau (☎03 83 17 27 37), near the intersection with rue Charles III.

Hospital: CHU Nancy, 29 av. de Lattre de Tassigny (☎03 83 85 85 85).

Internet Access: E-café, rue des 4 Eglises (☎03 83 35 47 34). 35F/€5.34 per hr. Open M-Sa 9am-9pm, Su 2-8pm.

Post Office: 8 rue Pierre-Fourier (☎03 83 39 27 10), behind the Hôtel de Ville and pl. Stanislas. Open M-F 8am-7pm, Sa 8am-noon. **Branch** on bd. des Aiguillettes, in Villers-lès-Nancy. **Poste Restante:** Nancy-RP 54039. **Postal code:** 54000.

ACCOMMODATIONS AND CAMPING

CROUS, 75 rue de Laxou, helps students find summer accommodations in university dorms. Call **Foreign Student Services** at 03 83 91 88 26 (open M-F 9am-5pm). There are several budget hotels around rue Jeanne d'Arc, behind the train station, all at least a 15-minute walk from pl. Stanislas. The hostel is lovely but far.

Centre d'Accueil de Remicourt (HI), 149 rue de Vandoeuvre (☎03 83 27 73 67; fax 03 83 41 41 35), in Villers-lès-Nancy, 4km southwest of town. From the station, take bus #122 to "St-Fiacre" (dir: "Villiers Clairlieu," 2 per hr., last bus at 8pm; be sure to ask the driver if he goes to St-Fiacre as there are two paths to part of the route). Just downhill from the bus stop, turn right onto the bending uphill rue de la Grange des Moines, which turns into rue de Vandoeuvre. Look for the signs pointing to "Château de Remicourt," which is the site of the hostel. Hilltop views, some over the garden, make up for an institutional interior. Breakfast included. Reception 9am-9pm. 3- and 4-bed dorms 82F/€12.51; doubles with bath 97F/€14.79. MC/V.

Hôtel Le Jean Jaurès, 14 bd. Jean Jaurès (☎03 83 27 74 14; fax 03 83 90 20 94). The prettiest rooms in town for the price–colorful, elegant, and scrupulously maintained. Some overlook a garden, others (with sound-proof glass) a busy street; all have cable TV. Breakfast 29F/€4.42. Reception 7am-11pm. Singles with bath 230F/€35.07; doubles with bath 260F/€39.64; triples with bath 290F/€44.21. AmEx/MC/V.

Hôtel de l'Académie, 7 rue des Michottes (☎03 83 35 52 31; fax 03 83 32 55 78). Convenient location between the station and pl. Stanislas. 29 humble but tidy rooms around a meager, skylit atrium and trickling fountain. Breakfast 22F/€3.36. Reception 24hr., except Su noon-4:30pm. Singles and doubles with shower 140-160F/€21.35-24.39, with bath 165-200F/€25.16-30.49. Extra bed 40F/€6.10. MC/V.

Campsites: Camping de Brabrois, av. Paul Muller (☎03 83 27 18 28), near the Centre d'Accueil. Take bus #125 or 122 to "Camping" (dir: "Villiers Clairlieu"). Sweeping, spacious hilltop site overlooks the town. Showers, mini-tennis court, volleyball, playground, and grocery store. Access to woodland trails. Reception June-Aug. 7:30am-12:30pm and 1:30-10pm; Apr.-May and Sept.-Oct. 7:30am-12:30pm and 1:30-9pm. Open Apr.-Oct. 15. Two people with tent 58F/€8.85; extra adult 20F/€3.05, child age 2-7 10F/€1.53. Electricity 18F/€2.74.

FOOD

Nancy's signature *bergamote* is a bitter hard candy flavored by the orangey spice used in Earl Grey tea. Off rue St-Dizier in pl. Henri Mengin is the **marché central** (Tu-Th 7am-6pm, F-Sa 7am-6:30pm). There's a **Shopi supermarket** at 26 rue St-Georges (☎03 83 35 08 35; open M-F 8:30am-7:30pm, Sa 8:30am-7pm), and a larger **Casino** in the Centre Commercial St-Sebastian on rue Notre-Dame (open M-Sa 8am-8:30pm). Restaurants pack **rue des Maréchaux,** spilling over onto pl. Lafayette and up along Grande Rue to pl. St-Epvre. For afternoon snacks, there are waffle and crêpe stands behind pl. Stanislas on the **Terrace de la Pépinière.** You might want to reserve ahead at **Aux Délices du Palais,** 69 Grande Rue. Locals love this hip sandwich joint, so come early at lunchtime or you'll be crowded out. Swivel on a cowprint stool and munch on meat- or veg-packed monsters (23-28F/€3.51-4.27). (☎03 83 30 44 19. Open Tu-Sa noon-2:30pm and 7-9:30pm. Cash only.) **Aux Croustillants,** 10 rue de Maréchaux (☎03 83 30 44 19), is at your service as the only 24-hour bakery in town, perhaps in all of Lorraine. Get luscious pastries (9F/€1.37), mini-pizzas (12F/€1.83), and fresh warm quiches (11F/€1.68) any time between 5:30am on Tuesday and 10pm on Sunday.

SIGHTS

PLACE STANISLAS. If you see nothing else in Nancy, you'll leave happy having walked through the *place*. Its three neoclassical pavilions and the gilt iron fences between them were commissioned in 1737 by Stanislas Lesczynski, former king of

Poland and new duke of Lorraine, to honor his nephew, Louis XV. On summer nights, light from the balconies and fountain pools illuminates the curlicues of the moldings and statues lining the roofs. *Son-et-lumière* spectacles gild the lily nightly at 10pm in July and August. From pl. Stanislas, pass through the five-arch **Arc de Triomphe** to the tree-lined **pl. de la Carrière,** a former jousting-ground rebuilt by Stanislas with Baroque architecture and wrought-iron ornaments.

MUSEE DE L'ECOLE DE NANCY. One of the most striking and delightful museums around illustrates the development of the Nancy School, the city's contribution to the turn-of-the-century Art Nouveau movement. Sculpture, glasswork, and furniture by Emile Gallé, creator of the Paris Métro signs, and his contemporaries leave you itching to redecorate. Additional Art Nouveau elements can be found on buildings scattered throughout Nancy; the tourist office distributes a guide with walking tours. *(36-38 rue du Sergent Blandan. Take bus #123 (dir: "Vandoeuvre Cheminots") to "Nancy Thermal." ☎03 83 40 14 86. Open M 2-6pm and W-Su 10:30am-6pm. 30F/€4.57, students 15F/€2.29. Students free W, everyone free the first Su of each month 10am-1:30pm. Tours F-Su at 3pm, 40F/€6.10.)*

MUSEE DES BEAUX-ARTS. This excellent museum is housed in a stately Baroque building. The collection of paintings and sculptures stretches from 1380 to the present, and includes gems by Rubens, Delacroix, Monet, Modigliani, Rodin, and Picasso. Especially noteworthy are the fantastical creations of 20th-century sculptors Lipchitz and Laurens and the collection of Art Nouveau Daum glasswork. *(3 pl. Stanislas. ☎03 83 85 30 72; fax 03 83 85 30 76. Open W-M 10am-6pm. 30F/€4.57, students and children 15F/€2.29, combined with Musée de l'Ecole de Nancy 40F/€6.10, tours 40F/€6.10. Students free W and first Su of each month 10:30am-1:30pm.)*

PARC DE LA PEPINIERE. Peacocks preen in the zoo while people pose in the outdoor café. Portals of pink roses lead into the deliciously aromatic **Roseraie,** a collection of gaudy blooms from around the world. *(Just north of pl. de la Carrière. Open June-Aug. daily 6:30am-11:30pm; May and Sept. 1-14 6:30am-10pm; Mar.-Apr. and Sept. 15-Nov. closes at 9pm; Dec.-Feb. closes at 8pm. Free.)*

OTHER SIGHTS. The late-19th-century **Basilique St-Epvre** has brilliant windows from around the world and free evening concerts of classical and organ music. *(Just off Grande Rue at pl. St-Epvre. Open daily 2-6pm.)* The innovative little **Musée du Téléphone,** on a quiet street off pl. Stanislas, traces the history of man's quest to reach out and touch someone, from telegraph stations to the cordless wonders of today. Surf the web for 25F/€3.81 per hour. *(11 rue Maurice Barrès. ☎03 83 86 50 00. Open Tu-F 10am-7pm, Sa noon-7pm and first Su of the month 2-6pm. 20F/€3.05, students 10F/€1.53.)*

ENTERTAINMENT

In summer, nightly concerts of all kinds float from the Roseraie at **parc de la Pépinière.** In mid-October, the **Jazz-Pulsations** festival beats from dusk to dawn in the park. **Pl. Stanislas** lights up on summer evenings with a free historical sound-and-light show (July-Aug. daily 10pm). The respected **Opéra de Nancy et de Lorraine** resides in one of the three big buildings on the *place.* The 2002 season includes Wagner's Tannhauser in late April and early May. (☎03 83 85 33 11. Open M-F 8am-noon and 1-7pm; stop in for tickets Tu-F 1-7pm. Tickets 40-320F/€6.10-48.80, students 30-255F/€4.57-38.88.) The **Festival International de Chant Choral** promises 2000 singers from France and around the world. (May 8-12. Concerts free, check in tourist office for details and locations. **CCN Ballet de Lorraine,** 3 rue Henri Bazin, is also big, with shows at the opera house throughout the year. (☎03 83 36 72 20. Office open M-F 10am-1pm and 2-6pm.)

For more frivolous fun, soak up the evening beauty of illuminated pl. Stanislas at its ritzy cafés, or grab a cheaper drink on rue Stanislas. Check out www.nancybynight.com for updates on bars, clubs, concerts and theater events. An old *cave* gone slickly mod, **Le Blue Note III,** 3 rue des Michottes, blasts disco, funk, and house (F-Sa plus Su after 2am), and offers a piano bar (Tu). There's live music on the first Thursday of every month. (☎03 83 30 31 18. Open Tu-Th and Su 11:30pm-

4am, F-Sa 11:30pm-5am. Cover 60F/€6.15 F-Sa after 12:30pm, includes one drink.) Nancy's boys gather at **Les Pietons,** 7 Grande Rue, a lively gay watering hole near pl. Stanislas. (☎03 83 37 32 08. Open Tu-Su noon-2pm and 6pm-2am.) **Be Happy Bar,** 23 rue de Gustave Simon, is packed with locals, billiards, and jukeboxes. (☎03 83 35 56 41. Open M-F noon-2am, Sa-Su 6pm-2am. MC/V.)

METZ

Metz (pop. 200,000; pronounced mess) is a stroller's city, a place of fountains, cobblestones, and canals, whose architecture and layout reflects its mixed Franco-German parentage. The Esplanade is a huge draw for locals and tourists alike. Extending all the way to the river Moselle, it is huge and impressive in a courtly way, with immaculately clipped bushes and flowers in large patterns. Though a fabulous cathedral and a major university add some life and noise, Metz remains refreshingly calm and slow for a city of its size.

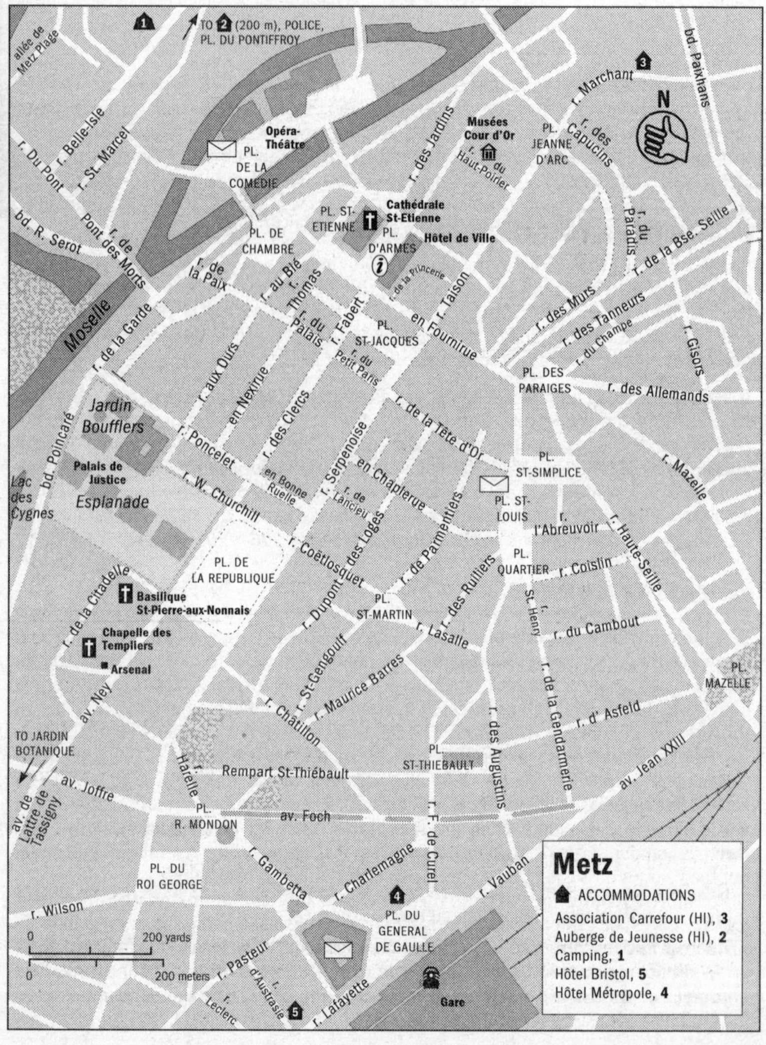

TRANSPORTATION

Trains: pl. du Général de Gaulle. To: **Luxembourg** (45min., 12 per day, 68F/€10.37); **Lyon** (5hr., 6 per day, 279F/€42.55); **Nancy** (40min., 31 per day, 52F/€7.93); **Nice** (10-12hr., 5 per day, 509F/€77.62); **Paris** (3hr., 10 per day, 238F/€36.30); and **Strasbourg** (1½hr., 7 per day, 116F/€17.69). Info office open M-F 8:30am-7:30pm, Sa 8:30am-6pm.

Buses: Les Rapides de Lorraine, 2 rue de Nonnetiers (☎03 87 75 26 62; for schedules ☎03 87 36 23 34); take the underpass to the right of the station below the tracks, and then go left. To **Verdun** (1hr., 7 per day, 69.10F/€10.54) and tiny regional towns. Ticket window open M-Th 7:30am-noon and 2-5:30pm, F 7:30am-noon and 2-4:30pm.

Local Transportation: TCRM, 1 av. Robert Schumann (☎03 87 76 31 11; open M-F 7:30am-6:30pm, Sa 8:30am-12:30pm), runs every 10-20min. 6:30am-8pm, Sa-Su less often. Tickets 5.50F/€0.84, 2 trips 10.80F/€1.65, *carnet* of 6 26.20F/€3.99. Late-night bus (10pm-midnight).

Taxis: (☎03 87 56 91 92), at the train station.

Car Rental: Avis (☎03 87 50 60 30), at the train station. Two-day rentals from 605F/€92.26 (weekends) and 930F/€141.83 (week), 500km included. 25+. Open M-F 8am-12:15pm and 1:30-7pm, Su 4:30-8:30pm, closed Sa. AmEx/MC/V.

Bike Rental: Vélocation, at the train station and on the Esplanade. 20F/€3.05 per half-day, 30F/€4.57 per day; ID deposit. Open daily 10am-6pm.

ALSACE

ORIENTATION AND PRACTICAL INFORMATION

The honey-colored *vieille ville* is mostly off-limits to cars. The cathedral dominates the skyline of the **pl. d'Armes;** the tourist office is just across the way in the Hôtel de Ville. To get there from the station, turn right and then left onto rue des Augustins. At pl. St-Simplice, turn left onto the pedestrian rue de la Tête d'Or, then right onto rue Fabet. You can also take bus #11 (dir: "St-Eloy") or #9, (dir: "J. Bauchez") from pl. Charles de Gaulle directly to pl. d'Armes. Metz is a big city; use cosmopolitan caution.

Tourist Office: pl. d'Armes (☎03 87 55 53 76; fax 03 87 36 59 43; tourisme@ot.mairie-metz.fr), facing the cathedral. English-speaking staff makes hotel reservations (10F/€1.53, must be done in person) and distributes maps. Ask for *Metz en Fête* for detailed listings of musical, artistic, and theatrical activities. Free **Internet access. Currency exchange.** Open July-Aug. M-Sa 9am-9pm, Su 11am-5pm; Mar.-June and Sept.-Oct. M-Sa 9am-7pm, Su 11am-5pm; Nov.-Feb. M-Sa 9am-6:30pm, Su 11am-5pm.

City Tours: Organized by the tourist office. M-Sa 3pm; 45F/€6.86, under 10 22.50F/€3.43; in French. Audioguides available in English (45F/€6.86). **Taxi tours** last 1hr. (3-4 people; 155F/€23.64).

Budget Travel: Agence Wasteels, 3 rue d'Austrasie (☎08 03 88 70 47). Student rates and passes. Open M-Th 9am-noon and 2-6pm, F 9am-noon and 2-7pm, Sa 9am-noon.

Youth Center: Centre Régional d'Information Jeunesse, 1 rue de Coëtlosquet (☎03 87 69 04 50). Open M-F 10am-noon and 1:30-6pm. Info on everything: hiking, religious organizations, concerts, travel, and employment.

Laundromat: 22 rue du Pont-des-Morts (☎03 87 63 49 57). Open daily 7am-7pm.

Police: 45 rue Belle Isle (☎03 87 16 17 17), near pl. de Pontiffroy.

Hospital: Centre Hospitalier Regional Metz-Thionville, 1 pl. Phillipe de Vigneulles (☎03 87 55 31 31), near pl. Maud Huy.

Internet Access: Free at **Espace Multimedia,** 6 rue Four de Cloître, near the cathedral (☎03 87 36 56 56). Open M and Th-Sa 9am-5pm, Tu-W 9am-8pm. Also **Net Café,** 1-3 rue Paul Bezanson (☎03 87 76 30 64), in cour St-Etienne near the cathedral. Student rate 30F/€4.57 for 30min. Open M-Sa 1-6pm.

Post Office: 9 rue Gambetta (☎ 03 87 56 74 23). **Currency exchange.** Open M-F 8am-7pm and Sa 8:30am-noon. **Branch office** (☎03 87 30 38 58), next to the theater on rue Pierre-Hardy. Open M-F 9am-5pm, Sa 8am-4pm. **Poste Restante:** 57037. **Postal code:** 57000.

ACCOMMODATIONS AND CAMPING

Hotels in the heart of the pedestrian district are expensive and hard to come by. Turn left from the train station onto **rue Lafayette** to find several large, impersonal, hotels in the 150F/€22.90 range.

Auberge de Jeunesse (HI), 1 allée de Metz Plage (☎03 87 30 44 02; fax 03 87 33 19 80), by the river. Walking is possible, but tricky and tiring (30min.). From the station, take bus #3 (dir: "Metz-Nord," last bus 8:30pm) or #11 (dir: "St-Eloy;" last bus midnight) to "Pontiffroy." Small, cozy rooms and friendly staff. Free **bike loans.** Laundry service (45F/€6.86). Kitchen. Breakfast included. Sheets 17F/€2.59. Reception 7:30-10am and 5-10pm. No curfew or lockout. Reserve ahead. 2- to 6-bed dorms 70F/€10.67 per person. **Non-members** pay a 19F/€2.90 supplement per night. MC/V.

Association Carrefour/Auberge de Jeunesse (HI), 6 rue Marchant (☎03 87 75 07 26; fax 03 87 36 71 44). From the station, turn right onto rue Vauban, which becomes av. Jean XXIII, and follow it around as it becomes bd. Maginot and bd. Paixhans. Rue Marchant will be on your left after 20min. Or take minibus line "B" from the station to "Ste-Ségolène" (every 15min. 7:30am-7:15pm, 5.30F/€0.81), and take a left up the hill. Mostly locals in serviceable but spartan digs. Larger, more central, and less congenial than the other hostel. Breakfast included. Meals 40F/€6.10. Laundry 21F/€3.20. Paper sheets 19.50F/€2.97, cloth ones (2+ nights) 26F/€3.97. 3- and 4-bed dorms 74F/€11.29 per person. Singles and doubles 85F/€12.96. Reception 24hr. **Non-members** pay a 19F/€2.90 supplement for each of the first 6 nights. MC/V.

Hôtel Métropole, 5 pl. du Général de Gaulle (☎03 87 66 26 22; fax 03 87 66 29 91). Pleasant stationside behemoth with spacious, elegant rooms. Breakfast 30F/€4.57. Reception 24hr. Singles from 145F/€22.11, with shower 160-290F/€24.39-44.21; doubles with shower 160-290F/€24.39-44.21. Extra bed 30F/€4.57. AmEx/MC/V.

Hôtel Bristol, 7 rue Lafayette (☎03 87 66 74 22; fax 03 87 50 67 89), a small, serviceable backup near the train station. The larger rooms–some with minibar–are cheerier. Breakfast 29F/€4.42. Reception 24hr. Singles with bath 150-290F/€22.90-44.21; doubles with bath 170-320F/€25.93-48.80. AmEx/DC/MC/V.

Campsite: Metz-Plage, allée de Metz-Plage (☎03 87 68 26 48; fax 03 87 32 61 26), by the Moselle and the hostel. Enter from rue de la Piscine, behind the hospital on rue Belle Isle. Campsites, almost all with caravans, line the river. A beautiful view, but very little privacy. Showers, grocery store, washing machines, TV room, and fishing. Reception 7am-8:30pm. Pedestrian access 24hr. 16F/€2.44 per person, 16F/€2.44 per tent, 11F/€1.68 per car, 37-55F/€5.64-8.39 per trailer including electricity.

FOOD

Bakeries, sandwich shops, and other cheap eateries cluster near the hostel on **rue du Pont des Morts,** in the **pedestrian district,** and toward the station on **rue Coislin.** The Centre St-Jacques (a mall off pl. St-Jacques) contains a number of specialty stores and cheap eateries, as well as an **ATAC supermarket** (open M-Sa 8:30am-7:30pm). The biggest **markets** (Th and Sa 7am-1pm) are next to the cathedral or on pl. St-Jacques (Oct. to mid-Apr.). 20F/€3.05 kebab shops sprout like mushrooms on every street corner. Locals flock to the **Crêperie St-Malo,** 14 rue des Clercs, which serves hundreds of stuffed galettes (23-57F/€3.51-8.69) and crêpes (from 13.50F/€2.06) on a tiny terrace and in its crammed dining room. (☎03 87 74 56 85. Open M-Sa 11:45am-11pm, closed M evenings. MC/V.)

SIGHTS

CATHEDRALE ST-ETIENNE. This golden-colored cathedral is the third tallest in France, the result of a competitive bid for prestige by 13th- to 16th-century Metz. The cathedral is actually a late-medieval fusion of two churches; you can recognize the older parts by their simple pillars. The most spectacular stained-glass windows here are the modern ones; several in the western transept are by Chagall. *(Pl. d'Armes. ☎03 87 75 54 61. Open M-Sa 9am-7pm, Su 1-7pm. Tours in French available at 10am, 2, and 4pm. 15F/€2.29, 25F/€3.81 including a tour of the crypt.)*

ESPLANADE AND GARDENS. At the other end of rue des Clercs from pl. d'Armes lies the Esplanade, a broad, formal garden overlooking the Moselle Valley. Metz's patchwork of gardens and promenades offers a refreshing green alternative to the urban core; it's one of the very best things about this city. The tourist office publishes a map with trails up to 10km long. Down the steps from the Esplanade, shady paths wend their way through wooded parkland along the **Lac aux Cygnes.** Paddle or pedal your way across the lake with a boat rented at **La Flotille.** *(1 quai des Régates. ☎03 87 36 86 71. Rowboats 59F/€9, motorboats 96F/€14.64 for 30min.)* In summertime, watch the fountains spurt to music from J.S. Bach to Louis Armstrong. *(Mid-June through Aug. F-Su at 10:30pm. Free.)* Swans preen at the **Jardin Botanique,** a taxonomist's heaven packed with flowerbeds and tagged trees. In the center, a greenhouse nurtures ferns and palm trees. *(Open May-Sept. M-F 9:45am-6:45pm, Sa-Su 9-11:30am and 2-6:45pm; Oct.-Apr. M-F 9:45am-4:45pm, Sa-Su 9-11:30am and 2-6:45pm.)*

BASILIQUE ST-PIERRE-AUX-NONNAINS. This tiny ancient church, the oldest in France, is half hidden in the green beyond the Esplanade. It was built by the Romans in the 4th century as part of a large set of baths, and has since been rebuilt four times—see if you can figure out where. There are temporary exhibits and good monthly concerts in the sprawling pavilion next door. *(☎03 87 74 16 16. Open Tu-Su 2-6:30pm, closed winter weekends.)*

MUSEES DE LA COUR D'OR. A huge collection of historical artifacts, from old surgical tools to Renaissance fireplaces, is so badly lit that you'd have trouble making it out even if you could find the thing you wanted to see. Bring a flashlight and compass. The top two floors are dedicated to the less comprehensive Musée des Beaux-Arts, in which the best works are by locals. Napoleon-lovers might like the even smaller military history museum. *(2 rue du Haut-Poirier, in the Cour d'Or. ☎03 87 68 25 00. Open daily 10am-noon and 2-6pm. 30F/€4.57, students 15F/€2.29, children under 12 free. Audioguide in 5 languages 15F/€2.29.)*

PL. DE LA COMEDIE. Built on a former swamp, the *place* served a less-than-comedic function during the Revolution, when the guillotine was its main attraction. Its centerpiece is the 1751 Opéra-Théâtre, the oldest still-functioning theater in France, which offers opera, ballet, dance, and drama performances. *(☎03 87 55 51 71. For tickets, call the Bureau de Location at 03 87 75 40 50. Ticket office open M-F 9am-12:30pm and 3-5pm, by phone M-F 1-6pm.)*

ENTERTAINMENT

After dark, be sure to stop by the cathedral to see the glowing stained-glass windows. In summer, a free **sound and light show,** complete with Vegas-style colored lights, fountains, and assorted tunes by Wagner, Elvis, and *Les Beatles* is held at dusk on the pond at the foot of the Esplanade (July-Sept. F-Su and holidays). **Arsenal,** av. Ney, is a concert hall and exposition space featuring classical music performances and dance (☎03 87 39 92 00; reservations ☎03 87 74 16 16). For bargain shoppers, Metz's monthly **marché aux puces (flea market)** is the second largest in France (outside of Paris). Ask tourist office for a brochure or call 03 87 55 66 00.

At night, students pack the bars and cafés at **pl. St-Jacques,** the central gathering point. Zebras await at **Les 2 Zèbres,** an impossibly hip bar on pl. St-Jacques that draws a young, chic crowd to its packed see-and-be-seen terrace. (☎03 87 76 24 00. Open Su-Th 8am-2am, F-Sa until 3am. MC/V.) Outdance the locals at leopard-crazy **Le Club Tiffany,** 24 rue Coëtlosquet, just outside pl. de la République. (☎03 87 75 23 32. Open W-M 11pm-5am. 70F/€10.67 weekend cover includes 1 drink. AmEx/MC/V.) **Le Tunnel,** 27 pl. Quarteau, is homey and low-key, and packs in likewise low-key locals. Take your pick of the big-screen TV or outside terrace. (☎03 87 36 62 99. Open Su-Th 10am-2pm, F-Sa 10am-3pm.)

VERDUN

France and Germany each lost almost 400,000 soldiers in the Battle of Verdun; that conflict, certainly the worst battle of WWI and according to some the worst in history, marks everything in and around the town. Eerie reminders surround the city: the 15,000 marble crosses in the National Cemetery; the Trench of Bayonets, where most of France's 137th Regiment perished; and Verdun's chosen symbol, a dove above a pair of clasped hands. Verdun (pop. 30,000) has painstakingly rebuilt itself since the war—its tourist literature likes to call it a "city in the country"—but despite modern spruce-ups and newly refurbished commercial streets, this city's main draw for French and foreign tourists will always be its tragic past.

TRANSPORTATION

Trains: pl. Maurice Genovoix. To: **Metz** (1½hr., 5 per day, 71F/€10.83). Ticket booth open M 4:45am-7pm, Tu-F 5:45am-7pm, Sa 9:45am-12:15pm and 2:15-7pm, Su 12:30-7:30pm.

Buses: pl. Vauban (☎03 29 86 02 71), at the other end of av. Garibaldi. To: **Metz** (2hr., 8 per day, 72F/€10.98). Open M-F 6am-8pm, Sa 6am-noon.

Car Rental: Grand Garage de la Meuse, 6 av. Colonel Driant (☎03 29 86 44 05). 21+. Open M-F 8am-noon and 1:30-7pm.

Bike Rental: Flavenot Damien, 1 Rond-Point des Etats-Unis (☎03 29 86 12 43), near the train station. 100F/€15.25 per day; passport deposit. Open M 2-7pm, Tu-Sa 9am-noon and 2-7pm.

ORIENTATION AND PRACTICAL INFORMATION

Verdun is split in two by the Meuse river, with the train station, the cathedral, and the hostel on one side, and the tourist office and war memorials on the other. To get to the **tourist office** from the station, walk straight ahead on av. Garibaldi (the street to the left) until you reach the bus station. Then turn right onto rue Frères Boulhaut and continue until you reach the Port Chaussée. Turn left and cross the bridge onto pl. de la Nation; the tourist office will be on your right.

Tourist Office: pl. de la Nation (☎03 29 86 14 18; fax 03 29 84 22 42). The staff offers a free map of the city center, a larger fold-out map (3F/€0.46), and info on the memorials as well as larcenous **currency exchange.** They also lead a daily 4hr. **tour** of major battlefields and monuments around the city. Tours in French depart May-Sept. daily 2pm, 145F/€22.11; call before noon to reserve a seat. Open July-Aug. M-Sa 8:30am-7:30pm, Su 9am-5pm; May-June and Sept. M-Sa 8:30am-6:30pm, Su 9am-5pm; Mar.-Apr. and Oct.-Nov. M-Sa 9am-noon and 2-6pm, Su 10am-1pm, except Apr. Su 9am-5pm; Dec.-Feb. M-Sa 9am-noon and 2-5:30pm, Su 10am-1pm.

Laundromat: av. de la Victoire (☎03 29 86 60 43). Open daily 6:30am-11pm.

Police: pl. du Gouvernement.

Hospital: 2 rue d'Anthouard (☎03 29 83 84 85).

Post Office: av. de la Victoire (☎03 29 83 45 58). Better **currency exchange** rate than the tourist office. Open M-F 8am-7pm, Sa 8am-noon. **Poste Restante:** 55107 Verdun, B.P. 729. **Postal code:** 55100.

ACCOMMODATIONS AND CAMPING

Auberge de Jeunesse (HI): pl. Monseigneur Ginisty (☎03 29 86 28 28; fax 03 29 86 28 82), at the "Centre Mondial de la Paix," next to the cathedral. From the train station, cross to the island with the Match supermarket in front of the station and turn right a little onto rue Louis Maury. When you reach the square, continue up on rue de la Belle Vierge. The hostel is at the end of the cathedral. Use the stairs in the corner of the parking lot in front of the cathedral to get down from the hill into the city center. Simple, renovated rooms in an elegant old building, with views of Verdun. 4- to 16-bed dorms, most with bath and dim lighting. Breakfast 19F/€2.90. Sheets 17F/€2.59. Reception M-F 7:30am-11pm, Sa-Su 8-10am and 5-11pm. Lockout 10am-5pm. No curfew. Bunks 51F/€7.78, ages 4-10 27F/€4.12. **Non-members** pay a 19F/€2.90 supplement for each of the first six nights. MC/V.

Le Montaulbain, 4 rue de la Vieille Prison (☎03 29 86 00 47; fax 03 29 84 75 70), in the heart of the *vieille ville.* Fairly large rooms decorated for lovers of gentle kitsch. Breakfast 25F/€3.81. Reception M-Sa 7:30am-10pm, Su 7:30am-noon and 6-10pm. Reserve in summer. Singles 140F/€21.35, with shower 160F/€24.39, with bath 180F/€27.44; doubles 150F/€22.90, with shower 180F/€27.44, with bath 210F/€32.02; triples with bath 240F/€36.59; quads with bath 270F/€41.16. MC/V.

Hôtel Les Colombes, 9 av. Garibaldi (☎03 29 86 05 46), around the corner from the train station. Homey, comfy rooms, some family-size. People in showerless rooms will not shower. Breakfast 35F/€5.34. Reception 9am-10:30pm. Singles 170F/€25.92, with bath 190-220F/€28.97-33.54; doubles with shower 220-250F/€33.54-38.12. Triples and quads with shower 190-250F/€28.97-38.12. MC/V.

Camping: Les Breuils, allée des Breuils (☎03 29 86 15 31; fax 03 29 86 75 76), past the Citadelle Souterraine on av. du Cinquième R.A.P. Take a right onto av. Général Boichut and then the first left. You'll be hemmed in by caravans, but tall bushes offer some privacy and spots by the river are pleasant. Facilities include a bar, grocery store, showers, and pool. Reception 7:30am-10pm. Open Apr.-Oct. 15. July-Aug. 24F/€3.66 per person, 20F/€3.05 per site; Apr.-June and Sept.-Oct. 15 22F/€3.36 per person, 20F/€3.05 per site. Electricity 21F/€3.20. MC/V.

ALSACE

FOOD

Verdun's contribution to confection is the *dragée,* made of almonds coated with sugar and honey. The treat was first engineered by an apothecary in the 13th century, when its medicinal powers were believed to ward off sterility. Today it is served at weddings and baptisms. Verdun's main **covered market** is on rue de Rû (Tu 7:30am-noon and F 7:30am-12:30pm). Stock up at the **Match supermarket,** in front of the train station on Rond-Point des Etats-Unis (open M-Sa 9am-7:30pm). Restaurants and cafés are in the pedestrian area along **rue Chaussée** and **rue Royeurs,** and by the canal along **quai de Londres.** You'll get a tasty and substantial meal at **Pile ou Face,** 54 rue des Royeurs, where they serve massive crêpes (20-40F/€3.05-6.10) and meal-worthy galettes (22-55F/€3.36-8.39) on the terrace or in the bustling dining room. (☎03 29 84 20 70. Open Tu-Su 10am-11pm. MC/V.)

SIGHTS

Built in 1200, the **Porte Chaussée,** quai de Londres, was a prison and a guard tower for river traffic; later it was a point of entrance for troops during WWI. At the other end of rue Frères Boulhaut, Rodin's bronze **Victory** guards the Port St-Paul. The **Monument à la Victoire** rises above a flight of 72 granite steps at the edge of the *haute ville;* a metal soldier on top aims bronzed cannons at the German front. The monument stands on an old chapel, the last remains of the Eglise de la Madeleine, built in 1049 and bombed beyond recognition in 1916. Inside the chapel are three volumes recording the names of those soldiers who fought here, signed by de Gaulle himself in 1948. (Open daily 9am-noon and 2-6pm.) At the top of the hill behind the monument is the

Musée de la Princerie. The creaky Renaissance building is a pleasure to wander around, but the collection is generally lackluster. A few treasures stand out: tiny portraits on semi-precious stones, an old jigsaw of the kings of France, and a 12th-century ivory comb engraved with scenes of Christ's passion. (☎ 03 29 86 10 62. Open W-M 9:30am-noon and 2-6pm. 10F/€1.53.) A few blocks away, the much-bombed **Cathédrale Notre-Dame** still has a fine set of stained-glass windows. (Open Apr.-Sept. daily 8am-noon and 2-7pm; Oct.-Mar. 8am-noon and 2-6:30pm.) **Parc Municipal Japiot,** across from the tourist office, rolls out the green carpet along the shady banks of the Meuse. (Open Apr.-Sept. 8:30am-8pm; Oct. and Mar. 9am-6pm; Nov.-Feb. 9am-5pm.)

The massive cement-and-stone **Citadelle Souterraine** (down rue de Rû) sheltered 10,000 soldiers on their way to the front. Its 4km of underground galleries were equipped to supply an army. Today, a small, chilly section of the tunnels can be visited in little carts on the official tour. Realistic talking holograms play out the life of hungry soldiers and worried generals underground. (30min. tours in French or dubiously dubbed English every 5min. Open July-Aug. daily 9am-7pm; Apr.-June and Sept. 9am-6pm; Nov.-Mar. 9:30am-noon and 1-5pm. 35F/€5.34, children 15F/€2.29.) Verdun also hosts a yearly **sound and light show** in June and July, recreating the battle with a cast of 300 actors and special effects from over 1000 projectors. (☎ 03 29 84 50 00 for info. 100F/€15.25, ages 12-18 50F/€7.62, children free.)

MEMORIALS NEAR VERDUN

Many sites to the east of Verdun commemorate the ten-month battle of 1916. As most are 5-8km away, they are difficult to reach without a car. The four-hour tourist office tour (see p. 392) visits all of the memorials mentioned below in rapid but thorough check-mark succession. The more contemplative may want to find their own transportation; a complete circuit is about 25km.

After Alsace and parts of Lorraine were annexed by Germany in 1871, Verdun found itself 40km from the German border and protected by 38 new French forts. These fortifications, the linchpin of France's northeastern defenses, were expressly targeted by General von Falkenhayn during the 1916 offensive, in which he hoped to make the French evacuate the right bank of the Meuse. The first to fall was also the strongest: the immense concrete **Fort de Douaumont,** covering three hectares and 3km of passageways, which had been left with only 57 soldiers after most of its arms and troops were transferred to weaker areas. The fortress was easily captured in February 1916, and housed over 3000 cramped German soldiers, who held on for a full eight months while the French frantically shelled their own fortress. In October 1916 a fire broke out and the Germans fled; a detachment of Moroccan troops walked in, and it was French again. The assault and defense of this militarily useless building caused over 100,000 French deaths altogether; in a sealed gallery are entombed 679 German soldiers, killed when some grenades accidentally went off. (☎ 03 29 84 41 91. Open July-Aug. daily 10am-7pm; Apr.-June 10am-6pm; Oct.-Dec. and Feb.-Mar. 10am-1pm and 2-5pm; Jan. 10:30am-1pm and 2-4:30pm. 16F/€2.44, under age 16 8F/€1.22.)

The central and most striking monument on the battlefields is the austere **Ossuaire de Douaumont,** a vast crypt crowned by a 46m granite tower that resembles a cross melded to an artillery shell. Inside the ossuary, vaults hold the remains of some 130,000 unknown French and German soldiers. Another 15,000, whose remains were identifiable, lie buried in the military cemetery that stretches out before it. Christian graves are marked by rows of white crosses, and Muslims lie beneath gravestones pointing toward Mecca. About 300m west of the building itself is a small monument to Jewish volunteers. (Open May-Aug. daily 9am-6:30pm; Sept. 9am-noon and 2-6pm; Mar. and Oct. 9am-noon and 2-5:30pm; Apr. 9am-6pm; Nov. 9am-noon and 2-5pm. Ossuary free; film and tower 20F/€3.05, children 12F/€1.83.) Nearby, the **Tranchée des Baïonettes** is the trench where a detachment of France's 137th infantry regiment was buried alive while taking shelter from heavy enemy fire. After the battle ended, the only visible sign of the men was the points of their bayonets protruding from the ground.

Fort de Vaux, the smallest of the fortifications, surrendered in June 1916 after seven days and nights of murderous hand-to-hand combat with gas, grenades, and flamethrowers in the fort's narrow passageways. Its defenders made numerous appeals for reinforcements to the Verdun garrison, but none came; inside the fort is a statue of a carrier pigeon named Valiant, who bore the last message out. (Open July-Aug. daily 9am-6:30pm; Apr.-June and Sept. 9am-6pm; Oct.-Mar. 9:30am-noon and 1-5pm. 16F/€2.44, children under 16 8F/€1.22.)

The little town of Fleury stood at the epicenter of the battle of Verdun; its demolition was so complete that afterwards there remained no trace of habitation or vegetation. The fighting was so intense in this area that Fleury changed hands 16 times in the summer of 1916 alone. Where the obliterated village's railway station once stood is now the grim **Musée de Fleury,** built by Verdun veterans in honor of their dead fellow soldiers. (Open Apr.-Sept. 16 daily 9am-6pm; Feb.-Mar. and Sept. 17-Dec. 9am-noon and 2-6pm. 30F/€4.57, under age 16 15F/€2.29.)

STRASBOURG

A few kilometers from the Franco-German border, cosmopolitan Strasbourg (pop. 260,000) seems to belong to both cultures—in some quarters as many *winstubs* line the squares as pâtisseries. When France annexed Strasbourg 30 years after the rest of Alsace in 1681, the townspeople demanded a charter as a free city. Since then, despite the bilingual street signs and prominent displays of civic culture, Strasbourg has cast its lot with the République; *La Marseillaise* was even composed here. The beautiful city serves as an administrative center for the European Union, hosting the European Parliament, the Council of Europe, and the European Commission for the Rights of Man. The 16th-century University of Strasbourg, with 35,000 students, prevents the town from sinking into a morass of policy papers and *choucroute garnie.* Besides serving as a capital to Europe and Alsace, Strasbourg has some of the most worthwhile sights this side of Paris; it is, for sheer size, import, and age, one not to miss.

TRANSPORTATION

Flights: Strasbourg-Entzheim Airport (☎03 88 64 67 67) is 15km from Strasbourg. **Air France,** 15 rue des Francs-Bourgeois (☎03 88 15 19 50), and other carriers send frequent flights to: **London** (student rates from 595F/€90.72 one way, 1102F/€168 round-trip); **Lyon** (student rates from 349F/€53.21 one way, 694F/€105.81 round-trip); and **Paris** (student rates from 263F/€40.10 one way, 522F/€79.59 round-trip). Shuttle buses (☎03 88 77 70 70) run from the airport to the Strasbourg tram stop "Baggarsee" (12min.; 3-4 per hr. 5:30am-11pm; 27F/€4.12, 49F/€7.47 round-trip).

Trains: pl. de la Gare (☎03 88 22 50 50, reservations ☎03 36 35 53 35). To: **Frankfurt** (3hr.; 3 direct per day, 18 total; 240F/€36.59); **Luxembourg** (2½hr.; 5 direct per day, 14 total; 165F/€25.16); **Paris** (4hr., 16 per day, 226F/€34.46); and **Zurich** (3hr.; 1 direct per hr., 3-4 total per hr.; 255F/€38.88). **Ticket office** open M 5am-9pm, Tu-Sa 5:30am-8:50pm, Su 6am-8:50pm.

Local Transportation: Compagnie des Transports Strasbourgeois (CTS), pl. Kléber (☎03 88 77 70 70). Open M-F 7:30am-6:30pm, Sa 9am-12:30pm and 1:30-5pm. Also at the central train station. Open M-F 7:15am-6:30pm. Extensive bus service. A single north-south tram line rumbles every 5-8min. 7am-7pm, less frequently 4:30-7am and 7pm-midnight. Tickets 7F/€1.07, *carnet* of 5 31F/€4.73, day pass 20F/€3.05; available at *tabacs*.

Taxis: Taxi 13, pl. de la République (☎03 88 36 13 13). 24hr. Also offers city tours (180F/€27.44 for 1-4 people) and service to the Route du Vin.

Car Rental: Europ'Car, 13 pl. de la Gare (☎03 88 15 55 66). Open M-F 8am-noon and 3-8pm, Sa 8am-noon and 2-5pm. From 470F/€71.66 per day or 540F/€82.33 for 2 weekend days. 21+. **Garage Sengler** (☎03 88 30 00 75), on rue Jean Giradow in Hautepierre. 199F/€30.34 per day, plus 1.30F/€0.20 per km over 50km; 550F/€83.85 for the weekend. 21+. Open M-F 8am-12:30pm and 2-6:30pm.

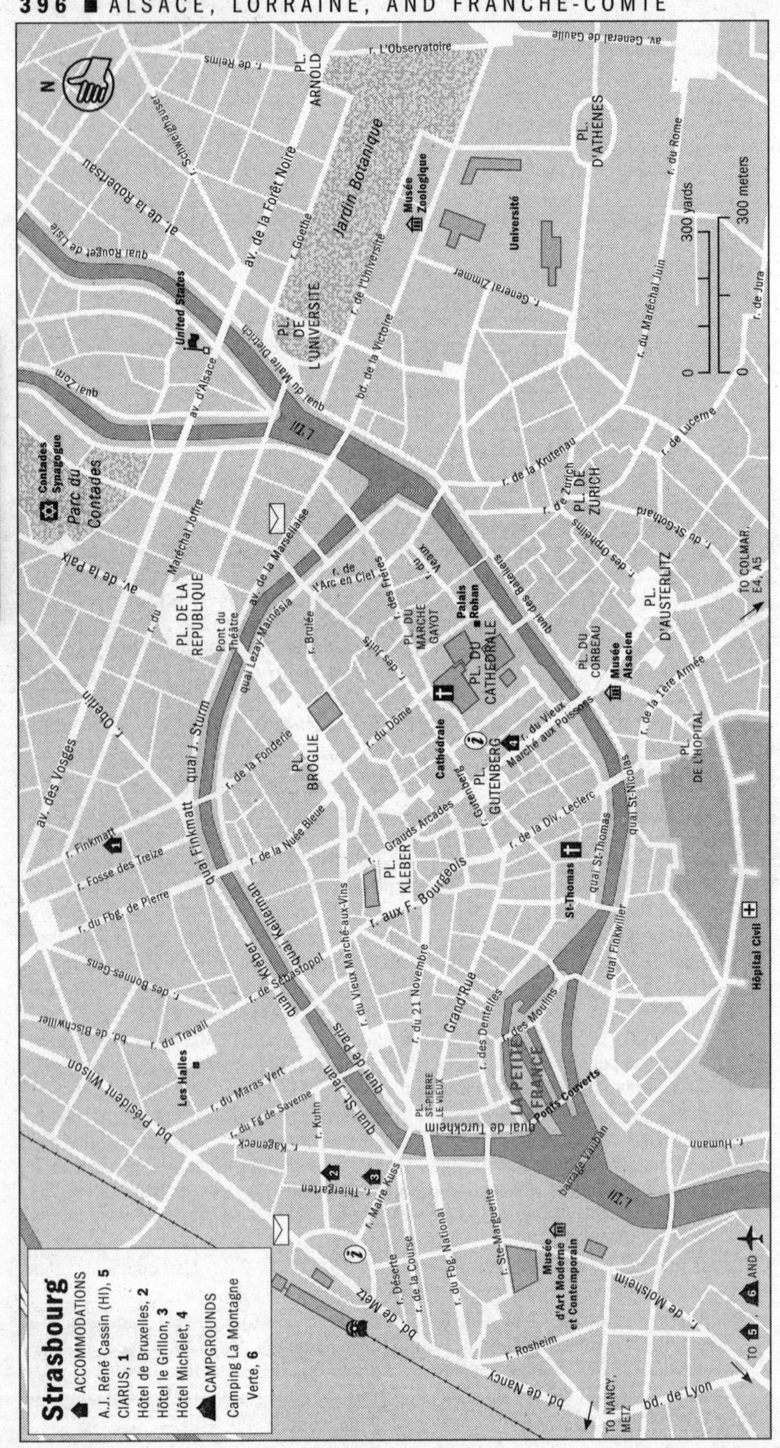
Strasbourg
ACCOMMODATIONS
A.J. Réné Cassin (HI), 5
CIARUS, 1
Hôtel de Bruxelles, 2
Hôtel le Grillon, 3
Hôtel Michelet, 4
CAMPGROUNDS
Camping La Montagne Verte, 6
N
300 yards
300 meters
PL. ARNOLD
Jardin Botanique
Musée Zoologique
Université
PL. D'ATHENES
PL. DE L'UNIVERSITE
United States
Contades Synagogue
Parc du Contades
PL. DE LA REPUBLIQUE
Pont du Théâtre
PL. DE ZURICH
PL. DU MARCHE GAYOT
Palais Rohan
PL. DU CATHEDRALE
Cathédrale
PL. GUTENBERG
PL. BROGLIE
PL. KLEBER
PL. DU CORBEAU
Musée Alsacien
PL. D'AUSTERLITZ
PL. DE L'HOPITAL
St-Thomas
Hôpital Civil
Grand'Rue
LA PETITE FRANCE
Ponts Couverts
barrage Vauban
Les Halles
PL. ST-PIERRE LE VIEUX
Musée d'Art Moderne et Contemporain
TO COLMAR, E4, A5
TO NANCY, METZ
TO 5, 6 AND
av. de la Forêt Noire
av. des Vosges
av. de la Paix
av. de la Marseillaise
quai Finkmatt
quai J. Sturm
quai Kléber
quai Kellermann
quai St-Jean
quai de Paris
quai de Turckheim
quai St-Thomas
quai St-Nicolas
quai des Bateliers
quai Finkwiller
bd. de la Victoire
bd. President Wilson
bd. de Metz
bd. de Nancy
bd. de Lyon
r. du 21 Novembre
r. des Dentelles
r. des Moulins
r. aux F. Bourgeois
r. de la Div. Leclerc
r. de la 1ère Armée
r. du Maréchal Juin
r. de la Krutenau
r. du Fbg. National
r. Ste-Marguerite
r. Rosheim
r. de Molsheim
r. Humann
r. du Dôme
r. des Juifs
r. Brûlée
r. de la Nuée Bleue
r. de la Fonderie
r. Finkmatt
r. Fosse des Treize
r. du Fbg. de Pierre
r. des Bonnes-Gens
r. du Travail
r. du Maras Vert
r. du Fg de Saverne
r. Kuhn
r. Thiergarten
r. Maire Kuss
r. Déserte
r. de la Course
r. Oberlin
r. de l'Observatoire
av. General de Gaulle
r. de Rome
r. de Lucerne
r. de Zurich
r. des Orphelins
r. du St-Gothard
r. de Jura
r. General Zimmer
r. de l'Université
r. Goethe
r. de Reims
al. de la Robertsau
quai Rouget de Lisle
quai Zorn
av. d'Alsace
quai du Maire Dietrich
r. Gutenberg
Grands Arcades
Marché aux Poissons
r. du Vieux
r. du Vieux Marché-aux-Vins
r. de Sebastopol
r. des Frères
r. de l'Arc en Ciel
quai Lezay-Marnésia
bd. de Bischwiller
r. Kageneck
L'Ill

Bike Rental: Strasbourg has been rated the most bike-accessible city in France. **Vélocation,** at 4 locations: 4 rue du Maire Kuss (☎03 88 43 64 30), near the train station, open M-F 6am-7:30pm, Sa 8am-noon and 2-7pm, Su 9am-noon and 2-7pm; 10 rue des Bouchers (☎03 88 43 64 40), in the town center, open M-F 8am-7pm, Sa-Su 9am-noon and 2-7pm; on pl. du Château (☎03 88 21 06 38), open Tu-F 9am-noon and 1:30-7pm, Sa-Su 9am-noon and 2-7pm; and 1 bd. de Metz (☎03 88 32 20 11), open M-F 7:30am-7pm. Bikes 20F/€3.05 per half-day, 30F/€4.57 per day. Tandems 40F/€6.10 per day. 300F/€45.74 deposit and xerox of ID card.

ORIENTATION AND PRACTICAL INFORMATION

The *vieille ville* is an eye-shaped island in the center of the city, bounded on the north by a large canal and on the south by the river Ill. To get there from the train station, go straight down rue du Maire-Kuss, cross pont Kuss, and make a quick right and then left onto Grande Rue, which becomes rue Gutenberg. Turn right at pl. Gutenberg and head down rue Mercière toward the cathedral. A right turn after the bridge from the station leads to **La Petite France,** a neighborhood of old Alsatian houses, restaurants, and narrow canals.

ALSACE

Tourist Office: 17 pl. de la Cathédrale (☎03 88 52 28 28), next to the cathedral. **Branches** at pl. de la Gare (☎03 88 32 51 49) and pont de l'Europe (☎03 88 61 39 23). Good free map; others 3-24F/€0.46-3.66. Hotel reservations 10F/€1.53 plus deposit. Pick up the free *Shows and Events* guide, *Strasbourg Actualités,* or *Strassbuch.* Open June-Sept. M-Sa 9am-7pm, Su 9am-6pm; Oct.-May daily 9am-6pm.

Tours: The tourist office organizes themed tours of the *vieille ville* and the cathedral, available in French for groups of 5 or more; 38F/€5.79, students 19F/€2.90. Tours offered July-Aug. daily 10:30am, Sa also 3pm; May-June and Sept.-Oct. Tu-W, F-Sa 3pm; Dec. daily 3pm, Su also 4:30pm. 1½hr. architectural, historic, and neighborhood theme tours Apr.-June and Sept.-Nov. Sa 2:30pm; July-Aug. M-Sa 6:30pm. Audioguides also available (in English) year-round at the same price as tours.

Budget Travel: Havas Voyages, 29 rue de la Nuée Bleue (☎03 88 52 89 00). Open M-F 9am-noon and 1:30-6:30pm, Sa 9am-noon and 2-5pm.

Consulates: US, 15 av. d'Alsace (☎03 88 35 31 04, cultural services ☎03 88 35 38 20), next to pont John F. Kennedy. Open M-F 9am-noon and 2-5pm.

Money: 24hr. automatic currency exchange at **Crédit Commerciale de France,** pl. Gutenberg at rue des Serruriers (☎03 88 37 88 00). **American Express,** 19 rue du Francs-Bourgeois (☎03 88 21 96 59). Open M-F 9:30am-noon and 2-5:45pm.

English Bookstore: Librairie Bookworm, 3 rue des Pâques, off rue du Fbg. de Saverne (☎03 88 32 26 99). Everything from science fiction to grammar guides, with a good second-hand selection. Open M 1:30-6:30pm, Tu-F 10am-4:30pm, Sa 10am-6pm.

Youth Center: CROUS, 1 quai du Maire-Dietrich (☎03 88 21 28 00; fax 03 88 36 77 79). Meal vouchers to university restaurants sold to students M-F 9am-1pm. 26F/€3.96 per meal. **Centre d'Information Jeunesse (CIJA),** 7 rue des Ecrivains (☎03 88 37 33 33), has info about jobs and lodging. Open M-Th 10am-noon and 1-6pm, F 10am-noon and 1-5pm.

Laundromat: Lavomatique, 10 rue de la Nuée Bleue (☎03 88 75 54 18). Open daily 7am-9pm. Also at 2 rue Deserte, near the train station.

Police: 11 rue de la Nuée Bleue (☎03 88 15 37 37).

Hospital: Hôpital Civil de Strasbourg, 1 pl. de l'Hôpital (☎03 88 11 67 68). South across the canal from the *vieille ville.*

Internet Access: Le Midi-Minuit, 5 pl. du Corbeau (☎03 88 36 09 92). Internet café and *salon de thé.* 30F/€4.57 for 30min. Open M-W 7am-7pm, Th-Sa 7am-10pm, Su 8am-7pm. Also at **Centre International d'Accueil** (see **Accommodations,** below). **Cybermaniak** (☎03 88 32 30 40), on rue du Fosse des Treize. *Centre d'Accueil* residents pay for first 30min. and get second 30min. free. Otherwise, 30F/€4.57 per hr. Open Tu, Th-Sa 2pm-midnight, Su 2-8pm, W 9am-noon.

Post Office: 5 av. de la Marseillaise (☎03 88 52 31 00). Open M-F 8am-7pm, Sa 8am-noon. **Branches** at cathedral (open M-F 8am-6:30pm and Sa 8am-6:30) and at 1 pl. de la Gare (open M-F 8am-7pm, Sa 8am-noon). All have **currency exchange. Poste Restante:** 67074. **Postal code:** 67000.

ACCOMMODATIONS AND CAMPING

Inexpensive hotels ring the train station. Make reservations early.

Centre International d'Accueil de Strasbourg (CIARUS), 7 rue Finkmatt (☎03 88 15 27 88; fax 03 88 15 27 89; ciarus@ciarus.com). From the station, take rue du Maire-Kuss to the canal, turn left, and follow quais St-Jean, Kléber, and Finkmatt. Take a left onto rue Finkmatt at the Palais de Justice; the hostel is on the left (15min.). Or take bus #10 (dir: "Brant Université") to "Place de Pierre." Large, spotless facilities and an international atmosphere. TV room, ping-pong, cafeteria, laundry, and **Internet access.** Breakfast included. Towels 8-15F/€1.22-2.29. Check-in 3:30pm, call ahead if arriving earlier. Check-out 9am. Curfew 1am. Reserve in advance year-round. 6- to 8-bed dorms 94F/€14.33; 3- to 4-bed dorms 105F/€16.01; 2-bed rooms 126F/€19.21; singles 211F/€32.17. Families 94F/€14.33 per person. Wheelchair access. MC/V.

ALSACE

Auberge de Jeunesse, Centre International de Rencontres du Parc du Rhin (HI), (☎03 88 45 54 20; fax 03 88 45 54 21), on rue des Cavaliers, on the Rhine. 7km from station, but less than 1km from Germany. From station, take bus #2 (dir: "Pond du Rhin") to "Parc du Rhin" (30min.). At the bus stop, facing the tourist office, go to the left; rue des Cavaliers is the street with flashing red lights on either side and with willow trees lining the right hand side. Use caution getting to and from here at night. Good facilities and great location overlooking the Rhine. Fills with school groups in summer. Volleyball and basketball courts, pool tables, disco and bar—all usually mobbed by hysterical teenagers. Internet access 1F/€0.15 per min. Breakfast and sheets included. Reception 7am-12:30pm, 2-7:30pm, 8:30pm-1am. Check-out 10am, curfew 1am. 3- to 4-bed dorms 114F/€17.38; singles 226F/€34.46; doubles 170F/€25.92. **Non-members** pay 19F/€2.90 extra a night up to six nights. MC/V.

Auberge de Jeunesse René Cassin (HI), 9 rue de l'Auberge de Jeunesse (☎03 88 30 26 46; fax 03 88 30 35 16), 2km from the station. Catch a bus just outside the train station to the right; take #2 (dir: "Illkirch") to the stop "Auberge de Jeunesse." To walk, turn right from the station onto bd. de Metz and follow it as it becomes bd. Nancy and bd. de Lyon. Turn right onto rue de Molsheim and go through the underpass. Be careful in this area at night. Follow rte. de Schirmeck 1km to rue de l'Auberge de Jeunesse, on the right (30min.). The setting by the canal and park is beautiful, but rooms are box-like and slightly worn. TV room, video games, kitchen, and cafeteria. Breakfast included. Sheets for dorms 17F/€2.59. Reception 7am-12:30pm, 1:30-7:30pm, and 8:30-11pm. Curfew 1am. Open Feb.-Dec. 3- to 6-bed dorms 75F/€11.43; singles 196F/€29.88; doubles 280F/€42.69 per person. Camping 42F/€6.40. **Non-members** pay a 19F/€2.90 supplement. MC/V.

Hôtel le Grillon, 2 rue Thiergarten (☎03 88 32 71 88; fax 03 88 32 22 01), 1 block from the station toward the city center. Spacious rooms reminiscent of an ski lodge, above a hip bar. Breakfast 32F/€4.88. Reception 6am-2am. Singles 180F/€27.44, with shower 240F/€36.59; doubles 230F/€35.06, with shower 280F/€42.69. Extra bed 70F/€10.67. MC/V.

Hôtel de Bruxelles, 13 rue Kuhn (☎03 88 32 45 31; fax 03 88 32 06 22). Just up the street from the train station, across the canal from the *vieille ville*. Lovely, bright breakfast nook downstairs, but ask to see your room before you take it; some are bigger and prettier than others. Breakfast 35F/€5.34. Showers 20F/€3.05. Reception 24hr. Singles 170F/€25.92, with bath 285F/€43.45; doubles 170F/€25.92, 285F/€43.45; triples and quads 285F/€43.45, 345F/€52.60. Extra bed 40F/€6.10. MC/V.

Hôtel Michelet, 48 rue du Vieux Marché-aux-Poissons (☎03 88 32 47 38). Dim hallways lead to equally dim but very clean rooms decorated with some care. Great location right around the corner from the cathedral. Breakfast 25F/€3.81. Reception 7am-8pm, otherwise call ahead. Singles 170/€25.92F, with bath 225F/€34.30; doubles 195F/€29.73, 275F/€41.93. MC/V.

Camping la Montagne Verte, 2 rue Robert Ferrer (☎03 88 30 25 46), just down the road from the René Cassin hostel (above). Spacious and shady riverside campsite. Car curfew 10pm. Reception July-Aug. 7am-12:30pm and 1:30-10:30pm; Apr.-June, Sept.-Oct. and Dec. 8am-noon, 4-7:30pm, and 8:30-9:30pm. 26F/€3.96 per site, 20F/€3.05 per person, 10F/€1.53 per child under 7, electricity 15-21F/€2.29-3.20. Tent and car included.

FOOD

The streets around the cathedral are filled with restaurants—particularly **pl. de la Cathédrale, rue Mercière,** and **rue du Vieil Hôpital.** A little farther away, off pl. Gutenberg, pretty cafés line **rue du Vieux Seigle** and **rue du Vieux Marché-aux-Grains.** Smaller restaurants can be found on and around **rue de la Krutenau.** All sorts swarm the cafés and restaurants of tiny **pl. Marché Gayot,** hidden off rue des Frères. In **La Petite France,** especially along rue des Dentelles and petite rue des Dentelles, you'll find small **winstubs** (VIN-shtoob)—classic Alsatian watering holes, traditionally affiliated with individual wineries, with timber exteriors and checkered tablecloths. Local restaurants are known for *choucroute garnie*, sauerkraut served with meats, but you also can find delicious 27F/€4.12 sausages at many stands throughout the city. **Markets** are held at bd. de la Marne (Tu 7am-1pm and Sa 7am-1pm), at pl. de Bordeaux (Tu 7am-1pm and Sa 7am-1pm), and pl. de la Gare (M 10am-6pm and Th 10am-6pm). Several **supermarkets** are also scattered around the *vieille ville*, including **ATAC,** 47 rue des Grandes Arcades, off pl. Kléber. (☎03 88 32 51 53. Open M-Sa 8:30am-8pm.) Peer down at canal locks over huge servings of seafood, salads (47F/€7.17), and sauerkraut from **Au Pont St-Martin,** 13-15 rue des Moulins, a consummately Germanic triple-decker *winstub* in La Petite France. (☎03 88 32 45 13. Mid-week lunch *menu* 60F/€9.15. Open in summer daily noon-11pm; in winter noon-2:30pm and 7-11pm. AmEx/MC/V.) Take a break from oily meats at the vegetarian **Poêles de Carrotes,** 2 pl. des Meuniers, with a lunch *menu* for 59F/€9. Dinner's actually a little cheaper: hearty salads 46F/€7.01; vegetable gratins 48-56/€7.32-8.54; pizzas 44F/€6.71; and pastas 39-49/€5.95-7.47. (☎03 88 32 33 23. Open M-Sa noon-2pm and 7-10:30pm. MC/V.)

SIGHTS

For info on exhibitions, concerts, and films, visit www.musees-strasbourg.org.

CATHEDRALE DE STRASBOURG. The ruddy, majestic Cathédrale de Strasbourg thrusts 142m into the sky from the belly of the city. Victor Hugo's favorite "prodigy of the gigantic and the delicate" took 260 years to build (it was completed in 1439) and today remains outstanding in form, decoration, and size. **Reliefs** around the three portals on the facade depict the life of Christ, with the left portal showing the Virtues stabbing the Vices with lances. Inside the southern transept, the massive wooden **Horloge Astronomique** is a testament to the wizardry of 16th-century Swiss clockmakers. At 12:30pm, tiny automated apostles troop out of the face, while a clockwork rooster greets a mechanical St. Peter. Get there at least half an hour early in July and August. The tiny automata inside an organ chest in the nave, with their movable joints and stern expressions, used to rant at the minister during services, much to the amusement of medieval parishioners. In front of the clock, the cathedral's central **Pilier des Anges,** decorated by a nameless 13th-century master from Chartres, depicts the Last Judgment. Goethe scaled the 330 steps of the tower regularly to cure his fear of heights. *(☎03 88 24 43 34. **Cathedral** open M-Sa 7-11:40am and 12:45-7pm, Su 12:45-6pm. Tours July-Aug. M-F 10:30am, 2:30, and 3:30pm; Sa 10:30am and 2:30pm; Su 2 and 3pm. 15F/€2.29. **Horloge** tickets (5F/€0.76) go on sale inside the cathedral at 8:30am, and at the south entrance at 11:45am. Hear choral rehearsals year-round Th 8-10pm, madrigals F 8-10pm, and Gregorian chants Su 8:45am. **Tower** open 9am-6:30pm. 20F/€3.05, children 10F/€1.53.)*

PALAIS ROHAN. This magnificent 18th-century building houses an excellent trio of small museums. The **Musée des Arts Décoratifs,** once a residence for cardinals, was looted during the revolution and then refurbished for Napoleon in 1805. Rooms don't get any more stylishly imperial than these; gold-encrusted ceilings, immense monochrome expanses of marble, and the bedroom of the Emperor himself are not to be missed. Upstairs, the **Musée des Beaux Arts** has a solid collection of art from the 14th to the 19th centuries, mostly Italian and Dutch, including works by Giotto, Botticelli, Raphael, Rubens, El Greco, and Goya. Hans Menling's polyptych *Vanity* shows a gruesome Death, entrails askew, beside a beautiful woman admiring herself in a mirror. The unusually appealing, comprehensive, and well-organized **Musée Archéologique** presents the history of Alsace from 600,000 BC to AD 800. *(2 pl. du Château. ☎03 88 52 50 00. Open M and W-Sa 10am-noon and 1:30-6pm, Su 10am-5pm. Museums 20F/€3.05 each; 40F/€6.10 for all 3, students 20F/€3.05.)*

MUSEE D'ART MODERNE ET CONTEMPORAIN. Opened in 1998, this steel and glass behemoth houses a small but impressive collection ranging from late 19th-century Impressionists to the work of Cubists and other 20th-century masters. Monet, Gauguin, Picasso, Dufy, Kandinsky, and Ernst are featured, and there's an entire room devoted to the work of regional artists Hans Jean Arp and Sophie Täuber. *(1 pl. Hans Jean Arp. ☎03 88 23 31 31. Open Tu-W and F-Su 11am-7pm, Th noon-10pm. 30F/€4.57, students and seniors 20F/€3.05, children under 15 free. Audio guide 20F/€3.05.)*

MAISON DE L'ŒUVRE NOTRE-DAME. This 14th- to 16th-century mansion and sometime headquarters of Strasbourg's cathedral builders, now holds a dry collection of Rhenish art from the 11th to the 17th centuries and various wonderful cathedral-related artifacts. Of particular note are statues originally from the cathedral's facade and some 12th- to 14th-century stained glass. A recreated Gothic garden awaits at the visit's end. *(3 pl. du Château. ☎03 88 52 50 00. Open Tu-Su 10am-6pm, Su 10am-5pm. 20F/€3.05; students, seniors, and large families 10F/€1.53; under 18 free.)*

LA PETITE FRANCE. This old tanners' district is tucked away in the southwest corner of the city center, an area of slender steep-roofed houses with carved wood facades. Tourists flock to this prettiest and least urban of neighborhoods, chatting in the sidewalk cafés over accordion music and the burble of water along the locks. Trust them on this one—it's unique and lovely.

L'ORANGERIE. Strasbourg's largest and most spectacular park was designed by Le Nôtre in 1692 after he cut his teeth on Versailles. It has all the attractions of a good municipal park: plenty of picnic room, ponds and waterfalls to be explored by rowboat, a stork-frequented mini-farm, go-carts, and Le Nôtre's original skateboard park. There are free concerts on summer evenings at the **Pavillon Joséphine.** *(Take bus #23, 30, or 72 to "l'Orangerie." Concerts Th-Tu 8:30pm.)*

BREWERIES. The **Kronenbourg** brewery provides a taste of Germany, with a free tour in French, English, or German, a look at different stages of brewing, a film, and a tasting session. *(68 rte. d'Oberhausbergen. Take the tram to "Ducs d'Alsace." ☎03 88 27 41 59; fax 03 88 27 42 06. Tours M-Sa 9-10am and 2-3pm, as well as 11am and 4-5pm in summer. Available in English.)* **Heineken** also offers free tours of its brewery in French, English, and German, for groups and by advance reservation only. *(4-10 rue St-Charles, Schiltgheim. ☎03 88 19 59 53. Call to schedule, M-F 8am-noon and 1:30-4:30pm.)*

PALAIS DE L'EUROPE AND THE PARLIAMENT. The Palais is the seat of the Council of Europe, while the European Parliament lies just opposite; both are on the northwest edge of the Orangerie. During sessions (one week per month Sept.-July), you may register at the desk to sit in the visitors' gallery, where headsets translate debates into several languages. *(Av. de l'Europe. Parliament ☎03 88 17 20 07 or 03 88 17 20 08. Bring your passport. 1hr. tours by advance request only.)*

NIGHTLIFE

Place Kléber and **pl. Maréchal** attract a student crowd. Slightly seedy—and all the better for it—is the area between **pl. d'Austerlitz** and **pl. de Zurich,** across the canal from the *vieille ville*. You may want to travel in a group. Numerous bars and cafés cluster there, particularly around the tiny **pl. des Orphelins.**

Les 3 Brasseurs, 22 rue des Veaux (☎03 88 36 12 13). A micro-brewery that serves a glass of each of the four home brews for 28F/€4.27. During happy hour (daily 5-7pm), two drinks go for the price of one. Open daily 11:30am-1am.

L'Elastic Bar, 27 rue des Orphelins (☎03 88 36 11 10). Easily one of the most energetic scenes in the city–get your drum'n'bass and house fixes here. Open M-Th 5pm-3am, F-Sa 5pm-4am.

Le Gayot, 18 rue des Frères (☎03 88 36 31 88). Its squished terrace opens onto lively pl. Maréchal; the bar draws a young crowd during the school year, when students frequently play jazz piano. Live music Sept.-June W-Sa. Open daily 10:30am-2am. MC/V.

Le Schutzenberger, 29-31 rue des Grandes Arcades (☎03 90 23 66 66). Everyone's checking everyone else out in this spare, blue-and-orange-lit warehouse of a bar. A porch overlooking pl. Kléber finds the black-sweater crowd seeing and eager to be seen. Open Su-Th 7:30am-3am, F-Sa 7:30am-4am.

Café des Anges, 5 rue Ste-Catherine (☎03 88 37 12 67), is most lively on the weekends. Spins funk, drum'n'bass or salsa several nights a week. No cover. Buzz to get in. Ground floor open Tu-W 9pm-3am, Th-Sa starting at 10pm.

ENTERTAINMENT AND FESTIVALS

Summer in Strasbourg is all about the **pl. de la Cathédrale,** the stage every afternoon and evening for a troupe of musicians, flame-eaters, acrobats, and mimes. The **cathedral** itself hosts organ concerts in summer (June 2-Aug. 26 F-Sa 9pm, July-Aug. also W. 34F/€5.18, students 17F/€2.59). Also on summer nights, but in pl. du Château this time, are the **Nuits de Strass,** a funny and free projection show. **Water-jousting** competitions take place on summer evenings on the river Ill outside the Palais Rohan. **Strasbourg Fluvial** sends boats out on 1¼hr. tours, including several at night in the summer. (☎03 88 84 13 13. 43F/€6.56, children 21.50F/€3.28.)

From October through June, the **Orchestre Philharmonique de Strasbourg** performs at the Palais de la Musique et des Congrès, behind pl. de Bordeaux. (☎03 88 15 09 09 for tickets, ☎03 88 15 09 00 for info. 50% student discount on all performances.) The **Théâtre National de Strasbourg,** 1 av. de la Marseillaise, has a season from September to May. (☎03 88 24 88 00. 100-140F/€15.25-21.35, students 75-100F/€11.43-15.25. Thursday shows 50F/€7.62.) The **Opéra du Rhin,** 19 pl. Broglie, features opera and ballet in its 19th-century hall. (☎03 88 75 48 23. Tickets 70-330F/€10.67-50.31, students half-price; rush tickets from 60F/€9.15, students 35F/€5.34.)

June brings the **Festival de Musique de Strasbourg,** a two-week-long extravaganza attracting some of Europe's best classical musicians. The **Festival de Jazz** spans the first two weeks of July and habitually draws giants of the jazz world to Strasbourg (tickets 160-230F/€24.39-35.06, students 130-150F/€19.82-22.90). For info on both festivals, contact **Wolf Musique,** 24 rue de la Mésange (☎03 88 32 43 10). **Musica** (☎03 88 23 47 23), a contemporary music festival from mid-September to early October, includes concerts, operas, and films.

NEAR STRASBOURG: SAVERNE

The 3rd-century Roman travel guide *Itinerarium Antonin* recommended Saverne as a "good place to rest." This 21st-century guidebook agrees. The town is located on a narrow pass through the Vosges mountains, a position which eight centuries of generals have coveted. Today the fat green mountains surrounding it give visitors to Saverne an indescribably soothing sense of physical isolation. There exists no better place than this for a morning stroll; have a pastry and a coffee, sit in the befountained square, and walk beside the town's canals and gardens.

ORIENTATION AND PRACTICAL INFORMATION. **Trains** leave from pl. de la Gare for **Metz** (1hr., 5 per day, 89F/€13.57); **Nancy** (1hr., 8 per day, 85F/€12.96); and **Strasbourg** (30min., 11 per day, 44F/€6.71). (☎03 88 91 33 66. Ticket office open M-F 6:30am-7:30pm, Sa 8:30am-6pm, Su 10am-8:30pm.) To get to the **tourist office,** 37 Grande Rue, from the train station, cross the square and turn right onto rue de la Gare. Cross the Zorn river and take a left onto Saverne's main street, **Grande Rue;** continue past the château on pl. de Gaulle and find the office on your left. A helpful staff dispenses town and trail maps, along with info on local sights and hiking. (☎03 88 91 80 47; info@ot-saverne.fr. Open May-Oct. and Dec. M-Sa 9am-12:30pm and 2-7pm, Su 10am-12:30pm and 2-5pm; Nov. and Jan.-Apr. M-Sa 9am-12:30pm and 2-7pm.) **Rent bikes** at **Cycles OHL,** 10 rue St-Nicolas. (☎03 88 91 17 13. Open Tu-F 9am-noon and 2-7pm, Sa 9am-noon and 2-6pm. Half-day 75F/€11.43, full day 95F/€14.48. MC/V.) The **police** are at 29 rue St-Nicolas (☎03 88 91 19 12), on the street veering right off the end of Grande Rue. **Hôpital Ste-Catherine** is at 19 côte de Saverne (☎03 88 71 67 67), east of the town center, near the forest. **Post office:** 2 pl. de la Gare. (☎03 88 71 56 40. Open M-F 8am-noon and 1:30-6:30pm, Sa 8am-noon.) **Postal code:** 67700.

ALSACE

ACCOMMODATIONS AND FOOD. The **Auberge de Jeunesse** occupies the fourth floor of the Château des Rohan, right in the center of town. Recently renovated rooms have great views, some over the statues and rose garden of the château's courtyard. (☎03 88 91 14 84; fax 03 88 71 15 97; aj.saverne@wanadoo.fr. Internet access. Breakfast 19F/€3.20. Sheets 17F/€2.70. Reception 8-10am and 5-11pm; ask for a key and the code to the front door if you plan to be out late. Lockout 10am-5pm. 8-bed dorms 52.50F/€8 per person; 19F/€2.90 extra for **non-members** the first 6 nights.

Camping de Saverne, rue du Père Libermann, is a rose-flowered three-star campground near tennis courts and trails to the Vosges, of which it has a particularly good view. (☎03 88 91 35 65. Reception Apr.-Sept. 7am-10pm. 15F/€2.29 per person, children 8F/€1.22; 10F/€1.53 per tent, 15F/€2.29 with car. Electricity 15F/€2.29. 2F/€0.30 daily residency tax and insurance.)

The Romans called Saverne "Tres Tabernae" (Three Taverns) for its hospitality and gut-warming cuisine. **S'zawermer Stuebel,** 4 rue des Frères, heir to this fine tradition, serves filling pasta (38-40F/€5.79-6.10) and pizzas (35-50F/€5.34-7.62) in a tiny converted wine cellar with vaulted ceilings and on the shaded terrace across the street. (☎03 88 71 29 95. Open daily 11:30am-2:30pm and 6:30-10pm. MC/V.) **Muller Oberling,** 66-68 Grande Rue, is a locally popular tea room that offers quiche, *tarte à l'oignon*, views of the *place*, and pizza (19.50F/€2.97), plus an exceptional range of baked goods. (☎03 88 91 13 30. Open M-F 7am-7pm, Sa 7am-6pm, Su 8:30am-12:30pm and 1:30-6pm. MC/V.) There are **ethnic options** on the Grande Rue, and a **Match supermarket** at 8 rue Ste-Marie, a 10-minute walk from the town center. (☎03 88 91 23 63. Open M-Th 8:30am-7:30pm, F 8:30am-8pm, Sa 8am-6:30pm.) Look for the pl. de Gaulle **market** on Thursday mornings.

SIGHTS. "Oh! What a lovely garden!" exclaimed Louis XIV upon visiting Saverne. The town's pride and joy is its **Roseraie,** a botanical garden that sprawls out to the left of Grande Rue, along the Zorn. Over 8500 blooms shimmy their pretty heads, giving Saverne the reputation of the "City of Roses." The first Saturday in August sees the **Cours de Greffe,** a contest for the most exquisite hybrid rose, while an exposition of new rose varieties takes place on the last Sunday of August. (Open June-Sept. daily 9am-7pm. 15F/€2.29, students 10F/€1.53.) The **Château des Rohan,** home to the bishop-princes of Strasbourg from the 15th century to the Revolution, spreads its elegant Neoclassical arms along pl. de Gaulle in the center of town. The château now hosts the **Musée du Château des Rohan** (☎03 88 91 06 28). In the archaeology wing are the requisite unspectacular Gallo-Roman remnants; it is worth visiting just to see the carved toads once placed as offerings at the Grotte St-Vic by women suffering gynecological problems (the toad was meant to represent a uterus). In the same building, the slick, self-important **Musée de Louise Weiss** is dedicated to the local feminist, journalist, and Resistance fighter. (Both open June 15-Sept. 15 W-M 10am-noon and 2-6pm; Mar.-June 14 and Sept. 16-Nov. 30 W-M 2-5pm; Dec.-Feb. Su 2-5pm. 16F/€2.44, students 11F/€1.68.)

HIKES. Saverne's greatest asset is its endless network of forested **hiking** and **biking trails. Club Vosgien** maintains phenomenal trails and also runs hikes in the area; ask the tourist office for info. Bikers can pick up the free brochure *Cyclo Tourisme*, with a map and suggested routes, from the tourist office. Even if you're not up for a long hike, try the 45-minute jaunt through shaded woods to the lovely 12th-century castle **Le Haut Barr;** pick up a map at the tourist office and follow rue du Haut Barr (D17) southwest. Nearby is the **Tour du Télégraphe Chappe,** the first telegraph tower along the Paris-Strasbourg line. (☎03 88 52 98 99. Open May Sa-Su noon-6pm; June-Aug. Tu-Su noon-6pm. 10F/€1.53, children 8F/€1.22.)

THE ROUTE DU VIN (WINE ROUTE)

The vineyards of Alsace flourish along a 170km corridor known as the Route du Vin that stretches along the foothills of the Vosges from Strasbourg to Mulhouse. The Romans were the first to ferment Alsatian grapes, but the locals, knowing a good thing when they taste it, have enthusiastically continued the tradition. Today over 150 million bottles are sold yearly. Hordes of tourists are drawn to the medieval villages along the route, with their picture-book half-timbered houses and numerous wineries offering free *dégustations* (tastings).

The Route includes nearly 100 towns, making for a lot of ground to cover. **Accommodations** tend to be expensive, so consider staying in Colmar (p. 407) or Sélestat (p. 405), larger towns which anchor the Route. **Buses** run frequently from Colmar to towns on the southern part of the Route, but many smaller towns are not well served by public transportation. **Car rental** from Strasbourg or Colmar is practical but pricey. **Biking** is a viable alternative, especially from Colmar, but the gentle yet persistent hills may challenge novices. Trails and turn-offs are very well marked. **Trains** connect Sélestat, Molsheim, Barr, Colmar, and Mulhouse. The best source of info on regional *caves* is the **Centre d'Information du Vin d'Alsace,** 12 av. de la Foire aux Vins, at the Maison du Vin d'Alsace in Colmar. (☎03 89 20 16 20, fax 03 89 20 16 30. Open M-F 9am-noon and 2-5pm.) Tourist offices in Strasbourg (p. 395) dispense regional advice, including the excellent *Alsace Wine Route* brochure.

If you only have the time or interest to cover one destination, *Let's Go* advises that you take the bus from the Colmar train station to **Kaysersberg** (see below), perhaps the Route's prettiest and most characteristic town. If you want to visit more than one place, find another means of transportation. Be warned that walking is not one—country roads have minimal sidewalks.

KAYSERSBERG

The exceptionally pretty and relatively untouristed Kaysersberg (pop. 2755) is a little town with a lot of history. Its name, from the Latin *Cæsaris Mons* (Caesar's Mountain), dates to Roman times, when it commanded one of the most important passes between Gaul and the Rhine Valley. More recently, Albert Schweitzer was born here and went on to win the Nobel Peace prize; his home has since been converted into the pastel-green **Musée Albert Schweitzer,** 126 rue Général de Gaulle, which contains copious memorabilia retracing the life and works of the good doctor. African art and photographs of his years in Africa are a welcome surprise in this rural Alsatian town. (☎03 89 78 22 78. Open May-Oct. daily 9am-noon and 2-6pm. 10F/€1.53, students 5F/€0.76.) Also noteworthy is the 12th- to 15th-century **Eglise St-Croix.** Between the church and the museum are the remains of the 15th- to 16th-century **fortified bridge.** Clamber up to see the ruined castle, now privately owned and not open to visitors, on the hill above the town.

The **tourist office,** 39 rue Général de Gaulle, is in the Hôtel de Ville; cross the bridge behind the bus stop and walk straight up the road to a little square with a fountain. (☎03 89 78 22 78; fax 03 89 78 27 44; www.kaysersberg.com. Open July-Aug. M-F 8:30am-6:30pm, Sa 9am-noon and 2-6pm, Su 10am-noon and 2-4pm; Sept.-June M-F 8:30am-noon and 1-5:30pm, Sa 9am-noon.) Kaysersberg has no train station, but **buses** run to **Colmar** (20min., M-Sa 1 per hr. 6am-7pm, 12.60F/€1.92).

RIQUEWIHR

Certainly the most visited village along the Route, the 16th-century walled hamlet of Riquewihr (pop. 1228) is the headquarters of a number of Alsace's best-known wine-shipping firms—but you may want to ship yourself somewhere less zoo-like in the summer months. The beautiful **Tour des Voleurs** (Thieves' Tower) contains a grisly torture chamber with audio commentary in English for those with shackled imaginations. (Open Apr.-Oct. daily 10am-noon and 1:30-6:15pm. 10F/€1.53, under 10 free.) The 13th-century **Tour du Dolder,** rue du Général de Gaulle, once served as a sentinel post and now houses a museum of local heritage. (Open July-Aug. daily 10am-noon and 1:30-6:15pm; Apr.-June and Sept.-Oct. Sa-Su only. 10F/€1.53, children under 10 free.) Summer nights bring free *son-et-lumière* (sound and light) shows. (July-Aug. Tu and F 10pm; mid-June to mid-Sept. F 10pm.) Riquewihr celebrates a number of alcohol-related holidays. The **Foire Aux Vins** takes place in nearby **Ribeauville** on the second-to-last weekend in July. On the first Sunday of September, music accompanies the clink of glasses during the **Minstrel's Festival.**

The **tourist office,** 2 rue de la Première Armée, leads free walking tours. (☎03 89 49 08 40. Tours July-Aug. daily 5pm. Office open M-Sa 9am-noon and 2-6pm.) You can pitch a tent at the small **Camping Intercommunal,** 1½km from the town center. (☎03 89 47 90 08. Reception 8:30-11am and 2-5pm. Open Apr.-Oct. 23F/€3.51 per person, under age 7 7F/€1.07. 26F/€3.96 per site. Electricity 25F/€3.81.)

LET'S GO: DEGUSTATION So you've swirled it around thoughtfully for a few seconds, you've taken a discerning sniff of the bouquet, you've sipped it with noisy flair, and you've finally nodded to the *garçon* in haughty approval. And yet you still have no idea what quality or even what kind of wine you've ordered, and whether it goes better with *flammekueche* or asparagus. Unique among French appellations, Alsatian wines are named for the grape varieties from which they are made rather than the area they are grown in. With the exception of the Pinot Noir, all the major Alsatian wines are white. Here's a basic run-down (*sans* flowery prose) on Alsatian wines:

Gewurztraminer: From a type of rosy Savagnin grape introduced by the Romans, this unpronounceable white wine has been called "The Emperor of Alsatian wines," known for a dry and very aromatic taste. Drink it as an *apéritif*, or with foie gras, "exotic" cuisine (Indian, Mexican, or Asian), and smelly cheeses.

Riesling: Considered one of the world's best white wines, Riesling is a very dry and somewhat fruity wine. Drink it with white meats, *choucroute*, and fish.

Sylvaner: From a grape variety with Austrian origins, Sylvaner is a light, fruity, and slightly sparkling white wine that goes great with seafood, charcuterie, and salads.

Muscat: A sweeter and highly fruity white wine which is often drunk as an *apéritif*.

The Pinot family: Pinot Blanc is a great all-purpose white wine for chicken, fish, and all sorts of appetizers. **Pinot Gris** is a "smoky," quite strong white wine that can often take the place of a red wine when eating rich meats, roasts, and game. **Pinot Noir** is the sole rose/red wine of the Alsatian bunch, tasting faintly like cherries and complementing red meats and charcuterie.

BARR

On the slopes of Mont Ste-Odile, Barr rests peacefully beneath vineyards stretching up the foothills of the Vosges. Of the Route du Vin towns, Barr seems most connected to its grapes; you can drink a glass of white wine here while walking between rows of plants two minutes from the town center. To get to the narrow, winding *vieille ville* from the industrial area around the train station, turn right onto the street just in front of the station (rue de la Gare), and take your first left onto av. des Vosges. Follow this past the round-about, and for several more blocks until you reach rue St-Marc. Take a right here, walk two winding blocks and turn right onto rue des Bouchers. From the pl. de l'Hôtel de Ville, a right on rue du Dr. Sultzer leads to several *caves*. To the left is the massive, unornamented **Eglise Protestante,** starting point for the **sentier viticole** (vineyard trail). Walkable alone or in a tour organized by the tourist office, the path winds 2km through fields of glistening grapes, past signs that illustrate the different types of grapes that grow. The second week of July sees the **Foire aux Vins,** and the **Fête des Vendanges** (Grape Harvest Festival) takes place the second weekend in October.

The **tourist office** is at pl. de L'Hôtel de Ville. (☎03 88 08 66 65; fax 03 88 08 66 51. Open Sept.-June M-F 8am-noon and 2-6pm, Sa 9am-noon and 2-4pm; July-Aug. M-F 9am-12:30pm and 2-7pm, Sa 9am-noon and 2-6pm, Su 10am-noon and 2-6pm.) **Trains** to Barr run from **Sélestat** (25min., 12 per day, 20F/€3.81) and **Strasbourg** (50min., 11 per day, 35F/€5.34).

ALSACE

OBERNAI

Obernai's lack of important sights is perhaps its biggest draw. The pleasures here are simple, and the town is best enjoyed in a twilight stroll around the 14th-century ramparts. The town (pop. 13,000) maintains a pristine Alsatian beauty despite a steady influx of tourists. Near where the ramparts meet rue Chanoine Gyss stands the Neogothic **Eglise Sts- Pierre et Paul,** the largest church in Alsace after the Strasbourg Cathedral. In the pl. du Marché behind the town hall, the **Fontaine de Ste-Odile** honors the patron saint of Alsace, whose father, a duke of Alsace, was born here. The **Hôtel-de-Ville,** first constructed in 1370, was decorated in 1610 with murals illustrating the ten commandments. The next to last weekend in July brings the **Hans im Schnokeloch** festival, in which costumed locals act out Alsatian legends. A **Foire Aux Vins** (wine fair) takes place the second weekend in August, and the **Wine Harvest Festival,** during the third week in October, features the election of a Grape Harvest Queen.

To get to the **tourist office** from the station, follow rue du Général Gouraud to pl. du Beffroi. Info awaits on beer and wine tastings, festivals, and over 200km of marked trails. (☎03 88 95 64 13; fax 03 88 49 90 84; ot.obernai@sdu.fr. Open June-Sept. M-Sa 9:30am-12:30pm and 2-7pm, Su 9am-12:30pm and 2-6pm; Oct.-May M-Sa 9:30am-noon and 2-5pm.) **Trains** run from **Sélestat** (35min., 9 per day, 25F/€3.81) and **Strasbourg** (45min., 20 per day, 30F/€4.57).

SELESTAT

Halfway between Colmar and Strasbourg, Sélestat (pop. 17,200) is often overlooked by tourists. As a result, it has avoided acquiring the looniness of some of the Route du Vin's more frequented towns. Part of the Holy Roman Empire starting in AD 1217 and a center of Renaissance humanism, Sélestat has painstakingly preserved its cultural heritage, including the ultimate in Rhineland bragging rights—the first-recorded Christmas tree. The area around town is the sloping wine country of the Route du Vin, grading into the Reid, a fertile and oft-flooded plain. This is an oasis of calm in a region that can be distressingly touristy.

ORIENTATION AND PRACTICAL INFORMATION. From pl. de la Gare, **trains** run to **Colmar** (15min., 16 per day, 24F/€3.66) and **Strasbourg** (30min., 15 per day, 42F/€6.40). The **tourist office,** 10 bd. Général Leclerc, in the Commanderie St-Jean, is north of the town center, a 10-minute hike from the train station. Go straight on av. de la Gare, through pl. Général de Gaulle, to av. de la Liberté. Turn left onto bd. du Maréchal Foch, which veers right and becomes bd. Général Leclerc after pl. Schaal. Continue on bd. du Général Leclerc; the office is a few blocks down on your right. The young, efficient staff can **change currency** and rent you a **bike.** (☎03 88 58 87 20; fax 03 88 92 88 63; www.selestat-tourisme.com. Open May-Sept. M-F 9am-12:30pm and 1:30-7pm, Sa 9am-noon and 2-5pm, Su 9am-3pm; Oct.-Apr. M-F 8:30am-noon and 1:30-6pm, Sa 9am-noon and 2-5pm, closed Su except in Dec. Bikes 50F/€7.62 per half-day, 80F/€12.20 per full day, 350F/€53.36 per week.) Find **Internet** at **Bazook'kafé,** 3 rue St-Foy. (☎03 88 58 47 59. 35F/€5.34 per hr., students 25F/€3.81 per hr.) The **police** are at bd. du Général Leclerc (☎03 88 58 84 22). The **hospital** is at 23 av. Pasteur (☎03 88 57 55 55), behind the train station. The **post office** is on rue de la Poste, near the Hôtel de Ville. (☎03 88 58 80 10. Open M-F 8am-noon and 1:30-6pm, Sa 8am-noon.) **Postal code:** 67600.

ALSACE

ACCOMMODATIONS AND FOOD. Sandwiched on a peaceful residential street in the *vieille ville*, the **Hôtel de l'Ill,** lies at 13 rue des Bateliers. From the train station, take av. de la Gare, turn right onto the large av. de Gaulle, and continue straight as it becomes av. de la Liberté, rue du 4e Zouaves, and rue du Président Poincaré. At the large intersection just before the river, veer to the left onto bd. Thiers; rue des Bateliers will be the second left. The hotel packs 15 cozy and colorful rooms with TV onto three floors presided over by a purring tabby cat. (☎03 88 92 91 09. Breakfast 30F/€4.57. Reception 7am-3pm and 5-11pm. Singles 140-165F/€21.35-25.16; doubles 180F/€27.44, with shower 240F/€36.59; triples with bath 400F/€60.98.) The small, shaded **Camping Les Cigognes** is outside the ramparts on the southern edge of the *vieille ville*, near public tennis courts, parks, and a willow-bordered lake. (☎03 88 92 03 98. Reception July-Aug. 8am-noon and 3-10pm; May-June and Sept.-Oct. 8am-noon and 3-7pm. Open May-Oct. 50-60F/€7.62-9.15 per person, 70-80F/€10.67-12.20 for 2-3 people. No credit cards.)

Bakeries, grocery stores, and the like are scattered throughout the *vieille ville*, especially on rue des Chevaliers and rue de l'Hôpital. Every Tuesday morning, a **market** fills the town center from 8am to noon with breads, meats, and produce, and there's a Saturday morning market for **regional specialties.** In a quiet square around the corner from the churches, **Au Bon Pichet,** 10 pl. du Marché-aux-Choux, prepares Alsatian favorites: large salads with *foie gras*, duck, or smoked salmon (48F/€7.32). The owner, a former butcher and Alsatian to the bone, can tell you everything you always wanted to know about meat but were afraid to ask. (☎03 88 82 96 65. Open Su-M 10am-2pm, Tu-Sa 10am-3pm and 6-10pm. MC/V.)

SIGHTS AND FESTIVALS. According to legend, Sélestat was founded by the giant Sletto. His massive thigh bone (a mere mammoth tusk, some claim) occupies Sélestat's extraordinary **Bibliothèque Humaniste,** 1 rue de la Bibliothèque, a storehouse for the products of Sélestat's 15th-century humanistic boom. There's a truly wonderful collection of ancient documents in this library, from Renaissance anatomy texts to 13th-century students' diligently annotated translations of Ovid, to the 16th-century *Cosmographie Introductio*, the first book ever to mention "America" by name. (☎03 88 58 07 20. Open M and W-F 9am-noon and 2-6pm, Sa 9am-noon; July-Aug. also Sa-Su 2-5pm. 20F/€3.05.)

Surrounded by ivy-covered homes, the 12th-century **Eglise Ste-Foy** rises above the *vieille ville* and the pl. Marché-aux-Poissons. Constructed by Benedictine monks and later taken over by Jesuits, Ste-Foy is one of the most beautiful Romanesque churches in the area. Hints of the imperial Hohenstaufen family (look for their insignia, a grimacing lion) contrast with striking floor mosaics of the Ganges and Euphrates, rivers of man's earliest civilizations, and the signs of the zodiac. Resentful of the monastery's power, the townspeople responded with the 13th- to 15th-century **Eglise St-Georges** across the square. Max Ingrand's vibrant 1960s stained glass complements the frescoes of the essentially Gothic church. The religious and political disorder of the 15th to 17th centuries have produced a more disturbing monument: originally built around 1300, the now-crumbling **Tour des Sorcières,** in front of pl. Maréchal de Lattre de Tassigny, held over 100 "witches" imprisoned by the Catholic church between 1403 and 1579, then again between 1629 and 1642 during the Thirty Years' War. It's no longer open to visitors.

Sélestat's major festival is its **Corso Fleuri,** or flower festival, on the second Sunday in August. Street artists perform, wine is tasted left and right, and wackily-clad gnomes, elves, and trolls invade the streets on floral floats; it all ends in a giant fireworks display. (40F/€6.10, students 20F/€3.05. Info at corso@ville-selestat.fr, or call the Service Culturel.)

ALSACE

NEAR SELESTAT: CHATEAU DE HAUT KOENIGSBOURG

Towering 757m over the town of Kintzheim, just east of Sélestat, this château was built in the 12th century by Frederic "One Eye" Hohenstaufen, duke of Swabia. Half-blind or not, the Duke knew a strategic spot when he saw it, and the castle stands at the crossroads of the major wine-wheat and salt-silver trade routes of its day. After a brief stint under Hapsburg ownership, the castle was pillaged and burnt by the Swedes in the Thirty Years' War, then left in ruins until Emperor Wilhelm II Hohenzollern rebuilt it at the beginning of the 20th century. The castle was wrested permanently from German possession by the Treaty of Versailles in 1919. An assortment of medieval arms can be found in the west wing. (☎03 88 82 50 60. Open July-Aug. daily 9am-6pm; May-June and Sept. 9am-5:30pm; Mar.-Apr. and Oct. 9am-noon and 1-5pm; Nov.-Feb. 9:30am-noon and 1-4pm. Audio tour, available in English, 25F/€3.81. 40F/€6.10, ages 18-25 25F/€3.81, under 18 free.)

COLMAR

Colmar (pop. 65,000) feels distinctly different from most French towns, a reminder that it hasn't always been part of France. In the city's former Dominican monastery and church are two superb works of German Renaissance art—Grünewald and Haguenauer's *Issenheim Altarpiece* and Schongauer's *Virgin in the Rose Bower*—which justify a visit in themselves. Whereas other touristy wine cities aim to convince you that this is how bucolic small-town existence must have been for centuries, with people wearing poofy traditional dresses or *lederhosen* and eating lots of *kugelhopf*, Colmar has a greater sense of historical and artistic profundity. Despite its popularity, Colmar's Alsatian character—stubby pastel houses, *choucroute* and all—is anything but fake.

TRUE LOVE Koenigsbourg has figured in tales of love as well as war; legend speaks of the Rathsamhausen and Tierstein families, who struggled against each other for control of the castle at the end of the 15th century. The Rathsamhausens appealed to Maximin of Ribeaupierre, asking him to tip the balance by marrying his daughter into one of the feuding families. Miffed that she hadn't been consulted, Isabella de Ribeaupierre disguised herself as a minstrel in order to sneak into the castle and catch a glimpse of Wilhelm de Tierstein, one of the prospective bridegrooms. Unbeknownst to her, however, Wilhelm had switched places with his valet Pépin and donned minstrel's garb as well, hoping thereby to uncover Isabella's true feelings toward him. A comedy of errors worthy of Shakespeare ensued, which is reenacted during the château's *Soirées Médiévales. (May-Oct and Nov.-Dec. F-Sa evenings. Reservations mandatory. 230F/€35.06, under 12 115F/€17.53, including a 4-course dinner. For further info, call 03 88 82 71 31.)*

TRANSPORTATION

Trains: pl. de la Gare. To: **Lyon** (5hr., 7 per day, 220F/€33.54); **Mulhouse** (30min., 15 per day, 42F/€6.40); **Paris** (5hr., 10 per day, 255F/€38.88); and **Strasbourg** (40min., 20 per day, 58F/€8.84). Office open M-F 6:30am-8pm, Sa 8:30am-6:30pm, Su 8:30am-8pm. Info office open M-F 9am-7pm, Sa 8:30am-6pm.

Buses: to the right as you exit the station, on pl. de la Gare. Numerous companies run to small towns on the Route du Vin. Pick up a schedule of bus times (in "Actualities Colmar") at the tourist office.

Local Transportation: Allô Trace (☎03 89 20 80 80), to the right of the tourist office in the covered *galerie* on rue Unterlinden. Open M-F 8:30am-12:15pm and 1:30-6:15pm, Sa 8:30am-12:15pm. Tickets 5.90F/€0.90, *carnet* of 10 42F/€6.40. Buses run 6am-8pm, night *Somnabus* M-Sa 9pm-midnight.

Taxis: pl. de la Gare (☎03 89 41 40 19 or 03 89 80 71 71). 24hr.

Bike rental is available at **La Cyclothèque,** 31 rte. d'Ingersheim (☎03 89 79 14 18). 50F/€7.62 per half-day, M-F 70F/€10.67 per full day, Sa-Su 130F/€19.82. Open M-Sa 8:30am-noon and 2-6:30pm.

PRACTICAL INFORMATION

To get from the station to the tourist office, take the first left onto av. de la République. Follow it as it becomes rue Kléber and curves right through pl. du 18 Novembre into the main pl. Unterlinden; the tourist office is straight ahead.

Tourist Office: 4 rue des Unterlinden (☎03 89 20 68 92; fax 03 89 20 69 14; info@ot-colmar.fr). The staff offers cash-only **currency exchange** and makes hotel reservations with a night's deposit. The free *Actualités Colmar* lists local events and bus schedules. **City tours** Apr. to Oct. Tours 25F/€3.81, children 12-16 15F/€2.29. Office open July-Aug. M-Sa 9am-7pm, Su 9:30am-2pm; Apr.-June and Sept.-Oct. M-Sa 9am-6pm, Su 10am-2pm; Nov.-Mar. M-Sa 9am-noon and 2-6pm, Su 10am-2pm.

Police: 6 rue du Chasseur (☎03 89 24 75 00).

Hospital: Hôpital Pasteur, 39 av. de la Liberté (☎03 89 80 40 00).

Post Office: 36-38 av. de la République (☎03 89 41 19 19), across Champs-de-Mars. **Currency exchange.** Open M-F 8am-6:30pm, Sa 8:30am-noon. **Postal code:** 68000.

ACCOMMODATIONS AND CAMPING

Colmar offers precious little in the budget range. The smattering of half-timbered one- and two-star hotels in the center of town are perfectly located but overpriced.

Auberge de Jeunesse (HI), 2 rue Pasteur (☎03 89 80 57 39). Take bus #4 (dir: "Europe") to "Pont Rouge." To walk, take the underground passage in the train station and exit to the right onto rue du Tir; follow it until it merges with av. du Général de Gaulle, bearing left when av. du Général de Gaulle bridges the railroad tracks. Follow the street you're on, rue Florimont, as it curves left into rue du Val St-Grégoire. Take a right on rue du Pont Rouge; continue through the intersection on the rte. d'Ingersheim to rue Pasteur (20min.). Plain rooms and common showers. Kitchen access in winter. Breakfast included. Sheets 20F/€3.05. Reception July-Aug. 7-10am and 5pm-midnight; Sept.-June 5-11pm. Lockout 9am-5pm. Curfew midnight. Reserve in advance in summer. Closed Dec. 15-Jan. 15. 6- to 8-bed dorms 71F/€10.82; singles 172F/€26.22; doubles 202F/€30.80. **Members only.** MC/V.

Hôtel Kempf, 1 av. de la République (☎03 89 41 21 72; fax 03 89 23 06 94). Large, simple rooms with a homey atmosphere in a perfect location. Breakfast 35F/€5.34. Reception 8am-midnight. Singles and doubles from 180F/€27.44, with shower 225-280F/€34.30; triples 350F/€53.36. 3F/€0.46 tax per person per night. MC/V.

La Chaumière, 74 av. de la République (☎03 89 41 08 99), around the corner from the train station, a 5min. walk from the center of town. Kind hostess lets pleasant rooms, some set around a cement balcony overlooking an inner courtyard. Breakfast 28F/€4.27. Reception 7am-11pm. Singles and doubles 170-180F/€25.92-27.44, with shower 240-260F/€36.59-39.64; triples 280F/€42.69. MC/V.

Camping de l'Ill, rte. Horbourg-Wihr (☎03 89 41 15 94), is 2 laurel-scented km from town on a wooded river in view of the Vosges. Take bus #1 (dir: "Horbourg-Wihr") to "Plage d'Ill." Reception July-Aug. 8am-10pm; Feb.-June and Sept.-Nov. 8am-8pm. Fills quickly in summer. Open Feb.-Nov., tents May-Sept. only. 18F/€2.74 per person, 10F/€1.53 under age 10. Site 20F/€3.05, tent 10F/€1.53. Electricity 15F/€2.29.

FOOD

There is a **Monoprix supermarket** at pl. Unterlinden. (Open M-F 8am-8pm, Sa 8am-7:55pm.) **Markets** are set up in pl. St-Joseph (Sa morning) and pl. de l'Ancienne Douane (Th morning), a popular café spot. Colmar boasts a number of viticulturists. A friendly welcome, a great selection of local wines (26F/€3.96 and up), and a 400-year legacy await at **Robert Karcher et Fils,** 11 rue de l'Ours, in the *vieille ville.* (☎03 89 41 14 42. Open daily 8am-noon and 2-6pm. MC/V.)

Tropic'ice, pl. des Dominicains, serves over 100 permutations of galettes, ice creams, and fresh salads. (☎03 89 41 31 36. Open daily 11:30am-midnight. MC/V.) **Brasserie Schwendi,** 23-25 Grande Rue, offers *tartes flambées* and other hearty Alsatian fare, as well as a great selection of local beers and wines. Meals (*plats* 55-85F/€8.39-12.96) are served late on a pleasantly vacant pedestrian street. (☎03 89 23 66 26. Open daily 10am-1am, hot food served 11:45am-11pm. MC/V.)

SIGHTS

The city's restored Alsatian houses glisten in fresh pastels; the best specimens are in the **quartier des Tanneurs** and down rue des Tanneurs, over a small canal, in **la petite Venise** (little Venice). Geraniums cluster in window boxes above cobblestone streets lining the canal. 105 grotesque stone heads adorn the 1609 **Maison des Têtes,** rue des Têtes, crowned with a 1902 Bartholdi statue. The **Musée d'Unterlinden,** 1 rue d'Unterlinden, is housed in a 13th-century Dominican convent. The centerpiece of this eclectic collection is Mathias Grünewald and Nikolaus Haguenauer's *Issenheim Altarpiece* (1500-1516), depicting the Crucifixion and other scenes from Christ's life in such complete iconographic detail that it is said, "Near Grünewald, all collapses." (☎03 89 20 15 50. Open Apr.-Oct. daily 9am-6pm; Nov.-Mar. W-M 10am-5pm. 35F/€5.34, students 25F/€3.81.)

The **Eglise des Dominicains,** pl. des Dominicains, is now little more than a showroom for Martin Schongauer's exquisite *Virgin in the Rose Bower* (1473), a lushly colored panel overwhelmed by an outrageous neo-Gothic frame. Delicate 14th-century stained glass illuminates the artwork with a golden glow. The German-captioned paintings on the wall date back to the German occupation of Alsace during the Franco-Prussian war; their return was a provision of the Treaty of Versailles. (Open Apr.-Dec. daily 10am-1pm and 3-6pm. 8F/€1.22, students 6F/€0.91.) The **Collégiale St-Martin,** pl. de la Cathédrale, feels more like a museum than a church. Despite its nondescript exterior, the church is actually full of interesting art, including a massive altarpiece transplanted from the convent that houses d'Unterlinden. (Open F-M and W 8am-6pm, Tu and Th 8am-6:30pm.)

Frédéric Auguste Bartholdi (1834-1904), best known for a 47m statue of his mother entitled *Liberty Enlightening the World* (known to some as the Statue of Liberty), has been memorialized in the engaging **Musée Bartholdi,** 30 rue des Marchands. The museum houses his personal art collection, drawings, and models of his monuments. Also here is your typical giant plaster ear, a full-scale study for Mrs. Liberty's *oreille.* (☎03 89 41 90 60. Open Mar.-Dec. W-M 10am-noon and 2-6pm. 26F/€3.96, students 15F/€2.29.)

ENTERTAINMENT AND FESTIVALS

The 10-day **Foire aux Vins d'Alsace** in mid-August is the region's largest wine fair. Concerts given by popular French and European musicians are held in the evenings at 9pm. (☎03 90 50 50 50; www.colmar.expo.fr. 10F/€1.53 until 5pm, 30F/€4.57 after 5pm. Concerts 60-100F/€9.15-15.25.) In the first two weeks of July, the **Festival International de Colmar** features two dozen concerts by classical musicians. (Tickets 90-340F/€13.72-51.84, students 45-130F/€6.86-19.82. For more info call 03 89 20 68 97 or festival-internation@ot-colmar.fr.) Eglise St-Pierre stages concerts from mid-August to early September. (Th 8:45pm. 45F/€6.86, under 21 25F/€3.81.) The Collégiale St-Martin's organists play on Tuesdays at 8:45pm at the **Heures Musicales** during July and August. (50F/€7.62, students 40F/€6.10.)

MULHOUSE

While this bustling town of 110,000 may not have Nancy's architecture or the gardens of Metz, Mulhouse atones for its indifferent buildings and occasional kitschy facades with a slew of fabulous museums on the city's periphery. A former industrial powerhouse for both mechanical and domestic goods, Mulhouse is today content with exploiting its productive past in the name of what is now a more powerful industry: tourism.

TRANSPORTATION AND PRACTICAL INFORMATION

Trains run from bd. Général Leclerc to **Basel,** Switzerland (20min., 6 per day, 36F/€5.49), **Belfort** (30min., 32 per day, 48F/€7.32), **Paris** (4½hr., 9 per day, 280F/€42.69), and **Strasbourg** (1hr., 14 per day, 87F/€13.26). Local **buses** run from Porte Jeune, north of the pedestrian district. (☎03 89 66 77 77. Most services 7am-7pm, evening routes 8:30-11:30pm. Tickets 7F/€1.07, *carnet* of 10 50F/€7.62, day pass 18F/€2.74; tickets available at the train station or on the bus.)

The **tourist office,** 9 av. Foch, lies two blocks straight ahead from the right-most edge of the train station, across from a park. They make hotel reservations, and have walking-tour maps and tours. (☎03 89 35 48 48; www.ot.ville-mulhouse.fr. Tours in French, in summer English also available; M, W and Sa 10am, 20F/€3.05. Office open July-Aug. M-Sa 9am-7pm, Su 10am-noon; Sept.-June M-F 9am-7pm, Sa 9am-5pm.) Rent **bikes** at **Cycles Beha,** pl. de la Concorde. (☎03 89 45 13 46. Open M 2-7pm, Tu-Sa 9am-noon and 2-7pm. 100F/€15.25 per day.) For a **taxi,** call 03 89 45 80 00. The **police** are at 12 rue Coehorn (☎03 89 60 82 00), off bd. de La Marseillaise, to the north of the city, and the **hospital** is behind the train station at 20 rue du Dr. Laënnec (☎03 89 64 64 64). **Internet access** is at **La Filature,** 20 allée Nathan Katz (☎03 89 36 28 28), or **Noumatrouff,** 57 rue de la Mertzau (☎03 89 32 94 10). The central **post office,** 3 pl. de Gaulle, offers **currency exchange.** (☎03 89 66 94 00. Open M-F 8am-7pm, Sa 8am-noon.) **Poste Restante:** 68074. **Postal code:** 68100.

ACCOMMODATIONS AND FOOD

Dirt-cheap rooms in town are elusive, but an assortment of comfortable two-stars compete for clients. Rates may drop on weekends. The newly refurbished **Auberge de Jeunesse (HI),** 37 rue d'Ilberg, offers 2- to 4-bed rooms with coed bathrooms. They're institutional and sparse, but cheap. Take bus #2 (dir: Coteaux; #S1 after 8:30pm) to Salle des Sports. (☎03 89 42 63 28. Breakfast 19F/€2.90. Linen 17F/€2.59. Reception 8am-noon and 5-11pm, until midnight in summer. No entrance after reception is closed. 53F/€8.08 per person. MC/V. **Members only.**) Homey, family-run **Hôtel St-Bernard,** 3 rue des Fleurs, conveniently located near the center of town, maintains bright, immaculate rooms. Included are showers and 32-channel TVs, not to mention free Internet and bikes, access to a small library, and, most importantly, a slobbery St. Bernard. (☎03 89 45 82 32; fax 03 89 45 26 32; stbr@evhr.net. Filling breakfast 38F/€5.79. Reception 7am-9:30pm. Singles and doubles with shower 180-300F/€27.44-45.74. AmEx/DC/MC/V.) **Hôtel de Bâle,** 19-21 Passage Central, is a practical backup. The common spaces are elegant and comfortable, but the same can't be said for all of the purely adequate rooms. (☎03 89 46 19 87. Breakfast 39F/€5.95. Reception 24hr. Singles from 175F/€26.68, with shower 185-195F/€28.21-29.73; doubles with bath 285F/€43.45, with bathtub 295-315F/€44.98-48.03. Extra bed 55F/€8.39. MC/V.) **Camping de l'Ill,** rue Pierre de Coubertin, has its own grocery store. (☎03 89 06 20 66. Reception 8am-1pm and 3-10pm. Open Apr.-Sept. 20F/€3.05 per person, car/tent 20F/€3.05. Electricity 20F/€3.05. Tax of 1F/€0.15 per person per day.)

Mulhouse *menus* go for Swiss (steep) prices, but the student community brings costs down on **rue de l' Arsenal.** A **Monoprix supermarket** lies on the corner of rue du Sauvage and rue des Maréchaux. (Open M-F 8:15am-8pm, Sa 8:15am-7pm.) A few doors down, **Le Globe** grocery sells delicacies from *pâté* to handmade marzipan animals. (☎03 89 36 50 50. Open M-Sa 9am-6:45pm.) Crêperies and Middle Eastern restaurants of varying quality abound. Get super-cheap gyros (20F/€3.05), salads (18-22F/€2.74-3.35), and desserts (15F/€2.29) at **Le Bosphore,** 13 av. de Colmar, the prettiest *doner* joint in town. (☎03 89 45 16 00. Open daily 10am-1am.) **Crampous Mad,** 14 impasse des Tondeurs, serves crêpes (13-43F/€1.98-6.56) and galettes (25-45F/€3.81-6.86) on a bright terrace beneath an oh-so-Alsatian facade. (☎03 89 45 79 43. Open M-F 11:30am-10pm, Sa 11:30am-11pm. MC/V.)

ALSACE

SIGHTS

Mulhouse's historical district centers around the festive **pl. de la Réunion,** named for the joyful occasions in 1798 and 1918 when French troops reunited the city with distant Paris. On the edge of town is a set of worthwhile museums focused on the technology of the city's past and present, from textile production to trains.

MUSEE NATIONAL DE L'AUTOMOBILE. The brothers Schlumpf once owned the 500-plus mint-condition autos of this gas-guzzling museum, whose staggering collection ranges from an 1878 steam-driven *Jacquot à Vapeur* to the bubbly electric cars of the future. Various celebrity cars include those which belonged to Charlie Chaplin and Emperor Bao Dai. *(192 av. de Colmar. Take bus #1, 4, 11, 13, or 17 north to "Musée Auto." ☎03 89 33 23 23. Open daily July-Aug. 9am-6:30pm; Mar. 26-June 30 and Sept.-Oct. 9am-6pm; Nov.-Mar. 25 10am-6pm. 65F/€9.91, students 47F/€7.17, ages 7-17 29F/€4.42, under 7 free.)*

MUSEE FRANÇAIS DU CHEMIN DE FER. A stunning collection of slick, gleaming engines and railway cars is kept in this warehouse-like museum. Peer into the perfectly restored compartments of such legends as the Orient Express. Every hour a massive 1949 steam engine (the last of its kind), chugs away in place so you can watch its gears and wheels spin and spin. Don't miss the awesome metal sculptures of rail-layers on the walkway to the one-room **Musée du Sapeur-Pompier.** *Sapeurs-Pompiers*, France's heroic firemen-cum-medics, consider themselves part of a grand tradition. *(2 rue Alfred de Glehn. Take bus #17, direction "Musées," from Porte Jeune Place or #18, direction "Technopole," from the train station; only 1 per hr. On Sundays use line "M." ☎03 89 42 25 67. Open daily Apr.-Sept. 9am-6pm; Oct.-Mar. 9am-5pm. 48F/€7.32, students and children 6-18 25F/€3.81, children under 6 free.)*

ELECTROPOLIS. This zippy new museum introduces kids to the wonderful world of energy through hands-on exhibits, films, and historical collections. It's everything you slept through in high school, only interesting. *(Next to the railway museum. ☎03 89 32 48 60. Open July-Aug. daily 10am-6pm; Sept.-June Tu-Su 10am-6pm. 48F/€7.32, students 23F/€3.51; combined ticket with railroad museum 78F/€11.89.)*

TEMPLE DE ST-ETIENNE. One of France's few Protestant Gothic cathedrals, St-Etienne casts a long shadow across the carousel and cafés on pl. de la Réunion. If the church seems distinctly modern, it's because the Protestants bought it lock, stock, and barrel from its Catholic owners in 1890, then tore the place down and built it back up again. The original stained-glass windows, some up to seven centuries old, were preserved and can be seen in the galleries above. *(☎03 89 66 30 19. Open May-Sept. W-M 10am-noon and 2-6pm, Sa 10am-noon and 2-5pm, Su 2-6pm. Free.)*

OTHER SIGHTS. Around the corner from the train station is the incongruously grand home of the **Musée de l'Impression sur Etoffes.** This happy marriage of technology, history, and aesthetics details the softer side of industry in Mulhouse, featuring miles of textile swatches from the last 250 years and from innumerable textile printers—everything from Indonesian scarves to *Back to the Future* t-shirts. *(14 rue J. J. Henner. ☎03 89 46 83 00. Open daily 10am-6pm. 36F/€5.49, students 18F/€2.74, children 12-18 15F/€2.29, under 12 free. Wheelchair access.)* To escape the ubiquitous machinery of Mulhouse, stop in the **Parc Zoologique et Botanique,** a collection of rare animals and plant life. *(Take bus #12, direction "Moenschsberg," to "Zoo." ☎03 39 31 85 10. Open May-Aug. 9am-7pm; Apr. and Sept. 9am-6pm; Mar. and Oct.-Nov. 9am-5pm; Dec.-Feb. 10am-4pm. Mar.-Oct. 48F/€7.32, Nov.-Mar. 24F/€3.66; students 24F/€3.66 year-round.)*

ALSACE

BESANÇON

Surrounded by the river Doubs on three sides and by a steep bluff on the fourth, Besançon (pop. 120,000) has intrigued military strategists from Julius Caesar to the great military engineer Vauban 1800 years later. Today, the city is known for its delightful setting, its fine parks, and its relative freedom from tourists. The home of a major university and an international language center, Besançon boasts a sizable student population and an impressive number of museums and discos.

TRANSPORTATION

Trains: av. de la Paix. To: **Belfort** (1hr., 8 per day, 79F/€12.04); **Dijon** (1hr., 6 per day, 75F/€11.43); **Lyon** (2½hr., 10 per day, 183F/€27.90); **Paris** (2hr., 7 per day, 269F/€41.01) via **Dole;** and **Strasbourg** (3hr., 10 per day, 165F/€25.16). Office open M-F 9am-6:30pm, Sa 10am-5:20pm.

Buses: Monts Jura, 9 rue Proudhon (☎03 81 63 44 44). To **Pontarlier** (1hr., 6 per day, 46.50F/€7.09). Office open M-Sa 9:30am-12:30pm and 2-6:30pm.

Local Transportation: CTB, 4 pl. du 8 Septembre (☎03 81 48 12 00). Open M-Sa 10am-12:45pm and 1:15-7pm. Tickets 6F/€0.91. *Carnet* of 10 51F/€7.78; 24hr. pass 20F/€3.05. Buy on bus.

Taxis: (☎03 81 88 80 80). 24hr. service. Minimum charge 30F/€4.57.

Bike Rental: Vélosphère, 18 av. Carnot (☎03 81 47 03 04). Open M-Sa 9am-noon and 2-7pm.

ORIENTATION AND PRACTICAL INFORMATION

Everything of interest in Besançon lies within a thumb-shaped turn of the Doubs river. To reach the tourist office, cross the train station's parking lot and head down the stairs. Follow the street in front of you heading downhill (**av. de la Paix,** which quickly turns into **av. Foch**), but stay to the right. At the corner of av. Foch and **av. Edgar Faure,** cross the street and continue to your right down av. Foch. When you reach the river it will continue to turn left and will turn into **av. de l'Helvétie,** which you should follow to **pl. de la Première Armée Française.** The office is in the park to your right, and the **vieille ville** is across the bridge (10min. total).

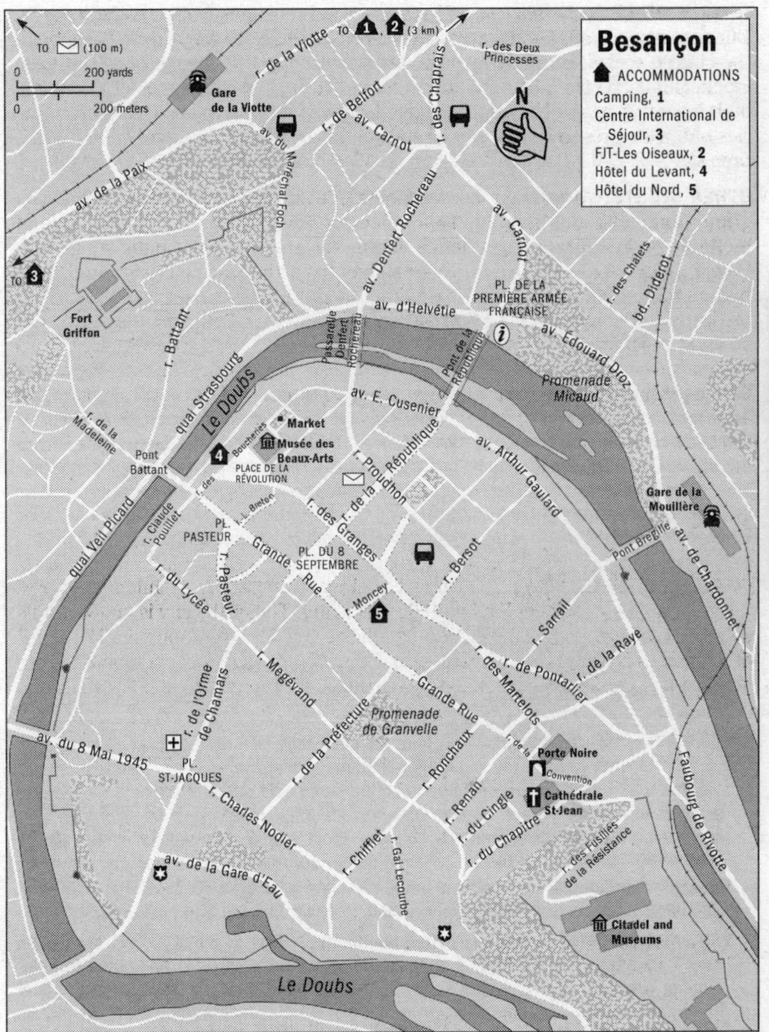

Tourist Office: 2 pl. de la 1ère Armée Française (☎03 81 80 92 55; fax 03 81 80 58 30; www.besancon.com). Free accommodations service; lists hotels and restaurants; provides info on excursions and festivals. Ask for a free copy of the student guide *La Besace.* **Tours** for individuals (in French; 38F/€5.79, students 28F/€4.27) and groups (in French, English, or German). Provides **currency exchange.** Open Apr.-Sept. M 10am-7pm, Tu-Sa 9am-7pm; June 15-Sept. 14 also Su 10am-noon and 3-5pm; Oct.-Mar. M 10am-6pm, Tu-Sa 9am-6pm; Sept 15-June 14 also Su 10am-noon. **Besançon Informations,** 2 rue Megevand (☎03 81 61 50 50). Info on sports, wheelchair facilities, lodging, and festivals. Open July-Aug. M-F 8:30am-noon and 1:30-5:30pm; Sept.-June M-F 8:30am-noon and 1:30-6pm, Sa 9am-noon. Grab the pamphlet *Culture Info.*

Laundromat: Blanc-Matic, 54 rue Bersot, near the bus station, and 57 rue des Cras, near the Foyer Mixte. Open daily 7am-8pm.

Youth Center: Centre Information Jeunesse (CIJ), 27 rue de la République (☎03 81 21 16 16; www.top-jeunes.com). Info on internships, jobs, events, and apartments. HI and ISIC cards. Free Internet access. Open M 1:30-6pm, Tu-F 10am-noon and 1:30-6pm, Sa 1:30-6pm.

Hiking Information: Club Alpin Français, 14 rue Luc Breton (☎03 81 81 02 77). Offers organized hikes and outdoor activities as well as info. Open Tu-F 5-7pm.

Police: 2 av. de la Gare d'Eau (☎03 81 21 11 22). Near pl. St-Jacques.

Hospital: Centre Hospitalier Universitaire, 2 pl. St-Jacques (☎03 81 66 81 66).

Internet Access: Free at the **CIJ** (see above). **Cyber Espace,** 18 rue de Pontarlier (☎03 81 81 15 74). 30F/€4.57 per hr. Open M-Sa 11am-midnight, Su 2-8pm.

Post Office: 23 rue Proudhon (☎03 81 65 55 82), off rue de la République. **Currency exchange.** Open M-F 8am-7pm, Sa 8am-noon. **Postal code:** 25019. **Main office** at 4 rue Demangel (☎03 81 53 81 12), in the new town. **Postal code:** 25000. **Poste Restante code:** 25031 Besançon-Cedex.

ALSACE

ACCOMMODATIONS AND CAMPING

Hostels here are a bargain and offer excellent facilities, but are quite a schlep from the *vieille ville*. Buses do run to both hostels, but daytime lines run only 6am-8pm, after which time you'll either have to find a different nighttime line, take a taxi. or burn a lot of shoe rubber. If you want to stay close to the action in one of Besançon's more central hotels, you'll need to make reservations ahead of time.

Foyer Mixte de Jeunes Travailleurs (HI), 48 rue des Cras (☎03 81 40 32 00; fax 03 81 40 32 01). Cross the parking lot of the train station and head down the stairs. Take the road in front of you that heads down slightly to the left (av. de la Paix), and keep to the left as the road bends and turns into rue de Belfort. After 10min., turn left on rue Marie-Louise, which becomes rue des Cras as you cross over the railroad tracks. Follow rue des Cras up a large hill and over a smaller one; the hostel entrance is just after rue Resal on your right (30min. total). Ask locals for "Foyer Les Oiseaux." Or for a mere 6F/€0.91, take bus #7 from pl. Flore (from rue de Belfort, turn right onto av. Carnot, walk for a block until you see the green lights of the pharmacy in pl. Flore; take a sharp left onto rue des Chaprais, and the stop is on the same side of the street as a Casino grocery). Take the bus from pl. Flore to Oiseaux (dir: "Orchamps", 3 per hr.). Large, bright, new rooms with private bathrooms. Concerts, movies, and other special events scheduled weekly. Breakfast included. Lunch or dinner 40F/€6.10. Reception 9am-8pm. No reservations, and only two rooms in the winter. Singles 100F/€15.25, 90F/€13.72 the 2nd night; doubles 80F/€12.20 per person, 70F/€10.67 the 2nd night. MC/V.

Centre International de Séjour, 19 rue Martin-du-Gard (☎03 81 50 07 54; fax 03 81 53 11 79). Take bus #8 (dir: "Campus") from the Foch stop near the station to Intermarché. To get to Foch from the station, cross the parking lot, go down the stairs, and head down the road that leads downward at a slight diagonal to the left (av. de la Paix which turns into av. Foch). The stop is half a block down on the left. A large, institutional hostel with many non-backpackers. Restaurant, TV room, and foosball. Breakfast 26.50F/€4.04. Meals start at 38F/€5.79. Reception 7am-1am. Check-in 3pm, check-out 9am. Singles 107F/€16.31, with bath 163F/€24.85; twins 67F/€10.22 per person, with bath 94F/€14.33; triples or quads 53F/€8.08 per person. MC/V.

Hôtel du Nord, 8 rue Moncey (☎03 81 81 35 56; fax 03 81 81 85 96), on a quiet but centrally located sidestreet in the heart of the old town. Carpeted, chandeliered lobby, attentive reception, and clean, full-sized rooms with cable TV—the lap of budget-travel luxury. Breakfast 30F/€4.20. Reception 24hr. Check-in and check-out noon. Reserve ahead. Singles with sink from €17, with bath, toilet, and TV from €25.80; doubles from €21.20, with bath, toilet, and TV €29; triples from €24.30. AmEx/DC/MC/V.

Hôtel du Levant, 9 rue des Boucheries (☎03 81 81 07 88), on pl. de la Révolution. A sedate old hotel with minimally decorated rooms. Good location. Breakfast 24F/€3.66. Reception 9am-3pm and 6:30-8pm. Singles 105F/€16.00, with shower 140F/€21.34; doubles 180F/€27.44 with shower. MC/V.

Camping de la Plage, rte. de Belfort in Chalezeule (☎03 81 88 04 26; fax 03 81 50 54 62), northeast of the city. Take bus #1 (dir: Palente) to the end (5min.). Pool shuttle bus (*navette*) leaves site 5 times per day (June 23-Sept. 2). Otherwise it's a 35min. walk down rte. de Belfort. 4-star municipal campground with free access to a pool from June 24-Aug. 9. Near a highway, but retains a certain bucolic charm. Breakfast 25F/€3.81. Reception open most of the day. Open Apr.-Sept. 21F/€3.20 per person, plus 30F/€4.57 per car or tent. Electricity 20F/€3.05.

FOOD

Restaurants along **rue Claude Pouillet** cater to Besançon's cosmopolitan students, while **rue des Boucheries** aims more at tourists. Pl. de la Révolution stages an outdoor **market** (Tu and F 6am-12:30pm, Sa 6am-7pm). Buy groceries at **Monoprix,** 12 Grande Rue (open M-Sa 8:30am-9pm). Sharp **comté cheese** is all over Besançon. Wash it down with **vin jaune,** one of the more famous Arbois wines. Charcuteries along rue des Granges sell *jambon de Haut Doubs*, a regional smoked ham. **La Boîte à Sandwichs,** 21 rue du Lycée, is near a popular student nightlife area off rue Pasteur. Exotic ingredients like heart of palm fill over 50 wittily named sandwiches (11-30F/€1.68-4.57), among them *La Geisha*, *La Bohémienne*, and *Le Communiste*, and every possible salad concoction, warm or cold. (☎03 81 81 63 23. Meals 15-35F/€2.29-5.34. Open M-Sa 11:30am-2:30pm and 6:30pm-midnight. MC/V.) **Au Gourmand,** 5 rue Megevand, serves up an astonishing array of hearty dishes at incredibly low prices. Rice and pasta dishes 35-50F/€5.34-7.62; omelettes 20-35F/€3.05-5.34; warm salads served with potatoes 30-40F/€4.57-6.10. With its canary-yellow walls, vintage chocolate advertisements, and collections of teapots and cat figurines, it'll remind you of that eccentric grandmother you never had. (☎03 81 81 40 56. Open Tu-F 11:30am-1:45pm and 6:45-9pm. Cash only.)

ALSACE

SIGHTS

Besançon's *vieille ville* is graced with remarkably well-preserved Renaissance buildings, though perhaps a visit to Vauban's citadel is more engaging than gazing at facades. The citadel, built during the reign of Louis "Sun King" XIV, sits high on the hill above the city and offers stunning views, several excellent museums, and zoos galore.

THE CITADEL. A gruelling trek uphill from the town, but worth every stitch in your side. While the Citad'in tour bus confirms this 17th-century stronghold as a conspicuous tourist spot, there is one great advantage to its status: detailed English translations of the extensive collections. The free first level includes a deer park, picnic lawns arrayed with cookie-cutter shrubs, and a view of the city below. Museums inside include the **Salle de Vauban,** an exhibit on the life and times of the Sun King, and the **Musée Comtois,** a collection of folk art and crafts from the Franche-Comté of days past.

Of special note is the **Musée de la Résistance et de la Déportation.** One hundred members of the French Resistance were shot at the citadel when the German troops occupied Besançon. The comprehensive collection of letters, artifacts, and often graphic photographs, chronicles the Nazi rise to power, the Holocaust, and the occupation of France. Ask a guard to open the exhibition room on the third floor, which contains a collection of sculptures and drawings by two local men who were deported to concentration camps. You can also pick up a 10F/€1.53 audio guide, available in English, which includes survivors' recorded accounts. *(☎03 81 65 07 55. Open summer 9am-6pm; winter 10am-5pm. No children under 10.)*

Sights sure to delight children include the **Musée d'Histoire Naturelle,** full of mammals, birds, and fish that fell victim to the taxidermist's tools; a small **aquarium** next door; and the **insectarium,** where a mock kitchen shows you all the little nasties that hide in your home. A **zoological park** sprawls out along the back wall of the citadel, and children can chase squawking chickens at a little hands-on farm. On the other side of the zoo, raccoons and nighttime creepy-crawlies lie in wait to scare kiddies in the pitch-black **noctarium.** *(The citadel is at the end of rue des Fusillés de la Resistance. ☎03 81 65 07 50. Open daily July-Aug. 9am-7pm; Apr.-June and Sept.-Oct. 9am-6pm; Nov.-Mar. 10am-5pm. 40F/€6.10, students 30F/€4.57, includes entrance to museums and all other facilities. Audio guide 10F/€1.53.)*

CATHEDRALE ST-JEAN. Perched beneath the citadel, the cathedral hides an interior that mixes architectural styles from the 12th to the 18th centuries. Look for the beautiful **Rose de St-Jean,** a circular altar of white marble dating from the 11th century, and the **Horloge Astronomique,** a 30,000-part clock housed within the cathedral and visible only by tour. Walking back into town on rue de la Convention, you pass through the **Porte Noire** (Black Gate), a stern if now-tarnished triumphal arch built during the reign of Marcus Aurelius. *(Cathedral ☎03 81 83 34 62. Open W-M 9am-7pm. Free. Horloge ☎03 81 81 12 76. Apr.-Sept. tours W-M at 9:50, 10:50, 11:50am, and 2:50, 3:50, 4:50, 5:50pm; Oct.-May tours Th-M. 15F/€2.29, 9F/€1.37 children.)*

ALSACE

MUSEE DES BEAUX-ARTS ET D'ARCHEOLOGIE. France's oldest public museum houses Egyptian mummies and statuettes, and an exceptional collection of more than 6000 works by Ingres, Van Dyck, Rubens, Matisse, Picasso, Renoir, and other masters. *(Pl. de la Révolution. ☎03 81 87 80 49. Open June-Oct. W-M 9:30am-6pm, Nov.-May W-M 9:30am-noon and 2-6pm. 21F/€3.20, free for students, and on Su and holidays.)*

MUSEE DU TEMPS. Far from an abstract Proustian elegy to things past, this brand-new museum—appropriately situated in the watch-making capital of France—takes a concrete approach to the grand question of time. The collection of the Musée du Temps will explore both proximate, cogs-and-gears conceptions of time, as well as more anthropological and archeological considerations. The museum itself, however, has a slightly relaxed notion of time; scheduled originally to open in 2000, it is now tentatively scheduled for the year 2002. Ask at the tourist office for more details. (*Palais Granvelle, 96 Grande Rue. ☎03 81 81 45 14.*)

BOAT TRIPS. Les Vedettes Bisontines runs boat cruises on the Doubs and the citadel canals from pont de la République, near the tourist office. *(☎03 81 68 13 25. June-Sept. 2hr.; 3 per day; 53F/€8.08, children 39F/€5.95.)* Or cross rue de la République to **Les Bâteaux Mouches'** "Le Pont Battant". *(☎03 81 68 05 34. Apr.-Oct. 4 per day; 49F/€7.47, children 39F/€5.95. Days and tours vary; call ahead.)*

NIGHTLIFE

The students of Besançon pack bars and discos until early morning most nights of the week. The area extending from **rue Claude Pouillet** to **Pont Battant** is perpetually jumping with night life. Small, friendly bars proliferate throughout the town, particularly on **rue Pasteur.**

Pop Hall, 26 rue Proudhon (☎03 81 83 01 90), across from the post office, is the hippest pool hall you'll ever see. Below its nondescript facade is everything from antique chandeliers to reappropriated cars from amusement park rides. The high point is the bathrooms, which feature faux-fur hand-dryers, bronze cowhead sinks, and a lamp made of a toilet bowl. Open M-Th 6pm-1am, Sa 3pm-2am, Su 6pm-2am.

Madigan's, pl. 8 Septembre (☎03 81 81 17 44), is full to bursting every night with a young crowd seeking the authentic Irish experience–i.e. 17F/€2.59 margaritas. Beer 12-17F/€1.83-2.59 on tap. Open M-Th 7am-1am, F-Su 7am-2am.

The Cactus Café, 79 rue des Granges (☎03 81 82 01 18), the closest thing in France to a frat party. Karaoke Th-Sa 10pm-2am. Beer 12F/€1.83 on tap. Open M-Th 9am-1am, F-Su 9am-2am. MC/V.

Le KGB, 8 av. de Chardonnet (☎03 81 61 17 49), about 1km from the tourist office, is the best of Besançon's dance clubs. A large dance floor with London Underground decor is surrounded by plush couches, two bars, and many drunken students. The street is not well lit; it's best to go in a group. Cover 50F/€7.62, F-Sa 60F/€9.10, students 25F/€3.81 W and Th. Open W-Th 10:30pm-4am, F-Sa 10:30pm-5am. MC/V.

Bannik, 10 chemin Mazagran. (☎03 81 51 40 05). With its cavern-like entrance, black dance floor, and huge mixing table, Bannik is the club for the a sophisticated gang. Take a taxi there like everyone else after the bars close; streets are not well lit and sidewalks perilously narrow. Open W-Th and Su 11pm-4am, F-Sa 11pm-5am. Cover W-Th and Su 50F/€7.62 including 1 drink, Th students 40F/€6.10, F-Sa 60F/€9.15. MC/V.

FESTIVALS

The tourist office publishes several comprehensive lists of events. In July and August, the city sponsors **Festiv'été,** with theater, music, dance, expositions, and a film festival. (Many events are free. Call the tourist office for info.) **Jazz en Franche-Comté** brings a flurry of concerts in June and July, uniting jazz musicians from across France and abroad. (☎03 81 83 39 09 for info; ticket hotline ☎08 92 68 36 22. Tickets from 80-130F/€12.20-19.82 student discounts, and some free events.)

The **Festival International de Musique** erupts during the middle two weeks of September with classical concerts nightly. Orchestras from across Europe perform well-worn favorites as well as more recent compositions in 85 concerts, 60 of which are free. (☎03 81 25 05 80; fax 03 81 81 52 15; contact@festival-besancon.com. Tickets 60-230F/€9.15-35.06 depending on the locale; up to 25% discount for students.) For more info on all three festivals, check out Besançon's website (www.besancon.com). The hostel (ASEP-FJT les Oiseaux, p. 414) sponsors an array of events each month; pick up a schedule at the tourist office.

BELFORT

Occupying a valley between the Vosges mountains to the north and the Jura to the south, Belfort (pop. 50,000) has been a favorite target of invading armies for centuries. Rather than dwelling on its impressive past, the old town has gained the reputation as an industrial powerhouse; it is the home to the factories of both the hi-tech TGV trains and the Peugeot automobile. Don't miss the Chapelle de Notre-Dame-du-Haut in nearby Ronchamp, one of Le Corbusier's masterpieces.

TRANSPORTATION AND PRACTICAL INFORMATION. **Trains** run to: **Besançon** (1hr., 10 per day, 79F/€12.04); **Mulhouse** (30min., very frequently, 48F/€7.32); **Paris** (4hr., 8 per day, 253F/€38.57); and **Strasbourg** (1½hr., 9 per day, 114F/€17.38). **CTRB,** pl. Corbis, offers extensive **local transportation** around Belfort. (☎03 84 21 08 08. Office open M-F 5:30am-8pm, Sa 9am-1pm and 3:15-6:30pm, Su 9am-1pm and 2:30-5pm. Most lines run 6am-8pm. Tickets 6.20F/€0.95, *carnet* of 10 51F/€7.78.) **Taxis Radio Belfortains** are at 44 rue André Parant (☎03 84 22 13 44).

To get from the station to the **tourist office,** 2bis rue Clemenceau, head left down av. Wilson and then bear right on fbg. de France. When the river comes into sight, turn left on fbg. des Ancêtres and follow it to rue Clemenceau; the office is the unexpectedly large building to the right across rue Clemenceau (to the right of the mammoth Caisse d'Epargne), set back from the road. Here, a young staff can outfit you with free maps, hotel and restaurant listings, and info on excursions to the countryside. Ask for *Le Petit Geni*, a comprehensive guide to Belfort that includes discounts at local stores and restaurants. (☎03 84 55 90 90; fax 03 84 55 90 99. Open June 15-Sept. 15 M-Sa 9am-7pm; Sept. 16-June 14 M-Sa 9am-12:30pm and 1:45-6pm.) There is an automatic **currency exchange** machine at **Caisse d'Epargne,** pl. de la Résistance (☎03 84 57 77 77). A **laundromat** is at 60 fbg. de Montbeliard. (☎03 84 21 84 10. Open daily 7am-9pm.) The **police** are at 1 rue du Monnier (☎03 84 58 50 00), the **hospital** at 14 rue de Mulhouse (☎03 84 57 40 00). **Internet access** is at **Cyberia Info,** 5bis. av. Wilson. (☎03 84 90 42 00. Open Tu-F 10am-noon and 2-7pm, Sa 10am-noon.) The **post office** is at 19 fbg. des Ancêtres. (☎03 84 57 67 56. Open M-F 8am-7pm, Sa 8am-noon.) **Postal code:** 90000.

ACCOMMODATIONS AND CAMPING. Belfort has a smattering of one- and two-star hotels that are rarely full in summer, but few truly budget places. The owners of **Hôtel Au Relais d'Alsace,** 5 av. de la Laurencie, might just be the sweetest people on the planet. All rooms feature phones and TVs, and have been cheerfully decorated in bright blocks of pastel color by the owners themselves. The top floor gives a prized view of the château. To get there from the train station, turn left onto av. Wilson, and right onto fbg. de France. After crossing the river, turn left onto quai Vauban and follow it until you reach pl. de l'Esperance. Turn onto av. de la Laurencie (to the right, after av. de l'Esperance), and the hotel will be on your left shortly after av. de la Miotte merges on the left. (☎03 84 22 15 55; fax 03 84 28 70 48. Breakfast 30F/€4.57; drink fresh-squeezed orange juice and draw a souvenir picture for the guest book as you eat. Reception 6:30am-midnight. Singles with shower from 160F/€24.39, doubles with shower from 210F/€32.02. Some 3- to 4-person rooms with shower available. MC/V.) **Résidence Madrid,** 6 rue Madrid, is a cheap option located near the station. Dorm-style facilities are serviceable, and the residents are a lively multinational bunch. There are sinks in every room, and co-ed toilets and showers on each floor. From the train station, turn left on rue Michelet, crossing over the railroad tracks. Take your second right onto rue Parisot which soon becomes av. Général Leclerc; rue Madrid will be on your left after about seven minutes. Be careful in the neighborhood at night. (☎03 84 21 39 16. Breakfast 15F/€2.29. Reception 8:30am-12:30pm and 2-7:30pm. 85F/€12.96 per person.) **Hôtel St-Christophe,** pl. d'Armes, scores the best location—right across from the cathedral in the heart of the *vieille ville.* The main hotel offers larger, more comfortable rooms, but the annex across the square is a better deal. (☎03 84 55 88 88; fax 03 84 54 08 77. Breakfast buffet 40F/€6.10. Reception 7am-11pm. Singles with bath 310F/€47.26; doubles with bath 350F/€53.36. Annex: singles 245F/€37.35; doubles 310F/€47.26. MC/V.)

The three-star **Camping International de l'Etang des Forges,** 4 rue du Général Bethouart, enjoys a delicious location on the Etang des Forges, a sparkling lake 10 minutes from the *centre ville.* The grounds offer little privacy but plenty of space, good views, and squeaky-clean bathrooms. (☎03 84 22 54 92; fax 03 84 22 76 55. Reception open 8am-12:30pm and 2:30-10pm. Open May-Sept. 2 people with tent 85F/€12.96; 12F/€1.83 per 5-10 year-old child. Electricity 15F/€2.29.)

FOOD. **Faubourg de France** cuts from the river to the train station, packed with cafés, bakeries, and anything else your rumbling stomach might demand. Cafés and restaurants, most in the 80F/€12.20-plus range, also cluster thickly in the old town, especially near **pl. des Armes.** The local pastry is the *belflore,* a rather generic raspberry pastry covered with almond paste. A **Casino** supermarket awaits by the hostel at 2 rue de Madrid. (☎03 84 21 02 13. Open M-F 8:30am-noon and 2:30-7pm, Sa 8:30am-12:15pm and 2-7pm.) The best place for people-watching is undoubtedly **Café Bruxelles** in the pl. des Armes. (Open M-F 9am-1am, Sa 9am-2am.) **Aux Crêpes d'Antan,** 13 rue du Quai, presents a formidable selection of creamy, aesthetically folded crêpes and galettes (25-50F/€3.81-7.62) in a provençal-decorated shop just around the corner from the cathedral. (☎03 84 22 82 54. Open noon-2pm and 7pm-midnight.) If you've overdosed on the Frenchie pancake, try a potato. **La Patate Gourmande,** 12bis rue des Ancètres, is like a cabin in the woods transplanted to a tiny alley off the bustling street; their diversely garnished baked and au gratin potatoes (45-75F/€6.86-11.43), as well as their elaborate salads (45-50F/€6.86-7.62), will leave you stuffed.

SIGHTS. Belfort's **château** has not yet been made into a playground for tourists. A circuit of the grounds affords a lesson in military history, as well as incomparable views of the countryside. The château, originally a medieval fortress, was expanded and refortified by the prolific Vauban when the French laid claim to Belfort after the Thirty Years War. Orange arrows direct you along a tour of the fort that leads up passageways, over walls, and through a cool, dank tunnel. The château lies above the *vielle ville* and can be reached by the winding road from pl. des Bourgeois. (Free tours available July-Aug. 10am-7pm. ☎03 84 54 25 51.)

A passageway on one of the lower levels leads to the viewing platform of the **Belfort Lion,** Bartholdi's monument to those fallen during the 1870 siege. Carved entirely of red sandstone, the Sphinx-ish reclining beast is both Belfort's most important monument and a symbol of national pride and resolve. (Platform open July-Sept. daily 9am-7pm, Apr.-June 9am-noon and 2-7pm, Oct-Mar. 10am-noon and 2-5:30pm. 6F/€0.91, under 18 free. Ticket (which includes the Musée d'Art et d'Histoire and the Donation Jardot 35F/€5.34, students 25F/€3.81.) The château at the heart of the fortifications houses the **Musée d'Art et d'Histoire.** There's something here for everyone, be they nostalgia-loving domestics or grenade-pin-spitting alpha males. (Open Apr.-Sept. daily 10am-6pm; Oct.-Mar. W-M 10am-noon and 2-5:30pm. 18F/€2.74, students 12F/€1.83; with entrance to Lion, 20F/€3.05, students 15F/€2.29.) The **terrace** above the museum is the best place for a look at the land below; diagrams at the northern, southern, and eastern sides point out landmarks. Along the route back into town, remnants of the octagonal fortifications that once surrounded the *vieille ville* are still intact, including several guard towers. **Tour 46,** on the corner of rue Bartholdi and rue Ancien Théâtre, hosts a variety of special exhibitions by great modern artists. (Open W-M 10am-6pm.)

The **Donation Maurice Jardot** on 8 rue de Mulhouse has an impressive collection of sketches and paintings by modern greats like Picasso, Braque, Léger, Chagall, and the architect Le Corbusier, all of which were donated in 1997 by Jardot to be housed in the beautifully renovated 19th-century house once belonging to the poet Deubel. (☎03 84 90 40 70. Open Apr.-Sept. W-M 10am-6pm, Oct-Mar. W-M 10am-noon and 2-5pm. 25F/€3.81, students €15/2.29.)

Back in the *vieille ville*, on rue des Mobiles, just on the other side of the ramparts of rue des Bons Enfants, Vauban's perfectly preserved 1687 **Porte de Brisach** bears the motto of the ever-humble Louis XIV: *Nec Pluribus Impar* ("Superior to all others"). The **Cathédral St-Christophe** presides over pl. des Armes in the heart of Belfort. Made of the same sandstone as the château, its graceful classical facade shelters a chilling transept paintings by Belfort native G. Dauphin.

ENTERTAINMENT AND FESTIVALS. Though its dance clubs are relegated to the suburbs, Belfort does have a number of bars. Check out the **Piano Bar,** 23 fbg. de France, for live rock and blues or karaoke. (☎03 84 28 93 35. No cover. Open M-Sa 8:30pm-2am.) Numerous **concerts** are held around town in July and August. The château hosts free jazz at around 8:30pm Wednesdays, and the cathedral hosts cheap classical concerts on Thursdays—the tourist office has details.

Every July, 80,000 enthusiastic music fans from all over Europe descend upon Belfort for **Les Eurockéennes,** France's largest open-air rock festival. The 2001 lineup, spread over three days, included Ben Harper, Wyclef Jean, Deftones, Iggy Pop, and 41 other acts from the entire spectrum of rock, rap, and any hybrid thereof. (☎08 92 69 23 92, 2.21F/€0.34 per min.; www.eurockeennes.fr. Tickets sold at FNAC stores.) At the end of May, musicians from around the world hit town for the **Festival International de Musique Universitaire,** a three-day extravaganza that offers over 200 concerts, many of them free, running the jamming gamut from classical to jazz and rock to world. Reserve accommodations well in advance; rooms are next to impossible to find the week of the event. (☎03 84 54 24 43) The last week of November brings **Entrevues,** a film festival showcasing fresh, young directors and retrospectives. (For info call Cinema d'Aujourd'hui 03 84 54 24 43.)

EXCURSIONS. With the Jura on one side and the Vosges on the other, Belfort is an ideal base for exploring the surrounding countryside. The tourist office has many pamphlets with nearby walks, hikes, and biking trails. *Country Walks* (available in English) includes a map and descriptions of hikable regions near the city. Bessoncourt, 4km to the east, is the departure point both for the daunting E5 trail that stretches from the Adriatic to the Atlantic and for many *petites randonnées* (short rambles), fragments of a larger circuit. Kids and the elderly should be able to handle the fairly flat 10-14km circuit (3-5hr.). To the north, the towering summit of the Ballon d'Alsace (1247m) is a meeting point for three major long-distance trails, the GR5, GR7, and GR59. The 7km hike to the peak is taxing and should only be tried by the fit, but the panorama over the glacial Doller valley and the Rhine and Saône valleys is well worth the sweat.

The warm **Lac de Malsaucy,** just west of Belfort, offers swimming, sunning, and outdoor performances. Throughout the summer, puppeteers, acrobats, comedians, and musicians perform here; in July, **Les Eurockéennes** (see above) makes the trek. Outdoor movies are shown on Thursday nights in late July and August.

Small boats, nautical bicycles, and mountain bikes can all be rented from the **Base de Loisirs du Malsaucy,** Rue d'Evette. The nearby Maison Départmentale de l'Environnement (☎03 84 29 18 12) offers expositions on everything from frogs to weather.

DAYTRIP FROM BELFORT: RONCHAMP

*To reach Ronchamp, hop on an SNCF **bus** or **train** at the SNCF station in **Belfort** (20min.; M-F 4 per day, 3 on Sa, 2 on Su; 26F/€3.96). The **tourist office** (☎03 84 63 50 82) is off rue le Corbusier, behind the church. (Open July-Aug. M-Sa 9:30am-noon and 2-5:30pm; Sept.-June M-F 9am-noon and 2-5pm.) To reach the chapel from the train station, follow the rue de la Gare, turn left onto rue le Corbusier, turn left again onto rue de la Chapelle, and lug yourself up the steep, winding road for 1½km. The prize at the top is worth the gruelling hike. If you are without a car, a bike, or legs of steel, Hôtel Pomme d'Or near the base of the hill will call a **taxi** for you (about 30F/€4.57 round-trip). A walk around the grounds of the chapel guarantees exceptional vistas of the valley below. (☎03 84 20 65 13. Open Apr.-Sept. daily 9:30am-6:30pm; Oct.-Mar. 10am-4pm. 10F/€1.53, children 5-12 6F/€0.91.*

Hidden in the hills to the west of Belfort, tiny Ronchamp (pop. 3000) would be living out its life in quiet provincial anonymity were it not home to one of the most unusual and striking buildings in all of France. Built on the site of a disastrous German attack in 1944, Le Corbusier's 1954 **Chapelle de Notre-Dame-du-Haut** is meant as a testament to hope in the wake of World War II. From afar, the chapel seems to sprout from the Bourlemont Hill, 472m above the town, like an overgrown mushroom. Up close, its typically Corbusierian elements become apparent: thick slabs of concrete, receding walls, and small panes of glass. With a sparsely-decorated candle-lit interior worship space as well as an exterior altar and pulpit, the chapel serves as both a place of shelter from and communion with the outside world. Next to the door are Le Corbusier's intentions for the chapel: "I wanted to create a space of silence, prayer, peace, and interior joy." The power of this building lies in its recognition of all that the war destroyed, and in the deliberacy of its moving-on; after such slaughter, the architect believed, any look backward would have been an act of bad faith.

THE JURA MOUNTAINS

France's forgotten mountain range, the Jura, is often overlooked by foreigners who flock to the Alps farther south. Much older than its neighbor, the Jura range has grown rounder and smoother with age and is covered with dense pine forests, sunny meadows, and countless trails for hiking, biking, and skiing.

LONS-LE-SAUNIER

Lons-le-Saunier is an agreeable mountain town, not quite so convenient a base as Pontarlier for exploration of the Jura, but far prettier and more pleasant. The town (pop. 22,000) is best known as the birthplace of Rouget de Lisle, composer of *La Marseillaise*. As an ancient spa site, Lons possesses its share of Roman ruins; still, one comes here more for the nearby mountains and the locals' highly developed *joie de vivre* than for any specific attraction.

ORIENTATION AND PRACTICAL INFORMATION. Trains run frequently to **Besançon** (73F/€11.13) and **Dole** (70F/€10.67). **SNCF** (☎08 36 35 35 35) also runs seven **buses** per day from the train station to **Dole.** Local buses run from Lons to the outlying villages; inquire at the tourist office for a schedule. **Taxis** (☎03 84 24 11 16) are available outside the station. You can rent **bikes** at **Dominique Maillard,** 17 rue Perrin. (☎03 84 24 24 07. Open M-F 9am-1pm and 2-6:30pm.) To get to the **tourist office,** pl. du 11 Novembre, cross the street in front of the station and head up rue Aristide Briand until it forks. Take the right fork (av. Thurel) to rue Rouget de Lisle and then take another left; the tourist office is in the old theater on your left, just to the right of the Café Strasbourg. They offer free maps, hotel and restaurant listings, guides to excursions in the Jura, and a mountain of friendly suggestions for what to do in town. (☎03 84 65 01; fax 03 84 43 22 59. Open M-F 8am-noon and 2-6pm, Sa 8am-noon and 2-5pm.) For info on countryside tours, contact **Juragence,** 19 rue Jean Moulin. (☎03 84 47 27 27. Open M-F 9am-12:30pm and 2-7pm, Sa 9am-noon and 2-5:30pm.) Hook up to the Internet at **Car'Com,** right next door to the tourist office in the old theater, for an unbeatable student rate of 25F/€3.81 per hr. (Regular rate 45F/€6.86 per hr. Open M-F 8am-noon and 2-6pm, Sa 10am-noon and 2-6pm.) There is a **laundromat** at 26 rue des Cordeliers. (☎06 80 92 08 37. Open daily 7am-9pm.) The **Commissariat de Police** sits at 6 av. du 44ème R.I. (☎03 84 35 17 10), and the **Centre Hospitalier** at 55 rue docteur Jean Michel (☎03 84 35 60 00). The **post office** is on av. Aristide Briand. (☎03 84 85 83 60. Open M-F 8am-7pm, Sa 8am-noon.) **Poste Restante:** 39021. **Postal code:** 39000.

ALSACE

ACCOMMODATIONS AND FOOD. Lons has no hostels, but there are a couple of decent cheap hotels near pl. de la Liberté. Be sure to get reservations, preferably a week in advance during the summer, for the **Hôtel les Glaciers,** 1 pl. Philibert de Chalon. From the train station, proceed on av. Aristide for four blocks until it abruptly turns left. Take this left and go one block, turning right onto rue St-Desiré. Walk one block and you'll be at pl. Liberté; diagonally across the *place* will be the arcaded rue du Commerce. Take this for two blocks to where it forks, then veer to the left and continue to the end of the block. The hotel will be on your right, across from the museum. Nine bright, simple, and fairly new rooms go for snap-'em-up budget rates. (☎03 84 47 26 89. Breakfast 30F/€4.57. Reception 7am-11pm. Singles 110F/€16.77, with shower 155F/€23.63; doubles 140F/€21.35, 175F/€26.68. Extra bed 40F/€6.10. Cash or traveler's checks only—ATM right down the block.) If Glaciers is full, try the **Hôtel des Sports,** centrally located at 21 rue St-Desiré. The hallways, which you must follow up past two floors of private rooms, are dark and cramped, but the rooms are surprisingly spacious and bright and have TVs. Roll out of bed and get breakfast at the daily local market just next door. (☎03 84 24 04 42. Breakfast at hotel 30F/€4.57. Reception M-Sa 6am-11pm, Su 6am-1pm and 5-11pm. Singles with shower 140F/€21.35; doubles with shower 210F/€32.02 for up to four people. AmEx/MC/V.)

Charcuteries, pâtisseries, and boulangeries live side by side on **rue du Commerce.** A produce **market** springs up there each Thursday morning. The rest of the week, find goodies at the local markets just surrounding the **pl. de la Liberté.** The small and cheerful **La Ferme Comtoise,** 23 rue St-Desiré (☎03 84 24 06 16) will help you find the perfect slice of *fromage de Comte*. If something still lacks from your picnic hamper, stock up at the **Casino supermarket** on rue du Commerce. (☎03 84 24 48 84. Open M-F 8:30am-12:30pm and 2:30-7:30pm, Sa 8am-7:30pm.) Drinkers leisurely sip their *kirs* at the **Grand Café de Strasbourg,** 4 rue Jean-Jaurès (☎03 84 24 18 45), next to the tourist office, quite possibly the classiest looking *fin de siècle* café you'll ever encounter. Check out the super-slick art-deco and neon interior at **L'Etoile,** pl. de la Liberté, featuring a metallic ceiling sprinkled with, you guessed it, stars. While their full meals are expensive, they serve regional nut-and-cheese salads for an affordable 45-50F/€6.86-7.62, and a variety of fruit-filled desserts for 25-30F/€3.81-4.57. (☎03 84 24 04 63. Open daily 7am-1am. MC/V.)

SIGHTS. All roads in Lons lead to **pl. de la Liberté,** site of the old theater. Following a devastating fire, the theater's rococo facade was reconstructed in 1901, and now a clock keeps time by chiming out a refrain from *la Marseillaise* every hour. Fire also played a part in the making of the pretty **rue du Commerce,** off the *place,* whose houses were rebuilt in stone after the great conflagration of 1637. Number 24, the birthplace of Rouget de Lisle, is now the **Musée Rouget de Lisle.** It houses a smattering of personal and *Marseillaise*-related memorabilia, including a recreation of his birth chamber and various editions of the famous song. (☎03 84 47 29 16. Open mid-June to late Sept. M-F 10am-noon and 2-6pm, Sa-Su 2-5pm. Free.) Following the rue du Commerce to its end and bearing left leads to the **Musée des Beaux Arts,** pl. Philibert de Chalon. This provincial museum boasts a splendid collection of Perraud statuary, a couple of nice Courbets, and precious little else. Even if you only have half an hour, stop in to get a glimpse of the incredible garden of human figures. (☎03 84 47 64 30. Open M-F 10am-noon and 2-6pm, Sa-Su 2-5pm. 10F/€1.53, students 5F/€0.76.)

ALSACE

To get to the **Musée d'Archéologie,** 25 rue Richebourg, veer right when the rue du Commerce forks and follow it as it becomes rue Trouillot, then turn right onto rue Richebourg. Housed in an old stone *fromagerie,* the museum features many exhibits excavated in or near Lons itself, including France's oldest dinosaur, the Plateosaurus. (☎03 84 47 12 13. Open W-M 10am-noon and 2-6pm, Sa-Su 2-5pm. 10F/€1.53, children 5F/€0.76; free W.) Between the museums, on rue Puits Salé and the corner of rue de l'Aubepin, you can see the off-kilter parabolic archway to the **Puits Salé,** the remains of the old saltwater baths that first drew the Romans to Lons. The spring is now connected via an underground canal to the **Thermes Ledonia** on the other side of town (☎03 84 24 20 34). This luxurious spa in the center of the shady green public **Parc des Bains** offers cures for ailments from rheumatism to cellulite; a full-scale cure can cost thousands of francs, but for 55F/€8.39 you can get yourself a dip in the pool and a sauna session. Following rue Richebourg back toward the center of town, you'll hit **place de la Chevalerie,** with the perpetually astonished-looking statue of Rouget de Lisle sculpted by Bartholdi. The sculptor recycled Rouget's stirring pose, one arm aloft, a few years later for a little lady now known as the Statue of Liberty.

EXCURSIONS. Just 10km from Lons slumbers the little town of **Baume-les-Messieurs.** The magnificent **abbey** there (☎03 84 44 61 41) was founded in the 6th century by St. Columban. Originally called Baume-les-moines (Baume-the-monks), by the 18th century the abbey attracted so many nobles *(messieurs)* that the name changed accordingly. There is no direct bus route between Lons and Baume, but you can take a bus from Lons to the very nearby Crançot and follow the signs to Baume. Ask at the tourist office for a current bus schedule. There is an extensive network of caves near the town, featuring underground lakes and vaults up to 80m high. (☎03 84 44 61 58. Caves open July-Aug. 9am-6pm; Apr.-June and Sept. 9am-noon and 2-6pm. 22F/€3.35, under 14 14F/€2.13.)

If you're seeking nature in all her splendor, the tourist office will happily bombard you with suggestions for exploration of the cascading waterfalls, crystal lakes, and green hills and forests of the Jura. Several hiking trails run near Lons, as well as paths for biking and horseback riding. Some tour operators guide trips through the Jura; try **Juragence,** 19 rue Jean Moulin (☎03 84 47 27 27).

DOLE

A pristine and provincial town, Dole is a good place for a quiet stopover and a transportation hub for the Jura area. Its beautiful canals, winding pedestrian passageways, flower-laden gardens, and tranquil atmosphere make for a splendid change of pace from the bustling student populations of Dijon and the foggy stupor of wine-tasting in Beaune.

TRANSPORTATION

Trains: pl. de la Gare (☎03 84 79 72 09). To **Besançon** (30min., 20 per day, 43F/€6.56); **Dijon** (30min., 25 per day, 45F/€6.86); **Paris TGV** (2hr., 6 per day, 236-286F/€35.98-43.60); **Pontarlier** (1hr., 4 per day, 77F/€11.74); **Strasbourg** (3½hr., 10 per day, 187F/€28.51).

Buses: Mosts Jura, 17 av. Aristide Briand (☎03 84 82 00 03; fax 03 84 82 46 88), up the street from the train station. Excursions to towns in the Jura and beyond. Office open M-Th 8am-noon and 2-6pm, F 8am-noon and 2-5pm, Sa 8am-noon.

Local transportation: Dolebus, 17 av. Aristide Briand (☎03 84 70 88 89). Tickets 5F/€0.76, *carnet* of 10 40F/€6.10. Office open M-F 9am-noon and 2-5pm.

Taxis: (☎03 84 82 13 70). Facing the train station. 7F/€0.76 per km.

Bike Rental: Griffon, 2 av. Léon Jouhaux (☎03 84 72 40 47), near the hostel. 120F/€18.30 per day, 300F/€45.74 per week. 2000F/€304.92 deposit. Open M-Sa 8am-noon and 2-7pm.

ORIENTATION AND PRACTICAL INFORMATION

Dole's center is **pl. Grévy,** a few blocks north of the river. Exiting the train station, turn left on av. Aristide Briand. Turn left again on bd. Wilson two blocks before you reach the pl. Grévy (you'll see the big globe fountain). Turn right at pl. Grévy and the **tourist office** will be on your immediate right.

Tourist Office: 6 pl. Grévy (☎03 84 71 11 22). Friendly staff, small office. Free map and hotel list. Brochures on Dole and Jura mountains. Pick up a copy of Passeport Intersites for discounts on sites throughout the Jura. In the same building, Jura Vert (☎03 84 82 33 01) offers expeditions in the Jura. Open Sept.-Apr. M-F 9am-noon and 2-6pm, Sa 9am-noon; May-Aug. M-Sa 9am-noon and 2-6pm.

Police: Local police, 1 rue du 21 Janvier (☎03 84 79 63 10). National police, 44 av. Jacques Duhamel (☎03 84 79 00 77). **Emergency:** ☎17.

Hospital: Centre Hospitalier Louis Pasteur, av. Léon Jouhaux (☎03 84 79 80 80). **Ambulance,** 44 rue des Arènes (☎03 84 82 66 33). **Emergency:** ☎03 84 82 36 36.

Post office: 33 rue Besançon (☎03 84 79 42 41). Poste Restante and **currency exchange.** Open M-F 8am-6:30pm, Sa 8am-1pm. **Postal code:** 39100.

ACCOMMODATIONS AND CAMPING

Dole has a number of inexpensive hotels clustered in front of the train station, as well as a youth hostel near the border of the town center. Be forewarned that almost all budget hotels in town are closed Saturday and Sunday evenings.

Auberge de Jeunesse le St-Jean (HI), pl. Jean XXIII (☎03 84 82 36 74; fax 03 84 79 17 69). Turn right out of the station and then left onto rue Jantet. Follow it to the end and make a right on bd. Wilson. Turn left onto av. Pompidou at the second big intersection, then take the next right onto rue Général Lachiche. Where the street makes a sharp left, walk straight into the hostel's gravel parking lot (15min.). Small, dark rooms. Breakfast 19F/€2.90. Lunch or dinner 50F/€7.62. Laundry. Reception M-F 8:30-11:30am and 4-8pm, Sa-Su 11:30am-2:30pm and 6-8pm. Call ahead. FUAJ members only (membership 70F/€10.67). Singles or doubles 66F/€10.07 per person.

Hôtel Moderne, 40 av. Aristide Briand (☎03 84 72 27 04), is the cheapest of the three pleasant, inexpensive hotels across from the noisy train station. Bar downstairs. Functional singles (2 can crowd in) 80F/€12.20, with bath 120F/€18.30. Larger rooms with bath 180F/€27.44. Reception 6am-midnight. AmEx/MC/V.

Camping du Pasquier (☎03 84 72 02 61), right on the canal. From the station, walk straight ahead on rue Aristide Briand, turn left onto bd. Wilson, right onto av. de la Paix. At pl. Grévy, turn onto av. Jaurès, and then right onto chemin G.V. Thevenot. It's an island in the middle of a quiet canal. Hot shower and laundry facilities. Reception in summer 7am-10pm; in winter 8am-noon and 3-10pm. Bungalows for long stays. Open Mar. 15-Oct.15 daily 7am-10pm. Call ahead. 1 person and tent 45F/€6.86; 2 people and tent 53F/€8.08; 2 people, car, and tent 63F/€9.61.

FOOD

Dole's canal no longer defends the Holy Roman Empire from France, but it does make a lovely site for a picnic. **Rue de Besançon** is rife with charcuteries, épiceries. The **Intermarché** supermarket on the corner of av. L. Johaux and av. Georges Pompidou has a large selection. (Open M-Th 8:30am-12:15pm and 2:30-7pm, F 8:30am-12:15pm and 2:30-7:15pm, Sa 8:30am-7pm.) **Marché de la Ville,** near the basilica, is sure to appease your grumbling stomach (every Tu, Th, and Sa 8am-noon).

La Bucherie, 14 rue de la Sous-Préfecture (☎03 84 82 27 61), serves excellent pizza (35-53F/€5.34-8.08) in a cheerful cave. Try the unusual and delicious *Franc-Comtoise pizza* with artichokes, snails, and bacon (50F/€7.62). Salads 20-46F/€3.05-7.01. Open Tu-F noon-2pm and 7-10pm, Sa noon-2pm and 7-11pm.

La Demi-Lune, 39 rue Pasteur (☎03 84 72 82 82), adjacent to Pasteur's birthplace. Cheerful, charming, dining room. Crêpes and galettes (12-75F/€1.83-11.43) with local specialties. Open daily noon-2pm and 7pm-whenever. MC.

SIGHTS

The **Maison Natale de Louis Pasteur** is the cream of Dole's crop. The house, 43 rue Pasteur, has been converted into a museum. Pasteur was not only a genius, a teacher at the Sorbonne, and an outspoken humanitarian, but also a gifted artist. A visit takes 45 minutes, with an English translation of the French legends available on request. (☎03 84 72 20 61. Open Apr.-Oct. M-Sa 10am-noon and 2-6pm, Su 2-6pm; Jan.-Mar. and Nov.-Dec. Sa 10am-noon and 2-5pm, Su 2-5pm.)

An arch to the right of the house leads to the **Canal des Tanneurs,** where Pasteur's father cured hides. Continue along the canal to your right to see the willow-lined estuaries and picture-perfect stone bridges, Dole's most endearing attractions. Kids and grown-ups will enjoy exploring an extensive network of **underground locks** and waterways. Look for the thankfully obsolete Fontaine des Lepreux (Fountain of Lepers). From Pasteur's house, go left on rue Pasteur, pass rue de Prelot, and walk 30 steps or so. Turn around. On your left, you should see a "hidden" stairway called **Passage Raynaud III,** an entrance to the underground canals. Explore the network of canals, paths, and gardens in the southern part of the *vieille ville*. In **Cours St-Marius,** across from the pl. Grévy, friendly *Dolois* often invite strangers to join the endless games of boules. The spire of **Basilique Notre-Dame,** the largest church in Franche-Comté, is visible from all points in the city.

ARBOIS

Although frequented by tourists, this idyllic wine-tasting town has not yet lost its regional flavor. Many of the locals still have that straight-from-the-vineyard look, and for every air-conditioned tour bus zipping by, there is a tractor rattling through the town. With vine-covered houses—all with blooming gardens that will make visitors with green thumbs even greener with envy—16th-century ramparts, and a river cascading through the town center, Arbois is well worth a visit.

ORIENTATION AND PRACTICAL INFORMATION. Trains and **SNCF buses** will take you to **Besançon** (9 per day, 47F/€7.17) and **Dole** (5 per day, 41F/€6.25). Bikes and other wheeled contraptions can be rented at **Butagaz,** 6 rue de Courcelles (☎03 84 66 04 48). The **train station** is a good 15-minute hike from the town center; go straight from the station onto av. de la Gare, take your second left onto av. Pasteur, and follow it straight into town as it becomes rue de Courcelles and, a block later, Grande Rue, and finally reaches the central **pl. de la Liberté.**

To get to the **tourist office** from the train station, follow the directions above to pl. de la Liberté. From there, turn right onto rue de l'Hôtel de Ville; the tourist office is on the left side of the Hôtel de Ville, with a SNCF office. Get yourself a free map, a list of hotels and restaurants, and a flood of brochures. Audio tours available in English 10F/€1.53. (☎03 84 66 55 50; www.arbois.com. Open M-Sa 9am-noon and 2-6pm, Su 10am-noon and 2-5pm.) The **police** can be reached at 03 84 66 14 25. The **hospital** is at 23 rue de l'Hôpital (☎03 84 66 44 00). The **post office** is on av. Général Delort (☎03 84 66 01 21). **Postal code:** 39600.

ACCOMMODATIONS AND FOOD. While the ritzy Arbois hotels often reach ungodly prices (from 700F/€106.72), there are also a surprising number of decent and centrally located budget options. **Hôtel Mephisto,** pl. Faramand, should be your first pick. Seven spacious, but slightly dark rooms, with classy furnishings and recently renovated bathrooms. Reserve in advance in the summer. (☎03 84 66 06 49. Breakfast 30F/€4.57. Bar downstairs. Reception 8am-10pm, later on weekends. Singles and doubles 140F/€21.35, with shower 190F/€28.97. MC/V.) Cheap but very basic is **Hôtel de la Poste,** 71 Grande Rue. (☎03 84 66 13 22. Breakfast 30F/€4.57. Shower on first floor, toilets on every floor. Reception 7am-11pm, closed Tu. Singles 110F/€16.77; doubles 140F/€21.35.) Slightly more expensive but well worth it is **Hôtel les Messageries,** 2 rue de Courcelles, which has bright white rooms with floral trimmings. (☎03 84 66 15 45. Reception 8am-noon and 5-9pm. Singles start at 175F/€26.68; doubles at 195F/€29.73; extra bed 50F/€7.62; under 10 stay free.) The three-star **Municipal des Vignes** campsite, av. du Général Leclerc, offers all modern amenities: hot showers, snack bar, electricity, nearby pool, laundry, and TV salon. (☎/fax 03 84 66 14 12. Open Apr.-Sept. July-Aug. 66F/€10.06 for 2 adults, camper, and pool access, 9F/€1.37 per child; Apr.-June and Sept. 60F/€9.15 for 2 adults, camper, and pool. Accepts bank cards and traveler's checks.)

The mysteriously compelling *vin jaune*, fermented with sauvignon grapes and walnuts, is the pride of Arbois, as is the even more elaborate *vin de paille*, made from grapes that have been dried on beds of hay. Many *caves* in Arbois will offer free *dégustations*, and many upscale restaurants have local wines by the glass. Not nearly so glamorous, but a fraction of the cost, are the fine wines of **Supermarché Casino,** 55 Grande Rue, which include a selection of *vins jaunes*. (☎03 84 66 05 92. Open M-Sa 8:30am-12:30pm and 3-7:15pm, Su 9am-noon.)

Cheap eats are a little difficult to find in Arbois, but there are a few good places. **La Cuisance,** 62 rue de Faramand, is full of locals and serves up reasonable but generous *plats* for lunch (40F/€6.10) and dinner (65F/€9.91); kids eat for 35F/€5.34. (☎03 84 37 40 74. Open Th-M 9am-3pm and 5pm-midnight, Tu-W 9am-3pm. MC/V.) For a quick bite, head to **Restaurant Agor Kebab,** 73 Grande Rue, which is a cheerful Middle Eastern oasis in a desert of expensive *coq-au-vin-jaune* eateries. Falafel and kebab sandwiches run 20-30F/€3.05-4.57, platters 45F/€6.86. (☎03 84 66 33 64. Open M-F noon-2pm and 6-10pm, Sa-Su 6pm-midnight.) Everybody's talking about **Hirsinger's Chocolatier and Salon de thé** on 38 Grande Rue. Acclaimed by glossy gourmet magazines and locals alike, the homemade ice cream simply begs to be eaten on the terrace overlooking pl. de la Liberté (☎03 84 66 06 97).

SIGHTS. If after your visit you just can't get Pasteur out of your thoughts, try getting him into your veins. The scientist's original vineyards at the **Maison de Pasteur,** 83 rue de Courcelles, where he made several crucial observations on the nature of alcoholic fermentation, continue to bottle wine under his name. (☎03 84 66 11 72. Open July-Aug. daily 9:45-11:45am and 2:15-6:15pm; Apr.-May and Oct. 2:15-5:15pm. 35F/€5.34, children 15F/€2.29.) If you want to know more about Arbois wine and its cultivation, head over to the **Musée de la vigne et du vin,** in Château Pécauld on rue des Fossés. (☎03 84 66 40 45. Open Apr.-Oct. daily 10am-noon and 2-6pm; Nov.-Mar. 2-6pm. 21F/€3.20.) **Eglise St-Just** and its tower as well as the nearby 16th-century ramparts offer an exquisite view of **La Cuisance** river.

PONTARLIER

The town of Pontarlier, 840m above most of Alsace, is a gateway to some of life's higher pleasures—namely, the oft-overlooked Haut-Jura mountains. Pontarlier's current status as a a friendly, slow, rather boring town belies its history as the absinthe capital of Europe (until the hallucinogenic liqeur was banned in 1915). Though full of tacky boutiques, Pontarlier's chalet-style houses just outside of town remind you that it's only 12km away from Switzerland, and the mountain views—well, those couldn't possibly be missed.

PRACTICAL INFORMATION. The **train station** is on pl. de Villingen-Schweningen. (☎03 81 46 56 99. Open M-F 5am-9pm, Sa-Su 7am-9pm.) Trains go to **Dijon** (1½hr.; M-F 6 per day, 7 Sa-Su; 113F/€17.22), **Dole** (1hr., 5 per day, 86F/€13.11), and **Paris** (3½hr., 6 per day, 350F/€53.36). **Monts Jura** buses go to **Besançon** (55min., 6 per day, 46.50F/€7.10). The **tourist office** is at 14bis rue de la Gare. From the train station, cross through the rotary and head left one block on rue de la Gare. The office is to the left of the bus station, down rue Michaud. The staff has info on hiking, skiing, and other outdoor sports. Ask for the free regional guides *Les Doubs: Massif de Jura* and *Guide Pratique*, which lists various cheap mountain lodgings. (☎03 81 46 48 33; fax 03 81 46 83 32. Office open July-Aug. daily 8:30am-noon and 2-7pm; Sept.-June closed Su.) **Cycles Pernet,** 23 rue de la République, rents **bikes.** (☎03 81 46 48 00. 60F/€9.15 per half-day, 80F/€12.20 per day. Passport deposit. Open M 3-6pm, Tu-Sa 9:30am-noon and 2-7pm. AmEx/MC/V.) The **police** are at 19 Rocade Pompidou (☎03 81 38 51 10); and the **hospital** is at 2 fbg. St-Etienne (☎03 81 38 54 54). The **post office** is across the street at 17 rue de la Gare. (☎03 81 38 49 44. Open M-F 8am-6:30pm, Sa 8am-noon). **Postal code:** 25300.

ACCOMMODATIONS AND FOOD. Expect to pay a 5F/€0.76 residency tax per person per night in Pontarlier. The cheapest place in town is the quiet, centrally located **Auberge de Pontarlier (FUAJ),** 2 rue Jouffroy. From the tourist office, go left on rue Marpaud; the hostel is the white stucco building on your left. The friendly folk at reception have no shortage of suggestions for things to do, and organize hiking and skiing trips. (☎03 81 39 06 57; fax 03 81 39 06 57. Breakfast 19F/€2.90. Sheets 17F/€2.59. Reception 8am-noon and 5:30-10pm. Reservations advised. Dorms 50F/€7.6, doubles 75F/€11.4. **Members only.**) TVs and a central location make up for the dim lighting and stale smell in the rooms of the **Hôtel de France,** 8 rue de la Gare. (☎03 81 39 05 20; fax 03 81 46 24 43. Reception 24hr. Singles 105F/€16, with shower 135F/€20.6; doubles 170F/€25.9, with shower 180F/€27.4; triples 210F/€32, triples or quads with shower from 320F/€48.8. MC/V.)

The most scenic option is the **campground** (☎03 81 46 23 33; fax 03 81 46 83 34) on rue du Tolombief. From the train station, turn right onto Rocade Georges Pompidou, cross the river, and bear left onto rue de l'Industrie. Take the first right onto av. de Neuchâtel and follow the signs (15min.). The grounds hold TV, ping-pong, a game room, and a bar. (July-Aug. 1 person and tent/car 65F/€9.91, 2 people and tent/car 83F/€12.65; Sept.-June 1 person and tent/car 58F/€8.84; 2 people and tent/car 64F/€9.76; children 7.50F/€1.14. Electricity 20F/€3.05. Châlets 300F/€45.74 per day for 2 people, extra person 20F/€3.05, 6 people max; weekly 2400F/€365.91; 8200F/€1250.19 per month; July-Aug. 1 week min. stay.)

The relaxed Pontarlier populace tends to eat at home, a fact reflected in the town's paucity of restaurants. Join the crowd at the **Casino supermarket** on rue de la République (open M-F 8am-12:30pm and 2:30-7pm, Sa 8:30am-7pm). Or try **Pizzeria Gambetta,** 15 rue Gambetta (off rue de la Gare), whose wood oven spins out over 20 varieties of pizza (from 45F/€6.86) with toppings ranging from simple pepperoni to eggs, tuna, and potatoes. Design your own for 55F/€8.4. The pizzas, along with regional meat dishes and pastas, can be made to go, but stay for the unimaginable chocolate mousse (24F/€3.66). (☎03 81 46 67 17. Open W-Su noon-2pm and 7-10pm.) **P'tit Delice,** on 10 rue de la République, is bright and centrally located with a large variety of galettes (36-49F/€5.49-7.47) and sweet crêpes (16-34F/€2.44-5.18). (☎03 81 46 57 74. Open Tu-Su noon-10pm. MC/V.)

SKIING, HIKING, BIKING, AND RIDING. The Jura mountains, best known for **cross-country skiing,** are covered with 60km of long-distance trails. Eight trails on two slopes (**Le Larmont** and **Le Malmaison**) cover every difficulty level. (Daily pass around 30F/€4.57, ages 10-16 20F/€3.05.) Le Larmont (☎03 81 46 55 20) is the alpine ski area nearest to Pontarlier. For ski conditions, call **Allo-Neige,** Massif de Jura (☎03 81 53 55 88). The Jura are much colder than the Alps, so wear your layers. **Sport et Neige,** 4 rue de la République, rents ski equipment. (☎03 81 39 04 69. 50F/€7.62 per day, 290F/€44.21 per week, children 40F/€6.10 per day, 210F/€32.02 per week. Open 9am-noon and 2-7pm. MC/V.) Prices all around are far cheaper than those in the Alps, but the snow's quality is less reliable. **Metabief Mont d'Or,** accessible by bus from Pontarlier, has day and night skiing. (☎03 81 49 13 81. Lift tickets 104F/€15.86 per day. 30min. shuttle ride 46.50F/€7.11; departs 4 times a day from Mont Jura bus station.)

In the summer, skiing gives way to fishing, hiking, and mountain biking. There are two mountain bike departure points in Pontarlier, one to the north just off rue Pompée and one to the south, about 2km west of Forges. Hikers can choose between a swath of the **GR5,** an international 262km trail, and the **GR6,** which leads to a narrow valley dominated by the dramatic **Château de Joux.** The thousand-year-old castle's collection of rare arms makes you wonder if the Franco-Swiss border has always been so peaceful. (☎03 81 69 47 95. Château open daily July-Aug. 9am-6pm; Feb.-June and Sept. 10-11:30am and 2-6:30pm; Oct.-Feb. 10-11:15am and 2-3:30pm; Nov. 15-Dec. 15 by request only.) The tourist office's map (15F/€2.29) marks departure points for biking and hiking around town, including one near the train station at pl. St-Claude. More detailed maps can also be found at the bookstore on rue de la Republique. **Le Poney Club,** 37 rue du Cret, adjacent to the campground, rents affectionate horses for riders of all skill levels. (☎03 81 46 61 67. 30F/€4.57 for 30min., 40F/€6.10 per hr. For organized rides, call at least eight days in advance.)

CHAMPAGNE

Brothers, brothers, come quickly! I am drinking stars!
—Dom Pérignon

John Maynard Keynes once remarked that his major regret in life was not having consumed enough champagne. Rolling through the vineyards and lush plains of Champagne, you can right Keynes' mistake while drinking in monuments to the region's rich history: the inspiring grandeur of the Reims Cathedral, the Roman ramparts of Langres, the half-timbered houses and crooked streets of Troyes.

According to European law, the word "champagne" may only be applied to wines made from grapes from this region and produced according to a rigorous, time-honored method which involves the blending of three varieties of grapes, two stages of fermentation, and frequent realignment of the bottles by *remueurs* (highly trained bottle-turners) to facilitate removal of sediment. So fiercely guarded is their name that when Yves Saint-Laurent brought out a new perfume called "Champagne," the powerful *maisons* sued to force him to change it—and won. You can see the *méthode champénoise* in action at the region's numerous wine cellars *(caves)*, at their best in the glitzy towns of Reims and Epernay. To sample the efforts of this rigorous process, partake in the tastings that cap most *cave* tours, or order a *coupe de champagne*, available in some cafés and bars. Even regional gastronomical specialities tend to center around a champagne base; try *volaille au champagne* (poultry) or *civet d'oie* (goose stew).

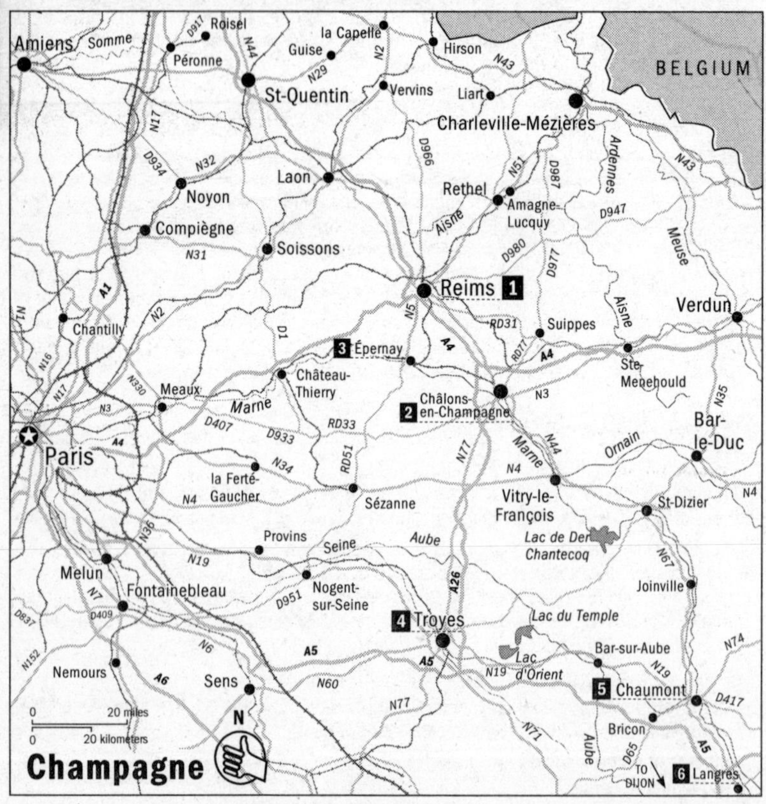

Today, small as it is, Champagne is strikingly diverse. The golden vineyards and *beaux arts* flavor of the north seem a world away from the quiet citadels and forests of the south. The grape-fed high life may buoy the whole region economically, but smaller towns both near and far from the vines have quite distinct characters.

TRANSPORTATION

Champagne is a great place for excursions into the countryside by car, bike, or foot. Drivers should follow any of the lovely *routes de champagne* through the Montagne de Reims, the Val de Marne, or the Côtes des Blancs. Tourist offices distribute road maps; ask for the free pamphlet *The Champagne Road.* Wander through the small villages and lakes that dot the region south and west of Epernay, or check out Champagne's two national parks, both ideal for hiking. The tourist office in Troyes has info on the Forêt d'Orient to the southeast, while the office in Reims sells a booklet of trails through the Parc Naturel de la Montagne de Reims (15F/€2.29). The Forêt de Verzy, a curious forest of twisted, umbrella-shaped dwarf beeches (*tortillards*) and the vast Forêt de Germaine are also worth visiting. Trains connect Reims and the larger towns to the rest of France, but you will have to rely on capricious bus schedules to reach the smaller villages.

1 **Reims:** Champagne, coronations, and flagrant public *joie de vivre* **(p. 429)**
2 **Châlons:** An uninspiring industrial town known for churches and gardens **(p. 434)**
3 **Epernay:** Where the wealthy (and you) go to drink champagne **(p. 434)**
4 **Troyes:** The best-preserved medieval town in its area; renowned Gothic churches **(p. 436)**
5 **Chaumont:** Lovely views and a mansion-studded *vieille ville* **(p. 440)**
6 **Langres:** One of France's most beautiful towns; eminently walkable ramparts **(p. 441)**

REIMS

Reims today (pronounced "rrrranhce") is an active, vibrant city (pop. 185,000), all champagne and nightlife. The city is famous for its celebrated cathedral, built on the site of Clovis' baptism in AD 496 (see p. 6). The cathedral has hosted the coronations of centuries of French monarchs; the most notable, the 1429 crowning of Charles VII, was Joan of Arc's greatest symbolic victory. The city also won the dubious honor of seeing Napoleon's last victory, the so-called "last smile of Fortune." Fortune frowned on another would-be conqueror on May 7, 1945, when the German army surrendered in Reims' little red schoolhouse. Scarred by the great wars of the 20th century, Reims has since been rebuilt to its 19th-century glory. For all its grape-draped surroundings, this is today as hip and lively a city as you'll find anywhere in the Northeast. Its bar-packed plazas and tree-lined avenues, built on bubbly, suit the comfortable lives and *joie de vivre* of the locals.

TRANSPORTATION

Trains: bd. Joffre (☎03 26 88 11 65). To: **Epernay** (20min., 11 per day, 34F/€5.18); **Laon** (1hr., 7 per day, 49F/€7.47); and **Paris** (1½hr., 11 per day, 123F/€18.75). Info desk M-F 8:30am-7pm, Sa 9am-6pm; ticket windows M-Sa 5:45am-9pm, Su 7am-9pm.

Local Transportation: Transport Urbains de Reims (TUR) buses stop in front of the train station. Info office at 6 rue Chanzy (☎03 26 88 25 38). Open M-F 7am-8pm and Sa 7am-7pm. 5F/€0.76 per ticket (available on bus); *carnet* of 10 36F/€5.49; day pass 13.50F/€2.06 available at info office. Most lines run 6am-8pm, some night routes have less frequent buses running until midnight.

Taxis: ☎03 26 47 05 05 or 03 26 02 15 02. 24hr.

Car Rental: Avis, cours de la Gare (☎03 26 47 10 08; fax 03 26 40 11 79). Open M-F 8am-noon and 2-7pm, Sa 8am-noon and 2-6pm.

Bike Rental: Cycles Hubert, 82 rue Neuchâtel (☎03 26 09 16 93). Open Tu-Sa 9am-noon and 2-7pm.

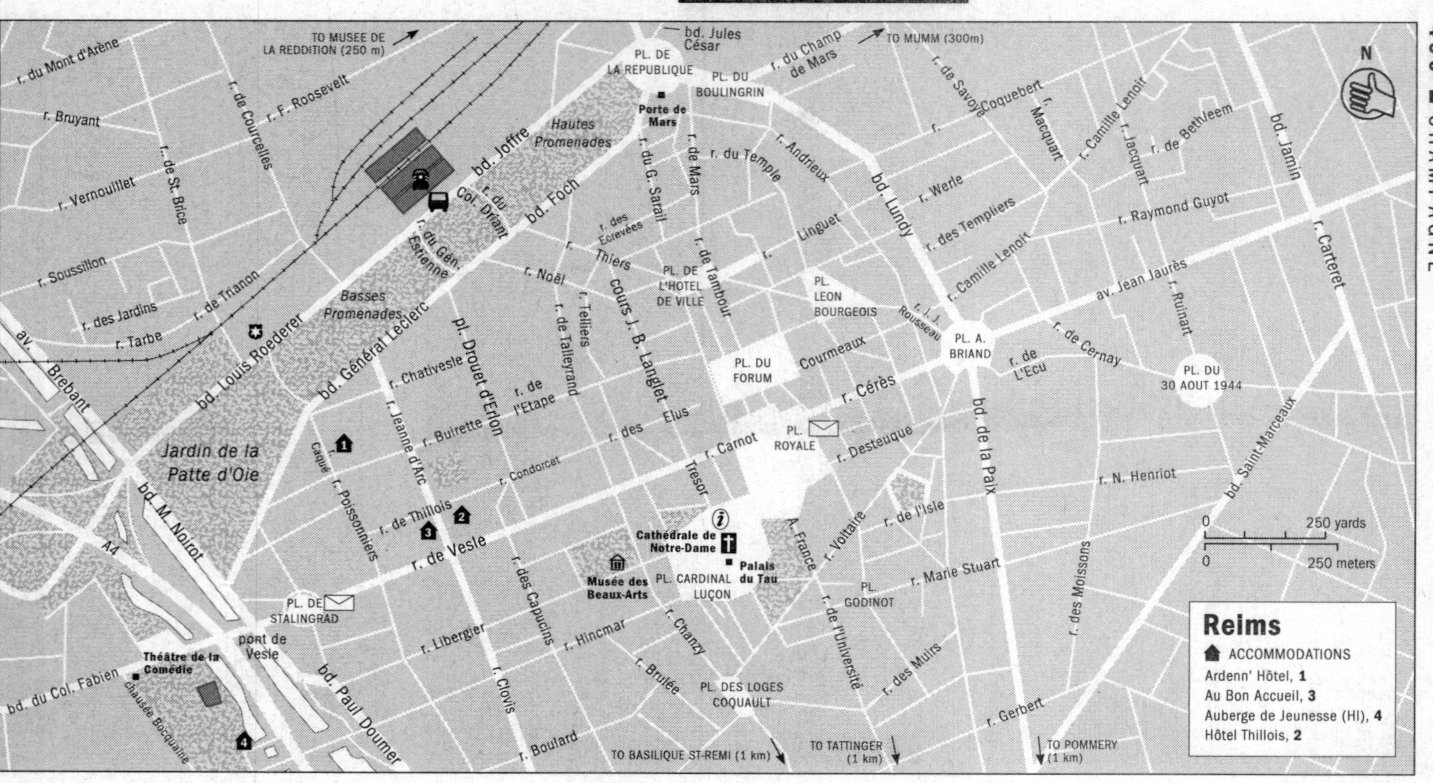
Reims
ACCOMMODATIONS
Ardenn' Hôtel, 1
Au Bon Accueil, 3
Auberge de Jeunesse (HI), 4
Hôtel Thillois, 2
0
250 yards
0
250 meters
N
TO MUSEE DE LA REDDITION (250 m)
TO MUMM (300m)
TO BASILIQUE ST-REMI (1 km)
TO TATTINGER (1 km)
TO POMMERY (1 km)
r. du Mont d'Arène
r. F. Roosevelt
r. Bruyant
r. de Courcelles
r. Vernouillet
r. de St. Brice
r. Soussillon
r. des Jardins
r. de Trianon
r. Tarbe
av. Brebant
bd. Louis Roederer
bd. Joffre
r. du Col. Driant
r. du Gén. Estienne
bd. Foch
Hautes Promenades
Basses Promenades
bd. Général Leclerc
Jardin de la Patte d'Oie
bd. M. Noirot
A4
Théâtre de la Comédie
chausée Bocquaine
bd. du Col. Fabien
pont de Vesle
bd. Paul Doumer
PL. DE STALINGRAD
r. Poissonniers
Caqué
r. Chativesle
r. Jeanne d'Arc
pl. Drouet d'Erlon
r. Buirette
r. de l'Etape
r. de Thillois
r. de Vesle
r. Condorcet
r. des Capucins
r. Clovis
r. Boulard
r. Libergier
r. Hincmar
r. Brulée
r. Chanzy
PL. DES LOGES COQUAULT
Musée des Beaux-Arts
PL. CARDINAL LUÇON
Cathédrale de Notre-Dame
Palais du Tau
A. France
r. de l'Université
PL. GODINOT
r. des Murs
r. Gerbert
r. Marie Stuart
r. Voltaire
r. de l'Isle
r. Desteuque
PL. ROYALE
r. Carnot
Tresor
r. des Elus
r. de Talleyrand
r. Telliers
cours J. B. Langlet
r. Noël
r. Thiers
r. des Ecrevées
r. du G. Sarail
r. de Mars
r. de Tambour
PL. DE L'HOTEL DE VILLE
PL. DU FORUM
Courmeaux
r. Cérès
PL. LEON BOURGEOIS
r. J. J. Rousseau
PL. A. BRIAND
bd. de la Paix
r. de L'Ecu
r. de Cernay
PL. DU 30 AOUT 1944
av. Jean Jaurès
r. Ruinart
bd. Saint-Marceaux
r. N. Henriot
r. des Moissons
PL. DE LA REPUBLIQUE
bd. Jules César
Porte de Mars
PL. DU BOULINGRIN
r. du Champ de Mars
r. du Temple
r. Andrieux
r. Linguet
bd. Lundy
r. Werle
r. des Templiers
r. Camille Lenoir
r. de Savoye
r. Coquebert
r. Macquart
r. Jacquart
r. de Bethleem
r. Raymond Guyot
bd. Jamin
r. Carteret

ORIENTATION AND PRACTICAL INFORMATION

Tourist Office: 2 rue Guillaume de Machault (☎03 26 77 45 25; fax 03 26 77 45 27; VisitReims@netvia.com), in a pint-sized ruin beside the cathedral. Free map with sights and *caves* and provides a free (with deposit), same-night **accommodations service.** Audioguides in 6 languages (50F/€7.62), as well as **tours** of the town. Ask for the student guide *Le Monocle;* for local events check out the weekly *Les Rendez-vous Rémois.* Office open mid-Apr. to mid-Oct. M-Sa 9am-7pm, Su 10am-6pm; mid-Oct. to mid Apr. M-Sa 9am-6pm, Su 10am-5pm.

Budget Travel: Wasteels, 26 rue Libergier (☎08 03 88 70 55). ISIC cards, cheap flights. Open M-Sa 9am-noon and 2-6pm.

Youth Center: Centre Régionale d'Information Jeunesse, 41 rue Talleyrand (☎03 26 79 84 79; fax 03 26 79 84 72). Oodles of info: jobs, local events, etc. Open M-Th 10:30am-12:30pm and 2-6pm, F 10:30am-12:30pm and 2-5pm.

Laundry: Laverie de Vesle, 129 rue de Vesle. Open daily 7am-9pm.

Police: 40 bd. Louis Roederer (☎03 26 61 44 00), by the train station.

Hospital: 45 rue Cognac Jay (☎03 26 78 78 78).

Internet Access: Clique & Croque, 27 rue de Vesle (☎03 26 86 93 92). 30F/€4.57 per hr. Open M-Sa 10:30am-12:30am, Su 2pm-9pm. Or try **Le Kraft** (see **Food,** below), where access is 25F/€3.81 per hr.

Post Office: rue Olivier-Métra (☎03 26 50 58 82), at pl. de Boulingrin, near the Porte Mars. Open M-F 8am-7pm, Sa 8am-noon. **Branch office,** 1 rue Cérès (☎03 26 77 64 80), on pl. Royale closer to the center of town. Open M-F 8:30am-6pm, Sa 8:30am-noon. **Poste Restante** 3F/€0.46 per item; specify "51084 Reims-Cérès" for branch. Another branch on rue de Veste close to hostel. **Postal code** (main office): 51100.

ACCOMMODATIONS AND CAMPING

Inexpensive hotels cluster west of pl. Drouet d'Erlon, in the area above the cathedral, and near the *mairie.* Reims is popular with travelers, so call ahead.

Au Bon Accueil, 31 rue Thillois (☎03 26 88 55 74; fax 03 26 05 12 38), off pl. Drouet d'Erlon. A sunny, civilized, spotless guest house. Reserve ahead and you may get a room nicer and cheaper than those at the hostel. Breakfast 25F/€3.81. Reception 24hr. Singles 80-150F/€12.20-22.90; doubles 140-220F/€2135-33.54. MC/V.

Ardenn' Hôtel, 6 rue Caqué (☎03 26 86 78 36; fax 03 26 09 48 56), near pl. Drouet d'Erlon and the station. 14 romantic, chandeliered, velvety rooms with showers, priced accordingly. Breakfast 35F/€5.34. Reception M-Sa 24hr., Su after 6pm. Singles and doubles 170-280F/€25.92-42.69; triples 300F/€45.74; quads 350F/€53.36. MC/V.

Centre International de Séjour/Auberge de Jeunesse (HI), chaussée Bocquaine (☎03 26 40 52 60; fax 03 26 47 35 70), next to La Comédie-Espace André Malraux. Cross the park in front of the station, following the right-hand side of the traffic circle. Turn right onto bd. Général Leclerc, follow it to the canal and cross the first bridge (Pont de Vesle) on your left. Bocquaine is the first left (10-15min.). Friendly staff. A mix of backpackers and hyperactive school groups. Small, tidy rooms off gloomy hallways. Breakfast 20F/€3.05. Kitchen. Laundry. Reception 24hr. Singles 89F/€13.57, with bath 149F/€21.34; doubles 65F/€9.91 per person, with bath 89F/€13.57; triples 59F/€8.99, with bath 79F/€12.04. **Non-members** pay one-time 10F/€1.53 fee. MC/V.

Hôtel Thillois, 17 rue Thillois (☎03 26 40 65 65), to the west of pl. Drouet d'Erlon. Medium-sized rooms are plain with good light and TVs. Breakfast 30F/€4.57. Singles and doubles with sink 130-150F/€19.82-22.90, with shower 150-170F/€22.90-25.92, with shower and toilet 160-180F/€24.39-27.44. MC/V.

FOOD

The heart of Reims' street life, day or night, **pl. Drouet d'Erlon** may also be its stomach; bakeries and sandwich shops squish side by side with cheap cafés and classier restaurants. A **Monoprix** supermarket occupies a 19th-century building on the corner of rue de Vesle and rue de Talleyrand (open M-Sa 8:30am-9pm); a smaller **Marché Plus** is on rue de Vesle (M-Sa 9am-9pm, Su 9am-1pm). The main **open-air market** is on pl. du Boulingrin near Porte Mars (W and Sa 6am-1pm).

Le Kraft, 5 rue Salin (☎03 26 05 29 29). In a class of its own—restaurant, bar, gallery, and cocktail lounge. The library is a perfect place to smoke, sip a 35F/€5.34 glass of champagne, and write edgy poetry while listening to Ella Fitzgerald. Entrees 40-60F/€6.10-9.15. Open M-F 11am-3am, Sa 6pm-3am. MC/V.

Le Petit Basque, 13 rue de Colonel Fabien (☎03 26 09 96 26), around the corner from the hostel, dishes out huge portions. The glorious *paella* (starting at 65F/€9.91) can be taken out, but the friendly owners and intimate atmosphere merit a sit-down meal. Lunch and dinner *menu* 55F/€8.39. Open Tu-Sa 11:30am-3pm and 7-11pm. MC/V.

SIGHTS

The most popular sights are around the center of town and are easily reached on foot. Other than the cathedral, the champagne *caves* are undoubtedly the biggest draw in town. Four hundred kilometers of *crayères* (Roman chalk quarries) and as many recently-dug tunnels wind under Reims, sheltering the bottled treasures of the great champagne firms. Many houses give tours by appointment only; the tourist office has info on hours and prices. It's not always cheaper to buy champagne at the houses; ask the advice of wine shops near the cathedral, look for sales on local brands—and check the prices at Monoprix (see **Food,** above). Good bottles start at 60F/€9.15, half the price of the same product sold abroad.

CATHEDRALE DE NOTRE-DAME. Three churches have stood on this spot, witness to the coronation of Clovis in 496 and of 25 French sovereigns between 816 and 1825. The present edifice (1211-1280) is built with blocks of golden limestone quarried from the *caves* now used to age champagne. Bombing during WWI destroyed most of the original stained glass, though some remains in the eastern part of the cathedral. More recently, this was the site of the 1962 reconciliation between President de Gaulle and German Chancellor Adenauer. The most spectacular element of the cathedral is a sea-blue set of replacement windows by Marc Chagall, integrating elements from Genesis with the baptism of Clovis. Outside, statues of local martyrs decorate the left porch, including the famous smiling angel of Reims—bring binoculars for the best views. For tours in English, consult the tourist office. *(☎03 26 77 45 25. Open daily 7:30am-7:30pm. Tours in French July-Aug. M-Sa 10:30am and 4:30pm, Su 11am; in English daily 2:30pm; less frequent tours in Oct. and late Mar. to mid-June. 35F/€5.34, ages 12-25 and seniors 20F/€3.05.)*

CHAMPAGNE CAVES. Of many tours offered, the most elegant by far is at the massive **Champagne Pommery.** Mme. Pommery became one of France's foremost vintners when she took over her late husband's business; since then she has brought art into the workplace, lining the *cave* walls with exquisite carvings by Gustave Navlet. The firm boasts the largest *tonneau* (vat) in the world, carved by Emile Galle and sent to the 1904 World's Fair in St. Louis as a 75,000-liter gesture of friendship to the USA. *(5 pl. du Général Gouraud. ☎03 26 61 62 56; fax 03 26 61 62 96. Tours Apr.-Oct. daily 11am-7pm. 46F/€7.01, students 23F/€3.51, children free.)* If caves are your thing, you'll love the gloom in **Taittinger's** spectacular spooky tunnels, dug by the Romans. Taittinger boasts an unbelievably informative tour, and M-Th, you can watch the *dégorgement* (sediment removal process) in person. *(9 pl. St-Nicaise. ☎03 26 85 45 35. Open Apr. to mid-Nov. M-F 9am-1pm and 2-5:30pm, Sa-Su 9-11am and 2-6pm, last tours start 1hr. before closing time; Dec.-Mar. closed weekends. 35F/€5.34.)* For an earthier take on the fermenting business, **Mumm's** the word. *(34 rue du Champ de Mars. ☎03 26 49 59 70. Follow the billboards from pl. de la République. 30F/€3.05. Tours Mar.-Oct. daily 9-11am and 2-5pm; Nov.-Feb. M-F 9-11am and 2-5pm, Sa-Su 2-5pm.)*

PALAIS DU TAU. This former archbishop's residence got its name from the original floor plan, which resembled a "T." Its dazzling collection includes reliquaries dating back to Charlemagne; the show-stopping highlights are the magnificent 16th-century tapestries and sumptuous 50-foot robes of Charles X. You can also view the massive original statues from the cathedral, many removed after WWI. *(Pl. du Cardinal Luçon. ☎03 26 47 81 79. Open July-Aug. daily 9:30am-6:30pm; Sept.-Nov. 14 and Mar. 16-June 9:30am-12:30pm and 2-6pm; Nov. 15-Mar. 15 M-F 10am-noon and 2-5pm, Sa-Su 10am-noon and 2-6pm. 26F/€3.96, students 21F/€3.20.)*

BASILIQUE ST-REMI. The basilica reposes on a bed of lavender at the other end of town from the cathedral, near the Pommery and Taittinger *caves*. This Romanesque church with Gothic tinges was built around the tomb of St-Rémi, the bishop who baptized Clovis. *(Pl. St-Rémi. Open daily 9am-7pm.* Son-et-lumière *spectacles held here July-Aug. Sa 9:30pm.)* Next door, the **Abbaye St-Rémi** shelters an extensive collection of religious art, military uniforms, and artifacts from the Merovingian and Carolingian eras. Look for the Enamels of St-Timothy, a fascinating series of engraved tiles depicting life under the oppressive Roman thumb. *(53 rue Simon. ☎03 26 85 23 36. Open M-F 2-6:30pm, Sa-Su 2-7pm. 10F/€1.53.)*

OTHER SIGHTS. The Germans signed their surrender to the Allies on May 7, 1945, in a schoolroom across the railroad tracks. That schoolhouse is now the small **Musée de la Reddition,** where a short film and several galleries of photos and timelines, more evocative than factual, lead up to the preserved (though glassed-off) room itself. The staff is helpful. *(12 rue Franklin Roosevelt. ☎03 26 47 84 19. Open W-M 10am-noon and 2-6pm. 10F/€1.53, children and students free.)* The largest arch in the Roman empire still crumbles over the modern pl. de la République. The **Porte Mars** is decorated with reliefs of Romulus and Remus, who gave the city its name.

CHAMPAGNE

ENTERTAINMENT AND FESTIVALS

The best entertainment is a stroll by the illuminated cathedral at night. The sidewalk leads to the **Comédie de Reims,** chaussée Bocquaine, which presents a wide variety of plays. (☎03 26 48 49 10. Tickets around 100F/€15.25, students 30F/€4.57.) **Opéra Cinémas,** 3 rue Théodore Dubois, shows a range of films, sometimes undubbed. (☎03 26 47 29 36. Tickets 35-46F/€5.34-7.01.) The **Grand Théâtre de Reims,** rue de Vesle, hosts primarily operas and ballets. (Box office on 13 rue Chanzy, ☎03 26 47 44 43. 48hr. before the show tickets 50F/€7.62.)

At night, the biggest concentration of people is in the cafés and bars of **pl. Drouet d'Erlon.** At **Le Kraft** (see **Food,** above) a window cut in the second floor looks down over a concert room which features jazz, salsa, blues, and world music. (Concerts free-70F/€10.67. Ask tourist office for schedule.) Hidden off rue de Vesle, tropical-style **Le Havana,** 27 rue de Vesle, is the most diverse watering hole in town; live Afro-Cuban music fills the bar every other Friday. (☎03 26 86 85 07. Happy hour daily 6-7pm, 2 beers for 14F/€2.13.) There are three **clubs** on two blocks of bd. Général Leclerc near the hostel. The best is the intimate **L'Aquarium,** 93 bd. du Général Leclerc, which blasts techno, house, and top 40. (☎03 26 47 34 29. No cover Su-Th, but 1 drink obligatory; weekend cover is 70F/€10.67 with 1 drink included. Open Su-Th 10:30pm-4am, F-Sa 10:30pm-5am. AmEx/V.) The enormous **L'Echiquier,** 110 av. Jean Jaurès, is just outside the pedestrian district—walk in a group. Three tiers of top 40, techno, and rock make for a flashy, pheromone-filled evening. (☎03 26 89 12 38. Cover 40F/€6.10. Open Th-Sa 10pm-5am. MC/V.)

Throughout July and August, Reims hosts the fantastic **Flâneries Musicales d'Eté,** with more than 100 free concerts in 60 days. For more fun, head to the cathedral every Friday and Saturday night in summer for **Cathédrale de Lumière,** a one-hour spectacle illuminating the cathedral and nearby buildings and culminating in a light show on the cathedral facade. (1hr. July 11pm, Aug. 10pm. 45F/€6.86, students 35F/€5.34, children 20F/€3.05. Buy tickets at the cathedral Th-Sa 2-7:30pm, or after 8:30pm the night of the show on the south side of the cathedral.)

DAYTRIP FROM REIMS: CHALONS-EN-CHAMPAGNE

***Trains** run from av. de la Gare to **Reims** (30min., 8 per day, 53F/€8.08) and **Paris** (1½hr., 7-10 per day, 123F/€18.75). To reach the **tourist office,** 3 quai des Arts, go left from the train station, and take another left at the roundabout onto av. Jean Jaurès and follow it across the river; the office is several blocks down, set back from the road on the left in a half-timbered mansion facing a canal (10-15min.). (☎03 26 65 17 89; fax 03 26 65 35 65. Open June-Aug. M-Sa 9am-noon and 1:30-6:30pm, Su 10:30am-12:30pm and 2:30-5:30pm; Sept.-May M-Sa 9am-noon and 1:30-6:30pm.)*

Having hidden out for years under the alias Châlons-sur-Marne, Châlons-en-Champagne (pop. 50,000) recently reverted to its original name, but not much else has changed here for centuries. As administrative center of Champagne, Châlons possesses little glamor or stunning scenery. Nevertheless, the churches and museum of this river-knit city make it a worthwhile daytrip from Reims.

Alongside the Mau canal, in one of the prettier areas of town, sits Châlons' pride, the graceful **Notre-Dame-en-Vaux.** Constructed in a mix of Romanesque and Gothic styles between 1157 and 1217, the church boasts the largest peal of bells—56—in all of Europe. (Open M-Sa 10am-noon and 2-6pm, Su 2-6pm.) Behind the church, the tiny **Cloître de Notre-Dame-en-Vaux,** rue Nicolas-Durand, displays statuary unearthed from the ancient church cloister, much of it dating from the 12th century. These statues are both beautifully detailed and virtually unique in the world. (☎03 26 64 03 87. Open Apr.-Sept. W-M 10am-noon and 2-6pm; Oct.-Mar. 10am-noon and 2-5pm. 26F/€3.96, students and children 16F/€2.44.) On the other side of the Marne River are the crypt and one remaining tower of the Romanesque **Cathédrale St-Etienne.** The remarkable stained glass ranges from the 13th to 20th centuries. (Open M-Sa 10am-noon and 2-6pm, Su 2:30-6pm.) Châlons is prettiest in the magnificently sculpted gardens along the Marne River. **Le Petit Jard,** a country garden in the style of Napoleon III, is famous for its fantastical floral clock, while the nearby **Grand Jard** is criss-crossed by vast tree-lined esplanades. Cross the bridge over the canal to reach the **Jardin Anglais,** an overgrown English-style garden. The **F'estival des Musiques d'ici et d'ailleurs** includes world, jazz, blues, and francophone music, and is held from July to mid-August at pl. de la République. (☎02 36 68 47 27; www.musiques-ici-ailleurs.com.)

EPERNAY

Situated at the juncture of three wealthy grape-growing regions, Epernay (pop. 30,000) is an appropriately ritzy town. The world's most distinguished champagne producers—Moët & Chandon, Perrier-Jouet, and Mercier, among others—have put their labels on the palatial mansions along av. de Champagne and buried their 700 million bottles of treasure in miles of subterranean tunnels. If you're just burning for bubbly, Epernay caters to connoisseurs and amateurs alike; tour a cave, raise a glass, and taste the stars. At the heart of the *Route Touristique du Champagne*, Epernay is also an excellent base for exploring the countryside. The **Champagne route** is a set of hikes through vineyards, châteaux, and mountains.

ORIENTATION AND PRACTICAL INFORMATION. Epernay loses no time introducing you to its biggest attraction; coming in by train from the east you encounter the colorful tiled roofs and blue enameled signs adorning the back of the de Castellane maison de champagne, which is situated on the self-explanatory av. de Champagne. The train station is two blocks from the central pl. de la République. **Trains** leave cours de la Gare for **Paris** (1¼hr., 18 per day, 109F/€16.62); **Reims** (25min., 16 per day, 34F/€5.19); and **Strasbourg** (4½hr., 3 per day, 223F/€34.01). (Ticket counters open Su-F 6am-8pm, Sa 6am-8pm. Info office open M-Sa 9am-6pm.) **STDM buses** (☎03 26 51 92 10) offer service to **Paris, Reims,** and many small towns in Champagne. **Local buses** are operated infrequently by **Sparnabus,** 30 pl. des Arcades. (☎03 26 55 55 50. Tickets 6.50F/€0.99, *carnet* of 10 42F/€6.41. Open M 2-6pm, Tu-F 9am-noon and 2-6pm, Sa 9am-noon.)

To get to the **tourist office,** 7 av. de Champagne, from the station, walk straight ahead through pl. Mendès France, passing a fountain, and go one block up rue Gambetta to **pl. de la République;** turn left onto av. de Champagne (5min.). The welcoming staff can outfit you with free maps, a list of hotels, info on Epernay's *caves*, and suggestions for *routes champenoises*. They also publish a free monthly guide, *On Sort?*, which lists local events and festivities. (☎03 26 53 33 00; fax 03 26 51 95 22. Open Easter-Oct. 15 M-Sa 9:30am-noon and 1:30-7pm, Su 11am-4pm; rest of year M-Sa 9:30am-12:30pm and 1:30-5:30pm.) Other services include: **currency exchange** at **Banque de France,** pl. de la République (M-F 8:45am-noon; no bills larger than US$50); the **police,** 7 rue Jean-Moët (☎03 26 56 96 60); and the **hospital,** 137 rue de l'Hôpital (☎03 26 58 70 70). Access the **Internet** at **l'Icone Café,** 25 rue de l'Hôpital Auban Moët. (☎03 26 55 73 93. 25F/€3.81 per first 30min., 20F/€3.05 next 30min. Open M noon-midnight, Tu-Th 10am-midnight, F-Sa 10am-1am, Su 3pm-midnight. MC/V.) The **post office,** pl. Hugues Plomb, has **currency exchange.** (☎03 26 53 31 60. Open M-F 8am-7pm, Sa 8am-noon.) **Postal code:** 51200.

ACCOMMODATIONS, CAMPING, AND FOOD. Epernay caters to the champagne set—budget hotels are rare. The closest hostel is in **Verzy** (20km), 14 rue du Bassin. (☎03 26 97 90 10. Breakfast included. Reception 7-10am and 5-10pm. Bunks 61F/€9.30.) For hostel-style accommodations without the ambience, try the **Foyer des Jeunes Travailleurs,** 2 rue Pupin, which maintains large, four-bed rooms with desks and sinks, laundry facilities, and a cafeteria (M-F lunch and dinner, Sa lunch only). From the station, cross the grassy square, turn left onto rue de Reims, and make an immediate right onto rue Pupin. There are only about five rooms available to travelers, so reserve ahead. (☎03 26 51 62 51; fax 03 26 54 15 60. Breakfast included. Meals 50F/€7.62. Laundry. Kitchen. Reception M-F 9am-8pm, Sa 10am-2pm. During meals, enter at 8 rue de Reims. Bunks 90F/€13.72. **Cash only.**) **Hôtel St-Pierre,** 14 av. Paul-Chandon, near pl. d'Europe, is cheap as can be. Luxuriously floral halls climb to three floors of spacious, antique-furnished rooms. (☎03 26 54 40 80; fax 03 26 57 88 68. Breakfast 29F/€4.42. Reception 7am-11pm. Singles 120-191F/€18.30-29.13; doubles 133-206F/€20.28-31.41. MC/V.) There is a **campground** about 1.5km from the station (dir: "Reims") at allée de Cumières. (☎03 26 55 32 14. Open mid-Apr. to mid-Sept. 7am-10pm. 16F/€2.44 per person, 8F/€1.22 per child, 19F/€2.90 per tent and car. Electricity 17F/€2.59.)

The pedestrian district around pl. des Arcades and pl. Hugues Plomb is dotted with delis and bakeries. There's a **Marché Plus** at 13 pl. Hugues Plomb. (☎03 26 51 89 89. Open M-Sa 7am-9pm, Su 9am-1pm.) Halle St-Thibault hosts a **market** (W and Sa 8am-noon). The cafeteria at the **Foyer** (see above) is open daily 11:30am-1:30pm. Walk your tipsy way from av. de Champagne into **Le Kilimanjara,** 15 pl. de la République. It's not a bit African, but they have a mountainous selection of salads (19-54F/€2.90-8.24), crêpes (32-62F/€4.88-9.46), pastas (45F/€6.86), and the most garish green-and-yellow decor this side of a pineapple skin. (☎03 26 51 61 60. Open W-Su noon-2pm and 7-10pm, Tu noon-2pm. MC/V.)

CONNING CONNOISSEURSHIP

Stare intently at your glass and swish dramatically before swallowing. Hold the flute by the stem to avoid warming the champagne. Refrain from smoking, wearing perfume, or eating pungent foods beforehand–anything that affects your sense of smell or taste will compromise your perception of subtle nuances. Wear warm clothes for the *caves*.

SIGHTS. The name says it all: **av. de Champagne** is a long, broad stripe of palatial *maisons de champagne* pouring out the bubbly to hordes of visitors every day. The tours below are all offered in French or English for walk-ins. All include a *petite dégustation* (ages 16+ only). *Caves* are usually around 10°C; bring a sweater. Each firm's tour may give more or less the same explanation of the process, but everything from the dress of the guides to the design of the lobby reflects the status and character of the producer. The grandpappy of them all and producers of Dom Perignon is **Moët & Chandon,** 20 av. de Champagne, who've been "turning nature into art" since 1743. You've come for old-money elegance, and you're going to get it. The 50-minute tour details the basic steps in champagne production, then gives an in-depth history of champagne and M&C in particular. The *caves* feel completely authentic, though the seven-minute film fairly tingles with pompous melodrama. (☎03 26 51 20 20. Open Apr.-Nov. 11 daily 9:30-11:30am and 2-4:30pm; Nov. 12-Mar. M-F only. Tour with one glass 40F/€6.10, two glasses 70F/€10.64, three glasses 100F/€15.25; ages 12-16 25F/€3.81, under 12 free.) Slightly less famous but equally swanky, **Mercier,** 70 av. de Champagne, is 10 minutes away, in the middle of a vineyard. The self-proclaimed "most popular champagne in France" certainly knows how to market itself. The film is little more than a slickly-scored advert, but their 30-minute tour, in roller coaster-style cars, is a kick. (☎03 26 51 22 22. Open Mar.-Nov. M-F 9:30-11:30am and 2-4:30pm, Sa-Su until 5pm; Dec. 1-19 and Jan. 13-Feb. Th-M only. 25F/€3.81, ages 12-16 20F/€3.04, under 12 free.) Across the street is **De Castellane,** 57 rue de Verdun, supplier to the famed Parisian restaurant Maxim's. Their tower has a magnificent view of the valley below, and roaring-20s lovers will dig their collection of posters from the age of flappers and before. (☎03 26 51 19 11. Open Apr.-Dec. 24 daily 10am-noon and 2-6pm, last tours 11:15am and 5:15pm. Full *cave* tour with tasting 35F/€5.34; tower and museum with tasting 20F/€3.05.) **Demoiselle Vranken,** 42 rue de Champagne, is a relatively new arrival. The lively, hip staff leads much smaller and more casual tours than the larger firms, accented with jazz recordings. (☎03 26 59 50 50. Open M-F 9am-noon and 2-5:30pm, Sa 9:30am-noon and 2-4:30pm, closed Sa Oct.-Apr. 20F/€3.05.)

For a laid-back and cheap, but nonetheless authentic, alternative to the big maisons, ask the tourist office about *l'esprit de champagne,* a free presentation and sampling given by several of the smaller companies directly in the tourist office from June to the end of October (F-Sa). Tickets must be obtained in advance.

ENTERTAINMENT. The city's watering holes are flooded with people until the wee hours. **Le Progrès,** 5 pl. de la République, draws a mix of 20-somethings and their elders for lingering, languorous champagne-sipping on its packed terrace. (☎03 26 55 22 72. Food served daily 11:20am-2:30pm, bar also 7-11pm.) From the end of June to the third week in August, free **concerts** are held at 7pm at the Château Perrier on av. de Champagne (classical Tu, jazz Th; occasional rock and world music at pl. Mendès France).

TROYES

With its principal roads cleverly forming the shape of the bouchon (cork) of a champagne bottle, Troyes (pronounced "trwah") may lead its visitors to wonder whether its city plan is a serendipitous historical quirk or a tourist gimmick. In any case, there is no denying the rich history of Troyes, a capital city dating back to the Middle Ages. Chrétien de Troyes wrote his *Parsifal* here, Rabbi Rachi translated the Bible and the Talmud, and a local shoemaker's son became Pope Urbain IV. Now Troyes has one of France's best-preserved old city centers, with distinctive half-timbered mansions dominating the *vieille ville.*

TRANSPORTATION

Trains: av. Maréchal Joffre (☎08 36 35 35 35 for info and reservations). To **Mulhouse** (3hr., 6 per day, 205F/€31.25) and **Paris** (1½hr., 10 per day, 120F/€18.30). **Info** open M-F 8:45-11:45am and 2-6:45pm, Sa 9:10-11:45am and 2-6:15pm. Station open M-Sa 4:30am-9pm, Su 6am-9:30pm.

Buses: Go left as you exit the train station and enter the door just around the corner labeled Gare Routière. **Courriers de l'Aube** (☎03 25 71 28 42) is located here. Info and tickets are also available here for **SDTM TransChampagne** (☎03 26 65 17 07), which goes to **Reims** (2hr., 2 per day, 112F/€17.08) and **Les Rapides de Bourgogne** (☎03 86 94 95 00), which goes to **Auxerre** (2½hr., M-Th 1 per day, 85F/€12.96).

Local Transportation: L'Autoville (☎03 25 70 49 00), in front of the market. Extensive and frequent service. Tickets 7F/€1.07, 3 for 18F/€2.74. Open M-Sa 8am-12:45pm and 1:30-7pm.

Taxis: Taxis Troyens (☎03 25 78 30 30), across the street from the station on the curb in front of the Grand Hôtel. Service Su-Th 4am-midnight, F-Sa 24hr.

Car Rental: Europcar, 6 av. President Coty (☎03 25 78 37 66). Open 7:30am-12:30pm and 1:30-6:30pm. **Budget,** 10 rue Voltaire (☎03 25 73 27 37). Open daily 8am-noon and 2-6:30pm.

ORIENTATION AND PRACTICAL INFORMATION

Troyes' train station is just three blocks from the *vieille ville*. The main tourist office is one block from the train station exit, on your right, at the corner of bd. Carnot; another is found near the town center on rue Mignard.

Tourist Office: 16 bd. Carnot (☎03 25 82 62 70; www.ot-troyes.fr) and rue Mignard off rue Emile Zola (☎03 25 73 36 88). Free detailed city map. Accommodations service with deposit. Both branches open M-Sa 9am-12:30pm and 2-6:30pm; rue Mignard branch also open Su 10am-noon and 2-5pm.

Cultural Center: Maison du Boulanger, 16 rue Champeaux (☎03 25 43 55 00; tickets and administration around the corner at 42 Paillot de Montabert). Info on festivals, exhibits, and concerts. Open M-F 9am-noon and 2-6pm, Sa 10am-noon and 2-5pm.

Money: Société Générale, 11 pl. Maréchal Foch (☎03 25 43 57 00; fax 03 25 43 57 57), has **currency exchange.** Open M-F 8:30am-12:20pm and 1:30-5:30pm. When banks are closed, the **tourist office** on rue Mignard (see above) will exchange currency.

Laundromat: 11 rue Clemenceau (☎03 25 73 93 46). Open daily 7:30am-8pm.

Police: ☎03 25 43 51 00. In an **emergency** dial 17.

Hospital: 101 av. Anatole France (☎03 25 49 49 49). For emergency medical service, call 03 25 71 99 00 or 15.

Post Office: 2 pl. Général Patton (☎03 25 45 29 00). From the train station, turn right onto bd. Carnot and walk down one block. Open M-F 9am-noon and 1:30-6:30pm, Sa 9am-noon. **Poste Restante:** 10013 Troyes-Voltaire. **Postal code:** 10000.

ACCOMMODATIONS AND CAMPING

Les Comtes de Champagne, 56 rue de la Monnaie (☎03 25 73 11 70; fax 03 25 73 06 02). On a quiet street just minutes from both the train station and city center. It's hard to imagine a nicer place to stay in Troyes than this 16th-century mansion. Reserve ahead. Breakfast 32F/€4.88. Most rooms have TVs. Reception 7am-11pm. Singles with shared shower 160F/€24.39, with private shower 200F/€30.49; doubles from 180F/€27.44, 220F/€33.54; triples 290F-360F/€44.21-54.89; quads 320F-380F/€48.79-57.94; some large rooms fit 5 or 6. Extra bed 32F/€4.88. DC/V.

Hôtel Ambassy Club, 49 rue Raymond Poincaré (☎03 25 73 12 03). With the town hall to your left, proceed down rue de la République as it becomes rue Raymond Poincaré. The hotel is 3 blocks down on the left, above a smoky brasserie. Breakfast 30F/€4.57. Reception (at bar) 7am-3am. Singles 135F/€20.58; one double and one triple 160F/€24.39 per person. AmEx/MC/V.

Camping Municipal, (☎03 25 81 02 64), on N60 2km from town. Take bus #1 (dir: "Pont St-Marie") to this 3-star site. Campers can enjoy all that nature stuff without forfeiting the creature comforts of showers, toilets, TV, and laundry. Open Apr. 1-Oct. 15. 25F/€3.81 per person, 30F/€4.57 per tent or car.

CHAMPAGNE

FOOD

The **quartier St-Jean** is the place to be for a meal and some local chatter; cafés, brasseries, and inexpensive crêperies line the pedestrian **rue Champeaux** on the way to pl. Alexandre Israël. On the other side of the *vieille ville*, reasonably priced international eateries can be found on **rue de la Cité** near the cathedral.

Les Halles, an English-style market behind the bus station (turn left down rue de la République from the town hall), offers a fresh selection of produce, meats, and baked goods from the Aube region. Try creamy *fromage de Troyes* or the *andouillette de Troyes*, a popular tripe sausage. (Open M-Th 8am-12:45pm and 3:30-7pm, F-Sa 7am-7pm, Su 9am-12:30pm. Many stalls take MC/V.) Grab generic grub at the **Monoprix** supermarket, 71 rue Emile Zola. (☎03 25 73 10 78. Open M-Sa 8:30am-8pm.) It would be a shame not to take full advantage of Troyes' beautiful parks—the pl. de la Libération is the perfect setting for a mid-afternoon snack.

Aux Crieurs de Vin, 4-6 pl. Jean Jaurès (☎03 25 40 01 01). This cool, minimalist eatery is part restaurant, part wine cellar. The knowledgeable staff will help you choose the perfect local wine. Open Tu-Sa 10am-2pm and 7:30-10:30pm; bar 11am-11pm; *cave* M 3-7pm, Tu-Sa 10am-9pm. MC/V.

Belle Epoque, 67 rue Urbain IV (☎03 25 73 49 84). The happily slapdash interior combines medieval timbering with a touch of *fin-de-siècle* class. 72F/€10.98 gets you a sampling of traditional favorites, including a warm salad of andouillette and brie. Open daily noon-2pm and 7-10pm. MC/V.

SIGHTS AND OUTDOORS

CATHEDRALE ST-PIERRE ET ST-PAUL. While the sheer verticality of the cathedral, with thin fluted pillars, is stunning, its largest attraction is the stained glass. Ranging in age from 100 to 700 years, the *vitraux* are in many cases as delicate as lace. Come in the late morning to see the kaleidoscopic light of the east rose window scattered on the floor. Although the cathedral has suffered invasions and natural disasters galore, its frequent rebuilding now provides a glimpse of the evolution of Troyen architecture. *(Pl. St-Pierre. Head down rue Clemenceau from the town hall until you reach the place. Enter the courtyard to the right of the cathedral; the entrance to the museum is on the right. ☎03 25 76 26 80. Open daily 10am-noon and 2-5pm.)*

MUSEE D'ART MODERNE. This collection of over 2000 works of French art from 1850 to 1950 is Troyes' cultural centerpiece. Alongside sculptures, paintings, and drawings by Degas, Rodin, Picasso, and Seurat is a collection of African and Oceanian sculpture, arranged to highlight its influence on 20th-century French art. The sculpture garden out back is not to be missed. *(Pl. St-Pierre; directions as above. Open Tu-Su 11am-6pm; 40F/€6.10, children 10F/€1.53; free W.)*

BASILIQUE ST-URBAIN. Walk by the basilica at night to see the spear-like spires illuminated against the sky, or visit in daylight to appreciate its flying buttresses. The archetypally Gothic 1261 structure, founded when Jacques Pantaléon became Pope Urbain IV, lies on the site of his father's cobbler shop. *(Walk down rue Clemenceau from the Hôtel de Ville. ☎03 25 73 37 13. Open daily 10am-noon and 2-5 pm.)*

MUSEE DES BEAUX-ARTS. Housed in the old Abbaye St-Loup, this museum displays an array of archaeological finds, medieval sculptures, and 15th- to 19th-century paintings. It also houses one of France's oldest libraries; many of the 85,000 volumes inside are 1300 years old. *(4 rue Chrétien-de-Troyes, near the cathedral. Walking from the canal along rue de la Cité, take a left on rue Mitantier; the entrance is on this street, to the left. ☎03 25 76 21 60. Open W-M 10am-noon and 2-6pm. 30F/€4.57, students and children 5F/€0.76, free W. Ticket includes access to Musée de la Pharmacie and Musée de Vauluisant.)*

OTHER SIGHTS. Troyes' museums are rich in local social history, particularly in the craft traditions that have put it on the map since medieval times. The **Maison de l'Outil et de la Pensée Ouvrière** is a beautifully restored 16th-century *hôtel*. Once the central workshop of the town's knitwear industry, it now houses over 7000 tools owned by 17th- and 18th-century craftsmen. *(7 rue de la Trinité, off rue Emile Zola. ☎03 25 73 28 26. Open M-F 9am-1pm and 2-6:30pm, Sa-Su 10am-1pm and 2-6pm. 40F/€6.10, students 30F/€4.57, families 100F/€15.25.)* The Musée de Vauluisant houses not only a collection of medieval Troyen sculpture but also the textile-oriented Musée de la Bonneterie and a history of tile-making in the cool cave below. *(4 rue de Vauluisant. ☎03 25 42 33 33. Open W-Su 10am-noon and 2-6pm.)* The 12th-century **Eglise Ste-Madeleine,** off ruelle des Chats (a covered alleyway so named because the houses are packed together tightly enough for cats to stroll from roof to roof), is home to an impressive stone screen separating the nave from the chancel. *(☎03 25 73 82 90. Open M-Sa 10am-noon and 2-5pm, Su 2-5pm.)*

EXCURSIONS. Troyes is near over 12,500 acres of freshwater lakes. The sunny waters of Lake Orient welcome sunbathers, swimmers, and windsurfers. Wilder Lake Temple is reserved for fishing and bird watching, and Lake Amance roars with speedboats, some tugging waterskiers. The **Comité Départemental du Tourisme de l'Aube,** 34 quai Dampierre, provides free brochures. *(☎03 25 42 50 00; fax 03 25 42 50 88. Open M-F 8:45am-noon and 1:30-6pm.)* The tourist office has bus schedules for the Troyes-Grands Lacs routes.

ENTERTAINMENT

Movie theaters, arcades, and pool halls neighbor chic boutiques on **rue Emile Zola.** On warm evenings, *Troyens* swarm the cafés and taverns of **rue Champeaux** and **rue Mole** near pl. Alexandre Israël. If you don't mind chain restaurants, the Alsatian brasserie **La Taverne de Maître Kanter,** 4 rue Champeaux, atones for its corporate aspects by having prime seating for summer concerts in front of the town hall. (☎03 25 73 25 60. Open daily 11:30am-midnight.) If you seek authentic local cuisine, head just up the road to the newly established **Café-Restaurant l'Union,** 34 rue Champeaux, which serves up traditional favorites to traditional folk on its private terrace. (☎03 25 40 35 76. Open noon-2pm and 7-11pm, bar 11am-3am.) The gregarious owner and loyal pub crowd at **Bar Montabert,** 24 rue Paillot de Montabert, like their beer. (☎03 25 73 58 04. Open daily noon-3pm and 6pm-3am.)

Outside of imbibing, Troyes offers a number of festivals and special events throughout the summer. **Le Chemin des Bâtisseurs de Cathédrales** is a free sound-and-light spectacle held in the Cathedral of St-Rémy on Friday and Saturday nights at 10pm, from the last weekend in June to the end of the summer. Troyes' **Ville en Musique,** a series of concerts held in churches or the open air, also occurs in the summer. (☎03 25 43 55 00 or stop by the Cultural Center for more info.)

MINI CHAMPAGNE GUIDE **Brut:** very dry; **Demi-sec:** somewhat sweet; **Sec:** sweet; **Nectar:** a very sweet champagne.

With these variations, it's not just a matter of adding a different amount of sugar before the final bottling, which is done in all cases, but there are actually different processes for each. The three types of grapes used are **Sauvignon** (a white grape), **Pinot Noir** (a red grape) and **Pinot Meunier** (also a red grape). Care must be taken in pressing the red grapes not to let the color of the skin infuse the juice. In the case of "rosé champagne," brut champagne is mixed with red wine.

Aging: Finished champagnes do NOT improve with age, so don't buy one as an "investment." A commercial champagne will be good for three years, a vintage for about five, Dom Perignon a maximum of ten. Champagnes continue to improve with age as long as they have sediment in them, but once they are degorged (sediment removed) and corked, they are already depreciating.

CHAUMONT

The lush panoramic view of the Marne and Suize valleys, seen from the train to Chaumont as it passes above a 19th-century aqueduct spanning the two valleys, is alone worth the trip to this quiet, steep-streeted town. Chaumont's mansion-studded *vieille ville* dates from the days when it was the seat of the Counts of Champagne. The 18th-century sculptor Jean-Baptiste Bouchardon was born and died in Chaumont, and his works still decorate the streets alongside the hip two-tone posters and experimental photography of the modern graphic design school.

ORIENTATION AND PRACTICAL INFORMATION. The heart of the *vieille ville* is a twisted knot of streets a few minutes' walk from the train station. To get there, walk straight ahead from the tourist office to the roundabout, and veer slightly to your right onto rue de la Tour Charton. From this road you will have the best panoramic view of the old city; continue to the end of the road and turn onto rue Mgr. Desprez; the Basilique St-Jean will be two blocks ahead. **Trains** (pl. du Général de Gaulle) roll to: **Paris** (8-10 per day, 171F/€26.07); **Reims** (5 per day, 135F/€20.58); and **Troyes** (8 per day, 78F/€11.89). Zip around town on *Le Bus*, the **local bus service,** 7 rue Jules Trefousse (☎03 25 01 88 42), or rent your own transport at: **Avis,** pl. Aristide Briand (☎03 25 32 00 79; open M-F 8:30am-noon and 2-6:30pm); **Europcar,** 9 rte. de Neuilly (☎03 25 31 50 19); or **Hertz,** rte. de Neuilly (☎03 25 32 66 06). Across from the station, the **tourist office,** pl. de la Gare, gives out a free map and an audio guide in English (25F/€3.81), and also **exchanges currency.** (☎03 25 03 80 80. Open July-Aug. M-F 9am-7pm; Sept.-June M-Sa 9:30am-12:30pm; Su year-round 10am-noon and 2-5pm.) **Société Générale,** rue Victoire de la Marne, also **changes currency.** (☎03 25 03 97 97. Open Tu-F 8:45am-noon and 1:40-6:15pm, Sa 8:45am-noon and 1:40-4:25pm.) Access the Internet at the **Net'Café,** 27 rue Champs du Mars, near pl. Aristide Briand. (☎03 25 02 92 76. 42F/€6.40 per hr. Open M-Sa 6am-8pm.) The **police** are at 1 and 3 av. Carnot (☎03 25 03 85 30), and the **hospital** at 2 rue Jeanne d'Arc (☎03 25 30 70 30). The **post office,** 39 rue Victoire de la Marne (☎03 25 30 66 81), is up the road from the town hall. **Postal code:** 52000.

ACCOMMODATIONS AND CAMPING. In Le Cavalier, a district south of the town center, there is an **Auberge de Jeunesse et Foyer des Jeunes Travailleurs (HI)** at 1 rue Carcassonne. From the train station, walk straight a block to pl. Gougenheim, take a sharp right onto rue du 21ème RIC, walk over the bridge above the train tracks, and cross the street (bd. Thiers). Turn right, and take the first left onto rue L. Alphandéry. Follow this road for about 1km, then turn left on rue du Cavalier; the foyer lies at the end of the road (15min.). *Le Bus* stops at the nearby stop "Suize"; call 03 25 01 88 42 for current schedule and bus number. This dorm-like building houses travelers and permanent residents in small, poorly-lit but clean rooms. (☎03 25 03 22 77. Breakfast included. Lunch and dinner 47.10F/€7.18. Sheets 17F/€2.59. Reception 9am-noon and 3-7pm. Singles or doubles 76F/€11.59 per person.) If you're not opposed to spending just a few more francs, the best value is the **Hôtel-Brasserie St-Jean,** 2 pl. Aristide Briand. Follow av. Victoire de la Marne to bd. Barotte and turn right. Take a left around the grassy sq. de Boulingrin and walk a block; the hotel will be on the corner to your right. Above a cheerful but quiet brasserie; bright, clean, pastel-colored rooms with TV. (☎03 25 03 00 79; fax 03 25 03 08 81. Breakfast 25F/€3.81. Singles 135F/€20.58, with bath 185F/€28.21; doubles with bath 230F/€35.07; triples with bath 300F/€45.74. MC/V.)

Rough it at **Camping Municipal,** rue des Tanneries. From the train station, follow rue de la Tour Charton from the roundabout in front of the station to sq. Bad Nauheim, then turn left onto rue des Tanneries (20min. on foot). (☎03 25 32 11 98; fax 03 25 02 59 50. 30F/€4.57 per tent, plus 12F/€1.83 per person, 6F/€0.91 per child under age 7. Electricity 13F/€1.98. Dogs 6F/€0.91. Open May-Sept.)

FOOD. Standard pâtisseries, cafés, pizzerias, and a smattering of brasseries, as well as a shameful amount of fast-food eateries, line **rue Victoire de la Marne** and **rue Verdun. Les Halles,** off rue Clemenceau, displays the bounty of nearby farms on Wednesdays and Saturdays. For your basic grocery needs, **Marché Plus** is centrally located on rue Victoire de la Marne. (Open M-Sa 7am-9pm, Su 9am-1pm.) **Bleu Comme Orange,** 11 rue St-Louis, off rue Victoire de la Marne, offers a rock-and-roll take on the traditional crêperie. Regional specialties like tripe sausage are served up in crêpes and galettes with names like Santana, Dylan, and Peter Gabriel. Take advantage of the express lunch: galette, crêpe, cider, and coffee for 50F/€7.62. (☎03 25 01 26 87. Open 11:45am-2pm and 7-11pm.) **Le Palmier,** 16 rue Victoire Mariotte, is a culinary crossroads, offering a variety of pizzas, couscous, and traditional French fare. (☎03 25 32 67 22. Open M-Sa noon-2pm and 7-11pm.)

SIGHTS. Chaumont retains a few monuments to its former medieval glory. The **Donjon** is all that remains of the castle of the Counts of Champagne. Built between the 11th and 12th centuries on a bluff overlooking the Suize Valley, the squat tower has served as a defensive outpost, a barracks, and a jail. The view of the lush hills below is unforgettable and free if you skip the climb to the top and take it in from the terrace at the base. (Tower open July-Sept. 15 M, W-Sa 2:30-6:30pm, Su 2:30-7pm. 5F/€0.76, students free.) Follow the steps down from the garden to the **Musée d'Art et d'Histoire,** which offers local goodies ranging from sexy 9th-century armor, to inevitable Bouchardons, to the amusingly anachronistic main gallery, in which a photograph of Mitterand gazes pensively at a sculpted 17th-century bishop. Both the Donjon and the museum are located at the end of rue du Palais, behind the Palais de la Justice. (Open July-Sept.15 W-M 2:30-6:30pm; Sept.16-June 30 W-M 2-6pm.) Walk up rue du Palais away from the Donjon and turn left on rue Desprez to reach the **Basilique St-Jean-Baptiste,** whose colorless glass windows shed light on Renaissance paintings and numerous wooden carvings by the celebrated J.B. Bouchardon. The students of the local Ecole de Musique make the most of the basilica's mighty organ pipes with free concerts throughout the year; schedules are available in the narthex and at the Ecole de Musique (12 rue Dutailly).

ENTERTAINMENT. Evening entertainment in Chaumont consists primarily of hopping between its several bars, most of which cluster around the streets near **pl. de la Concorde.** Be forewarned, however, that closing times may be early if the bars don't draw a good crowd. **La Concorde** (☎03 25 32 54 54), a brasserie just across from the Hôtel de Ville, offers a good eye- and earful of student life. For a more low-down, smoky, dart-throwing evening, try **Café le Khedive,** 32/34 rue Victoire Mariotte, off rue Verdun (☎03 25 03 62 77). This aspiring "Irish" pub offers the occasional cover band and plenty of good-humored ruckus.

Les Silos, 79 av. Foch, is by far the coolest cultural playground in Chaumont; this former agricultural co-op now houses a graphic design studio, *mediathèque* (multimedia library), and exhibition space. Visitors can use the extensive facilities, including books, newspapers, Internet access, CD-ROMs, CDs, and videos, for free. (☎03 25 03 86 86. Open Tu and Th-F 2-7pm, W and Sa 10am-6pm. Su 2-6pm exhibition space only.)

LANGRES

Perched prettily above the fertile Marne valley, tiny Langres (pop. 10,000) deserves its reputation as one of France's 50 most beautiful towns. Because of its height and central position between Champagne, Burgundy, and Franche-Comté, the town was a Roman stronghold. Years later, it became known as the birthplace of philosopher Denis Diderot, of encyclopedia fame (see p. 18). To walk on the well-preserved defensive ramparts of this friendly and charmingly proud little town is to feel, both literally and metaphorically, on top of the world.

CHAMPAGNE

ORIENTATION AND PRACTICAL INFORMATION. Langres sits 3km away—and half a kilometer up—from its train station. **Trains** roll north to **Paris** (3hr., 4 per day, 187F/€28.51) and west to **Reims** (2½hr., 5 per day, 153F/€23.33) and **Troyes** (1¼hr., 5 per day, 99F/€15.09). **Local buses** (5.50F/€0.84) run frequently between the station and the town center, so there's no need to make the sweaty hike. Schedules of departure times and stops are posted at the train station and are also available at the tourist office. The impatient can call a **taxi** (☎03 25 87 47 31), while the brave can **rent bikes** from **Diderot Cycles et Loisirs,** 67 rue Diderot (☎03 25 87 06 98; open Tu-Sa 8:30am-noon and 2-7pm). The **tourist office,** located in sq. Olivier Halle, is just across from the pl. Bel'Air bus stop. The friendly staff provides a free and very useful regional guide and reserves rooms for 5F/€0.76. (☎03 25 87 67 67. Open July-Aug. M-Sa 9am-12:30pm and 1:30-7pm, Su 10am-12:30pm and 2-6pm; May-June and Sept. M-Sa 9:30am-noon and 1:30-6:30pm, Su 10am-12:30pm and 2-6pm; Oct.-Apr. M-Sa 9:30am-noon and 1:30-6pm.) The tourist office provides **audio guides** in English (20F/€3.05). You can also rumble along the ramparts for an hour on the shameful *train touristique.* (Leaves from pl. Bel'Air, across from the tourist office. July-Aug. 7 departures daily 10am-6pm; May-June and Sept. 3 departures W and Sa-Su afternoons. Tickets 30F/€4.57, 20F/€3.05 for children.) The **police** are at the Hôtel de Ville on rue Charles Beligne (☎03 25 87 00 40). Medical care is available at the **Centre Hospitalier,** 10 rue de la Charité (☎03 25 87 88 88). On Mondays, the only **currency exchange** option is at the **post office,** rue Général Leclerc. (☎03 25 84 33 30. Open M-F 8am-noon and 1:30-6pm, Sa 8am-noon.) **Postal code:** 52200.

CHAMPAGNE

ACCOMMODATIONS AND CAMPING. Set right outside the Porte des Moulins by the tourist office, the **Foyer des Jeunes Travailleurs (HI),** pl. Bel'Air, offers pleasant, modern dorm rooms, kitchen access, and an adjoining cafeteria. It's slightly institutional, but it has outstanding views and is the best bargain in town. (☎03 25 87 09 69. Breakfast 17F/€2.59. Lunch daily 11:45am-1:30pm, dinner 7-11pm; *plats* 30F/€4.57. Sheets 17F/€2.59. Reception M-F 8:45am-12:45pm and 2-7pm, Sa 10:30am-noon. Singles 72F/€10.98; doubles 100F/€15.25. Discount after 4 nights. Cash only.) The **Hôtel de la Poste,** 8 & 10 pl. Ziegler, is a comfortable, inexpensive, and centrally located old hotel with 35 medium-sized rooms that would seem spacious were their ceilings not covered in garish wallpaper. (☎03 25 87 10 51; fax 03 25 88 46 18. Breakfast 30F/€4.57. Reception M-F 7am-1am, Sa-Su 7am-1:30pm. Singles 99-120F/€15.09-18.30, with shower 180F/€27.44; doubles and triples 130-220F/€19.82-33.54, 180-270F/€27.44-41.16. MC/V.) In a pinch, try the smaller and more expensive **Auberge Jeanne d'Arc,** 26 rue Gambetta, on pl. Jenson across from Eglise St-Martin, which has small but elegant rooms. (☎03 25 87 03 18. Breakfast 40F/€6.10. Reception 24hr. Singles with bath 180F/€27.44; doubles with bath 250-280F/€38.12-42.69; triples with bath 340F/€51.84. MC/V.)

Camping Navarre occupies prime hilltop space right next to the 16th-century Tour de Navarre at the edge of the old town, with fabulous views over the ramparts. (☎/fax 03 25 88 14 93. Reception July-Aug. 6-8am and 4-10:30pm; Sept.-June 6-8am and 4-8pm. Gates closed 10pm-6:30am. 11F/€1.68, 7F/€1.07 under 7, 23F/€3.51 with tent or car. Electricity 18F/€2.74.)

REINVENTING DIDEROT. For more than 40 years, the students of the local Collège Diderot have cheered on their graduation at the expense of their celebrated namesake and fellow Langrois. Each year at the end of May, the students dress poor Diderot in themed costumes to mark the end of their high school careers. "Zon Zon," as the statue is affectionately called, generally remains in costume for more than a week. In past manifestations, the hapless philosopher has become a hippie, a priest, and, because kids will be kids, he has also been endowed with a 1.5m phallus, complete with condom. This year he was dressed up as a member of *Loft Story*–one of the newest and most popular TV shows around, a variation of MTV's *Real World* in which 20-somethings live together until voted off the show.

FOOD. From fresh *foie gras* to the soft orange-cased *fromage de Langres* to the local sweet currant apéritif *rubis de groseilles*, Langrois' *specialités de terroir* are still made the old-fashioned way: on the farm. Many of these farms provide *dégustation* tours; the regional guide available at the tourist office provides contact info for these farms. For those who wish to stay within the city walls, there are a number of ways to delve into Langrois cuisine. The **market,** at pl. Jenson, is open Friday mornings, and cafés on the side streets near pl. Diderot offer plates of *fromage de Langres*. Look for cheap, generic goods just outside at **Aldi** supermarket, rue des Chavannes just before pl. Bel'Air. (Open M-F 9am-12:15pm and 2-7pm, Sa 9am-7pm.) Restaurants, like everything else in town, keep close to **rue Diderot. Café DeFoy,** pl. Diderot, serves up fresh local specials. Everybody orders the salad with walnuts and warm *fromage de Langres*, although you might not want to pass up the *formule rapide*, the dish of the day with dessert and coffee for 62F/€9.45. (☎03 25 87 09 86. Open daily until 11pm. MC/V.)

SIGHTS. The ramparts have been the soul of Langres for millennia, and you'll happen on a number of sights as you tramp along them. A good starting point is the squat **Tour de Navarre,** on the southeast corner. Opened in 1521 by François Ier, its 7m-thick walls and spiral ramp for moving artillery recall its effectiveness as a defensive outpost. (Tower open July-Aug. daily 10am-12:30pm and 2:30-7pm; May-June and Sept. Sa-Su 2:30-5:30pm. 15F/€2.29, students 10F/€1.53.) The first-century AD **Porte Gallo-Romane,** toward the center of the south wall, is the oldest of the seven gates piercing the fortifications; only from the outside, as you leave the ramparts, can you make out its arches. Farther clockwise stands the **Tour du Petit Sault,** which has an unobstructed view over the Marne Valley and the wooded Montagne Langroise. On the north wall one lonely and immobile train car remains as memorial to the **Old Cog Railway,** the first mechanical contraption devised by the Langrois to link their town to the valley below. **Place de la Crémaillère,** just after the railway, overlooks farmland and the glittering **réservoir de la Liez,** a nearby lake offering swimming, boating, and camping. A few steps ahead lies the **Table d'Orientation,** a fun 19th-century panel identifying visible landmarks as well as far-flung destinations like Moscow and Constantinople. Last is the zippy glass-and-steel **Panoramics,** a 20th-century answer to the cog railway, which whisks down to the parking lot and the road below at all hours of the day free of charge.

The best view in town is not from the ramparts but from the south tower of the **Cathédrale Mammès,** which dominates the center of town. Built between 1150 and 1196, the cathedral is an impressive combination of Burgundian-Romanesque and Gothic styles. It was given the name and patronage of St-Mammès when the relics of this poor disemboweled Roman shepherd were donated to Langres. Note the pillars in front of the altar, where you can peek at the two gold reliquaries housing the grisly remains of the saint. (Cathedral open daily 8am-7pm. Free. Tower and treasury open July-Aug. W-M 2:30-6pm. 10F/€1.53, students 8F/€1.22.) On Friday and Saturday nights in August, locals in full Renaissance costume divvy themselves into five groups to recreate the night watchman's patrol—the **Ronde des Hallebardiers**—of more turbulent times. If your French is up to par, get your cape, and gallivant about the town banishing the bandits and spooks of yore; otherwise chortle over the proceedings along the sidelines. It all ends in music and drink at a Renaissance tavern. (Begins at the cathedral cloister at 9:15pm.)

In the center of town sits the **Musée d'Art et d'Histoire,** pl. du Centenaire, with Egyptian artifacts and a Roman mosaic. Though the panels are in French, its impressive visuals make it worthwhile for non-French speakers. (☎03 25 87 08 05. Open W-M 10am-noon and 2-6pm. 21F/€3.20, students 11F/€1.68.)

FLANDERS AND THE PAS DE CALAIS

Even after five decades of peace, the memory of two world wars is never far from the inhabitants of northern France. Nearly every town bears scars from merciless bombing in World War II, and German-built concrete observation towers still peer over the dunes. Regiments of tombstones stand as reminders of the terrible toll exacted at Arras, Cambrai, and the Somme.

Flanders (on the Belgian border), the coastal Pas de Calais, and Picardy (farther inland) remain the final frontiers of tourist-free France. Although thousands traveling to and from Britain pass through the channel ports every day, few take the time to explore the ancient towns between the ports and Paris. This has left the countryside unspoiled by commercial traffic and the natives welcoming to travelers. Chalk cliffs loom over the beaches along the rugged coast, and cultivation gives way to cows and sheep grazing near collapsed bunkers. Once part of an independent state, the wooden windmills and gabled houses still show Flemish influence. In Picardy, seas of wheat extend in all directions, broken in spring and summer by eruptions of red poppies. As you flee the ferry ports, don't overlook the hidden treasures: the cathedrals of Amiens and Laon, the intriguing Flemish culture of Arras, the world-class art collections of Lille, and the rural charm of small towns like Montreuil-sur-Mer, whose imposing ramparts top a green valley.

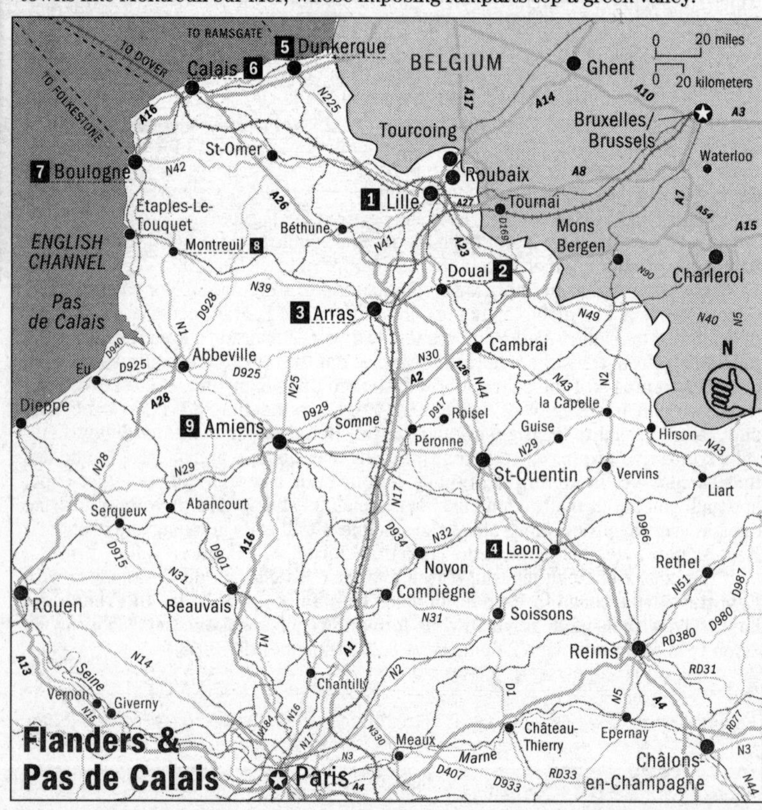

TRANSPORTATION

A logical base for a visit to the North is **Lille,** capital of the region and a major transportation hub. Getting to smaller towns often involves changing trains in **Amiens.** Ferries usually dock in the **Channel Ports,** where no one wants to linger; **Boulogne** is the most pleasant port of arrival. The **Channel Tunnel** connects France to Britain at Calais and provides a viable alternative to ferries (for more info, see **Getting There: By Channel Tunnel,** p. 62). The countryside is flat enough to allow bicycling, but towns are far apart. Consult local tourist offices for maps and routes.

1 **Lille:** Big city; lots of foreigners; untouristed for its size and appeal; great baroque **(p. 445)**
2 **Douai:** A quintessentially Flemish town, with a belfry and canal **(p. 449)**
3 **Arras:** Known for its gabled houses, chalk tunnels, and nearby WWI memorials **(p. 450)**
4 **Laon:** One of France's finest cathedrals–*really.* Check out the fabulous views **(p. 453)**
5 **Dunkerque:** Minor channel port famous for the Allied scramble there; don't go **(p. 457)**
6 **Calais:** Lively ferry port flooded with British tourists; don't stay **(p. 456)**
7 **Boulogne-sur-Mer:** Most genial of the Channel ports; exceptional fine-arts museum **(p. 454)**
8 **Montreuil:** A surprisingly stylish, art-loving, flower-lined little town **(p. 459)**
9 **Amiens:** More lively than most; known for its cathedral and floating gardens **(p. 460)**

LILLE

Lille (pop. 175,000) has been an international hub since the 11th century, and still accommodates tourists regularly. Charles de Gaulle's hometown retains a Flemish flavor, from its architecture to its inhabitants' rabid consumption of mussels and beer. France's fourth-largest city is much more inviting than the region's gaudy ports; shopping and strolling, drinking and thinking are all hassle-free in the *vieille ville* of this large, but simple city. Lille deserves a day or two on a northeastern itinerary, more for its urbanity than for any specific sights.

TRANSPORTATION

Flights: Aéroport de Lille-Lesquin (☎03 20 49 68 68). Cariane Nord **shuttles** (☎03 20 90 79 79; 5-6 per day M-F 5am-11pm, weekends according to flight times; 30F/€4.57) leave from rue le Corbusier at Gare Lille Europe.

Trains: Lille has two stations. One is **Gare Lille Flandres,** pl. de la Gare. To: **Arras** (40min., 19 per day, 54F/€8.23); **Brussels,** Belgium (1½hr., 20 per day, 135F/€20.58); and **Paris** (1hr., 21 per day, 212-287F/€32.32-43.76). **Currency exchange.** Info desk open M-Sa 9am-7pm. The other is **Gare Lille Europe,** rue le Corbusier (☎08 36 35 35 35), M: Gare Lille Europe. It services **Eurostar** (to **London** and **Brussels**) and all **TGVs** to the south of France, as well as to **Paris** (1hr., 4 per day, 212-287F/€32.32-43.76). **SOS Voyageurs** (☎03 20 31 62 12), on track 9 in Gare Lille Flandres, helps travelers in dire straits. Open M-F 9am-1pm and 2-6pm.

Local Transportation: The **Transpole** central **bus terminal** is next to the train station. **Métro (M)** and **trams** serve the town and periphery daily 5:12am-12:12am. Tickets 7.50F/€1.14, *carnet* of 10 65F/€9.91. Info at the tourist office or the office below Gare Flandres (☎03 20 40 40 40). Kiosks open M-F 7am-7pm, Sa 9am-5pm.

Taxis: Taxi Union (☎03 20 06 06 06).

Bike Rental: Peugeot Cycles, 64 rue Léon Gambetta (☎03 20 54 83 39). 50F/€7.62 per day. 1000F/€152.46 deposit. Open Tu-Sa 9am-12:30pm and 2-7pm. MC/V.

ORIENTATION AND PRACTICAL INFORMATION

Lille is easy to navigate, and has a métro, but get a map before tackling ***vieille Lille,*** a maze of narrow streets running from the tourist office north to the cathedral. The newer part of town, with wide boulevards and 19th-century buildings, culminates in the **Marché de Wazemmes.** Lille's largest shopping district is off **pl. du**

Théâtre. The areas around the train station and the Marché de Wazemmes may be unsafe at night. A word of **caution:** women may want to avoid the sidestreets between the Gare Lille Flandres and bd. Carnot, as well as rue Molinel.

Tourist Office: pl. Rihour (☎03 20 21 94 21; fax 03 20 21 94 20). M: Rihour. From Gare Lille Flandres, head straight down rue Faidherbe for 2 blocks and turn left through pl. du Théâtre and pl. de Gaulle. Beyond pl. de Gaulle, there's a huge war monument; the tourist office is behind it. Free maps, an essential mass transit guide, free **accommodations service.** Various tours. Unthrilling **currency exchange** rate. Sells the **Lille Metropole City Pass** (95F/€14.50), which buys you 1 day of unlimited transportation, entrance into museums and monuments, a panoramic tour, and additional discounts valid for one week. Open M-Sa 9:30am-6:30pm, Su 10am-noon and 2-5pm.

Budget Travel: Wasteels, 25 pl. des Reignaux (☎08 03 88 70 41). Open M-Th 9am-noon and 2-6pm, F 9am-1pm and 2-6pm, Sa 9am-noon.

Laundromat: 57 rue du Molinel. Open daily 8am-9pm.

Police: 10 rue Ovigneur (☎03 20 16 96 96).

Hospital: 2 av. Oscar Lambret (☎03 20 44 59 62). M: CHR-Oscar Lambret.

Internet access: NetPlayer Games, 25 bd. Carnot (☎03 20 31 20 29). 20F/€3.05 per hr. Open M-Sa 10am-1am, Su 2pm-midnight. **Agence France Télécom,** pl. Général de Gaulle, facing the Vieille Bourse (☎03 20 57 40 00). 1F/€0.15 per min., students half-price. Open M 2-7pm, Tu-Sa 9am-7pm.

Post Office: 8 pl. de la République (☎03 28 36 10 20). M: République. Decent rate of **currency exchange.** Open M-F 8am-7pm, Sa 8am-noon. **Poste Restante:** 59035 Lille Cédèx. **Branch** on bd. Carnot, near pl. du Théâtre. Open M-F 8am-6:30pm and Sa 8am-noon. **Postal code:** 59000.

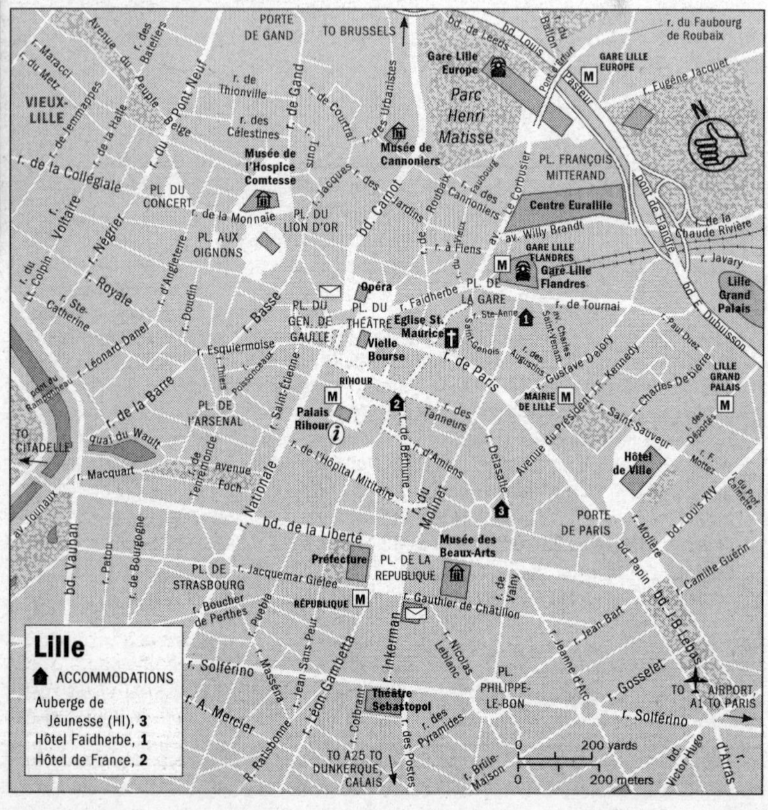

ACCOMMODATIONS AND CAMPING

Cheap university-run singles may be available in the summer from **CROUS,** 74 rue de Cambrai (☎03 20 88 66 00).

Auberge de Jeunesse (HI), 12 rue Malpart (☎03 20 57 08 94; fax 03 20 63 98 93; lille@fuaj.org). M: Mairie de Lille. From Gare Lille Flandres, circle around the station to the left and take a right onto rue du Molinel, then the second left onto rue de Paris and the third right onto rue Malpart. Friendly reception, international atmosphere, and spacious quarters. Co-ed bathrooms. Bar open 7:30pm-1am. Tiny breakfast included. Sheets 18F/€2.74. Kitchen, laundry. Check-out 10:30am, curfew 2am. Reception 7am-noon and 2pm-1am. Open Jan. 31-Dec. 17. 3- to 6-bed dorms (some with private shower) 75F/€11.43 per person; deposit of ID card or 50F/€7.62 required.

Hôtel Faidherbe, 42 pl. de la Gare (☎03 20 06 27 93; fax 03 20 55 95 38). M: Gare Lille Flandres. A tiny elevator and spackled halls lead to lovingly cared-for rooms with a splendid view of...the train station! Breakfast 27F/€4.12. Reception 24hr. 10% discount with *Let's Go.* Singles and doubles 170-260F/€25.92-39.64. Extra person 50F/€7.62; daily tax 2F/€0.30 per person. AmEx/MC/V.

Hôtel de France, 10 rue de Béthune (☎03 20 57 14 78; fax 03 20 57 06 01). TVs in all rooms, great location in the pedestrian district, but not much else. Price strongly correlates to quality; newly renovated rooms cost more, so ask to see your room ahead of time. Breakfast 27F/€4.12. Singles 170-350F/€25.92-53.36; doubles 260-385F/€39.64-58.70; triples 300-420F/€45.74-64.03. Extra bed 30F/€4.57. AmEx/MC/V.

Camping: Les Ramiers, 1 chemin des Ramiers (☎03 20 23 13 42), in Bondues. Take bus #35 (dir: "Halluin Colbras") or #36 (dir: "Comines Mairie") to "Bondues Centre," then follow rue Césair Loridan for 1km (25min.). Fences and garden plots divide spacious private spots. Reception 8am-7:30pm; call ahead if arriving later. Open mid-Apr. to Nov. 15F/€2.29 per site, 10F/€1.53 per person, 5F/€0.76 per car. Showers 6F/€0.91, electricity 12F/€1.83.

FOOD

Decently priced restaurants and cafés pepper the fashionable pedestrian area around **rue de Béthune.** Lille is known for *maroilles* cheese, *genièvre* (juniper berry liqueur), and, this being Flanders, mussels. Dusty **rue Léon Gambetta** is a paradise for picnickers, culminating in the enormous **Marché de Wazemmes,** pl. de la Nouvelle Aventure. Here you'll find **markets** both indoors (M-Th 7am-1pm, F-Sa 7am-8pm, Su 7am-3pm) and out (Su, Tu, and Th 7am-3pm). EuraLille, the big black shopping center next to the Eurostar station, has an enormous **Carrefour supermarket** with everything from Tintin towels to *camembert* (open M-Sa 9am-10pm). **Monoprix,** on rue du Molinel near Gare Lille Flandres (open M-Sa 8:30am-8pm), is a further testament to the glories of air-conditioned grocery shopping.

Le Maharajah, 4 rue du Sec Arembault (☎03 20 57 67 77), in the pedestrian district. Fabulous Indian food, from drool-worthy lamb to vegetarian plates (53-56F/€8.08-8.54). Dinner lines are long. Open M-Sa noon-2pm and 7-10:30pm. AmEx/MC/V.

Les 3 Brasseurs, 22 pl. de la Gare (☎03 20 06 46 25). Another branch of the microbrewery micro-chain. As a garnish for your beer, try a *tarte flambée* (from 32F/€4.88). *Menus* 67-69F/€10.22-10.52. Open Su-Th 11am-midnight, F-Sa 11am-1am.

SIGHTS

MUSEE DES BEAUX-ARTS. Housed in a 19th-century mansion, and surrounded by the lovely gardens of the pl. de la République, the museum holds one of the most respected collections in France, including an encyclopedic display of 15th- to 20th-century French and Flemish masters. Budget several hours; it is in no way a blow-through. An important Berthe Morisot exhibit will be displayed from March to May of 2002. *(Pl. de la République. M: République. ☎03 20 06 78 00. Open M 2-6pm, W-Th and Sa-Su 10am-6pm, F 10am-7pm. 30F/€4.57, students 20F/€3.05.)*

MUSEE D'ART MODERNE. More impressive from the outside than the inside, this museum houses works by Cubist and Postmodernist masters, including Braque, Picasso, Léger, Miró, and Modigliani. Temporary exhibitions can be interesting, but the museum is mostly for hard-core fans of Cubism. *(1 allée du Musée, in the suburb of Villeneuve d'Ascq. Take tram (dir: "4 Cantons") to "Pont du Bois" Then take bus #41 (dir: "Villeneuve d'Ascq") to "Parc Urbain-Musée." ☎03 20 19 68 68. Open W-M 10am-6pm. Tours Sa 3pm and Su 11am, 15F/€2.29. 43F/€6.56, 2nd adult 24F/€3.66; students 10F/€1.53; under age 12 free; free first Su of every month 10am-2pm.)*

VIEILLE BOURSE. Lille's old stock exchange epitomizes the Flemish Renaissance; the garland-like mouldings encircling the building give it the appearance of an elaborate, oversized wedding cake. *(Pl. du Général de Gaulle, between rue des Sept Acaches and rue Manneliers. Markets Tu-Su 9:30am-7:30pm.)* Nearby stands another masterpiece: the **Chamber of Commerce and Industry** and its tower on pl. du Théâtre.

THE CITADEL. This fortress on the city's north side was resculpted in the 17th century to Vauban's specifications. To tour the active army base, sign up at the tourist office. *(In French. May-Aug. Su 3-5pm, 45F/€6.86.)* Otherwise, enjoy some most civilian fun across the street at the **Jardin Vauban,** which has fields for frisbee-playing and picnicking, a carousel, and carnival games.

EGLISE ST-MAURICE. Deep in the heart of the pedestrian district and just steps from the train station, this church was begun in the 14th century but not finished until the 19th. A shrine to St. Maurice has stood on this spot since at least 1066. The forest of pillars inside, holding up the five naves, is characteristic of the *hallequerque* (Flemish for "market church"), a type of construction common in Flanders. *(Rue de Paris. M: Rihour. Open M-F 7:15am-7pm, Sa 8am-7pm, except during mass.)*

MUSEE DE L'HOSPICE. The hospital has existed since the 13th century, but underwent extensive renovations every other century or so. After the Revolution, it served as a hospice for the elderly and as an orphanage. Check out the fascinating *enseigne de la fille mal gardée*, a rather primitive sculpture of a young woman holding out a baby, designed as a moralistic lesson for children. The downstairs chapel is directly across the hall from the massive sick ward, so that the doors could be opened for patients to see the services from their beds. *(☎03 28 36 84 00. Open M 2-6pm, W-F 10am-12:30pm and 2-6pm, Sa-Su 10am-6pm. 15F/€2.29, students 5F/€0.76, children and students or teachers of art history free.)*

TEMPORARILY CLOSED. The **Musée Général de Gaulle,** the birthplace of the grand general, will re open sometime in 2002. *(9 rue Princesse; ☎03 20 31 96 03.)*

ENTERTAINMENT AND FESTIVE MARKETS

Partiers head to two separate neighborhoods. Around les Halles Centrales, pubs line **rue Solférino** and **rue Masséna.** To find the college crowd, pheromone cocktails, billiards, and 10F/€1.53 beer (!), head to **Gino Pub,** 21 rue Masséna. (☎03 20 54 45 55. Open daily noon-2am.) Down the street is the more intimate **Le Clave,** 31 rue Masséna (☎03 20 30 09 61), which pumps Afro-Cuban jazz and authentic tropical drinks (from 25F/€3.81). On the other end of town in the winding *vieille ville*, you can find tamer, more laid-back jazz at **L'Angle-Saxo,** 36 rue d'Angleterre, four or five nights a week. (☎03 20 51 88 89. Open daily 9pm-2am.) Find the art-school cuties at **L'Illustration,** 18 rue Royale, where you can drink in drum'n'bass and trip-hop as you philosophize about sex and Sartre over a candlelit martini (35F/€5.34). (☎03 20 12 00 90. Open M-Sa noon-2am, Su 7pm-2am.) Clubbers should seek out **Opera Night,** 84 rue de Trevise, which blasts "house-happy techno" (the owner's words) to a 20- and 30-something clientele. (☎03 20 88 37 25. No cover.)

The **Marché aux Fleurs** carpets the center of town at the end of April, while **La Braderie,** a centuries-old flea market, is held in the city's central squares on the first weekend of September. For a less materialistic dose of culture, contact the **Orchestre Nationale de Lille,** 30 pl. Mendes France. (☎03 20 12 82 40; www.onlille.com. Tickets 150F/€23, students 52F/€8.) The tourist office has info on **film festivals,** held at **Le Métropole,** rue des Ponts de Comines (☎08 36 68 00 73), and the **Majestic,** 54 rue de Béthune (☎03 28 52 40 40).

DOUAI

To stay a night in Douai (pop. 45,000) is to realize that a Flemish town is quite a different animal from a classically French one. The distinction is encapsulated in the almost surreally dawdling pace of life here. As the seat of the Flemish parliament from 1713 to the French Revolution, Douai acquired elegant mansions and government buildings that bear few scars of the onslaught suffered during both world wars; now they redeem the grungy, commercial blocks of the modern city.

ORIENTATION AND PRACTICAL INFORMATION. Douai is divided by the river Scarpe, with the shopping district and the tourist office on one side, the museum on the other. Trains speed to: **Arras** (15min., 20 per day, 27F/€4.12); **Lille** (30min., 32 per day, 35F/€5.34); and **Paris** (1hr., 18 per day, 177F/€26.99). Turn left from the train station; at the Porte de Valenciennes roundabout several blocks down take the third street (rue de Valenciennes) to the right and follow it for two blocks to reach **pl. d'Armes,** the center of town and home to the **tourist office,** 70 pl. d'Armes. The staff offers a map marking major sights, a list of hotels and restaurants, and a tour of the Hôtel de Ville (12F/€1.83). (☎03 27 88 26 79; fax 03 27 99 38 78. Open M-Sa 9am-noon and 2-6pm; in July-Aug. also Su 2-6pm.) **Local transport** is provided by **TUB.** (☎03 27 95 77 77. Tickets 6.40F/€0.98, *carnet* of 10 54F/€8.23. Office at pl. de Gaulle open M-F 9am-12:15pm and 1:30-5:30pm.) For a **taxi,** call 03 27 96 96 05. The **police** are at 150 rue St-Sulpice (☎03 27 92 38 38) and the **hospital** at rte. de Cambrai (☎03 27 99 61 61). **Net Gamer,** 64 rue St-Christophe, has **Internet access.** (☎03 27 88 69 85; 30F/€4.57 per hr.) The **post office** is on pl. Général de Gaulle. (Open M-F 8am-6:30, Sa 8am-1pm.) **Postal code:** 59500.

ACCOMMODATIONS AND FOOD. There's no reason to stay overnight in Douai rather than Arras or Lille. If you do so, **Le Carnot,** 47 pl. Carnot, has low prices and basic but homey rooms. (☎03 27 87 39 41. Breakfast 25F/€3.81. Reception M-Sa 7:30am-midnight, call in advance for Su. Reserve ahead. Singles 130F/€19.82; doubles with shower 170F/€25.92.) **Le Djurdjura,** 370 pl. du Barlet, just down the road from the pl. d'Armes, has airy, immaculate pastel rooms with baths. (☎03 27 88 74 65; fax 03 27 87 05 86. Reception 8am-midnight. Singles and doubles 170-250F/€25.92-38.12; triples 280F/€42.69. MC/V.)

Cheap cafés line the **pl. d'Armes** and **pl. Carnot.** Bakeries can be found on **rue de Bellain,** between the two. Get tender pasta or delicious pizzas pulled from a brick oven at **La Fata Morgana,** 68 rue des Ferronniers, off rue de Bellain. (☎03 27 88 60 95. Open daily noon-2pm and 7:30-10pm; June-Aug. closed Su. MC/V.)

SIGHTS AND FESTIVALS. The star attraction here is the fantastic, **Hôtel de Ville,** just up the road from pl. d'Armes. Popularized by Victor Hugo, its belfry rises to a height of 64m and is crowned with a delightfully gaudy assortment of tourelles and spires. Begun in the 14th century, it now holds 62 bells, possibly the largest collection in Europe. Every quarter hour the bells play a few notes of a tune, and there are concerts every Monday in July and August at 8:45pm. (Tours offered July-Aug. daily 10am-5pm; Sept.-June M-Sa 2-5pm, Su 10am-5pm. 12F/€1.83, children 6F/€0.91.) Following rue Gambetta to the right of the Hôtel de Ville, you'll arrive at the **Eglise St-Pierre.** From the outside, it appears to be two churches welded together, its 16th-century Gothic facade joined with a 1903 red-brick addition. (Open Tu-Sa 10-11:30am and 3-4:30pm, Su 3-5pm.) On the other side of the river, the **Musée de la Chartreuse,** 130 rue de la Chartreuse (☎03 27 71 38 80), inhabits an ancient monastery. The collection of painting and sculpture includes 16th-century Flemish altarpieces, Rodin bronzes, and an exceptional array of 17th-century Northern masters. Look for Jean Bellegambe's gruesome, yet provocative *Martyrdom of Ste. Barbara.* (Open M-Sa 10am-noon and 2-5pm, Su 10am-noon and 3-6pm. 20F/€3.05, students and seniors 10F/€1.53, under 18 free.)

Douai is most festive during the **Fête des Géants,** a tradition that began in 1479 with a procession through the streets to celebrate a Flemish victory over France. The first giant, constructed by basket makers, joined the procession in 1530, and the next year a wife was made to accompany him. Today Gayant (the Picardy *géant*) and his wife Marie Cagenon parade through the streets for three days along with their huge children. (First weekend in July; call tourist office for info.)

ARRAS

Rows of gabled townhouses, Flemish arcades, and the lilting melody of the belfry bells are a reminder of this city's vibrant past as capital of the Artois province. Arras (pop. 80,000) merits a short trip for its well-preserved collection of 17th- and 18th-century buildings. It was used as a base for the British and Commonwealth soldiers, and today, some of France's best museums and exhibits on front-line life during World War I lie nearby. Be warned, though—Arras is now a dull, humdrum city. Unless you love architecture or have a particular interest in the nearby war memorials, you probably won't want to stay here more than a day.

ORIENTATION AND PRACTICAL INFORMATION. Trains leave pl. Maréchal Foch for: **Amiens** (1hr., 12 per day, 60F/€9.15); **Dunkerque** (1½hr., 12 per day, 91F/€13.87); **Lille** (45min., 21 per day, 54F/€8.23); **Lyon** (3hr., 2 per day, 385F/€58.70); and **Paris** (50min., 13 per day, 166-222F/€25.31-33.85). (Info desk open M-F 8am-7pm, Sa 8am-6pm. Ticket counters open M-F 6am-8:30pm, Sa-Su 8am-8:30pm.) To get to the **bus station** from the train station, turn left onto rue du Dr. Brassart. At the end of the road, turn right; the bus station will be ahead to your left. (☎03 21 51 34 64. Open July-Aug. M-F 8am-noon and 4-6:30pm, Sa 10am-1pm; Sept.-June M-F 7am-7pm, Sa 7am-1pm.) **Local transportation** is operated by **STCRA** (☎03 21 58 08 58; tickets 6.60F/€1.01). **Arras Taxis** (☎03 21 23 69 69) wait at the train station (24hr.). **Avis Car Rental** is near the train station on 4 rue Gambetta. (☎03 21 51 69 03. Open M-F 8am-noon and 2-6pm, Sa 9am-noon and 4-6pm.)

To get to the **tourist office,** pl. des Héros, from the station, walk straight across pl. Foch, past the fountain, and onto rue Gambetta. Continue straight on Gambetta for five blocks until you reach rue Desiré Delansorne. Turn left and walk for two more blocks; the tourist office will be straight ahead in the elaborate Hôtel de Ville. The office is across pl. des Héros, inside the Hôtel de Ville. The bilingual staff offers a reservations service and a free map. (☎03 21 51 26 95; fax 03 21 71 07 34. Open May-Sept. M-Sa 9am-6:30pm, Su 10am-1pm and 2:30-6:30pm; Oct.-Apr. M-Sa 9am-noon and 2-6pm, Su 10am-12:30pm and 3-6:30pm.) The town's other main square, **Grand'Place,** is on the opposite side of pl. des Héros. **Crédit Agricole,** 9 Grand'Place, has the best rate of **currency exchange** as well as 24-hour exchange machines. (☎03 21 50 41 80. Open M 2-6pm, Tu-F 8:45pm-12:30pm and 2-6pm, Sa 8:45am-12:45pm.) Do your **laundry** at **Superlav,** pl. Ipswich, next to the Eglise St-Jean-Baptiste (open daily 7am-8pm). The **police station** is in the Hôtel de Ville (☎03 21 23 70 70), and the **hospital** at 57 av. Winston Churchill (☎03 21 24 40 00). The **post office,** 13 rue Gambetta, has **currency exchange.** (☎03 21 22 94 94. Open M-F 8am-6:30pm, Sa 8am-noon.) **Postal code:** 62000.

ACCOMMODATIONS AND FOOD. Arras has precious few budget hotels. During high season, it's wise to reserve in advance at the **Auberge de Jeunesse (HI),** 59 Grand'Place. Though the 2- to 7-bed rooms are spartan and tiny, they are cheerfully maintained and some have pleasant views over the *place*. The price and location are unbeatable. No locks on doors, but safes cost only 1F/€0.15. (☎03 21 22 70 02; fax 03 21 07 46 15. Breakfast 19F/€2.90. Sheets 17F/€2.44. Reception 8am-noon and 5-11pm. Lockout noon-5pm. Curfew 11pm. Open Feb.-Nov. Bunks 50F/€7.62. **Members only.**) If it's full, try the **Ostel des**

Trois Luppars, 47 Grand'Place, in the oldest house in Arras. Large, clean rooms with antiseptic decor follow the gorgeous lobby and dining room. (☎03 21 07 41 41; fax 03 21 24 24 80. Breakfast 40F/€6.10. Reception 9am-11:30pm. Singles 210-270F/€32.02-41.16, with bath 310F/€47.26; doubles 300F/€45.74, with bath 350F/€53.36; triples with bath 420F/€64.03; quads with bath 440F/€67.08. AmEx/MC/V.) Another option is the **OK Pub et Hôtel,** 8 pl. de la Vacquerie, behind the Hôtel de Ville, above a wild bar. The humble rooms differ greatly; ask to see yours before taking it. (☎03 21 21 30 60; fax 03 21 21 30 61. Breakfast 37F/€5.64. Singles 140-210F/€21.35-32.02; doubles 200-250F/€30.49-38.12. AmEx/MC/V.) The local **campsite,** 138 rue du Temple, is basically a parking lot with a few grassy plots. From the station, turn left onto rue du Dr. Brassart, then left on av. du Maréchal Leclerc. Cross the bridge; rue du Temple is on the left (10min.). (☎03 21 71 55 06. Reception 7am-10pm. Open Apr.-Sept. 16F/€2.44 per person; 9F/€1.37 per site; 11F/€1.68 per car or tent. Electricity 15F/€2.29.)

The pedestrian shopping area between the post office and the Hôtel de Ville bustles with bakeries and other specialty shops. There's a huge **Monoprix supermarket** across from the post office on rue Gambetta (open M-Sa 8:30am-8pm). The pl. des Héros springs to life during Arras' boisterous open-air **market** (W and Sa 8am-1pm). Inexpensive cafés skirt **pl. des Héros** and the pedestrian area; more elegant restaurants adorn the **Grand'Place.** You'll smell *Les Best Ribs in Town*—and probably the only ribs in town—all the way across the *place* at **Le Saint-Germain,** 14 Grand'Place, where France and America shake greasy hands. Gorge on a plateful of ribs (59.90F/€9.13) or grab 'em to go (50F/€7.62). Still low on animal fat? Try the all-you-can-eat *mousse chocolat* or *crème caramel* for 29.50F/€4.50. (☎03 21 51 45 45. Open daily noon-12:30am. AmEx/MC/V.)

SIGHTS AND ENTERTAINMENT. Arras' two great squares are framed by rows of nearly identical houses. **Grand'Place's** Flemish homogeneity is ruffled by a lone Gothic housefront (Ostel des Trois Luppars), which dates from 1430. A block away, shops, bars, and cafés line the smaller, livelier **pl. des Héros.** The current **Hôtel de Ville** is a faithful copy of the 15th-century original, which reigned over pl. des Héros until its destruction in 1914. You can peep into the municipal court, the obscenely ornate Gothic reception room, and the marriage chamber. The best view of Arras is had from the 75m-tall **belfry.** (Open M-Sa 10-11:45am and 2-5:45pm, Su 10am-12:15pm and 2-6:15pm. 15F/€2.29, students 10F/€1.53.) Beneath the town hall, the underground tunnels of **Les Boves** are an eerie subterranean maze first bored into the soft chalk as early as the 10th century. The tourist office leads fascinating tours. (☎03 21 51 26 95. 25F/€3.81, children and students 15F/€2.29.) A few blocks behind the Hôtel de Ville lies the **Abbaye St-Vaast.** Originally built in AD 667 on the hill where St-Vaast used to pray, the current gigantic structure dates from the 18th century. The church's traditional Gothic floor plan accommodates massive Corinthian columns with striking success. (Open daily 2:15-6:30pm; until 6pm in winter.) Inside the abbey, the sophisticated **Musée des Beaux-Arts** displays a collection of medieval architecture and tapestries. Look for the gruesome skeletal sculpture of Guillaume Lefranchois and his worm-infested entrails. (☎03 21 71 26 43. Open Apr.-Sept. M,W, and F-Sa 10am-noon and 2-6pm, Th 10am-6pm, Su 10am-2pm and 3-6pm; Oct.-Mar. M, W, F 10am-noon and 2-5pm, Th 10am-5pm, weekends same as rest of year. 25F/€3.81, students 12.50F/€1.91.)

Place des Héros, Grand'Place, and the surrounding pedestrian roads are the centers of local nightlife; just follow the young blood coursing into bars and cafés all over town. **Le Couleur Café,** 35 pl. des Héros (☎03 21 71 08 70), draws the college set with a house and drum'n'bass DJ. Take a break from the bars at cosmopolitan **Noroit,** 6-9 rue des Capuchins (☎03 21 71 30 12), which plays foreign artsy films and hosts several concerts and plays each month.

NEAR ARRAS

WORLD WAR I MEMORIALS AND BATTLEFIELDS

The green countryside around Arras, which saw heavy fighting during WWI, is dotted with war cemeteries, countless unmarked graves, and many powerful memorials. They're tricky to reach without a car, though a march along two-lane roads is feasible if you've got a good map. Consult Arras tourist office (☎03 21 51 26 95).

THE VIMY MEMORIAL. The Vimy Memorial, 12km northeast of Arras along N17, honors the more than 66,000 Canadian soldiers killed during WWI. The memorial itself is a vast limestone monument, consisting of two towering pylons rising from a rectangular base. Sculpted figures surround the edifice, the most poignant a sorrowful woman carved from a single 30-ton limestone block. The surrounding park, whose soil was shipped from Canada, is dedicated to the crucial victory at Vimy Ridge of April 1917. The land is morbidly beautiful here; tiny hills and large craters, carved out by shells and underground mines, are now covered in grass. Follow the path from the monument back toward the entrance and bear left to explore trenches, both Canadian and German, at times no more than 25m apart. Stay on the marked paths, as undetonated mines may still dot the area. The kiosk near the trenches is the starting point for an underground tour of the crumbling tunnels, which were dug by British and Canadian soldiers. Little details evoke the realities of life on the front lines: the registration room, the commander's desk, the little maple leaf chiseled in the chalk by an anonymous soldier. (☎03 21 58 19 34 or 03 21 48 98 97. Memorial open daily sunrise to sunset. Free tunnel tours May-Nov. 10am-6pm in English and French every 30min. Museum open daily 10am-6pm.)

The Vimy memorial is 2-3km from the town of **Vimy.** To reach it, the easiest, but most expensive, option is to catch a taxi in **Arras** (around 110-120F/€16.77-18.30, after 7pm 140-150F/€21.35-22.90). You can also catch one of seven daily **buses** from Arras to Vimy (20min., 14F/€2.13; none available Su).

NOTRE-DAME-DE-LORETTE. North of Neuville on D937 is the French cemetery, basilica, and museum of **Notre-Dame-de-Lorette.** The bodies of 22,970 unknown and 19,000 listed soldiers from the 1914-1915 Battle of Lorette rest here, arranged in eight ossuaries around the central Tour-Lanterne. Maréchal Pétain laid the first stone of the tower in 1921. The museum's first floor displays a touching collection of letters and photos sent by families. Unfortunately, Notre-Dame is quite impossible to reach without a car. Indomitable walkers can take bus #33 to the nearby town of Souchez and walk the 3km or so to Notre-Dame de Lorette, but don't try it without a good map or first consulting the tourist office in Souchez. (☎03 21 29 30 62. Basilica open mid-Mar. to Nov. daily 9am-6:30pm. Museum open daily 9am-8pm. 20F/€3.05, students 10F/€1.53.)

NEUVILLE-ST-VAAST. Farther west along D49, the largest cemetery in Europe holds the graves of over 44,000 German soldiers, marked by grim black crosses, each representing four soldiers. The Jewish graves, marked by simple inscribed headstones, stand out in stark contrast. There is also a large French cemetery and a small British one nearby. The **Musée La Targette,** across from the Monument au Flambeau, displays over 2500 painstakingly collected documents, uniforms, and objects used by soldiers; the sheer volume of the collection is overwhelming. The exhibits are the property of a collector whose grandfather was a Verdun veteran. Neuville-St-Vaast is accessible by bus from Arras (4 per day, 14F/€2.13). (☎03 21 59 17 76. Open daily 9am-8pm. 26.24/€4, students and children 13.12/€2.)

LAON

The cathedral of Laon, one of France's Gothic masterpieces, presides over the surrounding farmland from its hilltop berth. Residence in the fortified *haute ville* was reserved for kings when Laon was the capital of the mighty Carolingian Empire of the 9th and 10th centuries. The town (pop. 26,000) gave birth both to Charlemagne's mother and to the great folk hero Roland, the Emperor's nephew. There's no royalty here today, and the *basse ville* seems somewhat depressed; nevertheless, there are still some giddy thrills and glorious views to be had.

ORIENTATION AND PRACTICAL INFORMATION. Laon's *haute ville* is built around one main street, whose name changes from rue du Cloître by the cathedral to rue de Bourg by the Hôtel de Ville. **Trains** leave pl. de la Gare for: **Amiens** (1½hr., 7 per day, 86F/€13.11); **Paris** (1¼hr., 12 per day, 105F/€16.01); and **Reims** (50min., 9 per day, 49F/€7.47). (☎03 23 79 10 79. Ticket office open M-F 4:55am-9:15pm, Sa 6am-8:35pm, Su 6:45am-9:20pm.) The **POMA car** takes a roller-coaster ride every two minutes from the station to the *haute ville* and tourist office and allows a first breathtaking peek at the *basse ville* from above. (☎03 23 79 07 59. July-Aug. M-Sa 7am-8pm, Su 2:30-6pm; Sept.-June M-Sa only. Tickets 6.60F/€1.01, round-trip same price.) From the POMA station in the *haute ville*, exit straight out, cross the parking lot and turn left across pl. Gén. Leclerc onto rue Sérurier. Turn right when you reach the art center (old hospital) and walk one block to reach the **tourist office,** pl. du Parvis, occupying the Hôtel-Dieu, a squat 12th-century stone structure that served as France's first hospital. The staff organizes tours in French and English of the cathedral (daily 3pm) and the medieval city (summer Su 10:30am). (☎03 23 20 28 62; fax 03 23 20 68 11. Tours 35F/€5.34, students 20F/€3.05. Office open July-Aug. M-Sa 9am-1pm and 2-7pm, Su 10am-1pm and 2-7pm; Sept.-June M-Sa 9am-12:30pm and 2-6:30pm, Su 11am-1pm and 2-6pm.) The **police** are at 2 bd. de Gras Boncourt (☎03 23 20 28 62), and the **hospital** at rue Marcellin-Berthelot (☎03 23 24 33 33). There is a **post office** next to the station on pl. de la Gare, with **currency exchange.** (☎03 23 21 55 74. Open M-F 8am-7pm, Sa 8am-noon.) **Postal code:** 02000.

ACCOMMODATIONS AND FOOD. Popular with backpackers, the **Hôtel Welcome,** 2 av. Carnot in the *basse ville*, has simple rooms off a creaky hallway. (☎03 23 23 06 11. Breakfast 25F/€3.81. Reception M-Sa 7am-noon and 2-10pm, Su 7am-noon. Singles and doubles 140F/€21.35, with shower 155F/€23.63; triples 160F/€24.39; quads 180F/€27.44. MC/V.) Château-like **Les Chevaliers,** 3-5 rue Sérurier, has handsome, dark rooms just a block from the cathedral. (☎03 23 27 17 50; fax 03 23 23 40 71. Breakfast included. Reception 6:30am-8:30pm. Singles 190-302F/€29-46; doubles 276-380F/€42-58; triples 512F/€78. Extra bed 72F/€11. MC/V.) Rural **Camping Municipale,** allée de la Chênaie, about 3km from the train station, is mostly full of caravans but has some privacy for tents. (☎03 23 20 25 56. Reception 7am-10pm. Open May-Sept. 15F/€2.29 per person; 9.30F/€1.42 per site, 9.50F/€1.45 per car. Electricity 16F/€2.44. Cash only.)

The ever-reliable **Monoprix supermarket** lies on rue de Bourg (open M-F 8:30am-7pm, Sa 9am-noon and 2-7pm). **Rue Chatelaine,** which leads left from pl. Général Leclerc toward the cathedral, is the place to head for bakeries and cheap sandwich shops. **L'Aziza,** one block from the cathedral at 11 rue de la Herse, offers Moroccan couscous dishes (45-95F/€6.86-14.48), *tajines* (from 62F/€9.45), and fresh mint tea. Take an hour to say hello to the pleasant, conversational owners. (☎03 23 20 44 44. Open Tu-Su 10am-2:30pm and 7pm-midnight. MC/V.)

SIGHTS AND FESTIVALS. A maze of narrow, twisting alleys and medieval walls surrounds Laon's airy **Cathédrale de Notre-Dame,** one of the earliest and finest examples of Gothic architecture in France. Construction began in 1155 and was completed 80 years later. The striking white interior leads up to a simple, sumptuous rose window. Respect the carved oxen; they're miracle cows. Look for the winged hippopotamus, added during 19th-century renovations. (☎03 23 25 14 18. Open daily 9am-6:30pm. Tours 35F/€5.34, students 20F/€3.05.) The **ramparts** encircling the *haute ville* are excellent for a calm stroll, offering a panorama of the *basse ville* and the surrounding countryside. The lovely, cool **Eglise St-Martin,** the neglected sister of the cathedral, is open on weekend afternoons. Note the headless statues on the facade. Behind a lush courtyard on rue Georges Ermant are the tiny **Musée de Laon** and the crumbling 13th-century **Chapelle des Templiers.** The chapel holds the carved 14th-century cadaver of Laon native Guillaume de Harcigny, the celebrated physician to Charles VI, who cured the king of madness. The museum's collection of paintings and Greek and Egyptian antiquities shouldn't merit a detour. (☎03 23 20 19 87. Both open Apr.-Sept. W-M 10am-noon and 2-6pm; Oct.-Mar. 10am-noon and 2-5pm. Museum 20F/€3.05, students 15F/€2.29.)

Late September and early October bring Laon's acclaimed **Festival de Musique Française** (☎03 23 20 87 50). On the first weekend of May, **Les Euromédievales,** brings jousts, falconry, street performers, and medieval food. During the last week of March and first week of April there's the **Festival International du Cinéma Jeune Public,** an international film and animation festival aimed at kids. **Jazzitudes,** on the last weekend in June, brings jazz to a number of venues in Laon.

EXCURSIONS. To the south of Laon, the **Chemin des Dames** winds across the Aisne region, a scenic and historic route of great importance since Roman times, so named for the relatively recent journey of Louis XV's daughters. The route follows a 200m ridge whose value as a natural barrier was first noticed by Caesar when he conquered Northern Gaul in 57 BC. Later, the Chemin was the site of Napoleon's last victory before Waterloo and also a site of crucial strategic import during WWI, when the Germans held it from 1914 to 1918. Today the route is peppered with monuments to this turbulent history, including the **Caverne des Dragons,** a former quarry used by the Germans as a barracks, hospital, and chapel in WWI and later converted into a museum of remembrance. (☎03 23 25 14 18. Open July-Aug. daily 10am-7pm; Feb.-June and Sept.-Dec. 10am-6pm. 30F/€4.57, students and ages 6-18 15F/€2.29.) You'll probably need your own transportation.

THE CHANNEL PORTS (COTE D'OPALE)

They're big, they're bad, they're ugly. Such is the conventional wisdom regarding the sprawling ports that constitute the first taste of France for many travelers from Britain and beyond. Towns fronting the English Channel were wrangled over for centuries, but today's visitor has to wonder what made them such hot items; with soggy weather, schlocky boutiques, and cafés promising genuine steak and kidney pie, the ports seem to combine the worst of both worlds. No wonder many only get off the ferry long enough to stock up on cheap wine, beer, and cigarettes before heading back to Blighty. Scratch the surface, however, and these towns reveal a charm and a character uniquely their own, from Boulogne's ancient walled *haute ville*, to Dunkerque's gamey beach at Malo-les-Bains. Don't go out of your way to get here, but take some time as you pass through and you may be surprised.

BOATS TO BRITAIN. All three towns offer frequent service to the UK, though Calais is by far the busiest. **Eurostar** trains zip under the tunnel from London and Ashford, stopping outside Calais on their way to Lille, Brussels, and Paris; **Le Shuttle** carries cars between Ashford and Calais. **Ferries** from Calais cross to Dover, while Boulogne services Folkestone, Dunkerque, and Ramsgate. For details on operators, schedules, and fares, see **Getting There: By Boat** (p. 62) and **Getting There: By Channel Tunnel** (p. 62).

BOULOGNE-SUR-MER

By far the most attractive Channel port with a refeshing sea breeze and lavish floral displays, Boulogne balances its summer tourist flux with a large resident population of 46,000. The busy port cuts into the heart of town and unloads quantities of Britons seeking a continental getaway.

TRANSPORTATION. Trains leave **Gare Boulogne-Ville,** bd. Voltaire, for **Calais** (30min., 18 per day, 42F/€6.40); **Lille** (2½hr., 11 per day, 108F/€16.47); and **Paris-Nord** (2-3hr., 11 per day, 167-297F/€25.46-45.28). (Info office open M-Sa 8:15am-6:30pm.) **BCD** buses leave pl. Dalton for **Calais** (30min., 4 per day, 38F/€5.80) and **Dunkerque** (80min., 4 per day, 60F/€9.15). **TCRB** (☎03 21 83 51 51) sends **local bus #10** from the train station to the *haute ville;* or take any other line to pl. de France and transfer (tickets 6.50F/€0.99). **Taxis** (☎03 21 91 25 00) wait at the station.

ORIENTATION AND PRACTICAL INFORMATION. The river Liane splits Boulogne in two: the ferry terminal is on the west bank, and everything else on the east bank. The train station has a large map on its doors. To reach central **pl. de France** from Gare Boulogne-Ville, turn right on bd. Voltaire, and then take your first left onto bd. Danou for several blocks to pl. Angleterre; walk half a block more to reach pl. de France and the bus station hub, directly behind the post office. To get to the tourist office, continue past pl. de France and pl. Frédéric Sauvage onto rue Gambetta. On the other side of pl. de France, **Pont Marquet** leads to the **ferry port.** The streets between **pl. Frédéric Sauvage** and **pl. Dalton** form the busy town center.

The **tourist office,** 24 quai Gambetta, has bus info and makes hotel reservations; ask them for the fold-out town map. They also run **tours** of the port on Fridays (35F/€5.34, students and children 25F/€3.81). (☎03 21 10 88 10; fax 03 21 10 88 11; boulogne@tourisme.norsys.fr. Open July-Aug. M-Sa 9am-7pm, Su 10am-1pm and 3-6pm; Sept.-June M-Sa 8:45am-12:30pm and 1:30-6:15pm, Su 10am-12:30pm and 2:30-5pm.) **Crédit Agricole,** 26 rue Nationale, has a 24-hr. **currency exchange** machine. There's a **laundromat** at 62 rue de Lille in the *haute ville* (open daily 8am-7pm). The **police** are at 9 rue Perrochel (☎03 21 99 48 48), the **hospital** on allée Jacques Monod (☎03 21 99 33 33). The **post office** is on pl. Frédéric Sauvage. (☎03 21 99 09 03. Open M-F 8am-6:30pm, Sa 8am-12:30pm.) **Postal code:** 62200.

ACCOMMODATIONS. Many hotels in the 110-160F/€16.77-24.39 range are near the ferry terminal; the tourist office has a list. The **Auberge de Jeunesse (HI),** 56 pl. Rouget de Lisle, across from the train station, has pine cabin-esque 3- to 4-bed rooms, each with a bathroom. There's a lively, backpacker-packed bar and Internet access (30F/€4.57 per 30min.). (☎03 21 99 15 30; fax 03 21 80 45 62. Breakfast included. Late-night snack 30F/€4.57, served until 1am. Sheets 17F/€2.59. Wheelchair accessible. Reception 8am-1am, in winter till midnight. Check-in 5pm, check-out noon. Curfew 1am. Bunks 85F/€12.96, **non-members** 19F/€2.90 supplement per night up to six nights. MC/V.) The **Hôtel Au Sleeping,** 18 bd. Daunou, has spotless, lovingly decorated little rooms several minutes from the train station, above an old-man-filled brasserie. (☎03 21 80 62 79; fax 03 21 80 62 79. Breakfast 30F/€4.57. Reception 7am-10pm. Reserve ahead in summer. Singles 150-250F/€22.90-38.12; doubles 200-250F/€30.49-38.12; 3F/€0.46 tax per person per day. Prices around 20F/€3.05 lower in winter. AmEx/MC/V). The central **Hôtel de Londres,** 22 pl. de France, behind the post office, is a posh change of pace. (☎03 21 31 35 63; fax 03 21 83 50 07. Breakfast 32F/€4.88. Reception 7:30am-midnight. Rooms reserved must be taken by 7pm. Singles and doubles 250F/€38.12; triples or quads 390F/€59.46. Extra bed 50F/€7.62. Tax 4F/€0.61 per person per day. MC/V.)

FOOD AND ENTERTAINMENT. Restaurants, cafés, bakeries, and other food shops abound in the center of town. An excellent **market** is held on pl. Dalton (W and Sa 6am-1pm). A **Champion supermarket,** on rue Daunou near bd. de la Liane, is in the Centre Commercial de la Liane mall, up the road from the hostel (open M-Sa 8:30am-8pm). **Rue de Lille** is undoubtedly the most idyllic place to dine, but quaintness, as usual, has its cost. In the evening, check out the neon-blinking bars at **pl. Dalton.** Bars squish side by side on tiny **rue Doyen,** off pl. Dalton; drink a glass in memory of John-John and his dad at the **Pub "J.F. Kennedy,"** 20 rue du Doyen, which offers mounds of mussels (48F/€7.32) and beer (15F/€2.29). (☎03 21 83 97 05. Open daily 9am-1am. Food available 11am-3pm and 7-11pm.)

SIGHTS. Boulogne's *vieille ville* stands atop the hill where the Romans first settled. The ramparts have exhilarating views of the harbor, town, and countryside. The massive **Château-Musée,** rue de Bernet, dominates the east corner of the ramparts. Its collection is more striking for its size and variety than for any individual works, among them a bare-faced Egyptian mummy and Napoleon's second-oldest hat. (☎03 21 10 02 20, tours ☎03 21 80 56 78. Open M and W-Sa 10am-12:30pm and 2-5pm, Su 10am-12:30pm and 2:30-5:30pm. 20F/€3.05, children 13F/€1.98; tours 32F/€4.88, children 20F/€3.05.) Just down rue de Lille is the domed 19th-century **Basilique de Notre-Dame,** which sits above the labyrinthine crypts of a 12th-century edifice. The real treasure is the swirling, tapered dome behind the choir. (Basilica open Apr.-Sept 14 daily 9am-noon and 2-6pm; Sept. 15-Mar. 10am-noon and 2-5pm. Crypt open M-Sa 2-5pm, Su 2:30-5pm; 10F/€1.63.)

When the residents of Boulogne aren't catching fish or eating them, they're admiring them at the aquarium **Le Grand Nausicaä,** bd. Ste-Beuve. Climb a ladder down into the lagoons, or just admire the jellyfish tank. (☎03 21 30 99 99; www.nausicaa.fr. Open July-Aug. daily 9:30am-8pm; Sept.-June 9:30am-6:30pm. 68F/€10.37, ages 3-12 48F/€7.32.) Next to Nausicaä is the **beach,** where **Le Club de Voile** will rent you **windsurfers** (60F/€9.15 per hr., 600F/€91.48 for 10 2hr. sessions) and **catamarans** (300F/€45.74 for 2hr., 1500F/€228.69 for 10hr. sessions). (☎03 21 31 80 67. Open M-F 10am-5pm, Sa-Su 1-5pm. Cash only.)

CALAIS

Calais (pop. 80,000) is the most lively of the Channel Ports, and the least French; what with the Chunnel next door, you'll hear almost as much English as French on the streets. The town lacks charm, due in large part to the traumas it suffered in WWII, but as long as you're here for the day, check out Rodin's *Burghers of Calais,* or just sit and watch the white ships glide by the town's wide beaches.

TRANSPORTATION AND PRACTICAL INFORMATION. Free buses connect the ferry terminal and train station every 30 minutes. Avoid the area around the ferry terminal and harbor at night. **Eurostar** stops outside town at the new Gare Calais-Fréthun, but most **SNCF trains** stop in town at the Gare Calais-Ville, bd. Jacquard. They go to **Boulogne** (45min., 11 per day, 42F/€6.40); **Dunkerque** (1hr., 6 per day, 45F/€6.86); **Lille** (1¼hr., 12 per day, 86F/€13.11); and **Paris-Nord** (3¼hr., 6 per day, 220-292F/€33.54-44.52). (Ticket office open M-Sa 6:30am-8:30pm, Su 8:30-9:30am and 1:30-8:30pm.) **BCD buses** (☎03 21 83 51 51) theoretically stop in front of the station on the way to Boulogne (30min.; 6 per day, Sa 3 per day; 38F/€5.80) and Dunkerque (40min.; M-F 6 per day, Sa 3 per day; 40F/€6.10). **OpaleBus,** 22 rue Caillette (☎03 21 00 75 75), operates **local buses.** Line #3 (dir: "Blériot/VVF") from Gare Calais-Ville goes to the beach, the hostel, and campgrounds (M-Sa 7:15am-7:20pm, Su 10:30am-7:15pm; 5.20F/€0.79). For a **taxi,** call 03 21 97 13 14 (24hr.).

The **tourist office,** 12 bd. Clemenceau, is near the train station; cross the street, turn left, cross the bridge, and it's on your right. The staff will make reservations for free. (☎03 21 96 62 40; fax 03 21 96 01 92. Open M-Sa 9am-7pm, Su 10am-1pm.) **Exchange currency** at the ferry or Hovercraft terminals (both 24hr.), or more cheaply at the post office or banks. There's a **laundromat** at 34 rue de Thermes (open daily 7am-7:30pm). The **police** are on pl. de Lorraine (☎03 21 19 13 17), the **hospital** at 11 quai du Commerce (☎03 21 46 33 33). The **post office** is on pl. d'Alsace (☎03 21 85 52 72; open M-F 8:30am-6pm, Sa 8:30-noon); there's a **branch** on pl. du Reims (open M-F 8:30am-6pm, Sa 9am-noon). **Postal code:** 62100.

ACCOMMODATIONS AND FOOD. The few budget hotels fill up quickly in summer; call 10-14 days in advance. The tourist office provides a list of hotels and their prices. Better than any hotel is the modern, recently renovated **Centre Européen de Séjour/Auberge de Jeunesse (HI),** av. Maréchal Delattre de Tassigny, one block from the beach. From the station, turn left and follow the main road through various name changes past pl. d'Armes; cross the bridge and take a left at the roundabout onto bd. de Gaulle. Walk past the high-rise and go right on tiny rue Alice Marie; the white hostel is the third building on your left. Or take bus #3 to "Pluviose." From the ferry, take a shuttle bus to pl. d'Armes; your first right down the bus route is the main road, rue Royale. There are 42 bathrooms for the 84 doubles, some of which are even blessed with beach views. There's also a pool table, bar, library, and cafeteria (open M-F 7-9am, noon-1pm, and 5-7pm; Sa 7-9am and noon-1pm), **bike rental** (40F/€6.10 per day), and a warm, attentive staff. (☎03 21 34 70 20; fax 03 21 96 87 80. Breakfast and sheets included. Wheelchair accessible. Reception 24hr. Check-out 11am. Bunks 94F/€14.33 first night, 80F/€12.20 per extra night; singles 126F/€19.21. **Non-members** 10F/€1.53 supplement.)

One garrulous matron runs two hotels. The first, homey **Hôtel Bristol,** 15-13 rue du Duc de Guise, off the main road, has neat, quiet rooms and the reception for both establishments. (☎/fax 03 21 34 53 24. Breakfast 28F/€4.27. Reception 24hr. Singles 150-200F/€22.90-30.49; doubles 160-250F/€24.39-38.12; rooms for 3-5 people 270-380F/€41.16-57.94. MC/V.) The adorable **Hôtel Tudor,** 6 rue Marie Tudor, off rue Duc de Guise, has larger rooms. (☎03 21 96 08 15. Singles and doubles with bath 220F/€33.54; 3-5 people 270-380F/€41.16-57.94. Reserve ahead for both.)

Calais caters to that rare breed looking for boring food at middling prices. Morning **markets** are held on pl. Crèvecœur (Th and Sa) and pl. d'Armes (W and Sa). Otherwise, look for bakeries on **bd. Gambetta, bd. Jacquard,** and **rue des Thermes** or one of two supermarkets: **Match,** pl. d'Armes (open M-Th 9am-12:30pm and 2:30-7:30pm, F-Sa 9am-7:30pm), and **Prisunic,** 17 bd. Jacquard (open M-Sa 8:30am-7:30pm, Su 10am-7pm). The hostel and campsite cafeterias are also inexpensive options. Restaurants line **rue Royale** and **bd. Jacquard.** Try the outrageously fresh pies at **Le Napoli Pizzeria,** 2 rue Jean de Vienne. (☎03 21 34 49 39. Open Tu-F until 10:30pm, Sa-Su 11:30pm weekends; closed Sa afternoon. MC/V.)

SIGHTS. Rodin's evocative sculpture of **The Burghers of Calais** stands in front of the **Hôtel de Ville** at the juncture of bd. Jacquard and rue Royale. When Calais was captured during the Hundred Years' War, six of the town's leading citizens—the burghers in this statue—surrendered the keys to the city and offered their lives to England's King Edward III in exchange for those of the starving townspeople. Edward's French wife Philippa pleaded for mercy, and they were spared. The best part of Calais is its **beach;** follow rue Royale (of the many names) to rue de Mer until the road ends, then walk west along the shore away from the harbor.

A camouflaged German bunker in Parc St-Pierre houses the **War Museum,** a collection of battlefield models and airplane fragments. (☎03 21 34 21 57. Open Apr.-Sept. daily 10am-6pm; Oct.-Nov. and Feb.-Mar. W-M 10am-5pm. 25F/€3.81, children 20F/€3.05.) The **Musée des Beaux-Arts et de la Dentelle,** 25 rue Richelieu, houses a rather sexy exhibition on Calais' lace industry, along with Rodin sculptures, Flemish and Dutch paintings, and modern pieces by Picasso, Dubuffet, and Alechinsky. (☎03 21 46 48 40. Open M and W-F 10am-noon and 2-5:30pm, Sa 10am-noon and 2-6:30pm, Su 2-6:30pm. 15F/€2.29, students 10F/€1.53.)

DUNKERQUE

Dunkerque entered the history books in June 1940, when battleships, yachts, rowboats, and anything else British and waterborne gathered here to evacuate the last defenders of France. The last French city to be liberated, Dunkerque was over 80% destroyed before the Allies landed. Drab buildings are matched by a sort of gloom pervading the *dunkerquois* people. What fun there is to be had can be found in the lively beach area of Malo-les-Bains, a short bus ride away from the city center.

TRANSPORTATION AND PRACTICAL INFORMATION. **Trains** leave pl. de la Gare for **Arras** (1½hr., 15 per day, 91F/€13.87); **Calais** (1hr., 7 per day, 46F/€7.01); **Lille** (1¼hr., 14 per day, 74F/€11.28); and **Paris** (1½hr., 219-292F/€33.39-44.52). (Ticket windows open M-Sa 6am-7pm, Su 7am-7pm.) **BCD buses** (☎03 21 83 51 51) leave the train station for **Boulogne** (1hr.; M-F 5 per day, 2 on Sa; 60F/€9.15) and **Calais** (40min.; M-F 8 per day, 3 on Sa; 40F/€6.10). **Local transportation** is provided by **DK'BUS,** 12 pl. de la Gare (☎03 28 59 00 78; routes #3 and 3A connect the station and town center with the hostel and Malo-les-Bains every 10-20min. 6:30am-9pm; tickets 8F/€1.22, 4F/€0.61 students and children, *carnet* of 10 50F/€7.62) and **Taxibus** (every 30min. 10pm-midnight; tickets 8F/€1.22). **Taxis** wait at the train station, pl. de la République, and pl. Jean Bart (☎03 28 66 73 00; 24hr.).

Bd. Alexandre III connects pl. de la Gare and the town center, whose two main squares are **pl. Jean Bart** and **pl. Général de Gaulle.** Along the beach, **digue de Mer** turns into **digue des Alliés** on the west side, which is closer to the town center. To reach the **tourist office,** rue Amiral Ronarch, from the station, cross pl. de la Gare to rue du Chemin de Fer on the left, and follow the main road, bd. Alexandre III, which becomes rue Clemenceau at pl. Jean Bart. Here you'll find free maps and a lousy rate of **currency exchange.** (☎03 28 26 27 28; fax 03 28 63 38 34; dunkerque@tourisme.norsys.fr. Open July-Aug. M-Sa 9am-6:30pm, Su 10am-noon and 2-4pm; Sept.-June M-F 9am-12:30 and 1:30-6:30pm, Sa 9am-6:30pm, Su 10am-noon and 2-4pm.) For the **police,** call 03 28 23 50 50. A **hospital** is at 130 av. Louis Herbeaux (☎03 28 28 59 00). The **post office,** 20 rue du Président Poincaré, next to pl. de Gaulle, has good rates of **currency exchange.** (☎03 28 65 91 65. Open M-F 8:30am-6:30pm, Sa 8:30am-1pm.) **Postal codes:** Dunkerque 59140; Malo-les-Bains 59240.

ACCOMMODATIONS AND FOOD. The busy, uncongenial **Auberge de Jeunesse (HI),** pl. Paul Asseman in Malo-les-Bains, is right on the beachfront. From the station, take bus #3 or 3A to "Piscine." Turn left and walk past the pool and rink; the hostel will be on your right. Walking, follow bd. Alexandre III across town through its various name changes. At pl. de la Victoire, turn left onto av. des Bains, cross the bridge, and turn left onto allée Fenelon; pl. Asseman is on the right (30min.). The single-sex barracks are cramped, and the co-ed bathrooms are perpetually beach-grimy. (☎03 28 63 36 34; fax 03 28 63 24 54. Breakfast 19F/€2.90. Meals 43.50F/€6.63. Sheets 17F/€2.59. Reception 9am-noon and 6-11pm. Lockout noon-2pm. Curfew Sept.-June 11pm. In summer, entry but no check-in 11pm-6am. Bunks 50F/€7.62. **Non-members** pay 19F/€2.90 per night supplement up to 6 nights. **Members only** in summer.) Also on the beach is **Hôtel Eole,** 77-79 digue de Mer. Take bus #3 or 3A to pl. Turenne and walk past the church toward the beach, then turn right on digue de Mer; otherwise it's a 45-minute hike from the train station. (☎03 28 69 13 64; fax 03 28 69 52 57. Breakfast 30F/€4.57. Reception 10am-3pm and 6-10pm. Singles with bath 150-250F/€22.90-38.12; doubles with bath 180-300F/€27.44-45.74. AmEx/MC/V.) There's also **Hôtel le Lion d'Or,** 2 rue de Chemin de Fer, near the station. Rooms are well-sized, clean, and pretty. (☎/fax 03 28 66 08 24. Reception M-F 8am-midnight. Singles and doubles 185-240F/€28.21-36.59. MC/V.) You can camp near the sand at **Dunkerque Camping Municipal,** bd. de l'Europe. Take bus #3 or 3A to "Malo CES Camping" or follow av. des Bains east for 4km. (☎03 28 69 26 68. Reception 8am-8pm. Open Apr.-Nov. 1 person and tent 49.10F/€7.49, extra person 31.20F/€4.76; with car 97.20F/€14.82. MC/V.)

The cheapest pizzerias and crêperies flourish between #30 and 60 digue de Mer in Malo, but you'll get what you pay for. Various indistinguishable cafés offering lunchtime *formules* line bd. Alexandre III around pl. Jean Bart. Dunkerque's speciality is *potje vlesch,* a seemingly inedible gelatinous dish of rabbit, chicken, and lamb served cold in aspic. For something more recognizable, there's a **Monoprix** supermarket at pl. République (open M-Sa 8:30am-8pm). There is also a **market** at pl. Général de Gaulle (W and Sa 9am-4:30pm) and a smaller suburban version at pl. Turenne (in summer Tu 7am-2pm; in winter 7am-1pm).

SIGHTS AND ENTERTAINMENT. Opposite the tourist office on rue Clemenceau, the 15th-century **Eglise St-Eloi** has Flemish paintings within its spare spidery walls. Striking Flemish stained glass has replaced many of the bombed-out original windows. The church is the final resting place of Jean Bart (1650-1702), the famous swashbuckling local pirate knighted by Louis XIV after saving France from famine—his statue in the pl. Jean Bart is notable for its over-the-top foppishness. The church's 500-year-old **belfry** is open in the summer. The office-like interior of the **Musée des Beaux-Arts** houses a collection of 16th- to 18th-century paintings by French and Flemish artists and a few delightfully playful 19th-century works. (☎03 28 59 21 65. Open W-M 10am-12:15pm and 1:45-6pm. 20F/€3.05, couples 30F/€4.57, students 10F/€1.53, first Su of each month free.)

Although the coastline is marred by cranes and industrial buildings, the beach area of **Malo-les-Bains** is very active on sunny summer days. The boardwalk overflows with un-self-conscious tackiness. Rent **windsurfing** equipment at the **Office de Tourisme de la Plage,** 48bis digue de Mer. (☎03 28 26 28 88. 340F/€51.84 per 2hr.) In summer, the beachfront is an all-night party; everyone packs the bars along **digue de Mer** and **digue des Alliés.** Like clockwork, twenty-somethings pile into the **Milk Bar,** 46 digue de Mer, for milkshakes (22F/€3.35) and videogames. (☎03 28 59 12 52. Open daily 10am-2am.) For a faster pace, the nightclub **NASA,** 67 digue de Mer, launches reggae from 10pm until dawn (☎03 28 69 07 75).

MONTREUIL-SUR-MER

Though its name is misleading (not a drop of salt water has been seen here since the 13th century, when the ocean began to recede considerably), Montreuil could hardly be more idyllic if it were on the sea. The unmanicured *vieille ville* and the rough, peaceful hills outside bear no stains of tourism; next to the blighted Channel Ports, they're perfect. Montreuil merits a visit for its simple, honest appeal.

TRANSPORTATION AND PRACTICAL INFORMATION. The **train station** lies just outside the walls of the citadel. Trains go to: **Arras** (1½hr., 4 per day, 74F/€11.28); **Boulogne** (40min., 6 per day, 40F/€6.10); **Calais** (1hr., 3-4 per day, 71F/€10.82); **Lille** (2hr., 4per day, 91F/€13.87); and **Paris** via **Etaples** (3hr., 3 per day, 209F/€31.86). (☎03 21 06 05 09. Office open M-Sa 6am-9:30pm, Su 8:30m-9:15pm.)

To reach the **tourist office,** beside the citadel at 21 rue Carnot, climb the stairs across from the train station and turn right on av. du 11 Novembre. At the sign for the *Auberge de Jeunesse,* turn right onto quiet rue des Bouchers, then left onto the footpath at the shrine of Notre-Dame; the office is straight ahead. It distributes a map and brochures. (☎03 21 06 04 27; fax 03 21 06 57 85. Open Apr.-Oct. M-Sa 9:30am-12:30pm and 2-6pm, Su 10am-12:30pm and 3-5pm; Nov.-Mar. Su 10am-12:30pm only.) **BNP,** pl. Darnétal, **exchanges currency.** (Open Tu-W 8:30am-noon and 1:30-5:30pm, Th 8:30am-noon, F 1:30-5:30pm, Sa 8:45am-12:30pm.) Call the **police** at 03 21 81 08 48. The closest **hospital** (☎03 21 89 45 45) is in Rang du Fliers. The **post office** is on pl. Gambetta. (☎03 21 06 70 00. Open M-F 8am-noon and 2-5:30pm, Sa 8:30am-noon.) **Postal code:** 62170.

FLANDERS & CALAIS

ACCOMMODATIONS AND FOOD. The **Auberge de Jeunesse "La Hulotte" (HI),** is inside the citadel on rue Carnot. It offers rustic, summercamp-style accommodations, kitchen access, sweeping hilltop views, and freedom to wander around the medieval citadel after hours. (☎03 21 06 10 83. Open Mar.-Sept. 15 sun-drenched yellow-and-blue rooms in a petal-pink building on the central *place.* (☎03 21 06 04 95; fax 03 21 06 04 00. Breakfast 38F/€5.80. Reception 7:30am-11:30pm. Singles 200-250F/€30.50-38.10; doubles 200-300F/€30.50-45.75. 3F/€0.46 tax per person per night. AmEx/MC/V.) The **Renards,** at 4 av. du 11 Novembre, offer huge, old-fashioned **chambres d'hôte** at the top of the stairs from the train station. All rooms have fireplaces, rugs, and heavy old furniture; they may be the nicest accommodations, for their style and price, in northern France. (☎03 21 86 85 72. Breakfast included. Single with bath 180-200F/€28.97-30.49; double with bath 220-250F/€33.54-38.12. Extra bed 80F/€12.20.) The beautiful, forested **campground,** 744 rte. d'Etaples, is by the banks of the river and not far from a pool, restaurant, and tennis courts. (☎03 21 06 07 28. Reception 9am-noon and 2-6pm. 1 or 2 people with car or tent 38F/€5.80, extra person 9F/€1.37. Electricity 15F/€2.29.)

Restaurants crowd **pl. de Gaulle,** and there are bakeries on the adjacent streets. Picnic fare can be found at **Shopi,** pl. de Gaulle. (Open Tu-F 9am-12:15pm and 2:30-7:15pm, Sa 9am-7:15pm, Su 9am-12:15pm.) **La Crêperie Montreuil,** 3 rue du Clape en Bas, serves velvety crêpes and offers free, rock, jazz, and blues shows every summer Thursday at 9:30pm (open July-mid Sept. daily 4pm-midnight).

SIGHTS AND ENTERTAINMENT. A walk along the 3km-long **ramparts** is like the glorious minute after take-off. Green rivers cut through fields of wildflowers, grazing cows, and sooty red rooftops. Stop along the way to visit the1q6-th century **citadel,** on the site of the old royal castle. (Open July-Aug. W-M 10am-noon and 2-6pm; Sept.-June 10am-noon and 2-5pm. 15F/€2.29, children 8F/€1.22.)

Picture-perfect tumbledown cottages line the **rue du Clape en Bas** and the **Cavée St-Firmin;** the latter has actually been featured in several films, including the first version of *Les Misérables*. The liveliest streets are **rue d'Herambault** and those surrounding **pl. de Gaulle.** The **Chapelle de l'Hôtel Dieu** and the **St-Saulve Abbey,** are both heavily carved Gothic churches on pl. Gambetta. **Club Canoë Kayak,** 4 rue Moulin des Orphelins, across the canal from the train station, runs canoe and kayak excursions on the river Canche. (☎03 21 06 20 16. Open daily 10am-noon and 1:30-5pm. Sessions start at 55F/€8.39, different difficulty levels available.)

At the end of July, the townsfolk stage a big-time *son-et-lumière* behind the citadel. It's based on Victor Hugo's *Les Misérables*—in the book, it is as mayor of Montreuil that a newly reformed Jean Valjean flees from Inspector Javert to claim the child Cosette. (Contact tourist office. 90F/€13.72, children 60F/€9.15.) August 15 brings the **Day of the Street Painters,** an exuberant and artsy celebration.

AMIENS

Amiens, the capital of Picardy, is a friendly, livable place, more agreeable than any other city in the immediate area—and it has the added bonus of being extremely walkable. It's known for a fine Gothic cathedral, a twisting old quarter of streets and canals, and the tranquil *hortillonages,* former marshlands cultivated ever since the Romans set up camp here in 12 BC.

TRANSPORTATION AND PRACTICAL INFORMATION. Trains leave **Gare du Nord,** pl. Alphonse Fiquet, for **Boulogne** (1¼hr., 13 per day, 95F/€14.48); **Calais** (2hr., 10 per day, 120F/€18.30); **Lille** (1¼hr., 12 per day, 97F/€14.79); **Paris** (1¼hr., 20 per day, 100F/€15.25); and **Rouen** (1½hr., 3 per day, 94F/€14.33). (Ticket office open M-F 5am-9pm, Sa 6am-9pm, Su 6am-10pm; Info M-Sa 9am-6pm.) **Buses** leave from under the shopping center to the right of the station for **Beauvais** (1-1½hr., 5 per day, 44F/€6.71). **SEMTA,** left as you exit the station on 10 pl. Alphonse Figuet, provides **local transportation.** All buses stop at the train station; buy tickets on the bus or at the office. (☎03 22 71 40 00. Office open M-F 7am-7pm, Sa 8am-5:30pm. Buses run 6am-9pm, tickets 7.20F/€1.10.) For a **taxi,** call 03 22 91 30 03 (24hr.).

To get to the **tourist office,** 6bis rue Dusevel, turn right from the station parking lot, pass the mall, and turn left onto rue Gloriette. Continue through several name changes and pl. St-Michel; after the cathedral, turn left onto rue Dusevel; the office is on the left. The staff organizes tours (July-Aug. daily, Sept.-June weekends only; 30F/4.57, 25F/€3.81 students, children 20F/€3.05), takes care of **hotel reservations** (20F/€3.05, must be in-person), and has an excellent map of the town. (☎03 22 71 60 50; fax 03 22 71 60 51. Open Apr.-Sept. M-Sa 9am-7pm, Su 10am-noon and 2-5pm; Oct-Mar. M-Sa 9am-6pm, Su 10am-noon and 2-5pm.) **Net Express,** 10 rue André, is a laundromat, not a cybercafé. (☎03 22 72 33 33. Open daily 7am-9pm.) Surf the Internet at **Neurogame,** at rue St Martin aux Waides and rue du Marche Lanselle. (Open M-Sa 10am-10pm. 25F/€3.81 per hr.) **Hôpital Nord** is on pl. Victor Pauchet (☎03 22 66 80 00; take bus #10 (dir: "Collège César Frank"); #11 makes the return trip.) The **police** are at 1 rue Maré-Lanselles (☎03 22 71 53 00). The **post office** is at 7 rue des Vergeaux, down the block from the Hôtel de Ville. (☎03 22 44 60 00. Open M-F 8am-7pm, Sa 8am-12:30pm.) **Poste Restante:** 80050. **Postal code:** 80000.

ACCOMMODATIONS. Amiens has no youth hostel or nearby campgrounds. There is, however, a cluster of hotels in the 150-170F/€22.90-25.92 range near the train station. The tourist office publishes a list of hotels and price ranges. The spacious rooms at **Hôtel Puvis de Chavannes,** 6 rue Puvis de Chavannes, must have been pretty once, but are now quite worn-down. They're some of the cheapest around and are right by the Musée des Beaux-Arts. (☎03 22 91 82 96; fax 03 22 72 95 35. Breakfast 27F/€4.12. Shower 10F/€1.53. Reception 7:15am-8:30pm. Singles and doubles 130-200F/€19.82-30.49; triples 260F/€39.64. AmEx/MC/V.) The rooms at the **Hôtel Victor Hugo,** 2 rue l'Oratoire, are worn but pleasant and well-kept. (☎03 22 91 57 91; fax 03 22 92 74 02. Breakfast 28F/€4.27. Reception 24hr. Singles and doubles 220-250F/€33.54-38.12; triples 290F/€44.21. MC/V.) Snuggled in a prime location on a small street behind the cathedral, the **Hôtel le Prieuré,** 6 rue Porion, offers grandmotherly luxury: four-posters, and swirly floral wallpaper. (☎03 22 71 16 71. Breakfast 36F/€5.49. Reception Tu-Sa 8am-noon and 2-11:30pm. Singles from 250F/€38.12; doubles from 320F/€48.79; triples 350F/€53.36. MC/V.) The **Spatial Hôtel,** 15 rue Alexandre Fatton, between the train station and the cathedral, has impersonal but spacious rooms, all with TVs. (☎03 22 91 53 23; fax 03 22 92 27 87. Breakfast 30F/€4.57. Reception 7:30am-9:30pm. Singles 165-260F/€25.16-39.46; doubles 185-280F/€28.21-42.69; triples 320F/€48.80. Extra bed 45F/€6.86. MC/V.)

FOOD AND ENTERTAINMENT. There's plenty of food in the shops around the **Hôtel de Ville.** A **Match supermarket** is in the mall to the right of the station (open M-Sa 9am-8pm). Amiens' main **market** in pl. Pasmentier (Sa) sells vegetables grown in the *hortillonages* (see **Sights,** below). Smaller markets are held on pl. Beffroi (W and Sa). The **Restaurant Tante Jeanne,** 1 rue de la Dodane, serves a super *ficelles picardie* (thin crêpe, 40F/€6.10), along the waterfront in St-Leu. (☎03 22 72 30 30. Open daily noon-2pm and 7-10:30pm. V.)

At night, the gas-lit, cobbled **pl. du Don** and **rue Belu,** in the Quartier St-Leu, teem with energetic French students. The **Riverside Café,** 3 pl. du Don, is a self-dubbed "American 50s bar," packing kids in on the chrome stools inside and the terrace outside. (☎03 22 92 50 30. Happy hour 6-8pm: beer 10F/€1.53. Open daily 4pm-3am.) Across the street, **Le Zeppelin,** 2 rue des Bondes, is always full of partyers, cheap beer, and trip-hop. (☎03 22 92 38 16. Open M 2pm-3am, Tu-Su 10am-3am.)

SIGHTS. The **Cathédrale de Notre-Dame** was built in 1206 to house John the Baptist's head, brought home by a local who had fought in the Fourth Crusade. Its soaring 42m nave crowns a cathedral twice the size of its namesake in Paris. Look behind the choir for the small Weeping Angel, which became famous when WWI soldiers mailed thousands of postcards of it home to celebrate their victory in taking the town from the Germans. Before you go, pick up the surprisingly informative brochure from the tourist office. (Open Easter-Oct. M-Sa 8:30am-7pm, Su 8:30am-noon and 2:30-7pm; Nov.-Feb. M-Sa 8:30am-noon and 2-5pm, Su 8:30am-noon and 2:30-7pm. French tours July-Aug. daily at 3pm; Sundays all year at 3pm.)

Just north of the Somme River, the **Quartier St-Leu** is the oldest, most attractive part of Amiens. Built along a system of waterways and canals, its narrow, cobbled streets and flower-strewn squares make it the self-titled "Venice of the North." Nearby are the **hortillonages,** market gardens spread over the inlets created when the Romans built canals through the marshland. There is a daily antique market and countless small art studios on passage Belu.

The **Picardy Museum,** 48 rue de la République, houses a distinguished collection of French paintings and sculpture. Don't miss Pierre Coisin's sculpture of Daphnis embracing the nymph Naïs. (☎03 22 97 14 00. Open Tu-Su 10am-12:30pm and 2-6pm. 20F/€3.05, students and under 16 10F/€1.53.) Jules Verne (1828-1905) spent most of his life and wrote all of his novels in Amiens; his former house is now the **Centre de Documentation Jules Verne,** at 2 rue Dubois, near the cirque. A small but appropriately quirky museum, it has models of the Nautilus and a holographic head of Verne himself. (Open M-F 9am-noon and 2-6pm, Sa-Su 2-6pm. 20F/€3.05, students 15F/€2.29, under age 16 10F/€1.53.) Verne lies 0.00046 leagues under the earth in the **Cimitière de Madeleine,** a 20-minute walk from the center of town.)

NORMANDY (NORMANDIE)

In AD 911, Rollo, the leader of a band of Vikings who had settled around Rouen, accepted the title of Duke of Normandy from King Louis the Simple. After being baptized, Rollo assumed the name of Robert and over the next few centuries, Norman power grew beyond even Robert's wildest dreams. The most famous Norman achievement was the successful 1066 invasion of the island just across the Channel, celebrated in a magnificent tapestry that still hangs in Bayeux. Scarcely less remarkable is the seizure of southern Italy and Sicily by bands of roaming Norman Knights, how they came within a plague-ridden flea's breath of conquering the Byzantine Empire, and even won the crown of Jerusalem following the First Crusade. Occupied in 1346 by an English King Edward III in search of his Norman roots, their war-torn nation was by 1450 definitively incorporated into France. The English did not attempt another invasion until June 6, 1944, when they returned with American and Canadian allies to wrest Normandy from German occupation.

In the intervening centuries, Normandy exchanged its warlike reputation for a quiet agricultural role. Far removed from the border wars which raged between France and its neighbors, Normandy's towns and villages remained virtually unchanged from the Middle Ages—an architectural heritage mostly destroyed during the heavy fighting following the D-Day landings. Gustave Flaubert, Normandy's most famous author, set his tale of provincial woe, *Madame Bovary*, in his homeland. Later in the 19th century, a landscape painter from Honfleur, Eugène Boudin, persuaded a young Claude Monet to take up serious painting. Monet and his friends became regular visitors to the stormy coast and calm Seine estuary in the 1860s. In the 1930s, Jean-Paul Sartre served as a teaching assistant in Le Havre, which he renamed Bouville (Mudtown) in his first novel, *Nausea*.

TRANSPORTATION

Le Havre, Dieppe, Caen, and Cherbourg welcome travelers arriving by water from England and Ireland. Within Normandy, major towns are connected by rail; buses fill in the gaps. The largest bus operator in *Basse Normandie* (west of Rouen) is **Bus Verts du Calvados** (in Caen ☎02 31 44 77 44). They offer the **Carte Liberté,** allowing unlimited travel on their lines and on the Caen city bus system. Even if you don't opt for the *Carte*, ask about youth reductions. Since many spots lie off the main roads, a bike or car helps for extended touring. Cyclists should note that roads are hilly and coastal winds blow roughly west to east.

1 **Rouen:** Overgrown provincial town with everything Joan of Arc; grand Gothic cathedral **(p. 463)**
2 **Dieppe:** Dull seaside town full of Brits on holiday; pebbly beaches; great seafood **(p. 468)**
3 **Fécamp:** Best known for a healing liqueur; tucked among craggy cliffs **(p. 471)**
4 **Etretat:** Gem of the High Normandy coast; resort town with soaring chalk cliffs **(p. 470)**
5 **Le Havre:** A ferry hub, one of the ugliest places on Earth **(p. 471)**
6 **Honfleur:** Artists' haven—un-bohemian prices; fanciful museum honors Erik Satie **(p. 473)**
7 **Houlgate:** Quieter, more affordable seaside resort; sandy beaches with seashells **(p. 475)**
8 **Cabourg:** Marcel Proust spent his summers here; otherwise unexceptional **(p. 476)**
9 **Deauville:** Snootiness without glamor—prices to match; pleasant boardwalk **(p. 476)**
10 **Trouville:** Less wealthy and more welcoming than its twin across the river **(p. 476)**
11 **Caen:** Chic large city, rebuilt with skill and care; the best WWII museum in Normandy **(p. 478)**
12 **Bayeux:** Celebrated tapestries; good base from which to explore war memorials **(p. 482)**
13 **D-Day beaches:** Need and admit no summary **(p. 484)**
14 **Cherbourg:** Bleak coastal city; ferries and trains, and that's it **(p. 488)**
15 **Granville:** Bland base for visits to Mont-St-Michel and Channel Islands; silky beaches **(p. 489)**
16 **Mont-St-Michel:** Ancient fortified island shot through with tunnels and galleries **(p. 494)**
17 **Coutances:** Beautiful 13th-century cathedral; gorgeous surrounding countryside **(p. 491)**
18 **Avranches:** Extraordinary manuscripts in an ordinary town **(p. 492)**

ROUEN

However Gustave Flaubert may have criticized his hometown in *Madame Bovary*, Rouen (pop. 108,000) is no petty provincial town. From the 10th to the 12th century, it bloomed with Gothic architecture and half-timbered houses, as befitted the capital of the Norman empire. Joan of Arc was held prisoner here and tried for heresy by French clergy in 1431. The clerics passed down a life sentence which, under English pressure, was generously commuted to burning at the stake. The pathos of Joan's story, and the Gothic splendor of Rouen's churches, have always piqued the curiosity of artists and writers; in the 19th century, Victor Hugo dubbed it the "city of a hundred spires," and Monet's eye for the play of the light on the cathedral's facade made it a fixture in museums around the world. If post-WWII reconstruction didn't exactly beautify Rouen, it hasn't marred the architectural and historical appeal at its heart. A hip, young population has inherited the *vieille ville;* Madame B. would be jealous.

TRANSPORTATION

Trains: rue Jeanne d'Arc. To: **Caen** (2hr., 7 per day, 118F/€17.99); **Dieppe** (1hr., 13 per day, 57F/€8.69); **Le Havre** (1¼hr., 15 per day, 74F/€11.28); **Lille** (3hr., 5 per day, 163F/€24.85); and **Paris** (1½hr., every hr., 106F/€16.16). Info office open M-Sa 7:45am-7pm.

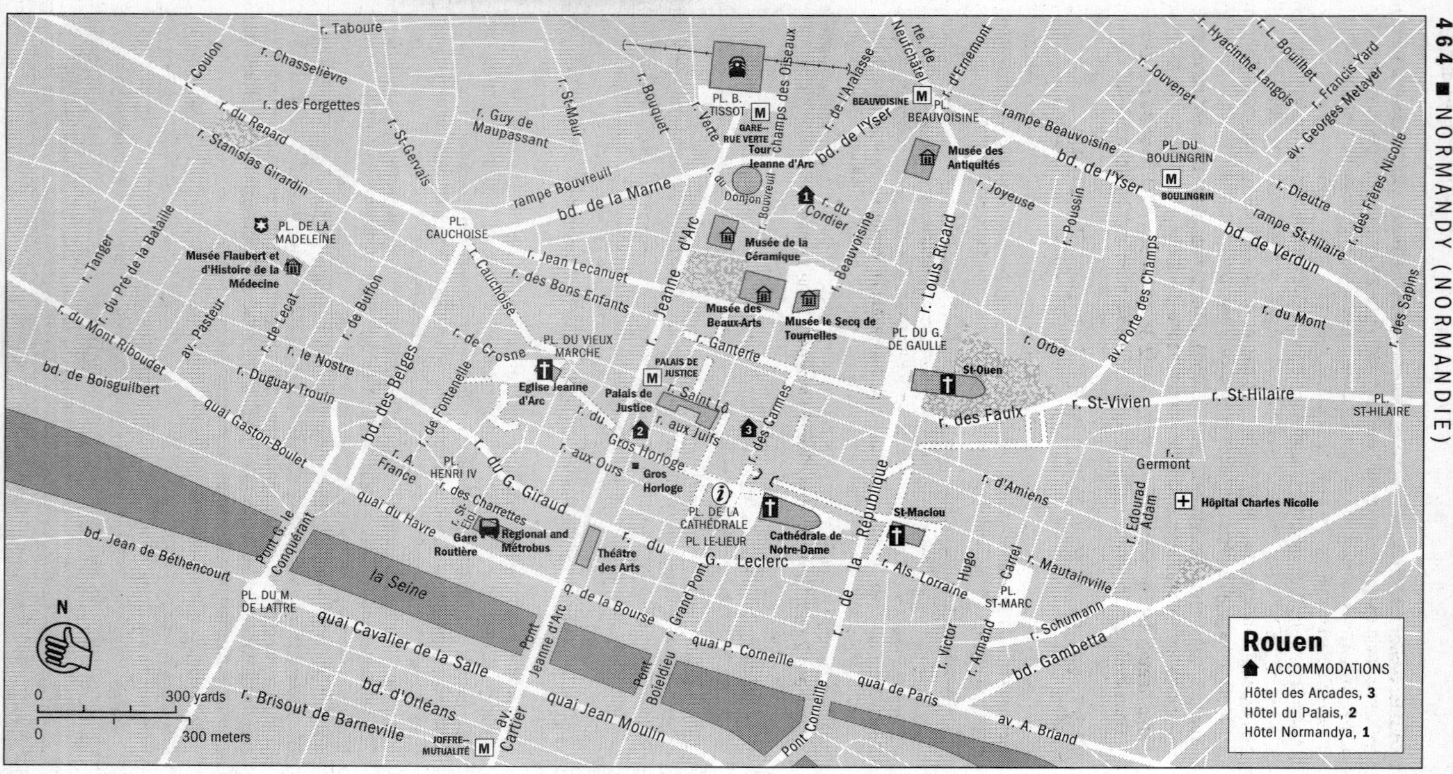
Rouen
ACCOMMODATIONS
Hôtel des Arcades, 3
Hôtel du Palais, 2
Hôtel Normandya, 1
Hôpital Charles Nicolle
Musée des Antiquités
Musée le Secq de Tournelles
Musée de la Céramique
Musée des Beaux-Arts
Musée Flaubert et d'Histoire de la Médecine
Palais de Justice
Gros Horloge
Théâtre des Arts
Eglise Jeanne d'Arc
Regional and Métrobus
Gare Routière
St-Ouen
St-Maclou
Cathédrale de Notre-Dame
Tour Jeanne d'Arc
Donjon
PL. DU BOULINGRIN
BOULINGRIN
PL. BEAUVOISINE
BEAUVOISINE
PL. B. TISSOT
GARE-RUE VERTE
PL. DU G. DE GAULLE
PL. ST-MARC
PL. DE LA CATHÉDRALE
PL. LE-LIEUR
PL. DU VIEUX MARCHE
PALAIS DE JUSTICE
PL. CAUCHOISE
PL. HENRI IV
PL. DE LA MADELEINE
PL. DU M. DE LATTRE
PL. ST-HILAIRE
JOFFRE-MUTUALITÉ
la Seine
bd. de Verdun
bd. de l'Yser
bd. de la Marne
bd. des Belges
bd. Gambetta
bd. d'Orléans
bd. de Boisguilbert
bd. Jean de Béthencourt
r. Jeanne d'Arc
r. de la République
r. St-Hilaire
r. St-Vivien
r. des Faulx
r. Louis Ricard
r. Beauvoisine
r. Ganterie
r. du Gros Horloge
r. du G. Giraud
r. du G. Leclerc
r. Grand Pont
r. Verte
r. du Donjon
r. Bouvreuil
r. Cauchoise
r. de Crosne
r. Jean Lecanuet
r. des Bons Enfants
rampe Bouvreuil
rampe Beauvoisine
rampe St-Hilaire
av. Porte des Champs
quai de Paris
quai P. Corneille
quai Jean Moulin
quai Cavalier de la Salle
quai du Havre
quai Gaston-Boulet
q. de la Bourse
Pont Corneille
Pont Boïeldieu
Pont Jeanne d'Arc
Pont G. le Conquérant
r. Brisout de Barneville
av. Cartier
av. A. Briand
r. du Mont Riboudet
r. Duguay Trouin
av. Pasteur
r. de Lecat
r. le Nostre
r. de Buffon
r. de Fontenelle
r. des Charrettes
r. A. France
r. Stanislas Girardin
r. du Renard
r. des Forgettes
r. Chasselièvre
r. Taboure
r. Coulon
r. St-Gervais
r. Guy de Maupassant
r. St-Maur
r. Bouquet
Champs des Oiseaux
r. de l'Aralasse
rte. de Neufchâtel
r. d'Ernemont
r. Joyeuse
r. Poussin
r. Orbe
r. du Mont
r. Dieutre
r. des Sapins
r. des Frères Nicolle
r. Francis Yard
av. Georges Metayer
r. L. Bouilhet
r. Hyacinthe Langlois
r. Jouvenet
r. Germont
r. Edouard Adam
r. d'Amiens
r. Mautainville
r. Armand Carrel
r. Victor Hugo
r. Als. Lorraine
r. Schumann
r. des Carmes
r. Saint Lô
r. aux Juifs
r. aux Ours
r. du Cordier
r. du Pré de la Bataille
r. Tanger
N
0
300 yards
0
300 meters

Buses: SATAR and **CNA,** office with Métrobus, below. Most buses depart from quai du Havre or quai de la Bourse. (☎02 35 52 92 00). To **Le Havre** (2½hr.; 6 per day in summer, 10 rest of year; 87F/€13.26), as well as various small towns in the **Seine Valley.** See office hours below.

Local Transportation: Métrobus, rue Jeanne d'Arc, in front of the Théâtre des Arts (☎02 35 52 52 52). Subway runs 5am-11pm, and most buses run 6am-8pm, some night lines until midnight. 1hr. ticket 8F/€1.22, *carnet* of 10 63F/€9.61. Day pass 20F/€3.05, 2-day 30F/€4.57. Info office open M-Sa 7am-7pm.

Taxis: 67 rue Jean Lecanuet (☎02 35 88 50 50). 24hr. stands at the train and bus stations, as well as the Palais de Justice on rue Jeanne d'Arc.

Bike Rental: Rouen Cycles, 45 rue St-Eloi (☎02 35 71 34 30). 120F/€18.30 per day. Deposit of the bike's value required. Open Tu-Sa 9am-noon and 2-7pm. AmEx/MC/V.

ORIENTATION AND PRACTICAL INFORMATION

To get to the city center from the station, exit straight out and follow **rue Jeanne d'Arc** several blocks. A left onto the cobblestoned rue du Gros Horloge leads to **pl. de la Cathédrale** and the tourist office; a right leads to **pl. du Vieux-Marché.**

Tourist Office: 25 pl. de la Cathédrale (☎02 32 08 32 40; fax 02 32 08 32 44). Free map; better one with index 31F/€4.73. Commission-free **currency exchange.** For info regarding excursions from Rouen, ask for the brochure *Day Trips around Rouen;* for a hip look at student favorites, pick up the student guide *Le Viking.* Open May-Sept. M-Sa 9am-7pm, Su 9:30am-12:30pm and 2-6pm; Oct.-Mar. M-Sa 9am-6pm, Su 10am-1pm.

Budget Travel: Wasteels, 111bis rue Jeanne d'Arc (☎08 03 88 70 57). Open M-F 9am-noon and 2-6pm, Sa 9am-noon. **Forum Voyages,** 72 rue Jeanne d'Arc (☎02 32 72 70 60). Open M-F 9:30am-7pm, Sa 10am-12:30pm and 2-6pm.

English Bookstore: ABC Bookshop, 11 rue des Faulx, behind Eglise St-Ouen (☎02 35 71 08 67). Windows display ads for au pairs and tutors for hire. Open Tu-Sa 10am-6pm; closes at 3pm in July. Usually closed late July through mid-August.

Youth Center: Centre Rouen Information Jeunesse (CRIJ), 84 rue Beauvoisine (☎02 35 98 38 75), helps find work and has info on activities. Open M-F 10am-5pm.

Laundromat: 73 rue Beauvoisine. Open daily 8am-8pm. Another on rue Cauchoise near pl. du Vieux Marché. Open daily 7am-9pm.

Police: 9 rue Brisout de Barneville (☎02 32 81 25 00), south of the river, off rue Barbey d'Aureyville.

Hospital: 1 rue de Germont (☎02 32 88 89 90), near pl. St-Vivien.

Internet Access: Place Net, 37 rue de la République (☎02 32 76 02 22), near the Eglise St-Maclou. 40F/€6.10 per hr. Open M-Sa 10am-midnight, Su 2-10pm. Also **Cybernetics,** pl. du Vieux Marché (☎02 35 07 02 77). 40F/€6.10 per hr. Open M and Th 11am-7:30pm, Tu-W and F-Sa 11am-midnight, Su 2-7pm.

Post Office: 45bis rue Jeanne d'Arc (☎02 35 15 66 73). **Currency exchange.** Open M-F 8am-7pm, Sa 8:30am-1:30pm. **Branch** at 122 rue Jeanne d'Arc, just left from the train station. Open M-F 8:30am-6:30pm, Sa 9am-noon. **Postal code:** 76000.

ACCOMMODATIONS AND CAMPING

Cheap lodgings lie on the side streets between the train station and the Hôtel de Ville; unfortunately, Rouen no longer has a hostel.

Hôtel Normandya, 32 rue du Cordier (☎02 35 71 46 15), near the train station off rue du Donjon. Owned by an exuberantly friendly, *Let's Go*-loving couple. Nicely decorated with excellent views of the city; a few dark, windowless rooms. Shower 10F/€1.53. Reception 8am-8pm. Singles and doubles 130-150F/€19.82-22.90. No credit cards.

Hôtel des Arcades, 52 rue de Carmes (☎02 35 70 10 30; fax 02 35 70 08 91). Bright, clean, highly color-coordinated rooms. Breakfast 32F/€4.88. Hall shower 15F/€2.29. Reception M-F 7am-8pm, Sa-Su 7:30am-8pm. Singles and doubles 157F/€24, with shower 223-262F/€34-40. AmEx/MC/V.

Hôtel du Palais, 12 rue Tambour (☎02 35 71 41 40), off rue du Gros Horloge. Homey, eccentrically decorated rooms in a prime location. Ask to see your room—some lack windows. Breakfast 25F/€3.81. Showers 15F/€2.29. Reception 24hr., closed Su noon-6pm. Singles 120F/€18.30; doubles 140F/€21.35, with shower 160-200F/€24.39-30.49, with bath 220-240F/€33.54-36.59. Extra bed 40F/€6.10. AmEx/MC/V.

Camping Municipal de Déville, rue Jules Ferry in Déville-les-Rouen (☎02 35 74 07 59), 4km from Rouen. Take the métro from the train station (dir: "Technopole" or "Georges Braque") to "Théâtre des Arts," transfer to line TEOR (T2), dir: "Mairie," and get off at "Mairie de Deville-les-Rouen." Rue Jules Ferry will be just up to your right. A few shady grass patches with a parking lot for caravans. Open June-Sept. for tents, year-round for caravans. 25F/€3.81 per person, 9.50F/€1.45 per tent, 9F/€1.37 per car, 17.50F/€2.67 per caravan, electricity 12.50F/€1.91, 1F/€0.15 tax per person per day.

FOOD AND ENTERTAINMENT

Outdoor cafés and brasseries crowd around **pl. du Vieux-Marché.** A **market** is held on the *place* itself (Tu-Su 6am-1:30pm). There are also plenty of eateries near the **Gros Horloge.** A **Monoprix supermarket** is at 73-83 rue du Gros Horloge (open M-Sa 8:30am-9pm), and a **Marché U** on pl. du Vieux-Marché (open M-Sa 8:30am-8pm). Vegetarianism and other organic obsessions are indulged at **Natural Gourmand'grain,** 3 rue du Petit Salut, off pl. de la Cathédrale. (☎02 35 98 15 74. *Plat* and salad 49F/€7.47. Restaurant open Tu-Sa noon-2pm; store open 10am-7pm. MC/V.) **Al Dente,** 24 rue Cauchoise, off pl. du Vieux-Marché, serves up tender pâté and crisp-crusted pizzas (both from 48F/€7.32). (☎02 35 70 24 45. 59F/€9 lunch menu. Open Tu-Su noon-2:30pm and 7-10:30pm. MC/V.)

The most active of Rouen's many indistinguishable bars is **Le Nash,** 97 rue Ecuyère, where beer is 15F/€2.29 and James Brown blasts from the porch. (☎02 35 98 25 24. Open M-F 10am-2pm, Sa 6pm-2am, Su 7pm-2am.) The best of the Rouen scene may be the gay and lesbian **Le Bloc House,** 138 rue Beauvoisine, where live DJs spin house Sa night. (☎02 35 07 71 97. Open M-Sa 7pm-2am. MC/V.)

SIGHTS

Sights in Rouen fall into three basic categories: museums, churches, and museums and churches related to Joan of Arc. The real show-stoppers are the cathedral, the Musée des Beaux-Arts, and Flaubert's former house. Sorry, Joan.

CATHEDRALE DE NOTRE-DAME. The cathedral is among the most important in France, and incorporates nearly every intermediate style of Gothic architecture. It also gained fame as the subject of a series of paintings by Monet. Many of the windows destroyed during WWII have been replaced with frosted glass, giving the cathedral the atmosphere of a very holy bathroom. Don't miss the stained glass in the **Chapelle St-Jean de la Nef** depicting the beheading of St. John the Baptist. To the left of Notre-Dame stands the 12th-century **Tour St-Romanus;** to the right stands the 17th-century **Tour de Beurre,** which was financed through dispensations granted to those who wanted to eat butter during Lent. The cathedral, whose central spire is the tallest in France (151m), is illuminated nightly in summer. *(Pl. de la Cathédrale. Open M-Sa 8am-7pm, Su 8am-6pm. Tours in French throughout the year Sa-Su at 3pm.)*

MUSEE DES BEAUX-ARTS. This renowned museum has one of France's most esteemed collections, a wallop of Dutch and Italian masters and a less impressive 19th- and 20th-century array. Monet's representation of the sun-drenched cathedral is a nice reprieve from the roomfuls of gloomy religious painting. *(Sq. Verdel, down rue Jeanne d'Arc from the train station. ☎02 35 71 28 40. Open W-M 10am-6pm; some exhibits closed 1-2pm. 20F/€3.05, ages 18-25 and groups 13F/€1.98, under 18 free.)*

MUSEE FLAUBERT ET D'HISTOIRE DE LA MEDECINE. Gustave Flaubert grew up on these premises, since converted into a fascinating museum. The building houses a few of Flaubert's possessions, as well as an old midwifery mannequin and a collection of gruesome medical instruments used by his father, a physician.

The union of literature and medical history seems less bizarre when you consider Flaubert's obsession with graphic literary realism, including Dr. Bovary's treatises on clubfeet. *(51 rue de Lecat, next door to the Hôtel-Dieu hospital. Follow rue de Crosne from pl. du Vieux Marché. ☎02 35 15 59 95. Open Tu 10am-6pm, W-Sa 10am-noon and 2-6pm. Free English brochure. 12F/€1.83; ages 18-25 8F/€1.22; seniors and students free.)*

EGLISE ST-MACLOU. St-Maclou's uniformly gothic facade, with a delicate free-standing flamboyant grille, may outgrace the cathedral's; inside, the elaborately carved friezes of the organ are the most stunning feature. Look for *les enfants pisseurs*, two urinating cherubs in the left corner of the facade. *(Concerts July and Aug. Tickets available 30min. before concert at the church. For more info, pick up a brochure at the church or call 02 35 70 84 90. 50F/€7.62, students 30F/€4.57.)* Beyond the church to the left, a poorly marked passage at 186 rue de Martainville leads to the **Aître St-Maclou.** This cloister served as the church's slaughterhouse and cemetery during the Middle Ages, including the years of the deadly plagues; hence the grisly 15th-century frieze that decorates the beams of the inner courtyard. The *Rouennais* entombed a live cat inside the walls to exorcise spirits; the shriveled feline is still suspended behind a glass panel for all to see. *(Pl. Barthélémy, behind the cathedral. Open M-Sa 10am-noon and 2-5:30pm, Su 3-5:30pm. Aître open daily 8am-8pm. Free.)*

EGLISE STE-JEANNE D'ARC. This massive structure was designed in 1979 to resemble an overturned Viking longboat. The interior "church in the round" is actually quite tiny; a wall of luminous stained glass, recovered from the Eglise St-Vincent, which was destroyed during WWII, provides a moment's relief from the drabness of poured cement. A 6½-meter cross outside marks the spot where Joan was supposedly burned, although the exact location is much-contested. *(Pl. de Vieux Marché. Open M-Th and Sa 10am-12:30pm and 2-6pm, F and Su 2-6pm.)*

TOUR JEANNE D'ARC. This is the last remaining tower of the château which confined Joan of Arc before she was burned at the stake in 1431, in the pl. du Vieux-Marché. For all but true fans of Joan, there isn't that much to see. *(To the left of the station on rue du Donjon. Due to renovations, the entrance is on rue Bouvreuil. Open Apr.-Sept. W-M 10am-12:30pm and 2-6pm, Su 2-6:30pm; Oct.-Mar. W-M 10am-12:30pm and 2-5pm, Su 2-5:30pm. 10F/€1.53, students free.)*

OTHER SIGHTS. The **Musée des Antiquités** houses a rambling, rummage sale-style collection of Gallo-Roman to Renaissance objects from carvings to tapestries and exquisite transplanted stained glass. *(198 rue Beauvoisine, in Cloître Ste-Marie. ☎02 35 98 55 10. Open M and W-Sa 10am-12:15pm and 1:30-5:30pm, Su 2-6pm. 20F/€3.05, seniors 10F/€1.53, students free.)* Built into a bridge across rue du Gros Horloge, the ornately gilded **Gros Horloge** ("Big Clock") is charmingly inaccurate; look up when passing under at the friezes of the Lamb of God. The belfry is scheduled to be repaired by January 2002; visitors will be able to ascend for a view of the 14th-century clockwork and the rooftops of Rouen. Under the war-marked Palais de Justice stands the 11th-century **Monument Juif** (Jewish Monument), uncovered in the 1970s. Hebrew graffiti on the walls confirmed that the structure had been a Jewish one, perhaps dating as far back as 1100, though whether a synagogue, Talmudic school, or private house is unknown. *(Call tourist office two days in advance for a tour in French.)*

NEAR ROUEN: THE SEINE VALLEY

The lazy Seine unwinds toward the sea, trailing behind it natural and historic gems: castles, abbeys, and national parks spread among rolling farmland and craggy cliffs. You can theme-trek along the river on an Impressionist route, an Emma Bovary route, a route of major castles and mansions, or the best-known itinerary, the Route des Abbayes. The first you'll encounter out of Rouen is the still-functioning **Abbaye St-Martin de Boscherville,** but the star of the bunch is the **Abbaye de Jumièges,** founded by St. Philibert in 654. A fixture in local history and legend since Merovingian times, the abbey became a stone quarry during the Revolution, but was bought and restored by the state in 1947. Now it's a splendid ruin, set in lush grounds that incorporate a 17th-century French garden. (☎02 35 37 24 02. Open Apr. 15-Sept. 15 daily 9:30am-7pm and Sept. 16-Apr. 14 9:30am-1pm and 2:30-5:30pm. Tours available in French every hr. 26F/€3.96, students 16F/€2.44, under age 18 free.) The **Parc Naturel Régional de Brotonne** sprawls across the Seine midway to Le Havre; before you hit the concrete jungle, get in some green time on this network of trails (inquire at the Rouen tourist office). The town of **Caudebec-en-Caux,** easily accessible by bus from Rouen or Le Havre, makes an excellent base to explore the park. A bit farther on toward the sea, the town of **Villequiers,** the site of the tragic drowning of Victor Hugo's daughter Léopoldine and her husband Charles Vacquerie, now houses the **Musée Victor Hugo,** rue Ernest Binet (☎02 35 56 78 31). The museum holds memorabilia from the Hugo and Vacquerie families, as well as drawings and first editions by Hugo himself. Cap off your tour of the valley with an eye at the enormous **Pont de Normandie,** the stark, futuristic bridge that joins the northern and southern banks of the Seine just above Le Havre.

It's easiest to get around the valley by car, but **CNA buses** (☎02 35 28 40 00) hit most of the major sites. Line #30A runs from Rouen's bus station to several of the abbeys, including Jumièges (45min., 4 per day, 35F/€5.34). Change buses at Caudebec-en-Caux to reach Villequiers and the Musée Victor Hugo. Biking is feasible as well, though distances are great. The Rouen tourist office can provide you with info on excursions and a map detailing all the major sights along the valley; its publication *Day Trips around Rouen* may prove helpful as well.

DIEPPE

Somewhere between the mixed bag of the Channel Ports and the concrete block of Le Havre is Dieppe (pop. 36,000), a longtime vacation spot for British and Parisian vacationers. They come for the beach, for Dieppe has little to offer beyond its seaside strip. Though an impressive château and some WWII monuments deserve a look if you're waiting to catch a ferry, nothing here merits a detour.

NORMANDY

ORIENTATION AND PRACTICAL INFORMATION. Hoverspeed ferries leave for **Newhaven,** England (☎08 20 00 35 55; 2hr.; 2-3 per day; 190F/€28.97, with car 642F/€97.88). Ferry ticket holders can take a free shuttle between the ferry terminal and the train station, bd. Clemenceau (☎02 35 06 69 33). **Trains** go to **Rouen** (1¼hr., 10 per day, 57F/€8.69), where you can change for other major destinations. (Ticket office open M-F 5:35am-7:30pm, Sa 6:15am-7:30pm, Su 7:15am-8:50pm.) **CNA buses** (☎02 35 84 21 97), next to the train station, go to **Rouen** (2hr., 4 per day, 73F/€11.13). Buy tickets on board. (Info office open M-Sa 8am-12:15pm and 2-6:30pm.) **Stradbus,** 56 quai Duquesne (☎02 32 14 03 03), runs **local buses** (tickets 6.40F/€0.98, *carnet* of 10 42F/€6.40). For a **taxi,** call 02 35 84 20 05 (24hr.).

A courtesy bus runs from the ferry terminal to the **tourist office,** pont Ango. Otherwise, follow the fishy smell to the waterfront in the town center, taking quai Berigny straight out from the train station until you reach the Pont Ango on your right. The multilingual staff book rooms (20F/€3.05) and provide maps and info about the town. (☎02 32 84 16 92; fax 02 32 14 40 61. Open July-Aug. M-Sa 9am-1pm and 2-8pm, Su 10am-1pm and 3-6pm; May-June and Sept. M-Sa 9am-1pm and 2-7pm, Su 10am-1pm and 3-6pm; Oct.-Apr. M-Sa 9am-noon and 2-6pm.) Check out the biweekly *Les Informations Dieppoises,* which lists local happenings and hotspots (published Tu and F, 6.60F/€1.01 at tabacs). There's a **laundromat** at pl. Nationale, behind the Eglise St-Jacques (open daily 7am-9pm). The **police** are on bd. Clemenceau, next to the station (☎02 32 14 49 00), and the **hospital** on av. Pasteur (☎02 35 14 76 76). **Le Cybercabine de Dieppe,** 48 rue de l'Epée, has **Internet** access. (☎02 35 84 64 36. 10F/€1.53 per visit plus 60F/€9.15 per hr. Open Tu-Sa noon-7pm, Su 2-6pm.) The **post office,** 2 bd. Maréchal Joffre, has **currency exchange.** (☎02 35 06 99 20. Open M-F 8-6pm, Sa 8am-12:30pm.) **Postal code:** 76200.

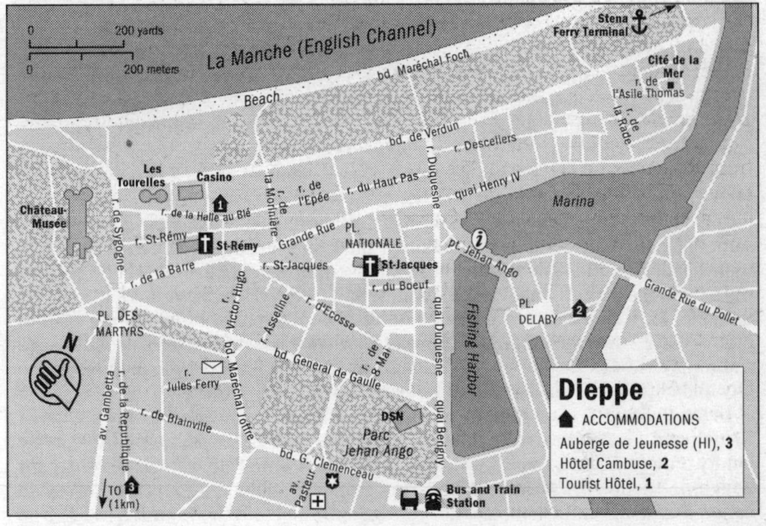

ACCOMMODATIONS AND FOOD. Inexpensive hotels are scattered throughout town, although truly cheap rates are hard to come by. There are more expensive two-stars all along the beach. Reserve well in advance for August.

The **Auberge de Jeunesse (HI),** 48 rue Louis Fromager, has spacious, modern, single-sex rooms with bunk beds. To get there, take bus #2 (dir: "Val Druel") from the Chambre de Commerce, 200m down quai Duquesne from the station, to "Château Michel." Walk back down the hill 200m and take the first left. To walk there from the station, turn left onto bd. Clemenceau, which becomes rue de Blainville. At the end of the street, turn right on rue de la République and make a sharp left on rue Gambetta. Climb the hill and keep going. Turn right at the roundabout onto D925, and left again 200m up the hill (rue Louis Fromager). The hostel is on your right (30min.). **Women should not walk here alone at night.** (☎02 35 84 85 73. Breakfast 19F/€2.90. Sheets 17F/€2.59. Reception 8-10am and 5-10pm. Bunks 50F/€7.62. **Members only.**) The **Tourist Hôtel,** 16 rue de la Halle au Blé, is just behind the beach. From quai Duquesne, turn left onto rue du Haut Pas, which becomes rue de l'Epée and eventually rue de la Halle au Blé. The rooms are roomy and the owner welcoming. (☎02 35 06 10 10; fax 02 35 84 15 87. Breakfast 33F/€5. Singles and doubles with toilet 151F/€23; with shower 141-253F/€21.50-38.50. **Hôtel Cambuse** is at 42 rue Belle Teste, across the Pont Ango, near the tourist office. From pl. Delaby on the other side of the bridge, take a left onto rue Belle Teste. Sparely furnished but spotless and well-maintained. (☎02 35 84 19 46. Breakfast 30F/€4.57. Reception 7am-10pm. Singles and doubles 180-250F/€27.44-38.12. MC/V.)

Inexpensive brasseries, bakeries, and crêperies are on Grande Rue, quai Henri IV, and around Eglise St-Jacques. The sidestreets hold small restaurants that proudly serve up local fish specialties: *harengs marinés* (marinated herring), *soupe du poisson* (fish soup), and *marmite dieppoise* (a fish and shellfish chowder). **Shopi** has two supermarkets, one on Grande Rue, the other near the hostel on rue Gambetta (both open M-Sa 8:30am-12:30pm and 3-7:30pm, Su 9:30am-noon). If canned tuna gets you down, check out the **marché de poissons** in front of the tourist office when the weather is good enough for fishing boats to go out (M-Sa 8am-noon). There's a **market** surrounding the Eglise St-Jacques (Tu and Th mornings), and a larger one takes over the town center all day Saturday.

SIGHTS AND ENTERTAINMENT. Most of Dieppe's summer visitors come to roast on the long pebbly beach, bordered by cliffs to the west and the port to the east. Atop these cliffs rises an imposing 15th-century **château,** now a civic museum housing a hodgepodge of navigational dials, antique planospheres, ivory carvings, and paintings by Renoir, Dufy, and Braque. (☎02 35 84 19 76. Open June-Sept. daily 10am-noon and 2-6pm; Oct.-May W-M 10am-noon and 2-5pm. 15F/€2.29, children and groups 7.50F/€1.91.) In town, the stone **Eglise St-Jacques** has been undergoing repairs, but still displays some beautiful modern stained glass, and a weird set of 16th-century ethnological wall carvings. A somber testament to more recent events is the chillingly beautiful **Canadian Cemetery** in nearby **Hautot-sur-Mer.** Thousands of Canadians died in the famous Allied raid on Dieppe (August 19, 1942); today each identified gravestone bears an inscription in English. To get there, turn right from the hostel, walk for 20 minutes, and turn right at the cross and sign. Or take bus #2, which leaves every 20 minutes from the tourist office. In the eastern part of town, atop the cliffs, the **Chapelle de Notre-Dame-de-Bon-Secours** commands a stunning view of the harbor. It's a long way, but you'll get terrific pictures of the city and cliffs. Take bus #1 (dir: "4 Poteaux") or #8 (dir: "Puys").

Le Brunswick, 19 rue St-Rémy, known as "Le Bronx" among locals, draws a young British and French crowd with booming techno and billiards, though it's pretty empty on weeknights. (☎02 35 40 10 71. Open daily 9pm-2am.) The best refuge for a night in Dieppe is **L'Abordage,** 3 bd. de Verdun, a club that pumps the Eurotrash canon Th-Su nights till 4am, and hosts *soirées* throughout the summer. (☎02 35 82 33 60. Occasional cover 60F/€9.15 includes drink.) Other bars cluster on **Grande Rue** and **rue du Haut Pas.**

THE HIGH NORMANDY COAST

ETRETAT

Heading southwest along the coast from Fécamp, you'll arrive at the small, touristy town of Etretat (pop. 1640), whose natural beauty overpowers its chintzy feel. A favorite destination of British and French vacationers, Etretat occupies perhaps the most spectacular spot on the channel coast, its pebble beach sandwiched between soaring chalk cliffs. The arching western cliff, known as the **Falaise d'Aval,** was likened by Guy de Maupassant to an elephant dipping its trunk into the sea. Climb the stairs on the west end of the promenade (to the left facing the sea) to ramble along the clifftop, which has spectacular views. Perched atop the eastern cliff (Falaise d'Amont) is the tiny **Chapelle Notre Dame de la Garde,** constructed by the Jesuits in 1854; note the spitting dolphins at the gutters on the roof. Behind it sits the **Musée Nungesser et Coli** and a monument dedicated to the first aviators to attempt a trans-Atlantic flight; their plane was lost off the coast of Etretat in 1927. (☎02 35 27 07 47. Open June 15-Sept. 15 daily 10am-noon and 2-6pm; Sept. 16-June 14 Sa-Su only. 6F/€0.91, children 4F/€0.61.) The town itself is just a handful of crooked streets wending between the main avenue, Georges V, and the beach. Stowed among them are the former house and gardens of crime novelist Maurice Leblanc, who created Arsène Lupin, the original "gentleman burglar." **Le Clos Lupin,** 15 rue de Maupassant, now hosts a murder mystery—with the help of headphones, you can foil Lupin in the rooms of the antique home (☎02 35 27 55 45).

There are plenty of hotels in town, but no truly budget ones; the closer to the beachfront, the higher the rates. Reservations are crucial in summertime. **Hôtel l'Angleterre,** steps from the beach on 35 av. Georges V, may not be cheap, but it's the best you can do in Etretat. (☎02 35 27 01 34; fax 02 35 27 76 28. Reception 8am-8pm at the Hôtel de la Poste down the street. Singles and doubles with bath 260F/€39.64; triples and quads with bath 380F/€57.94; lower prices Sept.-Easter. MC/V.) Campers can bed down at the **town campsite,** straight down rue Guy de Maupassant from the tourist office. It's dirt-cheap, probably because it's the only place in town far from the beach. (☎02 35 27 07 67. Reception 9am-noon and 3-7pm. Open Easter-Sept. 15. 14F/€2.13 per person, 7F/€1.07 per child; 14F/€2.13 per tent, 16F/€2.44 per car; electricity 24F/€3.66.)

The **tourist office,** just behind the bus stop, can outfit you with a free map, a **bike** (50F/€7.62 for 2hr.), and a **tour.** (☎02 35 27 05 21; fax 02 35 28 87 20. Open June 15-Sept. 15 daily 10am-7pm; Sept. 16-Nov. and Apr.-June 14 10am-noon and 2-6pm; Dec.-Mar. Sa-Su only.) **Les Autocars Gris** (☎02 35 27 04 35) runs from **Fécamp** (35min., 9 per day, 29F/€4.42) and **Le Havre** (1hr., 10 per day, 39F/€5.95) to the center of Etretat.

FECAMP

Tucked among craggy cliffs, Fécamp (pop. 22,000) is one of the jewels of the High Normandy coast, well worth a daytrip from Dieppe or Rouen. Fécamp first found fame as a pilgrimage site in the 6th century, when some drops of *précieux-sang* (Christ's blood) allegedly washed ashore in a fig-tree trunk. Few pilgrims still come to adore the holy plasma, which is held in the **Eglise Abbatiale de la Trinité,** rue des Forts. According to legend, the bishops were arguing over the church's dedication when an angel appeared to command patronage to the Holy Trinity; the footprint he left behind can still be seen to the right of the altar. At the eastern end of the nave sits a gold box containing the *précieux-sang*.

Most visitors to Fécamp are after a different precious liquid entirely—*Benedictine*. Between the 16th and 18th centuries, Fécamp's Benedictine monks created a mysterious concoction of 27 local plants and Asian spices for use as a healing agent. Local wine merchant Alexandre Le Grand rediscovered the recipe, which had been lost during the Revolution, and built a palace in 1888 to distill the spirit, named after the monks who invented it. Today the magnificent **Palais Bénédictine,** 110 rue Alexandre Le Grand, remains the town's greatest draw; follow up a visit to the excellent collection of medieval and Renaissance artifacts and contemporary art with a swill of the fiery liqueur. (☎02 35 10 26 10. Open daily July-Sept. 2 9:30am-7pm; Sept. 3-30 10am-1pm and 2-6:30pm; Oct.-Dec. and Feb. 3-28 10am-12:15pm and 2-6pm; Mar.-June 10am-1pm and 2-6:30pm. 30F/€4.57, under age 18 15F/€2.29, family 70F/€10.67.) The palace is half-price with the **Musée des Terre-Neuvas et de la Pêche,** 27 bd. Albert 1er, dedicated to the adventures of local cod fishermen, and the excruciatingly dull **Musée Centre-des-Arts,** near the abbey at 21 rue Alexandre Legros, with furniture, carvings, and ceramics. (Pêche ☎02 35 29 76 22. Centre ☎02 35 28 31 99. Both open July-Aug. daily 10am-7pm; Sept.-June W-M 10am-noon and 2-5:30pm. 20F/€3.05, students 10F/€1.53.)

If you plan on spending the night, try the **Hôtel Martin,** 18 pl. St-Etienne, which has clean, large rooms and a delightful restaurant. (☎02 35 28 23 82; fax 02 35 28 61 21. Reception 7:30am-11pm, closed Su evening and M. Singles and doubles 150-205F/€22.90-31.25. Extra bed 30F/€4.57. AmEx/MC/V.) For supplies, there's a **Marché-Plus** supermarket at 83 quai Berigny (open M-Sa 7am-9pm, Su 9am-1pm).

The town center is behind Eglise St-Etienne, across the street from the station and up the stairs. To reach the **tourist office,** 113 rue Alexandre Le Grand, turn right onto rue Gambetta, which becomes quai Berigny. Turn left onto rue du Domaine, and then right onto rue le Grand; it's across the street from the Palais Bénédictine. They dispense maps and book rooms for 10F/€1.53. (☎02 35 28 51 01; fax 02 35 27 07 77. Open July-Aug. M-F 10am-6pm; May-June and Sept. M-F 9am-12:15pm and 1:45-6pm, Sa 10am-noon and 2:30-6:30pm, Su 10am-noon and 2-6pm; Oct.-Mar. M-F 9am-12:15pm and 1:45-6:30pm, Sa 10am-noon and 2:30-6:30pm.) Fécamp is accessible by train from **Le Havre** (45min., 5 per day, 44F/€6.71); **Paris** (2½hr., 6 per day, 152F/€23.17); and **Rouen** (1¼hr., 6 per day, 71F/€10.82); and by **CNA bus** (☎02 35 84 21 97) from **Dieppe** (2hr., 4 per day, 77F/€11.74).

LE HAVRE

Everybody comes through Le Havre (pop. 200,000), but few stay. Founded in 1517 by François 1er, the town can boast of being the largest transatlantic port in France, and of little else. Le Havre's answer to WWII's devastation was to call in architect Auguste Perret, who spewed reinforced concrete everywhere, compounding the unsightliness of the already utilitarian harbor. The town is trying desperately to improve its image with a good museum and a few tree-lined boulevards, but is best as a stopover; get in, get out, and nobody gets hurt.

NORMANDY

PRACTICAL INFORMATION

To get to the tourist office from the station, follow bd. de Strasbourg across town as it changes to av. Foch; turn left onto bd. Clemenceau, and the tourist office will be on your left. From the ferry terminal, walk left down quai de Southampton and then right up bd. Clemenceau; the office will be on your right. **Beware of walking anywhere alone at night,** especially around the train station and harbor.

Trains: cours de la République. To: **Fécamp** via **Etretat** (1hr., 9 per day, 44F/€6.71); **Paris** (2hr., 8 per day, 154F/€23.48); and **Rouen** (50min., 13 per day, 74F/€11.28). (☎08 36 35 35 35. Info office open M-Sa 9:30am-6:15pm.) The **bus station** is by the train station on bd. de Strasbourg (☎02 35 26 67 23). **CNA** runs to **Rouen** (3hr.; M-Sa 7 per day, 2 on Su; 82F/€12.50).

Buses: Bus Verts (☎08 01 21 42 14) goes to **Caen** (1½hr.; 5 per day; 106F/€16.16, students 86F/€13.11) and **Honfleur** (30min.; 4 per day; 37.10F/€5.66, students 30.10F/€4.56). See p. 478, for Caen-Le Havre express info. **Autocars Gris** (☎02 35 28 19 88) runs to **Fécamp** via **Etretat** (45-100min.; 10 per day; 46F/€7.01, 50% reduction on same-day return). **Bus Océane,** 115 rue Jules Lecesne (☎02 35 19 75 75), runs **locally** (tickets 8F/€1.22, *carnet* of 10 50F/€7.62, day pass 20F/€3.05.)

Ferries: P&O European Ferries, av. Lucien Corbeaux (☎08 03 01 30 13; www.poportsmouth.com), leave from Terminal de la Citadelle (☎02 35 19 78 78) for **Portsmouth** (see **Getting There: By Boat,** p. 62, for details). Ticket and info office open M-F 8:30am-7pm, Sa 9am-5pm. Terminal closes at 11pm.

Taxis: Radio-Taxis wait at the train station (☎02 35 25 81 81). 24hr.

Tourist Office: 186 bd. Clemenceau (☎02 32 74 04 04; fax 02 35 42 38 39; www.lehavretourism.com). Info on outdoor activities, a list of hotels and restaurants, and a free, easy-to-read map. Open May-Sept. M-Sa 9am-7pm, Su 10am-12:30pm and 2:30-6pm; Oct.-Apr. M-Sa 9am-6:30pm, Su 10am-1pm.

Hospital: 55bis rue Gustave Flaubert (☎02 32 73 32 32).

Police: 16 rue de la Victoire (☎02 32 74 37 00).

Internet Access: Cybermetro, cours de la République (☎02 35 25 40 43), across from the train station. 30F/€4.57 per 30min., 45F/€8.86 per hr.; students 20F/€3.05 per 30min., 35F/€5.34 per hr. Open daily 11am-10pm. Or try the **library,** 17 rue Jules Lecesne (☎02 32 74 07 40). By appointment only, but you can use a computer when people (often) don't show up. Open July-Aug. Tu-W and F-Sa 10am-5pm, Th noon-5pm; Sept.-June Tu, F 10am-7pm; W, Sa 10am-6pm; Th noon-6pm.

Post Office: 62 rue Jules Siegfried (☎02 32 92 59 00). **Internet** kiosk. Open M-F 8am-7pm, Sa 8am-noon. **Postal code:** 76600.

NORMANDY

ACCOMMODATIONS AND CAMPING

Cheap one-star hotels, offering mostly singles, line the seedy cours de la République across from the train station. Pricier and marginally prettier two-star establishments line bd. de Strasbourg. **Hôtel Jeanne d'Arc,** 91 rue Emile Zola, offers freshly redecorated rooms in a truly homey atmosphere. (☎02 35 21 67 27 or 06 08 43 56 86; fax 02 35 41 26 83. Breakfast 20F/€3.05. Singles 135F/€20.58, with shower 149F/€22.72; doubles 150-160F/€22.90-24.39, with shower 164-200F/€25-30.49. Prices may rise after renovations; call ahead to check when they reopen. MC/V.) **Hôtel Le Monaco,** 16 rue de Paris, near the ferry terminal, has spacious rooms with classy, countryside decor above a popular brasserie (3-course *menu* 65F/€9.91). (☎02 35 42 21 01. Reception 6:30am-11pm. Breakfast 30F/€4.57. Showers 15-25F/€2.29-3.81. Singles 150F/€22.90, with bath 185-220F/€28.21-33.54; doubles 175F/€26.68, with bath 230-270F/€35.06-41.16; extra bed 40F/€6.10. AmEx/MC/V.)

Le Havre has no shortage of cheap eateries, but don't set your sights too high. Restaurants crowd **rue Victor Hugo** near the Hôtel de Ville, while the streets between **rue de Paris** and **quai Lamblardie** frame a range of neighborhood restaurants frequented by locals. Stock up for the ferry at **Monoprix,** 38-40 av. René Coty, in the *Espace Coty* shopping center (open M-Sa 8:30am-9pm). There's also a **Super U,** bd. François 1er, almost a full turn around the block from the tourist office (open M-Sa 8:30am-8:30pm), and a **Marché Plus** near the Volcan on rue de Paris (open M-Sa 7am-9pm, Su 8:30am-12:30pm). For unusually fresh food, try the morning **market** at pl. Thiers by the Hôtel de Ville (M, W, F) or the all-day market on cours République (Tu, Th, Sa).

SIGHTS AND ENTERTAINMENT

The skyscraper visible from practically everywhere in town is actually the **Eglise St-Joseph,** yet another chapter in Perret's sermon on the wonders of concrete. The quiet shade of the weeping willows in the **Jardin Sarraute,** off av. Foch, provides a refreshing counterpoint to the town's griminess, as do the ivy-covered walkways and sparkling fountains on **pl. de l'Hôtel de Ville.** The new **Sculptures Avenue Foch** is a display of funky modern art on the street's sidewalks. Check out the burned-out Renault entitled "Hooligan art."

That's actually not a giant felled mushroom in the middle of the city; it is Le Havre's center of performing arts. Nicknamed "Le Volcan," the **Maison de la Culture du Havre,** in pl. Gambetta, looks like the unholy union of a nuclear power plant and an overturned toilet bowl, and houses a state-of-the-art theater for renowned orchestras and plays, as well as a cinema that screens new releases and classics. (☎02 35 19 10 10. Closed July 20-Aug.)

The **Musée des Beaux Arts André Malraux,** 2 bd. Clemenceau, features an impressive collection of pre-Impressionist works. Everyone from Pissarro to Monet to Boudin has painted every cow in Normandy and every one of those paintings is here. (☎02 35 19 62 62. Open M and W-F 11am-6pm, Sa-Su 11am-7pm. 25F/€3.81, students 15F/€2.29, under 18 free.)

THE COTE FLEURIE

In contrast to Normandy's working port cities, the smaller villages along the northeastern coast of Lower Normandy, known as the Côte Fleurie, are decidedly playful. Doubling as resort towns and thalassotherapy centers, these coastal towns have served as weekend destinations for Paris' elite since the mid-19th century. Today, they cater to a more international crowd, which means that they won't turn up their noses at your French—but they might take exception to your attire. The Côte's reputation as the "Norman Riviera" stems mostly from its fixation on wealth and style, and the budget lifestyle is little accommodated. Caen's hotels or hostels can make good budget bases, and Bus Verts provides regular connections between coastal towns and to Caen and Bayeux. Consider their *Carte Liberté* bus passes if you'll be doing a lot of touring (see p. 462).

HONFLEUR

Among the picturesque, carefully-preserved towns in northwestern France, Honfleur (pop. 6000) stands out as a true gem of culture and architecture. The town emerged from WWII miraculously unharmed, and its narrow, multicolored houses surrounding the old port look precisely the same as they have for centuries. The beautiful wilds around the town have attracted a close-knit community of artists, whose works can be seen in the many local galleries. A day in Honfleur, the painters say, holds all the colors of the seasons—the morning is spring, the mid-afternoon summer, the evening fall, and the night winter.

PRACTICAL INFORMATION. The **bus station** is located at the end of quai Lepaulmier, near the Bassin de l'Est. **Bus Verts** (☎08 10 21 42 14) connects Honfleur to **Caen** (1½hr.; 15 per day; 63.60F/€9.70, students 51.60F/€7.87) and **Le Havre** (30min.; 4 per day; 37.10F/€5.66, students 30.10F/€4.56). To get to the **tourist**

office, 33 pl. Arthur Boudin, turn right out of the bus station and follow quai de la Tour along the avant Port until you see a glass library on your left, at rue de la Ville. The office is in the stone section of the library. The *guide pratique* (10F/€1.53) has a good town map that lays out 4 walking tours (2½-7km) in the streets of the town and the surrounding forests. (☎02 31 89 23 30; fax 02 31 89 31 82. Open July-Aug. M-Sa 9:30am-7pm, Su 10am-5pm; Oct.-Easter M-Sa 9:30am-noon and 2-6pm; Easter-June and Sept. M-Sa 9:30am-12:30pm and 2-6:30pm, Su 10am-5pm.)

ACCOMMODATIONS AND FOOD. The budget-conscious should make Honfleur a daytrip—hotels here have more stars than most constellations. That said, **Les Cascades,** 17 pl. Thiers, on cours des Fossés, offers comparatively inexpensive rooms in an ideal location right next to the port. Huge begonia-filled boxes adorn the windows of comfortable rooms, some with skylights and half-timbered walls. You may be asked to take dinner *(demi-pension)* at the hotel restaurant in summer. (☎02 31 89 05 83; fax 02 31 89 32 13. Breakfast 35F/€5.34. Open Feb.-Nov. Doubles with bath 200-300F/€30.49-45.74; triples 250-350F/€38.12-53.36; quads 360F/€54.89. AmEx/DC/MC/V.) The seaside **Le Phare** campsite rests at a quiet location 300m from the town center at the end of rue Haute. It gets crowded in summer, so arrive early to get a shady spot. (☎02 31 89 10 26. Reception July-Aug. 8am-10pm; otherwise varies. Car curfew 10pm-7am. Open Apr.-Sept. Shower 8F/€1.22. July-Aug. 30F/€4.57 per person, child under 7 20F/€3.05, day visitor 30F/€4.57; Apr.-June and Sept. 27F/€4.12, child under 7 19F/€2.90, day visitor 27F/€4.12; Apr.-Sept. 35F/€5.33 per tent and car. Electricity 25-36F/€3.81-5.49.)

For a sweet splurge, the homemade ice cream at **Aimé Stéphan,** 60 quai Ste-Catherine, is worth the price. (☎02 31 89 55 25. 1 scoop 12F/€1.83, 2 scoops 20F/€3.05. Open daily 11am-11pm.) For groceries, drop by the **Champion supermarket,** pl. Sorel. (Open July-Aug. M-F 8:30am-1pm and 2:30-7:30pm, Sa 8:30am-7:30pm, Su 9am-1pm; hours slightly shorter Sept.-June.) The conventional **market** goes up in pl. Ste-Catherine, in front of the church (Sa morning), while pl. St-Léonard sees an organic **Marché Bio** (W morning). Be sure to pick up some *pain Breton.*

NORMANDY

SIGHTS. Honfleur is for the curious; the city's tight corners and tucked-away streets hide lesser-know architectural marvels and any number of delights. Part of the ramparts that once surrounded the village, the **Porte de Caen** at the end of quai Ste-Catherine is the only remaining gate through which the king would ride into the fortified town. A block away from the Bassin's waters is the 15th-century **Eglise Ste-Catherine.** The largest wooden church in France, it was built hurriedly and cheaply by pious sailors after the first one burned down in 1450. The result is a splendidly carved church that resembles a cross between an ornamented market hall and a half-timbered house. (Open July-Aug. daily 8am-8pm; Sept.-June 8:30am-noon and 2-6pm.) The belltower across the street is open for climbing; despite fears to the contrary. (Open Mar. 15-Sept. daily 10am-noon and 2-6pm; Oct.-Nov. 11 M-F 2:30-5pm, Sa-Su 10am-noon. Included with Musée Eugène Boudin.)

Worth the trip to Honfleur alone is the **Maisons Satie,** 67 bd. Charles V, the 1866 birthplace and museum of composer, musician, artist, and author Erik Satie. Breathtaking, fanciful, and a little psychedelic, this maze of rooms feels like a stroll through the mind of an artist. Expect starry ceilings, indoor rainshowers, and the whimsical *laboratoire des émotions.* (☎02 31 89 11 11. Open May-Sept. W-M 10am-7pm; Oct.-Dec. and Feb. 16-Apr. 10:30am-6pm. 30F/€4.57, students and seniors 20F/€3.05. *Pass Musées* gives access to all 4 of Honfleur's museums and bell tower; 50F/€7.62, students and children 30F/€4.57, under 10 free.)

Paintings of Honfleur by Eugène Boudin and his circle became popular in the 19th century and are considered by many critics the precursors of Impressionism. A vast collection is displayed at the **Musée Eugène Boudin,** pl. Erik Satie, off rue de l'Homme de Bois. (☎02 31 89 54 00. Open Mar. 15-Sept. W-M 10am-noon and 2-6pm; Oct.-Mar. 14 M and W-F 2:30-5pm, Sa-Su 10am-noon and 2:30-5pm. 30F/€4.57, students and children 20F/€3.05, under 10 free.) The wonderful **Musée d'Ethnographie et d'Art Populaire,** quai St-Etienne, consists of two 15th-century houses, decorated as they would have been during Honfleur's glory days. For the full maritime treatment, check out the **Musée de la Marine,** quai St-Etienne, in the former Eglise St-Etienne. The tiny, informative museum tells the tale of Honfleur's affair with the sea engagingly enough for even the most earthy landlubber. (☎02 31 89 14 12. Both open July-Aug. daily 10am-1pm and 2-6:30pm; Apr.-June and Sept. Tu-Su 10am-noon and 2-6pm; Feb. 15-Mar. and Oct.-Nov. 15 Tu-F 2-5:30pm, Sa-Su 10am-noon and 2-5:30pm. Closed Nov. 16-Feb. 14. 15F/€2.29, students and children 10F/€1.53; with Musée d'Ethnographie: 25F/€3.81, students 15F/€2.29.)

The shaded **public gardens** on the bd. Charles V, just beside the port, make the perfect spot for a picnic. Flower beds, swingsets, a wading pool, and a waterfall should help while away the hottest hours of the day. (☎02 31 81 77 00.) A spectacular photo opportunity of the looming Pont de Normandie awaits at the peak of **Mont-Joli.** Fill your water bottle and follow rue du Puits from pl. Ste-Catherine to a steep asphalt ramp sloping up to the right (1½km). In mid-September, Honfleur invites comedians for the newest of its festivals, the **Estuaire en Rire.**

HOULGATE

Quieter and more affordable than its eastern neighbors, Houlgate (pop. 2000) was one of the first resorts to appear on the Norman coast. It has a remarkable number of expensive villas, and 1½km of sandy, seashell-strewn beaches.

TRANSPORTATION AND PRACTICAL INFORMATION. **Bus Verts** #20 runs to **Caen** (1hr.; 12 per day; 37.10F/€5.66, students 30.10F/€4.56) via **Cabourg** (11min.; 10.60F/€1.62, students 8.60F/€1.31), as well as to **Le Havre** (80min.; 2 per day; 68.90F/€10.50, students 55.90F/€8.52). A tide table and walking tours are available at Houlgate's **tourist office,** on bd. des Belges, down the hill from the Bus Verts stop. (☎02 31 24 34 79; fax 02 31 24 42 27; www.houlgate.com. Open daily 10am-12:30pm and 2-6:30pm.) There's **Internet access** at **CyberCafé,** 5 rue des Bains. (☎02 31 28 19 92. 1F/€0.15 per min., 50F/€7.62 per hr. Open July-Aug. W-M 10am-1pm and 3-10pm.) The **post office,** at the corner of bd. des Belges and bd. de St-Philbert, **exchanges currency.** (☎02 31 28 10 05. Open M-F 9am-noon and 2-5pm, Sa 9am-noon.) **Postal code:** 14510.

ACCOMMODATIONS AND FOOD. The tourist office maintains a list of *chambres d'hôte*, one of the cheapest indoor options. The **Hôtel du Centre,** 31 rue des Bains, has the most affordable rooms in town, close to the supermarket and just one block from the beach. (☎02 31 24 80 40; fax 02 31 28 52 21. Doubles 180F/€27.44, with bath 230F/€35.06.) Three kilometers east of Houlgate and 276 steps up from the beach is the wonderful **Camping les Falaises,** rte. de la Corniche (D163). From the tourist office, head toward the beach and turn right on rue des Bains; continue straight ahead as it becomes rue Baumier, takes you up dozens of stairs, through the woods, then to the paved rue de la Corniche. In 30 minutes, you'll see the campsite on your left. This 450-spot campground has a restaurant and bar, market, heated pool, life-size chessboard, and—most importantly—huge sites with ocean views. (☎02 31 24 81 09; fax 02 31 28 04 11; camping.lesfalaises@voila.fr. Open Apr.-Oct. 25.50F/€3.89 per person, child under 7 16F/€2.44; car and tent 30F/€4.57. Electricity 22.50F-26.50F/€3.43-4.04. July-Aug. minimum total fee 100F/€15.25 per night.) If you like feeling the vibrations from the tent beside you, try the **Camping de la Plage,** 58 rue Henri Dobert. It's literally on the beach, just as you will be literally on top of your neighbor in high season. (☎/fax 02 31 28 73 07. Gates close at 10pm. Reception 7:30am-1pm and 2-8pm. Open Apr.-Sept. Shower 5F/€0.76. 23F/€3.51 per person, child under 7 18F/€2.74; 10F/€1.52 per car, 20F/€3.05 per tent; day visitors 20F/€3.05. Electricity 18F/€2.74.)

Restaurants abound on **rue de Bains** and **rue du Général Leclerc.** Shop at the **8 à huit supermarket,** 57 rue des Bains near the beach (open daily 7:30am-8:30pm), the **covered market,** rue Général Leclerc (open June 15-Sept. 15 M-F 8am-1pm; Sept. 16-June 14 Th and Sa-Su 8am-1pm), or the Thursday morning **market,** pl. de la Mairie.

SIGHTS AND ENTERTAINMENT. East of Houlgate, the sea swells crash into the **Vache Noir** (Black Cow) cliffs, so named because of the dark hue of the fossil deposits against the cliffs' exposed limestone. The cliffs and beach below offer a remarkable walk that alternates between lush verdure and moonscape (best taken at low tide). Houlgate is host to an annual **Festijazz** for a weekend in late July, but their main event is in mid-August. The **Course des Garçons de Café** sends waiters from all corners of France careening down the main roads trying not to spill the various drinks on their trays, and trying even harder to look suave.

CABOURG

Marcel Proust spent many summers in Cabourg, looking for himself and penning his *Remembrance of Things Past* at the **Grand Hôtel.** Posh, but not as pretentious as some of the other resort towns to the east, Cabourg is well-suited to the gambler, the *nouveaux riches*, and the budget traveler. Take a moment to stroll along the boardwalk and the streets that literally radiate from the hotel and casino, then move on in search of more wallet-friendly spots if the Grand Hôtel isn't quite within your range (rooms start at only 880F/€134.16 per night). The **tourist office,** Jardins du Casino, lies in front of the famous hotel at the edge of its formal gardens. They run tours or provide you with a map for self-guided hikes, as well as a *Programme des Manifestations*, an entertainment guide published every two weeks. (☎02 31 91 20 00; fax 02 31 24 14 49; www.cabourg.net. Open July-Aug. daily 9:30am-7pm; Sept.-June M-Sa 9:30am-12:30pm and 2-6pm, Su 10am-noon and 2-4pm.) Across the Dives River, the Dives-Cabourg **train station** (☎02 31 91 00 74) serves **Deauville/Trouville** (30min.; July-Aug. 7 per day, Sept.-June weekends only; 26.10F/€3.98). The train station has the cheapest **bike rental** on the Côte (VTTs 55F/€8.39 per day, passport deposit). **Bus Verts** (☎08 01 214 214) runs from any of five in-town stops (pl. du 8 Mai is closest to the beach and tourist office) to **Caen** (45min.; 31.80F/€4.85, students 25.80F/€3.93), **Honfleur** (1hr.; 37.10F/€5.67, students 30.10F/€4.59), **Houlgate** (11min.; 10.60F/€1.62, students 8.60F/€1.31), and **Le Havre** (1½hr.; 74.20F/€11.31, students 60.20F/€9.18). It stops most frequently at the Pasteur stop; from the stop, walk toward the gardens and turn right onto av. de la Mer. The hotel and tourist office are at the end of the street.

DEAUVILLE AND TROUVILLE

Deauville and Trouville are traditionally treated as a pair, with their twin casinos, beaches, and boardwalks, but each manages to retain a distinct identity on its own bank of the river Touques. Since its founding in 1861 by Napoleon's cousin, the Duc de Morny, **Deauville** (pop. 4518) has consistently drawn the Parisian elite to its sandy shores. Its innovation over other resort towns is in somehow attaining snootiness without the corresponding glamor or glitz. Prices, of course, are high; budget travelers, as the tourist office puts it, "should walk through Deauville only. Don't shop, just walk." Across the river, **Trouville**'s streets (pop. 5500) are smaller, its crowds less absurdly wealthy, its shops more artistic and less expensive, and its overall feel welcoming and lovely. If you're only in town for the day, you may want to drop off your pack at the train station and put on some spiffier clothes; grungy backpackers stick out like a sore thumb in these parts.

NORMANDY

DISORIENTATION AND PRACTICAL CONFUSION. These siamese twins are joined at the station. **Trains** (SNCF ☎08 36 35 35 35) go to **Caen** (1hr., 5 per day, 77F/€11.74); **Paris** (2hr., 5-6 per day, 160F/€24.39); and **Rouen** (2½-3hr., 3 per day, 107F/€16.31). **Bus Verts** (☎08 01 21 42 14) goes to **Cabourg** (20min.; 26.50F/€4.04, students 21.20F/€3.28), **Caen** (70min.; 53F/€8.08, students 43F/€6.56), **Honfleur** (20min.; 15.90F/€2.42, students 12.90F/€1.97), **Houlgate** (21.20F/€3.22, students 17.20F/€2.62), and **Le Havre** via **Honfleur** (1hr.; 58.30F/€8.89, students 47.30F/€7.21). **Agence Fournier,** pl. du Maréchal Foch in Trouville, runs **shuttles** between Deauville and Trouville (☎02 31 88 16 73; 10F/€1.53). The **Bac de Deauville/Trouville** ferries passengers across the canal from Deauville to Trouville's Monoprix when the tide is high enough. (Mar. 15-Sept. daily about 8:30am-6:45pm; 5.50F/€0.84.) For a **taxi,** call 02 31 88 35 33 or 08 00 51 41 41.

To get to **Trouville** from the train station, turn right and cross the bridge (Pont des Belges) onto the main bd. Fernand Moureaux; turn left and the **tourist office** is one minute away in the direction of the town center, at 32 quai Fernand Moureaux. The staff distributes *Le Guide: Trouville*, a heavy, complete vacationing guide; also available are two walking tours (map 3F/€0.46) and a town map. (☎02 31 14 60 70; fax 02 31 14 60 71; www.trouvillesurmer.org. Open July-Aug. M-Sa 9:30am-7pm, Su 10am-4pm; Apr.-June and Sept.-Oct. M-Sa 9:30am-noon and 2-6:30pm, Su 10am-1pm; Nov.-Mar. M-Sa 9:30am-noon and 2-6pm, Su 10am-1pm.)

To get to **Deauville** from the train station, turn left as you exit; at the second roundabout take the second right (rue Désiré le Hoc) and follow it two blocks to pl. Morny. Cut through the *place* and continue another block; the **tourist office,** pl. de la Mairie, will be in front of you (10min.). Info on town and prestigious film and music festivals, and frequent horse races and polo games. (☎02 31 14 40 00; fax 02 31 88 78 88; www.deauville.org. Open July-Sept. 9 M-Sa 9am-7pm, Su 10am-1pm and 3-6pm; Sept. 10-Apr. M-Sa 9am-12:30pm and 2-6:30pm, Su 10am-1pm and 2-5pm; May-June M-Tu and Th 9am-12:30pm and 2-6:30pm, W 10am-12:30pm and 2-6:30pm, F-Sa 9am-6:30pm, Su 10am-1pm and 2-5pm.) **Rent bikes** at **La Deauvillaise,** 11 quai de la Marine. (☎02 31 88 56 33. 25F/€3.81 per hr., 75F/€11.43 for 5hr., 250F/€38.12 per week. Open July-Aug. daily 9am-6:30pm, Sept.-June Tu-Su 9am-12:30pm and 2-6:30pm.)

ACCOMMODATIONS AND FOOD. You'll have to stay in Trouville if you want to sleep without pawning your pack. **Le Florian,** 30 rue de la Plage, is clean, comfortable, and at 30m from the beach, a water baby's dream come true. (☎02 31 88 17 40; fax 02 31 39 61 41. Breakfast 30F/€4.57. Reception 8:30am-11pm. Apr.-May, weekends in June, July-Sept. singles with toilet 220F/€33.54, with bath 240F/€36.59; doubles with toilet 230F/€35.06, with bath 330F/€50.30-340F/€51.83; triples with bath 380F/€57.93; quads with bath 500F/€76.22. Extra bed 60F/€9.15. Prices 20-60F/€3.05-9.15 lower Oct.-Dec., Feb.-Mar. and June weekdays. Closed Jan. MC/V.) **Camping Le Chant des Oiseaux,** 11 rte. d'Honfleur, is 2km from town on cliffs overlooking the sea; take Bus Verts (dir: "Honfleur") to "Camping." To walk from the tourist office, continue down bd. Moureaux until just before the Casino and turn right onto rue Victor Hugo, which becomes rue de la Chapelle. At the fork, go left, walk to the end of the beach, and climb the 76 steps through the dunes. (☎02 31 88 06 42; fax 02 31 98 16 09. Open Apr.-Nov. July-Aug. shower 3F/€0.46. Reception July-Aug. 8am-10pm; in Apr.-June and Sept.-Nov. someone is almost always nearby if not in the office. 26F/€3.96 per person, ages 2-7 16F/€2.44; 30F/€4.57 per tent; 16F/€2.44 per car.)

Since many of the restaurants along the beach face west, toward the setting sun, beachcombers and locals flock to Trouville's terraces to dine in the last light of the day. A number of seafood restaurants, pizzerias, and crêperies with reasonable *menus* line the pedestrian **rue des Bains.** There is a **Monoprix Supermarket** on bd. Moureaux. (Open July-Aug. M-Sa 9am-8pm, Su 9:30am-1pm; Sept.-June daily 9am-12:30pm and 2-7:30pm.) A **market** fills pl. Maréchal Foch (W and Su morning).

SIGHTS AND ENTERTAINMENT. The original and best attraction at both towns is the **beach.** Their boardwalk promenades are the pride of each town; in Trouville, a stroll along the wooden planks affords a view of the spectacular houses that inspired Flaubert, in Deauville, a path lined with names of movie stars.

The **Aquarium-Vivarium de Trouville,** on the boardwalk, feels more like a disturbed collector's house. The glass cases hold the stuffed and the breathing, and everything from finches to tarantulas, guinea pigs to geckos, dried larvae to preserved organs. (☎02 31 88 46 04. Open July-Aug. daily 10am-7:30pm; Sept.-Oct. 10am-noon and 2-7pm; Nov.-Easter 2-6:30pm; Easter-June 10am-noon and 2-7pm. 38F/€5.80, students and seniors 30F/€4.57, ages 6-14 25F/€3.81, ages 3-5 17F/€2.59.)

Trouville's casino, **Louisiane Follies,** pl. du Maréchal Foch (☎02 31 87 75 00), has an adjoining nightclub and cinema, and offers a more laid-back atmosphere than the **Casino de Deauville** (☎02 31 14 31 14). **Café Trouville,** a series of café-side concerts held in July and August (4-5 per week), can be enjoyed from the terrace of the café du jour or for free on the sidewalk. The third weekend in June sees both the **Festival Folklorique** in Trouville, with music and dance groups from all over the world, and the town's **Carnaval.** The wine bar/café **La Maison,** 66 rue des Bains in Trouville, offers a sophisticated and laid-back setting. Grass mats and wrought-iron furniture give a dreamy, Spanish flavor to the terrace. (☎02 31 81 43 10. Open July-Aug. daily 11am-1am; Sept.-May Th-M 11am-1am.)

Deauville is famous for activities involving its four-legged equine demi-god. The town has two hippodromes: **Clairefontaine,** dedicated to racing, and **La Touques,** where the polo games are held. Deauville also hosts a number of festivals, including **Swing'In Deauville** (third week of July) and the **American Film Festival** (Sept.).

CAEN

Caen suffered more during World War II than almost any other city in Normandy; by the end of the fighting, two-thirds of her citizens were homeless and three-quarters of her buildings reduced to dust. The city is notable for the skill and care with which it has rebuilt itself; today, the finely restored abbeys commissioned by William the Conqueror have returned to their stunning form of years past. Closer than Bayeux to a good third of the D-Day beaches, and equally convenient to the resort towns of the Côte Fleurie, Caen combines its central location with the assets of a chic student population and several good museums.

TRANSPORTATION

Trains: pl. de la Gare (SNCF ☎08 36 35 35 35). To: **Cherbourg** (1½hr.; 10 per day, 5 on Su; 100F/€15.25); **Paris** (2½hr., 12 per day, 170F/€25.92); **Rennes** (3hr., 3 per day, 166F/€25.31); **Rouen** (2hr., 5 per day, 118F/€17.99); and **Tours** (3½hr., 2 per day, 172F/€26.22). Info office open M-Sa 8am-7pm, Su 9:15am-6:30pm.

Buses: Bus Verts, to the left of the train station, and at pl. Courtonne in the center of town, cover the region (☎08 01 21 42 14). See p. 484 for coverage of the D-Day beaches. To **Bayeux** (1hr.; M-Sa 2-3 per day; 37.10F/€5.66, students 30.10F/€4.59) and **Le Havre** (2-3hr.; M-Sa 6 per day, Su 5 per day; 106F/€16.16, students 98F/€14.94). Also Caen-**Le Havre** express (1½hr., 2 per day, 125F/€19.06) stops in **Honfleur** (1hr., 2 per day, 89F/€13.57). Full-day **Carte Liberté** 105F/€16.01, 3 days 165F/€25.15, 7 days 283F/€43.14; accepted on CTAC. Office open M-F 7:30am-7pm, Sa 8:30am-7pm, Su 9am-2:30pm.

Local Transportation: CTAC, 15 rue de Geôle (☎02 31 15 55 55). Info booth around the corner from the tourist office, at pl. St-Pierre. Tickets 6.40F/€0.98; *carnet* of 10 54F/€8.23, day pass 17F/€2.59, family of 2-5 24F/€3.66. Open July 14-Aug. 15 M-Sa 8am-6pm; Aug. 16-July 13 M-F 7:15am-7:15pm, Sa 9am-12:30pm and 1-5pm.

Ferries: Brittany Ferries go to **Portsmouth, England** from Ouistreham, 13km north of Caen. See **Getting There: By Boat,** p. 62. Bus Verts #1 links Ouistreham to Caen's center and train station (40min., 8 per day, 19.40F/€2.96).

Taxis: Abbeilles Taxis Caen, 19 pl. de la Gare (☎02 31 52 17 89). 24hr.

ORIENTATION AND PRACTICAL INFORMATION

Caen's train station and youth hostel are on the south side of the Orne River, far enough from the center of town that you may want to take the bus. The city is in the midst of constructing a new tramway that causes traffic patterns and bus stop locations to change constantly. All of the buses leaving from the front of the train station stop in the vicinity of the Eglise St-Pierre and the city center. Ask about changes in bus routes at the CTAC kiosk near the tourist office. From the station, **av. du 6 Juin** and **rue St-Jean** run parallel to each other toward the city center and the lively commercial districts between **rue St-Pierre** and **rue de l'Oratoir.**

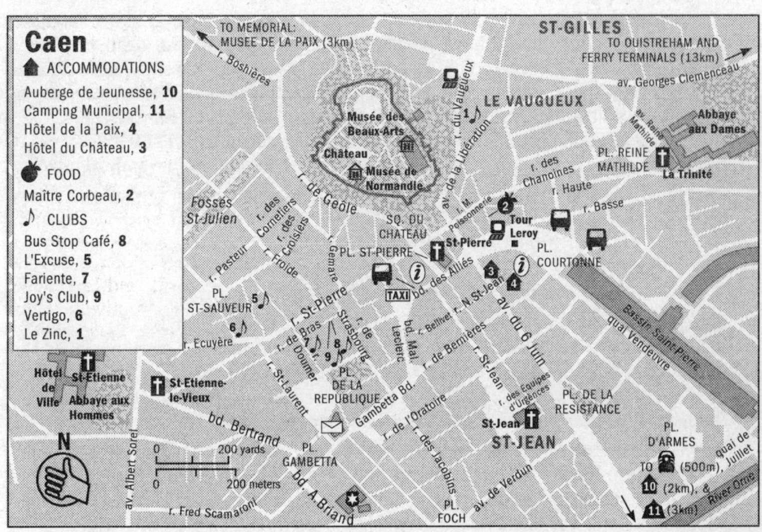

Tourist Office: pl. St-Pierre (☎02 31 27 14 14; fax 02 31 27 14 18; www.ville-caen.fr), by the Eglise St-Pierre. **Hotel booking** 10F/€1.53. Free map. *Le Mois à Caen* lists concerts and events. City **tours** by day from July-Sept. (1hr.; 25F/€3.81, students and children over 5 20F/€3.05). Theatrical visits at night in French from mid-July to Aug. (2hr.; 70F/€10.67, students and children over 5 50F/€7.62; reservations required). **Internet access** with France Telecom *télécarte*. Office open July-Aug. M-Sa 9:30am-7pm, Su 10am-1pm and 2-5pm; Sept.-June M-Sa 9:30am-1pm and 2-6pm, Su 10am-1pm.

Money: Currency exchange at the post office, and in most of the banks in the area.

Youth Center: Centre Information Jeunesse, 16 rue Neuve-St-Jean (☎02 31 27 80 80; fax 02 31 27 80 89; crij.bn@wanadoo.fr), off av. du 6 Juin next to the Hôtel de la Paix. Brochures on events, jobs, and lodging. Open M 1-6pm, Tu-F 10am-6pm.

Laundromat: rue de Geôle (☎06 60 55 75 60). Open daily 7am-9pm. Also 16 rue St-Pierre (☎06 80 96 08 26). Open daily 7am-8pm.

Hospital: Centre Hospitalier Universitaire, av. Côte de Nacre (☎02 31 06 31 06).

Police: rue Thiboud de la Fresnaye (☎02 31 29 22 22). Kiosk near the tourist office on rue Maréchal Leclerc.

Internet Access: At the **tourist office** (see above). 30 computers at **Espace Micro,** 1 rue Basse (☎02 31 53 68 68). 15F/€2.29 per 30min., 10F/€1.53 for less. Open Su-M 3-11pm, Tu-Sa 10:30am-11pm.

Post Office: pl. Gambetta (☎02 31 39 35 78). From pl. St-Pierre, take rue St-Pierre and turn left on rue St-Laurent. **Currency exchange.** Open M-F 7:30am-7pm, Sa 8am-12:30pm. **Poste Restante:** "14016 Gambetta." **Postal code:** 14000.

ACCOMMODATIONS AND CAMPING

There are many hotels in the center of Caen, but few go for under 150F/€22.90.

Auberge de Jeunesse (HI), Foyer Robert Reme, 68bis rue Eustache-Restout (☎02 31 52 19 96; fax 02 31 84 29 49). From the station, turn right and then left onto rue de Falaise. Walk up a block and look for the bus stop on your right. Take bus #5 or 17 (dir: "Fleury" or "Grace de Dieu") to "Lycée Fresnel." On foot, take a right out of the station and cross the street. Follow it until the road (now rue de Falaise) curves to the left and up the hill. Walk uphill until you reach the first major intersection, and then turn right onto bd. Maréchal Lyautey (to the left, it's called bd. Leroy) and continue about 10min.

Turn left onto rue Eustasche-Restout and continue 10min. through a residential area. The road turns right after a large school; the hostel will be on your right. Way away (3km) from where you want to be. Clean 4-person, single-sex rooms with showers and stoves. The hostel is within a foyer for young workers; the loitering residents can occasionally be a little *too* social. 24hr. guard. Breakfast 10F/€1.53. Sheets 15F/€2.29. Reception 5-10pm. Check-in 5-9pm. No lockout or curfew. Beds 62F/€9.45.

Hôtel de la Paix, 14 rue Neuve-St-Jean (☎02 31 86 18 99; fax 02 31 38 20 74), off av. du 6 Juin. Clean bathrooms, firm beds, and TVs right in the center of town. Breakfast 30F/€4.57. Reception 24hr. Singles 150F/€22.87, with toilet or shower 170F/€25.92, with bath 190F/€28.97; doubles 170F/€25.92, with shower or toilet 200F/€30.49, with bath 220F/€33.54; triples with shower 240F/€36.59, with bath 300F/€45.73; quads with bath 320F/€48.78; extra bed 30F/€4.57. MC/V.

Hôtel du Château, 5 av. du 6 Juin (☎02 31 86 15 37; fax 02 31 86 58 08). Exceptionally large, bright rooms (with TVs) on what will soon be a pedestrian street near the château. Breakfast 38F/€5.80. Reception 24hr. Singles 240F/€36.59; doubles 260F/€39.64, with sink 170F/€25.92; triples 310F/€47.26, quads 360F/€54.89, all with bath. Extra bed 50F/€7.62. Prices 20F/€3.05 lower Oct.-Easter. MC/V.

Campsites: Terrain Municipal, rte. de Louvigny (☎02 31 73 60 92). Take bus #13 (dir: "Louvigny") to "Camping." Pretty campground at a bend in the river at the edge of town, shaded by weeping willows. Reception 8am-1pm and 5-9pm. Gates closed 11pm-7am. Open June-Sept. 18F/€2.74 per person; child under 7 10.50F/€1.60; 10.50F/€1.60 per tent; 10.50F/€1.60 per car. Electricity 18F/€2.74.

FOOD

Crêperies, brasseries, and ethnic eateries abound in the **Quartier Vaugueux** near the château and are clustered between the Eglise St-Pierre and the Eglise St-Jean. Large **markets** are at pl. St-Sauveur (F) and on Sunday in front of the Eglise St-Pierre, on pl. Courtonne, and quai Vendeuvre. Smaller markets abound: Grace de Dieu and rue de Bayeux (Tu); bd. Leroy (W and Sa); La Guernière and Le Chemin Vert (F); all from 8am-1pm. There's a **Monoprix supermarket** at 45 bd. du Maréchal Leclerc (open M-Sa 9am-8:30pm), and a small **7-11** market at 1167 rue de Caen near the hostel (open Tu-Sa 9:15am-1pm and 3-11pm). Locals flock to **Maitre Corbeau,** 8 rue Buquet, to feast on *Fondue Normande* (with camembert and calvados, 75F/€11.43) amidst giant sunflowers and stuffed cows. It's so popular, in fact, that you'll probably have to reserve 2-3 days in advance just to get a table. (☎02 31 93 93 00. Open M and Sa 7-10:30pm, Tu-F noon-1:30pm and 7-10:30pm. Closed last week in Aug. and first week in Sept.) **La Vie Claire,** rue Basse, serves an ever-changing, ever-scrumptious 3-course vegetarian *menu* (45-57F/€6.86-8.69). (☎02 31 93 66 72. Open Tu-Sa noon-2pm; organic bakery and take-away store open 9am-7pm.)

NORMANDY

SIGHTS

Though pricey, some of Caen's sights are discounted with the purchase of a full-price ticket to other sights or museums in the area; the tourist office has details.

MEMORIAL DE CAEN. This memorial serves as a powerful reminder of the precious nature of peace and is without a doubt the best of Normandy's many WWII museums. It traces the "failure of peace" through spiralling galleries beginning with the end of WWI and incorporates a unique collection of WWII footage, high-tech audio-visual aids, and displays on pre-war Europe and the Battles of Britain and Normandy. The short, haunting testimonial to the victims of the Holocaust is particularly moving, as are the three striking films. Count on spending three hours here to see it all. *(Take bus #17 to "Mémorial." ☎02 31 06 06 44. Open July 13-Aug. 26 daily 9am-8pm; Feb. 3-July 12 and Aug. 27-Oct. 9am-7pm; Jan. 15-Feb. 2 and Nov.-Dec. 9am-6pm. Last entry 1¼hr. before closing. 76F/€11.59, students, seniors, and ages 10-18 66F/€10.06; W and Sa 43F/€6.56, students, seniors, and children 33F/€5.03.)*

ABBEYS AND CHURCHES. Caen got its start as the seat of William the Conqueror's duchy; the city's legacy of first-class Romanesque architecture is due chiefly to William's desperately guilty conscience. Despite the pope's explicit interdiction, William married his distant cousin Mathilda. To get themselves back on the gold-paved road to Heaven, the duke and his wife built several ecclesiastical structures, most notably Caen's twin abbeys. In 1066, William began the **Abbaye-aux-Hommes,** off rue Guillaume le Conquérant; the abbey now functions as Caen's Hôtel de Ville. *(☎02 31 30 42 81.)* The adjacent **Eglise St-Etienne** contains William's tomb and an enormous organ (which you can climb into). In one of the chapels off the choir, you'll find a small collection of photographs taken in Caen during and after the bombings. Many of the city's displaced citizens took shelter in the abbey; stunning photographs show upper-class women struggling for normalcy as they glance at the mirror by candlelight between the church's columns. *(Open daily 9:15am-noon and 2-6pm. 1¼hr. tours of church in French at 9:30am, 2:30, and 4pm; of Hôtel de Ville at 11am. 10F/€1.53, students 5F/€0.76, under 18 free.)* Across the street from the abbey's gardens are the tower and remaining arches of the **Eglise St-Etienne-le-Vieux,** a raw, unrestored reminder of the destruction of the bombings. The smaller **Eglise de la Trinité** of the **Abbaye-aux-Dames,** off rue des Chanoines, has two 16th-century towers and modern windows that illuminate Mathilda's trapezoidal tomb. To visit the crypt, go through the low doorway in the south transept. *(Open M-Sa 8am-5:30pm, Su 9:30am-12:30pm. Free 1hr. tours in French at 2:30 and 4pm.)*

CHATEAU. Centered between the two abbeys to its east and west sprawl the ruins of William's enormous **château.** Its construction began in 1060, but a community may have existed here since the first century AD. *(Open May-Sept. daily 6am-1am; Oct.-Apr. 6am-7:30pm. Free. 1hr. tours in French July-Sept. daily at 9:30am, 2:30pm, and 4pm; in English Tu-Sa at 11am and 4pm. 20F/€3.05, students 15F/€2.29.)* The château's outer walls hide the sparkling but confusingly laid-out **Musée des Beaux-Arts,** which contains a fine selection of 16th- and 17th-century Italian, French, Dutch, and Flemish painting, including works by le Perugin, Rubens, and van Dyck, Impressionist paintings of Normandy by Monet, Courbet, and Boudin, and an eclectic collection of 20th-century works. *(☎02 31 30 47 70. Open W-M 9:30am-6pm. 25F/€3.81, students 15F/€2.29, art history students and under age 18 free, W free. Joint ticket with Musée de Normandie 35F/€5.34, students 25F/€3.81.)* The small **Jardin des Simples** within the château holds a collection of plants used in the Middle Ages. *(Same hours as château.)*

OTHER SIGHTS. Just beyond the château is the **Musée de Normandie,** which traces the origins of Norman craftsmanship and farming. *(☎02 31 30 47 60. Open W-M 9:30am-12:30pm and 2-6pm. 10F/€1.52, students 5F/€0.76, under 18 free.)* For a break from the bustle of Caen's center, take a walk around the château walls on rue de Geôle, turning left on rue Bosnières, to reach the sheltered, romantic **Jardin des Plantes** on pl. Blot. *(Open June-Aug. daily 8am-sunset; Sept.-May 8am-5:30pm.)*

ENTERTAINMENT

Caen parties every night, especially during the school year. **Rue de Bras, rue des Croisiers, quai Vendeuvre,** and **rue St-Pierre** are packed with well-attended bars and clubs. Locals start the evening at **Vertigo,** 14 rue Ecuyère, crowding around outdoor tables to check out the multitudes at the neighboring bars. (☎02 31 85 43 12. Open July-Sept. M-W noon-1am, Th-Sa noon-2am; Oct.-June M-Sa noon-1am.) **Farniente,** 13 rue Paul Doumer, draws the young and the chic ready to warm up for the clubs as they grind to Latin music and throw back tequila. (☎02 31 86 30 00. Open M-W 6pm-1am, Th-Sa 6pm-2am.) **L'Excuse,** 20 rue Vauquelin, is adorned with funky, modern artwork, but bypass it for the dance floor where they work it to everything from house to arab-inspired techno. (☎02 31 38 80 89. Open June-Aug. Th-Sa 11pm-4am, Sept.-May Th-Sa 10pm-4am. Occasional 25F/€3.81 cover.) Steamy **Le Zinc,** 12 rue du Vaugueux, supplies a mixed gay and straight crowd with heart-pounding techno. (☎02 31 93 20 30. Open Tu-Th 6pm-2am, F-Sa 6pm-4am.) The posh **Joy's Club,** 10 rue Strasbourg, is Caen's only true nightclub; be prepared to pay to preserve your fashionably-late image. (☎02 31 85 40 40. Tu-Th 11pm-midnight women free; cover 60F/€9.15, 35F/€5.34 for students; after midnight, women 35F/€5.34. F-Sa 11pm-midnight cover 70F/€10.67, 35F/€5.34 for women and students; after midnight 70F/€10.67. Cover usually includes 1 drink. Open Tu-Sa 11pm-5am.) Around the corner from Joy's, there's inexplicably popular karaoke at the diner-style **Bus Stop Café,** 7 rue de Bras. (☎02 31 85 72 72. Open daily 7:30pm-4am.)

BAYEUX

Bayeux (pop. 15,000) was unharmed by Nazi occupation and Allied liberation; as a result, the town retains its original river-hugging architecture and resplendent cathedral. Bayeux is most visited for its celebrated 900-year-old tapestry, which narrates William the Conqueror's victory over England in 1066. Bayeux is a beautiful base for exploration of the D-Day beaches, but should not be treated as a stopover. Some visitors skip the tapestry to see the beaches, but this masterpiece narrates an equally significant invasion, a reverse D-Day of sorts.

PRACTICAL INFORMATION

Trains: pl. de la Gare (☎02 31 92 80 50). To: **Caen** (20min., 15 per day, 32F/€4.88); **Cherbourg** (1hr., 12 per day, 82F/€12.50); and **Paris** (2½hr., 12 per day, 174F/€26.53). Ticket counters open M-F 6am-8pm, Sa-Su 8am-8pm.

Buses: Bus Verts, pl. de la Gare (☎02 31 92 02 92) head west to small towns and east to **Caen** (1hr., M-Sa 2-3 per day, 37.10F/€5.66). See p. 484 for coverage of the D-Day beaches. Buy tickets from the driver or at the office. Open M-F 9:15am-noon and 1:30-6pm. **Bybus,** pl. de la Gare (☎02 31 92 02 92). In-town bus circuit runs about 9am-6pm. 5.60F/€0.85 or 4.25F/€0.65 9-11:30am and 2-4pm.

Taxis: Les Taxis du Bessin (☎02 31 92 92 40).

Tourist Office: pont St-Jean (☎02 31 51 28 28; fax 02 31 51 28 29; www.bayeux-tourism.com). To find it from the station, turn left onto the highway (bd. Sadi-Carnot), then bear right at the roundabout, still on bd. Sadi-Carnot, following the signs to the *centre ville.* Once there, continue up rue Larcher and turn right on rue St-Martin, Bayeux's commercial avenue. The office will be on your left, at the edge of the pedestrian zone. The staff offers **currency exchange** (Su and M only) and **Internet access** (25F/€3.81 per 15min., 50F/€7.62 per 50min., 100F/€15.25 for 100min.), and books rooms anywhere in Calvados for 10F/€1.53. Open June 15-Sept. 15 M-Sa 9am-7pm, Su 9:30am-12:30pm and 2:30-6:30pm; Sept. 16-June 14 M-Sa 9am-noon and 2-6pm.

Laundromat: 10 rue Maréchal Foch (☎06 08 24 69 98). Open daily 7am-9pm.

Police: 49 av. Conseil (☎02 31 92 94 00).

Hospital: 13 rue de Nesmond (☎02 31 51 51 51), next to the tapestry center.

Post Office: rue Larcher (☎02 31 51 24 90). **Currency exchange.** Open M-F 8am-6:30pm, Sa 8am-noon. **Postal code:** 14400.

ACCOMMODATIONS AND CAMPING

There are several inexpensive lodgings in Bayeux, but demand often outstrips supply, especially in summer. You'll need to plan with military precision to get a room around June 6, the anniversary of D-Day.

The Family Home/Auberge de Jeunesse (HI), 39 rue Général de Dais (☎02 31 92 15 22; fax 02 31 92 55 72), is right in the center of town. From the tourist office, turn right onto rue St-Martin (the name changes) and turn left onto rue Général de Dais. The hostel will be on your left (5min.). Or, from rue Larcher, turn left on rue L. Leforestier, then right onto rue Général de Dais; the hostel will be on the right. 1- to 7-person rooms in two old buildings around a courtyard. Your room will be adorable, though possibly less than spotless. Communal laundry, kitchen, and dining room make meeting other guests a cinch. Huge breakfast included. Reception hours inconsistent; there's usually someone around during the day. Beds 100F/€15.25, without HI membership 110F/€16.77.

Centre d'Accueil Municipal, 21 chemin des Marettes (☎02 31 92 08 19; fax 02 31 92 12 40). From the station, follow bd. Sadi-Carnot and bear left at the rotary onto bd. Maréchal Leclerc, which becomes bd. Fabien Ware (10-15min.). This *centre d'accueil* has the look of a 60s-era hotel, with clean, spartan singles inside. Don't expect a hostel atmosphere here; the center is huge and quite impersonal. Breakfast 16F/€2.44. Sheets included. Reception 8am-8pm; call if arriving late. Beds 78F/€11.89. It may close for 6 months of renovations, beginning in Sept. 2002.

Hôtel Notre-Dame, 44 rue des Cuisiniers (☎02 31 92 87 24; fax 02 31 92 67 11; hotel-notre-dame@welcome.to). Clean rooms, off winding old stairways and salons, some with amazing views of the cathedral. *Demi-pension* required Apr.-Oct. Breakfast 35F/€5.34. Reception 8am-midnight. Closed Nov. 15-Dec. 20. Singles and doubles 200F/€30.49 (220F/€33.54 with *demi-pension*), with bath 280F/€42.69 (280F/€42.69 with *demi-pension*); triples 360F/€54.89; family room (up to 6 people) 480F/€73.18. Prices lower Jan.-Mar. MC/V.

Le Maupassant, 19 rue St-Martin (☎02 31 92 28 53). 10 simple, clean rooms above a street and brasserie heavy with pedestrian traffic. Breakfast 35F/€5.34. Reception 8am-10pm. Singles with or without shower 170F/€25.92, doubles with shower or toilet 220F/€33.54, quads with bath 400F/€60.98.

Camping Municipal, bd. d'Eindhoven (☎02 31 92 08 43), is within easy reach of the town center and the N13. Follow rue Genas Duhomme to the right off rue St-Martin and continue straight on av. de la Vallée des Prés. The campground is on your right, across from a Champion Supermarket (10min.). Immaculate sites and shiny facilities next to the municipal swimming pool. Laundry, great showers. Gates closed 10pm-7am. Office open July-Aug. 7am-9pm; May-June and Sept. 8-10am and 5-7pm. Open May-Sept. 18.30F/€27.91 per person, children under 7 9.80F/€1.49, 22.60F/€3.45 per tent and car. Electricity 18.60F/€2.84. 10% reduction on stays of 5 or more days.

FOOD

Markets are on pl. St-Patrice on Saturdays, and rue St-Jean on Wednesdays, both about 7am-1pm. The area around the tourist office has small grocery stores and there is a **Champion** supermarket on bd. d'Eindhoven, near the campground. One of the heartiest and most engaging restaurants in the city is **La Table du Terroir,** 42 rue St-Jean, down the street from the tourist office. The jovial chef-owner and his family serve local meat dishes and delicious desserts at communal wooden tables. (☎02 31 92 05 53. *Menus* 60F/€9.15 and 98F/€14.94. Open Tu-Sa noon-2:30pm and 7-10pm, Su noon-2:30pm; Oct.-May F-Sa 7-10pm.)

NORMANDY

SIGHTS

TAPISSERIE DE BAYEUX. The exquisite tapestry illustrates in vibrant detail the events leading up to the Battle of Hastings. On October 14, 1066, William the Bastard earned himself a more sociable nickname by crossing the Channel with a large cavalry to defeat his cousin Harold who, according to the Norman version of the tale, had stolen something of William's—the English throne, to which he had been named. After pledging fealty to William (who'd rescued him from the nasty Guy de Ponthieu during a cross-channel sojourn that had gone awry), Harold decided to pre-empt William's coronation while Edward's body was still warm (an event cleverly shown in the otherwise chronological tapestry *before* Edward's death and funeral). William's victory, following a grueling 14-hour battle in which Harold was dramatically killed by an archer, would be the last successful invasion of England. A mere 50cm wide but 70m long, the tapestry, now over 900 years old, hangs in all its glory at the **Centre Guillaume le Conquérant,** rue de Nesmond. Take note of the horses, the soldiers flailing in quicksand at Mont-St-Michel (frames 16-17), Halley's comet (32-33), and poor Harold, with the fatal arrow in his eye (57). A lengthy, elaborate exhibit details the tapestry's contents; you'll miss out if you settle for the short refresher film on 11th-century history. Everything is translated into English. *(☎02 31 51 25 50. Open May-Aug. daily 9am-7pm; Mar. 15-Apr. and Sept.-Oct. 15 9am-6:30pm; Oct. 16-Mar. 14 9:30am-12:30pm and 2-6pm. 41F/€6.25, seniors 31F/ €4.73, ages 10-26 16F/€2.44, under 10 free; includes Musée Baron Gérard and Hôtel du Doyen, a religious art museum and center for lace production. Audio guide 5F/€0.76.)*

CATHEDRAL. Nearby is the original home of the tapestry, the **Cathédrale Notre-Dame.** Above the transept are Gothic arches with dizzyingly intricate carvings, while the 11th-century crypt beneath displays chipping 15th-century frescoes. To the left of the entrance is the *salle capitulaire*, which contains the only *chemin de Jerusalem* in France, a tile labyrinth on the floor that retraces the twists and turns of Jesus' *via crucis* (the route that he followed on the way to Calvary). *(Open July-Aug. M-Sa 8am-7pm, Su 9am-7pm; Sept.-June M-Sa 8:30am-noon and 2:30-7pm, Su 9am-12:15pm and 2:30-7pm. Informal tours of the cathedral July-Aug. Tu-F approximately 10am-noon and 3-7pm. Tours of the salle capitulaire July-Aug. M-F 1, 3, and 5pm. Free.)*

MUSEE BARON GERARD. Next to the cathedral, the **Musée Baron Gérard,** pl. de la Liberté, houses a large collection of porcelain, along with tapestries, 16th- and 17th-century paintings, and the delicate lace characteristic of Bayeux. Just before you enter the museum, glance at the enormous tree, planted in 1793 to commemorate the French Revolution, that fills the *place*. *(☎02 31 51 60 50. Oper June-Sept. 15 daily 9am-7pm; Sept. 16-May 10am-12:30pm and 2-6pm. Prices same as to the tapestry, but admission to tapestry gets you in free to Musée Baron Gérard.)*

LOCAL D-DAY SIGHTS. The events of the D-Day landing and the subsequent 76-day battle are recounted in the overwhelming **Musée de la Bataille de Normandie,** bd. Fabian Ware. American, English, French, and German newspapers of the time are presented, along with photos, weapons, and innumerable uniform-clad mannequins. It is impossible to cover the entire exhibit, though—there's just too much small type. *(☎02 31 92 93 41. Open May-Sept. 16 daily 9:30am-6:30pm, Sept. 17-Apr. 10am-12:30pm and 2-6pm. 30min. film in English approx. every 2hr. Closed last two weeks in Jan. 34F/ €5.19, students 16F/€2.44, under age 10 free.)* In contrast, the **British Cemetery** across the street is strikingly simple and a far more moving wartime record.

THE D-DAY BEACHES

By 1944, the German forces stationed along the northern coasts of France had been waiting for an Allied invasion for the four years since they had taken over the Republic. The area around Calais, at the English Channel's narrowest point, had been heavily fortified with batteries every 2mi. along the coast; Normandy was slightly less prepared for a full-scale invasion but still a treacherous landing zone, with batteries stationed at 10-mile intervals. Preparations for the attack began at the Québec Conference of 1943, when the Allied leaders concluded that the only way to defeat Hitler was to recapture what he had dubbed "Fortress Europe." The attack, a gamble from the outset, would come mostly from the sea, even though there had been only one successful amphibious assault in the past several centuries of warfare. Allied counterintelligence disseminated false attack plans, inflated dummy tanks near Norway, and flooded the radio waves with retired military men. Meanwhile, the British, Canadian, and American masterminds of "Operation Overlord" planned a landing on the Normandy coast between the Cotentin Peninsula and the Orne. In the pre-dawn hours of **June 6, 1944,** 16,000 British and US paratroopers tumbled from the sky; a few hours later, 135,000 troops and 20,000 vehicles landed in fog from a rough sea onto the beaches code-named Utah and Omaha (American), Gold and Sword (British), and Juno (Canadian). The D-Day landings caused devastating losses on both sides, but were undoubtedly a crucial precursor to great successes for the Allies. The Battle of Normandy raged on until August 21; on August 24 free French forces entered and liberated Paris; less than a year later, Allied forces rolled into Berlin, and Germany surrendered.

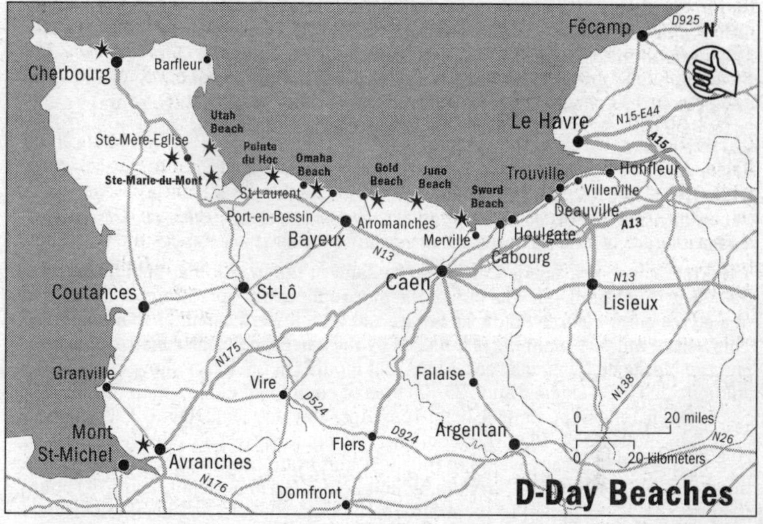

The **Voie de la Liberté** (Liberty Highway) follows the US army's advance from Utah Beach to Bastogne in Belgium. For a more complete description of the sites and museums which commemorate the battle, pick up *The D-Day Landings and the Battle of Normandy*, a brochure available from most tourist offices in the area. Today, the battle's traces are visible in remnants of German bunkers and the few unfilled bomb craters that dot the coast. Monuments, cemeteries, and museums commemorating the battle and its victims are strewn from Cherbourg to Le Havre. More striking, however, than the physical remnants are the memories of the citizens of this area, and despite a material rebirth, it may take yet another sixty years for Normandy to fully recover from the war.

TRANSPORTATION. Although the most convenient way to see the beaches is undoubtedly by car, most of the beaches and museums can be reached from Caen and Bayeux with the help of **Bus Verts** (☎08 10 21 42 14). Ask about the special **"D-Day" line** that runs from Arromanches to the Pointe du Hoc, stopping at the US Cemetery and Omaha Beach along the way. The bus leaves from Caen for Arromanches at 9:30am and returns at 6pm (unit ticket 74.20F/€11.31); from Bayeux take #75 in time for a 2pm departure from Arromanches (buy the 105F/€16.01 Carte Liberté). To get to **Benouville** and **Ouistreham,** take Bus Verts #1 from Caen; #20 links Caen to the British cemetery at **Ranville.** Line #70 (M-Sa 5 per day, 3 on Su) runs from Bayeux to **Pointe du Hoc,** the **American Cemetery,** and **Port-en-Bessin,** and #75 goes to **Arromanches** and **Ouistreham** (3 per day). You may want to buy a day-pass if you plan to make many stops (see **Normandy: Transportation,** p. 462, for more info). **Ste-Mère-Eglise** is accessible by **STN** bus (☎02 33 77 44 88) from **Carentan** (15min.; 1 per day leaving at 12:50pm, returning at 6:35pm; 18.20F/€2.77). Call the Carentan tourist office (☎02 33 42 74 01) for more info. To get to Carentan, you can take the train from Bayeux (30min., 10 per day, 43F/€6.56). **Utah Beach** and the **Musée du Débarquement** are only accessible by car, foot, or thumb from Ste-Mère-Eglise, though *Let's Go*, as always, does not recommend hitchhiking.

Before renting a car or heading off by bus, consider a **tour.** All three companies listed here include admission to the museum in Arromanches. **Bus Fly,** rue des Cuisiniers in Bayeux, runs tours with English-speaking guides. (☎02 31 22 00 08; fax 02 31 92 35 10; www.busfly.com. 4hr. tour 210F/€32.02, students 190F/€28.97, under 12 100F/€15.25; 8hr. tour 350F/€53.36, students 320F/€48.79, under 12 200F/€30.49. Pick-up 8:30am and 1:30pm from your hotel or hostel. Reservations required.) **Victory Tours** leads tours in English that leave from behind the tourist office in Bayeux. (☎02 31 51 98 14; fax 02 31 51 07 01; www.victory-tours.com. 4hr. tour departs at 12:30pm, 175F/€26.68. 8hr. tour departs at 9:15am, 300F/€45.74. Reservations required.) **Normandy Tours,** 26 pl. de la Gare, based in Bayeux's Hôtel de la Gare, runs flexible tours with less commentary in both English and French. (☎02 31 92 10 70; fax 02 31 51 95 99. 4hr. tour 200F/€30.49, starting at 8:30am or 1pm.) Tipping tour guides is gracious, but not mandatory.

BEACHES NEAR BAYEUX

Local tourist offices distribute a list of D-Day museums and sights that offer discounted admission with a full-price ticket to another museum or sight.

The Americans spearheaded the western flank of the invasion at **Utah Beach,** near Ste-Marie du Mont. Utah was one of the more successful operations of the day; all objectives were completed on schedule, and with fewer casualties than expected. This feat of military planning is honored by the **American Commemorative Monument** and the **Musée du Débarquement.** Films and models in the latter show how 836,000 soldiers, 220,000 vehicles, and 725,000 tons of equipment came ashore. (☎02 33 71 53 35. Open June-Sept. daily 9:30am-7pm; Apr.-May and Oct. 10am-12:30pm and 2-6pm; Nov.-Mar. Sa-Su 10am-12:30pm and 2-5:30pm. 30F/€4.50, ages 6-16 13F/€2.) Nearby **Ste-Mère-Eglise** was one of the most important targets of the invasion. The town was on the road to Carentan, which held a German depot, and Cherbourg, the port the Allies hoped to recapture. Many paratroopers had been misdropped because of German flak and strong winds; in the pre-dawn hours these soldiers fell directly into the town. The local church had just caught fire, and the paratroopers, illuminated by the glow of the flames, were easy targets for the Germans. Carrying twice their weight in equipment, many others drowned in the channel or in rivers before they could get out of their harnesses. All told, 16% were killed before they hit the ground. Even so, a badly outnumbered group of paratroopers broke through heavy German defenses after six hours of fighting. The parachute-shaped **Musée des Troupes Aéroporteés,** 14 rue Eisenhower, houses one of the planes that dropped them. (☎02 33 41 41 35. Open Apr.-Sept. daily 9am-6:45pm; Feb.-Mar. and Oct.-Nov. 9:30am-noon and 2-6pm; closed Dec.-Jan. and Nov. 5, 2002-Mar. 22, 2003 for construction. 33F/€5, ages 6-14 13F/€2.)

The most difficult landing was that of the First US Infantry Division at **Pointe du Hoc.** Not only was this the most strongly fortified of all the coastline strongholds, but it stood above 30m cliffs that had to be scaled with ropes and hooks. Of the 225 specially trained US Rangers who climbed the bluff, neutralized a key German position, and were left to defend it for two days until help arrived, only 90 survived. German losses were even heavier: only 40 prisoners were left among the 2000 stationed there. The Pointe is considered to be a military cemetery because so many casualties still remain there, crushed beneath collapsed 5m thick concrete bunkers. Dozens of unfilled bomb craters dive into the earth surrounding the rubble in one of the few areas that still represents the day's destruction.

Omaha Beach, next to Colleville-sur-Mer and just east of the Pointe du Hoc, is perhaps the most famous of all the beaches—often referred to as "bloody Omaha." Nothing went right here on D-Day: scouts had failed to detect a German presence, and aerial and naval bombardment of the fortifications had been entirely ineffective due to foggy conditions. What's more, the attacks had been unanswered by the Germans, furthering the impression of a scantily guarded region. The beach was protected by three veteran battalions, instead of the single motley division that the Americans had expected, was covered with "Rommel's asparagus," a mine-topped jack-and-pole device, and ended in concrete walls, anti-tank ditches, minefields, and barbed wire. The first waves of troops to hit the shores suffered casualties of nearly 100%, and of 40 amphibious tanks launched, only five made it ashore and one reached Bayeux. 6000 men of the initial wave of 35,000 died within the first hour of fighting, and an additional 8000 were killed the same day. After a heavy rain, pieces of 57-year-old German barbed wire can still be found peeking out of the sand near the grass at the back of the beach.

Overlooking Omaha beach, 9387 American graves stretch across a 172-acre coastal reserve. The **American Cemetery** contains rows of immaculate white crosses and stars of David, among them the graves of a father and his son and 38 pairs of brothers. A simple marble chapel and a 7m bronze statue, *The Spirit of American Youth Rising from the Waves*, face the soldiers' graves, while the Garden of the Missing, behind the memorial, lists the names of the 1557 individuals whose remains were never recovered. The cemetery contains only a fraction of all those killed here, as many soldiers were buried in the US instead. (☎02 31 51 62 00; fax 02 31 51 62 09; www.abmc.gov. Open Apr. 16-Sept. daily 8am-6pm; Oct.-Apr. 15 9am-5pm. The American staff at the office can help locate specific graves.)

Six kilometers west of Arromanches in tiny **Longues-sur-Mer,** the **Batteries de Longues** are an ominous reminder of the German presence (☎02 32 14 68 71). These four bunkers, constructed in 1944, still hold their original artillery, capable of firing 12km; one contains the only cannon in the region still loaded with its original ammunition. Only one gun was put out of commission on D-Day; the naval bombardment destroyed the town a kilometer inland, but left the bunkers intact for the most part. On June 7, British troops took the battery with essentially no resistance from the German and Polish troops stationed here. (Tours in French and English daily 10am-5:30pm, none Apr.-May M-Tu. 26F/€3.96, 23F/€3.51 with ticket stub from almost any other area museum.)

At **Arromanches,** a small town at the center of **Gold Beach,** the British used retired ships and 600,000 tons of concrete towed across the Channel to build **Port Winston,** the floating harbor that was to supply the Allied forces until Cherbourg was liberated months later. The hulking ruins of a port built in six days and designed to last 18 months remain 57 years later in a broken semicircle just off the coast. The **Musée du Débarquement** on the beach uses models to show how the port was built, towed, and assembled under fire. Two short, effective films and frequent tours make this one of the best museums in the area. (☎02 31 22 34 31; www.normandy1944.com. Open May-Aug. daily 9am-7pm; Sept. 9am-6pm; Oct. and Mar. 9:30am-12:30pm and 1:30-5:30pm; Apr. 9am-12:30pm and 1:30-6pm; Nov.-Dec. and Feb. 10am-12:30pm and 1:30-5pm. Opens at 10am on Sunday, except June-Aug (9am). Closed Dec. 30-Jan. 28. 35F/€4, students and children over 6 22F/€3.) The **Arromanches 360° Cinéma** shows a well-made and very interesting 18-minute film, *Le Prix de la Liberté* (*The Price of Freedom*), on its circular screen. The movie combines battle footage with peaceful images of pre-war Normandy. To reach the cinema from the museum, turn left onto rue de la Batterie and follow the steps to the top of the cliff. (☎02 31 22 30 30. Open June-Aug. daily 9:40am-6:40pm; May 15-31 and Sept. 1-14 10:10am-6:10pm; Sept. 15-Oct. 10:10am-5:40pm; Mar.-May 14 and Nov. 10:10am-5:10pm; Dec. and Feb. 10:10am-4:40pm. Closed Jan. Movies at 10 and 40min. past the hour. 24F/€3.66, children 10-18 21F/€3.20.)

Camping Reine Mathilde, in Etreham, near Port-en-Bessin, is 5km from the sea and Omaha Beach, 10km from Bayeux, and always packed. (☎02 31 21 76 55; fax 02 31 22 18 33; camping.reine-mathilde@wanadoo.fr. Open Apr.-Sept. Reception daily 8:30am-12:30pm and 2:30-7:30pm. 27F/€4.12 per person, children under age 7 11F/€1.68, 26F/€3.96 per tent and car, electricity 21F/€3.20, day visitors 20F/€3.05.) Bayeux's tourist office can help you find accommodations in *chambres d'hôte* or in one of the many campgrounds along the coast.

BEACHES NEAR CAEN

These eastern beaches were landing sites for the Canadian and British armies; German defenders fired on them from expensive stone vacation houses along the beach. The beaches have changed considerably since 1944. The bunkers of Juno, Sword, and Gold Beaches have been replaced by resorts, and the somber taboos against recreation which characterize the American sites are not maintained here. **Juno Beach,** east of Arromanches, was the Canadian battlefront. The last Canadian amphibious attack, in Sicily in 1942, had resulted in 75% casualties and ultimate failure; bent on revenge at Juno, they pushed their attacks through without air or naval support and despite terrible losses. The **Canadian Cemetery** is located at **Bény-**

sur-Mer-Reviers. The British anchored the easternmost flank of the invasion with their landing at **Sword Beach.** This enormously successful mission was accomplished with the help of the quirky "Hobart's Funnies," tanks outlandishly fitted with bridge-building, mine-sweeping, and ditch-digging apparatus.

At **Benouville,** British paratroopers of the 6th Airborne Division captured Pegasus Bridge within 10 minutes of landing and held it until their Scottish reinforcements arrived. The **Musée des Troupes Aéroportées,** also known as the **Memorial Pegasus,** in Benouville tells the story of the Parachute Brigades' operations on the Dives River. (☎02 31 44 62 54. Open May-Sept. daily 9:30am-6:30pm; Oct.-Nov. and Feb.-Apr. 10am-1pm and 2-5pm. 30F/€4.57, students 20F/€3.05.) One of the largest of the 16 British cemeteries is 1.5km away in **Ranville.** The only French troops involved in the D-Day landings came ashore at **Ouistreham,** at the mouth of the Orne River. They and Normandy's resilient citizens are memorialized in the **N°4 Commando Museum,** pl. Alfred Thomas. (☎02 31 96 63 10. Open mid-Mar. to Oct. daily 10:30am-6pm. 25F/€3.81, students and children 10 and over 15F/€2.29. Call well in advance for tours with a bilingual veteran of the landing.)

CHERBOURG

Strategically located at the tip of the Cotentin peninsula, Cherbourg (pop. 44,000) was the Allies' "Gateway to France," their major supply port following the D-Day offensive of 1944. Today, the town's numerous ferry lines shuttle tourists from France to England and Ireland. Don't go out of your way to visit Cherbourg; the city's a bit short on both sights and charm. But if you find yourself there on your way in and out of France, don't despair. There's just enough to keep you busy until the next train or ferry leaves.

PRACTICAL INFORMATION. Ferries leave from the *gare maritime*, northeast of the town center, along bd. Maritime (open daily 5:30am-11:30pm). Irish Ferries goes to **Rosslare** about every other day. P&O European Ferries go to **Portsmouth,** and Brittany Ferries to **Poole** (see **Getting There: By Boat,** p. 62). It is essential to both reserve ahead and check the most up-to-date ferry schedules; many travelers find themselves stranded in Cherbourg if they don't plan ahead. To get to the **tourist office** and the center of town, turn right from the terminal onto bd. Felix Amiot. At the roundabout, go straight and continue around the bend to the left. Make a right at the first bridge to cross the canal; you will see the tourist office ahead on your left (20min.). To reach the **train station,** go left at the roundabout onto av. Aristide Briand and follow it as it becomes av. Carnot. Turn right at the end of the canal onto av. Millet; the station will be ahead on the left (25min.).

Trains run to **Bayeux** (1hr., 8 per day in the afternoon, 82F/€12.50); **Caen** (1½hr., 10 per day, 100F/€15.25); **Paris** (3hr., 7 per day, 222F/€33.85); **Rennes** via Lison (3½hr., 3 per day, 174F/€26.53); and **Rouen** (4½hr., 4 per day, 186F/€28.36). (☎02 33 44 18 74. Station open daily 5:30am-7:30pm.) **STN** (☎02 33 88 51 00) sends **buses** around the region (open M-F 8am-noon and 2-6pm). You can **rent bikes** from the hostel or **Station Voile,** rue Diablotin, for 40F/€6.10 per half-day or 60F/€9.15 per day. (☎02 33 78 19 29. Open June 15-Sept. 15 daily 10am-6pm.)

The **tourist office,** 2 quai Alexandre III, leads hikes and tours in summer, and books rooms for free. (☎02 33 93 52 02; fax 02 33 53 66 97; www.ot-cherbourg-cotentin.fr. Open June-Aug. M-Sa 9am-6:30pm, Su 10am-12:30pm; Sept.-May M-Sa 9am-12:30pm and 2-6pm.) An **annex** at the *gare maritime* is open for ferry arrivals and departures. (☎02 33 44 39 92. Open daily approx. 7am-noon and 2-8pm; Sept.-May closes at 6pm.) There's **currency exchange** at the ferry terminal or at banks around **pl. Gréville. Internet access** is available at the **Forum des Halles,** pl. Centrale. (☎02 33 78 19 30. Open M 2-7pm, Tu-Sa 10am-7pm. 15F/€2.29 per 30min.) The **post office** is on rue de l'Ancien Quai. (☎02 33 08 87 00. Open M-F 8am-7pm, Sa 8am-noon.) There's a **branch** on av. Carnot near the ferry terminal. **Postal code:** 50100.

ACCOMMODATIONS AND FOOD. Cherbourg's few budget accommodations are often available, since most leave town as soon as they step off the ferry, but check the possibilities a few days in advance. The tourist office has lists of *chambres d'hôte* (around 150F/€22.90) and nearby campsites. The cheapest option is the **Auberge de Jeunesse (HI),** 57 rue de l'Abbaye. From the tourist office, go left onto quai de Caligny and then left again on rue de Port, which becomes rue Tour Carrée and then rue de la Paix. Bear left onto rue de l'Union, which feeds into rue de l'Abbaye; the hostel is on the left (10min.). From the station, take bus #3 or 5 to "Arsenal" (last bus around 7:30pm). The hostel has 100 beds in spotless 2- to 5-person rooms, each with a sink, shower, and lockers (bring your own lock), a kitchen, and bar. (☎02 33 78 15 15; fax 02 33 78 15 16; cherbourg@fuaj.org. Bike rental available. 51F/€7.78 per half-day, 81F/€12.35 per day. Sheets 18F/€2.74. Reception 8am-noon and 6-11pm. Lockout from 10am-6pm; can enter after 1pm if you've already checked in. No curfew. Bunks and breakfast 98F/€14.90 first night, 80F/€12.20 second night.) Opposite the station, **Hôtel de la Gare,** 10 pl. Jean Jaurès, lets large, colorful, lovingly tended rooms that seem miles away from the asphalt. (☎02 33 43 06 81; fax 02 33 43 12 20. Bacon and egg breakfast 35F/€5.34. Reception 24hr. One single without shower 115F/€17.53, singles and doubles with shower 170-185F/€25.92-28.21, with bath 210-260F/€32.02-39.64; triples and quads 300-360F/€45.74-54.89. MC/V.)

A huge **market** is held on pl. du Théâtre on Tuesday morning and on Thursday until 3pm. Stock up at the **Carrefour supermarket,** quai de l'Entrepôt, next to the station (open M-Sa 8:30am-9pm) or at the **Proxi,** rue de l'Union, near the hostel (open M-Sa 8:30am-1pm and 2:30-7:45pm, Su 9am-1pm and 5-7:45pm). **Rue de la Paix** is lined with inexpensive ethnic restaurants. **Crêperie Ty Billic,** 73 rue au Blé, is a tourist-free haven. Get two galettes, two crêpes, and one cider for 59F/€9. (☎02 33 01 11 90. Open daily noon-2:30pm and 7-11:15pm.)

SIGHTS AND ENTERTAINMENT. Founded by William the Conqueror's granddaughter—and Henry II's mother—Mathilda in 1145, the semi-ruined **Abbaye du Vœu** and its gardens are at the western edge of town, past the hostel. With intricate lacework and dark, angular windows in the transept, the **Basilique de la Trinité** has meshed centuries of architectural styles. Sixteenth-century carvings above the nave include a boogying skeleton on the left, who leads us through the ranks of man, from peasant to Pope, with the reminder that "death comes for us all." The **Musée de la Libération,** perched high on the **Fort du Roule** in the old citadel, covers occupation, liberation, and reconstruction in Cherbourg. (☎02 33 20 14 12. Open May-Sept. daily 10am-6pm; Oct.-Apr. Tu-Su 9:30am-noon and 2-5:30pm. 20F/€3.05, ages 7-16 10F/€1.53, free for students with ID.) Look for the upcoming **La Cité de la Mer,** opening in 2002, which will be an aquarium of sorts. (☎02 33 20 26 26.)

The streets around pl. Central are filled with bars and late-night eateries that are happy to help you drink away your layover. Multilingual crowds congregate nightly at **Art's Café,** 69 rue au Blé. (☎02 33 53 55 11. Open M-Sa 11am-1am; live DJ F-Sa). Or try mellow **Le Solier,** 52 rue Grande Rue, with cushy stools, Celtic music, and cheap cider. (Open June-Sept. M-Th 5:30pm-1am, F-Sa 5:30pm-2am; Oct.-May M-Sa 5:30pm-1am.) During the second week of October, Cherbourg hosts the **Festival des Cinemas d'Irlande et de Grande Bretagne,** a festival of Irish and British films.

GRANVILLE

In 1439, the expatriate Lord Jean d'Argouges sold his great-grandmother's dowry to the English. This dowry—the rocky peninsula of Granville—quickly became an entire fortified city, from which the English spent 30 years trying to take Mont-St-Michel. Now thoroughly pardoned by France, Granville (pop. 13,700) crams a lot of variety into a small area. The center is a bustling and attractive shopping district, and on the sea is a popular resort with rugged cliffs and ribbons of white sand. Granville's distance from Paris keeps it less crowded and less expensive than you might expect, and proximity to Mont-St-Michel and the Channel Islands, a great beach, and exceptional museums give the town a definite appeal.

ORIENTATION AND PRACTICAL INFORMATION. The **train station,** pl. Pierre Semard, off av. Maréchal Leclerc, has service to: **Bayeux** (2hr., 4 per day, 91F/€13.87); **Cherbourg** via Lison (3hr., 3 per day, 126F/€19.22); and **Paris** (3hr., 4 per day, 202F/€30.80). (☎08 36 35 35 35. Station open M-F 5:15am-12:30pm and 12:55-7:40pm, Sa 6am-12:30pm and 12:55-7pm, Su 1:30-8pm; July-Aug. Su also open 6am-12:30pm.) **SNCF buses** go to **Coutances** (30min., 3 per day, 42F/€6.40), and **STN,** on cours Jonville, to **Avranches** (1hr., 3 per day, 34.50F/€5.26). STN also runs a mostly extraneous **local bus** circuit. (☎02 33 50 77 89. Office open M-F 8:30am-noon and 1:30-6:30pm, Sa 9:15am-noon and 2:15-4:15pm.) **Emeraude Lines** (☎02 33 50 16 36), at the *gare maritime,* sails to: the **Chausey Islands** (1hr., 1-2 per day, 105F/€16.01, ages 3-14 65F/€9.91); **Guernsey** (2hr.; 3 per week; 360F/€54.89, ages 16-23 295F/€44.98, ages 4-15 215F/€32.78); and **Jersey** (1¼hr.; 3 per week; 299F/€45.60, ages 16-23 220F/€33.56, 4-15 180F/€27.44). Ask about family rates. **Vedette "Jolie France"** (☎02 33 50 31 81; fax 02 33 50 39 90; open daily 8:30am-12:30pm and 1:30-7pm) also sails to the **Chausey Islands** (50min.; 1-3 boats per day; 104F/€15.86, children ages 3-14 64F/€9.76; reserve 2 days ahead July-Aug.). There's **bike rental** at **Sport Evasion,** av. Maréchal Leclerc for 50F/€7.62 per day with a security deposit. Call in advance (☎02 33 68 10 00). Access the **Internet** at the post office.

To get to the center of town, leave the station and follow av. Leclerc downhill as it becomes rue Couraye (10min.). The **tourist office,** 4 cours Jonville, is around the corner on your right as soon as you reach the main *place.* They **reserve rooms** for free and offer **tours** of the city. Ask for a copy of the *Calendrier des manifestations* for a list of events in town. (☎02 33 91 30 03; fax 02 33 91 30 19; www.ville-granville.fr. Tours in French July-Aug. daily at 3pm, 10F/€2. Office open July-Aug. M-Sa 9am-1pm and 2-7:30pm, Su 10am-1pm; Sept.-June M-F 9am-12:15pm and 2-6:30pm, Sa 9am-12:30pm and 2-6:30pm; Easter-June and Sept. 1-15 open Su 11am-12:30pm.) Next door, the **post office** has **currency exchange.** (☎02 33 91 12 30. Open M-F 8am-12:30pm and 2:30-6:30pm, Sa 8:30am-noon.) **Postal code:** 50400.

ACCOMMODATIONS AND FOOD. In summer you're unlikely to find either solitude or a surplus of hotel rooms in Granville. To get to the **Auberge de Jeunesse (HI),** bd. des Amiraux Granvillais, from the train station, turn right onto av. Maréchal Leclerc and follow it downhill. Just before the town center, turn left onto rue St-Sauveur; head right when the road forks and look for "Centre Nautisme" signs. Part of a huge sailing center, it runs week-long camps during July and August. Comfortable and newly redone dorms. Be sure to reserve well in advance in the summer. (☎02 33 91 22 60; fax 02 33 50 51 99. Breakfast 18F/€2.74. Meals 57F/€8.69. Sheets 23F/€3.51. Office open 9am-noon and 3-7pm. Code for late entry. Singles 110F/€16.77; one bed in double 89F/€13.57; triple 77F/€11.74; quad 59F/€9. Prices 40% higher for non-members.)

To reach **Hôtel Michelet,** 5 rue Jules Michelet, from the tourist office, head straight across pl. de Gaulle onto rue P. Poirier. When that ends, take a right onto rue Georges Clemenceau (becomes av. de la Libération), then a sharp left up the hill onto rue Jules Michelet. Comfortable, modern rooms, some with balconies, in a calm location near the beach. (☎02 33 50 06 55; fax 02 33 50 12 25. Breakfast 30F/€4.57. Shower 15F/€2.29. Reception 7:30am-10pm. Doubles 140F/€21.35, with toilet 185F/€28.21, with shower and TV 240F/€36.59, with bath and TV 300F/€45.74. Extra bed 60F/€9.15. MC/V.) **Hôtel Terminus,** 5 pl. de la Gare, feels like a Victorian dollhouse. All rooms have toilet and TV. (☎02 33 50 02 05. Breakfast 25F/€3.81. Singles 125F/€19.06, with shower 160F/€24.39; doubles 165F/€25.16, with shower 195F/€29.73, with bath 215F/€32.79; triples 205-265F/€31.25-40.40; quads 235F/€35.83, with shower 280F/€42.69.)

There are **markets** on cours Jonville all day Saturday and pl. du 11 Novembre 1918 on Wednesday mornings. For more groceries, head to **Marché Plus,** 107 rue de Couraye (open M-Sa 7am-9pm, Su 9am-1pm). Restaurants in town are plentiful, but tend to be a bit pricey. Near the beach, you'll find kebab vendors and ice cream stands. The town also has an enormous number of boulangeries and pâtisseries. Near the hostel, **Monte Pego,** 13 rue St-Sauveur, serves delicious pastas, pizzas, and salads for 38-58F/€5.79-8.84. (☎02 33 90 74 44. Open July-Aug. daily noon-2:30pm and 7-10:30pm; Sept.-June closed Su-M. MC/V.)

SIGHTS AND ENTERTAINMENT. Granville's old English walled city, known as the *haute ville*, occupies the top of a point that stretches from the casino to the **Eglise de Notre-Dame** (where classical concerts are held on summer weekends). Stretching northward from the old city is Granville's most popular **beach,** but you'll also find quiet stretches of sand past the port on the opposite side of the point. Anchored at the edge of the *haute ville*, at the pl. de l'Isthme, is its most modern addition: the **Musée Richard Anacréon,** the area's only 20th-century art museum. The museum focuses on the first half of the century, and on Fauvism in particular. Temporary exhibitions supplement the permanent collection during the summer. (☎02 33 51 02 94. Open July-Sept. W-M 11am-6pm, Oct.-June W-Su 2-6pm. 10F/€1.53, students and children 6F/€0.91.)

You can take a coastal path from the beach promenade to the stairs that deposit you at the clifftop **Musée Christian Dior,** in the childhood home of Granville's most famous son. The museum's extravagant and impractical dresses are as flowery as the villa's immaculate gardens, designed from 1905 to 1930 by Dior and his mom. (☎02 33 61 48 21. Open May 20-Sept. Tu-Su 10am-12:30pm and 2-6:30pm. Gardens close at 9pm. 25F/€3.81, students and over 60 years 20F/€3.05, under 12 free.)

From May to September, boats leave daily for the **Chausey Islands,** a sparsely inhabited archipelago of 52 to 365 islets, depending on the tide (see **Orientation and Practical Information,** above for ferry info).

Nightlife is limited and pleasantly low-key; bar-hopping in your flip-flops will not earn you disapproving stares. The **Bar les Amiraux,** bd. des Amiraux, across from the hostel, pulls in relaxed, mid-summer crowds fresh off the beach. (☎02 33 50 12 83. Open June-Sept. M-Sa noon-2am, Su noon-1am; Oct.-May Su-Th until 1am, F-Sa until 2am.) **Les Bals des Oiseaux,** rue St-Sauveur, serves a laid-back, hemp-strung clientele and hosts occasional reggae and ska concerts. (☎02 33 51 35 51. Open Tu-Sa 10:30am-2am. Open M evening.) Granville hosts *Carnaval* every year on the Sunday before Mardi Gras and the **Fête des Marins** at the end of July. The **Eglise de Notre-Dame** also holds classical concerts on summer weekends.

COUTANCES

Miraculously unscathed by World War II, the 13th-century cathedral of Coutances (pop. 11,000) is second in beauty perhaps only to Chartres. Flanked by the churches of St-Pierre and St-Nicholas, the cathedral forms the centerpiece of the town's three-spired skyline, which is visible from miles into the surrounding countryside. The beautiful abbeys and châteaux, within walking distance of town, provide a true respite from the heavily touristed D-Day beaches and Mont-St-Michel.

ORIENTATION AND PRACTICAL INFORMATION. The **train station** (☎02 33 07 50 77) has service to **Avranches** (1hr., 3 per day, 45F/€6.86); **Caen** (1½hr., 8 per day, 84F/€12.81); **Cherbourg** (1½hr., 6 per day, 96F/€14.64); **Paris** (3½hr., 8 per day, 209F/€31.86); and **Rennes** (2hr., 3 per day, 110F/€16.77). **STN buses** (☎02 33 50 77 89 in Granville) run to **Granville** (30min., 3 per day, 42F/€6.40). To reach the cathedral from the train station, walk straight ahead to the roundabout and turn right onto bd. Legentil de la Galaisière and take your first left onto rue de la Mission. Take the second right onto rue Maréchal Foch, then your first left. From the front of the cathedral, you can take rue Tancrède to the right, down to rue St-Nicolas, the main commercial area of the town center. The **tourist office,** pl. Georges Leclerc, is one block from the front of the cathedral, behind the Hôtel de Ville. (☎02 33 19 08 10; fax 02 33 19 08 19; tourisme-coutances@wanadoo.fr. Open July-Sept. 15 M-Sa 10am-12:30pm and 1:30-7pm, Su 2-6pm; Sept. 16-June M-Sa 10am-12:30pm and 2-6pm; Oct.-Apr. closes Su at 5pm.) There's **currency exchange** at **Crédit Agricole,** pl. de la Poste, a block to the right as you leave the cathedral. (Open Tu-Sa 9am-noon and 1:30-6pm.) The **post office** is on pl. de la Poste. (☎02 33 76 64 10. Open M-F 8:30am-12:30pm and 1:30-6:30pm, Sa 8:30am-noon.) **Postal code:** 50200.

ACCOMMODATIONS, CAMPING, AND FOOD. Coutances is best seen as a daytrip from Granville, but there are a couple of decent budget options. Off the hospital-sterile hallways of **Hôtel de Normandie,** pl. du Général de Gaulle, are spacious and comfortable rooms, all with views of one steeple or another. (☎02 33 45 01 40; fax 02 33 46 74 54. Breakfast 28F/€4.27. Singles 120F/€18.30, with shower 175F/€26.68, with bath 200-220F/€30.49-33.54; doubles 160F/€24.39, with shower 210F/€32.02, with bath 250F/€38.12. Extra bed 60F/€9.15. MC/V.) The **Hôtel des Trois Pilliers,** 11 rue des Halles, near the cathedral, plans to renovate its already pleasant, modern rooms. The bar downstairs overflows with local teens. (☎02 33 45 01 31. Breakfast 27F/€4.12. Singles or doubles 130F/€19.82, with shower 140F/€21.35. Extra bed 30F/€4.57. MC/V.) **Camping Municipal Les Vignettes,** 27 rte. de St-Malo, lies just outside town, within walking distance of the town center. From the tourist office, head toward the Jardin des Plantes and down the hill to the right; take a sharp left at the bottom of the hill, then immediately bear right onto busy D44 (toward Agon). Walk downhill past the stadium; the camping's just past the municipal pool on the left (1km, 15-20min.). The well-spaced sites have privacy and ample facilities. (☎02 33 45 43 13. 16.50F/€2.52 per person, child under 7 10.50F/€1.60, 16.50F/€2.52 per tent. Electricity 12.50F/€1.91.)

On Thursday mornings, **markets** fill pl. de Gaulle (9am-1pm). The Champion **supermarket,** rue de la Verjustière, is at the bottom of the hill behind Eglise St-Nicolas (open M-F 9am-12:45pm and 2:30-7:30pm, Sa 9am-1pm and 2-7:30pm), but you can find smaller stores around the cathedral. There is a small supermarket near the campsite, across from the stadium (open M-Sa 9am-noon and 2-7pm). Restaurants around the cathedral tend to be reasonably priced.

SIGHTS. The carved, patterned spires of Coutances' grand **cathedral** are the foreground for its even more impressive lantern-tower, a three-tiered structure that catapults upward from the choir, filling it with light. Visitors can ascend to its galleries during tours. (☎02 33 45 00 41. Tours July-Aug. 3 per day in French, 2 per week in English; none Sa. Open daily 9am-7pm. Tours 30F/€4.57, ages 10-18 20F/€3.05. Under 10 not permitted.)

The **Jardin des Plantes,** near the tourist office, is among the oldest in France and has creative flowerbeds, including one arrangement in the shape of a ship. (Open July-Aug. daily 9am-11:30pm; Apr.-June and Sept. 9am-8pm; Oct.-Mar. 9am-5pm.) At the entrance is the **Quesnel-Morinière museum,** which houses temporary exhibits along with regional paintings and artifacts, including one of the best collections of ceramics in Normandy. Note the *Christ de la Mission*, a crucifix three times larger than life. (☎02 33 45 11 92. Open July-Aug. W-M 10am-noon and 2-6pm, closed Su morning; Sept.-June 10am-noon and 2-5pm. 15F/€2.06, students free.)

There are many treasures within 4 to 5km of town. If you are up for walking (there is no bike rental in Coutances), ask the tourist office for the brochure *Monuments et Lieux de Visite* (in English too), which covers a number of châteaux, manors, museums, and abbeys. The **Château de Gratot,** an easy 40- to 50-minute walk from Coutances, offers a look at the renovations old châteaux undergo. (☎02 33 45 18 49. Open daily 10am-7pm. 15F/€2.29, ages 10-18 10F/€1.53.) The week of Ascension Thursday (May 9, 2002), Coutances hosts **Jazz sous les Pommiers,** a week of more than 30 concerts in the streets and bars (☎02 33 76 78 61).

AVRANCHES

From its hilltop corner of the bay of Mont-St-Michel, Avranches (pop. 9000) watches proudly over the fortified island, satisfied that its residents have safeguarded the monastery's real treasures (its manuscripts) since the French Revolution. The town's link to the Mont goes back to its beginnings, when Bishop Aubert was visited here by the Archangel Michael. Apart from the exquisite manuscripts and such relics as Aubert's skull, Avranches offers an unexpected wealth of churches and beautiful vistas of the Mont from afar.

ORIENTATION AND PRACTICAL INFORMATION. The Caen-Rennes train line passes through Avranches' **train station** (☎02 33 58 00 77) at the bottom of the hill. Destinations include **Caen** (112F/€17.08); **Granville** (15min., 2 per day, 35F/€5.34); **Paris** (5hr., 2 per day, 225F/€34.30); and **Pontorson** (25min., 24F/€3.66). (Station open M-Th and Sa 8:45am-noon and 1:45-6:45pm; F 8:45am-noon, 2-7:45pm, and 8:30-10:05pm; Su and holidays 1:45-7:30pm and 8:30-9:05pm.) **STN,** 2 rue du Général de Gaulle (☎02 33 58 03 07), around the back of the tourist office, sends buses to **Granville** (70min.; M-F 3 per day, Sa-Su 2-3 per day; 34.50F/€5.26) and **Mont-St-Michel** (40min.; July-Aug. 1 per day, Apr., June, and Sept. W only; 27.40F/€4.18). (Office open M-F 10:15am-noon and 4-6pm.) **Rent bikes** from **Decathalon,** 2½km from town, for 70F/€10.67 per day. (☎02 33 89 28 50. Open July-Aug. M-Sa 9:30am-8pm; Sept.-June M-Sa 9:30am-7:30pm.)

To get to the center of town from the station, cross the highway via the footbridge to the right of the station and lean into the grueling hike uphill. At the top of the hill, head straight across rue du Général de Gaulle at the intersection. The **tourist office,** 2 rue du Général de Gaulle (☎02 33 58 00 22; fax 02 33 68 13 29; www.ville-avranches.fr), will be 250m ahead on the left (10min.). The office reserves rooms for 10F/€1.53 and gives out free town maps. There is a skimpier **annex** outside the Jardin des Plantes from July to August. (Annex ☎02 33 58 59 11. Open daily 10am-noon and 2-6pm. Main office: open July-Aug. M-Sa 9am-12:30pm and 2-7:15pm, Su 9am-12:30pm and 2-7:15pm; Sept.-June M-F 9am-noon and 2-6pm, Sa 9:30am-noon and 2-6pm, Su 10am-noon and 2-5pm.) **Le Point Information Jeunesse,** 24 pl. du Marché, between the market halls and to the left, offers **Internet access** when they're not running training workshops. (☎02 33 79 39 41. 10F/€1.53 per hr., plus a 10F/€1.53 membership fee. Open M-F 1:30-5:30pm; Tu-W and F also 9:30am-12:30pm; W closes at 6:30pm; call ahead.) The **post office** on rue St-Gervais has **currency exchange.** (☎02 33 89 20 10. Open M-F 8am-12:15pm and 1:30-6:15pm, Sa 8am-12:15pm.) **Postal code:** 50300.

ACCOMMODATIONS AND FOOD. The popular **Hôtel de Normandie,** bd. L. Jozeau-Marigné, sits at the end of the steep path you'll hit after crossing the footbridge to the right of the station. The ivy-covered building, run by three generations of the same family, has large and lovely rooms with fluffy eiderdowns, immaculate bathrooms, and views of the patchwork countryside. (☎02 33 58 01 33. Breakfast 30F/€4.57. Singles 150F/€22.90, with bath 180F/€27.45.; doubles 180F/€27.45, with bath 240F/€36.59. MC/V.) **Hôtel Valhubert,** 7 rue du Général de Gaulle, is opposite the tourist office. New owners let three freshly renovated top-floor rooms above a popular bar. (☎02 33 58 03 28. Breakfast 35F/€5.34. Reception M-Sa 8:15am-8pm. Doubles with shower and toilet or twin beds with shower 280F/€42.69; twin beds 240F/€36.59 for one person. Prices lower Oct.-May.) The tourist office lists *chambres d'hôte,* often the cheapest option (from 100F/€15.25).

A **market** is held on pl. du Marché (a.k.a. pl. des Halles), off rue des Chapeliers (Sa morning). You'll pass a **Champion supermarket** on the right side of rue du Général de Gaulle before you reach the tourist office. (Open M-Sa 9am-7:30pm, Su 9:30-11:45am.) Numerous cheap brasseries and restaurants surround the tourist office. **Pizzeria l'Anticario,** at pl. St-Gervais, serves up a creative lunchtime *formule* for 49F/€7.47, but dinner is the better time to make an appearance at this three-tiered candle-lit restaurant. (☎02 33 58 32 10. Open Tu-Sa noon-2pm and 7pm-midnight, Su 7pm-midnight.)

SIGHTS AND FESTIVALS. The town's treasures are the 10th- to 15th-century **manuscripts** copied and illuminated by the monks of Mont-St-Michel and now kept in the **Hotel de Ville's library,** in the square next to the tourist office. In a single silent room, 30 of the 200 surviving manuscripts are displayed each summer. Line after line of sharply executed script detail the finer points of theology, philosophy, astronomy, and music. Those who studied the books sometimes added their own notes in equally perfect script, making each a repository of centuries of thought.

(☎02 33 89 29 40. Open June-Sept. daily 10am-6pm. 20F/€3.05, students 10F/€1.53, under 12 free. Combined ticket with the museum and treasury: 30F/€4.57, students 15F/€2.29, under 12 free.) The **Musée Municipal,** rue d'Office, houses reproductions of local craftsmen's workshops and a rural Norman home. Downstairs is a replica of a medieval scriptorium (the room in which the manuscripts were created), where you can attempt the monks' trade. (☎02 33 58 25 15. Open Easter-Sept. daily 9:30am-noon and 2-6pm. 15F/€2.29, students 8F/€1.22, under 12 free.)

The granite 19th-century **Eglise St-Gervais,** pl. St-Gervais, has a stratospheric 74m bell-tower and a treasury containing one of the holiest heads this side of the Seine. After Avranches' Bishop Aubert twice refused the archangel Michael's command to build a church on the Mont, the exasperated angel scolded Aubert with a rap on the forehead emphatic enough to leave the future saint with a perfectly circular hole in his skull. The sacred cranium is in a monumental gold-plated reliquary, to the right as you enter the church. (Open June-Sept. daily 10am-noon and 2-6pm. Closed Su morning in June and Sept. 10F/€1.53, students 5F/€0.76, under 10 free.)

The **Jardin des Plantes,** pl. Carnot, is built around the remains of an 1803 Ursuline monastery destroyed in WWII. Rose gardens and lush grass ring the Romanesque arches. The garden provides a spectacular view of the distant Mont-St-Michel, directly in line with the winding river that appears to lead to its gates—a can't-miss sight on summer evenings when the island is illuminated. (Open daily 8:30am-11:30pm.) Down rue de la Constitution is the **Patton Memorial,** officially American soil. The huge obelisk commemorates Operation COBRA's successful break through the German front between St-Lô and Périers in July of 1944.

In the beginning of July, Avranches hosts **Musiques en Baie,** a concert series that covers the spectrum from Baroque to jazz. (3-concert pass 150F/€22.90, students 90F/€13.72. The tourist office has details.) The third weekend of June is the popular **Eclats de Rire,** during which comedians and actors take to the streets, devoting themselves entirely to the art of laughter.

NORMANDY

MONT-ST-MICHEL

The fortified island of Mont-St-Michel (pop. 42) rises from the sea like a vision from another world. It's one of a kind, a dazzling 8th-century labyrinth of stone arches, spires, and stairways that climb to an abbey overlooking both Brittany and Normandy, the disputed jewel of each. Pilgrims have flocked to the island for centuries, braving the area's fickle tides and quicksand to set foot in the eighth wonder of the occidental world. Modern, secular visitors arrive in RVs and double-decker tour buses, invulnerable to these natural trials, but invariably victimized by the holy isle's hawkers. With three million visitors annually, there are few chances to see the Mont as its peaceful Benedictine inhabitants must have known it; to avoid the crowds, arrive early or stay late. An exploration of the abbey at midnight, provides an unforgettable view of the heavens in perfectly pitch-black skies.

ORIENTATION AND PRACTICAL INFORMATION

Mont-Saint-Michel is at the northeastern tip of Brittany, or the southwestern tip of Normandy. **Pontorson,** 9km due south down D976, has the closest train station, supermarket, and affordable hotels. Just inside the Porte de l'Avancée, the only entrance to the Mont, lies the tourist office; **Grande Rue,** the town's major thoroughfare, is to the right. All hotels, restaurants, and sights are on this steep, spiraling street. There's no public transportation off the Mont late at night—you'll need a car. Biking from Pontorson takes about one hour on relatively flat terrain, though not always on bike-friendly roads; try the path next to the Couesnon river instead.

Trains: In Pontorson (☎02 33 60 00 35). To: **Dinan** (1hr., 2-3 per day, 46F/€7.01); **Granville** via Folligny (1hr.; 3 per day, Sa-Su 2 per day; 52F/€7.93); **Paris** (3½hr., 3 per day, 321F/€48.95 plus TGV supplement); and **St-Malo** via Dol (90min., 2-3 per day, 43F/€6.56). Open daily 8:40am-12:30pm and 12:45-7:30pm.

Buses: leave from Porte de l'Avancée, at the entrance to the Mont; buy tickets on board. **STN buses** (☎02 33 50 77 89 in Granville, ☎02 33 58 03 07 in Avranches) go to **Avranches** (40min.; July-Aug. 1 per day, Apr., June, and Sept. W only; 27.40F/€4.18); **Granville** (2hr.; 1 per morning to Mont-St-Michel, 1 per afternoon to Granville; 87.50F/€13.34 round-trip); and **Pontorson** (15min.; 8 per day until 7pm; 14.90F/€2.27, round-trip 23.90F/€3.64). **Courriers Bretons,** 104 rue Couesnon in Pontorson (☎02 33 60 11 43), run to **Rennes** (1½hr.; June-Sept. M-Sa 5 per day, Su 3 per day, Sept.-June 6 per day, 1 on Su; 65F/€9.91) and **St-Malo** (1½hr.; July-Aug. 3-4 per day, Sept.-June 1-2 per day; 57F/€8.69). Office open M-F 10am-noon and 4-7pm.

Bike Rental: Couesnon Motoculture, 1bis rue du Couesnon (☎02 33 60 40 11), in Pontorson. 45F/€6.86 per half-day, 80F/€12.20 per day, 150F/€22.90 for 2 days, 210F/€32.02 for 3 days. Open Tu-Sa 8:30am-noon and 2-7pm.

Tourist Office: Just behind the wall to your left after you enter the island (☎02 33 60 14 30; fax 02 33 60 06 75; OT.Mont.Saint.Michel@wanadoo.fr). Busy, but helpful, multilingual staff can set you up with info on sites and nearby lodging. Be sure to pick up a free *Horaire des Marées* (tide-table) before venturing into the bay. Hours vary in the off-season, so you may want to call first. Open July-Aug. daily 9am-7pm; Apr.-June and Sept.-Oct. 9am-12:30pm and 2-6pm; Nov.-Mar. 9am-noon and 2-5:30pm. **Tourist office in Pontorson:** pl. de l'Eglise (☎02 33 60 20 65; fax 02 33 60 85 67; MONT.ST.MICHEL.PONTORSON@wanadoo.fr) has maps and info on walking tours. Open July-Aug. M-F 9am-12:30pm and 2-6:30pm, Sa 10am-12:30pm and 3-6:30pm, Su 10am-12:30pm; Sept.-June M-F 9am-noon and 2-6pm, Sa 10am-noon and 3-6pm.

Laundromat: next to the Champion supermarket (see below). Open daily 7am-9pm.

Police: entrance just to the left of the Porte de l'Avancée before you enter (☎02 33 60 14 42). Open daily 11am-1pm and 5:30-7:30pm.

Hospital: Emergency services are in Avranches. There is a small **clinic** on the Mont, across from the post office.

Internet Access: SIDE Tech, 45 rue Couesnon (☎ 02 33 60 52 20). 30F/€4.57 for the first 30min., 20F/€3.05 every 30min. thereafter. Pro-rated prices (10F/€1.53 for 10min.). Open M-Sa 8:30am-12:30pm and 2-7pm.

Post Office: Grande Rue (☎02 33 89 65 00), about 100m to the right of Porte de l'Avancée. **Currency exchange** at tolerable rates. Open June-Aug. M-F 9am-5:30pm, Sa 9am-4pm; Mar.-May and Sept.-Oct. M-F 9am-noon and 2-5pm, Sa 9am-noon; Nov.-Feb. 9am-noon and 1:30-4:30pm. **Postal code:** 50116.

NORMANDY

ACCOMMODATIONS

Forget about actually staying on the Mont; unless St-Michel himself is bankrolling your visit, it's not going to happen. Your best bets for affordable indoor lodging are in Pontorson or further away in St-Malo and Avranches. There are also a number of campsites and *chambres d'hôte* near Beauvoir. Plan ahead to reserve a room you can afford, since prices climb faster than the spring tide.

Centre Duguesclin (HI), rue Général Patton (☎/fax 02 33 60 18 65; aj@ville-pontorson.fr). From the station, turn right onto the main road, then left after a block onto rue Couesnon. Take the third right onto rue St-Michel. When you see the tourist office on your left, cut diagonally across the square, following signs toward the church. Bear left in front of the church onto rue Hédou. Follow that to the end, then turn right on rue Gén. Patton. The hostel is on your left (10min.). Spotless dorm-style 3-, 4-, and 6-person rooms in a 1910 stone house; inviting lounge, kitchen, and dining area. Breakfast 19F/€2.90. Sheets 17F/€2.59. Reception July-Aug. 8am-9pm; Sept.-June 8am-noon and 5-9pm. Lockout Sept.-June noon-5pm. Open year-round. **Call at least 1 week ahead; 1 month in the summer.** Dorms 48F/€7.32; 55F/€8.39 without HI membership.

Hôtel le Grillon, 37 rue du Couesnon, on the right after rue St-Michel (☎02 33 60 17 80). 5 quiet, like-new rooms (all with showers), behind a perky crêperie/bar. Breakfast 30F/€4.57. Reception F-W 7am-11pm. Reserve 1-2 weeks ahead during July and August. Doubles 180F/€27.44, with toilet 210F/€32.02. Extra bed 30F/€4.57. MC/V.

Hôtel de L'Arrivée, 17 rue de Docteur Tizon, (☎/fax 02 03 60 01 57) right across the street from the station, on the other side of the Courriers Bretons office. Spacious, rooms with ample windows, some of which open onto a small flowered terrace. Breakfast 20-29F/€3.05-4.42. Reception 8am-10pm. Shower 15F/€2.29. Singles and doubles with sink 99F/€15.10, with sink and bidet 120F/€18.30, with shower 130-160F/€19.82-24.39; triples with shower 230F/€35.06; quads with shower 250F/€38.12. Extra bed 30F/€4.57. Prices drop slightly in the winter.

CAMPING

Camping Municipal "les Rives du Couesnon" at Pontorson, chemin des Soupirs (☎/fax 02 33 68 11 59; camping-monto@ville-pontorson.fr). Follow hostel directions to rue Hédou, then take a left on rue Général Patton and the first right onto chemin des Soupirs. The campsite will be 300m ahead on the left. Hedges and cornfields hide this well-kept, 3-star site from the road and the nearby Couesnon river. Clean, extensive central bathrooms and showers. Reception June 15-Sept. 15 7:30am-10pm; Apr.-June 14 and Sept. 16-30 8-10am and 6-7pm. June 15-Sept. 15: 15F/€2.29 per person, 8F/€1.22per child; 15F/€2.29 per tent; 10F/€1.53 per car; electricity 15F/€2.29. Apr.-June 14 and Sept. 16-30 10F/€1.53 per person, 7.50F/€1.14 per child, 10F/€1.53 per tent, 5F/€0.76 per car, electricity 13F/€1.98. Handicapped-accessible.

Camping du Mont-St-Michel is a mere 1.8km from the Mont at the junction of D275 and N776 (☎02 33 60 22 10; fax 02 33 60 20 02). More like a small town with 350 spots and many dependent businesses. They also **rent bikes** (30F/€4.57 per hr., 50F/€7.62 per 4hr., 100F/€15.25 per 8hr.). May-Sept. 15: 23F/€3.51 per person, 52F/€7.93 per site; Feb. 15-Apr. and Oct. 42F/€6.41 per site, 18.50F/€2.82 per person. Electricity included.

Camping St-Michel, rte. du Mont-St-Michel (☎02 33 70 96 90), is by the bay in Courtils. This 3-star campground is a bit far from the Mont (9km). It was named the most garden-like campsite in the *département*–flowers surround the heated swimming pool, common room, grocery store, breakfast room (20F/€3.05), and snackbar. They **rent bikes** for 30F/€4.57 per half-day, 50F/€7.62 per day. July-Aug. 22F/€3.36 per person, 10F/€1.53 per child under 7, 20F/€3.05 per car and tent; Mar. 15-June and Sept.-Oct. 15 19F/€2.90 per person, 8F/€1.22 per child,19F/€2.90 per tent.

FOOD

If you dare invest in more than a postcard and sandwich on the Mont, look for local specialties such as *agneau du pré salé* (lamb raised on the surrounding salt marshes) and *omelette poulard*, a fluffy soufflé-like dish (about 65-90F/€9.91-13.72). **Chapeau Rouge,** Grande Rue, serves these delicacies at lower prices than most (lamb 50F/€7.62), in a homey wood-furnished dining room. (☎02 33 60 14 29. 3-course *menus* 69-149F/€10.52-18.63. Open daily 11:30am-2:30pm and 7-9pm. Sometimes closed at night.) To eat in a room with a view, walk along the ramparts and take your pick; all restaurants sport terraces or glass walls. You could be lured to a sticky end at **La Sirène,** Grande Rue, past the post office—bind yourself to avoid the temptation of chocolate-banana crêpe (31F/€4.73), stuffed to bursting and topped with a *mont* of chocolate sauce. (☎02 33 60 08 60. *Menu* 60F/€9.15. Open daily 11am-9pm.) If you plan to picnic, arrive prepared as there are no grocery stores within the walls. Pontorson has a morning market (W) on rue Couesnon and at pl. de la Mairie. Or stop by the **Champion supermarket,** just across the street from the rue St-Michel STN bus stop outside Pontorson. (☎02 33 60 37 38. Open July-Aug. M-Sa 9am-7:30pm; reduced hours in the off-season.)

SIGHTS

Grande Rue is quite a spectacle in itself—jam-packed with restaurants and shops selling everything from Breton biscuits to postcards showing the bay's "native" dolphins leaping over the Mont. For a structured visit, pick up one of the murderously expensive (and generally unnecessary) guides sold along Grande Rue (28-

200F/€4.37-30.49). While you're free to explore the bay, don't wander off too far on the sand without company—the broad expanses are riddled with quicksand, and the bay's tides, changing every six hours or so, are the highest in France. During the bi-monthly spring tides, the *mascaret* (initial wave) rushes in at 2m per second, flooding the beaches along the causeway. To see this spectacle, you must be within the abbey two hours ahead of time. New surprises await in every nook and cranny on the Mont, and it's near-impossible to get lost.

HISTORY. Legend holds that the Baie de St-Michel was created by a tidal wave that flooded the surrounding forest and left three islands: Tombelaine, Mont Dol, and Mont Tomba (meaning "mound" or "tomb"). So appealing was the latter island that heaven wanted a piece of it. As the *Revelation ecclesiae sancti* recounts, in 708, the Archangel Michael appeared to St. Aubert, Bishop of Avranches, instructing him to build a place of worship on the barren island. The doubting bishop ignored the angel not just once but twice; on the third visit, the frustrated Michael pointed a fiery finger at Aubert that drilled a hole into his cranium. Construction of the hill-top church began when Benedictine monks from Fontenelle were sent to the Mont in 966 at the request of Richard I, the third duke of Normandy. Four crypts were built, one at each cardinal point, to support the base of a church on Tomba's 80m high point. These became the monastery's first chapels, beginning with Notre-Dame-sous-Terre later in the 10th century. The Mont became an increasingly important destination for pilgrims, comparable in importance to Rome and Jerusalem; every king of France spent time here, except for Louis XIV (too busy building Versailles) and Louis XVI (too busy being beheaded). In the 14th and 15th centuries, it was fortified against a 30-year English attack with ramparts designed by Abbot Jolivet; and the Benedictines continued their life-long work, the copying and illumination of the *manuscrits du Mont-St-Michel*, now on display in nearby Avranches (see p. 492). In 1789, the Revolutionary government turned the island into a prison, first jailing 600 monks, followed by Robespierre and 14,000 others who ranged from royalists to ordinary criminals. The prison was closed in 1863, and shortly thereafter, in 1874, Mont-St-Michel was classified as a national monument. In 1897, the church was topped with a neo-Gothic spire identical to the one atop Ste-Chapelle in Paris, and a copper and gold leaf statue of St-Michel. Around that time a new dike made the island a peninsula, facilitating tourist access. Today the abbey is again home to a small community of monks. The last three Benedictine monks who made their home on the Mont for 30 years were replaced on June 24, 2001 by a group of nine monks from Jerusalem.

ABBEY AND CRYPTS. The twisting road and ramparts end at the abbey entrance, the departure point for five one-hour English tours daily during the summer (free). French tours leave every half-hour. Mass is held daily at 12:15pm; entry to the abbey church for the service only is free noon-12:15pm. The **church,** with its exterior lace-work stairways is the most ornate portion of the abbey. The interior's hodgepodge of architectural styles is the result of reconstruction following the collapse of half of the nave in 1103, the Romanesque choir in 1421, and 13 separate fires over the past 1000 years. The adjacent cloister is the center of **La Merveille** ("the Marvel"), the 13th-century gothic monastery. Beneath the church and the cloister are the Mont's frigid **crypts,** which can only be seen on tours. The descent passes through the **refectory,** where the monks took their meals in silence as St. Benedict's rules were read recto-tono. Below, in the Chapelle St-Etienne, deceased monks' naked bodies were displayed before interment. Prisoners held on the Mont's **treadmill** during the Revolution would walk on the wheel for hours, as their labor powered an elaborate pulley system that carried supplies up the side of the Mont. Many actually volunteered for the grueling task, since it meant they got more food to keep them strong. The **Crypte des gros piliers** is directly under the choir and was built at the same time; its pillars, 6m in circumference, were described by Victor Hugo as a forest of palm trees. The narrow abbey gardens, clinging to the side of the rock, surround the compound's exit. *(☎02 33 89 80 00. Open July 13-Aug. daily 9am-7pm; May-July 12 and Sept. 9am-5:30pm; Oct.-Apr. 9:30am-*

4:30pm, until 5pm during school holidays. Closed Jan. 1, May 1, Nov. 1 and 11, and Dec. 25. 42F/€6.41, ages 18-25 26F/€3.96; Oct.-Mar. first Su of the month free. A 2hr. conference tour with a guide (only in French) leaves once a day at 2pm (July-Aug. 4 times per day) and costs 25F/€3.81, 20F/€3.05 for ages 12-25. Audio tour 30F/€4.57.)

MUSEUMS. Several museums on Mont-St-Michel offer moderately interesting summaries of its history and a hodgepodge of "artifacts." Near the top of Grande Rue is the **Logis Tiphaine,** (☎02 33 60 23 34) 14th-century home of Bertrand du Guesclin and the most worthwhile of the museums. Guesclin, born so ugly that his mother rejected him, went on to become governor of Pontorson and marry the beautiful young *savante* Tiphaine. He built this four-story villa in 1365 to protect his wife from the English while he was fighting in Spain. The *logis* now displays well-preserved 14th- to 17th-century furniture, fireplaces, and objects of everyday use. The **Archéoscope** (☎02 33 89 01 84), presents the island's legend and history with film, opera, and an intricate model that rises from the water. The **Musée Maritime** (☎02 33 60 14 09) has a collection of 250 antique model boats. *(All open daily July-Aug. 9am-at least 6pm; Sept.-June until at least 5pm. Closed Nov. 12-Dec. 19 and Jan. 5-Feb. 6. Each separately 45F/€6.87, children 30F/€4.58; all 4 combined 90F/€13.72, students 75F/€11.43, children 60F/€9.15, under 10 free.)*

SPECTACLES. Nightly illumination transforms the Mont into a glowing jewel best seen either from the causeway entrance or from across the bay in Avranches. *(Illumination June-Sept. from 9 or 10pm.)* Dusk is also the time to revisit the crypts of the Abbey. **Songes de nuit** immerses the sanctuary's corridors in a flood of light and music. *(☎02 33 89 80 00. July 13-Aug. M-Sa and Sept. F-Sa 9pm-1am, last entry at midnight. 52F/€7.93, ages 12-25 36F/€5.49, under 12 free; last entry at midnight.)* On Sunday, May 5, 2002, the Mont will celebrate the **St-Michel de Printemps** folk festival, when costumed men and women parade through the streets and re-enact local traditions. The **St-Michel d'Automne** festival, held on the Sunday before Michaelmas (late September), is similar but more religious.

BRITTANY (BRETAGNE)

Brittany tugs away from mainland France, maintaining its Celtic traditions despite Paris' centuries-old effort to Frenchify the province. In recent years the government has softened its stance, allowing schools to teach in Breton; it is still, however, illegal to advocate independence. Present-day Breton culture has its roots in the 5th-7th centuries, when Britons fled Anglo-Saxon invaders for this beautiful, wild peninsula. But reminders of earlier inhabitants are plentiful: Neolithic people, who settled here before the Gauls, erected the thousands of megaliths visible today. The Romans, who conquered the area in 56 BC, decorated some of these monuments and incorporated them into their own rituals. In the centuries that followed the exodus to its shores from Britain, Brittany fought for and retained its independence from Frankish, Norman, French, and English invaders, uniting with France only after the last Duchess ceded it to her husband, François I, in 1532.

Brittany is lined with spectacular beaches and misty, almost apocalyptic headlands. If you dislike crowds, beware of visiting in summer. In the off-season, some coastal resorts such as St-Malo, Quiberon, and Concarneau close down, but the churches, beaches, and cliffs are as eerie and romantic as ever. The traditional costume of Breton women—a black dress and an elaborate white lace *coiffe* (head-dress)—appears in folk festivals and some markets, and lilting *Brezhoneg* is spoken energetically at pubs and ports in the western part of the province.

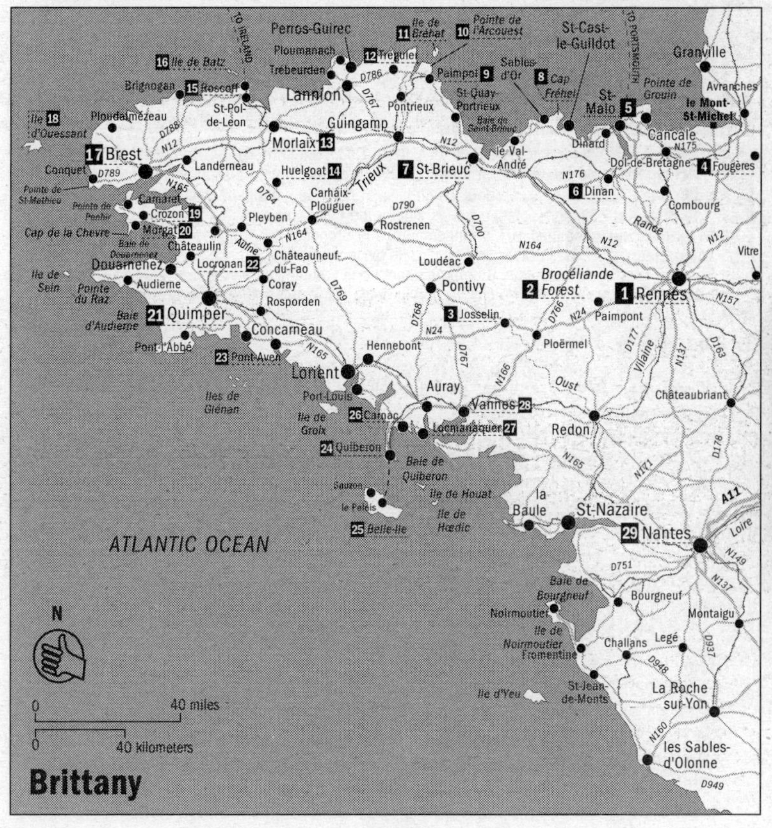

TRANSPORTATION

High-speed trains leave Paris' Gare Montparnasse and arrive in Rennes and Brest two and four hours later, respectively. Getting around Brittany is more difficult. The main train lines connect Rennes to Brest and Quimper, and Nantes with Quimper. Less frequent trains and SNCF buses connect other cities to rail hubs. Private bus lines connect towns that trains miss, but are infrequent and almost nonexistent in the off-season. Cycling is a good option, especially since the most beautiful sights are the least accessible by public transport. The relatively flat terrain gets a bit hillier in the interior. Hikers can try the long-distance footpaths **GR341, GR37, GR38, GR380,** and the spectacular **GR34** along the northern coast.

1 **Rennes:** Breton student town; great nightlife **(p. 500)**
2 **Brocéliande Forest:** Misty, mysterious woodlands and moors roamed by Arthur **(p. 506)**
3 **Josselin:** A private château open to visits, in a pleasant little medieval town **(p. 507)**
4 **Fougères:** Huge solid thousand-year-old bastard of a fortress, half in ruins **(p. 509)**
5 **St-Malo:** A popular seaside getaway and a well-reconstructed walled city **(p. 510)**
6 **Dinan:** The best-preserved medieval town in Brittany; dignified despite the crowds **(p. 515)**
7 **St-Brieuc:** Nothing to see here, but a good base for daytrips to the countryside **(p. 518)**
8 **Cap Fréhel:** Picture-perfect terrain: rust-hued, sea-beaten cliffs thick with flowers **(p. 520)**
9 **Paimpol:** Fishing town with restaurants, bars; access to islands, cliffs, and hiking trails **(p. 520)**
10 **Pointe de l'Arcouest:** Pink granite peninsula with great sea kayaking **(p. 523)**
11 **Ile de Bréhat:** Tiny little wisp of an island; walk end to end in an hour **(p. 523)**
12 **Tréguier:** Well-known cathedral here houses the tomb of St. Yves **(p. 523)**
13 **Morlaix:** Medieval town criss-crossed by mossy stairways; good base for excursions **(p. 524)**
14 **Forêt d'Huelgoat:** Part of the ancient Breton woodlands; full of strange boulders **(p. 526)**
15 **Roscoff:** Spa town and Île de Batz embarkation point; ferries to Ireland and England **(p. 527)**
16 **Ile de Batz:** Few locals, no street names, and many rocky little beaches **(p. 528)**
17 **Brest:** Major port and university town; ugly, though, and not too many sights **(p. 530)**
18 **Ile d'Ouessant:** Beautiful, windswept, flower-strewn little island **(p. 533)**
19 **Crozon:** Main island of the peninsula; the place to rent bikes and buy groceries **(p. 535)**
20 **Morgat:** A better base for outdoor adventures; access to beaches, trails, and caves **(p. 535)**
21 **Quimper:** Principal city of western Brittany and a center of Breton culture **(p. 537)**
22 **Locronan:** Perfect medieval city feels like a Celtic fairy tale **(p. 540)**
23 **Pont-Aven:** So beautiful that its woods and streams inspired a school of painters **(p. 541)**
24 **Quiberon:** Rugged peninsula popular with hikers and bikers; near spectacular Belle-Ile **(p. 542)**
25 **Belle-Ile:** High cliffs, crashing seas, heathered fields; big enough for a good cycle **(p. 544)**
26 **Carnac:** Huge neolithic rock arrangements, à la Stonehenge, arranged in lines **(p. 546)**
27 **Locmariaquer:** A small port town proud of its oysters and neolithic rocks.
28 **Vannes:** Lots of characteristic Breton architecture in a sleepy, mid-sized town **(p. 550)**
29 **Nantes:** Historically important city, Breton in spirit though quite far south **(p. 552)**

RENNES

Rennes (pop. 210,000) tempers its Parisian sophistication with the relaxed Breton spirit and college town revelry. During the day, its *vieille ville* of half-timbered houses seems frozen in time; but come 4pm, locals flock to the cafés and bars, the narrow streets are filled with traffic, and students are drawn to the city's sizzling nightlife. Rennes is a popular stopover for medieval folklore enthusiasts traveling to the mysterious and mythical forests of King Arthur's clan, as well as for those heading to Mont-St-Michel (p. 494) and St-Malo (p. 510) to the north, and to the beaches on the western coast. Everything can be squeezed into a couple of jam-packed days, but save some energy for the super-charged club scene.

TRANSPORTATION

Trains: pl. de la Gare (☎02 99 29 11 92). To: **Brest** (2-2½hr., at least 1 per hr., all TGV 175F/€26.68); **Caen** (3hr., 8 per day, 167F/€25.46); **Nantes** (1¼-2hr., 7 per day, 114F/€17.38); **Paris** (2hr., 1 per hr., 289-349F/€44.06-53.20); **St-Malo** (1hr., 15 per day, 70F/€10.67); **Tours** via **Le Mans** (2½-3hr., every 2-3hr., 180F/€27.44). **SNCF** info and ticket office open M-Sa 8:45am-7:45pm, Su and holidays 11am-7:45pm. Info booth open M-F 7am-9pm, Sa 8am-5pm, Su 1-9pm. **SOS Voyageurs,** under the escalator by the north exit, is open M-F 9am-noon and 4-7pm.

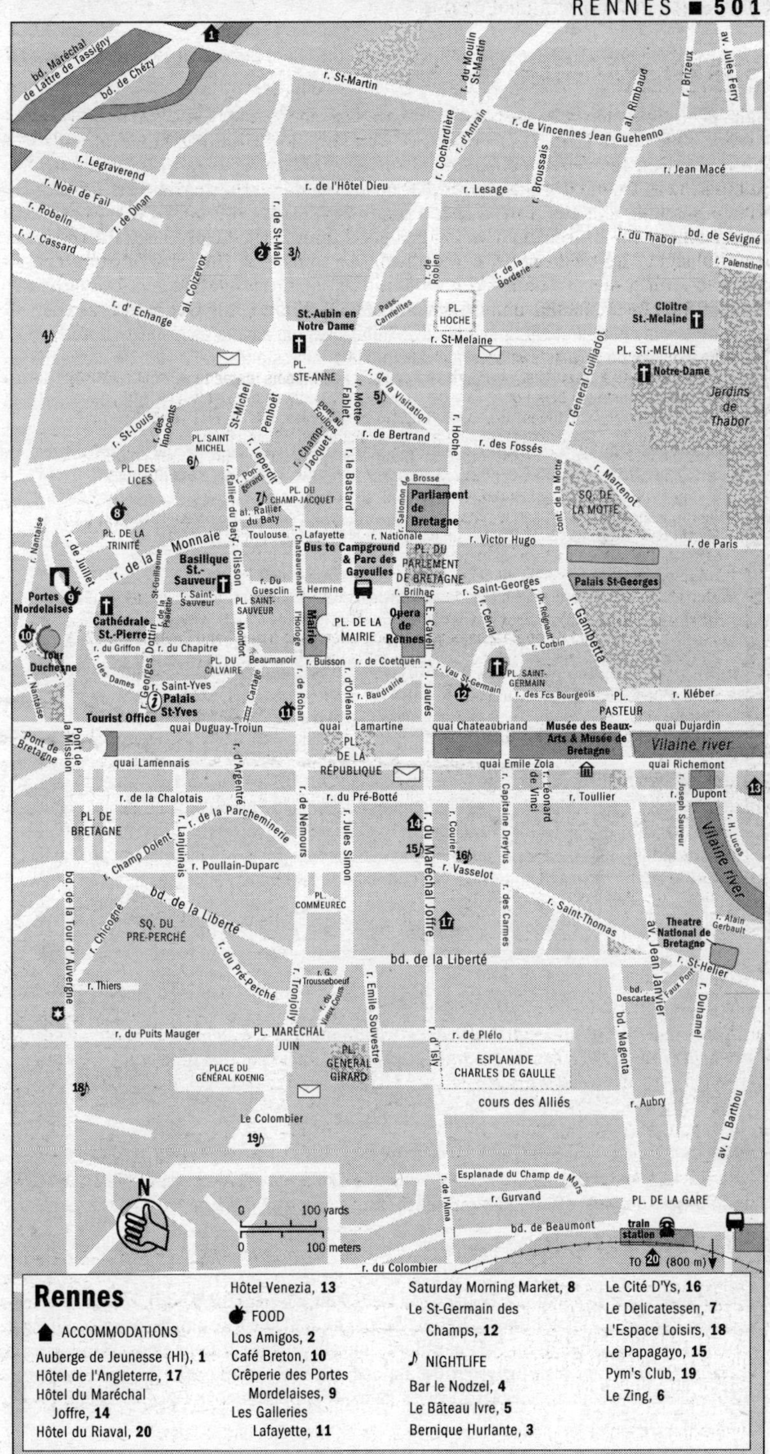

Rennes

ACCOMMODATIONS

Auberge de Jeunesse (HI), **1**
Hôtel de l'Angleterre, **17**
Hôtel du Maréchal Joffre, **14**
Hôtel du Riaval, **20**
Hôtel Venezia, **13**

FOOD

Los Amigos, **2**
Café Breton, **10**
Crêperie des Portes Mordelaises, **9**
Les Galleries Lafayette, **11**
Saturday Morning Market, **8**
Le St-Germain des Champs, **12**

NIGHTLIFE

Bar le Nodzel, **4**
Le Bâteau Ivre, **5**
Bernique Hurlante, **3**
Le Cité D'Ys, **16**
Le Delicatessen, **7**
L'Espace Loisirs, **18**
Le Papagayo, **15**
Pym's Club, **19**
Le Zing, **6**

Buses: 16 pl. de la Gare (☎02 99 30 87 80), to the left of the train station as you face its north entrance. **Dinan** (1¼hr.; M-Sa 6-7 per day, Su 3 per day; 50F/€7.62); **Fougères** (1hr.; M-F at least 10 per day, Sa 3 per day, Su 2 per day; 53F/€8.08); **Paimpont,** location of the Brocéliande Forest (1¼hr.; M-F 3-4 per day, Sa 2 per day; 17F/€2.59); and **St-Malo** (3hr.; 1 per day, 2 on W, no service on Su; 58F/€8.84) are all serviced by **Cars 35** (☎02 99 26 11 11). **Nantes** (2hr.; M 3 per day, Tu-Th and Sa 2 per day, F 4 per day; 95F/€14.48) is covered by **Cariane Atlantique** (☎02 40 20 46 99, 08 25 08 71 56 in Nantes). **Anjou Bus** (☎02 41 69 10 00) goes to **Angers** (2½-3hr.; 3-4 per day; 98F/€14.94, express 122F/€18.60). **Mont-St-Michel** (2½hr., 1-2 per day, 64F/€9.76) is served by **Les Courriers Bretons** (☎02 99 19 70 70).

Local Transportation: Star, 12 rue du Pré Botté (☎ 02 99 79 37 37). Buses run daily from as early as 5am until 8pm, although some lines run as late as midnight based on demand. Purchase tickets in advance from office or newsstands (6.5F/€0.99, *carnet* of 10 55F/€8.38, 1-day pass 20F/€3.05). Office open M-Sa 7am-7pm.

Taxis: 4 rue Georges Dottin, at the train station (☎02 99 30 79 79). 24hr.

Bike Rental: Guedard, 13 bd. Beaumont (☎02 99 30 43 78), by the station. 80F/€12.20 per day. Open M-F 9am-12:30pm and 2-7pm, Sa closes at 6:30pm.

ORIENTATION AND PRACTICAL INFORMATION

The **Vilaine river** cuts the city in two, with the train station to the south and most of the historic sights in the north. **Av. Jean Janvier,** directly in front of you as you leave the station from the north exit, will take you into the center of town (where the Vilaine lies). Once across the river, the old city begins about 5 blocks to your left. Most of the clubs, bars and other nightlife can be found around **pl. Ste-Anne, pl. des Lices,** and **pl. St-Michel** just north of the *vieille ville*, but there are also a number of hotspots on the southern bank. To the east and west lie Rennes' modern, sometimes architecturally abysmal sectors, and its suburbs.

Tourist Office: 11 rue St-Yves (☎02 99 67 11 11; fax 02 99 67 11 10). From the station, take av. Jean Janvier to quai Chateaubriand. Turn left and walk along the river until you reach rue George Dottin. Turn right, and then right again on rue St-Yves. The office is on the right, just past the church on the corner. Everything the main office provides, including maps, directions, and lists of hotels and restaurants, and shops, is free, with the exception of hotel reservations (5F/€0.76). Call in advance to reserve tours of the Parliament (1½hr.; offered July-Aug. daily, Sept.-June 1-3 times per week; 40F/€6.10, 20F/€3.05 for students), the *vieille ville*, the *Jardin du Thabor,* and themed visits to historical houses. Open Apr.-Sept. M-Sa 9am-7pm, Su and holidays 11am-6pm, Oct.-Mar. M-Sa 9am-6pm, Su and holidays 11am-6pm.

Hiking and Biking Information: France Randonnée, 9 rue des Portes Mordelaises (☎02 99 67 42 21). Info on **GR trails.** Open M-F 10am-6pm, Sa 10am-1pm.

American Consulate, 30 quai Duguay-Trouin (☎02 23 44 09 60; fax 02 99 35 00 92). Offers information about visas, but does not issue them.

Laundromat: 25 rue de Penhoet. Open daily 8am-10pm. Also at 45 rue St-Malo (☎02 99 36 11 80). Both open daily 9am-noon and 2-7pm.

Police: 22 bd. de la Tour d'Auvergne (☎02 99 65 00 22). **Emergencies:** ☎17.

Hospital: Rennes has a number of hospitals. In an **emergency,** dial 16. The most central is on Pontchailloux, past rue St-Malo.

Internet Access: Cyberspirit, 22 rue de la Visitation (☎02 99 84 53 30). 5F/€.76 per 10min., 15F/€2.29 per 30min., 30F/€4.57 per hr. Half-price 2-3pm, 6-7pm, and after 9pm. Open July-Aug. Tu-Su 2-10pm; Sept.-June M 2-9pm, Tu noon-9pm, W-F noon-10pm, Sa 2-10pm. Also **Cybernet Online,** 22 rue St-Georges (☎02 99 36 37 41). 10F/€1.53 per 10min., 25F/€3.81 per 30min., 45F/€6.86 per hr. Open M 2-8pm, Tu-Sa 10am-8pm. Closed Aug 1-20.

Post Office: 27 bd. du Colombier (☎02 99 01 22 11), 1 block left of the train station exit. **Postal Code:** 35032. **Branch office,** pl. de la République (☎02 99 78 43 35), on the quai. From the station, walk up av. Jean Janvier and turn left onto the quai three blocks over. **Currency exchange,** 2.5% commission, minimum 20F/€3.05. **Western Union** at branch only. Open M-F 8am-7pm, Sa 8:30am-12:30pm. **Postal code:** 35000.

ACCOMMODATIONS AND CAMPING

You must reserve for the first week of July during the *Tombées de la Nuit* festival, but many hotels recommend reservations year-round. A number of moderately priced hotels lie to the east of av. Jean Janvier between quai Richemont and the train station. Most of the budget hotels, unfortunately, are not central.

Auberge de Jeunesse (HI), 10-12 canal St-Martin (☎02 99 33 22 33; fax 02 99 59 06 21; rennes@fuaj.org). From the train station, take av. Jean Janvier straight to the canal, where it becomes rue Gambetta. Go 5 blocks, then take a left onto rue des Fossés. Take rue de la Visitation to pl. Ste-Anne, hugging the right side of the church as you approach it. Follow rue de St-Malo (on your right) down the hill and through its intersection with rue Dinan and rue St-Martin. Cross the canal and immediately turn right into a gravel parking lot. The hostel is ahead on the left (30min.). Or, take bus #1 (dir: "Chêne Germain") to the Mairie and change to #18 (dir: "St-Grégoire") to the "Auberge de Jeunesse," just before the canal (see above). Kitchen, common room, cafeteria, and Internet access. Discount bus fares to Mont-St-Michel and St-Malo. Breakfast included. Showers in rooms. Lockers in most rooms. Bottom sheet and blanket provided, but top sheet 17F/€2.59. Laundry. Handicapped-accessible. Reception 7am-11pm. No lockout. Singles 129F/€19.67; doubles, triples, and quads 74F/€11.28 per person. MC/V.

Hôtel d'Angleterre, 19 rue Maréchal Joffre. (☎02 99 79 38 61; fax 02 99 79 43 85). See directions for Hôtel Maréchal Joffre, below. Rooms with views of the street or a courtyard surpass the standards of other single-star establishments. Breakfast 31F/€4.73, 36F/€5.49 in bed. Reception 7am-10:30pm, Su 7am-noon and 6-10:30pm. Singles 140F/€21.35; doubles 160F/€24.39, with shower and TV 197F/€30.03, with toilet and TV 220F/€33.54, with bath, toilet, and TV 230F/€35.06; room with twin beds 195F/€29.73, with shower and TV 250F/€38.11, with toilet and TV 270F/€41.16, with bath, toilet, and TV 280F/€42.69. MC/V.

Hôtel Maréchal Joffre, 6 rue Maréchal Joffre (☎02 99 79 37 74; fax 02 99 78 38 51). From the train station's north entrance, proceed along av. Jean Janvier to bd. de la Liberté. After 3 blocks, take a right on rue Maréchal Joffre; the hotel is 2 blocks up the street on the left (15min.). Tiny, cheerful rooms in a fabulous location, with a few dingy carpets. Breakfast 30F/€4.57. Reception 24hr. Closed last week of July and 1st week of Aug. Singles 120F/€18.30, with shower and toilet 175F/€26.68; doubles 130F/€19.82, with shower 175F/€26.68, with shower and TV 195F/€29.73, with shower, TV, and toilet 220F/€33.54; room with twin beds 200-220F/€30.49-33.54; triples with shower and TV 220F/€33.54, with shower, toilet, and TV 260F/€39.64. MC/V.

Hôtel Riaval, 9 rue Riaval (☎02 99 50 65 58; fax 02 99 41 85 30). Leave the train station through the southern "Cour d'Appel" doors; walk across the open plaza and down the metal stairs. Take a left at the bottom of the steps onto rue de Quineleu, and proceed until the first intersection. Across the street, rue de Quineleu becomes rue Riaval. Cross the street onto rue Riaval and follow the sign to the hotel, 100m ahead on the left. Although hardly central, the rooms are clean and in a quiet neighborhood. Breakfast 28F/€4.27. Showers 15F/€2.29. Reception M-F 7am-10pm, Sa-Su 8am-1pm and 8-10pm. Reserve ahead. Singles and doubles 135F/€20.58, with shower 170F/€25.92; triples and quads (or twin beds) 170-270F/€25.92-41.16. MC/V.

Hôtel Venezia, 27 rue Dupont des Loges (☎02 99 30 36 56; fax 02 99 30 78 78). From the train station's north entrance, walk up av. Jean Janvier for about 10min. Turn right onto rue Dupont des Loges (one street before quai Richemont), and cross the bridge; the hotel is on the left. On an island surrounded by the Vilaine River, the Venezia has spectacular views of the canal. Rooms have an old-world (and sometimes just old) feel. Breakfast 30F/€4.57. Reservations recommended. Singles 145F/€22.11, with shower, toilet, and TV 190F/€28.97; doubles 180F/€27.44, 240F/€36.59. MC/V.

Camping: Municipal des Gayeulles, in Parc des Gayeulles (☎02 99 36 91 22; fax 02 23 20 06 23). Take bus #3 (dir: "Gayeulles/St-Laurent") from pl. de la Mairie to "Piscine/Gayuelles," the 3rd stop once you reach the park (last bus 8:30pm). Follow the path around the swimming pool dome until you see a paved road. Turn left and follow the signs to the campground. Turn right once you reach the large sign for the camping and proceed to the *accueil* (100m ahead on the left). The campground lies deep within the lush Parc des Gayeulles (see **Excursions,** p. 505). Reception June 15-Sept. 15 7:30am-1pm and 2-8pm; Sept. 16-June 14 9am-12:30pm and 4:30-8pm. Gates close at 11pm June 15-Sept. 15; 10pm off-season. Open year-round. 20F/€3.05 per person, 10F/€1.53 per child under 10. 10F/€1.53 per car. Electricity 17F/€2.59. MC/ V.

FOOD

Traditional crêperies, cafés, kebab stands, Chinese restaurants, and even Pizza Hut can be found side by side on **rue St-Malo, rue St-Georges,** or in **pl. St-Michel.** There is a huge **market** every Saturday (6am-1pm) in pl. des Lices that should not be missed. Flowers, fresh fruit and vegetables, baked goods, cheeses, meats, and other culinary delights abound. There are also two **supermarkets:** one in the **Galeries Lafayette** on quai Duguay-Trouin, and a **Marché Plus** in the apartment complex on the left side of rue de St-Malo as you walk from rue de l'Hôtel Dieu to the youth hostel (both open M-Sa 9am-8pm).

Café Breton, 14 rue Nantaise (☎02 99 30 74 95). An ever-changing menu of Breton cuisine in an upscale atmosphere, minus the upscale prices. *Plats* 46-52F/€7.01-7.93; desserts 23-26F/€3.51-3.96. Open M and Sa 9am-5:30pm, Tu-F 9am-11pm.

Le St Germain des Champs (Restaurant Végétarien-Biologique), 12 rue du Vau Saint Germain (☎02 99 79 25 52). The organic restaurant's chef-owners welcome guests to their open kitchen and bamboo-accented dining room. *Menus* 70-90F/€10.67-13.72. Open M-Sa noon-2:30pm and Th-Sa 7-10pm. Closed in Aug. MC/V.

Los Amigos, 13 rue de St-Malo (☎02 99 36 86 86), across from #40. Savor an evening drink at the fur-lined bar, followed by heaping platters of local oysters or duck hearts. Six *plats du jour* each 65-85F/€9.91-12.96. Open M-Sa 8pm-midnight.

Crêperie des Portes Mordelaises, 6 rue des Portes Mordelaises (☎02 99 30 57 40). Below the old city walls, this crêperie is one of the best in the city. Galettes and crêpes 25-40F/€3.81-6.10. Open M-Sa 11:30am-2pm and 6:30-11pm, Su 6:30-11pm.

SIGHTS AND EXCURSIONS

SIGHTS. On the surface, Rennes' *vieille ville* bears a striking architectural resemblance to medieval villages throughout much of Western Europe. Excellent examples of these buildings can be found throughout the old city on **rue St-Georges,** in **pl. Ste-Anne,** and **pl. St-Michel.** Upon exiting the tourist office, turn left on rue St-Yves and right on rue Georges Dottin. One block ahead, to the right, rue du Chapitre has some appealing examples. Continuing on rue Georges Dottin, one finds another example on **rue de la Psalette** which becomes **rue St-Guillaume.** At the end of rue St-Guillaume, turn left onto rue de la Monnaie, which becomes rue de la Cathédrale, to visit the Cathédrale St-Pierre (on the left).

The imposing **Cathédrale St-Pierre** seen today was constructed beginning in 1787, following the demolition (or crumbling) of a pagan temple, Roman church, and Gothic cathedral that each occupied the same plot. The fifth and last chapel houses one of the cathedral's treasures: a delicately-carved, glass-encased 16th-century altarpiece tracing the life of the Virgin Mary. (Open daily 9:30am-noon and 3-6pm. Closed to visitors during high mass Su 10:30-11:30am.) Across the street from the cathedral, tucked in an alleyway bearing the same name, are the **Portes Mordelaises,** former entrance to the city and some of the last vestiges of the medieval city walls. The **Tour de Duchesne,** another medieval holdover, is attached to the Portes by the original wall and best viewed from pl. du Maréchal (from the entrance to rue des Portes Mordelaises, head to your right down rue de la Monnaie until you see the tower and park on your right).

The **Musée des Beaux-Arts,** 20 quai Emile Zola, the highlights of the 17th-century French, Flemish, Pont-Aven, and modern/surrealist collections, respectively. (☎02 99 28 55 85 Open W-M 10am-noon and 2-6pm. 26F/€3.96, students and the unemployed 13F/€1.98, free for children under 18.)

Rennes' **Jardin du Thabor** is among the most beautiful gardens in France. Its lush grounds contain sculptures, fountains, a carousel, a massive bird cage, and the "caves of hell," while the rose garden alone holds an amazing 1700 types. Concerts are often held here, and there's a rotating exhibit of local artwork in a small gallery on the north side. (Garden open daily June-Sept. 7am-9:30pm.) Adjacent is the understated **Eglise Notre Dame;** inside are the remnants of a 15th-century fresco and the blazing colors of the choir's stained glass.

EXCURSIONS. The **Parc des Gayeulles,** a 15-minute bus ride from the center of Rennes (see directions to the campground under **Accommodations** for bus info). Gayeulles' forests are interspersed with an indoor pool, several lakes (with paddle-boats in the summer), sports fields, tennis courts, mini-golf, and a campground. Many walking paths and bikepaths cut through the park. (Check the maps posted in the park to be sure you're cycling legally.) The park is also home to a working farm and animal reserve. The farm, an instructional facility where local youngsters are taught about gardening, milking cows, and feeding horses, is open to guests of the campground who are accompanied by a parent. (☎02 99 36 71 73. Open July-Aug. M-F 9am-5:30pm; Sept.-June Tu, Th-F 4:30-6pm. Free.)

NIGHTLIFE

With enough bars for a city twice its size and a collection of clubs that draws students from Paris and beyond, Rennes is *the* partying mecca of northwestern France. After the sun sets (as late as 10:30pm in the summer) the city's visible population seems to double, and the kids don't disappear until the sun comes up again. Much of the action centers around **pl. Ste-Anne, pl. St-Michel,** and the radiating streets, but don't limit yourself—there are hot nightspots all over the city, including a few great bars and *discothèques* to the south of the Vilaine. In 2001, new laws (accompanied by protests) changed the closing times for *bars de nuit* from 3am to 2am, and for discos from 5am to 4am. But don't fret: the laws don't seem to have cramped the average reveler's style.

If you do choose to go out, begin your action-packed evening at one of the earlier-closing bars. Swing by **Bar le Nozdei,** 39 rue de Dinan, where you can sip cider (13F/€1.98) and admire the prominent disco ball hanging amidst centuries-old timbered walls. (☎02 99 30 61 64. Open M-Sa 11am-1am.) **Le Bateau Ivre,** 28 rue de la Visitation (☎02 99 38 76 93), filled with eclectic decorations and patrons, or the intimate **Bernique Hurlante,** 40 rue de St-Malo (☎02 99 38 70 09), are also great options for starting out the evening right.

BARS

Le Zing, 5 pl. des Lices (☎02 99 79 64 60). Zing's 2 floors and 8 rooms are packed with the young and the beautiful, who look all the more mysterious in the seductively dim red lighting. Beer 14F/€2.13 before midnight, 20F/€3.05 after. Opens at 2pm; picks up from around midnight until the crowd heads for the discos at 2am.

Le Papagayo, 10 rue Maréchal Joffre (☎02 99 79 65 13). An unassuming tapas bar by day, this place is transformed to a wild, raging party—especially on tequila nights, when dancers crowd the bartops. Open until 1am.

La Cité D'Ys, 31 rue Vasselot (☎02 99 78 24 84), is so truly Breton that the regulars refuse to speak French. 2 floors, decorated with Celtic knots and crosses, with an equally fabulous variety of traditional music. Open M-Sa 11am-1am.

CLUBS

Delicatessen, 7 allée Rallier du Baty (☎02 99 78 23 41), tucked around the corner from pl. St-Michel in a former prison, is one of the hottest clubs in town. Open Tu-Sa midnight-5am. Cover Th-Sa 80F/€12.20, Tu-W 60F/€9.15, students 60F/€9.15.

L'Espace Loisirs, 45 bd. La Tour d'Auvergne (☎02 99 30 21 95). From 2am on, L'Espace plays host to writhers of all sexual orientations, who fill its stage and dance floor as house music blasts through the cavernous hall. (F and Sa 40-50% gay, mostly mixed students on W and Th). Upstairs is **L'Endroit,** which attracts a more relaxed, mixed crowd, reclining on wicker furniture and grooving to techno. Both open Th 11pm-4am, F-Sa 11pm-5am, Su-W midnight-4am. Cover 60F/€9.15, students 40F/€6.10.

Pym's Club, 27 pl. du Colombier (☎02 99 67 30 00). Look for the signs for Colombier, not Colombes, from pl. Maréchal Juin, and ask for the cinema; the club's just below it. The most posh of Rennes' discothèques; 3 rooms filled with scarlet benches and couches, occupied only by the most chic clientele. **Planête** draws the largest, youngest crowd with its techno sounds; **Le Salon's** mellow music caters to an older set; and **Club's** hits from the 80s and 90s attract a mix of the two. Cover F-Sa 85F/€12.96, Su-Th 65F/€9.91. For students, F-Sa 50F/€7.62 before 1am, 65F/€9.91 after 1am; Su-Th free until 1:30am, 50F/€7.62 after. Open daily 11pm-5am (music stops at 4am).

ENTERTAINMENT AND FESTIVALS

For a more sedate evening, search out theater, dance, and classical music performances in *Contact Hebdo Le Guide-Loisirs*, available at the tourist office or hostel. For information on **Orchestre de Bretagne** concerts, call 02 99 27 52 83.

The best-known of Rennes' summer festivals, **Les Tombées de la Nuit,** is a nine-day riot of music, theater, mime, and dance (complete with a 14-hour traditional Breton dancefest) in early July. For information, contact the Office de Tourisme, Festival de Tombées de la Nuit, 11 rue St-Yves (☎02 99 67 11 11; www.ville-rennes.fr). The **Festival Transmusicales** (www.transmusicales.com) fills the city from mid-May to late June, featuring local artists and international bands.

DAYTRIP FROM RENNES: BROCELIANDE FOREST

BRITTANY

***TIV** buses leave from Rennes (1hr.; M-F 3-4 per day, Sa 2 per day; 17F/€2.59) and stop in the village of **Paimpont,** in the middle of the forest.*

Brocéliande, just an hour from Rennes, is one of the most legend-saturated spots in Europe. Its associations with King Arthur and his knights are almost innumerable; a 75km road through the forest passes such sights as Merlin's Tomb, the Fountain of Youth, and the Valley of No Return. Adulterers can visit the field where Lancelot confessed his love for Guinevere and stole the kiss that ended an age. Many of the forest's supposedly Arthurian structures are the remnants of stone-age megaliths (à la Stonehenge) dating from 3000 to 2000 BC; they're so worn down that there's not much to see of them nowadays. They're also fenced in, and heavily touristed by the chronically hopeful. Though the Tomb of Merlin is covered in bouquets and notes from people seeking his aid, the real magic here is the misty forest, with trees up to 6000 years old and terrain ranging from dense wood to mystical moor.

To get a real sense of the forest, you might want to camp, or stay in a nearby *gîte.* If you don't have a car, rent a mountain bike at **Le Bar Brecilien,** 1 rue Général Charles de Gaulle, behind the tourist office. (☎02 99 07 81 13. 60F/€9.15 per half-day, 90F/€13.72 per day. Open July-Aug. daily; Sept.-June Tu-Sa.)

From the Paimpont bus stop, turn around and walk back in the direction from which the bus came (about 200m). Before the road crosses the water, you should see a sign for the "Syndicat d'initiative" on the left. Turn left and proceed toward

NO LAUGHING MATTER When Olivier de Clisson rebuilt Josselin's château in 1370, its citizens just had to celebrate their new freedom from attack. They decided to rename a street; that street, whose name actually appears in quotation marks, leads into pl. Notre Dame and is called the ruelle de "Haha." Why that name? It's meant to imitate the sound of invading knights pouring down that very road, swords drawn, chopping off (ha) the heads (ha) of retreating townspeople.

the old abbey ahead (now half Presbyterian church, half *mairie*). The **tourist office** is next to the abbey. The tourist office provides information on bike and car routes and local accommodations, as well as maps of the forest (57F/€8.69). In July and August, it also offers guided tours of the major sites in the forest to those with their own cars. Tours, usually in French, leave from the tourist office M-Tu, Th-F, and Su 2pm (40F/€6.10 per person for 4hr.); W and Sa 10am-12:30pm (25F/€3.81 per person) or 2-6:30pm (40F/€6.10 per person). Call ahead to reserve a place. They also offer pedestrian tours that involve 7-10km hikes (July12-Aug. 16 Tu 9:30am-1pm) for 40F/€6.10 per person. (☎02 99 07 84 23. Open Feb.-Dec. M-F 10am-noon and 2-5pm, Sa-Su 10am-noon and 2-6pm.)

NEAR RENNES

JOSSELIN

The village of Josselin (pop. 2636), with both flowers and charm to spare, seems to have undergone little change since its medieval beginnings. While kids here are up on the latest looks, the pace of life still seems to match the speed of the canal that meanders past the château, for which the town is famous.

TRANSPORTATION AND PRACTICAL INFORMATION. CTM buses (☎02 97 01 22 10) run to **Rennes** (1¼hr.; M-Th and Sa 4 per day, F 6 per day, Su 2 per day in the evening; 66F/€10.06; some 33F/€5.03 student rates—ask the driver). The first bus from Rennes to Josselin usually doesn't leave until noon, while buses from Josselin to Rennes tend to run mostly in the morning. The same number of buses go to Rennes and to Josselin each day. Buses stop at pl. de la Résistance.

To get to the **tourist office,** pl. de la Congrégation, take your first right upon exiting the bus onto rue Olivier de Clisson and head downhill to pl. Notre-Dame. Turn left on rue des Vierges; the office is at the intersection with rue de Château, on the left side of the latter street before the château's entrance. The office has free maps, information on activities and accommodations, and sells maps of local and regional bike routes with explanations in English (10-20F/€1.53-€3.05). Walkers and bikers alike can enjoy the beautiful paths along the canal. (☎02 97 22 36 43; fax 02 97 22 20 44. Open July-Aug. daily 10am-6pm; Apr.-June and Sept.-Oct. M-Sa 10am-noon and 2-6pm, Su 2-6pm; Nov.-Mar. M-F 10am-noon and 2-6pm, Sa 10am-noon.) The **police** (☎02 97 22 20 26) are at the top of town on the corner of rue de Pont Mareuc and rue de Carouges. The **hospital** (☎02 97 73 13 13) is on rue St-Jacques. The **post office,** rue Olivier de Clisson, has **currency exchange.** (☎02 97 22 20 00. Open M-F 9am-noon and 2-5pm, Sa 9am-noon.) **Postal code:** 56120.

ACCOMMODATIONS AND FOOD. The *gîte d'étape* **L'Ecluse 35 de Josselin** houses guests in orange- and blue-accented rooms inside a brightly lit, impeccably clean restored farmhouse. From the bottom of the château, proceed to the left along the canal and through the parking lot until you reach a small cluster of houses that face one of the canal's lochs—then ask for the *gîte*. They have a kitchen, dining room, one single, two doubles, and 12 dorm-style beds. (☎02 97 75 67 18 or 02 97 22 24 17. 49F/€7.47 per person, 52F/€7.93 in winter.) A 25-minute walk from Josselin, **Camping du Bas de la Lande** is situated on the canal; the site has beautiful views and fishing, as well as the natural joys of laundry, ping pong, and mini-golf. No buses run here; from the château, proceed to the right along rue de Canal (the actual road, not the path along the canal, which should be on your left) and continue ahead when it becomes rue Glatinier. Take a left at the first roundabout and then a right after the bridge. The campsite is on the left, across from the mini-golf course. (☎ 02 97 22 22 20; fax 02 97 73 93 85. Reception July-Aug. 9:30am-noon and 3-9pm; Apr.-June and Sept.-Oct. 9:30am-noon and 2:30-8pm. Open Apr.-Oct. 20F/€3.05 per person, 13F/€1.98 per car, 18F/€2.74 per tent; Apr.-June and Sept.-Oct. 15F/€2.29 per person, 10F/€1.53 per car, 12F/€1.83 per tent.)

The **Crêperie du Centre,** 9 pl. Notre Dame, in Josselin's central square, is perfect for people-watching. Sample as many scrumptious galettes and omelettes (30-40F/€4.57-6.10) as you can handle. (☎ 02 97 22 20 98. Open daily 11am-9pm.)

SIGHTS AND ENTERTAINMENT. The stately **château** which dates back to 1008 (when it bore the name Goscelinus), still presides over the Canal de Nantes à Brest under the stewardship of a descendant of the first Josselin de Rohan. England's King Henry II razed the original wooden structure in 1168 to punish the feudal Bretons for opposing his attempted takeover of the duchy. Olivier de Clisson he rebuilt the château in 1370 and expanded it to its present form, adding three main towers, a 26m-diameter keep (which became his residence), a gatehouse, and a fourth tower across from the first three that served as a prison. Clisson's grandson later added a longhouse, whose design included intricate granite lacework. The construction was not complete without the prominent display of the Rohan motto, "A PLUS" (without equal), on its facade and its interior fireplaces. In spring and summer, the gardens, complete with 300-year-old cedar tree, are a must-see. Since the castle is still a private home, you can only see its interior by taking a tour, available in impeccable English (45min., July-Aug. 11am and 2:30pm; June and Sept. 2:30pm). The château's former stables are now home to the **Musée de Poupées,** 3 rue des Trente, a 19th- and 20th-century doll collection. (Château and museum ☎ 02 97 22 36 45. Open July-Aug. daily 10am-6pm; June and Sept. 2-6pm; Apr.-May and Oct. W and Sa-Su 2-6pm. Château 35F/€5.34, children 25F/€3.81; museum 33F/€5.03, children 24F/€3.66; both 65F/€9.91, children 45F/€6.86.)

The **Basilique Notre Dame,** a Romanesque structure dating back to the 9th century, is in a *place* bearing the same name, on the way from the bus station to the château. There's a toothpick-sized remnant of the statue of the Virgin (in a reliquary to the left of the choir) that reportedly inspired the church's construction.

Bastille Day (July 14) brings the **Festival Médiéval** to Josselin, complete with period-clad dancers, troubadours, jugglers, plays, and medieval delicacies. Festivities include jousting tournaments, a banquet, fireworks, and a medieval market (10am-7:30pm). (Admission to the town during the festival 30F/€4.57, children under 14 and those in costume free. Call tourist office for more info.)

SNAKE WOMAN One of the stained-glass windows in Fougères' Eglise St-Sulpice (on the right as you face the altar—look hard) bears the image of a beautiful woman with long blond hair, a mirror in her hand, and the lower body of a snake. Fougères' seigneurs claimed descent from Mélusine, daughter of the King of Albania, who killed her father when she discovered him abusing her mother. As punishment, she was turned into a serpent-woman every Saturday. On these days, she would hide herself in the château's underground passages. One day, however, her husband became suspicious of his wife's frequent absences and peered through the keyhole of her hiding place. There he beheld his bride in her bath, brushing her long hair, while her scaly extremities flailed about. Understandably upset, he burst into the room, only to have Mélusine scream in terror and slither into their castle's subterranean passages, never to be seen again. Legend has it that her screams can be heard in Fougères on the eve of any tragedy, and have foretold not only plagues but also the beginning of the World War II bombardments in 1944.

FOUGERES

The medieval town of Fougères (pop. 23,000) sits high atop a hill overlooking the Nançon Valley, its gardens and steep, winding streets cascading toward the fortress-like château and river below. It was first settled by a succession of feudal lords and ladies, then became the home of craftsmen, and later a haven for artists and authors. Today, Fougères is a modern town with a perfectly preserved historic center. The town demonstrates its dedication to culture today through its focus on carefully maintained museums, and the international music festival, **Voix des Pays,** that occurs at the beginning of July just outside the grounds of the château.

TRANSPORTATION AND PRACTICAL INFORMATION. Fougères is 50km from Rennes. No trains run here; the station only serves buses. **TIV buses** (☎ 02 99 99 02 37 in Fougères) run from **Rennes** (1hr.; M-F 10 per day, Sa 4 per day, Su 2 per day; 53F/€8.08). Get off at the "Fougères Jean Jaurès" stop for the historic center of the city. For the return trip, it's easiest to leave from the **bus station** (☎ 02 99 99 08 77), pl. de la République. From the stop where you were dropped off, walk downhill on bd. Jean Jaurès for about seven minutes until you reach the fountain in the center of the traffic circle. The station is on the left side of the fountain. (Open M-Sa 9:30am-noon and 2-7pm.) **Les Courriers Bretons** (☎ 02 99 19 70 70; www.lescouriersbretons.fr) run from **St-Malo** (2¼hr., 2 per day, 82F/€12.50) via **Pontorson** (1hr., 2 per day, 45.50F/€6.94).

To get to the tourist office, pl. Aristide Briand, walk uphill on bd. Jean-Jaurès and at the traffic circle (a four-pronged fork), choose the second curve from the right, rue de Paris. Follow it to the end and you'll see pl. Aristide Briand on your right, with the **tourist office** at the far end. The office provides maps and information of accommodations and local activities. They also sell maps of bike routes (forest of Fougères map 20F/€3.05, regional map 57F/€8.69). (☎ 02 99 94 12 20; fax 02 99 94 77 30. Open July-Aug. M-Sa 9am-7pm, Su and holidays 10am-noon and 2-4pm; Sept.-June M-Sa 9:30am-12:30pm and 2-6pm, Su and holidays 1:30-5:30pm.) The **hospital** is at 133 rue Forêt. A **clinic/pharmacy** can be reached at 02 99 94 17 17. **Police:** ☎ 02 99 94 25 25. The **post office** on av. Général de Gaulle has **currency exchange.** (☎ 02 99 99 24 24. Open M-F 8:30am-6:30pm, Sa 8:30am-noon.) **Postal code:** 35300.

FOOD. Fougères' public squares and beautiful gardens beg for a picnic. Pick up fresh fruit (apples 8.50F/€1.30 per kg), veggies, and cheese where the locals do: **Au Panier Garni,** 6 pl. Aristide Briand. (☎ 02 99 99 15 94. Open Tu-Sa 7am-7pm.) Then grab a baguette at any of the bakeries in the *place* or lining rue Pinterie.

SIGHTS. To reach the château from pl. Aristide Briand, turn left onto rue Porte Roger (near the tourist office) and go to the right of the fountain (up one block), rue de la Pinterie, the main artery of the medieval city. Proceed downhill until a view of the château opens up ahead. You can proceed directly to the castle, or make a detour into the garden immediately to the left. The ruined ramparts are full of nooks and spiral staircases leading nowhere.

As you exit the garden, bear right at the fork to stay on rue de la Pinterie. Just ahead, you will see the tri-towered, moat-traversing entrance to Fougères' awe-inspiring **château,** sitting on a promontory flanked by rock walls and the Nançon river. The construction of its three levels began around AD 1000, as part of a plan to reinforce the entire Breton duchy. Steady expansion continued for the next 500 years, as this prominent stronghold on the Breton-French border was captured, destroyed, and rebuilt five times. Despite the château's current state of disrepair, a number of architectural ingenuities have been left standing, including the behemoth **Tour Mélusine,** built by the Lusignans of Poitou in honor of their half-human ancestor (see Snake Woman, below). It stands 30m high, with 3m-thick walls and a dungeon to boot (peer through the trap door for a bird's-eye view). (☎ 02 99 99 79 59. Open June 15-Sept. 15 daily 9am-7pm; Sept. 16-Oct. and Apr.-June 14 9am-6pm; Nov.-Dec. and Feb.-Mar. 10am-noon and 2-5pm. Tours July-Aug. on the hour 10-11am and 2-5pm. English tours leave 5min. later. 23F/€3.51, students 18F/€2.74, ages 10-16 12F/€1.83, under 10 free. Tower 18F/€2.74.)

Right outside the castle walls (from the château, walk back to the fork between rue de la Pinterie and rue le Bouteiller and go downhill on the latter street) is the **Eglise St-Sulpice.** This, the town's oldest church, expanded from the 15th to 18th centuries as the chateau's chapel (built from 1050 to 1060) became too small for the town's population. The large Chapelle de Notre-Dame to the left of the altar (not to be confused with the smaller one in the rear of the church that bears the same name) presents the rare image of Mary breast-feeding Christ.

Look for signs to the **Jardin Public,** which has a breathtaking panoramic view of the château, the Eglise St-Sulpice, and surrounding countryside. The garden also honors the writers (among them, Hugo, Balzac, Guéhenno, and Chateaubriand) who have found inspiration in Fougères. (Open Apr. 16-Oct. 15 daily 8am-midnight; Oct. 16-Apr. 15 8am-10pm.) There's an even better view from the top of the tower of **Eglise St-Léonard,** St-Sulpice's larger, younger sibling. (Access to tower June 15-Sept. 15 except during daily mass at 10:30 am. 11F/€1.68.) Turn left out of the church doors and down to 51 rue Nationale, to a 17th-century half-timbered house that is now the **Musée Emmanuel de la Villeon.** The museum displays sixty works by de la Villeon (1858-1944), a little-known artist from Fougères who was among the last of the Impressionists. (Open June-Aug. daily 10:30am-12:30pm and 2-6pm; Sept.-May 10am-noon and 2-5pm. Free.)

ST-MALO

St-Malo (pop. 52,000) is the ultimate seaside getaway—and everybody knows it. The city's combination of fabulous beaches with the history within its old walls (*intra-muros*) will justify your fun in the sun with intellectual fortification. Although 80% of the city was destroyed in World War II, St-Malo has been rebuilt so thoughtfully that it's difficult to distinguish the old from the new. Within its towering stone walls, a web of cobblestone streets winds among 15th- to 17th-century-style buildings, where artisans' workshops have been replaced by the Body Shop and Lacoste, and more than a few merchants vie to sell you sailor suits.

TRANSPORTATION

Trains: pl. de l'Hermine (☎02 99 40 70 20). Trains run, all via Dol, to: **Caen** (3½hr., 8 per day, 148F/€22.56); **Dinan** (1hr., 5 per day, 48F/€7.32); **Paris** (5hr., 3 per day, 321F/€48.94); **Pontorson** (45min., 5 per day, 43F/€6.56); and **Rennes** (1hr., 8-12 per day, 69F/€10.52). Station open M-Sa 5:30am-8pm, Su 7:30am-8:25pm. Info and reservations daily 9:30am-7pm.

Buses: Esplanade St-Vincent. **Tourisme Verney** (☎02 99 82 26 26) runs to: **Cancale** (30min., 3 per day, 22.50F/€3.44); **Dinard** (30min., 11 per day, 21.50F/€3.28); and **Rennes** (1½hr.; M-F 4 per day, Sa 2 per day, Su 1 per day; 61.50F/€9.38). Offices in the train station and opposite the tourist office open July-Aug. M-Sa 8:30am-12:30pm and 1:30-7pm; Sept.-June M-F 8:30am-noon and 2-6:30pm, Sa 8:30am-noon. **Courriers Bretons** (☎02 99 19 70 80; www.lescouriersbretons.fr) to: **Cancale** (45min., 4 per day, 23.50F/€3.58) and **Mont-St-Michel** (1½hr.; M-Sa 4 per day, Su 3 per day; 57.50F/€8.77). Buses also stop at the hostel. Tours in summer to **Cap Fréhel** (5hr.; 95F/€14.48, ages 4-11 55F/€8.39); **Dinan** (5hr.; 95F/€14.48, ages 4-11 55F/€8.39); **Ile de Bréhat** (full day; 165F/€25.16); and **Mont-St-Michel** (half-day 115F/€17.53, ages 4-11 70F/€10.67; full-day 130F/€19.82, ages 4-11 70F/€10.67). 10% student discount. Office open July-Aug. M-F 8:30am-6:30pm; Sept.-June 8:30am-12:15pm and 2-6:15pm.

Ferries: Gare Maritime de la Bourse. **Brittany Ferries** (☎02 99 40 64 41; www.brittany-ferries.fr) serves **Portsmouth** (9hr.; 1 per day in summer, less frequently in the winter; 330F/€50.31). See **Getting There: By Boat** (p. 62) for details. **Condor Ferries** (☎02 99 200 300; www.condorferries.co.uk) to **Jersey** (70min.) and **Guernsey** (1¾hr.; 4 per day; round-trip 299F/€45.59, 460F/€70.13 for stays over 24hr.). **Emeraude Lines** (☎02 33 180 180; fax 02 99 18 15 00; www.emeraudelines.com) runs to the same

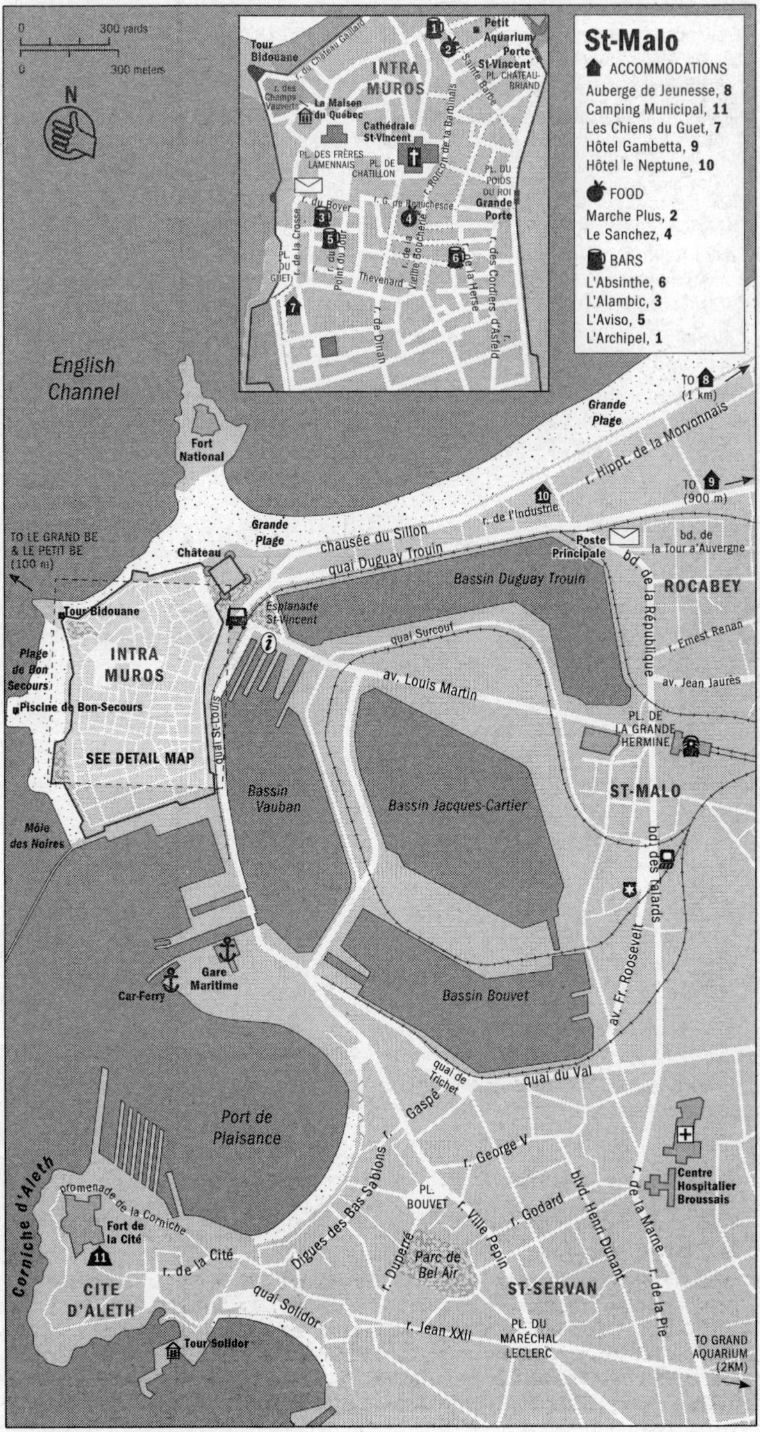

St-Malo

ACCOMMODATIONS
- Auberge de Jeunesse, **8**
- Camping Municipal, **11**
- Les Chiens du Guet, **7**
- Hôtel Gambetta, **9**
- Hôtel le Neptune, **10**

FOOD
- Marche Plus, **2**
- Le Sanchez, **4**

BARS
- L'Absinthe, **6**
- L'Alambic, **3**
- L'Aviso, **5**
- L'Archipel, **1**

0 300 yards
0 300 meters
N

INTRA MUROS
Tour Bidouane
r. du Château Gaillard
r. des Champs Vauverts
La Maison du Québec
Cathédrale St-Vincent
PL. DES FRÈRES LAMENNAIS
PL. DE CHATILLON
Petit Aquarium
Porte St-Vincent
PL. CHÂTEAUBRIAND
r. Sainte Barbe
r. Broussais
r. Porcon de la Barbinais
PL. DU POIDS DU ROI
Grande Porte
r. du Boyer
r. G. de Beauchesne
r. de la Crosse
r. du Point du Jour
PL. DU GUET
Thevenard
r. de la Vieille Boucherie
r. de la Herse
r. des Cordiers
r. d'Asfeld
r. de Dinan

English Channel
Fort National
Grande Plage
TO 8 (1 km)
r. Hippt. de la Morvonnais
TO 9 (900 m)
r. de l'Industrie
chaussée du Sillon
TO LE GRAND BE & LE PETIT BE (100 m)
Château
quai Duguay Trouin
Poste Principale
bd. de la Tour a'Auvergne
Bassin Duguay Trouin
bd. de la République
ROCABEY
Tour Bidouane
Esplanade St-Vincent
quai Surcouf
r. Ernest Renan
Plage de Bon Secours
INTRA MUROS
av. Louis Martin
av. Jean Jaurès
Piscine de Bon-Secours
quai St-Louis
PL. DE LA GRANDE HERMINE
SEE DETAIL MAP
Bassin Vauban
Bassin Jacques-Cartier
ST-MALO
Môle des Noires
bd. des Talards
Gare Maritime
Car-Ferry
Bassin Bouvet
av. Fr. Roosevelt
quai de Trichet
quai du Val
Gaspé
Port de Plaisance
r. George V
Centre Hospitalier Broussais
Corniche d'Aleth
promenade de la Corniche
PL. BOUVET
r. Ville Pepin
r. Godard
blvd. Henri Dunant
r. de la Marne
Fort de la Cité
Digues des Bas Sablons
r. Duperré
Parc de Bel Air
r. de la Cité
CITE D'ALETH
quai Solidor
ST-SERVAN
r. de la Pie
r. Jean XXII
PL. DU MARÉCHAL LECLERC
TO GRAND AQUARIUM (2KM)
Tour Solidor

BRITTANY

islands (3 per day; round-trip within 72hr. 480F/€73.18, ages 16-23 330F/€50.31, ages 4-15 290F/€44.21, more for longer stays) and has all-inclusive vacation packages. Bikes 50-60F/€7.62-9.15 round-trip; call for car prices.

Public Transportation: St-Malo Bus (☎02 99 56 06 06), in the bus office pavilion. Buses run July-Aug. daily 8am-midnight; Sept.-June 8am-7pm. The tourist office and the hostel have free copies of the master map and schedule. Tickets 7F/€1.07 (valid 1hr.), *carnet* of 10 50F/€7.62, 24hr. pass 20F/€3.05.

Taxis: Allô Taxis Malouins (☎02 99 81 30 30) leave from St-Vincent and the station.

Bike Rental: Diazo, 47 quai du Duguay-Trouin (☎02 99 40 31 63), has bikes and mountain bikes. 60-65F/€9.15-9.91 per half-day, 80-85F/€12.20-12.96 per day. 500F/€76.23 or passport deposit. Open in summer daily 9am-noon and 2-6pm.

Moped Rental: M'Road, 2 pl. de l'Hermine (☎02 99 40 13 15; fax 02 99 40 97 24), in front of the train station. Open Tu-Sa 9am-12:15pm and 2-7pm.

Windsurfer Rental: Surf School St-Malo, 2 av. de la Hoguette (☎02 99 40 07 47; fax 02 99 56 44 96). Walk along Grande Plage until you see signs. 150F/€22.90 per hr., 250F/€38.12 per half-day; subsequent rentals 100F/€15.25 per hr., 200F/€30.49 per half-day. 5 2½hr. lessons 870F/€132.64. Open daily 9am-noon and 1:30-6pm.

ORIENTATION AND PRACTICAL INFORMATION

The small walled city (*intra-muros*) is the westernmost point of St-Malo and the heart of the shopping and restaurant district. The train station is closer to the town center, which holds nothing of interest to tourists. The area from four blocks to the west of the train station down to the old city is prime beach territory. To get to the *intra-muros*, as you exit the train station, cross bd. de la République and follow av. Louis-Martin straight to the tourist office (10min.), or take bus #1, 2, 3, 4, or 6 (every 20min., 7F/€1.07) from the stop on bd. de la République to St-Vincent. To get to the tourist office from the ferry terminals, turn left onto quai St-Louis as you leave the *gare maritime;* the office is beside the port and the bus station.

Tourist Office: Esplanade St-Vincent (☎02 99 56 64 48; fax 02 99 56 67 00; www.saint-malo-tourisme.com), near the entrance to the old city. Cross bd. de la République and follow esplanade St-Vincent to the office (10min). Free map (or a very detailed one for 5F/€0.76) and list of accommodations. Open July-Aug. M-Sa 8:30am-8pm, Su 10am-7pm; June and Sept. M-Sa 9am-12:30 and 1:30-7pm, Su 10am-12:30pm and 2:30-6pm; Oct.-Easter M-Sa 9am-12:30pm and 1:30-6pm; Easter-May M-Sa 9am-12:30pm and 1:30-7pm, Su 10am-12:30pm and 2:30-6pm.

Money: Exchange currency at **Banque de France,** rue d'Asfeld at the southeast corner of the walled city. Exchange desk open M-F 9am-noon.

Laundromat: 27 bd. de la Tour d'Auvergne. Open daily 7am-9pm. Also *intra-muros* on Halle aux Blés (☎02 99 81 59 16).

Hospital: Centre Hospitalier Broussais, 1 rue de la Marne (☎02 99 21 21 21).

Police: 5 av. Louis Martin (☎02 23 18 18 18).

Internet Access: Ultima, 75 bd. des Talards (☎02 23 18 18 23). 30F/€4.57 per 30min., 40F/€6.10 per hr. Open Tu-Sa 10:30am-1pm and 2-7pm.

Post Office: 1 bd. de la Tour d'Auvergne (☎02 99 20 51 70), at the intersection with bd. de la République. Open M-F 8am-7pm, Sa 8am-noon. **Poste Restante code:** 35401. **Postal code:** 35400. **Branch office,** pl. des Frères Lamennais in the *vieille ville* (☎02 99 40 89 90). Open M-F 8:45am-12:15pm and 1:30-5:45pm, Sa 8:45am-noon. **Postal code:** 35402.

ACCOMMODATIONS AND CAMPING

Reserve up to six months in advance to stay in the *vieille ville* in July and August. The extremely popular hostel doesn't take phone reservations; book by fax or letter—and well in advance—to stay there in summer. Don't sleep on the beach unless you want a soggy sleeping bag—tides swallow the sands twice daily.

Auberge de Jeunesse/Centre Patrick Varangot/Centre de Rencontres Internationales (HI), 37 av. du Révérend Père Umbricht (☎02 99 40 29 80; fax 02 99 40 29 02; reservation.ajcri@wanadoo.fr). From the train station, take bus #5 (dir: "Paramé" or "Davier") or bus #1 (dir: "Rothéneuf") to "Auberge de Jeunesse" (last bus 7:30pm). You can also take bus #1 from St-Vincent and the tourist office. From July to Aug. 25, #1 runs about once per hr. 8-11:30pm. By foot, follow bd. de la République to the right from the front of the station. After 2 blocks, turn right onto av. Ernest Renan. When it ends, turn left onto av. de Moka. Turn right on av. Pasteur, which becomes av. du Rév. Père Umbricht, and keep right at the sign saying "Auberge de Jeunesse" (30min.). The professional staff runs an enormous establishment, more hotel than hostel. Clean 2- to 6-person rooms with new furniture, sinks and bathrooms. Athletic facilities. 3 blocks from the beach. Kitchen with individual refrigerators (10F/€1.53). Laundry. Sheets 17F/€2.59. After 10:45pm guard in the neighboring Foyer des Jeunes Travailleurs can let you in. M-F meals 40F/€6.10. Handicapped-accessible. Reception 24hr. 4- to 6-person rooms with sink 72F/€10.97; 2- to 3-person rooms with shower 74F/€11.28; 2- to 5-person rooms with bunk beds, toilet, and shower 81F/€12.34; 2- to 3-person rooms with toilet and shower 89F/€13.56. Prices go up 3F/€0.45 Apr.-Oct.

Les Chiens du Guet, 4 pl. du Guet (☎02 99 40 87 29; fax 02 99 56 08 75). Fabulous location *intra-muros;* direct access to beach and promenade. Bright rooms with elegant furnishings. Just 5min. from the restaurants and bars, and well-worth the extra money. Breakfast 28F/€4.27. July-Aug. doubles 200F/€30.49, with shower 250F/€38.12, with bath 290F; triples 220F/€33.54, with bath 360F/€54.89; quads with bath 430F/€65.56. Prices fall 30-90F/€4.57-13.72 off-season. Closed Nov. 12-Jan. MC/V.

Hôtel le Neptune, 21 rue de l'Industrie (☎02 99 56 82 15). 5min. from beach, station, and *vieille ville* in an unappealing industrial sector. From the station, turn right onto bd. de la République and bear left when it ends, passing the post office on your right. Keep straight; rue de l'Industrie will be on the left. New owner has renovated all rooms. Breakfast 30F/€4.57. Reception 8am-midnight. Singles and doubles 130F/€19.82, with shower 160F/€24.39, with bath 180F/€27.44; quads with shower 210F/€32.02, with bath 230F/€35.06; quint with shower 260F/€39.64. MC/V.

Hôtel Gambetta, 40 bd. Gambetta (☎02 99 56 54 70). Follow directions to hostel and look for bd. Gambetta to the right, off av. du Rév. Père Umbricht. Charming owner lets bright rooms with big windows that look out over a small garden. Quiet location, somewhat far from the old city and beach. Breakfast 30F/€4.57. Showers 16F/€2.52. July-Aug. singles €23; doubles €27, with bath €45; triples with bath €68; quads with bath €69. Sept.-June prices drop €3-23, depending on the size of the room.

Camping Municipal La Cité d'Alet, at the western tip of St-Servan (☎02 99 81 60 91). Buses #1 and 6 run to "Alet" about twice per day. From the bus stop, head uphill and bear left; the campground is 50m away. 350 spots adjacent to the ruins of a 4th- to 10th-century cathedral, partly occupying a recently decommissioned 18th-century fort. Reception July-Aug. 8am-9pm, Sept.-June 11am-noon and 2-7:30pm. Gates closed 11pm-7am. 2 people and tent 65F/€9.91, 2 people and caravan with electricity 89F/€13.57. 31F/€4.73 per person, ages 2-7 15F/€2.29.

FOOD

Restaurants are thick and almost indistinguishable along the main roads of *intra-muros*, particularly along rue Jacques Cartier; there are less generic and less populated spots along the side streets. **Outdoor markets** (8am-12:30pm) are on pl. Bouvet in St-Servan, not far from the campsite at the Marché aux Légumes *intra-muros* on Tuesdays and Fridays, and on pl. du Prieuré in Paramé on Wednesdays and Saturdays. There is an under-ground **Marché Plus,** 9 rue St-Vincent, just as you enter the city walls through the Porte St-Vincent. (☎02 99 40 94 14. Open M-Sa 7am-9pm and Su 9am-1pm.) A **Champion supermarket** is on av. Pasteur near the hostel. (☎02 99 56 04 88. Open M-F 8:30am-1pm and 3-7:30pm, Sa 8:30am-7:30pm, Su 9:30am-noon. Longer hours July-Aug.) Sweet-toothed travelers might as well accept it now—you *will* end up at **Le Sanchez,** pl. du Pilori, for an irresistible scoop (10F/€1.53) or two (16F/€2.52) of homemade "Italian" gelato. The massive four-scoop cones topped with *chantilly* (whipped cream) make it hard to pass up this caloric treat. (☎02 99 56 67 17. Open daily about 11am-11pm.)

SIGHTS

St-Malo's miles of **beaches** attract sun-bathing beauties, volleyball and sand soccer enthusiasts, and brave cold-blooded swimmers. Just outside the city walls, you'll find the area's warmest water in the large, square **Piscine de Bon-Secours,** a pool filled by the sea at high tide and by local youth at all other times. To the east of the city, **Grand Plage** is the most popular beach; further up the coast is the slightly calmer, couple-filled **Plage Rochebonne.**

The best view of St-Malo is from its **ramparts,** which kept invaders (and still keep the sea) from entering the *intra-muros*. All entrances to the city have stairways leading up to the old walls. From the northern side of the city, you can see a series of small islands drifting out into the sea. The three largest, Fort National, Le Grand Bé, and Le Petit Bé, can be reached at low tide over a sandy, pebbly, squelching path strewn with stranded mollusks. **Fort National** (look for the French flag) was built in 1689 by the military's master-architect, Vauban, to protect St-Malo from the English. It's not really worth paying for a tour of the empty, stony fortresses, but if you do, you'll at least be satisfied by the fabulous view of the bay and the city from the top. (Open June-Sept. daily; Easter-May Sa-Su only. Hours depend on the tides; call the tourist office for a schedule. Tours in French every 20min; written explanations in English. 20F/€3.05, children 6-15 10F/€1.53.) The other two islands, west of the Fort and off the shore near the Piscine de Bon-Secours, are worth a visit for their strange rocky seclusion. **Le Grand Bé,** the closer of the two, holds the grave of native son **Chateaubriand** (1768-1848), who asked to be buried amid the wind and waves that inspired his books. "Bé" means "tomb" in Breton; on that note, don't set out for **Le Petit Bé** if the sea is within 10m of the walkway.

The **Grand Aquarium** displays an impressive marine bestiary hailing from Atlantic to Amazonian climes, as well as a frightening robotic creature that welcomes you to the site. The new Nautibus gives visitors an up-close look at underwater treasures and the giant wrap-around CineMerScope will get you as close to the sharks as you'll want to be. Take bus #5 (dir: "Moinerie" or "Grassinais") from the station, the tourist office, or the hostel; in summer, ask about the special A line straight there from the tourist office (7F/€1.07). (☎02 99 21 19 00; fax 02 99 21 19 01; www.aquarium-st-malo.com. Open July-Aug. daily 9:30am-8pm; Apr.-June and Sept. 9:30am-7pm; Oct.-Mar. 10am-6pm. 75F/€11.43, ages 4-17 58F/€8.84.)

St-Malo native Jacques Cartier, who discovered Canada, is buried in the 12th-century **Cathédrale St-Vincent,** which suffered heavy damage in WWII, but has been carefully restored. Most interesting today are the funky 20th-century altar and pulpit. (Open June-Aug. daily 8am-7pm; Sept.-May 8am-noon and 2-7pm.) During July and August, the cathedral presents a series of classical and choral music concerts through the **Festival de Musique Sacrée** to commemorate the completion of the restoration in 1972. (☎02 99 56 05 38, reservations 06 08 31 99 93.)

ENTERTAINMENT AND FESTIVALS

L'Absinthe, 1 rue de L'Orme, is a great place to meet locals, world-class sailors, and beach bums, who stand elbow-to-elbow in the large front room downing anything and everything from beer to mojitos. As the night goes on, the clientele spreads out to three surrounding rooms of tatami-style tables, red velvet couches, and movie-theater seats. (☎02 99 40 85 40. Open daily 2pm-2am, 4pm-2am if it's sunny. Closed M off-season.) **L'Alambic,** 8 rue du Boyer, looks like a brewery with its brass lamps, stone walls, and timbered ceilings, but funky wire-wicker stools add a beachy feel. (☎02 99 40 86 41. Open July-Aug. daily 10am-2am; Sept.-June 10am-1am.) **L'Aviso,** 12 rue Point du Jour, sells 300 different beers (17F/€2.59), 12 whiskeys, and more kinds of juice than you're interested in drinking. (☎02 99 40 99 08. Open July-Aug. daily 6pm-3am; Sept.-June 6pm-2am.) Intimate, cave-like **L'Archipel,** 18 rue Sainte Barbe, sees a chic crowd of regulars around just a few tables and the wood-paneled bar. (☎02 99 56 75 10. Beer 13F/€1.98. Open July-Aug. daily 4pm-2am; Sept.-June noon-2am.)

St-Malo draws even more crowds during its many festivals. **Etonnants Voyageurs,** the preeminent international literary festival in France, will bring travel and adventure writers to the city May 16-20, 2002, to celebrate the theme of *L'Afrique.* The **Festival des Folklores du Monde** brings international folk musicians and dancers in the first week of July. The **Route du Rock** draws about 20 bands to the city in the second weekend of August. The **Quai des Bulles,** during the last weekend in October, is a great way to meet the creators of some of your favorite comic strips. The **Route du Rhum,** named for its participants' beverage of choice, is a sailing race that begins in St-Malo in November and ends in the French Antilles.

DINAN

Tranquil Dinan (pop. 10,000) may be the best-preserved medieval town in Brittany, and shows all the signs of a town that has reaped the benefits of its tourist-friendly status. Its spectacular *vieille ville* teeters 66m above the river Rance, and its 15th-century streets house artisans and postcard hawkers in roughly equal numbers. During the Hundred Years' War, Dinan was caught in the medieval tug-of-war between England and France. In 1364 its fate turned on the outcome of a duel—Bertrand du Guesclin overpowered Sir Thomas of Canterbury, and the English forces honorably withdrew across the Channel. In spite of the tourist hordes, Dinan maintains a quiet dignity, and its scenery will take you back centuries.

TRANSPORTATION

Trains: pl. du 11 Novembre 1918 (☎02 96 39 22 39). Office open M-Th 6am-7pm, F-Sa 7:10-7pm, Su 9am-8pm. To: **Morlaix** via St-Brieuc (1½hr., 2-3 per day, 48F/€7.32); **Paris** (3hr., 8 per day, 323F/€49.25); **Rennes** (1hr., 8 per day 72F/€11); **St-Brieuc** (1hr., 2-3 per day, 66F/€10); and **St-Malo** via Dol (1hr., 7 per day, 48F/€11).

Buses: CAT/TV buses (☎02 96 39 21 05) leave from train station and pl. Duclos. Office open M-F 8am-noon and 2-6pm. To **St-Malo** (45min., M-Sa 5 per day, Su 3 per day; 34F/€5.18). July-Aug. **tours** of **Mont-St-Michel** (1-2 per week, 110F/€16.77). **TAE buses/Cars 35** (☎02 99 26 16 00), leave from the station. To **Dinard** (30min., 7 per day, 11.50F/€1.75) and **Rennes** (70min., 7 per day, 53F/€8.08).

Taxis: ☎02 98 39 06 00.

Bike Rental: Cycles Scardin, 30 rue Carnot (☎02 96 39 21 94). Bikes 50F/€7.62 per day, 300F/€45.74 per week; mountain bikes 80F/€12.20 per day, 480F/€73.18 per week. 500-800F/€79.28-121.97 deposit. Open Tu-Sa 9am-noon and 2-7pm. MC/V.

Canoe and Kayak Rental: Port de Dinan, **Club de Canoë** (☎02 96 39 01 50), across from rue du Quai. Canoes 100F/€15.25 per half-day, 150F/€22.90 per day. Kayaks 80F/€12.20 per half-day, 120F/€18.30 per day. Passport deposit. Open July-Aug. daily 10am-noon and 2-5:30pm.

ORIENTATION AND PRACTICAL INFORMATION

To get from the station to the **tourist office,** rue du Château, bear left across pl. du 11 Novembre 1918 onto rue Carnot, then right onto rue Thiers, which brings you to pl. Duclos. Turn left to go inside the old city walls, and immediately bear right onto rue du Marchix, which becomes rue de la Ferronnerie. Pass the parking lots on pl. du Champ and pl. Duguesclin to your left; the tourist office is ahead on the right.

Tourist Office: rue du Château (☎02 96 87 69 76; fax 02 96 87 69 77; www.dinan-tourisme.com). Provides free walking tour map of city and offers historical guide with circuits in the city and region for 15F/€2.29. Tours Apr.-Sept. daily 25F/€3.81, children 15F/€2.29. Open June 15-Sept 15 M-Sa 9am-7pm, Su 10am-12:30pm and 2:30-6pm; Sept. 16-June 14 M-Sa 9am-12:30pm and 2-6:15pm.

Laundromat: 19 rue de Brest (☎02 96 39 71 35), off rue Thiers on rue des Rouairies, which becomes rue de Brest. Open M 2-7pm, Tu and Th 8:30-noon and 2-7pm, W and F-Sa 8:30am-7pm.

Police: 16 pl. du Guesclin (☎02 96 39 03 02), near the château.

Hospital: rue Chateaubriand (☎02 96 85 72 85), in Léhon.

Internet Access: Arospace Cybercafé, 9 rue de la Chaux (☎02 96 87 04 87), off rue de l'Horloge. 20F/€3.05 for the first 30min., 10F/€1.53 for each additional 15min. Open Tu-Sa 10am-7pm.

Post office, pl. Duclos (☎02 96 85 83 50), has **currency exchange.** Open M-F 8am-6:30pm, Sa 8am-noon. **Postal code:** 22100.

ACCOMMODATIONS AND CAMPING

The best place to **camp** is at the hostel in a shaded field behind the main building (27F/€4.12). The tourist office lists other, more urban sites.

Auberge de Jeunesse (HI) Moulin du Méen (☎02 96 39 10 83; fax 02 96 39 10 62; dinan@fuaj.org), slightly outside town in Vallée de la Fontaine-des-Eaux. Turn left out of train station, turn left again across tracks, then turn right and follow tracks and signs downhill for 1km. Eventually turn right and continue through wooded lanes for 0.5km until you reach the hostel on the right (30min.). Beautiful old stone house by a brook. Small, clean 2- to 8-bed rooms. Summer photo workshops and equestrian activities. Breakfast 19F/€2.90. Dinner 50F/€7.62. Kitchen access. Lockers. Sheets 17F/€2.59. Laundry. Reception 8am-noon and 5-8pm. Curfew 11pm. Beds 54F/€8.23.

Hôtel du Théâtre, 2 rue Ste-Claire (☎02 96 39 06 91), above quiet bar of same name, has bright rooms, some with large windows, in the heart of the *vieille ville*. Breakfast 25-35F/€3.81-5.34. Singles 90F/€13.72; doubles 130-140F/€19.82-21.35, with shower 170F/€25.92; triples with shower and toilet 225F/€34.30.

Hôtel de l'Océan, pl. du 11 Novembre 1918 (☎02 96 39 21 51; fax 02 96 87 05 27), nowhere near its namesake, but right across from the station. Spacious, bright, and clean rooms about a 10min. walk from the historic quarter. Breakfast 28F/€4.27. Reception 6:30am-10pm. Singles and doubles 115F/€17.53, with TV 135F/€20.58, with shower 160F/€24.39, with bath 190F/€28.97; triples with shower 190F/€28.97; quads with bath 250F/€38.12. Extra bed 30F/€4.57. MC/V.

FOOD

Simple bars and brasseries line the streets linking rue de la Ferronnerie with pl. des Merciers, especially on narrow **rue de la Cordonnerie. Monoprix supermarket** is on rue de la Ferronnerie (open M-Sa 9am-7:30pm). There is also a **Marché Plus,** 28 pl. Duclos, near the post office. (☎02 96 87 50 51. Open M-Sa 7am-9pm, Su 9am-1pm.) Buy a picnic of fruit and crêpes at the outdoor **market** on pl. du Champ and pl. du Guesclin in the *vieille ville* (Th 8am-noon). Small restaurants cluster in the cobbled streets just outside the ramparts and along the port.

SIGHTS

Dinan's city walls and its churches and houses within make the town a sight unto itself. The tourist office provides two separate walking tours which guide your visit of the ramparts and the *intra muros*.

On the ramparts, the 13th-century **Porte du Guichet** is the entrance to the **Château de Dinan.** Its former dungeon in the Tour de la Duchesse Anne houses a decent museum of local art and history. At the top of the 34m tower and its 150 steps, you'll be greeted with a great view of the town and a congratulatory sign for making it to the top. On the same ticket, and definitely worth the money, is the 15th-century **Tour de Coëtquen,** just outside the dungeon walls. Along with the occasional temporary exhibit, its dank, drafty basement possesses a fine collection of funerary ornaments—seven spotlit stone slabs portray 14th-century noblemen clutching shields, wives, and weapons. It's terrifying. (Open June-Sept. daily 10am-6:30pm; Oct.-Nov. 15 and Mar. 16-May W-M 10am-noon and 2-6pm; Nov. 16-Dec. and Feb. 7-Mar. 15 W-M 1:30-5:30pm. 25F/€3.81, ages 12-18 10F/€1.53.) The **Jardin du Val Cocherel,** on the ramparts far from the château, begins hilly, twisting, and dense, but gives way to huge bird cages, a rose garden, a checkerboard for life-sized chessmen, a small zoo, and a children's library. (Garden open daily 8am-7:30pm. Library open daily 10am-noon and 1:30-6:30pm.)

The **Basilique St-Sauveur** was built by a local man grateful to have been spared in the Crusades. The Romanesque facade, including the lion and bull above the doorway and the four statues in the side arches, date back to 1120. Within is the heart of the unfortunate Bertrand du Guesclin (see box, **Rest in Pieces**).

REST IN PIECES As his dying wish, Bertrand du Guesclin made a simple request: he wanted to be buried next to his wife, Tiphaine, in the Dominican monastery in Dinan. Unfortunately, he had breathed his last in Chateauneuf; in 1380, refrigerated flatcars were still some years down the line. Guesclin's friend built him a tomb on the spot where he had died, then loaded his body on a cart and headed east. As the corpse decayed, his friends removed, burned, and buried Bernard's entrails along the road to slow the decomposition. Then they did they same with his skin. Then his bones. Finally, nothing remained but Guesclin's heart, preserved in alcohol, which his friends diligently interred in the abbey. The Revolutionaries who destroyed the abbey had enough heart to spare Guesclin, who was re-interred in the Basilica. Guesclin is the only man in this book, perhaps even in France itself, to have five tombs.

The **Maison d'Artiste de la Grande Vigne,** 103 rue du Quai, past the port, is the former home of painter Yvonne Jean-Haffen (1895-1993). The whole house is a work of art—everything from bathroom to study is decorated in the artist's whimsical, delicate style. (☎02 96 87 90 80 or 02 96 39 22 43. Open June-Sept. daily 10am-6:30pm. 16F/€2.52; students and ages 12-18 10F/€1.53.)

The **Eglise St-Malo,** on Grande Rue, contains a remarkable 19th-century organ with blue and gold pipes and a massive Baroque altar. If you're willing to excuse "the nauseating gifts left by the pigeons" (as a sign calls them), the 30m 15th-century **Tour de l'Horloge,** on rue de l'Horloge, commands a brilliant view of Dinan's jumbled streets and the countryside. Before you reach the stairway, you'll pass through the stone rooms that once held the town archives, now a museum of Arthurian legend and lore. (☎02 96 87 02 26. Open June-Sept. daily 10am-6:30pm. 16F/€2.44, ages 12-17 10F/€1.52.) If you're planning to see all of these sights, you may want to take advantage of the "Clés pour Dinan" ticket: the keys to the Tour de l'Horloge, Château, and Maison d'Artiste de la Grande Vigne, as well as the Maison du Gouverneur, can be yours for 35F/€5.34, family 85F/€12.96. Every two years (next in 2002), Dinan hosts the two-day **Fête des Remparts** during the second half of July, when the whole town dons medieval garb for jousting tournaments, markets, and merrymaking.

ST-BRIEUC

As most locals will tell you, St-Brieuc (pop. 48,000) is much more of a commercial center than a tourist trap; its small *vieille ville* and city center are surrounded by an industrial port and economically diverse suburbs. The university students enliven the city, and make for a lively bar scene. However, the main reason most visit St-Brieuc is its situation between the Côte d'Emeraude and the Côte de Granite Rose. It's a perfect launch pad for daytrips, particularly stunning Cap Fréhel.

TRANSPORTATION

Trains: bd. Charner (☎02 96 01 61 64). To: **Dinan** (1hr., 2-3 per day, 84F/€12.81); **Morlaix** (1hr., 8-11 per day, 120F/€18.29); **Rennes** (1hr., 15 per day, 132F/€20.12); and **Vannes** (2hr., 6 per day, 132F/€20.12). Info and reservations M-Sa 8am-7pm, Su 9:30am-7pm. Ticket office open M-Th 5:30am-9pm, F 5:30am-10pm, Sa 5:30am-8:30pm, Su 5:30am-1pm.

Buses: CAT is at both the train station and the **bus station** at rue du Combat des Trente (☎02 96 68 31 20), next to the main intra-city bus terminal at Champs de Mars. To: **Cap Fréhel** (1½hr.; July-Sept. M-Sa 6 per day, Su 3 per day, Oct.-June 3 per afternoon; 45F/€6.86, students 36F/€5.49) and **Paimpol** (1½hr.; M-Sa 8 per day, Su 5 per day; 45F/€6.86, students 36F/€5.49). **TUB,** 8 rue Jouallan (☎02 96 68 14 87) runs throughout the city about every 15min. 6:30am-8pm; **NOCTUB** runs for line #3 every 30min. from 8-11:15pm. Tickets 6F/€0.91, *carnet* of 10 52F/€7.93.

Bike Rental: at the **hostel** (see below).

ORIENTATION AND PRACTICAL INFORMATION

To get to the center of town from the station, walk straight ahead onto rue de la Gare. When you reach rue du 71*ème* Régiment d'Infanterie, the main intra- and inter-city bus terminals will be to the right at pl. du Champ de Mars. Continue straight on rue de la Gare (through name changes) until the road forks; to the left, up rue St-Gilles, is the cathedral; to the right, is the **tourist office.**

Tourist Office: 7 rue St-Gouéno (☎02 96 33 32 50; fax 02 96 61 42 16; www.mairie-saint-brieuc.fr). From July 3-Aug. 25, they have 80min. guided tours of the cathedral and old quarters (M-F at 10:30am and 3pm; meet outside of the cathedral; 17F/€2.59). Pick up the free *Le Griffon* for info on regional events. Open July-Aug. M-Sa 9am-12:30pm and 2-7pm, Su 10am-1pm; Sept.-June M-Sa 9am-12:30pm and 2-6pm.

Currency Exchange: banks line pl. Champ de Mars.

Laundromat: Behind the cathedral in pl. du Martray (☎06 08 05 29 84). Has a terrifying automatic locking system. Open Apr.-Sept. daily 7am-9pm; Oct.-Mar. 7am-8pm.

Police: 17 rue Joullan (☎02 96 33 36 66).

Hospital: rue Marcel Proust (☎02 96 01 71 23).

Internet Access: MediaCap, 4 rue Joullan (☎02 96 68 90 31). 20F/€3.05 per hr. Open M-F 9:30am-7:30pm.

Post Office: pl. de la Résistance (☎02 96 61 10 60). Open M-F 8am-noon and 2-6pm, Sa 8am-noon. **Postal code:** 22000.

ACCOMMODATIONS AND FOOD

Decent budget accommodations are extremely hard to come by in town. Most inexpensive hotels are cheap for a reason. To escape from the dingy city feel, try the **youth hostel,** 3km outside town in a 15th-century house surrounded by fields and hiking trails. From the train station, cross the street and take bus #2 (dir: "Centre Commercial les Villages") and get off at the last stop. You can also go to the bus terminal at pl. du Champs de Mars and take bus #3 (same direction as #2), which stops at the hostel about half of the time and at les Villages the other half. From the bus stop at the Centre Commercial les Villages, turn right along bd. de l'Atlantique and take your second left onto rue de Brocéliande. After 300m that dead-ends; turn left onto rue du Vau Meno and then right onto rue de la Ville Guyomard, where you'll find the hostel on the left. Tennis, bike rental, sea kayaking, and horseback riding are all available. Call ahead, as they are often full. (☎02 96 78 70 70. Breakfast included. Hearty meals 49F/€7.47. Sheets 17F/€2.59. Bikes 68F/€10.37 per day with 500F/€76.23 or passport deposit. No lockout or curfew. Reception 8am-noon, 2-4pm, and 8-10pm, but someone is always around. Bunks 75F/€11.43. MC/V.) **Hotel de l'Arrivée,** 35 rue de la Gare, has small, clean rooms on a busy street 250m from the train station and 500m from the bus terminal, only a ten-minute walk from the cathedral and tourist office. (☎02 96 94 05 30. Breakfast 32F/€4.88. Reception 7am-3pm and 5-9:30pm. Singles 200F/€30.49; doubles 220F/€33.54, twin beds 250F/€38.12; triples 270F/€41.16. Extra bed 50F/€7.62. V.)

Bars and outdoor cafés cluster in the *vieille ville* behind the tourist office; rue des Trois Frères le Goff is lined with inexpensive Moroccan, Italian, Chinese, Mexican, and Indian restaurants. There's a **Monoprix supermarket** on pl. de la Résistance (open M-Sa 8:30am-7:15pm). The ginormous **Géant** supermarket (open M-Sa 8am-9pm) is at the Centre Commercial Les Villages near the hostel. The public **market** sells all things cloth, leather, and beaded around the cathedral, and edible merchandise in front of the post office (W and Sa 8am-1pm).

SIGHTS, ENTERTAINMENT, AND FESTIVALS

St-Brieuc doesn't offer much in the way of sights, but it's worth visiting the **Cathédrale St-Etienne,** pl. de Gaulle, a multi-century work of art. Christians tried to evangelize this area's Druid populations as early as the 6th century AD, but didn't build the first wooden monastery here until 848. A second was constructed in 970 after the original was destroyed by Viking invaders, but it too was soon toppled. Construction of the stone edifice began in 1180 and was more or less complete by the 14th century, but additions continued for the next 500 years. Of particular interest are the 12th-century column capital on the left of the south transept, and a 1950s-era set of stations of the cross that mixes modern art with the flatness of icon painting. Guided visits offered by tourist office (see above) give a good sense of the history of the cathedral and the region. For a better sense of old St-Brieuc, ask the tourist office for the **Circuit de découverte du centre historique,** a self-guided walking tour past the city's monuments and older neighborhoods.

St-Brieuc's bars accommodate a large range of ages and types; on any given night, the same place may be filled with a chic student crowd or a familiar group of middle-aged shopkeepers. **Chez Rollais,** 25 rue du Général Leclerc, first opened its carved oak door in 1912; locals still sip Loire wines (7-17F/€1.07-2.59 a glass) under the frescoed ceiling of this beautiful old wine bar. (☎02 96 61 23 03. Open Tu-Sa 9am-11pm.) St-Brieuc's most popular lounge is **Le Piano Bleu,** 4 rue Fardel. The front room sees frequent concerts; the back has cushy couches and padded benches. During the summer, young businessmen lounge alongside students halfway into the narrow street at outdoor tables. (☎02 96 33 41 62. Open daily 5pm-3am.) **Café del Mar,** 37 rue des Trois Frères le Goff, looks like a concrete bunker from the outside. Behind the doors, a young crowd dances to DJed music in a single huge room wrapped halfway around by the bar. Outside, the sandy patio is backed by a flower-covered stretch of the ancient city wall. (☎02 96 62 29 17. Beer or rum 15F/€2.29. Open daily 10pm-3am.) **Le Chapeau Rouge,** 13 rue Fardel, welcomes a loyal, partly gay clientele (whose photos decorate the walls) into a single, intimate wood-paneled room in one of the oldest buildings in St-Brieuc. In the summer months, the outdoor tables have a great view of the other bars' patios down the hill. (☎02 96 33 83 13. Open daily 6pm-2am.)

St-Brieuc's innovative festivals include **ArtRock,** a combined music and street art festival held on the last weekend in May or first weekend in June. Every Thursday and Friday in July and August, **L'Eté en Fête** brings at least three street concerts or presentations to pl. du Martray, near the tourist office.

NEAR ST-BRIEUC: CAP FREHEL

To get to the Cap, you'll need to catch a ***CAT bus*** *from* ***St-Brieuc*** *(1½hr.; July-Sept. M-Sa 6 per day, Su 3 per day, Oct.-June 3 per afternoon; 45F/€6.86, students 36F/€5.49). In low season, buses are scheduled so that you only have an hour to visit the Cap; consider spending the night, or renting a bike.*

When landscape artists go to sleep at night, they dream of Cap Fréhel. The plant life here is reason enough to come: green expanses dotted by royal purple spiny petals and wild orchids. Add rust-hued cliffs, which drop 70m to inlets beaten by a raging sea, and you'll begin to understand why this peninsula is so popular with hikers, postcard photographers, and those in search of self. The Cap does not offer much solitude in the summer, as hundreds flock here to hike the well-marked **GR34 trail** that follows the peninsula's edge. Wander off the trail, and you're bound to find a less crowded set of winding paths and nooks. However, be sure not to get too adventurous—the terrain can be challenging and there are several fatalities every year. At the northernmost point (easily accessible from the Cap Fréhel bus stop) there's a great view from the **light house,** set in the middle of an ornithological reserve (access to the point free, 10F/€1.53 per car). An easy walk southwest leads to a breathtaking, secluded little beach. You can also take a scenic walk to the **Fort de La Latte,** a 13th-century castle complete with drawbridges. (90min.) (☎02 96 41 40 31. Open June-Sept. with daily tours 10am-12:30pm and 2:30-6:30pm; Oct.-May no tours M-F 2:30-5:30pm. 22F/€3.35, under age 12 11F/€1.68.)

If you want to nap on the Cap, try the **Auberge de Jeunesse Cap Fréhel (HI),** la Ville Hadrieux, Kerivet, near the town of Plévenon. Get off the bus one stop after Cap Fréhel at "Auberge de Jeunesse," or stay on for one more to stock up at the small grocery store in town (open approximately M-F 9am-noon and 3:30-6pm). Take the only road that cuts away from the "Auberge de Jeunesse" bus stop and follow the inconspicuous signs with the fir-tree hostel symbol down the road for ten minutes to a right-hand turn. The hostel will be ahead shortly on your left (12min. total). The hostel's two-tiered eight-person rooms are clean and perfectly acceptable, but some prefer to sleep in the three tents beyond the bonfire pit outside, where they can be closer to the sandbox, the goats, the horses, and, of course, the Chinese pigs. It's very popular with groups, so be sure to call ahead. The hostel also **rents bikes** (48F/€7.32 per half-day) and has maps of the GR34. (☎02 96 41 48 98; Sept. 16-Apr. ☎02 98 78 70 70. Breakfast 19F/€2.90. Dinner 50F/€7.62. Sheets 17F/€2.59. Lockout noon-5:30pm. Open May-Sept. 45F/€6.86 inside or out.)

PAIMPOL

Anchored on the border of the Côte de Granite Rose and the Côte de Goëlo, Paimpol (pop. 8200) once fueled its economy with fishing expeditions to Newfoundland and Iceland. There remains a strong connection between the locals (or "*islandais*") and the rod and reel, but the port now harbors a string of snazzy bars, restaurants, and yachts. Although Paimpol itself has few sights, the town provides easy access to the surrounding islands, cliffs, beaches, and hiking trails.

TRANSPORTATION

Trains: av. Général de Gaulle. To: **Pontrieux** (18min., 4 per day, 18F/€2.75). At Guingamp (☎02 96 20 81 22), there are connections to **Morlaix** (1¼hr., 4 per day, 68F/€10.37) and **St-Brieuc** (1hr., 4-5 per day, 70F/€10.67). Office open M-Sa 6:40-7:10am and 8am-7pm, Su and holidays 9am-7pm.)

Buses: CAT (☎02 96 22 67 72) scurries from the train station to **Pointe de l'Arcouest** (15min.; M-Sa 7 per day, Su 5 per day; 11F/€1.68) and **St-Brieuc** (1¼hr.; 8 per day; 45F/€6.86, students 36F/€5.49). The same well-organized bus system runs throughout the Côtes d'Armor and serves the campground and **Tréguier** (see below).

Bike Rental: Cycles du Vieux Clocher, pl. de Verdun. (☎02 96 20 83 58). 40F/€6.10 per half-day, 70F/€10.67 per day. Open M-Sa 8:30am-12:30pm and 2-7:30pm, Su 8am-noon.

CAUGHT RED-HANDED While geologists may claim to know what gives the cliffs of Cap Fréhel their vibrant red color, locals know the real reason. In the 5th century, Irish monks evangelizing along the Côte d'Emeraude ran into opposition from powerful druids. One monk demonstrated his faith to a group of villagers by cutting off a finger. As soon as the first drop of blood hit the earth, the entire coast turned red; to this day, the cliffs retain that color as a reminder of the monk's sacrifice.

ORIENTATION AND PRACTICAL INFORMATION

To reach the port, the center of town, and the tourist office on **pl. de la République,** go straight onto rue du 18 Juin as you exit the train station, turn right onto rue de l'Oise which becomes rue St-Vincent, and continue on to the *place;* the office will be on the right (5min.).

Tourist Office: pl. de la République (☎02 96 20 83 16; fax 02 96 55 11 12; tourisme.paimpol@wanadoo.fr). They have a map of the hiking trails that lead from Paimpol to the Pointe de l'Arcouest, and *La Presse d'Armor,* a local publication with a schedule of events (5.50F/€0.84). Open July-Aug. M-Sa 9am-7:30pm, Su 10am-1pm; Sept.-June Tu-Sa 10am-12:30pm and 2:30-6pm.

Currency exchange: Société Générale, 6 pl. de la République (☎02 96 20 81 34).

Hospital: chemin de Malabry (☎02 96 55 60 00), off the right side of the port.

Police: rue Raymond Pellier, the third road on the roundabout at the non-portside end of pl. de la République (☎02 96 20 80 17).

Laundromat: Au Lavoir Pampolais, 23 rue du 18 juin (☎02 96 20 96 41), near the station, also rents sheets. Open daily 8am-8pm; last wash 7pm.

Internet Access: Cybercommune, Centre Dunant, near the church (☎02 96 20 74 74). 0.69F/€0.11 per min. Open July-Aug. M-F 9:30am-1pm and 4:30-8pm; Sept.-June M-F 3-8pm, Sa 2-6pm.

Post Office: av. du Général de Gaulle (☎02 96 20 82 40). **Currency exchange.** Open M and W-F 8am-noon and 1:30-5:30pm, Tu 8am-12:30pm and 1:30-5:30pm; Sa 8am-12:30pm. **Postal code:** 22500.

ACCOMMODATIONS

The **Auberge de Jeunesse (HI),** Château de Kéraoul (☎02 96 20 83 60), has been completely renovated for 2002. From the train station, turn left onto av. du Général de Gaulle, right onto rue du Marne at the first light, and left at the next light onto rue Bécot. When the road forks, veer right onto rue de Pen Ar Run. Turn left when the street ends and the hostel will be on your right (20min. uphill). The hostel provides beds in 2- to 6-person rooms at the western edge of town. Breakfast 19F/€2.90. Lunch or dinner 50F/€7.63. There's no lockout and no curfew, but no new guests are admitted after 6pm. Sheets 17F/€2.59. Dorms 48F/€7.32. **Camping** 27F/€4.12. **Hôtel Berthelot,** 1 rue du Port (☎02 96 20 88 66). From the tourist office, walk straight ahead toward the port and turn left after several blocks onto rue du Port. You'll see a bright blue "H" on the right at the hotel's entrance. On a quiet side street, it has friendly reception and large, comfy rooms with big windows. Breakfast 27F/€4.12. Singles and doubles 160F/€24.39, with toilet 170F/€25.92, with bath 230F/€35.08, with TV 240F/€36.60. The very popular sea-side **Camping Municipal de Cruckin,** off the plage de Cruckin (☎02 96 20 78 47), is right by the Abbaye de Beauport. From the train station, turn right onto av. du Général de Gaulle and take the third option, rue du Général Leclerc, at the roundabout. Follow the street as it twists through four name changes. Rue de Cruckin branches off to your left from rue du Commandant le Conniat. The entrance will be 150m down the hill, on the right (25min.). Alternatively, you can take the CAT bus (dir. "St-Brieuc") from the train station to "Kerity" (5min., 8 per day, 11F/€1.68). (Reception June 11-Aug.

daily 8am-10pm; Apr.-May 15 and Sept. M-Sa 8am-noon and 4-8pm, Su 9-11am and 7-8pm; May 16-June 10 M-Sa 8am-noon and 4:30-8:30pm, Su 9-11am and 7:30-8:30pm. Gates close to cars in summer 10pm-6am, but there's a night watchman July-Aug.; off-season gates closed 10pm-7am. Open Apr.-Sept. Handicapped-accessible. 1 person and tent 43.85F/€6.67, 2-3 people and tent 73.25F/€11.18, students 26F/€1.70. 16.55F/€2.52 per extra person. Electricity 14.45-17.60F/€2.62-2.68.)

FOOD

Picnickers can find supplies either at Paimpol's Tuesday morning **market,** held in squares throughout the town, or at the **Marché Plus,** rue St-Vincent, across from the tourist office (open M-Sa 9am-9pm, Su 10am-noon). Seafood fans will be happy at portside **Le Terre-Neuvas,** quai Duguay-Trouin, where there is elegant food at backpacker prices. The specialties of the house are *moules frites* (50F/€7.26, 80F/€12.20 with entree and dessert) and, in July and August, five *grandes assiettes gourmandes* are served with grilled and seasoned bread, catch of the day, salad, vegetables, and a side dish for 58-75F/€8.85-11.44. (☎02 96 55 14 14; fax 02 96 20 47 66. Open July-Aug. daily noon-2pm and 7-10pm, Sept.-June closed M.)

SIGHTS

Hidden from the road by vegetation, the ruins of the **Abbaye de Beauport,** chemin de l'Abbaye, look dreamily out to sea from their spot east of Paimpol. The now-roofless church has flowers sprouting from its flying buttresses. Dating from 1202, the abbey is celebrating its 800th birthday in 2002 with an expanded list of festivities. To get there, take the scantily-marked **GR34** along the coast from the port (1½hr.); follow the red-and-white striped blazes. For a shorter, more direct walk, you can follow directions to the campground, then follow signs from Kerity for 30 minutes (☎02 96 20 97 69. Open June 15-Sept. 15 daily 10am-7pm; Sept. 16-June 14 W-M 10am-noon and 2-5pm. English tours available July-Aug. daily 11am. 3-4 tours in French per day, beginning at 10:30am. 25F/€3.81, students and seniors 20F/€3.05, ages 11-18 10F/€1.52, ages 5-10 5F/€0.76.)

The **Musée de la Mer,** rue de Labenne, on the opposite side of the roundabout from the tourist office, is the town's tribute to its Icelandic fishing industry. Nautical experts will likely take the plunge and see the two 50-minute films and all the black-and-white photos of local fishermen, as well as the cramped cubbies in which they supposedly slept. (☎02 96 22 02 19 or 02 96 20 83 16. Open July-Aug. daily 10:30am-1pm and 2:30-6:30pm; Apr. 9-June and Sept. 1-17 10am-noon and 3-6pm. 25F/€3.81, students 13F/€1.98.) For a more domestic look at Breton culture, the miniscule **Musée du Costume,** rue R. Pelletier, displays a wide range of costumes, from baptismal gowns to wedding gowns, amidst dozens of coiffes. (Open July-Sept. 15. Same hours as the Musée de la Mer. 15.50F/€2.36, students 7F/€1.07. Joint ticket with the Musée de la Mer 33F/€5.03, under 18 16F/€2.44, under 8 free.)

ENTERTAINMENT

The port is boxed in by bars and restaurants on all sides except on the water, where it's overrun by private yachts. As the sun sets, the crowds head across the port to bars along quai de Kernoa. **La Falaise,** 2 quai de Kernoa, blasts house music. (☎02 96 20 89 79. Open daily 10am-1am, F-Sa until 2am.) To get back to your Breton roots, walk a few doors down to the **Tavarn An Tri Martolod** (Tavern of the Three Sailors), 11 quai de Kernoa. (☎02 96 20 75 15. Open July-Aug. Su-Th 11am-1am, F-Sa 11am-2am; Sept.-June W-M 11am-1am.) Nearby sidestreets have even more interesting options. Just around the corner from Hôtel Berthelot, **Le Corto Maltese,** 11 rue du Quai, draws locals and tourists of all ages. (☎02 96 22 05 76. Open July-Aug. M-F 10am-1am, Sa-Su 10am-2am; Sept.-June Tu-Su 10am-1am.) For a cozier atmosphere, try **Le Cargo,** 15 rue des 8 Patriotes, with its plaid-draped windowsills and chunky wooden tables. (☎02 96 20 72 46. Open Su-Th 12:30pm-1am, F-Sa

12:30pm-2am.) Whether you're starting at the *Cargo*, the *Corto*, or by the port, you'll probably end up at Paimpol's most popular (and only) late-night bar. Set back from the street in an alley, **La Ruelle,** 26 rue des 8 Patriotes, doesn't get going until other bars close, but it stays open until 3am, sending the sounds of ska and reggae out through open doors into the street. (☎02 96 20 56 96. Beer 12F/€1.83. Open July-Sept. daily 6:30pm-3am; Oct.-June Th-Sa 6:30pm-3am, Su 10:30pm-3am.)

The **Festival du Chant de Marin** (next in 2003) draws sailor-musicians from the world to the port of Paimpol in August. For three days the city dedicates itself to dancing, boating, and general merriment. Call the tourist office for more info.

DAYTRIP: POINTE DE L'ARCOUEST AND ILE DE BREHAT

To reach the Pointe, take a ***CAT bus*** *(☎02 96 68 31 20) from Paimpol (12min.; M-Sa 8 per day, 7 on Su; 11F/€1.68; last bus from the Pointe 5:20pm). Drivers can follow the clearly marked* ***GR34*** *from the Paimpol port.* ***Les Vedettes de Bréhat*** *(☎02 96 55 79 50) sends boats from the Pointe to the island (10min.; 10-15 per day 7:20am-7:30pm; round-trip 40F/€6.10, children 4-11 years 34F/€5.19; passenger and bike 90F/€13.72, must leave before 10am and return before 4pm; tours 70F/€10.67, ages 4-11 50F/€7.62).*

Six kilometers north of Paimpol, the peninsula ends in the tumble of pink granite that is the **Pointe de l'Arcouest.** The archipelagos and blue-green waters flowing around this point provide some of France's best sea kayaking. Two kilometers across the water is the Ile de Brehat, a mesh of rocky beaches, flower-covered mansion-like homes, and fields of elbow-high grasses. Only 3.5km in length, cinched to a little bridge in the middle, the idyllic **Ile de Bréhat** (pop. 450) is divided into the rugged northern half, with a lighthouse, and the southern half, where the *bourg* and the port lie. What most refer to as the Ile de Bréhat is actually the largest landmass in an archipelago of 96 islets, some of them so minute that they essentially amount to single rocks. If you can, take the first boat of the day, then head north to avoid the crowds. Empty, isolated beaches dot the coastline; be sure to bring a mat since most of Bréhat's beaches are rocky. The view from the white **Chapelle St-Michel,** on the west side of the island, is unparalleled—except by that from the **Phare du Paon,** a lighthouse at the island's northern tip (a 40-50min. walk from the center of town). The *bourg* is a fifteen-minute walk from the port, which is at the southernmost point of the island and has restaurants, a **post office,** and a 8 à Huit **supermarket** (open M-Sa 8:30am-8pm, Su 9am-1pm). To get to the **tourist office,** follow the main road toward the *bourg*, passing the 8 à Huit, until you reach the large square. Turn right and it will be in front of you, before the church. (☎02 96 20 04 15. Open M-Tu and Th-Sa 10am-12:30pm and 2-5:30pm.)

TREGUIER

Descending from the east bank of the wide and languorous Jandy river, medieval **Tréguier,** once the seat of the Breton monarchy, seduces visitors with its multicolored *maisons à colombage* and magnificent **cathedral.** The cathedral, a short walk uphill from the port, mixes Romanesque and early Flamboyant Gothic styles. Construction in the 14th century was disrupted by the Hundred Years' War and the Wars of Breton Succession, as evidenced by the diversity and irregular spacing of the pillars. The elaborate tomb of St. Yves, aesthete and lawyer, lies in the first chapel to the left of the choir. To its left, the Chapelle de St- Sacrement was added by Duc Jean V so that he could be buried next to St-Yves. The treasury holds the bones of St-Yves and the adjacent cloister, filled with flowers, has magnificent latticework on every arch. (Open July-Aug. daily 9:30am-6:30pm; Sept.-June 10am-noon and 2-6pm. Cathedral free. Cloister and treasury 17F/€2.59, under 14 free.)

If you'd like to explore the area further, try **Le Syet,** a *gîte d'étape* about 20 minutes from the town center. Coming out of the tourist office, turn right and right again onto rue Colvestre; follow it straight out of town until you see signs for Le Styvel. (☎02 96 92 31 79. Breakfast 25F/€3.81, *gîte* 50F/€7.62 per person.)

Tréguier works best as a day excursion from Paimpol. **CAT buses** (☎02 96 22 67 72) connect Tréguier to **Paimpol** and **Lannion** (20min.; 3 per day; 25.50F/€3.89, students 20.50F/€3.13). Buses drop you off in pl. de Gaulle on the port. Rue St-André, the left-most of the two options, leads from the bus stop to the **cathedral.** To reach the **tourist office,** pl. Général Leclerc, walk past the cathedral and turn right to walk around the far side. The office will be just past the cathedral, on the left. Accommodations info, maps, and self-guided walking tours are all free. (☎02 96 92 30 19. Open July-Aug. M-Sa 10am-12:30pm and 2-7pm, Su 11am-1pm and 5-7pm; Sept.-June M-Sa 10am-noon and 2-6pm.)

MORLAIX

A half-dozen stone stairways and two rivers descend sharply from the hills on either side of Morlaix (pop. 17,000) and pour cars, water, and people into the squares and port of the narrow town center, giving it a fast-paced, crowded, big-city feel. Founded in Gallo-Roman times, when Armorican Celts built a fort here called "Mons Relaxus" (Mount of Rest), the town was continually invaded during the Middle Ages by the Duchy of Brittany, the French crown, and the British, all of whom sought to control Morlaix's enviably located port. British invaders ransacked the town in 1522, but made the mistake of celebrating their victory to drunken excess. When Morlaix's avenging citizens returned, the British were caught napping. From this event came Morlaix's name and motto: *"S'ils te mordent, mords-les!"* ("If they bite you, bite them back!"). Luckily, their ancestors re significantly less blood-thirsty.

TRANSPORTATION

Train Station: rue Armand Rousseau. To: **Brest** (45min., 8-10 per day, 53F/€8.08); **Paimpol** (1¼hr., 5 per day, 85F/€12.96); **Quimper** via Landerneau (2hr., 5-7 per day, 97F/€14.79); **Roscoff** (30min., 2 per day, 29F/€4.42); and **St-Brieuc** (45min., 6-10 per day, 74-82F/€11.29-12.51). (☎08 36 35 35 35 for SNCF info line; office open daily 5:05am-8:20pm.)

Buses: SNCF also leaves from the train station for **Roscoff** (30-45min., 4 per day, 29F/€4.42). **CAT** (☎02 98 72 01 41) goes to **Huelgoat** (1hr., 2-3 per day, 36F/€5.49), **Quimper** (2hr., 3-5 per week, 64F/€9.76), and **Roscoff** (30-45min.; M-Sa 3-4 per day, 1 on Su; 45F/€6.86). You can catch some buses at the Morlaisiennes stop, in front of the Monoprix on rue d'Aiguillon, or at the station.

Public Transportation: TIM, pl. Cornic (☎02 98 88 82 82). Tickets 6F/€1.07, *carnet* of 10 54F/€8.24. Buses run 7:30am-7pm.

Taxis: Radio Taxis are usually at pl. des Otages and the station (☎02 98 15 12 73).

ORIENTATION AND PRACTICAL INFORMATION

All roads run downhill from the station to the port and up into the surrounding hills. There are three ways to get down to the town center. The most direct route is **rue Courte,** also known as the Cent Marches, a set of 100 steps interspersed with a series of ramps. From the station, walk straight ahead on **rue Gambetta** for 100m and turn left onto the stairs, which lead directly to the central **pl. Emile Souvestre.** The switchbacking **rue Gambetta** and the steep **rue Longue** (the next road to the left after rue Courte) get you to the same place without stairs. If you climb up any of the three, be aware that you may be using muscles you didn't know existed. To get from the station to the **tourist office,** follow the directions above to pl. Emile Souvestre. Turn left and you will shortly be in **pl. des Otages.** The tourist office is in the far right hand corner of the *place*, in front of the viaduct.

Tourist Office: pl. des Otages (☎02 98 62 14 94; fax 02 98 63 84 87). Maps and a complete city guide. Open July-Aug. M-Sa 10am-noon and 2-7pm, Su 10:30am-12:30pm; Sept.-June Tu-Sa 10am-noon and 2-6pm.

Laundromat: 4 rue de Lavoirs or pl. Charles de Gaulle (both ☎02 98 63 83 19). Both open daily 8am-8:30pm.

Police: 17 pl. Charles de Gaulle (☎02 98 88 17 17).

Hospital: Hôpital Général, 15 rue Kersaint Gilly (☎02 98 62 61 60).

Internet Access: at the **post office.** You can also surf the web for free for 1hr. at the **public library,** 5 rue Gambetta (☎02 98 15 20 60). Open Tu and F 1:30-6pm; W 10am-noon and 1:30-6pm; Sa 10am-5pm.

Post Office: 15 rue de Brest (☎02 98 88 93 22). **Currency exchange.** Open M-F 8:30am-6:30pm, Sa 8:30am-noon. **Postal code:** 29600.

ACCOMMODATIONS

Morlaix is small enough that few areas are undesirable or inconvenient. Ask the tourist office about local *gîtes d'étape* (around 50F/€7.62) or *chambres d'hôte* (100-200F/€15.25-30.49).

Auberge de Jeunesse (HI), 3 rte. de Paris (☎02 98 88 13 63; fax 02 98 88 81 82). Far from the train station but not from sights, nightlife, and a lovely canal. From the station, follow the directions in **Orientation,** above, to pl. Emile Souvestre, and bear slightly to the right onto rue Carnot. Take a right onto rue d'Aiguillon (the sign for the hostel will be one among many), which becomes rue de Paris as it bears left 200m ahead. Proceed another 200m and take a left at the roundabout onto rte. de Paris. The road immediately curves to the right and goes up the hill. You'll find the hostel 250m ahead, just after the road curves to the right again (25min.). The hostel has bright, simple 2- to 9-bed rooms, a kitchen, and a huge dining room. Breakfast 20F/€3.05. Dinner 49F/€7.47. Sheets 20F/€3.05. Reception M-F 8-10am and 5-8pm, Sa-Su 6-10pm. Lockout 10am-6pm. Curfew off-season 11pm; ask for a key if you'll be late. Dorms 49F/€7.47.

Hôtel des Halles, 23 rue du Mur (☎02 98 88 03 86; fax 02 98 63 47 96). In the middle of the *centre ville,* overlooking the marketplace at pl. Allende. From the train station, walk to pl. Emile Souvestre (see **Orientation,** above). Bear slightly to the right onto rue Carnot and take the first right onto rue du Mur. The hotel is on the right, at the entrance to pl. Allende. The rooms are being renovated; ask for a newer one. Breakfast 32F/€4.88. Singles 180F/€27.44, with shower 200F/€30.49; doubles 200F/€30.49, with shower 220F/€33.55. Extra bed 40F/€6.10 and extra person 20F/€3.05. MC/V.

Hôtel du Port, 3 quai de Leon (☎02 98 88 07 54; fax 02 98 88 43 80). As its name indicates, is directly across the street from the town's port, on the quieter side of the viaduct. Follow directions to pl. Emile Souvestre and turn left toward pl. des Otages. Hug the left-hand sidewalk and pass under the viaduct. Staying to the left, you'll pass through pl. Cornic and pl. de Gaulle. As soon as you see the water, the hotel is immediately on the left (20min.). Bright, spiffy rooms, all with full bathrooms and satellite TVs, some with great views of the port. Breakfast 30F/€4.57. Singles 185-210F/€28.21-32.02; doubles 210-230F/€32.02-35.06. Extra bed 40F/€6.10.

Camping à la Ferme, in Croas-Men (☎/fax 02 98 79 11 50). Worth the 7km walk. From the center of town, follow signs first to Plouigneau and then to Garlan, and then look for the sign. The campsite will be past Garlan on your left. The owners, 3rd-generation farmers of this land, want you to love their farm. To this end, they offer breakfast in the 1840s farmhouse, a petting farm, tractor rides for kids, and sell fresh yogurt and cider. Reception 8am-10pm; gates open 24hr. Open Apr.-Oct. 25F/€3.81 per site, 16F/€2.44 per person, children under 7 13F/€1.98. Electricity 16F/€2.44. Pets 5F/€0.76.

FOOD

There are many places to eat in **quartier St-Mathieu** and on **rue Ange de Guernisac.** For crêperies and inexpensive restaurants, head to **rue au Fil.** Saturday brings an all-day **market** that stretches from pl. des Otages to pl. Allende, spilling over into neighboring streets where local craftsmen sell their wares. A Marché Plus **supermarket** is on rue de Paris (open M-Sa 7am-9pm, Su 9am-noon).

SIGHTS AND ENTERTAINMENT

The **Circuit des Venelles,** a walking tour through medieval Morlaix, is the best way to see the city. The steep, sometimes stairwayed alleys (*venelles*) were the city's main thoroughfares in ancient times. They lead you past Morlaix's churches, wooden architecture, and views, along with all the sights listed here. The tourist office has a map of the circuit and theatrical tours of the *venelles* in summer.

The **viaduct,** 58m high and 285m long, is Morlaix's most visible sight. Though the airy walkway is now closed to the public, you can get a good view of steep, near-vertical Morlaix from its gates. **La Maison de la Duchesse Anne,** across pl. Allende on rue du Mur, commemorates the Queen's 1505 visit to the city. The house is a prime example of a Morlaisienne *maison à pondalez* (lantern house). (☎02 98 88 23 26. Open July-Aug. daily 10am-6:30pm; Apr.-May Tu-Sa 10am-noon and 2-5:30pm; June and Sept. 10am-noon and 1-6pm. 10F/€1.53, ages 10-18 5F/€0.76, under 10 free.) The collection at the **Musée des Jacobins,** in the 13th-century Jacobin church on pl. des Jacobins, mixes traditional Bretonalia like *lits-clos* (cabinet-like beds used from the 17th to early 20th centuries) with works by Rodin. The museum contains one of the few existing statues of Ankou (the Breton figure of death) as well as a mummy, though you may want to steer clear of the sarcophagi if you have a weak stomach. (☎02 98 88 68 88. Open July-Aug. daily 10am-12:30pm and 2-6:30pm; Easter-June and Sept.-Oct. W-M 10am-noon and 2-6pm, Sa 2-6pm; Nov.-Easter W-M 10am-noon and 2-5pm, Su 2-5pm. 26F/€3.97, students 13F/€1.98, children under 12 free. Families 40F/€6.10. Joint ticket with Maison 30F/€4.57, students 20F/€3.05.)

The **Ty Coz** pub, 10 venelle au Beurre, is close to everything of interest in Morlaix. If Brittany produced "Brocéliande II: The Bar," this would be it; there's Breton music, Breton beer, and the tables are thick cylindrical sections of trees. (☎02 98 88 07 65. Open M-Sa 11am-1am, closed Th mornings.) The bar-brasserie **Café de L'Aurore,** 17 rue Traverse, attracts those of all ages and has an **Internet** kiosk with *télécarte* access (1F/€0.15 per min.). (☎02 98 88 03 05. Open M-Sa 7:30am-1am.)

NEAR MORLAIX

FORET D'HUELGOAT

Although **Argoat** (ar-gwah) means "wooded country" in Breton, centuries of clearing have made this one of the least forested regions in France. Only a few scattered plots remain of the great oak and beech forest where menhir-carvers once lived. Brocéliande (see p. 506), Merlin's legendary stronghold, is one; Huelgoat (wel-gwaht), meaning "high forest" in Breton, is another. The boulder-strewn, rugged forest enjoys significant governmental protection as part of the **Parc Régional d'Armorique,** which stretches 70 hectares eastward from the coast. On the eastern edge of a sparkling lake, the tiny village of the same name (pop. 1700) serves as a pit stop for hikers; the area's too hilly and rough for comfortable biking. The park service has excellent topographic maps (available at the tourist office for 6F/€0.92) that include hiking tours. There are scrupulously marked trails from one *gîte* to the next (about 50F/€7.62 per night).

The forest's marvels include the **Mare au Sangliers** (Pond of Boars), a tree-lined pool at the base of an intricate rock structure, and the **Roche Tremblante,** a 137-ton rock monster balanced precariously on the hillside. Guides (July-Aug. only) somehow set the entire thing a-trembling with a tap in just the right place. Most impressive is the **Grotte du Diable** (Devil's Grotto), a cave formed by building-sized boulders that hang over the raging Argent river.

In town, you'll find the **tourist office** beside the **Moulin du Chaos,** a mill next to a tumble of boulders along the Argent river. From the bus stop, facing the 8 à Huit, turn right, take your first left, and the office will be on your right (2min.). The office has a list of *chambres d'hôte* (150-250F/€22.90-38.13) within 15km of town. They also have regional maps and information on the grottoes. (☎02 98 99 72 32. Open July-Aug. M-Sa 10am-noon and 2-5pm; Sept.-June until 4pm.)

Huelgoat is best visited as a daytrip, but if you decide to stay, check out the in-town **Camping Municipal du Lac,** rue du Général de Gaulle. From the bus stop, facing the 8 à Huit supermarket, turn left and go to the end of the square. Take the first right onto rue du Docteur Jaco, then left onto rue du Général de Gaulle (the road closest to the lake); the campsite is past the lake on the right (10min.). It has 75 some lake sites and a pool in summer. (☎02 98 99 78 80. Reception M-Sa 9am-11am and 4:15-7:30pm, Su 9-10:30am and 5:45-7:30pm, but you can get a spot at any hour. Open June 15-Sept. 15. 17F/€2.59 per person, children under 7 10F/€1.53. 20F/€3.05 per tent. Electricity 11F/€1.68.) Huelgoat's **market** is on pl. A. Briand and along rue du Lac (1st and 3rd Th of the month, 8am-1pm); the alternate Thursdays host a smaller version. Across from the bus stop on pl. A. Briand is a small 8 à Huit **supermarket** (open M-Sa 8am-12:30pm and 2:30-7:15pm, Su 9am-noon).

CAT buses (☎02 98 93 06 98) go to **Morlaix** (1hr.; M-Sa 2-3 per day, one on Su with no return until M; 36F/€5.49) and **Quimper** (70min., 3-5 per week, 43F/€6.56), stopping by the church on pl. A. Briand. The **post office** is on rue de Cieux. (☎02 98 99 73 90. Open M-F 9am-noon and 2-5pm, Sa 9am-noon.) **Postal code:** 29690.

ROSCOFF

Although the ferries streaming into Roscoff (pop. 3688) are its longtime livelihood, the town has completely evaded "harbor blight." The turreted houses of the port area and the attractive beaches on either side of the town are noteworthy, but Roscoff's prime location and famous thalassotherapy (spa treatments involving fresh, heated seawater) centers are its true prizes. Roscoff is also the prime embarkation point to the nearby gem Ile de Batz, which is tantalizingly close.

ORIENTATION AND PRACTICAL INFORMATION. Roscoff's port is the center of the action. Turn right after fully exiting the bus station and make an immediate right onto rue Ropartz (unmarked). Follow the scent of the sea and the signs to the *centre ville* (you'll be bearing left more than right). **Brittany Ferries** (☎02 98 29 28 00; www.brittany-ferries.fr) sends boats to **Plymouth, England** and west to **Cork, Ireland,** while **Irish Ferries** (☎02 98 61 17 17; fax 02 98 61 17 46; shamrock@wanadoo.fr) serves **Rosslare, Ireland** (see **Getting There,** p. 63, for details of service). Both offer Eurail discounts of up to 50%. **SNCF trains** and **buses** go from the station to **Morlaix** (30-45min., 7-11 per day, 46F/€7.02 for train) with connections to **Brest** and **Paris. CAT buses** (☎02 98 90 68 40) go to **Morlaix** (30-45min.; M-Sa 3-4 per day, 1 on Su; 45F/€6.86) and **Quimper** (2hr., 2 per day, 100F/€15.25).

The **tourist office,** 46 rue Gambetta, set back slightly from the center of the port, has transportation schedules, walking tours, maps, info on *chambres d'hôte,* plus a shiny visitor's guide. (☎02 98 61 12 13; fax 02 98 69 75 75. Open July-Aug. M-Sa 9am-12:30pm and 1:30-7pm, Su 10am-12:30pm; Sept.-June M-Sa 9am-noon and 2-6pm.) A **laundromat** is at 23 rue Jules Ferry. (☎02 98 78 32 13. Open daily 9am-8pm.) Though you shouldn't need a **bike** in Roscoff itself, you can rent one at **Cycles Desbordes,** 13 rue Brizeux. (☎02 98 69 72 44. Bikes 40-60F/€6.10-9.15 per day.) The **post office,** on 17 rue Gambetta, offers **currency exchange.** (☎02 98 69 71 28. Open July-Aug. M-F 9am-12:30pm and 1:30-5:30pm, Sa 9am-12:15pm; Sept.-June M-F 9am-noon and 2-5:30pm, Sa 9am-12:15pm.) **Postal code:** 29680.

ACCOMMODATIONS, CAMPING, AND FOOD. Budget hotels are in short supply in Roscoff, so you might do best to head straight to the youth hostel on the Ile de Batz (see below), which is only 15 minutes away by ferry. If you decide to spend the night on the mainland, there are two excellent options. The **Hôtel d'Angleterre,** 28 rue Albert de Mun, is in an old mansion that has retained its original Breton furniture and stained-glass windows in the restaurant downstairs. An adjacent sunroom looks onto the enormous, beautiful backyard garden. (☎02 98 69 70 42; fax 02 98 69 75 16. Breakfast 35F/€5.34. Singles and doubles 188F/€28.67, with toilet 230F/€35.06, with bath 295F/€44.99; 3- to 4-person rooms 248F/€37.82, with toilet 290F/€44.23, with bath 355F/€54.14. Apr.-May and Sept.-Oct. prices 15-20F/

€2.29-3.05 lower. Open Apr.-Oct.15. AmEx/MC/V.) **Camping de Kérestat Peoc'h,** rue de Pontigou, is on the estate of a 15th-century manor. With a 19th-century labyrinth for a backyard, a tower built under Louis XIV, remnants of Gallo-Roman walls, and flower-tufted wilds stretching to the sea, this campground is almost reason enough to visit Roscoff. The estate and its tennis courts are open to campers. (☎/fax 02 98 69 71 92. Open June 28-Sept. 2. Reception 10am-noon and 5-8pm. 35F/€5.34 per person, 40F/€6.10 per tent. With car: 24F/€3.66 per person, under age 16 12F/€1.83, 40F/€6.10 per tent, 14F/€2.13 per car. Electricity 16F/€2.44.)

Restaurants serving seafood *menus* (80-100F/€12.20-15.25) line the port, and there is a **market** every Wednesday morning on quai Auxerre, but those in the know head for **Ti Saozon,** 30 rue Gambetta, an upscale crêperie with good prices (12-46F/€1.83-7.02). (☎02 98 69 70 89. Open Tu-Sa 6:30-9:30pm. MC/V.)

SIGHTS. This spa town was not made for the budget-conscious—sitting by the port is probably the cheapest activity around, but there are a few worthwhile free sights. The 16th-century **Eglise Notre-Dame de Kroaz-Batz,** with its turreted spires, two-tiered belfry, and massive, golden Baroque choir, merits a look. (Open daily 9am-noon and 2-7pm.) For fans of alternative agriculture, the new **Algoplus factory,** zone de Bloscon, and the **Thalado Comptoir des Algues,** rue Victor Hugo, harvest seaweed for the production of cooking products and cosmetics. Each provides free tours of their facilities with slightly different emphases: Algoplus' 45-minute visits cater to consumers with a brief video and general explanation of the beach-to-table process. (☎02 98 61 14 14. Tours July-Aug. M-F 10, 11am, 3, 5pm; Sept.-June call for info. Open M-F 9am-noon and 2-6pm.) Thalado's workshops focus on tidal impact, biodiversity of local algae, the uses of seaweed, and cooking lessons. Both offer tastings at the end. (Thalado ☎02 98 69 77 05. Workshops M-Th 5:45pm, available in English. Call first. Open M-Sa 9am-noon and 2-7pm.)

On the far right of the port is the **Pointe St-Barbe,** a tall rock outcropping wrapped in spiralling stone steps and crowned with a white chapel, which provides a wonderful panoramic view of the coast, the port, and the Ile de Batz. To get a better sense of the environs of Roscoff, which are well worth the minimal effort involved in a visit, take one of the 1½-3hr., or 6-12km, walking tours explained in the free *Circuits Pedestre* brochure, available at the tourist office.

ILE DE BATZ

Just 15 minutes off the coast from Roscoff, this tiny, wind-battered island has an unmistakable appeal. Thanks to unusual meteorological phenomena, Batz experiences quite temperate weather. So as clouds build over Roscoff, the skies over Batz often stay deep blue and cloud-free. This intimate isle shows few signs of civilization, making it ideal for anyone searching for a profound sense of serenity.

ORIENTATION AND PRACTICAL INFORMATION. Two **ferry** companies connect Roscoff and Batz in 10 to 15 minutes. (**Armein** ☎02 98 61 77 75 and **CFTM** ☎02 98 61 78 87.) Boats leave from the port during high tide or from the long walkway extending into the harbor (extra 5min. walk) at low tide. (June 26-Sept. 10 departs Roscoff 8am-8pm, Batz 7am-7:30pm, every 30min.; Sept. 11-June 25 8-9 each way per day. 38F/€5.80 round-trip, ages 4-12 19F/€2.90.) On the island, there are free trail maps at the **tourist office,** in the *mairie;* turn left out of the port and follow the signs. (Open Sept.-June daily 9am-noon and 2-5pm; **annex** at port open July-Aug. M-Sa 9am-1pm and 2-5pm.) The **laundromat** is in a private home 50m to the left as you face the supermarket (open daily 8am-9pm). The **post office** is up the hill in the center of town; look for the signs. (☎02 98 99 73 90. Open M-F 9:30am-noon and 1:30-4:30pm, Sa 9:30am-noon.) **Postal code:** 29253.

ACCOMMODATIONS AND FOOD. To reach the **Auberge de Jeunesse Marine** after leaving the ferry, face the Hôtel Roch Ar Mor and take the road that goes sharply uphill immediately to the left of the hotel. There are clearly marked signs leading to the hostel in about five minutes, uphill and eventually on your right. Perched on a hill, the five-building hostel has amazing views of Roscoff as well as access to a private beach down the hill. In July and August, the hostel doubles as a sailing school–call ahead to enroll in a course. (☎02 98 61 77 69; fax 02 98 61 78 85. Breakfast 20F/€3.05. Dinner 49F/€3.47. Sheets 20F/€3.05. No lockout or curfew. Reception 6:30-7:30pm. Open Apr.-Oct. Beds 49F/€7.47, bunk cots in big tent 39F/€5.95, camping 33F/€5.03.) Overlooking the port, **Ti Va Zadou** is expensive, but a good value. From the ferry, head left toward town and follow the signs. The stone house with light blue shutters is at the top of the hill, on the right fork just before the church. The four guest rooms are decorated with lovely old dark wood furniture. (☎02 98 61 76 91. Breakfast included. All rooms with bath. Open Mar.-Nov. 15. Singles 230F/€35.08; doubles 300F/€45.75; 2-room family suite 390-450F/€59.48-68.63. Reserve at least a month in advance July-Aug.) The **Hôtel Roch Ar Mor,** facing the port, lets ten spacious singles and doubles, some with magnificent views, as well as larger family rooms for up to six people. The dock-side location makes up for the scarcity of showers; there's exactly one. (☎02 98 61 78 28; fax 02 98 61 78 12. Breakfast 35F/€5.34. Reception 8am-8pm. Rooms 225F/€34.31. Extra bed 65F/€9.91.) The grassy, wind-scoured **Terrain d'Hébergement de Plein Air,** on the beach near the lighthouse, is the only legal campground on the island. Head toward the town center, keeping it to your right and the water to your left, then follow the signs to the campsite or to the *phare*, or lighthouse (45min.). As there are no official sites, finding a spot is sort of a free-for-all, but there's plenty of room. There are three little beaches but only two toilets, two sinks, and one shower. (☎02 98 61 75 70. 6F/€0.92 per person, 3F/€0.46 per child, 6F/€0.92 per tent.)

At the highest point in town is a **8 à Huit supermarket.** (☎02 98 61 78 79. Open July-Aug. M-Sa 9am-1pm and 2:30-8pm, Su 9am-12:30pm; Sept.-June Tu-Sa 9am-12:30pm and 2:30-7:30pm, Su 10am-12:30pm.) **A l'Abri du Vent,** 50m from the hostel and overlooking the channel on the other side of the island, serves crêpes and galettes with a heftier filling than most (11-34F/€1.68-5.19). Try the creamy *bord de mer* with shrimp and calamari (34F/€5.19), with some delicious cider (23F/€3.51 per half-liter) to wash it down. (☎02 98 61 79 31. Open July-Aug. daily noon-3pm and 7:30-10:30pm; Easter-June and Sept.-Oct. closed Tu. MC/V.)

SIGHTS AND HIKES. The best way to see the Ile de Batz is to take the *sentier côtier*, 14km of trails that follow the coastline. The tourist office has maps, but the trails are well-marked, and on an island this size, it's hard to get lost. The trails are technically private property, but that doesn't stop most from using them. They run past the *côte sauvage* on the west side of the island, along small white sandy beaches, over massive rocks, and beside inland lakes. The hike is easy and well worth the four hours it takes. You can find the trails from any point on the island by heading toward water or by following signs from the port.

West of the town center is a **lighthouse** with great views of the island, Roscoff, and the occasional ferry Channel ferry. Be ready for a workout–there are 190 steps to the top, where you'll likely brave the howling wind. (Open July-Sept. 15 daily 1-5:30pm; June and Sept. 16-30 Th-Tu 2-5pm. 10F/€1.53, children over 6 5F/€0.76.) At the southeast tip of the island, a **botanical garden** is named for Georges Delaselle, a Parisian transplant who decided in 1897 that Batz needed a little exotic plantlife. (☎02 98 61 75 65. Open July-Aug. daily 1-6pm; Apr.-June and Sept. W-M 2-6pm; Oct. Sa-Su 2-6pm. Guided visits Su at 3pm 33F/€5. 26F/€4, students and seniors 23F/€3.5, children 13F/€2.)

Slightly inland, to the west of the garden, stand the ruins of the 12th-century **Chapelle Ste-Anne,** first the site of a Viking structure in AD 878. During the **Fête de Ste-Anne,** on the last Saturday in July, everyone on the island comes out to light a massive bonfire on the dunes as part of the largest celebration of the year. The festivities are followed by a more solemn mass in the chapel the next morning, perhaps to atone for the previous night's festivities.

BREST

Brest was transformed into a somber wasteland after its 1944 destruction by Allied bombers as they drove out the occupying German flotilla. Now home to the French Atlantic Fleet, Brest (pop. 156,217) has slowly replaced its toppled historic buildings with concrete ones. But despite its reputation as one of the dreariest places in Brittany, the city is slowly being rejuvenated, with an active downtown and a summer concert series. Brest now combines the pleasures of a major port and a university town, and possesses one of the largest aquariums anywhere.

TRANSPORTATION

Trains: pl. du 19*ème* Régiment d'Infanterie (☎02 98 31 51 72). To: **Morlaix** (64F/€9.76); **Nantes** (244F/€37.21); **Paris** (382F/58.26 or 444F/€67.69); **Quimper** (30min., 5 per day, 45F/€6.86); **Rennes** (1½hr., 15 per day, 170F/€25.93). Info and reservations M-F 8:30am-7:30pm, Sa 8:30am-7pm, Su 9:30am-7pm.

Buses: in front of the train station (☎02 98 44 46 73). To: **Crozon** and **Camaret** (1½hr.; M-Sa 2 per day, Su 1 per day; 58F/€8.85); **Quimper** (1¼hr.; 4 per day, 1 on Su; 88F/€13.42); and **Roscoff** (30-45min., 7-11 per day, 29F/€4.42). Open July-Aug. M-F 7am-12:30pm and 1-7pm, Sa 7:15-11am and 1-6:30pm, Su 8:45-10:15am, 1-2pm, and 5:15-7:45pm; Sept.-June M-F 7am-12:30pm and 1-7pm, Sa 8am-1:15pm and 2:30-6:30pm, Su 6-7pm.

Ferries: For ferry lines serving Brest, see **Ouessant** (p. 533) or **Crozon** (p. 535).

Local Transportation: Bibus, 33 av. Georges Clemenceau (☎02 98 80 30 30). Service from about 6am-8pm after which erratic service by a special letter-designated route runs until about 10pm, F-Sa until midnight. Buses run infrequently, particularly in the summer months, so plan ahead. Ask at the tourist office or the Bibus *"point d'accueil"* at the Hôtel de Ville (M-F 8:15am-12:15pm and 1:15-6:45pm, Sa 9am-noon and 1:30-6pm) for a bus map and a book-sized schedule. Buy tickets on the bus: 6.50F/€0.99, *carnet* of 10 52F/€7.93, full-day 19F/€2.90, students 51F/€7.78 for one week.

Taxis: Allô Taxis, 234 rue Jean Jaurès (☎02 98 42 11 11).

ORIENTATION AND PRACTICAL INFORMATION

To the right of the train station, av. Georges Clemenceau leads to the tourist office and the central **pl. de la Liberté,** the main terminal for the city's internal bus system. **Rue Jean Jaurès,** to the north of the *place,* is prime shopping territory, but exercise caution at night. **Rue de Siam,** to the south of the *place,* is the city's most vibrant street. Bookshops, clothing stores, markets, and bars spill out onto the thoroughfare overlooking the water. The city's only remaining **old quarter** is across the space-age Pont de Recouvrance (Bridge of Recovery) at the end of rue de Siam.

Tourist Office: pl. de la Liberté (☎02 98 44 24 96; fax 02 98 44 53 73), near the Hôtel de Ville. Can make hotel and ferry reservations. Free map and info on food, sights, and tours, *Jeunes à Brest* for young people. Open June 15-Sept. 15 M-Sa 9:30am-12:30pm and 2-6:30pm, Su 2-4pm; Sept. 16-June 14 M-Sa 10am-12:30pm and 2-6pm.

Laundromat: Point Blue, 7 rue de Siam (☎02 98 46 27 08). Open daily 8am-9:30pm. **Bleu Ocean,** 140 rue Jean Jaurès (☎06 07 33 03 53). Open M 12:45-9pm, Tu-Sa 8am-9:30pm.

Police: 15 rue Colbert (☎02 98 43 77 77).

Hospital: av. Foch (☎02 98 22 33 33).

Internet Access: @cces.cibles, 31 av. Clemenceau (☎02 98 46 76 10). Cyberdeath-seeking pre-pubescent males. 20F/€3.05 per hr. Open M-Sa 11am-1am, Su 2-11pm.

Post Office: rue de Siam, near the tourist office on pl. Général Leclerc (☎02 98 33 73 07). **Currency exchange.** Open M-F 8am-7pm, Sa 8am-noon. **Poste Restante code:** 29279. **Postal code:** 29200.

ACCOMMODATIONS AND CAMPING

Brest is a haven for the budget traveler, with oodles of inexpensive hotels and one of the swankiest hostels in France. Call 2-3 weeks ahead in July and August.

Auberge de Jeunesse (HI), 5 rue de Kerbriant (☎02 98 41 90 41; fax 02 98 41 82 66), about 4km from the train station, near Océanopolis, next to the artificial beach in Le Moulin Blanc. Leave the train station, walk past the bus station, cross the street, and head left down the street to the bus stop. Take bus #7 (6.50F/€0.99) to its final stop at "Port de Plaisance" (M-Sa first bus 6:45am, last 7:30pm; Su first bus 2pm, last 5:45pm). With your back to the bus stop, go left toward the beach, take an immediate left, and follow signs to the hostel; look for a sign in Breton reading "ostaleri ar yaouankiz." Looks like an IKEA ad set in the tropics. Rémy, the renaissance man/caretaker, can answer any and all questions. Ping-pong, foosball, and TV room. Kitchen. Breakfast included. Dinner 49F/€7.47. Reception M-F 7-9am and 5-8pm, Sa-Su 7-10am and 6-8pm. Lockout 10am-5pm. July-Aug. curfew midnight; Sept.-June 11pm; ask for a key if you'll be late. Beds 74F/€11.29.

Hôtel Astoria, 9 rue Traverse (☎02 98 80 19 10; fax 02 98 80 52 41), off rue de Siam. From the station, walk straight ahead, across av. Georges Clemenceau, onto av. Amiral Reveillre, which bears slightly to the left at the first intersection to become rue Voltaire. Take your fourth right onto rue Traverse. The hotel will be on your right (8min.). Central, quiet, and spotless. Modern rooms and helpful staff. Call ahead, especially July-Aug. Local discounts. Breakfast 36.08F/€5.50. Shower 26.24F/€4. Reception M-Sa 7am-11pm, Su 8am-noon and 6-11pm. Singles and doubles 150.87F/€23, with shower 249.26-282.06F/€38-43, with bath 288.62F/€44; triples 301.74F/€46. MC/V.

Abalis Hôtel, 7 av. Georges Clemenceau (☎02 98 44 21 86; fax 02 98 43 68 32). Exit the train station, turn right onto av. Georges Clemenceau, and the hotel will be directly on your right. Warm welcome at the front desk and great views of the Jardin Kennedy and the sea from the 3rd- and 4th-floor flower-boxed windows. The 3 simplest rooms share a full bathroom in a quiet annex, next to a little garden behind the central building. Wheelchair-accessible. Breakfast 35F/€5.34. Bar downstairs. Reception 7am-1am. Singles 140F/€21.34, with shower 240F/€36.59, with bath 260F/€39.64; doubles 160F/€24.39, with shower 265F/€40.40, with bath 285F/€43.45; "regal" quarters 400-450F/€60.98-68.62. Extra bed 40F/€6.10. MC/V.

Hôtel de la Rade, 6 rue de Siam (☎02 98 44 47 76; fax 02 98 80 10 51). The hotel's giant windows open onto the lively bar and restaurant scene of the rue de Siam near the water and the château. 44 immaculate and identically cheery rooms; quieter ones lie port-side. Breakfast buffet 35F/€5.34. All rooms have showers or baths. Singles 250F/€38.12; doubles 280F/€42.69; triples 310F/€47.26. MC/V.

Camping du Goulet (☎/fax 02 98 45 86 84), 7km from downtown Brest in Ste-Anne du Portzic; take bus #14 (dir: "Plouzané") to "Le Cosquer." Follow signs 100m down the side road to this large, often crowded site. Clean facilities, free hot showers, and glimpses of the ocean. Reception M-F 10am-noon and 3-7:30pm, Sa 9am-noon, longer hours July-Aug. Laundry 18F/€2.74. 22F/€3.35 per person, 13F/€1.98 per child under 7, 25F/€3.81 per tent. Electricity 11-16F/€1.68-2.44.

FOOD

Markets are held every day in various locations; the traditional and organic market on rue du Moulin à Poudre is notable (Tu 4-8pm and Sa mornings). Every Sunday morning, the area around St-Louis is closed down for an enormous market that sells everything from *moules* to melons at decent prices. There is a slightly pricey **indoor market** at Les Halles St-Louis, a block from rue de Siam (daily 7am-1pm and 4-7:30pm). Bakeries, pâtisseries, and vegetable stores can be found on and around rue de Siam, as can a **Monoprix supermarket,** at #49. (Open M-Sa 8:30am-7:30pm.)

L'Abri des Flots, 8 quai de la Douane, at the Port de Commerce, will satisfy all with its jovial ambiance, huge portions, and relatively low prices. They serve everything from galettes and crêpes (10-36F/€1.53-5.49) to seafood couscous (90F/€13.72). (☎02 98 44 07 31. *Menus* 95-145F/€14.48-22.11. Open noon-2pm and 7pm-midnight.) Brest is full of East Asian restaurants—for one with a French twist at some of the low prices, try **L'Eurasie,** 48 rue de Lyon. (☎02 98 44 78 00. 3-course lunch *menu* 59F/€9. Open M noon-2pm, Tu-Sa noon-2pm and 7-11pm.)

SIGHTS AND ENTERTAINMENT

Brest's **château** was the only major building to survive the bombings of World War II. In over 1700 strife-laden years, through Roman, Breton, English, French, and German occupations, no attacker has ever taken the château by force; it now holds the distinction of being the world's oldest active military institution. You can only enter the château through the **Musée de la Marine,** which occupies most of the sprawling fortress. Its dungeons are multiple massive towers that are filled with exhibits ranging from early copper scuba gear to torpedoes to a display chronicling the invention of the comic book pirate. (☎02 98 22 12 39. Open Apr.-Sept. Tu 2-6pm, W-M 10am-6:30pm; Oct.-Mar. W-M 10am-noon and 2-6pm. 30F/€4.57, students 20F/€3.05, ages 6-18 15F/€2.29, under 6 free.) In an unlikely site on a plot of land just above the port and its dozens of modern vessels stands the lone 14th-century tower that is the **Musée de la Tour Tanguy,** pl. Pierre Péron. The museum houses dioramas of historic (pre-1939) *Brestois* architecture and culture. (☎02 98 45 05 31. Open June-Sept. daily 10am-noon and 2-7pm; Oct.-May W-Th 2-5pm and Sa-Su 2-6pm. Free.) The rose-tinted **Monument Américain,** on rue de Denver, overlooks the Port du Commerce, a reminder of the Americans' landing in 1917. Locals joke that you need a passport to visit this American-built monument to the US, guarded by American officers on American-owned soil.

Océanopolis, port de Plaisance, welcomes you into its temperate pavilion, which emphasizes Brittany's marine life (much of it in tidal tanks) and the Iroise Sea (which surrounds the Ile d'Ouessant). There's a polar pavilion with a 3-D theater that opens onto the penguin playland, and a tropical pavilion, complete with coral reef, accessible by glass elevator. Océanopolis is huge and can have massive lines; don't expect to spend less than a day here. (From the Liberty terminal, take bus #7, dir: "Port de Plaisance," to "Océanopolis." Buses about every 30min. M-Sa until 7:30pm, 6.50F/€0.99. Aquarium ☎ 02 98 34 40 40; fax 02 98 34 40 69. Open Apr.-Sept. 16 daily 9am-7pm; Sept. 17-Mar. 9am-6pm. 90F/€13.72, ages 4-12 70F/€10.67, under 4 free.) Five minutes away is the beautiful **Conservatoire Botanique de Brest** park, with a trail stretching lengthwise through 3km of exotic plantlife, bamboo groves, and trickling brooks that seem miles away from the city.

Nightlife centers around the Port de Commerce, the pont de Recouvrance end of rue de Siam, and, to a lesser extent, the streets near pl. de la Liberté. You may want to avoid the neighborhoods on the other side of pl. de la Liberté after dark. Be aware that you have to walk through a deserted railyard to get to the Port de Commerce from the center of town. The popular **Jeudis du Port** concerts dominate the Port with the sounds of Breton music, rock, and jazz on Thursdays (July-Aug. 7:30pm-midnight). Locals pack **Aux Quatres Vents**, quai de la Douane, rocking the boat-bar from 10pm to 1am. (☎ 02 98 44 42 84. Open M-Sa 10am-1am, Su 2pm-1am.) The similarly sea-themed **Le Tour du Monde,** port du Moulin Blanc, near the aquarium, is owned by a famous navigator and draws crowds with cheap beer, mussels, and great port views. (☎ 02 98 41 93 65. Open daily 11am-1am.) The young, fresh crowd in **Casa Havana,** 2 rue de Siam, munches tapas and mingles amidst tropical plants and pounding Latin music. (☎ 02 98 80 42 87. Cuban cocktails 25F/€3.81; beer 20F/€3.05. Open daily noon-2:30pm and 7:30-11:30pm; bar open 10am-1am.)

ILE D'OUESSANT

As the westernmost point in France, windswept Ouessant (pop. 951; *Enez Eussa* in Breton) is an isolated haven for hikers and naturalists, an hour's boat ride from the nearest point of mainland Brittany. Ouessant's jagged rock formations mysteriously rise up in the middle of grazing grounds covered in miniature wildflowers and grazing sheep.

PRACTICAL INFORMATION. Two **ferry** companies offer service to Ouessant. Buy tickets at the port or at the Brest tourist office, and reserve in advance in summer. **Penn Ar Bed** sails year-round between **Ouessant** and **Le Conquet** (1¼hr.), on the western end of the peninsula, and then a further hour on to **Brest.** It also serves the islands of Molène and Sein. (☎ 02 98 80 80 80; www.penn-ar-bed.fr. Leaves Brest 1-2 times per morning, and the Ile d'Ouessant 1-2 times per evening. July-Aug. departs from and returns to Le Conquet 4-6 times per day. Brest-Ouessant round-trip 189F/€28.81, students 168F/€25.62, children 114F/€17.38; Le Conquet-Ouessant 159F/€24.24, students 135F/€20.59, children 96F/€14.64. Reservations required; arrive 30min. before departure.) **Finist'mer's** "fast ferries" connect Ouessant to **Camaret** (1hr.), and **Le Conquet** (30min.). (☎ 02 98 89 16 61; www.finist-mer.fr. Depart Camaret July-Aug. 9:30am; Apr.-June and Sept. 8:45am; return leaves 5:30-6:15pm. Le Conquet to/from Ouessant July-Aug. 4-6 times per day; Apr.-June and Sept. 2-3 times per day. 152-180F/€23.17-27.44, students 130-154F/€19.82-24.70, children 4-16 86-102F/€13.11-15.55. Some 60F/€9.15 one-way tickets available July-Aug.) To get to **Le Conquet,** take the **Cars de St-Mathieu bus** (☎ 02 98 89 12 02) from **Brest** (40min., 27F/€4.12). It's very difficult to coordinate the bus schedule with Finist'mer departures. Both ferry companies charge 40F/€6.10 each way for bikes, so consider renting on the island.

Boats dock at **Port du Stiff,** 3.5km from **Lampaul,** the main town on the Ile d'Ouessant. **Riou** (☎ 02 98 48 81 57) and **Jean Avril** buses (☎ 02 98 48 85 65) await the boats' arrival at the port and take you into town in a few air-conditioned minutes (both 10F/€1.53). On foot it's a 45-minute stroll. Four companies **rent bikes** at the port (60F/€9.15 per day). You can rent by the hour in Lampaul (15-25F/€2.29-3.81).

Lampaul's **tourist office,** near the church in the center of town, sells a pedestrian guide (15F/€2.29) to the island with 4 routes that cover every inch of the coastline in 1½-3hr. hikes. They also sell a separate guide to the island's bike paths since cycling is forbidden on the foot paths. The office also houses the only **cash machine** on the island. (☎02 98 48 85 83; fax 02 98 48 87 09; www.ot-ouessant.fr. Office open July-Aug. M-Sa 9:30am-6pm, Su 9:30am-12:30pm; Apr.-June and Sept. M-Sa 10am-noon and 2:30-6pm, Su 10am-noon; Oct.-Mar. M-Sa 10am-noon and 2:30-5pm.) **Police** only operate on the island in July and August (☎02 98 48 81 61). The **post office** (☎02 98 48 81 77) is to the left of the church and 30m downhill. (Open June 15-Sept. 15 M-F 9:15am-12:30pm and 2-5:15pm, Sa 9-12:15am; Sept. 16-June 14 M-F 9:30am-noon and 2-5pm, Sa 9am-noon.) **Postal code:** 29242.

ACCOMMODATIONS AND FOOD. It's a good idea to make hotel reservations in advance, as tourism is slowly but incessantly encroaching on the island. The **Auberge de Jeunesse d'Ouessant** is just a five-minute walk from the tourist office and the center of Lampaul. Take the stairs to the right of the SPAR supermarket across from the church and turn right onto the first road the stairs bring you to (not at the top of the stairs). The hostel is on your right up the hill, across from a garage. 48 beds in sunny, clean 2- to 6-person rooms, a communal kitchen, and a dining area with views of the water. (☎02 98 48 84 53 or 06 81 23 72 95; fax 02 98 48 87 42. Breakfast included. Sheets 20F/€3.05. Dorms 80F/€12.20, students and under age 25 70F/€10.67.) The **Centre d'Etude du Milieu Ouessantin,** an environmental studies and ornithological center, doubles as a hostel. From Lampaul's tourist office, bear right onto the road just past the supermarket and follow the signs for the Musée des Phares. Continue on the same road to the center, which is at Keridreux on the left, the last major building before you reach the lighthouse (30min., in addition to the hike to Lampaul). The beds and facilities aren't as spiffy as those at the Auberge, but it's just down the road from the lighthouse and the spectacular coast. In July and August, you can also reserve a place in one of their nature hikes by calling in advance. (☎02 98 48 82 65; fax 02 98 48 87 39. Reception M-F 8:30am-noon and 1:30-5:30pm. Sheets 20F/€3.05. Reserve early, especially for July. Beds in 4-5 person rooms 72F/€10.98, students 58F/€8.85, children under 15 56F/€8.54. For each additional night up to 5, price is reduced 3F/€0.46.) **Roc'h Ar Mor** has spacious blue and yellow bedrooms and bathrooms, in a prime seaside location in the center of Lampaul. (☎02 98 48 80 19; fax 02 98 48 87 51. Breakfast 48F/€7.31, 35F/€5.33 for children. Singles and doubles with bath 290-450F/€44.21-68.60; triples 350-450F/€53.36-68.60; quads 420F/€64.03; discounts Oct.-Dec. Extra bed 50F/€7.64. Handicapped-accessible.) **Camping Municipal** is 2km from the port on the main road, on the left about 300m before the church in Lampaul. (☎02 98 48 84 65. Laundry 15F/€2.29. Reception July-Aug. 7am-10pm; call ahead in the off-season. Open Apr.-Sept. 16.50F/€2.52 per person, under 7 8F/€1.22; 16.50F/€2.52 per tent, 20F/€3.05 bed in communal tent.)

A **SPAR supermarket** is next door to the tourist office (open M-Sa 8:30am-7:30pm, Su 9:30am-12:30pm). There is also a small market, **Le Marché des Iles,** 50m from the campground. (☎02 98 48 88 08. Open M-Sa 8:30am-7:30pm, Su 8:30am-12:30pm.)

SIGHTS. You really have to walk Ouessant to appreciate the rugged simplicity of its landscape. Some bike trails exist, but for safety reasons, it is strictly forbidden to bike along the coast. A good hiking companion is the complete and accurate tourist booklet of coastline paths (15F/€2.29), which contains details of all of the ruins and rocks along each route. If you only have time to choose one path, take the 14km northwest trail to the **Pointe de Pern,** whose breathtaking rock formations rising from the ocean are the westernmost point in Europe.

The northwest path takes you past Ouessant's two museums, which, unlike the coast, are easily accessible by bike. The **Musée des Phares et Balises,** in du Créac'h, once Europe's most powerful lighthouse, is devoted to the history of lighthouses and maritime signaling. The exhibit includes two short films on lighthouses in Brittany and their caretakers, and displays dozens of intricate lights that have now been retired from use. (☎02 98 48 80 70. Open May-Sept. daily 10:30am-6:30pm; Oct.-Mar. Tu-Su 2-4pm; Apr. Tu-Su 2-6:30pm. 25F/€3.81, children 8-14 15F/€2.29, under 8 free. Joint ticket with Ecomusée 40F/€6.10, children 8-14 25F/€3.81.) The **Ecomusée and Maison du Niou,** 1km northwest of Lampaul, is comprised of two buildings: the first contains traditional local women's clothing, and the second is a replica of a traditional *ouessantine* home. (☎02 98 48 86 37. Hours same as Musée des Phares. 20F/€3.05, children 8-14 12F/€1.83.)

CROZON PENINSULA

Jutting out into the ocean between Léon to the north and La Cornouaille to the south, the virtually uninhabited *Presqu'île de Crozon* (Crozon Peninsula) tempts outdoorsmen of every persuasion. Its rugged, sloping interior tumbles toward a coastline alternating between vast sandy beaches and unusual rock formations. A dense web of trails lined with *gîtes d'étape* facilitates hiking, which is the best way to explore the forest and coastline. Cycling opportunities abound, though the hilly turf makes for a demanding ride. Scuba diving, snorkeling, and kayaking are also options on the tiny peninsula. The tourist offices sell maps of *circuits de randonnées* (hiking trails) for specific parts of the region for 5F/€0.76 (all 14 routes 77F/€11.74). Hitchers report easy success all over the peninsula, but *Let's Go* does not recommend hitchhiking.

The peninsula's major towns are **Crozon, Morgat,** and **Camaret.** Most sights accessible from a town are in or near Morgat; Camaret, the most urban, has good campgrounds and the wonderful Hôtel Vauban. Most locals consider Crozon-Morgat as a single town, the latter being just a 2.5km walk. The two towns share multiple services and you'll likely need to stop by both before you head out on (or off) the road. From Brest, **Vedettes Armoricaines** sails to **Le Fret** on the peninsula (4km from Crozon, 6km from Camaret) and then shuttles passengers to the towns. (☎02 98 44 44 04. 45min.; Apr.-Oct. 3 per day; 50F/€7.62, with shuttle bus 57F/€8.69. Office open daily 9am-noon and 2-5pm.) **Société Maritime Azenor** runs between Le Fret and Brest at similar times and also offers tours of Brest and dinner cruises. (☎02 98 41 46 23. 30min.; July-Aug. 4 per day, June and Sept. 3 per day; 50F/€7.62, round-trip 90F/€13.72l; children 4-16 30F/€4.57, round trip 60F/€9.15; children under 4 free. Bike charge 25F/€3.81; round-trip 40F/€6.10. MC.) **Effia Voyageurs** (☎02 98 93 06 98) connects **Crozon** and **Camaret** to **Brest** (1½hr.; 2-3 per day, 1 on Su; 58F/€8.85) and **Quimper** (1¼hr., 2-5 per day, 58F/€8.85). Getting from town to town is more difficult. **Buses** run between **Camaret** and **Crozon** on their way to and from Quimper (4-6 per day, 11F/€1.68), but you need to walk or bike from Crozon to **Morgat.**

CROZON AND MORGAT. The somewhat industrial-looking town of Crozon (pop. 7900) holds little of cultural interest, but has enticing glimpses of the Bay of Douarnenez, which laps up against the cliffs upon which the town is perched. Extending from the base of Crozon's cliffs (and from the end of the inter-town road), the pebbly Plage de Portzic pushes into the larger, sandy Plage de Morgat. The adjacent bd. de la Plage leads to Morgat's town center, a half-kilometer down the beach. Buses to Crozon stop at the **tourist office,** which has road and trail maps and lodging information. (☎02 98 27 07 92; fax 02 98 27 24 89; crozon.maison.du.tourisme@wanadoo.fr. Open July-Aug. M-Sa 9:30am-7pm, Su 10am-12:30pm; Sept.-June M-Sa 9:15am-noon and 2-6pm.) Morgat's summer-only tourist office, pl. d'Ys, offers the same map and same info as Crozon's. (☎02 98 27 29 49. Open July-Aug. M-Sa 10am-7pm; Sept.-June M-Sa 10am-noon and 3-6pm.)

Crozon has a large number of supermarkets per capita. The most central is the **Shopi,** a sizable market despite its tiny facade on rue Alsace-Lorraine. (Open M-Sa 8:30am-12:30pm and 2:30-7:30pm, Su 9am-12:30pm; July-Aug. M-Sa 8:30am-8pm, Su 9am-1pm.) E. Leclerc, Intermarché, and Casino are all a five-minute walk from the center of town on Bd. de Pralognon. The only market in Morgat is the modest **Proxi** at 4 pl. d'Ys, near the tourist office. (Open July-Aug. M-Sa 8am-1pm and 2-8pm; Sept.-June M-Sa 8am-12:30pm and 3-7:30pm.) On the road from Crozon to Morgat (literally at the town line at the bottom of the hill), you can rent bikes at **Nature Evasion,** 79 bd. de la France Libre. (☎02 98 26 22 11. 50F/€7.62 per half-day, 70-80F/€10.68-12.20 per day, 350-490F/€53.38-74.73 per week. Open June-Sept. daily 9am-8pm; Oct.-May 9am-7pm.) A huge **laundromat** is at 50 rue Alsace-Lorraine. They can even press and fold your camping gear, if you so desire. (☎02 98 26 19 28. Open July-Aug. M-Sa 8:30am-12:30pm and 2-8pm; Sept.-June Tu-Sa 9am-noon and 2-7pm.) The **police** are on rte. de Camaret (☎02 98 27 00 22). The small **Centre Medical St-Yves** is on rue St-Yves, near the tourist office (02 98 27 08 10). Morgat is home to the only public computer on the *presqu'île.* This crusty keyboard is in the beach-side bar **Le Relais des Pêcheurs,** bd. de la Plage, just before the port. (☎02 98 27 04 02. 1F/€0.15 per min., minimum 10F/€1.53. Open daily 10am-midnight.) The spiffy, new Crozon **post office,** at 55 rue Alsace-Lorraine has **currency exchange.** (☎02 98 27 06 39. Open M-F 9am-noon and 2-5:15pm, Sa 9am-noon.) **Postal code:** 29160.

The **Hôtel du Clos St-Yves,** 61 rue Alsace-Lorraine, has the most reasonably-priced (though mildly musty) rooms in town. (☎02 98 27 00 10; fax 02 98 26 19 21; www.presquile-crozon.com/le-clos-saint-yves. Breakfast 35F/€5.34. Reception June-Sept. 7am-10:30pm; Oct.-May 7am-9pm. Doubles 150F/€22.88, with shower or bath and toilet 250F/€38.13; triples 330F/€50.31. MC/V.)

A few kilometers south of Morgat, down rue de la Cap de la Chèvre, in the village of St-Hernot, is the plush **Gîte St-Hernot.** Near the trailhead for the Cap de la Chèvre, this *gîte* rents private doubles with fully stocked kitchens and immaculate three-part bathrooms. (☎02 98 27 15 00. Breakfast 27F/€4.12. Doubles 55F/€8.39.) About 2km outside of Crozon, on the way to Camaret, is the **Gîte de Lescoat.** Head towards Ronscanvel from Crozon and look for the white sign for Lescoat on your left, along with a little brown bed sign. There are two *meublés* to be rented by groups for a week or longer, and a *gîte de randonnée,* rented by the bed and by the night. (☎06 03 28 83 23. *Gîte* 50F/€7.62 per night. *Meublés* 1800F/€274.43 per week for 2-4 people, 2800F/€426.89 per week for 5 people. Open June-Sept.)

The **Centre de Plongée ISA,** at the port de Plaisance in Morgat, past the beach and to the left, offers scuba diving (day and night), snorkeling lessons, and tours. Medical certificate may be required. (☎02 98 27 05 00; www.perso.club-internet.fr/centrisa. Daily excursions 115-230F/€17.54-35.06. Open daily 9am-noon and 2:30-6pm, later with advance notice.) Next door is the **Centre Nautique de Crozon and Morgat (CNCM),** which rents anything a waterbaby could want: windsurfers (160F/€24.39 per 2hr.; the recreational devices, not the suntanned beach boys); "fun boards" (200F/€30.49 per 2hr.); catamarans (360F/€54.89 per 2hr.); kayaks single (110F/€16.77 per 2hr.) and double (150F/€22.90 per 2hr.). (Main office ☎02 98 16 00 00; fax 02 98 16 00 01. Open Tu-Su 2-7pm.)

The smooth **Plage de Morgat** spans up to ¼km of sand and shells. The **Plage du Porzic,** a quick walk from the main beach, has access to the smaller caves and to a hiking trail that leads to the top of **Pointe des Menhirs.** The menhirs themselves were unfortunate casualties of WWII. For devotees of rocks and blacklights, the **Maison des Minéraux,** rte. de Cap de la Chèvre, about 4km out of town on D155 just before St-Hernot, has the largest European collection of funky fluorescent minerals. The museum also organizes half-day hikes to many interesting rock formations in the region. Call ahead to reserve. (☎02 98 27 19 73. Open July-Sept. 15 daily 10am-7pm; Sept. 16-Apr. M-F 2-5:30pm; May-June M-Sa 10am-noon and 2-5:30pm, Su 2-5:30pm. 26F/€3.96, students 20F/€3.05, ages 8-14 16F/€2.44.)

A highlight of this peninsula is the spectacular **Cap de la Chèvre,** at the end of the peninsula, linked to Morgat Port by a 14km series of paths. You can stick to the main path (the "circuit"), or find a smaller trail running toward the water and follow the clearly blazed *"sentier côtier"* (coastal path), more challenging but twice as rewarding. The trail passes through young pine forests, along pebbly cliffs overlooking the ocean, and around the natural springs and coves of the peninsula. You can get to the trail from almost any point between Morgat and the Cap; look for the numerous access signs along the road. Tuesdays from mid-July through August bring rock and jazz to the beach for the *Mardis de Morgat* concert series.

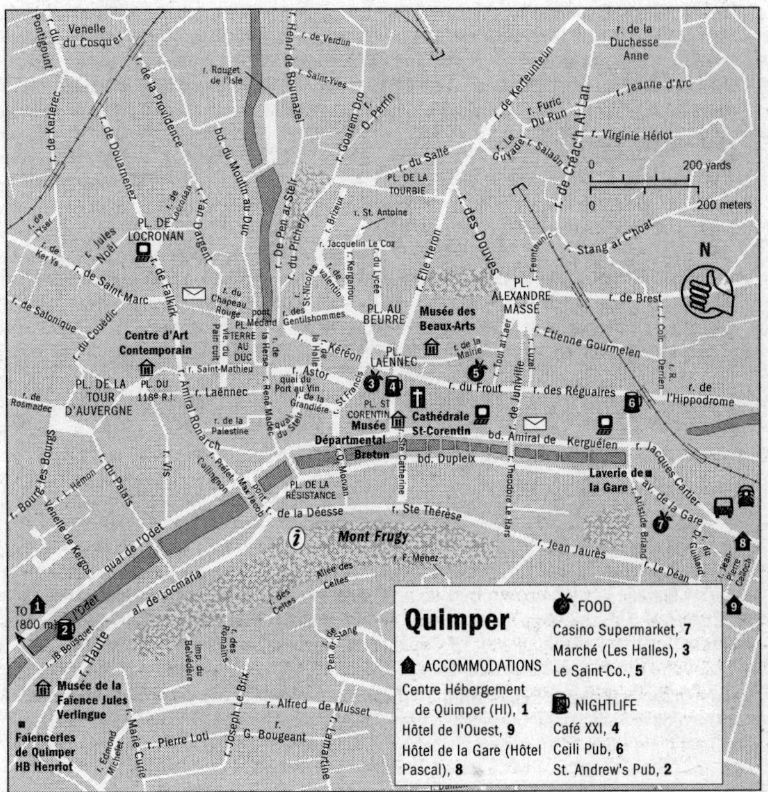

QUIMPER

Quimper (kem-PAIR, pop. 63,000), ancient capital of the Cornouaille kingdom, is reminiscent of Paris, with its central waterway lined by stately homes, and its theater and cathedral occupying opposite banks of the river Odet. However, Quimper (or "Kemper" in Breton), is also among the most aggressively Breton cities in the region. Many street signs appear in both languages, most masses are conducted in Breton, and one high school even teaches exclusively in the old tongue. Breton *faïencerie* (stoneware) is hand-painted in Quimper just as it was 300 years ago, and each year between the third and fourth Sundays of July, the city celebrates its links to tradition in the *Festival de Cornouaille*.

TRANSPORTATION

Trains: av. de la Gare (☎08 36 35 35 35, the main SNCF information line). To: **Auray** (1hr., 83F); **Brest** (1½hr., 4 per day, 84F/€12.81); **Nantes** (2¾hr., 4 per day, 172F/€26.22); **Paris** (4¾hr., 8 TGVs per day, 391F/€59.61 or 454F/€69.22); **Rennes** (2¼hr.; 10 per day, 4 TGV; 178F/€27.14 plus 10F/€1.53 TGV reservation); and **Vannes** (95F/€14.48). Info office open M-Sa 8:15am-7pm.

Buses: next to the train station (☎02 98 90 88 89). To: **Brest** (1¼hr.; M-Sa 4 per day, 2 on Su; 82F/€12.50); **Pointe du Raz** (1½hr.; M-Sa 2-4 per day, 2 on Su; 80F/€12.20 round-trip); **Pont-Aven** (1¼hr.; M-Sa 3 per day, 2 on Su; 59.50F/€9.07); and **Roscoff** (2hr., July-Aug. 1 per day, 140F/€21.35).

Local Transportation: QUB, 2 quai Odet (☎02 98 95 26 27). **Buses** (tickets 6F/€0.91; day pass 19F/€2.90; *carnet* of 6 33F/€5.03; *carnet* of 10 50/€7.62F) run 6am-7:30pm. Bus #1 serves the hostel and campground. The office has schedules and a map of the bus lines. Open M-F 8am-12:15pm and 1:30-6:30pm, Sa 9am-noon.

Taxis: ☎02 98 90 21 21. In front of the station.

Car Rental: Hertz (☎02 98 53 12 34, reservations ☎08 03 86 18 61), across the street from the train station. Open M-F 8am-noon and 2-7pm, Sa 8am-noon and 2-6pm.

Bike Rental: MBK s.a. Lennez, 13 rue Aristide Briand (☎02 98 90 14 81), off av. de la Gare. Bikes 60F/€9.15 per half-day, 80F/€12.20 per day. Passport deposit. Open Tu-Sa 9am-noon and 2-7pm. **Torch'VTT,** 58 rue de la Providence (☎02 98 53 84 41) has more bikes. 50F/€7.62 per half-day, 100F/€15.25 per day. Open Tu-Sa 9:30am-12:30pm and 2:30-7pm.

ORIENTATION AND PRACTICAL INFORMATION

Quimper is in the heart of the Cornouaille region; rich farmland separates it from the sea and port towns about twenty kilometers to its south and west. The center of town is to the west of the train station, which is on the edge of town; from the train station, go right onto av. de la Gare and follow the river Odet (keeping the river and its numerous footbridges to your right). It will become bd. Dupleix and lead to pl. de la Résistance. The tourist office will be on your left, the *vieille ville* across the river to your right (10min.).

Tourist Office: 7 rue de la Déesse (☎02 98 53 04 05; fax 02 98 53 31 33; www.bretagne-4villes.com), off pl. de la Résistance. Free, detailed map. **Tours** of city in English (1½hr.; July-Aug. 1 per week; call to reserve). Office open July-Aug. M-Sa 9am-7pm, Su 10am-12:45pm and 3-5:45pm; Apr.-June and Sept. 9am-12:30pm and 1:30-6:30pm; Oct.-Mar. 9am-12:30pm and 1:30-6pm.

Laundromats: Laverie Repasserie, 47 rue de Pont l'Abbé, about 5min. from the hostel. Open daily 8am-10pm, but you can't start machines after 8:45pm. **Laverie de la Gare,** 2 av. de la Gare. Open daily 8am-8pm.

Police: 1 rue de Pont l'Abbé (☎02 98 55 09 24).

Hospital: Centre Hospitalier Laënnec, 14bis av. Yves-Thépot (☎02 98 52 60 60).

Internet Access: CyberCopy, 3 bd. A. de Kerguelen (☎02 98 64 33 99), is close to the station. 30F/€4.57 per hr. Open M-Sa 9am-7pm. **CyberVideo,** 51 bd. A. de Kerguelen (☎02 98 95 31 56). 20F/€3.05 per 30min., 30F/€4.57 per hr. Open M-Sa 10:30am-noon and 2-8pm.

Post Office: 37 bd. A. de Kerguelen (☎02 98 64 28 28). **Currency exchange.** Open M-F 8am-6:30pm, Sa 8am-noon. **Branches** on chemin des Justices, 2min. from hostel, and on rue Châpeau Rouge. **Poste Restante:** 29109. **Postal code:** 29000.

ACCOMMODATIONS AND CAMPING

As lovely as the city center and river Odet are, don't count on being able to see them from your hotel room. Most budget travelers will find themselves relegated to declining neighborhoods on the outskirts of town, not always the safest or most appealing environment. Travelers should be particularly careful at night (and even on smaller streets during the day); Quimper's a big city with big-city problems. To skirt some of these problems, you may want to ask the tourist office about private homes offering bed and breakfast (doubles usually 150F/€22.90). In July and August, it's a good idea to make reservations in writing as early as possible.

Hôtel de l'Ouest, 63 rue le Déan (☎02 98 90 28 35), is your best bet in terms of price, location, and safety. Clean rooms and a welcoming atmosphere, in a lively part of an otherwise undesirable neighborhood. At night, stick to crowded streets when walking here from the train station. Breakfast 30F/€4.57. Shower 15F/€2.29. Singles 100F/€15.25; doubles with bath 190F/€28.97; quads with bath 250F/€38.12. MC/V.

Centre Hébergement de Quimper (HI), 6 av. des Oiseaux (☎02 98 64 97 97; fax 02 98 55 38 37). Take bus #1 from pl. de la Résistance (dir: "Kermoysan"). The hostel will be 50m up the street on your left. On foot, cross the river from pl. de la Résistance and go left on quai de l'Odet. Turn right onto rue de pont l'Abbé and continue past two major intersections until the roundabout; continue straight for 100m and the hostel will be on your left. Clean facilities. The hostel's at the end of a questionable street on the edge of town and, although the building is secure from the outside, individual rooms don't have locks. Breakfast 19F/€2.90. Sleepsack 15F/€2.29, sheets 20F/€3.05. Reception 8-11am and 5-9pm; call if arriving later. Bunks 50F/€7.62; singles 64F/€9.76.

Hôtel de la Gare (Hôtel Pascal), facing the train station (☎02 98 90 00 81). Modern, freshly redone rooms are set back from the noise and the traffic of the street and face an inner courtyard/parking lot. Nearly all rooms have bath, TV, and kitchenette. Breakfast 30F/€4.57. Singles 190F/€28.97; doubles 270F/€41.16; triples 300F/€45.74.

Campsite: Camping Municipal, av. des Oiseaux (☎/fax 02 98 55 61 09), next to the hostel. From the hostel, turn left and follow signs to the campground. A forested area with plenty of shade trees. Reception M-Tu, Th, and Sa 8-11am and 3-8pm; W and Su 9am-noon; F 9-11am and 3-8pm. 18.60F/€2.82 per person, 9.50F/€1.45 per child; 7.10F/€1.08 per car; 4.10F/€0.63 per tent. Electricity 16.40F/€2.50.

FOOD

The lively **covered market (Les Halles),** off rue Kéréon on rue St-François, always has some shops open to provide good bargains on produce, seafood, meats, and cheeses (as well as fabulous crêpes), but the earlier you get there the better. (Open M-Sa 7am-8pm, Su 9am-1pm.) An **open market** is held twice a week. (W in Les Halles, Sa outside Les Halles and in pl. des Ursulines; both open June-Aug. 9am-6pm, Sept.-May 9am-1pm.) A **Casino supermarket** is on av. de la Gare. (Open M-Sa 8:30am-7:30pm, Su 9:30am-1pm and 5-7:30pm.) On a quiet street just around the corner from the cathedral, the classy, modern bistro **Le Saint Co.,** 20 rue Frout, offers a tasteful (and tasty) variety of steak *plats* (60-90F/€9.15-13.72; 65-110F/€9.91-16.67 *menu*). If steak isn't your thing, try one of their creative and filling salads (38-60F/€5.79-9.15); omelettes (20-50F/€3.05-7.62); or mussels (45-50F/€6.86-7.62.) (☎02 98 95 11 47. Open July-Aug. daily 11:30am-midnight; Sept.-June 11am-2pm and 6pm-midnight. MC/V.)

SIGHTS AND ENTERTAINMENT

The unmistakable, magnificent dual spires of the **Cathédrale St-Corentin,** built between the 13th and 15th centuries, mark the entrance to the old quarter from the quai. St-Corentin, Quimper's patron, is one of dozens of Breton saints not officially recognized by the Church. (Open M-Sa 8:30am-noon and 1:30-6:30pm, Su 8:30am-noon, except during mass, and 2-6:30pm.) **Mont Frugy,** next to the tourist office, offers an amazing view of the cathedral spires and some relief from the bustle of the city center. It's an easy hike, with numerous wooded walking trails.

The **Musée Départemental Breton,** 1 rue du Roi Gradlon, is housed in the former episcopal manor and may be entered through the cathedral garden. Finistère's history, archaeology, and ethnography are presented in clever exhibits. An elaborate display of traditional Breton clothing is a highlight. (☎02 98 95 21 60. Open June-Sept. daily 9am-6pm; Oct.-May Tu-Sa 9am-noon and 2-5pm, Su 2-5pm. 25F/€3.81, students 12F/€1.83, under 11 and on Su free. Tours July-Aug., at least 1 per day, 10F/€1.53; call for details and reservations.) The **Musée des Beaux-Arts,** 40 pl. St-Corentin, holds a collection of large-scale interpretations of Breton folktales and the joys and trials of everyday life. A fascinating exhibit about the poet and artist Max Jacob, a Quimper native killed in the Holocaust, contains portraits by several of his friends, including Picasso. (☎02 98 95 45 20. Open July-Aug. daily 10am-7pm; Sept.-June W-M 10am-noon and 2-6pm. Tours daily July-Aug.; call for information. 25F/€3.81, ages 18-26 and over 60. 15F/€2.29, under 18 free.) The **Musée de la**

Faïence, 14 rue J-B Bousquet has a permanent exhibit on Quimper's characteristic earthenware as well as temporary exhibits (☎02 98 90 12 72. Open Apr.-Oct. 27 M-Sa 10am-6pm.) But for a more hands-on experience, head to **Faïenceries de Quimper H. B. Henriot,** rue Haute. Henriot's studio allows visitors to tour the facilities and watch potters at work. (☎02 98 90 09 36. Open M-F 9-11:15am and 1:30-4:45pm; July-Aug. tours every 15min., Sept.-June every 30min. Closed F in June. Call in advance for English tours. 20F/€3.05, children 8-14 10F/€1.53, under 8 free.)

Come evening, *Quimpérois* of all stripes pour into the boisterous **Céili Pub,** 4 rue A. Briand. It's the kind of place where everybody knows your name and you'll be treated to the occasional live concerts of Breton music. (☎02 98 95 17 61. Open M-Sa 10:30am-1am, Su 5:30pm-1am.) The 21st century meets the 11th in glittering **Café XXI,** 38 pl. St-Corentin, across from the cathedral and next to the Musée des Beaux Arts. This popular daytime people-watching venue doubles as a glam night-spot, serving its "XXI" specialty (white rum, curaçao, and fresh citrus juice; 21F/€3.20) to its sophisticated clientele. (☎02 98 95 92 34. Open daily 8:30am-11pm.) **St. Andrew's Pub,** 11 pl. Styvel, is just across the river from rue de Pont l'Abbé. A breezy terrace next to the Odet is the perfect setting for a relaxed drink or snack, served by the pub's friendly managers. (☎02 98 53 34 49. Open daily 11am-1am.)

Those who miss the *Festival de Cornouaille* (see **Introduction**) can still catch Breton cultural celebrations. Every Thursday from late June to early September, the cathedral gardens, next to the Odet, fill with **Breton dancers** in costume, accompanied by lively *biniou* (bagpipes) and *bombarde* (similar to an oboe) players (9pm, 20F/€3.05). Quimper holds its **Semaines Musicales** during the first three weeks in August. Orchestras and choirs perform nightly in the Théâtre Municipal and cathedral, and during the last half of August brass bands fill the streets for the **Festival Extérieurs Cuivres;** call the tourist office for more information.

DAYTRIP FROM QUIMPER: LOCRONAN

***Effia Voyageurs** (☎02 98 93 06 98) drop in from **Quimper** (20min., 3 per day, 22F/€3.35). The **tourist office** is at pl. de la Mairie (☎02 98 91 70 14; fax 02 98 51 81 20; www.locronan.org.) Map of town and of the* circuit pédestre, *a walking path which passes by the principal sights. (Open July-Aug. daily 10am-7pm; Sept.-June M-F 10am-12:30pm and 2:30-7pm.) **Crédit Agricole** has a 24-hour **ATM** on rue du Prieurié.*

About 20km northwest of Quimper, medieval Locronan (pop. 827) sits high on a hill above the countryside, overlooking 16th-century houses, farms, and the ocean, and attracting 21st-century tourists and filmmakers alike. Stepping into the town's main square (the **Grand Place**) is like walking into a Celtic fairy tale. Its 14 sculpted and flower-studded houses, former homes of the town's wealthiest merchants and officials, have been the setting for more than twenty films. Locronan first established a successful sail-making industry, which outfitted the Spanish Armada and the East India Company, but the city now relies on the unstoppable patronage of tourists. Its past extends back to its ties to druidism, still celebrated by **Tromenie,** processions through the countryside that occur on the second Sunday of July.

NATURE LOVERS The black-and-white Breton flag bears a striking resemblance to the Stars and Stripes, which it long predates. Where the American flag has stars, the Breton flag has a mysterious figure: a trio of small diamonds at the top and an elongated one at bottom. These represent a caped ermine, symbol of the king of Brittany. Legend tells that the first king came across an ermine while hunting, and, taken by its beauty, pursued it to the edge of a bog. There the unfortunate animal turned around and declared that it would rather face death than the prospect of soiling its coat. Struck by the animal's gallantry—though not struck enough to save its life—the king insisted on placing its hide before him at every meal.

On the northern edge of the Grand Place is the **Eglise Priorale,** a 15th-century church around which the town is centered. Down the hill from the Grand Place, past the tiny stone houses on rue Moal, sits the smaller **Chapelle Notre-Dame de Bonne Nouvelle** (15th-16th century). The chapel used to be surrounded by the weavers' guilds in the liveliest quarter of Locronan and still guards a freshwater spring. Poster buffs will get a kick out of the **Musée de l'Affiche,** on venelle des Templiers, at the top of the hill above the church. The beautiful views of the countryside and nearby mansions make the uphill trek well worth it. (☎02 98 51 80 59. Open July-Aug. daily 10am-1pm and 2-6pm; Sept.-Oct. 11am-noon and 2-6pm. 20F/€3.05.) The chapel-capped **Montagne de Locronan,** 4km east of town, offers a stunning view of the countryside and the deep blue sea beyond.

NEAR QUIMPER: PONT-AVEN

Between Quimper and Quimperlé lies Pont-Aven (pop. 3000), a jewel immortalized on countless canvases, its air of the surreal unspoiled even by the tourists who descend upon the town in search of inspiration. The first to paint the town was Paul Gauguin (1848-1903), who, fed up with mainstream Impressionism, came here in 1886. Inspired by Gauguin, the Pont-Aven School, comprising 20 artists, developed into a movement emphasizing pure color, absence of perspective, and simplified figures. The town now claims some of the finest art galleries and museums in France, along with acres of woodland that inspired their contents.

The tourist office provides maps detailing a number of short hikes in the surroundings, many of them passing through places where these artists congregated. In the town center, you can follow the **Promenade Xavier Graal,** a series of bridges hovering over the swift river Aven on their way to the **Chaos de Pont-Aven,** a set of flat rocks around which the river swirls. A path through the tranquil **Bois d'Amour** (Lover's Wood) meanders along the Aven beneath the rich, dappled load of gnarled old trunks. The most enticing part of the walk in the woods is closest to town and runs next to the river. If you choose to do the entire circuit (about 40min.), you may want to start from the Chapelle de Trémalo, since it's all downhill from there! Above the woods, amidst thriving farmland, is the **Chapelle de Trémalo.** This simple 16th-century church has crumbling granite walls and a wooden roof, edged with lively, cherubic faces and one irreverent rear end. The chapel also houses the 17th-century polychrome crucifix that inspired Gauguin's "Yellow Christ." The **Musée de L'Ecole de Pont-Aven,** pl. de l'Hôtel de Ville, up the street to the left when facing the tourist office, showcases the works of Gauguin, Serusier, and many of the school's other artists. Those familiar with the northwestern tip of Brittany may experience a pleasant sense of *déjà vu*—canvases depicting the cliffs of Ile d'Ouessant and other regional attractions are prominently displayed on the museum's walls. (☎02 98 06 14 43. Open July-Aug. daily 10am-7pm; Apr.-Oct. 10am-12:30pm and 2-6:30pm; Feb.-Dec. 10am-12:30pm and 2-6pm. 25F/€3.81, off-season 20F/€3.05, students and those 13-20 15F/€2.29, under 12 free.)

Pont-Aven's few hotels cater to the same crowd that comes to town for the express purpose of leaving with less money and more paintings than they started with. So you might do best to make Pont-Aven a daytrip from Quimper or Concarneau. If you're willing to splurge a little to stay in a restored farm house, Mme. Larour's **gîte d'étape** on rue Kermentec (a mere 600m walk from the town or the chapel) is the perfect place. Surrounded by enough flowers to inspire any artist, the *gîte* has a kitchen, common areas, and large, exquisitely furnished, sky-lit bedrooms. (☎02 98 06 07 60. Breakfast included. 3 doubles, each 270F/€41.16. Children 80F/€12.20.) The tourist office may also be able to help you find less expensive *chambres d'hôte* (160-200F/€24.39-30.49), depending on the season.

Pont-Aven is connected by **Transports Caoudal buses** (☎02 98 56 96 72) to **Quimper** (1¼hr., 3 per day, 38F/€5.79, 59.50F/€9.07 round-trip) and nearby towns. The **tourist office,** pl. de l'Hôtel de Ville, is a block from the bus stop on pl. Gauguin (turn away from the river and walk toward the square and the museum, beyond; the office is on the right side of the street). The staff sells a walking-tour guide (2F/€0.30), and organizes **tours** of the town and museum. The office can also provide information on the "Fleurs d'ajonc" folk **festival** on the first Sunday of August. (☎02 98 06 04 70; fax 02 98 06 17 25. Tours June-Sept. at 11am and 4:30pm; town 37F/€5.64, under 20 25F/€3.81; museum 32F/€4.88, under 20 20F/€3.05. Call to inquire about tours in English. Open July-Aug. M-Sa 9:30am-7:30pm, Su 10am-1pm and 3-6:30pm; Apr.-June and Sept. M-Sa 9:30am-12:30pm and 2-7pm, Su 10am-1pm; Oct.-Mar. M-Sa 10am-12:30pm and 2-6pm.)

QUIBERON

Connected to the mainland by just a narrow strip of land, this peninsula is almost overwhelmed in summer with tourists who come to sun themselves on the smooth stretch of the Grande Plage on the southern tip, or to surf, kayak, and sail on the smaller, but spectacular, beaches on the eastern side of the peninsula. Stunning Belle-Ile is only a 45-minute ferry ride away, but the countryside of Quiberon (pop. 4500) offers many opportunities for excursions. Save time for a hike or bike ride along the peninsula's wave-battered, seaward-facing coast, the Côte Sauvage.

TRANSPORTATION AND PRACTICAL INFORMATION. To take the train toward Quiberon, you'll have to stop at **Auray** (☎02 97 24 44 50) and take a bus from there. Trains run through Auray on their way to **Brest, Paris,** and **Quimper** (schedules vary; call 08 36 35 35 35 for info). **TIM buses** run M-Sa from **Auray** (1hr., 7-9 per day, 31F/€4.73), **Carnac** (30min., 7-9 per day, 22F/€3.35), and **Vannes** (2hr., 7-9 per day, 52F/€7.93). For info, call **Cariane Atlantique** in Vannes (☎02 97 47 29 64). **Quiberon Voyages,** 21 pl. Hoche (☎02 97 50 15 30), runs trips all over the province, including an afternoon excursion to **Carnac** and **Vannes** (130F/€19.82) and one full-day trip to **Concarneau, Pont-Aven,** and **Quimper** (220F/€33.54). **CMNN,** in Port Maria, serves **Belle-Ile** from the **gare maritime,** quai de Houat. (☎08 20 05 60 00; fax 02 97 31 56 81. 5-13 per day; round-trip tickets 127.50-141F/€19.44-21.50, students 79.50-87.50F/€12.12-13.34, seniors 88.50-97.50F/€13.49-14.87. Bikes 65F/€9.91, cars 615-996F/€93.76-151.85.) Cruise the beachfront or explore the Côte Sauvage on **bikes,** tandems, pedal carts, or scooters from **Cyclomar,** 47 pl. Hoche (☎02 97 50 26 00). In July and August, there is an **annex** at the train station. (Bikes 39-59F/€5.95-9 per half-day, 52-83F/€7.93-12.65 per day, 224-352F/€34.15-53.67 per week. Scooter 157F/€23.94 per half-day, 234F/€35.68 per day (plus insurance). Moped 93F/€14.18 per half-day, 147F/€22.41 per day. 10% off with ISIC card or a note from the youth hostel. Credit card, personal ID, or passport deposit. Open July-Sept. daily 7:30am-9pm; Oct.-June 8:30am-12:30pm and 1:30-7:30pm. Annex open July-Aug. daily 8:30am-8pm.)

To find the **tourist office,** 14 rue de Verdun, turn left from the train station and walk down rue de la Gare. When you see the church ahead on your left, bear right down rue de Verdun (5min.). The staff distributes a detailed guide to six pedestrian tours of the peninsula. (☎02 97 50 07 84; fax 02 97 30 58 22; www.quiberon.com. Open July-Sept. M-Sa 9am-12:30pm and 2-7pm, until 8pm from Aug. 1-15, Su 9:30am-12:30pm and 3-7pm; Nov. and Feb.-June M-Sa 9am-12:30pm and 2-6pm; Dec.-Jan. M-Sa 9am-12:30pm and 2-5pm.) The **Centre Hospitalier du Pratel** (☎02 97 29 20 20) in Auray is the nearest hospital, but only has 24hr. service during July and August (Sept.-June, open until 8pm). The **Centre Hospitalier Bretagne Atlantique** in Vannes (bd. Maurice Guillaudot, ☎ 02 97 01 41 41) has year-round emergency service. The **post office,** pl. de la Duchesse Anne, has **currency exchange.** (☎02 97 50 11 92. Open July-Aug. M-F 9am-12:30pm and 2-5:30pm, Sa 9am-noon; Sept.-June M-F 9am-noon and 2-5pm, Sa 9am-noon.) **Postal code:** 56170.

ACCOMMODATIONS AND CAMPING. Quiberon is generally expensive, but the small, comfy, personal **Auberge de Jeunesse (HI),** 45 rte. du Roch-Priol, will silence any complaints. From the station turn left and take rue de la Gare toward the beach and the church. Turn left onto rue de Port-Haliguen, then right onto bd. Anatole France, and left on rte. du Roch-Priol. The hostel, will be on your left (12min.). Guillaume, the manager, lets 8-person rooms with a woodsy feel that'll take you back to summer camp. With the outdoor eating area, communal kitchen, and tents in the garden, you'll be making fast friends in no time. (☎02 97 50 15 54. Breakfast 19F/€2.90. Sheets 17F/€0.44. Reception 8:30-10am and 6-8:30pm. Open May-Sept. Bunks 51F/€7.78. Camping 32F/€4.88 per person, tents 7F/€1.07.) The central **Hôtel de l'Océan,** 7 quai de l'Océan, offers plain, bright, florally decorated rooms, some facing the harbor. An enormous sunny salon with views of the quai makes for a lovely place to people watch or just take in the scenery. (☎02 97 50 07 58; fax 02 97 50 27 81. Breakfast 36F/€5.49. Shower 10F/€1.53. Singles and doubles 180-200F/€27.44-30.49, with shower 250F/€38.12, with bath 280-300F/€42.69-45.74. Extra bed 80F/€12.20. MC/V.)

The campsite closest to the city is **Camping Municipal du Goviro.** Windswept and consequently a little dusty, it nonetheless provides the best access available to the quiet, intimate beach across the street that bears the same name. Make reservations, as it's almost always full in high season. (☎02 97 50 13 54. Reception July-Aug. M-Sa 8:30am-7:30pm, Su 9am-7pm; June and Sept.-Oct. 5 M-Sa 9am-12:30pm and 2-6pm, Su 9am-noon. Reservation deposit 224F/€34.15. Open Mar. 16-Oct. 14. 25F/€3.81 per tent, 12.50F/€1.91 per car; 18F/€2.74 per person, children under 10 12.50F/€1.91. Electricity 18F/€2.74. 10% reduction with *Carte Jeune*.) Just a bit farther from the beach, behind Goviro, is the slick, spacious, snack bar endowed, and well-landscaped **Camping Bois d'Amour.** (☎02 97 50 13 52; off-season ☎04 42 20 47 25. Reception July-Aug. 8:30am-8pm; Apr.-May and Sept. 9:30am-12:30pm and 2-6:30pm. Tent or caravan with car 40-81F/€6.10-12.35, tent without car 19-40F/€2.90-6.10; 25-45F/€3.81-6.86 per person, children under 10 15-25F/€2.29-3.81. Electricity 23F/€3.51.)

FOOD. Quiberon's many port-side eateries are prime territory for two particular gastronomic delights: as many kinds of seafood and shellfish as you can fit on your plate, and the lollipop-topped, caramel-like *niniche* candy. For a little taste of the sea or a biblical-size blowout, try **La Criée,** 11 quai de l'Océan. The fish are displayed in grisly ice cascades as you walk through the door. The *plateau gargantua*, an awesome array of oysters, crab, and other ocean-dwellers (295F/€44.98), is perfect for a large group. Otherwise, try the 88F/€13.42 three-course *menu*. (☎02 97 30 53 09. Open July-Aug. daily noon-2pm and 7-10:30pm; Sept.-Dec. and Feb.-June Tu-Sa noon-2pm and 7-9:30pm, Su noon-2pm. MC/V.) Down the quai toward the Grande Plage is **L'Elfenn,** 1 rue de Kervozes, a slightly less expensive alternative, with has great views of the port upstairs. (☎02 97 30 40 43, MC/V.)

The **Marché Plus** on rue de Verdun (open M-Sa 7-9pm, Su 9am-noon), and the **Casino supermarket,** closer to the hostel on rue de Port Haliguen (open M-F 9am-8pm, Sa 9am-noon), vie for your non-fish food dollars. There are also fresh produce **markets** Saturday mornings in pl. du Varquez, and Wednesday mornings at Port Haliguen from June 15-Sept.15.

BEACHES. The craggy Côte Sauvage is aptly named; this "savage" coastline stretches a wild and windy 10km along the western edge of the Quiberon peninsula. Though it seems as if the amazing views from the easy road cannot be surpassed, you must drop your car and take to the foot paths to fully enjoy these boulder-strewn beaches and eroded bedrock archways. But heed the signs marked *Baignades Interdites* ("swimming forbidden"); many have drowned in these tempting but treacherous waters. The flag system is as follows: green=safe supervised bathing; orange=dangerous but supervised bathing; red=bathing prohibited. There are SOS posts dotting the coastline with flotation devices attached. The weather here can be both as brutal and as fleeting as the crashing waves; storms assault the coast and then leave it to dry as quickly as they came.

Grande Plage is the most popular beach, while the small, rocky **plage du Goviro** appeals to those who prefer solitude over boardwalks. To reach it from the port, follow bd. Chanard east along the water as it becomes bd. de la Mer and then bd. du Goviro. The east side of the peninsula is dotted with a number of sandy beaches, perfect for sunbathing after a quick dip in the cool waters.

ENTERTAINMENT AND FESTIVALS. The beaches don't empty until it's too dark to see the volleyball. About 45 minutes later, a newly sand-free and still energized crowd heads to **L'Hemisphère Sud,** 4 rue du Phare, off pl. Hoche, the hottest bar in town. It's packed with young *Quiberonnais*, who shoot pool, drink, and dance until 2am. Wash that sand off carefully—black lights illuminate fluorescent murals covering every surface, including the bar. (☎02 97 30 51 76. Open July-Aug. daily 10pm-2am; Oct.-Apr. F-Su only.) **Le Nelson,** pl. Hoche, the local "rhumerie," (rum joint) may have walls covered with naval paraphernalia, but the boisterous crowd is more surfer than sailor, inundated with giddy teenage girls rather than hardened fishermens' wives. A zillion types of rum (18-50F/€2.74-7.62) and fabulous punch for 25F/€3.81. (☎02 97 50 31 37. Open daily noon-2am, closed Su from Oct.-Easter.) During the second week in August a **festival** called "La Flibuste," takes the town by storm, complete with dance, music, plays, and even pirates.

BELLE-ILE

The coast of Belle-Ile, just 45 minutes away from Quiberon, is even more breathtaking than that of its neighboring presqu'île. At least five boats depart daily from Quiberon's Port-Maria for Belle-Ile, an island also known as "Le Bien-Nommé" (the well-named). Throughout their long history, Belle-Ile's high cliffs, crashing seas, and heathered fields have attracted residents of all sorts, from menhir-carvers to monks, from pirates to German POWs. At 20km in length, Belle-Ile (pop. 4824) is large enough to make bike rental or a few shuttle rides necessary.

TRANSPORTATION. Boats dock on the northern coast at **Le Palais,** the island's largest town. The ferry ride takes 45 minutes, and you can take your bike along (round-trip 110F/€16.77). The other main towns—**Bangor, Locmaria,** and **Sauzon**—lie in the center, on the east coast, and on the northwest tip respectively. A shuttle system linking the four ports makes travel between them much easier, though there are fewer routes and buses in June and September than July and August. (**Le Palais** to **Bangor** 33min., 7 per day; to **Locmaria** 30min., 5 per day; to **Sauzon** 15-25min., 10 per day. Single ticket 16F/€2.44, 2-day pass 60F/€9.15; children 4-12 years old 10F/€1.53, 35F/€5.34. Tickets available on the bus or at **Point Taoi Mor,** quai Bonelle in Le Palais, ☎02 97 31 32 32; fax 02 97 31 33 31.) **Cars Verts,** Gare Maritime at Quiberon, runs one-day bus tours of the island, beginning in Le Palais and rapidly exploring all major towns and coastal hot spots before returning to Le Palais in the evening. (☎02 97 50 11 60. 70F/€10.67, students 60F/€9.15, children 5-14 years old 55F/€8.39, not including ferry to the island.) There is a clearly marked, well-kept trail running along much of the coast. Alternate bike routes are well-marked on smaller, more scenic, and occasionally unpaved roads. The most spectacular area, the island's own Côte Sauvage, is also accessible by boat (see **Quiberon Beaches,** p. 543, for safety info).

PRACTICAL INFORMATION: LE PALAIS. The **tourist office** is on the left end of the dock. The energetic staff distributes a thorough guide to the island (5F/€0.76), a comprehensive French brochure with hiking and biking plans, and a map (45F/€6.86) essential for exploring the island on foot or bike. They also have info on sailing, sea kayaking, and numerous other island activities. (☎02 97 31 81 93; fax 02 97 31 56 17; www.belle-ile.com. Open July-Aug. M-Sa 9am-8pm, Su 10am-12:30pm; Apr.-June and Sept.-Nov. M-Sa 9am-1pm and 2-6pm, Su 10am-12:30pm.) **Rent bikes** and mountain bikes at **Cyclotour,** quai de Bonnelle, near the tourist office. (☎02 97 31 80 68. Bikes 40-70F/€6.10-10.67 per half-day, 60-80F/€9.15-12.20

per day. Passport deposit. Open July-Aug. daily 8:30am-7pm; Sept.-June M-Sa 9am-noon and 2-7pm.) Those 14 and over can rent **mopeds** at **Au Bonheur des Dames,** quai Jacques Le Blanc. (☎02 97 31 80 52. 150-200F/€22.90-30.49 per half-day, 200-280F/€30.49-42.69 per day. Open daily 9am-7pm.) The **police** are at Les Glacis (☎02 97 31 80 22); the **hospital** (☎02 97 31 48 48) is in Le Palais. There is a **pharmacy** on rue de l'Eglise (☎02 97 31 81 30; fax 02 97 31 49 06). The **post office,** on quai Nicolas Foucquet across from quai Gambetta, has **currency exchange.** (☎02 97 31 80 40. Open M-F 9am-12:30pm and 2-5pm, Sa 9am-noon.) **Postal code:** 56360.

ACCOMMODATIONS AND CAMPING. The tourist office in Le Palais can help you find cheap rooms, and has info about the island's *chambres d'hôte*, rudimentary *gîtes d'étape*, and numerous campsites. Both the Palais campground and the hostel are near the citadel, a 5-minute walk, followed by a 5-minute uphill hike from Le Palais' port. Upon debarking from the ferry, look for rue J. Simon (it should be directly in front of you, perpendicular to the quai) and walk about a block to pl. de la République, where you'll see quai J. Le Blanc and the water ahead to your right. Follow quai Le Blanc to the first footbridge (it leads to the citadel). Cross the bridge, go up the steep hill directly ahead, and follow the road as it turns to the left. Keep going through the parking lot and take a right at the end; **Camping Les Glacis** will be on your right. You can also take the shuttle bus (5F/€0.76) from the port to the "Les Glacis" stop, which is not on the schedule. Perched on a hillside, the campground offers several sites with beautiful views of the port and the citadel. (☎02 97 31 41 76; fax 02 97 31 57 16. Reception July-Aug. 8am-8pm; Apr.-June and Sept. 9am-noon and 4-6:30pm. Reservation required July-Aug., recommended at all times. Open Apr.-Sept. 12.50-25F/€1.91-3.81 per tent, 12.50F/€1.91 per car, 4.50F/€0.69 per bike; 18F/€2.74 per person, 12.50F/€1.91 children under 10. Electricity 18F/€2.74. 10% reduction with *Carte Jeune.*) The large **HI hostel** is another seven minutes' walk up the same road on the right, just past the *gendarmerie* and down its own driveway to the right—follow the signs. The shuttle system also has an "Auberge de Jeunesse" stop (ticket 5F/€0.76). Suited to large groups, this hostel has fantastic facilities. The manager leads week-long hiking tours of the island that involve day hikes, which return to the hostel in the evening. To camp on the lawn, you must rent a tent. (☎02 97 31 81 33; fax 02 97 31 58 38; belle-ile@fuaj.org. Breakfast 19F/€2.90. Luggage storage (unlocked). Sleepsack 17F/€2.59, sheets 21F/€3.20. Reception 8:30am-noon and 6-8pm; July-Aug. 6-10pm. Open Mar.-Sept. and Nov.-Dec. Doubles 53F/€8.08 per person. Camping 42F/€6.40 per person.) **La Frégate,** quai de l'Acadie, in front of the dock, has small, cheap, and sunny, if somewhat musty, rooms, each individually named and decorated. Downstairs, a bright, gigantic sitting room has fabulous views of the port. (☎02 97 31 54 16. Breakfast 35F/€5.34. Reception Apr.-Nov. 15 8am until just after the last boat from Quiberon. Singles and doubles 140-190F/€21.35-28.97, with bath 250F/€38.12; triples with bath 290F/€44.21. MC/V.)

FOOD. A small **market** is held every morning in Le Palais at pl. de la République; on Tuesday and Friday it takes over the *place* (8am-1pm). There is a Super U **supermarket** on rue de l'Eglise. (Open M-Sa 8am-12:30pm and 3:30-7pm, Su 8am-noon; July-Aug. M-Sa 8am-1pm and 3-8pm, Su 8am-12:30pm.) **Traou-Mad,** 9 rue Willaumez in Le Palais, means "good things" in Breton, and offers plenty of them. Among the favorites are *galettes complètes* (7-74F/€1.07-11.28), dessert crêpes (*beurre-sucre* 11.50F/€1.75), and giant salads (42F/€6.40). (☎02 97 31 84 84. Open Apr.-Sept. daily 11am-2pm and 6-10pm. MC/V.)

SIGHTS AND FESTIVALS. The massive **Citadelle Vauban,** built in 1549 by Henri II to protect monks from pirates, grew to an impressive network of snaking passageways between 30-foot walls. Today, they protect a grass-roofed museum that dishes up the latest on Sarah Bernhardt, Monet, 400 German POWs housed here during WWI, and other celebs who have spent time on Belle Ile. (☎02 97 31 84 17. Open July-Aug. daily 9am-7pm; Apr.-June and Sept.-Oct. 9:30am-6pm; Jan. 11-Mar. 9:30am-noon and 2-5pm. 40F/€6.10, ages 7-16 20F/€3.05, under 7 free.)

Belle Ile's natural treasures lie scattered along the coastline. The **plage de Donnant** on the western coast, with its expansive dunes and mysterious stone facade, is the widest and most popular beach. Equally gorgeous are the pristine **plage Port-Maria,** on the eastern shore, and the powder-white **plage Grands Sables,** southeast of Le Palais. To see the more rugged side of the island's coastline, head 6km northwest from Le Palais to postcard-like **Sauzon.** The narrow port fills with sailboats, rocking gently on the turquoise water beneath. Gentle breezes (the remnants of gusts of wind softened by the nearby hills) bring salt-tinged air into the crisp white houses with multicolored shutters that line the port and face the mossy rock cliffs on the other side. Massive rock formations rise over the thunderous **Grotte de l'Apothicairerie,** southwest of **Pointe des Poulains** on the northern tip of the island, and at the **Aiguilles de Port Coton,** where needle-like rock formations shoot up through electric-green water.

From late July to mid-August, the **Festival Lyrique** brings Mozart concerts and several operas to the island (☎02 97 31 49 50; fax 02 97 3 42 78; www.belle-ile.net).

CARNAC

> I would express the irrefutable, indisputable, irresistible...Here is my opinion: the stones of Carnac are big stones.
>
> —Gustave Flaubert

Carnac (pop. 4487) is home to one of the world's most impressive series of ancient megalithic monuments, collectively the oldest prehistoric site in Europe. Carnac's rock formations come in various shapes and sizes, and many still go by their ancient Breton names. Here's a little glossary to get you going: **menhir:** from the ancient Celtic, a large upright stone (men = stone, hir = long); **dolmen:** a table-like structure which was used as a funeral chamber. Some are attached to **dolmen corridors,** which allowed the living to visit with the dead; **cairn** or **tumulus:** a pile of stones that may be on top of one or many dolmens. If you get confused, don't worry. If miles of monster rocks aren't your style, try small granular ones—the smooth stretch of beach is a great place to frolic and unwind.

TRANSPORTATION AND PRACTICAL INFORMATION. To get to Carnac, take the **TIM bus** (☎02 97 21 28 29, in Vannes) from **Auray** (30min., 9 per day, 23F/€3.51), **Quiberon** (30min., 7 per day, 22F/€3.35), or **Vannes** (1¼hr., 9 per day, 39F/€5.95). You can also take the **train** to **Plouharnel** and catch a bus from there (5min., 9 per day, 5F/€0.76). There are two bus stops (corresponding to two tourist offices): "Carnac-Ville" is convenient for the town and its sights; "Carnac-Plage" is close to the beach, in front of the main **tourist office,** 74 av. des Druides. (☎02 97 52 13 52; fax 02 97 52 86 10. Open July-Aug. M-Sa 9am-7pm, Su 3-7pm; June M-Sa 9am-12:30pm and 2-6:30 pm; May 9am-noon and 2-6pm.) To walk back to the town center, leave the tourist office and turn left onto av. des Druides. It will curve to your right and become av. de la Poste, which will lead to the **tourist office annex** at pl. de l'Eglise, just behind the church. (No phone or fax. Open Apr.-Sept.) **Bikes** are useful in this area; go to **Cycles Lorcy,** 6 rue de Courdiec. (☎02 97 52 09 73. 28-35F/€4.27-5.34 per half-day, 35-60F/€5.34-9.15 per day, 180-230F/€27.44-35.07 per week. Deposit 700F/€106.72 or passport. Open July-Aug. Tu-Sa 8:30am-noon and 2-7pm, Su 8:30am-12:15pm; Sept.-June Tu-Sa only.) For those who fare better on four wheels, the **Tatoovu bus** shuttles visitors from major sites to Carnac-Ville and Carnac-Plage. (Buses run June-Sept. daily 9:15am-1pm and M-Sa 2:30-8pm. Tickets 5F/€0.76 or 11 for 50F/€7.62, purchased on the bus. Ask tourist office for schedules.) The **police station** is at 40 rue St-Cornély (☎02 97 52 06 24). The **post office,** av. de la Poste, just outside the town center, has **currency exchange.** (☎02 97 52 03 90. Open July-Aug. M-F 9am-6pm, Sa 9am-noon; Sept.-June M-F 9am-noon and 2-5pm, Sa 9am-noon.) **Postal code:** 56430.

A REVERSAL OF FORTUNES At the beginning of the 20th century, the wealthiest inhabitants of Carnac lived in houses near the church in Carnac-Ville, where the land was best for farming, while the poor farmers near the beach lived on what little they could earn growing carrots and onions in the sandy soil. The growth of the tourism industry has brought with it an interesting twist of fate: the poor farmers have sold all of their land for the construction of beach-front property and are independently wealthy, while the fertile areas inland are now protected as part of the alignment sites. So, for once, the rich got poorer and the poor got richer.

ACCOMMODATIONS AND FOOD. Carnac is best as a daytrip, since hotel prices rise in summer. B&Bs and *chambres d'hôte* are the cheapest housing option; the tourist office has a list (doubles run 100-150F/€15.25-22.90). The most reasonably-priced, coziest hotel is **Hôtel Chez Nous,** 5 pl. de la Chapelle. From the Carnac town center bus stop, facing the road, turn left and head down rue St-Cornély toward pl. de l'Eglise. A block before the church, turn left onto rue de Courdiec, then right onto rue Kervarail. The hotel will be on your left, though you may have to go across the street to the right to find the exceptionally friendly owner. The two-room triples are beautifully decorated and perfectly clean. (☎02 97 52 07 28. Breakfast 36F/€5.49. Singles and doubles with shower 210-280F/ €32.02-42.68, July-Aug. 250-340F/€38.12-51.84; doubles with full bath 270F/€41.16, July-Aug. 310F/€47.26; triples 320-350F/€48.79-53.36, July-Aug. 370-390F/€56.41-59.46. MC/V.) **Camping Kerabus,** allée des Alouettes, off rte. d'Auray, is 10 minutes from the Alignements de Kermario. Hedges separate each campsite, and paths lead to the menhirs. (☎/fax 02 97 52 24 90. Bring your own toilet paper. Reserve well in advance July-Aug. Open Apr.-Sept. 15. Gates close at 10:30pm. 50F/€7.62 per person without car, July-Aug. 60F/€9.15. With car 17F/€2.59 per person, under 7 9F/€1.37. 29F/€4.42 per car, July-Aug. 36F/€5.49. Electricity 15F/€2.29.)

There's a **Marché U supermarket,** 68 av. des Druides, next to the beach and tourist office, and a **Casino** on av. des Salines, close to the city. (Both open M-Sa 8:30am-8pm, Su 8:30am-noon.) There's also a **Proxi** on rue St-Cornély, between the church and the Carnac *centre ville* bus stop. (Open Tu-Sa 8am-1pm and 3-7:30pm, Su 8:30am-1pm.) At the **market** behind the church at pl. du Marché, vendors sell clothing, in addition to meat, fish, fruits, and veggies. (W and Su 8am-1pm.)

SIGHTS. In the center of town, behind the church, is the **Musée de Préhistoire,** 10 pl. de la Chapelle. The museum showcases an impressive collection of tools, burial chamber contents, jewelry, and artifacts illuminating Brittany's history from 450,000 BC to the early Middle Ages. (☎02 97 52 22 04. Open June-Sept. M-F 10am-6:30pm, Sa-Su 10am-noon and 2-6:30pm; Oct.-May W-M 10am-noon and 2-5pm. 30F/€4.57; Oct.-Mar. 25F/€3.81; students 15F/€2.29; children under 10, unemployed, and disabled free. Combined admission to museum and tour of alignments 45F/€6.86, museum and Table des Marchands in Locmariaquer 30F/€4.57.)

The **Archéoscope,** just across the street from the Alignements du Ménec, provides a flashy, dramatic introduction to the region's dozens of megalithic sites, through the use of lasers, films, and life-size moving menhirs. From the museum, go back toward the church, take a right on rue St-Cornély, and another right a block later onto rue de Courdiec. Walk directly up the street (about 1km), then turn left onto route des Alignements and the Archéoscope will be ahead on your left. (☎02 97 52 07 49. Open July-Aug. daily 9am-6pm; mid-Feb. to mid-Nov. 10am-noon and 1:30-5pm. Showings in French every 30min., July-Aug. in English at 10:30am, 2:30, 6pm; call for off-season showings. 45F/€6.86, students and ages 13-18 30F/€4.57, ages 6-12 25F/€3.81, under 6 free.)

The alignments at Carnac are the most prominent example of the neolithic monuments that are scattered throughout the area. Built from 4500 to 2500 BC, Carnac's 3000 menhirs stretch along the horizon for 4km, steadily increasing in height as they extend to the west. Their origins have been traced back to a

Celtic myth, the legend of St. Cornély (who turned a Roman legion to stone as he fled from these persecutors of Christianity), and, more recently, archeo-astronomic indicators of important sunrises and sunsets. In any case, the closest menhirs to town are the **Alignements du Ménec,** the largest single collection of menhirs in the world. More than 1000 menhirs, some over 3m tall, stretch over 2km in a line along the horizon. The **Alignement de Kermario** stands adjacent to the **Géant du Manio** (a big rock) and the **Quadrilatère** (rocks in a square). Due to concerns about receding vegetation and erosion that could destabilize their foundations, fences have been constructed around them. Sheep still roam unfazed among the wonders, but most tourists keep to the observation boardwalk and surrounding hills. Call the **Centre d'Accueil** to reserve a spot in one of the guided tours. (☎02 97 52 89 99. Open July-Aug. daily 9am-10pm; Mar.-June and Sept.-Oct. 9am-6pm; Nov.-Feb. 10am-5:30pm. All hours are likely to change, so call in advance to check. Tours in French; occasionally in English. 25F/€3.81, students 20F/€3.05, under 12 free.)

LOCMARIAQUER

The port of Locmariaquer (pop. 1400) lies on the eastern base of a 4km peninsula that reaches out toward Arzon, across the Auray river, in an attempt to seal off the Gulf of Morbihan. Some of the world's oldest and most impressive neolithic structures can be found here, clustered between the port and the Grande Plage on the southwestern side of the peninsula. The town and its oyster industry have grown up around the lesser known of these monuments, leaving lone menhirs next to beaches and oyster farms, and surrounding dolmens with gardens and swing-sets.

TRANSPORTATION AND PRACTICAL INFORMATION. Getting here takes planning. There's one bus to town each evening and one that leaves early the next morning (except on market days, when there are two). Your best bet might be to take the bus to **Chat Noir** (4km to the north) and call one of Locmariaquer's two **taxi** drivers, Mlle. LeBayon (☎02 97 57 31 31) or Lucien Burguin (☎02 97 57 31 17) to pick you up (about 50F/€7.62). **Buses** run to **Chat Noir** from **Auray** (7 per day), **Quiberon,** and **Vannes** (7 per day) with the same frequency as those from **Carnac,** since it's on the same route. (**Cariane Atlantique** in Vannes: ☎02 97 47 29 64.)

Once in town, you can get to the major megalithic site with a mere five-minute stroll out of town. To get to some of the other dolmens scattered around the peninsula, or the Grande Plage on its southwestern shore, you may want to rent a bike at the **Elf Garage,** 7 rte. d'Auray, just up the street from the tourist office. (☎02 97 57 32 52. Open July-Aug. M-Sa; Sept.-June Tu-Sa. Half-day 25-37F/€3.81-5.64, full day 35-55F/€5.34-8.39, week 140-280F/€21.35-42.69.) Locmariaquer only has a **police** department from July to August (☎02 97 57 39 09); otherwise call Carnac's police (☎02 97 52 06 24). The nearest **hospital** is in Auray. The **post office** is at pl. de la Mairie. (☎02 97 57 13 00. Open M-F 9am-noon and 2-5pm, Sa 9am-noon.) Around the corner from the post office, you'll find the **tourist office,** 1 rue de la Victoire. The extraordinarily helpful staff will gladly give you a map and info on *chambres d'hôte,* campsites, and tours of the gulf. From June to September, they also run tours of the oyster park (*visites ostréicoles*) that can be combined with visits to the megaliths. (Call for tours. ☎02 97 57 33 05; fax 02 97 57 44 30. Open July-Aug. daily 9am-1pm and 2-6pm, Mar.-June and Sept. 10am-noon and 2-5pm.)

ACCOMMODATIONS AND CAMPING. Locmariaquer's six hotels offer only one real budget option. **Hôtel du Menhir,** 7 rue Wilson, provides very simple rooms (with sinks) above a quiet bar and restaurant about three minutes from the center of town. (☎/fax 02 97 57 31 41; le.menhir@wanadoo.fr. Breakfast 35F/€5.34. Reception 9am-9pm. Closed Feb. Singles 135F/€20.58; doubles 200F/€30.49. AmEx/MC/V.) The more central **Hôtel Lautram,** pl. de l'Eglise, has clean, bright rooms that face the church, as well as an annex with views of a garden. (☎02 97 57

31 22; fax 02 97 57 37 87. Breakfast 37F/€5.64. Open Apr.-Oct. Reception 8am-10pm. Double (only one) 200F/€30.49, with shower and toilet 310-360F/€47.26-54.89; quads 330-450F/€50.33-68.61. MC/V.) At **L'Escale,** all 12 rooms have some view of the water. Though the rooms are unexciting, the rustic restaurant has the nicest waterfront location in town. (☎02 97 57 32 51; fax 02 97 57 38 87. Breakfast 36F/€5.49. Open Mar. 28-Sept. Doubles 220F/€33.54, with shower 248F/€37.82, with shower and toilet 318F/€48.50; twin beds 352-370F/€53.68-56.43. MC/V.)

One and a half kilometers away from the center of town, **Camping Municipal "La Falaise"** has two hundred sites across the street from the beach. From the tourist office, head down rue de la Victoire toward the church. This becomes rue Wilson; proceed straight ahead at the multi-road intersection on to rte. de Kerpenhir. Continue past the hotel and the Marché Utile on your left, and Camping Kerpenhir on your right. La Falaise is on the right at the end of the street, just before you reach the beach. (☎02 97 57 31 59. Open Apr.-Sept. Reception June-Sept. 9am-noon and 4-6pm; call otherwise. 18F/€2.75 per person, under age 7 9F/€1.37. Site for tent 10.90F/€1.66. Car 8.60F/€1.31. Electricity 13.50F/€2.06.)

FOOD. Locmariaquer is proud of its *huîtres* (oysters). The only place you'll probably see them, though, is at the restaurant downstairs from your hotel room, or one of the two restaurants at the port. For the same view at a price you can stomach, head to **Le Relais des Mousquetaires,** rue de la Victoire. (Open July-Aug. daily 9am-8pm; Sept.-June M 10am-12:30pm and 4-7:30pm, Tu-Sa 9am-12:30pm and 3-7:30pm, Su 9am-12:30pm.) Or try **Spar Marché,** rue de la Plage. (Open July-Aug. daily 8am-1pm and 3-8pm; Sept.-June M-Sa 8:30am-12:30pm and 3-7:30pm, Su 9am-12:30pm.) If a picnic on the beach floats your boat, stop at the large **Marché Utile,** on the way to the campsite. (Open July-Aug. daily 8am-1pm and 2:30-8pm; June-Sept. M-Sa 8am-12:30pm and 2:30-7:30pm, Su 8am-12:30pm.)

SIGHTS. Locmariaquer's three greatest neolithic monuments lie side by side in an otherwise unremarkable field on a hill, half a kilometer inland from the port. The **Grand Menhir Brisé** (Great Broken Menhir), known by Bretons as the "men-er-gran," or "fairy stone," has a mysterious past that is gradually being uncovered by archaeologists. The once upright monolith stood a staggering 18m in height and weighed nearly 280 tons—but the stone from which it was made, orthogneiss, can't be found on the Locmariaquer peninsula. That's right, neolithic man had to drag the stone from somewhere else and erect this giant obelisk, only to have it come crashing down a thousand years later, at least 500 years ago. The precise origins of its dramatic tumble are unknown; it's currently believed that it may have been dismantled during an early cultural revolution.

Just north of the menhir is the **Table des Marchands,** a passage grave with detailed engravings of an axe on the capstone of the dolmen. In the form of a giant table earlier this century, the chamber's cairn (the stones that covered it) has been restored to its original state, leaving a nearly house-like structure in view, while the decorated slabs can only be seen from inside the chamber.

The **d'Er Grah Tumulus,** the third structure in this compact compound, was constructed in three stages that transformed it from a modest bovine burial ground to a 140m-by-25m closed chamber. These three monuments are in such close proximity that one almost wonders whether the adjacent **Archaeological Information Center** moved them to attract tourists. The center shows a concise, informative twelve-minute video with the price of admission. (☎02 97 57 37 59. Video shown 11am-6pm on the hr., French viewings at 15 and 45 past. Combined tickets available. 1hr. tours July-Aug. 5 per day (1 in English); May-June and Sept. 3 per day. Open June-Sept. daily 10am-7pm; Oct.-Dec. 19 and Jan. 11-Mar. 2-5pm; Apr.-May 10am-1pm and 2-6pm. July-Aug. 32F/€4.88, Sept.-June 25F/€3.81, students 15F/€2.29.)

VANNES

Few natives still call Vannes (pop. 54,000) by its Breton name, Gwened, but this town by the Bay of Morbihan clings to its Celtic roots, for reasons perhaps as much economic as sentimental. Vannes was a major maritime center and the ducal seat of Brittany until the dukes moved to Nantes in 1450 and the port's traffic shifted to Lorient. Vannes struggled for much of the next 500 years to regain its economic footing, and ultimately resorted to its rich architectural past as a means of generating income. Like many coastal towns, it brims with tourists in July and August, but sleeps in a state of under-employment during the winter months. What sets Vannes apart, however, are its incomparable collection of Breton wooden furniture and its city center, with spectacular ramparts and 180 *maisons à colombage*, houses remarkable for their prominent, colorful wooden beams.

TRANSPORTATION

Trains: To: **Paris** (3¼hr., 5 per day, 338F/€51.53); **Quimper** (1hr. 20min., 8 per day, 106F/€16.16); and **Rennes** (1¼hr., 6 per day, 107F/€16.31). Consult schedules, as timetables change during the summer months. **Cariane Atlantique** (☎02 97 47 29 64) runs one line which stops in **Auray** (50min., 22F/€3.35), **Carnac** (1¼hr., 39F/€5.95), and **Quiberon** (2hr., 52F/€7.93). There are 7 per day.

Local Buses: TPV serves the city and surrounding areas. Get a schedule at the tourist office or at **Infobus,** pl. de la République (☎02 97 01 22 23).

Taxis: At the train station, cross the street to the small booth marked "taxis" and press the *"appel taxis"* button on the wall for a direct line to service. Or, call 02 97 54 34 34.

Bike Rental: Cycles le Mellec, pl. de la Madeleine (☎02 97 63 00 24).

ORIENTATION AND PRACTICAL INFORMATION

To reach the tourist office from the train station, turn right on av. Favrel et Lincy. At the roundabout, turn left, and stay right when the street splits immediately after the turn (av. Victor Hugo). Follow av. Victor Hugo across bd. de la Paix, up the hill, to the intersection with a Monoprix on the left and a modern fountain in the middle. Bear right onto rue Joseph le Brix, and turn left onto rue Thiers. Follow the road past the post office; the tourist office is a large brown building on the right.

BRITTANY

Tourist Office: 1 rue Thiers (☎02 97 47 24 34; fax 02 97 47 29 49; www.pays-de-vannes.com/tourisme). Ask for a detailed city map (the standard one does not have all of the street names). Hotel reservations 5F/€0.76. **Tours** (in French) leave from Musée de la Cohue mid-Apr. to June W and Sa at 3pm; July-Aug. daily (except Su morning) at 10:30am and 3pm (30F/€4.57, students 20F/€3.05, under 12 free). Open July-Aug. M-Sa 9am-7pm, Su 9:30am-6pm; June and Sept. M-Sa 9:30am-12:30pm and 2-6pm.

Laundromat: Laverie Automatique, 5 av. Victor Hugo (☎02 97 47 15 80). Open June-Sept. daily 7am-9pm; Oct.-May 7am-8pm.

Police: 2 pl. de la République (☎02 97 54 75 00).

Hospital: bd. Maurice Guillaudot (☎02 97 01 41 41).

Internet Access: Cybercafé "Le Seven," 15 pl. du Général de Gaulle (☎02 97 54 04 72). 25F/€3.81 per 30min. Open M-Sa 3pm-1am.

Post office: pl. de la République (☎02 97 68 30 20). **Currency exchange. Postal code:** 56000.

ACCOMMODATIONS AND CAMPING

Hotels in Vannes tend to the expensive side, but there are a number of cheaper options scattered throughout town. Besides the following accommodations, many reasonably-priced *chambres d'hôte* are listed at the tourist office.

Foyer des Jeunes Travailleuses, 14 av. Victor Hugo (☎02 97 54 33 13; fax 02 97 42 57 73). Residents will enthusiastically welcome you into their home to join them in such activities as kayaking and photo workshops. TV room with video library, piano room, and billiard hall. Breakfast 14F/€2.13. Lunch and dinner M-F 55F/€8.39. Sheets 28F/€4.27. Reception 7am-11pm (guard on duty 11pm-7am); ring bell until 1am lockout. Reserve ahead July-Aug. Singles 90F/€13.72, students 75F/€11.43.

Hôtel Anne de Bretagne, 42 rue Olivier de Clisson (☎02 97 54 22 19; fax 02 97 42 69 10), near the train station. Everything from the bathrooms to the breakfast room is like new and in perfect, sparkling order. TVs in all rooms. Breakfast 35F/€5.34. Reception 7am-10:30pm. Singles and doubles with toilet 190-220F/€28.97-33.54; singles with bath 250-290F/€38.12-44.21; doubles 280-340F/€42.69-51.84; triples 360-390F/€54.89-59.46; quads 400-430F/€60.98-65.56. DC/MC/V.

Hôtel Le Richemont, 26 pl. de la Gare (☎02 97 47 12 95; fax 02 97 54 92 79). Rooms with individual character, and a breakfast room reminiscent of the Middle Ages. Breakfast 35F/€5.34. Showers 15F/€2.29. Reception 24hr. Singles with sink 120F/€18.30, with toilet 170F/€25.92; doubles with sink 150F/€22.90, with toilet 170F/€25.92, with bath 230-260F/€35.07-39.64; triples 200F/€30.49, with shower 265F/€40.40, with bath 295F/€44.98; quads 300F/€45.74. MC/V.

Camping Municipal de Conleau. Continue on rue Thiers past the tourist office. It will become rue du Port and then av. Maréchal Delattre de Tassigny. Just past the bridge, take the right fork onto av. du Maréchal Juin; the campground will be on the right (25min.). Or take bus #2 (D on Su) from Hôtel de Ville (dir: "Square du Morbihan or "Conleau") to "Camping." (Note that buses to sq. du Morbihan finish their routes 1 stop before this. Continue along av. du Maréchal Juin to reach the campsite.) Last bus around 8pm. Good facilities deep in the gulf, next to a path-laced wildlife reserve. Open Apr.-Sept. 26F/€3.96, under 12 16F/€2.44. Tent 53F/€8.08. Electricity 17F/€2.59.

FOOD

Vannes' selection of restaurants caters to a range of tastes, from traditional Breton fare to a surprisingly broad variety of ethnic cuisine. The extraordinarily narrow **rue des Halles** has a number of pizzerias and crêperies. Just outside the walls of the *vieille ville*, on rue de la Fontaine in the **Quartier St-Patern's,** you'll find Vietnamese, Afghan, Indian, and Moroccan restaurants, to name a few. The port is also, naturally, strong on seafood. On Wednesday and Sunday mornings, the **market** in the pl. du Poids Public brings vendors selling everything from sole to sunflowers (7am-1pm). If you miss the market, **Maison Le Luherne,** 4 pl. Général de Gaulle, is filled with mountains of fresh produce. (☎02 97 47 15 02. Open M 7am-12:30pm and 3-7:30pm, Tu-Sa 7am-12:30pm and 2:30-7:30pm, Su 9am-12:30pm.)

Chez La Mère 6 Sous, 11 rue de Closmadeuc, has a large, festive terrace among dozens of flowers, red parasols, checked tablecloths, and mannequins in Breton outfits. (☎02 97 54 05 83. Pizzas 42-62F/€6.40-9.45, *plats* 78-88F/€11.89-13.42. Open Easter-Sept. Tu-Su noon-2pm and 7:30-10:30pm; Oct.-Easter closed Su-M.) If you just can't seem to get enough of those crêpes and galettes, try **Dan Ewen,** 3 pl. du Général de Gaulle, where the Breton music never stops and the customers still live in Gwened—not Vannes. (☎02 97 42 44 34. Open July-Aug. M-Sa 11:30am-2pm and 6:30-10:30pm, Su 6:30-10:30pm; Sept.-June Tu-Sa 11:30am-2pm and 6:30-9:30pm. Closed 15 days in mid-Sept.)

SIGHTS

The size of Vannes' city center makes it an ideal area to explore on foot, though you may want to bike or take the bus to some of the newer sights like the aquarium. The most striking feature of Vannes' architecture are its *maisons à colombage*, found in the city center. The houses in **pl. St-Pierre** still bear the bold colors that served as addresses before Louis XIII mandated a numbering system. Stroll along the old city's periphery on rue François Decker, separated from the **17th-cen-**

tury ramparts by a moat and painstakingly manicured lawns and flower-gardens. Overlooking the ramparts is the **Jardin de la Garenne,** dedicated to the soldiers of the world wars, and the diverse and fabulous **Jardin de la Prefecture.**

CATHEDRALE ST-PIERRE. Looms over the *place*, with its 19th-century neogothic facade and adjoining north tower that dates back to 1143. Lining the nave are ten chapels; the fourth on the left contains the tomb of St-Vincent Ferrier and a tapestry relating the events of his life beneath a Renaissance-style rotunda. *(Open June-Sept. M-Sa 8am-7pm; Oct.-May 8am-noon and 2-7pm.)*

LA COHUE. This museum, opposite the cathedral and formerly the site of a covered market, holds a permanent collection of Parisian salon paintings and rotating exhibits on art in Brittany. *(Pl. St-Pierre. ☎ 02 97 47 35 86. Open June 16-Sept. daily 10am-6pm; Oct.-May W-Su 10am-noon and 2-6pm. Closed Su morning. 26F/€3.96, students 16F/€2.44, under 12 free.)*

AQUARIUM DE VANNES. The aquarium houses a variety of tropical fish, giant turtles, sharks, and the legendary crocodile found in the Paris sewers in 1984 (following the mysterious disappearance of the rat population), which now lounges, fat and miserable, in a depressingly tiny tank. Kids may be enthralled by the gangplank over the shark tank, but parents, be warned: the path to it involves a trip *through* the gift shop. *(Follow directions for campground (see above), but go straight (left side) when av. du Maréchal Juin forks to the right. Or take bus #2 (dir: "Conleau" or "sq. du Morbihan") from pl. de la République, and ask the driver for the aquarium stop. ☎ 02 97 40 67 40. Open July-Aug. daily 9am-8pm. 52F/€7.93, ages 5-12 32F/€4.88, under 5 free.)*

JARDIN DES PAPILLONS. A large tropically-climatized room (read 80% humidity) brims with 400 butterflies of at least 25 species at any time. Step carefully, and watch out for giant teal caterpillars the size of candy bars. *(Parc du Golfe, down the street form the aquarium, to the right (just past the hotel). ☎ 02 97 46 01 02. Open July-Aug. daily 10am-6pm; Apr.-June and Sept. 10am-12:30pm and 1:30-6pm. 38F/€5.79, children 28F/€4.27, under 5 free. 10% off with aquarium.)*

ENTERTAINMENT AND FESTIVALS

Nightlife in Vannes tends to be on the tame side. Come evening, everyone crowds into the bars that line the old port near **pl. Gambetta.** The most club-like of the bars is **Le Colonial,** Port de Plaisance, with its blasting techno, tropical plants, and sombreros. (Open daily 3pm-2am.) A few doors down, **Paddy O'Doud's** (☎ 02 97 47 87 81), fills with those looking for a little Celtic flare. Slightly away from the water is **Tavarn le Gwenn Ha Du,** 19 rue de la Boucherie. *Gwenn ha du* means white and black, the colors of the Breton flag and of the tavern walls. (☎ 02 97 47 17 16. Coreff 12F/€1.83. Open daily 11:30am-1am.)

At the beginning of August, the city hosts the **Jazz à Vannes** festival in the Jardin de Limur. (☎ 02 97 01 81 21; www.vannes-bretagne-sud.com. Tickets 140F/€21.35, students and under 18 110F/€16.77; at least one night free, call for details.)

NANTES

Nantes (pop. 550,000) tastefully blends the distinct flavors of its modern high-tech industry, the lively pedestrian district with a touch of big-city class, and the historical sights reminiscent of its glorious, if gory, past. Nantes' château hosted both Henri IV's famous Edict and the infamous pirate Bluebeard (the Maréchal de Retz). Between the 16th and 18th centuries, Nantes established itself as a nexus of the slave trade, a grisly business which bolstered the local economy and made this city France's largest port. During the Revolution, not even the guillotine could keep pace with the march of death as hundreds of people, stripped and bound in pairs, were drowned in the Loire. Today, just down the street from the modern, gargantuan train station and towering buildings, the winding cobblestone streets of the pedestrian district are lined with numerous cafés, and 15th- and 16th-century wood-paneled houses. Locals gather throughout the town to hear the street musicians who perform in the central squares nightly in summer.

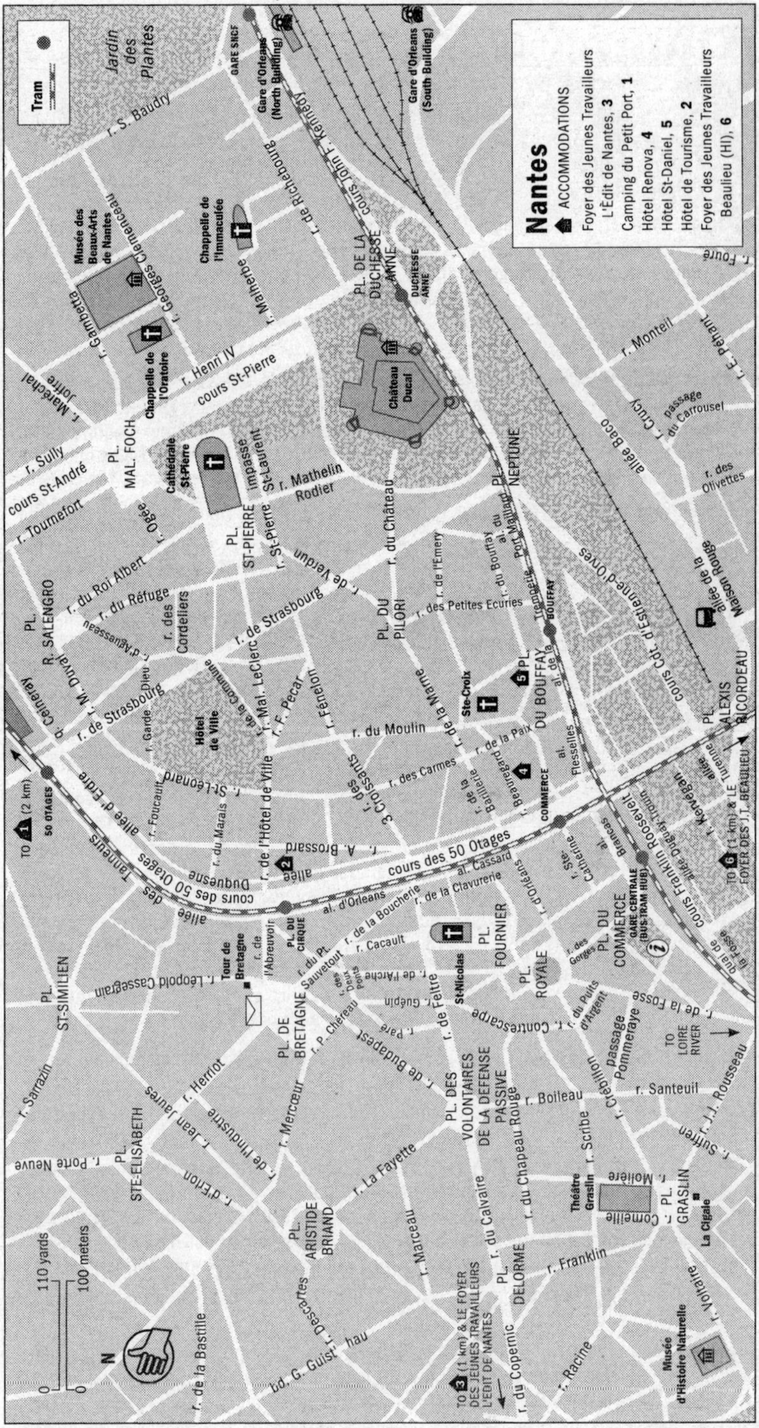

Nantes

ACCOMMODATIONS

Foyer des Jeunes Travailleurs L'Édit de Nantes, 3

Camping du Petit Port, 1

Hôtel Renova, 4

Hôtel St-Daniel, 5

Hôtel de Tourisme, 2

Foyer des Jeunes Travailleurs Beaulieu (HI), 6

TRANSPORTATION

Flights: The airport is 10km south of Nantes (☎02 40 84 80 00). **Air Inter** (☎02 51 88 31 08) flies daily to **Lyon, Marseille, Nice,** and **Paris. Air France** (info ☎02 40 47 12 33; reservations ☎08 02 80 28 02) sends at least 6 flights per week to **London.** A **Tan Air** shuttle (☎02 40 29 39 39) runs from pl. du Commerce and the station (25min., M-F 13 shuttles per day, Sa 8, Su 3). Tickets 38F/€5.80, *carnet* of 4 100F/€15.25.

Trains: There are two entrances to the train station: Nord (north), 27 bd. de Stalingrad, and Sud (south), across the tracks on rue de Loumel. Information and tickets are at the northern entrance. To: **Angers** (40min., about 20 per day, 84F/€12.81); **Bordeaux** (4hr., 6-8 per day, 224F/€34.16); **La Rochelle** (2hr., 8-11 per day, 128F/€19.52); **Paris** (2-4hr., about 20 per day, 299-372F/€45.60-56.73); **Rennes** (2hr.; M-Sa 10 per day, 3 on Su; 114F/€17.39); and **Saumur** (70min., 7 per day, 100F/€15.25).

Buses: Cariane Atlantique, 5 allée Duquesne (☎02 40 20 46 99), sends buses to **Rennes** (2hr.; Sept.-June 2 per day in winter only, none July-Aug.; 98F/€14.95) and **Vannes** (1½hr., 1 per day, 119F/€18.15). Buses leave from the train station's south entrance and from the bus station (☎02 40 47 62 70) on allée Baco. Office open M-F 8am-noon and 2-7pm.

Local Transportation: TAN (☎08 01 44 44 44) runs buses and two tram lines until 8pm. Ticket 8F/€1.22, 2 for 15F/€2.29, 5 for 32F/€4.88, 10 for 56F/€8.54. Day pass 21F/€3.20, week 69F/€10.52. Info booth at 3 allée Brancas, opposite pl. du Commerce. Open M-F 7:15am-7pm, Sa 9am-7pm.

Taxis: Allô Radio-Taxis Nantes Atlantique (☎02 40 69 22 22), at the station. 24hr. 50-80F/€7.62-12.20 to the hostel in Beaulieu.

ORIENTATION AND PRACTICAL INFORMATION

Nantes is a tangle of neighborhoods, hills, and pedestrian streets spread along the north bank of the Loire. Shadowed by a modest skyscraper, the Tour Bretagne, the city axes run east-west along **cours John Kennedy,** which becomes **cours Franklin D. Roosevelt** and later quai de la Fosse, and north-south along **cours des 50 Otages.** To get to the city center and the **tourist office,** turn left out of the north exit *(accès nord)* of the train station onto allée du Charcot, which becomes cours John Kennedy. After the château and pl. Bouffay, cross cours des 50 Otages and continue past the buses. The tourist office is on your right, at the end of the bus port, in the FNAC building (20min.). By bus, take the free shuttle from the train station to pl. du Commerce (line #10, dir: "François Mitterrand," across the street from *accès nord*). At pl. du Commerce, walk one block up in the direction of the bus, and the FNAC building and tourist office will be across the street on your right.

Tourist Office: pl. du Commerce (☎02 40 20 60 00; fax 02 40 89 11 99; www.reception.com/Nantes). Excellent maps and tours. Daily **city tour** (French) 40F/€6.10, students 20F/€3.05; reservations recommended. Open M-Sa 10am-7pm. **Branch** at the château entrance open July-Aug. daily 10am-6pm; Sept.-June Su only 10am-6pm.

Budget travel: Voyage au Fil (☎02 51 72 94 60), at CRIJ. Ground and air tickets. Matches travelers with drivers. Hours as for CRIJ, closed 12:30-1:30pm. AmEx/MC/V. **SMEBA travel,** 7-8 allée Duguay Trouin (☎02 40 35 90 90; fax 02 40 35 90 87), between pl. Franklin D. Roosevelt and pl. du Commerce. Open M-F 9am-6pm.

Money: Best **currency exchange** rates at **Change Graslin** (☎02 40 69 24 64), on rue Rousseau in pl. Graslin right next to *La Cigale.* Open M-F 9am-noon and 2-6pm, Sa 10am-noon and 2-5pm.

Laundromat: 3 rue de Bouffay. Open M-Sa 9am-7pm. Also at 7 Hôtel de Ville, open daily 7am-8:30pm. **Laverie de la Madeleine,** 11 rue Chaussée de la Madeleine (☎02 40 47 10 17). Open M-Sa 9am-8pm. 24-40F/€3.66-6.10 per load.

Youth Information: Centre Régional d'Information Jeunesse (CRIJ), 28 rue du Calvaire (☎02 51 72 94 50). Info on youth discounts and employment opportunities. Open Tu-F 10am-6:30pm, M and Sa 2-6:30pm.

Hospital: Centre Hospitalier Régional, pl. Alexis Ricordeau (☎02 40 08 33 33).

Police: pl. Waldeck-Rousseau (☎02 40 37 21 21).

Internet Access: Welcome Services Copy, 70 rue Maréchal Joffre (☎02 51 81 96 25). 35F/€5.34 per hr. Open M 2:30-7pm, Tu-F 9am-12:30pm and 2-7pm, Sa 10am-noon and 2:30-6pm. **Cyberkebab,** 30 rue de Verdun, serves falafel and kebabs. 16F/€2.44 per 30min., 22F/€3.36 per hr., reduced for students. Open until 2am. Or try: **Cyber House,** 8 quai de Versailles (☎02 40 12 11 84); **Cybercity,** 14 rue de Strasbourg (☎02 40 89 57 92); or **Virus.com,** 22 rue Paul Bellamy (☎02 40 35 53 51).

Post Office: 4 rue du Président Edouard Herriot, at pl. de Bretagne (☎02 40 12 62 74), near Tour Bretagne. **Currency exchange.** Open M-F 8am-7pm, Sa 8am-noon. **Postal code:** 44000.

ACCOMMODATIONS AND CAMPING

Nantes has plenty of good hotels and lots of student dorm space in the summer. Most budget places are within a 10-minute walk or bus ride of pl. du Commerce.

Hôtel St-Daniel, 4 rue du Bouffay (☎02 40 47 41 25; fax 02 51 72 03 99), just off pl. du Bouffay, in the heart of the peppy pedestrian district. Immaculately clean rooms with comfy comforters. Breakfast 25F/€3.81. Singles and doubles 160F/€24.39, with shower and toilet 180F/€27.44; triples and quads 230F/€35.06. AmEx/MC/V.

Foyer des Jeunes Travailleurs L'Edit de Nantes, 1 rue du Gigant (☎02 40 73 41 46; fax 02 40 69 11 55). Hop on the #21, 23, 24, or 56 bus, which will take you to "Edit de Nantes," across the street from the hostel. The #24 and #56 buses have more accessible pickup points; both stop at pl. du Commerce, a 2min. tram ride from the train station. 60 beds in barren double rooms with shower and toilet; lively *foyer* with friendly residents and pleasant cafeteria. Minimum 2-night stay. Lunch or dinner 40F/€6.10. Reception M-F 9am-9pm. Call ahead for winter stays. Beds 60F/€9.15.

Foyer des Jeunes Travailleurs Beaulieu (HI), 9 bd. Vincent Gâche (☎40 12 24 00; fax 02 51 82 00 05). From the station, take the free shuttle bus from *accès sud* to pl. du Commerce (bus #10, dir: "Francois Mitterrand") and switch to the tramway (line #2, dir: "Trocardinet," to "Vincent Gâche"). Bd. Vincent Gâche is ahead on the left (12min.). By foot, exit via *accès nord* and turn left onto cours John F. Kennedy. Turn left onto av. Carnot and continue straight for about 10-15min. until you cross the river. Vincent Gâche will be one block up on the left, past the Holiday Inn (20min.). 200 beds in 1- to 4-person rooms with baths. Singles cost the same as the larger rooms. Though perfectly adequate, the foyer is housed in a dingy, industrial-style building. Breakfast 14F/€2.14. Meals 40F/€6.10. Sheets 17F/€2.59. Reception 8am-9pm; call ahead if arriving later. No lockout or curfew. Beds 60F/€9.15, non-members 135F/€20.59.

Hôtel Renova, 11 rue Beauregard (☎02 41 4 57 03; fax 02 51 82 06 39), off cours des 50 Otages. Rooms get stuffier but less expensive as you go up. Incredibly central location. Breakfast 17F/€2.59. Singles and doubles 115-135F/€17.54-20.59, with shower 165F/€25.16, with bath 185-225F/€28.21-34.31; triples with bath 275F/€41.93. Those in rooms without showers won't shower. AmEx/MC/V.

Hôtel du Tourisme, 5 allée Duquesne (☎02 40 47 90 26; fax 02 40 35 57 25). Pretty, tiled stairs lead up to 20 clean, attractive rooms, all with TV and phone. Free bike storage. Breakfast 28F/€4.27. Reserve ahead. Singles and doubles with shower 190F/€28.97. 3-4 person rooms 225F/€34.31. Extra bed 50F/€7.62. MC/V.

Camping du Petit Port, 21 bd. du Petit Port (☎02 40 74 47 94; fax 02 40 74 23 06; camping-petit-port@nge-nantes.fr). 10min. tram ride from pl. du Commerce (take line 2 north to "Marhonnière"). Superb 4-star site with activities to keep children busy. Laundry and pool access. Reception 9am-9pm. Reserve in writing or arrive early in summer. 18F/€2.74 per person, 26F/€3.97 per tent, 37F/€5.64 per tent and car, 49F/€7.47 per caravan and car. Electricity 18F/€2.74. Prices lower in off season.

FOOD

Local specialties include seafood *au beurre blanc* (with butter sauce) and *canard nantais* (duck prepared with grapes), as well as Mouscadet and Gros Plant white wines. *Le Petit Beurre* cookies are a local invention, as are *muscadines* (chocolates filled with grapes and Muscadet wine). Explore the streets behind **pl. du Bouffay,** where the crêperies are especially good.

The biggest **market** in Nantes is at the **Marché de Talensac,** along rue de Bel-Air near pl. St-Similien behind the post office (Tu-Sa 9am-1pm). A smaller market has the same hours on **pl. du Bouffay,** while another stretches down pl. de la Petite Hollande opposite pl. du Commerce (Sa 8am-1pm). **Monoprix** is off cours des 50 Otages at 2 rue de Calvaire, down from the Galeries Lafayette. (Open M-Sa 9am-9pm. MC/V.) **La Cigale,** 4 pl. Graslin, opposite the Théâtre Graslin, is one of the most beautiful brasseries in France. It's a classified historical monument as well as a not-to-be-missed dining experience. The art nouveau mosaics, gold detail, and huge mirrors complement dishes like lobster soup (42F/€6.41). *Menus* are expensive, but snacks are available all day for under 50F/€7.62. (☎02 51 84 94 94. Open daily 7:30am-12:30am. Reserve for supper. MC/V.)

SIGHTS

Ask the tourist office about the ***Nantes City Card,*** *a pass to the château museums, the Musée des Beaux-Arts, the Musée d'Histoire Naturelle, and the Musée Jules Verne. The pass includes free access to trams and buses, and a guided tour with the tourist office. Except for the planetarium, Nantes' museums are* ***free on Sundays.***

Nantes' elaborate 19th-century facades are fashioned with wrought-iron balconies; a walk around the city gives you a good view. Make sure to see **Passage Pommeraye,** an unusual shopping arcade accessible from pl. du Commerce.

CHATEAU DES DUCS DE BRETAGNE. Currently under renovation, this château has seen as much history as any in the Loire. Its imposing walls once held Gilles de Retz, the original Bluebeard, who was convicted of sorcery in 1440 for sacrificing hundreds of children in gruesome rituals. In 1598, Henri IV composed the Edict of Nantes here in an effort to soothe national tensions. All of the château's museums but one are closed until 2004, but the interim **Musée du Château des Ducs de Bretagne** hosts a number of temporary exhibits. The château grounds, surrounded by a lovely moat and ramparts, are open, however. *(☎02 40 41 56 56. Courtyard open for free visits July-Aug. daily 10am-7pm; Sept.-June 10am-6pm. Free guided tour takes you inside the castle. Museum open July-Aug. daily 10am-6pm; Sept.-June closed Tu. 20F/€3.05, students 10F/€1.53, under 18 free. Free after 4:30pm.)*

CATHEDRALE ST-PIERRE. Step inside to appreciate the soaring 38m Gothic vaults and the elaborate tomb of Francois II in the south transept, commissioned by his daughter, Anne de Bretagne. Built from 1434 to 1891, the cathedral has seen its fair share of low periods: it was pillaged during the Revolution, bombed during WWII, and suffered a fire in 1972. Fortunately, a restoration has masterfully undone the ravages of time—except for the dearth of stained glass; all but one of the original windows were shattered in WWII. The largest stained-glass window in France (25m) is above François' tomb. *(Open daily 10am-7pm.)*

MUSEE DES BEAUX-ARTS. This collection prompted Henry James to reflect on provincial museums: "The pictures may be bad, but…from bad pictures, in certain moods of the mind, there is a degree of entertainment to be derived." James' assessment notwithstanding, the collection includes works by Delacroix, Ingres, and Kandinsky. *(10 rue Clemenceau. Take bus #11 or 12 to "Trébuchet." ☎02 40 41 65 65. Open M and W-Sa 10am-6pm, Su 10am-6pm; F until 8pm, with free entry 6-9pm. 20F/€3.05, students 10F/€1.53, free first Su of the month.)*

MUSEE JULES VERNE. The innovative museum recreates Verne's wonderful world through novels, letters, and photographs. *(3 rue de l'Hermitage. ☎02 40 69 72 52. Open M and W-Sa 10am-noon and 2-5pm, Su 2-5pm. 8F/€1.22, students 4F/€0.61.)*

OTHER SIGHTS. The **Planetarium** allows you to relax to galactic vistas and an exploration of the solar system. *(8 rue des Acadiens, off pl. Moysan. ☎02 40 73 99 23. Shows M-F 10:30am, 2:15, and 3:45pm. Su shows at 3 and 4:30pm. 26F/€3.97, students 13F/€1.98.)* The **Musée d'Histoire Naturelle,** with live pythons and stuffed mammals, is great for kids; don't miss the skeleton of the baby blue whale. *(12 rue Voltaire. Take bus #11 to "Jean V." ☎02 40 99 26 20. Open W-M 10am-6pm. 20F/€3.05, students 10F/€1.53; free third Su of every month.)* The **Jardin des Plantes,** behind the Musée des Beaux Arts, is full of grassy hills and duck ponds; more exotic flavors are housed in the northern section's huge greenhouse. *(Open daily 8am-7:45pm. Tours every hr. Su 2-5pm.)*

ENTERTAINMENT AND FESTIVALS

A good deal of nightlife is listed in the weekly *Nantes Poche* (3F/€0.46 at any *tabac*). **The Katorza,** 3 rue Corneille (☎08 36 68 06 66), projects nightly independent films in their original languages. The **Apollo Theatre,** on rue Racine, shows movies nightly for 10F/€1.53 with an occasional English selection. Nearby **rue Scribe** is full of late-night bars and cafés. A favorite of the young and funky, **quartier St-Croix,** near pl. Bouffay, has about three bars per block and just as many cafés. At **Buck Mulligan's Irish Pub,** 12 rue du Château, pull up a chair and enjoy the Irish cheer. (☎02 40 20 02 72. Open daily 11am-2am.) Another Irish pub, **Le John McByrne,** 21 rue des Petites Ecuries, has live Irish music on Friday nights. (☎02 40 89 64 46. Open daily noon-2am.) On the other side of town, **La Maison,** 4 rue Lebrun off rue Maréchal Joffre, has cantina lighting and a party atmosphere filled with mostly young people. (☎02 40 37 04 12. Open daily 3pm-2am.) **Le Canotier,** 21 quai de Versailles, hosts local musicians 3-4 times a week, with blues, jazz, and French music on weekends and a nightly piano bar. (☎02 40 12 06 29. Open Tu-Su 2pm-2am.)

Clubs are a bit farther out. **Le News,** 4 pl. Emile Zola off bd. Pasteur (☎02 40 58 01 04), spins house and garage in one room and new jack, funk, and dance in another. A few blocks to the south, **Le Paradiso,** 17 rue de la Convention, opens up its doors to all and the dance floor to those in their prime. **Le Temps d'Aimer,** 14 rue Alexandre Fourny (☎02 40 89 48 60) is Nantes' favorite gay disco. From pl. de la République on Ile Beaulieu, follow rue Victor Hugo until rue Fourny on the left.

Eastern Orthodox chanters, blues rockers from Mali, and masqueraders from Trinidad and Tobago perform at the international **Festival d'Eté,** which takes place each year in early July. Up-and-coming Asian, African, and South American filmmakers are featured in the **Festival des Trois Continents** in late November and early December (☎02 40 69 74 14). Locals boast that their **Carnaval** (info ☎02 40 35 75 52) is one of the biggest in France, with parades and an all-night party on Mardi Gras.

LOIRE VALLEY (VAL DE LOIRE)

The Loire, France's longest river, drifts toward the Atlantic through a landscape of vineyards and châteaux. Though its source lies far away in the mountains of the Massif Central, the *pays de la Loire* is commonly understood to be that part of the country drained by the river and its tributaries, between Orléans and Nantes. Famed for its châteaux, the Loire also raised some of the brightest stars of French thought, including Rabelais, Descartes, and Balzac; the French spoken on its banks is considered the purest in the country. Loire vineyards produce some of France's best wines, and the soil is among the country's most fertile. It is hardly surprising that a string of French (and English) kings chose to station themselves by these waters rather than in the dirt and noise of their capital cities.

The history of the châteaux goes back to the 9th century, when a splintered France was crumbling under Viking invasions. Local communities, under the leadership of feudal lords, erected fortresses to protect important landholdings from the new invaders. Later the region was a focal point of the incessant Anglo-French wars, beginning when Henry Plantagenêt, Duke of Anjou and local strongman, inherited the English crown. During the Hundred Years' War, the region was one of the few to effectively resist the English; it was at Chinon (p. 581) in 1429 that Joan of Arc persuaded the Dauphin to give her an army with which to liberate Orléans. With the introduction of effective artillery in the 16th century, the age of the defensive fortress was over and battles moved into the plains. Most of the surviving castles were converted into comfortable palaces, adapting the new Italian style to fit local sensibilities. These elegant Renaissance homes, reflected in pools and framed by spectacular gardens, were heaped with masterworks of fine art and design, fostering an opulence hardly imagined before or since.

The valley was scarred by the 16th-century Wars of Religion, which culminated in the Duc de Guise's massacre of Protestants at Amboise (p. 572) in 1560, avenged 18 years later with the duke's own assassination in Blois (p. 569). The Loire settled down for a political nap in the 17th century when Louis XIV summoned the nobles to court at Versailles, but awoke once again during the Revolution when rural peasants violently protested Republican policies, provoking an uprising that ended with the wholesale massacre of civilians by the Revolutionary armies.

TRANSPORTATION

Faced with such widespread grandeur, many travelers plan over-ambitious itineraries that result in hazy memories of highways and big stone houses. Two châteaux a day is a good limit. Trains don't reach many châteaux, and those that do are scheduled inconveniently. Tours (p. 573), connected to 12 châteaux, is the region's best rail hub. Many stations distribute the useful booklet *Châteaux pour Train et Vélo*, with train schedules, distances, and info on bike and car rental. Of the châteaux included in *Let's Go*, Sully-sur-Loire, Chambord, Cheverny, Beauregard, and Ussé are *not* accessible by train. Bikes are the best way to see the most of this flat but beautiful region. Distances between châteaux and hostels tend to be short, and many small roads cut through fields of brilliant poppies and sunflowers. The Michelin map of the region and tourist biking guides will steer you away from truck-laden highways and onto delightful country roads. Alternatives include buses, cars, or tour bus circuits that require the purchase of half-day or full-day passes; a group of four renting a car can generally undercut tour bus prices. Nature buffs should request the excellent (and free) bilingual booklet *Loisirs and Randonnées of the Val de Loire* from tourist offices. This has info on regional hiking and biking paths, canoe trips, and horse-riding areas, as well as contact info for outdoor activities like rock climbing and parachuting.

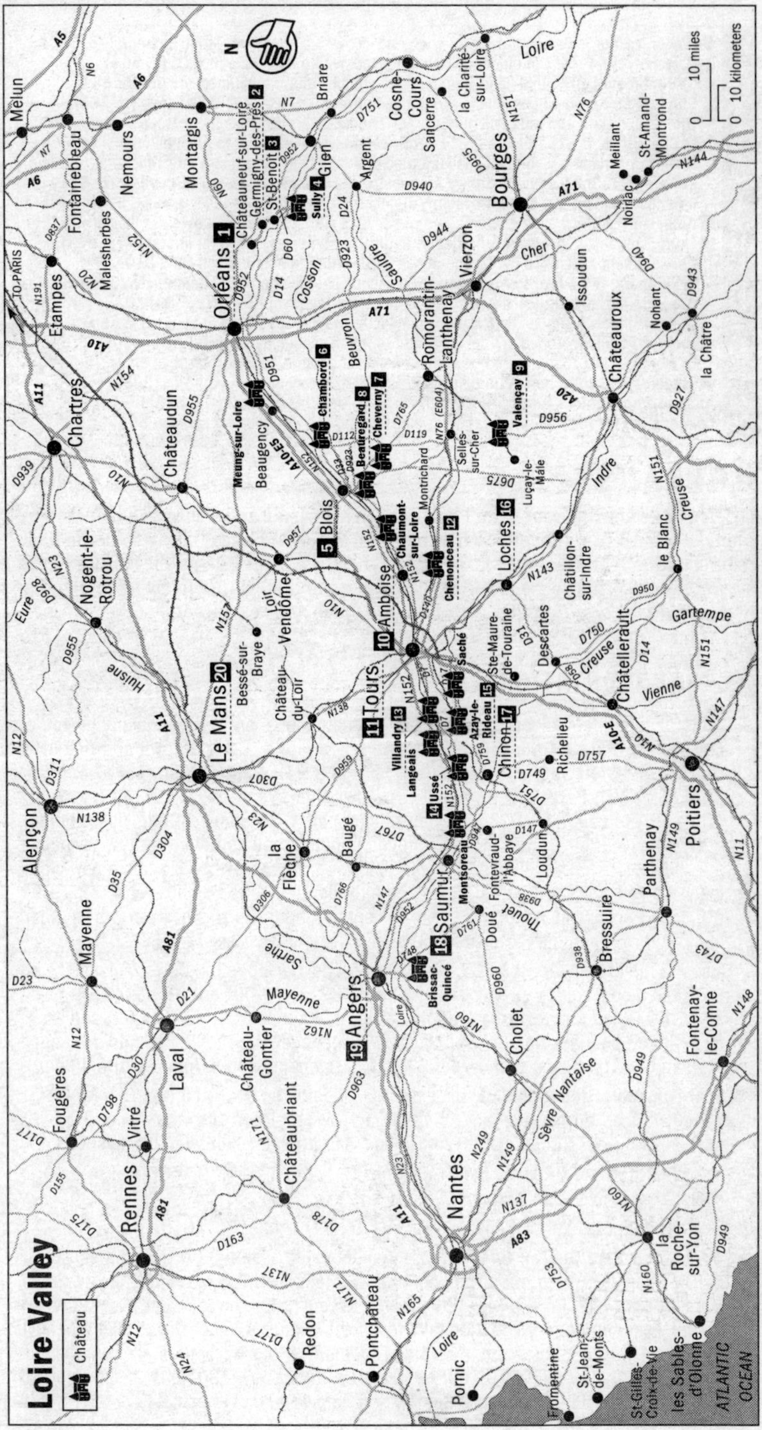

Loire Valley

Château

0 10 miles
0 10 kilometers

1 **Orléans:** Joan of Arc's hometown, an energetic city with a luminous Gothic cathedral **(p. 560)**
2 **Germigny-des-Près:** The oldest church in France, with a Byzantine mosaic **(p. 564)**
3 **St-Benoît-sur-Loire:** Arch-filled Romanesque church, with marble mosaic floor **(p. 564)**
4 **Sully-sur-Loire:** Small castle with the requisite towers, turrets, and drawbridge **(p. 564)**
5 **Blois:** Blue slate and red brick outside, rich chocolate inside; base for château visits **(p. 565)**
6 **Chambord:** *The* château; a lavish, many-chimneyed testament to royal egomania **(p. 569)**
7 **Cheverny:** Low-key, modest castle; a precious vase here, an ancient tapestry there **(p. 570)**
8 **Beauregard:** Small château known for housing the world's largest portrait gallery **(p. 571)**
9 **Valençay:** Château of the 18th-century statesman and survivalist Talleyrand **(p. 571)**
10 **Amboise:** Small city, big château; lots of Da Vinci stuff. Bizarre troglodyte dwellings **(p. 572)**
11 **Tours:** Low-key, convenient, affordable; a rollicking university city near châteaux **(p. 573)**
12 **Chenonceau:** A delicate river-spanning château with a feminine touch **(p. 579)**
13 **Villandry:** Three levels of recreated Renaissance gardens no one should miss **(p. 580)**
14 **Ussé:** Spired, turreted castle inspired the fairy tale *Sleeping Beauty* **(p. 580)**
15 **Azay-le-Rideau:** Flamboyant Renaissance castle rivaling Chambord in beauty **(p. 580)**
16 **Loches:** Fortified, storied citadel with Joan of Arc associations **(p. 581)**
17 **Chinon:** Quaint, good-natured village; tunnel-riven château-rubble on a ridge above **(p. 581)**
18 **Saumur:** Odd collection of unrelated attractions in a very beautiful town **(p. 583)**
19 **Angers:** World-famous tapestries are the reason to visit this pretty city **(p. 588)**
20 **Le Mans:** An OK place with a beautiful *vieille ville*; annual 24-hour car race **(p. 592)**

ORLEANS

Orléans' location, an hour from Paris, is both a blessing and a curse. Considered by many a suburb of the capital, Orléans (pop. 200,000) clings tightly to its history, mainly to that which involves Joan of Arc; there are at least 45 public statues of the savior of 1429. This sense of a defined past, combined with a lively shopping district and a *vieille ville* filled with intimate cafés and restaurants, makes it a perfect transition from Paris into the Loire.

TRANSPORTATION

Trains: 2 separate stations. Most trains make both stops, but a few routes only stop at Les-Aubrais. **Gare d'Orléans,** on pl. Albert 1er, is in the center of town and better for tourists. To: **Blois** (30min., 12 per day, 54F/€8.24); **Nantes** (2hr., M-F 3 per day, 194F/€29.59); **Paris** (1¼hr., about 3 per hr. 4am-10pm, 94F/€14.34); and **Tours** (1hr., 12 per day, 91F/€13.88). Info office open M-Sa 9am-7:30pm. Ticket booths open daily 5:30am-9pm. There is a huge shopping mall complete with supermarket attached to the train station, so you can grab food, buy sneakers, or acquire new clothing while you wait for the train. **Gare Les-Aubrais,** rue Pierre Semard (☎02 38 79 91 00), is a 30min. walk north from the town center. A train **shuttles** new arrivals stranded at Les-Aubrais from quai 2 to Gare d'Orléans. The journey costs 7F/€1.07.

Buses: 2 rue Marcel Proust (☎02 38 53 94 75), connected to the Gare d'Orléans by an overpass. **Les Rapides du Val de Loire** (☎02 38 61 90 00) and **TransBeauce** (☎02 37 18 59 00, in Chartres) run to **Blois** (1½hr., M-Sa 1 per day, 50F/€7.62) and **Chartres** (2hr.; 3 per day, 1 on Su; 68F/€10.37, under age 20 34F/€5.19). Info desk open M-Tu and Th 10am-1pm and 4-7pm, W and F 10am-1pm and 3-7pm, Sa 10am-1pm.

Local Transportation: SEMTAO, 2 rue de la Hallebarde (☎02 38 78 01 20 or 08 00 01 20 00), off pl. du Martroi. Tickets 7.80F/€1.19 (good for 1hr.), *carnet* of 10 68F/€10.37, day pass 20F/€3.05. Free city bus map available here and at tourist office.

Taxis: Taxi Radio d'Orléans, rue St-Yves (☎02 38 53 11 11). 35-40F/€5.34-6.10 to hostel from train station. 24hr.

Car Rental: Ecoto, 19 av. Paris (☎02 38 77 92 92). From 100F/€15.25.

Scooter and Bike Rental: CAD, 95 fbg. Bannier (☎02 38 81 23 00). Scooters 180F/€27.44 per day. Open M-Sa 9am-noon and 2-7pm. **Rent bikes** at **Kit Loisirs,** 1720 Marcel Belot (☎02 38 63 44 34), in nearby Olivet, 15min. on the tram. From the train station, take the tram (dir: "L'Hôpital") to "Victor Hugo." At Victor Hugo, take bus #14 (dir: "Foch") to "Pressoir Aubry" (10min.). Alternatively, it's a 15min. walk from the Victor Hugo tram stop. Bikes 70-100F/€10.67-15.25 per day. 1300F/€198.20 deposit. Open M-F 10am-12:30pm and 2-6pm, Sa-Su 9am-7pm. Call ahead M-F.

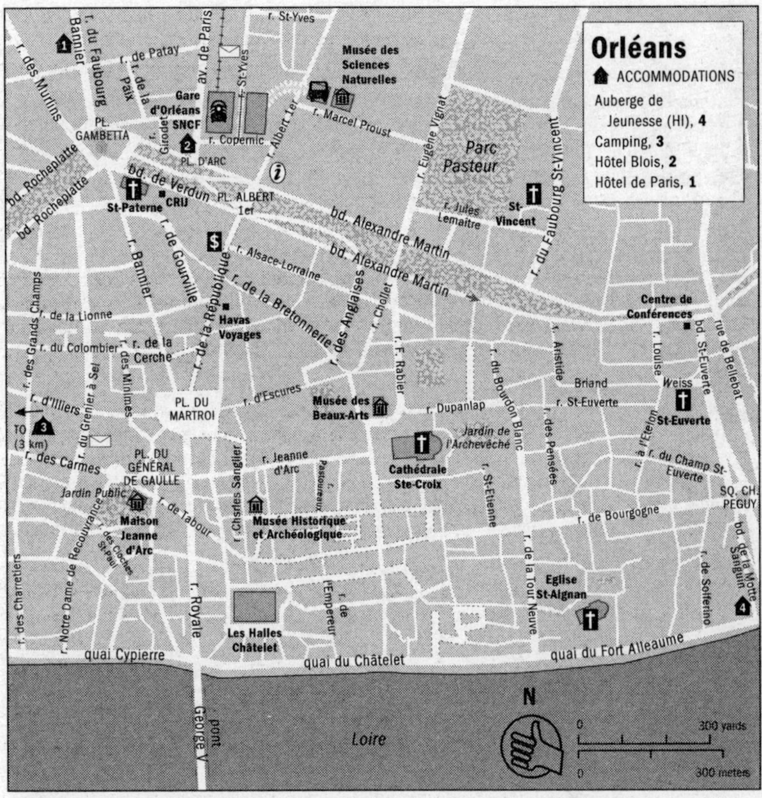

ORIENTATION AND PRACTICAL INFORMATION

Most places of interest in Orléans are on the north bank of the Loire, a five-minute walk south of the train station. Leave the station and go left under the tunnel to pl. Jeanne d'Arc; the tourist office will be across the street to your right. To get to the city center from the station, turn right onto **rue de la République,** which leads to **pl. du Martroi.** Here, rue de la République becomes **rue Royale** and runs to the river, intersecting **rue de Bourgogne** and **rue Jeanne d'Arc,** two pedestrian-dominated streets where most of the city's sights, restaurants, and bars are located.

Tourist Office: 6 pl. Albert 1er (☎02 38 24 05 05; fax 02 38 54 49 84). Maps (2F/€0.31) and excellent walking tour guide of the *vieille ville*. For 13F/€1.98, you can buy a tour book containing info and maps of all of the museums and tourist sites in town. The tourist office also runs French tours (daily at 2:30pm). Tours (free-25F/€3.81). Open July-Aug. M-Sa 9am-7pm, Su 9:30am-12:30pm and 3-6:30pm; Apr.-June and Sept. M-Sa 9am-7pm, Su 10am-noon; Oct.-Mar. M-Sa 9am-6:30pm, Su 10am-noon.

Budget Travel: Havas Voyages, 34 rue de la République (☎02 38 42 11 80). Open M-F 9:30am-12:30pm and 2-6:30pm, Sa 9am-noon and 2-6pm.

Money: Banks are on rue de la République and pl. du Martroi. ATMs are everywhere.

English Bookstore: Librairie Loddé, 41 rue Jeanne d'Arc (☎02 38 65 43 43), off rue Royale. Good selection. Open M-Sa 9am-12:30pm and 1-7pm. MC/V.

Youth Information: Centre Régional d'Information Jeunesse (CRIJ), 5 bd. de Verdun (☎02 38 78 91 78; fax 02 38 78 91 71). Very friendly and helpful staff. Open M, Th 10am-6pm; Tu, F 10am-1pm and 2-6pm; W 10am-6pm; Sa 2-6pm.

Laundromat: Laverie, 26 rue du Poirier (02 38 88 23 84). Open daily 8am-9:30pm.

Police: 63 rue du fbg. St-Jean (☎ 02 38 24 30 00). Emergency ☎ 17.

Hospital: Centre Hospitalier Régional, 1 rue Porte Madeleine (☎ 02 38 51 44 44).

Internet Access: Médiathèque, pl. Gambetta (☎ 02 38 65 45 45). Three free computers. Wait of up to 30min. Open July-Aug. Tu and F 1-7pm, W-Th and Sa 1-6pm; Sept.-June Tu and F 11am-7pm, W 10am-6pm, Th 2-6pm, Sa 11am-6pm.

Post Office: pl. du Général de Gaulle (☎ 02 38 77 35 14). **Currency exchange.** Open M-F 8am-7pm, Sa 8am-noon. **Postal code:** 45000.

ACCOMMODATIONS AND CAMPING

Inexpensive hotels are hard to find in Orléans; the few that exist are spread throughout the city. They fill up by early evening in July and August, and many have an annual closure in August; call ahead.

Auberge de Jeunesse (HI), 1 bd. de la Motte Sanguin (☎ 02 38 53 60 06). A 15min. walk from the train station, 20min. from the *vieille ville*. Turn left out of the train station onto bd. Alexandre Martin, and follow the road straight down for about 15min. Just after the convention center, turn right onto bd. St-Euverte and go down two blocks. Stay to the right when the road splits; veer right onto bd. de la Motte Sanguin and the hostel is three buildings down on the right. By bus: from pl. d'Arc, bus "RS" (dir: "Rosette") or "SY" (dir: "Concyr/La Bolière") will get you to "Pont Bourgogne" (7.50F/€1.14; until 8pm). From the train station, take #4 and tell the driver you want to get off by the auberge. Once you exit the bus, follow the boulevard straight down; the hostel is in the middle of the road on your right. Press-and-repeat showers. 70 beds in bare 2-4 person rooms. Kitchen facilities and bike storage. Breakfast 22F/€3.36. Sheets 21F/€3.20. Reception 9am-noon and 5-10pm, though staff tend to be around during the afternoon as well, and if you call in advance they will be happy to accommodate you at any point during the day. Dorms 61F/€9.30; singles 100F/€15.25.

Hôtel de Paris, 29 rue du fbg. Bannier (☎ 02 38 53 39 58). 13 light, simple, renovated rooms in a pleasant area off pl. Gambetta. Brasserie on the ground floor. Breakfast 25F/€3.81. Singles and doubles with toilet 150F/€22.90, with shower 180F/€27.44; triples 190-240F/€28.97-36.59. Extra bed 40F/€6.10. AmEx/MC/V.

Hôtel Blois, 1 av. de Paris (☎/fax 02 38 62 61 61). Conveniently located across the street from the train station. Clean yet unexciting rooms overlook a busy intersection. The front door locks around 10pm—be sure to get the code from the owner. Breakfast 28F/€4.27. Singles and doubles 130F/€19.82, with shower and bath 200F/€30.49.

FOOD

In late summer and autumn, locals feast on *gibier* (game) freshly procured in the nearby forests. Specialty sausages include the *andouillettes de Jargeau*, while *saumon de Loire* is grilled fresh from the river. Orléans' most important culinary contribution is its tangy wine vinegars, which you can taste on salads and in marinades at many local brasseries. The local cheeses are *frinault cendré*, a savory relative of camembert, and a mild *chèvre*. Wash it all down with Gris Meunier or Auvergnat wines, or nearby Olivet's pear and cherry brandies.

Les Halles Châtelet, pl. du Châtelet, is an indoor market attached to Galeries Lafayette (Tu-Sa 7am-7pm, Su 7am-1pm). Though there are many supermarkets, you'll gravitate to the massive **Carrefour** that occupies the back of the mall at pl. d'Arc (open M-Sa 8:30am-9pm). Just three blocks from the hostel is a **Marchéplus supermarket,** on the corner of rue de la Manufacture and rue Alexandre Martin (open M-Sa 7am-9pm, Su 9am-1pm). Pedestrian **rue de Bourgogne** offers an endless string of affordable brasseries, pizzerias, and bars. **Rue Ste-Catherine** has several quality restaurants, including **Le Ste-Catherine,** number 64, a classic brasserie with heaping portions of traditional cuisine. (☎ 02 58 53 42 87. *Menus* from 78F/€11.90; *plats* 60-120F/€9.15-18.30; salads 45-65F/€6.86-9.91. Open daily noon-2:30pm and

7-11:30pm. MC/V.) **Les Alpages**, 182 rue de Bourgogne, serves traditional French cuisine with seasonings and prices that will keep you coming back for more. (☎02 38 54 12 34. Open M-Sa 7-10pm. Salads 16-48F/€2.44-7.32, *plats* 56-68F/€8.54-10.37, desserts 19-34F/€2.90-5.19, *menus* 92-135F/€14.03-20.58.)

SIGHTS

Most of Orléans' historical and architectural highlights are near **pl. Ste-Croix.** In 1429, having liberated Orléans from a seven-month siege, Joan of Arc triumphantly marched down nearby **rue de Bourgogne,** the city's oldest street; the scene is vividly captured in *Jeanne d'Arc*, at the Musée des Beaux-Arts. There are 11th- to 15th-century churches spread throughout the city; the **Eglise St-Paterne,** pl. Gambetta, is a particularly massive showcase of modern stained glass. *(The "Pass Orléans" at the tourist office gives free admission to almost all sites in town, and includes walking tours (60F/€9.15). Passes go on sale June 1 and are valid until the end of Sept.)*

CATHEDRALE STE-CROIX. With towering Gothic buttresses, an intricate facade, and slender, dramatic interior arches, the cathedral is the most prominent building in Orléans. On May 8, 1429, Joan of Arc came here to join the first procession of thanks for the deliverance of the town from the English. A series of 19th-century stained glass windows in the nave depict her life's story, down to the flames that consumed her. *(Pl. Ste-Croix. Open July-Aug daily 9:15am-noon and 2:15-7pm; Apr.-Sept. 9:15am-noon and 2:15-6pm; Oct.-Mar. 9:15am-noon and 2:15-5pm. Free. Tours of the upper sections of the cathedral are organized by the tourist office.)*

HOTEL GROSLOT D'ORLEANS. Built in 1550 by bailiff Jacques Groslot, this Renaissance mansion served as the king's local residence for two centuries. In 1560, François II died here amid scandal after opening the Estates Général; Charles IX, Henri III, and Henri IV were also guests here. Now an annex to the town hall, the *hôtel* opens its sumptuously decorated rooms and romantic garden to the public and the occasional wedding. *(Pl. de l'Etape. ☎02 38 79 22 30. Open daily 9am-6pm. Ask the tourist office about free English tours.)*

MUSEE DES BEAUX-ARTS. This fine collection of Italian, Flemish, and French works displays painting, sculpture, and *objets d'art* from the 15th to the 20th centuries. An exceptional *salle des primitifs* awaits on the second floor, while the first floor holds a collection of 18th-century French portraits. Good modern art and archaeological exhibitions come through regularly. *(1 rue Fernand Rabier, to the right as you exit the cathedral. ☎02 38 79 21 55; fax 02 38 79 20 08. Open Th-Sa 10am-6pm, Tu and Su 11am-6pm, W 10am-8pm. 20F/€3.05, students 10F/€1.53, under age 16 free.)*

MUSEE D'ORLEANS. Different wings of the museum are based around different animal groups or environmental regions. Shiny rocks, minerals, dinosaur skeletons, and a small aquarium are a few of the attractions. *(6 rue Marcel Proust. ☎02 38 54 61 05. Open daily 2-6pm. 20F/€3.05, students and under age 16 10F/€1.53.)*

PARC LOUIS PASTEUR. Large grassy areas with flowered borders for relaxed picnicking or lazing around. Great jungle gym for kids. *(Rue Jules Le Maitre, 10min. from the tourist office in the direction of the youth hostel, on a side street that runs perpendicular to the main bd. Alexandre Martin—turn left onto rue Eugène Vignat to get to Jules Le Maître. Open Apr.-Sept. daily 7:30am-8pm; Feb.-Mar. and Oct. 7:30am-6:30pm; Nov.-Jan 6am-5:30pm.)*

OTHER SIGHTS. The **Maison de Jeanne d'Arc** is a reconstruction of the original house where the medieval *mademoiselle* stayed, consisting of fragments of other 15th-century houses. *(3 pl. de Gaulle. ☎02 38 52 99 89. Open May-Oct. Tu-Su 10am-noon and 2-6pm; Nov.-Apr. 2-6pm. 13F/€1.98, students 6.50F/€0.99, under age 16 free.)* **Musée Historique et Archéologique de l'Orléanais** displays the treasure of Neuvy-en-Sullias, a remarkable set of Gallo-Roman statues discovered in 1861, along with relics from the Middle Ages to the Neoclassical period. *(Sq. Abbé Desnoyers. ☎02 38 79 25 60. Open July-Aug. daily 10am-6pm; May-June and Sept. 2-6pm; Oct.-Apr. W and Sa-Su 2-6pm. 15F/€2.29, students 7F/€1.07, under age 16 free.)*

ENTERTAINMENT AND FESTIVALS

Most locals head to Paris for action, but the bars along **rue de Bourgogne** and near **Les Halles-Châtelet** keep the home front happy. **Paxton's Head,** 264 rue de Bourgogne, features live jazz on Saturday nights in a jolly British pub. (☎02 38 81 23 29. Open daily 3pm-3am.) The only regularly packed bar in town is the **Havana Café,** 28 pl. du Châtelet, a tropical playland. (☎02 38 52 16 00. Open daily 3pm-3am.) Even Orléans can be snotty—check the scene at exclusive **KOA,** Les Halles Châtelet, on the corner of rue Ducereau and pl. du Châtelet. (☎02 38 53 08 79. Open daily 11pm-5am.) **Karaoke bar St-Marcelin,** 31 rue M. Berthelot cranks out the karaoke every night until 1am, 2am in the summer months. (☎02 38 84 03 77. Open M-Sa.) **Bowling,** 2 rue Moreau, proves that the smoke, cheap beer, and good fun of bowling is universal. (☎02 38 66 31 55. Open M-Th 2pm-1am, F 2pm-2am, Sa 2pm-midnight.) For a more grandiose night out, **Cabaret Restaurant L'insolite**, 14 rue du Coq St. Marceau, serves dinner with a cabaret show. (☎02 38 51 14 15. *Menus* from 70F/€10.67. Dinner 8:30pm, show begins at 10:30pm. Open F-Sa, groups only Su-Th.)

Select-Studios, 45 rue Jeanne d'Arc, shows a few first-run English language movies and French films. (☎02 38 62 00 88. 30-48F/€4.57-7.32, matinee 25F/€3.81.) There's also **Cinema des Carmes,** just up the block at 7 rue des Carmes. The last week of June and the first week of July see a **jazz festival** (tickets 40F-150F/€6.10-22.90). On weekends in November and December, the **Semaines Musicales Internationales d'Orléans (SMIO)** brings in the Orchestre National de France.

NEAR ORLEANS: GERMIGNY, ST-BENOIT, AND SULLY

A day's drive eastward along the Loire takes in these three small towns, each dating from a different era of the Middle Ages. About 30km southeast of Orléans lies the squat Carolingian church of **Germigny-des-Près,** heavily restored but nonetheless the oldest in France. The private chapel preserves a restored 9th-century Byzantine-style mosaic. Call to request a tour in French. (☎02 38 58 27 97. Open Apr.-Sept. daily 8:30am-7pm; Oct.-Mar. 8:30am-6pm. Free.)

The prize of **St-Benoît-sur-Loire,** 35km southeast of Orléans, is an exquisite 11th- to 12th-century Romanesque basilica. Originally part of the Abbaye de Fleury, the church was destroyed during the French Revolution. Its charms now include its Romanesque mosaic floor, intricate carvings, and 75 arched pillars supporting a barrel vault. Twice daily, sung services set the whole church ringing. (☎02 38 35 72 43; fax 02 38 35 77 71. Masses M-Sa noon, Su 11am; vespers daily 6:10pm. Church open daily 6:30am-10pm. Tours Easter-Sept. in French Tu-Sa 10am and 3pm, Su 3:15 and 4:15pm. Call ahead for English tours.)

The 14th-century fortress of **Sully-sur-Loire** lies 42km from Orléans, dominating the countryside from the southern bank of the Loire. The château commands a regal presence on the wooded grounds that guard the intersection of four major roads. At one time it required three drawbridges to protect the main residence. The white-turreted castle housed a somnolent Charles VII, a frustrated Joan of Arc, a fleeing Louis XIV, and an exiled Voltaire. Inside the castle, visitors are invited to participate in interactive activities, such as designing their own coat of arms, or trying their hand at a round of chess on a life-sized board. Intricate tapestries tell the story of Psyche, who fell in love with Cupid, and horse and carriage rides are available around the grounds. (☎02 38 36 36 86. Open Apr.-Sept. 15 daily 10am-6pm; Feb.-Mar. and Oct.-Dec. 10am-noon and 2-5pm; closed Dec. 25-Feb. 1. Hours may vary in June. English tours July 12-Aug. 16 M at 1:30pm. 30F/€4.57, students and children 20F/€3.05, 10F/€1.53 extra for tours.) Sully's sprawling, grassy grounds and wooded pathways are perfect for picnics and walks. (Park open daily 9am-nightfall.) **Camping Sully-sur-Loire,** chemin de la Salle Verte, surveys the château from the riverbank. (☎02 38 36 23 93. Reception M-Sa 9am-noon and 2-7pm. Open Apr.-Sept. 8F/€1.22 per site; 12.70F/€1.94 per person, under age 8 6.30F/€0.96. 5.80F/€0.88 per car. Electricity 9-17F/€1.37-2.59.) The **tourist office** is in the center of town on pl. de Gaulle. (☎02 38 36 23 70; fax 02 38 36 32 21. Open July-Aug. M 9am-12:30pm and 2-7pm, Tu-F 9am-12:30pm and 2-7pm, Sa 9am-7pm, Su 10:30am-1pm; Sept.-June M-Sa 9am-noon and 2-6:30pm.)

The same **bus** from **Orléans** serves the three towns (**Germigny** 45min., 45F/€6.86; **St-Benoit** 50min., 47F/€7.17; **Sully** 1hr., 57F/€8.69), but comes around only three times a day (none Su). Although bus travel between the towns is difficult, the walk from St-Benoît to Germigny only takes about 45 minutes, while a trek from Sully to St-Benoît takes about 75 minutes. The adventurous may choose to make the challenging 45km **bike ride** to Sully from Orléans, with a scenic route that winds along the south bank of the Loire and passes tiny villages and sunflower fields along the way. **Driving,** take eastbound 152, which becomes the D955, in the direction of Châteauneuf-sur-Loire; signs point you to the D60, which will take you to the towns.

BLOIS

Blois (pop. 60,000) is one of the Loire's must-see cities. Its great château, one of the most important in France, is an architectural mélange of four wings, each built in a different style by four generations of the royal family. In the town itself blue slate roofs, red-brick chimneys, and narrow cobblestone lanes evoke the simple beauty of a Vermeer village. Blois is the best base for a visit to Chambord and Cheverny, arguably the most important châteaux in the Loire Valley; each is just an hour's bike trip or a 20-minute bus ride away. The tourist office has excellent maps of bike paths in the area, the most popular being a 45km bike ride that passes the châteaux and takes approximately four hours.

TRANSPORTATION

Trains: pl. de la Gare. To: **Angers** via Tours (3hr., 10 per day, 118F/€18); **Orléans** (30min., 14 per day, 54F/€8.24); **Paris** via Orléans (1¾hr., 8 per day, 125F/€19.06); and **Tours** (1hr., 10 per day, 57F/€8.69). Info office open daily 9am-6:30pm.

Buses: Point Bus, 2 pl. Victor Hugo (☎02 54 78 15 66). Info on buses to châteaux. Open M 1:30-6pm, Tu-F 8:30am-noon and 1:30-5:30pm, Sa 9am-noon. **Transports Loir-et-Cher** (TLC; ☎02 54 58 55 44) sends buses to nearby **châteaux** and **Vendôme** (1¼hr., 4 per day, 35F/€5.34). Buses leave from the station and pl. Victor Hugo.

Taxis: Taxis Radio, pl. de la Gare (☎02 54 78 07 65). 55F/€8.39 to hostel near Blois; 70F/€10.67 with baggage. 24hr.

Bike Rental: Cycles Leblond, 44 levée des Tuileries and 17 rue de Sanitas (☎02 54 74 30 13; fax 02 54 74 06 07). About 1km down the river from the city center, near the "Verdun" bus stop on line #4. 30-80F/€4.57-12.20 per day. Passport deposit. Open daily 9am-9pm.

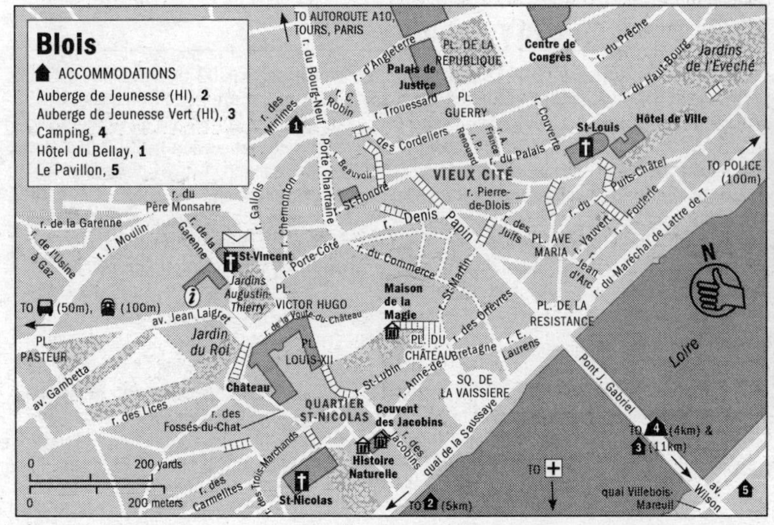

Canoe Rental: la chaussée St-Victor (☎02 54 78 67 48). Open daily 9am-6pm. 132F/€20.12 per half-day, 305F/€46.50 per day.

ORIENTATION AND PRACTICAL INFORMATION

The train station is five to ten minutes north of the château and the town center. Leaving the station, go straight down av. Jean Laigret; the tourist office will be on the left, near the bottom of the hill before sq. Augustin-Thierry. The city center is three minutes farther. The **rue Porte-Côté** leads to the bustling café-lined pedestrian quarter. When in doubt, descend, as all roads lead down to the city center.

Tourist Office: 3 av. Jean Laigret (☎02 54 90 41 41; fax 02 54 90 41 49; www.loiredeschateaux.com), in Anne de Bretagne's Renaissance pavilion. The free walking tour map in English is invaluable, as are the maps of bike paths in the area. Complete info on châteaux, including tickets for bus circuits and shows. **Currency exchange** with a 3% commission. **Accommodations service** 15F/€2.29. Open Apr. 15-Sept. Tu-Sa 9am-7pm, Su-M and holidays 10am-7pm; Jan.-Mar. and Oct.-Dec. M 10am-12:30pm and 2-6pm, Tu-Sa 9am-12:30pm and 2-6pm, Su 9:30am-12:30pm. MC/V. **Branch office,** pl. de la Voûte du Château (☎02 54 74 41 32), tucked underneath the château, provides info and hotel reservations. Open July-Aug. daily 10am-7pm. Around the corner, **Maison du Loir-et-Cher,** 5 rue de la Voûte du Château (☎02 54 57 00 41; fax 02 54 57 00 47), provides info and brochures on events, festivals, lodging, and camping. Open Apr.-Oct. daily 9am-7pm; Nov.-Mar. 9am-noon and 2-6pm.

Money: In summer, stores displaying the *No Francs, No Problem* sign accept currencies from dollars to yen at no commission—but check rates. **Banque de France,** 4 av. Jean Laigret (☎02 54 55 44 00), is on the right as you walk down the hill to the tourist office. Currency exchange available M-F 9am-12:15pm.

Laundromat: 11 rue St. Lubin, pl. Louis XII (☎02 54 74 89 82). Open daily 7am-10pm.

Youth Center: Bureau Information Jeunesse de Loir-et-Cher, 7 av. Wilson (☎02 54 78 54 87). Brochures, job info, and cheap train tickets. Open M-F 9am-12:30pm.

Police: 42 quai St-Jean (☎02 54 55 17 99).

Hospital: Centre Hospitalier de Blois, mail Pierre Charlot (☎02 54 55 66 33).

Internet Access: Bibliothèque Abbé Grégoire, pl. Jean Jaurès (☎02 54 56 27 40). 2F/€0.31 per 5min. Open M-Tu and F 1-6:30pm, W 10am-6:30pm, Sa 10am-6pm.

Post Office: 2 rue Gallois (☎02 54 57 17 17). **Currency exchange.** Open M-F 8am-6:30pm, Sa 8am-noon. **Postal code:** 41000.

ACCOMMODATIONS AND CAMPING

Auberge de Jeunesse (HI), 18 rue de l'Hôtel Pasquier (☎/fax 02 54 78 27 21), 5km west of Blois in Les Grouets. From the tourist office, follow rue Porte Côté, bear right, following rue Denis Papin down to the river, and take bus #4 (dir: "Les Grouets") to "Auberge de Jeunesse." The hostel is atop a small hilly driveway. An SNCF bus also goes there each evening around 7pm; ask at the train station. Two 24-bed, single-sex dorms in a pretty, shady setting. Excellent kitchen facilities and hot showers in bathroom complex outside. Breakfast 19F/€2.90. Reception 6:45-10am and 6-10:30pm. Lockout 10am-6pm. Curfew 10:30pm. Open Mar.-Nov. 15. Bunks 45F/€6.86.

Auberge de Jeunesse Verte (HI), levée de la Loire, off D951 in Montlivault close to Chambord (☎02 54 78 27 21—this telephone number is for the auberge in Blois, ask to be transferred to Montlivault; fax 02 54 78 27 21), 11km east of Blois. Take the TLC bus #1 (dir: "Beaugency," 22.40F/€3.42) from the station and ask the driver to drop you off by the Auberge de Jeunesse in Montlivault. Cross the highway, follow the dirt road into the field, and take a sharp left at the small FUAJ sign at the bottom. The hostel is 50m ahead under a clump of trees to the right. This rustic old stone lodging has over 32 beds in clean, painted dorms. Bright bathrooms, kitchen facilities, and a fireplace. Sleeping bags or sheets 17F/€2.59. Reception (loosely interpreted) 6-8pm; calling ahead is mandatory. Open July-Aug. only. Bunks 45F/€6.86. Camping 27F/€4.12.

Hôtel du Bellay, 12 rue des Minimes (☎02 54 78 23 62; fax 02 54 78 52 04), at the top of porte Chartraine, 2min. above the city center. Family-run establishment offers cozy, carpeted rooms overlooking a quiet back street. Breakfast 25F/€3.81. Closed Jan. 5-25. Singles and doubles 135-185F/€20.58-28.20; triples 240F/€36.59; quads 280F/€42.69. Call ahead. MC/V.

Hôtel Renaissance, 1 rue de la Garenne (☎02 54 78 02 63; fax 02 54 74 30 95; hotel.renaissance@wanadoo.fr). From the train station, follow av. Jean Laigret and turn left at the first big intersection; the hotel is on your left at the bottom of the hill. Carpeted, color-coordinated rooms in an unexciting 2-star hotel that is conveniently close to the train station. Breakfast 27F/€4.12. Singles with shower 149F/€22.71, with bath 239F/€36.44; doubles 169-259F/€25.76-39.48; triples and quads 259F/€39.50. Prices rise about 50F/€7.62 July-Aug.

Le Pavillon, 2 av. Wilson (☎02 54 74 23 27; fax 02 54 74 03 36), overlooking the Loire. 20min. from train station. Busy streets surround this hotel with bright, pretty rooms. Breakfast 35F/€5.34. Singles and doubles 120-240F/€18.30-36.59; doubles with bath 240F/€36.59; quads 300F/€45.74. Extra bed 60F/€9.15. MC/V.

Campsite: Lac de Loire (☎02 54 78 82 05; fax 02 54 78 62 03). From the station or city center, take bus #S7 to "Lac de Loire" (20min., 3 per day, 7F/€1.07). 2-star site. Open July-Aug. Tent and 1 person 85F/€12.96, 15F/€2.29 per extra person, 10F/€1.53 per child. Electricity 20F/€3.05. MC/V.

FOOD

Blois coats its citizens in chocolate. Locals have been perfecting *le chocolat blésois* ever since Catherine de Medici brought her own pastry-makers from Italy. Sumptuous *pavés du roi* (chocolate-almond cookies) and *malices du loup* (orange peels in chocolate) peer invitingly from pâtisseries along **rue Denis Papin.** For those who cling to the dinner-before-dessert convention, homey restaurants are along **rue St-Lubin** and around **pl. Poids du Roi.** For inexpensive Chinese and Greek restaurants try **Rue Drussy;** bakeries and fruit stands are in the central pedestrian area. An **Intermarché supermarket** is at 16 av. Gambetta (open M-Th 9am-12:30pm and 3-7:15pm, F-Sa 9am-7:15pm), and a **Utile** at 6 rue Drussy (open M-Sa 9am-9pm, Su 9:30am-noon and 5-9pm). Place Louis XII holds an open-air **market** (Sa 8am-12:30pm), and pl. du Château a **gourmet market** (July-Aug. Th 11am-6:30pm). **Le Castelet,** 40 rue St-Lubin, offers regional delicacies for vegetarians (*menu* 92F/€14.03), children (50F/€7.62), and everybody else (*formules* from 20F/€3.05). (☎02 54 74 66 09; fax 02 54 56 18 77. Entrees from 45F/€6.86, salads 18-32F/€2.75-4.88. Open July-Aug. M-Tu and Th-Sa noon-2pm and 7:30-10pm, W and Su 7:30-10pm; Sept.-June M-Tu and Th-Sa noon-2pm and 7:30-10pm. MC/V.)

SIGHTS

CHATEAU DE BLOIS. Brilliantly decorated with gold trimming, carved pillars, and stained glass, this château is unique among those in the Loire. Home to the French monarchs Louis XII and François Ier, Blois' château was as influential in the late 15th and early 16th centuries as Versailles was in later years. François Ier (1494-1547), whose motto "Nutrisco et extingo" (I feed on fire and I extinguish it) explains the abundance of carved and painted fire-breathing salamanders, invited artists and scientists to his court. He also enforced unprecedented respect for court women. Though not as grandiose as other châteaux of the Loire, Blois was meticulously restored by 19th-century architect Félix Duban. Housed in the château are three excellent museums: the recently renovated **Musée de Beaux-Arts,** with a remarkable 16th-century portrait gallery in the former apartments of Louis XII; the **Musée d'Archéologie,** displaying locally-excavated glass and ceramics; and the **Musée Lapidaire,** preserving sculpted pieces from nearby 17th-century châteaux. *(☎02 54 78 06 62. Open July-Aug. daily 9am-7:30pm; Apr.-June and Sept. 9am-6pm;*

Jan.-Mar. and Oct.-Dec. 9am-12:30pm and 2-5:30pm. Tours May-Sept. approx. every 30min., English tours (30min.) describe the architecture of the courtyard, while French tours (1hr.) begin in the courtyard and continue into the rooms of the château. 38F/€5.80, students under 25 and ages 6-11 20F/€3.05, ages 12-17 28F/€4.27. Tours of the city (45min.) 30F/€4.57, ages 2-12 20F/€3.05. Son-et-lumière show July-Aug. 15 daily 10:15pm; Aug. 16-31 10pm, English show on W. Joint tickets with the Musée de la Magie are available. 70F/€10.67 for museum and château; 95F/€14.48 includes the son-et-lumière. MC/V.)

VIEILLE VILLE. Blois holds its own in a land of monuments and cathedrals, but you're likely to most enjoy a its hilly streets and ancient staircases, outlined on the tourist office's walking guide. **Rue St-Lubin** and **rue des Trois Marchands** are lined with inviting bars and bakeries en route to the 12th-century Abbaye St-Laumer, now the **Eglise St-Nicolas.** *(Open daily 7:30am-6pm.)* East of **rue Denis Papin** are the most beautiful streets of all, lined with timber-framed houses narrowing into intimate alleys and courtyards. The 12th- to 19th-century **Cathédrale St-Louis,** whose 11th-century crypt is open for viewing upon demand, is a fascinating mix of architectural styles thanks to centuries of additions. (*Open daily 7:30am-6pm; crypt open July-Aug.)* At sunset, cross the Loire and turn right onto **quai Villebois Mareuil** for a view of the château rising above the homes of the commonfolk.

OTHER SIGHTS. The **Musée de la Résistance, de la Déportation et de la Libération** is not an easy museum to take in, even if it takes only 14 minutes to walk through. *(1 pl. de la Grève. ☎/fax 02 54 56 07 02. Open M-Sa 2-6pm. 20F/€3.05, students and children 5F/€0.76.)* The **Musée d'Histoire Naturelle** features minerals, flora, and fauna from the Loire region, plus tropical specimens. *(Past the château off rue Anne de Bretagne. ☎02 54 90 21 00; fax 02 54 90 20 01. Open Tu-Su 2-6pm. 15F/€2.29, students and children 5F/€0.76.)* The **Musée Diocésain des Arts Religieux,** one floor lower, displays religious objects dating back to the 15th century. *(☎02 54 78 17 14. Open Tu-Sa 2-6pm. Free.)* The **Maison de la Magie,** next to the château, entertains children with its mostly simple tricks. One amateur trickster was so impressed by the museum's godfather, Blois native Jean-Eugène Robert-Houdin, that he adopted his name: Houdini. *(1 pl. du Château. ☎02 54 55 26 26. Open July-Aug. daily 10am-12:30pm and 2-6:30pm; Apr.-June W-Su 10am-noon and 2-6pm. Live shows once per morning, and 1-2 times per afternoon. Call for off-season hours. 48F/€7.32, ages 12-17 42F/€6.40, ages 6-11 34F/€5.18.)*

ENTERTAINMENT

Blois may seem like a tame city, but there is nightlife to be found. Move from Point A, the cafés of **pl. de la Resistance,** to the modern, swanky **Z 64,** 6 rue Maréchal de Tassigny, near the center of town. It's a combination discothèque, pub, and karaoke bar. (☎02 54 74 27 76. Cocktails 25-50F/€3.81-7.62. Open Tu-Su 8:30am-4am.) Near the *place* is **Le Blue Night,** 15 rue Haute, serving over 80 international beers for 12-55F/€1.83-8.39. (☎02 54 74 82 12. Open daily 6pm-4am.) Down the street at #12, gay-frequented **L'Insomniaque** softly vibrates with house and techno (open Tu-Su 5pm-2am). **L'Elite Club**, 19 rue des Ponts Chartrains, rocks all night long with disco music. (☎02 54 78 17 73. Open Th-Sa 11pm-5am.)

In July and August, for **Le Soleil a Rendez-Vous avec la Lune,** the city holds free concerts in the street almost nightly including jazz, classical, and traditional French music. Complete schedules and locations available at the tourist office.

CHATEAUX NEAR BLOIS

Blois would be the perfect base from which to explore surrounding châteaux, were it not for the problem of transportation; all those listed below are inaccessible by train. On the bright side, **Point Bus** in Blois sends inexpensive **TLC buses** to the castles. TLC also runs a special **châteaux circuit** to **Chambord** and **Cheverny,** giving you two hours at each. Buses leave from outside the Blois train station. Keep your bus ticket, as it knocks 25% off admission to each castle. (May 15-Aug. Buy tickets at the station, at the tourist office, or on the bus.)

CATHOLIC GUISE ARE EASY In its long spell as a royal residence, Blois saw its fair share of scandals and intrigue. The most famous is the murder of the fanatically Catholic duc de Guise, who was committed to stamping out the Protestant heresy in France. When Henri III recognized a Protestant (Henri de Navarre) as the legitimate heir to the throne, de Guise was outraged. As de Guise advanced on Paris, the unpopular king fled Paris and the duke found himself in control of the capital. Emboldened, he called for a meeting of the Estates General at Blois, which he stacked with his own supporters to depose the king and elect himself. Henri had other plans for the duke. On the morning of December 23, 1588, following a meeting of the governing council, de Guise was invited to discuss some points in private with the king. On his way to the royal chamber, the king's bodyguards fell on the seven-foot duke with knives. When the drama was over, Henri stepped out from behind a tapestry and exclaimed coolly, "He looks even bigger dead than alive." The next day, the duke's brother was dispatched in a similar manner. Unfortunately for Henri, he didn't have long to enjoy his newly-won freedom; he himself was murdered by a monk eight months later. You can go to the scene of the duke's murder on your visit to the castle (see château above); the stabbing occurred in the King's Chamber, room no. 12.

If you'd prefer to travel on your own, the châteaux are within easy biking range over beautiful terrain. From Blois, it's 10km to **Cheverny** and only 6km to **Beauregard.** Bikers should start by crossing the Loire in central Blois and riding to the roundabout 1km down av. Wilson. The châteaux and towns are well-marked along the roads. Cyclists are advised to stay off the major—and narrow—French highways. The **tourist office** branch at the Châteaux de Blois has small maps of routes which will lead you safely and efficiently to the châteaux of your choice. Pay attention to route numbers on road maps: roads are marked by their destination. The **Regional Tourism Committee** (☎02 54 78 62 52) offers one-week cycling packages which include bike rental, meals, accommodations, and admission to châteaux.

CHAMBORD

*Take **TLC bus #2** from **Blois** (45min., 20F/€3.05) or enjoy the hour-long **bike** ride. Take route D956 south for 2-3km followed by a left onto D33. **Château:** ☎02 54 50 40 00. Open July-Aug. daily 9am-6:45pm; Sept. 9am-6:15pm; Oct.-Mar. 9am-5:15pm; Apr.-June 9am-6:15pm. Last entry 30min. before closing. 42F/€6.40, ages 18-25 26F/€3.96, under 18 free.*

Built by François Ier between 1519 and 1545 for his hunting trips and orgiastic fêtes, Chambord is the largest and most extravagant of the Loire châteaux. With 440 rooms, 365 chimneys, and 83 staircases, the castle is a realization of the ambitious king's most egomaniacal fantasies and compares in grandiosity to Versailles. The Greek cross floor design used for the keep was formerly reserved for sacred buildings, but François liked the idea of using it for his mansion; to complete his blasphemy, in the center of the castle, where the altar would stand in a church, he built a spectacular double-helix staircase whose design is attributed to Leonardo da Vinci. Not to leave his purpose underemphasized, François stamped Chambord with 70 of his trademark stone salamanders, commissioned 14 four-meter tall tapestries depicting hunting conquests, and left his initials splayed across the forest of stone chimneys on the rooftop terrace. Despite all this, François stayed at Chambord only 42 days.

While rooms in the château are adequately labeled in English, the experience is enhanced by a free, 90-minute architecturally-focused English tour; alternatively, you can rent a CD headset for 25F/€3.81. In summer, visitors are given lanterns to visit the castle on incomparable **night tours** that feature whispering voices, mysterious eyes peeking through the castle walls, dancing shadows, and colorful frescoes projected onto the outer walls of the castle. Visitors go through the castle at their own pace. However, though exciting, the night tour only takes you through the empty front foyers of the castle, so be sure to do the day tour to see specific castle rooms complete with furniture, tapestries, and François's personal posessions. (Night tours July-Aug. daily 10:30pm-1am, last entry midnight. 80F/€12.20, ages 12-25 50F/€7.62, under 12 free).

Chambord's **tourist office,** pl. St-Michel, next to the château, gives info on travel through the rest of the region. (☎ 02 54 20 34 86; fax 02 54 74 81 79. Open Apr.-Sept. daily 10am-7pm.) There is no currency exchange in the small town, but an **ATM** awaits outside the tourist office. While the stretch of forlorn lawn in front of the château is less than inspiring, the lush forest that surrounds it begs to be explored. **Boat** and **bike rentals** are available from a little shelter in front of the château. (☎ 02 54 33 37 54. 2-person boats 70F/€10.67 per hr., electric boats 40F/€6.10, children 35F/€5.34 for 55min.; bikes 30F/€4.57 per hr., 55F/€8.39 per half day, 70F/€10.67 per day, 60F/€9.15 each additional day. Open June-Sept. daily 10:30am-8pm; Oct.-Apr. 11am-6pm, closed Nov.-Feb.) Campers can trek to **Camping Huisseau-sur-Cosson,** 6 rue de Châtillon, about 5km southwest of Chambord on D33. (☎ 02 54 20 35 26. Open May-Sept. 21F/€3.20 per person, children 12F/€1.83, tent and 2 people 35F/€5.34.) Or try **Camping des Châteaux,** between Chambord and Cheverny in **Bracieux.** (☎ 02 54 46 41 84; fax 02 54 46 09 15. Open Apr.-Oct. 15 daily 8am-8pm. Tent and 1 person 41F/€6.25; extra adult 18F/€2.75, under age 7 8F/€1.22. Electricity 10F/€1.53.) The **Montlivault hostel** (see p. 566) is but 3.5km from Chambord.

CHEVERNY

***Buses** leave **Blois** for Cheverny at 12:30pm and return at 6pm (45min., 19F/€2.90). To **bike** to the château, take D956 south for 45min. **Château:** ☎ 02 54 79 96 29. Open July-Aug. daily 9:15am-6:45pm; Apr.-June and Sept. 1-15 9:15am-6:15pm; Oct. and Mar. 9:30am-noon and 2:15-5:30pm; Nov.-Feb. 9:30am-noon and 2:15-5pm. 38F/€5.80, students 25F/€3.81, ages 7-14 17F/€2.60. MC/V. Four-star **Camping Les Saules** is 2km away on the road to Contres. (☎ 02 54 79 90 01; fax 02 54 79 28 34. Open Apr.-Sept. 8:30am-8:30pm. 25-34F/€3.81-5.19 per person depending on the season, ages 3-11 17F/€2.59; 32-40F/€4.88-6.10 per tent.)*

Privately owned by the Hurault family since its completion in 1634, Cheverny and its impeccable grounds radiate a style unique among the major châteaux, and at times more extravagant. While perhaps lacking the royal intrigues of others, Cheverny retains magnificent furnishings. With murals, armor, and elegant tapestries covering every inch of its wall space and telling stories of Greek gods, ancient wars, or touting Latin axioms about love and bravery, Cheverny is a picture of decadence. Fans of Hergé's *Tintin* books may recognize Cheverny's Renaissance facade as the inspiration for the design of Captain Haddock's mansion. Cheverny housed the *Mona Lisa* in its Orangerie while German artillery shelled Paris during WW II. Animal lovers may want to skip the kennels, which still host 70 mixed English-Poitevin hounds who stalk stags in hunting expeditions (Oct.-Mar. every Tu and Sa). The **soupe des chiens** is not a dubious regional dish but a bizarre opportunity to see these hounds gulp down bins of ground meat in less than 60 seconds (daily except Tu and Sa when the dogs are out on hunting trips; feeding times subject to change). Next to the kennels, thousands of antlers poke out of the ceiling of the **trophy room,** around a striking stained glass window depicting a hunt.

SOUND...LIGHTS...ACTION! In 1952, Chambord witnessed the first *son-et-lumière* spectacular the world had ever seen. The whole affair was conceived by Paul Robert-Houdin, the curator of the château. The idea caught on quickly, and now nary a castle or cathedral in France abstains from a sound-and-light show to draw in nighttime crowds. The spectacles have come a long way from their spotlight-and-historical-narration beginnings, and some approach full-scale theatrical productions. Sit back and enjoy live-action games, duels, concerts, and fireworks—much as François and his courtiers did back in the good old days. Chambord and Azay-le-Rideau in particular merit a nocturnal visit.

BEAUREGARD

No buses go here, but it's 30min. by ***bike*** *from Blois. Off D956, en route to Cheverny. Ask when you rent your bike for more detailed directions. A* ***taxi*** *from Blois costs 80F/€12.20;* ***hitchhikers*** *report easy success (but don't trust those rascals).* ***Château:*** *☎ 02 54 70 36 74 or 02 54 70 40 05; fax 02 54 70 36 74. Open July-Aug. daily 9:30am-6:30pm; Apr.-June and Sept. 9:30am-noon and 2-6:30pm; Oct.-Jan. 9:30am-noon and 2-5pm; Feb. 8-Mar. 9:30am-noon and 2-5pm. 40F/€6.10, students and children over 7 30F/€4.57, under 7 free. Gardens only 30F/€4.57.*

Before François Ier unleashed his fancy on Chambord, he designed Beauregard as a hunting lodge for his uncle René. Located 6km south of Blois, Beauregard is cozier than its flashy cousin. Paul Ardier, treasurer to Louis XIII, commissioned Jean Mosnier to paint what was to become the world's largest portrait gallery. This collection of over 300 paintings is a *Who's Who* of European powers from Philippe de Valois (1378) through Louis XIII (1638), including all of the Valois monarchs, Elizabeth I, Thomas Moore, and Columbus. The floor's 5616 hand-painted Delft tiles, undergoing a 20-year restoration project, portray Louis XIII's army solemnly marching to war. Outside the château, the ruins of a 14th-century chapel invite a walk into the woods. Tours are available in French and English; times vary depending on the season and the availability of tour guides. Call ahead to check tour times. English sheets are available when tour guides are not.

VALENÇAY

Trains *run from rue de la Gare to* ***Salbris,*** *which connects to* ***Orléans*** *(2hr.; M-Sa 7 per day, 2 on Su; 97F/€14.79) and* ***Paris*** *(3hr.; M-Sa 7 per day, 2 on Su; 159F/€24.25).* ***Buses*** *go to* ***Blois*** *(1½hr.; Sept.-July 2 per day, 1 on Su; 46F/€7.02). To get to the château from the bus stop at pl. de la Halle, continue straight down rue de l'Auditoire and take your second right into pl. Talleyrand.* ***Château:*** *☎ 02 54 00 10 66. Open July-Aug. daily 9:30am-7:30pm; Apr.-June and Sept.-Oct. 9:30am-6pm; call ahead for schedule Nov.-Mar. 50F/€7.62, students and 7-17 38F/€5.80; July-Aug. and weekends in May-Sept. 53F/€8.08, students and children 43F/€6.56. Free shows in French feature actors in traditional dress. The* ***tourist office*** *is on av. de la Résistance (☎ 02 54 00 04 42).*

Midway between the châteaux of the Loire to the west and the castles of the Route Jacques Cœur to the east, the majestic château of Valençay has Renaissance and Neoclassical architecture to match any of them. Dominating the quiet town and ripe vineyards that surround it, the luxurious château was built in 1540 on the site of an earlier 12th-century fortress. Its rich owner Jacques d'Etampes intended it to compete with the likes of Chambord and Chenonceau.

The château today preserves the traditions of its 19th-century owner, the cunning Charles-Maurice Talleyrand-Périgord. Even though Talleyrand began his career under Louis XVI, he survived the Revolution and was made Minister of Foreign Affairs by Napoleon. It was the Emperor who bought the château for Talleyrand, desiring that he entertain important guests here as extra insurance for the empire's popularity. After Napoleon deposed King Ferdinand VII of Spain in 1808, he sent the Spanish royal family to Talleyrand at Valençay. Here the princes and at least 50 ladies-in-waiting remained until 1814, when Ferdinand was reinstated as monarch. The exquisite interior contains a number of remarkable items, including the table used for the Congress of Vienna and a sumptuous dining room in which some of the most celebrated culinary creations in all of Europe slipped down the throats of Talleyrand's guests four nights a week.

Admission to the château comes with a free audio guide in English and includes visits to the wine cellars, the underground kitchens, and the animal park complete with peacocks, ponies, goats, hens, and horses. Don't mistake the wallabies for kangaroos. In summer, costumed actors perform duels and short spectacles.

AMBOISE

Amboise's postcard-perfect location has enticed royalty for 500 years. Neither as ornate as Chambord nor as charming as Chenonceau, the château has a medieval, fortress-like character which is appealing in its own right. Charles VIII, Louis XI, Louis XII, and the bacchanalian François Ier ruled France from this hillside château, enjoying its extraordinary panorama of the river valley below, while Leonardo da Vinci spent his last years in the town. Not to be missed are the life-size versions of da Vinci's unrealized projects in his home/museum.

ORIENTATION AND PRACTICAL INFORMATION. **Trains** run from bd. Gambetta to: **Blois** (20min., 15 per day, 35F/€5.34); **Orléans** (1hr., 14 per day, 76F/€11.59); **Paris** (2¼hr., 5 per day, 147F/€22.42); and **Tours** (20min., 14 per day, 28F/€4.27). (☎ 02 47 23 18 23. Ticket office open M-Sa 6am-9:30pm, Su 7:30am-9:30pm. Station closes 10:15pm.) **Fil Vert buses** leave the tourist office for **Chenonceau** (30min., 3 per day, round trip 40F/€6.10) and **Tours** (25min., 3 per day, 13F/€1.98). To **rent bikes,** head out to **V.T.T. Cycles Richard,** 2 rue de Nazelles, on the north bank by the first bridge as you walk away from the station. (☎ 02 47 57 01 79. 90F/€13.72 per day. Passport or 800F/€122 deposit. Open Tu-Sa 9am-noon and 2:30-7pm.) To reach the **tourist office,** follow rue Jules-Ferry from the station and cross both bridges past the residential Ile d'Or. The office is 30m to the right of the bridge, on quai du Général de Gaulle (15min.). The staff has info about bus tours to nearby châteaux. (☎ 02 47 57 09 28; fax 02 47 57 14 35. Open July-Aug. M-Sa 9am-8pm, Su 10am-6pm; Sept.-June M-Sa 9am-12:30pm and 2-6:30pm, Su 10am-noon.) The **police** are on bd. A. France (☎ 02 47 57 26 19), and the **hospital** is on rue des Ursulines (☎ 02 47 23 33 33). The **post office** sits at 20 quai du Général de Gaulle, three blocks down the street to the left as you face the tourist office; it offers **currency exchange.** (Open M-F 8:30am-noon and 1:30-6:15pm, Sa 8:30am-noon.) **Postal code:** 37400.

ACCOMMODATIONS AND FOOD. Your best bet is the **Centre International de Séjour (HI) Charles Péguy,** Ile d'Or. Follow rue Jules-Ferry from the station and head downhill to the right after the first bridge onto Ile d'Or (10min.). The industrial feel is offset by a quiet setting; ask for a room with a view of the Loire and the château. The youth-center facilities are conducive to socializing. (☎ 02 47 30 60 90; fax 02 47 30 60 91. Breakfast 15F/€2.29. Sheets 19F/€2.90. Reception M-F 3-7pm. Beds 54F/€8.24.) **Ile d'Or camping** has clean, well-maintained facilities and a spectacular view of the Loire and the château. (☎ 02 47 57 23 37. Open Apr. 6-Sept. 23 8am-10pm; Sept.-June 8:30am-12:15pm and 3-7pm. 13F/€1.98 per person, 24F/€3.66 per site, children under 12 years 8F/€1.22. Electricity 10F/€1.53.)

A cheap picnic with a great view of the Loire can be had by climbing the hill to **ATAC supermarket,** at pl. de la Croix Bernard, at the intersection of rue Grégoire de Tours. (Open M-F 8:30am-12:30pm and 2:30-7:30pm, Sa 8:30am-7:30pm, Su 9:30am-12:30pm.) There's also a **Netto** on av. de Tours. (☎ 02 47 57 00 98. Open M-Th 9am-12:30pm and 2:30-7:30pm, F-Sa 9am-7:30pm, Su 9am-noon.)

SIGHTS. The battlements of the 15th-century **château** that six paranoid French kings called home stretch out above the town like protective arms. In 1498, as the four-foot-tall Charles VIII rushed out with his queen to watch a tennis match, he bumped his head on a low door and died a few hours later. Less slapstick was the response to a failed Protestant conspiracy against the influential, arch-Catholic de Guise family in 1560; Huguenots were thrown into the Loire in sacks and others killed on the château balcony, now described by smiling tour guides as the "Balcony of the Hanging People." In the **Logis de Roi,** the main part of the château, intricately carved 16th-century Gothic chairs stand over 6 ft. high in order to prevent surprise attacks from behind. A beautiful rosewood-veneered 1832 pianoforte in the music room was a gift from the king of Brazil, whose daughter married into King Louis Philippe's family. The jewel of the grounds is the **Chapelle St-Hubert,** outside the château, the final resting place of Leonardo da

Vinci. In summer, people flock to the "Court of King François" *son-et-lumière* (July-Aug. W and Sa), while Renaissance games and entertainment are held at the nearby park. (☎02 47 57 00 98. Château open July-Aug. daily 9am-8pm; Sept.-Nov. 9am-6pm; Dec.-Jan. 9am-noon and 2-5pm; Mar.-Nov. 9am-noon and 2-5:30pm; Apr.-June 9am-6:30pm. Nearby park open same hours as château. 41F/€6.25, students 34F/€5.19, ages 7-14 22F/€3.36; *son-et-lumière* 80F/€12.20, children 40F/€6.10.)

Just beneath the château, the **Caveau de Dégustation,** rue Victor Hugo, offers free tastings of the region's wines, cheeses, and pâté. (☎02 47 57 23 69. Open Apr. 30-Sept. daily 11am-7pm.) From the château, follow the cliffs along rue Victor Hugo beside centuries-old **maisons troglodytiques,** houses hollowed out of the cliffs and still inhabited today. Four hundred meters away is **Clos Lucé,** the manor where Leonardo da Vinci spent the last four years of his life. Inside are his furnished bedroom, library, drawing room, and chapel, but the main attraction is a collection of 40 unrealized inventions, recently built with the materials that would have been available to da Vinci at the time. Long before their respective "inventions," Leo had developed everything from the helicopter to the machine gun. (☎02 47 57 62 88; fax 02 47 30 54 28. Open July-Aug. daily 9am-8pm; Mar. 23-June 9am-7pm; Sept.-Nov. 12 9am-7pm; Nov. 13-Dec. 9am-6pm; Jan. 10am-5pm; Feb.-Mar. 22 9am-6pm. 40F/€6.10, students 32F/€4.88, ages 6-15 20F/€3.05. MC/V.)

TOURS

After Roman Cæsardom was wiped off the map by a barbarian invasion in the 3rd century, three separate towns made use of the site until the Hundred Years' War (1337-1453) compelled them to unite into one city—Tours. In the 15th and 16th centuries, Tours was the heart of the French kingdom, and although the government has long since migrated north, the city is still the urban mouthpiece of the Loire region. The birthplace of Balzac looks firmly toward the future, yet rather than cater to its growing industry, the modern day city caters to the 30,000 students who call Tours (pop. 250,000) home, and feels more like a college town than a bustling industrial center. Clothing stores, coffee shops, bakeries, and shoe racks line the wide boulevards filled with young people; warm spring and summer evenings see joggers and musicians along the strollable paths lining the Loire River. The prettiest view is at sunset, when the bridges are illuminated above the rushing waters. Tours is conveniently located near about half of the Loire châteaux, and budget travelers should use it as a base; it also offers rollicking nightlife and a good collection of sights in its own right.

TRANSPORTATION

Trains: 3 rue Edouard Vaillant, pl. du Maréchal Leclerc. Many non-local destinations require a change at **St-Pierre-des-Corps,** 5min. outside Tours; check schedule. To: **Bordeaux** (2½hr., 6 per day, 229F/€34.92); **Paris** (2¼hr., 7 per day, 160F/€24.39; TGV via St-Pierre 1hr., 6 per day, 215-280F/€32.79-42.69); and **Poitiers** (45min., 7 per day, 80F/€12.20). Ticket windows open M-Sa 6am-10pm, Su 7am-10pm.

Local Transportation: Fil Bleu (☎02 47 66 70 70). Tickets 6.90F/€1.05, *carnet* of 10 57F/€8.69. Day pass 27F/€4.12. Buses run throughout the city 7am-8:30pm; map available from the tourist office or Fil Bleu office near the train station.

Taxis: Artaxi (☎02 47 20 30 40) is available 24hr. 70F/€10.67 from the station to the hostel on weekdays, 100F/€15.25 on weekends.

Car Rental: The tourist office has a list of companies in town. **Avis** (☎02 47 20 53 27; fax 02 47 66 70 70) is by the station. 525F/€80.06 per day including 300km, insurance, and fees. 144F/€21.96 per day supplement for ages 21-24. 21+ only. Open M-F 8am-noon and 1:15-7pm, Sa 8am-noon and 2-6pm. AmEx/DC/MC/V. Similarly priced agencies include **Europcar,** 76 rue B. Palissy (☎02 47 64 47 76) and **Hertz,** 57 rue Marcel Tribut (☎02 47 75 50 00). The cheapest cars in town begin at 99F/€15.10 per day from **Ada,** 49 bd. Thiers (☎02 47 64 94 94).

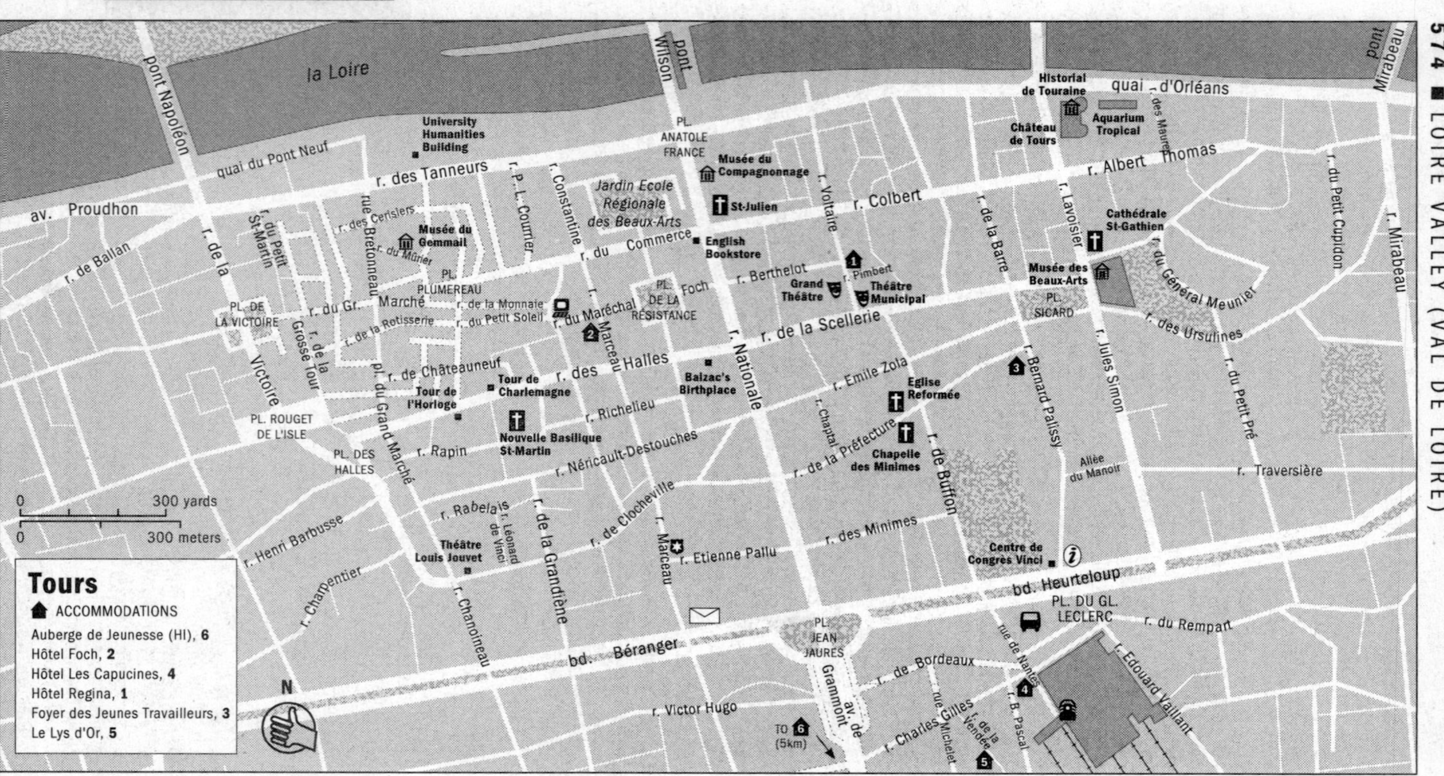

LOIRE VALLEY

Bike Rental: Amster Cycles, 5 rue du Rempart (☎02 47 61 22 23; fax 02 47 61 28 48). 85F/€12.96 1st day, 40F/€6.10 thereafter. Passport or credit card deposit. Open M-Sa 9am-12:30pm and 1-7:30pm, Su 9am-12:30pm and 5-7pm. AmEx/MC/V.

ORIENTATION AND PRACTICAL INFORMATION

Place Jean-Jaurès, vertex of four major boulevards, is the main thoroughfare. **Rue Nationale,** once part of the main road between Paris and Spain, runs north to the Loire, while **av. de Gramont** runs into the Cher river to the south. **Bd. Béranger** and **bd. Heurteloup** run west and east, respectively, from pl. Jean Jaurès. The mostly pedestrian *vieille ville*, the lively **pl. Plum',** and the tourist draws are northwest of pl. Jean Jaurès, toward the Loire. To reach the **tourist office** from the station, cross the park across from the station, and turn right at bd. Heurteloup. The office is the glass building on the left, past the futuristic Centre des Congrès.

Tourist Office:78-82 rue Bernard Palissy (☎02 47 70 37 37; fax 02 47 61 14 22; www.ligeris.com). Free maps and info booklets; finds rooms. Arranges **châteaux tours.** 2hr. historical walking tour departs daily at 10am and 2:30pm Apr.-Oct. (30F/€4.57, children 6-12 years 25F/€3.81). Call in advance to arrange English tours. The best tours are the 1½hr. walking illuminated **city tours,** every F July-Aug. Leave from tourist office at 9:30pm. 50F/€7.62, children 40F/€6.10. Office open mid-Apr. to mid-Oct. M-Sa 8:30am-7pm, Su 10am-12:30pm and 2:30-5pm; mid-Oct. to mid-Apr. M-Sa 9am-12:30pm and 1:30-6pm, Su 10am-1pm.

Money: Best rates at **Banque de France,** 2 rue Chanoineau (☎02 47 60 24 00), off bd. Heurteloup. Exchange desk open Tu-Sa 8:45am-noon.

English Bookstore: La Boîte à Livres de l'Etranger, 2 rue du Commerce (☎02 47 05 67 29). Open M 2-7pm, Tu-Sa 9:30am-7pm. MC/V.

Police: 70-72 rue de Marceau (☎02 47 60 70 69).

Hospital: Hôpital Bretonneau, 2 bd. Tonnelle (☎02 47 47 47 47).

Laundromat: Cyber-Laverie, 16bis pl. de la Victoire. **Internet access available** while you wait for laundry. Open daily 9am-7pm. **Lavo 2000,** 17 rue Bretonneau (☎02 47 73 14 69). Open daily 7am-8:30pm.

Internet access: Cyber Gate, 11 rue de Président Merville (☎02 47 05 95 94). 5F/€0.76 per 15min. Open M 1pm-midnight, Tu-Sa 11am-midnight, Su 2pm-midnight. **Cyber Micro Touraine,** pl. de la Victoire (☎02 47 38 13 13). 10F/€1.53 per 15min., 15F/€2.29 per 30min., 20F/€3.05 per hr. Open M-Sa 9am-7pm. **Net@ccess,** 21 rue de Marceau has an American keyboard. Open M 2pm-midnight, Tu-Sa 11am-midnight, Su 2-7pm; 13F/€1.98 per ½hr. 25F/€3.81 per hr.

Post Office: 1 bd. Béranger (☎02 47 60 34 20). **Currency exchange.** Open M-F 8am-7pm, Sa 8am-noon. **Branch** office on 92 rue Colbert. **Postal code:** 37000.

ACCOMMODATIONS AND CAMPING

The hostel's inconvenient location is a drawback for those wanting to stay close to the city center. Luckily, many good, cheap hotels can be found within a 10-minute walk of the station. In peak season, call a day or two in advance. **CROUS** (☎02 47 60 42 42) can provide info about discount meals and long-term housing for students.

Foyer des Jeunes Travailleurs, 16 rue Bernard Palissy (☎02 47 60 51 51). Centrally located. Meals 48F/€7.32. More availability in summer. One-time 20F/€3.05 membership. Singles with bath 100F/€15.25; doubles with bath 160F/€24.39.

Hôtel Regina, 2 rue Pimbert (☎02 47 05 25 36; fax 02 47 66 08 72). Hosts make you feel like family. The hostess might throw in a free knitting lesson. Near beautiful river strolls and good restaurants. Spotless hallway showers. Breakfast 27F/€4.12. Singles 130-180F/€19.82-27.44; doubles 140-240F/€21.35-36.59. MC/V.

Auberge de Jeunesse (HI), av. d'Arsonval in parc de Grandmont (☎02 47 25 14 45; fax 02 47 48 26 59). Bus #6 is the most direct line, although #3 and 11 also stop at the hostel. Buses leave from pl. da Vinci outside the train station to "Auberge de Jeunesse." Turn left across the busy street and follow the signs. Cheapest option for solo travelers, but too far from town to walk. TV, game room, laundry, and kitchen facilities. Breakfast included. Dinner 50F/€7.62. Sheets 17F/€2.59. Reception 7-11am and 4-10pm. Bunks 70F/€10.67; singles 109F/€16.62. MC/V.

Hôtel Foch, 20 rue du Maréchal Foch (☎02 47 05 70 59; fax 02 47 20 95 10). Just off pl. Plumereau. 14 large rooms. Unbeatable location, and a friendly proprietor eager to help you plan your day. Most rooms have shower; no hallway showers are available. Breakfast 30F/€4.57. Singles 130-220F/€19.82-33.54; doubles 150-300F/€22.90-45.74; triples 240-380F/€36.59-57.95; quads 330-380F/€50.33-57.95. MC/V.

Le Lys d'Or, 23 rue de la Vendée (☎02 47 05 33 45; fax 02 47 64 19 00), 5min. from the station—turn left and follow the signs. 15 large but dreary rooms in a dimly lit neighborhood. Breakfast 27F/€4.12 (20F/€3.05 with *Let's Go*). Singles and doubles 90F/€13.72, singles with shower 140F/€21.35, doubles with shower 120-175F/€18.30-26.68; triples with bath 235F/€35.84; quints with bath 355F/€54.14. AmEx/MC/V.

Hôtel Les Capucines, 6 rue Blaise Pascal (☎02 47 05 20 41; fax 02 47 05 20 41), just 1min. from train station. Turn left out of train station, and cross rue Nantes. Rue Blaise Pascal is next left. Dingy hallways lead to spacious, newly renovated rooms with bathrooms, showers, and TVs. Breakfast 25F/€3.81. Singles 170-180F/€25.92-27.44; doubles 195-210F/€29.73-32.02; triples and quads with bath 240F/€36.59. MC/V.

Camping: Tourist office lists campsites within 30km. The closest is **Camping St-Avertin,** 63 rue de Rochepinard in St-Avertin (☎02 47 27 27 60), accessible by bus #5 from Tours. Ask for stop nearest campsite, and follow signs (5min. walk). Tennis, volleyball, pool. Open Apr.-Oct. 15. 15F/€2.29 per person, 8.50F/€1.30 per child under 7, 15F/€2.29 per site, 8.50F/€1.30 per car. Electricity 13-21F/€1.98-3.20. **Camping Azay-Le-Rideau,** at Le Sabot (☎02 47 45 42 72). Open Easter-Oct. TV, laundry, tennis, minigolf, swimming, fishing. Pets allowed. 13.30F/€2.03 per person, 7.10F/€1.08 per child, 48F/€7.32 per site. Electricity 12.20F/€1.86.

FOOD

Tours is full of affordable restaurants serving everything from traditional *tourangelle* cuisine to ethnic fusion. **Rue Colbert** has dozens of pleasant outdoor options serving *menus* under 70F/€10.67. Look out for melt-in-your-mouth macaroons, and anything *aux pruneaux* (with prunes). Connoisseurs esteem such local wines as the light, fruity whites of *Vouvray* and *Montlouis*.

Budding chefs can browse the **indoor market,** pl. des Halles, which spreads outdoors Wednesdays and Saturdays (M-Sa 6am-7:30pm, Su 6am-1pm). The first Friday of the month brings the **Marché Gourmand** to pl. de la Résistance, an epicurean's daydream (4-10pm). **Supermarkets** are all over town. **ATAC,** 7 pl. Maréchal Leclerc, faces the train station (open M-Sa 8:30am-8pm, Su 9:30am-12:30pm). **Monoprix** is in the Galeries Lafayette on the corner of rue Etienne Pallu and rue Nationale, just north of pl. Jean Jaurès (open M-Sa 9am-7:30pm).

La Souris Gourmande, 100 rue Colbert (☎02 47 47 04 80). More cheese than a 1970s disco night with your parents. Dive into a melting pot of fondue, crêpes, omelettes and more at this excellently-priced restaurant. Staff is happy to suggest regional wines that complement the fondue options. Open Tu-Sa noon-2pm and 7-10:30pm.

Le Charolais Chez Jean Michel, 123 rue Colbert (☎02 47 20 80 20; fax 02 47 66 66 25). Regional French cuisine, exceptional regional wines, big portions, and good prices. 62F/€9.46 and 74F/€11.29 3-course lunch *menus*. Dinner *menus* 89-130F/€13.57-19.82. Open M 7:30-10:30pm, Tu-Sa noon-2pm and 7:30-10:30pm. MC/V.

SIGHTS

*A 50F/€7.62 **Carte Multivisite** includes admission to seven museums and the 2:30pm city tour. Available at the tourist office.*

Those in search of peace and quiet can leave the city behind at the beautiful **Lac de la Bergeonnerie** (also called Lac de Tours), a 10-minute ride away (bus #1), on the banks of the Cher.

CATHEDRALE ST-GATIEN. Several centuries' worth of architectural caprice have gone into the wildly intricate facade. Solid Roman columns were embellished with delicate Gothic micro-carvings in the Middle Ages, and graceful turrets were added to church spires during the Renaissance. The cathedral is celebrated for its balanced arrangement of windows and for one of the most dazzling displays of stained glass in the Loire. *(Rue Jules Simon. ☎02 47 70 21 00. Cathedral open daily 9am-7pm. Cloister open Easter-Sept. 9:30am-12:30pm and 2-6pm; Oct.-Mar. W-Su 9:30am-12:30pm and 2-5pm. Mass on Su 10am and 6:30pm.)*

MUSEE DU GEMMAIL. Works by Picasso, Braque, and Cocteau glow in rooms of dark velvet. A fusion of *gemmes* (shards of brightly colored glass) and *émail* (enamel) result in works of glass that are illuminated from behind with colored lights. *(7 rue du Murier. Off rue Bretonneau, near pl. Plumereau. ☎02 47 61 01 19; fax 02 47 05 04 79. Open Apr.-Nov. 15 Tu-Su 10am-noon and 2-6:30pm; Nov. 16-Mar W-Su Sa-Su 10am-noon and 2-6:30pm. 30F/€4.57, students 20F/€3.05, under 10 10F/€1.52.)*

MUSEE DES BEAUX-ARTS. The upper floors of the museum house primarily 17th- and 18th-century French paintings, but a few works by Degas, Monet, Delacroix, and Rodin add variety. The *primitif* collection downstairs includes two paintings by Andrea Mategna, astoundingly well-preserved since the 1430s. The Lebanese cedar outside was planted during Napoleon's reign. *(18 pl. François Sicard, next to the cathedral. ☎02 47 05 68 73; fax: 02 47 05 38 91. Open W-M 9am-12:45pm and 2-6pm. 30F/€4.57, students 15F/€2.29. Gardens open in summer daily 7am-8:30pm; off-season 7am-6pm.)*

MUSEE DE COMPAGNONNAGE. The museum houses the works of *compagnons*, or "companions," members of artisans' guilds dating back to the Middle Ages. Arm yourself with a copy of the *International Herald Tribune* article "The Aristocrats of Manual Labor" and view, with informed appreciation, such curios as an impressively detailed cathedral model and miniature spiral staircases carved in wood. *(8 rue Nationale. ☎02 47 61 07 93; fax 02 47 21 68 90. Open June 16-Sept. 15 daily 9am-12:30pm and 2-6pm, Sept. 16-June 15 W-M 9am-noon and 2-6pm. 25F/€3.81, students and seniors 15F/€2.29, under 12 free.)*

THE TWIN TOURS OF TOURS. The **Tour de l'Horloge** and the **Tour de Charlemagne,** flanking rue des Halles, are fragments of the 5th-century Basilique St-Martin, a gargantuan Romanesque church that first fell to fire in 994 and then collapsed again in 1797, a few years after Revolutionary looters removed its iron reinforcements. St-Martin himself, the city's first bishop, was carried here following his death in Candes-St-Martin and now slumbers on undisturbed in the **Nouvelle Basilique St-Martin,** a *fin-de-siècle* church in the popular Neo-Byzantine style. *(Rue Descartes. ☎02 47 05 63 87. Open daily 8am-noon and 2-6:45pm. Closed Jan.-Dec. Mass held daily at 11am.)*

ENTERTAINMENT AND FESTIVALS

Pl. Plumereau (or just plain **pl. Plum'**) is the *place* to be, with cheerful students sipping drinks and chattering at countless cafés and bars. Three clubs on the square are stacked one above the other. A bust of the Sun King keeps an older crowd in line upstairs at **Louis XIV;** even higher is the chill, jazzy **Duke Ellington.** (All 3 open daily until 2am; only Louis XIV open July-Aug.) Find more jazz a few blocks off the *place* in **Le Petit Faucheux,** 23 rue des Cerisiers. (☎02 47 38 67 62. Live combos play Tu and Sa-Su until 2:30am. 100F/€15.25, students 60F/€9.15.) Low-key **Le Café** is on 39 rue Bretonneau. (☎02 47 61 37 83. Open daily noon-2am.)

In late June Tours hosts the **Fêtes Musicales en Touraine,** a 10-day celebration of voices and instruments playing selections from Saint-Saëns to Gershwin. (☎02 47 21 65 08. 80-280F/€12.20-42.69 per night.) The end of September sees the annual **Jazz en Touraine** jazz festival, while the end of October offers the **acteurs-acteurs** festival of film and theater. Call the tourist office for more info. There's theater yearround at the **Théâtre Louis Jouvet,** 12 rue Leonardo da Vinci (☎02 47 64 50 50), and the **Théâtre Municipal,** 34 rue de la Scellerie (☎ 02 47 60 20 00).

DAYTRIP FROM TOURS: CHATEAUDUN AND VENDOME

***Trains** and **SNCF buses** run from **Tours** through **Vendôme** (1hr.; 5 per day, 3 on Su.; 60F/€9.15) to **Châteaudun** (1¾hr;, 88F/€13.42, 42F/€6.41 from Vendôme). The Vendôme station is on bd. de Tremault (☎02 54 23 50 04); Châteaudun's is at pl. Armand Lhullery (☎02 37 45 00 54).*

Northeast of Tours is the small **Loir Valley,** the rocky older brother of the Loire. The hilly countryside, dotted with troglodyte cave dwellings and strained by crisscrossing brooks, makes for easy ambling. The Gothic château of **Châteaudun** presides over the valley from a bluff 60m above the river. Joan of Arc's companion Jean Dunois, the Bastard of Orléans, rebuilt the castle in the 1450s, adding Gothic touches to the 12th-century structure; 15 pillars in the Ste-Chapelle raise 15 perfectly preserved statues from Dunois's additions. Fifty years later, Dunois's grandson began the Longueville wing, whose flamboyant Gothic facade is lined with nasty-looking gargoyles. Beside the château is the 12th-century **Eglise de la Madeleine,** pl. Cap de la Madeleine, perched 20m above the southern edge of the town center. The church was never completed and suffered severe fire damage during WWII. Its sparse white interior is now eerily empty. (Open daily 10am-noon and 2-5pm.) Down the road are the chilling and attractive **Grottes du Foulon,** 35 rue des Fouleries. A one-hour French tour takes you through the caves all the way beneath the center of town, call in advance to arrange English tours. (☎02 37 45 19 60. Open May-Sept. 10am-noon and 2-6pm, Oct.-Apr. Sa-Su 2-6pm. 30F/€4.57, students 20F/€3.05, ages 6-14 15F/€2.29.) The **tourist office,** 1 rue de Luynes, has brochures with helpful walking tours taking you past some of the city's prettiest houses and oldest alleyways, dating back to the 16th century. (☎02 37 45 22 46; fax 02 37 66 00 16; www.eureetloirtourism.com.)

Vendôme, the village of Balzac's childhood, would be unremarkable (by the Loire's blooming, bubbling standards) were it not for the **Abbaye de la Trinité,** rue de l'Abbaye, built after Geoffrey Martel's vision of three burning spears piercing into what would become the abbey grounds. The **Eglise Abbatiale** is everything but a cathedral, lacking only a bishop to claim the title. Its prickly 1506 facade is the definition of High Gothic and inside remains an elaborate shrine to the Holy Tear, empty since its lachrymose contents were appropriated by Rome in the 19th century. The 12th-century belltower has been pealing a pleasant tune ever since the Hundred Years' War. The cloister today holds the **Musée Municipal de Vendôme,** which features a number of mural paintings from Loir churches along with religious and archaeological artifacts. The **tourist office,** Hôtel du Bellay in parc Ronsard, can give you plenty of info about the entire valley. (☎02 54 77 05 07; fax 02 54 73 20 81; www.tourisme.fr. Open M-Sa 10am-12:30pm and 2-6pm, Su 10am-1pm.)

CHATEAUX NEAR TOURS

Dozens of beautiful, historic châteaux lie within 60km of Tours; though we cover all of the most popular sites, do yourself a favor and visit some of the equally appealing, lesser-known châteaux. **Driving** is by far the most convenient, though generally the most expensive, way to travel; highways are well-marked with arrow-shaped signs to most châteaux. **Biking** along the Loire between châteaux is enchanting, although **bus tours** are more efficient. You can travel in air-conditioned luxury on one of the many minibuses which leave Tours every day; expect to shell out 100-300F/€15.25-45.74, which normally includes admission fees to the châteaux. The best deal is **Valleybus** (www.touring-france.com.), which offers English day-excursions. The price includes one or two châteaux and museums, lunch, and transportation. Daytrips vary in prices, beginning at 135F/€20.58. For other tour companies, contact **Saint-Eloi Excursions** (☎02 47 37 08 04), **Touraine Evasion** (☎06 07 39 13 31), **Acco-Dispo Excursions** (☎02 47 57 67 13), or **Sillonne Val** (☎02 47 59 13 14). **Service Touristique de la Touraine** (☎02 47 05 46 09) sits right in Tours' train station, but is the most expensive. All tours have English-speaking guides. (The château of Villandry is relatively inaccessible; the only way to get there is by **taxi shuttle** (☎02 47 70 37 37) that runs daily in July at 10am and 2:30pm and returns at 2 or 6 pm. 100F/€15.25 for 1-2 people, 90F/€13.72 for 3-4 people, 75F/€11.43 for 5-7 people, contact the tourist office for more info.) Most châteaux have free tours (with printed translations or English guides), as well as various performances and special events which take place during the summer. Sound and light shows are lots of fun, and worth at least one attendance, especially if daylight visits are beginning to feel a bit dry. On your way, don't neglect the wine cellars offering free *dégustations*. **Vouvray**'s 30 cellars, 9km east of Tours on the N152, specialize in sweet white wine (☎02 47 52 75 03). By bus, take #61 from pl. Jean Jaurès to "les Patis" (20min., M-Sa 14 per day, 18F/€2.75). In **Montlouis,** across the river to the south (20min., M-Sa 3 per day, 15F/€2.29; and accessible by train from Tours). 10 *caves* pour forth wonderful dry whites. See transportation info in Tours (p. 573).

CHENONCEAU

Perhaps the most exquisite château in France, Chenonceau arches gracefully over the Cher river, flanked by shaded woods and gardens. The site of many outrageous parties in the Renaissance, the château owes its beauty to centuries of female designers. Royal tax-collector Thomas Bohier originally commissioned a château on the ruins of a medieval mill on a tiny island in the Cher river. While he fought in the Italian Wars (1513-21), his wife Catherine oversaw its practical design, which features four rooms radiating from a central chamber and straight (rather than spiral) Italian-style staircases. In 1547, Henri II gave the château to his mistress, Diane de Poitiers, who added symmetrical gardens and constructed the arched bridge over the Cher so she could hunt in the nearby forest. When Henri II died in 1559, his widow Catherine de Medici kicked Diane out of her beloved castle and designed her own set of gardens and the most spectacular wing of the castle: the two-story gallery atop the bridge, spanning the Cher. In the 18th century, Mme. Dupin employed Jean-Jacques Rousseau as her son's tutor, prompting him to write his monumental work on children's education, *Emile*. (☎02 47 23 90 07. Open daily Mar. 15-Sept. 15 9am-7pm. Call for off-season hours. 50F/€7.62, students 40F/€6.10. From late July-Aug., *son-et-lumière* at 10:15pm; 50F/€7.62, students 40F/€6.10. Entry to Château des Dames wax museum 20F/€3.05.)

There's wine at **La Cave Cellar** (open 11am-7pm; free) and you can rent 4-person **boats** for the remarkably reasonable price of 10F/€1.53 per half-hour (open July-Aug. 10am-7pm). Chenonceau's idyllic setting makes it a tempting stopover. Of the few hotels in the area, **Hostel du Roy,** 9 rue Bretonneau, is the best deal. (☎02 47 23 90 17; fax 02 47 23 89 81. Breakfast 35F/€5.34. Singles and doubles 150-300F/€22.90-45.74. MC/V.) A tiny **campground** is a few blocks left of the entrance to the château. (☎02 47 23 90 13. Open Apr. 15-Sept. 13F/€1.98 per person, 9F/€1.37 per site, 11F/€1.68 with car. Electricity 13.50F/€2.06.) Trains run to **Tours** (45min., 3 per day, 36F/€5.49); the station is 2km from the château. Don't follow the mob; cross the tracks and turn right, where a blue sign directs you to the château. Continue straight past the campground. **Fil Vert buses** leave for Chenonceau from **Amboise** (30min., 3 per day, round-trip 40F/€6.10) and **Tours** (25min., 2 per day, 13F/€1.98).

VILLANDRY

Villandry lives up to its claim to be *"le plus beau des jardins du jardin de la France"* ("the most beautiful of gardens of the garden that is France"). Built on the banks of the Cher by Jean le Breton, minister to François Ier, the château was bought in 1906 by Dr. Joachim Carvallo, the present owner's great-grandfather. He went about renovating the decaying structure and reconstructing the surrounding gardens, which had been redone in the popular English style. Today, the formal French gardens have not only become Villandry's main attraction, but are considered the most beautiful in the Loire Valley. Be sure to stroll underneath the romantic covered arbors and get lost in the passageways of the recently opened hedgerow maze. The grounds have three levels: the kitchen garden, designed like that of an Italian monastery, is so productive that its bounty is given away. The middle level is the most artistic, using hedges and flowers to form patterns. The peaceful upper level offers lime groves, swan pools, waterfalls, and a view of all the grounds. Inside, don't miss the medieval Moorish ceiling constructed from 3000 gold-leafed wooden pieces. (☎02 47 50 02 09. Gardens open July-Aug. daily 9am-7:30pm; Sept.-June 9am-7pm. Château open July-Aug. daily 9am-6:30pm; mid-Feb. to June and Sept. to mid-Nov. 9am-6pm. Château and gardens 46F/€7.02, students 32F/€4.88. Gardens only 33F/€5.03, students 22F/€3.36.)

Fifteen kilometers from Tours, Villandry is one of the closest châteaux, but it is still hard to reach via public transportation. Take one of the infrequent **trains** to **Savonnières** (10min., 2 per day, 19F/€2.90) and walk or bike the remaining 4km along the Loire; the train times work out best for Saturday visits. Many **minibus** tour agencies include Villandry in their full-day and half-day tours (see above). From Tours, **cyclists** should follow the tiny D16, a narrow marvel that winds along the bank of the Cher past Villandry to Ussé; **drivers** should stick to the D7.

USSE

Though no king ever laid a head on the fancy four-poster bed of Ussé's *chambre du Roi*, the fairy-tale spires awoke inspiration in one 17th-century visitor: Charles Perrault, who penned the tale of *Sleeping Beauty* during his stay here in 1697. It's now billed as the *château de la belle au bois dormant*, and a bizarre sub-Disneyesque experience awaits in a corner turret where costumed mannequins illustrate the story's unfolding—watch out for the Beauty's fancy lace underwear. The rest of the 15th- to 16th-century château can be seen during a 50-minute English tour. While waiting, explore Le Nôtre's fabulous gardens, the follow-up to his work at Versailles. You can also check out the Gothic chapel, wine *caves*, and stables. A small door leads from the moat to the prison, a single tiny room deep within the walls; graffiti scratched by former prisoners looks almost too well-preserved.

Ussé is easiest to get to as part of a château minibus tour; the nearest **train station** is at **Langeais** (a fine feudal château-town west of Tours) from which one can bike the remaining 13km. (☎02 47 95 54 05. Open June-Aug. daily 9am-6:30pm; Apr.-May and Sept. 9am-6:30pm; Oct.-Nov. 15 and Feb. 15-Mar. 10am-noon and 2-5:30pm. Tours only. 59F/€9, ages 8-16 19F/€2.90.)

AZAY-LE-RIDEAU

Azay-le-Rideau gazes peacefully at its reflection from an island in the Indre. Surrounded by acres of breeze-ruffled trees and grass, the present château was built on the ruins of an earlier fortress. The town acquired the nickname "Azay-le-Brulé" (Azay the Burned) in 1418 after Charles VII razed the village in revenge against a Burgundian guard who had refused to let him in. The corrupt financier Gilles Berthelot bought the land in 1518, and his wife Philippa set about designing a new castle. Though smaller than François Ier's Chambord, the château which rose from the ashes was intended to rival its contemporary in beauty and setting; the Berthelots succeeded so well that François seized the château before its third wing was completed. On the exterior walls, salamanders without crowns mark the castle as a non-royal residence built under François. Azay's flamboyant style is apparent in the furniture and the ornate Italian second-floor staircase, the latter carved with the faces of 10 Valois kings and queens and lit through open, glassless windows. Azay's *son-et-lumière* is among the highest rated in the Loire. (☎ 02 47 45 42 04. Open July-Aug. daily 9:30am-7pm; Apr.-June and Sept.-Oct. 9:30am-6pm; Nov.-Mar. 9:30am-12:30pm and 2-5:30pm, last entrance 45min. before closing. 36F/€5.49 ages 18-25 23F/€3.51, under 18 free. Audio commentary available in English 26F/€3.97. *Son-et-lumière* July daily 10:30pm; Aug 10pm, 60F/9.15. Joint ticket for night show and daytime visit 80F/€12.20, 18-25 50F/€7.62, under age 18 35F/€5.34.)

Trains run from **Tours** (30min., 3 per day, 28F/€4.27) to the town of Azay-le-Rideau, a 2km walk from the château. Turn right from the front of the station and head left on the D57. **Buses** run from the **Tours** train station to the tourist office (45min.; M-Sa 3 per day, Su 1 per day; 30F/€4.57; pay on bus). The **tourist office,** pl. de L'Europe, 1km from the train station along av. de la Gare, can give you a small map and help with rooms, although few are cheap. (☎ 02 47 45 44 40; fax 02 47 45 31 46. Open Apr.-Oct. Su-F 9am-1pm and 3-7pm, Sa 10am-1pm and 2-7pm; Nov.-Feb. M-Sa 2-6pm.) Rent **bikes** at **Le Provost,** 13 rue Carnot. (☎ 02 47 45 40 94; fax 02 47 45 91 48. 50-60F/€7.62-9.15 per half-day, 65-90F/€9.91-13.72 per day. Passport deposit. Open Tu-Sa 8:30am-12:30pm and 2-7pm, also Su and M 9am-noon in June-Aug., but you can arrange to return bikes anytime in the day or evening.) You can stay at the **Camping Parc de Sabot,** across from the château on the banks of the Indre. (☎ 02 47 45 42 72. Open Easter-Oct. 50F/€7.62 per 2 people with tent, 14F/€2.14 each additional person, children 8F/€1.22. Electricity 13F/€1.98.)

LOCHES

It was in the state room of Loches that Joan of Arc, on the heels of her Orléans victory over the English in 1429, told the indifferent Dauphin that she had cleared the way for him to travel to Reims to be crowned king. Surrounded by a walled medieval town whose ramparts and 15th-century church merit a visit in themselves, the château consists of two distinct structures at opposite ends of a hill. To the north, the 11th-century keep and watchtowers switched from keeping enemies out to keeping them in when Louis XI turned them into a state prison. The posh cell of art-lover Ludovico Sforza is perfectly preserved, its frescoes slightly peeling around the latrine and heating system. Additional curiosities include a torture chamber, galleries 20m underground, and a replica of the suspension cages used to hold revolutionary prisoners. The **Logis Royal** pays tribute to the famous ladies who held court here. It was in Loches that Agnès Sorel, lover of Charles VII, became the first woman to hold the official title of Mistress of the King of France, and here she has been entombed since her early death at age 28. Anne de Bretagne later added a lacy, stone chapel in the logis. The terrace atop the round tower offers a magnificent view of the medieval city. (☎ 02 47 59 01 32; fax 02 47 59 17 45. Open Apr.-Sept. daily 9am-7pm; Oct.-Mar. 9:30am-12:30pm and 2-5pm. Donjon or Logis Royal 24F/€3.66, students 17F/€2.59; both 32F/€4.88, students 22F/€3.36. *Son-et-lumière* F-Sa and occasionally once a week in July at 10:30pm and Aug. 10pm, call for specific dates; 70F/€10.67, ages 6-12 40F/€6.10.)

Buses drive the 40km from **Tours**'s train station (50min., 4 per day, 49F/€7.47; pay on board). **Trains** also make the journey (1hr., 9 per day, 49F/€7.47). The **tourist office** is in a pavilion near the station on brasserie-lined **pl. de la Marne.** (☎ 02 47 91 82 82; open June-Aug. daily 9:30am-7pm; Sept.-May 9:30am-12:30pm and 2-6pm.) Two blocks from the tourist office is an **ATAC supermarket,** 5 rue Descartes. (Open M-Sa 9am-12:30pm and 2:30-8pm. Open without break W and Sa.)

CHINON

High above Chinon looms the crumbling, majestic château where Richard the Lionheart drew his last breath and Joan of Arc first addressed the Dauphin. Chinon (pop. 9117) is one of the best-natured and quaintest of the Loire villages. With its medieval houses, artisan's studios, and glorious château, it makes an ideal daytrip from Tours.

PRACTICAL INFORMATION. **Trains** and **SNCF buses** run to **Saumur** via St-Pierre-des-Corps (1½hr., 2 per day, 70F/€10.67) and **Tours** (45min.; 10 per day M-Sa, 5 on Su; 47F/€7.17). A train runs from **Saumur** to **Port Boulet** (40min., 5 per day, 19F/€2.90) where you can then take a bus to **Chinon** (15min., 5 per day, 14F/€2.14). From the station (☎02 47 93 11 04), walk along quai Jeanne d'Arc, and turn right at Café de la Paix to get to pl. de l'Hôtel de Ville. Then, turn right onto the little road at the back of the square to get to pl. d'Hofheim and the **tourist office.** (☎02 47 93 17 85; fax 02 47 93 93 05. Open May-Sept. daily 10am-7pm; Oct.-Apr. M-Sa 10am-noon and 2-6pm.) The best **currency exchange** rates are at **Crédit Agricole,** 2 pl. de l'Hôtel de Ville. (☎02 47 39 88 88. Open Tu-F 8:45am-12:30pm and 2-5:15pm, Sa 9am-12:30pm and 2-4pm.) The **post office** is at 80 quai Jeanne d'Arc. (Open M-F 8am-noon and 1:30-5:45pm, Sa 8am-noon.) **Postal code:** 37500.

ACCOMMODATIONS AND FOOD. The **Auberge de Jeunesse (HI),** rue Descartes, is five minutes from town along quai Jeanne d'Arc, around the corner from the train station, but it is indefinitely closed for renovations with no set date to reopen. The big rooms at **Hôtel du Point du Jour,** 102 quai Jeanne-d'Arc, are a good value, despite the noisy street. (☎02 47 93 07 20. Breakfast 30F/€4.57. Reservations recommended. Singles and doubles 130F/€19.82, with shower 160-180F/€24.39-27.44; quads 290-310F/€44.21-47.26.) The pleasant but crowded two-star **Camping de l'Ile Auger,** across the river at Ile Auger, off N749, provides a stunning view of the château. (☎02 47 93 08 35. Open mid-Mar.-Oct. 15. 11F/€1.68 per person, 8F/€1.22 per child, 26F/€3.97 per tent. Electricity 11F/€1.68.) There is a **Shopi supermarket** at 22 pl. de l'Hôtel de Ville (open M-Sa 9am-1pm and 2:30-7pm) and an **open-air market** every Thursday on pl. Jeanne d'Arc. Find the best cheap meals around **rue Voltaire** and **pl. de l'Hôtel de Ville.**

SIGHTS. The **château** presides in august rubble on a hilltop overlooking the Vienne River. First erected in the 10th century, the château has crumbled not under attack but by neglect; the stone walls nevertheless convey a sense of history and past glory unexpected for their partially crumbled state, and capture the imagination more than even some of the fully renovated châteaux in the region. The three-part château has recently-discovered tunnels which originally connected each fortress during sieges; additional tunnels, just wide enough for a man to crawl through on his stomach, lead to the main well and the town center. Thanks to a belief that anyone who captured the **Tour Marie-Javelle** would die a horrible death, the 14th-century belltower has withstood the Hundred Years' War, the Wars of Religion, and the French Revolution without a blemish—and has proudly struck every half-hour since 1399. A wonderful **Joan of Arc Museum** occupies the top floor with an English audio-visual presentation about Joan's military travels and numerous artistic tributes to the young warrior, as well as a copy of her 14th-century signature. (Open Apr.-Sept. daily 9am-7pm; Oct.-Mar. 9:30am-12:30pm and 2-5:30pm. 29F/€4.42, students 20F/€3.05.) Just as great a tribute is in **pl. de Jeanne d'Arc,** where a dynamic 1893 monument by Jules Colleau honors the saintly youngster. Less forbidding tunnels than those of the château dig into the hillside at **Maison Plouzeau,** 94 rue St. Maurice, where M. Plouzeau's sons conduct free tours and pour their superb red wines in a *cave* beneath the château. (☎02 47 93 16 34. Open Easter-Aug. Tu-Sa 11am-1pm and 3-7pm.) The **Musée Animé du Vin et de la Tonnellerie,** 12 rue Voltaire, illustrates wine-making from grape-crushing to barrel building; costumed automata in bad wigs lace the 20-minute tour with Rabelais quotes, exhorting you to "drink always and never die." Their free *dégustations* of wine and wine jam are sure to lift your spirits. (☎02 47 93 25 63. Tours in French and English. Open Apr.-Sept. daily 10:30am-12:30pm and 2-7pm. 25F/€3.81.) Finally, the tourist office organizes 90-minute **walking tours** of the city. (July-Aug. Tu-Th, F-Su 3:30pm; July 13-Aug. 11 additional morning tours at 9:30am; June and Sept. W, Sa, Su 3:30pm. Tours leave from the tourist office. Call in advance for English tours. 30F/€4.57, students and children 15F/€2.29, children under 12 free.)

SAUMUR

Saumur (pop. 30,000) is known for both its wines and its equestrian tradition. Samur is home to the national cavalry school, whose elite *Cadre Noir*—Black Corps—has trained the country's best riders since the 18th century. As a refreshing break from the usual castle-heavy Loire and with an enchanting old quarter, it's not hard to see why Saumur has won a spot on *le pôle touristique*, the official government list of eight places in France you simply must see. Munch a mushroom and enjoy, as Balzac did, "the essential strangeness of the place."

TRANSPORTATION

Trains: av. David d'Angers. To get to station from pl. Bilange in town center, take bus A (dir: "St-Lambert" or "Chemin Vert"). Local bus costs 7.50F/€1.14. To: **Angers**

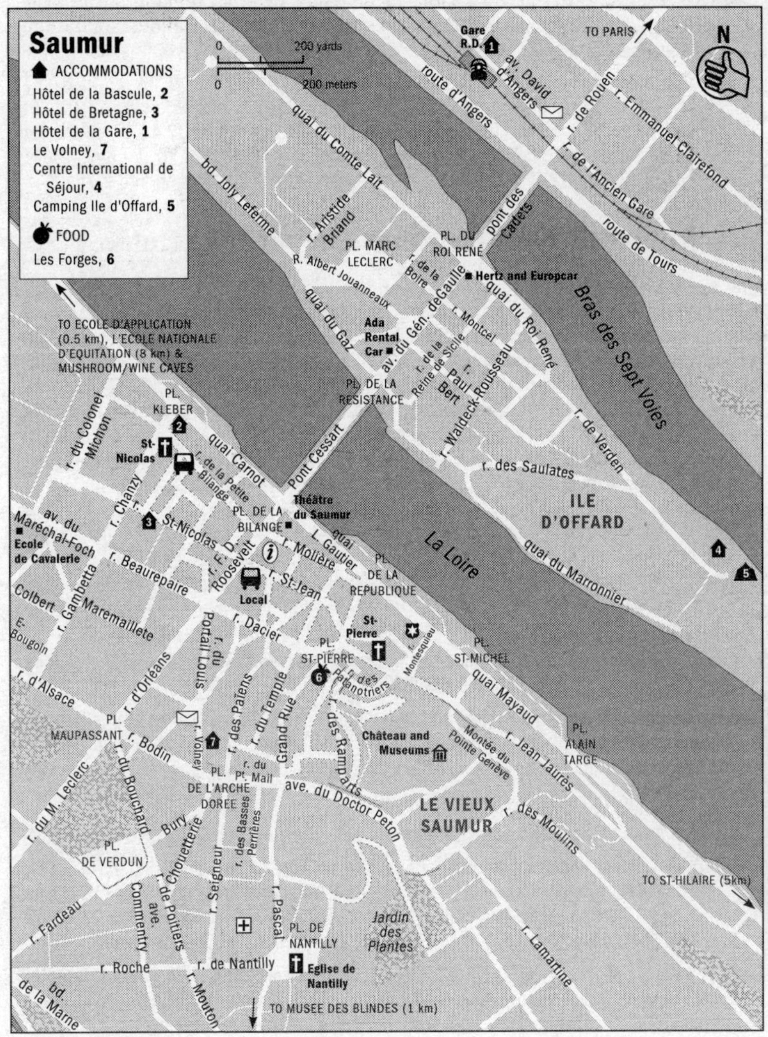

(30min., 23 per day, 43F/€6.56); **Nantes** (1hr., 9 per day, 100F/€15.25); **Paris** (1½hr., 8 per day, 248F/€37.82); **Poitiers** (2½hr., 6 per day, 135F/€20.59); and **Tours** (45min., 21 per day, 57F/€8.69). Luggage storage available. Ticket office open until 9:30pm, station open until midnight.

Buses: pl. St-Nicolas (☎02 41 51 11 87 local, ☎02 41 81 49 72 intercity), across from St-Nicolas church. Departures from here or rue F. Roosevelt to **Angers** (1½hr., 6 per day, 34F/€5.19). **SNCF buses** leave from train station to **Le Mans** (110min., 10 per day, 103F/€15.71) and **Nantes** (3½hr., 2 per day, 132F/€20.13).

Local Transportation: Bus Saumur, 19 rue F. Roosevelt (☎02 41 51 11 87). Buses run M-Sa 7am-7:30pm; schedules are unreliable in July and Aug. Tickets 7.50F/€1.14. Office open M-F 9am-12:15pm and 2-6pm, Sa 9am-noon and 2-5pm.

Car Rental: Cheapest at **Ada,** 29 av. Général de Gaulle (☎02 41 50 46 77). From 99F/€15.10 per day. Open M-F 8am-noon and 2-6:30pm, Sa 9am-noon and 3-6:30pm, closes W 6pm. **Hertz,** 78/80 av. Général de Gaulle (☎02 41 67 20 06), Open M-F 8am-noon and 2-7pm, Sa 8:30am-noon and 2-5:30pm. From 276F/€42.09 with 200km included, under 21 fee of 144F/€21.96 per day.

Bike Rental: Camping Municipal, on Ile d'Offard (☎02 41 40 30 00; fax 02 41 67 37 81). 45F/€6.86 per half-day, 70F/€10.67 per day, 315F/€48.03 per week. Passport or 1000F/€152.46 deposit. **Cycles Cesbron,** 79 rue d'Orléans (☎02 41 67 69 32; fax 02 41 38 68 61), on the road to the mushroom caves. 80F/€12.20 per day, 450F/€68.61 per week. 1000F/€152.46 deposit. Open M-Sa 9:30am-noon and 2-7pm.

ORIENTATION AND PRACTICAL INFORMATION

The tourist office and most sights are on the left bank of the Loire, a 10- to 15-minute walk from the train station, which is on the right bank; the hostel sits on an island between the two. To reach the hostel and campsite, cross pont des Cadets and turn left immediately onto rue Roi De Sicile and continue straight for 10 minutes. The hostel and camping are at the same site on the left hand side of the road. Don't be confused when you pass bd. de Verdun on the right on your way to rue de Verdun which is farther down the road. Continue straight on av. Gén. de Gaulle to reach the city center. The tourist office will be to your left, at the corner of quai Lucien Gautier. Bus A also goes all the way there from the train station.

Tourist Office: pl. de la Bilange (☎02 41 40 20 60; fax 02 41 40 20 69). Multilingual staff books beds (5F/€0.76). Free maps. Tours suggestions. "14 Sites/14 Privileges" card, guarantees free gift when you visit a pictured site. Open July-Aug. M-Sa 9:15am-7pm, Su 10:30am-12:30pm and 2:30-5:30pm; June-Sept. M-Sa 9:15am-12:30pm and 2-6pm, Su 10:30am-5:30pm; mid-Oct. to mid-May Su 10am-noon.

Currency Exchange: Best rate generally at the **Banque de France,** 26 rue Beaurepaire (☎02 41 40 12 00). Open M-F 8:45am-noon.

Laundromat: 12 rue Maréchal Leclerc. Open daily 7am-9:30pm. Also at 16 rue Beaurepaire, open daily 7:30am-9:30pm, till 10pm in the summer, and at 74 rue du Général de Gaulle, open daily 7am-9pm. 22-44F/€3.36-6.71 per load.

Police: rue Montesquieu (☎02 41 83 73 00).

Medical Assistance: Centre Hospitalier, rue de Fontevraud (☎02 41 53 30 30).

Internet Access: Welcome Services Copy, 20 rue Portail-Louis (☎02 41 67 75 15). 35F/€5.34 for up to 1hr. Open M 2:30-7pm, Tu-F 9am-12:30pm and 2-7pm, Sa 10am-noon and 2:30-6pm; June-Aug closed M. **Internet Café,** 37 rue Rabelais (☎02 41 52 72 72). Open daily 12:30-8:30pm. 20F/€3.05 per 30min., 35F/€5.34 per hr.

Post Office: rue Volney (☎02 41 40 22 05). **Currency exchange.** For **Poste Restante,** address to "Saumur Volney 49400." Open M-F 8am-6:30pm, Sa 8am-noon. There is another office across from the train station. **Postal code:** 49400.

ACCOMMODATIONS AND CAMPING

Le Volney, 1 rue Volney (☎02 41 51 25 41; fax 02 41 38 11 04; contact@le-volney.com), on a quiet street in the town center, one block off rue d'Orléans. Friendly young proprietor rents large, beautifully furnished rooms at reasonable prices. Bed-and-breakfast feel. Breakfast 35F/€5.34. Singles and doubles with TV, telephone, and toilet 160-170F/€24.39-25.92; with shower 220-270F/€33.54-41.16. MC/V.

Centre International de Séjour, rue de Verdun (☎02 41 40 30 00; fax 02 41 67 37 81). Hostel on Ile d'Offard, between station and tourist office. Adequate rooms. 2-person rooms especially nice. Helpful English-speaking staff. Pool, TV, pinball, and laundry. Breakfast and sheets included. Reception 8am-8pm; until 9pm in summer. Closed Dec. 15-Jan. 15. 2- to 8-bed dorms 85F/€12.96; 2- to 4-bed dorms with shower 150F/€22.90 for first person, 60F/€9.15 for each additional person. Ask at reception for free tickets to Grottien and Meyer *caves*.

Hôtel de la Gare, 16 av. David d'Angers (☎02 41 67 34 24), across street from train station. Streaky painted hallways and ragged carpets lead to bright, clean, decent rooms. Minimal noise. Breakfast 30F/€4.57. Singles and doubles 140F/€21.35, with shower 190F/€28.97; triples and quads 250F/€38.12. MC/V.

Hôtel de la Bascule, 1 pl. Kléber (☎02 41 50 13 65), near Eglise St-Nicolas on quai Carnot. For those willing to spend a few more francs, these rooms are worth it. Newly renovated with spotless bathrooms. All rooms have TV and showers. Many overlook the river. Breakfast 33F/€5.03. Reception closed Su Oct.-June. Singles and doubles 200F/€30.49; one big room for 2-4 people 244F/€37.21. Extra bed 40F/€6.10, MC/V.

Hôtel de Bretagne, 55 rue St-Nicolas (☎02 41 51 26 38). Conveniently situated in the town center. Adequate rooms. Breakfast 34F/€5.19. Singles and doubles 145F/€22.11, with micro-shower or toilet 165F/€25.16, with shower and toilet 195F/€29.73; triples with the works 250F/€38.12. Extra person 55F/€8.39. MC/V.

Camping de l'Ile d'Offard (☎02 41 40 30 00; fax 02 41 67 37 81), same site as hostel. 4-star site with pool, laundry, tennis, snack shop, minigolf, and TV. Reception 8am-8pm. Closed Dec. 15-Jan. 15. June-Aug. 110F/€16.77 for 2 people with car, 80F/€12.20 without car, 25F/€3.81 for each additional person; Sept.-May 80F/€12.20 for 2 people with car, 40F/€6.10 without car. Electricity 17-19F/€2.59-2.90.

FOOD

Saumur is renowned for its sparkling *crémant de Loire* wine and its mountains of mushrooms, grown in caves hollowed out along the riverbank. Stock up on fungi at the indoor **market** at the far end of pl. St-Pierre (Su-F until 1pm, Sa until noon), or its outdoor brethren on pl. de la République (Th morning) and pl. St-Pierre (Sa morning). The **ATAC supermarket,** 6 rue Franklin D. Roosevelt, sits inside the shopping center across from the Printemps department store, with a back entrance on rue St-Nicolas. (☎02 41 83 54 54. Open M-Th 9am-7:30pm, F until 8pm, Sa until 7pm. MC/V.) An assortment of cheap restaurants are sprinkled along **rue St-Nicolas;** while the town sleeps Sunday away, **pl. St-Pierre** and its offshoots are a great option for light food and drinks. **Les Forges,** 1 pl. St-Pierre, specializes in grilled meats. House specialty *steak tartare* served with a crazy assortment of condiments. The sparkling *saumur rouge* goes for 15F/€2.29 per glass. (☎02 41 38 21 79. 3-course *menus* 75F/€11.43 and 105F/€16.01. Open W-M noon-2pm and 7-10pm; closed Sundays in winter. MC/V.)

SIGHTS

The impressive number of museums and festive *caves* will keep you busy all day, but that doesn't mean you can't enjoy the city's quieter gems as well. Already housing three 12th- to 15th-century **churches** in its main district, Saumur also tucks a very pretty **Jardin des Plantes** between rue Docteur Peton and rue Marceau, on the other side of the château. The picturesque **Pont Cessart** has a fantastic view, and the promenades along the river are nice for sunset strolls.

CHATEAU. Saumur's 14th-century château is best known for its cameo appearance in the famous medieval manuscript "*Les très riches heures du duc de Berry*" and lives up to its reputation as "the very image of a fairy tale château." For two centuries, Huguenots studied at the prestigious Protestant academy inside before the château was pillaged, abandoned, and finally converted into a prison. It now houses two small museums. The **Musée des Arts Décoratifs** has a collection of medieval and Renaissance painting and sculpture, 15th- and 16th-century tapestries, and brightly decorated *faïence* (stoneware). The horse-crazy **Musée du Cheval** holds tack from all over the world and traces the evolution of man's second best friend. *(Château and museums ☎02 41 40 24 40. Open July-Aug. daily 8:30am-10:30pm; June-Sept. 9:30am-6pm and 8:30-10:30pm; Oct.-May W-M 9:30am-noon and 2-5:30pm; Oct.-Mar. closed Tu. English tours (70min.) June-Sept. All three 38F/€15.79, students 27F/€4.12. Castle gardens half-price.)*

GRATIEN ET MEYER. Saumur's wines have been prized since the 12th century, when Plantagenêt kings took their favorite casks with them to England. The popular Gratien et Meyer offers tastings and tours (15F/€2.29) that describe the wine making process from grape harvest until it hits your tongue. The site also houses the **Musée de la Figurine-Jouet,** a collection of 20,000 toy soldiers. The small collection of figurines in the *cave's* office should be enough for most. *(Rte. de Montsoreau. ☎02 41 83 13 32. Take bus D from pl. Bilange to "Beaulieu." Both open June 15-Sept. 15 daily 9am-6:30pm; Sept. 16-June 14 9am-noon and 2-6pm; Nov.-Mar. M-F 9am-noon and 2-6pm, Sa-Su 10am-12:30pm and 3-6pm. Tour 15F/€2.29, museum 25F/€3.81, children 15F/€2.29.)*

MUSEE DU CHAMPIGNON. This is what you'd expect—a dark, dank cave full of exotic mushrooms. Tours in English trace the history of the mushroom, with emphasis on its cultivation in France, the world's third-largest mushroom producer. The mushroom grill outside serves gourmet *hors d'oeuvres* (30-46F/€4.57-7.02) from noon-3pm. *(Rte. de Gennes, St-Hilaire-St-Florent. ☎02 41 50 31 55. Open Feb. 3-Nov. 11 daily 10am-7pm. 40F/€6.10, students 30F/€4.57, children 6-14 25F/€3.81.)*

L'ECOLE D'APPLICATION DE L'ARME BLINDEE ET DE LA CAVALERIE. Saumur is famous for its equestrian associations, of which this 18th-century mouthful is the most notable. In 1939, its lightly-armed cadets deemed surrender dishonorable and held back the mighty Wehrmacht for three days. These stables served as the training grounds for Saumur's celebrated equestrian troops until 1984, but now only house their uniforms, weapons, and horse tackle in **Musée de la Cavalerie.** *(Pl. Charles de Foucauld. June-Aug. ☎02 41 83 92 10, off-season ☎02 41 83 93 15. Open May 26-July 22 Tu-Su 10am-noon and 3-6pm. Tours last 1hr., but are by appointment only. 15F/€2.29.)*

ECOLE NATIONALE D'EQUITATION. The spectacular Cadre Noir tradition is kept up within this civilian national riding school. The palatial 20th-century premises, 15 minutes from the center of town, boast over 50km of training grounds, 400 fine purebreds, and the world's best veterinarians. Tradition demands unwavering obedience from the horses and irreproachable decorum from the riders, who have, since 1825, donned "black dress decorated with gold, and 'lampion' hats worn ready for battle." Tours discuss facilities and the rigorous demands of equestrianism; morning visits include a half-hour viewing of daily training. *(☎02 41 53 50 60. Take bus D to "Alouette;" continue along the road in the same direction until signs direct you the remaining 3km. Visits with a peek at equestrian drills Apr.-Sept. Tu-Sa 9:30-11am (last tour at 11). Visits without drills M-F 2:30-4pm (last tour 4pm), Sa morning visits only. Shows last 90min. in the morning, 1hr. in the afternoons, though the morning tours are worth the extra 30min. Mornings 40F/€6.10, children 20F/€3.05; afternoons 30F/€4.57, children 15F/€2.29.)*

MUSEE DU MASQUE. In the commune of St-Hilaire-St-Florent, this museum displays a collection of carnival masks in thematic scenes. The exhibit pays tribute to Saumur's carnival-mask factory, the largest of its kind in Europe. *(Rue de l'Abbaye. ☎02 41 50 75 26, off-season ☎02 41 50 26 54; fax 02 41 50 28 71. Open Easter-Oct. 15 daily 10am-12:30pm and 2:30-6:30pm; Mar. 15-Easter 2-6pm; Oct. 15-Dec. 15 Sa and Su only 2-6pm. Tours last 45 min. 25F/€3.81, children 15F/€2.29.)*

MUSEE DES BLINDES. Displays of over 150 guns and armored cars from 15 different countries. Keep an eye out for the camouflaged Tiger I, a monstrous German cruiser, and the Leclerc, France's first tank. Once a year, in mid-July, French soldiers drive the unwieldy tanks around like bumper cars. *(1043 rte. de Fontevraud. ☎02 41 53 06 99. Take bus A or C to "Musée." Visit lasts 90min. Open May-Sept. daily 9:30am-6:30pm; Oct.-Apr. 10am-5pm. 25F/€3.81, children 15F/€2.29.)*

ENTERTAINMENT AND FESTIVALS

The **Théâtre de Saumur** (☎02 41 83 30 85), next to the tourist office, hosts everything from *galas de danse* to jazz and classical concerts in its 19th-century hall. **Le Blues Rock Magazine,** 7 rue de la Petite Bilange, features live nightly concerts, from jazz to the unidentifiably uproarious, 6:30-9:30pm; dancing takes over 11pm-4am. (☎02 41 50 41 69. Cover 40-50F/€6.10-7.62; drinks 25-30F/€3.81-4.57. Open May-Sept. daily; Oct.-Apr. Tu-Su. MC/V.) For a few games of pool, head to **Le Général,** 67 av. de Général de Gaulle. (☎02 41 67 31 77. 5F/€0.76 per game, 13F/€1.98 per beer. Open M-Sa 6:30am-10pm, Su 8am-1pm.) Late-night lingerers loiter in **pl. St-Pierre** beside the illuminated cathedral, while livelier crowds and louder music beat around the Irish pubs in **pl. de la République.**

In the first week of July, the three-day **Estivales de Saumur** bring a fun, festive atmosphere to rue St-Nicolas with vendors, outdoor dining, music, and free food. The **International Festival of Military Music** bugles in late June every other year, with the next one occurring in 2003. Alternating years, during the same time slot, there's the **Festival des Géants,** a march of over-sized puppets that pays tribute to Saumur's eternal fascination with carnivals. In late July, the cavalry school and the local tank school join forces in the celebrated **Carrousel.** After two hours of graceful equestrian performances, the spectacle degenerates (or evolves) into a three-hour motorcycle show and dusty tank parade. (Info and reservations ☎02 41 40 20 66. Tickets 120F/€18.30.) Saumur annually hosts dozens of (often free) equestrian events. The tourist office has the information.

DAYTRIP FROM SAUMUR: FONTEVRAUD-L'ABBAYE

*The **#16 bus** makes the 14km trip from **Saumur**'s train station (25min., 3 per day, 14F/€2.14). The **tourist office** can give you a free map of the town, which also houses the Gothic **Eglise St-Michel.** (☎02 41 51 79 45. Open Apr.-Oct. 15 daily 10am-noon and 2:30-6:30pm.) One stop before Fontevraud, in **Montsoreau,** are curious **troglodyte cliff dwellings.** Call the tourist office in Montsoreau (☎02 41 51 70 22) for info.*

The **Abbaye de Fontevraud,** the largest monastic complex in Europe, has awed nine centuries of visitors. The founder of this now-defunct community, Robert d'Arbrissel, settled in the forest of Fontevraud in 1101. To increase the humility of his monks, he placed a woman at the head of the order. Of its 32 abbesses, 16 were of royal blood; under their rule the abbey became a place of refuge for women of all classes—from reforming prostitutes to princesses escaping unhappy marriages. Following the Revolution the abbey became a prison, and so it remained from 1804 until 1963. The 12th-century abbey church serves as a Plantagenêt necropolis; **Eleanor of Aquitaine,** who lived out her days here after being repudiated by her second husband, **Henry II,** now lies next to him along with their son **Richard the Lionheart.** The British government has repeatedly sought to transfer the royal remains to Westminster, but the French insist that the Plantagenêts were dukes of Anjou first, kings of England second. The walls of the abbey's **chapter house** are painted with scenes that depict Christ's last hours. The most notable decoration is the carving of God holding the world in his hands that sits above one of the carved archways in the Abbey; throughout the centuries, part of the timeline has been obstructed by intruding nuns—seven abbesses have had themselves added to the wall paintings. Outside, the gardens are organized into patches of legumes, tubers, greens, and medicinals; they bloom behind the abbey kitchen, whose spire-like chimney led 19th-century restorers to take it for a chapel. Be sure not to miss the 12th-century kitchens and the ceiling models' fascinating architecture of a square superimposed inside an octagon, that culminates in a circle at the top. An English booklet and signs help visitors along; don't bother waiting for one of the hour-long English tours. The themed visits put a different spin on life in the abbey and are worth the extra price, but are only available in French. (☎02 41 51 71 41. Abbey open June-Sept.16 daily 9am-6:30pm; Sept. 17-May 9:30am-12:30pm and 2-5:30pm. Tours last 1¼hr. 36F/€5.49, students 23F/€3.51; theme tours 10F/€1.53.)

ANGERS

From behind the imposing walls of their fortress in Angers (pop. 220,000), the medieval dukes of Anjou ruled over the surrounding territory and a certain island across the Channel. The 13th-century château remains well preserved, although the rest of the valley now blooms with shops, museums, and gardens. Angers today offers inexpensive restaurants and a youthful atmosphere that keeps the town hopping well into the night. But the city's traditions haven't been forgotten; café-lined streets link a remarkable array of museums, while two medieval edifices housing Angers' world-famous tapestries provide another reason to visit.

TRANSPORTATION

Trains: rue de la Gare. To: **Le Mans** (30min., 6-7 per day, 89F/€13.57); **Nantes** (1hr., 5 per day, 84F/€12.81); **Orléans** (3-4hr.; 6 per day, change at St-Pierre des Corps; 150F/€22.90); **Paris** (2-4hr., 3 per day, 254-320F/€38.74-48.80); **Poitiers** (2-2½hr.; 4-5 per day, change at St-Pierre or Tours; 152F/€23.18); and **Tours** (1hr., 7 per day, 86F/€13.12). Ticket office open daily 5:45am-9:30pm.

Buses: pl. de la République (☎02 41 88 59 25). To **Rennes** (3hr., 2 per day, 97F/€14.79). Open M-Sa 6:15am-7:15pm.

Local Transport: COTRA buses (☎02 41 33 64 64). Buses leave from pl. Kennedy or pl. Ralliement 6am-8pm. Limited night service 8pm-midnight. Tickets 6.60F/€1.01.

Taxis: Angers Taxi-Anjou Taxi (☎02 41 87 65 00). **Accueil Taxi Radio-Angers Taxi** (☎02 41 73 98 20). Open daily 5am-11pm; call ahead for a taxi outside these hours. 50F/€7.62 from the train station to the hostel.

Bike Rental: Maison du Port, Cale de la Savatte. 50F/€7.62 per half-day, 70F/€10.67 per day. ID or credit card deposit. Open daily 10:30am-noon and 2-6:30pm.

ORIENTATION AND PRACTICAL INFORMATION

To reach the château and tourist office, leave the train station walking straight onto rue de la Gare. Turn right at the roundabout one block from the train station, at pl. de la Visitation, onto rue Talot. At the traffic light, a left onto bd. du Roi-René leads to the château at pl. du Président Kennedy. The **tourist office** is on the right across from the château. To get to the city center, walk past the office onto rue Toussaint, which leads to **pl. du Ralliement,** the center of town. Go left, and one block down is **rue St-Laud,** the pedestrian-only zone of shops and pâtisseries. If taking a bus from the train station, exit the station and turn right; as you walk up the hill, you'll pass two stops on the route of most bus lines.

Tourist Office: pl. Kennedy (☎02 41 23 50 00; fax 02 41 23 50 09; accueil@angers-tourisme.com). Staff organizes trips to châteaux, reserves rooms, sells tickets to local events, hands out free maps, and **exchanges currency.** Open June-Sept. M-Sa 9am-7pm, Su 10am-6pm; Oct.-May M-Sa 9am-6pm. Offers **walking tours** of the city every Sa June-Sept. at 3pm, french only (☎02 21 23 50 10; fax 02 41 23 50 29; christine.thinon@angers-tourisme.com). 30F/€4.57, students 20F/€3.05.

Money: Banque de France, 13 pl. Mendès-France (☎02 41 24 25 00), has good rates of **currency exchange.** Exchange desks open M-F 9am-noon.

Youth Services: Centre d'Information Jeunes, 5 allée du Haras (☎02 41 87 74 47). Job and student info, discount services. Open M-F 1-3:30pm, Sa 10am-noon.

Laundromat: Laverie du Cygne, pl. de la Visitation (☎02 41 86 11 20). **Laverie des Justices,** 10 pl. Justices (☎02 41 47 24 22). Both open daily 8am-noon and 2-8pm.

Hospital: Centre Hospitalier, 4 rue Larrey (☎02 41 35 36 37).

Police: Gendarmerie, 33 rue Nid de Pie (☎02 41 73 56 10). For emergencies, dial 17.

Internet Access: Cyber Espace, 25 rue de la Roë (☎02 41 24 92 71). 15F/€2.29 per 30min. 25F/€3.81 per hr. Open M-Th 10am-10pm, F-Sa 10am-midnight.

Post Office: 1 rue Franklin Roosevelt (☎02 41 20 81 81), just off Corneille near rue Voltaire. **Currency exchange.** For **Poste Restante** mark "Angers-Ralliement 49052." Open M-F 8am-7pm, Sa 8:30am-12:30pm. **Postal code:** 49052.

ACCOMMODATIONS AND CAMPING

Auberge de Jeunesse Darwin (HI), 3 rue Darwin (☎02 41 22 61 20; fax 02 41 48 51 91). Take bus #6 (dir: "St-Sylvian") or #1 (dir: "Belle-Beille") to "Bull"; walk past the Bull Factory on av. General Patton, and signs on the right-hand side will point you to the hostel; the #6 is faster (20min.). The night bus #11 1/S (dir: "Belle-Beille/Lac de Maine") runs to pl. Ralliement until 12:10am. Dark 1-, 2-, and 3-bed rooms with poorly-kept hall showers and bathrooms. Unwelcoming, industrial setting and architecture make the hostel feel like a factory. Kitchen facilities, TV, ping-pong, billiards. Breakfast 20F/€3.05. Sheets 22F/€3.36. Reception until 10pm. Dorms 50F/€7.62; singles 65.50F/€9.98. 8-10F/€1.22-1.53 more for non-members.

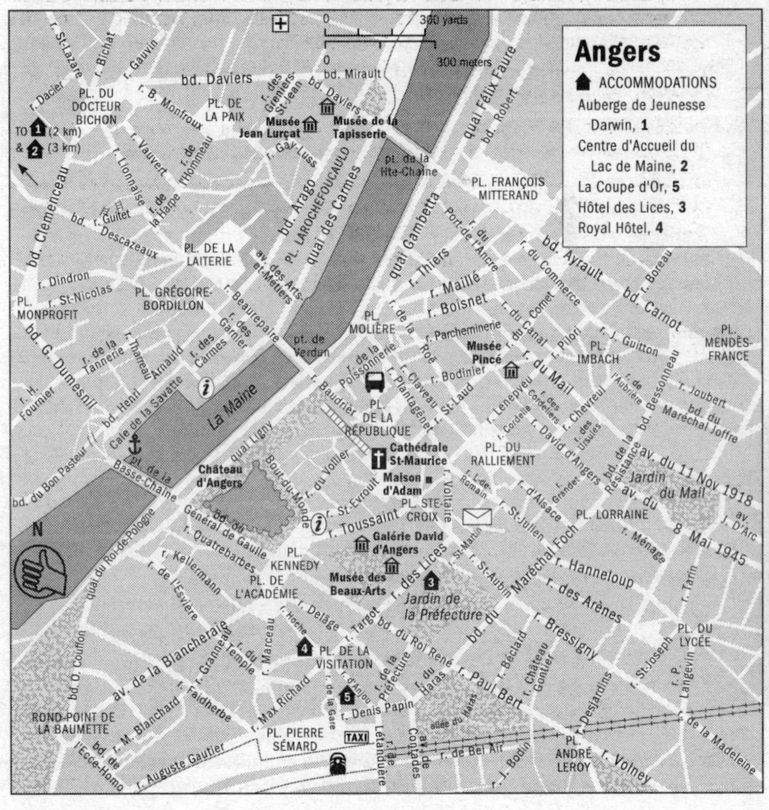

Royal Hôtel, 8bis pl. de la Visitation (☎02 41 88 30 25; fax 02 41 81 05 75). Walk straight down rue de la Gare for one block and the hotel will be ahead of you, on the corner of rue d'Iena. 40 spacious, high-ceilinged rooms with big windows and TVs will make you feel like a king. Breakfast 30-32F/€4.57-4.88. Reception M-Sa 6:45am-midnight, Su 7:45am-midnight. Singles 110-138F/€16.77-21.05, with shower 200-260F/€30.49-39.64; doubles 260F/€39.64; quad 280F/€42.69. AmEx/MC/V.

Hôtel des Lices, 25 rue des Lices (☎02 41 87 44 10), near the château. From the train station follow the directions to the tourist office, but instead of turning left onto rue du Roi-René, continue straight ahead onto rue des Lices. 13 plain, clean rooms above a pleasant bistro in a great location. Don't worry about the name–it refers to jousting, which is what you'll have to do to get a room in summer. Breakfast 28F/€4.27. Showers 10F/€1.53. Reception M-F 7am-9pm, Sa-Su 4:30-9pm. Singles and doubles 130F/€19.82, with bath 180F/€27.44; triples 190-240F/€28.97-36.59.

La Coupe d'Or, 5 rue de la Gare (☎02 41 88 45 02; fax 02 41 78 31 59), 200m from the train station. Charming owner maintains 18 small, comfy, worn rooms with TVs at the top of a narrow winding staircase. Breakfast 30F/€4.57. Showers 15F/€2.29. Singles and doubles 100-189F/€15.25-28.82; triples 240F/€36.59. MC/V.

Centre d'Accueil du Lac de Maine (HI), 49 av. du Lac de Maine (☎02 41 22 32 10; fax 02 41 22 32 11; angers.lac@wanadoo.fr). Take bus #6 or 16 to "Accueil Lac de Maine," turn around, cross the busy road, and follow signs on the right-hand side to the Centre d'Accueil. A lakeside setting, extensive sporting facilities, and a mini-golf course justify the 10-15min. ride. Call ahead to make sure there's space; school groups often book the Centre in summer. Breakfast included. Singles 177F/€26.98; doubles 120F/€18.30; quads 85F/€12.96. **Members only.**

Camping du Lac de Maine, av. du Lac de Maine (☎02 41 73 05 03; fax 02 41 73 02 20), near the Centre d'Accueil on CD 111, rte. des Pruniers. Take bus #6 to "Camping Lac de Maine." Camp on a sandy lakeside beach at a 4-star campsite. Open Mar. 25-Oct. 10. 86F/€13.12 for 2 people, tent, and car; July-Aug. 89F/€13.57. Electricity 18.50F/€2.82.

FOOD

Because of its student population, Angers offers lots of cheap and international food, especially on **rue St-Laud.** There is a **covered market** with inexpensive produce and baked goods in the basement of **Les Halles,** on rue Plantagenêt behind the cathedral, down the street from pl. du Ralliement (Tu-Sa 7am-8pm, Su 7am-1:30pm). There's a grocery store in the basement of **Galeries Lafayette** at the corner of rue d'Alsace and pl. du Ralliement (open M-Sa 9am-7pm). If you have a university ID, you can eat inexpensively at the **Université de Clous,** 35 bd. Roi-René (☎02 41 25 45 80), near the tourist office, and the **Université de Belle-Beille,** bd. Lavoisier, near the hostel. (☎02 41 48 45 76. Salad, main course, and dessert 25F/€3.81. Open Sept. 7-July 10 M-Sa 11:30am-1pm and 6:30-8pm.)

SIGHTS

A 28F/€4.27 ticket gives admission to 5 museums; the 50F/€7.62 ***billet jumelé*** *also includes château. Both are sold at the tourist office and at museums.*

Angers is famous for its cherished woven works, which are found in many of the city's main sights. The town has a lot of small museums not listed here, such as the Musée de Vin, Musée des Beaux Arts, Musée d'Histoire Naturelle, and the Slate museum, which will take you through an old-fashioned slate mine.

CHATEAU D'ANGERS. Composed of 17 towers and a 900m-long, 15m-high wall surrounding its perimeter, the château was built by St-Louis from 1228 to 1238. The inner courtyard was designed to protect the inhabitants of the city and was constructed under Angers' Duke René in the 15th century—he made it a meeting place for artists and used the central courtyard as the town marketplace. During the Wars of Religion, Henry III ordered the château's demolition; fortunately, his subjects had only diminished the towers by one story when he died; the moat has blossomed into a colorful garden populated by deer, and the northernmost tower offers a spectacular view of the city. *(2 promenade du Bout du Monde, pl. Kennedy. ☎ 02 41 86 81 94. Open June-Sept. 15 daily 9:30am-7pm; Sept. 16-Oct. and Mar. 16-May 10am-6pm; Nov.-Mar. 15 10am-5pm. Tours leave from the chapel 5 times daily (French) and 1-3 times daily (English). 36F/€5.49, students 23F/€3.51, under 18 free. Last entrance 45min. before closing.)*

LA TAPISSERIE DE L'APOCALYPSE. Inside the château is the largest tapestry of its quality in the world. It was commissioned by Duke Louis I, who was inspired by an illuminated manuscript of the Book of Revelations. Executed by master weaver Robert Poinçon, the tapestry was completed in 1382 and measured 133m by 6m. The current 103m by 4m fragments hang in a gallery space beyond the chapel-museum. The six segments of the tapestry mirror the life of St-John in his battle against evil, subtly weaving in references to the war between France (represented by John himself) and Britain, the evil aggressor. The work is full of monsters and beasts, including a seven-headed Satan gobbling down babies, and heavenly armies preparing for battle. *(Same hours as château; included with château.)*

GALERIE DAVID D'ANGERS. This gallery houses the 19th-century sculptor's work in the beautifully restored and glass-topped 13th-century Toussaint Abbey. Among the impressive pieces are a scale replica of David's masterwork for the Panthéon facade in Paris, as well as many of the 30 statues he designed for city squares. *(37bis rue Toussaint. ☎ 02 41 87 21 03. Open mid-June to mid-Sept. daily 9:30am-6:30pm; late Sept. to early June Tu-Su 10am-noon and 2-6pm. 12F/€1.83, under age 16 free.)*

MUSEE JEAN LURCAT. You'll find Angers' second woven masterpiece in this former 12th-century hospice. The 80m-long *Chant du Monde* ("Song of the World") is a symbolic journey through human destiny. Lurçat, inspired by the Apocalypse tapestry, abandoned his career as a painter and turned to weaving; he completed this surprisingly modern work in the 1930s. Filled with blazing colors, the tapestry represents life's joys and sorrows in 10 enormous panels. *(4 bd. Arago. ☎ 02 41 24 18 45. Open mid-June to mid-Sept. daily 9:30am-6:30pm; late Sept. to early June Tu-Su 10am-noon and 2-6pm. 20F/€3.04, under age 16 free.)*

MUSEE DE LA TAPISSERIE CONTEMPORAINE. In the same building as the Musée Jean Lurçat is this stunning permanent collection of textile and tapestry, including pieces by the renowned cloth sculptor Magdalena Abakanowicz. *(☎ 02 41 24 18 48. Open mid-June to mid-Sept. daily 9:30am-6:30pm; late Sept. to early June Tu-Su 10am-noon and 2-6pm. 20F/€3.05, under age 16 free.)*

CATHEDRALE ST-MAURICE. The 12th-century building is all kinds of old: there's a Norman porch, a 13th-century chancel intersecting a 4th-century Gallo-Roman wall, and some of the oldest stained-glass windows in France, dating to the 12th and 15th centuries. Linger long enough, and you might get a free tour in English from the lovely local nuns. *(Pl. Monseigneur Chappoulie. ☎ 02 41 87 58 45. Open July-Aug. daily 8:30am-7pm; Sept.-June 8:30am-5:30pm.)*

VIELLE VILLE. To the left of the cathedral and a few blocks from the château, pl. du Ralliement holds numerous stores and cafés, alongside a magnificent **theater,** rebuilt in the 19th century and decorated by local painter Lenepveu. The area also holds many old, low-roofed, stone houses from the 16th century, including the oldest house in Angers, **La Maison d'Adam,** a beautiful timber-framed house from the beginning of the 16th century, just behind the cathedral on pl. Ste-Croix.

ENTERTAINMENT AND FESTIVALS

Although the discos are way out in the suburbs, nightlife in Angers remains lively. The cafés along **rue St-Laud** are always packed, while a few bars on student-dominated **rue Bressigny** get down even before the sun does. International students pack **Dupont,** 43 rue Toussaint, where the English language prevails. (☎ 02 42 88 15 64.

Open daily 11pm-2am.) Shoot a game, drink a beer, and stay for a while in the spacious and bright **Paquebot,** 45 rue St-Laud. (☎02 41 81 06 20. Open daily 11am-2pm.) Just across the street, **Le Sunset,** 44 rue Saint-Laud, is dimmer but no less popular, with its smooth tropical punch (Le Sun) and its young, hip crowd. (☎02 41 87 85 58. Open daily noon-2am.) In Angers' "philosophical cafés," guests are encouraged to enjoy a drink while sharing their opinion on philosophical matters. These include **Le Carpe Diem,** 15 rue St. Maurille (☎02 41 87 50 47), and **Le Petit Anjou,** 6 rue Thiers (☎02 41 88 70 50). Feel free to dress in black and wear a beret.

At the end of June and beginning of July, Angers hosts the **Festival d'Anjou.** One of the largest summer theater festivals in France, it attracts renowned French comedy and dramatic troupes to the château; Albert Camus once staged a play in front of a nationwide TV audience here. (Info at 1 rue des Arènes. ☎02 41 88 14 14; www.angers.ensam.fr/festanjou. 170F/€25.92 per show, students 100F/€15.25.)

LE MANS

Le Mans (pop. 150,000) is best known today for the 24-hour car race which has stormed around the city's circuit each summer since 1923. Charles VI went mad when he tried to leave Le Mans in 1392—and you'd be mad not to come, since you're already in the Loire Valley; Le Mans has possibly the most beautiful *vieille ville* in France, and is worth a night for its unique sights and zippy nightlife.

TRANSPORTATION

Trains: bd. de la Gare, off pl. du 8 Mai 1945 (☎08 36 35 35 35). To: **Nantes** (1hr., 7 per day, 141F/€21.50); **Paris** (1-3hr., 12 per day, 151-255F/€23.03-38.88); **Rennes** (1hr., 7 per day, 133F/€20.28); and **Tours** (1hr., 6 per day, 79F/€12.05). Tickets sold M-F 5am-10:30pm, Sa 6am-10:30pm, Su 5am-11pm.

Buses: SNCF (☎02 43 25 30 12) sends buses to **Saumur** (1½hr.; 3 per day M-Sa, 1 on Su) from the station.

Public Transportation: SETRAM buses, 65 av. Général de Gaulle (☎02 43 24 76 76), run 5:30am-8 or 9pm (depending on the bus line), after which the city's four **Hi'bus** lines take over until 2am. Pick up a bus map at the SETRAM office or tourist office if you're planning on moving and shaking. Ticket 6F/€0.91, *carnet* of 10 49F/€7.47. Info office open M-F 7am-7pm, Sa 8:30am-6:30pm.

Taxis: Radio Taxi (☎02 43 24 92 92). 24hr.

Bike Rental: Top Team, 9 pl. St-Pierre (☎02 43 24 88 32). From 100F/€15.25 per day. 2000F/€304.92 and ID deposit. Open Tu-Sa 9:30am-noon and 2-7pm. MC/V.

ORIENTATION AND PRACTICAL INFORMATION

Place de la République is the center of modern Le Mans. The sights and restaurants of the *cité médiévale* are propped up by Roman walls on the bank of the Sarthe. To get to the **tourist office** from the station, cross bd. de la Gare and head about 1km up av. du Général Leclerc; the road plows through several squares, curving to the right of the large Caisse d'Epargne and becoming av. François Mitterrand. Two blocks past the intersection with av. du Général de Gaulle is the house-shaped black glass front of the office (25min.). Or head up rue Gastelier across from the post office and take bus #5 (dir: "Villaret") to "Etoile." Cross pl. Lecouteux and head down rue de l'Etoile; the office will be two blocks down to the left.

Tourist Office: rue de l'Etoile (☎02 43 28 17 22; fax 02 43 28 12 14), in the 17th-century Hôtel des Ursulines. The staff distributes maps and info booklets. Historical **walking tours** in French depart from the cathedral fountain (1½-2hr.; July-Aug. M-F 3pm; 35F/€5.34, students 20F/€3.05). Open June-Aug. M-Sa 9am-6pm, Su 10am-12:30pm and 2:30-5pm; Sept.-May M-Sa 9am-6pm, Su 10am-noon.

Money: Best currency exchange rates are at **Banque de France,** 2 pl. Lionel Lecouteux (☎02 43 74 74 00). Exchange desks open M-F 8:45am-noon.

English Bookstore: Thuard Librairie, 24 rue de l'Etoile (☎02 43 82 22 22), has bestsellers and some classics in English. Open M-Sa 8:30am-7:30pm. MC/V.

Laundromats: Lav'Ideal, 4 pl. l'Eperon (☎02 43 24 53 99). Open daily 7am-9pm. **Laverie Libre Service,** 4 rue Gastelier (☎02 43 43 99 18).

Youth Information: Ville du Mans Service Jeunesse, 13 rue de l'Etoile (☎02 43 83 00 09), near the tourist office. Offers student discounts and has job and housing info. Open M and W-F 9am-noon and 1-5pm, Tu 1-5pm. **SMEBA,** 34 av. François Mitterrand (☎02 43 39 90 20), is a student travel agency which arranges discount tickets and offers health insurance for foreign students in France. Open M-F 9am-6pm.

Police: Commissariat Central, 6 rue Coeffort (☎02 43 61 68 00).

Hospital: Centre Hospitalier, 194 av. Rubillard (☎02 43 43 43 43).

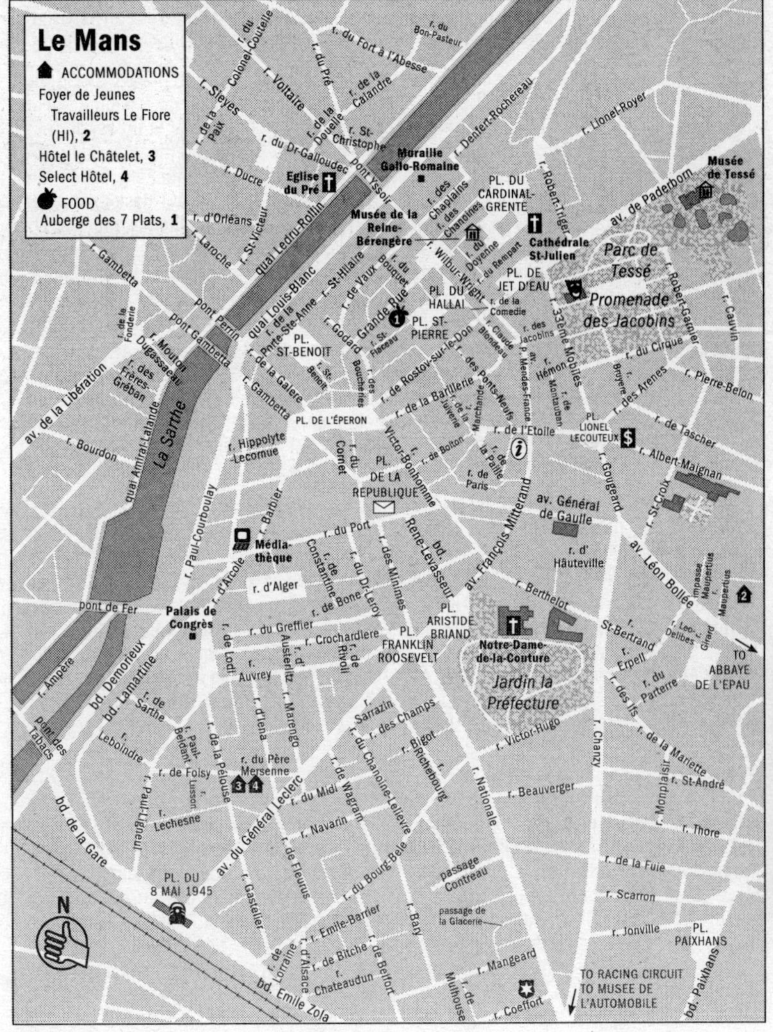

Internet Access: Médiathèque, 54 rue du Port (☎02 43 47 48 74). 5F/€0.76 per 15min. Open July-Aug. Tu-F 2-6pm, Sa 10am-noon and 2-5pm; Sept.-June Tu-W and F 10am-6:30pm, Th 1:30-6:30pm, Sa 10am-5pm. **Cyberville,** 8 rue d'Alger (☎02 43 43 90 90), charges 50F/€7.62 per hr. or about 1F/€0.15 per min. Open M 9:30am-noon and 1:30-9:30pm, Tu-F 9am-noon and 1:30-9:30pm, Su 9:30am-noon and 1:30-8:30pm. Get free Internet access at the **hostel** (see below).

Post Office: 13 pl. de la République (☎02 43 21 75 00). **Currency exchange.** Open M-F 8am-7pm, Sa 8am-noon. **Branch office,** 1 pl. du 8 Mai 1945, right by the station. Same hours and services. **Poste Restante** (at main office): "République, 72013 Le Mans Cedex 2." **Postal code:** 72000.

ACCOMMODATIONS AND CAMPING

It's a good idea to call ahead in Le Mans, as spontaneous renovations and closings seem to be favorite sports of local hotel proprietors. The row of gaudy establishments across from the station faces noisy pl. du 8 Mai 1945 and is surprisingly expensive; you'll find better deals on the quieter streets up the hill.

Foyer de Jeunes Travailleurs Le Flore (HI), 23 rue Maupertius (☎02 43 81 27 55; fax 02 43 81 06 10; florefjt@noos.fr). From the train station, cross pl. du 8 Mai and head up av. du Gén. Leclerc. Follow directions to tourist office, but turn right up av. du Gén. de Gaulle, and cross the next intersection to av. Leon-Bollée. Continue straight; rue Maupertius is the third street on your left (35min.). Or take bus #5 from the station (dir: "Villaret") to "de Gaulle," walk down a block to the bright red SETRAM kiosk near pl. de la République, and catch the #4 (dir: "Gazonfier") or #12 (dir: "Californie") to "Erpell." The hostel is across the street and down rue Maupertius to the right. Blissfully clean and quiet *foyer* near the Jardins des Plantes, close to the tourist office and the city center. The modern building has doubles, triples, and quads, plus kitchen, laundry, and free Internet access. Breakfast included. Sheets 19F/€2.90. Bunks 68F/€10.37, Sa 49F/€7.47 (no breakfast Su). **Members only.** Wheelchair accessible.

Hôtel le Châtelet, 15 rue du Père Mersenne (☎02 43 43 92 36). From station, head up av. du Gén. Leclerc and turn left onto rue de la Pélouse; rue du Père Mersenne is the second on the right. 9 beautiful, newly-carpeted rooms make you wonder if the owners realize what a bargain they're offering. Breakfast 25F/€3.81. Singles 150F/€22.90, doubles 200F/€30.49; triples 290F/€44.21. Weekend stays require advance notice.

Select Hôtel, 13 rue du Père Mersenne (☎02 43 24 17 74), just up the street from le Châtelet. 15 rooms in fairly good condition off darkly wallpapered halls. Breakfast 25F/€3.81. Shower 13F/€1.98. Singles and doubles with sink 135F/€20.59, with sink and micro-shower 160F/€24.39; triples 290F/€44.21. MC/V.

Campsites: The tourist office has a list of campsites in the Sarthe region. The closest is the two-star **Camping Le Vieux Moulin,** 9km away in Neuville-sur-Sarthe (☎02 43 25 31 82; fax 02 43 25 38 11). Take the train from Le Mans (8min., 4 per day, 16F/€2.44). The riverside site has bikes (40F/€6.10 per day), laundry, a pool, and tennis courts. Open June-Sept. 2 people and site 70F/€10.67, 20F/€3.05 per extra person. Electricity 20F/€3.05. MC/V.

FOOD

Renowned for its poultry, regional cuisine commonly includes dishes of *pintade* (guinea fowl) and *canard* (duck). Taste tiny tidbits or go for the kill—the succulent *marmite sarthoise*, a warm casserole of rabbit, chicken, ham, carrots, cabbage, and mushrooms, bubbling in a bath of Jasnière wine, is an omnivore's dream. The best *menus* are in the brasseries that line **pl. de la République,** a favorite area for midday meals and late-evening lounging. Pleasant, affordable restaurants settle along Grande Rue and behind pl. de l'Eperon in the *vieille ville*. The **indoor market** sells portable goodies in **Les Halles,** pl. du Marché, while an **outdoor market** waits in pl. des Jacobins (W and Su 7am-12:30pm, F 7am-6pm). There is a

Prisunic supermarket at 30 pl. de la République (open M-Sa 9am-8pm). The eponymous seven *plats* of **Auberge des 7 Plats,** 79 Grande Rue, lend themselves to diverse combinations in the 87F/€13.27 *à la carte menu.* (*Menus* 47-67F/€7.17-10.22. Open Tu-Sa 10:15am-2:15pm and 6:15-11pm, Su 7-11pm. MC/V.)

SIGHTS

*The combined **billet couple** includes visit to two of the following: Musée de Tessé, Musée Vert, or Musée de la Reine-Bérengère. 26F/€3.97, students 13F/€1.98. **Billet triple** covers all three (34F/€5.19, students 17F/€2.59). Note that all are free on Sunday.*

Roman walls, medieval streets, a Gothic cathedral, and a 20th-century race-car museum make Le Mans a city to savor. Le Mans also holds a remarkable set of beautiful **churches,** sprinkled throughout the city, including the **Maison-Dieu** founded by Henry Plantagenêt. The tourist office brochure *Les Plantagenêts* maps out all the churches, accompanied by detailed descriptions.

THE VIEILLE VILLE. Rising up behind thick Roman walls and the river Sarthe, Le Mans' *vieille ville* is considered one of the most picturesque in France, though the city becomes a bit of an eyesore outside the central downtown area. The winding streets and alleys, in which *Cyrano de Bergerac* was filmed, are lined with 15th- to 17th-century houses. Before you set out strolling, stop at the tourist office for the English-language *Le Mans: An Art and History Town*, which will allow you to identify the houses as they go by. If your French is up to it, join the **tour** that meets at the cathedral fountain. *(2hr.; daily 3pm; 35F/€5.34, students 20F/€3.05.)* The drab **Musée de la Reine-Bérengère,** 9 rue Reine-Bérengère, inside a 1460 residence in the *vieille ville*, occasionally has a good exhibition. *(Open M-Sa 9am-noon and 2-6pm, Su 10am-noon and 2-6pm. 18F/€2.74, students and children 9F/€1.37.)*

CATHEDRALE ST-JULIEN. One of France's most famous cathedrals, this great fireball of Romanesque and Gothic architecture was originally constructed in the 11th and 12th centuries. The sculpted front of the south porch, dating from this time, is considered one of Europe's finest. After a fire destroyed the town in 1134, the cathedral was repaired using Gothic techniques, hence the pointed arch reinforcements you can see on either side in the nave. The great chancel with twelve chapels was added on in the 13th century, doubling the size of the cathedral and necessitating the tangle of flying buttresses which encircle the exterior. A great torrent of color, the chapel still retains its original 14th-century paint job, including dark violet walls and a blood-red ceiling upon which angels float in painted plasma. *(Pl. des Jacobins. Open daily 9am-noon and 2-6pm.)*

MURAILLE GALLO-ROMAINE. The stocky 4th-century Roman walls which hug the city's southwestern edge are Le Mans' pride and joy, and rightly so. Punctured with arched gates and fortified with massive towers, the 1.3km-long *muraille* is the longest and perhaps best preserved in all of France. Pink mortar gives the entire structure an earthy orange glow.

RACING CIRCUIT AND MUSEE DE L'AUTOMOBILE. Those who are really into cars can gawk at the 13.5km stretch of racetrack that lies south of the city. Since 1923, the circuit has held the annual *24 Heures du Mans*, a gruelling feat of either endurance or misused patience. The race is held in the second week of June, but other events take place during the summer. *(Tickets ☎ 02 43 40 24 75 or 02 43 40 24 77. 10F/€1.53 to enter and walk around track.)* Just outside the track's main entrance is the massive **Musée de l'Automobile,** which traces the evolution of motor vehicles all the way up to the present, including scores of shiny racing cars and cycles of premium vintage. Check out the slick Ford GT40, the only one of its kind. *(From bd. Levasseur off pl. de la République, take bus #6 to "Raineries," the end of the line (25min.). Continue on foot down rue de Laigne, following signs to the track and museum (12min. walk). ☎ 02 43 72 72 24. Open June-Aug. daily 10am-7pm; Oct.-Dec. and Feb.-May 10am-6pm; Jan. Sa-Su 10am-6pm. 40F/€6.10, students and ages 12-18 30F/€4.57, ages 7-11 10F/€1.53.)*

MUSEE AND PARC DE TESSE. Housed in the former 19th-century bishops' palace, this fabulous collection celebrates over 600 years of art. The modern interior displays 17th- to 19th-century painting and sculpture, temporary exhibits of modern art, and an Egyptian collection in which a mummy lies supine next to its full-body X-ray. The highlight is a 12th-century enamel portrait of Geoffrey Plantagenêt that originally decorated his tomb in the Cathédrale St-Julien. When you've seen the collection, bask in the sun in the beautiful **Parc de Tessé,** with a fountain, a waterfall, shady trees, and acres of grass. *(2 av. de Paderborn, a 15min. walk from pl. de la République. Take bus #3 (dir: "Bellevue") from rue Gastelier by the station or from av. du Gén. de Gaulle, a block down from pl. de la République, to "Musée." Bus #9 (dir: "Villaret") also goes there from av. du Gén. de Gaulle. ☎ 02 43 47 38 51. Open May-Oct. daily 9am-noon and 2-6pm; Nov.-Apr. Tu-Su 9am-noon and 2-6pm. 18F/€2.74, students 9F/€1.37, free Su.)*

ENTERTAINMENT AND FESTIVALS

Le Mans packs most of its nocturnal revelry in and around **pl. de la République.** Crowds of 20- and 30-somethings sip drinks at relaxed *place*-side brasseries like **Le Moderne,** 23 pl. de la République. (☎02 43 28 40 88. Open daily 7am-2am.) The younger, funkier scene is down **rue du Dr. Leroy,** whose bars resonate with techno or rock. **Paris Texas Café,** 21 rue du Dr. Leroy, is a little club with 1950s decor. (☎02 43 23 71 00. Open daily 11am-2am.) **Le Bakoua,** 5 rue de la Vieille Porte, off pl. de l'Eperon, feels like a beach party, complete with calypso music and tropical drinks. (☎02 43 23 30 70. Open June-Sept. daily 6pm-2am; Oct.-May 5pm-2am.) Several discothèques are right in town, including **Le Select,** 44 pl. de la République, with wild strobe lights and good beats. (☎02 43 28 87 41. Open Th-Su 11pm-5am. Cover 50F/€7.62 with drink.) There's also the gay-friendly **La Limite,** 7 rue St-Honoré, in the *vieille ville.* (☎02 43 24 85 54. Cover 35F/€5.34. Open Th-Su.)

Cannes film festival winners roll nightly in *v.o.* at the *vieille ville's* ultra-cool **Ciné-Poche,** 97 Grande Rue (☎02 43 24 73 85). For the entire month of April, the city attracts contemporary jazz artists of every creed for the **Europa Jazz Festival.** (Info and tickets from 9 rue des Frères Greban, ☎02 43 23 78 99.) On the first weekend of July, over 40 theater companies hit the streets for **Les Scénomanies,** a festival presenting over 100 different shows on the streets of old Le Mans. The excitement brings out all sorts of street entertainment, including international music, dance, and acrobatics. If you've missed *Les Scénomanies,* worry not—throughout July and August, **Les Soirs d'Eté** feature free theater, musical comedy, and music performances in the streets. Pick up a *L'Eté au Mans* schedule from the tourist office.

POITOU-CHARENTES

Poitou-Charentes could be France's best-kept secret. The Côte d'Azur may be tops in topless beaches, and the Loire Valley may be the king of châteaux, but no other region of France has so impressive a collection of both. Poitou-Charentes is a brilliant collage of pristine natural sights and coastal towns, tucked away on the western shore of France.

With the acceptance of Christianity in the 4th century, the area emerged as an influential political and religious center. The 8th century saw Charles "the Hammer" Martel fend off Moorish attempts to conquer the region. With the marriage of Eleanor of Aquitaine and Henry II of England in the 12th century, possession of the region in the Middle Ages was tossed to the other side of the Channel, where it remained for 300 years. In the 17th century, Cardinal Richelieu laid siege to the Protestant stronghold of La Rochelle, relegating it to a century of obscurity until trade with Canada restored it to prosperity.

TRANSPORTATION

Trains run to all major towns, and buses fill in the gaps. The **Comité Régional de Tourisme,** 62 rue Jean Jaurès, in Poitiers, has info on hiking, biking, and other modes of transport (☎05 49 50 10 50).

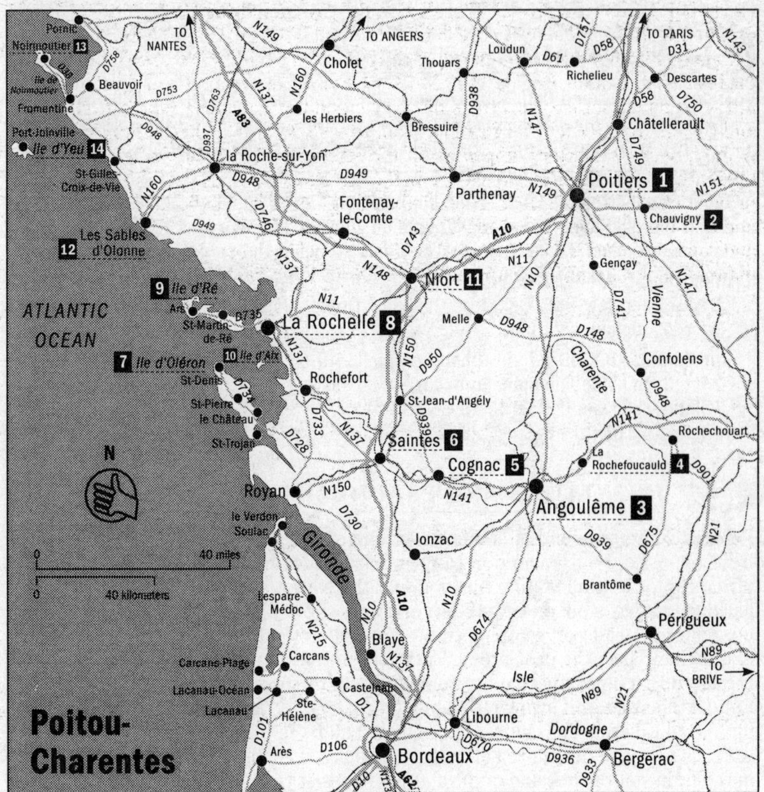

POITIERS

Poitiers' many beautiful and renowned churches—like Notre-Dame-la-Grande and the Cathédrale St-Pierre—are witness to the growth of Church power in the early Middle Ages. It was here that Clovis struck a blow for Christianity in defeating the Visigoths in 507, and Charles Martel beat back invading Moors in 732. In 1432, when Poitiers (pop. 83,000) was the capital of France, Charles VII established the Université de Poitiers. As beautiful as the famous façades of Poitiers may be, this city has lost the tranquil atmosphere that characterizes the rest of Poitou-Charentes. Poitiers is now a bustling, get-up-and-go kind of city, whose claim to fame is not breathtaking scenery but the ultra-modern Futuroscope cinematography theme park 10 km outside of town (see p. 602).

TRANSPORTATION

Trains: bd. du Grand Cerf. To: **Bordeaux** (2hr., 8 per day, 175F/€26.68); **La Rochelle** (1¾hr., 8 per day, 120F/€18.30); and **Paris** (2hr., 6 per day, 265F-330F/€40.40-50.33); and **Tours** (1hr., 5 per day, 98F€14.95). **SNCF office** open M-Sa 6am-9:45pm, Su 7am-11:10pm.

Local Transportation: S.T.P., 6 rue du Chaudron-d'Or (☎05 49 44 77 00). Buses crisscross the city 7am-8:30pm. Night buses on 2 central lines run until 1am. Timetables at tourist office and train station. Tickets 8F/€1.22, valid 1hr. *Carnet* of 5 27F/€4.12.

Bike Rental: Atelier Cyclaman, 60bis bd. Pont Achard (☎05 49 88 13 25). 85F/€12.96 per day, 55F/€8.39 per half-day. Open M-F 9am-12:30pm and 3-7pm, Sa 9am-12:30pm and 2-7pm.

Car Rental: ADA, 19 bd. du Grand Cerf (☎05 49 50 30 20). From 249F/€37.97 for 24hr. Open M-Sa 9am-6pm. **Europcar,** 48 bd. du Grand Cerf (☎05 49 58 25 34). **Avis,** 135 bd. du Grand Cerf (☎05 49 58 13 00).

Taxis: Radio Taxis, 22 rue Carnot (☎05 49 88 12 34). 65F/€9.91 to hostel. 24hr.

ORIENTATION AND PRACTICAL INFORMATION

Poitiers centers around **pl. Maréchal Leclerc** and **pl. Charles de Gaulle.** Buses run from opposite the train station to the central **Hôtel de Ville.** To get to the tourist office from the train station on foot, exit the station and cut straight across the parking lot. Cross bd. du Grand Cerf and bear slightly to your right. Turn left onto bd. Solférino as it curves uphill to the left. Climb the long staircase and take rue Arthur Ranc past the post office. Turn left on rue Gambetta, which you'll follow for about two blocks before turning right onto the pedestrian rue des Cordeliers. Follow this road as it swings to the left, curving into rue du Marché, which opens up into pl. Charles de Gaulle. Notre Dame will be in front of you, and the tourist office is opposite the church (10min.). Maps are available at the information desk in the train station; ask one of the staffers to assist you.

Tourist Office: 45 pl. Charles de Gaulle (☎05 49 41 21 24; fax 05 49 88 65 84). Well-labeled maps (3F/€0.46), and lists of hotels and campgrounds. **City tours** (1½hr.) run July-Sept. at 3 and 5pm in French; English tours on demand. 35F/€5.34, under 25 20F/€3.05 (ask for the brochure *Laissez-vous conter Poitiers*). Hotel reservations 15F/€2.29. Open June 21-Sept. 16 M-Sa 9:30am-11pm, Su 10am-6pm; Sept. until 10pm; late Sept.-June M-Sa 10am-6pm. For current info on events, snag the free *Affiche.*

English Books: Librairie de l'Université, 70 rue Gambetta (☎05 49 41 02 05), off pl. M. Leclerc. Open M-Sa 9am-7:30pm. MC/V.

Youth Information: Centre Regionale Information Jeunesse (CRIJ), 64 rue Gambetta (☎05 49 60 68 68), near pl. Leclerc. Help with jobs, lodging, budget travel, activities, etc. Open M-F 10am-6pm. **Internet access** for students only 5F/€0.76 per 30min.

Laundromat: 2bis rue de le Tranchée. Open daily 7am-8:30pm. Or 182 Grande Rue, open daily 8am-9pm.

Police: 38 rue de la Marne (☎05 49 60 60 00).

Hospital: 350 av. Jacques Caire (☎05 49 44 44 44), on the road to Limoges.

Internet Access: France Télécom, rue du Marché, free email. Open M 2-6:30pm, Tu-F 9am-6:30pm, Sa 9:30am-12:30pm and 2-6:30pm. **Centre Regionale Information Jeunesse (CRIJ).** Email for students for 5F/€0.76 per 30min. **Cybercafé LRM,** 171 Grande Rue (☎05 49 39 51 87). 47F/€7.17 per hr. Open M-Th 10:30am-10:30pm, F-Sa 10:30am-11pm, Su 4-8pm.

Post Office: 16 rue A. Ranc (☎05 49 55 50 00). **Currency exchange.** No commission. Open M-F 8:30am-7pm, Sa 8:30am-noon. **Postal code:** 86000.

ACCOMMODATIONS AND CAMPING

The hostel and campgrounds are far from the city center, but respectable, cheap hotels in the town center and near the train station make good alternatives; travelers in pairs or larger groups will find a cheaper deal at hotels than at the hostel.

Auberge de Jeunesse (HI), 1 allée Tagault (☎05 49 30 09 70; fax 05 49 30 09 79). Catch bus #3 by the traffic light ahead of the station (dir: "Pierre Loti") to "Cap Sud" (M-Sa every 30min. until 7:50pm, 8F/€1.22). If walking, turn right at station and follow bd. du Pont Achard to av. de la Libération. Then, take right-hand fork onto rue B. Pascal, turn right on rue de la Jeunesse, and turn left onto allée Tagault. Hostel ahead on left (3km, 35min.). Irksome press-and-repeat showers. Perfectly adequate. Breakfast 19F/€2.90; lunch 45F/€6.86; dinner 49F/€7.47. Sheets 17F/€2.59. Reception 7am-noon and 4pm-midnight. No curfew, no lockout. **Members only.** Beds 53F/€8.08. Pitched **tents** in backyard for 30F/€4.57 (groundpad included).

Hôtel Jules Ferry, 27 rue Jules Ferry (☎05 49 37 80 14; fax 05 49 53 15 02). From train station, turn right onto bd. Pont Achard, and walk up street (and slightly uphill). Turn left onto rue J. Brunet and left again onto rue Jules Ferry. Hotel is on the right in front of you. Carpeted rooms with narrow but spotless showers awaits. Breakfast 28F/€4.27. Reception M-Sa 7am-11pm. For Su reservations, call ahead. Get door code if you plan to return late. Singles and doubles 140F/€21.35, with shower 180F/€27.44.

Campsites: Le Porteau, (☎05 49 41 44 88), on rue de Porteau 2km out of town. Take bus #7 (dir: "Centre de Gros," 8F/€1.22) and get off at "Porteau." Tiny, rock-hard field encircled by roads. Open June-Sept. Site fee 47F/€7.17 (2 people) and 57F/€8.69 (3 people); extra person 16F/€2.44, child 10F/€1.53. Electricity 15F/€2.29. **Camping St-Benoît,** rte. de Passelourdin (☎05 49 88 48 55), 5km from Poitiers, is slightly better (there's grass), but very hard to reach by public transport. Take bus #2 (dir: "Les Sables") from the station; the campgrounds are about 2km from the bus stop. Taxi from train station to campgrounds about 85F/€12.96. Open July-Aug. 53F/€8.08 per 2-person site, extra person 15F/€2.29. Electricity 15F/€2.29.

 FOOD

Lamb from nearby Montmarillon, *chèvre* (goat cheese), macaroons, and the wines of Haut-Poitou can be found on local *menus*. The problem is finding a *menu* that fits your budget—most hover around 100-200F/€15.25-30.49. Many hotel bars post adequate 3-course *menus* for 70-90F/€10.67-13.72. Inexpensive pizzerias line the pedestrian streets between pl. Leclerc and Notre-Dame-la-Grande. There is a **market** at **Les Halles,** on pl. Charles de Gaulle (M-Sa 7am-1pm), which expands beyond your wildest dreams on Saturdays. **Monoprix supermarket,** at Ile des Cordeliers on rue des Grandes Ecoles, fills you up for less (open M-Sa 9am-7:30pm). **Buffet Grill,** 11 rue Lebascles, off pl. Leclerc, is an oasis of refreshment for hungry travelers, with both fresh and sweet all-you-can-eat buffets (49F/€7.47 for one, 61F/€9.30 for both). (☎05 49 01 74 00. Open daily 11:30am-2pm and 7-10:30pm. MC/V.)

SIGHTS

Poitiers' churches date back to the conversion of France in the 4th century. All are open daily 9am-6pm, all are free, and many hold organ concerts in the summer; check the *Guide des Manifestations* or call *Les Nuits en Musique* (☎05 49 41 21 24) or *Les Concerts du Marché* (☎05 49 41 34 18) for schedules.

NOTRE-DAME-LA-GRANDE. Despite its modest proportions, this is one of France's most important Romanesque churches. The 12th-century facade's statuary stands in a double row. Inside, an original fresco on the choir ceiling depicts Christ in glory, the Virgin and Child, and the Lamb of God in a cruciform; the rest of the interior was originally also decorated this way, but unfortunate restoration attempts have resulted in garish designs. In the summertime, the original polychrome detail is projected onto the facade with special lights, reviving all of the original colors and details of the cathedral in all of its splendor. Do not miss this event, at 10:30pm each night. *(On pl. de Gaulle, off Grande Rue. Projections June-Aug. at 10:30pm, Sept. 1-16 until 9:30pm.)*

CATHEDRALE ST-PIERRE. The 1162 construction was funded by Eleanor of Aquitaine and her husband King Henry II Plantagenêt, who lived in Poitiers in the current Palais de Justice. The church is celebrated for its elaborate Cliquot classical organ (1787-1791), and its central stained-glass window, one of the oldest crucifixion scenes in France. Look carefully at the column capitals and where the wall meets the ceiling; 267 of the church's original carvings, human and bestial in subject, remain to this day. *(On pl. de la Cathédrale, off rue de la Cathédrale.)*

EGLISE STE-RADEGONDE. The church's belltower porch was built on the ravaged foundations of a 6th-century chapel founded by the saint herself. A few original stained-glass windows remain, putting to shame the gaudy 19th-century replacements. Besides the tomb of Radegondé, the church boasts another sacred relic—in AD 587, Christ appeared to Radegondé on this site and foretold her imminent death, reassuring her that she was "one of the most precious diamonds in His crown." He helpfully left a footprint in the stone floor before vanishing, providing the nun with proof and the abbey with pilgrims and income for centuries to come. *(Off rue de la Mauvinière, down the street from the cathedral.)*

BAPTISTERE ST-JEAN. This 4th-century baptistry is the oldest Christian structure in France. No longer a sacred building, the Baptistère is now a museum of Roman, Merovingian, and Carolingian sarcophagi and capitals. The earliest Christians kept these fragments when they destroyed Poitiers' fine Roman baths, arches, and amphitheater—buildings they would imitate in the future, but never with the pagans' skill or success. *(On rue Jean Jaurès, near the cathedral. Open July-Aug. daily 10am-12:30pm and 2:30-6pm; Apr.-June and Sept.-Oct. daily 10:30am-12:30pm and 3-6pm; Nov.-Mar. W-M 2:30-4:30pm. 4F/€0.61, under 12 2F/€0.31.)*

SISTER ACT Ste-Radegondé (520-587) was a Thuringian princess carried off as booty by the Frankish son of Clovis. When he demanded that she marry him, Radegondé fled to the church and strong-armed a priest into making her a nun. She went on to found one of the first women's abbeys, Ste-Croix, and, according to myth, killed a villager-eating dragon who lurked in Poitiers' network of underground tunnels. Radegondé was not the only woman to stick out her neck to save the city: the Virgin herself took matters into her own hands in 1202, during the English siege of Poitiers. A traitor planned to give the invaders the keys to the city gates, only to find out that the keys had disappeared. The English retreated, claiming to have seen terrible visions of a queen, a bishop, and a nun outside the city (the Virgin, 4th-century bishop St. Hilaire, and Ste-Radegondé, of course). The "lost" keys were discovered in the wooden hands of the Statue of Mary in Notre Dame la Grande.

ESPACE MENDES FRANCE. Next to the cathedral, but a millennium younger, this sleek hands-on science museum presents temporary science and technology exhibits most often geared toward children and adolescents (only in French). The Center also has a small planetarium and airs educational wide-screen features. *(1 pl. de la Cathédrale. ☎05 49 50 33 08; www.pictascience.org. Planetarium shows 5pm July-Aug. daily and Sept.-June Su. Museum open Sa-M 2-6pm and Tu-F 9:30am-6:30pm. Planetarium 35F/€5.34, 17 and under 20F/€3.05; museum 26F/€3.97, 8 and under 16F/€2.44.)*

PARC DE BLOSSAC. This 18th-century park is one of the most beautiful in the region. A classic *jardin à la française* (French-style garden), it is criss-crossed by perfectly rectilinear paths and planted mostly with Dutch linden trees. The park's small zoological garden houses goats and a few birds, the highlight of which are the numerous varieties of duck swimming in the pond. *(Rue de Blossac, down rue Carnot, near the river Clain. Open Apr.-Sept. daily 7am-10:30pm; Oct.-Mar. 7am-9:30pm. Jardin Anglais open Apr.-Sept. daily 7am-8pm; Oct.-Mar. 8am-dusk.)*

OTHER SIGHTS. The **Musée Ste-Croix** holds relics of Poitiers' Bronze Age, Roman inscriptions, some melodramatic Camille Claudels, and an early Mondrian. Summer events include special exhibits, guest lectures, and concerts; check the bulletin outside for details. Visit the **Musée Rupert de Chièvres** for its collection of Dutch, Flemish, and Italian paintings, and its display of scientific antiquities, among them one of the earliest Diderot encyclopedias. *(Musée Ste-Croix: 3bis rue Jean Jaurès. ☎05 49 41 07 53; fax 05 49 88 61 63. Musée Rupert de Chièvres: 9 rue Victor Hugo. ☎05 45 41 07 53 or 05 49 41 42 21. Both open June-Sept. M 1:15-6pm, W–F 10am-noon and 1:15-6pm, Sa-Su 10am-noon and 2-6pm; Oct.-May M 1:15-5pm, Tu 10am-5pm although the Musée Rupert de Chièvres is closed Tu noon-1:15pm, W-F 10am-noon and 1:15-5pm, Sa-Su 2-6pm. Admission to both 20F/€3.05; students free, and everybody free on Tu and the first Su of each month. Guided tours in French on Tu.)*

ENTERTAINMENT AND FESTIVALS

Poitiers is quiet in the summer, but livens up during the school year. **Pl. Leclerc** is generally the liveliest square in town, and pubs and restaurants are densest in the streets that branch from it. **Le Pince Oreille,** 11 rue des Trois Rois, hosts a blues or jazz band almost every W, Th, and F night; the mood of the club varies with the band. The armchairs and painted walls create a welcoming and decorative atmosphere from which to kick back and enjoy the show. The dimly-lit social bar is full of students almost every night of the week. Stop by in the winter on Sundays and join their "philosophical cabaret."(☎05 49 60 25 99. Cover 20F-30F/€3.05-4.57, occasionally free. Open M-Th 5pm-2am, F 5pm-3am, Sa 9pm-3am, and Su for the cabaret.) **Auberge "Le Pilori,"** 9 pl. de la Liberté, opens up two bars and a disco to its mostly student clientele; the three chambers create some variation in scene, though the mellow, pleasantly social ambience is a constant. (☎05 49 88 09 14. Open M-Th 9am-2am, F 9am-3am, Sa 8pm-3am; closed July 7-Aug. 24.)

Le George Sand, 25 rue St-Pierre le Puellier, is packed with locals of all sexual orientations; the active disco is officially gay but draws in a diverse crowd looking for house music and a great dance scene. (☎05 49 55 91 58. No cover. Open daily 11pm-4am; W and Sa 11pm-5am.) **La Grande Goule,** 46 rue du Pigeon Blanc, is a mainstay of Poitiers nightlife; the disco brings in older teens early on, then an older crowd. (☎05 49 50 41 36. Open Tu-Sa 11pm-4am. 50F/€7.62 cover includes one drink; students 40F/€6.10; free for women before midnight.) The booklet *Café-Concerts*, *Bars avec Animations* is available from the tourist office.

The **Festival du Cinéma** in March draws film students from international schools all over the world and features much of their work, both artsy and mainstream. Throughout July and August, rock, opera, jazz, and fireworks thunder through town for the **Places à l'Eté** festival. Concerts, mostly free, begin around 9pm 3-4 nights per week. A new annual festival, **La Nuit des Orgues,** was begun in 2000; this series of organ performances in various local churches runs from May to October and is largely free of charge. Contact the tourist office for tickets and details. In late August and early September there is a more formal organ festival, **Voix Orgues,** featuring organ players from all over the region. Tickets should be booked in advance, and range 40F-100F/€6.10-15.25. (☎05 49 47 13 61; fax 05 49 60 37 62.)

DAYTRIPS FROM POITIERS

FUTUROSCOPE

10km north of Poitiers near Chasseneuil. ☎05 49 49 30 80; fax 05 49 49 59 38; www.futuroscope.com. Open Apr.-Aug. daily 9am-11pm; Sept.-Mar. 9am-6pm. Prices vary day to day; in general, Apr.-Aug. 210F/€32.02, kids 5-16 145F/€22.11; Oct.-Mar. 145F/€22.11, kids 100F/€15.25; night ticket 100F/€15.25, kids 60F/€9.15.

Silvery, slick, and stylish, the Futuroscope amusement park amounts to a collection of high-tech film theaters—spherical and hemispherical screens, virtual reality, and high-definition 3-D trickery. All video attractions are included in the admission price, but video games, in the park's Cyber Avenue, require additional tokens. A **night ticket** (after 6pm) is significantly cheaper than normal admission and gets you into the fantastic laser show. A **translating headset** from the Maison de Vienne near the entrance switches many films' narration into English.

To get there, take bus #16 or 17 from Poitiers (20min., 18 per day, 8F/€1.22). You can catch the bus at the Hôtel de Ville or across the street from the train station, in front of the Printania Bar-Hôtel. Bus schedules available at the hotel or at the tourist office. Buy tickets can be bought at the newsstand in the hotel or from the bus driver. Get off at the "Parc De Loisirs" stop, walk up the path across the green, down the stairs, and follow the path under the bridge. The path will curve to the right, leading you to the park entrance. Buses also return from the park to the train station or the Hôtel de Ville every 30-60min. By car, follow A10 (dir: "Paris-Châtellerault") and take Exit 18. The park is also accessible by **TGV** from **Bordeaux** (100min., 1-2 per day, 200F/€30.49); and **Paris** (80min., 2-3 per day, 200F/€30.49).

CHAUVIGNY

Buses leave Poitiers for Chauvigny from outside the station (dir: "Châteauroux"; 30min., 5 per day, 27F/€4.12). To get to the tourist office, 5 rue St-Pierre, in the cité médiévale, take rue de Château up the hill from pl. de la Poste and walk down rue St-Pierre keeping pl. du Donjon on your right; the tourist office is at the bottom of the road to the right. (☎05 49 46 39 01. Open July-Aug. daily 10am-7pm; Sept.-June 10:30am-12:30pm and 2-6pm. Tours July-Aug. W-M 2pm and 4pm; 20F/€3.05. Call 05 49 46 35 45 in advance for English tours.)

Twenty-three kilometers east of Poitiers, Chauvigny's beauty belies its bloody history; it was taken and retaken four times during the Hundred Years' War, burnt down during the Wars of Religion, and shelled by a retreating Wehrmacht in 1944. Today the town's miniature medieval citadel, and a collection of pretty restaurant-lined walkways encircling tranquil pl. du Donjon, makes a worthwhile half-day escape from bustling Poitiers.

Five ruined 11th- to 15th-century châteaux give Chauvigny a striking skyline. Farther down, the 12th-century **Eglise St-Pierre** is celebrated for its choir capitals, engraved with dragons, vultures, and images of Satan. The ultra-modern **Espace d'Archéologie Industrielle** nestles in the ruins of the Gouzon keep and showcases regional quarrying, porcelain-firing, milling, and steam-engine activity. There's a great view of the city and countryside below from the museum's glass elevator. (☎05 49 46 35 45. Open June 15-Sept. 15 daily, year-round Sa-Su. 30F/€4.57, students 20F/€3.05, under 14 free.) Your ticket to the Espace entitles you to enter the decidedly minor **Musée d'Ethnologie et d'Archéologie,** right behind the dungeon and beside Eglise St-Pierre. (Open June-Aug. daily 10:30am-12:30pm and 2:30-6:30pm; Sept.-May 2-6pm. 20F/€3.05, under 14 free.) **Les Géants du Ciel** (☎05 49 46 47 48; fax 05 49 44 10 45), once home to Chauvigny's bishops, now houses 60 eagles, falcons, vultures, owls, and buzzards. All that remains of the castle are some crumbling, roofless walls, but you can poke around inside or watch birds swoop in from above. (Open Apr.-Nov. 4. May-Aug. 4 shows per day; Apr. and Sept.-Nov. 3 shows per day. 45F/€6.86, students 40F/€6.10; ruins only 20F/€3.05.) For a truly unique view of the countryside, take a ride on the **Vélo-Rails,** contraptions on rails which allow up to five people to pedal along the viaduct that traverses the Vienne river; a 17km loop extends from Chauvigny's train station around the valley. Reservations must be made one day in advance. (☎05 49 46 39 01. Open July-Aug. daily 10am-9pm; Sept., and May-June 2-7pm; Oct.-Nov. and Mar.-Apr. 2-6pm; Dec.-Feb. by reservation. July-Aug. 2hr. ride 140F/€21.35, off season 120F/€18.30. July-Aug. 3 per day, off-season 2 per day.)

In summer, the **Festival d'Eté** (☎05 49 45 99 10) fills the city with jazz, dance, and theater. Purchase tickets in advance at the tourist office; some performances free.

ANGOULEME

High on a plateau, Angoulême (pop. 46,000) affords a magnificent view of the Charente river and the surrounding countryside. The cradle of the French paper industry in the 1600s, the town and its ready supply of writing pads brought Jean Calvin here in 1534. The revocation of the Edict of Nantes in the 1600s sent the primarily Protestant paper-makers packing to Holland. Today, Angoulême has emerged as the capital of French comic strip production, with countless Lucky Luke and Astérix volumes rolling off the town's presses. Today, the *vielle ville* does not have the traditional charm of its geographical neighbor; instead its winding hilly streets are filled with modern stores, restaurants, and movie theaters. Several of the museums lie on the outskirts rather than within the city itself.

TRANSPORTATION

Trains: pl. de la Gare (☎05 45 69 91 65). To: **Bordeaux** (55min., 8-10 per day, 113F/€17.23); **Paris** (2¾hr., 7 per day, 316-385F/€48.19-58.71); **Poitiers** (1hr., 5 per day, 99F/€15.10); and **Saintes** (1hr., 4-5 per day, 68F/€10.37). Open M-F 9:30am-7pm, Sa 9:30am-6:30pm.

Buses: Autobus Citram, rue Louis Pergaud (☎05 45 25 99 99). To **Cognac** (1hr., 8 per day, 45F/€6.86) and **La Rochelle** (3hr., 3 per day, 104F/€15.86). Buses stop at pl. du Champ de Mars. Buy tickets on board. Info at the **Cartrans** office, pl. du Champ de Mars (☎05 45 95 95 99). Open July to mid-Aug. M-F 2-6:15pm; mid-Aug. to June M-F 9:15am-12:15pm and 2-6:15pm. **CFTA Périgord** (☎05 53 08 43 13), goes from the train station to **Périgueux** (1½hr.; M-Sa 2 per day, 1 on Su; 76F/€11.59).

Local Transportation: STGA, 554 rue de Bordeaux (☎05 45 65 25 25), is in a kiosk on pl. du Champ de Mars. Maps available. Open July-Aug. M-F 1-5pm; Aug. 20-June M-F 1-6pm, Sa 9am-12:30pm. Tickets 7.50F/€1.14, *carnet* of 10 53F/€8.08. Buses run M-Sa 6am-8pm, and are a good way to get to many of the museums on the edge of town.

Taxis: Radio Taxi (☎05 45 95 55 55; fax 05 45 65 91 99), in front of the train station. 45F/€6.86 to hostel. 24hr.

Car Rental: Ada, 19 pl. de la Gare (☎05 45 92 65 29), offers the best deals, with cars starting at 99F/€15.10 per day, 145km included. Open M-Sa 8am-noon and 2-7pm. **National Rent-A-Car** is right across from the train station at 21 pl. de la Gare (☎05 45 37 39 49). Open M-Sa 8am-noon and 2-7pm. Cars start at 265F/€40.40. Must be 21 to rent. MC/V). A few doors down at 15 pl. de la Gare is **Europcar** (☎05 45 92 02 02), which sometimes has special student reductions. Cars start at 295F/€44.98. Must be 21+. Additional charge of 100F/€15.25 per day for those under 25. Open M-F 8am-noon and 2-7pm, Sa 8am-noon and 2-6pm. AmEx/MC/V.

ORIENTATION AND PRACTICAL INFORMATION

Angoulême lies halfway down the TGV line between Bordeaux and Poitiers. The *vieille ville* sits among the ramparts just south of the Charente and southwest of the train station. It is easy to get lost in this maze of streets, so grab a map from the tourist office branch outside the station. To get to the main **tourist office** at pl. des

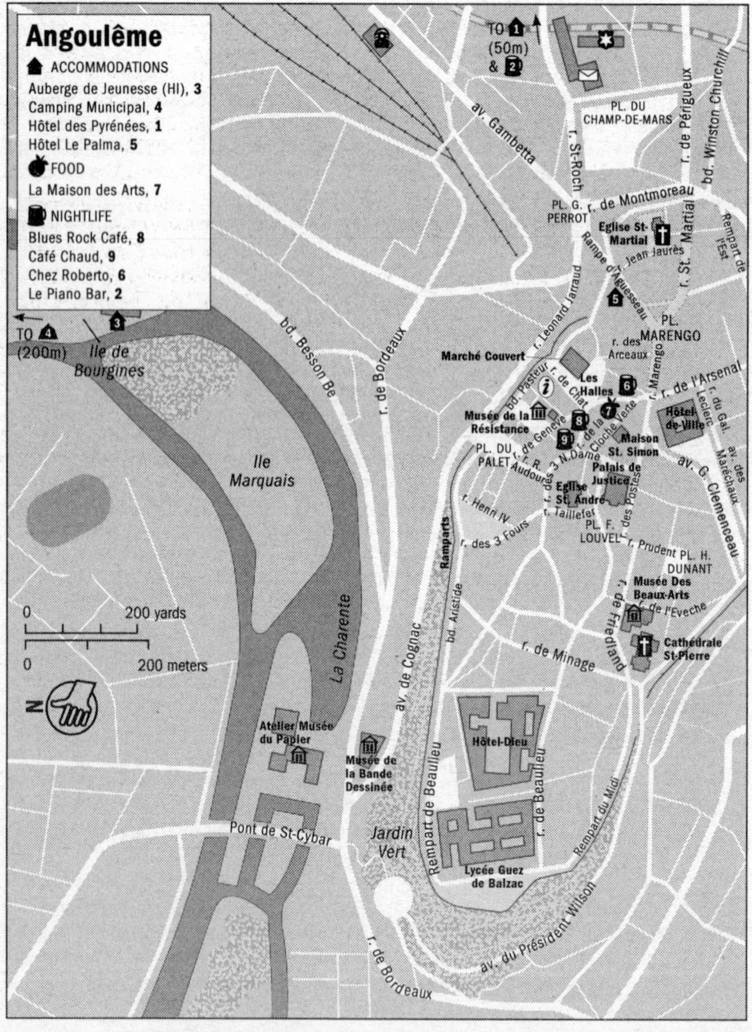

Halles, follow av. Gambetta right and uphill to pl. G. Perrot, and continue straight up the rampe d'Aguesseau and turn right onto bd. Pasteur, keeping close to the railing overlooking the valley, pass the market building on your left, and turn left beyond the market onto rue du Chat; the office will be on your right.

Tourist Office: 7bis rue du Chat, pl. des Halles (☎05 45 95 16 84; fax 05 45 95 91 76). Makes hotel reservations free of charge. Distributes an indispensable city guide, including restaurants, hotels, museums, and outdoors activities; available only in French with a few English paragraphs available to describe the main tourist sites in the *vieille ville*. Open July-Aug. M-Sa 9:30am-7pm, Su 10am-noon and 2-5pm; Sept.-June M-F 9:30am-6pm, Sa 10am-noon and 2-5pm, Su 10am-noon. **Kiosk** (☎05 45 92 27 57), by the train station. Open daily M-Sa 9am-noon and 2-6:30pm.

City Tours: Day and night tours offered through the Hôtel de Ville's **Service Patrimoine** (☎05 45 38 70 79). Day trips leave daily at 4pm and in July-Sept. 4 times a day. Tours leave from the Hôtel de Ville. Call the Service Patrimoine or tourist office for more info. 30F/€4.57, children 20F/€3.05. English tours available, call in advance.

Budget Travel: Voyages Wasteels, 2 pl. Francis Louvel (☎05 45 92 56 89; fax 05 45 94 01 31). 20-30% savings on train and plane tickets. Open M-F 9am-12:30pm and 2-6:30pm, Sa 10am-12:30pm and 2-5:30pm. MC/V. **Jet tours,** 5bis rue de Perigeux (☎05 45 92 07 94), can also arrange cheap trips with excellent deals on airfare. Open M-Sa 9:30am-12:30pm and 2-6:30pm, closes Sa 6pm.

Money: Good rates at **Banque de France,** 1 rue de Général Leclerc (☎05 45 97 60 00), on pl. de l'Hôtel de Ville. Exchange desk open M-F 8:40am-noon. Post office also has good rates and no commission for US dollars.

Youth Center: Centre Information Jeunesse, L'Espace Franquin, 1*ter* bd. Bertholet (☎05 45 37 07 30; fax 05 45 38 65 51), around the corner from the Hôtel de Ville. Friendly staff provides info on jobs and events, cheap concert tickets, and general advice. Open July-Aug. M-F 9am-12:30pm and 2-6pm; Sept.-June M-F 9am-6pm, Sa 2-6pm. Email access also available for 10F/€1.53 per 30min., 15F/€2.29 per hr.

Laundromat: Lavomatique, 3 rue Ludovic Trarieux, near the Hôtel de Ville. Open daily 7am-9pm. Dry cleaning service and laundry at **Washmatic,** 11 rue St-Roch (☎05 45 95 19 44). Open M-Sa 9am-7pm. 20F/€3.05 per load.

Police: pl. du Champs de Mars (☎05 45 39 38 37), next to the post office.

Hospital: Hôpital de Girac, rte. de Bordeaux (☎05 45 24 40 40). Closer to town is the private **Clinique St-Joseph,** 51 av. Président Wilson (☎05 45 38 67 00).

Internet Access: Café Arobase, 121 rue de Bordeaux (☎05 45 38 65 65), inside the CNBDI (see p. 607). Open Sept.-June Tu-F 10am-6pm, Sa-Su 2-6pm; July-Aug. 10am-7pm, Sa-Su 2-7pm. 20F/€3.05 per hr. for students. Be prepared to wait in line. If you come to CNBDI when the Café is closed, the receptionist might let you use the museum computers for free. Museum open July-Aug. M-F 10am-7pm, Sa-Su 2-7pm; Sept.-June Tu-F 10am-6pm, Sa-Su 2-6pm. The best deal in town is at the **Centre Information Jeunesse,** see above, 10F/€1.53 per 30min., 15F/€2.29 per hr.

Post Office: pl. du Champs de Mars (☎05 45 66 66 00; fax 05 45 66 66 17). **Currency exchange.** Open M-F 8am-7pm, Sa 8am-noon. **Branch office,** pl. Francis Louvel, near the Palais de Justice (☎05 45 90 14 30). Open M-F 8am-6:45pm, Sa 8:30am-12:30pm. **Postal code:** 16000.

ACCOMMODATIONS AND CAMPING

Cheap hotels cluster near the intersection of av. Gambetta and the pedestrian district, which slopes downhill from the *vieille ville*. The hostel and campground are on the Ile de Bourgines, an island in the Charente 2km from the town center.

Auberge de Jeunesse (HI) (☎05 45 92 45 80; fax 05 45 95 90 71), on Ile de Bourgines. To walk, turn left out of the train station onto av. de Lattre de Tassigny and take the first left onto bd. du 8 Mai 1945. Just before the big bridge, turn left onto bd. Besson Bey and cross the footbridge. Follow the dirt path beside the river to the left; the hostel is just ahead (30min.). To get there by bus, leave the station, turn right onto av. Gambetta, and right again onto rue Denis Papin, which crosses over the tracks. Continue straight onto Passage Lamaud, a pedestrian shortcut that leads to rue de Paris (5-10min.). Turn right onto rue de Paris and take bus #7 (dir: "Le Treuil," last bus 8pm) to "St-Antoine." Gorgeous location along the Charente. 15 bright 2- to 6-bed rooms with skylights and sinks in a modern building; fiendish press-and-repeat showers get warm when they want to. Breakfast 19F/€2.90. Meals 28-55F/€4.27-8.39. Sheets 17F/€2.59. No lockout. No curfew. Call ahead in summer. Dorms 53F/€8.08.

Hôtel Le Palma, 4 rampe d'Aguesseau (☎05 45 95 22 89; fax 05 45 94 26 66), near the Eglise St-Martial, about 3 blocks up the hill from the train station. Ten large, bland, but perfectly sufficient rooms lie along a narrow winding staircase. Quiet atmosphere with excellent location–5min. from both the train station and the center of town. Breakfast 28F/€4.27. Reception M-Sa only; call in advance for Su. Singles 130F/€19.82, with shower 160F/€24.39; doubles 160-180F/€24.39-27.44. AmEx/DC/MC/V.

Hôtel des Pyrénées, 80 rue St-Roch (☎05 45 95 20 45; fax 05 45 92 16 95), off pl. du Champ de Mars. From the train station, follow rue Gambetta until the second large intersection, and take a very sharp left. Bright, spacious, well-kept rooms with spotless bathrooms. Breakfast 30-35F/€4.57-5.34. Singles and doubles 150-170F/€22.90-25.92, with shower and TV 210-280F/€32.02-42.69. Extra bed 50F/€7.62. MC/V.

Camping Municipal, on Ile de Bourgines (☎05 45 92 83 22; fax 05 45 95 91 76; campingangouleme@wanadoo.fr). 3-star camping next to the youth hostel. In forested surroundings beside the Charente, removed from the bustle of the city. Picnic tables, swimming pool, telephones, ping-pong. Handicapped-accessible. Reception 7am-12:30pm and 2:30-9pm. Open Apr.-Sept. 16F/€2.44 per person, 8F/€1.22 per child, 27F/€4.12 per site with vehicle; 56F/€8.54 per 2 people, tent, and car.

FOOD

The local specialty, *cagouilles à la charentaise* (snails prepared first with garlic and parsley, then with sausage, smoked ham, and spices; 45-50F/€6.86-7.62), can be found in the restaurants of the *vieille ville*. A favorite sweet is the flower-shaped *marguerite* chocolate, named for François Ier's sister, Marguerite de Valois. Bars, cafés, and bakeries line rue de St-Martial and rue Marengo, but the food becomes funkier and the crowds more interesting as you weave your way into the narrow streets of the quadrant formed by Les Halles, pl. du Palet, Eglise St-André, and the Hôtel de Ville. **Letuffe Chocolatier,** 10 pl. Francis Louvel, gives free samples. (☎05 45 95 00 54. 72F/€10.98 per 250g. Open M-F 9am-6pm. MC/V.) **La Maison Des Arts,** 24 rue de la Cloche Verte, is perfect for diners with a flare for the artistic. The restaurant displays glass and ceramic pottery and paintings by local artists. Meals are served in the courtyard in summer under the shade of trees and plants strung with lights; in the winter the tables and plants are moved inside to create a winter garden inside the gallery. Salads (35F/€5.34) are especially good. (☎05 45 93 91 77. Open Tu noon-8pm, W-Sa 10am-11pm.) The recently renovated covered **market** on pl. des Halles sells the town's freshest produce two blocks down rue de Gaulle from the Hôtel de Ville (daily 7am-12:30pm). There is a **Stoc supermarket,** 19 rue Périgueux, right by the Champ de Mars. (Open M-Sa 8:30am-7:15pm, Su 9am-noon. MC/V.). Be prepared to wait in line.

SIGHTS

CATHEDRALE ST-PIERRE. The splendid 12th-century cathedral of Angoulême is textbook Romanesque, but for one missing element: the structure was built without internal columns, to permit an uninterrupted view of the interior. Even the ones that line the walls are purely ornamental. The original 6th-century structure also lacked vertical windows; before Byzantine renovations bathed the transept in pale blue light, it was lit only by lanterns. The edifice exerted a considerable influence, not only on other churches in the diocese, but also on more distant buildings like Fontevraud in the Loire and Notre-Dame-la-Grande of Poitiers. A splendid facade depicts the Ascension of Christ and scenes from the Last Judgment. Other notable features include the distinguished capitals below the belfry, the graceful arch-lined walls, and a four-domed nave characteristic of the region. *(Pl. St-Pierre. ☎05 45 95 20 38. Open daily 9am-7pm.)*

MUSEE DE LA BANDE DESSINEE. Housed in the **Centre Nationale de la Bande Dessinée et de L'Image (CNBDI),** this museum is a tribute to Angoulême's leading role in the development of computerized graphics and the *B.D.—la bande dessinée* (comic strips). Here you'll find French cartoons from the 19th and 20th centuries, including favorites like *Popeye. (121 rue de Bordeaux. From pl. du Champ de Mars and pl. de l'Hôtel de Ville, take bus #3 or 5 to "Nil-CNBDI." ☎05 45 38 65 65; cnbdi@cnbdi.fr. Open July-Aug. M-F 10am-7pm, Sa-Su 2-7pm; Sept.-June Tu-F 10am-6pm, Sa-Su 2-6pm. 30F/€4.57, students 20F/€3.05, children 6-14 10F/€1.53, under 6 free.)*

MUSEE DES BEAUX-ARTS. Inhabiting a restored 12th-century bishop's palace, the museum displays a pleasing mélange of media. A labyrinth of 16th to 19th-century paintings, 19th-century *charentais* archaeological digs, North and West African pottery, and locally created sculptures surrounds one of the museum's prized possessions, Etienne Barthélémy's *Grief of Priam's Family* (1800). *(1 rue Friedland, behind the cathedral. ☎05 45 95 07 69; fax 05 45 95 98 26. Open M-F noon-6pm, Sa-Su 2-6pm. 15F/€2.29, students 5F/€0.76, children under 18 free; free to everyone noon-2pm.)*

EGLISE ST-ANDRE. The 12th-century church, originally Romanesque, was reworked in a Gothic style. It combines paintings from the 16th to the 19th centuries with a massive altarpiece and a superb baroque oak pulpit. The facade was redone in the early 19th century, but the church still retains its original tower and entrance. *(8 rue Taillefer, on the pl. de Palet in the town center. Open daily 9am-7pm.)*

GARDENS AND WATER SPORTS. Angoulême's ramparts and green riverside areas are a refreshing escape from the medieval gloom of its interiors. At the bottom of av. du Président Wilson, the flowers and waterfalls of the **Jardin Vert** soothe tourists. The 4th-century ramparts that surround the town provide a view of the red-roofed houses and green countryside. To canoe or kayak on the Charente, call SCA Angoulême (☎05 45 94 68 91). The tourist office has lots of info on sports (both water and non-) in the area including canoeing, kayaking, water skiing, and tennis. For water skiing, call **CAM's water skiing** (☎05 45 92 76 22). Open June 15-Sept. 15 daily noon-8pm. The Bourgines Olympic **swimming pool,** next to the hostel, for splashing under the blue sky. *(☎05 45 95 21 70. Open July-Aug. daily 10am-8pm.)*

OTHER SIGHTS. The **Atelier-Musée du papier** consists of two open-air rooms, illustrating the history of Charente's paper-making industry, and the other that explains the industrial history of the area, in French. *(134 rue de Bordeaux. ☎05 45 92 73 43; fax 05 45 92 15 99. Across from the CNBDI. Open Sept.-June Tu-Su 2-6pm; July-Aug. Tu-Sa noon-6:30pm. Free.)* The **Musée de la Résistance et de la Déportation** has taken over the one-time home of 16th-century religious reformer Jean Calvin, and now chronicles Angoulême's experience under Nazi occupation, particularly the development and courage of the French resistance fighters, many of whom were captured and tortured to death by the Nazis, but whose invaluable work was recognized by General Eisenhower as central to the success of the war. The exhibits are all in French, with limited English texts available. *(34 rue de Genève. ☎05 45 38 76 87; fax 05 45 93 12 66. Open July-Aug. M-Sa 9am-noon and 2-6pm; Sept.-June Tu-Sa 2-6pm. 15F/€2.29, children and students free.)* Built by the Souchet family in the early 16th century, the **Maison St-Simon** cherishes its Renaissance facade; within, the **Fonds Régional d'Art Contemporain** displays avant-garde art. *(15 rue de la Cloche Verte. ☎05 45 92 87 01. Open Tu-Sa 10:30am-noon and 2-7pm. Free.)* The **Musée Archéologique** displays regional treasures from Gallo-Roman times. *(44 rue Montmoreau. ☎05 45 94 90 75. Open M-F 9-noon. Free.)*

ENTERTAINMENT AND FESTIVALS

As the sun sets, folks move toward the cafés on rue Massillon and pl. des Halles, and av. Gambetta comes alive with numerous bars and restaurants. Have a hot coffee or a cold drink at **Café Chaud,** 1 rue Ludovic Trarieux. The lively music, wooden spiral staircase, and cushioned wicker seats hold mostly locals. (☎05 45 38 26 32. Occasional live music. Open M-Th noon-2am, F-Sa noon-4am, Su 3pm-2am.) **Blues Rock Café,** 19 rue de Genève, packs the square outside with drinks, smoke, laughter, and, occasionally, live music. (☎05 45 94 05 98. Open daily 11am-2am, F-Sa 11pm-3am.) Live concerts almost nightly make worthwhile the hike out to **Le Piano Rétro Club,** 210 rue St-Roch. (☎05 45 92 87 11. Open Tu-Sa 10:30pm-2am.) **Chez Roberto,** 6 rue de Genève, packs its room full of beer, smoke, and loud laughter. This restaurant is a bar by night, with happy hour beginning at 7pm, later evolving into loud Mexican music and dancing. Occasional concerts, theme nights, and even a sporadic striptease. (Open daily 11am-2am, busiest on Th-Sa nights.) Enjoy a slightly calmer drink on av. Gambetta at **Lieu dit** or **Koda Koda.**

The world-famous **Salon International de la Bande-Dessinée** (☎05 45 97 86 50; www.bdangouleme.com) breezes into town the last weekend in January (Jan. 25-28, 2002). Over 200,000 visitors spend four days admiring comic-strip exhibits throughout town (60F/€9.15 for all four days), where Astérix and Obélix can occasionally be sighted. The **Festival Musiques Métisses,** 6 rue du point-du-Jour, features French-African and Caribbean music each year during Pentecost (☎05 45 95 43 42). The popular **Circuit des Remparts,** 2 rue Fontgrave, revs its engine in mid-September, as antique cars hold races and exhibitions for three days in the town center (☎05 45 94 95 67). International pianists of all genres participate in the two-week **Festival International de Piano, "Piano en Valois,"** in late September and early October. Some concerts are free, but most cost 50-80F/€7.62-12.20 (☎05 45 94 74 00). In November enjoy **Gastronomades,** a celebration of culinary arts, and **Ludoland,** which pays homage to video games. Call the tourist office for more info. Finally, like many French cities, Angoulême welcomes all sorts of artistic festivity in the summertime; call the tourist office after mid-June for information about the **Eté au Ciné,** a series of outdoor films shown evenings during the summer and the **Jeux de Rue,** an open air theater festival with free outdoor performances.

For those who love to wine and dine with the gentle sway of the river, **Les Croisières au pays d'Angoulême** are a series of themed nighttime cruises that run July to August. Themes include the paper cruise with a stop at the paper museum, the wine cruise, and the chocoholic cruise. The themes tend to change each summer, but may include fireworks, or a Spanish fiesta. Prices, depending on the cruise, range from 80-205F/€12.20-31.26, children 35-145F/€5.34-22.11. Call the tourist office to make reservations or for more info.

DAYTRIP FROM ANGOULEME: LA ROCHEFOUCAULD

Get to La Rochefoucauld by ***train*** *(M-Sa 5 per day, 3 convenient ones, Su 3 per day; 30F/€4.57). At the train station, walk around the back and across the parking lot to the traffic circle. Go halfway around the traffic circle and keep walking straight for 4 blocks through the town center. The château will be straight ahead (8min.). The* ***tourist office*** *is at 1 rue des Tanneurs. (☎05 45 63 07 45. Open M-Sa 9:30am-12:30pm and 2:30-7pm.)*

La Rochefoucauld has been home to the aristocratic Foucauld family for over 1025 years; more than 43 generations have resided there. The present **château,** known as the "pearl of Angoumois," was built by Duke Francis II in 1528 on a feudal-era foundation, with twin towers, a medieval fortress, and an elegant chapel on a plateau overlooking the town. The magnificent central spiral staircase, built in 1520, is a perfect work of renaissance art and was designed by Leonardo Da Vinci. The classical music playing in the inner courtyard adds a touch of humanity to the stone building. (☎05 45 62 07 42. Open M-Sa 10am-7pm, Su and holidays 2-7pm.) The surrounding village, which takes its name from the family ("La Roche à Foucauld" or "The Rock of Foucauld"), preserves a Gothic cloister, **Le Couvent des Carmes,** built in 1329 and in surprisingly good shape, and a church, dating to 1266.

COGNAC

Comely Cognac (pop. 20,000) rises along the banks of the Charente, which Henry IV called the "gentlest and most beautiful river in France." According to French law, the crops produced in the Cognac region are the only crops in the world fit to become the liquor that bears the Cognac name; trade megaliths Hennessy, Martell, Rémy Martin, and Otard offer a look inside their distilleries and a sampling of the sweet liqueur. An ideal daytrip from Saintes and Angoulême, Cognac offers a budget opportunity to taste this rarest of *digestifs*.

ORIENTATION AND PRACTICAL INFORMATION. Trains come from **Angoulême** (40min., 5 per day, 47F/€7.17) and **Saintes** (20min., 6 per day, 29F/€4.42). To get to the **tourist office,** 16 rue du 14 Juillet, follow av. du Maréchal Leclerc out of the train station to the first circle and take a right, following signs to the town center. Turn right on rue Bayard and go straight across pl. Bayard onto rue du 14 Juillet (15min.). You'll find information, maps, and a free accommodations service. The office arranges tours of the city, including nocturnal trips (July 12-Aug. Th at 9:30pm; 40F/€6.10, under 12 30F/€4.57), and *petit train* tours for 30F/€4.57. (☎05 45 82 10 71; fax 05 45 82 34 47; office.tourisme.cognac@wanadoo.fr. Office open July-Aug. M-Sa 9am-7pm, Su 10:30am-4pm; Sept.-June M-Sa 9am-12:30pm and 2-6:15pm.) Find the **Banque de France,** 39 bd. Denfert-Rochereau, for the best rates. (☎05 45 82 25 10. Open M-F 8:45am-noon.) The **post office,** 2 pl. Bayard, also has **currency exchange.** (☎05 45 36 31 82. Open M-F 8am-6:30pm, Sa 8:30am-noon.) **Postal code:** 16100.

ACCOMMODATIONS AND CAMPING. Unfortunately, there is no hostel in Cognac. **Le Saint Martin,** 112 av. Paul Firino Martell, about 1km from the center of town, has the cheapest rooms in town. To get here, turn left onto av. Martell from pl. Martell. Singles and doubles, recently redone, are cozy and accommodating, and kept very clean. (☎05 545 35 01 29; http://perso.wanadoo.fr/hotel.stmartin. Singles 130F/€19.82, with shower 155F/€23.63; doubles with shower 160-185F/€24.39-28.21.) Three-star **Cognac Camping,** bd. de Châtenay, on rte. de Ste-Sévère, is a 30-minute walk from the town. A bus (4F/€0.61, 6-trip *carnet* for 20F/€3.05, under 18 2F/€0.30) runs twice daily from pl. François 1er (☎05 45 82 01 99; June 16-Sept. 4). Get off at "Camping." (☎05 45 32 13 32. Pool. Laundry. Open May-Oct. July-Aug. 2 people with site, showers, and electricity 70F/€10.67; Sept.-June 65F/€9.91. 3 people with site 70-80F/€10.67-12.20.)

FOOD. Tasting Cognac's famous product doesn't necessarily mean drinking it. Restaurants around **pl. François Ier** serve pricey local specialties drenched in the stuff. Right in the town center, **La Boune Goule,** 42 allées de la Corderie, is at the intersection of rue Aristide Briande. The name is a *charentais* expression for good taste, appropriate when "nothing except the fries is frozen." Huge, fresh portions of local cuisine, with 30F/€4.57 omelettes. (☎05 45 82 06 37. 70F/€10.67 lunch *menu*. Open daily noon-2:30pm and 7-11:30pm. MC/V.) More basic needs can be satisfied at **Supermarket Eco,** on pl. Bayard, right down the street from the tourist office (open M-Sa 9am-12:30pm and 3-7:30pm, Su 9-11:45 am). There is an **indoor market** at pl. d'Armes (Tu-Su 7am-1pm), and a lively **outdoor market** brightens pl. du Marché on the second Saturday of each month.

COGNAC DISTILLERIES. The joy of visiting Cognac lies in making your way from one brandy producer to the next, touring warehouses, watching films on the history of each house, and collecting nip bottles. If a nip is not enough, Otard offers its "Extra" in a gold-trimmed black porcelain bust of François 1er for 1530F/€233.27, while Hennessy's "Timeless" Cognac, created especially for the millennium with the best stock of the past century and bottled in pure crystal, costs a mere 21,000F/€3201.70. If you want the drink, you'll have to take the tour. In the summer, most houses regularly give tours in English; English tours are less frequent in the winter, but Cognac houses want to accommodate customers and will gladly arrange a tour—even a private one—if you call in advance.

Hennessy, quai Richard Hennessy (☎05 45 35 72 68; fax 05 45 35 79 49). The industry's biggest player has the longest, most technically involved, most detailed, and most interesting presentation, which includes barrel-making displays, a trip to "paradise," where the oldest cognacs are kept, and a short boat ride along the Charente river. If you have time for only one, this should be it, and in any case it is best to visit this one first as it will give the best background before visiting some of the other producers with less detailed tours. This tour is the most expensive, but also the most elegant. Open June-Sept. daily 10am-6pm; Mar.-May and Sept.-Dec. 10am-5pm; Jan.-Feb. call ahead for a reservation. Several excellent English tours per day, call ahead for times. 50F/€7.62, students 30F/€4.57, under 16 free.

Otard and the Château Francois Ier, 127 bd. Denfert-Rochereau (☎05 45 36 88 86), is housed in the Château de Cognac, the 1494 birthplace of François Ier. Dressed in medieval costumes, the tour guides are as proud of the history of the house as they are of the distillation within–the 50min. tour begins with the history of the building, ending with a tour of the damp castle cellar where the cognac is produced and stored. Be sure to notice the fungus growing on the walls–it consumes in vapors the equivalent of 23,000 bottles each year. Open July-Aug. daily 10am-7pm; Apr.-June and Sept.-Oct. daily 10am-noon and 2-6pm; Nov.-Dec. M-Th 11am-noon and 2-5pm, F 11am-noon and 2-4pm; Jan.-Mar. call ahead for a visit (groups only). Last tours leave 1hr. before closing. 25F/€3.81, 18 and under 15F/€2.29, under 12 free.

Martell, pl. Edouard Martell (☎05 45 36 33 33), was founded by an Englishman in 1715 and is the oldest of the major cognac houses, and ships to cities around the world. Today, it is the only tour that will take you into the bottling room itself, where you can see its 11 automatic assembly lines that with clockwork computer precision fill, wrap, and package over 10,000 bottles of Cognac a day. Open June-Sept. M-F 9:30am-5pm, Sa-Su noon-5pm; Oct., Mar.-May M-Th 9:30am-noon and 2:30-5pm, F 9:30am-noon; Nov.-Feb. call ahead to reserve. English tours given daily, call ahead to arrange. 25F/€3.81, children 15F/€2.29.

Camus, 29 rue Marguerite de Navarre (☎05 45 32 28 28; fax 05 45 32 17 11). The smallest of the Cognac distillers, the family-owned Camus attributes its fine blending to the superior taste buds of its members. Open July-Aug. M-F 10am-noon and 1:45-4:30pm; June and Sept.-Oct. M-F 10am-noon and 2-4:30pm; May M-F 10am-12:30pm and 1:45-5:45pm. Call ahead for an English tour.

Rémy Martin, rte. de Pons D732 (☎05 45 35 76 55), does much the same 5km outside of town in Merpin, but adds a little train ride to the vines. No buses access the site and it's a long hike. Open Apr.-Nov. 4 by reservation 10am-5pm. Tour 30F/€4.57, students 20F/€3.05, under 18 free.

THE ANGELS' SHARE Discovered by Charentais wine makers in 1598 during an economic crisis, cognac has kept Cognac solvent for four centuries. Strict government labeling regulations separate the cognacs from common brandies. The only fine liquor in the world limited to a specific production region, cognac must be made from grapes in six small concentric regions, the heart of which is Grande Champagne (in which Cognac itself is located). Cognac is produced from the white *unis blanc* grape through a short fermentation period (5-10 days) followed by a double distillation that brings the alcohol level to 70%. This *eau de vie* is then aged for 5-100 years, under the careful direction of the cellar master. During the aging period the alcohol level falls to around 40% due to evaporation through the oak storage barrels (which contribute the amber tint to an otherwise colorless brandy). This lost portion is known as the "angels' share." Cognac is enjoyed most frequently as a *digestif,* straight up, in a snifter or tulip glass, but Charentais custom also supports its consumption as a "long drink" or *apéritif,* on the rocks or in tonic or water.

SIGHTS. The **Musée Municipal du Cognac,** 48 bd. Denfert-Rochereau, details the history of Cognac and cognac through regional clothing, ceramics, and viticulture tools, and displays Marie Curie's cognac bottle bust. (☎05 45 32 07 25. Open June-Sept. W-M 10am-noon and 2-6pm; Oct.-May 2-5:30pm. 13F/€1.98, students 6F/€0.91, under 18 free.) Despite all the cognac mania, a stroll through the friendly, pedestrian center of town, full of flowers and marketware in the summertime, is always worthwhile. Step into the **Eglise Saint Léger,** off rue Aristide Briand, to admire its restored 12th- to 14th-century architecture. The church houses two grand 18th-century tableaux that complement the gold-lined altar, and arches carved with stunning precision. (Open daily 8am-7pm.)

FESTIVALS. In early April, Cognac hosts the **Festival du Film Policier,** hauling 10 cop flicks in front of a grand jury. (35F/€5.34 per film. Call tourist office for details.) The **Blues Passions** concerts of late July have showcased artists such as B.B. King and Otis Rush. For info, visit 9A pl. Cagouillet. (☎05 45 32 17 28; fax 05 45 32 66 33. Tickets 30F/€4.57, under 18 100F/€15.25.) Mid-July brings in the annual **Fête du Cognac,** which features boat races and fireworks on the Charente.

OUTDOOR PURSUITS. Cognac's valley provides great hiking among vineyards, fields, groves, and forests. The tourist office provides four *Sentiers de Randonnées* maps (12F/€1.83 each) with paths in and around Cognac; off-trail surprises include abbeys, historic ruins, and châteaux. For information about canoeing, call 05 45 82 46 24. Parks in Cognac include the **Jardin de l'Hôtel de Ville** around the museum (open June-Sept. daily 7am-10pm; Apr.-May and Oct. 7am-9pm; Nov.-Mar. 7am-7pm) and the large, tree-lined **Parc François I**[er] (open 24hr.), northwest of the city center between allée Bassée and allée des Charentes.

SAINTES

Gracefully bisected by the Charente river and named for the local Gallic Santon tribe, the ancient city of *Mediolanum Santonum* was founded by Romans in the first century AD. Connected by a major road to Lyon, the city served as the capital of Aquitaine for nearly 100 years; today Saintes retains an assortment of first-century ruins, bearing testimony to the Roman city's importance. Alternately sacked and plundered by pyromaniacal Gallic tribes from the 3rd to the 10th centuries Saintes was also subject to such niceties as the Black Plague, the Hundred Years' War, and the wars of religion. In the 11th century, after St-Eutrope evangelized the region, two major Benedictine abbeys in the Romanesque style popped up; the Cathédrale St-Pierre, the bell-tower of the Eglise St-Eutrope, and the present municipal library reflect the later Gothic style. Modern Saintes (pop. 27,000) rewards visitors' curiosity with a quiet charm that even the rampaging Gauls would have appreciated.

TRANSPORTATION

Trains: pl. Pierre Senard. To: **Bordeaux** (1½hr., 5 per day, 97F/€14.79); **Cognac** (20min., 5 per day, 29F/€4.42); **La Rochelle** (50min., 5 per day, 66F/€10.06); **Niort** (1hr., 5 per day, 65F/€9.91); **Paris** (2¼hr., 6 per day, 352-400F/€53.67-60.98); **Poitiers** (2hr., 6 per day, 144F/€21.95); and **Royan** (30min. 6-7 per day, 38F/€5.79). Train station open 5:30am-9:30pm; ticket booths open M 5:40am-8pm, Tu-F 8am-8pm, Sa 8am-7pm, Su 8am-9:30pm.

Buses: Autobus Aunis et Saintonge, 1 cours Reverseaux (☎05 46 97 52 03). To: **Royan** (1hr., 8 per day, 35F/€5.34); **Le Château** and **St-Pierre d'Oléron** on the Ile d'Oléron (1½hr., 2 per day, 61-71F/€9.30-10.82). Office open M-F 9am-noon and 2-6pm. **Océcars** (☎05 46 99 23 65), in Rochefort, goes to **La Rochelle** (2½hr., 1-2 per day, 57F/€8.69). An operator answers calls M-F 8:30am-noon and 2-7pm.

Local Transportation: Buses cross the city regularly (5.50F/€0.84). Schedules at tourist office or Boutique Bus, in the Galerie du Bois d'Amour (☎05 46 93 50 50).

Car Rental: Budget, 51 av. de la Marne (☎05 46 74 28 11). Cars start at 330F/€50.31 with 200km included. Drivers must be 21+, no extra fee for those under 25. Open M-Sa 8am-noon and 2-6:30pm. **Europcar,** 43 av. de la Marne (☎05 46 92 56 10). Drivers must be 21+, those under 25 pay a one-time fee of 100F/€15.25. Cars start at 415F/€63.27 with 200km included. Open M-F 8am-6:30pm, Sa 8am-noon and 2-6:30pm.

Taxis: at the train station (☎05 46 74 24 24). 6-7F/€0.91-€1.07 per km.

Bike Rental: Groleau, 9 cours Reverseaux (☎05 46 74 19 03). 50-55F/€7.62-8.39 per day. Open Tu-Sa 9am-12:15pm and 2-7pm. MC/V.

ORIENTATION AND PRACTICAL INFORMATION

Saintes lies on the Charente river, along the La Rochelle-Bordeaux railway line and 25km from Cognac. To get to the **tourist office,** take a sharp left upon leaving the train station and follow av. de la Marne until you hit hopping av. Gambetta. Turn right and follow it to the river; the Arc Germanicus will be on your left. Cross the bridge over the river at pont Palissy and continue straight on leafy green **cours National.** The tourist office is on your right in a villa set back from the street (20min.). The hub of the mellow pedestrian district is **rue Victor Hugo,** three blocks to the left after the bridge.

Tourist Office: 62 cours National (☎05 46 74 23 82; fax 05 46 92 17 01), in Villa Musso. Free maps and pamphlets. Organizes walking tours of the city, *abbaye,* and Roman ruins. Office open July-Aug. M-Sa 9am-1pm and 2-7pm, Su 10am-1pm and 2-6pm; Sept.-June M-Sa 9am-12:30pm and 2-6pm. Tours June-Sept. M-Sa. 37F/€5.64 for one tour, 65F/€9.91 for two, 85F/€12.96 for all three.

Banks: Banque de France, 1 cours Lemercier (☎05 46 93 40 33). **Currency exchange** desk open M-F 8:45am-12:15pm and 2-3:30pm.

Laundromat: Laverie de la Saintonge, 18 quai de la République (☎05 46 74 47 18). Open M-Sa 8:30am-7pm, Su 2-6pm. **Laverie et Cie,** 46ter cours Reverseaux (☎05 46 74 34 79; fax 05 46 82 05 50).

Police: rue de Bastion (☎05 46 90 30 40), or **Gendarmerie,** 17 rue du Chermignac (☎05 46 93 01 19).

Hospital: pl. du 11 Novembre (☎05 46 92 76 76).

Internet Access: Accès Micro, 74 rue Arc de Triomphe (☎05 46 92 85 10; fax 05 46 92 85 11), one block away from the hostel. 1F/€0.15 per min. **France Telecom,** 22 rue Alsace-Lorraine, has one terminal available. *Télécarte* necessary. Open M 1:30-6:30pm, Tu-Sa 9:30am-12:30pm and 1:30-6:30pm.

Post Office: 6 cours National (☎05 46 93 84 50). **Currency exchange.** Open M-F 8:30am-7pm, Sa 8:30am-noon. **Postal code:** 17100.

ACCOMMODATIONS AND CAMPING

Hotels fill for the early to mid-July festivals; otherwise rooms should be easy to find. Most of the cheap beds cluster on the train station side of the Charente.

Auberge de Jeunesse (HI), 2 pl. Geoffrey-Martel (☎05 46 92 14 92; fax 05 46 92 97 82), next to the Abbaye-aux-Dames. From the station, take a sharp left onto av. de la Marne and then turn right onto av. Gambetta, left onto rue du Pérat, and right onto rue St-Pallais; 25m up at pl. St-Pallais, turn left through the archway into the courtyard of the abbey. Go straight through the courtyard and out through the arch at the back, and the hostel will be on your right (15min.). A clean, renovated building that feels like part of the abbey itself. Cozy, pine-scented, cabin-like rooms. Breakfast included. Sheets 17F/€2.59. Camping 27F/€4.12, with breakfast 37F/€5.64. No lockout or curfew. Reception 7am-noon and 5-11pm; Oct.-May until 10pm. Dorms 69F/€10.52.

Le Parisien, 35 rue Frédéric-Mestreau (☎05 46 74 28 92), by the train station. Owner can recite the entire train schedule plus a "highlights of Saintes" speech in one breath. The floral arch over the main entrance leads to small, friendly rooms with bright, mismatched bedcovers. Breakfast 15-25F/€2.29-3.81. Hall showers 15F/€2.29. Call several weeks ahead for July-Aug. June-Aug. singles or doubles 160F/€24.39; Sept.-May 130F/€19.82. Extra bed 45F/€6.86. AmEx/MC/V.

Camping Au Fil de L'Eau, 6 rue de Courbiac (☎05 46 93 08 00; fax 05 46 93 61 88), 1km from the center of town. From the train station, follow directions to hostel until av. Gambetta and turn right onto quai de l'Yser after crossing the bridge (25-30min.). Signs mark the way. By bus, take #2 (dir: "La Recluse") from the train station; get off at "Théâtre" and catch the #3 (dir: "Magezy"), to "Courbiac" (25min., 6F/€0.91). Three-star site by the Charente, next to municipal pool (free for campers) and mini-golf (25F/€3.81). Individual lots are crowded, but enhanced by an on-site market and brasserie. Reception July-Aug. 8am-1pm and 3-9pm; May 15-June and Sept. 1-15 9:30am-noon and 4-8pm. 32F/€4.88 per person, 10F/€1.53 per child; 27F/€4.12 per site; car included. Electricity 19F/€2.90. MC/V. Certain buildings are handicapped-accessible.

FOOD

Menus in Saintes flaunt the region's seafood as well as *escargot* dishes and *mojettes* (white beans cooked in Charenté). Start things off with *pineau*, a sweeter relative of Cognac. Saintes is blessed with plenty of family-run restaurants and bars, especially in the pedestrian district by rue Victor Hugo. Saintes holds **markets** on cours Reverseaux (Tu and F), near Cathédrale St-Pierre (W and Sa), and on av. de la Marne and av. Gambetta (Th and Su), all 8am-12:30pm. On the first Monday of every month **Le Grand Foire** open-air market stretches from the cours National to av. Gambetta. A huge **Leclerc supermarket** and general store are on cours de Gaulle near the hostel (open M-Th and Sa 9am-7:15pm, F 9am-8:15pm). A smaller **Co-op** supermarket can be found on both rue Urbain Loyer, off cours National (open M-Sa 8:30am-12:45pm and 3-7:45pm), and at 162 av. Gambetta, near the train station (open Tu-Sa 8:30am-1pm and 3:30-8pm, Su 8:30-11am). For sit-down fare, try the friendly **Le Gourmandin,** av. de la Marne. In nice weather, the outdoor seating at Le Gourmandin takes the prize. Sit under an umbrella in a quiet courtyard next to a small manmade waterfall. (☎05 46 93 27 60. Entrees 48-80F/€7.32-12.20, salads 35-65F/€5.34-9.91. Open daily noon-2:30pm and 7-10pm.) For a cheap, hot meal, try **Cafétéria du Bois-d'Amour,** 7 rue du Bois-d'Amour, off cours National in the Galérie Marchandise, a serve-yourself, pay-by-the-plate cafeteria, offering 5-28F/€0.76-4.27 entrees and 24-41F/€3.66-6.25 *plats*. (☎05 46 97 26 54. Open daily 11:30am-10:30pm; hot food available 11:30am-12:30pm and 6:30-9:45pm. 5% student discount. MC/V.)

SIGHTS

International flags line both sides of the **pont Bernard Palissy,** which looks out onto most of Saintes' sights. Built in AD 18 as the entrance to the city, the Roman **Arc Germanicus** rises on the left bank of the river to honor Emperor Tiberius of Gaul and his nephew Germanicus. First located at the entrance to a bridge that crossed the Charente, the Arc tried to become an aqueduct as the river widened over the centuries. The bridge was extended, but around its 1800th birthday the Arc began to lose stability. The bridge was demolished in 1843, and replaced by the pont Bernard Palissy slightly to the north, but the Arc was spared and moved to the right bank of the river, 15m from its original location.

Behind the Arc, the **Jardin Public** offers refuge on shaded benches next to colorful flower beds. A peaceful mini-zoo in the center houses a few small goats, deer, rabbits, and birds. In July and August, the garden hosts free Sunday afternoon performances, ranging from traditional folk dancing to—grab your Stetson—country line-dancing. Next door, on esplanade André Malraux, the popular **Musée**

Archéologique displays the remains of architecture and chariots from the first-century city. A partially finished puzzle of Roman columns, friezes, and cornices, most dating from the demolition of the town's ramparts in the 4th century, lies in another chamber. A comprehensive guide in English and French explains the Roman craftsmanship. (☎05 46 74 20 97. Open May-Sept. Tu-Su 10am-noon and 2-6pm; Oct.-Apr. Tu-Sa 10am-noon and 2-5:30pm, Su 2-6pm. Free.)

Rue Arc de Triomphe (which becomes rue St-Pallais) leads to the Romanesque **Abbaye-aux-Dames.** Built in 1047, the abbey led a quiet life for a while—some Gothic touch-ups here, another gallery there—until plagues, fires, and wars prompted centuries of constant construction and reconstruction. During the anti-religious fervor of the Revolution, the abbey was shut down and turned into a prison. Today, it serves as the musical and cultural center of Saintes. Frequent exhibitions by local artists brighten the pale stone walls of the **Salle Capitulaire,** which was once the daily meeting place of Benedictine nuns. The pinecone-shaped belltower of the **Eglise Notre-Dame** dates from the 12th century, when Eleanor of Aquitaine gave the nuns some friendly pointers during renovations. Climb to the top to scan the stunning horizon or check out contemporary tapestries depicting the six days of the Creation. Unlocked doors, winding stairways, and isolated passageways welcome leisurely wanderers. See the *L'Abbaye aux Dames: Eté* pamphlet at the tourist office for summer concerts. (☎05 46 97 48 48. Exhibition and ramparts open July-Sept. 15 daily 10am-12:30pm and 2-7pm; Sept. 16-June Th F and Su-Tu 2-6pm, W and Sa 10am-12:30pm and 2-7pm. Church free. Abbey 20F/€3.05, students and under age 16 free. French tours 37F/€5.64. Concerts 80-280F/€12.20-42.69.)

Cross the flower-lined pedestrian bridge as you head for the **Cathédrale St-Pierre** on rue St-Pierre. With its metal helmet, the cathedral hovers over the town, visible from almost anywhere. The 12th-century church was redone in Gothic style from the 15th to 18th centuries, but the steeple and portal were left unfinished. (☎05 46 93 09 22. Open daily 10am-7pm. Free.) Turn away from the center of town and descend the steps of less traveled rue St-Eutrope, which crawls through tree-lined fields to the crypt of the saint who names the road. Known as the saint of recovery, **St. Eutrope** lies in a **crypt** treasured for its healing powers by many, including Joseph de Compostela, who paid a visit on his way to Santiago. (Open daily 9am-7pm. Free.) Follow the path as it curves to the left and turn right onto rue de La Croix Boisnard. The road leads to the **Arènes Gallo-Romaines,** now a crumbled and peaceful amphitheater in a residential neighborhood. Built in AD 40, the structure seated 20,000 spectators who flocked to see gladiators battle wild animals or each other to the death. Don't bother paying the 5F/€0.76 admission: you can see just as well from outside the fence. (Open Apr.-Oct. daily 9am-7pm; Nov.-Mar. Tu-Su 10am-12:30pm and 2-4:30pm.)

ENTERTAINMENT AND FESTIVALS

Come nightfall, unwind with an evening of conversation and sunset-watching in a Saintes café or pub. Try your game (5F/€0.76) at **Billiard Santais,** 126 av. Gambetta, accompanied by 12F/€1.83 beers. (☎05 46 93 74 71. Open W-M 2pm-2am.) Where rue Gambetta runs into pont Palissy you'll find **Bar Le Palissy,** a gathering place for students who listen to jazz or rock, or sing to classics on Thursday karaoke nights. (☎05 46 74 30 65. Occasional live music. Open W-Su 9pm-2am.) If you've got a car, you can dance up a storm with partying students at the **Le Santon** club, Ste-Vegas, on rte. de Royan. In summer, the adjoining **swimming pool** provides a respite from steamy body heat. (☎05 46 97 00 00. Cover 67F/€10.22. Open daily 10:30pm-3am.)

In mid-July, **La Fête des Pays du Monde** brings diversity to Saintes with a ten-day celebration of international folk music, food, and dance. The Arènes Gallo-Romaines host the opening and closing events. Some events are free; most cost 40-200F/€6.10-30.49, and a 200F/€30.49 passport gets you into a selected program of events. (For info call ☎05 46 74 47 50, or stop by 43 rue Gautier.) At the same time, be sure to join the **Académies Musicales** celebration, in which more than thirty classical music concerts are packed into ten days at the Abbaye aux Dames. (☎05 46 97 48 48; fax 05 46 92 58 56. Tickets 80-280F/€12.20-42.69.)

ILE D'OLERON

Hovering only a couple of miles from the mainland, Oléron is the second-largest French island after Corsica, but not easily accessible from mainland France. Some of France's most renowned oyster beds, first cultivated by the Romans, encircle the island; the 90km coastline also includes 20km of fine beaches. A 3km bridge links the island to the continent, and is perhaps best traversed by buses that circulate between Saintes or Rochefort-sur-Mer and **Le Château,** the main town on the southern end of the island and the best base from which to explore it. For the ultimate escape, rent a bike in Le Château and pedal through the **Marais aux Oiseaux** bird sanctuary in the middle of the island to **St-Pierre d'Oléron,** the main town in the north, then into the evergreen **Forêt des Saumords** in the northeast corner. Return by way of the coastal villages, and leave yourself plenty of time, as bike trails are not clearly marked and do not always offer direct paths between towns.

ORIENTATION AND PRACTICAL INFORMATION (LE CHATEAU). Buses leave for **Le Château** from 1 cours Reverseaux (☎05 46 97 52 03) in **Saintes** (1½hr., 3-4 per day, 65F/€9.91), and from **Rochefort's** bus station (☎05 46 99 98 97; 1hr., 6-8 per day, 45F/€6.86), and train station (☎05 46 93 21 41). Ask your driver or check a bus schedule to see whether the bus continues on to other parts of the island; if it does, stay on until the next stop, in the center of town right next to the tourist office. If the bus ride ends at the port in Le Château, turn your back to the water, and follow av. du Port and the signs to the town center. Turn right onto bd. Victor Hugo and head up the hill toward the **tourist office,** pl. de la République, for a chock-full info packet, free maps of the island and the city, and hotel reservations. (☎05 46 47 60 51; fax 05 46 47 73 65. Open July-Aug. M-Sa 9:30am-12:30pm and 3-7pm, Su 10am-12:30pm; Sept.-June M-Sa 9:30am-12:30pm and 3-6:30pm.) **Rent bikes** at **Cycles-Peche Locavente,** 5 rue Maréchal Foch, just off pl. de la République. (☎05 46 47 69 30. 35-50F/€5.34-7.62 per half-day, 45-65F/€6.86-9.91 per day; deposit 650F/€99.10. Open July-Aug. daily 9am-12:15pm and 2-7:15pm; Sept.-June Tu-Sa 9am-12:30pm and 2-7pm, Su 9am-12:30pm. MC/V.) **Crédit Maritime,** near the tourist office on bd. Thiers, charges 15F/€2.29 to change foreign traveler's checks. (☎05 46 47 62 23. Open M-Sa 8:30am-12:15pm and 1:30-5pm.) Le Château's **post office** is on bd. Victor Hugo. (☎05 46 47 61 99. Open M-F 9am-noon and 1:30-4:30pm, Sa 9am-noon.) **Postal code:** 17480.

From Le Château, a **shuttle bus** runs to: **Grand Village,** near the beaches (20min.; M-Sa 5-6 per day, Su 2 per day; 10F/€1.53); **St-Denis** (1hr., 3 per day, 32F/€4.88); and **St-Pierre-d'Oléron** (45min.; M-Sa 6-8 per day, Su 4 per day; 17F/€2.59).

ACCOMMODATIONS AND CAMPING. Reserve several weeks in advance if you want a cheap place to crash. In Le Château, **Le Castel,** 54 rue Alsace-Lorraine, lets cheerful, spotless rooms, which would be spacious were it not for all the furniture. (☎05 46 75 24 69; fax 05 46 75 25 41. Breakfast 35F/€5.34. Reception 9am-noon and 6-10pm. Singles and doubles with bath 170-260F/€25.92-39.64. Extra bed 35F/€5.34. MC/V.) In the center of town near the tourist office, **Le Jean-Bart,** pl. de la République, offers four barren, white stucco rooms with a great view. Wake up to the sounds of the morning market. (☎05 46 47 60 04. Breakfast 34F/€5.18. Doubles with shower 160F/€24.39 and 210F/€32.02. Extra bed 50F/€7.62. MC/V.)

Most people on a budget take tents, since 34 **campsites** are spread along the coast. Two-star **Les Remparts,** on bd. Philippe Daste, is also in Le Château, right next to the beach. It's the most convenient site for those without a car, but also more crowded. (☎05 46 47 61 93; fax 05 46 47 73 65. Open Mar.-Oct. June 15-Sept. 15 car and tent 88F/€13.42; off-season 75F/€11.43.) Two and a half kilometers northeast of Le Château, on rte. des Huitres, reigns the four-star **La Brande,** with 199 luxury sites, a pool, tennis courts, and a waterslide. (☎05 46 47 62 37; fax 05 46 47 71 70. Reception 8:30am-10pm. Open Mar. 15-Nov. 15. July-Aug. 128F/€19.52 for 2 people; Sept.-June 90F/€13.72. Extra person 38F/€5.79. Electricity 20F/€3.05. MC/V.) Near **Grand-Village** and the beaches lies **Camping Municipal des Pins,** on allée des Pins. With 340 sites, this campground can hold as many people as the nearby town. Campgrounds are a bit crowded, but tall trees help keep an isolated feeling. (☎05 46 47 50 13. Open Easter-Sept. July-Aug. 2-person site 90F/€13.72, Easter-June and Sept. 80F/€12.20; 26F/€3.96 per person. Electricity 21F/€3.20. MC/V.)

FOOD. Each town has a Sunday morning **market,** and many have weekday morning versions as well. In **Le Château,** vendors fill the covered building across from the tourist office in pl. de la République (Tu-Su 7:30am-12:30pm). **The Coop,** 3 rue Reytre Frères, right behind Hôtel Jean-Bart off pl. République, is a modest grocery just across from the market square. (Open M-Sa 8:30am-12:30pm and 4-7:30pm, Su 9am-1pm.) **Super U Supermarché,** 15 av. d'Antioches, 250m out of Le Château, has a larger selection. (Open M-Sa 8:30am-8pm, Su 9am-12:30pm.) St-Pierre's **Lidl,** on av. de Vel Air (the main route from Le Château), is less expensive than **STOC. Grand Village** also has a large **Super U** in its commercial center. (Both open July-Aug. M-Sa 8:30am-8pm, Su 9am-12:30pm; Sept.-June M-Sa 9am-12:30pm and 3-7:30pm, Su 9am-12:30pm.)

Larger towns have some nightlife. In **Le Château, La Cigale,** on rue Clemenceau, has a lively crowd. (☎05 46 47 61 37. Open daily 7am-2am.) **St-Denis** is home to **Le Panoramic,** 3 bd. d'Antioche, a relaxed jazz and blues bar. (☎05 46 75 98 18. Open daily 8am-2am.) In **La Cotinière,** a city that stays up late in summer, check out **Café de la Marine,** on rue du Port. (☎05 46 47 10 38. Open 10am-2am.)

ISLAND TOWNS AND SIGHTS. The mighty but crumbling **citadel** in Le Château was built on the ruins of a medieval fortress. In 1621, following a revolt in La Rochelle, skittish Louis XIII had it destroyed to prevent its falling into Protestant hands, only to rebuild it nine years later; the current structure dates to this 1630 reconstruction. Louis XIV and Richelieu were some of its more famous guests; WWI German POWs were some of the more infamous. Allied bombs destroyed much of the citadel in 1945 to keep German squadrons left on Oléron from regrouping. The fortress ruins have since been taken over by grass and picnickers. Various exhibits come and go in the more habitable chambers; call 05 46 75 53 00 for hours and activities, some of which take place in pl. de la République. (Exhibits open daily 10am-7pm. Free.)

St-Pierre d'Oléron, with a bustling pedestrian sector, is the island's geographic and administrative center; it also houses the tomb of French writer and naval officer Pierre Loti. The staff of the St-Pierre **tourist office,** pl. Gambetta, is all-knowing. (☎05 46 47 11 39; fax 05 46 47 10 41. Open July-Aug. M-Sa 9am-7pm, Su 10am-1pm; Sept.-June M-Sa 9:15am-12:30pm and 2-6pm.) A lively, brightly colored port graced by a modern chapel makes **La Cotinière** the most picturesque of the island towns. **Le Grand Village,** 4km southwest of Le Château, is the inappropriately named smallest town, with 910 locals and the island's glitziest, most **flamboyantly topless** beach, **Les Allassins.** (Tourist office ☎05 46 47 58 00; fax 05 46 47 42 17.) Another beach, **Plage du Vert Bois,** near Grand Village and separated from the main road by a thick pine forest, feels almost like an island itself. Near the northwestern tip, **St-Denis** invites tourists to climb the 54m lighthouse and peer down at the colorful collage below. (Open daily 10am-noon and 2-6:30pm; Sept.-June 10am-noon and 2-6pm. 10F/€1.53, children 7-12 5F/€0.76, under 7 free.) The **tourist office** on bd. d'Antioche has more information (☎05 46 47 95 53; fax 05 46 75 91 36).

LA ROCHELLE

Though it cannot boast of beautiful beaches or sandy shores, La Rochelle does have one great claim to fame—fish, and lots of it. La Rochelle's position as one of France's best-sheltered seaports helped to create its fortune, and later helped to nearly destroy it. France and England fought over it during the Hundred Years' War, and Cardinal Richelieu was so upset with the city's support of England during the 17th-century invasion of the Ile de Ré that he had the town besieged for fifteen months, during which time three quarters of its citizens starved. La Rochelle didn't really recover until 20th-century vacationers discovered its medieval architecture, proximity to some of the most perfect isles off the French coast, and its superlative seafood restaurants.

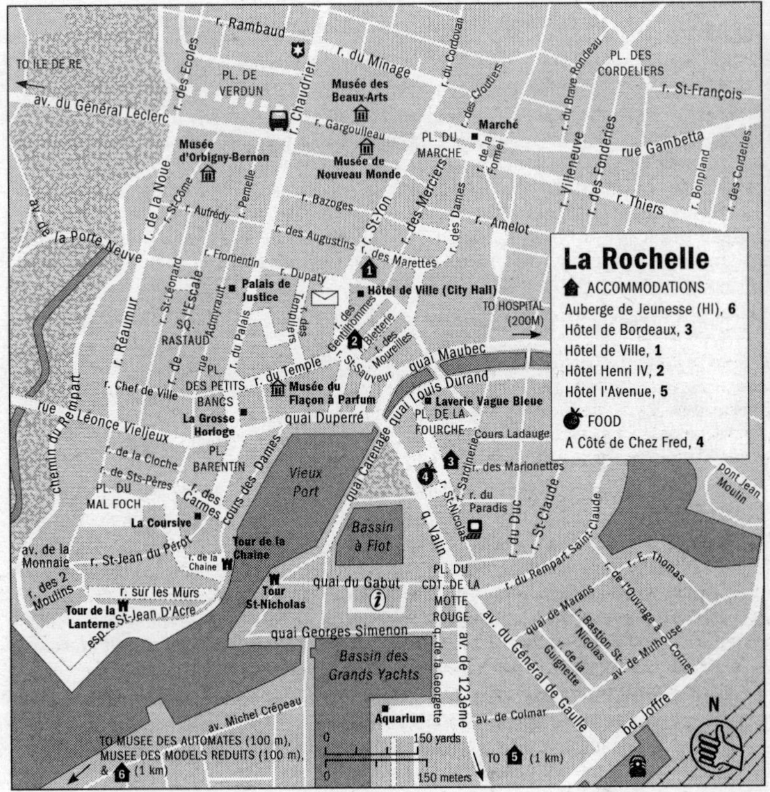

TRANSPORTATION

Trains: bd. Maréchal Joffre. To: **Bordeaux** (2hr., 5 per day, 136F/€20.73); **Nantes** (2hr., 5 per day, 128F/€19.52); **Paris** (5hr., TGVs 3hr.; 1 per day, 5 TGVs per day; 326F/€49.70, TGVs 393F/€59.92); and **Poitiers** (2hr., 8 per day, 120F/€18.30). Ticket office open daily 5am-10:30pm, info desk open 9am-6:45pm.

Ferries: Boats run to **Ile d'Aix** (see p. 624). **Bus de Mer** (☎05 46 34 02 22) shuttles between the old port and les Minimes until 12:10am (11F/€1.68).

Buses: Citram, 30 cours des Dames (☎05 46 50 53 57), goes to **Angoulême** (3½hr., 2 per day, 105F/€16.01). Open M 2-6:45pm, Tu-F 9am-12:15pm and 2-6:45pm, Sa 9am-12:15pm. **Océcars** (☎05 46 00 21 01), in pl. de Verdun, sends buses to **Royan** (1¼hr., 3 per day, 73F/€11.13) and **Saintes** via Rochefort (3-5 per day, 57F/€8.69). For all buses, buy tickets from driver.

Public Transportation: Pick up a schedule at the pl. de Verdun main office (5F/€0.76). **Autoplus** (☎05 46 34 02 22) serves the campgrounds, hostel, and town center (8F/€1.22).

Taxis: pl. de Verdun (☎05 46 41 55 55 or 05 46 41 22 22). 45F/€6.86 to hostel.

Bike Rental: Vélos Municipaux Autoplus, off quai Valin or in pl. de Verdun near the bus station (☎05 46 34 02 22). Free with ID deposit for 2hr., 6F/€0.91 per hr. thereafter. Quayside location open May-Aug. M-Sa 7:30am-7pm, Su 1-7pm.

ORIENTATION AND PRACTICAL INFORMATION

La Rochelle spreads out from the *vieux port*, where many cafés line **Quai Duperré**, to the boutique-filled *vieille ville* just inland. To get from the train station to the **tourist office,** head up av. du Général de Gaulle to the first square, pl. de la Motte Rouge, and turn left onto the quai du Gabut. The tourist office is on the left, in the **Quartier du Gabut,** a zone of shops, seafood, and pan-Asian restaurants of dubious authenticity (5min.). To reach the center of town directly from the station, take av. du Général de Gaulle through pl. de la Motte Rouge until it becomes quai Valin, which will lead you straight to quai Duperré. For those staying in town, the beach nearest the hostel by the aquarium and the port de Plaisance is nicer than the stony strand west of the old port.

Tourist Office: pl. de la Petite Sirène, quartier du Gabut (☎05 46 41 14 68; fax 05 46 41 99 85; www.ville-larochelle.fr). Multilingual staff sells informative maps in French (3F/€0.46) and decent ones in English (1F/€0.14). Pick up the free entertainment magazines *Tenue de Soirée* and *Sortir* for current festivities. Daily city **tours** by foot and horse carriage, 2hr. walking, 90min. by carriage. Walking tours cost 35F/€5.34, children 25F/€3.81. Horse-and-carriage tours are 50F/€7.62, children 30F/€4.57. July-Aug. weekly **night visits** led by costume-clad locals leave from the tourist office at 8:30, 9, and 9:30pm, 45F/€6.86, students and children 35F/€5.34. Most tours are in French, although English tours can sometimes be arranged in advance. Hotel **reservation service** 10F/€1.53. Open July-Aug. M-Sa 9am-8pm, Su and holidays 11am-5pm; May-June and Sept. M-Sa 9am-7pm, Su 11am-5pm; Oct.-Apr. M-Sa 9am-noon and 2-6pm, Su 10am-noon.

Money: Banque de France, on rue St-Come (☎05 46 51 48 00). Good rates. Open for exchange M-F 8:30am-noon. In a pinch, 24hr. **exchange machines** at **Crédit Lyonnais,** 19 rue du Palais.

Youth Center: Centre Départemental d'Information Jeunesse (CDIJ), 2 rue des Gentilshommes (☎05 46 41 16 36 or 05 46 41 16 99; fax 05 46 41 50 35). BIJ tickets. Boards list apartments and jobs. Open M 2-6pm, Tu-F 10am-12:30pm and 1:30-6pm. closed Sa and Su. **Internet** 10F/€1.53 per hr.

Laundromat: Laverie Vague Bleue, 4bis quai Louis Durand, corner of rue St-Nicolas (☎05 46 50 67 91). Open daily 8:30am-8:30pm. Take advantage of "happy hour" (W 8:30am-1:30pm) when prices are reduced by 5-10F/€0.76-1.53 per load.

Police: 2 pl. de Verdun (☎05 46 51 36 36).

Hospital: rue du Dr. Schweitzer (☎05 46 45 50 50).

Internet Access: Cyber Squat, 63 rue St-Nicolas (☎05 46 34 53 67). 5F/€0.76 connection fee, 0.68F/€0.10 per min. Open M-Sa 11am-about midnight. One email terminal is also available at the **Auberge de Jeunesse** with a phone card, and the cheapest email in town is at the **Centre Departemental d'Information Jeunesse** (see above).

Post Office: 6 pl. de l'Hôtel de Ville (☎05 46 30 41 30). **Currency exchange.** Main office at 52 av. Mulhouse, by the train station. Open M-F 8am-7pm, Sa 8am-noon. For **Poste Restante:** address to "Hôtel de Ville, 17021 La Rochelle." Open M-F 8:30am-6:30pm, Sa 8am-12:30pm. **Postal code:** 17000.

ACCOMMODATIONS AND CAMPING

Cheap beds in town are limited; make reservations now. The huge industrial port-side hostel fills fast in July and August, as do the many two-stars near pl. du Marché in the *vieille ville*.

Centre International de Séjour (HI), Auberge de Jeunesse (HI), av. des Minimes (☎05 46 44 43 11; fax 05 46 45 41 48). Take bus #10 (dir: "Port des Minimes") from av. de Colmar, 1 block from the station, to "Lycell Hotelier" (M-Sa every 20min. until 7:15pm,

8F/€1.22). Continue walking in direction of bus up to traffic circle, and take left-most turn off traffic circle. Follow this road for about 15min. Hostel set back from road on the right hand side. Or enjoy the waterside walk–great view, and you can't get lost. Keep to the port edges and watch for the hostel on your left, at the end of the boardwalk (30min. from station). Enormous, hospital-like hostel with 2- to 6-bunk dorms. Breakfast included. Laundry. Reception July-Aug. 8:30am-11pm; Sept.-June 8am-12:30pm, 1:30-7:30pm, and 8:30-10pm. Lockout 10am-2pm. Doors locked after 11:30pm, but there's a code. Reserve ahead. Dorms 75F/€11.43; singles 110F/€16.77.

Hôtel Henry IV, 31 rue des Gentilshommes (☎05 46 41 25 79; fax 05 46 41 78 64), on pl. de la Caille off rue du Temple, in the heart of the *vieille ville*. Cozy wood-paneled floral rooms reminiscent of a bed and breakfast, 1970s tiled bathrooms in brown and orange; cheery dining room with sunflower mural. Breakfast 35F/€5.34. Singles and doubles 220F/€33.54 June-Sept.; 185F/€28.21 off-season, with shower 195-210F/€29.73-32.02; 2- to 4-person suites with shower 360-440F/€54.89-64.08. MC/V.

Hôtel de Bordeaux, 43 rue St-Nicolas (☎05 46 41 31 22; fax 05 46 41 24 43; www.rivages.net/bordeaux), right off quai Valin, 5min. from station. A great location, with 22 renovated rooms above a café. Breakfast 33F/€5.03. Reception 8am-9:30pm. Singles and doubles July-Aug. 295-360F/€44.98-54.89; Sept.-June 170-235F/€25.92-35.83; 70F/€10.67 for each additional person. AmEx/MC/V.

Bar de l'Hôtel de Ville, 5 rue St-Yon (☎05 46 41 30 25). Hotel-bar in the center of town houses students during the year and offers its fading pastel rooms and linoleum floors to travelers from mid-June to the end of August. Feel just like an impoverished, overworked French grad student, complete with the occasional smoky smell. One studio apartment, complete with bathroom and fully stocked kitchenette, is available for 350F/€53.36 per day, although it is usually rented by the week. Reception closed Su and after 8pm weeknights. Mid-June to Aug. doubles 190-230F/€28.97.

Hôtel l'Avenue, 109 rue Emile Normandin (☎05 46 44 26 10). Cramped, carpeted rooms a 15min. walk from the city center. Breakfast 27F/€4.12. Singles and doubles with sink 185F/€28.21, with bath 210F/€32.02; triples with shower 250F/€38.12, with bath 290F/€44.21; quads 300F/€45.74. Extra double bed 80F/€12.20. MC/V.

Camping Municipal du Soleil, av. Michel Crépeau (☎05 46 44 42 53). A 10min. walk from the city center past the old port along the quai, following av. Marillac to the left at its junction with allée des Tamaris, or catch bus #10. Crowded, friendly campground along the water. Open mid-May to Sept. 15; reserve in advance to ensure a spot. One person and car 43F/€6.56, extra person 19F/€2.90. The tourist office has a list of more distant campsites and info on more beautiful, but remote, island camping.

FOOD

The *fruits de mer* are always ripe in La Rochelle; follow the fishy smell to the stands of the **covered market** at pl. du Marché for fresh seafood, fruit, and vegetables (daily 7am-1pm). **Monoprix,** on rue de Palais, near the clocktower, sells the usual (open M-Sa 8:30am-8pm), as do the **Co-ops** which have sprung up around town; two are at 41 rue Sardinerie and 17 rue Amelot (both open daily 9am-1pm and 3:30-8pm). Restaurants crowd the *vieille ville* along **rue St-Jean** and the quai.

A Côté de Chez Fred, 30-32 rue St-Nicolas (☎05 46 41 65 76). This little seafood place physically surrounds its supplier, Poissonnerie Fred; you can watch the fish being prepared through an open window. *Plats* 40-110F/€6.10-16.77. Don't skip the fish soup (39F/€5.95). Open M-Sa noon-2:30pm and 7-10:30pm. AmEx/MC/V.

La Provençale Pizzeria, 15 rue t. Jean du Perot (☎05 46 41 43 68). Opt for the French cuisine rather than the pizza, and you're in for a solid meal. This friendly restaurant serves many local favorites including mussels, duck, and the ever-popular rabbit. 3-course *menu* 69F/€10.52. Open M-Sa noon-2pm and 7-9pm, Su 7-9pm.

SIGHTS

THE OLD TOWN. The pedestrian *vieille ville*, dating from the 17th and 18th centuries, stretches beyond the whitewashed townhouses of the harbor to a glitzy inland shopping district sprinkled with museums. Stroll by the 14th-century **grosse horloge** (great clocktower), but skip the archaeological exhibit inside. Check out the Renaissance **Hôtel de Ville,** with its prominent statue of Henry IV, who built it. *(45min. French tours of the interior July-Aug. daily 3 and 4pm; Sept.-May daily at 3pm, June Sa-Su 3pm. 20F/€3.05, students 10F/€1.53.)*

TOUR ST-NICOLAS AND TOUR DE LA CHAINE. The 14th-century towers guarding the port guaranteed La Rochelle's safety from attack—essential in a city which served as a giant warehouse for both France and England. When hostile ships approached, guards could bar the harbor by linking a chain between the two towers. Now unfit even for that use, the 800-year-old chain lines the path leading from rue de la Chaîne to the tower. Today, La Rochelle's citizens are more worried about getting out themselves than about keeping invaders from the city, as the harbor has begun to silt up dangerously. Tour St-Nicolas, on the left as you face the harbor, has impressive fortifications and narrow, dizzying staircases; in the Tour de la Chaîne is a historical exhibit with a model of the town in Richelieu's day. *(St-Nicolas ☎05 46 41 74 13; Chaîne ☎06 46 34 11 81. Both towers open Apr.-Sept. daily 10am-7pm; Oct.-Mar. W-M 10am-12:30pm and 2-5:30pm. 26F/€3.96, ages 18-25 16F/€2.44, under 18 free. Combined ticket including Tour de la Lanterne 45F/€6.86, ages 18-25 30F/€4.57.)*

TOUR DE LA LANTERNE. Accessible from the Tour de la Chaîne by a low rampart, this 58m-high tower was France's first lighthouse. The 15th-century tower has a morbid history—it became known as the *Tour des Prêtres* after 13 priests were thrown from the steeple during the Wars of Religion. In 1822, four sergeants were imprisoned here before being executed in Paris for conspiring against the monarch. The 162 steps to the top hold intricate graffiti scrawled by other 19th-century detainees. At the summit, only three inches of stone separate you from your own 45m free-fall, but you can see all the way to the Ile d'Oléron on sunny days. *(☎05 46 34 11 81. Same hours and prices as the Tour St-Nicolas.)*

MUSEE DU FLACON A PARFUM. In the shopping district near la Grosse Horloge, this tiny tribute to scent is on the second floor of the Saponaire perfume shop. A private collector has amassed thousands of perfume bottles, including *crème parfum* flasks produced by the Ku Klux Klan in 1933, which look like tiny white Lego people, and bottles designed by Cocteau, Dali, and Miró. One 1937 bottle is modeled on Mae West's torso. Descriptions available in English. *(33 rue du Temple. ☎05 46 41 32 40. Open M 2:30-7pm, Tu-Sa 10:30am-noon and 2-7pm; July-Aug. also open Su and holidays 3-6pm 27F/€4.12, students 24F/€3.66, under 10 free.)*

AQUARIUM. The newly reopened aquarium is home to hundreds of the world's most exotic fish. The octopus is especially graceful and surprisingly shy, unlike the piranhas in the simulated rainforest. The tanks are built against stone and coral backdrops to make the exhibits as realistic as possible—after a few minutes it's hard to forget that you're not 20,000 leagues under the sea. To avoid the crowds, go in the afternoon or evenings. *(Bassin des Grande Yacht, across from the Musée Maritime. ☎05 46 34 00 00. Open July-Aug. daily 9am-11pm; Apr.-June and Sept. 9am-8pm; Oct.-Mar. 9am-8pm. 65F/€9.91, students and children 45F/€6.86.)*

MUSEE DES AUTOMATES. The crown jewel of this collection is a miniature Montmartre with artists, pharmacists, drunkards, and a lingerie store—watch out for the street performers and dancers. A model train loops around the **Musée des Modèles Réduits.** The best of their many miniature scenes is the *Bataille Navale*, in which ships maneuver through a tiny sea clouded by cannon smoke. *(Automates on Rue de la Desirée, off av. Marillac. ☎05 46 41 68 08; fax 05 46 41 68 82. Modèles Réduits around the corner on rue Desirée. ☎05 46 41 64 51. Both open June-Aug. daily 9:30am-7pm; Sept.-Oct. and Feb.-May 10am-noon and 2-6pm; Nov.-Jan. 2-6pm. 65F/€9.91 for both, children under 10 35F/€5.34; for one museum 40F/€6.10, children 25F/€3.81. MC/V.)*

MUSEE D'ORBIGNY-BERNON. A very respectable collection of European and Chinese decorative arts and ceramics, including special exhibits on Japanese samurai and 19th-century Chinese life and ancient musical instruments from Southeast Asia. The museum also covers local history—they've got a wonderful display of 84 pharmaceutical vases from the old Aufredi hospital. *(2 rue St-Côme. ☎05 46 41 18 83. Open M and W-Sa 10am-noon and 2-6pm, Su 2-6pm. 22F/€3.35, students and under 18 free. 43F/€6.56 buys combined admission to the Musées d'Orbigny-Bernon, Nouveau Monde, Beaux-Arts, and Histoire Naturelle. Joint ticket available at tourist office, valid for one month.)*

OTHER SIGHTS. The outdoor **Neptunéa Musée Maritime de la Rochelle** consists of seven decks' worth of exhibits on two large fishing boats; special exhibits include a wind tunnel (for storm simulations), a display on locals fishing techniques, and a submarine. *(Pl. Bernard Moitessier. ☎05 46 28 03 00. Open Apr.-Sept. daily 10am-6:30pm, closes 7:30pm in July and Aug.; Oct-Mar. 2-6pm; closed from late Nov.-Jan. Last entry 1½hr. before the closing of the museum. 50F/€7.62, students and children 35F/€5.34.)* Two less sea-centric museums have, between them, a very worthwhile collection of art. There are paintings by Rembrandt and Delacroix in the **Musée des Beaux Arts,** along with a nice Fromentin series—those last being the ones on postcards all over town. Look for Signac's 18th-century painting of the bustling city harbor. *(28 rue Gargoulleau. ☎05 46 41 64 65. Open W-M 2-5pm. 22F/€3.35, students and children under 18 free.)* In a 1740s mansion, the interesting **Musée du Nouveau-Monde** studies France's role in the New World. It's pretty clear that the French thought new-worlders were bestial savages. *Plus ça change...* *(10 rue Fleuriau. ☎05 46 41 46 50. Open W-M 10:30am-12:30pm and 1:30-6pm, Su 3-6pm. 22F/€3.35, students and children under 18 free.)*

ENTERTAINMENT AND FESTIVALS

La Coursive, 4 rue St-Jean-du-Perot, hosts operas, jazz and classical music concerts, traditional and experimental plays, dance performances, and art films. (☎05 46 51 54 02; fax 05 46 51 54 03. Open M 5-9pm, Tu-Sa 1-8pm, Su 2-6:30pm.) On summer evenings, **quai Duperré** and **cours des Dames** are closed to cars and open to magicians, mimes, jugglers, musicians, and an open market (July-Sept.). Bars and pubs fill up during the evening *apéritif* hours; **rue St-Nicolas** and **rue de la Chaîne** overflow with jovial pub-goers, but slow down later in the night. Local youths hang out around the **cour du Temple,** a lively square tucked away off rue des Templiers. Try relaxed **Le Mayflower** (☎05 46 50 51 39) for its 18F/€2.74 rum concoction. Or toss a serious game of darts before a Saturday concert at **Le Piano Pub** (☎05 46 41 03 42); the dark dance floor upstairs at **Café Tribal** draws a young and active crowd. (All three open daily 6pm-3am.) Decked with mirrors, brass, and lacquer, **The Triolet,** 8 rue des Carmes, gets a lot of yuppies very silly on 94 different kinds of whiskey. (☎05 46 41 70 16. Cover 110F/€16.77. Open daily 11pm-5am.) The crowd is even younger at the **Oxford and Papagayo Discothèque,** plage de la Concurrence. (☎05 46 41 51 81. Cover 30F/€4.57, 60F/€9.15 with drink. Open daily 11pm-5am.)

La Rochelle's wildly popular festivals attract art-loving, sun-seeking mobs like nowhere else. During the last week of June and the first week of July, the city becomes the Cannes of the Atlantic with its **Festival International du Film de La Rochelle.** (All 100 films 490F/€74.71; 3 films 90F/€13.72; one film 35F/€5.34; under 21, 10 films for 170F/€25.92. For tickets, write to 16 rue St-Sabin, 75011 Paris. ☎05 46 51 54 00.) Without batting an eyelash, La Rochelle turns right around and holds its **FrancoFolies,** a massive six-day music festival in mid-July that brings francophone performers from around the world. (Call 05 46 28 28 28 or the tourist office. Event tickets 55-175F/€8.39-26.68.) And to round out the month, July ends with a ten-day **theater festival** on quai Simenon (☎05 46 34 33 75). During the second week of September, hundreds of boats in the Port des Minimes open their immaculate interiors to the public for the **Grand Pavois,** a festival and boat competition, known as "the foremost floating boat show in Europe" (☎05 46 44 46 39). The **marathon** (☎05 46 44 42 19) runs through town at the end of November.

ISLANDS NEAR LA ROCHELLE

ILE DE RE

Ile de Ré, dubbed "Ré La Blanche" for its 70km of fine, white sand beaches, is a sunny paradise just 10km from La Rochelle. Connected by a bridge to the mainland, the 30km-long island contains one of Europe's largest nature preserves, extensive paved bike paths, pine forests, farmland, bustling towns, and huge stretches of untouched sand. Though only 15,000 lucky people live on the island year-round, July and August bring crowds to the southern half and to the main town, St-Martin-de-Ré, in the middle of the north coast.

TRANSPORTATION. The island is easily accessible by bus. Driving across **pont La Pallice** costs a ridiculous 110F/€16.77 round-trip in tolls from June to September (60F/€9.15 Oct.-May; 15F/€2.29 for motorcycles and scooters). **Walking** and **biking** are easy options, and the cycle from La Rochelle to Sablanceaux takes less than an hour. The ride is a bit tough going up the bridge, but once you get there, the trails on the island are marvelous, with great coastal views. From pl. de Verdun in La Rochelle, head west on rue Maréchal Leclerc and follow road signs to Ile de Ré until the bike path with the same label appears on the left. If that thought makes your calves quiver, try a bus. Lines #1 and 50 go from pl. de Verdun to the beach at the foot of the bridge—make sure your bus goes all the way to "Sablanceaux" (dir: "La Pallice," 32 per day July-Aug., 10F/€1.53). If you'd like to venture beyond Sablanceaux, try **Rébus** (☎05 46 09 20 15), which runs between pl. de Verdun and every stopping place on Ré, including **St-Martin** (45min., 8 per day, 29.50F/€4.50) and **Les Portes,** at the northern tip (1½hr., 8 per day, 51.50F/€7.85).

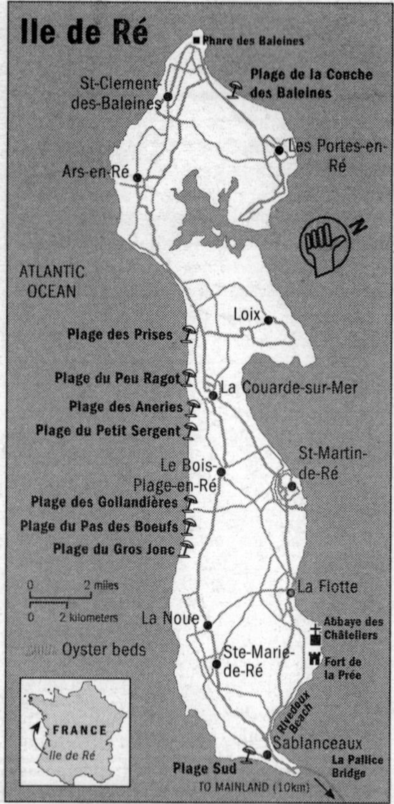

PRACTICAL INFORMATION: ST-MARTIN-DE-RE. Though it's a good idea to pick up the free tourist booklet in La Rochelle, you can get a free bike path map and guide at St-Martin's **tourist office,** on quai Nicolas Baudin. (☎05 46 09 20 06; fax 05 46 09 06 18; ot.st.martin@wanadoo.fr. Open July-Aug. daily 10am-8pm; May-June and Sept. 10am-1pm and 2-7pm, Oct.-Apr. 10am-noon and 2-6pm, closed Su afternoon.) **Cycland,** impasse Sully, off rue du Sully, rents cheap **bikes,** with branches in Sablanceaux, La Flotte, Ars, Les Portes, St-Clément, and La Couarde. (☎05 46 09 08 66. Bikes 18-40F/€2.74-6.10 per hr., 36-60F/€5.49-9.15 per half-day, 45-75F/€6.86-11.43 per day. ID deposit. Open July-Aug. daily 9am-7:30pm; Sept.-June 9:30am-1pm and 2:30-7pm. AmEx/MC/V.) The best **currency exchange** rates, despite a 40F/€6.10 commission, are at **Crédit Agricole,** 4 quai Foran, on the port. (☎05 46 09 20 14. Open Tu-F 9am-12:15pm and 1:30-5:45pm, Sa 9am-noon.) The **post office** is on pl. de la République (☎05 46 09 38 20). **Postal code:** 17410.

ACCOMMODATIONS AND CAMPING. Prices go way up in the summer. St-Martin's **Hôtel Le Sully,** 19 rue Jean Jaurès, has bright rooms—the island's cheapest—a block up from the port on a rowdy pedestrian street. (☎05 46 09 26 94; fax 05 46 09 06 85. Breakfast 30F/€4.57. June-Sept. singles or doubles with shower 240F/€36.59, with bath 290F/€44.21; Oct.-May with shower 190F/€28.97, with bath 240F/€36.59. Extra bed 50F/€7.62. MC/V.) There are also places to stay in smaller towns. In **La Flotte,** 4km east of St-Martin and 9km north of Sablanceaux, is **l'Hippocampe,** 16 rue Château des Mauléons, with small, comfortable, but aging rooms. (☎05 46 09 60 68. Breakfast 30F/€4.57. Shower 15F/€2.29. Reserve ahead. Singles and doubles 180F/€27.44, with bath 250F/€38.12. MC/V.) Gorgeous **Camping Tamaris,** 4 rue du Comte D'Hastre, right near **Rivedoux's** center, is a thickly forested site in one of the island's best spots. (☎05 46 09 81 28. Open Easter-Sept. 1-3 people 70F/€10.67, extra person 25F/€3.8, under age 7 12.50F/€1.91. Electricity 20F/€3.05.) **La Plage,** 408 rte. du Chaume, near St-Clément, is beachside on the north coast. (☎05 46 29 42 62. Open Apr.-Sept. 2 people with tent 80F/€12.20.)

FOOD AND ENTERTAINMENT. Island restaurants are pricey, but most towns have pizzerias and crêperies as well as **morning markets,** which are listed in full in Ré's tourist packet. St-Martin's **market** is indoors off rue Jean Jaurès, by the port (daily approx. 8am-1pm). Two supermarkets, **Intermarché** and **Super U,** are just east of St-Martin on the road to La Flotte (open July-Aug. daily 8am-8pm; Sept.-June M-Sa 9am-noon and 3-7:30pm).

St-Martin has a surprisingly good nightlife for its size. Port-side vendors stay open until 11pm or midnight during the summer to please the late-night tourists, and locals shuttle between the bars and discos all night. **Le Cubana** (☎05 46 09 93 49) and **Boucquingham** (☎05 46 09 01 20), both on Venelle de la Fosse Bray, are intimate piano bars tucked behind the quai, across from the tourist office. (Both open M-Th 5pm-2am, F-Sa 5pm-3am. 60F/€9.15 cover with one drink most nights. MC/V.) The versatile **Le Bastion,** cours Pasteur, across town with a great view of the sea, is a wild all-purpose grill, pizzeria, nightclub, and disco. It hosts weekly theme nights in summer. (☎02 46 09 21 92. Open Tu-Sa 5:30pm-5am.) Farther down the island, on Rivedoux plage, **Le Réseu Club,** pl. de la République, cranks it out from 11pm-5am every Friday and Saturday night. (☎05 46 09 30 90; 60F/€9.15 cover.)

TOWNS AND SIGHTS. Between Sablanceaux and beachy La Flotte are the ruins of the 13th-century **Abbaye des Chateliers.** First built in 1156, the abbey was destroyed during the Wars of Religion as Ré passed between Catholic and Protestant hands. The monks abandoned the abbey in 1574, and many of its stones were then taken in 1625 to build the Prée Fort. The ruins now stand in an isolated field, visible from the bus from Sablanceaux or Rivedoux to La Flotte. If you're biking the northern coast, signs point to the massive, derelict building, now little more than a set of crumbling walls. **La Flotte** (pop. 2700) is the island's most typical fishing town, with a very lively port and pedestrian area. It is home to the **EcoMusée La Maison du Platin,** av. du front de Mer, 4 cours Felix Fauré, devoted to the history of the town's maritime life. (☎05 46 09 61 39. Open Apr. to mid-Nov. 20F/€3.05, ages 7-18 12F/€1.83.) The museum hosts daily walking tours in French (25F/€3.81) of the town, island, and surrounding attractions. Schedules vary; call for info.

The island's largest commercial town, **St-Martin** (pop. 2650), holds a port built by Vauban and a citadel built by Louis XIV to protect Ré from the invading English; the citadel is now an active prison, with around 500 inmates. The 15th- to 17th-century Renaissance gallery of the **Hôtel Clerjotte,** on av. Victor-Bouthilier, houses the **Musée Ernest Cognac,** which is filled with model ships, old paintings, and archaeological finds. (☎05 46 09 21 22. Open July-Sept. daily 10am-1pm and 2-7pm; Oct.-June W-Su 10am-noon and 2-5pm. 25F/€3.81, students 15F/€2.29.) Climb up the hill from the quai to the imposing 15th-century **Eglise St-Martin,** originally Romanesque but built and destroyed so many times in religious wars (five) that its outside and interior now have no stylistic relation. (Open daily 10am-6:30pm, until midnight in July-Aug.) On your way up the island, stop by **Ars** to admire its 17 windmills, dismantled in the 19th century when the phyloxera plague wiped out the island's chief crop. The mill outside St-Martin is the only one to have kept its wings. As you near **St-Clément-des-Baleines,** keep your eye out for the blinking red light of the 1854 **Phare des Baleines;** flashing once every 15 seconds, the lighthouse is watched by boats over 60km away. You can climb its 167 stairs for a view of the ocean. (Open June-Sept. daily 10am-noon and 2:30-5pm; Oct.-May 11am-noon and 3-5pm. 10F/€1.53.) Also near St-Clément are the **écluses à poissons,** fishing devices used in medieval times. The stone walls were erected so that fish would be trapped when the tide went out. (☎05 46 30 22 92. Call for info. Wear boots!)

BIKES AND BEACHES. It's easy to rent a bike in any island town and pedal along the bike paths, coastal sidewalks, and wooded lanes spread out across the island. Although everybody and his grandmother bikes the southern half of Ile de Ré to St-Martin, crowds thin out as you travel north. The *Guide des Itinéraires Cyclables*, available from island tourist offices, describes five 10-22km paths. One of the island's best trails begins in Le Martray, just east of Ars, and runs along the northern coast through the island's trademark salt marsh and bird preserve, a wetlands sanctuary humming with the songs of the rare blue-throated thrush and heron. The marsh is worth visiting in the summer, but winter's really the time to see it—20,000 birds stop by on their migration from Siberia and Canada to Africa. Rent a bike in Ars to pedal this trail. Other bike paths lead you through forests, beside beaches, and past other island landmarks.

The major attraction of the island is, of course, its splendid beaches. Slather yourself with sunscreen and shake off all inhibitions at the **Plage du Petit Bec** in clothing-optional Les Portes. If you want to avoid that full-body glow, head to the pine-fringed dunes of **la Conches des Balaines,** near the lighthouse just off the Gare Bec. Both beaches, at the northern tip of the island, are huge and empty of the crowds that fill beaches on the western coast. The sea off the exposed north coast tends to be dangerous, and the shores rocky; for better swimming, try the long strip of beach along the southern shore, beginning at **La Couarde.**

ILE D'AIX

Smaller and less accessible than Ré, Aix (pop. 200) sees fewer tourists and makes an unbeatable daytrip on a sunny day. Just 3km long and barely 600m wide, the island has backwoods trails perfect for quiet hiking, and tiny coves set in the rocky, shell-covered coastline. The best beaches are along the southwest edge near the lighthouses. There are almost no cars on Aix, because it's one of the only coastal islands with no highway to the mainland. To get here, it's ferry or bust.

Once on the island, stop for a free map and brochure at the **Point Accueil,** on your right as you leave the port. The info center also organizes guided **historical tours** of the island in French (1hr.; 3 per day; 25F/€3.81, under age 12 free). **Horse carriages** do the same number of rounds from one block farther up. (☎05 46 84 07 18. 50min.; 40F/€6.10, under age 10 30F/€4.57.) To explore the island, **rent bicycles** from crêperies and snack shops in town (approx. 20F/€3.05 per hr., 40F/€6.10 per half-day, and 50F/€7.62 per day), or take the smaller coastal paths on foot—a stroll about the perimeter of the island only takes about two hours, and paths are clearly indicated on the guide distributed by the Point Accueil.

Napoleon's last three post-Waterloo days in France were spent here before he surrendered to the British, a fact celebrated in the island's two museums. The **Musée Africain** and **Musée Napoléonien** house their small but impressive collections in the island's tiny town center, surrounded by a sprinkling of public buildings, flower-laced bungalows, and little shops. The Musée Africain presents an ethnographical and zoological exhibition on Napoleon's Egyptian campaign, the highlight of which is his (preserved) dromedary. The Musée Napoléonien has a vast collection of portraits, bric-a-brac, and war memorabilia, including a facsimile of the emperor's totally illegible surrender to the British. (☎05 46 84 66 40. Both open June-Sept. daily 9:30am-6pm; Apr. and Oct. 9:30am-noon and 2-6pm; Nov.-Mar. 9am-noon and 2-5pm. Separate admission 20F/€3.05, ages 18-25 15F/€2.29, under 18 free. Combined admission before 4:30pm 25F/€3.81, ages 18-25 20F/€3.05.)

Ile d'Aix's only hotel is outrageously expensive, but **Camping le Fort de la Rade** is quiet and cheap; stone walls and purple lilacs surround your tent. (☎05 46 84 28 28; fax 05 46 84 00 44. 32-45F/€4.88-6.86 per tent, 25F/€3.81 per person, 16F/€2.44 per child.) The few restaurants on Aix tend to be pricey, but that doesn't mean you have to pack cereal. The **bakery,** on your right as you walk up rue Gourgaud, sells cheap sandwiches, and there's a little grocery store with all the essentials just across the street. The cheerful **Pressoir,** in the middle of the island on rue Le Bois Joly, is run by a bunch of young fisherman types with perpetual five-o'clock shadows. Their 56F/€8.54 lunchtime mussels-and-potatoes dish will put some meat on those spindly bones of yours. (☎05 46 84 09 37. Open daily noon-3pm and 7-11pm.)

In the summer ferries link Aix to **La Rochelle. Inter Iles,** 14 cours des Dames, runs 2-4 ferries per day to the island via the fascinating Fort Bayard. (☎05 46 50 51 88. 1½hr., round-trip 88-100F/€13.42-15.25. MC/V.) Similar service is provided by **Croisières Océanes.** Their booth is on the cours des Dames in La Rochelle. (☎05 46 50 68 44. 1hr.; 90-110F/€13.72-16.77 round-trip, ages 4-12 60F/€9.15. Ask about *Journées Promotion*, when prices dip to 75F/€11.43. MC/V.)

THE MARAIS POITEVIN

Stretching west from Niort to the Atlantic just north of La Rochelle, this natural preserve has been nicknamed *"la Venise Verte"* (the Green Venice) for the serene canals which wind through its wetlands and forests. Biking along the banks, or punting on the canals, you'll pass weeping willows, purple irises, herons, and the occasional rustic home. At its start by the Sèvre Niortaise River, graceful trees form a canopy overhead and duckweed carpets the water's surface, making the canals look like grassy paths. Toward the coast, the lush greenery gradually gives way to the dry marsh. The canals enhance agriculture and control flooding and small-scale farming remains the region's primary industry.

Though well worth the trouble of getting there, the Marais is not a very convenient daytrip; consider spending a night if you come. Most towns are tiny and inaccessible by public transport, so the local hub of **Niort** is the best base from which to explore the region. From Niort it's easy to get to **Coulon,** where you can hire bikes or boats to get into the Marais. Both Niort and Coulon's tourist offices provide info and maps and sell an excellent walking and biking map for 32F/€4.88.

JUST A SPOONFUL OF SUGAR The Angelique plant, native to the Marais region and recognizable by its white, parachute-shaped bulbs, gives new meaning to the term "all-purpose flower." It is used as an antiseptic, digestive, natural stimulant, *apéritif,* and even perfume. After the tree grows to be two years old, it can be harvested and each part of it processed for a different purpose. The bright green stems and roots are eaten raw and coated with sugar to help with digestion and upset stomach; the leaves are ground up and mixed with Cognac to create an after-dinner liquor; and the sweetly scented flower is used as an *eau de toilette*. Other plants of the Marais are also used for homeopathic purposes, especially the ever lovable "pissenlit" (dandelion) that is crushed and kept at 12° Celsius, until its natural juices ferment and create an acidic dandelion wine. Both dandelion and Angelique can also be eaten raw in salads, or made into jelly, usually sugar-coated to mask their natural bitter taste. To sample the stuff, head to La Libellule Boutique and La Maison des Marais Mouilles in Coulon.

NIORT

Niort's greatest attribute is its prime location, just a 20-minute bus ride from Coulon, and an easy entrance to the Marais. Its many narrow, twisting streets and low flat-fronted houses have a drab feeling—that of a city steeped in apathy. Though Niort does boast the Sèvre Niortaise River, numerous restaurants, and even a few nightclubs, all of these attractions suffer from the same apparent lack of energy.

PRACTICAL INFORMATION. Niort is easily accessible by **train** from **La Rochelle** (45min., 5-6 per day, 59F/€9); **Poitiers** (1hr., 6-8 per day, 69F/€10.52); **Royan** (1¼hr., 6-7 per day, 86F/€13.12); and **Saintes** (45min., 6-7 per day, 65F/€9.91). Niort has numerous **car rental** agencies all within one block of the train station. Choose from **Budget, Hertz, Europcar, National,** and **Avis.** The **tourist office** is at 16 rue du Petit St-Jean, just behind the Hôtel de Ville. They can provide you with maps and info on the Marais and Niort. (☎05 49 24 18 79; fax 05 49 24 98 90. Open July-Aug. M-F 9:30am-7pm, Su 10am-1pm; Oct.-Mar. M-F 9:30am-6pm, Sa 9:30am-12:30pm, Apr.-June and Sept. M-Sa until 6:30pm.) **Marché Plus,** on rue Victor Hugo, is just past the Pilori (open M-Sa 7am-9pm). To reach the **police,** dial 17; the **hospital** is at 40 av. Charles de Gaulle (☎05 49 32 79 79). There's **Internet access** at **Medi@click,** 9 rue Mellaise, near pl. St. Jean d'Angely. (☎05 49 28 31 31. Open Tu-Sa 9am-noon and 2-6pm.) The **post office** is at 4 rue Ernest Perochon. (☎05 49 24 38 15. Open M-F 8:30am-6:30pm, Sa 8:30am-noon.) **Postal code:** 79000.

ACCOMMODATIONS AND FOOD. The **Foyer des Jeunes Travailleurs,** 63 rue St. Jelais, near the town center, is almost always full. Call ahead for a place in one of its 65 tidy dorms, each with bath. (☎05 49 24 50 68; fax 05 49 24 34 41. Reception M-F 9am-1pm and 2-7pm. No lockout. No curfew. Bunks 110F/€16.77.) The *foyer* has a cafeteria, open to the public, which serves a 35-45F/€5.34-6.86 *menu.* (Open Sept.-July daily 6-9:30am, noon-1pm, and 7:30-8:30pm.) Try the **Hôtel St-Jean,** 21 av. St-Jean d'Angely, halfway between the train station and the center of town. From the station, walk straight up rue de la Gare until the traffic circle and bear left; and the hotel is one block up on the left (8min.). A cheery owner and large, well-lit rooms await. (☎05 49 79 20 76; fax 05 49 35 03 27; hotelsaintJean@wanadoo.fr. Breakfast 23F/€3.50. Singles 118F/€18, with shower 138F/€21, with bath 157.50F/€24; doubles 131F/€20, with shower 151F/€23, with bath 177F/€27; triples 151F/€23, with shower 177F/€27, with bath 197F/€30; quads 216F/€33. MC/V.) Just across from the train station, **Hôtel de L'Univers,** 22 rue Mazagran, offers rooms that are slightly more expensive and luxurious. (☎05 49 24 41 70; fax 05 49 77 09 52. Breakfast 29F/€4.42. Singles with shower 160-170F/€4.40-26.92, with bath 195F/€29.73; doubles with shower 185-195F/€28.20-29.73, with bath 220F/€33.54; triples 210-245F/€32-37.35.) **Camping Municipal,** 21 bd. Salvador-Allende, is a grassy campsite along the river 2km from town. Take bus #2 from pl. de la Breche to "Tour Chabut" (7.50F/€1.14 per person, *carnet* of 10 55F/€8.39). Reserve ahead in July and August. (☎05 49 79 05 06; fax 05 49 79 05 06. 17F/€2.60 per person, 10F/€1.53 per child, tent rental 7F/€1.07, 9-19F/€1.37-2.90 per car.)

Locals congregate in **rue Victor Hugo** and **rue Ricard,** and at the covered **market** in Les Halles (Tu-Su 9am-1pm, larger version Th and Sa). Health nuts, vegetarians, or neither of the above will find good choices including tofu, seitan, and steak at **Les Deux Chèvres,** 19 rue Basse. (☎05 49 05 10 44. *Menu* 98F/€14.95. Open M 7-10pm, Tu-Sa noon-2pm and 7-10pm.) Niort has two discothèques: **Le Cubana,** 43 rue St-Gelais (☎05 49 17 17 25); and **Le Malibu,** 113 rue de l'Aérodrome (☎05 49 28 35 00).

SIGHTS. The center of town is bordered on one side by the elegant Gothic **Eglise St-André** and the Renaissance **Hôtel de Ville** (also known as **Le Pilori**), and on the other by the 14th-century **Eglise Notre-Dame** and the bold **Donjon,** all that remains of Richard the Lionheart's former castle. The well-preserved keep in the latter has an archaeological and historical museum, and its battlements provide a remarkable view. (Open May 2-Sept. 15 W-M 9am-noon and 2-6pm; Sept. 16-May 9am-noon and 2-5pm. Th-Tu 17F/€2.59, W free; students and seniors free.)

COULON

Tiny Coulon's (pop. 2200) winding streets and bridges run alongside the canals of the Marais, making it the ideal spot from which to take a boat into the Marais. **CASA Autocars,** 11-13 chemin du Fief Binard (☎05 49 24 93 47), come from **Niort's** bus station, pl. de la Brèche, or its train station (30min.; M-Sa 4-5 per day, Su and holidays 2-3 per day; 11F/€1.68, bus #20, dir: "Coulon/Maurais Poitevin"). **SNCF buses** also run from the train station (20min.; M-Sa 4 per day, 2 on Su; 19F/€2.90).

Once here, the most practical way to get farther into the Marais is by boat or bike, though many hitch (NOT recommended). Head to the **tourist office,** rue Gabriel Auchier, for general info about the Marais' offerings; there are bike, canoe, and punt rental locations all over the town. (☎05 49 35 99 29. Tourist office open July-Aug. daily 10am-1pm and 2-7pm; call for off-season hours.)

Though more expensive than bikes, boats are well worth the extra money and are the only way to truly experience the Marais. Guides will fill you in on the marsh's history and secrets. Stirring the waters also releases methane gas trapped below; your guide will prod the water to light a fire right on the surface. In Coulon, **Le Trigale,** 6 rue de l'Eglise (☎05 49 35 14 14), will set you up with a private boat and boatsman (1-2½hr., 1-7 people, 165-420F/€25.16-64.05). To sign up for a boat tour, call **La Pigouille,** quai Louis Tardy, just along the water's edge. (1½hr.; 3 per day; 65F/€9.91, children 55F/€8.38. Private canoe rentals 65F/€9.91 per hr., 110F/€16.77 per 2hr.) It's also possible to rent a boat from numerous vendors along the water's edge (from 70F/€10.67 per hr.).

Hotels are expensive here. **Le Central,** 4 rue d'Autre-mont, has singles and doubles beginning at 240F/€36.59. Campers should try the three-star **Camping de la Venise Verte,** 2km outside of town, and embedded in luscious greenery. Follow the river west from Coulon to get to the campground. (☎05 49 35 90 36; fax 05 49 35 84 69. 50 canal-side sites, a pool, and canoe and bike rental. Open Apr.-Sept. June 23-Sept. 2 adults, car, tent, and electricity 100F/€15.25; off-season 85F/€12.96.)

The little village of **La Garette** is 3km south of Coulon. Easily reached by foot from Coulon or by the infrequent **Autoplus bus,** Garette is a starting point for an 8km hike through marshy forests, past the two-door houses (one for land, one for water) unique to the area. Signs indicate the path from Coulon to La Garette, where there's a small **campground.** (☎05 49 35 00 33. Open May-Sept., 17F/€2.59 per person, 12F/€1.83 per child, 10F/€1.53 per car. Electricity 15F/€2.29.)

OTHER SIGHTS OF THE MARAIS

About 35km from Niort, the ruins of the 12th-century **Abbaye St-Pierre de Maillezais** peer out from among the trees. Within the crumbled walls, driven into uneven and shifting marshland, are the 13th-century monks' ruined kitchen and living quarters, as well as the tombs of several dukes of Aquitaine. To get to the abbey from Niort, follow the national highway or take the **SNCF buses** that leave from the train station (dir: "Fontenay-le-Comte" 3-6 per day). About seven minutes after you pass the town of Oulmes, signs point to the parking lot for the abbey on the left. (☎02 51 00 70 11 or 02 51 50 43 00. Open July-Aug. daily 10am-7pm; Sept.-June M-Sa 9:30am-6pm, Su 10am-7pm. 15F/€2.29. Tours available in French.) Farther west, just north of La Rochelle, is the little inlet known as the **Baie de l'Aiguillon,** one of the largest shellfish-producing regions of France; oyster- and mussel-collecting are still its livelihood. Bordered on the east by a nature reserve and by sparkling water on the west, **Aiguillon-sur-mer** is a little vacation resort amid the salt marshes and the swamps. Aiguillon is serviced by **Sovetours** (☎02 51 95 18 71) and is accessible by bus from Niort and La Rochelle. Just east of Aiguillon sits a **nature reserve** at St-Denis-du-Payre, with trails to the winter residence of greylag geese, wigeons and teels, and the summer home of storks, redshanks, and the occasional spoonbill. Thousands of birds drop by in spring and autumn during the migratory periods. Aiguillon has several campsites, which can serve as a base both for the bay and the nature reserve. The **municipal campgrounds,** rte. de Lyon, are just outside of town on a lake. (☎02 51 56 40 70. Open Apr.-Sept. 23F/€3.51 per person, 16.50F/€2.52 per child, 25F/€3.81 per site.) Right at the end of the Sèvre Niortiase river, just east of La Rochelle, is the picturesque town of **Charron,** where mussel farms run along the coast to Charron's southern neighbor Esnandes.

LES SABLES D'OLONNE

Les Sables d'Olonne (pop. 16,500) is a beach town popular with vacationing families. Once a port attached to Olonne, the region's capital, Sables d'Olonne became useless for shipping when its harbor began to silt up.

ORIENTATION AND PRACTICAL INFORMATION. The station on av. de Gaulle sends **trains** to: **La Rochelle** via La Roche-sur-Lyon (2hr., 5 per day, 108F/€16.47); **Nantes** (1½hr., 6-7 per day, 98F/€14.95); and **Paris** (5hr., 6 per day, 351F/€53.53). At the **bus** station next door, **Sovetours** sends buses to **La Rochelle** (3¼hr., 1 per day, 98F/€14.95) and **Nantes** (2hr., 2 per day, 98F€14.95). (☎02 51 95 18 71. Office open M-F 8:30am-12:30pm and 2:30-6:30pm, Sa 9:30am-noon.) To **rent bikes,** visit the beachfront **Cyclotron,** 66 promenade Clemenceau (☎02 51 32 64 15; open June-Sept. daily 9am-midnight), or **Le Roch,** 65 rue Nationale (☎02 51 32 04 46; open daily 9am-7pm; bikes 40F/€6.10 per day, 180F/€27.44 per week, scooters 110F/€16.77, motorbikes 300F/€45.74; 600F/€91.50 deposit).

To get to the **tourist office,** 1 promenade Joffre, turn right outside the station and then right again into av. de Gaulle. Follow it to pl. de la Liberté (ignore the signs!) and walk past the winged statue on your right. Head for the fountain straight ahead in the small pl. du Poilu de France, and turn left behind it onto rue de la Réunion, which will lead you up the hill to the seafront. At the seafront, turn right on prom. de l'Amiral Lafargue and continue straight until the end of the strip. The road will lead you to the glass-fronted Les Atlantes building, which houses the tourist office in its front entrance to the right (15min.). The friendly staff has excellent regional and local maps. The *Randonées* brochure is full of info on hiking and bike excursions in the area. (☎02 51 96 85 85; fax 02 51 96 85 71; info@ot-lessables-dolonne. Open July-Aug. daily 9am-7pm; Sept.-June 9am-12:15pm and 2-6:30pm.) **Banque de France,** 6 av. du Général de Gaulle, offers **currency exchange** at good rates. (☎02 51 23 81 00. Open M-F 8:45am-noon.) The **police** are at 1 bd. Blaise Pascal (☎02 51 21 19 91, or dial 17 for emergencies). The **hospital** is at 75 av. d'Aquitaine (☎02 51 21 85 85). The **Centre Information Jeunesse,** housed in the Hôtel de Ville at pl. Du Poilu, has everything from Internet access (with télécarte) to apartment listings. (☎02 51 23 16 83. Open M-Th 9am-noon and 2-6pm, F 9am-noon and 2-5pm.) The **post office,** on av. Nicot, has **currency exchange.** (☎02 51 21 82 82. Open M-F 8:30am-5:45pm, Sa 8:30am-noon.) **Postal code:** 85100.

ACCOMMODATIONS AND FOOD. The best deals in town are the 14 well-kept rooms of **Hôtel de Départ,** near the train station at 40 av. de Gaulle. (☎02 51 32 03 71; fax 02 51 32 03 71. Breakfast 30F/€4.57. Doubles 165F/€26; triples 220F/€33.54.) As you exit the train station, the street running to your left contains **Hôtel les Voyageurs,** 16-17 rue de la Bauduere at pl. de la Gare, which has modern, spacious rooms with wood floors and bright furniture. (☎02 51 95 11 49; fax 02 51 21 50 21. Breakfast 30F/€4.57. Singles and doubles with bath 195-220F/€29.73-33.54, triples with bath 265-300F/€40.40-45.74. MC/V.) Several smaller hotels offer a few rooms starting at 150F/€22.90 per person, but availability is a crapshoot. Ask the tourist office for a complete list. There are dozens of **campgrounds** in and around Les Sables, also listed at the tourist office.

There's a **covered market** in the 19th-century Art Nouveau **Les Halles,** between rue des Halles and rue du Palais (June 15-Sept. 15 daily 8am-1pm; Sept. 16-June 14 Tu-Su 8am-1pm). To reach the enormous **Intermarché supermarket,** on bd. de l'Ile Vertime, continue past the train station on av. Général de Gaulle. Then turn right on rue Nicot, right at the post office, and right again just after the train tracks. It will be on your left. There's also a more central, slightly smaller Intermarché on bd. de Castelnau. (Both open July-Aug. M-Sa 8:30am-8pm, Su 8:30am-1pm; Sept.-June daily 9am-6pm.) The quays and seaside walkways near the Porte de Pêche overflow with **restaurants** serving whatever the boats brought in that morning.

SIGHTS. Les Sables has a few interesting sights hidden among the postcard racks and bright plastic sea pails. **La Chaume,** the body of land across the channel from the center of town, houses four historical monuments in a row, notably the 18th-century **Tour d'Arundel,** which houses the restored **Prieuré St-Nicolas,** converted to a fort in 1779, and the **Musée de la Mer,** a museum with exhibits on naval life and fishing techniques of the past (Open Easter-Oct. daily 10:30am-12:30pm and 3-7pm; 15F/€2.29, children 8F/€1.22). On the mainland, **Notre-Dame-de-Bon-Port,** pl. de l'Eglise, is a rare blend of Gothic and Baroque styles. The mid-1600s nave rises behind Gothic arches, which themselves are supported by Corinthian columns. The **Musée de l'Abbaye Ste-Croix,** on rue de Verdun, inhabits one wing of a restored 17th-century Benedictine abbey and presents a hodgepodge of regional prehistory, as well as folk and contemporary art, of which the last two sets of Victor Brauner and Gaston Chaissac canvases are noteworthy. (☎ 02 51 32 01 16. Open June 15-Sept. Tu-Su 10am-noon and 2:30-6:30pm; Oct.-June 14 2:30-5:30pm. 30F/€4.57, children 15F/€2.29; first Su of every month free.) The **Musée du Coquillage,** 8 rue du Maréchal Leclerc near Porte de Pêche, is the only one of its kind in Europe, and displays over 200 different kinds of shells and corals from a private collection gathered by a local deep sea diver. (☎ 02 51 23 50 00. Open July-Aug. daily 9:30am-11pm; Sept.-June 9:30am-noon and 2-7pm, closed Sa and Su morning Nov.-Apr. 30F/€4.57, under age 12 20F/€3.05).

EXCURSIONS AND BEACHES. Outdoor activities abound in Les Sables. **Sables Tours** books excursions, sports, and entertainment in the region (☎ 02 51 96 85 71). The tourist office has a free 5-ft. foldout brochure of the area's hiking and biking trails (*randonnées*), covering the dunes, forest, and beach. In July and August, they also post daily listings in the front entrance of the office with local activities including tennis tournaments, daily concerts, and organized beach volleyball. Nightly in the summer, *Les Remblais*, the widest strip of the boardwalk, is closed to cars and becomes a pedestrian walkway with organized nightly concerts, outdoor theater, jugglers, clowns, or marionette shows. The tourist office has the complete schedule of events. The closest hiking trail to Les Sables starts about 1km north of the train station. From the station, follow rue Georges Clemenceau until its intersection with rue du Doctor Charcot; signs there indicate the beginning of an 18km trail leading through the Vendée countryside and many tiny villages to a beautiful church at Olonne sur Mer. Guided boat trips, canoeing, surfing, sailing, diving, and other water sports are also readily available. Ask at the tourist office for a complete listing. When it comes to beaches, **Plage du Remblai** is the largest, most commercial, and most crowded of Les Sables' offerings. If solitude is worth it to you, catch bus #1 or 2 to nearby La Chaume's **Plage de la Paracou.** Following the coastline north from Paracou, you'll get to two other uncrowded beaches with great surf. **Plage de Sauveterre** is about 1½km north of Paracou, and **Plage des Granges** is north another kilometer; in between, all is nudity. Adventurers may enjoy heading into the **Forêt Domaniale d'Olonne,** just east of these beaches, where huge dunes tumble from dry woodlands into the sea.

NOIRMOUTIER AND ILE D'YEU

Noirmoutier and Ile d'Yeu are two pinprick islands, just off the mainland between Nantes and Les Sables d'Olonne. Noirmoutier is beachy and touristy; Ile d'Yeu is the jewel of the French coast, a wild expanse of woods, dunes, and rocky little inlets. You can get to Noirmoutier by bus, car, or bike, since it's linked to the mainland by a bridge, while Yeu requires a ferry crossing. Both bridge and ferries leave the mainland from **Fromentine,** and unless you book well in advance, you'll probably have to sleep here.

TRANSPORTATION AND MAINLAND INFORMATION. Your first task is to get to **Fromentine.** Do this by **CTA** bus (☎02 51 68 51 98) from **Nantes** (1½-2hr., 3-5 per day, 86F/€13.12). **Sovetours** buses also run to Fromentine from **Les Sables** but take much longer (2hr., 4 per day, 66F/€10.07). More conveniently, you can now get from Les Sables to Yeu directly by **SABIA** boats. (☎02 51 23 54 88; fax 02 51 21 33 85. 1hr., 2 per day. Boats leave from quai A. Gerbaud in the Port de Plaisance. 145F/€22.11, round-trip 215F/€32.79, children 92F/€14.03, round-trip 145F/€22.11. Reservations necessary through the SABIA office or tourist office.) To get from Fromentine to Noirmoutier, change to the CTA bus to **Noirmoutier en l'Ile** (25-45min., 4 per day, 20F/€3.05). Two ferry companies shuttle visitors from Fromentine to the **Ile d'Yeu: Compagnie Yeu Continent,** stationed near the *gare maritime* (☎02 51 49 59 69. 1hr., day return 165F/€25.16, child rates and student discounts 125-145F/€19.06-22.11; AmEx/MC/V), and **Vedettes Inter-Iles Vendéenes (VIIV)** (☎02 51 39 00 00; day return 165F/€25.16, students 140F/€21.35; MC/V). VIIV also connects the two islands, running from **Fosse,** on Noirmoutier, to **Yeu** (45min., 165F/€25.16 round-trip, students 140F/ €21.35). For more info, plus a map of the area, stop in at Fromentine's **tourist office,** in front of the bus station. (☎02 51 68 51 83. Open June-Sept. daily 9:30am-12:30pm and 3-6pm; call for off-season hours.)

MAINLAND ACCOMMODATIONS. Hôtel de Bretagne, 27 av. de l'Estacade, is the cheaper of two hotels. Spacious, high-ceilinged rooms with great adjoining bathrooms. (☎02 51 68 50 08; fax 02 51 68 20 18. Breakfast 32F/€4.88. Singles and doubles with bath 160-220F/€24.39-33.54; triples 260F/€39.64; quads 290F/€44.21. Extra bed 40F/€6.10. AmEx/MC/V.) Next door, **Hôtel de la Plage,** 29 av. de l'Estacade, has huge rooms with clean bathrooms and a small pool. (☎02 51 68 52 05; fax 02 51 68 46 87. Breakfast 35F/€5.34. Mid-June to Aug. singles and doubles 200-290F/€30.49-44.21; off-season 175-255F/€26.68-38.88. Extra bed 90-100F/€13.72-15.25. MC/V.) There are seven **campsites** in Fromentine; the tourist office has a list.

NOIRMOUTIER

Despite the wizened mussel-seekers wading at low tide near fleets of tiny fishing boats, Noirmoutier's fortune was made through salt farming and tourism. In the 16th and 17th centuries, the island was the salt capital of France, exporting the vital preservative and seasoning to all of Europe. Today, the saline industry has become the sailing industry, as Germans and Dutch flock to Noirmoutian waters to fasten their halyards.

NOIRMOUTIER-EN-L'ILE. There's a well-preserved 12th-century **château** on pl. d'Armes, which repelled foreign invaders for centuries. Today it welcomes them into its artifacts museum; climb to the top for a sweep of the salt marshes below. (☎02 51 39 10 42. Open June 15-Sept. daily 10am-7pm; Apr. 10-June 14 10am-6pm; Oct.-Nov. and Mar. W-M 10am-12:30pm and 2:30-6pm; closed Dec.-Jan. 20F/€3.05, children 10F/€1.53.) In the **Eglise St-Philbert,** rue de l'Eglise, two ornate 18th-century altars flank the main platform; directly below, a restored crypt was the original resting place of St-Philbert in the 7th century. The small **Musée de la Construction Navale,** across the quai, explains ship-building methods and the town's seafaring history. (☎02 51 39 24 00. Hours same as château, but closed M rather than Tu.) Hikers and cyclists explore the salt puddles of the **Natural Bird Preserve,** marshlands just south of town and off-limits to automobiles. Guides from the **Maison de la Reserve** can turn your stroll through the bird sanctuary into an ornithology lesson. (☎02 51 35 81 16. Open June-Sept. daily 10am-1pm and 5-7pm. Tours 30F/€4.57, students 20F/€3.05, children 10F/€1.53; July-Aug. free guided bird observation at the end of each morning and afternoon.)

Pick up a free map and island guide from the **tourist office** on rue St-Louis, in the small square behind pl. de la République. (☎02 51 39 80 71. Open daily 9am-12:30pm and 2-6pm.) You can **exchange currency** at a good rate at **Crédit Agricole,** 4 rue du Rosaire, along the quai on pl. de la République. (Open Tu-F 9am-12:30pm and 2-5:15pm, Sa 9am-12:30pm and 2-4pm.) The **post office** is on rue du Puits Neuf (open M-F 9am-noon and 2-5pm, Sa 9am-noon). The **postal code** is 85330.

There are few cheap beds, especially in August. Try **Chez Bébert,** 37 rue Joseph Pineau, a 10-minute walk from town. Follow the signs to the *centre ville*. Then, follow signs to Plage Des Dames taking rue Joseph Pineau. Bébert lets sunny, simple rooms; ask for rooms on the far side to eliminate street noise. (☎02 51 39 08 97. Breakfast 30F/€4.57. Open June-Dec. 22. Singles 130-165F/€19.82-25.16; doubles 185-220F/€28.21-33.54.) **Hôtel Esperanza,** 10a rue du Grand Four, offers pricier rooms with a pretty countryside view. (☎02 51 39 12 07. Breakfast 32F/€4.88. Singles and doubles 185-200F/€28.21-30.49, with shower 230F/€35.07, with bath 265F/€40.40. Extra bed 55F/€8.39. MC/V.) Two kilometers east of town, along a beach, the two-star **Campsite La Vendette,** rte. des Sableaux, has 600 sites. (☎02 51 39 06 24; fax 02 51 35 97 63. Open Apr.-Sept. Two people and tent or caravan 88F/€13.42; off-season 80F/€12.20. 25F/€3.81 per extra person, 12F/€1.83 per extra child. Electricity 12.50F/€1.91.) Just inland, **Le Clair Matin,** rte. des Sableaux, maintains a green, pretty, beach-less campsite. (☎02 51 39 05 56. Open Easter-Oct. July-Aug.: 3 people, car, and tent 71F/€10.83; off-season 67F/€10.22. 12F/€1.83 per extra person. Shower 5F/€0.76. Electricity 12F/€1.83. MC/V.) The **Cours des Halles grocery store,** 3 rue de la Prée au Duc, is rivaled by a **market** in pl. de la République (F 8 or 9am-1 or 2 pm; summer also Tu and Su).

THE REST OF THE ISLAND. Noirmoutier's **Passage du Gois** has attracted European tourists since its discovery in 1942. This 3km road connecting Noirmoutier to the continent is flooded with one to four meters of water during high tides, but becomes fully exposed and walkable twice daily during low tide. The passage is open to pedestrians and cyclists about one hour before and after low tide. Daredevils who take on the forces of nature and get stuck can find safety in one of eight tall *refuges* along the path. The passage begins in the island's southern town, Barbatre. (Consult tourist office at 02 51 39 08 97 for low-tide times.)

Free shuttles make the rounds to the island's northern villages and beaches, but you'd do better to rent a **bike** in Noirmoutier-en-l'Ile. It's the only way of visiting the island's marshy, salty center, where cars aren't allowed. Try **Le Temple des Loisirs,** 18 rue de Rosaire. (☎02 51 39 80 71 or 02 51 39 12 42. 40-68F/€6.10-10.37 per half-day, 45-80F/€6.86-12.20 per day. Credit card deposit. Open July-Aug. daily 9am-7pm; rest of the year M-Sa 9am-12:30pm and 1:30-7pm; arrange in advance if you would like to return your bike after 7pm. MC/V.)

A short pedal away from town down av. Joseph Pineau gets you to **plage des Dames,** the island's most popular beach. This beach serves as a gateway to the north coast's more Mediterranean beaches; turn left onto the labeled bike path next to plage des Dames and roll along the beach-view path until you find an inlet to your liking. Two kilometers from des Dames, you'll hit **plage de la Clère,** a lovely if slightly crowded beach overlooking sailing and fishing vessels in the harbor.

Surrounding Noirmoutier-en-l'Ile are the sparkling white piles of the salt marshes, the island's most exotic biking terrain. West of the town you can ride around in the **salt mines.** East from Noirmoutier-en-l'Ile, in the direction of "Les Sableaux," is a marsh where bucket-toting locals and tourists search ankle-deep water for shellfish, mussels, and the occasional lobster. Potato farms on the right, and salt marshes on the left, line the path to the fishing village of **L'Herbaudière,** northwest of Noirmoutier-en-l'Ile, as far as the eye can see. Thirty *saumiers* (salt farmers) have revitalized a long-dormant industry; several offer French tours to the public, explaining how they collect and isolate pure salt from the ocean.

The island's southern beaches lie just beside the inland forests, with a line of pine trees extending onto the sand. **Plage de l'Epine** in **La Bosse** (4km southwest of Noirmoutier) is a pleasant place to relax under the shadow of an evergreen.

ILE D'YEU

Ile d'Yeu (pop. 5000) is, in a word, idyllic. Bordered on all sides by the clear reflection of the water, the island has a vast array of landscapes—dense mini-forests border wide, flat beaches, and stony bike paths lead to areas of the island where waves crash on the jagged rocks. Since the island is not really accessible by car, tourists get the sense that they are in the last preserved wilderness of the French landscape. Check out the marine-wear boutiques and retiree-filled restaurants in Port-Joinville, the island's largest town, and do visit the deservedly popular ports, but accept the island's silent urging to step off that beaten path.

Biking is the best way to explore the island; you can cover the whole thing in four to five hours if you resist the temptation to stop and swim. The many paths range from sandy to boulder-strewn; fortunately, bikes in Port-Joinville are built for the back roads. Expect to pay 35-45F/€5.34-6.86 for half-day rental or 50-85F/€7.62-12.96 per day. Most rental places will store your bags and give you a xeroxed map of suggested routes, but stop at the **tourist office,** on rue du Marché, before planning your route. They distribute biking and hiking itineraries of varying lengths, with extensive directions and description of sights in English and French. (☎02 51 58 32 58. Open July-Aug. M-Sa 9am-6:30pm, Su 9am-12:30pm; Apr.-June and Sept. 9am-12:30pm and 2-6pm; Oct.-Mar. 9am-12:30pm and 2-5:30pm.)

There are four easy **bike circuits** of the island, all starting in Port-Joinville. The smallest takes you to the island's southern port and back in 2½ hours; its highlight is **Port Meule,** just south of Joinville, with its gorgeous sea cliffs and moss-grown marshy inlets. The longest route (5½hr.) takes you all around the island, passing Renaissance churches and picturesque ports. One of the most popular bike itineraries (4½hr.) includes a stop 2km southeast of Port-Joinville at the 18th-century church in St-Sauveur. A chlorine-blue door and bright stained-glass windows illuminate its dark, musty interior. Working your way eastward and southward, you'll come across flat, sparkling **plage des Sapins,** which is very popular with windsurfers, followed by **plage de la Conche,** a stretch of beach that allows plenty of space for each bronzer. The route curves around to the south coast, where cliffs rise in all directions, resulting in rocky steep paths and rest stops at the beginning of the **Côte Sauvage.** In the early afternoon, **plage Anse des Soux,** surrounded by looming cliffs, may be the best place on the island to lounge. The 4½-hour path then leads back to Joinville, but you can continue west to the **Grand Phare,** the 20m-tall lighthouse on the island's tallest "hill," for a birds-eye view of the island (☎02 51 58 30 61; open for climbing daily 9am-5pm; donations encouraged), and to the **Pointe du Châtelet,** a jutting cliff which bears a rusted commemorative cross built in 1934 for sailors lost at sea. Near the cross, the 14th-century **Vieux Château,** used as a fortress in the 16th century and later abandoned by Louis XIV, crumbles on a craggy coast. The remarkable remnants stand alone on the edge of the ocean, accessible by bike path alone. (Tours July-Aug. daily 9:30am-6:30pm; late June and Sept. 11am-5:30pm. 12F/€1.83, children 6F/€0.92.)

The island's one crowded **campground** is near the beach at Pointe de Gilberge, 1km from the port. (☎02 51 58 34 20. 57-60F/€8.69-9.15 for 4 people and 2 tents, 16F/€2.44 per car. 9F/€1.37 per extra person.) In summer many camp illegally all over the island. Fresh, cheap food is available at the **outdoor market** on quai de la Mairie (M-Sa 9am-noon or 1pm). **Casino supermarket** is on rue Calypso, two minutes from the port. (Open Tu-F 9am-1pm and 2:30-7pm, F until 7:30pm, M and Sa 9am-7:45pm, Su 9:30am-12:30pm. MC/V.)

PERIGORD

The name summons up an intoxicating set of images: green countryside splashed with yellow sunflowers, white chalk cliffs, plates of black truffles, and the smell of warm walnuts. The area around Les Eyzies-de-Tayac has turned up more stone-age artifacts—tools, bones, weapons, cave paintings, and etchings—than any other place on earth. The painted caves of Lascaux are the most extensive and best preserved in the world, but they were closed to the public in 1963; a replica, Lascaux II, was opened 150m away in 1983. Today, the Grotte de Font de Gaume in Les Eyzies-de-Tayac and the Grotte du Pech-Merle, 25km from Cahors, contain extraordinary original paintings still accessible to the public. The caves open into spectacular countryside, including feudal châteaux, poplar-lined rivers, and valleys carpeted with sunflowers and wheat fields.

1 **Périgueux:** Small city with many ruins; good base for visits to prehistoric caves **(p. 634)**
2 **Les Eyzies-de-Tayac:** Close to most of the great Neolithic art, though not Lascaux **(p. 639)**
3 **Sarlat:** Beautifully restored, film-worthy medieval architecture **(p. 637)**
4 **Lascaux:** Site of the most spectacular cave paintings—and their duplicates **(p. 641)**
5 **Bergerac:** Celebrated red and sweet white wines; village in fertile Dordogne valley **(p. 643)**
6 **Castelnaud-la-Chapelle:** Well-restored castle with 100 Years' War museum **(p. 639)**
7 **Beynac:** A fortress sheathed in greenery above a stony ancient town **(p. 644)**
8 **Domme:** Walled village on a high rock dome; its towers imprisoned 70 Templars **(p. 644)**
9 **Bretenoux:** Base for two or three towns near the upper stretches of the Dordogne **(p. 646)**
10 **Castelnau-Prudhomat:** Triangular château with burnt-red ramparts; tapestries inside **(p. 646)**
11 **Beaulieu:** Medieval village with terrifying apocalyptic church sculpture **(p. 647)**
12 **Brive-la-Gaillarde:** A major rail junction and solid base for exploring the Quercy region **(p. 649)**
13 **Rocamadour:** Pilgrimage town built, astoundingly enough, into a cliff face **(p. 647)**
14 **Collonges-la-Rouge:** Slow, exquisite red-rock village **(p. 651)**
15 **Cahors:** Relaxed, remote isthmus town; monumental bridge; good stopover for cyclists **(p. 652)**
16 **St-Cirq-Lapopie:** Cliff-edge village on the Lot; full of artisans, flowers, and tourists **(p. 653)**
17 **Grotte du Pech-Merle:** Best-preserved of all the prehistoric caves; less accessible **(p. 654)**
18 **Château Cénevières:** Italianate castle with many quirky attractions **(p. 654)**

TRANSPORTATION

Big towns like Périgueux and Brive have good rail connections, but you'll need a car or bike to get to the smaller towns, châteaux, and vineyards. Bike trails tend to be hilly but manageable. The Bordeaux-Sarlat line stops at Bergerac, but Périgueux makes a better base for the Dordogne valley.

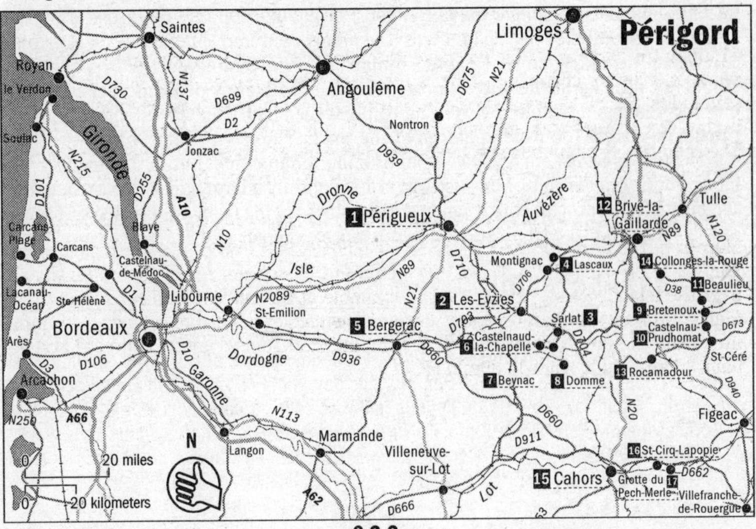

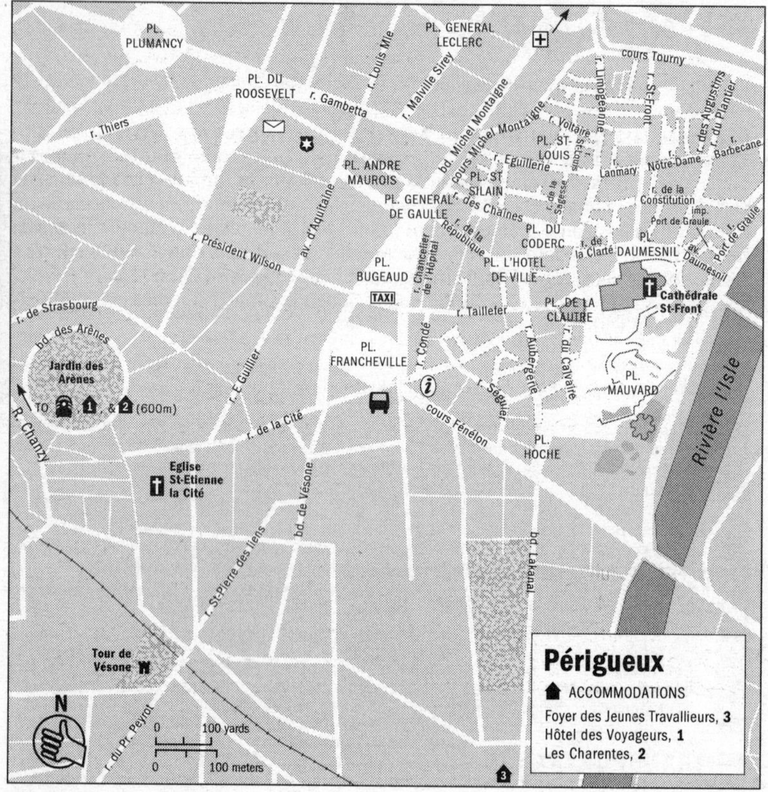

PERIGUEUX

The towering steeple and five massive cupolas of the Cathédrale St-Front dominate Périgueux from above the Isle River. Périgueux (pop. 37,700) arose from the 13th-century union of two rival towns: the abbey-centered Cité de Puy-St-Font and the Gallo-Roman Vésone. Plagued by barbarian invasions in the 3rd century, Huguenot attacks in the 16th century, and the Jacqueries peasant uprisings, the city has managed despite everything to preserve significant architecture in both the medieval and the Roman halves of the town. The town center, paved in white cobblestones, can seem as dead as its Roman monuments, but in the evening the city's youth crawls out of its historic cracks and into bars and clubs throughout the city. Travelers with cars might consider daytripping from here to see the caves of the Périgord rather than staying in the more expensive Les Eyzies.

TRANSPORTATION

Trains: rue Denis Papin. To: **Bordeaux** (1½hr., 7 per day, 99F/€15.09); **Brive** (1hr., 7 per day, 64F/€9.76); **Limoges** (1-1½hr., 6 per day, 82F/€12.50); **Lyon** (6-8hr., 5 per day, 282F/€42.99); **Paris** (4-6hr., 12 per day, 277F/€42.23) via Limoges; **Sarlat** (1½hr., 4 per day, 75F/€11.43); and **Toulouse** (4hr., 8 per day, 183F/€27.90). Info office open M 4:50am-8:50pm, Tu-Th 5:40am-8:05pm, F 5:40am-10:15pm, Sa-Su 6:15am-10:15pm.

Buses: pl. Francheville (☎05 53 08 43 13). To **Angoulême** (1½hr.; M-Sa 3 per day, 1 on Su; 92F/€14.03) and **Sarlat** (1½hr., F-Sa 2 per day, 50F/€7.62). Office open M-Th 8:30-11:30am and 2:30-5:30pm, F 8:30-11:30am and 2:30-4:30pm.

Taxis: Taxi Périgueux, pl. Bugeaud (☎05 53 09 09 09). 24hr.

ORIENTATION AND PRACTICAL INFORMATION

To get to the *vieille ville* and tourist office from the train station, turn right on rue Denis Papin and bear left on rue des Mobiles-de-Coulmiers, which becomes rue du Président Wilson. On your right, you'll pass rue Guillier, which leads to the **Roman ruins.** Take the next right (just after the Monoprix) and walk down one block. The **tourist office** is on the left, beside the round stone **Mataguerre Tower** (15min.).

Tourist Office: 26 pl. Francheville (☎05 53 53 10 63; fax 05 53 09 02 70). Free map; walking, *petit train,* and boat tours. Open July-Aug. M-Sa 9am-7pm, Su 10am-6pm; Sept.-June M-Sa 9am-6pm. The annex, **Point "i,"** pl. de Général de Gaulle, is a good source of assistance for late arrivals. Open June 15-Sept. 15 daily 9am-10pm.

Espace Tourisme Périgord, 25 rue Wilson (☎05 53 35 50 24). Info on Périgord, lists of campgrounds, *gîtes,* and *chambres d'hôte,* and excellent topographic maps (40F/€6.10). Open M-F 8:30am-noon and 2-6pm.

Money: Banque de France, 1 pl. du Roosevelt (☎05 53 03 30 44), has **currency exchange.** Exchange desk open M-F 8:45am-12:15pm.

Laundromat: Lav'matic, 20 rue Mobiles de Coulmiers, near Rondpoint Lanxade. **La Lavendiere,** 61 rue Gambetta, near pl. Plumency.

Police: rue du 4 Septembre (☎05 53 08 10 17), near the post office.

Hospital: Centre Hospitalier, 80 av. Georges Pompidou (☎05 53 07 70 00).

Internet Access: No Internet cafés in this godforsaken town! The **post office** has one terminal, accessible with a télécarte, as does the **Monoprix** (see **Food,** below).

Post Office: 1 rue du 4 Septembre (☎05 53 53 60 82), offers **currency exchange.** Open M-F 8am-7pm, Sa 8am-noon. **Poste Restante:** 24017. **Postal code:** 24070.

ACCOMMODATIONS AND CAMPING

Hôtel des Voyageurs, 26 rue Denis Papin (☎/fax 05 53 53 17 44), right across from the train station. 15 clean, bright rooms at great prices, tended by a friendly couple. Rooms that face the station can be noisy when windows are open. Breakfast 21F/€3.20. Singles 80F/€12.20; doubles 90F/€13.72, with shower 110F/€16.77.

Les Charentes, 16 rue Denis Papin (☎05 53 53 37 13), facing the train station. Dark wood hallways papered with Victorian designs lead to slightly worn rooms. Breakfast 30F/€4.57. Reception 7am-11pm; call ahead if arriving outside those hours. Closed first week of Nov. and Dec. 23-Jan. 4. Singles with shower 145F/€22.11, with TV 175F/€26.68, with toilet 205F/€31.25. Extra person 30F/€4.57. AmEx/MC/V.

Foyer des Jeunes Travailleurs Résidence Lakanal, rue des Thermes (☎05 53 06 81 40; fax 05 53 06 81 49). From the train station, turn right onto rue Denis Papin and follow it as it becomes rue Chanzy. Turn left onto av. Cavignac, and on the far side of the St-Etienne church, turn right down rue Emile and left down rue des Thermes (25min.). The hostel, in an industrial section of town, is mostly a residence for young workers. 4-bunk rooms are cramped; singles, harder to get, are very nice. Breakfast 7F/€1.07, lunch and dinner 35F/€5.34. Reception 24hr., except Sa-Su 3-5pm. Reserve ahead. Dorms 73F/€11.13. Singles with bath 88F/€13.42.

Barnabé-Plage, 80 rue des Bains (☎05 53 53 41 45), 1.5km outside Périgueux in Boulazac. From cours Montaigne, take bus #8 (dir: "Cité Belair," last bus about 7:30pm, 7F/€1.07) to "Rue des Bains." Riverside site packed in summer. Reception 8:30am-midnight. 17F/€2.59 per person, 16.50F/€2.52 per tent, 25.50F/€3.89 per car.

FOOD

Charcuteries along rue Limogeanne are palaces of *foie gras*, walnuts, *cèpe* and *girolle* mushrooms, and fruit liqueurs. The area southwest of the cathedral around pl. Hoche and rue Aubergerie has diverse and wallet-pleasing restaurants. **Au Bien Bon,** 24 rue Aubergerie, serves cuisine at the height of regional cooking, and has lunch *menus* from 65-85F/€9.91-12.96. (☎05 53 09 69 91. Open M 7:30-10pm, Tu-Sa noon-2pm and 7:30-10pm.)There's a daily morning **market** on pl. du Coderc, and a larger one on pl. de la Clautre, near the cathedral (mid-Nov. to Mar. W and Sa 8am-1pm). The behemoth **Monoprix,** on pl. de la République in the town center, is impossible to miss (open M-Sa 8:30am-8pm).

SIGHTS

Périgueux en Bateau offers 50-minute **boat tours** of the city from Easter to October, departing from the base of Cathédrale St-Front (40F/€6.10). The tourist office gives out an excellent walking-tour guide to medieval-Renaissance and Gallo-Roman Périgueux. To get inside the *hôtels particuliers* and monuments, you'll have to take one of their tours (June 15-Sept. 15 M-Sa at 10:30am, 2:30, and 4pm).

OLD PERIGUEUX

The **Cathédrale St-Front** is somewhere between a monstrosity and a masterpiece. Nearly 1500 years of rebuilding, restoration, and revision have produced an ungainly edifice that dominates the skyline above the river, along with five immense Byzantine cupolas in the shape of a cross. In the late 1800s, Paul Abadie took inspiration from it for an equally controversial project: the Basilique Sacré-Coeur in Paris. (Open daily 8am-7:30pm.)

Across the street from the cathedral stands the modest but elegant **Maison Daumesnil,** 7 rue de la Clarté. Yrieix Daumesnil, born here in 1776, joined the French army at age 15, participating in the great battles of the Directorate and eventually rising to the rank of general in Napoleon's armies. He lost a leg during his greatest victory at Wagram in 1809. A peg-legged statue of the man himself stands in the park on cours Montaigne, on the other side of the *vieille ville.*

Down the rue St-Front from the Maison and the cathedral, the **Musée du Périgord,** 22 cours Tourny, is home to one of France's most important collections of prehistoric artifacts, including fossils from Les Eyzies, 2m-long mammoth tusks, and an Egyptian mummy whose toes peek out from crusty coverings. (☎05 53 53 16 42. Open M and W-F 11am-6pm, Sa-Su 1-6pm. 20F/€3.05, students 10F/€1.53, under 18 free.) Retrace your steps to the tourist office, where you'll find the crumbling **Tour Mataguerre.** It takes its name from an English captain who was kept prisoner in its dungeons for 17 years during the Hundred Years' War.

VERY OLD PERIGUEUX

The few crumbling remains of Gallo-Roman Périgueux lie to the west of the *vieille ville*, down rue de la Cité from pl. Francheville. Perhaps the most impressive is the towering **Tour de Vésone,** built in the first century AD and once the centerpiece of a brilliant Roman colony. The tower itself was a *cella*, the center of worship in a Roman temple, though now it's little more than three-quarters of a crumbling stone tube. About a fourth of the weighty structure was knocked down completely, supposedly by the last fleeing demons of paganism, expelled by St. Front in the 5th century. (Park grounds open Apr.-Sept. daily 7:30am-9pm; Oct.-Mar. 7:30am-6:30pm.) The **Villa de Pompeïus** next door was once the lavish home of a wealthy Roman merchant. Back across the bridge from the Tour de Vésone and to the left down rue Romaine, you'll find a cluster of architectural vestiges of the first century through the high Middle Ages. The **Château Barrière,** a late Gothic castle, preserves four floors of stone walls but is gutted on the inside. The Romanesque house next door is an example of the use of *spolia*—chunks of ruins incorporated decoratively into new buildings. Both buildings were constructed on the remains of the Roman wall which surrounded Vésone, built in AD 275 to protect the city against the first Norman and barbarian attacks. Just a couple of meters away, the **Porte Normanne** remains, a fragment of this wall.

Up rue Romaine, the 11th-century **Eglise St-Etienne-de-la-Cité** was the first Christian edifice in Vésone, and the seat of the bishopric until Calvinist attackers in 1669 destroyed all but the choir and one-third of the nave. Barely 40m beyond the church, up rue de l'Ancien Evêché, the Roman amphitheater has been transformed into a public park, complete with sagging archways, rubble, and palm trees. (Garden open Apr.-Sept. daily 7:30am-9pm; Oct.-Mar. 7:30am-6:30pm.)

ENTERTAINMENT AND FESTIVALS

While the streets may be sleepy, the *places* have no intention of calling it a night. **Pl. St-Silain** and **pl. St-Louis** are nightlife centers, while **pl. du Marché** hosts frequent concerts. **Gordon Pub,** 12 rue Condé, off rue Taillefer near the tourist office, is an Irish-style pub with a terrace. (☎05 53 35 03 74. Beer on tap 13F/€1.98. Open July-Oct. M-F 11am-2am, Sa 2pm-2am; Nov.-June M-F 11am-1am, Sa 2pm-2am.)

Macadam Jazz presents free outdoor jazz concerts once or twice a week throughout July and August. **Son-et-Lumière de Périgueux: La Légende de Saint-Front** illuminates the Cathédrale St-Front every summer on Wednesday nights at 10:30pm from the end of July through the middle of August. (☎05 53 53 18 71. 80F/€12.20, students 60F/€9.15.) The town quiets down during the first week of August for **Mimos,** the best mime festival in the world. Mime companies from the far corners of the world come to give performances that push the bounds of this art beyond the imagination. The big events cost money, but free performances take place on the street corners, and impromptu heckling workshops pop up all over town. (☎05 53 53 18 71. Ticketed events 100F/€15.25, students 70F/€10.67.)

SARLAT

Until 1962, Sarlat (pop. 10,700) was a quiet hamlet with little to distinguish it from nearby towns. That's when Minister of Culture André Malraux, inspired by the old city's architectural unity and lack of modernization, chose it for a massive restoration project. Three years later, the new Sarlat emerged—handsomely restored and surprisingly medieval. Since then it has provided the setting for films such as *Cyrano de Bergerac* and *Manon des Sources.* Flea markets, paintings, dancing violinists, acrobats, and the purveyors of *foie gras, gateaux aux noix*, and golden Monbazillac wines fill the narrow streets. Sarlat certainly merits a day's meandering before you spring into the châteaux and scenery of the valley beyond; it's also the only good base for a visit to the prehistoric site of Lascaux (see p. 641).

ORIENTATION AND PRACTICAL INFORMATION. Trains (☎05 53 59 00 21) rumble from av. de la Gare to **Bordeaux** (2½hr., 4 per day, 122F/€18.60) and **Périgueux** (3hr., 1 per day, 75F/€11.43) via le Buisson. (Info booths open daily 6am-12:30pm and 1:15-7pm.) **CFTA** (☎05 55 86 07 07 in Brive) and **Trans-Périgord** run **buses** from the train station to **Brive** (1½hr., 1 per day, 40F/€6.10) and **Périgueux** (1½hr., 1 per day, 64F/€9.76). To rent **bikes,** try **Peugeot Cycles,** 36 av. Thiers. (☎05 53 28 51 87; fax 05 53 30 23 90. 70F/€10.67 for 24hr. Open Tu-Sa 9:30am-7pm. MC/V.) There's also **Cum's Bikes,** 8 av. de Selves, a block from the youth hostel. (☎05 53 53 31 56. Open M-Sa 2-7pm, arrange in advance to return your bike on a Sunday.)

To get to the town center and the **tourist office** on rue Tourny, follow av. de la Gare downhill to the left and turn right on av. Thiers, which becomes av. Général Leclerc. Past the small pl. du 14 Juillet, the road becomes rue de la République, which bisects the *vieille ville.* Bear right on rue Lakanal, past the church-turned-restaurant, and left onto rue de la Liberté, which leads to the Cathédrale St. Sacerdos. The **tourist office** is in the Ancien Evêché, just across from the cathedral (2km). The staff offers an accommodations service, **currency exchange** when banks are closed, and **tours.** (☎05 53 31 45 45; fax 05 53 59 19 44. Open May-Sept. M-Sa 9am-7pm, Su 10am-noon and 2-6pm; Oct.-Apr. M-Sa 9am-noon and 2-7pm. 1-2 English **tours** weekly Apr.-Sept.; call in advance to arrange. 25F/€3.81, children 15F/€2.29. 1-3 tours per day in French.) There's an **ATM** just opposite the entrance to the Bishop's Palace on rue Tourny, and a **laundromat** at 24 av. de Selves (open daily 7am-9pm). The **police** are at pl. Salvador Allende (☎05 53 59 10 17); the **Centre Hospitalier** on rue Jean Leclaire (☎05 53 31 75 75). Access the **Internet** at **France Télécom,** 41 av. Gambetta. (30F/€4.57 per hr. Open M-F 8am-noon and 2-6pm, Sa 8am-noon.) The **post office,** pl. du 14 Juillet, has **currency exchange.** (☎05 53 31 73 10. Open M-F 9am-5:30pm, Sa 9am-noon.) **Postal code:** 24200.

ACCOMMODATIONS AND FOOD. Hotels are expensive (240-400F/€36.59-60.98 per night), and the hostel is often filled in summer. There are *gîtes*, farms, and many campgrounds in the surrounding countryside, but you'll need a car to get to them. Ask the tourist office for a list. The small, affable **Auberge de Jeunesse,** 77 av. de Selves, is 40 minutes from the station, but only five to ten minutes from the *vieille ville.* Follow rue de la République until it becomes av. Gambetta; go for another 100m, then bear left at the fork onto av. de Selves. It has 32 bunks in three rooms, one co-ed and two single-sex, as well as a grassy yard for **campers.** (☎05 53 59 47 59 or 05 53 30 21 27. Kitchen access. Sheets 16F/€2.79. No lockout or curfew. Reception 6-8:30pm. Reserve ahead. Open Mar. 15-Nov. Bunks 60F/€9.15, 55F/€8.39 subsequent nights. Camping 35F/€5.34 per night.) The **Hôtel des Récollets,** 4 rue Jean-Jacques Rousseau, off rue de la République, is in a 14th- to 15th-century hillside house with bright and well-renovated rooms. (☎05 53 31 36 00; fax 05 53 30 32 62. Breakfast 38F/€5.79. Reception 8am-9pm. Reserve ahead. Singles and doubles with bath begin at 250F/€38.12, with shower 390F/€59.64; triples with bath 350F/€53.36; quads with bath 450F/€68.61. MC/V.) For tent-packers, there are countless **campsites** in the area. The three-star **Le Montant** is 4km from town on D57 toward Bergerac, with a bar, laundry and pool. (☎05 53 59 18 50 or 05 53 29 45 85; fax 05 53 59 37 73. Open Easter-Sept. Reception 9am-8pm. 28F/€4.27 per person, 36F/€5.49 per tent, including vehicle. Electricity 15F/€2.29.)

Meals here are marvelous but expensive. Most of the regional delicacies—*foie gras, confit de canard,* truffles, mellow red and sweet white Bergerac wines—can be bought directly at the farms for much less. Pâtisseries and confiseries sell decorated breads, walnut-and-chocolate tarts, *gateaux aux noix* (walnut cookies), and chocolate-dipped meringue *boules* the size of grapefruits. The city **market** takes over the city (Sa 7:30am-2pm), while Wednesday mornings see a smaller version on pl. de la Liberté. **Champion supermarket** sits near the youth hostel on rte. de Montignac; follow av. de Selves away from the town center. (Open M-Sa 9am-7:30pm, Su 9am-noon. MC/V.) Stock up in the heart of the *vieille ville* at **Petit Casino,** 32 rue de la République. (Open M-Sa 8am-7:30pm, Su 8am-12:30pm.)

SIGHTS AND ENTERTAINMENT. Malraux's little project in the 60s certainly did the trick; the spotless golden stone buildings of Sarlat's *vieille ville* are the most interesting aspect of the city. Most of the sights—and all of the tourists—are to the right off rue de la République as you enter the town from the station.

The surprisingly dilapidated **Cathédrale St-Sacerdos,** to the right after you leave the tourist office, is in the 16th-century neo-Gothic style. It is closed for renovations until January 2002. Behind the cathedral, the conical **Lanterne des Morts** (Lantern of the Dead) has served as a chapel, charnel-house, a site for electing city consuls, and finally as a powder magazine after the French Revolution.

Across the street from the bishop's palace, and similarly ornamented, is the **Hôtel de la Boétie,** a tall, gabled house with stone flourishes. Its carved pilasters and detailed window transoms are typical of the Italian Renaissance, which was in full bloom when it was built. The windows are worth closer inspection, intricately composed themselves of hundreds of tiny panels of glass. On November 1, 1550, the building saw the birth of writer Etienne de la Boétie, Montaigne's friend and a key figure in late Renaissance efforts to reconcile Catholics and Protestants. Finally, the **public gardens** in pl. Maurice Albe are perfect for a picnic.

Every weekend, street performers and musicians converge on pl. de la Liberté, making cafés crowded and boisterous. Around 11pm, young locals meet in the well-polished **Le Bataclan,** 31 rue de la République, a boisterous bar that opens onto the street, with the standard techno and noisy rock in the background. (☎05 53 28 54 34. Open daily 7am-2am.) In the last two weeks of July and the first week of August, Sarlat hosts the well-attended **Festival des Jeux du Théâtre.** (☎05 53 31 10 83; fax 05 53 30 25 31. Tickets 100-165F/€15.25-25.16.)

DAYTRIP FROM SARLAT: CASTELNAUD AND LES MILANDES. Ten kilometers southwest of Sarlat, the town of **Castelnaud-la-Chapelle** snoozes in the shadow of its pale yellow stone château. The largest and perhaps best restored castle in the region, it looks solid enough now, with its massive round towers and exterior wall; nonetheless, Castelnaud was won and lost seven times during the Hundred Years' War. To visit the castle, leave your car or bike at the foot of the hill in the post office parking lot, right by the bridge over the Dordogne, and mount the steep but much more direct path by foot through the village, following signs for *piétons* (10min.). It's furnished in simple 15th-century military style, and houses a museum of war aimed mostly at children and families. The **Musée de la Guerre du Moyen-age** comes equipped with a 13th- to 17th-century armory, including a behemoth catapult. (☎05 53 31 30 00. Open July-Aug. daily 9am-8pm; May-June and Sept. daily 10am-7pm; Mar.-Apr. and Oct.-Nov. 15 daily 10am-6pm; Nov. 16-Feb. Su-F 2-5pm. July-Aug. 6 French tours a day, 2-3 English tours a day. Call in advance off-season for English tours. Château and museum 28F/€4.27, ages 10-17 19F/2.90, under 10 free.) Castlenaud and Les Milandes are not accessible by bus, but the bike trip from Sarlat (10km and 15km respectively) follows level riverbanks.

The elegant Renaissance **Château Les Milandes,** 8km from Castelnaud, was built by François de Caumont of Castelnaud in 1489. Centuries later, Josephine Baker fell in love with the neglected château's steep pointed roofs and gables, bought the place, and created a world village, where she cared for a dozen children between 1954 and 1969. The tour through two floors of her homey living space includes a museum devoted to her life and times; a falconry show, complete with handlers dressed in medieval garb, takes place 2 to 4 times per day on the lawns outside. (☎05 53 59 31 21. Open July-Aug. daily 9:30am-7:30pm; Apr.-June and Sept. 10am-6pm; Oct.-Mar. 10am-noon and 2-5pm. Tours off-season only. Falconry show June-Sept. 48F/€7.32, students 40F/€6.10, ages 4-15 35F/€5.34.)

LES EYZIES-DE-TAYAC

Les-Eyzies-de-Tayac is the carless traveler's best base for a visit to most of the Vézère valley's famous cave paintings (although it is still a distance from Lascaux). A huge number of the region's most stunning caves are less than a 20-minute walk from the center of town. With two important museums and the official information center for the region's prehistoric sites, it's also a good place to start learning about Neolithic art. Each of the 760 people that live here has his own Neanderthal-themed hotel, duck-filled restaurant, or fossils 'n' *foie gras* knick-knack boutique, to which hordes of camcorder-toters rush all summer long. Arrive early if you want to get into the caves—visits are limited. If Les Eyzies is more than a daytrip for you, book your rooms even earlier or you'll be sleeping under a postcard rack.

ORIENTATION AND PRACTICAL INFORMATION. Trains to: **Paris** (6-8hr., 4 per day, 294F/€44.82); **Périgueux** (30min., 4 per day, 40F/€6.10); and **Sarlat** (1hr.; 3 per day, change at Le Buisson; 47F/€7.17). (☎05 53 06 97 22. Open M 5:10am-6:10pm, Tu-F 6am-6:15pm, Sa noon-6:15pm, Su noon-7:15pm.) With your back to the train station, turn left and walk 1km down the village's only street to reach its center (5min.). The best resource for detailed information about the area's prehistoric sites is the **Point Accueil Préhistoire,** directly across from the post office on the main street through town (D47). (☎06 86 66 54 43. Open daily 9:15am-1:30pm and 3-7pm.) But if you want to get out and see the caves yourself, the **tourist office,** at pl. de la Mairie, can help. Offers summer tours to sights outside of walking distance (call ahead), keeps a list of caves and **gîtes d'étapes,** and **rents bikes** and **canoes.** (Bikes 50F/€7.62 per half-day, 90F/€13.72 per day. 100F/€15.25 deposit.) **Internet access** (40F/€6.10 per hr.) and **currency exchange** without a commission. (☎05 53 06 97 05; fax 05 53 06 90 79. Open July-Aug. M-Sa 9am-8pm, Su 10am-noon and 2-6pm; Mar.-June and Sept.-Oct. M-Sa 9am-noon and 2-6pm, Su 10am-noon and 2-6pm; Nov.-Feb. M-F 10am-noon and 2-6pm.) The **police** are in nearby St-Cyprien (☎05 53 29 20 17). The **post office,** is on the main street, past the tourist office as you walk away from the train station. **Currency exchange.** (☎05 53 06 94 11. Open M-F 9am-noon and 2-5pm, Sa 9am-noon.) **Postal code:** 24620.

ACCOMMODATIONS AND FOOD. Rooms are expensive. The tourist office has a list of private B&Bs in the surrounding area (160-200F/€24.39-30.49 for 1-2 people), and travelers by bike or car will notice signs along the main roads advertising *fermes* (farms) with camping space (20-45F/€3.05-6.86). Some village homes rent rooms for 150-300F/€22.90-45.74 during the summer. Your best bet for these is to go by the sign that appeals to you most, although the tourist office can provide some names and numbers. In town, the **Hôtel des Falaises** is on the main street. On your way to the caves, leave your pack in these lovely rooms. (☎05 53 06 97 35. Breakfast 25F/€3.81. Reception in the bar downstairs 8am-8pm. Doubles with bath 180-200F/€27.44-30.49; twins 190F/€28.97; triples 250F/€38.12. MC/V.) The hotel also offers more private and homey lodging in the **annex,** about 100m down the road toward Font-de-Gaume in a large half-timbered building. (One small single 150F/€22.90; doubles 180-200F/€27.44-30.49; triples 260-290F/€39.64-44.21.) For **Camping La Rivière,** rte. de Périgueux, turn left as you step out of the tourist office toward Périgueux on D47. Follow the road straight for about five minutes, cross the bridge, and take another left when you reach the Citroën/Elf gas station (10min.). (☎05 53 06 97 14; fax 05 53 35 20 85. Snack bar, restaurant, bike rental, and a pool. Breakfast 28F/€4.27. Reception 8am-10pm. Open Apr. 4-Oct. 4. July-Aug. 26.50F/€4.04 per person, 42F/€6.40 per site; Apr.-June and Sept.-Oct. 22.10F/€3.37 per person, 32.30F/€4.92 per site. Electricity 18F/€2.74. Doubles with shower 195F/€29.73; quads with shower 280F/€42.69. MC/V.)

Most restaurants in Les Eyzies are expensive and extremely good. A **market** runs the length of town every Monday (9am-1pm). **Halle des Eyzies,** just past the center of town on rte. de Sarlat, is a building full of expensive boutiques hawking *foie gras* and walnut products. Here you can find wonderful nut wines, oils, cookies, cakes, and every duck, goose, and pork product imaginable. (Open June 15-Sept. daily 9am-1pm and 2:30-7pm.) A large convenience store, **Relais de Mousquetaires,** sells groceries by the bridge on the Périgueux edge of town. (Open daily 8:30am-7:30pm, Su 9am-1pm.) **La Grignotière,** just to your right as you leave the tourist office, serves very cheap drinks, sandwiches all day long (16-25F/€2.44-3.81), and regional, duck-filled three-course *menus* at mealtimes (60-86F/€9.15-13.11). (☎05 53 06 91 67. Open daily 8:30am-midnight. MC/V.)

SIGHTS. The **Musée L'Abri Pataud** sits on what was once the property of a local farmer, Monsieur Pataud, whose plot consisted of bones, stone tools, and precious little arable land. As it turned out, his farm was built on an *abri* (shelter), where several groups of reindeer hunters lived over a span of 20,000 years. The museum now gives an in-depth explanation of the archaeological methods used in the Périgord area. The 18,600-year-old remains of a teenage girl found on the site represent a possible transitional link between Neanderthal and Cro-Magnon man. (☎05 53 06 92 46; pataud@mnhn.fr. Open July-Aug. daily 10am-6:30pm; Sept.-June by reservation only; visits every half-hr. 30F/€4.57.)

The **Musée National de Préhistoire,** in the cliff above the village, is being renovated until 2003, at which point they hope to open a bigger museum. The remains of the old museum are still worth seeing, mainly for the 30,000 year-old petrified rhinoceros who lies in the position he was found in one of the main rooms. (☎05 53 06 45 45. Open July-Aug. daily 9:30am-7pm; Mar. 15-June and Sept.-Nov. 15 W-M 9:30am-noon and 2-6pm; Nov. 16-Mar. 14 9:30am-noon and 2-5pm. 1hr. tours: 3 per day in French; 1 per day in English at 1:30pm. 24F/€3.66, students 16F/€2.44.)

CAVES OF THE VEZERES VALLEY

NEAR SARLAT: LASCAUX

The most famous and spectacular prehistoric cave paintings yet discovered line the ceilings of **Lascaux,** aptly christened "the Sistine Chapel of prehistory." A couple of teenagers stumbled upon these "prehistoric frescoes" in 1940 while looking to retrieve their clumsy dog. Lascaux was closed to the public in 1963—the humidity from millions of tourists' oohs and aahs fostered algae, and micro-stalactites ravaged the paintings that nature had preserved for 17,000 years. Today, only five archaeologists per day, five days a week, are allowed into the original caves.

Instead, Disney-style, visitors queue to see **Lascaux II,** which duplicates practically every inch of the original. The new paintings of 5m-tall bulls, horses, and bison are brighter than their ancient counterparts, yet were created with identical natural powders, taken from the soil in the original caves. While there is a distinct lack of ancient awe and mystery, Lascaux II does inspire a sense of wonder at 20th-century tourism and pre-historic art. Their guided tour is among the best cave tours in the valley, engagingly introducing the figures that gallop and trot across the ceiling. You'll see a deer whose eyes appear to follow you, a horse sprawling on his back on a rock nearby, and a herd of galloping elk.

The Lascaux twins are 2km from the town of **Montignac,** 25km north of Sarlat along D704, and 23km northeast of les Eyzies along D706. The Montignac **tourist office** on pl. Bertram-de-Born shares a building with the **ticket office** for Lascaux II. (M-F ☎05 53 35 50 10, Sa-Su ☎05 53 51 95 03.) Tickets go fast—reserve a week or two ahead, or arrive early in the morning. (Tourist office ☎05 53 51 95 03. Ticket office open from 9am until tickets sell out. Advance booking May-Aug. daily 9am-7pm; Sept.-Oct. and Apr. Tu-Su 9am-6pm; Nov.-Mar. Tu-Su 10am-12:30pm and 2-5:30pm. 40min. tours in French and English 50F/€7.62, ages 6-12 25F/€3.81.)

The train station nearest Montignac is at **Le Lardin,** 10km away. **CFTA** (☎05 55 86 07 07 for info office in Brive) runs buses from **Brive** (1½hr., 1 per day, 35F/€5.34), **Périgueux** (1½hr., 1 per day, 40F/€6.10), and, most conveniently, from **Sarlat** (20 min., 3 per day, 30F/€4.57), leaving in the morning or afternoon and returning in the early evening. Buses run into Montignac center. The caves are 2km outside the city center and can be reached by foot, cab, bike, or car. Buses come and go from pl. du 14 Juillet, which faces the church. The trip by bike isn't too steep, besides a sharp incline out of Sarlat. Since most visitors return to nearby towns, those with cars are sometimes willing to give lifts to those without. The **Camping Municipal,** with 91 spots, is just outside town on D65. (☎05 53 52 83 95. Open Apr.-Oct. 15. 20F/€3.05 per person, 15F/€2.29 per site, 13F/€1.98 per car.)

NEAR LES EYZIES-DE-TAYAC

CAVES WITHIN WALKING DISTANCE OF LES-EYZIES. The **Grotte de Font-de-Gaume,** on the D47 1km east of Les Eyzies (10min.), has the most important paintings still open to tourists. The faded but spectacular 15,000-year-old friezes were completed over hundreds of years and are technically advanced—for example, using the natural contours of the cave for relief. This is the last cave in the Aquitaine basin with polychrome (mixed-color) paintings still open to the public. Though locals discovered the paintings in the 18th century, they did not realize their importance until two centuries later, by which time several murals had decayed and been defaced by graffiti. To find the most brilliant colors, head to the farther reaches of the cavern. Notice the scene of a black reindeer licking the nose of a kneeling red reindeer. The *vôute* (vault), where 12 bison stampede on the ceiling, is the undisputed highlight. *(☎05 53 06 86 00; fax 05 53 35 26 18. Open Apr.-Sept. daily 9am-noon and 2-6pm; Mar. and Oct. 9:30am-noon and 2-5:30pm; Nov.-Feb. 10am-noon and 2-5pm. Reservations obligatory; July-Aug. reserve 15 days in advance; Sept.-June 1 week in advance. 36F/€5.49, ages 18-25 23F/€3.51, under 18 free. 45min. tours available in English.)*

PERIGORD

Unlike Font-de-Gaume, the **Grotte des Combarelles,** 2km farther down the road, has lost its paintings to humidity, and only etchings remain. But the "Lascaux of engravings" is no less spectacular without color. More than 600 carvings depict a large variety of species, including donkeys, cave lions, and rhinoceri. Fifty human figures keep watch from the narrow halls of the cave. The small six-person tours are more personalized than the larger groups at Font-de-Gaume, and the tourguides are wonderfully flexible. Reserve far in advance for the summer. *(☎05 53 06 97 72. For tickets and reservations, call the Font-de-Gaume office at 05 53 06 86 00. Hours and prices same as Font de Gaume; 1hr. tours in French only.)*

The **Gorge d'Enfer,** just upstream from Grand Roc and 2km from Les Eyzies, is full of waterfalls, lagoons, and blooming flora. Inside it is the **Abri du Poisson,** a shelter which contains the oldest drawing of a fish in France—a 25,000-year-old, meter-long "beaked" salmon. The rendering is so detailed that you can make out its upturned jaw, a sign of exhaustion after spawning. *(☎05 53 06 86 00. Open Apr.-Sept. daily 9am-noon and 2-6pm; Mar. and Oct. 9:30am-noon and 2-5:30pm; Nov.-Feb. 10am-noon and 2-5pm. 15F/€2.29, under 18 free.)*

NEARBY CAVES WITHOUT PAINTINGS. Many caves have natural decoration as fascinating as anything ancient man created. Most interesting is the **Grotte du Grand Roc,** 1½km northwest of town along the road to Périgueux. The cave lies halfway up the chalk cliffs and commands a blistering view of the valley and Tayac's fortified church. The cave is filled with millions of stalactites, stalagmites, and *eccentriques*—small calcite accretions that grow neither straight down nor straight up. The most eccentric of these are a vaguely ostrich-like form and an eroded column that resembles Bigfoot's foot. The cave is naturally a constant 16°C (nice) and 95% humidity (not nice). *(☎05 53 06 92 70. Open July-Aug. daily 9:30am-7pm; Apr.-June and Sept.-Oct. 10 9:30am-6pm; Nov.-Dec. and Feb.-Mar. 10am-5pm. 30min. tour in French only, but many explanatory signs are in English. 40F/€6.10, children 21F/€3.20.)*

Those interested in more recent cavemen should head for the **Musée Spéléologie,** 91 rue de la Grange-Chancel, just 1km north of Les Eyzies. Located in the Fort de Roc, a niche in a cliff high above the Vézère Valley, it was dug by English soldiers during the Hundred Years' War. The museum narrates the region's cave history with models, documents, and equipment. *(☎05 53 06 97 15. Open June 15-Sept. daily 11am-6pm. 20F/€3.05, under 16 10F/€1.53.)*

CAVES ACCESSIBLE BY CAR OR BIKE. Fifteen kilometers northwest of Les Eyzies in Rouffignac, on the road to Périgueux, **La Grotte de Rouffignac,** also known as **La Grotte aux Cent Mammouths,** houses 250 engravings and paintings. Among etchings of rhinoceri, horses, and bison, the shaggy mammoths are most striking. This is one of the longest caves in the area. The guided tour (via train) lasts an hour. *(☎05 53 05 41 71; fax 05 53 35 44 71. Open July-Aug. daily 9-11:30am and 2-6pm; Apr. 5-June and Sept.-Oct. 10-11:30am and 2-5pm. 30F/€4.57, children 10F/€1.53.)*

Only 12 figures are visible at the sculptured frieze **Abri du Cap-Blanc,** 7km northeast of Eyzies on D48, but they are outstandingly preserved. 15,000 years ago, hunters drew horses, bison, and reindeer onto the thick limestone walls. The carvings are not as detailed as those in Font-de-Gaume, but the quality of preservation fully compensates. The exhibit's centerpiece is a 2m-long herd of shuffling animals. It's wise to call for tickets at least one to two weeks in advance, or else arrive early. *(☎05 53 59 21 74; fax 05 53 29 89 84. Open July-Aug. daily 9:30am-7pm; Apr.-June and Sept.-Oct. 10am-noon and 2-6pm. 34F/€5.18, children 25F/€3.81. 45min. tours in French.)*

Northeast of Les Eyzies on route D66, the **Roque St-Christophe** is the most extensive cave dwelling yet to be discovered. Its five floors of terraces stretch over 400m. From 40,000 BC until the Middle Ages, this fascinating sanctuary served as a defensive fort and home to over 3000 people. You'll visit an 11th-century kitchen and peer over the 60m-high cliff where Protestants sought shelter from a Catholic army in 1580. A 45-minute tour allows you to check out the cave's ovens, monastic remains, and military defenses. *(☎05 53 50 70 45. Visits in summer daily 10am-6:30pm; Nov. 11-Feb. 11am-5pm; closed Jan. 36F/€5.49, students 28F/€4.27, ages 5-13 19F/€2.90.)*

THE LOWER DORDOGNE VALLEY

Steep cliffs and poplar thickets overlook the slow-moving waters of the Dordogne, which served in the Hundred Years' War as a natural boundary between France and English Aquitaine to the south. The châteaux, built to keep watch on the enemy, are numerous, if not as regal as those of the Loire. In summer the valley overflows with tourists in canoes, on bikes, and in cars; by avoiding the major towns, it is still possible to find solitude. *Chambres d'hôte* provide cheap farmhouse rooms near the historic sites; ask at any tourist office for a list.

TRANSPORTATION. The valley stretches from Bergerac west, passing 15km south of Sarlat. To get there and get around you'll need to rent a car or be prepared for a good bike workout. **Hertz** car rental is right in front of the train station in Périgueux; see Brive for information on its branch. Hitching, though never safe, is reportedly easy, although most family-filled cars have no room to spare.

Many outfits along the Dordogne rent **canoes** and **kayaks.** At the Pont de Vitrac, near Domme, you can find them at **Canoës-Loisirs** (☎05 53 28 23 43) and **Périgord Aventure et Loisirs** (☎05 53 28 23 82). **Canoës-Dordogne** (☎05 53 29 58 50) and **Canoë Vacances** (☎05 53 28 17 07) are at La Roque Gageac. **Le Sioux** (☎05 53 28 30 81) is near Domme and Cénac (open July-Sept. 15). Get schedules and info from tourist offices; prices average 70F/€10.67 per person for a half-day and 105F/€16 for a full day. When you finish your course down the river, many rental organizations will pick you up in a bus and bring you back to your starting point free of charge.

BERGERAC

Until the early 20th century, when trains started rolling into Bergerac's newly built station, the Dordogne defined the town culturally and economically. Flat-bottomed boats, known as *gabarres*, departed from the Quai Salvete, trading lumber, wine, and all the other necessities of life with Bourdeaux and Libourne. The *vieille ville*, with its 14th- and 15th-century houses close to the docks, was the heart of town. Now the trade takes place in the fabulous town markets instead of on the river. Locals of Bergerac participate in the new industry of "living well." Perfect produce is available every day, and the fertile land along the riverbanks breeds red and sweet white wines that have been pressed here since the 11th century. The chapels, vine-covered roofs, and winding streets of the now-quiet *vieille ville* perfectly accompany a Côtes de Bergerac or a golden Monbazillac.

ORIENTATION AND PRACTICAL INFORMATION. The train station on av. du 108*ème* R.I., is a 10-minute walk from the *vieille ville* along what is first rue Ste-Catherine and then cours Alsace-Lorraine. Trains leave for **Bordeaux** (1½hr., 7 per day, 80F/€12.20) and **Périgueux** via Buisson (1½-2hr., 3 per day, 78F/€11.89) and via Libourne (2hr., 6 per day, 115F/€17.53). (☎08 36 35 35 35. Office open M-Sa 7am-7pm, Su 8:30am-12:30pm and 1:50-10:30pm.) **Rent bikes** at **UCAR Cycles,** 31 bd. Victor-Hugo, just between the train station and pl. de la République. (☎05 53 61 08 16; fax 05 53 57 72 48. 60F/€9.15 per day, 85F/€12.96 per weekend. Scooters 200-300F/€30.49-45.74 per day; motor bikes 350-1150F/€53.36-175.33 per day. Open M-Sa 8am-noon and 2-7pm.) **Taxis:** ☎05 53 57 17 06.

Services include: the main **tourist office** at 97 rue Neuve d'Argenson, which offers one-hour **tours** of the town (1 per day, 25F/€3.81). (☎05 53 57 03 11; www.bergerac-tourisme.com. Open July-Aug. M-Sa 9:30am-7:30pm, Su 10am-1pm and 2:30-7pm; Sept.-June M-Sa 9:30am-7pm.); the **hospital** (☎05 53 63 88 88) at 9 av. du Prof. Albert Calmette; the **Police Nationale Commissariat** at 37 bd. Chanzy (☎05 53 74 66 22), and the **post office** at 36 rue de la Resistance. (☎05 53 63 50 00. Open M-F 8:30am-6:30pm, Sa 8am-noon.) **Postal Code:** 24100.

ACCOMMODATIONS AND FOOD. Accommodations can be atrociously expensive, but **Hôtel Pozzi,** 11 rue Pozzi, offers 11 reasonable rooms at fair prices. (☎05 53 57 04 68. Breakfast 28F/€4.27. Reception 7am-midnight; closed Su. Reserve one week in advance. Singles 100F/€15.25; doubles 130F/€19.82; quads 190F/€28.97.) Restaurants, especially in the *vieille ville*, can also be expensive. Stick with the plentiful bakeries, pâtisseries, and charcuteries which seem to line every street, and the **Marché Couvert** at pl. du Marché Couvert. Wednesday and Saturday mornings a spectacular **market** spreads from the pl. du Marché Couvert to completely surround the Eglise de Notre Dame with fruit and wine vendors.

SIGHTS AND ENTERTAINMENT. Get an introduction to wine at **La Maison du Vin,** 2 pl. du Docteur Cayla. (☎05 53 63 57 57. Open Apr. and Oct. daily 10am-7pm; May-Sept. 10am-12:30pm and 2-6pm. Free; includes a movie and a tasting of 3 or 4 Bergerac wines.) Just a few blocks away in the Maison Peyrarède, a stately Renaissance mansion houses the **Musée du Tabac.** The museum presents a 3000-year history of tobacco; don't miss the intricate ivory cigar holder on the top floor, containing a sculpted Sicilian wedding, complete with frolicking lovers, a horse-drawn carriage, and serenading musicians. (☎05 53 63 04 13. Open Tu-F 10am-noon and 2-6pm, Sa 10am-noon and 2-5pm, Su 2:30-6:30pm. 18F/€2.74, students free, although children ages 10-17 without a student card must pay 8F/€1.22.)

La Fête des Vendanges, from the last week of September through the first week of October, celebrates Bergerac's vineyards and the crucial role that the Dordogne played in the 19th-century wine industry. An opening day parade kicks off the festivities as all the local wine makers converge on Vieux Pont, bearing their banners. Some arrive on foot, others by horse-drawn carriage. They pile into the *gabarres* and set off symbolically for a few hundred meters down the Dordogne toward Bordeaux. On the river banks, spectators cheer while drinking free-flowing wine.

BEYNAC-ET-CAZENAC

The fortress at **Beynac** is perhaps the most picturesque one in the lower Dordogne. It perches 150m above the river, sheathed in misty clouds and greenery, overlooking a town of ancient stone houses decorated with wrought-iron balconies and flowered terraces. In 1214, when Simon de Montfort invaded the lower Dordogne, he sacked the castles of Domme, Castelnaud, and Beynac in turn, allegedly in pursuit of Cathar heretics and sympathizers. The lord of Beynac, a good Catholic and supporter of the French King, put up no resistance when Montfort decided to "humiliate" the castle by pruning the tops of the ramparts. Beynac has enjoyed a topsy-turvy history since then, with only one thing certain throughout: it was always at odds with its neighbor, siding with the French after Castelnaud sided with the English during the Hundred Years' War. (☎05 53 29 50 40. Castle open Mar.-Sept. daily 10am-6:30pm; Oct.-Nov. 10am-noon and 2pm-dark; Dec.-Feb. 11am-dark. 40F/€6.10, ages 5-11 17F/€2.90.) The Gauls never left the **Parc Archéologique de Beynac,** just below the château. Thatch huts with mud walls, a 5000-year-old *dolmen* (sacrificial table), and many historic sheep are scattered throughout this reproduction of an ancient Gaulish village. (☎05 53 29 51 28. Open to individuals July 3-Sept. 15 Su-F 10am-7pm. 30F/€4.57, ages 6-16 20F/€3.05.)

The **tourist office** sits by the river at the bottom of Beynac's steep hill. (☎05 53 29 43 08. Open July-Aug. daily 10am-noon and 2-6pm.) The 19 cheapest beds around are in two large dorm rooms at the **Gîte d'Etape de Beynac,** 2km from town toward Castelnaud. In July and August, reserve at least a week in advance. (☎05 53 29 40 93; if there's no answer, call the *mairie*, ☎05 53 31 34 00. Open year-round. 50F/€7.62 per person.) **Camping Le Capeyrou** is just out of town on the riverbank, by the entrance to the city. (☎05 53 29 54 95. Open May 15-Sept. 15. 25F/€3.81 per person, 12F/€1.83 per child, 35F/€5.34 per site. Electricity 15F/€2.29.)

DOMME AND LA ROQUE GAGEAC

Built by King Philip the Bold in 1280 on a high dome of solid rock, Domme is the best-defended of the Dordogne villages. Enter through any one of the three crumbling gates on the lower side of the town, and make your way up tiny alleys and past limestone homes and *foie gras* stores to the main square, pl. de la Halle. Excellent guided tours in French take you into one of the towers guarding the town's main gate, the dilapidated **Porte des Tours.** Seventy Templar Knights were imprisoned there in 1307 and tortured for nearly 20 years by King Philip IV, who wanted the secret of their hidden treasure. The graffiti they scratched into the walls with their teeth, hands, and fingernails still remain; they combine Islamic and Jewish motifs encountered by the Templars in the Holy Land with an idiosyncratic Christian iconography. Astrological signs and images of stars abound, along with representations of Christ, the Virgin Mary, and the Templar cross. Their chief persecutors, Pope Clement V and Philip IV, appear as well, represented as monsters. (Consult tourist office for tours. 1hr.; 1 per day, July-Aug. 2-3 per day. 25F/€3.81, children 18F/€2.74.) Back in the center of town, a *tour des grottes* (cave tour) descends from pl. de la Halle into the intricate cavern network of the stalagtite-bristling **Grottes de la Halle,** some of the largest caves in Europe. (☎05 53 31 71 00. Cave tours in French and English July-Aug. every 30min. 10:15am-7pm; Apr.-June and Sept. every 45min. 10:15am-noon and 2-6pm; Feb.-Mar. and Oct. every hr. 2-5pm. 35F/€5.34, students 30F/€4.57, children 20F/€3.05. Ticket includes entrance to the Musée des Arts et Traditions Populaires de Domme.)

At the other end of the pl. de la Halle, the uninspired **Musée des Arts et Traditions Populaires de Domme** displays costumes and artifacts from 17th- to 19th-century Périgord. (☎05 53 31 71 00. Open July-Aug. daily 10:30am-7pm; Apr.-May and Sept. 2-5pm; June 10:30am-12:30pm and 2:30-6pm. 18F/€2.74, students 14F/€2.13, ages 5-14 12F/€1.83. Free entrance if combined with the Grottes de la Halle.)

The **tourist office,** pl. de la Halle, lists *chambres d'hôte* (doubles 150-230F/€22.90-35.06), and leads tours. (☎05 53 31 71 00; fax 05 53 31 71 09. Open July-Aug. daily 10am-7pm; Sept.-June 10am-noon and 2-6pm; phone ahead for Jan.) The **Nouvel Hôtel,** rue Malville at pl. de la Halle, lets 14 well-equipped rooms. (☎05 53 28 36 81. Reception 8am-10pm. Open Easter-Dec. Singles and doubles with bath 250F/€38.12; triples with bath 300F/€45.74; quads with bath 350F/€53.36. MC/V.) The **Camping Municipal Cénac St-Julien** sits near the river 1½km out of Domme on the way to La Roque Gageac on D46. (☎05 53 28 31 91. Reception July-Aug. 8am-noon and 12:30-8pm; June and Sept. 9:15-11:45am and 1:30-8pm. Reserve ahead. Open June-Sept. 15. 21.10F/€3.22 per person, 26.30F/€4.01 per tent. Electricity 14.70F/€2.24.) **Canoë Cénac** (☎05 53 28 22 01) rents kayaks near the campground. (140F/€21.35 per 2hr., 150F/€22.90 per half-day, 240F/€36.59 per day.)

After you pass the campsite and cross the river on D46, turn left onto D703. Four kilometers downstream, **La Roque Gageac** juts out from the base of a sheer cliff, with steep, twisting streets lined with medieval-style stone houses. For a perfect view of the many châteaux along the Dordogne, take a **boat.** They leave from the dock beyond the town's big parking lot. (1hr.; every 15min. 10am-6pm. English-speaking guides available. 45F/€6.86, children 25F/€3.81.) The 12th-century **Fort Troglodytique Aérien,** high above La Roque, commands a spectacular view of the Dordogne river valley. Its height and position within the rock made it ideal; it withstood all British assaults during the Hundred Years' War, even outlasting the château it protected, until neglect felled it. It's accessible only by bike or foot. (☎05 53 31 61 94. Open July-Aug. daily 10am-7pm; Apr.-June and Sept.-Nov. 11 Su-F 10am-6pm. 25F/€3.81, students 20F/€3.05, ages 10-16 10F/€1.53, under 10 free.)

THE UPPER DORDOGNE VALLEY

This fertile area south of Brive is home to hilltop châteaux, lazy rivers, and tiny hamlets that have never seen a tour bus. A world away from the lower reaches of the valley, this region ranges from deep valleys nestled between rolling hills, canopies of trees, towering cliffs of white rock, and fields of tall grass and rolls of hay. You can bike it, but you'll probably want to rent a car. Bretenoux, Rocamadour, Padirac, Gourdon, Souillac, and Gramat are serviced by trains, but there are few buses. Sites of interest are invariably far from stations, so bring your hiking shoes.

TRANSPORTATION. Trains run to **Bretenoux** from **Brive** (45min., 4-5 per day, 45F/€6.86). **Castelnau, Montal,** and **Beaulieu** are accessible by bike from Bretenoux, but just barely. You'll need to invest at least a whole day or two if you want to visit them all. The train station is 2km from **Bretenoux;** shuttle buses run from the train station to Bretenoux (10min.) and **St-Céré** (15min., 3-4 per day, 15F/€2.29; schedule posted outside the train station). It's probably easier to make the clearly marked 25-minute walk to Bretenoux; from there it's a flat 3km southwest to Castelnau, 8km southwest to St-Céré, and 9km north to Beaulieu.

BRETENOUX

This 13th-century town is useful as a transportation hub from which to explore the upper valley. The **tourist office,** in the Manoir du Fort on av. de la Libération, has maps and info on hiking. (☎05 65 38 59 53; fax 05 65 39 72 14. Open daily 9am-noon and 2-6pm.) An immense **supermarket** sits near the traffic light by the train station (☎05 65 10 22 00. Open M-F 8:30am-7:30pm, Sa 8:30am-7:15pm); another one can be found one block down from the tourist office, av. de la Libération. (☎05 65 38 58 70. Open M 3-7:30pm, Tu-Sa 7:30am-12:30pm and 3-7:30pm, Su 8:45am-12:30pm.) An **open-air market** is held behind the tourist office (Tu and Sa 8am-noon).

Three-star **Camping de Bourgnatelle** is a beautiful site straddling the river that runs through the town. (☎05 65 38 44 07 or 08 35 33 75 68; bougnatel@aol.com. Reception 9am-1pm and 3-8pm. Reserve in advance. July-Aug. 21F/€3.20 per person, children under 7 11F/€1.68, 21F/€3.20 per site; May-June and Sept. 16.50F/€2.52 per person, children 8F/€1.22, 16.50F/€2.52 per site. Electricity 14F/€2.13. MC/V.) You can **rent bikes** in Bretenoux from **Cycles Bladier,** av. de la Libération. (☎05 65 38 41 56. 50F/€7.62 per day, price lowers with longer rentals. Mountain bikes 60F/€9.15 per half-day, 80F/€1.220 per day. 500F/€76.23 deposit or passport. Open Tu-Sa 8am-noon and 2-7pm.) There are numerous places to rent kayaks and canoes all along the Dordogne river, but some of the best bargains on rentals and lessons are at the non-profit **Canoe Kayak-Bretenoux.** (☎05 65 35 91 59. Open July-Aug. daily 9am-noon and 2-5pm. 30F/€4.57 per person for 90min., 70F/€10.67 per person for half day, 90F/€13.72 per person for full day.)

NEAR BRETENOUX: CASTELNAU-BRETENOUX AND ST-CERE

The burnt-red ramparts of Castelnau-Prudhomat, 3km southwest of Bretenoux, have kept an eye on the valley below for 900 years. The château was built in the shape of a triangle, flanked by three corner towers. In the central *cour d'honneur*, the medieval Tour Sarrazin, commands a view that extends for miles. Famed 19th-century opera singer Jean Mouliérat restored the château after an 1851 fire, poking large windows into the protective walls. Today, Aubusson and Beauvais tapestries are displayed beside modern operetta scores and 15th-century stained glass in the oratory. The true charm of the castle comes from its dried moat and crumbling walls. (☎05 65 10 98 00. Open July-Aug. daily 9:30am-6:45pm; Apr.-June and Sept. daily 9:30am-12:15pm and 2-6:15pm; Oct.-Mar. W-M 10am-12:15pm and 2-5:15pm. Last entry 45min. before closing. Tours in French with English pamphlets every 30min., July-Aug. every 15min. 36F/€5.49, ages 18-25 23F/€3.51, under 18 free.)

Château de Montal rests 8km southwest of Bretenoux and 2km from St-Céré. To get there, follow the signs to St-Céré; the château will be on your right just before you enter the city. The biggest attraction is the carved staircase in which the underside of each step is uniquely decorated. Otherwise, this château offers more of the same tapestries, wooden furniture, and renaissance fireplaces as others in the area. From 1941 to 1945, the artwork of the Louvre, including the *Mona Lisa*, was kept at Montal for safekeeping. (☎05 65 38 13 72. Open Mar.-Oct. Su-F 9:30am-noon and 2:30-6pm. Tours in French every 45min.; last tour 45min. before closing. 30F/€4.57, students 25F/€3.81, children 7-15 12F/€1.83.) The nationally acclaimed **Festival Saint-Céré** is a series of classical music and dance performances, including at least one full-fledged opera, that takes place from late July to August 14. Venues include the courtyard of the Château de Castelnau and the Théatre de l'Usine, an old factory in St-Céré. (For tickets (available after May 3) and information call 05 65 38 28 08. 100-260F/€15.25-39.64, students 70-230F/€10.67-35.06.)

Ten kilometers southwest of St-Céré lie the mysterious caverns and subterranean river known as **Le Gouffre de Padirac.** The 90-minute tour takes visitors first by boat and then by foot through the twisting caves and great domed rooms of gargantuan stalagtites and stalagmites, formed by millions of years of calcium deposits carried by the water. Little English translation is available, although the natural grandeur of the 103m-underground formations transcends language barriers. (☎05 65 33 64 56. Open Apr.-June and Sept.-Oct. daily 9am-noon and 2-6pm; July 1-July 9 8:30am-noon and 2-6:30pm; July 10-July 31 8:30am-6:30pm, Aug. 8am-7pm. 49F/€7.47, under 12 32F/€4.88. Last tours leave 90min. before closing. Boats leave as soon as they are filled.) The closest train station is in Padirac; Le Gouffre is accessible by cab, car, or bike from the station.

BEAULIEU-SUR-DORDOGNE

Ten kilometers north of Bretenoux on route D940, the medieval village of Beaulieu-sur-Dordogne is home to the 13th-century **Abbaye Bénédictine St-Pierre.** The abbey is known for its medieval painting and sculpture, particularly the stone sculpted tympanum above the south portal. Here, a chillingly expressionless Jesus dwarfs the angels and apostles around him, his arms spread wide, while tiny condemned human beings and demons get squashed under the weight of heaven. Inside the abbey, the narrow room leads to the altar, above which the Virgin Mary appears to conduct a chamber orchestra of cherubs while the twelve apostles point at her. (Open daily 8am-7:30pm.) All the way down rue de la Chapelle, along the banks of the river, is the 12th-century **Chapelle des Pénitents,** pl. de Monturu. Even if the chapel is closed, the view of the river is worthy of the trip down there. (Hours vary.) Overlooking the river is the popular **Auberge de Jeunesse (HI),** pl. de Monturu, the only inexpensive place to stay indoors in the region. (☎05 55 91 13 82; fax 05 55 91 26 06; beaulieu@fuaj.org. Breakfast 19F/€2.90. Sheets 17F/€2.59. Kitchen access. Reception 6-8pm. Reserve 2-3 weeks in advance July-Aug. Open Apr.-Sept. 2- to 6-bed dorms 48F/€7.32. **Members only.**) The **tourist office** is in the central square. (☎05 55 91 09 94; fax 05 55 91 10 97. Open daily 9:20am-12:30pm and 2-7pm.) Guided **tours** of Beaulieu leave once a week from the tourist office. (M 9:45am. 15F/€2.29 per person, under 12 free.) For a **taxi,** call 05 55 91 02 83 or 05 55 91 00 76. There is a **Banque Populaire du Centre** on rue Général de Gaulle. (☎05 55 91 93 30. Open Tu-F 8:30am-noon and 1:30-6pm, Sa 8:30am-12:30pm.) There are no trains or buses between Beaulieu and Bretenoux, but **buses** from Brive arrive at pl. de Champ de Mars (1hr., 1-2 per day, 40F/€9.15). Otherwise, you'll have to bike, hike, or hitch (*Let's Go* does not recommend hitchhiking). The Auberge de Jeunesse will try to match you up with free space in a car if you call them in advance.

ROCAMADOUR

The tiny town of Rocamadour is a "verticity," built into a mountainside in three sections, one above the other. The private château at the peak of the cliff is connected to the village at the bottom by the winding road that runs through the *Cité Religieuse* in the middle. The town (pop. 638) was of no consequence until 1166, when the perfectly preserved body of St. Amadour was unearthed near the town's chapel. It was reputed that St. Amadour was actually the biblical Zacchaeus, a tax collector who altered his ways after dining with Jesus. As the story grew, so did the miracles, and the town became an important pilgrimage site. Today, Rocamadour's visual splendor is what draws travelers visiting Brive.

PRACTICAL INFORMATION.

Trains run from **Brive** (40min., 3 per day, 61F/€9.30) to Rocamadour, stopping at the old train station, 4km from town on route N140. The station at Rocamadour has no ticket office or information booth; tickets can be purchased on the train. From the station, a flat, winding road leads directly to the top of town (45min.). Hitching, never safe, is tough, as most cars are already full. For a **taxi,** call 05 65 33 63 10 or 05 65 33 73 31. Separate **tourist offices** serve the cliff's top (☎05 65 33 22 00; fax 05 65 33 22 01) and bottom (☎05 65 33 62 59; www.rocamadour.com). Each distributes a list of hotels and restaurants, books rooms, sells maps (5F/€0.76), and **exchanges currency** at nefarious rates. The lower office is in the old Hôtel de Ville, the upper in **l'Hospitalet,** rte. de Lacave. (Both open Sept.-June 10am-12:30pm and 1:30-6:30pm; July 9-Aug. 24 9:30am-7:30pm.) **Bikes** can be rented from the upper tourist office for 55F/€8.39 per day. The **police** (☎05 65 33 60 17) are only around on weekends in May and June, but are available daily in July and August. The **post office** is near the lower tourist office. (☎05 65 33 62 21. Open M-F 9:30-11:30am and 2-4pm, Sa 9am-noon.) **Postal code:** 46500.

ACCOMMODATIONS AND FOOD. Prices at Rocamadour hotels make daytripping almost mandatory; luckily, one inexpensive accommodation does exist, with a prime location in the clifftop castle that offers one of the most beautiful views in this part of France. **Relais de Remparts** caters mainly, but not exclusively, to pilgrims. Their 44 bare rooms are available for private meditation or for a night's sleep, saggy mattresses notwithstanding. (☎05 65 33 23 23; fax 05 65 33 23 24. Breakfast 30F/€4.57, elaborate lunch 85F/€12.96, dinner 75F/€11.43. Reception M-F 9am-8pm, Sa-Su 10am-7pm. Singles with sink 110F/€16.77, with bath 130F/€19.82; doubles with sink 190F/€28.97, with bath 210F/€32.02; twins with sink 200F/€30.49, with bath 220F/€33.54.) A bit pricier are the calm, elegant rooms with private baths of the **Hôtel du Roc,** on the main street in the lower town. (☎05 65 33 62 43; fax 05 65 33 62 11; www.verthotel.fr. Reception 6am-midnight. Open mid-Feb. to Nov. Singles 190-220F/€28.97-33.54; doubles 200-265F/€30.49-40.40; twins 235-295F/€35.83. Discount on subsequent nights. AmEx/MC/V.)

Not surprisingly, all the restaurants in town have tourist-adjusted prices. Tiny stores line Rocamadour's main street, hawking *noix* (nuts), *truffes* (truffles), *foie gras*, and *cabécou* (a mild, nutty local goat cheese). Several stores at the far end of the pedestrian road offer free tastings of a sweet walnut *apéritif*, a specialty of the Quercy region. Most stores also offer free samples of other nutty delights, such as grilled, caramel-coated walnuts or a crumbly hazelnut cake. Bakeries and grocery stores are pricey, so it's a good idea to bring your own groceries to town—the scenery is perfect for picnicking.

SIGHTS. Millions of believers, from beggars to kings, have crawled on their knees up the **Grand Escalier,** which rises steeply up the cliffside beside the town's main street. King Henry II of England visited in 1170, and Blanche de Castille dragged her son St. Louis (Louis IX) along in 1244, just before he led a crusading army into the Holy Land. Today some pilgrims still kneel in prayer at each step, but you're more likely to see tourists kneeling to retrieve film. The Grand Escalier winds up to the 12th-century **Cité Réligieuse,** which is actually not a city but an enclosed courtyard that encompasses seven chapels, two of which can be visited without a guide. Its nucleus is the **Chapelle Nôtre-Dame,** a dark, quiet place of prayer. Within, you'll find a black ship model, honoring all victims of shipwrecks, under the watchful eye of a 12th-century Black Madonna. (Chapel ☎05 65 33 23 23. Cité open July-Aug. daily 9am-6pm and 6:30-10pm; Sept.-June 8am-6pm. Mass daily 11am.) Under Notre-Dame lies the **Crypte St-Amadour,** where the saint's body rested until a Protestant tried unsuccessfully to set it ablaze during the Wars of Religion. The body finally succumbed to the assailant's axe. What remains is now under wraps next door in the **Musée d'Art Sacré,** which also houses paintings, colorful statues, illuminated manuscripts, and other relics of religious art. (☎05 65 33 23 30. Open June 15-Sept. 15 daily 9:30am-6pm; Apr.-June 14 and Sept. 16-Nov. 11 10am-noon and 2-6pm. 30F/€4.57, students 17F/€2.59.) Adjacent to the chapel, the **Basilique St-Sauveur** is home to a gilt wooden altar. A **tour** takes visitors to the Crypte St-Amadour and the Chapelle St-Michel, which has several large frescoes. (Basilica ☎05 65 33 62 61. Open Apr.-Oct. M-Sa 9am-noon and 2-6pm. 20F/€3.05. 3 French tours per day; in English July-Aug. Call ahead to reserve.)

Next to the Cité is the zigzagging **Chemin de Croix,** which depicts the 14 stations of the cross in vivid relief. The weak-kneed can ride an elevator for 15F/€2.29 round-trip. At the summit is the 14th-century **château,** inhabited by the chaplains of Rocamadour, which is not open to the public. The view from the **ramparts** isn't as good as that from the road, but you'll feel as if you're floating in midair as you walk the walls that hang over the village below. (Open daily 8am-8pm. 15F/€2.29.)

Signs from the upper tourist office point the way (300m) to **La Féerie du Rail,** a singing, dancing miniature world created by one man after 45,000 hours of work, detailed down to the last doorknob. Go early as shows tend to sell out. The 45-minute show is in French with English subtitles. (☎05 65 33 71 06; fax 05 65 33 71 37. June-Aug. 5-8 shows per day; off-season usually 2 per day. Tickets sold July 13-Aug. 22 daily 9am-noon and 2-7pm; Aug. 23-Nov. 11 and Easter-July 12 10am-noon and 2-6pm. 40F/€6.10, children 25F/€3.81.) On the **Rocher des Aigles,** which shares the plateau with the castle, there's a 45-minute show featuring trained birds of prey. (☎05 65 33 65 45. Open July-Aug. daily noon-6pm, 5 shows per day; Apr.-June and Sept. M-Sa 1-5pm, Su 1-6pm, 3 shows per day; Oct.-Nov. M-Sa 2-4pm, Su 2-5pm, one show per day. 40F/€6.10, children 25F/€3.81.) If Rocamadour in July isn't enough of a zoo, walk 200m down the road to the **Forêt des Singes,** 2km from l'Hospitalet, the home of Barbary macaques from the Atlas mountains. (☎05 65 33 62 72. Open July-Aug. daily 10am-7pm; Apr.-June and Sept. 10am-noon and 1-6pm; Oct. M-Sa 1-5pm, Su 10am-noon and 1-5pm; Nov. 1-11 W and Sa-Su 10am-noon and 1-5pm. 40F/€6.10, children 25F/€3.81.)

BRIVE-LA-GAILLARDE

Brive received its nickname, *"la Gaillarde"* (the Bold), when its courageous citizens repelled English forces during the Hundred Years' War. Continuing this tradition, Brive was the first town in France to liberate itself from the German occupation in 1944. Apparently Brive (pop. 53,000) reserves such outbursts for special occasions; to the modern visitor it seems a quiet, unpretentious industrial city, free from the crowds of tourists so common in the area. With its 1970s high-rises, Brive is no postcard star, yet it is certainly not painful to the eyes and makes an inexpensive base for exploring the Quercy region, particularly if you have a car.

TRANSPORTATION

Trains: av. Jean Jaurès. To: **Bordeaux** (2½hr., 2 per day, 140F/€21.35); **Cahors** (1hr., 5 per day, 81F/€12.35); **Limoges** (1hr., 5 per day, 82F/€12.50); **Paris** (4hr., 5 per day, 277F/€43.23); **Sarlat** (1hr., 3 per day, 59F/€9 for train and bus combo via Souillac); and **Toulouse** (2½hr., 8-10 per day, 146F/€22.26). Info office open M-F 9am-9:30pm, Sa 9am-6:30pm.

Buses: office at pl. du 14 Juillet (☎05 55 74 20 13), next to the tourist office. Info desk open M-Sa 8:15am-noon and 2-6:30pm. Buses also stop at the train station and in pl. de Lattre de Tassigny, next to the post office. **STUB** runs within the city; **CFTA** to surrounding areas. To **Sarlat** (1½hr.; 1 per day, 2 on W and Sa; 45F/€6.86) and smaller towns. **Trans-Périgord** buses (☎05 53 09 24 08). To **Sarlat** via Souillac (1½hr., 1 per day, 59F/€9). Buy tickets on board.

Taxis: ☎05 55 24 24 24. 24hr.

Car Rental: Avis, 56 av. Jean Jaurès (☎05 55 24 51 00), has cars from 400F/€60.98 per day. 23+. Open M-F 8am-noon and 2-6:30pm, Sa 9-11:30am and 2:30-5:45pm. **Hertz,** 54 av. Jean Jaurès (☎05 55 24 26 75), from 150F/€22.90 per day with very limited mileage. 21+. Open M-F 8am-noon and 2-6:30pm, Sa 8am-noon and 2-6pm. If closed, call the reservation center at 01 39 38 38 38. **Europcar,** 52 av. Jean Jaurès (☎05 55 74 14 41). 25+. **National Rent-a-Car,** 24bis av. Edouard Herriot (☎05 55 17 22 23; fax 05 55 17 01 68. 24hr. reservation line).

ORIENTATION AND PRACTICAL INFORMATION

Tourist Office: pl. du 14 Juillet (☎05 55 24 08 80; fax 05 55 24 58 24). From the train station, go straight down av. Jean Jaurès to the Collégiale St-Martin, cut diagonally across the courtyard of the Collégiale and veer left onto rue Toulzac, which becomes av. de Paris. The office is 300 feet up on the right through the large parking lot. Open July-Aug. M-Sa 9am-7pm, Su 10am-1pm; Sept.-June M-Sa 9am-noon and 2-6pm.

Money: Banque de France, bd. Gén. Koenig (☎05 55 92 37 00), at pl. de la République, **exchanges currency.** Exchange counter open M-F 9:30am-noon.

Police: 4 bd. Anatole France (☎05 55 17 46 00).

Hospital: bd. Docteur Verlhac (☎05 55 92 60 00).

Internet Access: Ax'tion, 33 bd. Koenig (☎05 55 17 14 15). 0.85F/€0.13 per min., 50F/€7.62 per hr. Open M 11am-7pm, Tu-Sa 9am-7pm. Closed week of Aug. 15.

Post Office: pl. Winston Churchill (☎05 55 18 33 10). **Currency exchange** with no commission on US dollars. Open M-F 8am-6:45pm, Sa 8am-noon. **Postal code:** 19100.

ACCOMMODATIONS AND CAMPING

Auberge de Jeunesse (HI), 56 av. du Maréchal Bugeaud (☎05 55 24 34 00; fax 05 55 84 82 80; ag@wanadoo.fr). From the train station, walk the length of av. Jean Jaurès past the St-Sernin church, crossing the street at the bottom. Take rue de l'Hôtel straight into the old town, turn right just before you reach Eglise St-Martin, and follow rue du Docteur Massenat out again. Take a few steps left on bd. du Salan, and turn right onto av. du Maréchal Bugeaud. The hostel will be on your right. Small, bare, 2- to 4-bunk rooms. A battered patch of grass outside is covered in tables, full of lively twenty-somethings. Breakfast 19F/€2.90. Lunch and dinner 50F/€7.62. Reception M-F 8am-10pm, Sa-Su 9am-noon and 6-10pm. No lockout or curfew. Members 50F/€7.62. Non-members must buy membership: 100F/€15.25, under 26 70F/€10.67. MC/V.

Le Majestic-Voyageurs, 67 av. Jean Jaurès. (☎05 55 24 10 20), to the right of the station. Inexpensive, if slightly musty and creaky rooms. Breakfast 25F/€3.81. Reception until midnight. Closed Dec. 15-Jan. 15. Singles with sink 85-120F/€12.96-18.30; doubles 120F/€18.30; twins with bath 140F/€21.35.

Hôtel-Restaurant l'Andréa, 39 av. Jean Jaurès (☎05 55 74 11 84; fax 05 55 17 25 73). Bright, newly renovated rooms for twice the price of the Majestic. Breakfast 25F/€3.81. Reception 7am-midnight. Doubles with toilet 200F/€30.49, with bath 220F/€33.54; quad 300F/€45.74. MC/V.

Camping Municipal des Iles (☎/fax 05 55 24 34 74), beyond the youth hostel on bd. Michelet, borders the Corrèze river. Reception 7am-9pm. 18F/€2.74 per person, 16F/€2.44 per tent. Electricity 15-33F/€2.29-5.03. **Lac du Causse-Correzien,** 32 quai Baluze (☎08 20 90 19 19; fax 05 55 29 98 77; slacorreze@infonie.fr.), 10km outside of Brive. To get there, head out of the city toward Bordeaux. At the traffic circle on the outskirts of the city, follow the signs to Lac du Causse-Correzien. Woodsy, with a lake and waterskiing, organized sports, ping-pong, and a communal lounge.

FOOD

Brive's **market** occupies pl. du 14 Juillet, just outside the tourist office. The food is dirt cheap and the shopping serious (Tu, Th, and especially Sa 8am-noon). A **Casino supermarket** lies at the intersection of bd. Gén. Koenig and av. de Paris (open M-Sa 9am-7:30pm). The few cheap restaurants are concentrated around **pl. Anatole Briand** and the cathedral side of **pl. Charles de Gaulle.** Family-run **Le Corrèze,** 3 rue Corrèze, in a narrow building in the old town, prepares gourmet regional fare at great prices. Four-course *menus* start at 65F/€9.91 with more extravagant choices up to 130F/€19.82. (☎05 55 24 14 07. Three-course meals 40-65F/€6.10-9.91. Open M-Sa noon-2pm and 7-10pm. MC/V.)

SIGHTS

The 12th-century **Eglise Collégiale St-Martin,** pl. Charles de Gaulle, is named for the iconoclastic Spaniard who introduced Christianity to Brive in the 4th century. Its high crossed arches and pale, thin stone columns mark the center of town. Martin was beheaded after interrupting the feast of Saturnus, loudly proclaiming his faith and smashing idols; his sarcophagus is visible along with reliquaries, polychrome statues, and other tombs in the crypt beneath the nave. The **Musée Labenche,** 26bis bd. Jules Ferry, in a beautiful Renaissance building, spans art, science, and interior decorating in exhibits that include ancient coins, a turn-of-the-century accordion collection, and 17th-century English tapestries. All explanations in French. (☎05 55 92 39 39. Open W-M Apr.-Oct. 10am-6:30pm; Nov.-Mar. 1:30-6pm. 27F/€4.12, students 13.50F/€2.06, under 16 and last Su of the month free.)

From pl. de la République, rue Emile Zola leads to the **Centre National de la Résistance et de la Déportation Edmond Michelet,** 4 rue Champanatier, honoring the Brive native. Take bd. Koenig to the pl. de la République, turn right on rue Emile Zola, then left on rue Hue, and right onto rue Champanatier. Michelet, a Resistance leader, endured the concentration camp at Dachau for more than a year and later became a minister under de Gaulle. Photos of women and children on their way to the gas chambers, heartbreaking last letters to loved ones, and other mementos tell the story of the French Resistance and the Nazi concentration camps. There are no English texts available, but the photographs speak for themselves. (☎05 55 74 06 08; fax 05 55 17 09 44. Open M-Sa 10am-noon and 2-6pm. Free.)

ENTERTAINMENT AND FESTIVALS

After midnight, twenty-somethings fill **La Charette,** 33 av. Ribot, which plays techno and disco. (☎05 55 87 65 73. Cover 60F/€9.15, women free Th-F. Open Tu-Sa until 3am.) **Pub le Watson** livens the otherwise lukewarm rue des Echevins with boisterous beer-drinkers spread among outdoor tables and indoor booths. (☎05 55 17 12 09. Open Tu-Sa 5pm-2am.) **Havane Café,** 9 rue des Cloutiers (pl. de la Jauberlie), offers sangria, salsa, and a chance to practice your Spanish. (Beer 13F/€1.98. Open July-Aug. daily 1pm-2am; Sept.-June 6pm-2am. AmEx/MC/V.)

In mid-August, **Orchestrades Universelles** brings young orchestras, bands, and choirs from all over the world to Brive for a festival of classical, traditional, and jazz music. All performances are free until 9pm on the last evening, when a final gala featuring 750 young musicians echoes across Perigord from l'Espace de Trois Provinces. (☎05 55 92 39 39. Tickets 20-100F/€3.05-15.23.) For three days during the first weekend in November, the pl. du 14 Juillet and Salle Georges Brassens are filled with authors, writers, and books from all over France for the **Foire des Livres** (☎05 55 92 39 39). Four times a year, from December to February, the streets of Brive host **La Fois Grasses,** a market with the delicacies that make Brive famous: *champignons* (mushrooms), truffles, chocolates, and foie gras, among others.

DAYTRIP FROM BRIVE: COLLONGES-LA-ROUGE

Twenty kilometers southeast of Brive is the red-rock village of Collonges-la-Rouge, so exquisite it's hard to believe it's real. Cylindrical towers dangle tangled grapevines, all surrounded by rolling pastures and orchards basking in the afternoon sunlight. There's nothing to do here but look, really. If you're bent on visiting sights, the **Maison de la Sirène** contains a beautiful 18th-century painting of a blonde siren clutching a mirror in one hand and a comb in the other. The 12th-century **church** in the town center received a facelift during the 16th-century religious wars; a Gothic steeple now rises majestically above 3m of thick fortressed walls. Collonges is accessible by bus from Brive (30min., 2 per day, 20F/€3.05).

CAHORS

Cradled in the horseshoe-shaped curve of the Lot river, Cahors is notable as a city in which to find cheap beds and a base for daytrips into the scenic Lot Valley. The town itself, however, is a little too big (pop. 20,000) to take advantage of the natural beauty of the surroundings and a little too small to possess an urban appeal. There is enough in the town to fill a day, but you might feel impatient for the villages, vineyards, cliffs, and caves of the surrounding Lot Valley.

PRACTICAL INFORMATION. **Trains** leave from av. Jean Jaurès for **Brive** (1½hr., 10 per day, 81F/€12.35); **Limoges** (2½hr., 6 per day, 142F/€21.65); **Montauban** (45min., 10 per day, 56F/€8.54); **Paris** (5-7hr., 7 per day, 320F/€48.79); and **Toulouse** (1½hr., 9 per day, 89F/€13.57). (Info booth open M-Th and Sa 6am-8:30pm, F 6am-9:30pm, Su 8am-10:20pm.) **Voyages Belmon Buses,** 2 bd. Gambetta (☎05 65 35 59 30; fax 05 65 35 22 55), runs full-day **bus excursions** to nearby sights daily (100-210F/€15.25-32.03). **Cycles 7,** 417 quai de Regourd, **rents bikes.** (☎05 65 22 66 60. 50F/€7.62 per half-day, 80F/€12.20 per day. Passport deposit. Open Tu-Sa 9am-noon and 2-7pm.) You can **rent cars** near the train station; **Avis** is at 512 av. Jean Jaurès. (☎05 65 30 13 10. Open daily 9am-12:30pm and 2-7pm.)

To get to the **tourist office,** pl. Mitterrand, leave the station, cross the street, and head up rue Anatole France. At the end of the street, turn left onto rue du Président Wilson and then right onto **bd. Gambetta,** the main thoroughfare separating the *vieille ville* from the rest of Cahors. The office will be just around the corner on your right (15min.). The staff finds rooms, gives outdoors advice, and offers **city tours** in French (Tu, Th 5pm, F 10:30am). (☎05 65 53 20 65; fax 05 65 53 20 74. Open July-Aug. M-F 9am-6:30pm, Sa 9am-6pm, Su 10am-noon; Sept.-June daily 9am-noon and 2-6pm.) Do your **laundry** at **GTI Lavarie-Pressing,** 208 rue Clemenceau. Open daily 7am-9pm. **Internet access** is at the **Bureau Information Jeunesse,** in the **Foyer des Jeunes,** 20 rue Frédéric Suisse (see below; 20F/€3.05 per hr.; open M-F 9am-noon and 1-6pm, Sa until 5pm). The **post office,** 257 rue Wilson, has **currency exchange.** (☎05 65 23 35 00. Open M-F 8am-7pm, Sa 8am-noon.) **Postal code:** 46000.

ACCOMMODATIONS AND CAMPING. The hostel in Cahors is amenity-laden, but the rooms are unimpressive. There are a few budget hotels in the *vieille ville.* The **Foyer des Jeunes Travailleurs Frédéric Suisse (HI)** resides at 20 rue Frédéric Suisse. From the train station, ignore the Auberge de Jeunesse sign and bear right onto rue Anatole France, then turn left onto rue Frédéric Suisse (10min.). This 17th-century building contains coed rooms host up to ten guests in a room. Amenities include TV, ping-pong, and laundry. (☎05 65 35 64 71; fax 05 65 35 95 92. Breakfast 20F/€3.05. Lunch or dinner 49-50F/€7.47-7.62. Sheets 20F/€3.05. Reception 24hr. except closed 12:30-2pm; call ahead if arriving late. 8- to 12-bunk dorms 53F/€8.08 for members; singles and doubles 53F/€8.08 per person.)

To get to **Hôtel Aux Perdreaux,** 137 rue de Portail Alban, from the train station, follow rue Joachim to bd. Gambetta. Cross the street and proceed down rue Portail Alban. Perdreaux has airy, linoleum-tiled rooms with showers but shared toilets, some with balconies. (15min.). (☎05 65 35 03 50. Breakfast 25F/€3.81. Reception 8am-10pm. Reserve July-Aug. Singles 150F/€22.90; doubles 170F/€25.92; triples and quads 220F/€33.54. MC/V.) For easy access to the markets (and early morning noise), stay at the **Hôtel de la Paix,** 30 pl. St-Maurice, by the cathedral. Follow the directions to the hostel, but continue on rue Frédéric Suisse through the arch at the end of the street and turn right down rue Caviole. Turn left on rue du Président Wilson, cross bd. Gambetta, and take your second right off rue Maréchal Joffre (15min.). (☎05 65 35 03 40; fax 05 65 35 40 88. Breakfast 30F/€4.57. Shower 10F/€1.53. Reception M-Sa. Singles 150F/€22.90; doubles 160-190F/€24.39-28.97, with shower 200-210F/€30.49-32.02, with bath 220-230F/€33.54-35.06. MC/V.)

Camping "Rivière de Cabessut," rue de la Rivière, is an idyllic three-star campground, near the center of town on the riverbanks. Take city bus #5 from the train station to the "Stade" (8min., 7F/€1.07) and walk the remaining 10 minutes along the riverbank. (☎05 65 30 06 30; fax 05 65 23 99 46. Reception 8am-10pm. Reserve ahead in summer. Open Apr.-Oct. 12F/€1.83 per person, 50F/€7.62 per site.)

FOOD. **Open-air markets** liven up pl. Chapou (W and Sa 8am-noon). On the first and third Saturdays of the month, produce and flowers swamp the *vieille ville*. The more modest **covered market** is just off the square (open Tu-Sa 8am-12:30pm and 3-7pm, Su 9am-noon). Two **supermarkets** compete for customers: **Casino,** pl. Gén. de Gaulle (open M-Sa 9am-12:30pm and 3-7:30pm, Su 9am-12:30pm; Sept.-June closed Su); and **Champion,** pl. Emilien-Imbert, just off bd. Gambetta (open M-Th 9am-12:25pm and 2:30-7:10pm, F-Sa 9am-7:10pm). The new *"bar à vins,"* **Le Dousil,** 124 rue Nationale, at the corner of rue Clemenceau, has an excellent 58F/€8.84 lunch *menu* with salad, bread and hot cheese, wine, and coffee. Local wines go for 16F/€2.44 a glass. (☎05 65 53 19 67. Open Tu-Sa 10am-2am. AmEx/MC/V.)

PERIGORD

SIGHTS AND ENTERTAINMENT. Like many other churches in Périgord, the 12th-century **Cathédrale St-Etienne,** pl. Chapou, is topped by three cupolas of Byzantine inspiration. The northern wall's sculpted 1135 tympanum depicts Christ's ascension. (☎05 65 35 27 80. Open Easter-Oct. daily 8am-7pm; Oct.-Easter 8:30am-6pm. Cloister and chapel 15F/€2.29, pilgrims and students 10F/€1.53.)

With its six massive stone arches and three towering turrets, the monumental 14th-century **Pont Valentré,** credited with repelling invaders during the Siege of Cahors in 1580, remains the city's most impressive sight. Legend holds that its architect, dismayed by construction delays, bargained with the devil to exchange his soul for building materials. When it came time to give the devil his due, the architect slit the throats of all the town's roosters; the unannounced dawn took Beelzebub by surprise, turning him to stone with the first rays of the sun. Today, if you look carefully, you can still see the devil clutching a corner of the central tower. On the far side of the bridge, stone steps precede a 1km path to the viewing platform of **Mont St-Cyr** (20-30min.). The path doesn't stay as steep as it starts out. From the hilltop, there is a spectacular view of Cahors and the picturesque bridge.

Back in town, the grim **Musée de la Résistance, de la Déportation, et de la Libération du Lot,** in the former Bessières barracks in pl. du Gén. de Gaulle, catalogues Cahors' role in France's shames and triumphs during WWII. The reams of newspaper clippings, transcripts of speeches, and photographs are well worth seeing. Each room is dedicated to a local resident who lost his life in the war. (☎05 65 22 14 25. Open daily 2-6pm. Free.) The **Musée Henri Martin,** 792 rue Emile Zola, has a number of small modern art exhibits, including Pointillist interpretations of Cahors by Henri Martin. (☎05 65 30 15 13. Open M and W-F 11am-6pm, Su 2-6pm.)

For one week at the end of July, Cahors taps its toes to American blues during the **Festival de Blues.** Afternoon and early evening blues "appetizers" in coffee shops and bars throughout town are free, as are many of the formal concerts. For big-name concerts, buy tickets in advance. (☎05 65 35 55 55. Available after July 3. Tickets 100-150F/€15.25-22.90. Reduced student tickets available for 50F/€7.62.)

THE LOT VALLEY

The emerald-green Lot Valley snakes its way from Cahors to Cajarc between steep cliffs, sheltering sunflowers and vineyards. Long a favorite of bikers and hikers, the river Lot has recently been opened to boaters for a 70km stretch near Cahors. Though buses pass through the valley on their way from Cahors to Figeac, stops are few and far between, and inevitably involve some hiking—often upwards of 5km. But roads shadow the river, making car rental an option. **Quercyrail,** pl. de la Gare in Cahors (☎05 65 23 94 72), also runs several tourist trains to various sights in the valley on day excursions, including train-and-boat combos (160F/€24.39). The Cahors tourist office sells hiking maps for the entire Lot Valley for 30F/€4.57.

ST-CIRQ-LAPOPIE

> St-Cirq-Lapopie...appeared to me like an impossible rose in the middle of the night. I succumbed to its singular enchantment...I no longer wished to be elsewhere.
>
> —André Breton

Breton's rhetoric aside, many Frenchmen cite the tiny St-Cirq-Lapopie as one of the most beautiful villages in France. Built on a cliff ledge, along streets so steep that the roof of one house begins where its neighbor's garden ends, St-Cirq-Lapopie hangs high over the Lot valley, 36km east of Cahors. The picturesque stone houses, along narrow streets, date from the 17th century. Sadly, the village's renown has spread—you *will* be joined by carloads of tourists. The view from the ruins of **Château Lapopie,** the highest point in town, extends over the river, cliffs, and plains below. The village's cultural center, the **Maison de la Fordonne,** contains a museum chronicling the rocky history of St-Cirq, including a display devoted to Breton. (☎/fax 05 65 31 21 51. Open June-Sept. daily 10:30am-12:30pm and 1:30-7:30pm; Mar. 16-May 10:30am-noon and 2-6pm; Sept.-Nov. 14 2-6pm. 10F/€1.53.)

To get to St-Cirq-Lapopie by car, follow D653 out of Cahors; turn right on to D662 when you reach Vers. **SNCF buses** run past St-Cirq-Lapopie from **Cahors** on the way to Figeac (35min., 5 per day, 30F/€4.57). Ask to be let off at Tour de Faure, Gare. The town is across the bridge and a beautiful 2km walk uphill (30min.). The **tourist office,** pl. de Sombral, in the main square, has a self-guided tour in English, and French walking tours. (July-Aug. 1 per day F-Su; 22F/€3.35). (☎05 65 31 29 06. Open June-Aug. daily 10am-1pm and 2-7pm; Sept.-May 10am-1pm and 2-6pm.)

The best place to stay is the *gîte d'étape* **La Maison de la Fourdonne.** Spotless, pine-paneled 3- to 5-bed rooms all have baths; some have balconies. (☎/fax 05 65 31 21 51. Reservations obligatory July-Aug. Reception same as museum hours. Bring your own sheets or sleepsack. 65F/€9.91 per night.) Between the town and the bus stop is the riverside **Camping de la Plage,** with many opportunities for hiking or kayaking. (☎05 65 30 29 51; fax 05 65 30 23 30; camping.laplage@wanadoo.fr. 30F/€4.57 per person; July-Aug. 30F/€4.57 per site, Sept.-July 20F/€3.05 per site.)

GROTTE DU PECH-MERLE

A few kilometers past the turn-off for St-Cirq-Lapopie on the road from Cahors is the turn-off for D653 and the **Grotte du Pech-Merle,** one of the best-preserved prehistoric caves still open to the public. Unfortunately, the nearest bus stop is 7km away in Caberets. Discovered by local teenagers in 1922, the 4km-long gallery contains paintings from 18,000 to 30,000 years ago, and a natural sideshow of core mineral formations. Bring a jacket—it gets chilly 60m underground. The cave has a daily visitor limit of 700, so arrive early or call ahead to reserve. Admission includes the adjoining museum. English pamphlets are available at the entrance. (☎05 65 31 27 05; museum ☎05 65 31 23 33; fax 05 65 30 21 26. Open Apr.-Oct. daily 9:30am-noon and 1:30-4:45pm. 50min. max. visit. French tours July-Aug. every 30min. 46F/€7.01, children 30F/€4.57.) *Gîtes d'étape* and campgrounds line the route to Pech-Merle. Hitching is said to be easy, though it's not recommended by *Let's Go*.

CHATEAU CENEVIERES

Flotard de Gourdon, a local 16th-century nobleman, traveled to Italy and returned eager to transform his castle. Today, elegant chimneys, classical columns, narrowing staircases that play with perspectival illusions, and a modest "alchemy room" all attest to his success. The Château Cénevières, resting on top of a cliff barely 7km from St-Cirq-Lapopie, also displays a fascinating collection of correspondence from such notables as Henri IV and Talleyrand in the 13th-century **Tour de Gourdon.** The current owners of the château run excellent guided tours. Don't neglect the glorious views of the valley from the back. (☎05 65 31 27 33. Open Easter-Sept. daily 10am-noon and 2-6pm; Oct. 2-5pm. Admission and 1hr. tour 28F/€4.27, children 14F/€2.13.) The most convenient way to reach the château is by the **Quercyrail** excursion from the Cahors train station. (☎05 65 23 94 72. July-Aug. M and Th 1:30-6:30pm. 120F/€18.30, château tour included.)

AQUITAINE, THE PAYS BASQUE, AND GASCONY

In this southwest corner of France, the earth is generous with itself. The vineyards of Aquitaine sprawl into the forest of the Landes, which give way to the strip of sand known as the Côte d'Argent. Further south, the forests recede and the mountains of Gascony begin, shielded from the Atlantic by the coast of the Pays Basque. To enjoy this region, you must taste it—in the pungent wine of its vineyards, the salty sea air of its coast, the fog on its icy mountains. It is after smelling earthy truffles and red wine in Bordeaux, watching the shepherds of St-Jean-Pied-de-Port in the fields, and standing in the gardens of Pau as the orange sun dips behind the dark Pyrenees, that you will know this corner of France has become part of you.

This geographical extremity of the Hexagon has long tugged away from France. Aquitaine remained in English hands from the 12th to 15th century, while Gascony and the Pays Basque were part of independent Basse-Navarre until their ruler inherited the French throne in 1598 as Henri IV. Basque separatists maintain that their *Euzkadi* homeland is independent, and part of neither France nor Spain. You may sympathize with them when attending one of the colorful Basque festivals, with folk dancing accompanied by the sounds of the *ttun ttun* (snare drum) and *tchirulä* (vertical flute).

TRANSPORTATION

You'll quickly find that Bordeaux is the hub from which all its trains begin. To get to the Pays Basque, take the Bordeaux-Dax line through the immense forest of the Landes. If, however, you're heading for the sunlit Côte d'Argent, buses are your best bet. Though Bayonne, Anglet, and Biarritz are so close to one another that they are known together as BAB, transportation is centered around Bayonne, and it's almost always cheaper to base longer journeys here. Local STAB buses conveniently connect the three towns. Getting into and around the central Pyrenees will normally require a change in Lourdes. Lourdes and Pau are regular stops on the Toulouse-Irun line, permitting easy travel to the Pays Basque and Languedoc. SNCF buses run from Lourdes to Cauterets and Luz.

1 **Bordeaux:** Celebrated wines; a stately 18th-century city worth anyone's visit (p. 656)
2 **St-Emilion:** Medieval village with legendary vineyards and châteaux (p. 663)
3 **Arcachon:** Best of the Côte d'Argent; Europe's highest sand dune; huge sandbar (p. 664)
4 **Biarritz:** Gambling; crowded beaches among cliffs; royalty's preferred vacation spot (p. 671)
5 **Anglet:** Surfing capital of France; little more than fun-filled beaches (p. 666)
6 **Bayonne:** Necessary base for Basque country, pretty but unremarkable in itself (p. 667)
7 **St-Jean-de-Luz:** Small, vibrant port; typical Basque town with exceptional seafood (p. 675)
8 **St-Jean-Pied-de-Port:** Pyrenean village, Basque stronghold; lovely ruined fortress (p. 678)
9 **Pau:** Incredible château and extensive gardens; grand views of the distant Pyrenees (p. 680)
10 **Lourdes:** Pilgrimage destination, healing center, and Roman Catholic Disneyworld (p. 682)
11 **Cauterets:** Sleepy little town with access to long-range mountain hikes in the Parc (p. 686)
12 **Parc National des Pyrénées:** Two parks in one: lush French, barren Spanish sides (p. 688)
13 **Luchon:** Cosmopolitan town with tree-lined boulevards and glorified baths (p. 690)

BORDEAUX

Bordeaux's aromatic wines, grown on the bords d'eaux (riverbanks) of the Garonne and Dordogne, are some of the best in the world. But wine is not a new obsession here—without it, Bordeaux (pop. 714,000) might never have been born. The sandy, rocky land around the city was useless until someone, probably an ancient Roman, discovered that the soil was perfect for growing grapes. Today, the city provides a base for tours of the châteaux of legendary nearby vineyards like St-Emilion, Médoc, Sauternes, and Graves, and wine festivals fill its summer months. Note that "château" in Bordeaux means the headquarters of a vineyard, not a castle. Finally, it's position as a university town makes for great nightlife.

TRANSPORTATION

Flights: Airport 11km west of Bordeaux in **Mérignac** (☎05 56 34 50 00.) A shuttle bus connects the airport to the train station and tourist office (☎05 56 34 50 50; 45min.; M-F every 30min. 6am-10:45pm, Sa-Su every 45min. 5:30am-10pm; 37F/€5.64, students 27F/€4.12.) **Air France** (☎08 02 80 28 02) flies to **London** daily.

Trains: Gare St-Jean, rue Charles Domercq (☎05 56 33 11 83). Buy tickets downstairs to: **Lyon** (7-8hr., 4 per day, 331F/€50.47); **Marseille** (6-7hr., 12 per day, 351F/€53.51); **Nantes** (4hr., 4 per day, 224F/€34.15); **Nice** (9-10hr., 5 per day, 436F/€66.47); **Paris** (TGV: 3-4hr., 15-25 per day, 359F/€54.73); **Rennes** (6hr., 1 per day, 290F/€44.21); and **Toulouse** (2-3hr., 11 per day, 179F/€27.29).

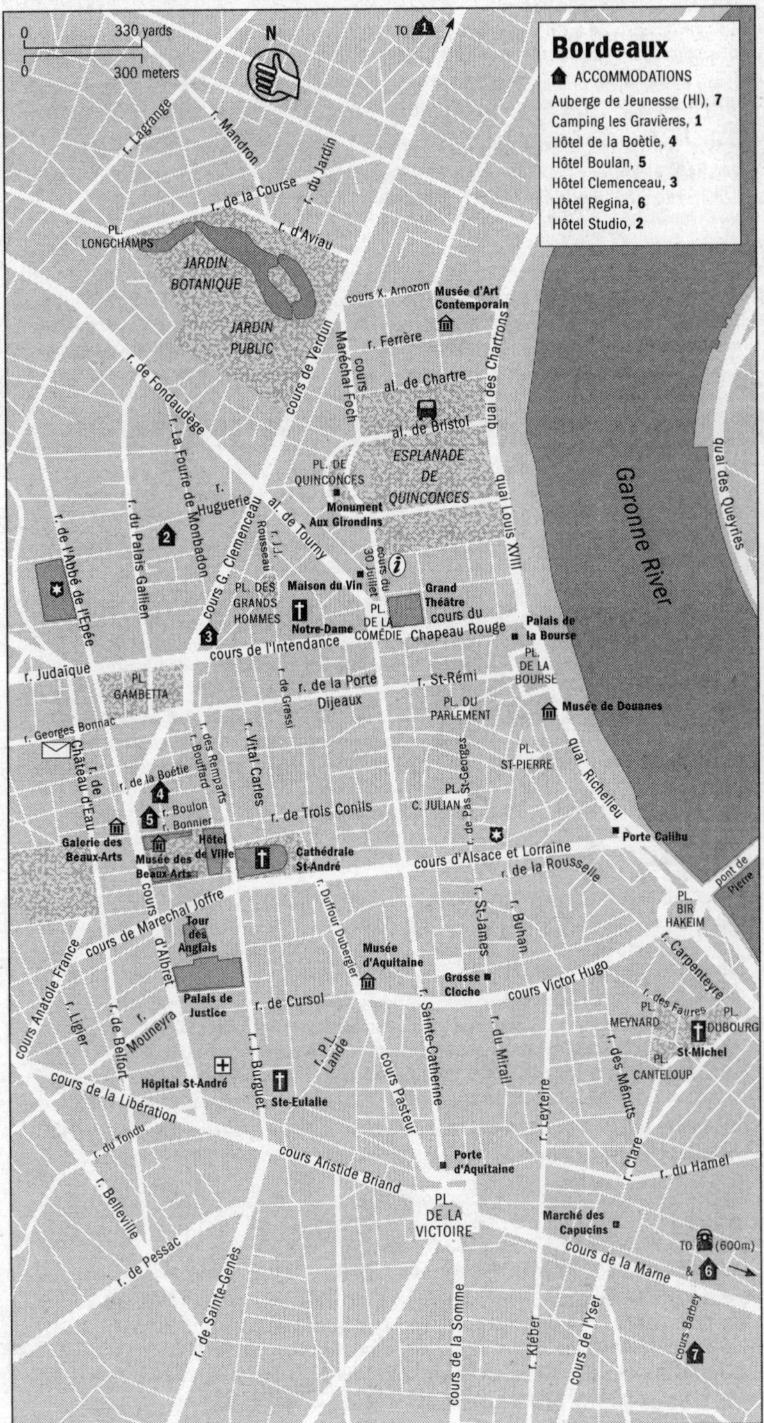
Bordeaux
ACCOMMODATIONS
Auberge de Jeunesse (HI), 7
Camping les Gravières, 1
Hôtel de la Boètie, 4
Hôtel Boulan, 5
Hôtel Clemenceau, 3
Hôtel Regina, 6
Hôtel Studio, 2
0 330 yards
0 300 meters
N
TO 1
JARDIN BOTANIQUE
JARDIN PUBLIC
ESPLANADE DE QUINCONCES
Garonne River
Musée d'Art Contemporain
Monument Aux Girondins
Maison du Vin
Grand Théâtre
Notre-Dame
Palais de la Bourse
Musée de Douanes
Porte Calihu
Galerie des Beaux-Arts
Musée des Beaux-Arts
Hôtel de Ville
Cathédrale St-André
Tour des Anglais
Palais de Justice
Musée d'Aquitaine
Grosse Cloche
St-Michel
Hôpital St-André
Ste-Eulalie
Porte d'Aquitaine
Marché des Capucins
PL. DE LA VICTOIRE
TO (600m) & 6
PL. LONGCHAMPS
PL. DE QUINCONCES
PL. DES GRANDS HOMMES
PL. DE LA COMÉDIE
PL. DE LA BOURSE
PL. GAMBETTA
PL. DU PARLEMENT
PL. ST-PIERRE
PL. C. JULIAN
PL. BIR HAKEIM
PL. MEYNARD
PL. DUBOURG
PL. CANTELOUP
r. Lagrange
r. Mandron
r. de la Course
r. du Jardin
r. d'Aviau
cours X. Arnozon
r. Ferrère
cours Maréchal Foch
cours de Verdun
al. de Chartre
al. de Bristol
quai des Chartrons
quai Louis XVIII
quai des Queyries
r. de Fondaudège
r. La Fourre de Monbadon
r. Huguerie
al. de Tourny
cours G. Clemenceau
r. J.J. Rousseau
cours du 30 Juillet
r. du Palais Gallien
r. de l'Abbé de l'Epée
cours du Chapeau Rouge
cours de l'Intendance
r. Judaïque
r. de Grassi
r. de la Porte Dijeaux
r. St-Rémi
r. Georges Bonnac
r. de Château d'Eau
r. des Remparts
r. Bouffard
r. Vital Carles
r. de la Boëtie
r. Boulan
r. Bonnier
r. de Trois Conils
r. de Pas St-Georges
quai Richelieu
cours d'Alsace et Lorraine
r. de la Rousselle
pont de Pierre
cours de Marechal Joffre
cours d'Albret
r. Duffour Dubergier
r. St-James
r. Buhan
r. Carpenteyre
r. des Faures
cours Victor Hugo
cours Anatole France
r. Ligier
r. de Belfort
r. Mouneyra
r. de Cursol
r. J. Burguet
r. P. L. Lande
cours Pasteur
r. Sainte-Catherine
r. du Mirail
r. des Ménuts
r. Leyteire
r. Clare
r. du Hamel
cours de la Libération
r. du Tondu
cours Aristide Briand
r. Belleville
r. de Pessac
r. de Sainte-Genès
cours de la Somme
r. Kléber
cours de l'Yser
cours de la Marne
cours Barbey

AQUITAINE

Local Transportation: The **CGFTE bus system** (☎05 57 57 88 88) crosses the city and suburbs. Maps at the train station and in info offices at 4 rue Georges Bonnac and pl. Jean-Jaurès. Open M-Sa 9am-7pm. The *Carte Bordeaux Découverte* allows **unlimited city bus use** (1 day 23F/€3.51, 3 days 54F/€8.23); otherwise, fare is 7.50F/€1.14.

Taxis: Aquitaine Taxi Radio (☎05 56 86 80 30). About 100F/€15.25 to the airport.

Car Rental: Europcar, 35 rue Charles Domercq (☎05 56 31 20 30; fax 05 56 31 26 94), facing the train station. From 438F/€66.78 per weekend. Minimum age 21. Open M-F 7am-10pm, Sa 7am-8pm, Su 10am-11:30pm. AmEx/MC/V.

Bike Rental: Free at the tourist office (June-Sept. only, plus the 1st Su of each month at pl. des Quinconces). Call 05 56 10 20 30 for info. **Bord'eaux Vélos Loisir,** quai Louis XVIII, facing the pl. des Quinconces (☎05 56 44 77 31), rents bikes, in-line skates, and "talking bikes" that give directions to major landmarks in 4 languages. Bikes and in-line skates 50F/€7.62 per half day, 90F/€13.72 per day. Open May-Oct. daily 9:30am-8pm, Nov.-Apr. 2:30-6:30pm.

ORIENTATION AND PRACTICAL INFORMATION

It takes about 30 minutes to walk from the train station to the *centre ville*, the oldest and most picturesque part of town. Follow **cours de la Marne** from the station. This busy thoroughfare will take you past the **Marché des Capucins** on your right and into the **pl. de la Victoire,** with the huge stone arch of the **porte d'Aquitaine** towering above the surrounding bars and clubs that serve crowds of students coming from the nearby **Domaine Universitaire** every night. From here, turn right under the arch of the *porte* onto the pedestrian **rue Sainte Catherine.** The patterned brick sidewalks bring you into *vieux Bordeaux*, the hub of the city, where shops and restaurants draw tourists and locals alike. After about 10 to 15 minutes, you'll cross the wide **cours de l'Intendance** and enter the **pl. Comédie** as the street you're on becomes the **cours du 30 juillet.** The **tourist office** is ahead on the right, just beyond the Grand Théâtre. The **bus depot** is right in front of the station. Both buses #7 and 8 run from the train station to pl. Gambetta (dir: "Grand Théâtre;" every 10min., less frequently after 10pm, last bus 11:30pm; 7.50F/€1.14). **Pl. Gambetta,** a splash of greenery with park benches, lawns, and trees in the middle of the old town, is a good landmark and a place to catch the #7 or 8 bus back to the train station. Bordeaux is a big city; guard yourself and your wallet, especially at night.

Tourist Office: 12 cours du 30 juillet (☎05 56 00 66 00; fax 05 56 00 66 01; www.bordeaux-tourisme.com). Well-stocked with maps and brochures. Open May-Oct. M-Sa 9am-7pm, Su 9:30am-6:30pm; Nov.-Apr. M-F 9am-6:30pm, Su 9:45am-4:30pm. **Branch** at the train station (☎05 56 50 44 70). Open Nov.-Apr. M-F 9:30am-12:30pm and 2-6pm; May-Oct. M-Sa 9am-noon and 1-6pm, Su 10am-noon and 1-3pm.

Tours: Several in French and English are offered by the **tourist office. City tours:** By foot, Apr. 15-Nov. 15 daily except W and Sa. Tours given Nov. 16-Apr. 14 daily at 10am. Also at 3pm July 15-Aug. 31. 40F/€6.10, students 35F/€5.34. Bus tours Apr. 15-Nov. 15 W and Sa at 10am. 60F/€9.15, students 55F/€8.34.

Local vineyards: May-Oct. half-day bus tour leaves daily 1:30pm; Nov. 16-Apr. 14 W and Sa only. Daily Apr. 15-Nov. 15. 160F/€24.39, students and seniors 140F/€21.35.

Budget Travel: Wasteels, 13 pl. de Casablanca (☎08 03 88 70 32; fax 05 56 31 91 48), across the street from the station, sells BIJ tickets and books charter flights. Open M-F 9am-noon and 2-7pm, Sa 9am-1pm and 2-6pm. MC/V.

Consulate: UK, 353 bd. du Président Wilson (☎05 57 22 21 10, emergency ☎06 60 28 21 10; fax 05 56 08 33 12). Open M-F 9am-12:30pm and 2:30-5pm.

American Express: 14 cours de l'Intendance (☎05 56 00 63 36). Open M-F 8:45am-noon and 1:30-5:30pm. 24hr. refund assistance (☎08 00 90 86 00).

Youth Center: Centre d'Information Jeunesse d'Aquitaine, 5 rue Duffour Dubergier (☎05 56 56 00 56). Information about activities and jobs. Open M-F 9am-6pm.

Laundromat: 203 cours de la Marne. Also at 27 rue de la Boétie and at 43 cours de la Libération. All open daily 7am-9pm.

Police: 87 rue de l'Abbé de l'Epée/rue Castéja (☎05 56 99 77 77). Branch at station.

Hospital: 1 rue Jean Burguet (☎05 56 79 56 79).

Internet Access: France Télécom, 2 rue Château d'Eau (☎08 00 35 23 19). Close to pl. Gambetta. Walk in the opposite direction from the river on rue Judaique. 30F/€4.57 per hr., students 20F/€3.05. Open M-F noon-7pm. **Netzone,** 209 rue Ste-Catherine (☎05 57 59 01 25), near pl. de la Victoire. 35F/€5.34 per hr., students 30F/€4.57. Open M-Sa 10am-8pm, Su 2-7pm.

Post Office: 52 rue Georges Bonnac (☎05 57 78 88 88), off pl. Gambetta. **Currency exchange.** Open M-F 8am-7pm, Sa 8am-noon. **Postal code:** 33065.

ACCOMMODATIONS AND CAMPING

Bordeaux's main hostel has recently reopened after a long renovation. In a somewhat unsavory area near the train station, it's convenient for those getting off a train with a heavy backpack, but a long walk from the town center. Private rooms in Bordeaux are numerous, but often expensive. A few deals can be found on the side streets around the pl. Gambetta and the cours d'Albret, but be forewarned—these fill fast. Reserve at least a few days to a week in advance in summer.

AQUITAINE

Hôtel Studio, 26 rue Huguerie (☎05 56 48 00 14; fax 05 56 81 25 71; studio@hotel-bordeaux.com), is a backpacker favorite for good reason. Walk 1 block down rue Clemenceau from pl. Gambetta, and half a block left on rue Huguerie. The clean, sunny rooms have showers, telephones and cable TV, at the lowest prices around. Reserve early. Rooms are a little dark on the lower floors, but with all the perks and the comfortable beds, you might not even notice. Breakfast 20F/€3.05. Singles with shower or bath 98F/€14.94, larger bed 135F/€20.58; doubles with bath 120F/€18.30, 160F/€24.39; triples 180F/€27.44. Quads and quints 200-250F/€30.49-38.12.

Hôtel Boulan, 22 rue Boulan (☎05 56 52 23 62; fax 05 56 44 91 65). Take bus #7 or 8 from the train station to cours d'Albret. It's right around the corner from the Musée des Beaux Arts. 18 rooms with hardwood floors and cable TVs; some with balconies overlooking quiet rue Boulan. Breakfast 20F/€3.05. Singles 110F/€16.77, with shower 130F/€19.82; doubles 130F/€19.82, 150F/€22.90. MC/V.

Auberge de Jeunesse (HI), 22 cours Barbey (☎05 56 33 00 70; fax 05 56 33 00 71). A smaller branch has opened at 208 cours de l'Argonne (☎05 56 94 51 66; fax 05 56 94 51 66). With the doors newly open after renovation, both hostels are still working out the kinks. But they compensate for the constantly slamming doors and difficult-to-use key system with spotless rooms and a friendly staff. The main one, near the station, is in a neighborhood filled with seedy characters who make the 30min. walk from the city center feel dangerous at night. Breakfast 15F/€2.29. Sheets included. Curfew 3am. Dorms 80F/€12.20. Non-members can pay an extra 10F/€1.53 to stay 1 night.

Hôtel de la Boétie, 4 rue de la Boétie (☎05 56 81 76 68; fax 05 56 81 24 72). Check-in is at Hôtel Bristol around the corner, 4 rue Bouffard. Run by the same family as Hôtel Studio, La Boétie offers similar amenities. Each room comes with shower, cable TV, and telephone. One single 120F/€18.30; other singles 135F/€20.58; doubles 135F/€20.58, 160F/€24.39 for separated beds. Larger rooms available as well.

Hôtel Clemenceau, 4 cours Georges Clemenceau (☎05 56 52 98 98; fax 05 56 81 24 91). In the heart of old Bordeaux, barely 20m from where buses #7 and 8 stop in pl. Gambetta. This 2-star hotel is a bit expensive, but has sizable rooms, views of pl. Gambetta, A/C, and small refrigerators. Breakfast 25F/€3.81, 35F/€5.34 in bed. Reception until 1am; ask for the code to get in later. Su-Th singles 170F/€25.92, doubles 200-230F/€30.49-35.07; F-Sa singles 150F/€22.90, doubles 170F/€25.92.

Hôtel Regina, 34 rue Charles Domercq (☎05 56 91 66 07), just opposite the train station. Perfect for late arrivals and those just passing through, with clean and new rooms. Noise from the street and the station may bother some. Singles with shower 145F/€22.11, with bath 185-205F/€28.21-31.25; doubles 185F/€28.21, with bath 205-225F/€31.25-34.30.

Campsite: Camping les Gravières, 35 av. Mirieu de Labarre in Villeneuve d'Ornon (☎05 56 87 00 36). Take the infrequent bus B (dir: "Courrégean," 5-6 per day, 30min.) from pl. de la Victoire to the end. By car, take Exit 20 ("Begles") toward Courrégean from Rocade A630. A large and pretty campsite, but very difficult to reach and far away from any worthwhile sights. Only worth the stay if you can't afford to do otherwise–and even then, reconsider. 22F/€3.35 per tent, 19F/€2.90 per person, children 12F/€1.83. Tent and car 30F/€4.57. Open all year. MC/V.

FOOD

Center of the self-proclaimed "région de bien manger et de bien vivre" (region of fine eating and living), Bordeaux takes its food as seriously as its wine. Local specialties include oysters, *foie gras*, and beef braised in wine sauce. Most restaurants are scattered around the **rue St-Rémi** and **pl. St-Pierre.** Here, candlelit tables spill out of restaurants, filling the alleyways that converge on **pl. du Parlement.** For Middle Eastern specialties, try the area around **St-Michel.** Most *Bordelais* don't eat before 9pm in the summer, and restaurants usually serve until 11pm or midnight.

There's fruit at the **market** in pl. des Grands Hommes (open M-Sa 7am-7pm), fish at the **marché des capucins,** and organic food in the **marché biologique** on pl. St-Pierre (open Th 5am-5pm). For prepackaged goods, try the enormous **Auchan supermarket,** near the Maison des Etudiantes at the huge Centre Meriadeck on rue Claude Bonnier. (☎05 56 99 59 00. Open M-Sa 8:30am-10pm.)

Restaurant Chez le Chef, 57 rue Hugherie (☎05 56 51 92 71). This beautifully formal restaurant seats guests in a hidden garden. The traditional dishes are some of the best Bordeaux has to offer–fresh salmon with basil, cassoulet, duck preserve–and the prices are lower than many of Bordeaux's *sandwicheries*. Price *formules* begin at 60F/€9.15. Dress formally to fit in with the other diners.

La Casuccia, 49 rue St-Rémi (☎05 56 51 17 70). Light, romantic restaurant, perfect for an intimate candle-lit *tête-a-tête* or an outing with friends. Filling *menus* start at 65F/€9.91. Open for lunch daily at 11:30am, 7pm-midnight for dinner. MC/V.

Le Marhaba, 27 rue des Faures (☎05 57 59 10 63). The nicest of the cafés in the area around St-Michel, Le Marhaba is both a restaurant and a *salon de thé*. Algerian specialties such as couscous and *merguez* (spiced beef sausage). Many people just come for the *thé à la menthe*, a sweet warm mint tea served in small decorated glasses. Prices for a full meal start as low as 30F/€4.57.

SIGHTS

Admission to all museums in Bordeaux is free on the first Su of every month.

CATHEDRALE ST-ANDRE. Nearly 900 years after its consecration by Pope Urban II, this building is still the centerpiece of Gothic Bordeaux. Built between the 11th and 16th centuries, and heavily renovated in the 19th century. On the facade of the church are statues of angels and apostles—many apparently deranged or deformed—surrounding reliefs from the life of Christ. Its bell-tower, the **Tour Pey-Berland,** juts 50m into the sky, with a large statue of Notre-Dame d'Aquitaine on top for good measure. The tower was placed 15m away from the cathedral, Italian-style, because its masons feared that the vibrations of the massive bells might make the cathedral collapse. Climb the 229 spiraling steps for the view of your life. *(Pl. Pey-Berland. ☎05 56 52 68 10. Cathedral open Apr.-Oct. daily 7:30-11:30am and 2-6:30pm; Nov.-Mar. M-F same hours. In summer, free organ recital every other Tu at 6:30pm. Belltower open July-Aug. daily 10am-7pm; Sept. and Apr.-June 10am-6pm; Oct.-Mar. 10am-5pm. 25F/€3.81, under 25 and seniors 15F/€2.29.)*

ST-MICHEL. You can see even more of the world sitting in one of the many cafés that surround the church or browsing the different markets (open 9am-1pm daily) that fill the courtyard each morning. As one inhabitant of the area describes the area, "here we have a bit of Portugal, a bit of Morocco, a bit of Algeria and bit of Aquitaine." This is the most Bohemian district of Bordeaux, the place where students hang out and sip mint tea with their friends. *(Open June-Sept. 15F/€2.29.)*

PLACE DE LA BOURSE. The construction of the pl. de la Bourse, with its pillars and pilasters, fountain and wrought-iron facades, was the most important step in the 18th-century modernization of Bordeaux overseen by royal agents under Louis XV. The town's grand buildings, squares, gardens, and promenades spread outward from this spot. The building on the left houses the surprisingly interesting **Musée National des Douanes,** or National Customs Museum. Come here to feed your obsession with customs, or to awaken the passion for excise taxation that you never knew you had. *(☎05 56 48 82 82. Open Apr.-Sept. daily 10am-noon and 1-6pm; Oct.-Mar. M-Sa 10am-noon and 1-5pm. 20F/€3.05, students and seniors 10F/€1.53.)*

MONUMENT AUX GIRONDINS. Several avenues in Bordeaux converge on pl. de Quinconces, at whose center is a much-adorned pole topped by a stone Lady Liberty. The monument commemorates a group of revolutionary leaders from towns bordering the Gironde river. The Girondins, as they were called, had the misfortune of being far more moderate than the deranged Montagnards, who ended up beheading them. Before losing their heads though, they produced the Revolution's most important document, the **Declaration of the Rights of Man** (see p. 8); that event is commemorated in the bicentennial date inscribed on the monument's side (1989). The hundred-year-old monument is laden with symbolism: the three women on the side facing town represent Bordeaux, the Dordogne, and the Garonne, and empty pedestals facing the river remind us of the murdered Girondins—most famously poor Pierre Vergniaud, who argued so eloquently for the King's life. The rest of the figures are mostly of the Virtue-trampling-Vice sort.

GRAND THEATRE. The colonnaded neoclassical facade of this 18th-century opera house conceals a breathtaking interior. It's probably the most strictly classical opera house in the world, and one of the most impressive. Attend an opera, concert, or play, or take a daytime tour. *(On pl. de la Comédie. Tickets ☎05 56 00 85 95. Tours through tourist office ☎05 56 00 66 00. 30F/€4.57, students 20F/€3.05.)*

MUSEE DES BEAUX ARTS. This small, unimpressive museum was originally used to display Napoleon's captured war booty; later additions, acquired through purchase rather than invasion, are mostly 17th- through 19th-century works by European artists, including Titian, Rubens, and Van Dyck. *(20 cours d'Albret, near the cathedral. ☎05 56 10 20 56. Open W-Su 11am-6pm. 25F/€3.81, students free.)*

VINORAMA DE BORDEAUX. Although this is the best of Bordeaux's wine museums, it is hardly worth the trek from the city center to the Chartron district (where most Bordeaux wine traders were once based). Visitors carry around a tape recorder with the voice of Bacchus narrating the history of mannequins involved in the wine-making process. The tour ends with a brief wine-tasting session, including samples of wine made from an ancient Roman recipe, a wine from around 1850, and a modern wine. *(12 cours du Médoc. Near the river just off the quai des Chartrons. ☎05 56 39 39 20. Open June-Sept. Tu-Sa 10:30am-12:30pm and 2:30-6:30pm, Su 2-6:30pm; Oct.-May Tu-F 2-6:30pm, Sa 10:30am-12:30pm and 2:30-6:30pm. 35F/€5.34, children 15F/€2.29.)*

OTHER SIGHTS. The grim, sooty Entrepôt Laine houses Bordeaux's **contemporary art museum** and, upstairs, its **museum of architecture.** Exhibits in both rotate and are sometimes worth seeing; pick up a copy of *Dans les Musées de Bordeaux* at the tourist office or any museum to find out what's on exhibition. *(7 rue Ferrère, two blocks from cours de Maréchal Foch. ☎05 56 00 81 50. Both open Tu-Su 11am-6pm, W 11am-8pm. 30F/€4.57, students 20F/€3.05, seniors free.)* The **Musée d'Aquitaine** is a historic and ethnographic display of the classical and folk art of Aquitaine from prehistory to the present. Don't miss the giant Gothic rose window near the end of the exhibit. *(20 cours Pasteur. ☎05 56 01 51 00. Open daily 11am-6pm. Booklet and video presentations in English. 20F/€3.05.)* Near the **pont de Pierre,** the city's oldest bridge, stands the 15th-century slate-roofed **Porte de Cailhau.** A few blocks down cours Victor Hugo on rue St-James is the imposing 16th-century **Grosse Cloche.** Two angels preside over the Big Clock, whose golden hands still keep good time.

WHY WINE IS GOOD FOR YOUR HEART A marathon *à la bordelaise* is enough to make anyone feel like hitting the pavement. Runners here quaff wine from crystal glasses to quench their thirst, indulge in an oyster bar at mile 24, and snack on buffets of meats and cheeses *en route*. For many participants, the excitement is not so much in crossing the finish line as in actually finding it.

ENTERTAINMENT

For an overview of nightlife, grab a free copy of *Clubs and Concerts* at the tourist office, or purchase the biweekly magazine *Bordeaux Plus* (2F/€0.3) at any magazine stand. **Pl. de la Victoire** and **pl. Gambetta** are mobbed by 70,000 students during the school year, and continue to serve as the hotspots for entertainment during the summer. **St-Michel** has a more mellow atmosphere, with locals gathering at the café tables around 6pm and often staying until midnight. Closer to the train station, the pubs and dance clubs in **quai Ste-Croix** and **quai de Paludate** are always packed with leather-clad revelers. After the clubs close, you can eat and drink at **pl. Marché des Capucins** and hang out with early-morning market workers. Bordeaux has—after Paris—one of the best-developed gay scenes in France.

Le Plana, 22 pl. de la Victoire (☎05 56 91 73 23). The hottest bar around pl. de la Victoire. Tables outside and inside this swank nightspot are occupied every night of the week by locals and foreigners of all ages. On Saturdays, current hits spun by a DJ set many dancing. Free live jazz concerts begin at 10:30pm Su-M. Open daily 7pm-2am.

O'Ventilo, 34 cours de l'Argonne (☎05 56 92 33 98), near pl. de la Victoire. Look for the inverted triangles on the doors of this funky "Elektronic café." Young crowd arrives after 11pm most nights, and most rave parties get their second wind here in the early morning hours. Live DJs Th-Sa. Open Tu-Sa 9pm-2am; reopens at 5am on weekends.

BHV (Bar de l'Hôtel de Ville), 4 rue de l'Hôtel de Ville (☎05 56 44 05 08), across from the Hôtel de Ville. Flashing lights spin off the mirrors in this small gay bar, filled most nights of the week. Drag shows every other Su Sept.-June. Open daily 6pm-2am.

Chica Cafe, 3 rue Duffour Dubergier (☎05 56 01 12 08), in the shadow of the cathedral. A friendly, boisterous bar and dance venue where you can mingle with young locals. Open M-Sa 9pm-2am.

WINERIES AND VINEYARDS

A HISTORY OF CLARET

Bordeaux's reputation for wine is the product of 20 centuries of shameless (but justified) self-promotion. The wines were of variable color and quality until Louis IX snatched the port of La Rochelle from the English in 1226. Not to be deprived of his claret (as the English call red Bordeaux wine), King Henry II bestowed generous shipping rights on English-ruled Bordeaux, making it England's wine cellar. At first the citizens simply shipped out wines produced further up the river Garonne, but the money from this trade sparked a local planting mania. Soon Bordeaux's port began refusing to accommodate other wines. In the 18th century, the vineyards spread from the Médoc region to areas south of the Dordogne, including St-Emilion. Today, the wines of Bordeaux flow into 500 million bottles a year.

TASTING IN BORDEAUX

If you're just in town for a day or two and are desperate for the full wine experience, head to the **Maison du Vin/CIVB,** 1 cours du 30 juillet, where there's a wine bar, professionals on hand to tell you what you're drinking, and even a tasting course. The two-hour "Initiation to Wine Tasting" course, available in English, teaches the gentle art of oenophilia through comparative tasting; you'll leave confident enough to waltz into any four-star restaurant. The staff can give you a list of local châteaux and recommend vineyards. Ask about a 15-minute video on Bordeaux wines. (☎05 56 00 22 66; fax 05 56 00 22 82; www. vins-bordeaux.fr. Open M-Th 8:30am-6pm, F 8:30am-5:30pm. Wine tasting course offered twice weekly, 100F/€15.25.) Locals buy their wine at **Vinothèque,** 8 cours du 30 juillet (☎05 56 52 32 05; open M-Sa 9:15am-7:30pm), and classy **L'Intendant,** 2 allées de Tourny (☎05 56 48 01 29; open M-Sa 10am-7:30pm).

VISITING THE CHATEAUX

It's easiest to explore the area with a car, but some vineyards are accessible by train—St-Emilion and Pauillac in particular make good daytrips—and the tourist office gives afternoon **tours.** (Apr. 15-Nov. 15 daily 1:30pm, Nov. 16-Apr. 14, W and Sa 1:30pm. Tours W and Su to St-Emilion, Th and Sa to Médoc, F to Graves and Sauternes. 160F/€24.39, students and seniors 140F/€21.35.) Bring a good map if you're biking or walking, because local roads are hard to navigate. The owners of the châteaux are usually happy to give private tours, but call ahead or ask the tourist office to call for you. Finally, all of the châteaux offer direct sales.

ST-EMILION. The viticulturists of St-Emilion, just 35km northeast of Bordeaux, have been refining their technique since Roman times; theirs is, not surprisingly, among the best appellations in France. Today they gently crush 12,850 acres of grapes to produce 23 million liters of wine annually. Quite apart from its wine, the medieval village's stone buildings, twisting narrow streets, and café-lined *places* are a pleasure to visit. Beneath the streets there is another part of St-Emilion, accessible only through a tour from the **tourist office** (see below). The **Eglise Monolithe,** carved by Benedictine monks over three centuries, is the largest subterranean church in Europe. The underground **catacombs** nearby served as the burial place for a series of Augustine monks when the cemetery became too small. The monks were lowered by rope through a conduit into the natural underground grotto. The tour also stops at the hermitage of **St-Emilion** himself, a Benedictine monk originally from Brittany, who left for undeveloped Aquitaine when his miracles brought him unwanted celebrity status.

The **Maison du Vin de St-Emilion,** pl. Pierre Meyrat, offers a one-hour course on local wines. Their wine shop has wholesale prices and a free exhibit. (☎05 57 55 50 55. Open Mar.-July and Sept.-Nov. M-Sa 10am-12:30pm and 2-6:30pm, Su 10am-12:30pm and 2:30-6:30pm; Aug. daily 10am-7pm; Dec.-Feb. daily 10am-12:30pm and 2:30-6pm. Wine course offered mid-July to mid-Sept. 11am; 110F/€16.77.)

The **tourist office,** near the church tower at pl. des Créneaux, gives out the *Grandes Heures de St-Emilion*, a list of **classical concerts** and **wine tastings** hosted by nearby châteaux. (☎05 57 55 28 28; fax 05 57 55 28 29. Open July-Aug. daily 9:30am-7pm; Sept.-Oct. and Apr.-June 9:30am-12:30pm and 1:45-6:30pm; Nov.-Mar. 9:30am-12:30pm and 1:45-6pm.) As well as renting **bikes** (60F/€9.15 per half-day, 90F/€13.72 per day), they also offer tours in English to local châteaux (July-Aug. at 2 and 4:15pm; June and 1st week of Sept. 3pm.; 51F/€7.78). **Trains** come here from Bordeaux (30min., 2 per day, 66F/€10.06). Plan on spending the whole day; trains arrive in the morning and don't leave until 6:30pm. It's the second stop from Bordeaux and the tiny station is poorly marked—don't miss it! To get to the tourist office, take a right on the main road from the station; when you reach town, head straight up rue de la Porte Bouqueyre toward the tower (2km).

MEDOC, GRAVES, SAUTERNES. Though St-Emilion is probably the best vineyard for a first visit—it's accessible and attached to a beautiful village—there are other worthwhile regions near Bordeaux. The **Médoc** region lies north of Bordeaux, between the Gironde estuary and the ocean—its name comes from the Latin *medio-acquae*, meaning "between the waters." This area is home to some of the world's most famous red wines: Lafite-Rothschild, Latour, Margaux, Haut-Brion, and Mouton-Rothschild. Book an organized tour, or take the Citram bus from the depot to Pauillac, the most renowned village of the region. The **tourist office** can rent bikes, suggest routes, and help make reservations to visit local châteaux. (☎05 56 59 03 08; fax 05 56 59 23 38. Open July 1-Sept. 15 9am-7pm; Sept. 16-June 30 9:30am-12:30pm and 2-6:30pm.)

ROTTING TO PERFECTION A climatic quirk gives Sauternes wines their particular taste. When the weather cools here in September, a morning fog rises from the confluence of the Ciron and Garonne rivers, allowing a fungus—*Botrytis Cinerea* or "Noble Rot"—to breed on the grapes. Water evaporates as the grapes shrivel up, leaving a high concentration of sugar and a rich, complex taste. Each grape is picked only when it has been well covered in "rot"; the selection requires several careful harvests. Unlike other regional whites, these sweet wines take many years to reach their peak, and are only cultivated during years when the climate cooperates; vineyards here are famous for rejecting entire vintages that they consider below their standards.

South of the Garonne is the **Graves** region, named for its gravelly topsoil. Graves' dry and semisweet wines were the drink of choice in the time of Eleanor of Aquitaine, before the reds of Médoc overtook them 300 years ago. In the southeastern end of Graves is the **Sauternes** region, celebrated for its sweet white wines.

ARCACHON

Arcachon is one of the best in a chain of beach towns on the Côte d'Argent (Silver Coast), that thin strip of sand which runs along 200km of France's southern Atlantic seaboard. It's known in particular for two silicon landmarks: the **Dune du Pyla,** Europe's highest sand dune, even by those who only make Arcachon a daytrip from nearby Bordeaux, and the **Banc d'Arguin,** a 1000-acre sand bar. Arcachon is a resort town at heart, full of vacationing families in summer and inhabited during the off-season only by senior citizens and despondent hotel owners. When it's running, though, the town is great fun; easygoing, unpretentious, and unusually well-endowed with natural beauty.

ORIENTATION AND PRACTICAL INFORMATION. Trains, pl. Roosevelt, go only to **Bordeaux** (45min.-1hr.; 10-20 per day; 54F/€8.23, 25 and under 41F/€6.25. Last train M-Sa 9:05pm, Su and holidays 9:50pm.) **City bus** #611 runs from a stop in front of the train station to Pyla-sur-Mer where the Dune is (☎15 57 72 45 00; 20 min.; July-Aug. 15 per day, Sept.-June 2 per day; 17F/€2.59.) Sometimes the bus will not stop at Pyla; the Haitza stop is only a 10-minute walk from the dune. Walk uphill between the two hotels and take the wooden stairway down to the sea when you reach the three-star hotel at the bend in the road. **Locabeach 33,** 326 bd. de la Plage, rents two-wheeled transportation. (☎05 56 83 39 64. Open July-Sept. Tu-Sa 9am-midnight. Bikes 40-60F/€6.10-9.15 per half-day, 60-80F/€9.15-12.20 per day; 800-1000F/€121.97-152.46 or passport deposit. Scooters and motorcycles 150F/€22.90 per day. MC/V.)

Arcachon's **tourist office,** pl. Roosevelt, is about three blocks left of the station. (☎05 57 52 97 97; fax 05 57 52 97 77; tourisme@arcachon.com. Open Oct.-May M-Sa 9am-12:30pm and 2-6pm, Apr.-May Su 9am-1pm also.) There's an **annex** on the corner of bd. Mestrezat and rue des Pêcheries. (Open July-Aug. daily 9am-7pm.) Wash beach towels at the **laundromat** on the corner of bd. Général Leclerc and rue Molière. The **police** (☎05 57 72 29 30) are on pl. de Verdun. The **hospital** (☎05 57 52 90 00) is on allée du Dr. Jean Hameau. The **post office,** 1 pl. Franklin Roosevelt, opposite the tourist office, has **currency exchange** and a **Western Union** desk. (☎05 57 52 53 80. Open July-Aug. M-F 8:30am-7pm, Sa 8:30am-noon; Sept.-June M-F 8:30am-6:15pm, Su 8:30am-noon.) **Postal code:** 33120.

ACCOMMODATIONS. Rooms here start at 240F/€36.59 for a double in the summer; even in the off-season, the prices begin at 175F/€26.68. A mellow summer hostel, camping, or cheap bunks in Bordeaux are your best options. **The Auberge de Jeunesse (HI),** 87 av. de Bordeaux, is in Cap-Ferrat. To get there, take a ferry from Arcachon's Jetée Thiers on av. Gambetta. (☎05 56 54 60 32. At least one per hour. 35F/€5.34, round-trip 60F/€9.15.) From the Cap-Ferrat ferry pier, take av. de l'Océan and continue as it becomes rue des Bouvreuils after the roundabout (15min.). Turn left onto av. de Bordeaux, and the hostel will be on your right after a few minutes. (☎05 56 60 64 62. **HI members only.** Reception 8am-1pm and 6-9pm. 45F/€6.86. Open July-Aug. only.) In Arcachon, the very social **Camping Club d'Arcachon,** 5 allée de la Galaxie, 2km from the beach, has a two-tiered pool, billiards, and a bar-restaurant. (☎05 56 83 24 15; fax 05 57 52 28 51. Check-out noon. Site fees for 1-3 people and car: Aug. 1-20 140F/€21.35; July 1-13 and Aug. 21-31 140F/€21.35; July 13-31 135F/€20.58; June and Sept. 80F/€12.20; May and Oct. 70F/€10.67; Nov.-Mar. 60F/€9.15. Extra person 20-30F/€3.05-4.57. Electricity 20-25F/€3.05-3.81. AmEx/MC/V.) Once you get there, ask about their shortcut for getting to town and back. There are five campsites within a few km of each other in **Pyla-sur-Mer** along the rte. de Biscarrosse. It's quite a trek to any of these; the closest, for what it's worth, is **Camping de la Dune,** 300m from the beach on rte. de Biscarrosse. (☎05 56 22 72 17. Open May-Sept. 2 people with car 140F/€21.35, extra person 22F/€3.35; off-season prices 20-40F/€3.05-6.10 lower.)

FOOD. It would be a crime to leave Arcachon without savoring a few ounces of the 15,000 tons of oysters gathered here annually. Beach cafés line **av. Gambetta** and **bd. de la Plage,** offering copious seafood platters and 60F/€9.15 *moules frites* (mussels-'n'-fries). **La Marée,** 21 rue du Mal de Lattre de Tassigny, is not only a restaurant; it's also a fish shop where local fishermen deliver their catch. Starting with a *menu formule* of 75F/€11.43, La Marée offers good deals on great meals. (☎05 56 83 24 05. Open noon-2:30pm and 7pm-midnight.) A cheaper option is to imitate the French tourists, most of whom load up on bread from one of the many *boulangers artisanals* and produce from the **Marché Municipal** (rue Jehenne, open daily during the summer 8am-1pm) for a picnic to bring to the beach.

SIGHTS AND ENTERTAINMENT. Rising suddenly from the edge of a pine forest, the 117m **Dune du Pyla** looks more like a transplanted section of the Sahara than a French beach. Wind and sand race across the face of the dune while smaller humps of sand provide some sheltered spots. For courageous souls who are willing to cross the entire dune, there is a protected area at the edge where wading is possible, although a fierce undertow makes deeper swims too dangerous. Further along the water, there are separate beaches for the clothed and the nude. From the bus stop in Pyla-sur-Mer, head down bd. de l'Océan and take the first right. Follow the same road for about 20 minutes; the Dune area will be on your right. The **Ecole Professionnelle de Vol Libre du Pyla (EPVLP)** has **hang gliding** from the dune; ask at the tourist office. (☎05 56 22 15 02. 400F/€60.98 per flight, 2500F/€381.16 per week.)

Arcachon's bird sanctuaries and nature parks attract flocks of tourists. **UBA boats** (☎05 56 54 60 32 or 05 56 54 83 01) take two-hour excursions to the **Arguin Sandbar** from the Jetée Thiers pier at 10:45am, 2:30, and 3pm, weather permitting. (75F/€11.43, children 55F/€8.39.) The same company also offers trips to the oyster beds (55F/€8.39) and around an island bird sanctuary (daily 2:30pm, 70F/€10.67). About 15km out of town, the **Parc Ornithologique du Teich** shelters 260 species of birds in one of France's most important sanctuaries. (☎05 56 22 69 43. Open in summer daily 10am-10pm; off-season 10am-8pm. 33F/€5.03.)

In the hilly town of Arcachon itself, **Ville d'Hiver,** an arboreal district of turn-of-the-century villas, lies across from the **Parc Mauresque** north of the beach. Doctors designed the neighborhood's curving streets to protect invalids from the ocean winds; this "winter village" is 2°C warmer on average than its beachfront counterpart. Now the fairy-tale villas, which range in style from faux-Swiss chalet to pseudo-Gothic castle, make up a quiet suburban neighborhood, removed from the tourist rat-race below. The village is accessible on foot or via **tours** in a tourist office mini-train. (June-Sept. 3 per week, 1½hr tour, 10:30am; call for reservation. 25F/€3.81.) The **Ste-Cécile** observatory, across the park on the way back from the Ville d'Hiver, offers a stunning view of Arcachon. The spiral staircase is not easy to climb, and worse to descend (Open 9am-7pm. Free.)

Arcachon's kids run to several beachfront discothèques as soon as night falls. There's also the **Casino d'Arcachon,** bd. de la Plage (☎05 56 83 41 44), a fairy tale-creation containing, besides the obvious, several bars and a nightclub.

ANGLET

Eleven beaches, separated by rock jetties—there is nothing more to the town of Anglet. But these beaches are enough to bring out France's best to surf their waves each year. Anglet is the surfing capital of France, a town inundated with sweaty, smoking, surfing youngsters. Serious surfers won't want to leave, but others may feel a little out of place in the hostel and campground here, and might enjoy the town as a daytrip from nearby Bayonne and Biarritz.

PRACTICAL INFORMATION. The well-equipped **tourist office,** 1 av. de la Chambre d'Amour in pl. Général Leclerc, is a good 10- to 15-minute walk from the sea. (☎05 59 03 77 01; fax 05 59 03 55 91. Open July-Sept. M-Sa 9am-7pm; Oct.-June M-F 9am-12:45pm and 1:45-6pm, Sa 9am-12:15pm.) There is an **annex** closer to the shore on av. des Dauphins (open July-Sept. daily 10:30am-7:30pm). **STAB** buses (7.50F/€1.14) run about every 15 minutes, but less frequently on Sundays and holidays. Get a map or schedule if you can. The #2 or "B" bus in Biarritz or Bayonne, the #7 in Bayonne, and the #9 or "C" from Biarritz to La Barre (Aug. only) all go to Anglet. The #2 and 9 buses stop near the youth hostel. **BNP,** pl. Leclerc, has **currency exchange** at decent rates. (☎08 02 35 58 63. Open Tu-Sa 8am-noon and 1:45-5pm.) You can rent **bikes** near the beach at **Sobilo,** pl. des Docteurs Gentilhe. (☎05 59 03 37 56. Open M-Sa 10am-7pm.) For laundry, head to **Lavomatic,** at plage Chambre d'Amour, 21 av. du Rayon Vert (open daily 7am-10pm). In the absence of **lifeguards** (they're on duty 10am-7pm), dial 18 to get the **police** and **fire department** for beach emergencies. The **post office** is inconveniently located near the *mairie* at 7 rue du 8 Mai (☎05 59 58 08 40). There's a **branch** at pl. Général Leclerc, next to the tourist office (☎05 59 03 88 63). **Postal code:** 64600.

ACCOMMODATIONS, CAMPING, AND FOOD. It's hard to find a spot in summer, so you might consider spending the night in Biarritz or Bayonne. The **Auberge de Jeunesse (HI),** 19 rte. des Vignes, lies 600m directly uphill from plage de Marinella. From Biarritz, take bus #9 or "C" to "Auberge" (dir: "La Barre," every 50min.). This well-equipped and care-free hostel is a hub of French surfing subculture. It includes spots for camping as well as 99 clean rooms. The hostel even has its own surf club, not to mention board and wet-suit rental. Though a great place to meet people and make friends, with an Irish pub open every night, the hostel lacks privacy, and its amenities trail a little behind those of its sister hostel in Biarritz. (☎05 59 58 70 00; fax 05 59 58 70 07. Breakfast included. Dinner Easter-Oct. 28-50F/€4.27-7.62. Sheets 17F/€2.59. Kitchen Sept.-Mar. Reception 8:30am-10pm. Check-out 10am. Reservations accepted April-June. Bunks 75F/€11.43. Camping 51F/€7.78. **HI members only** (others can purchase card).) Shaded **Camping Fontaine Laborde,** 17 allée Fontaine Laborde, close to the beach, caters to young surfers with foosball tables, an extensive bar, and a pinball machine. Take bus #4 to Fontaine Laborde, just down the road from the hostel or walk up the av. des Maïlhouns to the allée de Fontaine Laborde from the beach. (☎05 59 03 48 16. Reception July-Aug. 9am-noon and 3-9pm; Sept.-June 9am-noon and 3-8pm. 99 spots available at 32F/€4.88 per person, 29F/€4.42 per site, 20F/€3.05 per car.)

Other than the **Italian ice cream** sold by vendors all along Anglet's beaches, food comes low on the list of priorities in Anglet. Sandwiches are available from stands behind most of the beaches. For a real meal, the strip behind the **Plage des Sables d'Or** along the **av. des Dauphins** offers a large number of cafés and restaurants, and the town's bars. Follow the direction of the glowering Indian figurine to **El Mexicano,** one of the hottest bar-restaurants on the Sables d'Or. (☎05 59 03 14 88. Open daily noon-3pm and 7pm-1am.) Walk one street farther to the **Havana Café** for loud music on a shaded balcony. (☎05 59 03 77 40. Open daily noon-3pm and 7pm-1am.)

BORN TO BE BASQUE Over the millennia, the Basque gene pool has drifted quite far away from the rest of Europe. For one thing, over 70% of Basques have perfect pitch; Basque choirs seldom use pitch pipes. For another, Basques tend to have uncanny senses of direction. Both Columbus and Magellan sailed around the world with Basque navigators. Basque culture is different in many other respects from those that surround it; their language, for example, is a Stone Age tongue with no known modern relatives. Even Basque customs tend to be of ancient and inexplicable origin; every flock of Basque sheep must include one black sheep, and Basques always paint their houses before June 24th.

SURF'N'TURF. Anglet's *raison d'être* is its 4km of fine-grained white sand, parcelled out into nine beaches, each beach with its own name and personality. The waves are strongest at the **Plage des Cavaliers** where most of Anglet's surfing competitions are held. The smaller **Plage des Sables d'Or** has beach volleyball and topless sunbathers. Swimmers should know about the strong cross-current undertow. When in doubt, swim near a lifeguard (they're on all the beaches except the Plage du Club and the Plage des Dunes). There are walking trails covered with pine needles at the **Fôret du Chilberta,** along with a newly-constructed adventure and ropes course. Contact **Evolution 2 Pays Basque,** 33 rue de Madrid. (☎05 59 41 18 81. Open May 15-Nov. 1.) To get there, take STAB line #7 or 9 to "Pignada."

Professional surf competitions are all free for spectators. In March, both surfers and skateboarders compete in the **Quik Cup.** Mid-August brings the three-day **France Championship,** while the traveling **O'Neill Surf Challenge** takes up residence for five days at the end of August, around the same time as the **Europe Bodyboard Championship.** The last major event of the year is the **WCT Quiksilver ProFrance,** which runs from the end of September into October. You can prepare for your title challenge by renting a board and taking lessons at one of the many surf shops along the beaches. The prices are all similar. Try **Rip Curl/Ecole Française de Surf,** av. des Dauphins. (☎05 59 23 15 31. Boards 60F/€9.15 for a half-day or 100F/€15.25 full-day with a passport deposit. 2hr. lessons 220F/€33.54 for 1 person; 550F/€83.85 for 3 people; 1000F/€152.46 for 6 people.)

BAYONNE

Although Bayonne (pop. 43,000) is only a few kilometers from the center of Biarritz, it seems to be hundreds of years removed from its more fashionable neighbor. This is a city where the pace of life has not changed since the 17th century—here the verb for "walk" is *flaner*—meaning "stroll"—rather than *marcher* or *se promener*. Bayonne rises early, as lively markets crowd the banks of the Nive, but takes a long siesta when things heat up in the afternoon and life slows down as people retreat indoors behind exposed wooden beams and colorful shutters. Towering above it all, the grand Gothic cathedral marks the leisurely passing of time with the tolling of its bells. It is only in the middle of July and August that things pick up, when hurried tourists flock to Bayonne in droves to catch the traditional Basque festivals, bullfights, and sports matches.

ORIENTATION AND PRACTICAL INFORMATION

Ernest Hemingway, in a fit of wordy enthusiasm, once wrote that "Bayonne is a nice town. It is like a very clean Spanish town, and it is on a big river." His observation was nearly correct. Bayonne is on two rivers that join to split the city into three sections. The train station is in **St-Esprit,** on the northern side of the wide river **Adour.** From here, the pont St-Esprit, usually lined with fishermen, connects to budget-friendly **Petit-Bayonne,** home of Bayonne's museums and smaller restaurants. Five small bridges from Petit-Bayonne cross the much narrower Nive to Grand-Bayonne on the west bank. This, the oldest part of town, has a buzzing pedestrian zone where red-shuttered houses (*arceaux*) perch over ground floor shops and pâtisseries. The center of town is manageable on foot, and an excellent bus system makes Anglet and Biarritz a snap to reach. To get to the **tourist office** from the train station, follow the signs to the *centre ville*, crossing the main bridge, pont St-Esprit, to Petit-Bayonne, and continuing through pl. Réduit across the next bridge (pont Mayou) to Grand-Bayonne. Turn right onto rue Bernède, which soon becomes av. Bonnat. The tourist office is on your left (10min.).

Trains: pl. de la République (☎05 59 50 83 42; schedules 08 36 35 35 35). To: **Biarritz** (10min., 11 per day, 13F/€1.98); **Bordeaux** (1½hr., 9 per day, 130-138F/€19.82-21.04); **Paris** (5hr., 7 TGVs per day, 406-456F/€61.90-65.52); and **Toulouse** (4hr., 5 per day, 200F/€30.49). Also to **San Sebastian, Spain** (1½-2hr.; M-F 6 per day, Sa-Su 5 per day; 154F/€23.48, under 26 77F/€11.74). Info office open daily 9am-7pm.

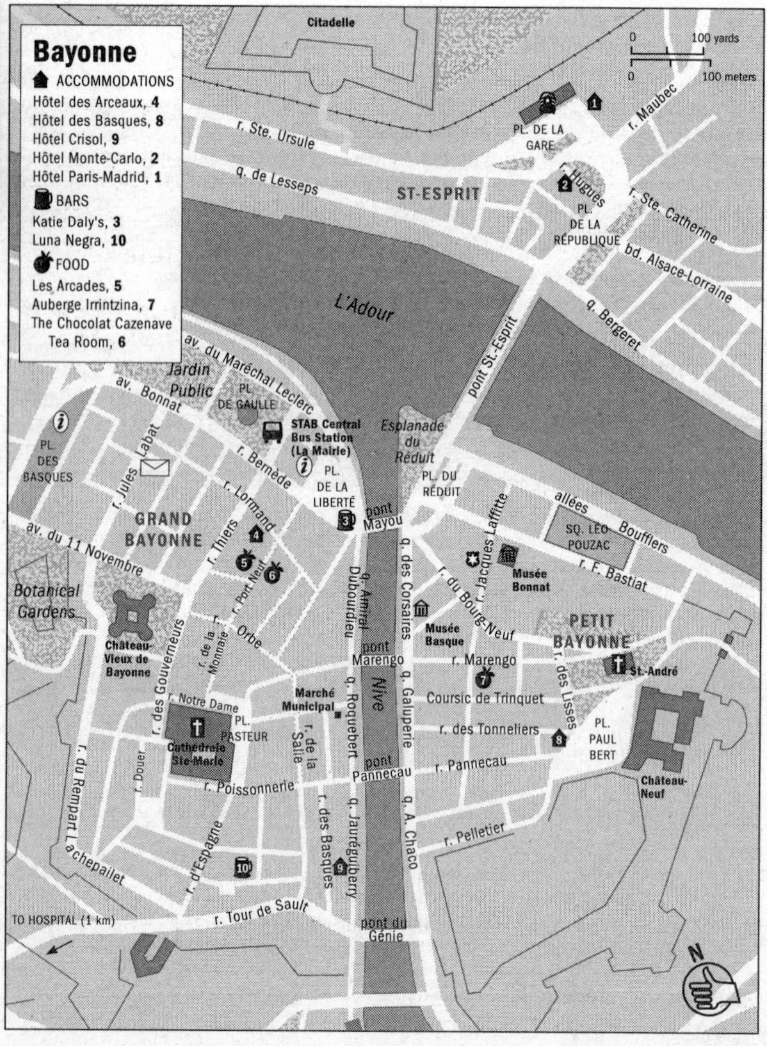

Local Transportation: STAB, Hôtel de Ville (☎05 59 59 04 61). Open M-Sa 8am-noon and 1:30-6pm. Buses run every 20-30min. Lines #1, 2, and 6 serve **Biarritz.** Lines #1 and 2 also stop in the center of **Anglet.** Line #4 follows the river Adour through **Anglet.** Last bus in any direction around 8pm (7pm on Su). 1hr. ticket 7.50F/€1.14; *carnet* of 10 62F/€9.45, 52F/€7.93 for students during the school year.

Taxis: Radio Taxi (☎05 59 59 48 48). **Taxi Gare** (☎05 59 55 13 15). Both 24hr.

Tourist Office: pl. des Basques (☎05 59 46 01 46; fax 05 59 59 37 55). Free city map; help finding rooms; the free *Fêtes en Pays Basque* and *Les Clés de la Ville.* Open July-Aug. M-Sa 9am-7pm, Su 10am-1pm; Sept.-June M-F 9am-6:30pm, Sa 10am-6pm.

Tours: The tourist office organizes 2hr. walking tours of Bayonne's neighborhoods in the summer. (July-Aug. daily 10am, 30F/€4.57). Tours given in English on Th. For a different perspective, **Bateau Le Bayonne** (☎06 80 74 21 51) runs 2hr. boat trips along the Adour river. Departures July-Aug. 10am, 2, and 5pm; 80F/€12.20, children ages 5-12 50F/€7.62, children 5 and under free.

Budget Travel: Pascal Voyages, 8 allées Boufflers (☎05 59 25 48 48). Open M-F 8:30am-6:30pm, Sa 9am-noon.

Money: Or et Change, 1 rue Jules Labat (☎05 59 25 58 59), in Grand-Bayonne. No commission, good rates. Open M-Sa 10am-12:30pm and 1:30-7pm.

Laundromat: In Grand Bayonne, use **Salon Lavoir,** 7 rue Douer at pl. Montaut. Open Tu-W and F-Sa 9am-12:45pm and 2-6:45pm, Th 10:30am-12:45pm and 2-6:45pm. Closer to the train station is **Laverie St-Esprit,** 16 bd. Alsace-Lorraine. Open July-Aug. daily 8am-10pm; Sept.-June 8am-8pm.

Police: av. de Marhum (☎05 59 46 22 22).

Hospital: 13 av. Interne Jacques Loëb, St-Léon (☎05 59 44 35 35).

Internet Access: In St-Esprit, **Cyber-net Café,** 9 pl. de la République (☎05 59 55 78 98). 40F/€6.10 per hr., students and children 30F/€4.57. Open daily 7am-2am.

Post Office: 11 rue Jules Labat (☎05 59 46 33 60), Grand-Bayonne. **Currency exchange.** Open M-F 8am-6pm, Sa 10am-noon. **Branch office,** bd. Alsace-Lorraine, has same hours. **Poste Restante** (at main branch): 64181. **Postal code:** 64100.

ACCOMMODATIONS AND CAMPING

In **St-Esprit,** reasonably-priced lodgings dot the train station area. The hotels in **Grand-Bayonne** are usually more expensive; in **Petit-Bayonne,** hunt around **pl. Paul Bert,** but expect a noisy night, thanks to the high concentration of Basque bars. Every hotel in Bayonne fills during the festival season in July and August—reserve up to a month ahead. The closest hostels are in Anglet (see p. 666) and Biarritz (see p. 673), each a 20-minute bus ride away.

Hôtel Paris-Madrid, pl. de la Gare, to the left of the station (☎05 59 55 13 98; fax 05 59 55 07 22), a 3min. walk from Petit-Bayonne. More like a home than a hotel, and a great base for getting to know the region. Large, individualized rooms; space for families. Gracious husband and wife speak excellent English and are more knowledgeable and forthcoming than 20 tourist offices. TV/reading room. Breakfast 25F/€3.81. Hall shower 5F/€0.76. Reception 6am-12:30am. Singles and doubles 95-135F/€14.48-20.58, with shower 150-160F/€22.90-24.39, with shower and toilet 170-180F/€25.92-27.44; triples and quads with bath 235-250F/€35.83-38.12. MC/V.

Hôtel des Arceaux, 26 rue Port Neuf (☎05 59 59 15 53). Follow the directions to the tourist office, but turn left from rue Bernède onto rue Port Neuf at pl. de la Liberté in Grand-Bayonne. In the process of being refurbished, this hotel has an unbeatable location and friendly reception in the center of Grand-Bayonne, but relatively high prices. Breakfast 30F/€4.57. Reception M-F 7:30am-10pm, Sa-Su 8:30am-10pm. In-season singles and doubles 150-160F/€22.90-24.39, with TV and bath 170-250F/€25.92-38.12; larger rooms from 220F/€33.54 for two people. Extra person 40F/€6.10.

Hôtel Crisol, 19 rue des Basques, on a quiet street in Grand-Bayonne (☎05 59 59 30 23). Cross pont Panneceau into Grand-Bayonne; take the second left onto rue des Basques. 12 simple rooms tended by a feisty Italian proprietress. Usually completely booked during winter season by older men. Breakfast 25F/€3.81. Reception 7am-10pm. Call ahead if arriving late. Singles with shower 150F/€22.90; doubles 200F/€30.49.

Hôtel des Basques, 4 rue des Lisses (☎05 59 59 08 02), in Petit-Bayonne. Big, minimalist rooms overlook pl. Paul Bert and local bars. Breakfast 30F/€4.57. Reception until 9:30pm; call ahead if arriving later. Singles and doubles 140-170F/€21.35-25.92, with TV and bathroom 180F/€27.44, extra person 30-60F/€4.57-9.15; triples 180F/€27.44; triples and quads with TV and bathroom 230F/€35.06.

Hôtel Monte-Carlo, 11 rue Hugues, to the right of the train station (☎05 59 55 02 68). Check in at the bar next door. Clean but absolutely bare rooms. Singles 130F/€19.82; doubles 150F/€22.90, with shower 170F/€25.92; quads with shower 250F/€38.12.

FOOD

The narrow streets of Petit-Bayonne and St-Esprit offer 50-60F/€7.62-9.15 *menus* of *jambon de Bayonne* (dry cured ham) and *poulet à la basquaise* (chicken wrapped in large peppers). Grand-Bayonne, the city's cloth-napkin zone, serves regional specialties in a less budget-oriented atmosphere. Vendors sell meats, fish, cheese, and produce at the **marché municipal,** on quai Roquebert (Tu-Th 7am-1pm, F 7am-1pm and 3:30-7pm, Sa 6am-2pm). There is a **Monoprix supermarket** at 8 rue Orbe. (☎05 59 59 00 33. Open M-Sa 8:30am-7:30pm. MC/V.)

Auberge Irrintzina, 9 rue Marengo (☎05 59 59 02 51). Authentic Basque cuisine with a home-cooked feel. Meals from 65F/€9.91. Four courses of Basque specialties 125F/€19.06. Open noon-2:30pm and 7-11pm. MC/V.

Les Arcades, 40 rue Port Neuf (☎05 59 59 33 66). Outdoor tables on the popular rue Port-Neuf make a perfect spot for people-watching. Lunch from 60F/€9.15 and includes a number of regional specialties. Open daily 7:30am-7pm.

Chocolat Cazenave Tea Room, 19 rue Port Neuf (☎05 59 59 03 16). Since 1854, the Cazenave has served chocolate under the arches of the rue Port-Neuf, with a degree of luxury nearly unimaginable. Dark frothy chocolate with freshly whipped cream (26F/€3.96) is served between mirrored walls. Open M-Sa 9am-noon and 2-7pm. MC/V.

SIGHTS

The 13th-century **Cathédrale Ste-Marie,** pl. Pasteur, whose spiny steeples bite the sky above Bayonne, feels disproportionately tall in relation to the town it serves. Although the church has endured sporadic fires, weathered a brief stint as a cemetery, and suffered massive destruction during the secularizing zeal of the Revolution, renovations have completely erased all traces of decay. (Church open M-Sa 7am-noon and 3-7pm, Su 3:30-10pm. Cloister open daily 9:30am-12:30pm and 2-5pm; Easter-Oct. 9am-6pm. Free.) The prison block of the **Château-Vieux de Bayonne** on nearby rue des Gouverneurs has held such notorious villains as Don Pedro of Castille (1367) and certain out-of-favor kings. The avenue continues to Bayonne's vast, grassy **fortifications,** where you can lose yourself among the shaded lawns. Around the corner on av. du 11 Novembre, Bayonne's refreshing **botanical gardens** flourish atop the battlements with 1000 species of Japanese flora, including a miniature bamboo forest. (Open Apr. 15-Oct. 15 daily 9am-noon and 2-6pm.)

The reopening of the **Musée Basque,** 37 quai des Corsaires, in 2001, has been deemed the "cultural event of the year." The refurbished collection will include everything Basque, from traditional religious objects to sporting and fishing equipment. (Open May-Oct. Tu-Sa 10am-6:30pm; Nov.-Apr. 10am-12:30pm and 2-6pm. 35F/€5.34, students 20F/€3.05.) Nearby, the works of Bayonnais painter Léon Bonnat (1833-1922) are displayed along with his extensive art collection at the

Musée Bonnat, 5 rue Jacques Laffitte. The walls are hardly large enough to hold all the paintings in this Bonnat-designed museum, and the masterpieces by painters such as Degas, Darer, Ingres, and Goya are often lost among more mediocre works. (Open Tu-Su 10am-6:15pm. 35F/€5.34, students 20F/€3.05.) On Sundays at 11am, the **Eglise St-André** gives a traditional Basque mass with Basque chants that are worth hearing even for those who find the religion unappealing.

For sandy and more secluded delights than you'll find on the crowded beaches of Anglet or Biarritz, try the **Metro plage** in Tarnos; take bus #10 from the train station. The water is only swimmable during July and August when coast guards line the beach, but the 2km walk is beautiful throughout the year.

ENTERTAINMENT AND FESTIVALS

In this quiet town of long afternoons and short evenings, nightlife is nearly nonexistent. The main bars that are grouped on the streets running between **pl. Paul Bert** and **quai Galuperie** in Petit-Bayonne cater mostly to aging local men. Travelers seeking a more lively atmosphere often take the ten-minute bus ride to Biarritz or even head for the border to San Sebastian, where the evening begins at midnight and doesn't end until around 8am. In Bayonne, the Irish pub **Katie Daly's,** 3 pl. de la Liberté, serves expensive pints to animated crowds on the weekends. Irish bands fly in to play (Th-F), local ones walk in (Sa). (☎05 59 59 09 14. Pints of Guinness 37F/€5.64, 29F/€4.42 during happy hour 7-9pm.) Bayonne's cultural education is taken care of by **La Luna Negra,** in an alleyway between rue Poissonnerie and rue Tour de Sault. Wednesday is blues night in this cabaret-style bar and stage. Thursday through Saturday, entertainment ranges from mimes to storytellers to classical concerts. (Open W-Sa starting at 9:30pm. Prices vary.) **L'Atalante,** 7 rue Denis Etcheverry, in St-Esprit, shows artsy international films in their original language. (☎05 59 55 76 63. 37F/€5.64, students 25F/€3.81; closed late July-early Aug.)

Preparation for Bayonne's festivals occupies most of the early summer, and at the end of June the season begins, lasting through September. June 21, the longest day of the year, brings the **Fête de la Musique.** Rock bands, jazz ensembles, breakdancers, and Basque crooners all contribute and, for one night, there are no volume restrictions on live performances or radios. In mid-July, **Jazz aux Remparts** begins, with some of the world's most famous jazz artists flying in to play on Bayonne's battlements. (Contact the **Théâtre Municipale** at 05 59 59 07 27. Ticket office open Tu-Sa 1-7pm. 160-210F/€24.39-32.02 per night, students 50-160F/€7.62-24.39, under 12 30F/€4.57.) The orchestra **Harmonie Bayonnaise** stages jazz and traditional Basque concerts in the pl. de Gaulle gazebo (July-Aug. Th 9:30pm; free). After the first Wednesday in August, unrestrained hedonism breaks out with the **Fêtes Traditionelles,** as the locals immerse themselves in five days of concerts, bullfights, fireworks, and a chaotic race between junk heaps masquerading as boats. From July through September, Bayonne holds several bullfights or *corridas* in the **Plaza de Toros** (☎05 59 46 61 00). Seats (75-470F/€11.43-71.66) sell out fast, but the cheap, nose-bleed section usually has seats available on fight days.

BIARRITZ

Once a whaling village at the base of the Pyrenees, Biarritz became the playground of crowns in the mid-19th century. Napoleon III, Alphonse XIII of Spain, Nicholas of Russia, and the Shah of Persia all visited its shores, drawn by its natural beauty. Biarritz still glistens with money. Hardly a city at all in the traditional sense, it is a theme park for a select few and a museum of wealth and glamour for everyone else—a tantalizing glimpse into the life of the filthy rich. In the daytime, when luxury cars prowl the narrow streets and everyone turns their envious stares on everyone else, the city becomes too fashionable for its own good and visitors might feel the need to flee to the nearby beaches of Anglet.

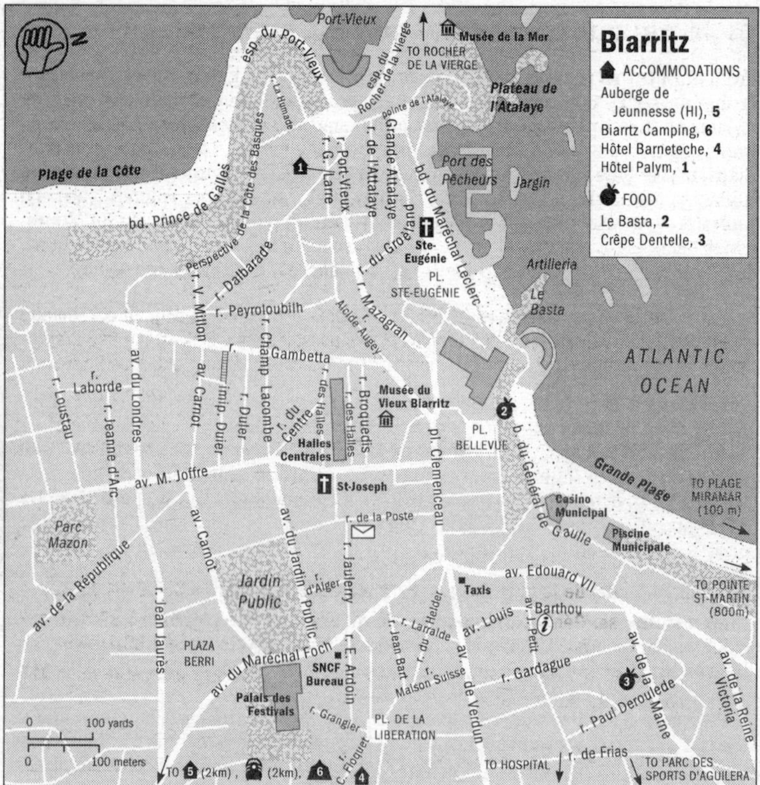

TRANSPORTATION

Flights: Aéroport de Parme (☎05 59 43 83 83), 7 Esplanade de l'Europe. M-Sa take bus #6 from Hôtel de Ville to "Parme Aéroport" (every 30min. 7am-7pm), Su take bus B. **Ryanair** (UK ☎01 279 680 500) has flights to **London.**

Trains: Biarritz-la-Négresse (☎05 59 23 04 84), 3km from town. To: **Bayonne** (10min.; 17 per day; 13F/€1.98; TGV 23F/€3.51); **Bordeaux** (2hr.; 7per day; 133F/€20.28, TGV 153F/€23.33); **Paris** (8hr., 5hr. TGV; 5 per day; 392F/€59.77, TGV 442F/€67.39); **Pau** (1½hr., 4 per day, 90F/€13.72); and **Toulouse** (4hr., 5 per day, 204F/€31.10). **SNCF office,** 13 av. Foch (☎05 59 24 00 94). Open daily 8am-8pm.

Buses: ATCRB (☎05 59 26 06 99), main office in St-Jean de Luz. Bus stops on rue Joseph Petit, next to the tourist office. Buy tickets on the bus.

Local Transportation: STAB (☎05 59 52 59 52). Office with maps and schedules on rue Louis-Barthou, near the tourist office. 20min. to Bayonne (bus #1 or 2); 10min. to Anglet (bus #7, 9, or 4). 7.50F/€1.14 tickets good for 1hr., *carnet* of 10 62F/€9.45, students during school year 52F/€7.93.

Taxis: Atlantic Taxi Radio (☎05 59 03 18 18). 24hr.

Bike and Scooter Rental: SOBILO, 24 rue Peyroloubilh (☎05 59 24 94 47). Bikes 80F/€12.20 per day. Scooters 200F/€30.49 per day. Motorbikes 350-450F/€53.36-68.61 per day. Open daily 8am-7pm.

Surfboard Rental: Rip Curl Surf Shop, 2 av. Reine Victoria (☎05 59 24 38 40), 1 block from Grande Plage. 60F/€9.15 per half-day, 100F/€15.25 per day; 2000F/€304.92 and ID deposit. Open July-Aug. M-Sa 10am-8pm, Su 3-7pm; Sept.-June M-Sa 10am-12:30pm and 3-7pm. For **lessons,** contact **Rip Curl** at 05 59 24 62 86. 1 person for 2hr. 220F/€33.54, 3 people for 2hr. 550F/€83.85, 6 people 1000F/€152.46.

ORIENTATION AND PRACTICAL INFORMATION

From most towns near Biarritz, buses are more convenient than trains. Even from farther away, the best option is a train to Bayonne and then a bus to Biarritz. Bus #2 runs to the city center, the tourist office, and the hostel. From farther away, trains only service **Biarritz-la-Négresse,** 3km from the center. To get to the center of Biarritz, take blue bus #2 (dir: "Bayonne via Biarritz;" in summer every 20-40min. 6:30am-9pm) or green bus #9 (dir: "Biarritz HDV;" in summer 6:30am-7pm). To walk into town from Biarritz-la-Négresse (40min.), turn left onto allée du Moura, which becomes av. du Président Kennedy. Turn left a few kilometers later onto av. du Maréchal Foch, which continues to **pl. Clemenceau,** Biarritz's main square.

Tourist Office: 1 sq. d'Ixelles (☎05 59 22 37 00; fax 05 59 24 14 19), off av. Edouard VII. Staff tracks down same-night rooms or campsites for free. Pick up the free *Biarritz-scope* for monthly events listings. Open July-Aug. daily 8am-8pm; Sept.-June 9am-6pm.

Money: Change Plus, 9 rue Mazagran (☎05 59 24 82 47). No commission. Open July-Aug. M-Sa 9am-8pm, Su 10am-1pm; Sept.-June M-F 9am-12:30pm and 2-7pm.

Laundromat: Le Lavoir, 4 av. Jaulerry (☎05 59 24 57 23), by the post office. Open daily 7am-9pm.

Beach Emergencies: Grande Plage ☎05 59 22 22 22. **Plage Marabella** ☎05 59 23 01 20. **Plage de la Milady** ☎05 59 23 63 93.

Police: rue Louis-Barthou (☎05 59 24 68 24).

Hospital: Hôpital de la Côte Basque, av. Interne Jacques Loëb (☎05 59 44 35 35).

Internet Access: Génius Informatique, 60 av. Edouard VII (☎05 59 24 39 07). 1F/€0.76 per min., 50F/€7.62 per hr. Open Tu-Sa 10am-12:30pm and 1:30-7:30pm.

Post Office: 17 rue de la Poste (☎05 59 22 41 10). **Currency exchange** open M-F 8:30am-7pm, Sa 8:30am-noon. **Postal code:** 64200.

AQUITAINE

ACCOMMODATIONS AND CAMPING

Bargains do exist, but you may want to plan a month ahead in July and August or enlist the help of the tourist office. The best priced hotels are off rue Mazagran, around rue du Port-Vieux. The youth hostel is newly-renovated but far from the city center; all other hotels listed are centrally located.

Hôtel Barnetche, 5bis rue Charles-Floquet (☎05 59 24 22 25; fax 05 59 24 98 71; www.hotel-barnetche.fr), in the center of town. From pl. Clemenceau, take rue du Helder through pl. Libération to rue Charles Floquet. 12-bed dorm room is the best deal in town; larger rooms great for families. No-nonsense, energetic owner keeps everything ship-shape. Obligatory breakfast included. In Aug., obligatory (and tasty) *demi-pension* 100F/€15.25 extra. Reception 7:30am-10:30pm, until 11pm July-Aug.; reservations by phone or web recommended. Open May-Sept. Dorms 110F/€16.77 per person, no meal obligation. Doubles 380F/€57.94; triples and quads 160F/€24.39 per person.

Auberge de Jeunesse (HI), 8 rue de Chiquito de Cambo (☎05 59 41 76 00; fax 05 59 41 76 07), a 40min. walk or a 15min. bus ride to the center of town. Consider renting a bike or scooter. Take bus #2 to "Bois de Boulogne." Walking, take av. Maréchal Foch and continue through as it becomes av. du Président J.F. Kennedy. Turn right on rue Ph. Veyrin and the hostel is at the bottom of the hill on your right. Well-equipped, with Internet, laundry, ping-pong, surfboard rentals, and a bar. Dinner 50F/€7.62 or 28F/€4.27 for only a main course. Sheets 17F/€2.59. Breakfast included. Dorms 78F/€11.89 per person. **HI members only** (others can purchase card).

Hôtel Palym, 7 rue du Port-Vieux (☎05 59 24 16 56; fax 05 59 24 96 12). Beautiful wood furnishings in clean, airy rooms. Bar and terraced pizzeria span 2 streets below. Some rooms come with TVs. Breakfast 30F/€4.57. Reception 8am-midnight. Singles 180F/€27.44; doubles 240F/€36.59, with shower 300F/€45.74; triples 240F/€36.59, with shower 400F/€60.98. Prices 10% lower Sept.-June. MC/V.

Camping: Biarritz, 28 rue d'Harcet (☎05 59 23 00 12; biarritz.camping@wanadoo.fr). Calm and within 1km of Milady beach. A 45min. walk from town. Take the Navette-des-Plages bus (#9) or walk down av. Kennedy from the station following signs (30min.). Caters to surfers, but not as exclusively as Anglet does. July-Aug. 110F/€16.77; Sept.-June 75F/€11.43 for 2 people with tent.

FOOD

In dining, as with everything in Biarritz, style trumps substance. Expect impressive elegance and high prices around **Grande Plage** and **pl. St-Eugénie.** More mid-priced eateries can be found on **av. de la Marne** as it splits from av. Edouard VII. Expect 60-80F/€9.15-12.20 *menus* and oceans of chintz floral ruffles. Cheap crêpes and sandwiches can be found along **rue du Port-Vieux** and **rue Mazagran.** The **Marché Municipal** on rue des Halles offers local produce and an abundance of specialties (open daily 7am-1:30pm). Next door is a **Shopi supermarket,** 2 rue du Centre. (☎05 59 24 18 01. Open M-Sa 8:45am-12:25pm and 3-7:10pm.)

AQUITAINE

Le Basta, 31 Blvd. du Général de Gaulle (☎05 59 22 22 58), under the pl. St-Eugénie. An inexpensive view of the Port des Pêcheurs and the Eglise St-Eugénie. *Moules frites* 53F/€8.08. Open daily noon-5pm and 7-11pm. Cash only.

La Crêpe Dentelle, 6 av. de la Marne (☎05 59 22 28 29). Filling crêpes served with Breton cider. 62F/€9.45 lunch *menu.* Open daily noon-3pm and 7-11pm.

SIGHTS AND BEACHES

All of Biarritz is designed in consideration of its beaches. The **Grande Plage** is nearly covered in summer by thousands of perfect bodies and plainer onlookers. This is also the beach of choice for the surfers who stop in Biarritz. On the walkway behind the beach, the immaculate, white **Casino Municipal** draws a few high rollers to its slot machines and roulette tables. (☎05 59 22 44 66. Open daily 10am-3am.) Walk to your right along the Grande Plage through the tunnel under the jetty to the less crowded **Plage Miramar,** at the base of the cliffs, where bare bathers relax. The stairs from the end of Plage Miramar lead up the cliff. Turn left along av. de l'Impératrice to reach the **Pointe St-Martin** and the tall lighthouse, **Le Phare de Biarritz.** From here, it is possible to see the sands of the Landes separating from the rocky coast of the Basque country. Inland, the **Hôtel Du Palais** sits overlooking the Plage Miramar. Constructed in 1845 by Emperor Napoleon III for Princess Eugenia, the E-shaped palace has since been converted into a hotel but retains all the luxury of Napoleon III's era. Rooms begin at 1,700F/€259.19 in high season, but stop at the terrace café for a cup of coffee and soak in the atmosphere of Biarritz's best four-star hotel. Across av. de l'Impératrice is the site of the old **Hôtel Continental,** where Russian nobles fled after the Bolshevik Revolution in 1817.

On the other side of the Grande Plage, jagged rock formations provide a sheltered spot in the **Port des Pêcheurs** to harbor small fishing craft. **BASC Subaquatique,** near Plateau de l'Atalaye, organizes scuba excursions. (☎05 59 24 80 40. Open July-Aug. 110-150F/€16.77-22.90.) Walk from the point out over the steel bridge and through the **Rocher de la Vierge,** a tooth-like rock with a statue of the Virgin Mary, to gaze at magical sunsets. Next to the bridge to the rock, the **Musée de la Mer,** 1 esplanade du Rocher de la Vierge, includes an aquarium with local fish and displays on the Basque fishing industry. (☎05 59 22 75 40. Open daily 9:30am-12:30pm and 2-6pm. Open until midnight July-Aug.) Finally, the **Plage des Basques** stretches on the other side of the jetty. Endless paths cut into the flowered coast two minutes from the town center, but check the tides before traipsing onto the rocks. At low tide, this deserted beach has the cleanest water and sand in town.

Finally, trek out of town to the **Musée du Chocolat,** 14-16 av. Beaurivage, which contains the private collection of the proprietor of **Henriet,** the chocolate shop on pl. Clemenceau. Getting to see elaborate chocolate sculptures being created, and the free *cadeau,* are convincing lures. (☎05 59 41 54 64. Open July-Aug. Tu-Sa 10am-7pm; Sept.-June 10am-noon and 2:30-6pm. 30F/€4.57, students 25F/€3.81.)

ENTERTAINMENT AND FESTIVALS

Casino Municipal gloats over the Grande Plage in all its art-deco glory. Curse Lady Luck as you and up to 700 of your little friends blow a month's worth of baguettes on the greedy slot machines. (☎05 59 22 44 66. Open daily 10am-3am.) Jeans and sneakers are fine for slot machines, but you'll need to look snazzier to get upstairs. Hang out around the **Port des Pêcheurs** until 11pm or midnight, when the rich and reckless strap on their party boots. Things pick up early at the **Ventilo Caffé,** 30 rue Mazagran, a bar with a heavenly theme where young people drink and talk while sitting in exotic red velvet chairs. (☎05 59 24 31 42. Open July-Aug. daily 8pm-3am; Sept.-June 8pm-2am.) Dress up before heading to the **Brasilia Copacabana,** 24 av. Edouard VII. (☎05 59 24 65 39. Cover about 60F/€9.15.) On weekend nights, many head for cheaper, wilder **San Sebastian** just over the border in Spain.

The **International Festival of Biarritz** takes over in the first week of October. Throughout September, **Le Temps d'Aimer** will please the culturally inclined with music, ballet, and art exhibits (tickets 100-180F/€15.25-27.44; student discounts). In July and August, *pelote* and Basque dancing hit **Parc Mazon** Mondays at 9pm. Two *cesta punta* tournaments animate the Fronton Euskal-Jai, Parc des Sports d'Aguiléra: for two weeks in mid-July, Biarritz hosts the international **Biarritz Masters Jai-Alai** tournament, while for three weeks in mid-August the town is taken over by the **Gant d'Or,** a tournament among big-name players. The winning teams of each tournament compete for the **Trophée du Super Champion** in September. (For all three, call tourist office at 05 59 22 37 00. Tickets 60-120F/€9.15-18.30.)

ST-JEAN-DE-LUZ

The village of St-Jean-de-Luz (pop. 13,000; Basque name *Donibane Lohitzun*) has always lived off the sea. Its early wealth came from whaling and the Basque *corsaires* (pirates) who raided the British merchant marine throughout the 1600s. These high-seas riches are responsible for the finest examples of Basque architecture, from the octagonal belltower above Maurice Ravel's birthplace to a church built like a fishing boat. St-Jean is one of the area's most perfectly Basque towns, worth a visit for its regional architecture and a nets-by-sunset port-town charm.

TRANSPORTATION

Trains: bd. du Cdt Passicot. To: **Bayonne** (30min.; 7 per day; 25F/€3.81, TGV 35F/€5.34); **Biarritz** (15min.; 10 per day; 16F/€2.44, TGV 26F/€3.96); **Paris** (5hr.; 10 per day; TGV 453F/€69.07); and **Pau** (2hr.; 5 per day; 98F/€3.51). Info office open M-F 10am-12:30pm and 2-6:30pm.

Buses: across from the station. **ATCRB** (☎05 59 26 06 99) runs to: **Bayonne** (7-13 per day, 23F/€3.51); **Biarritz** (7-13 per day, 18F/€2.74); and **San Sebastian,** Spain (1¼hr.; 2 per day June 16-Sept. 25 M-Sa; Sept. 26-June 15 Tu, Th, and Sa; 45F/€6.86). Buy tickets on bus. Office open M-Sa 9am-7pm. **Pullman Basque,** 33 rue Gambetta (☎05 59 26 03 37), runs excursions to St-Jean-Pied-de-Port, the Basque villages, Spain, and elsewhere. Half-day tours to La Rhune (F). Ticket office open July-Sept. daily 8:30am-12:30pm and 2:30-7:30pm; Oct.-June 9:30am-12:15pm and 2:30-7:15pm.

Taxis: at the train station (☎05 59 26 10 11).

Bike Rental: Sobilo (☎05 59 26 75 76), at the station. Bikes 80F/€12.20 per day. Scooters 200F/€30.49 per day. Motorbikes 350-450F/€53.36-68.61 per day. Open daily 8am-7pm.

ORIENTATION AND PRACTICAL INFORMATION

From the train station, bear left diagonally across the rotary onto bd. du Commandant Passicot. The **tourist office,** pl. Foch, is on your right, just past the second rotary. From pl. Foch, rue de la République runs two short blocks to **pl. Louis XIV,** the center of town. The beach is one minute farther, along a restaurant-studded alley, and the pedestrian **rue Gambetta** runs perpendicular to the right past the church and endless shops. **Ciboure,** the section of St-Jean-de-Luz on the other side of the river **Nivelle,** can be reached by crossing the pont Charles de Gaulle.

Tourist Office: pl. Foch (☎05 59 26 79 63; fax 05 59 26 21 47). Maps and info on accommodations, events, and excursions. English tours of the town July-Aug. Tu, Th, Sa at 10am; 30F/€4.57. Tours in French given the rest of the year Sa 3pm.

Money: Change Plus, 31 rue Gambetta (☎05 59 51 03 43). Fair rates; no commission. Open July-Aug. M-Sa 9am-8pm; Sept.-June M-Sa 9am-12:30pm and 2-7pm. **Branch** open July-Aug. in the Maison Louis XIV.

Laundromat: Automatique, 3 rue Chauvin Dragon. Open daily 8am-10pm.

Surf shop: Le Spot, 16 rue Gambetta (☎05 59 26 07 95). 2hr. lesson 230F/€35.06. Rentals: wet-suit 40F/€6.10 per half-day, 60F/€9.15 per day; bodyboard 50F/€7.62 per half-day, 80F/€12.20 per day. Open Jan.-Oct. daily 9:30am-9pm; Nov.-Dec. Su 10am-7:30pm. MC/V.

Police: av. André Ithurralde (☎05 59 51 22 22).

Hospital: av. André Ithurralde (☎05 59 51 45 45). 24hr. emergency service at the private hospital **Polyclinique,** 10 av. de Layats (☎05 59 51 63 63).

Post Office: 44 bd. Victor Hugo (☎05 59 51 66 54). Open July-Aug. M-F 9am-6pm, Sa 9am-noon; Sept.-June M-F 9am-noon and 1:30-5:30pm, Sa 9am-noon. **Postal code:** 64500.

ACCOMMODATIONS AND CAMPING

Hotels are expensive and fill up rapidly in summer. Arrive early, especially in August. You may do best to commute from Bayonne or Biarritz. However, if you do stay in St-Jean-de-Luz, you can expect nice rooms and service for the prices.

Hôtel Verdun, 13 av. de Verdun (☎05 59 26 02 55), across from the train station. Well-kept, pastel-colored rooms for what are sadly the lowest prices in St-Jean. July-Sept. singles and doubles 220F/€33.54 (obligatory *demi-pension* adds around 60F/€9.15); Jan-Apr. and Oct.-Dec. 150F/€22.90; May-June 160F/€24.39. MC/V.

Hôtel Bolivar, 18 rue Sopite (☎05 59 26 02 00; fax 05 59 26 38 28), on a central but quiet street near the beach. Sparkling rooms with shining floors, some with balconies. Breakfast 36F/€5.5. Reception 7am-9:30pm. Open May-Sept. Singles 197-210F/€30-32, with shower 275-302F/€42-46; doubles 203-243F/€31-37, with shower 302-367F/€46-56; triples with bathroom 361-400F/€55-61. AmEx/MC/V.

Campsites: There are 14 sites in St-Jean-de-Luz and 13 more nearby. All are slightly separated from the city center, behind the plage Erromandi. The tourist office has info. To walk to most of the campsites, take bd. Victor Hugo, continue along av. André Ithurralde, then veer left onto chemin d'Erromardie (20min.). Or take an ATCRB bus headed to Biarritz or Bayonne and ask to get off near the *camping*. For a quiet and sheltered location, continue 200m around the bend to **Camping Iratzia** (☎05 59 26 14 89), chemin d'Erromardie. Reception 9am-8pm.

FOOD

St-Jean-de-Luz has the best Basque and Spanish specialties north of the border. The port's famous seafood waits on ice in every restaurant along the rue de la République and pl. Louis XIV. For these meals, expect to pay upwards of 85F/€12.96. There is a large **market** at pl. des Halles (Tu and F-Sa 7am-1pm). For groceries, stop at the **Shopi supermarket,** 87 rue Gambetta (open M-Sa 8:30am-12:30pm and 3-7:15pm, Su 8:30am-12:30pm), or **8 à Huit,** 46 bd. Victor Hugo (open M-Sa 8:30am-1pm and 3:30-8pm; July-Aug. also Su 8:30am-12:30pm).

The neighborhood restaurant, **Buvette de la Halle,** bd. Victor Hugo-Marché de St-Jean-de-Luz, serves regional specialties for the best prices in St-Jean. At this café on the side of the marketplace (during market hours, they operate inside the market), the staff chats with diners while serving grilled sardines and *gambas*, *gâteaux Basques*, and apéritifs of wild prune *Patxaran* (pronounced "padsharan"). (☎05 59 26 73 59. Open June-Sept. daily noon-3pm and 7-11pm).

The Hôtel Verdun's restaurant, **Relais de St-Jacques,** 13 av. de Verdun, across from the train station, is the best deal in St-Jean-de-Luz. The ever-changing 70F/€10.67 *menu* includes a cauldron of soup, a main course, and an all-you-can-eat dessert tray. (☎05 59 26 02 55. Open July-Aug. daily noon-2pm and 7-8:45pm; Sept.-June M-F noon-2pm and 7-8:45pm, Sa noon-2pm. MC/V.) **Chez Etchebaster,** 42 rue Gambetta, caters to sweet tooths with cream-filled *gâteaux basques.* (☎05 59 26 00 80. Open Tu-Sa 8am-12:30pm and 3-7:30pm, Su 8am-1pm and 4-7pm. MC/V.)

AQUITAINE

SIGHTS AND FESTIVALS

To see St-Jean-de-Luz at its most striking, follow the walkway on the beachfront away from the river Nivelle to the end of the Grande Plage. The path up toward the **Chapelle Van Bree** takes you on a *balade à pied* (footpath) along the edge of St-Jean's layered cliffsides. From the lookout points, gaze out across the river Nive and to Hendaye and the Spanish border beyond. In town, the 15th-century **Eglise St-Jean-Baptiste,** rue Gambetta, looks plain from the outside, but is filled within by elaborate gilt wood carvings of saints and apostles. (Open daily 8:30am-noon and 2-6:30pm). This was the church where Louis XIV married the Spanish king's daughter Maria-Teresa, according to the terms of the 1659 Treaty of the Pyrenees. The treaty was worked out after months of negotiations by Cardinal Mazarin and the Spanish prime minister on the nearby *île des faisans* or "island of conferences," a "no man's land" jointly owned by France and Spain.

At the pl. Louis XIV, the **Maison Louis XIV** has inside decoration and furnishing frozen in time, seemingly awaiting the return of its most famous boarder. It was here that Louis XIV stayed while Mazarin negotiated, and here that he consummated his marriage with Maria Teresa. Unlike the average royal marriage, this one proved successful; upon the queen's death, the king lamented, *"C'est le premier chagrin qu'elle me cause"* ("this is the first sorrow she has caused me"). (☎05 59 26 01 56. Open July-Aug. M-Sa 10:30am-noon and 2:30-6:30pm, Su 2:30-6:30pm; Sept.-June until 5:30pm. 25F/€3.81, students 20F/€3.05. 30min. recorded tour in French leaves every 30min. Written explanations in English upon request.)

SWIMMING WITH THE FISHES

From 1954 to 1956, St-Jean-de-Luz was France's premier supplier of tuna. Fishing boats still leave regularly from quai de l'Infante and quai Maréchal Leclerc. To get in on the fun at sea level, stop by the docks, where **Mairie Rose** offers a four-hour fishing trip from 8am to noon. (☎05 59 26 39 84; www.bateau-marierose.com. 160F/€24.39). If you prefer to leave the fish alive, **Promenade Jacques Thibaud,** sheltered by protective dikes, provides some of the best sailing and windsurfing in the Basque region. Farther on, the best surfing in St-Jean-de-Luz is beyond the more popular beaches on **Plage d'Erromardi.**

FESTIVALS

Summer is packed with concerts, Basque festivals, and a championship match of *cesta punta*, one of the many variations on the game of *pelote basque*, a game played like jai alai or lacrosse. (*Cesta punta* July-Aug. Tu and F at 9:15pm. Tickets 50-120F/€7.62-18.30 at the tourist office.) The biggest annual festival is the three-day **Fête de St-Jean,** held the last weekend in June, when singing and dancing fill

FRONTON CENTER In the Pays Basque, the term *pelote basque* refers to a number of games. One of them, *cesta punta* (or jai alai), is the world's fastest ball game. Burly players hurl a hard ball at a wall at speeds of up to 200km per hour at a wall by means of a *chistera* (basket appendage) laced to the wrist. Outdoor *fronton* arenas and indoor *trinquets* bear witness to local players' speed and skill. Spreading beyond its homeland, *pelote basque* fever has caught on in such places as Cancun, Cuba, and Connecticut. But watch out, ladies: so far, only men have played.

the streets. Nearly perpetual performances by amateurs and professionals alike liven the *fronton* (arena), with sangria and barbecued Basque dishes with names like *Taloak* and *Txartelak.* **Toro de Fuego** heats up summer nights in pl. Louis XIV with pyrotechnics, dancing, and bull costumes. (July-Aug. W 10:30pm, Su 11:30pm.) At the **Fête du Thon** (the first Sa in July), the town gathers around the harbor to eat tuna, toss confetti, and pirouette (60F/€9.15). The madness continues the last Saturday of July with the all-you-can-eat **Nuit de la Sardine** at the Campos-Berri, next to the *cesta punta* stadium. The fabulous **Fête du Ttoro** features all manner of exciting activities involving *ttoro* (fish soup). The *fête* takes place on an early Saturday in September; the next day, residents can sheepishly confess to the priests whom they pelted with fish guts hours earlier.

DAYTRIP FROM ST-JEAN-DE-LUZ: LA RHUNE

***Basque Bondissant** (☎05 59 26 30 74) runs buses to **Col de St-Ignace** from the green-rimmed bus terminal facing the train station in **St-Jean-de-Luz** (30min.; July-Aug. M-F 2 per day that meet train to La Rhune, Sept.-June M-Tu and Th-F 1 per day; 25F/€3.81 round-trip to the base of the mountain, 89F/€13.57 with train to the top.)*

Ten kilometers southeast of St-Jean-de-Luz, the miniscule village of **Col de St-Ignace** serves as a gateway to the Basque country's loveliest vantage point. From here, an authentic 1924 *chemin de fer* (railroad) crawls at a snail's pace up the mountainside to the 900m summit of **La Rhune.** Each tortuous turn reveals a postcard-perfect display of forests hovering above sloping farmland, as *pottoks* (wild Basque ponies) return your curious stares and sheep bound down the mountainside. At the peak, chilling air and gusty winds prevail even in summer. (Trains operated by **SHEM.** ☎05 59 54 20 26; www.basque-explorer.com/rhune.htm. July-Oct. daily every 35min. from 9am; May-June and Oct.-Nov. 15 Sa-Su, and holidays 10am and 3pm. 60F/€9.15 round-trip.) La Rhune *(Larun)* is Spanish soil; shopowners slip easily between French and their native tongue. If you decide to walk back down from La Rhune, safety warrants a longer, roundabout route; loose rocks on the path make for treacherous footing. Take the well-marked trail to the left of the tracks down to the village of **Ascain,** instead of trying to return directly to St-Ignace, and hike the remaining 3km on D4 back to Col de St-Ignace (1½hr.); or set out directly for St-Jean-de-Luz from Ascain along the busy highway (5km).

ST-JEAN-PIED-DE-PORT

St-Jean-Pied-de-Port is the last stop before the tortuous mountain pass of Roncevaux on the pilgrimage to the tomb of St-Jacques in Santiago de Compostela, Spain. Pilgrims have been making the trek ever since the 10th century, their routes intersecting in this medieval village surrounded by the red Pyrenean hills. In the village, a single cobblestone street marks the steep ascent through the *haute ville* to the dilapidated fortress, offering ever expanding vistas of the rolling hills and red-tiled roofs of the surrounding villages. First built by Sancho the Strong in the 13th century, the walls of St-Jean-Pied-de-Port have withstood attack from Visigoths, Charlemagne's men, the Moors, and the Spanish army. Outside the walls, visitors can set off on numerous hikes into the French and Spanish mountains. The Fôret d'Iraty, a mecca for hikers and cross-country skiers, is only 25km away.

PRACTICAL INFORMATION. **Trains** leave for **Bayonne** (1hr.; 5 per day, last train leaves July-Aug. 6:50pm; Sept.-June Su-Th 4:33pm, F 4:56pm, Sa 6:50pm; 47F/€7.17) from the station on av. Renaud (☎05 59 37 02 00; open daily from 5:40am). **Rent bikes** at **Garazi Cycles,** 1 pl. St-Laurent. (☎05 59 37 21 79. 50F/€7.62 per half-day, 120F/€18.30 per day, 150F/€22.90 per weekend, 400F/€60.98 per week. Passport deposit. Open M-Sa 8:30am-noon and 3-6pm.) From the station, turn left and then immediately right onto av. Renaud, follow it up the slope, and turn right at its end to reach the **tourist office,** 14 av. de Gaulle, which gives out small hiking maps for the surrounding region. (☎05 59 37 03 57; fax 05 59 37 34 91; saint.jean.pied.de.port@wanadoo.fr. Open July-Aug. M-Sa 9am-12:30pm and 2-7pm, Su 10:30am-12:30pm and 3-6pm; Sept.-June M-F 9am-noon and 2-7pm, Sa 9am-noon and 2-6pm.) The **police** are on rue d'Ugagne (☎05 59 37 00 36). The **post office** (☎05 59 37 90 00), rue de la Poste, has **currency exchange** (open M-F 9am-noon and 2-5pm, Sa 9am-noon). **Postal code:** 64220.

AQUITAINE

ACCOMMODATIONS, CAMPING, AND FOOD. St-Jean offers pretty rooms at ugly prices; you won't find much under 160F/€24.39 per night. The best option is to stay at Mme. Etchegoin's *gîte d'étape*, a popular stopover for pilgrims following the chemin de St-Jacques. The lodging is just outside the city walls, 9 rte. d'Uhart. From the tourist office, walk downhill, crossing the bridge, and take your first right on the opposite bank. The street becomes rte. d'Uhart after you pass through the city gates (5min., follow signs to Bayonne). Twelve spartan bunks, divided among three white rooms, await in an 18th-century house, as do six attractive *chambres d'hôte* with flowered pillows and hardwood floors. (☎05 59 37 12 08. Breakfast 25F/€3.81. Reception 8am-10pm. Sheets or sleeping bag 17F/€2.59. Dorms 50F/€7.62. Doubles 200-220F/€30.49-33.54.) **Hôtel des Remparts,** 16 pl. Floquet, has 14 large and beautifully clean rooms on the same road as Mme. Etchegoin's *gîte*, but inside the city walls. (☎05 59 37 13 89; fax 05 59 37 33 44. Breakfast 34F/€5.18. Reception Apr.-Sept. 9:30am-10pm; Oct.-Mar. M-F only. Singles and doubles 230-270F/€35.06-41.16; triples 300F/€45.74. MC/V.) A block uphill from the tourist office, opposite the old town wall, **Hôtel Itzalpea,** 5 pl. du Trinquet, has ten institutional-looking rooms, some without windows. (☎05 59 37 03 66; fax 05 59 37 33 18. Breakfast 40F/€6.10. Singles and doubles with shower, TV, and telephone 220F/€33.54; triples and quads 300-350F/€45.74-53.36. MC/V.)

Quiet **Camping Municipal** rests against a low ivy-encrusted stone wall by the Nive, close to the center of town. For its price, the campsite has the most central and convenient location of any lodging in St-Jean. From the porte St-Jacques, follow the river upstream 50m to the next bridge. When you cross the river, the site will be on your left on av. du Fronton (5min.). (☎05 59 37 11 19. Open Apr.-Oct. daily 8-10am and 5-8pm. 13F/€1.98 per person, 8F/€1.22 per tent, 8F/€1.22 per car.)

Farmers bring *ardigazna* (tangy, dry, sheep's-milk cheese) to the **market** on pl. de Gaulle (M 9am-6pm). In July and August, there are also local fairs that bring produce from all the villages nearby; ask for the dates at the tourist office. Bread, cheese and wine are all available at any one of the many small shops that line **rue d'Espagne.** For everyday food, there is the **Relais de Mousquetaires supermarket,** also on rue d'Espagne. (☎05 59 37 00 47. Open M, W, and F-Sa 9:30am-12:30pm and 4-7:30pm.) None of the inexpensive restaurants in St-Jean-Pied-du-Port are spectacular, but there are a number of cafés and crêperies along the main strip past the tourist office that each are good for a cheap meal and refreshing sangria.

SIGHTS AND ENTERTAINMENT. St-Jean's streets and mountain location make for wonderful explorations. The ancient *haute ville*, bounded by **Porte d'Espagne** and **Porte St-Jacques,** consists of one narrow street, **rue de la Citadelle,** bordered by houses made from regional crimson stone. The well-preserved remains of St-Jean-Pied-de-Port's **Citadelle de Vauban** lie at the top of narrow rue de la Citadelle, which originates in the trinket frenzy of the *haute ville*. Although the interior of this fortress is now an elementary school, visitors enjoy unlimited access to the fortified grounds. The present edifice, built by the knight Antoine Deville, dates back to 1628, but you'll also notice signs of renovations begun in 1680 by Vauban, chief military architect and planner under Louis XIV. Return to the *haute ville* by the partially concealed staircase that runs along the ramparts. It will be on your right as you complete a counter-clockwise tour of the grounds.

The staircase returns you to the steep main street, which takes you past the 13th-century **Prison des Evêques,** 41 rue de la Citadelle. Once a municipal prison, the building sat next to the medieval headquarters of local bishops. At some point, the names were combined and the "prison of the bishops" was formed. The museum now documents information on the pilgrimage of St-Jacques and the game of *pelote basque.* (Open Apr.-Oct. 15 daily 10am-12:15pm and 3-6:15pm. 15F/€2.29.) Rue de la Citadelle returns you to the rear of the **Eglise Notre-Dame-du-Bout-du-Pont,** fused with the **Porte St-Jacques** on the banks of the Nive. Once a fortress, the church betrays its past with rocky, low-lit crevices instead of side chapels. Carefully patterned stained glass casts a mist of light over the rest of the simple edifice. (Open daily 7am-9pm.) A wooded walk to the left of the church along the river leads to the stone arches of the postcard-popular **Pont Romain** (about 10min.).

In summer, *bals* (street dances) and concerts offer free frivolity, while Basque choirs and *pelote* add local color. (*Pelote* June-Sept. F at 5pm at the *fronton municipal* by the campground.) Thursday nights in July and August, traditional Basque folkdances are held in different locations around the town. Once in July and once in August, Basques get buff for the **Force Basque** competition, which includes gritty tug-of-war matches and the hoisting of 150-pound hay bales. Admission around 40F/€6.10, but you can peer through vines from the fence for free.

HIKE: THE PILGRIM'S ROUTE. The Spanish border is only a four- to five-hour walk from St-Jean-Pied-de-Port along a clearly marked trail. The **GR65** leads you through the Pyrenees toward the Pass of Roncevaux, and eventually almost 800km later to Santiago de Compostela and St-Jacques' tomb. To get on the trail from St-Jean, take the rue d'Espagne out from the Porte de l'Eglise. Continue straight ahead as it becomes rte. de St-Michel and then rte. Napoleon. You will start to see painted red and white stripes on the telephone poles, the symbol of the GR65. The narrow paved road slopes up the mountainside, past family farms and then into the Pyrenees, where cows, sheep, and wild horses wander. The **Fontaine de Roland** and the **col de Bentarte** signal entry onto Spanish land. The round-trip hike takes about eight hours; if it becomes too late to turn back, there is lodging near the pass of Roncevaux, about a two-hour walk past the Fontaine de Roland.

PAU

Pau, once the seat of the kings of Navarre, clings tightly to this heritage and the memory of its native son Henry IV of France, who ended the Wars of Religion with the Edict of Nantes in 1598. But although Henry's castle is in near-perfect condition, the surrounding city (pop. 78,000) has begun to show some signs of wear. There is fairly little to see besides the château, but Pau benefits from the good weather that slopes off the nearby Pyrenees and its proximity to many mountain sports. And its position as the capital of the Béarn region has made it the capital of Béarnais cuisine—the city now holds more than 150 restaurants, each serving delicacies that 17th-century epicures agreed were the best in the kingdom.

ORIENTATION AND PRACTICAL INFORMATION. The **train station,** on av. Gaston Lacoste, is at the base of the hill by the château. Trains go to: **Bayonne** (1¾hr., 7 per day, 82F/€12.51); **Biarritz** (2hr., 6-7 per day, 84F/€12.81); **Bordeaux** (2hr., 9 per day, 186F/€28.37); **Lourdes** (30min., 14 per day, 40F/€6.10); **Paris** (5hr., 8 per day, 458F/€69.85); and **St-Jean-de-Luz** (1¾hr., 4 per day, 98F/€14.95). (Info desk open M-F 9:30am-6:40pm, Sa 9am-6pm.) **CITRAM,** 30 rue Gachet, runs **buses** to **Agen** (1¾hr., 1 per day, 164F/€25.01). (☎05 59 27 22 22. Office open M 2:30-6:15pm, Tu-F 8:40am-12:15pm and 2:30-6:15pm, Sa 8:40am-12:15pm.) **Société**

TPR, 2 pl. Clemenceau, heads to **Bayonne** (2¼hr., 2 per day, 78.50F/€11.97); **Biarritz** (2½hr., 2 per day, 84.50F/€12.88); **Lourdes** (1¼hr., 5 per day, 36F/€5.49). (☎05 59 82 95 85. Office open M-F 8am-noon and 2-6pm.) **STAP,** rue Gachet, runs **local buses** (tickets 6F/€0.92). (☎05 59 14 15 16.) For a **taxi,** call 05 59 02 22 22 (24hr.). **Pedegaye Cyclesport,** 3 chaussée de la Plaine, **rents bikes.** (☎05 59 77 82 30. 100F/€15.25 per day, 250F/€38.13 per week. Deposit 1000F/€152.46. Open M 2-7pm, Tu-Sa 9am-noon and 2-7pm. MC/V.)

To get to the tourist office and town center from the station, ride the free **funicular** to bd. des Pyrénées (every 3min., M-Sa 6:45am-12:10pm, 12:35-7:30pm, and 7:55-9:40pm; Su 1:30-7:30pm and 7:55-9pm), or climb the steep zigzagging path outlined in white fences to the top of the hill. At the top, the **tourist office** is at the far end of pl. Royale, across the tree-lined park from the funicular. Ask for their free map, *Pau—Ville Authentique.* They also have a free accommodations service, and give out copies of *Béarn Pyrénées,* with *gîtes* and camping info. (☎05 59 27 27 08; fax 05 59 27 03 21. Office open M-Sa 9am-6pm, Su 9:30am-1pm.) **Service des Gîtes Ruraux,** 20 rue Gassion, in the Cité Administrative, gives advice on mountain lodgings and will make reservations. (☎05 59 11 20 64. Open M-F 9am-12:30pm and 2-5pm.) Other services include: **police,** rue O'Quin (☎05 59 98 22 22); the **hospital,** 4 bd. Hauterive (☎05 59 92 48 48); and a **laundromat,** rue Gambetta (open daily 7am-10pm). Access the **Internet** at **C Cyber,** 20 rue Lamothe, past the post office. (☎05 59 82 89 40. Open M-Sa 11am-2am, Su 2-11pm. 5F/€0.76 per 10min.) The **post office,** on cours Bosquet at rue Gambetta, has **currency exchange.** (☎05 59 98 98 98. Open M-F 8am-6:30pm, Sa 8am-noon.) **Postal code:** 64000.

AQUITAINE

ACCOMMODATIONS, CAMPING, AND FOOD. Near the château and on a side street that runs directly from the front door of the St-Martin church, **Hôtel d'Albret,** 11 rue Jeanne d'Albret, has huge and peaceful rooms for the lowest prices in Pau. Turn right as you exit the tourist office; the hotel is on the second right along rue Henri IV. (☎05 59 27 81 58. Breakfast 18F/€2.74. Showers free. Reception 7:30am-10:30pm. Singles and doubles 90F/€13.72, with shower 120F/€18.30, with bath 145F/€22.11; triples 125F/€19.06, with bath 155F/€23.63.) There is a **Logis des Jeunes** hostel 3km from the train station, outside Pau in Gelos. Take bus #1 (dir: "Larrious Mazeres-Lezon") to "Mairie de Gelos." A limited number of frequently filled beds and kitchen facilities await (☎05 59 06 53 02. No reservations; give them a call from the train station to see if they have any vacancies. Dorms 84F/€12.81, HI members 54F/€8.24.) **Hôtel de la Pomme d'Or,** 11 rue Maréchal Foch, between the post office and pl. Clemenceau, has smaller, dimmer, and stuffier rooms than the Albret, off a dingy hallway. The hotel is only a few blocks from the tourist office in the opposite direction from Hôtel d'Albret. Turn left out of the tourist office along rue Louis Barthou and left again on rue A. de-Lassence. Walk through pl. Clemenceau and turn right on rue Maréchal Foch. (☎05 59 11 23 23; fax 05 59 11 23 24. Breakfast 20F/€3.05. Reception 24hr. Singles 95F/€14.48, with shower 125F/€19.06; doubles 115F/€17.53, with shower 120-160F/€18.30-24.39; triples 210F/€32.02; quads 225-240F/€34.31-36.59.) **Camping Municipal de la Plaine des Sports et des Loisirs** is a 6km trek from the station. Take bus #7 from the station to pl. Clemenceau (dir: "Trianon" or "Pl. Clemenceau") and switch to bus #4 (dir: "Bocage Palais des Sports"). Get off at the final stop. (☎05 59 02 30 49. Open May 5-Sept. 22. 17.40F/€2.65 per person; 33.50F/€5.11 per tent.)

The region that brought you tangy *béarnaise* sauce has no *pau*city of specialties: salmon, pike, *oie* (goose), *canard* (duck), and *assiette béarnaise,* a succulent platter that can include gizzards, duck hearts, and asparagus. The area around the château, including **rue Sully** and **rue du Château,** only has elegant regional restaurants. Down the hill, the *quartier du hédas* offers more expensive fare in a fancier setting. Inexpensive pizzerias and ethnic eateries can be found on **rue Léon Daran** and adjoining streets. The Olympic-sized **Champion supermarket** sits in the new **Centre Bosquet** megaplex on cours Bosquet (open M-Sa 9am-7:30pm). The enormous **market** at **Les Halles,** pl. de la République, is a maze of vegetable, meat, and cheese stalls (M-Sa 6am-1pm). The **Marché Biologique,** pl. du Foirail, offers organic produce to the health-conscious (W and Sa 7:30am-12:30pm). Near Les Halles, the beautiful and modern **Le Saint Vincent,** 4 rue Gassiot, serves 44F/€6.71 *moules frites* and 96F/€14.64 *escargots.* (☎05 59 27 75 44. Open M-Sa 7:30am-9:30pm.) On a cobblestone street by the château, **Au Fruit Defondu,** 3 rue Sully, serves nine kinds of fondue—many including typical Béarnaise fare, such as duck hearts. (☎05 59 27 26 05. Open daily 7pm-12:30am.)

SIGHTS AND ENTERTAINMENT. Formerly the residence of *béarnais* viscounts and Navarrese kings, the 12th-century **Château d'Henri IV** is now a national museum. Glorious Gobelin tapestries, preserved royal chambers, and ornate ceilings and chandeliers grace a castle that doesn't seem to belong to any particular age—partly because Napoleon and Louis-Philippe both remodeled it to suit their needs. Today, the military fortress of the 12th century seems lost among the long balconies and large windows that made life nicer for kings from the 15th century onward. Interminable-feeling French tours of the château leave every 15 minutes and last an hour. (☎05 59 82 38 00. Open daily 9:30am-12:15pm and 1:30-5:45pm. Last tour 1hr. before closing. English brochure available. 25F/€3.81, under 18 free.) It becomes clear that Henry IV is a local obsession when you visit the **Musée des Beaux-Arts,** on rue Mathieu Lalanne, where the marble staircase leads first to an enormous tableau of his birth and then to a wall-length depiction of his 1598 coronation. The rest of this uneven museum contains a small collection of modern art and a rather more impressive collection of 17th- to 19th-century European paintings. (☎05 59 27 33 02. Open W-M 10am-noon and 2-6pm. 12F/€1.83, students 6F/€0.92.) The mild climate makes Pau conducive to botanical flights of fancy, and for a good part of the year the town is covered in flowers and trees of every color and origin, from America to Japan. The best place to sample some of this biodiversity is around the pond in the **parc Beaumont.** Follow the bd. des Pyrénées away from the castle to the Palais Beaumont; the park is just behind the Palais.

Clubs in the town center cater to an older and more sedate crowd. The real action is 7km across town in **La Noche,** av. de Pau, home to serious dancing and partying. You'll need your own wheels, a taxi, or the help of some locals to make it that far. In town, a lively foreign bar scene illuminates the bd. des Pyrénées at night. Two Irish bars, an Australian bar, and a Russian café serve a stylish mixed crowd of youngsters and thirty-somethings. For those looking for more excitement, **Le Contre-temps** has laser lights, a live DJ, and pounding techno music. (☎05 59 98 40 74. Open M-Sa 9am-2:30am; closed M nights. DJs Th-Sa.) **Cinéma le Méliés,** 6 rue Bargoin, shows some artsy films, some in English. (☎05 59 27 60 52, listings ☎08 36 68 68 87. Tickets 35F/€5.34, students 28F/€4.27. Closed Aug.)

In mid-March, the **Festival de Flamenco** comes to town with an impressive array of dancers and musicians. Starting in mid-June, the **Festival de Pau** brings a month of theater, music, ballet, and poetry to the château courtyard and to the Théâtre St-Louis. (Reservations ☎05 59 27 27 08 or 05 59 98 90 00.) A Formula 3 **Grand Prix de Pau** is held the weekend of Pentecost. In the first week of August, the **Festival International des Pyrénées,** 35km south of Pau in Oloron, brings in 45 folk ballet troups from 25 countries (info and tickets ☎05 59 39 98 00 or 05 59 80 77 50). Trains and SNCF buses run to Oloron from Pau's train station (30-35min., 14 per day, 40F/€6.10).

LOURDES

In 1858, 14-year-old Bernadette Soubirous reported seeing the first of what would total 18 visions of the Virgin Mary in the Massabielle grotto in Lourdes. Over time, "The Lady" made a spring appear beneath Bernadette's fingers, told her to repent, drink, and wash in a nearby stream, and instructed her to "go tell the priests to build a chapel here so that people may come in procession." Bernadette may have gotten more than she bargained for. Today, over five million visitors from 100 countries come to Lourdes (pop. 16,300) annually, filling the 18,000 rooms that make Lourdes second only to Paris in total hotel capacity. Toting rosaries, hoping for miracles, and filling bottles with holy water from Bernadette's spring, the faithful and the gawking flock to the Blessing of the Sick here. Lourdes is a gateway to the Pyrenees (Cauterets is just a 50-minute bus ride away), and a world center for pilgrimages. But even pilgrims shouldn't miss its secular wonders. The medieval fortress rising from the center of town and the panoramic views from the summit of nearby Pic du Jer rival any nearby city's attractions.

TRANSPORTATION

Trains: 33 av. de la Gare (☎05 62 42 55 53). To: **Bayonne** (2hr., 5 per day, 108F/€16.47); **Bordeaux** (3hr.; 7 per day; 176F/€26.83, TGV 186F/€28.36); **Paris** (7-9hr.; 5 per day, TGV 523F/€79.74); **Pau** (30min.; 16 per day; 40F/€6.10, TGV 50F/€7.62); and **Toulouse** (2½hr., 8 per day, 127F/€19.36). Info office open daily 6am-8:50pm.

Buses: SNCF runs from the station to **Cauterets** (50min., 3-6 per day, 39F/€5.95).

Local Buses: Buses run from all points in the city to the Grotto. Buses also run to the Pic du Jer (from which the funicular departs) and to the Lac de Lourdes. Buses run about every 20min. Easter-Oct. daily 7am-6:30pm. Tickets 10F/€1.53.

Taxis: Taxi Lourdais at the train station (☎05 62 94 31 30) and grotto (☎05 62 94 31 35; Easter-Oct.).

Bike Rental: Cycles Antonio Oliveria, 14 av. Alexandre Marqui (☎05 62 42 24 24), near the train station. Open Tu-Sa 9:30am-7pm. 60F/€9.15 per half-day, 120F/€18.30 per day, 480F/€73.18 per week.

AQUITAINE

ORIENTATION AND PRACTICAL INFORMATION

The train station is on the northern edge of town, ten minutes from the town center. To get from the station to the **tourist office,** turn right onto av. de la Gare, then bear left onto busy av. Maransin at the first intersection, cross a bridge above bd. du Lapacca, and proceed gently uphill. The office is in a modern glass complex on the right (5min.). To get to the **grotto** and most other sights, follow av. de la Gare through the intersection, turn left on bd. de la Grotte, and follow it as it snakes right at pl. Jeanne d'Arc. Cross the river Gave to reach the Esplanade des Processions, the Basilique Pius X, and the grotto (10min.).

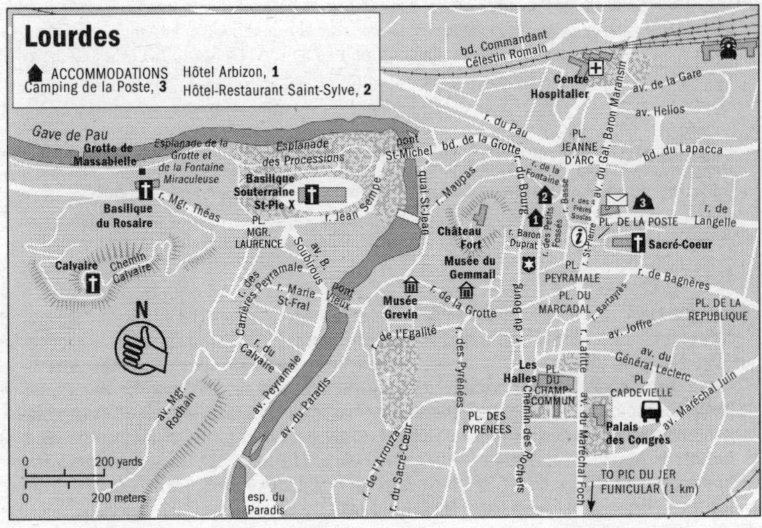

Tourist Office: pl. Peyramale (☎05 62 42 77 40; fax 05 62 94 60 95; lourdes@sudfr.com). Friendly polyglot staff distributes maps, info on religious ceremonies, and a list of hotels. Open May-Oct. M-Sa 9am-7pm; Nov. 1-15 9am-noon and 2-7pm; Nov. 16-Mar. 15 9am-noon and 2-6pm; Mar. 16-Apr. 9am-noon and 2-7pm. Bernadette-related sights are managed by the Church-affiliated **Sanctuaires de Notre-Dame de Lourdes** (☎05 62 42 78 78), which has a **Forum d'Info** to the left, in front of the basilica. Open daily 8:30am-12:30pm and 1:30-7pm.

Youth Center: Forum Lourdes/Bureau Information Jeunesse, in pl. de Champ Commun beyond Les Halles (☎05 62 94 94 00). Open M-F 9am-noon and 2-6pm.

Laundromat: Laverie GTI, 10 av. Maransin. Dry-cleaning too. Open daily 8am-7pm.

Police: 7 rue Baron Duprat (☎05 62 42 72 72). Open daily 9am-noon and 3-8pm.

Hospital: Centre Hospitalier, 3 av. Alexandre Marqui (☎05 62 42 42 42). At the intersection of av. de la Gare, av. Marqui, and av. Maransin. **Medical emergency:** 2 av. Marqui (☎05 62 42 44 36).

Information for people with disabilities: A Catholically-inclined guide to facilities entitled *Guide de Lourdes* (20F/€3.05) is available from the **Association Nationale Pour Integration Handicapés Moteurs,** on bd. du Lapacca. Call first (☎05 62 94 83 88).

Internet Access: In the social and cultural center in pl. du Champ Commun (☎05 62 94 94 00). 20F/€3.05 per hr. Open daily 9am-noon and 2-6pm.

Post Office: 31 av. Maransin (☎05 62 42 72 00). **Currency exchange** machine takes bills only. Open M-F 8:30am-6:30pm, Sa 8:30am-noon. **Postal code:** 65100.

AQUITAINE

ACCOMMODATIONS AND CAMPING

Lourdes is a city of pilgrims—you should have no problem finding a room at 160F/€24.39, or even below. The city's massive healing industry has induced most proprietors to improve wheelchair accessibility as well as facilities for the visually and hearing impaired, though this is less true in the cheapest hotels.

Hôtel Saint-Sylve, 9 rue de la Fontaine (☎/fax 05 62 94 63 48). Follow av. Helios away from the train station as it curves down the hill. Bear right and under the bridge in front of you on bd. du Lapacca. Take your first left after the bridge uphill onto rue Basse; rue de la Fontaine is the second right. Spare, uninspired rooms overlook a side street beside the town center and close to the grotto. Breakfast 25F/€4. Reception until 11:30pm; call ahead if arriving late. Closed Oct. 31-Mar. 30. Singles 80F/€13; doubles 180F/€28; triples 220F/€34.

Hôtel Arbizon, 37 rue des Petits Fossés (☎/fax 05 62 94 29 36). Follow directions to Saint-Sylve, but take your first left off rue Basse. Centrally located, with small but sufficient rooms at low prices. Pleasant, welcoming owner. Breakfast 25F/€3.81. Reception 7am-midnight. Open Feb. 9-Nov. 11. *Demi-pension* and *pension* from 130-150F/19.82-22.90. Singles 90F/€13.72; doubles 120F/€18.30; triples 150F/€22.90.

Camping de la Poste, 26 rue de Langelle (☎05 62 94 40 35), has about 12 large spaces with grass and shade trees in a backyard 2min. beyond the post office. Open Easter-Oct. 15. Hot shower 8F/€1.22. 15F/€2.29 per person, 23F/€3.51 per site. Electricity 16F/€2.44.

FOOD

Groceries along the processional route will gladly feed you for outrageous prices. Find relief at **Casino supermarket,** 9 pl. Peyramale (☎05 62 94 03 87; open Tu-F 7:30am-1pm and 3:30-8pm, Sa 7:30am-1pm and 3-8pm, Su 8am-1pm), or at the bigger **Prisunic supermarket,** 9 pl. du Champ Commun (☎05 62 94 63 44; open M-Sa 8:30am-12:30pm and 2-7:30pm, Su 8am-noon). Produce, flowers, second-hand clothing, and books are all sold daily at the **market** at **Les Halles,** pl. du Champ Commun (daily 8am-1pm, every other Th until 5pm).

Restaurants not affiliated with hotels are few and far between in Lourdes. On the main strip of the **bd. de la Grotte,** many similar restaurants charge similar prices for meals. The meal, surrounded by religious souvenir shops, will cost from 60-80F/€9.15-12.20. Slightly lower priced *plats du jour* and *menus* can be found around the tourist office and on **rue de la Fontaine;** don't expect gourmet fare or pay more than 70F/€10.67—quality varies little with price here. To escape the rush of tourists, head away from the grotto toward the cheap pizzerias of **Les Halles.**

SIGHTS

Passeport Visa Lourdes *(169F/€25.77) provides access to seven activities: admission to four Bernadette-related museums, the Fortified Castle and its museum, the funicular to Pic du Jer, and a tourist train ride through town. Ask for details at the tourist office.*

GROTTE DE MASSABIELLE. It was in this cavern at the edge of town that the Virgin Mary appeared to Bernadette. Visitors to Lourdes come for even just a glimpse of these holy rocks and the spring that flows beneath. In the afternoon rush, hundreds shuffle past this small dark crevice in the mountainside, touching its cold rock walls, whispering prayers, and waiting to receive a blessing from the priest on duty. Nearby, water from the spring where Bernadette washed her face is available for drinking, bathing, and bringing back home. The cave lies by the river on the right side of two superimposed churches, the Basilique du Rosaire and the upper basilica. *(No shorts or tank tops. Fountain and grotto open daily 5am-midnight.)*

THE BASILICAS. The **Basilique du Rosaire** and **upper basilica** were built double-decker style above Bernadette's grotto. In the **Rosaire,** completed in 1889, an enormous Virgin Mary strikes a maternal pose. The **upper basilica,** consecrated in 1876 has a more traditional interior. If you're looking for **the Basilique St-Pius X,** you're probably standing on it. It's underground, in front of the other two basilicas and to the left of the Esplanade des Processions—a stadium-sized concrete echo chamber designed in the form of an upturned ship. It won an international design prize in 1958 despite closely resembling the parking garage of the Starship Enterprise. Covering 12,000 square meters, its concrete cavern fits 20,000 souls with room to spare. Super-electric stained-glass rectangles—appropriately Cubist versions of the traditional sunlit model—are placed at 10m intervals. *(All 3 open Easter-Oct. daily 6am-7pm; Nov.-Easter 8am-6pm, excluding masses.)*

PROCESSIONS AND BLESSINGS. The **Procession of the Blessed Sacrament** and the **Blessing of the Sick** are huge affairs held daily at 5pm, starting in the Basilica Pius X; fight for bench space or watch from the upper basilica's balcony. As a one-day pilgrim, you can join the procession and march along the esplanade behind rolling ranks of wheelchairs. *(Meet other pilgrims July-Sept. at 8:30am at the "Crowned Virgin" statue in front of the basilica.)* A solemn **torchlit procession** in six languages blazes from the grotto to the esplanade nightly at 8:45pm. Add to the glow by lighting a long-burning candle, available for a few francs in the booths by the river Gave. *(Mass in English Apr.-Oct. daily at 9am at the Hémicycle, just across the river from the cave in a cavernous concrete building.)*

MUSEUMS. The **Musée de Gemmail** reproduces famous works of art in the thick multi-layered stained-glass technique that gives the museum its name. If you like stained glass, check out the equally large annex near the pont St-Michel. *(72 rue de la Grotte. ☎05 62 94 13 15. Open Apr.-Oct. daily 9-11:45am and 2-6:45pm. Annex on bd. Père Rémi Sempe. Free.)* Down the street, 100 wax figures in the **Musée Grevin** act out the lives of Bernadette and Jesus. Most impressive is the life-size wax replica of Leonardo da Vinci's *Last Supper*. *(87 rue de la Grotte. ☎05 62 94 33 74. Open July-Aug. daily 9-11:30am, 1:30-6:30pm, and 8:30-10pm; Apr.-June and Sept.-Oct. 9-11:30am and 1:30-6:30pm. 35F/€5.34, students 28F/€4.27.)*

CHATEAU FORT. Practically the only sight in town without a religious connection, the feudal castle overlooks Lourdes from atop a rocky crag. A shuttlecock in territorial disputes between France and England during the Middle Ages, the current building dates principally from the 14th century. The high square tower and well-preserved walls of the château now offer unequaled panoramas of surrounding Lourdes, and guard the strange displays of the **Musée Pyrénéen.** The museum displays a series of regional objects including wine barrels, decorated plates, and butter churns. *(☎05 62 42 37 37. Enter by elevator. Open Apr. 15-Oct. 15 M-Sa 9am-noon and 1:30-6:30pm, Su 11am-6pm; Oct. 16-Apr. W-M 9am-noon and 2-6pm. 32F/€4.88.)*

FUNICULAIRE. From just outside of town, a track climbs 1000m up the **Pic du Jer.** Local buses lead to the bottom of the track. Take this six-minute ride and walk the extra way (10min.) up to the observatory at the summit for a stunning 360° view of the surrounding countryside and the town below. More energetic folk can hike up or down with a map available from the ticket booth. Beware of rapidly descending mountain bikes. *(☎05 62 94 00 41. Daily every 30min. 9am-noon and 1:30-6:30pm. 44F/€6.71, children 22F/€3.36. Depot on the southern edge of town, at the base of the mountain. Follow the main road (called rue St-Pierre at first) 2km from the center of town by the tourist office. There's also a bus from the ticket booth at the intersection of rue de la Grotte and rue de la Tour de Brie. Round-trip bus ticket 20.40F/€3.11.)*

AQUITAINE

LAC DE LOURDES. Local bus #7 leads to a large, peaceful lake 4km away from the center of town, where locals flip off the dock or eat ice cream in the slightly overpriced café on the water. A blessed relief from the bustle of town, the lake is close enough for an afternoon after visits to the grotto and sanctuaries. To walk to the lake, take av. Maransin toward the train station and turn left on the bd. Romain. The street becomes first av. Béguere and then rte. de Pontacq. A left turn on the Chemin du Lac leads right to the water (about 30min.).

THE WESTERN PYRENEES

CAUTERETS

The people of tiny Cauterets (pop. 1300) seem friendlier than anywhere else in France. The explanation lies either in the sugared vapors coming from the candy stores or simply in the soothing influence of the town's location. Nestled 930m up in a narrow, breathtaking valley among near-vertical peaks, sleepy Cauterets wakes up in May and June to the sounds of a turquoise river rushing beneath its bridges. The melting snows of early summer bring wilderness lovers here, to the edge of the Parc National des Pyrénées Occidentales. For those up to the challenge, the wildly contrasting French and Spanish sides of the Pyrenees are both accessible from Cauterets, but there are plenty of rewarding opportunities for day hikes ranging from 1½-8 hours as well. When the hiking becomes overly taxing, the *thermes*, in addition to the arduous "cure," offer a relaxation program of *remise en forme* to bring you back to your former self.

ORIENTATION AND PRACTICAL INFORMATION. Cauterets runs lengthwise along the river Gave and is small enough to walk across in three minutes. It is accessible only by bus from Lourdes. From the bus station, turn right and follow av. Général Leclerc up a steep hill to the tourist office at pl. Foch. **SNCF buses** run from pl. de la Gare to **Lourdes** (1hr.; 6 per day; 39F/€5.95, students 30F/€4.57). (☎05 62 92 53 70. Office open daily 9am-12:30pm and 3-7pm.) You can rent **bikes,** as well as in-line skates and ice skates, at **Skilys,** rte. de Pierrefitte, on pl. de la Gare. (☎05 62 92 52 10. Mountain bikes with guide 110-185F/€16.77-28.21 per half-day, 250-350F/€38.12-53.36 per day, 1500-2500F/€228.69-381.16 deposit; without guide 60F/€9.15 per half-day, 100F/€15.25 per day, ID deposit. Open daily 9am-7pm; in winter 8am-7:30pm. AmEx/MC/V.) **Bernard Sports-tifs,** 2 rue Richelieu, next to the tourist office, offers good prices on **alpine ski rentals** and discounts for American students. (☎05 62 92 06 23. 70-100F/€10.67-15.25 per day for boots, skis, and poles; 380-540F/€57.95-82.33 for six days.)

The **tourist office,** pl. Foch, has a list of hotels, a useful map, and a *Guide Pratique.* (☎05 62 92 50 27; fax 05 62 92 59 12; www.cauterets.com. Open July-Aug. daily 9am-7pm; Sept.-June 9am-12:30pm and 2-6:30pm.) For hiking info, drop by the **Parc National des Pyrénées** office (see p. 688). The **police** are on av. du Docteur Domer (☎05 62 92 51 13). For **medical emergencies,** call 05 62 92 14 00. Access the **Internet** at **Pizzeria Giovanni,** 5 rue de la Raillère. (☎05 62 92 57 80. 40F/€6.10 per hr. Open July-Aug. daily; Sept.-June Th-Su only.) The **post office,** at the corner of rue Belfort and rue des Combattants, has **currency exchange.** (☎05 62 92 53 93; fax 05 62 92 08 83. Open July-Sept. 12 M-F 9am-6pm, Sa 9am-noon; Sept. 13-June M-F 9am-noon and 2-5pm, Sa 9am-noon.) **Postal code:** 65110.

ACCOMMODATIONS, CAMPING, AND FOOD. For the real mountain traveler, the best accommodations in town are at the **Gîte d'Etape UCJG,** av. du Docteur Domer, close to the center of town (200m). From the Parc National office, cross the parking lot and street and turn left uphill underneath the funicular depot. The *gîte* is just beyond the tennis courts. Gloriously located with welcoming hosts, this *gîte* has 60 beds in every sort of set-up, from a canvas barracks to the eaves of an attic, as well as leafy campsites. (☎05 62 92 52 95. Kitchen, shower, and sheets included. Reception daily, but hours vary. Open June 15-Sept. 15. Dorms 45-55F/€6.86-8.39; camping 20F/€3.05.) Every room at **Hôtel Bigorre,** 15 rue de Belfort, has a balcony that looks out on the surrounding mountains. The rooms are spacious, although some have peeling wallpaper and cracking paint. Rue de Belfort runs between pl. de la Gare and pl. Foch, where the tourist office is. (☎05 62 92 52 81. Breakfast 30F/€4.57. Singles 100F/€15.25, with shower 150F/€22.90; doubles 150F/€22.90, with shower 200F/€30.49; triples or quads 190-280F/€28.97-42.69.) **Hôtel Christian,** 10 rue Richelieu, offers a view of the Pyrenees, darts, and bocce for somewhat high prices. Make sure to spend time talking to the incredibly gracious owner, whose family has been running the hotel for generations. Cheaper rooms on the top floor are stuffy and darker than the others. (☎05 62 92 50 04; fax 05 62 92 05 67; http://perso.wanadoo.fr/hotel-christian. Breakfast included. Closed Oct. 10-Dec. 20. Singles 200F/€30.49, with shower 228F/€34.77, with TV 255F/€38.89; doubles 236F/€35.99, with shower 272F/€41.48, with TV 320F/€48.80; triples with shower and TV 423F/€64.51, quads with shower and TV 512F/€78.08. MC/V.)

The beautifully old-fashioned **Halles market,** a few doors down from the tourist office on av. du Général Leclerc, has fresh produce (daily 8:30am-12:30pm and 2:30-7:30pm). An **open-air market** is held in the parking lot at pl. de la Gare (June 15-Sept. F 8am-5pm). The local specialty is the *berlingot,* a hard sugar candy originally used by patients visiting the *thermes* to contribute to "the cure." You can watch 35 flavors of the candies being prepared by hand and cranked through a magical candy-making machine at **A la Reine Margot,** pl. de la Mairie Crown. (9-10F/€1.37-1.53 per 100g. Open daily 10am-midnight.) The husband and wife team at **Chez Gillou,** 3 rue de la Raillère, specialize in blueberry and almond cakes known respectively as *tourtes myrtilles* and *pastis des Pyrénées* (each 35F/€5.39). (☎05 62 92 56 58. Open July-Aug. and Feb.-Mar. daily 7am-1pm and 3:30-7:30pm; Sept., Dec., and Apr.-June Th-Tu 7:30am-12:30pm and 4-7pm.) Get regional jam, Basque cider, and cheap quiche with local flavorings just up the street at **Au Mille Pâtes,** 5 rue de la Raillère. (☎05 62 92 04 83. Open daily 8am-12:30pm and 4-7pm.)

SIGHTS. From the center of town, the **Téléphérique du Lys** cable car (☎05 62 92 50 27) races above the clouds every half-hour into the nearby mountains. From here, trails lead across the ridge and eventually to the breathtaking Lac d'Ilhéou (1½hr.). In July and August and ski season, the **Télésiege du Grand Barbat** chairlift takes you onto the **Crête du Lys,** over 1000m above Cauterets. (29F/€4.42 round-trip, 20F/€3.05 one-way.) You can hike back down from **Crête du Lys,** passing Lac d'Ilhéou on the way (1½hr.).

Cauterets' natural sulfur springs have been credited over the years with curing everything from sterility to consumption. But it's no bubble bath—the doctors and nurses here have taken to heart the maxim of "no pain, no gain." Separate sterilized rooms each offer different contraptions for "enjoying" the full effects of the water. You'll be given protective plastic covering for your shoes if you want to see the inhalation chambers and hosing rooms. For info on the *thermes*, contact **Thermes de Cesar,** av. Docteur Domer. (☎05 62 92 51 60. Open M-F 9am-12:30pm and 1:30-6pm, Sa 9am-12:30pm.) The *thermes* also offer a relaxing program of massage for those who don't have what it takes to undergo the full process.

ENTERTAINMENT. For a couple of days in early to mid-August, locals turn out for the **Festival des Terroirs Pyrénéens,** a festival with changing themes that usually include some aspect of historical Cauterets. Mainly an excuse to celebrate, it culminates in a grand outdoor ball in the evening (☎05 62 92 50 27 for information). In general, though, the town's nightlife tends to lack spice. Esplanade des Oeufs offers a **cinema** (☎05 62 92 52 14) playing French and foreign films (the latter are mostly popular American imports in their original language) and a **casino** (open May-Oct. daily 11am-3am). The **patinoire** (skating rink) hosts skating nights year-round, mostly near the end of the week, according to an complicated schedule given out by the tourist office. The rink itself can be reached through the parking lot of the train station. (30F/€4.57, children 13F/€1.98; skate rental 15F/€2.29.)

PARC NATIONAL DES PYRENEES OCCIDENTALES

One of France's seven national parks, the **Parc National des Pyrénées** holds endangered brown bears and lynxes, 200 threatened colonies of marmots, 118 lakes, and 160 unique plant species in its snow-capped mountains and lush valleys. Punctuated with sulfurous springs and unattainable peaks, the Pyrenees change dramatically with the seasons, never failing to awe a constant stream of visitors. To get a full sense of the extent and variety of the mountain range, you really have to experience both the lush French and barren Spanish sides of the Pyrenees (a 6- to 7-day round trip hike from Cauterets). But there are plenty of more modest opportunities as well, in case you're just looking to get your feet wet in the wilderness.

PRACTICAL INFORMATION AND SERVICES. Touch base with the friendly and very helpful staff of **Parc National Office,** Maison du Parc, pl. de la Gare, before braving the wilderness. They have loads of free info on the park and 15 different trails beginning and ending in Cauterets. The trails in the park are designed for a range of aptitudes, from rugged outdoor enthusiasts to those just discovering a love of nature. The **Haute Randonnée Pyrénées (HRP)** trails offer a more challenging mountain experience. Talk with the folks at the Parc National Office before attempting them. Documentary films (in French) 2-3 times a week featuring aerial views of the local mountains can turn you on to various hikes (55F/€8.39, children and students 10F/€1.53). (☎05 62 92 52 56; fax 05 62 92 62 23; www.parc-pyrenees.com. Open June-Aug. daily 9:30am-noon and 3-7pm; Sept.-May M-Tu and F-Su 9:30am-12:30pm and 3-6pm, Th 3-6pm.)

The **maps** sold at the Parc National office are probably sufficient (regional maps 42F/€6.41, day-hike maps 58F/€8.85). For the Cauterets region, use the #1647 Vignemale map published by the Institut de Géographie Nationale (IGN), sold at **La Civette bookstore,** 12 pl. Clemenceau. (☎05 62 92 53 87. Open July-Aug. and ski season daily 8:30am-1pm and 2:30-8pm; otherwise 9:30am-12:30pm and 3:30-7:30pm.) The **Bureau des Guides,** on tiny rue Verdun in Cauterets, runs tours and guides for rock-climbing, canyoning, hiking, and skiing. Medium-difficulty tours cost 90-200F/€13.72-30.49 per person; harder ones go for 300-900F/€45.74-137.22. Tours leave as early as 5am from the Cauterets tourist office. (Summer ☎05 62 92 62 02, winter ☎05 62 92 55 06. Open daily 10am-12:30pm and 3:30-7:30pm.)

Gîtes in the park average 75F/€11.43 a night and are strategically placed in towns along the GR10. Reserve at least 2 days ahead, especially in July and August, when the mountains flood with hikers. The Parc National office in Cauterets will help you plan an itinerary and make *gîte* reservations, as will the **Service des Gîtes Ruraux** (☎05 59 80 19 13) in Pau. The general rule is that you can camp anywhere in the wilderness for one night, provided you are more than an hour's hike from the nearest highway. Long-term camping in one place is not allowed. You can find a camp zone near a *refuge* if you want to stay in one place for a couple of days. Listen to **Météo-Montagne** for a weather forecast in French for nearby mountains (☎08 36 68 02 65; updated twice daily). For **Mountain Rescue,** call 05 62 92 75 07.

SKIING. The Cauterets tourist office has free *plans des pistes*—maps of ski paths for all skill levels. Many area resorts are accessible by SNCF **bus** from Cauterets or Lourdes. **Luz-Ardiden** offers downhill and cross-country skiing. (☎05 62 92 30 30; fax 05 62 92 87 19. 135F/€20.59, student reductions available.) Farther away are **Barèges** (☎05 62 92 16 01) and **La Mongie** (☎05 62 95 81 81), the two biggest ski stations in the Pyrenees (joint ticket 153F/€23.33 per day).

HIKING. The **GR10** meanders across the Pyrenees, connecting the Atlantic with the Mediterranean and looping through most major towns. Both major and minor hikes intersect with and run along it; for either level of trail, pick up one of the purple maps at the park office (58F/€9). The most spectacular local hikes begin at the **Pont d'Espagne** (a 2½-hr. walk or 20min. drive from Cauterets). Several **buses** run daily in July and August (every 2hr. 8am-6pm, 25F/€3.81); inquire at **Bordenave Excursions** (☎05 62 92 53 68). During the rest of the year, call a **taxi** (☎06 12 91 83 19; around 110F/€16.78). One of the most spectacular and popular trails follows the GR10 to the turquoise **Lac de Gaube** (1hr.) and then to the end of the stony glacial valley (2hr. past the lake) where you can spend the night 2km in the air at **Refuge des Oulettes.** (☎05 62 92 62 97. Open June-Sept. 80F/€12.20.) A greener hike lies one valley over along the **Vallée du Marcadau,** which also offers shelter at the **Refuge Wallon Marcadau.** (☎05 62 92 64 28. Open June-Sept. 15. 80F/€12.20.) Both hikes are popular as daytrips. In May or June, when the melting snow swells the streams, the **Chemin des Cascades** (waterfall trail), which leads from the Pont d'Espagne to La Raillère, is sensational. This four-hour round-trip from Cauterets makes a good, short hike—if you lose the path, keep the river on your left as you go up. The **Circuit des Lacs** is a marathon eight-hour hike that includes the Vallée du Marcadau as well as three beautiful mountain lakes.

THE CIRCUIT DE GAVARNIE. From Cauterets, the GR10 connects to Luz-St-Sauveur (Luz tourist office: pl. du 8 Mai 45; ☎05 62 92 30 30) over the mountain and then on to Gavarnie, another day's hike up the valley; the round-trip from Cauterets to Gavarnie and back is known as the **"circuit de Gavarnie."** These towns are also accessible by **SNCF bus** (6 per day from Cauterets to Luz, 39F/€5.95; 2 per day from Luz to Gavernie, 35F/€5.34). Circling counter-clockwise from Cauterets to Luz-St-Sauveur, the **Refuge Des Oulettes** (see above) is the first shelter past the Lac de Gaube. Dipping into the Vallée Lutour, the **Refuge Estom** rests peacefully near Lac d'Estom. (Summer ☎05 62 92 72 93, winter ☎05 62 92 75 07. 60-70F/€9.15-10.67 per night.) The **Refuge Jan Da Lo** (☎05 62 92 40 66) in Gavarnie, near the halfway mark of the loop, costs 48F/€7.32 per night. From Gavarnie, you can hop on a horse (90F/€13.72 round-trip) for a two-hour trek to the grandiose, snow-covered **Cirque de Gavarnie** and its misty waterfall. During the third week in July, the **Festival des Pyrénées** animates the foot of the Cirque. Nightly performances begin as the sun sets over the mountains; afterwards, torches are distributed to light the way back to the village. (Tickets 130F/€19.82, students under 25 110F/€16.77.)

INTO SPAIN AND BACK. To get a full sense of the diversity of these mountains, you must experience both the Spanish and French sides of the range. The desiccated red rock of the Spanish side and the misty forests of the French side are accessible in a 6- to 7-day hike from Cauterets. Confer with the tourist office in Ainsa, Spain (☎34 974 50 07 07), for reservations at the Spanish *refuges* before attempting this trek. A 2- to 3-day hike from Pont d'Espagne will take you up and over the Spanish border. Descend the far side of the Pyrenees to the village of Torla where you can hop on one of the frequent buses to the *refuge de Goriz* (call ahead to reserve ☎34 974 34 12 01). A magnificent hike to **Brèche de Roland,** with its snow-capped mountain peaks, perched on the edge of the cirque de Gavarnie, will start your return to France the following day. You can cut your hike short here at 4-5 days and take a bus back from Gavernie to Luz and then to Cauterets; otherwise, it's another rewarding 2-day trek back to Cauterets. Climb from the Vallée d'Ossoue to camp among the clouds of the *Refuge de Bayssellance* in view of mount Montferrat, before returning to Cauterets along the Vallée de Lutour.

LUCHON

More grandiose and cosmopolitan than other Pyrenean mountain towns, Luchon (pop. 3000) has attracted the rich and famous to its celebrated *thermes* for over two centuries. The baths are the town's main attraction, and the number of senior citizens in the tourist population is correspondingly large. But you'll also find women in Chanel and cigarette-toting teenagers on the boulevards, all enjoying the same serene atmosphere. Hikers will appreciate that the numerous trails in the surrounding mountains are less crowded than those of the Parc National. A *télécabine* (gondola) ferries skiers and hikers from the town center to Superbagnères.

ORIENTATION AND PRACTICAL INFORMATION. The **train station,** av. de Toulouse, runs **trains** and SNCF **buses** to **Montréjeau** (50min., 4-5 per day, 36F/€5.49), from which you can connect to **Bayonne, Paris, St-Gaudens, Toulouse,** and other cities. Trains also run directly to **Toulouse** (2hr., 1-2 per day, 105F/€16.01). (☎05 61 79 03 36. Info office open daily M-F 6am-8:15pm, Sa-Su 6am-9pm.)

From the station, turn left on av. de Toulouse and then bear right at the fork to follow av. M. Foch. At the lions, cross the rotary and bear left, following signs for the *centre ville.* You will arrive at the main **allée d'Etigny,** which unfolds to your left. A few blocks down on your right is the **tourist office,** 18 allée d'Etigny, which can give you a list of nearby hikes and mountain biking trails and a map of the town. (☎05 61 79 21 21; fax 05 61 79 11 23; www.luchon.com. Open M-F 9am-noon and 2-7pm, Sa-Su 9am-7pm.) For more ambitious outdoor experiences, check in at the **Bureau des Guides,** next to the tourist office also at 18 allée d'Etigny. Stop by for a schedule and a list of possible activities, including bike excursions, hiking, rock climbing, canyoning, and canyon hiking nearby and in Spain. Hiking runs around 800F/€121.97 per day for a group of 12; canyoning and climbing 1500F/€228.69. (☎05 61 79 69 38; bureaudesguides@free.fr. Open July-Sept. daily 10am-noon and 3-7pm; May-June M-Sa 10am-noon and 3-7pm.) Other services include: a **laundromat,** 66 av. M. Foch (open daily 8am-8pm); **police,** at the Hôtel de Ville (☎05 61 94 68 81); the **medical emergency center,** 5 cours de Quinconces (☎05 61 79 93 00); and **Internet access** at **Ecriture et la Communication,** 34 rue Lamartine (open M-F 9:30am-noon and 2-6pm; 60F/€9.15 per hr.). The **post office** is on the corner of allée d'Etigny and av. Gallieni. (☎05 61 94 74 50. Open M-F 8:45am-noon and 2-5:45pm, Sa 8:45am-noon.) **Postal code:** 31110.

ACCOMMODATIONS AND FOOD. The closest *gîte,* **Gîte Skioura,** is 3km uphill from the tourist office en route to Superbagnères. If you call ahead, they might be able to pick you up. Otherwise, follow cours des Quinconces out of town and up the mountain. During the week, it's more convenient to catch the *car thermal* from the train station to the *thermes* and get off at the camping stop (1hr., 30F/€4.57). Five large rooms contain 40 beds and a fireplace big enough to heat a castle. Some privacy is afforded by cloth partitions between every two beds. During the high season, the *gîte* is dominated by groups. (☎05 61 79 60 59 or 06 84 23 97 80. Breakfast 25F/€3.81. Sheets 15F/€2.29. Open all year. 80F/€12.20.) Another 2km up the road from Gîte Skioura, **La Demeure de Venasque** offers dorm accommodations in a large house in the middle of an open field along with every kind of facility, including a basketball court, foosball, and a music room. (☎05 61 94 31 95; fax 05 61 94 31 96. Breakfast 26F/€4. Dorms 72F/€11.) Across from the train station, the **Hôtel du Baliran,** 1 av. de Toulouse, has first-rate rooms and ornate tiles in modern bathrooms. (☎05 61 79 27 95; fax 05 61 94 31 64. Breakfast 30F/€4.57. Reception 24hr. Closed June. Singles and doubles with shower 190F/€28.97; triples 235F/€35.84; quads 315F/€48.04. MC/V.) There's a huge **Casino supermarket** at 45 av. M. Foch on the way from the train station (open M-Sa 8:30am-12:30pm and 3-7:30pm). Inexpensive 50-70F/€7.62-10.67 *menus* can be found at any of the brasseries and restaurants that line **allée d'Etigny**.

SIGHTS AND HIKES. The tourist office can tell you about hiking paths (1-2½hr.) that leave from the **Parc Thermal,** just behind the *thermes* at the end of allées d'Etigny on Superbagnères. There are also mountain bike trails. The **télécabine** will transport hikers and bikers to the top of Superbagnères. (One-way 28F/€4.60, round-trip 43F/€7. Open Apr.-Sept. Sa-Su 1:30-5pm; July-Aug. daily 9:45am-12:15pm and 1:30-6pm; ski season daily 8:45am-5:30pm.) The tourist office has two free maps—one for hikers, the other for bikers—that show the way back down. Also see the Bureau des Guides (above). Treat yourself to a soak in the **thermes,** housed in the appropriately lavish white marble building at the end of allées d'Etigny. 80F/€12.20 buys access to the 32°C pool and the **Vaporarium,** a natural underground sauna. For this and other programs, ask at **Vitaline,** 66 allées d'Etigny. (Open mid-Dec. to mid-Oct. daily 4-7pm. Closed mid-Oct. to mid-Dec.). Tours of the adjacent 18th-century *thermes* leave June-Sept. Tu and Th at 2pm (20F/€3.05).

CURATIVE POWER Taking "the cure" in hot sulfur springs was done not for pleasure but for health, and the doctors who presided over the proceedings in the 19th century did little to make it easier. The cure included everything from having your sinuses cleaned with small brushes to taking the water up through the nose and expelling it out the mouth. Around the 1840s, some doctors decided that the healing process was helped along if the patient held a morsel of sugar in the mouth while gargling the hot water. The change stuck around, mostly as a way to make the cure more bearable, and France's *thermes* were surrounded by *confiseries*, turning out the hard sugar candies known as *berlingots*. The *thermes* have since refined their techniques so that the *berlingot* is no longer a necessary component, but the candies are now savored by many as a "cure" in their own right.

LANGUEDOC-ROUSSILLON

An immense region called Occitania once stretched from the Rhône valley to the foothills of the Pyrenees. Its people spoke the *langue d'oc*, a Romance language whose name comes from their word for "yes," *oc*, and which was distinct from the *langue d'oïl* spoken in the north (*oïl* meaning yes in that tongue). While independent of France and Spain, the area was a fiefdom of the Count of Toulouse. In the mid-12th century, Occitania's nobles and peasants alike adopted the heretical Cathar brand of Christianity. Disturbed by the loss of Occitan believers—and revenues—the Church launched the Albigensian Crusade (named for the Cathar stronghold of Albi) against the "heretics;" the slaughter that followed resulted in Occitania's political and linguistic integration into France. Up to the Revolution, most of the population clung to their old language, but by the late 19th century it had all but died out. Roussillon, in the far southwest corner, was historically separated from France as a part of Catalonia—Perpignan even served as the capital of the Kings of Majorca—and today cultural links across the Spanish border remain strong, with locals looking to Barcelona rather than Paris for inspiration. Many here speak Catalan, a relative of the *langue d'oc* which sounds like a hybrid of French and Spanish.

TRANSPORTATION

Toulouse may be the hub city of the gods. Frequent train service, a city metro, a modern bus station, and cheap accommodations make daytrips a simple pleasure. Unfortunately, its convenience has led the SNCF to neglect direct connections between surrounding cities; you'll find yourself constantly doubling back between towns. **Perpignan** and **Montpellier** are each a short distance from the beaches and nightlife of the Côte Catalane, though buses stop running too early for clubbers.

Tourist offices throughout the region distribute itineraries which follow *Les Traces des Cathares* (tracks of the Cathars) and ancient Roman roads. The Canal du Midi connects the Atlantic to the Mediterranean, passing through Toulouse and Perpignan and linking some towns in the region. The hilly countryside makes **biking** difficult, but the villages strewn along the way make the effort worthwhile.

TOULOUSE

Just when all French towns start to look alike, you discover Toulouse, or "la ville en rose"—the city in pink. The city's magnificent buildings, from the stately homes of 16th-century pastel merchants to the striped Capitole, are built of local rose-colored bricks, a distinctive shade lighter than the red ones of Albi and less ochre-tinged than those of Montauban. Many of them are trimmed with white marble, giving Toulouse a grandeur befitting the fourth-largest city (pop. 350,000) in France. Politically, Toulouse has always been a free-thinking, headstrong place. Its powerful counts made life miserable for French kings in the Middle Ages, and it wasn't until the Revolution that France finally got a firm grip on the *capitouls* (town councillors) of its unique 12th-century government. Still pushing the frontiers of knowledge, this university town, where Thomas Aquinas made Aristotle palatable to medieval theologians, now serves as the capital of France's aerospace industry. During the school year, 100,000 students flood the pizzerias of rue du Taur, the city's countless museums, and the quays of the Garonne. But even during the sweltering summer months, you'll find yourself bumping friendly elbows on the narrow pink sidewalks of the *vieille ville.*

TRANSPORTATION

Flights: Aéroport Blagnac: (☎05 61 42 44 00). **Air France** (☎08 02 80 28 02) flies to **London** (2 per day, from 1360F/€207.35 round-trip) and **Paris** (25 per day, from 730F/€111.33 round-trip). **Navettes Aérocar** (☎05 34 60 00; www.navettevia-toulouse.com) serves the airport from the bus station and allée Jean Jaurès (30min., every 20min.; under 25 18F/€2.75).

Trains: Gare Matabiau, 64 bd. Pierre Sémard. To: **Bordeaux** (2-3hr., 14 per day, 169F/€25.77); **Lyon** (6½hr., 3-4 per day, 310F/€47.28); **Marseille** (4½hr., 8 per day, 246F/€37.52); **Paris** (8-9hr., 4 per day, 450F/€68.61); and **Perpignan** (2½hr., 6 per day, 146F/€22.27). Tickets M-Sa 9am-7:30pm.

Buses: Gare Routière, 68-70 bd. Pierre Sémard (☎05 61 61 67 67), next to the train station. Open M-Sa 7am-7pm, Su 8am-7pm. To: **Albi** (1½hr., 4 per day, buses run by two companies, cheapest ride through Bel Buses 63F/€9.61); **Carcassonne** (2¼hr., 63F/€9.61); **Foix** (2hr., 1 per day, 55F/€8.39); and **Montauban** (70min., 4 per day, 40F/€6.10). Buy tickets on the bus. **Eurolines** (☎05 61 26 40 04; www.eurolines.fr) with an office in the station, runs buses to most major cities in Europe. Prices shift around, but there are usually worthwhile package deals to big traveler destinations. Open M-F 9:30am-6:30pm, Sa 9:30am-5pm.

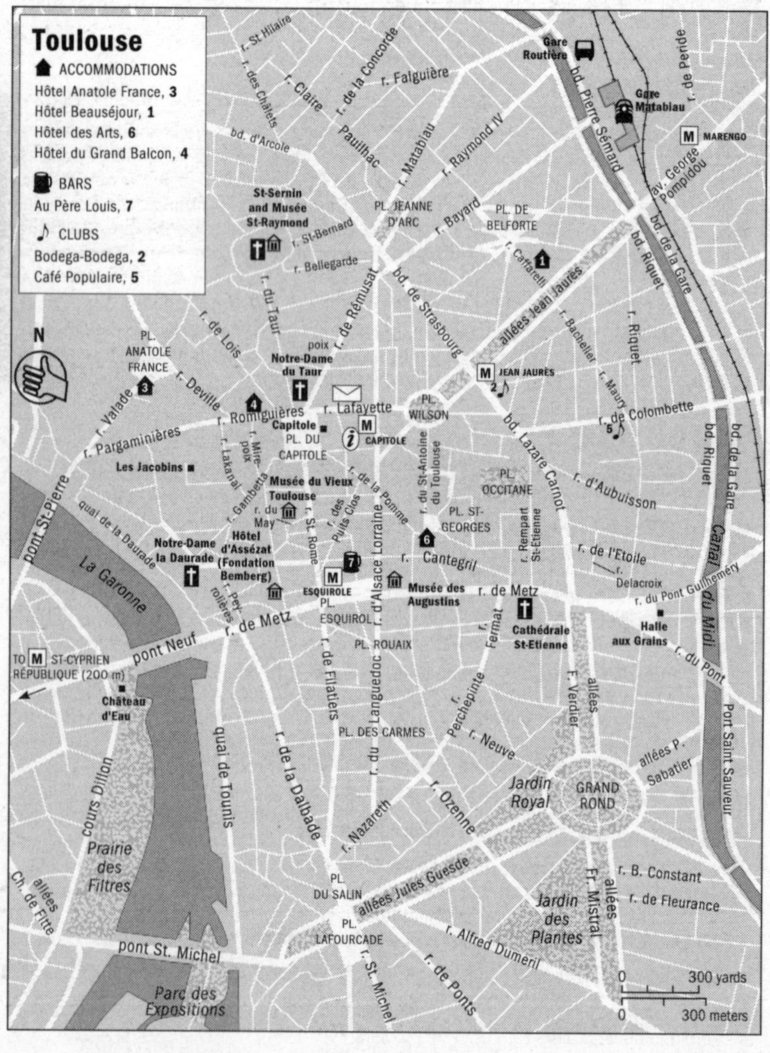

Metro: SEMVAT, 49 rue de Gironis (☎05 61 41 70 70 or 05 62 11 26 11). Buy tickets just inside the stations (8.60F/€1.31 for 1 zone, 10F/€1.53 for 2 zones). Maps at ticket booths and tourist office. Open daily 8am-midnight.

Taxis: Taxi Bleu (☎05 61 80 36 36). 100-130F/€15.25-19.82 to the airport. 24hr.

Bike Rental: Temps Libre, 14 rue F. Magendie (☎05 61 53 51 83). 80F/€12.20 per day.

ORIENTATION AND PRACTICAL INFORMATION

Toulouse sprawls on both sides of the Garonne, but the museums and sights are mostly within a small section east of the river, bounded by rue de Metz in the south and by bd. Strasbourg and bd. Carnot to the north and east. The métro is useful for reaching your hotel from the train station, but after you've dropped off your pack, there should be no need to venture underground again. Even the walk from the train station to the main part of town takes only about 15 minutes. The center is the huge stone plaza known as the Capitole.

Tourist Office: Donjon du Capitole, rue Lafayette, sq. Charles de Gaulle (☎05 61 11 02 22; fax 05 61 22 03 63; www.mairie-toulouse.fr), in the park behind the Capitole. From the station, take the métro to Capitole or turn left along the canal and then right onto allée Jean Jaurès. Walk two thirds of the way around pl. Wilson (bearing right), then take a right onto rue Lafayette. The office is in a small park on the left of the intersection with rue d'Alsace-Lorraine. **Accommodations service.** City tours in English (July-Sept. Sa at 3pm, 50F/€7.62; in French M-F 3 per day, 50-65F/€7.62-9.91). Office open May-Sept. M-Sa 9am-7pm, Su 10am-1pm and 2-6:30pm; Oct.-Apr. M-F 9am-6pm, Sa 9am-12:30pm and 2-6pm, Su and holidays 10am-12:30pm and 2-5pm.

Budget Travel: OTU Voyage, 60 rue de Taur (☎05 61 12 54 54). Cheap fares for students. Open M-F 9am-6:30pm, Sa 10am-1pm and 2-5pm. **Nouvelles Frontières,** 2 pl. St-Sernin (☎05 61 21 74 14, national ☎08 25 00 08 25), has cheap flights for all. Open M-Sa 9am-7pm. MC/V.

Consulates: Canada, 30 bd. de Strasbourg (☎05 61 99 30 16). Open M-F 9am-noon. **UK,** c/o Lucas Aerospace, Victoria Center, Bâtiment Didier Daurat, 20 chemin de Laporte (☎05 61 15 02 02). Open M-Tu and Th-F 9am-noon and 2-5pm.

Currency Exchange: Banque de France, 4 rue Deville (☎05 61 61 35 35). No commission, good rates. Open M-F 9am-12:20pm and 1:20-3:30pm.

English Bookstore: The Bookshop, 17 rue Lakanal (☎05 61 22 99 92). Extensive collection of novels, French history books, and travel guides. Open M 2-7pm, Tu-Sa 10am-7pm. Closed first 2 weeks of August.

Youth Center: CRIJ (Centre Regional d'Info Jeunesse), 17 rue de Metz (☎05 61 21 20 20). Info on travel, work, and study. Open July 13-Sept. 16. M-Sa 10am–6pm; Sept. 17-July 12 M-Sa 10am-1pm and 2-7pm.

Laundromat: Laverie St-Sernin, 14 rue Emile Cartailhac. Open daily 7am-10pm.

Hospital: CHR de Rangueil, chemin de Vallon (☎05 61 32 25 33).

Police: Commissariat Central, bd. Embouchure (☎05 61 12 77 77).

Internet Access: l'@fterbug, 10 pl. St-Sernin (☎05 61 22 19 19), near the student quarter. 25F/€3.81 per hr. Open M-F noon-2am, Sa noon-5am, Su 2-10pm. **Espace Wilson Multimédia,** 7 allée du Président Roosevelt, at pl. Wilson (☎05 62 30 28 10). 20F/€3.05 per hr. Open M-F 10am-7pm and Sa 10am-6pm.

Post Office: 9 rue Lafayette (☎05 62 15 30 00). **Currency exchange** with good rates. Open M-F 8am-7pm, Sa 8am-noon. **Poste Restante:** La Poste Capitole, Poste Restante, 9 rue Lafayette, 31049 Toulouse Cedex. **Postal code:** 31000.

ACCOMMODATIONS AND CAMPING

Hotels line the blocks near the train station, but most aren't worth staying in. Cheaper, more comfortable hotels can be found in the center of the city, away from the noise and traffic, on the outskirts of town. Toulouse has no youth hostel, but the low-priced hotels are friendly and welcoming.

Hôtel des Arts, 1bis rue Cantegril (☎05 61 23 36 21; fax 05 61 12 22 37), at rue des Arts near pl. St-Georges. Take métro (dir: "Basso Cambo") to "pl. Esquirol." Go down rue de Metz, away from the river; rue des Arts is on the left. Low prices in a perfect location. Spacious rooms wind around a plant-filled, sunlit staircase. Breakfast 25F/€3.81. No curfew. Reception 7am-11pm. Singles 95-135F/€14.48-20.59, with shower 145F/€22.11; doubles 160F/€24.39, 165F/€25.16. Extra bed 30F/€4.57. MC/V.

Hôtel du Grand Balcon, 8 rue Romiguières (☎05 61 21 48 08; fax 05 61 21 59 98), on a corner of pl. du Capitole. Worn 1920s luxury overlooking the bustle of the pl. du Capitole. This is the official hotel of the French airborne postal service; Antoine de St-Exupéry stayed in room #32 whenever his piloting assignments brought him to Toulouse, and so can you for 205F/€31.26. The whole thing–facade, high-ceilinged reception room, and rickety elevator–is classified as a historical monument by UNESCO. Breakfast 25F/€3.81. St.-Exupéry's room 205F/€31.26; singles and doubles 180F/€27.44, with shower 230F/€35.07, with bathroom 240F/€36.59; triples with bath 270F/€41.16; quad without bath 210F/€32.02.

Hôtel Beauséjour, 4 rue Caffarelli (☎/fax 05 61 62 77 59), just off allée Jean Jaurès, close to the station. Bright rooms with new beds at the lowest prices in Toulouse. Call ahead; reserve if arriving after 4pm. Breakfast 23F/€3.51. Shower 10F/€1.53. Reception till 11pm. Ask about tiny singles that usually go to long-term guests (85F/€12.96). Huge singles and doubles 115F/€17.54, with shower 140F/€21.35, with toilet 155F/€23.64. Extra bed 50F/€7.62. AmEx/MC/V.

Hôtel Anatole France, 46 pl. Anatole France (☎05 61 23 19 96; fax 05 61 21 47 66). In a calm *place* next to the university and student quarter. Rooms are airy and bright. Breakfast 25F/€3.81. Singles and doubles 125F/€19.06, with shower 145F/€22.11, with TV and toilet 185-190F/€28.21-28.97. Extra bed 30F/€4.57.

Campsites: Pont de Rupé, 21 chemin du Pont de Rupé (☎05 61 70 07 35; fax 05 61 70 00 71), at av. des Etats-Unis (N20 north). Take bus #59 (dir: "Camping") to "Rupé." Restaurant, bar, and laundry. 50F/€7.62 per person, 60F/€9.15 per person, 17F/€2.59 per additional person. **La Bouriette,** 201 chemin de Tournefeuille (☎05 61 49 64 46), 5km outside Toulouse along N124 in St-Martin-du-Touch. Take bus #64 (dir: "Colomiers") and ask for "St-Martin-du-Touch." 25F/€3.81 per person, 18-26F/€2.75-3.97 per site. Car included. Open year-round.

FOOD

Any budget traveler should head directly to the **rue du Taur** in the student quarter, where cheap, spirited eateries serve meals for 50-60F/€7.62-9.15. The choices include typical café fare as well as low-priced foreign meals. The brasseries that crowd pl. Wilson offer 50-80F/€7.62-12.20 *menus* on a busy thoroughfare. Lebanese, Chinese, and Mexican restaurants coexist on rue des Filatiers and rue Paradoux. On Wednesdays, **pl. du Capitole** transforms into an open-air department store and on Saturday mornings it hosts an **organic market.** Other markets are held at **pl. Victor Hugo, pl. des Carmes,** and **bd. de Strasbourg** (Tu-Su 6am-1pm). There's a **Monoprix supermarket** at 39 rue Alsace-Lorraine (☎05 61 23 39 80; open M-Sa 8:30am-9pm) and a **Casino** near pl. Occitane at the Centre Commerciale St-Georges (☎05 61 22 50 66; open M-Sa 9am-7:30pm). Students who need a good, hot meal at student rates should head to the **Restaurants Universitaires.** For info on the 14 student cafeterias scattered around the Toulouse area, head to the **CROUS,** 58 rue du Taur. (☎05 61 12 54 00. Open M-F 8:30am-5:30pm; cafeterias open 11:30am-1:30pm and 6:30-8pm.) The nearest student cafeteria to town is the **Arsenal Restaurant Universitaire,** 2 bd.

Armand Duportal (☎05 61 23 98 48), near rue du Taur. A good student hang-out for dinner is **Jour de Fête,** 43 rue du Taur. This relaxed brasserie serves a large *plat du jour* for 42F/€6.41. (☎05 61 23 36 48. Open daily for lunch and dinner.) The seafood in Toulouse comes from the nearby port towns and is prepared in restaurants on either side of bd. Lazare Carnot as it leaves allée Jean Jaurès. For dinner, though, you should expect to pay upwards of 90F/€13.73 for a full meal at one of these restaurants. **Le Carré Vert,** 3bis bd. de Strasbourg, on the corner of bd. Lazare Carnot and allée Jean Jaurès, serves a 59F/€9 seafood lunch *menu* that includes three courses, coffee, and wine. (☎05 61 21 25 79. Open M-Sa noon-2pm and 7-11:30pm.)

SIGHTS

Most of Toulouse's museums are free to students. For others, museum passes are available for multiple visits: 20F/€3.05 gives entry to any three museums, 30F/€4.57 to six. Passes are sold at all museums.

From local artists to canonized painters, the diversity of Toulouse's art makes for a nice afternoon of museum-hopping. The city also has some of France's most distinctive religious monuments. Toulouse's red-brick construction often has more to do with economics than aesthetics; not so with the **stone mansions** of the town's wealthy 15th- and 16th-century dye merchants. An excellent way to see these is the tourist office's two-hour French **tour.** (50F/€7.62. July-Sept. M-Sa at 10am.)

LA CAPITOLE. The city's most prominent monument is this brick palace next door to the 16th-century defense tower, archive, and dungeon that presently goes by the name of "Office de Tourisme." The huge stone plaza in front provides the perfect ambience for an afternoon of people-watching. As early as the 11th century, the bourgeois *capitouls* (rather than the counts of Toulouse) were beginning to take over the running of the city; this *place* has been the center of city government ever since, though the building itself is much more recent. The **Salle des Illustres,** filled with Roman-style sculptures, is right next to the Mairie and sees all the marriages in Toulouse pass through its doors. **La Salle Henri Martin,** next door, includes 10 post-Impressionist *tableaux* by Henri Martin representing Toulouse in all four seasons. *(Salles open M-F 8:30am-noon and 1:30-7pm, Sa and Su 10am-noon and 2-6pm. Free.)*

EGLISE NOTRE-DAME-DU-TAUR. This unrestored church was originally named St-Sernin-du-Taur after Saturninus, the first Toulousian priest, martyred in AD 250. Legend has it that disgruntled pagans tied him to the tail of a wild bull that dragged him to his death. The building marks the spot where Mr. Saturninus' wild ride finally ended—the enormous fresco over the altar recalls the event. *(12 rue du Taur. ☎05 61 21 41 57. Open July-Sept. daily 9am-6:30pm; Oct.-June 8am-noon and 2-6pm.)*

BASILIQUE ST-SERNIN. An enormous brick steeple rises over Toulouse in five ever-narrowing double-arched terraces, like the king of all wedding cakes. Quite apart from the height of its central tower, St-Sernin happens to be the longest Romanesque structure in the world. **St. Dominic,** responsible for the Dominican order of friars, made the church his base in the early 13th century, though his philosophy ran directly counter to the idea of friars' squirreling themselves away in hidden monasteries and lavish cathedrals. Behind the left side of the altar in the back of the church, the **crypt** conceals a treasure trove of holy relics, from engraved silver chests to golden goblets, gathered since the age of Charlemagne. *(**Church** open July-Sept. M-Sa 9am-6:30pm, Su 9am-7:30pm; Oct.-June M-Sa 8:30-11:45am and 2-5:45pm, Su 9am-12:30pm and 2-7:30pm. Free. Tours in French July-Aug. 2 per day, 35F/€5.34. **Crypt** open July-Sept. M-Sa 10am-6pm, Su 12:30-6pm; Oct.-June M-Sa 10-11:30am and 2:30-5pm, Su 2:30-5pm. 10F/€1.53.)*

REFECTOIRE DES JACOBINS AND CHURCH. The final resting place of St. Thomas Aquinas is this 13th-century church, built in the Southern Gothic style. The ashes of St. Thomas Aquinas take center stage in an elevated, underlit tomb, but there is no crypt; crypts ran contrary to the principles of elevation, exposure, and lighting that guided Gothic architecture in the era when the church was built. *(Rue Lakanal. Open daily 9am-7pm. Weekly summer piano concert tickets 80-140F/€12.20-21.35 available at the tourist office. Cloister 14F/€2.14.)* The **Réfectoire des Jacobins** presents regular exhibitions ranging from archaeological artifacts to modern art. *(69 rue Pargaminières. ☎05 61 22 21 92. Open daily, during expositions, 10am-7pm; same hours as church without exposition. 20F/€3.05.)*

HOTEL D'ASSEZAT. The striking hôtel has been restored and opened to the public. The Fondation Bemberg inside displays 28 Bonnards and a modest collection of Dufys, Pissarros, and Gaugins, but the building itself is more interesting. *(Pl. d'Assézat. ☎05 61 12 06 89; fax 05 61 12 34 47. Fondation ☎05 61 12 06 89. Open Tu and F-Su 10am-6pm, Th 10am-9pm. Groups 18F/€2.75, temporary exhibits 20F/€3.05.)*

MUSEUMS. The huge **Musée des Augustins** displays an unsurpassed assemblage of Romanesque and Gothic sculptures, including fifteen snickering gargoyles. The display is presented in a gorgeous redone Augustine monastery, complete with an inner cloister and vegetable garden. *(21 rue de Metz, off rue des Arts. ☎05 61 22 21 82. Open W-M 10am-6pm. On W, the museum stays open until 9pm with a free organ concert beginning at 8:30pm. 14F/€2.14, students free)* The best collection of archaeological finds in the area is at the **Musée St-Raymond.** Especially fascinating is the hall of Roman emperors, where visitors can confront the proud stares of hundreds of stone sculptures. *(Pl. St-Sernin. ☎05 61 22 31 44. Open June-Aug. daily 10am-7pm; Sept.-May 10am-6pm. 14F/€2.14, students 7F/€1.07.)* The jumbled fragments of Toulouse's past come together at the **Musée de Vieux Toulouse** in a garage-sale hodgepodge of artifacts, from conventional landscapes and portraits to plaster busts and yellowing newspaper ads. Carnival broadsides advertise the talents of commander Mazius Cazeneuve, a famed conjurer and confidant of the queen of Madagascar; a model of the gymnasium of Jules Leotard, inventor of the flying trapeze, recalls his pivotal place in circus history. Check out the enlarged photograph of a woman being dunked in the Garonne for running a whorehouse. *(7 rue de May, off rue St-Rome. ☎05 61 13 97 24. Open June-Sept. M-Sa 3-6pm; Oct.-May only by appointment, call F afternoon. Lengthy explanatory pamphlet available in English. 10F/€1.53, students 5F/€0.76.)*

OTHER SIGHTS. Opened in 1997, the super-duper **Cité de l'Espace** park is devoted to Toulouse's space programs, complete with interactive games and a planetarium. *(Take A612 exit 17 to Parc de la Plaine, av. Jean Gonord or bus #19 to pl. de l'Indépendance and follow the signs. ☎05 62 71 64 80. Open June 15-Sept. 15 Tu-Su 9:30am-7pm; Sept. 16-June 14 Tu-Su 9:30am-6pm. 69F/€10.52, children 49F/€7.47, planetarium 15F/€2.29.)* It's necessary to call ahead for a tour of the **Airbus Factory,** but the visit will let you see how planes are constructed and view the sleek Concorde. *(10 av. Guynemer. ☎05 61 18 06 01. Open M-F 9am-12:30pm and 2-6pm, Sa 9am-12:30pm. 58F/€8.85, students 48F/€7.32.)* The **Galerie du Château d'Eau,** just across from the town center on the Pont Neuf, contains photography exhibits. *(Pl. Laganne. ☎05 61 77 09 40; fax 05 61 42 02 70. Open W-M 1-7pm. 15F/€2.29, students and seniors 10F/€1.53.)* For greener pastures, head to the shady **Jardin Royal** and the less formal **Jardin des Plantes** across the street. For cyclists, the **Grand Rond** unfurls into allée Paul Sabatier, which just keeps rolling along to the **Canal du Midi.**

ENTERTAINMENT AND FESTIVALS

Toulouse has something to please almost any nocturnal whim, although the city is at its liveliest from October to May when the students come out in full force. The numerous cafés, *glaciers*, and pizzerias flanking **pl. St-Georges** and **pl. du Capitole** are open late, as are the bars off **rue St-Rome** and **rue des Filatiers.** During the school year, students head to the **pl. St-Pierre** to watch rugby in one of the small bars while drinking *pastis*. From September to June, the weekly *Flash* gives restaurant and bar info and keeps Toulouse up on the ever-changing club scene (7F/€1.07 at *tabacs*). Unfortunately, the July-August issue *Flash Eté* is little more than a festival listing. CD and book megalith **FNAC,** at the intersection of bd. Strasbourg and Carnot, has cultural pamphlets, club advertisements, and tickets to large concerts. (☎05 61 11 01 01. Open M-Sa 10am-7:30pm.)

The wine bar, **Au Père Louis,** 45 rue des Tourneurs, is always packed by well-dressed crowds who drink the regional wines by the glass and the bottle. The "maison" (with a lunchtime restaurant) has been around since 1889. (☎05 61 21 33 45. Open M-Sa 8:30am-3pm and 5-10:30pm. Lunch noon-3pm.) More informal evenings begin at the smoky **Café Populaire,** 9 rue de la Colombette. Groups come here for the cheapest beer in Toulouse. A box of 13 beers can be had for 120F/€18.30. (☎05 61 63 07 00. Open M-F 9pm-2am, Sa 3pm-6am.) **La Ciguä,** 6 rue de la Colombette, just off bd. Lazare Carnot, is a friendly gay bar and a great place to ask about the discos du jour. Every night, a different DJ plays the same hard rock. (☎05 61 99 61 87. Open Tu-F and Su 9pm-2am, Sa 9pm-4am.) The best dancing is at **Bodega-Bodega,** 1 rue Gabriel Péri, just off bd. Lazare Carnot. There's no cover charge for the large bar and dance floor, although it's hard to guard your money since the poker chips they give as change make it so easy to buy the next drink. Tapas are served until midnight. (☎05 61 63 03 63. Open Su-F 7pm-2am, Sa 7pm-6am.)

Cave Poésie, 71 rue du Taur (☎05 61 42 91 34, reservations 05 61 23 62 00), hosts plays and performances. The full moon is the catalyst for an "open door" night of comedians, poets, musicians, or whatever else the Cave can dig up. Stop by for a schedule; events begin at 9pm. **Cour de l'Ecole des Beaux Arts,** quai de la Daurade, stages classic plays with a modern twist (☎05 61 23 25 49 or 05 61 23 25 45). Most of Toulouse's **movie theaters** are around pl. Wilson. **UGC,** 9 allée du Président Roosevelt, plays mostly American new releases, some dubbed, some not (☎05 62 30 28 30). Everything is shown in its original language at **Utopia Cinemas,** 23 rue Montardy, which shows artsy films from around the world (☎05 61 23 66 20).

July through September, **Musique d'Eté** brings classical concerts, jazz, gospel, and ballet to a variety of outdoor settings. Tickets are sold at concert halls and the tourist office (80-140F/€12.20-21.35). Traditional music and dance groups parade through the streets on the last Sunday in June for the festival known as the **Grand Fénétra** (info ☎05 61 49 18 36). The **Festival International de Piano aux Jacobins** tickles Toulousian ivories every couple of days during September at the Jacobins cloister. (8:30pm. Tickets available at the tourist office or through the Bureau du Festival, ☎05 61 22 40 05. 100-140F/€15.25-21.35, students 60F/€9.15.)

DAYTRIPS FROM TOULOUSE: CASTRES

The city of Castres (pop. 48,000) muddled through history until it acquired the 11th-century bones of St. Vincent. The holy relics made the town an essential stopover for pilgrims en route to Santiago de Compostela, until the saint was dumped in the river and his basilica destroyed during the Wars of Religion. With relics in short supply, the city has compensated by constructing two museums, each worth their own brief pilgrimages. The Musée Goya contains France's second-largest collection of Spanish art and a huge number of Goya engravings. The Musée Jaurès has assembled effluvious quantities of pamphlets, drawings, photographs, and avenues dedicated to native son Jean Jaurès, a great humanist and committed socialist who worked for peace until his assassination shortly before WWI. Make Castres a daytrip from Toulouse, as hotels are exorbitantly expensive and the city itself is not impressively picturesque.

In front of the shrubs of the perfectly-groomed ornamental **Jardin de l'Evêché,** the **Musée Goya,** houses a terrific spread of Spanish painting dating back to the 14th century, along with Catalan and Aragonese masters. The display inside the ancient Episcopal palace constructed in 1673 includes four series of Goya's sardonic engravings, bearing witness to the horrors of war as well as the humors of everyday interaction. (☎05 63 71 59 27. Open July-Aug. daily 10am-12:30pm and 1:30pm-6pm; Sept.-June Tu-Sa 9am-noon and 2-5pm, Su 10am-noon and 2-5pm. July-Aug. 20F/€3.05, students 10F/€1.53; rest of the year 15F/€2.29, students 8F/€1.22.)

The **Musée Jaurès,** 2 pl. Pélisson, is packed with political cartoons, photographs, and newspaper articles that recount the spirited life and rhetoric of the man himself. A brilliant scholar and professor of philosophy at Albi and Toulouse, Jaurès leapt into prominence as leader of the striking glass-workers of Carmaux in 1896 and later joined Emile Zola's vehement defense of Alfred Dreyfus, the Jewish officer framed as a traitor by the army. (☎05 63 72 01 01. Open July-Aug. daily 10am-12:30pm and 1:30-6:30pm; Sept-June Tu-Su 9am-noon and 2-6pm. 10F/€1.53, students 5F/€0.76.) For two weeks in mid-July, the **Festival Goya** celebrates international Hispanic culture with concerts, exhibitions, flamenco and ballet performances, and more. Many events are free; tickets to others are available at the tourist office or by calling the **Théâtre Municipale.** (☎05 63 71 56 57. Open M-F 10:30am-12:30pm and 3-6:30pm. Tickets 40-150F/€6.10-22.90, reductions for students and groups of 10 or more.)

When hunger strikes, you can avail yourself of the **markets** on **pl. Jean Jaurès** (Tu and Th-Sa 7:30am-1pm) and **pl. de l'Albinque** (Tu-Su 8:30am-1pm). **Monoprix,** rue Sabatier at pl. Jean Jaurès, delivers the usual supermarket fare (open M-Sa 8:30am-7:30pm). There are a few bakeries and butcher shops on **rue Gambetta** and **rue Victor Hugo** in the town center, while restaurants surround the **Pont Vieux** and continue to **pl. Jean Jaurès** and near **rue Villegoudou.** Traditional *Nougatines Castraises* can be found at **Cormary,** 13 rue Victor Hugo, which also sculpts fine chocolates, marzipan, and pastries into animal shapes. (☎05 63 59 27 09. Open M-F 6am-1pm and 1:30-7:30pm, Sa 6am-5:30pm, Su 6am-1pm.)

In exchange for a passport or driver's license, the **tourist office** at 3 rue Milhau Ducommun, loans **bikes** for up to two hours. To get there from the station, turn left onto av. Albert 1er and then bear right onto bd. Henri Sizaire. At pl. Alsace-Lorraine, continue straight over the bridge, ignoring signs for the *centre ville.* Turn left onto bd. Raymond Vittoz, then turn left onto rue Villegoudou and veer right onto rue Leris. It's on the right at the very end of the street (20min.). From the bus station, walk across pl. Soult and continue straight on rue Villegoudou, veering right onto rue Leris. The tourist office is on the right (5min.). (☎05 63 62 63 62; fax 05 63 62 63 60. Open July-Aug. M-Sa 9am-12:30pm and 1:30-7pm, Su 10:30am-noon and 3-5:30pm; Sept.-June M-Sa 9am-noon and 2-6:30pm, Su 3-5pm.) The **train station,** av. Albert 1er (☎05 63 72 29 91), has service to **Toulouse** (1hr., 8 per day, 72F/€10.98). Though trains from Albi do eventually arrive in Castres, **buses** are cheaper and more direct. They run from the **bus station,** pl. Soult (☎05 63 35 37 31), to **Albi** (45-55min., 8 per day, 36F/€5.49) and **Toulouse** (1½hr., 7 per day, 60F/€9.15).

MONTAUBAN

Montauban (pop. 55,000) sits on the wide river Tarn 50km north of Toulouse, indifferent to the ebb and flow of the tourist industry. Its ochre-tinted medieval architecture dates back to a spat between the townspeople and the wealthy, oppressive abbey at Montauriol ("golden mountain"). The Count of Toulouse incited the enraged artisans to sack the abbey in 1144 and use its remains to start construction of the present town, then known as "Mount Alba." Never on good terms with mainstream Catholicism, Montauban was one of the last bastions of Protestantism in France following the revocation of the Edict of Nantes in 1685. Today, Montauban's surest claim to fame is as birthplace of the celebrated 19th-century painter Jean-Auguste Dominique Ingres (1780-1867). Less than an hour from Toulouse, the impressive Musée Ingres makes the town an art-lover's daytrip.

PRACTICAL INFORMATION. **Trains** roll from av. Chamier to **Bordeaux** (2hr., 9 per day, 142F/€21.65); **Paris** (5½hr.; 7-9 per day; 344F/€52.45, TGV 438F/€66.78); and **Toulouse** (25min., every hr., 48F/€7.32). Info office open M-Sa 7am-7:45pm. **Buses** leave from pl. Lalaque; **SNCF** goes to **Albi** (1¼hr., 2 per day, 64F/€9.76) and **Jardel** (☎05 63 03 18 95) runs to **Toulouse** (1hr., 4 per day, 40F/€6.10). **Local buses** are run by **Transports Montaubanais,** bd. Midi-Pyrénées (☎05 63 63 52 52; 5F/€0.76).

To get to the tourist office in the town center, walk down av. Mayenne from the station, cross pont Vieux, and continue uphill on côte de Bonnetiers. On the far side of the Eglise St-Jacques, turn right on rue Princesse, which runs into the central **pl. Nationale.** Follow rue Fraîche out of the far corner and turn left two blocks later onto rue du Collège. The **tourist office,** 4 rue du Collège (main entrance on pl.

Prax-Paris), gives out a free self-guided tour map in English and runs **tours** in French of the town and its museums. Ask for the free practical guides to Montauban and the entire area of the Tarn-et-Garonne. (☎05 63 63 60 60; fax 05 63 63 65 12. Open July-Aug. M-Sa 9am-7pm, Su 10am-noon and 2-6pm; Sept.-June M-Sa 9am-noon and 2-6pm. Tours July-Aug. 2:30pm; 30F/€4.57, students 15F/€2.29, couples 45F/€6.86.) **Crédit Mutuel,** 8 bd. Midi-Pyrénées, has **currency exchange.** (☎05 63 91 74 74. Open M-F 8:45am-noon and 1:30-5pm, Sa 8:30am-noon and 1:30-4pm.) The **police station** is at 50 bd. Alsace-Lorraine (☎05 63 21 54 00), and the **hospital** at 100 rue Léon Cladel (☎05 63 92 82 82). **Internet access** is at **3D Gamma,** 103 fbg. Lacapelle. (☎05 63 91 00 91. 30F/€4.57 per hr. Open M-F 11am-midnight, Sa 2pm-midnight.) The **post office** is at 6 bd. Midi-Pyrénées. (☎05 63 68 84 84. Open M-F 8am-7pm, Sa 8am-noon.) **Postal code:** 82000.

ACCOMMODATIONS AND FOOD. With Toulouse so nearby, there is little reason to stay the night in overpriced Montauban. If you choose to stay, hotels by pl. Nationale and on av. Mayenne, between the old town and the train station, are your best bet. The **Hôtel du Commerce,** 9 pl. Roosevelt, has cheap rooms, but hidden costs like the 35F/€5.34 obligatory breakfast in high season and 10F/€1.53 showers. The walls are paper-thin and the smell of stale smoke hangs in the air. After pont Vieux, turn right on rue de l'Hôtel de Ville. Follow it uphill to pl. Roosevelt, in front of the cathedral. (☎05 63 66 31 32; fax 05 63 03 18 46. Almost obligatory breakfast (30F/€4.57) in off-season. Singles 110-120F/€16.77-18.30; doubles 140-150F/€21.35-22.90, with shower 185-320F/€27.44-48.79; triples 185F/€27.44; quads with shower 200-250F/€30.49-38.12. MC/V.) One **market** is held regularly on pl. Nationale (Tu-Su 8am-12:30pm); another goes on at pl. Prax-Paris under the Halles Ligou (Sa 9am-1pm). A **Champion** supermarket is across pl. Prax-Paris from the tourist office (open M-Sa 9am-7:30pm and Su 9am-12:30pm).

SIGHTS AND FESTIVALS. Overlooking the river and the Pont Vieux, the **Musée Ingres** is housed in the Bishop's palace. The upper floors of the museum spotlight several hundred Ingres sketches and some minor paintings, while below, in the excavated fort, the town's archaeological finds are displayed. (☎05 63 22 12 91. Open July-Aug. daily 9:30am-noon and 1:30-6pm; Sept.-June Tu-Su 10am-noon and 2-6pm. 25F/€3.81; students free; first Su of every month free.) Just after revoking the Edict of Nantes, Louis XIV spitefully constructed Montauban's baroque **cathedral.** Four enormous sculptures of the Evangelists keep solemn watch over *Le Voeu de Louis XIII*, one of Ingres' largest and most impressive religious works. Commissioned by the Ministry of the Interior in 1820, the painting was part of an attempt to reforge the link between France and the Church after the iconoclasm of the Revolution. (Open daily 9am-noon and 2-6pm.)

Across pl. Bourdelle, the small **Musée d'Histoire Naturelle Victor Brun,** quai Montmurat, presents stuffed ostriches, crocodiles, armadillos, and the obligatory preserved tarantula. (☎05 63 22 13 85. Open Tu-Sa 10am-noon and 2-6pm, Su 2-6pm. 15F/€2.29; 20F/€3.05 during exhibits, students free.) Next door, the **Musée du Terroir,** 2 place Antoine Boudelle, showcases old-fashioned rural life in Languedoc. (☎05 63 22 13 85. Open Tu-Sa 10am-noon and 2-6pm, Su 2-6pm. 10F/€1.53, students free.) The **Musée de la Résistance,** 33 Grand rue Villenouvelle, has permanent exhibits on Nazi occupation and the internment camps in the region. (☎05 63 66 03 11. Open Sept.-July Tu-Sa 9am-noon and 2-6pm. 10F/€1.53, students free.) A pass to all four museums costs 25F/€3.81.

Montauban has two annual music festivals. **Alors Chante** plays traditional French tunes, for one week at the end of May and beginning of June. (☎05 63 63 02 36. Tickets 70-200F/€10.67-30.49.) A **Jazz Festival** swings through town the third week of July. The big names are all ticketed events, but between the 17th and 21st of July the streets of the *vieille ville* ring out with free concerts, usually given at noon and 7pm. (Info ☎05 63 63 60 60. Tickets for the festival available at the tourist office for 100-180F/€15.25-27.44; some student discounts.)

ALBI

Dominated by its magnificent Cathédrale Ste-Cécile, Albi is a town of narrow cobblestone streets twisting down to the tree-lined river Tarn. Native son Henri de Toulouse-Lautrec left this town for the lights of Paris and the Moulin Rouge, a decision that seems unfathomable on a summer afternoon, when the setting sun sparkles off the brick tower of the cathedral and filters through into the maze of the city center. Next to the cathedral, the former Bishop's palace has been transformed into a museum in Toulouse-Lautrec's name. Albi remains as yet relatively unfrequented by American tourists, although the English and the French flock here to savor the town's natural beauty. Those who come planning to see only the cathedral and museum often end up staying longer, entranced by the peaceful city.

ORIENTATION AND PRACTICAL INFORMATION. Trains run from av. Maréchal Joffre to: **Castres** via St-Sulpice (1½hr., 3 per day, 80F/€12.20); **Paris** (7hr.; approx. 8 per day, some via Toulouse, some via Bordeaux; 478-620F/€72.88-94.53); and **Toulouse** (1hr., 15 per day, 65F/€9.91). **Buses** leave from pl. Jean Jaurès (☎05 63 54 58 61) for **Castres** (1hr., M-Sa 8 per day, 34F/€5.18) and **Toulouse** (5 per day, 1 on Su; 63F/€9.60). **Local transportation** is provided by **Espace Albibus,** 14 rue de l'Hôtel de Ville. (☎05 63 38 43 43. Tickets 5F/€0.76. Buses run roughly 7:30am-7:30pm.) **Albi Taxi Radio** (☎05 63 54 85 03) awaits at the station. **Rent bikes** at **Cycles Andouard,** 7 rue Séré-de-Rivières. (☎05 63 38 44 47. 80F/€12.20 per half-day, 100F/€15.25 per day, 500F/€76.23 per week. Deposit 2000F/€304.92. Open Tu-Sa 9am-noon and 2-7pm. MC/V.)

To reach the **tourist office,** Palais de la Berbie, at pl. Ste-Cécile, turn left from the station onto av. Maréchal Joffre and left again onto av. du Général de Gaulle. Bear left over pl. Lapérouse to the pedestrian *vieille ville.* Rue de Verdusse leads toward pl. Ste-Cécile, from where signs point the way (10min.). The office offers an accommodations service (10-15F/€1.53-2.29); city tours in French (June 15-Sept. 15; 27F/€4.42, students 25F/€3.81). (☎05 63 49 48 80; fax 05 63 49 48 98. www.tourisme.fr/albi. Open July-Aug. M-Sa 9am-7:30pm, Su 10:30am-1pm and 3:30-6:30pm; Sept.-June M-Sa 9am-12:30pm and 2-6pm, Su 10:30am-12:30pm and 3:30-5:30pm.) There's a **laundromat** at 8 rue Emile Grand, off Lices Georges Pompidou (open 7am-9pm). The **police** are waiting at 23 Lices Georges Pompidou (☎05 63 49 22 81). The **Centre Hospitalier** is on rue de la Berchère (☎05 63 47 47 47). Access the **Internet** at **Ludi.com,** 62 rue Séré de Rivière. (☎05 63 43 34 24. 36F/€5.49 per hr. Open M-Sa 11am-midnight.) The **post office,** pl. du Vigan, offers **currency exchange.** (☎05 63 48 15 63. Open M-F 8am-7pm, Sa 8am-noon.) **Postal code:** 81000.

ACCOMMODATIONS AND CAMPING. Arrive early or reserve ahead in Albi, especially for summer weekends. For info on *gîtes d'étape* and rural camping, call **ATTER** (☎05 63 48 83 01; fax 05 63 48 83 12. Open M-F 8am-12:30pm and 2-6pm). Even the budget hotels are expensive for solo travelers, but the antiqued **Hôtel La Régence,** 27 av. Maréchal Joffre, is a good deal. On av. Maréchal Joffre, near the train station, the hotel is close to the center of things. (☎05 63 54 01 42; fax 05 63 54 80 48. Breakfast 33F/€5.03. Singles and doubles with TV 145F/€22.11, with shower 171-256F/€26.07-39.03. Extra bed 53F/€8.08. MC/V.) If they're full, try the well-equipped **Hôtel du Parc,** 3 av. du Parc. From the station, follow av. Maréchal Joffre, veering left. It becomes bd. Carnot. The hotel is on the left across from Parc Rochegude. (☎05 63 54 12 80; fax 05 63 54 69 59. Breakfast 35F/€5.34. Reception 24hr. Singles 170F/€25.92; doubles with shower 220F/€33.54, with bathtub 250-290F/€38.12-44.21; quads with shower 330F/€50.31. AmEx/MC/V.)

Those on a tight budget will have to try to book a room at the **Maison des Jeunes et de la Culture,** 13 rue de la République, which is often filled by groups. From the bus station, walk across the parking lot toward the Théâtre Municipale. Bear left onto the wide Lices Jean Moulin and turn right onto rue de la République before the bridge. The entrance is on rue Jules Rolland, through formidable steel doors. It's 15 minutes farther from the train station: follow av. Maréchal Joffre, bear left on av. Général de Gaulle, and turn right on rue Hippolyte Savary to reach the pl. Jean Jaurès bus station. The hostel has institutional co-ed dorms and co-ed bathrooms. (☎05 63 54 53 65; fax 05 63 54 61 55. Breakfast 15F/€2.29. Meals 40-50F/ €6.10-7.62. Sheets 18F/€2.74. Laundry. Key deposit 20F/€3.05. Reception only M-F 9am-1pm and 7-9pm, Sa-Su 8-9pm, so catch them when you can. Often booked long in advance, so call ahead. Dorms an unbelievable 31F/€4.73.)

You can **camp** near a pool at **Parc de Caussels,** 2km east of the center of town, toward Millau on D999. To get there, take bus #5 from pl. Jean Jaurès to "Camping" (every hr. until 7pm). On foot, leave town on rue de la République and follow the signs (30min.). (Open Apr.-Oct. 15. 50F/€7.62 for 2 people, 66F/€10.06 for 2 people with car; extra person 19F/€2.90.)

FOOD. Next to Albi stretches the vast region of **Gaillac,** where *vignoble* estates prepare some of the best wines of the Southwest. Red, white, and rosé wines are all available from the Gaillac estates. They can be tasted and bought, at **Confidences Du Terroir,** 1 pl. Ste-Cécile, across from Albi's tourist office. (☎05 63 54 05 78. Open daily 10am-12:30pm and 2-7pm.) Markets are held indoors at **pl. du Marché** near the cathedral (Tu-Su 8am-12:30pm), outdoors at **pl. Ste-Cécile** (Sa 8am-12:30pm), and organically at **pl. du Jardin National** (Tu and Th 5-7pm). Cheap meals and groceries await at **supermarket/cafeteria Casino,** 39 rue Lices Georges Pompidou. (Open M-Sa 8:30am-7:30pm. Cafeteria open daily 11:30am-9:30pm. Dishes 24-49F/€3.66-7.47.) For a truly romantic dinner, descend the stairway by the pont Neuf to riverside **Le Robinson,** 142 rue Edouard-Branly. This elegant Eden, with dripping vines, romantic lighting, and tables on outdoor terraces, offers a peek at the Tarn as it flows under the bridge. Try delicately flavored *menus* for 100-160F/ €15.25-24.39. (☎05 63 46 15 69. Open Tu 7:30-10pm, W-Su noon-2pm and 7:30-10pm. MC/V.) Specialties of the region are served with exquisitely fresh fruits and vegetable garnishes at **La Tête de l'Art,** 7 rue de la Paille. Try the local tripe flavored with saffron. Enormous wine glasses allow the *Gaillac* to flow freely. (☎05 63 38 44 75. *Menus* 75-160F/€11.43-24.39. Open July and Aug. daily noon-2pm and 7:30-10pm; Sept.-June Th-M same hours.) **Le Tournesol,** rue de l'Ort en Salvy, is a popular vegetarian restaurant coincidentally situated behind the pl. du Vigan, with healthy concoctions of grains and heavenly homemade desserts. (☎05 63 38 38 14. Open Tu-Th and Sa noon-2pm, F noon-2pm and 7:30-9:30pm.)

SIGHTS. The pride of Albi, eclipsing even the Lautrec museum, is the **Cathédrale Ste-Cécile.** With its massive, sloping walls, high stained-glass windows, and graphic frescoed representations of hell, it is the physical manifestation of the Catholic Church's power. It was built to enforce the "one true religion" after the Church's "Albingensian Crusade" wiped out the Cathar heresy that had taken root in Albi. Inside, magnificent stone carvings line the walls of the choir in patterns so intricate they almost look like lace. The enormous fresco of the Last Judgment that presides over the altar is thought to be the work of the celebrated German painter Hieronymus Bosch. The church's **organ** bursts into song on Wednesdays at 5pm and Sundays at 4pm in July and August. (☎05 63 49 48 86. Open June-Sept. daily 8:30am-6:45pm; Oct.-May 8:30-11:45am and 2-5:45pm. Choir 5F/€0.76. Two tours daily June 15-Sept. 15. 27F/€4.12, students 23F/€3.51. Evening tours 30F/ €4.57, students 20F/€3.05. English audioguide available. 11am services.)

Born with a congenital bone disease to the Count of Toulouse and the Count's cousin and wife, **Henri de Toulouse-Lautrec** (1864-1901) was left quite a bit shorter than average. "Whenever he appeared at a crowded dance hall or smoke-filled café, he caused a sensation," wrote Maurice Joyant. "Astonished, people stared at this dwarf with two deformed legs, his over-size head, his malicious eyes peering through spectacles astride his huge nose, his bulbous lips and tousled bushy black beard." Lautrec led a life of debauchery in the cafés, cabarets, and brothels of Paris, and with his keen sense of caricature, satiric wit, and accomplished brush, left behind a lasting homage to Parisian nightlife in oil paint and ink. The collection of works ferreted away by his mother and assembled in the **Musée Toulouse-**

LANGUEDOC

Lautrec, in the 13th-century Palais de la Berbie, includes all 31 of the famous posters of Montmartre nightclubs. Upstairs, a fine collection of art includes sculptures and paintings by Degas, Dufy, Matisse, and Rodin. (☎05 63 49 48 70. Open June-Aug. daily 9am-6pm; Sept. 9am-noon and 2-6pm; Apr.-May 10am-noon and 2-5:30pm; Oct.-Mar. W-M 10am-noon and 2-5pm. 30F/€4.57, students 20F/€3.05. Tourist office gives tours June 15-Sept. 15 for 38F/€5.80, students 26F/€3.96.) Don't miss the **courtyard** behind the museum, with an ornamental garden and views of the river Tarn. Toulouse-Lautrec's family still owns his birthplace, the **Hôtel du Bosc,** 14 rue Toulouse-Lautrec in old Albi. You can visit the 12th-century **Château du Bosc,** where he spent childhood vacations, in a forest 45km northeast of Albi. Drive up the N88 toward Rodez or take the train to the **Naucelle** station, 4km from the château. (☎05 65 69 20 83; fax 05 65 72 00 19. Open daily 9am-7pm.)

ENTERTAINMENT AND FESTIVALS. You'll have no problem finding a crowd along **pl. de l'Archevêché** in front of the Palais de la Berbie and at the late-night bar-restaurants on **Lices Georges Pompidou** near pl. du Vigan. Innovative plays run at the **Théâtre de la Croix Blanche,** 14 rue de Croix Blanche (☎05 63 54 18 63 for schedules, around 70F/€10.67). The **Centre Culturel de l'Albigeois,** on the felicitous pl. de l'Amitié Entre les Peuples, off bd. Carnot and opposite Parc Rochegude, often shows foreign art films in *v.o.* (☎05 63 54 11 11. Open Tu-F 2-7pm, Sa 10am-noon and 2-7pm. 41F/€7.01, students and seniors 29F/€4.42.) Albi brings in the noise with an abundance of celebrations, all listed in *Sortir à Albi*, available at the tourist office. In the last two weeks of May, **Jazz dans le Tarn** brings harmony to the streets. The **Festival Théâtral** takes place in the last week of June and the first week of July. (Tickets 115F/€17.53, students 100F/€15.25.)

NEAR ALBI: CORDES-SUR-CIEL

> The traveler who looks at the summer night from the terrace at Cordes knows that he need go no further, and that if he wishes it, the beauty of the place, day after day, will banish solitude.
>
> —Albert Camus, 1954

Poking its church steeple above the morning mists and overlooking the far-off yellow valleys of St-Cérou, medieval Cordes-sur-Ciel often looks as good as its name—a celestial city, perched among the clouds, where an alienated Camus found the courage to believe that "estranged lovers would finally embrace, love and creation achieve perfect equilibrium." Located 24km north of Albi, this fairy tale of a city is bounded by a crumbling double wall that sprouts flowers and sometimes entire gardens. The tiny city rises to a summit and descends the other side by a single steep cobblestone street, twisting through multiple gates that have regulated its commerce for the better part of a millennium.

PRACTICAL INFORMATION. The best transportation from **Albi** is the buses of **Sudcar Rolland** (☎05 63 54 11 93). Two buses run M-F from **Albi's** bus station to Cordes (30F/€4.57; last bus from Cordes to Albi 5:15pm). **Trains** from **Albi** go via Tessonnières to **Vindrac** (1 hr., 2 per day, 37F/€5.64), where you can call the **Barrois minibus** (☎05 63 56 14 80) to take you the 5km to Cordes (28F/€4.27). If the minibus is unavailable, getting from the train station to Cordes can be a nightmare of a 5km walk. Though it's not recommended by *Let's Go*, many choose to hitch, but don't count on catching a ride; families on vacation, which account for the majority of the traffic, seldom pick up hitchhikers.

The **tourist office,** pl. de Halle in Maison Fontpeyrouse, can help find accommodations and offers daily tours of the city at 11am (25F/€3.81). (☎05 63 56 00 52; fax 05 63 56 19 52; www.cordes-sur-ciel.org. Open July-Aug. daily 10am-7pm; Sept.-June 10:30am-12:30pm and 2:30-6pm.) An **annex** in the lower city is in the Maison du Pays Cordais. (Open daily 10:30am-12:30pm and 2-6pm.) A **market** takes place at the bottom of the hill (Sa 8am-noon). A **navette** shuttles between the *haute ville* and the lower part of Cordes, leaving from in front of the tourist office. (Departs daily every 12min. 10am-1pm and 2-6pm. 13F/€1.98, children 8F/€1.22.)

SIGHTS AND ENTERTAINMENT. Located in Portail Peint as you first approach the upper town from pl. de la Bouteillerie, **Musée Charles Portal** displays archaeological finds and pictures of the city through the ages. (Call tourist office for info at 05 63 56 00 52. Open July-Aug. daily 10am-12:30pm and 3:30-6:30pm; Apr.-June and Sept.-Oct. Su and holidays 3-6pm. 15F/€2.29, students 7F/€1.07.) A few steps farther down Grande Rue Raymond VII is the **Musée de l'Art du Sucre,** a sweet tooth's dream, which sells all kinds of candied concoctions in its boutique and displays intricate models, all made entirely of sugar. (☎05 63 56 02 40. Open Feb.-Dec. daily 9:30am-12:30pm and 2-7:30pm. 15F/€2.30.) Next door is the **Musée Yves Brayer,** with the drawings, paintings, and garb of the artist who left occupied Paris for Cordes in 1940. (☎05 63 56 14 79. Open Feb.-Dec. daily 10:30am-12:30pm and 2-6pm. 20F/€3.05, children 10F/€1.53.)

At Cordes' summit is **Eglise St-Michel,** the highest point in town; right beside it is the flat, open **pl. de la Bride.** Apparently the extensive fortifications that ring the city never had a central fort or château. Instead, Cordes had pl. de la Bride—an ideal platform for all kinds of stone-flinging machinery, used to halt the advance of invaders from below. This is also the site of the **Puits de la Halle,** the 114m long well constructed in 1222 along with the town. Albi had other sources of water and no pressing need to perform this feat by tunnelling through the entire mountain, but the well in the center of town provided absolute security in the event of a siege. On the way down the far side of the hill on Grande Rue Raymond VII, take a moment to stop and look at the facade of **La Maison du Grand Ecuyer,** marked with a plaque just beyond the tourist office. Staring stone carved faces set among columns, pilasters, delicately wrought foliage, and snarling gargoyles survey the passing scene.

For four days surrounding the 14th of July, fire-eaters play to costumed crowds at the medieval market during the **Fête du Grand Fauconnier,** which offers plays, concerts, and magic shows within the *vieille ville.* Gnaw a drumstick at one of the Fête's banquets. (☎05 63 56 00 52 for reservations and info. Costume rentals 100F/€15.25; 1000F/€152.46 deposit. Entrance 30F/€4.57; free if costumed.)

CARCASSONNE

Carcassonne from afar is breathtaking. Approaching the city, you realize that you have reached the place where Cinderella lost her glass slipper, where Beauty nursed the Beast, and where Jack's giant lived out a happy life until the beanstalk episode. Round towers capped by red tile roofs guard the entrance to the city, while an undulating double wall protects against intruders. As you enter the stone portals, the ramparts still seem to resound with the screams of battle and the clash of the armored knights who defended the city in the 11th and 12th centuries.

The illusion fades fast once you clear the city walls; the 'battle sounds' are actually the grunts and exclamations of thousands of photo-taking visitors who crowd the city's narrow streets each year. Carcassonne has become one of France's best tourist traps, a place where families and school groups load up on cheap plastic swords and shields from souvenir shops. The city should not be missed but, if you can, daytrip away from Carcassonne's hostel during the middle of the day and return late in the evening, when the streets are clear of crowds and the floodlit fortress echoes with free animations and concerts.

TRANSPORTATION

Trains: ☎04 68 71 79 14, behind Jardin St-Chenier. To: **Lyon** (5½hr., 2 direct per day, 271F/€41.34); **Marseille** (3hr., every 2hr., 205F/€31.26); **Montpellier** (2hr., 14 per day, 115F/€17.54); **Narbonne** (1hr., 10 per day, 54F/€8.24); **Nice** (6hr., 5 per day, 303F/€46.21); **Nîmes** (2½hr., 12 per day, 142F/€21.66); **Perpignan** (2hr., 10 per day, 94F/€14.34); and **Toulouse** (50min., 24 per day, 75F/€11.43). Info office open M-Sa 9am-noon and 1:30-6:15pm.

Buses: Catch all buses near the train station. Check posted schedules at the station or ask tourist office. To: **Foix** (1hr., 2 per day, 33F/€5.03); **Narbonne** (3hr., 1 per day, 44F/€6.71); and **Toulouse** (2½hr., 3 per day, 52F/€7.93). **Cars Teissier** (☎04 68 25 85 45) has service to **Lourdes** (150F/€22.90).

Local Transportation: A free **shuttle** (*navette*) takes you from sq. Gambetta (in the lower city) to the citadel gates. (☎04 68 47 82 22. M-Sa only; every 15 min.,) **CART,** sq. Gambetta (☎04 68 47 82 22), runs **buses** throughout the city, from the train station to the citadel gates and the campground. To get from the station to the *cité,* take bus #4 (dir: Gambetta) and then bus #2 (dir: La Cité). M-Sa only; every 20-40min., approx. 7am-7pm, 5.90F/€0.90.

Taxis: Radio Taxi Services (☎04 68 71 50 50). At the train station or across the canal by Jardin Chenier. 24hr.

ORIENTATION AND PRACTICAL INFORMATION

The **bastide St-Louis,** once known as the *basse ville* (lower town), recently changed its name to recruit daytrippers who might otherwise skip the lower town entirely. In it are shops, hotels, the **train station,** and most importantly, the **shuttle** and **TOUC,** either of which will get you to the citadel (see **Transportation**). Otherwise, it's a pleasant but steep 30 minute hike. To get from the station to the *cité,* walk straight away down what is first Av. de Maréchal Joffre and then rue Clemenceau. Just past the clearing of Pl. Carnot, turn left onto rue Verdun, which leads

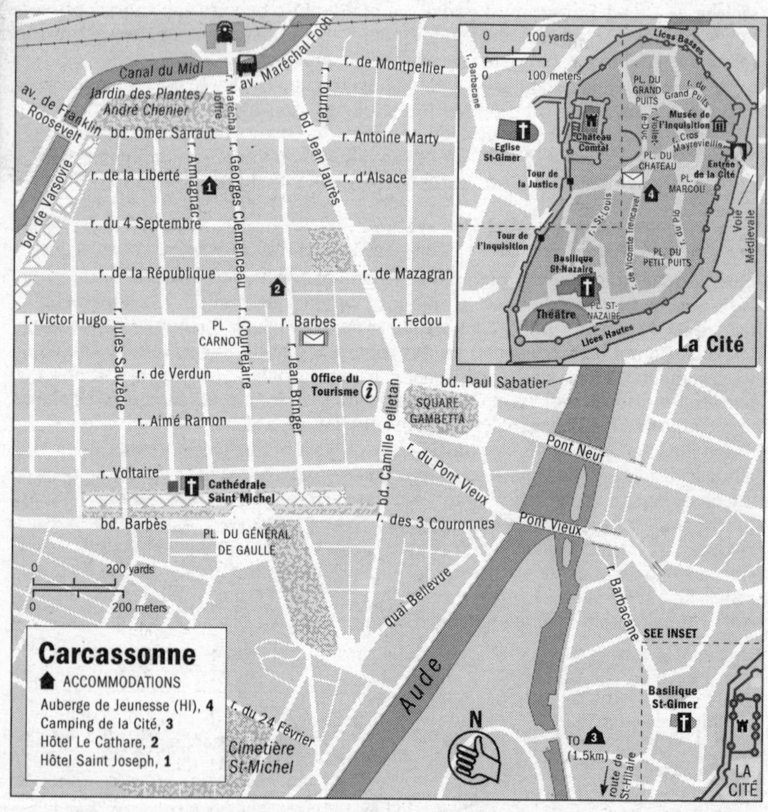

you to Square Gambetta and the **tourist office**. Bear right through the square and turn left up the narrow road that leads to Pont Vieux. Continue straight up the hill to the *cité*. The **tourist office annex** will be on the right as you enter the castle.

Tourist Office: 15 bd. Camille Pelletan, sq. Gambetta (☎04 68 10 24 30; fax 04 68 10 24 38). Open daily July-Aug. 9am-7pm; Sept.-June 9am-12:15pm and 1:45-6:30pm. Annex in the *cité's* porte Narbonnaise (☎04 68 10 24 36). Open daily July-Aug. 9am-7pm; Sept.-June 9am-1pm and 2-6pm. Also an annex near the train station on av. de Maréchal Joffre (☎04 68 25 94 81. Hours same as *cité* annex.)

Money: Banque Nationale, 50 rue Jean-Bringer (☎08 02 35 01 03), offers **currency exchange** at decent rates.

Internet: Alerte Rouge, 73 rue de Verdun (☎04 68 25 20 39). 40F/€6.10 for first hour, 20F/€3.05 for following hours. Open M-Sa 8:30am-1am.

Police: La Comissariat, 4 bd. Barbès (☎04 68 11 26 00).

Medical Assistance: Centre Hospitalier, rte. de St-Hilaire (☎04 68 24 24 24).

Post Office: 40 rue Jean Bringer (☎04 68 11 71 00). **Currency exchange.** Open M-F 8am-7pm, Sa 8am-noon. **Branch office** (☎04 68 47 95 45) also offers currency exchange on rue de Comte Roger and rue Viollet-le-Duc in *la cité*. **Poste Restante:** 11012. **Postal code:** 11000.

LANGUEDOC

ACCOMMODATIONS AND CAMPING

Carcassonne's comfortable hostel is a gift to budgeteers, with 120 beds smack dab in the middle of the *cité*. Hotels in the Bastide St-Louis are surprisingly cheap, and those in the *cité* ferociously expensive. For those who find the crowds unbearable, the Sidsmums hostel is in beautiful countryside 10km outside the city.

Auberge de Jeunesse (HI), rue de Vicomte Trencavel (☎04 68 25 23 16; fax 04 68 71 14 84; carcassonne@fuaj.org), in the *cité*. The only place worth staying if you want to see the castle late at night. Bunked beds with shower and sink. Breakfast included. Kitchen. Sheets 17F/€2.59. Bike rental 50F/€7.62 per day. Laundry. Internet access 28F/€4.27 per hr. Reserve a few days ahead, more in July and August. Reception 24hr. Lockout 10am-3pm. Bunks 76F/€11.59. **Members only.** MC/V.

Sidsmums Travellers Retreat, 11 chemin de la Croix d'Achille, town of Preixan (☎04 68 26 94 49). 10km outside Carcassonne, this recently opened 10-bed hostel is situated in some of Southern France's most beautiful countryside. Sid and his Mum will give advice on the best walks and bike rides in the area or drive you into Carcassonne. Call for pick-up from the station. Open year-round. Bikes 50F/€7.62 per day. Sheets 15F/€2.29. One double for 200F/€30.49; bunks 75F/€11.43.

Hôtel Le Cathare, 53 rue Jean Bringer (☎04 68 25 65 92; fax 04 68 47 15 02), near the post office in the lower town. 4 tiny, aging singles for 90F/€13.72; bright, well-renovated rooms are worth the extra money. Breakfast 27F/€4.12. Singles and doubles 115F/€17.54, with shower 160-170F/€24.39-25.92; triples 200F/€30.49. MC/V.

Hôtel Saint Joseph, 81 rue de la Liberté (☎04 68 71 96 89; fax 04 68 71 36 28), offers 37 rooms in a charming, bright building on a calm street near the train station. Take av. Maréchal Joffre across the canal, and across bd. Omer Sarraut; continue for one block on rue G. Clemenceau before turning right onto rue de la Liberté. Breakfast 28F/€4.27. Reception 7am-11pm. 4 Singles without shower 115F/€17.54; Singles/doubles with shower and TV 185F/€28.21, triples with shower and TV 245F/€37.35, quads with shower, TV 285-305F/€43.46-46.51. MC/V.

Camping de la Cité, rte. de St-Hilaire (☎04 68 25 11 77), has plenty of wide open grassy space across the Aude; from the lower town, turn right immediately after you cross Pont Vieux down rue du Jardin and follow the footpath for a long time (30min. from train station, 20min. from *Cité*). Or take the shuttle from the train station (15min.). Pool, tennis, and a grocery store. Reception 8am-9pm. Open Apr.-Sept. 95F/€14.49 per site and 1 person, 28F/€4.27 for each extra person. Cheaper Apr.-May.

FOOD

Carcassonne's specialty is the inexpensive *cassoulet*, a stew of white beans, herbs, and meat (usually duck or pork, sometimes pigeon). There is a food **market** on pl. Carnot (open Tu, Th, and Sa 7am-1pm) and a **Monoprix** on rue G. Clemenceau at rue de la République (open M-Sa 8:30am-7pm). Restaurants on **rue du Plo** tend to have 55-60F/€8.39-9.15 *menus;* save room for dessert at one of the outdoor *crêperies* on **pl. Marcou.** Restaurants in the *cité* tend to close in winter. Simple and affordable restaurants line **bd. Omer Sarraut** in the lower city. **Les Fontaines du Soleil,** 32 rue du Plo, in the *cité*, is one of Carcassonne's most popular restaurants, a sunny garden courtyard with a fountain. During the week, 59F/€9 lunch menu gets a salad, cassoulet and a pitcher of wine. (☎04 68 47 87 06. Open 11:30am-3pm and 7-10:30pm. Closed Nov. 15-Feb. 15. MC/V.)

SIGHTS

It's no surprise that Carcassone's **fortifications** date back to the first century; this hill above the sea road to Toulouse has always been a strategically valuable spot. An early Visigoth fortress here repelled Clovis in AD 506, and only after many centuries of unsuccessful siege was the town finally taken, falling with Languedoc during the Albigensian Crusade. The *cité* eventually passed under the control of the French crown, and it was King Louis IX who built the second outer wall, copying the double-walled fortress design he had seen in Palestine as a crusader. The city was left untended during the 1700s, until the architect Viollet-le-Duc took it upon himself to begin restoration in 1844.

Originally built as a palace in the 12th century, the **Château Comtal,** 1 rue Viollet-le-Duc, was transformed into a citadel following Carcassonne's submission to royal control in 1226. Entrance to the outer walls is free, but you can enter the château only on a paid tour. The **Cour du Midi,** included in the visit, contains the remains of a Gallo-Roman villa, former home to the troubadours for which Carcassone's court was famous. The **Tour de la Justice's** treacherous staircase leading nowhere was a stairway to heaven (or hell) for ill-fated invaders, who on penetrating the fortress, rushed upstairs and found themselves trapped. Tours in French run continuously, with 3 daily in English June 15-Sept. 15. (☎04 68 25 01 66; fax 04 68 25 65 32. Open daily June-Sept. 9am-7:30pm; Apr.-May and Oct. 9:30am-6pm; Nov.-Mar. 9:30am-5pm. Visits 1hr., 36F/€5.49, ages 18-25 23F/€3.51.)

The *cité* of Carcassonne is filled with small museums, most of which should be skipped. An exception is **Le Musée de l'Ecole,** 3 rue du Plo, in the city's old schoolhouse, which showcases a fascinating display of textbooks, certificates and letters from the late 1800s, just when the French education system was being entirely transformed by Jules Ferry. (☎04 68 25 95 14. Open July-Aug. daily 10am-7pm, Sept-June daily 10am-6pm.) Outside the city walls, across the parking lot from the main entrance over the pont Levis, the **Musée Mémoires Moyen Age,** chemin des Anglais, combines a uninformative video presentation with an intricate model of Raymond de Trencavel's 1240 countersiege of Carcassonne, complete with battle towers, catapults, and grimacing soldiers. (☎04 68 71 08 65. Open daily June-Sept. 10am-8pm, otherwise 9am-6pm. 25F/€3.81, students 20F/€3.05, children 15F/€2.29.) The multimedia presentation of the Cathare crusade at the **Imaginarium** is drawn out, but visitors do get 15 min. of free **Internet access** at the end. (☎04 68 47 78 78. Open July-Aug. daily 10am-9pm, rest of year 10am-6pm.)

The lower town—the **Bastide St-Louis**—was born when Louis IX, afraid enemy troops might use them for shelter, razed the houses clinging to the city's outside walls and relocated their residents, whom he gave their very own walled fortifications and church. Turned into a fortress after the Black Prince destroyed Carcassonne during the Hundred Years' War in 1355, the *basse ville*'s **Cathédrale St-Michel,** rue Voltaire, still sports fortifications on its southern side, facing bd. Barbès. Don't miss the gargoyles that snarl down from their high perches. (Open M-Sa 7am-noon and 2-7pm, Su 9:30am-noon.)

ENTERTAINMENT AND FESTIVALS

The evening is the best time for wandering the streets of the *cité*, and sitting in the cafés in **pl. Marcou**. Bars and cafés along **bd. Omer Sarraut** and **pl. Verdun** remain open until midnight. At the base of the *cité's* battlements, locals dance the night away at **La Bulle,** 115 rue Barbacane. (☎04 68 72 47 70. Open F-Sa until dawn; 60F/€9.15 cover includes first drink.)

In July, the month-long **Festival de Carcassonne** brings dance, opera, theater, and concerts to the Château Comtal and the ancient amphitheater. (160-300F/€24.39-45.74; student reductions available. Info and reservations ☎04 68 11 59 15.) The **Festival Off** showcases smaller bands as well as more far-out comedy and dance performances in the *places* of the *cité* and in the Bastide St-Louis (free). On **Bastille Day,** deep red floodlights and smoke set the entire *cité* ablaze in remembrance of the villages burned when the Tour de l'Inquisition here was the seat of the inquisitorial jury. The firework display is the second best in France. For two weeks in early August, the entire *cité* returns to the Middle Ages for the **Spectacles Médiévaux** (www.terredhistoire.com). People dressed in medieval garb talk to visitors, display their crafts, and pretend nothing has changed in eight centuries. At 5:30pm an equestrian show including mock-jousting and pitched battles enlivens the town. French speakers will enjoy the nightly 9:30pm *spectacle*—a huge multimedia drama bringing to life the 13th century. For ticket info, contact Carcassonne Terre d'Histoire, Club Hippique, Chemin de Serres (☎04 68 71 35 35).

LANGUEDOC

FOIX

Il était une fois, as French fairy tales begin, that a town grew up at the base of a large castle surrounded by mountains. Little has changed in Foix. The towers of the magnificent château look down on the busy marketplace below, cobblestone streets lead through a maze of red-roofed houses, and nearby caves and grottoes still bear the marks and drawings of the prehistoric peoples who made the Ariège region their home. In the summer, the whole town turns out for an enormous medieval spectacle (see **Festivals,** below) to remember the days of yore. The city also provides a base for a large number of nearby hiking and kayaking opportunities. Consider renting a car, or at least a bike; the Château de Montségur, prehistoric caves, and serene Ariège passes are poorly served by public transportation.

PRACTICAL INFORMATION. The **train station,** av. Pierre Sémard, is north of town off the N20. Trains go to **Toulouse** (1hr., 10 per day, 70F/€10.67). (☎05 61 02 03 64. Info and reservation desk open M-Sa 8:10am-12:20pm and 1:25-8:30pm, Su 8:15am-1:55pm and 2:15-10:20pm.) **Salt Autocars,** 8 allées de Villote (☎05 61 65 08 40), also runs to **Toulouse** (1¼hr., 2 per day, 50F/€7.62). **L.C.F. Motos,** 16 rue Labistour, rents **bikes** for 95F/€14.48 per day. (☎05 61 05 29 98. Open M 2-7pm, Tu-Sa 9am-noon and 2-7pm.) To reach the **tourist office,** 29 rue Théophile Delcassé, leave the train station and turn right. Follow the street until you reach the main road (N20). Follow this highway to the second bridge, cross it, and follow cours G. Fauré for about three blocks. Rue Théophile Delcassé is on your right and the tourist office is right on the corner. (☎05 61 65 12 12; fax 05 61 65 64 63; www.mairie-foix.fr. Open July-Aug. M-Sa 9am-7pm, Su 10am-12:30pm and 3-6:30pm; June and Sept. M-Sa 9am-noon and 2-6pm, Su 10am-12:30pm; Oct.-May M-Sa 9am-noon and 2-6pm.) For **police,** call 05 61 05 43 00. The **hospital** is 5km out of town in St- Jean de Verges (☎05 61 03 30 30). In an emergency, dial 112. For **Internet access,** drop by the **Bureau d'Information Jeunesse (BIJ),** pl. Parmentier. (☎05 61 02 86 10. 20F/€3.05 per hr. Open M 1-5pm, Tu and Th-F 10am-5pm, W 10am-6pm.) There is a **laundromat** at 32 rue de la Faurie (open daily 8:30am-9:30pm). The **post office,** 4 rue Laffont, has **currency exchange.** (☎05 61 02 01 02. Open M-F 8am-7pm, Sa 8am-noon.) **Poste Restante:** 09008. **Postal code:** 09000.

CATHARISM 101 The terms by which we know the Cathars today are largely the terms of its enemies. The Cathar priests were mockingly named *"perfecti"* by the records of the Inquisition; the term "Cathar" also has a Catholic origin, deriving from the Greek word for "purity," and used derisively. Catharism was a heretic movement out of the Catholic church that claimed that the institutionalized, bureaucratic church had lost contact with its spiritual essence. Most notably, they rejected the Old Testament entirely (as too grounded in the material world); they rejected baptism of the new-born (as too young to choose their faith); they even rejected the universal Christian symbolism of the cross (as nothing more than a torture device). Their ultimate rejection was of the material, temporal world, a world seen as evil and false. When the movement gained the backing of nobles in the Ariège region, it became increasingly threatening, and the pope inaugurated a series of crusades against all Cathars. The taking of Montségur fully wiped out the sect, and many Cathars (disregarding the temporal world as false), flung their bodies into the fires of Montségur as a last act of faith.

ACCOMMODATIONS, CAMPING, AND FOOD. The best option for budget travelers is unquestionably the **Foyer Léo Lagrange,** 16 rue Peyrevidal. To get there, turn right onto cours Gabriel Fauré out of the tourist office and turn right again onto rue Peyrevidal just after the Halle Aux Grains; the *foyer* will be on your right. A cross between a nice hotel and a friendly hostel, it offers privacy and sociability in 22 1- to 4-bed rooms, each equipped with a sink, closet, desk, and private shower. Rooms facing the street in back have impressive views of the château. (☎05 61 65 09 04; fax 05 61 02 63 87. Free Internet access. Kitchen available. Reception 8am-11pm; call ahead if arriving late. 90F/€13.72 per person.) Opposite the Foyer is **Hôtel Eychenne,** 11 rue Peyrevidal, which rents large rooms above a smoky but lively bar. (☎05 61 65 00 04; fax 05 61 65 56 63. Breakfast 30F/€4.57. Singles and doubles with shower 180F/€27.44, with toilet 230F/€35.06; triples or quads with shower 280F/€42.69. MC/V.) Classy **La Barbacane du Château,** 1 av. de Lérida, is just past the flowered roundabout to the right on rue Gabriel Fauré from the tourist office. It offers a higher level of elegance for a higher price. Several rooms have excellent views of the château. (☎05 61 65 50 44; fax 05 61 02 74 33. Breakfast 38F/€5.80. Open Apr.-Oct. 7am-11:30pm. Singles and doubles 195F/€29.73, with bath 220F/€33.54. MC/V.) **Camping du Lac/Labarre** is a three-star site on a lake 3km up N20 toward Toulouse. Rent canoes and kayaks from lakefront **Base Nautique** (half-day 50F/€7.62). Buses from Toulouse stop at the camp; from the train station, head left along N20 until you see the signs for the campground on your left. (☎05 61 65 11 58; fax 05 61 05 32 62; camping.du.lac@wanadoo.fr. Open Apr.-Sept. July-Aug. tent and 1 person 55F/€8.39; tent, car, and 2 people 76F/€11.59. Apr.-June and Sept. 40F/€6.10, 60F/€9.15. Electricity 15F/€2.29.)

Foix's restaurants serve specialties of the Ariège region. Try *truite à l'ariègeoise* (trout), *cassoulet* (a white-bean and duck stew), or the wonderfully messy *écrevisses* (crayfish). Restaurants serving moderately priced local specialties line **rue de la Faurie.** For regular supplies, head to **Casino** supermarket, rue Laffont (open M-Sa 9am-7pm). On Fridays, an **open-air market** sprouts all over Foix, with meat and cheese at the Halle aux Grains, fruits and vegetables at pl. St-Volusien, and clothing along the allées de Villote (food 8am-12:30pm, clothes 8am-4pm). For good prices on regional food, try the **Restaurant Vanille&Chocolat,** 19 rue des Marchands, which serves 55-75F/€8.39-11.43 *menus* on a terrace near pl. St-Volusien. (☎05 61 65 36 90. Open M-Sa 11:30-10pm.) For those who want to escape the cassoulet glut, **l'Atlas,** 14 pl. Pyrène, serves many varieties of couscous and *tagines* (a steaming casserole of lamb or chicken and vegetables) in a vibrant setting of Moroccan tapestries. (☎05 61 65 04 04. Open daily 11:30am-3pm and 7-10:30pm.)

SIGHTS AND EXCURSIONS. The **Château de Foix** is everything a medieval castle should be, with three stunning towers perched protectively on a high point above the city. Inside the well-preserved castle, the small **Musée de l'Ariège** displays a collection of armor, stone carvings and artifacts from the Roman Empire to the Middle Ages. Be sure to take the free, English-language tour. The towers of the castle offer an impressive panoramic view of the Pyrenean foothills from the tower. (☎05 34 09 83 83. Both open July-Aug. daily 9:45am-6:30pm; June and Sept. 9:45am-noon and 2-6pm; Oct.-May W-Su 10:30am-noon and 2-5:30pm. Tours in French every hr., 1 per day in English at 1pm. 25F/€3.81.)

The Ariège region boasts some of the most spectacular **caves** in France. The **Grotte de Niaux** would be a stunning cave in its own right, but it becomes spectacular when the guide's lantern illuminates the prehistoric wall drawings of bison, horses, and ibex that date from around 12,000 BC. Reservations are required to enter the cave. 20km south of Foix, the grotto is only accessible by car. (☎05 61 05 88 37. Open Apr.-Oct. daily; Nov.-Mar M only. 60F/€9.15, students 35F/€5.34.) An hour-long boat ride navigates the **Rivière Souterraine de Labouiche,** the longest navigable underground river in Europe. The small metal boat cruises through galleries of stalagtites and stalagmites, pulled along by wisecracking guides who can give the tour in both French and English. There is no public transportation to this site; consider biking the 6km from Foix. Don't be discouraged—it's all downhill on the way back. (☎05 61 65 04 11. Open July-Aug. daily 9:30am-6pm; Apr.-May 24 M-Sa 2-6pm, Su 10am-noon and 2-6pm; May 25-June and Sept. daily 10am-noon and 2-6pm; Oct.-Nov. 11 Su 10am-noon and 2-6pm. 46F/€7.02, children under 12 34F/€5.18.)

FESTIVALS. Every weekend at 10pm from the end of July though the end of August, an extravagant medieval spectacle, **Il était une Foix...l'Ariege,** enlivens the area around Foix's château. Villagers wrestle bears, fight pitched battles, and shoot off more fireworks than on your average Bastille Day. (For info and tickets call the Théâtre de Verdure de l'Espinet, ☎05 61 02 88 26. 70-140F/€10.67-21.35, under 12 35-70F/€5.34-10.67.) In the second week of July, the **Résistances** festival brings 100 art films—many the same as those shown in Cannes—to Foix. (☎05 61 05 13 30; www.cine-resistances.com. 80F/€12.19 per day; 400F/€60.97 per week.)

NEAR FOIX: CHATEAU DE MONTSEGUR

Rocky Montségur was the Cathars' last stand; their final refuge before complete extinction. The castle on the highest point of a spur of rocks known as "the pog" belonged to a devout Cathar lord; as the pressure of the papal assault against the sect intensified, the Cathar bishop of Toulouse, Guilhabert de Castres, chose Montségur ("Secure Mount") as the new, permanent home for Catharism. A bloody Cathar raid at Avignonet in retaliation for the Inquisition provoked an equally violent and far more final raid by the Catholic church. The siege of Montségur lasted from May 1243 till March 1244, as the crusaders made slow advances up the *pog*, establishing footholds first at the **tower rock** and then, after a bloody confrontation, at the **barbican** or outer tower. When the castle keep finally succumbed, the remaining Cathars were given a choice between renouncing their beliefs and being burnt at the stake. On March 16, 1244, more than 200 unrepentant Cathars flung themselves onto a pyre at the base of the *pog*. Legend enshrouds the events of the night preceding the fire, when the Cathar bishop entrusted their treasure to four *perfecti*, who escaped into the mountains. Today, a few massive, crumbling walls and a broken vault are all that's left of the château of Montségur, but the setting, history, and archaeological finds make for a breathtaking experience. (Open May-Sept. daily 9am-7:30pm; Oct.-Mar. 10am-4pm. 22F/€3.36. Tours in French; July-Aug. 4 per day, May-June and Sept. 2 per day. 25F/€3.81, ages 8-14 13F/€1.98.)

A nameless **gîte d'étape** in the center of the village offers a line of small beds. To get in, follow the signs to Hôtel Costes, and knock on Mr. Massera's door, 90 rue du Village. (☎05 61 01 08 57; marylok@club-internet.fr. Reservations only. Bunks 60-70F/€9.15-10.67.) Next to the *gîte*, the **Hôtel Costes** has large, comfortable rooms. (☎05 61 01 10 24. Breakfast 38F/€5.80. Reception Apr.-Nov. 15 8am-8pm. Doubles with shower 200-250F/€30.49-38.12; triples 270F/€41.18. MC/V.) If Hôtel Costes is full, **Hôtel Couquet,** 51 rue Priucefale, has six huge quads at good prices. (☎05 61 01 10 28. Rooms 180-200F/€27.44-30.49.) Also in the heart of the village, the Germa family's **chambre d'hôte,** 46 rue du Village, has a room for 2 to 5 people and a homemade breakfast for around 250F/€38.12 per night (☎05 61 02 80 70).

Montségur's **tourist office** provides info on the château and on various hiking and biking trails, including the **Massif de St-Barthélémy** and the **Massif de la Frau.** (☎05 61 03 03 03. Open July-Sept. daily 10am-1pm and 2-7pm.) To see the results of archaeological excavations at Montségur, visit the small **Musée de Montségur** just down the street. (Open May-Aug. 10am-12:30pm and 2-7:30pm. Free.) Montségur is 35 kilometers southeast of Foix along the D9. During the school year, five **Sovitour buses** (☎05 61 01 02 35) run daily from Foix's Centre Culturel Olivier Carol to Lavelanet (25F/€3.81). Ask the driver to drop you at the turn-off to Montségur, and follow the signs through Villeneuve d'Olmes to Montférrier (5km). From here it's another 5km uphill to the château. The rest of the year you'll need to plan quite carefully; only four buses run daily.

VILLEFRANCHE-DE-CONFLENT

Deep in the mountains of the Conflent range, hidden within the shadow of Vauban's military masterpiece, Fort Liberia, the miniscule Villefranche-de-Conflent (pop. 260) occupies a once-prized position. For almost 300 years, the walled city kept an active garrison to protect the borders arbitrated by Louis XIV in the 1659 Treaty of the Pyrenees. With the low red sun baking its cobblestone streets, Villefranche makes an ideal afternoon stopover for travelers en route from Perpignan to Toulouse via the scenic Train Jaune line.

PRACTICAL INFORMATION. The **train station** is just outside the town walls off the highway. From the station, take the only road to the highway and turn right toward Villefranche (3min.). **Trains** (☎04 68 96 56 62) run to **Perpignan** (50min., 8 per day, 45F/€6.86). The station is also the terminus of the scenic **Train Jaune** route (see **Outdoors,** below). The **tourist office,** 32bis rue St-Jacques, has lodging info and sells IGN hiking maps for 60-70F/€9.15-10.67. (☎04 68 96 22 96; fax 04 68 96 07 24. Open July-Aug. daily 10am-6:30pm; Sept.-Dec. and Feb.-June 2-5pm.) **Hiking** info is also available through the **Direction Départementale de la Jeunesse et des Sports** (☎04 68 35 50 49). For info about hiking locally and throughout the Pyrenees, and a more extensive (and expensive) collection of IGN hiking maps (70F/€10.67), contact **Editions et Diffusions Randonnées Pyrénéennes,** BP 88, 09200 St-Girons (☎04 61 66 71 87). This region is IGN map #10: "Massif du Canigou."

ACCOMMODATIONS. Villefranche has few cheap hotels, and even the expensive ones fill quickly during the summer. **Hôtel Le Terminus,** just to the right of the train station, offers six pastel rooms with wooden floors. (☎04 68 96 11 33. Breakfast 30F/€4.57. Call ahead. Singles and doubles 180F/€27.44, with shower 200F/€30.49, with bath 230F/€35.06.) The *mairie* (town hall) on pl. de l'Eglise operates **gîtes communaux,** but you must stay for a full week (Sa-Sa)—or at least pay the weekly rate. (☎04 68 96 10 78. Town hall open M-F 8am-noon and 2-6pm.) If you succumb completely to the lure of the Pyrenees and of the tiny Train Jaune, continue on from Villefranche to the stop "Thues/Caranca" (30min., 7 per day, 32F/€4.88 from Villefranche). The *gîte-camping* **Mas de Bordes** is perched beside a crumbling stone church in a canyon nook, right by a natural hot spring. (☎04 68 97 05 00. 60F/€9.15 with kitchen access; camping 25F/€3.81 per person, 6F/€0.92 per tent.) The *gîte* is a three-hour walk from an entrance to the **GR10,** the hiking trail which stretches from the Atlantic to the Mediterranean.

SIGHTS AND OUTDOORS. Built into the mountainside high above the town, Vauban's masterpiece, the 17th-century **Fort Liberia** takes the form of two overlapping hexagons. (☎04 68 96 34 01. 30F/€4.57, students 25F/€3.81.) To reach its fortified heights, hike (20min.) or catch the *navette* from Porte de France (20F/€3.05). In the fort, there are towers to climb and passageways to navigate, but it is the view of the impossibly picturesque Villefranche from above that makes the trip worthwhile. There are actually only 832 steps in the subterranean passage, known as the "staircase of 1000 steps," that leads back down to the city. But the disparity feels small as the unending marble passageway unfolds before you.

The walled fortifications of Villefranche offer more rock passageways within which to lose yourself. But the **remparts,** accessible from the tourist office, look better from the outside. If you choose to enter them, follow the red and blue arrows carefully. (☎04 68 96 22 96. Open July and Aug. daily 10am-7:30pm; June and Sept. 10am-6:30pm; Oct.-May 2-5pm. 20F/€3.05, students 15F/€2.29. Cassette tour in English or French available for 15F/€2.29.)

Running 63km through the Pyrenees, the tiny **Train Jaune** links Villefranche to **Latour-de-Carol** (2½-3hr., 5 per day, 97F/€14.80). The roofless train runs over deep mountain valleys on spectacular viaducts, stopping at many towns along the way. A trip to Latour and back will take a day and cost 194F/€29.59, or you can continue on to **Toulouse** (3hr. from Latour-de-Carol, 3 per day, 170F/€25.92). Shorter trips can be made (from 15F/€2.29). Get started early so as not to be caught unawares by the train schedule. (☎08 36 35 35 35; http://ter.sncf.fr/train-jaune/default.htm.) In winter, the Train Jaune hauls **skiers** to fashionable **Font-Romeu** (3-4 per day, 70F/€10.67). Equipped with snow machines and ski lifts, this resort offers first-rate skiing. Call the **tourist office** in Font Romeu 04 68 30 68 30 for info.

LANGUEDOC

FESTIVALS. On June 23, the **Fête des Feux de St-Jean,** celebrated throughout the Catalonian region, burns brightly in Villefranche. Torches lit on the Canigou mountain bring sacred fire back to the village, where locals dance the traditional *sardane*, drink wine, and hop over bonfires. People dressed as giants also appear in the village every Sunday in April in recognition of **Pâques.** Instead of Bastille Day, Villefranche-de-Conflent celebrates the **Fête de St-Jacques** from July 20-22.

The biggest festival in the area is in the nearby city of **Prades,** which for 23 years was home to the great Catalan cellist Pablo Casals during his political exile from Franco's Spain. The annual **Festival Pablo Casals,** from the last week of July through the middle of August, attracts an array of international musicians for three weeks of chamber music and workshops. Tickets (150-180F/€22.90-27.44) are available after May 15 from the **Association Pablo Casals,** rue Victor Hugo. (☎04 68 96 33 07; fax 04 68 96 50 95. Open M-F 9am-noon and 2-6pm. MC/V.)

COLLIOURE

Collioure (pop. 2770) lounges at the very spot where the Pyrenees tumble through emerald vineyards and orchards into the concave lip of the Mediterranean. The rocky harbor of this small port captured the fancy of Greeks and Phoenicians long before it modeled for a then-unknown Matisse, who baptized the town an artists' mecca in 1905. He was soon followed by Dérain, Dufy, Dalí, and Picasso. You'll understand the town's draw after a glimpse at the expansive sea and stone lighthouse tower bathed in the late afternoon sun. Collioure is a land of plenty where the farmers and fishermen offer direct sales of produce. Apricots and peaches fresh from the orchards are sold alongside anchovies and regional Banyul wines.

PRACTICAL INFORMATION. The **train station** (☎04 68 82 05 89), at the top of av. Aristide Maillol, sends trains north to **Narbonne** (1hr., 12 per day, 75F/€11.43) and **Perpignan** (20min., 15 per day, 29F/€4.42). You can also go south to **Spain:** trains run to **Barcelona** (3½hr., 5 per day, 79F/€12.05) and **Port Bou** (6 per day, 19F/€2.90). For info on the coastal bus routes, call **Cars Inter 66** (☎04 68 35 29 02) or inquire at the **tourist office,** pl. du 18 Juin. They can help you plan dayhikes. (☎04 68

82 15 47; fax 04 68 82 46 29; contact@collioure.com; www.collioure.com. Open July-Aug. daily 9am-8pm; Sept.-June M-Sa 9am-noon and 2-6:30pm.) **X-Trem Bike,** 7 rue de la Tour d'Auvergne, keeps strange hours but has good prices on **bike rentals.** (☎06 15 97 83 74. Open daily 8:30am-12:30pm, 1:30-2:30pm, 6:30-8:30pm. Half-day rental 50F/€7.62, full day 90F/€13.72, week 390F/€59.48.) **Exchange currency** at **Banque Populaire,** 16 av. de la République. (☎04 68 82 05 94. Open M-F 8am-noon and 1:30-5pm.) The **police station** is on rue Michelet (July-Aug. ☎04 68 82 25 63; Sept.-June ☎04 68 82 00 60). The **post office** is on rue de la République. (☎04 68 98 36 00. Open M-F 9am-noon and 2-5pm, Sa 8:30-11:30am.) **Postal code:** 66190.

ACCOMMODATIONS AND FOOD. Collioure fills its hotels and beaches to the brim during July and August. **Hôtel Triton,** 1 rue Jean Bart, is on the waterfront 10 minutes from the center of town. The rooms have A/C, TVs, and showers, for comparably low prices. (☎04 68 98 39 39; fax 04 68 82 11 32. Breakfast 37F/€5.64. Reserve rooms as early as possible. Doubles 200F/€30.49, with toilet 280F/€42.69. AmEx/MC/V.) The **Hostellerie des Templiers** is on av. Camille Pelletan (mailing address: 12 quai de l'Amirauté), facing the château. Tiled stairways lead to hallways covered top to bottom with over a thousand original paintings, gifts of such lodgers as Matisse, Picasso, and Dalí (see **Sights,** below). The simple rooms come equipped with original works of art. The hotel also has two annexes in the back that offer cheaper rooms. (☎04 68 98 31 10; fax 04 68 98 01 24; info@hotel-templiers.com. Breakfast 38F/€5.80. Reception 8am-11pm. In summer, doubles with bath 335-395F/€51.09-60.24, quads with bath 605F/€92.26. In winter, doubles with bath 290-350F/€44.23-53.36, quads with bath 500-515F/€76.23-78.54. In annex, in summer, doubles with bath 315F/€48.04; in winter 250F/€38.12. AmEx/MC/V.) **Camping Les Amandiers,** 28 rue de la Démocratie, Plage de l'Ouilla, is a 20-minute walk north of town on the N114 road, but only 150m from the beach. The campgrounds are crowded with cars and tents, but the price includes hot showers. (☎04 68 81 14 69; fax 04 68 81 09 95. Open Apr.-Sept. 125F/€19 for 2 people and tent.)

Local produce is sold at a fantastic **market,** centered on pl. du Maréchal Leclerc and spilling out along the canal toward the Château Royal (W and Su 8am-1pm). Reasonably priced crêperies, bakeries, and cafés crowd **rue St-Vincent** near the port. For the greatest selection, head to the **Shopi supermarket,** 16 av. de la République. (Open M-Sa 8:30am-12:30pm and 4-7:30pm, Su 8:30am-12:30pm.) The **Petit Casino** on pl. Maréchal Leclerc has more extensive hours. (Open mid-June to mid-Sept. M-Sa 7am-7:30pm, Su 7am-3pm; mid-Sept. to mid-June M-Sa 7am-7pm.)

SIGHTS. Extending from pl. du 8 Mai 1945 to the port, the hulking stone **Château Royal** housed the kings of Majorca in the 13th century, and was later fortified by both French and Spanish kings to serve as a battlement in the unending border wars. The château is worth the climb just to lean over its thick walls and survey the brilliant blue harbor below. (☎04 68 82 06 43. Open June-Sept. daily 10am-5:15pm; Oct.-May 9am-4:15pm. 20F/€3.05, students and children 10F/€1.53.) From the château, the most picturesque view looks out onto the oft-painted red-domed tower of the 17th-century **Notre-Dame-des-Anges.** The tower of the church rises majestically from foundations built directly into the sea. The steeple is actually much older than the rest of the church; it doubled as a fortified stone lighthouse for the harbor of Collioure in the Middle Ages. The tower is not open for climbing, and the inside of the church itself is much less impressive. (Open daily 7:30am-noon and 2-6pm. Free.) The two stone châteaux on the hill are private, but a 30-minute hike through the **Parc Pams,** behind the Musée d'Art Moderne off rte. de Port-Vendres, will give a good view of the 16th-century **Fort Saint Elme,** built by Spain's Charles V. Back across the bay, on the northern end of town, a walkway built into the bottom of the cliffs leads a few kilometers north to **Argelès** along the isolated coastline. Hikers can get info from the tourist office on these and a number of other trails in the magnificent hills above the Mediterranean.

To retrace the tracks of Matisse and Dérain, follow the **Chemin du Fauvisme.** Most of the sights lie clustered along the shorefront, reaching out to the Chapelle St-Vincent on the peninsula. The *chemin* begins and ends in the "Espace Fauve" in front of the tourist office, where you can pick up a map and itinerary. Over a thousand of the artists' originals are displayed on the walls of the **Hostellerie des Templiers** (see above), 12 quai de l'Amirauté, where they were given as gifts. Proprietor Jo Pous was only a child when Matisse and Picasso set up easels in the living room. Even visitors who are not staying in the hotel are welcome to view the paintings at any time. Less impressive is the small collection at the **Musée d'Art Moderne-Fonds Peské,** Villa Pams, rte. de Port-Vendres. The two floors contain some paintings of Collioure as well as ceramics collected from the Hispano-Mauresque period. (☎04 68 82 10 19. Open July-Aug. daily 10am-noon and 2-7pm; Sept. and June 10am-noon and 2-6pm; Oct.-May W-M 10am-noon and 2-7pm. 12F/€1.83, students 8F/€1.22.)

Those with a taste for the harbor should stop by **Les Etablissements Desclaux,** 3 rte. d'Argelès. Besides selling anchovies, the store escorts visitors into the back where they can watch the salty product being prepared and taste a series of anchovies preserved in vinegar with flavors like lemon, curry, and pimento.

EXCURSIONS AND FESTIVALS. The **Centre International de Plongée,** 15 rue de la Tour d'Auvergne, provides numerous nautical services and entertainments, including windsurfing (2hr. rental or 1hr. mini-course 100F/€15.25), scuba diving (initiation course 450F/€68.61, with scuba card 120F/€18.30), and boat rides aboard a traditional 11m Catalan *barque* built in 1908 (2hr., 180F/€27.44). (☎04 68 82 07 16; fax 04 68 82 44 74; www.cip-collioure.com. Open Apr.-Nov.)

From August 14 to 18, the streets of Collioure fill with dance and music for the **Festival de St-Vincent.** Midway through the festival, on August 16th, a **corrida** (bullfight) at the arena (5pm) is followed by a **fireworks** display over the sea (10pm).

PERPIGNAN

The hot and crowded city of Perpignan (pop. 130,000) is only a few kilometers from the transparent waters of the Mediterranean, but the distance feels large enough when you're stuck in the midst of this congested city. Although the Catalan influence permeates the town, with brilliant "blood and gold" flags hanging everywhere, there is little to see or do in central Perpignan. Even the streets of the old city, heralded by the towers of the Castillet, are notable only for their restaurants. What makes Perpignan worthwhile are cheap hotels and a good transportation system; the town can provide a reasonably-priced home base for visits to the more expensive and more beautiful towns of Collioure, Céret, or Canet-Plage.

TRANSPORTATION

Flights: Aéroport de Perpignan-Rivesaltes, 10km northwest of the town center, just outside of town along the D117 (info and reception desk ☎04 68 52 60 70). **Ryanair** (☎04 68 71 96 65; www.ryanair.com) offers the cheapest flights to **London** (from 750F/€114.35). **Hertz** rents **cars** at the airport (☎04 68 61 18 77).

Trains: rue Courteline, off av. de Gaulle. To: **Carcassonne** (1½hr.; 2 per day, change at Narbonne; 70-80F/€10.67-12.20); **Lyon** (4-5hr., 4-5 per day, 268F/€40.87); **Montpellier** (2hr., 8-10 per day, 100-120F/€15.25-18.30); **Nice** (6hr., 3 per day, 299F/€45.60); **Paris** (6-10hr., 4 per day, 439-505F/€66.95-77.01); and **Toulouse** (2½-3hr.; 15 per day, some change at Narbonne; 143F/€21.81). Open M-Sa 8am-6:30pm.

Buses: 17 av. Général Leclerc (☎04 68 35 29 02). **Car Inter 66** (☎04 68 35 29 02) runs 4 buses to the beaches from **Le Barcarès** (to the north) to **Cerbère** (to the south). Schedules at both tourist offices. They offer a **tourist pass** good for 8 days within the *département* (150F/€22.90). Office open M-Sa 6:45am-7:15pm.

Local Transportation: CTP, pl. Gabriel-Péri (☎04 68 61 01 13). Tickets 6.50F/€0.99; *carnet* of 10 50F/€7.62.

Taxis: A.B.S. Taxi (☎06 14 55 84 36). 24hr. Catch them at the train station.

Bike Rental: Cycles Mercier, 20 av. Gilbert Brutus (☎04 68 85 02 71). 250F/€38.12 for 5 days. 8000F/€1219.70 deposit. Open M-Sa 9am-12:30pm and 2:30-7:30pm.

ORIENTATION AND PRACTICAL INFORMATION

Perpignan's train station, once referred to as "the center of the world" by a rather off-center Salvador Dalí, is almost constantly packed with weary travelers, making connections to Catalonia, Spain, 50km to the south, and to the Pyrenees, whose foothills begin rolling 30km to the west. The city itself stretches out for a long way from the station, but most of the action takes place in the small *vieille ville* just past the tower of the red **Castillet.** The area makes a triangle, bounded on the far side by the regional tourist office, the **pl. de la Victoire** up the canal toward the train station, and the **Palais des Rois de Majorque.** Be thankful for the bus shelters' useful maps, as the *vieille ville* is a labyrinth. Most of Perpignan's gypsy population lives on the hilltop past the *vieille ville* in the **Quartier St-Jacques,** near the intersection of bd. Jean Bourrat and bd. Anatole France. In the daytime, this neighborhood buzzes with activity—on hot days, most residents sit outside, chatting noisily—but it may be best to avoid it at night.

Tourist Office: Palais des Congrès, pl. Armand Lanoux (☎04 68 66 30 30; fax 04 68 66 30 26; www.perpignantourisme.com), at the opposite end of the town center from the train station. Follow av. de Gaulle to pl. de Catalogne, then take bd. Georges Clemenceau across the canal past Castillet as it becomes bd. Wilson. Follow the signs along

the park (promenade des Platanes) to the glass-paneled Palais des Congrès (20min. walk from train station). Offers several comprehensive **tours** (in French) June-Sept. (2½hr., 25F/€3.81). For tours in English, call 04 68 22 25 96. Open June-Sept. M-Sa 9am-7pm, Su 10am-noon and 2-5pm; Oct.-May M-Sa 9am-noon and 2-6pm.

Laundromat: Laverie Foch, 23 rue Maréchal Foch. Open daily 7am-8:30pm.

Youth Center: Bureau d'Information Jeunesse, 35 quai Vauban (☎04 68 34 56 56), near the hostel. Open June-Aug. M-F 9:30am-12:30pm and 2-5pm; Sept.-May M-F 9:30am-12:30pm and 1:30-6pm, Sa 2-5pm.

Police: av. de Grande Bretagne (☎04 68 35 70 00).

Hospital: av. du Languedoc (☎04 68 61 66 33).

Internet Access: Hôtel Méditerranée, 62bis av. de Gaulle (☎04 68 34 87 48). 40F/€6.10 per hr.; after 8pm or before noon, 30F/€4.57 per hr. Open daily 7am-2am. **Arena Games,** 9bis rue Pous (☎04 68 34 26 22). 40F/€6.10 per hr., students 35F/€5.34. Open daily 11am-11:30pm.

Post Office: quai de Barcelone (☎04 68 51 99 12). **Currency exchange.** Open M-Tu and Th-F 8am-7pm, W 9am-7pm, Sa 8am-noon. **Poste Restante:** 66020. **Postal code:** 66000.

ACCOMMODATIONS AND CAMPING

The cheapest hotels are near the train station on av. Général de Gaulle. From these hotels, it's only about a 10-minute walk to the city center. The bare Auberge de Jeunesse is also in this section of the city.

Hôtel de l'Avenir, 11 rue de l'Avenir (☎04 68 34 20 30; fax 04 68 34 15 63; avenirhotel@aol.com), off av. du Général de Gaulle. Colorful rooms and hallways, terraces, and a rooftop garden give the feel of a beautiful summer home. The lowest-priced rooms fill quickly, so reserve ahead. Breakfast 25F/€3.81. 15F/€2.29 for key to shower. Singles 90F/€13.72; doubles and larger singles 120-130F/€18.30-19.82, with toilet 140F/€21.35, with shower 160-190F/€24.39-28.97; quads 250F/€38.12. Prices for everything except singles drop 10-20F/€1.53-3.05 in the off-season. AmEx/MC/V.

Auberge de Jeunesse La Pépinière (HI), rue Marc-Pierre (☎04 68 34 63 32; fax 04 68 51 16 02), on the edge of town, between the highway and the police station. From the train station, take a few steps down av. de Gaulle and turn left onto rue Valette. Turn right onto av. de Grande Bretagne, left on rue Claude Marty (rue de la Rivière on some maps) just before the police station, and right onto rue Marc-Pierre (10min.). Small metal bunks are crowded into each room of this barrack-like hostel. Squat toilets and trough sinks are nearby. Music begins playing at 8am and the proprietors run through the hostel calling everyone to breakfast. Small kitchen available 4-11pm. Breakfast included. Sheets 18F/€2.74. Strictly enforced 11am check-out. Lockout 10am-5pm. Closed Dec. 20-Jan. 20. Bunks 70F/€10.67. **Members only.**

Hôtel Express, 3 av. de Gaulle (☎04 68 34 89 96). A block from the train station. Clean, functional rooms include table and chair. Breakfast 20F/€3.05. Shower 15F/€2.29. Often full; call ahead. Singles and doubles 100F/€15.25, with shower 124F/€18.91; triples or quads 184-254F/€28.06-38.74. MC/V.

Camping Le Catalan, rte. de Bompas (☎04 68 63 16 92). Take "Bompas" bus from train station and ask to be let out at *"camping catalan"* (15min., 2 per day, 12F/€1.83). Pools, hot showers, and 94 spots. 2 people July-Aug. 86F/€13.12; Mar.-June 63F/€9.61. Extra person 16-24F/€2.44-3.66.

FOOD

Perpignan's best quality is its spread of reasonably priced restaurants serving Catalan specialties. If you've been waiting to try *escargots*, don't slither an inch farther; *cargolade* is a serving of your shell-wearing garden friends smothered with garlic *aïoli.* The specialty *touron* nougat is available in many flavors. **Pl. de la**

Loge, pl. Arago, and **pl. de Verdun** in the *vieille ville* are filled with restaurants that stay lively at night. For candle-lit tables, take the **rue des Fabriques Couvertes** from pl. de Verdun. Pricier options line **quai Vauban** along the canal. Try **av. de Gaulle,** in front of the train station, for cheaper alternatives. You'll find barrels and baskets of specialties that don't stick around long at the **open-air markets** on pl. de la République (daily 6am-1pm) and pl. Cassanyes (Sa-Su 8am-1pm). Pl. de la République also holds an assortment of fruit stores, charcuteries, and bakeries, as well as the **Marché République** (open Tu-Su 7am-1pm and 4-7:30pm). **Casino supermarket** stockpiles food on bd. Félix Mercader. (☎04 68 34 74 42. Open M-Sa 8:30am-8pm.) The best location in the city is taken by the **Restaurant St-Jean,** 1 rue Cité Bartissol, which sets its tables in the courtyard of the cathedral. Enjoy the *pause terroir* (55F/€8.39), grilled bread smothered with cheese and toppings such as onions, potatoes and anchovies. (☎04 68 51 22 25. Open daily noon-2:30pm and 7-10pm.)

SIGHTS

A museum passport, valid for one week (40F/€6.10), allows entrance to four museums including the Musée Hyacinthe Rigaud, the Casa Pairal, the Musée Numismatique Joseph Puig, 42 av. de Grande-Bretagne (☎04 68 34 11 70), and the Musée d'Histoire Naturelle, 12 rue Fontaine Neuve (☎04 68 35 50 87).

An uphill walk across the *vieille ville* brings you to the sloping red-rock walls of Perpignan's 15th-century Spanish **citadel.** Concealed inside is the simple, square 13th-century **Palais des Rois de Majorque,** where the Majorcan kings used to breed lions in the castle ditches. The courtyard now serves as a concert hall, sheltering plays and jazz and classical concerts in summer at 9pm; tickets at the door. Enter from av. Gilbert Brutus. (Palais ☎04 68 66 38 83. Open June-Sept. daily 10am-6pm; Oct.-May 9am-5pm. Tours every 30min. in French. 20F/€3.05, students 10F/€1.53. Ticket sales end 45min. before closing.) Back in the *vieille ville*, the **Musée Hyacinthe Rigaud,** 16 rue de l'Ange, contains a small but impressive collection of paintings by 13th-century Spanish and Catalan masters; canvases by Rigaud, court artist to Louis XIV and one of the 17th century's great portraitists; and works by Ingres, Picasso, Miró, and Dalí. (☎04 68 35 43 40. Open W-M noon-7pm. 25F/€3.81, students 10F/€1.53.) Guarding the entrance to the city's center, **Le Castillet** holds the small **Casa Pairal,** a museum of Catalan domestic ware. (☎04 68 35 42 05. Open June 15-Sept. 15 W-M 9:30am-7pm; Sept. 16-June 14 W-M 9am-6pm. 25F/€3.81, students 10F/€1.53.) A paragon of Gothic architecture, the **Cathédrale St-Jean** at pl. Gambetta is partly supported by a macabre pillar depicting the severed head of John the Baptist. (☎04 68 51 33 72. Open 9am-noon and 3-7pm. Free.)

ENTERTAINMENT AND FESTIVALS

Perpignan is a big city that keeps small-town hours. Everything seems to shut down by 8pm, and even the restaurants usher out their last customers around 10:30pm. If you're looking for a night on the town, prepare yourself for a calm and café-centric experience. Traditional Catalonian dancing in front of **Le Castillet** (Tu, Th, and Sa) makes for a lively scene around pl. de Verdun, especially in summer. The open-till-dawn clubs lining the beaches at nearby **Canet-Plage** (p. 719) constitute the wildest nightlife, but unless you can make the night last until 6:25am (9:26am on Sunday morning), getting back to Perpignan will mean taking a taxi.

Procession de la Sanch takes over the streets of the *vieille ville* on Good Friday. Although the hooded, solemn ceremony feels a little like the rites of some secret society, anyone who wants to can join the "Friends of the Brotherhood" and participate. As in most of southwestern France, sacred fire is brought down from Mt. Canigou on June 23 for the **Fête de St-Jean.** Dance the *sardana*, munch powdered-sugar *rouquilles*, and pour down the sweet *muscat* wine. In July, the **Estivales de Perpignan** brings world-renowned theater and dance to Perpignan. Get info about the 2002 acts to the right of the tourist office in the Palais de Congrès. During the first two weeks in September, Perpignan hosts **Visa Pour l'Image,** an international festival of photojournalism.

DAYTRIP FROM PERPIGNAN: CERET

*Car Inter 66 (☎04 6 8 39 11 96 in Céret; ☎04 68 35 29 02 in Perpignan; fax 04 68 87 00 56) runs **buses** to Céret from Perpignan (45min., every hr., 35F/€5.34). From the bus stop on av. Clemenceau, the **tourist office,** 1 av. Georges Clemenceau (☎04 68 87 00 53; www.ot-ceret.fr.), is 2 blocks up the hill on the right. Make sure your bus stops in the town center. The office offers a free map of easy hikes and tours (2hr., 20F/€3.05). Open July-Aug. M-Sa 9am-12:30pm and 2-7pm, Su 10am-12:30pm; Sept.-Oct. M-F 10am-noon and 2-5pm, Sa 10am-noon.*

Céret, in the foothills of the Pyrenees, blossoms in the spring—the first cherries of each season from Céret's prized orchards are sent to the President of France. The town square is not just known for its cherry markets but also for being the "Cubist Mecca" beloved by Chagall, Picasso, Manolo, and Herbin. Céret is now home to one of the best museums in southwestern France. Far enough into the hills to allow spectacular hiking, Céret has plenty to offer any naturalist or artist.

The **Musée d'Art Moderne,** 8 bd. Maréchal Joffre, is up the hill from the tourist office. The collections in this graffiti-covered building are composed primarily of personal gifts to the museum by artists including Picasso, Braque, Chagall, and Miró. (☎04 68 87 27 76. Open June 15-Sept. 15 daily 10am-7pm; May-June 14 and Sept. 16-30 10am-6pm; Oct.-Apr. W-M 10am-6pm. July-Sept. 45F/€6.86, students 30F/€4.57; Oct.-June 35F/€5.34, students 20F/€3.05, under 16 free.)

According to legend, the **pont du Diable** (Bridge of Satan), which links the town center to its outskirts, couldn't be successfully built until the devil agreed to aid in its construction. But he claimed the right to the first soul to cross the bridge, so the villagers sent a black cat across it. In the town center, admire the marble fountain in **pl. des Neuf Jets** (Place of Nine Jets). The Castilian lion was kept as a symbol of France's victory over Spain in taking Céret in 1659. The **Porte de France,** on rue de la République, is a remnant of the 19th-century city walls. In place of thse that have crumbled, tremendous plane trees have been planted. The 200-year-old trees mark the boundary of the *vieille ville.*

In late May, Céret celebrates the **Grande Fête de la Cerise** with two days of cherry markets and Catalan songs. The town then gears up for July when all hell breaks loose. The most raucous *fèria,* **Céret de Toros,** occurs every year over the second weekend in July. At 3:30pm, young cows are released into the crowd for anyone to wrestle to the ground. The street show serves as an appetizer for the grand performances, when two bullfights satisfy local bloodlust. A *novillada* without picadors lets young matadors practice on young bulls. Afterwards, music continues in the streets well into the night. (☎04 68 87 47 47. Tickets 125-425F/€19.06-64.81.) In the last weekend in July, crowds gather for the **Festival de la Sardane,** commemorating the traditional Catalan folkdance. It includes a contest of Sardane groups as well as nearly continuous dancing in the streets. (Entrance to contest 80F/€12.20.)

NEAR PERPIGNAN: CANET-PLAGE AND THE COTE CATALANE

Perpignan residents commute to **Canet-Plage,** a 30-minute bus ride from the main city. There are trampolines, miniature golf courses and over 20 beach clubs on the long sandy beaches of this rollicking town. Inland, the streets are lined with cafés and a daily market.

TRANSPORTATION AND PRACTICAL INFORMATION. CTP Shuttles (☎04 68 61 01 13) runs buses to Canet-Plage; catch the #1 in Perpignan at pl. Catalogne (at the top of av. Général de Gaulle) or at promenade des Platanes on bd. Wilson. (30min.; every 30min.; 13F/€1.98, round-trip 24F/€3.66. Last bus from Canet around 9pm, last from Perpignan around 8:30pm.) **Bus Interplages** connects the Côte Catalane resorts from Le Barcarès to Cerbère (☎04 68 35 67 51; one-way 60F/€9.15, round-trip 108F/€16.47). **Taxis** are on av. Méditerranée where it hits the beach. (☎04 68 73 14 81. 95-110F/€14.48-16.77 to Perpignan.) Rent **bikes** at **Sunbike,** 122 Promenade Côte Vermeille. (☎04 68 73 88 65. Bikes 50F/€7.62 for 2hr., 90F/

€13.72 for 8hr., 290F/€44.21 per week. Open July 14-Aug. 20 daily 8am-midnight; June 13-July 13 and Aug. 21-Sept. 9am-8pm, Oct.-May Tu-Sa 9am-noon and 2-6pm.) The Canet-Plage **tourist office,** pl. de la Méditerranée, doles out free brochures and maps. (☎04 68 73 61 00. Open July-Aug. daily 9am-7pm; Sept. and June M-F 9am-noon and 2-6:30pm, Sa-Su 9am-12:30pm and 3-6:30pm; Oct.-May M-F 9am-12:30pm and 2-6:30pm, Sa 9am-12:30pm and 3-6pm, Su 10am-noon.)

ACCOMMODATIONS AND FOOD. Unless you are camping or can claim one of the 24 rooms in the well-priced **Hôtel Clair Soleil,** 26 av. de Catalogne, it's worth the trouble to commute from Perpignan. Internet access is free, and all rooms come with balconies. (☎/fax 04 68 80 32 06; clair-soleil@wanadoo.fr. Breakfast 25F/€3.81. Singles, doubles, or triples with shower 205F/€31.25, with toilet 250F/€38.11. Additional bed 50F/€7.62. 15% student discount. Prices lower Sept.-June. AmEx/MC/V.) Three-star **Camping Club Mar-Estang,** A 25-minute walk from the tourist office, hosts the most lively social scene in Canet-Plage. It has tennis courts, water-slides, and its own disco, which holds foam parties every Monday. They organize excursions to both Carcassonne (160F/€24.39) and Figuères, in Spain (170F/€25.92). (☎04 68 80 35 53; fax 04 68 73 32 94. Open Apr. 28-Sept. Reception 7am-midnight. July 28-Aug. 25 2 people and car 148F/€22.57, Apr. 28-July 27 and Aug. 26-Sept. 128F/€19.52. 30% discount for 4 or more nights.)

On the beachfront, it's not hard to find a good, cheap meal. **Gallerie Cassanyes,** leading away from the Espace Méditerranée, is packed with sandwich shops and restaurants that improve in quality the farther you get from the plaza. Pizzerias have pizzas or pasta for around 45F/€6.86. The **market** near the beach on pl. Foment de la Sardane sells produce and cheap clothes (Tu-Su 7:30am-12:30pm). There is another **market** in the village, 45 minutes from the beach, at pl. St-Jacques (W and Sa 7:30am-noon). Pick up supplies at the **Casino supermarket,** 12 av. de la Méditerranée. (Open July-Aug. daily 8am-1pm and 3:30-5pm; Sept.-June M-Sa 8am-12:30pm and 3:30-7:30pm, Su 8am-12:30pm and 4-7:30pm.) Bakeries and charcuteries cluster along the same avenue toward the port.

ENTERTAINMENT. At night the beachfront shimmers with neon lights. Vendors line the boardwalk, children crowd onto the musical carousels in the Espace Méditerranée, and parents sit in one of the surrounding cafés, most of which bring in live music after 8pm. The **casino,** at the edge of the Espace Méditerranée, also contains the **La Rose** discothèque. (☎04 68 80 14 12. Casino open July-Aug. daily 10am-4am; Sept.-June Su-Th 10am-2am, F-Sa 10am-4am. Disco open July-Aug. W-Su 11pm-dawn; Sept.-June F-Sa 11pm-dawn.) A 20-minute walk away from the beach toward Canet, the discothèque complex **La Luna,** in the Colline des Loisirs, is packed with young people once the bars close around 2am. The disco for those under 30 is called **Voice&BDF**—groups can call ahead for a bus from Perpignan. (☎04 68 73 31 01. Open July-Aug. daily midnight-6am, Sept.-June F-Sa midnight-6am. 80F/€12.20.)

NARBONNE

Though Narbonne is a relatively minor city now, it wasn't always so. Rome's first colony in France, it was at one point the capital of a duchy that included Nîmes, Toulouse, and four other cities. Narbonne quickly fell off the map when its port silted up around 1340; most of its fine Roman architecture was subsequently destroyed, and only the huge, unfinished cathedral remains today as a reminder of its past. Narbonne never really recovered; today it's a quiet, elegant provincial town, with few attractions. Most tourists here are French vacationers headed for the popular sands of Narbonne-Plage and Gruisson-Plage, both half-hour bus rides away. The city's crime rates are higher than might be imagined for a peaceful-looking town; lock doors and try not to walk alone at night.

PRACTICAL INFORMATION

Trains: av. Carnot (☎04 67 62 50 50). To: **Béziers** (15min., 19 per day, 28F/€4.27); **Carcassonne** (30min., 15 per day, 54F/€8.24); **Montpellier** (1hr., 12 per day, 79F/€12.05); **Perpignan** (70min., 14 per day, 57F/€8.69); and **Toulouse** (1½hr., 13 per day, 112F/€17.08). Ticket office open daily 5:40am-8pm.

Tourist Office: pl. Salengro (☎04 68 65 15 60; fax 04 68 65 59 12; www.mairie-narbonne.fr). Turn right onto av. Carnot, which becomes bd. F. Mistral, and then left up the stone staircase onto passage Rossell. Continue across rue de l'Ancienne Porte Neuve up the stone ramp and you will come out at pl. Salengro (5min.). Free tourist guide in a number of languages. Open June 15-Sept. 15 M-Sa 8am-7pm, Su 9:30am-12:30pm; off-season M-Sa 8:30am-noon and 2-6pm. **City tours** (☎04 68 90 30 66) in French and English leave June 15-Sept. 15 every 30min. from in front of the museums and include the price of museum entry. 30F/€4.57, students and seniors 20F/€3.05.

Police: bd. Général de Gaulle (☎04 68 90 38 50).

Internet Access: Versus, 73 rue Droite (☎04 68 32 95 27). 5min. free, 40F/€6.10 per hr. Open M-F 10am-10pm, Sa 2-4pm, Su 2-7pm.

Post Office: 19 bd. Gambetta (☎04 68 65 87 00). **Currency exchange.** Open M-F 8am-7pm, Sa 8:30am-noon. **Postal code:** 11100.

ACCOMMODATIONS

Centre International de Séjours, pl. Salengro (☎04 68 32 01 00; fax 04 68 65 80 20; cis.narbonne@wanadoo.fr), near the tourist office. The well-staffed hostel gives priority to groups that have reserved ahead, but there's often extra space in the 3- to 5-bed dorm rooms. No reservations for individuals. Breakfast included. Reception 8am-7pm, night guard 24hr. 2nd-floor rooms with wooden bunks 70F/€10.67; more spacious 3rd-floor rooms with showers 90F/€13.72; singles 120-140F/€18.30-21.35.

Hôtel de la Gare, across from the train station on av. Pierre Sémard (☎04 68 32 10 54). Friendly owner, clean rooms with showers, and low prices. Breakfast 22F/€3.36. Singles and doubles 120F/€18.30; quads 180F/€27.44, with bath 220F/€33.54; one room rented to students 100F/€15.25.

Hôtel de France, 6 rue Rossini, off bd. du Dr. Ferroul near the pont de la Liberté (☎04 68 32 09 75; fax 04 68 65 50 30). This two-star hotel has a calm atmosphere and an excellent location just off the canal. Breakfast 35F/€5.34. Reception 7:30am-10pm. Reserve July-Aug. Singles and doubles 150-160F/€22.87-24.39, with shower 260-280F/€39.64-42.69; triples and quads 320-400F/€48.78-60.98. MC/V.

Hôtel de Paris, 2 rue du Lion d'Or (☎04 68 32 08 68). Small and musty rooms, but situated directly in the town center. Follow the directions to the tourist office and turn onto rue Lion d'Or from rue Chennebier. Breakfast 25F/€3.81. Reception 24hr. Singles and doubles 150F/€22.90, with shower 180-200F/€27.44-30.49; quads 300F/€45.74; quints 250F/€38.12. Prices lower Sept.-May. MC/V.

Campsites: Beachside campgrounds abound in the area. In summer, about 6 buses per day head to the campsites from Narbonne's train station (14.80F/€2.26). **Camping des Côtes des Roses** (☎04 68 49 83 65) offers tennis, horseback riding, mini-golf, and the Mediterranean. Open Easter-Sept. 77F/€11.74 for 2 people, 97F/€14.79 with electricity. **Camping le Soleil d'Oc** (☎04 68 49 86 21) rents spots from Apr.-Oct. 94F/€14.34 for 2 people, 112F/€17.08 with electricity.

FOOD

Most of Narbonne's restaurants cluster in the area surrounding the cathedral, near the adjoining **rue Droite.** These are almost uniformly pricey and mediocre for dinner, although some offer worthwhile lunch specials. Grab a bite from the canal-side vendors lining **cours de la République,** or pick up picnic items at the **market** on plan (not *place*) St-Paul Thursday mornings (9am-noon). The **covered market** at **Les Halles,** along the canal on cours Mirabeau, is open daily 6am-1pm. **Monoprix,** pl. Hôtel de Ville, satisfies all other food needs (open M-Sa 8:30am-7:30pm). For lunch, the best deal is at **Le Chat Botté,** 72 rue Droite. The 73F/€11.13 *menu de meunier* buys an unlimited portion from an extensive buffet of *hors d'oeuvres* as well as two more courses and a carafe of wine at lunch. (☎04 68 65 34 50. Open M-Sa noon-2pm and 7-10:30pm, Su 7-10:30pm. AmEx/MC/V.)

SIGHTS

Narbonne's monuments are all either in or next to the cathedral, on rue Gauthier, near the tourist office. It's easy to make a quick round before heading to the beach.

CATHEDRALE ST-JUST ET ST-PASTEUR. The cathedral is one of the city's most central and prominent landmarks. Inside, flying buttresses encircle the massive walls of the choir, but end abruptly—the cathedral is only half as large as its architects intended it to be. Construction began in 1272, but stopped in 1340 during a dispute between the archbishops and the city government. If you walk around the outside to the park off rue Fabre, you can still see the point where the cavernous vault was suddenly walled over. Free summer concerts (Su 9pm) showcase the bombastic pipe organ.

PALAIS DES ARCHEVEQUES. Accessible through the entrance to the cathedral, the opulent and beautifully restored palace testifies to the power of the former archbishops of Narbonne. *(☎04 68 90 30 66.)* Within its walls, the **Musée Archéologique** displays a complete collection of Roman artifacts. Across the atrium, the **Musée d'Art et d'Histoire** has French, Flemish, and Italian 17th-century paintings in the exquisite former apartments of the archbishops. The most surprising part of the exhibit is its European Orientalist collection. The hazy dunes, swarthy Saracens, sultry maidens, and overburdened camels that fill these canvases seem plucked straight out of the Arabian Nights. *(All museums ☎04 68 90 30 54. Open Apr.-Sept. daily 9:30am-12:15pm and 2-6pm; Oct.-Mar. Tu-Su 10-11:50am and 2-5pm. Museums and L'Horreum (below) 30F/€4.57, students and seniors 20F/€3.05.)*

L'HORREUM. In front of the palace, in pl. Hôtel de Ville, a little segment of an exposed commercial Roman road built in 120 BC (but not discovered until 1997) points the way to **l'Horreum,** a Roman grain warehouse and the city's only surviving structure from antiquity. *(Same hours and phone number as museums.)*

ENTERTAINMENT AND FESTIVALS

Narbonne-Plage, the town's best asset, lies 15km to the east. **Buses** (☎04 68 90 77 64) leave from across the parking lot to your right from the train station or from the terminal on quai Victor Hugo (35min.; July-Aug. 8 per day, Sept.-June 2-4 per day; 14.80F/€2.26). **Le Coche d'Eau du Patrimoine** covers 20 centuries of history in several hours on its **boat tour** of the Canal de la Robine, an offshoot of the Canal du Midi. (☎04 68 90 63 98. Tours July-Aug.) **Nightlife** in Narbonne is almost nonexistent. One option is to take the **Carte JINS** bus that runs Friday and Saturday nights in the summer to and from the town of **Gruissan** where there is a strip of **discothèques.** (☎04 68 32 68 69. Buses leave Narbonne in front of the JINS office, 60 bd. Général de Gaulle, at 11:30pm, returning from Gruissan at 4am. Bus runs June 29-Sept. 1.)

Narbonne's biggest event is the **Le Théâtre: Scène Nationale de Narbonne** festival, which keeps January to May packed with cultural acts of all shapes and sizes. (☎04 68 90 90 20; www.narbonne.com/letheatre. Performances at 2 av. Domitius; usually 8:45pm; tickets 90-160F/€13.72-24.39. Reserve early.) Free amateur performances can be found at Narbonne's **17th Annual Amateur Theater Festival** for one week in early July. (☎04 68 32 01 00. Entrance is free for most events.)

BEZIERS

More welcoming than Narbonne, Béziers is the archetypal provincial city in Languedoc-Roussillon. It has been a city of passage: Celts, Iberians, Phoenicians, Greeks, Romans, Arabs, and Franks all settled here for a time. Each civilization left its mark, and although Béziers has no spectacular monuments or ruins, the past has left the city laden with hidden surprises. It is also in Béziers that the Canal du Midi begins. This man-made waterway links with the river Garonne to provide a channel between the Atlantic and the Mediterranean—the only one other than the Strait of Gibraltar before the construction of the Suez canal.

PRACTICAL INFORMATION. Frequent **trains** leave from the station, bd. Verdun, for **Montpellier** (40min., 25 per day, 62F/€9.45); **Narbonne** (15min., 20 per day, 28F/€4.27); and **Toulouse** (1½hr., 6 per day, 126F/€19.21). Station open M-Sa 6am-9:15pm. From in front of the station, take the underpass and climb the steep rue de la Rotonde to the top of the hill, where you'll find the long tree-lined allées Paul Riquet. A left on allées Paul Riquet leads to an immense statue of Riquet himself, with his back turned toward av. St-Saëns and the **tourist office,** 29 av. St-Saëns (15min.). The office can direct you to the local wineries or to nearby beaches. (☎04 67 76 47 00; fax 04 67 76 50 80. Open July-Aug. M-F 9am-7pm, Su 10am-noon; Sept.-June M 9am-noon and 2-6pm, Tu-F 9am-noon and 2-6:30pm, Sa 9am-noon and 3-6pm.) **Banque Courtois,** 24 allées Paul Riquet, has **currency exchange** (open M-F 9am-12:45pm and 3:45-5pm). Other services include: **police,** 14 bd. Maréchal Leclerc (☎04 67 35 17 17); the **hospital** at ZAC de Montimaran (☎04 67 35 70 35); and **Internet** access at **Cyberia,** 7 rue Solférino. (☎04 67 62 99 91. 5F/€0.76 per 15min. M-Sa 8am-midnight, Su 2pm-midnight.) The **post office** is on pl. de Gabriel Péri. (☎04 67 49 86 00. Open M-F 8am-7pm, Sa 8am-noon.) **Postal code:** 34500.

ACCOMMODATIONS AND CAMPING. The **Hôtel Cécil,** 5 pl. Jean Jaurès, at the center of town off allées Paul Riquet, has the cheapest prices around for small but cozy rooms. One room is rented to students for 80F/€12.20. (☎04 67 28 48 55. Reception 7am-1am. Curfew 1am. Reserve ahead July-Aug. Singles with sink 100F/€15.25, larger ones with shower 140F/€21.35; doubles 130F/€19.82, with shower 170F/€25.92; twins 220F/€33.54.) The **Hôtel Angleterre,** 22 pl. Jean Jaurès, off allées Paul Riquet, rents 22 tastefully decorated rooms, each one unique. The hotel is close to the busy cafés but away from the noise. (☎04 67 28 48 42; fax 04 67 28 61 53. Breakfast 30F/€4.57. Reserve in summer. Singles 120-140F/€18.30-21.35; doubles 150F/€22.90, with shower 160F/€24.39; quads with bath 280F/€42.69.) **Hôtel Le Revelois,** 60 av. Gambetta, is one block past the train station above a bar on a noisy street. The 17 large rooms are slowly being renovated; ask to see yours first. (☎04 67 49 20 78; fax 04 67 28 92 28. Breakfast 30F/€4.57. Reception until 1am. Reserve July-Aug. Singles and doubles 155F/€23.63, with shower 195F/€29.73, with toilet 235F/35.83, with bath 250F/€38.12; doubles and triples with shower 220-275F/€33.54-41.93; prices lower in winter.) Info on **beach camping** at Valras (July-Sept.) is available at the tourist offices in Béziers or Valras (☎04 67 32 36 04).

FOOD AND ENTERTAINMENT. *Biterrois*, the local sweet specialty cake, is flavored with almonds and filled with a pâté of grapes and wine in pastry. There's an indoor **market** at **Les Halles,** allées Paul Riquet (Tu-Su 8am-noon). Across the street, on the corner of allées Paul Riquet and rue Flourens, the **Frio Supermarché** has a reasonable selection (open M-Sa 8am-8pm, Su 8am-1pm). There is a larger **Monoprix** at 5 allées Paul Riquet (open M-Sa 8:30am-7pm). As allées Paul Riquet progresses toward the Théâtre Municipal, its sides become a giant blur of restaurants and cafés. These are all reasonably priced and great for people-watching—however, many are open only for lunch. For dinner, elegant—and surprisingly inexpensive—restaurants line the small av. Viennet that runs between La Poste (pl. G. Péri) and the Cathédrale St. Nazaire (pl. de la Révolution).

The biweekly magazines *Pau's Café* and *Olé* list clubs and bars, as well as upcoming concerts, exhibits, and spectacles in Béziers and the surrounding area. *Exit* magazine details the disco scene. After 10pm, many of the cafés on allées Paul Riquet draw crowds with pounding music inside their small bar areas. A fashionable set frequents the **Ness Café,** 36 allées Paul Riquet, where the bartenders sometimes dress in drag. (☎04 67 49 07 19. Open Su-F 9am-1am, Sa 9am-2am.) **Le Dollar** draws a slightly older clientele. (☎04 67 28 20 84. Open daily 7am-1am.)

In mid-August, a **féria** that has earned Béziers the nickname "the French Seville" fills the town with *corridas* (bullfights) and *flamenco* dancing. Tickets are available at the arena on av. Emile Claparede. (☎04 67 76 13 45. 100-450F/€15.25-68.61.)

SIGHTS. Le Musée du Biterrois, pl. St. Jacques, is a set of displays that pulls together regional objects and curios spanning the period from the Roman Empire until WWII. These fascinating collection includes ancient farm instruments, a 1913 Renault driven by *"le plus jeune chauffeur du monde"* ("the youngest driver in the world"—4-year-old Jean Lovign), and documents testifying to both French collaboration and resistance during WWII. (☎04 67 36 71 01. Open M 2-5pm, Tu-F 9am-noon and 2-5pm. 15F/€2.29, students 10F/€1.53.) A pass will let you into the museum, as well as the town's two others: the **Musée des Beaux-Arts,** pl. de la Révolution (☎04 67 28 38 78), and the **Espace Paul Riquet,** rue Massol (☎04 67 28 44 18).

The **Cathédrale St-Nazaire,** built on the ruins of a pagan temple in pl. de la Révolution, was destroyed with the rest of the city in 1209 but rebuilt in the 14th century. The best view around is from atop the belltower, which overlooks the countryside arching across the horizon. (Open M-Sa 9am-noon and 2:30-7pm.) Follow rue des Albigeois from the cathedral to bd. d'Angleterre, take a right onto rue St-Vincent, and walk around the Collège St-Madeleine to find **l'Eglise de la Madeleine.** The Romanesque structure is supported by a pillar scorched when an earlier church, full of Cathar martyrs, was razed by Abbot Arnaud Amalric in 1209. (Open M-Sa 9am-noon and 2:30-6:30pm.) Paul Riquet's **Canal du Midi,** which links the Atlantic to the Mediterranean via the river Garonne, lies at the base of the city, down quai Port Neuf. The canals are still used to irrigate the town and to transport tourists.

EXCURSIONS. 15km from Béziers, the one-time fishing village of **Valras** has become a family beach resort complete with water slide and Ferris wheel. To get there, take bus #401 from pl. du Général de Gaulle (☎04 67 36 73 76; 30min.; 10 per day in summer, last return 8pm; round-trip 27F/€4.12).

For those blessed with their own transportation, most of the nearby private vineyards and *caves cooperatives*, central outlets for local wineries, give tours ending with samples of their wines. **Le Club des Grands Vins des Châteaux du Languedoc** will provide info on *dégustations* of the region's acclaimed *appellations:* Minervois, St-Chinian, Faucères, and a spicy red Cabrières. Contact the club's offices at the Château du Raissac, 2km west of Béziers. The cellars of the château itself are open to visitors year-round, provided they can get there with a car. (☎04 67 49 17 60. Open M-Sa 9am-noon and 2:30-7pm.)

SETE

Sète (pop. 42,000) sprang to life in 1666 when Louis XIV's minister Colbert pointed to the "Cap de Cette" as a new port. At the turn of the 20th century, most of the population of the Italian village of Gaet immigrated to Sète to escape the Italian depression. A hybrid Italian-French culture has emerged here as a result, producing unique cuisine, strange maritime festivals, and a charming *Sètois* accent, made famous by folk singer Georges Brassens. Spread along a narrow strip of land cordoning off the Bassin Thau from the Mediterranean, the town is now France's largest Mediterranean fishing port. Modern commercial fishing has added heavy machinery to Sète's otherwise postcard-perfect shoreline, but there is a certain industrial poetry in the rusty ships and screeching gulls—appropriately enough, since the town gave birth to Paul Valéry, one of France's greatest modern poets.

PRACTICAL INFORMATION. The **train station,** quai M. Joffre, serves those headed to **Béziers** (30min., approx. 2 per hr., 43F/€6.56); **Montpellier** (20min., 1 per hr., 29F/€4.42); **Narbonne** (50min., 2 per hr., 62F/€9.45); and **Toulouse** (2hr., approx. 10 per day, 149F/€22.72). Info office open M-F 9am-noon and 2-5:50pm. The **bus station,** 13 quai de la République (☎04 67 74 66 90 for Montpellier station info desk), services **Montpellier** (1hr.; 11 per day M-Sa, 3 on Su; 34.50F/€5.26). La Sétoise **local buses** run until 7:30pm (☎04 67 74 18 77; 6F/€0.91). Bus #3 goes from the train station to the tourist office, #4 from quai de la Résistance to both beaches. **Cycles Estopina,** 4 rue Voltaire, rents **bikes.** (☎/fax 04 67 74 74 77. 60F/€9.15 per half-day, 90F/€13.72 per day. ID and 2000F/€304.92 deposit. Open Tu-Sa 9am-7:30pm. MC/V.) Find a **taxi** at the train station (☎04 67 48 62 98).

Sète's **tourist office,** 60 rue Mario Roustan, behind quai Général Durand, has good maps. To walk from the station, go straight onto pont de la Gare, cross the canal, and turn right onto quai Pavois d'Or. Turn the corner and cross the first bridge on the right, then turn left and walk down quai de Lattre de Tassigny past Pont Virla and Pont de la Civette until rue Roustan veers off to the right (20min.). (☎04 67 74 71 71. Open July-Aug. daily 9am-8pm; Sept.-June M-Sa 9am-noon and 2-6pm; Apr.-May also Su 10am-noon and 2-6pm.) **Change currency** here (M-F 10am-1pm and 3-7pm, Sa 9:30-noon). For **Internet access,** stop at **Le Cyber-Snack,** 10 av. Victor Hugo. (☎04 67 46 14 36. Open M-F 10am-7pm and Sa 2-7pm. 40F/€6.10 per hr.) To reach the **hospital** on bd. C. Blanc (☎04 67 46 57 57), take bus #2, 3, or 5 to "Hôpital." The **police** are at 50 quai de Bosc (☎04 67 46 80 22). The **post office** is on bd. Danièle Casanova. (☎04 67 46 64 20. Open M-F 8:30am-12:30pm and 1:30-6pm, Sa 8:30am-noon.) **Poste Restante:** 34207. **Postal code:** 34200.

LANGUEDOC

ACCOMMODATIONS. The **Auberge de Jeunesse "Villa Salis" (HI),** rue du Gén. Revest, is at the top of one of the steepest roads in France. Follow the directions to the tourist office, then at pont de la Civette turn right onto rue Gén. de Gaulle and follow the signs to the *auberge* around the Parc du Château d'Eau and up the steep hill to the coral-colored inn (20min.). Here you'll find 90 spartan beds in tight 4- to 5-bed single-sex rooms. (☎04 67 53 46 68; fax 04 67 51 34 01. Breakfast included. Dinner required July-Aug. Sheets 17F/€2.59. Reception 8am-noon and 6-10pm. Check-out 10am. Curfew 4am. Reservations recommended. Bunks 70F/€10.67, with dinner 119F/€18.14. Camping 50F/€7.62. MC/V. **Members only.**) The **Hôtel Tramontane,** 5 rue Frédéric Mistral, off the quai de la Résistance, has clean, cheery rooms and sparkling bathrooms directly in the center of town. (☎04 67 74 37 92. Breakfast 30F/€4.57. Reception until 10pm. Singles and doubles 150-170F/€22.87-25.92, with shower 260-270F/€39.64-41.16; triples 230-280F/€35.06-42.69; quads 260-300F/€39.64-45.73. AmEx/MC/V.) Two-star **Hôtel le Valéry,** 20 rue Denfert-Rochereau, is just minutes from the train station. Walk across the bridge and continue straight onto rue Victor Hugo and then left on rue Denfert-Rochereau. A wide staircase leads to large, light, airy rooms. (☎04 67 74 77 51; fax 04 67 46 12 84. Breakfast 25F/€3.80. Reception 8am-11pm. Reserve July-Aug. Singles and doubles 140-160F/€21.35-24.40, with shower 160-220F/€24.40-33.55; triples 180F/€27.45, with shower 230F/€35.05; quads 220F/€33.55, with shower 280F/€42.70. MC/V.)

FOOD. Head to the **Prisunic supermarket** at 7 quai de la Résistance (☎04 67 74 39 38; open M-Sa 8:30am-8pm, Su 9am-noon) or the **daily market** at **Les Halles,** just off rue Alsace-Lorraine (7am-noon). Vendors on the canal hawk fresh *tielles* (squid and tomato pizzas) for about 13F/€1.98, though inland bakeries sell somewhat less authentic versions for 7F/€1.07 or so. The restaurants lining **Promenade J.B. Marty,** at the end of rue Mario Roustan near the *vieux port*, serve the catch of the day any way you can imagine for 60F/€9.10 and up. Cheaper pizza, pasta, and seafood await in the less touristy eateries on **rue Gambetta** and its offshoots.

WETTING YOUR LANCE The history of water jousting is long and glorious, according to the research of Sète's Musée Paul Valéry. Jousts were held on boats in ancient Greece and Rome. Pictures of water jousts have even been found in a 14th-century English manuscript. In Sète, the jousts began when some Crusaders with too much time on their hands decided to demonstrate their skills aboard boats rather than horses. Although Sète sees fewer crusaders these days, nautical jousting continues to be popular, particularly among local fishermen. The rules are simple: red and blue boats represent two different neighborhoods in Sète, and the object of the competition is to remain high and dry. Each boat is rowed and maneuvered by *chevaliers* (knights), while two opponents duel with wooden shield and lance. The loser is the one who makes friends with the fish of the Royal Canal, much to the mirth of the crowd.

SIGHTS. The **Société Nautique de Sète,** one of France's oldest yacht clubs, lounges on Môle St-Louis, at the southern end of town. Throughout the summer, yacht races, including the prestigious Tour de France à la Voile, set sail from the Môle. The **plage de la Corniche** in the southwest corner of town marks the beginning of 12km of sandy yellow beaches, accessible by bus #6 or a summer shuttle from quai de la Résistance at stops marked "La Plage" (both 6F/€0.91).

A walk to the *vieux port* and up the hill along rue Haute leads to the **maritime cemetery** that inspired Valéry's poem *Le Cimetière Marin.* The poet himself lies interred here. (Open Apr.-Sept. daily 7am-noon and 2-7pm; Oct.-Mar. 8am-noon and 2-6pm.) The modern building above the cemetery, the **Musée Paul Valéry,** rue François Desnoyer, displays a huge collection of model ships as well as exhibits on local archaeology, history, and even water-jousting. The best part is the room devoted to the poet himself, with original drafts illuminated with doodles and ink sketches. (☎04 67 46 20 98. Open July-Aug. daily 10am-noon and 2-6pm; Sept.-June W-M 10am-noon and 2-6pm. July-Aug. 30F/€4.57; Sept.-June 20F/€3.05.) On the other side of the city is **L'Espace Georges Brassens,** 67 bd. Camille Blanc, a multimedia museum that pays homage to the irreverent folk singer from Sète. The museum provides a wonderful introduction to the man and his music. (Buses #2 and 3. ☎04 67 53 32 77. Open July-Aug. daily 10am-noon and 2-7pm; Sept.-June 10am-noon and 2-6pm; Oct.-May. closed M. 30F/€4.57, students 10F/€1.53.)

If you can, climb chemin de Biscan-Pas from the hostel to the top of **Mont St-Clair** (183m) for a great view of Sète, its canals, and the sea (15min.). The church **Notre Dame de la Salette,** with wall murals from the 1950s, brings fishermen's wives to this summit on a pilgrimage every September 19 for the *Feu de la St-Jean.*

ENTERTAINMENT AND FESTIVALS. Every evening popular **La Bodega,** 21 quai Noel Guignon, has live music from Brazilian blues to rock. (☎04 67 74 47 50. Open daily 5:30pm-3am; Oct.-May closed Su.) In late August, locals celebrate **La Fête de St-Louis,** when Sète holds its animated **Tournois de Joutes Nautiques,** in which participants joust from oversized rowboats. Arrive in the morning to secure a spot on quai de la Résistance for the final competition on Monday at 2pm. Most other summer weekends, at 2:30pm, the gladiators prepare for the tournament and impress tourists with exposition battles. On Wednesdays, any novice can go to the Quilles quarter for a jousting lesson. **La Fête de St-Pierre** occurs on the first weekend in July. Mornings involve solemn religious rites, while the nights are loud and festive. On Sunday morning, during the **Bénédiction de la Mer,** fishermen allow the crowds to walk over their decorated boats. They then throw of flowers into the water in memory of those lost at sea.

The first weekend in August (starting on Thursday), Sète holds its annual jazz festival, **Jazz à Sète.** The festival manages to draw a few big names. (Call the tourist office for info. Tickets 130F/€19.82, students 110F/€16.77.)

MONTPELLIER

Montpellier (pop. 211,000), Languedoc's capital, is a student town that behaves like one. It is one of the most light-hearted places in the south. There are little theatrical performances going up everywhere you look, the bookstore-browsing prospects are superb, and every year the town hosts an avant-garde dance festival. During the summer, many students stick around and the city floods with tourists, but the wide avenues and sunny streets leave the it feeling open and airy. Cafés on pl. de la Comédie, fondly known as *l'Oeuf* (the egg), offer expensive coffee and hours of five-star people-watching. Come sundown, the student population puts down its books and hits the bars and *boîtes* around pl. Jean Jaurès.

TRANSPORTATION

Trains: pl. Auguste Gibert (☎04 67 34 25 10). To: **Avignon** (1hr., 20 per day, 80F/€12.20); **Perpignan** (1½hr., 10 per day, 117F/€17.84); **Marseille** (1¼-1½hr.; 8 per day; 127F/€19.36, TGV 147F/€22.41); **Toulouse** (2½hr.; every 2hr.; 164F/€25, TGV 174F/€26.53); **Nice** (5hr., 5 per day, 236F/€35.98); and **Paris** (4½hr., 10 TGVs per day, 496F/€75.62). Info office open M-F 8am-7pm, Sa 9am-6pm. **Currency exchange** (☎04 67 58 00 55) with no commission. Open M-Sa 8am-7pm, Su 10am-5:30pm.

Buses: pl. du Bicentenaire (☎04 67 92 01 43), on the 2nd floor of a parking garage next to the train station. **Les Courriers du Midi** (☎04 67 06 03 78) go to **Béziers** (2hr.; M-Sa every hr., Su 4 per day; 76F/€11.59) and **Nîmes** (2hr., M-Sa 2 per day, 59F/€9). Info office open M-Sa 8am-noon and 1:45-6:45pm, Su 2-7pm.

Local Transportation: TAM, 6 rue Jules Ferry (☎04 67 22 87 87), handles both the local buses and the new tramway that connects the city center to its outskirts. Trams every 10min. 5am-1am; buses more irregular and only until 8pm. 7F/€1.07 tickets for both good for 1hr., weekly pass 63F/€9.61. Buy bus tickets from the driver, and tram tickets from automated dispensers in tram booths. **Petitbus** serves the city center from the train station M-Sa 7:20am-7:30pm; **Rabelais** runs 9pm-12:30am.

Taxis: TRAM (☎04 67 58 10 10) and **Taxi A** (☎04 67 20 35 20). Both 24hr.

Bike Rental: Vill' à velo (TAM), at the bus station (☎04 67 92 92 67).

ORIENTATION AND PRACTICAL INFORMATION

Radiating out from the train station, **rue Maguelone** leads to fountain-filled **pl. de la Comédie,** Montpellier's modern center and the best starting point for a visit to the city. To find the tourist office upon reaching the *place*, turn right and walk past the cafés and street vendors. It's located behind the right-hand corner of the Pavillon de l'Hôtel de Ville (10min. from the station). Continuing on in this direction will lead to the huge mall shopping center whose two buildings are named Le Triangle and Le Polygone. The *vieille ville* is bounded by bd. Pasteur and bd. Louis Blanc to the north, esplanade Charles de Gaulle and bd. Victor Hugo to the east, and bd. Jeu de Paume to the west. From pl. de la Comédie, **rue de la Loge** leads from uphill to the center of the *vieille ville*, **pl. Jean-Jaurès.**

Tourist Office: 30 allée Jean de Lattre de Tassigny (☎04 67 60 60 60; fax 04 67 60 60 61). Free maps and same-night hotel reservation service. Has the weekly *Sortir à Montpellier* and *L'INDIC,* a student guide that comes out in July. Daily **city tours** in French July-Sept. 39F/€5.95, students 34F/€5.18. Tours in English Tu 10:30am. Office open M-Sa 9am-7:30pm, Su 10am-6pm. **Branch office** at the train station (☎04 67 92 90 03). Open July-Aug. M-Th 9am-1pm and 3-7pm, F 10am-1pm and 3-7pm.

Budget Travel: Wasteels, 1 rue Cambacares (☎04 67 66 20 19), and 6 fbg. de la Saunerie (☎04 67 58 74 26), offers good plane, train, and bus prices. Open M-F 9am-12:30pm and 2-6:30pm, Sa 9am-12:30pm and 2-5:30pm. MC/V.

English Bookstore: BookShop Montpellier, 4 rue de l'Université (☎04 67 66 09 08). Best-sellers, classics, and travel guides. Open M-Sa 9:30am-1am and 2:30-7pm.

Internet Access: Point Internet, 54 rue de l'Aiguillerie, near the Auberge de Jeunesse (☎04 67 54 57 60). 10F/€1.53 per hr. Open M-Sa 9am-midnight, Su 10am-midnight. **Station Internet/France Télécom,** 6-8 pl. du Marché au Fleurs (☎08 00 35 25 15). 40F/€6.10 per hr., students 30F/€4.57 per hr. Open M 2-8pm, Tu-Sa 10am-8pm.

Laundromat: Lav'Club Miele, 6 rue des Ecoles Laïques. Open daily 7:30am-9pm.

Hospital: 191 av. Doyen Gaston Guiraud (☎04 67 33 67 33).

Police: 13 av. du Prof. Grasset (☎04 67 22 78 22).

Post Office: pl. Rondelet (☎04 67 34 50 00). From pl. de la Comédie, follow rue Jean Moulin, cross bd. Observatoire onto rue de Fbg. de la Saunerie, then follow rue Rondelet. **Currency exchange.** Open M-F 8am-7pm, Sa 8am-noon. **Branch office** at pl. des Martyrs de la Résistance (☎04 67 60 03 60). Open M-F 8:30am-6:30pm and Sa 8:30am-noon. **Postal code:** 34000 (central).

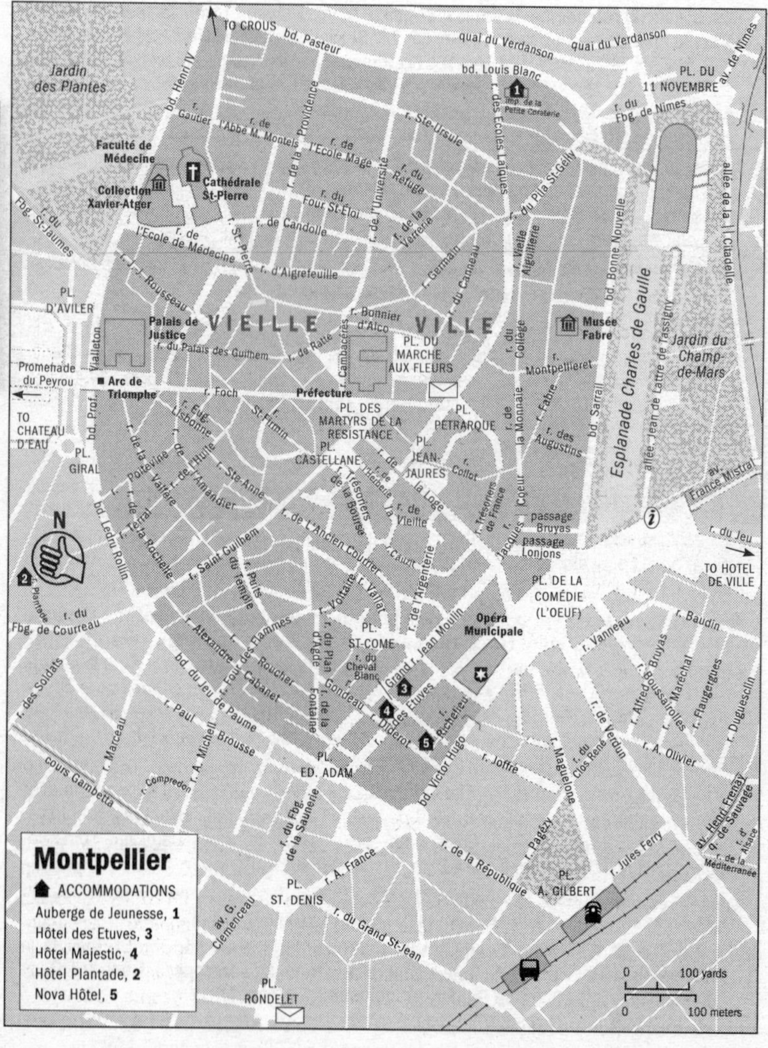

ACCOMMODATIONS

Except for the campsite, all listings are in the large *vieille ville*—even the youth hostel. If you're traveling in a group, it is usually cheaper and more convenient to stay in a hotel (with no curfew, a private room) than in the overcrowded youth hostel. But the hotels fill fast too. Search **rue Aristide Olivier, rue du Général Campredon** (off cours Gambetta and rue A. Michell), and **rue A. Broussonnet** (off pl. Albert 1er) for other reasonably priced hotels.

Hôtel Plantade, 10 rue Plantade (☎04 67 92 61 45). Bear left out of the train station on rue de la République. The large street changes to first bd. de l'Observatoire, then bd. du Jeu de Paume and then bd. Ledru-Rollin. Follow it up to a left turn on rue du Fbg. du Courreau. Take a right onto rue Plantade (10min.). A somewhat dingy hallway leads to clean, colorful rooms. This is the lowest-priced hotel in town, if you approach the owner with the right attitude. Breakfast 18F/€2.74. Singles 90-135F/€13.72-20.58; doubles 105-150F/€16.01-22.90; triples 165F/€25.16. Those staying for only 1 night might have to pay 12F/€1.83 for a shower and 10F/€1.53 room surcharge, but these fees are only for those who make too much work for the owner.

Nova Hôtel, 8 rue Richelieu (☎04 67 60 79 85; fax 04 67 60 89 06; olivier.granier@wanadoo.fr). From the train station bear left on rue de la République; turn right on bd. Victor Hugo, left on rue Diderot, and right on rue Richelieu (5min.). Welcoming, comfortable rooms. 5% discount for students with *Let's Go*. Breakfast 30F/€4.57. Reception 7am-11:30pm. Reserve a week in advance. Singles 125F/€19.06; doubles 150F/€22.90, doubles with shower 170-210F/€25.92-32.02; triples with shower 250F/€38.12; quads with bath 321F/€48.94. AmEx/MC/V.

LANGUEDOC

Hôtel Majestic, 4 rue du Cheval Blanc (☎04 67 66 26 85). From the train station, follow directions to Nova Hôtel, then turn left off rue Richelieu onto rue du Cheval Blanc. Simple, clean rooms–some shower-less ones may be window-less, too. Breakfast 25F/€3.81. Shower 20F/€3.05. Reception until 11pm. Singles 115F/€17.53; doubles 150F/€22.90, with shower 190F/€28.97; triples 220-300F/€33.54-45.74. MC/V.

Hôtel des Etuves, 24 rue des Etuves (☎/fax 04 67 60 78 19; hoteldesetuves@wanadoo.fr). From the train station, follow directions to Nova Hôtel. Turn left off rue Richelieu onto rue du Cheval Blanc and right onto rue des Etuves. This personable little hotel has 13 fresh, spacious rooms, all with showers, most with TV. Breakfast 27F/€4.12. Reception 7am-11pm, closed Su 3-6:30pm. Reserve one week in advance. Singles with shower 130F-180F/€19.82-27.44; doubles with shower 200-240F/€30.49-36.59.

Auberge de Jeunesse (HI), 2 impasse de la Petite Corraterie (☎04 67 60 32 22; fax 04 67 60 32 30). To walk to the hostel from the train station (better than the circuitous tram route), walk straight out on rue Maguelone and continue across pl. de la Comédie onto rue de la Loge. Turn right onto rue Jacques Cœur and proceed straight to pl. Notre Dame. Bear left out of the *place* onto rue l'Aiguillerie and follow it through its name change to rue des Ecoles Laïques. The hostel is on the right, just before bd. Louis Blanc. This overcrowded, understaffed hostel may not be worth the trouble. Call ahead to reserve, but expect frustrations. The enforced 2am curfew means you'll miss out on a lot of local nightlife. 80 beds in 4- to 9-person single-sex rooms. Breakfast included. Sheets 17F/€2.59 per week. Co-ed bathrooms. Reception 8am-10am and 1pm-midnight. Lockout 10am-1pm. Curfew 2am. Bunks 69F/€10.52. MC/V.

Campsites: 3km away in coastal **Lattes, L'Eden,** rte. de Palavas (☎04 67 15 11 05; fax 04 67 15 11 31). To reach L'Eden, take bus #17 from the bus station to "Oasis Palavasienne" (20min.). 4-star camping with tennis courts, a pool, and a restaurant. Provides free shuttle service to the beach and back (15min.). Open May-Aug. 1 or 2 people 74-134F/€11.28-20.43; 3 people 90-165F/€13.72-25.16; 4 people 106-196F/€16.16-29.88; most expensive in July.

FOOD

Montpellier is a town of students and tourists, and reasonably priced restaurants are everywhere. Standard French fare awaits on the many *places* of the *vieille ville*, but don't neglect the many ethnic possibilities. **Rue des Ecoles Laïques** in the old city has a variety of choices, including Greek, Egyptian, Italian, and Lebanese fare. During the school year, students can be found munching in the eateries on **rue de Fbg. Boutonnet**. Contact **CROUS,** 2 rue Monteils, for info about the four **university restaurants.** None are conveniently located, but 17.50F/€2.67 gets you a full meal. (☎04 67 41 50 00. Open Sept.-June M-F lunch and dinner, Sa on a rotating basis. July-Aug., the CROUS at the "Boutonnet" tram stop stays open.) Relatively unimpressive morning **markets** are held at pl. Cabane and bd. des Archeaux (daily), and pl. de la Comédie (M-Sa). The super-duper **supermarket INNO,** in the basement of the Polygone commercial center, just past the tourist office, has great bargains (open M-Sa 9:30am-8pm). For other staples, Montpellier is filled with convenience stores, many of which stay open late (until 2am).

Pepe Carvalho, 2 rue Cauzit (☎04 67 66 10 10), near pl. St-Ravy. Named for the Catalan hero of Manuel Vásquez Montalbán's detective stories. Enjoy the lively atmosphere and cheap tapas (16F/€2.44). 59F/€9 *menu* includes 5 tapas. Four-person special gives you 12 tapas and 1L of wine for 189F/€28.82. Sangría 12F/€1.83. Open M-Sa noon-3pm and 7pm-1am, Su 7pm-1am. AmEx/MC/V.

La Case du Saloum, 8 rue Ecole de Pharmacie (☎04 67 02 88 94), serves Senagalese specialties on a quiet street. Most plates are served with a delicious onion melange. *Plats* offered for 45F/€6.86 and 70F/€10.67. Open daily 11am-3pm and 7pm-1am.

The Patchwork Café, 15 rue St. Firmin (☎04 67 60 75 35). A pizzeria with theme nights. On Monday nights, your fortune will be told as you eat, Tuesday is caricature day, and free henna tattoos are given on Wednesday. Pizza toppings range from cheese to meats like kangaroo and ostrich. Open daily noon-3pm and 7pm-1am.

SIGHTS

The humongous **Musée Fabre,** 39 bd. Bonne Nouvelle, near the esplanade, holds one of the largest collections of fine art outside of Paris. Six floors of paintings interspersed with occasional sculptures cover Western art since the Renaissance. The museum will close in September 2002 for renovations; until 2006, only the small pavilion annex will be open, displaying a sample of the museum's collection. (☎04 67 14 83 00. Open Tu-F 9am-5:30pm, Sa-Su 9:30am-5pm. 20F/€3.05, students 10F/€1.53.) The **Collection Xavier Atger,** 2 rue de l'Ecole de Médecine, was donated by Jean François Xavier Atger. A series of bureaus contain anatomical drawings, etchings, and sketches by Fragonard, Watteau, and Caravaggio. (☎04 67 66 27 77. Open Sept.-July M, W, F 1:30-5pm. Free.)

The old city's pedestrian streets and bookstores, as well as the sprawling pl. de la Comédie, have some of the best entertainment in Montpellier, all of it free. Hidden behind grandiose oak doors, the secret courtyards and intricate staircases of 17th- and 18th-century *hôtels particuliers* block out the bustle outside. Particularly notable are the **Hôtel de Varennes,** 2 pl. Petrarque, with its medieval-style rooms, and the **Hôtel des Tresoriers de France,** rue Jacques Cœur. The tourist office distributes a walking guide, and their tours let you into some of the 100-odd *hôtels*. Rue Foch, off pl. des Martyrs in the northwest corner of the old city, leads to the **promenade du Peyrou.** The promenade links the **Arc de Triomphe,** erected in 1691 to honor Louis XIV, to the **Château d'Eau,** the arched terminal of a modern aqueduct built on a Roman model. Misguided locals may tell you it dates back to antiquity, but it's actually a little over a century old. Bd. Henri IV leads to the **Jardin des Plantes,** France's first botanical garden. (☎04 67 63 43 22. Open Apr.-Sept. M-Sa 9am-noon and 2-7pm; Oct.-Mar. 10am-noon and 2-5pm. Free.) If you're still inside when the noon closing bell rings, you'll spend the next two hours wilting with the plants in the sun. Back across pl. de la Comédie and through the modern Polygone shopping center, ancient Greece meets postmodernism in the **Antigone** low-income housing complex.

If you're oversaturated in culture, the sandy **plage de Palavas** is only a twenty-minute bus ride away. To get there, take the #17 bus from Montpellier's bus station (*gare routière*) and get off at the *gare routière* stop in Palavas.

ENTERTAINMENT AND FESTIVALS

At night, the most animated bars are at **pl. Jean-Jaurès.** Once stores have closed, **rue de la Loge** becomes a street of vendors, musicians, and stilt-walkers. At the always-packed **Barberousse "Bar A Shooters,"** 6 rue Boussairolles, just off pl. de la Comédie, you can down 73 different flavors of rum for 10F/€1.53 each. (☎04 67 58 03 66. Open M-Sa 6pm-1am). The dance spot **Rockstore,** 20 rue de Verdun, hosts a crowd of teens and twenty-somethings dancing to metallic hits. (Bar ☎04 67 06 80 06. Open July-Aug. M-Sa until 6am; Sept.-June M-Th until 4am, F-Sa until 6am. No cover; beer 22F/€3.35.) **Fizz,** 4 rue Cauzit, is the other shaking club in the city, with dancing below and a space to hang out above. (☎04 67 66 22 89. Open daily 11pm-4am. Cover 50F/€7.62 with 2 drinks; students 40F/€6.10 during the week.)

Gay nightlife abounds in Montpellier. The best discos, such as **La Villa Rouges** (☎04 67 06 52 15) in Lattes, lie on the outskirts of town, inaccessible at night without a car. Gay bars, on the other hand, are sprinkled throughout the *vieille ville*, with a few dance clubs too. A young, chic crowd rocks the house late into the evening at **THT,** 10 rue St-Firmin, off rue Foch. (☎04 67 66 12 52. Open daily 9am-1am.) A mixed clientele surveys the scene outside the popular, gay-friendly **Café de la Mer,** 5 pl. du Marché aux Fleurs (☎04 67 60 79 65. Open daily until 1am.)

The **Corum,** at the far end of Esplanade Charles de Gaulle, houses the local opera and philharmonic orchestra. (☎04 67 61 67 61. 80-140F/€12.20-21.35; discounts for students and seniors.) **Cinéma Le Diagonal,** 18 pl. St-Denis, shows new-release films in their original languages. (☎04 67 92 91 81. Films 37F/€5.64.) Check with the music school, **JAM** (Jazz Action Montpellier), 100 rue de Lesseps, to see if any jazz artists are gigging (☎04 67 58 30 30). The *café-théâtre* **L'Antirouille,** 12 rue Anatole France, has international music and rock concerts W-Sa nights. (☎04 67 58 75 28. Open Apr.-Aug. M-Sa 9pm-2am; Sept.-Mar. 8pm-1am. 20-80F/€3.05-12.20.)

The last two weeks of June and the first week of July bring the **Printemps des Comédiens pac Euromédecine,** an open-air theater festival. For details, contact the Opéra Comédie, pl. de la Comédie. (Info ☎04 67 60 19 99, reservations ☎04 67 63 66 66. Tickets 40-140F/€6.10-21.35, under age 25 and seniors 40-120F/€6.10-18.30.) In the first two weeks of July, the **Festival International Montpellier Danse** brings performances, workshops, and films to local stages and screens. For details contact Hôtel d'Assas, 6 rue Vieille Aiguillerie. (Info ☎04 67 60 83 60; reservations ☎04 67 60 07 40. 25-180F/€3.81-27.44.) The rest of July is taken up by the **Festival de Radio France et de Montpellier,** with performances of opera, jazz, and classical music. (Info and tickets ☎04 67 02 02 01; contact@festival-rfmontpellier.com. 70-220F/€10.67-33.54; discounts for those under 26 and seniors.)

CONQUES

Stashed away amidst verdant hills in the heart of the Aveyron, the tiny village of Conques (pop. 314) was a major pilgrimage stop between Le Puy-en-Velay and Moissac on the road to Santiago de Compostela. Though its monastery dates back to the early 9th century, it was only when one of their monks pulled off a daring relic heist—snatching the remains of the child martyr Ste-Foy from Agen—that Conques made its mark. The robbery was immediately justified by a string of miracles, and countless streams of pilgrims made their way here between the 11th and 13th centuries. Today the restored abbey rests among medieval houses and lush greenery. Be sure to bring enough cash to tide you over—there are no ATMs in this town, though the post office will extend cash advances with a Visa card.

PRACTICAL INFORMATION. There are no trains to Conques and only occasional buses. The easiest way to get there is by car; otherwise plan bus travel carefully, which will require a change at **Rodez.** In summer, a bus goes to Rodez in the morning and returns in the afternoon (1hr., M-F, 39F/€5.95). The rest of the year, there is a daily afternoon bus from Rodez to Conques, which returns the following morning. **Rodez's bus station** (☎05 65 68 11 13) is located at the Esplanade Foirail in the town center. From the bus stop, follow the main street past the post office and head toward the church. The **tourist office** is to the right of the church facade and distributes a free map, a *guide pratique*, and info on accommodations. (☎05 65 72 85 00; fax 05 65 72 87 03. Tours in French of the abbey and cloister July-Aug. Contact office for times or to make a reservation for a tour in English. Open July-Aug. daily 9am-7pm; Sept.-June 9am-noon and 2-6pm.) For a **taxi,** call Annie Lample (☎05 65 72 84 76). The **post office** has **currency exchange.** (Open M-F 9am-12:30pm and 2-5pm, Sa 9:30-11:30am.) **Postal code:** 12320.

ACCOMMODATIONS AND FOOD. Conques can easily be seen in a morning, but the bus schedule may force you to stay the night. Alas, prices are high and hotels fill quickly in summer. The most economical option is the **gîte d'étape communale,** in a stone courtyard off rue Emile Roudie at the top of the village, which has one crowded dormitory with a communal kitchen, squat toilets, and showers. (☎05 65 72 85 56. Reserve ahead. Open Apr.-Oct. Beds 40F/€6.10; pay on the honor system.) **L'Auberge Saint-Jacques,** rue Gonzague Florens on the way to the church, has comfortable rooms with splendid views. Reserve well in advance—this hotel is almost always full. (☎05 65 72 86 36; fax 05 65 72 82 47. Breakfast 40F/€6.10. Doubles with bath 200-320F/€30.49-48.79; triples with bath 300-320F/€45.74-48.79, quads 330-360F/€50.21-54.89. MC/V.) The closest **campsite** is the three-star **Beau Rivage,** 300m from Conques via rue Charlemagne on the wooded banks of the Dourdou. It has a pool, restaurant, and laundry. (☎05 65 69 82 23. Open Apr.-Sept. Reception June-Aug. 8am-midnight; Apr.-May and Sept. 7-9:30pm. 23F/€3.51 per person; 20F/€3.05 per tent, 13F/€1.98 per car. Electricity 15F/€2.29.)

Food is hard to come by in this tiny hamlet. Try the **bakery** on rue de Charlemagne on the way to the church, where in addition to bread and pastries you can get ready-made sandwiches for 15-18F/€2.29-2.74 (open daily 7am-8pm). **Restaurant Au Parvis** offers a great view of the church and the heavenly ranks passing judgement on your choice between *tripoux* (tripe) and *aligot.* (☎05 65 72 82 81. Lunch *menu* 55F/€8.39, other *menus* 69F/€10.53, 89F/€13.57. Open Apr.-Nov. 15 daily 10:30am-11:30pm; Nov. 16-Mar. weekends only. Reserve in advance. MC/V.)

SIGHTS AND FESTIVALS. The main attraction in Conques is the **Eglise Abbatiale Ste-Foy,** an elegant example of Romanesque architecture, built between 1050 and 1120. Before entering, admire the carved **tympanum,** which depicts a faded Last Judgment with a gaping Mouth of Hell ready to gobble up the wicked. The barrel-vaulted interior, unusual for its airy proportions, is flooded with light, thanks to the deceptively simple stained glass designed in 1987. The precious relics, revered for their ability to cure the blind and to free prisoners, were partly concealed in an opulent, gem-studded statue now displayed with much reverence in the **trésor** next door. The treasury has a superb collection of medieval reliquaries and liturgical instruments. One prized relic is the bizarre, silver-plated "A" of Charlemagne, supposedly given to Conques by the emperor, but actually from the 11th century. Newer and less precious goods are relegated to the **trésor II,** behind the tourist office. (Church open daily 8:30am-8pm. Free. *Trésors* open July-Aug. daily 9am-noon and 2-7pm; Sept.-June 9am-noon and 2-6pm. 32F/€4.88, students with ID 24F/€3.66, children 12F/€1.83. Tickets can be used for both *trésors.*)

The **Centre Européen d'Art et de Civilisation Médiévale,** at the top of the town, is a cultural center for medieval studies which organizes free exhibitions. (☎05 65 71 24 00. Open M-F 9am-noon and 2-6pm.) Classical concerts are given in the abbey during the **Festival de la Musique** in early August. (Tickets at tourist office 60-130F/€9.15-19.82, students 40-110F/€6.10-16.77.)

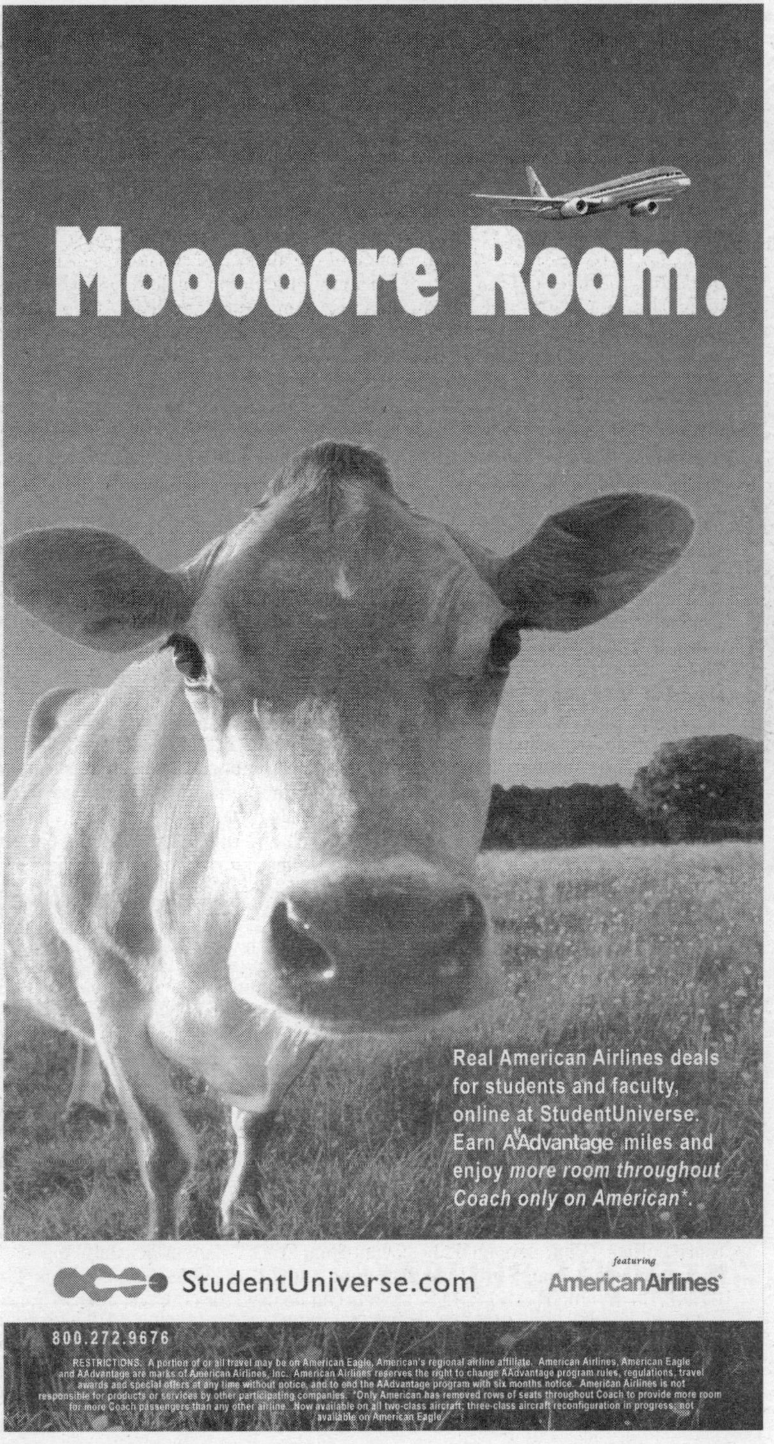
Moooore Room.
Real American Airlines deals for students and faculty, online at StudentUniverse. Earn AAdvantage miles and enjoy *more room throughout Coach only on American**.
StudentUniverse.com
featuring
AmericanAirlines
800.272.9676
RESTRICTIONS: A portion of or all travel may be on American Eagle, American's regional airline affiliate. American Airlines, American Eagle and AAdvantage are marks of American Airlines, Inc. American Airlines reserves the right to change AAdvantage program rules, regulations, travel awards and special offers at any time without notice, and to end the AAdvantage program with six months notice. American Airlines is not responsible for products or services by other participating companies. *Only American has removed rows of seats throughout Coach to provide more room for more Coach passengers than any other airline. Now available on all two-class aircraft; three-class aircraft reconfiguration in progress; not available on American Eagle.

APPENDIX

CLIMATE

The chart below gives average temperatures and rainfalls for major French cities. For a conversion chart from °C to °F, see the inside back cover; for a rough estimate, double the Celsius and add 32.

Av. Temp. (lo/hi), Precipitation	January			April			July			October		
	°C	°F	mm	°C	°F	mm	°C	°F	mm	°C	°F	mm
Ajaccio	4/13	39/55	7.5	9/19	48/66	5.5	18/29	64/84	7.0	13/22	55/71	9.5
Bordeaux	1.6/9	35/48	6.8	7/17	45/63	6.5	14/27	57/81	5.0	8/19	46/66	9.5
Brest	4/8	39/46	8.8	7/13	45/55	6.3	13/21	55/70	5.0	9/16	48/61	9.0
Cherbourg	4/8	39/46	8.3	6/12	43/54	5.0	14/19	57/66	4.8	10/15	50/59	11.5
Lille	0.5/6	33/43	5.0	4/14	39/57	7.0	13/24	55/75	7.0	7/15	45/59	7.5
Lyon	-1/5	30/41	5.3	6/16	43/61	7.0	14/27	39/81	7.0	7/16	45/61	7.8
Marseille	3/12	37/54	5.0	5/15	41/59	1.5	14/26	57/79	1.5	13/24	55/75	9.3
Paris	0/6	32/43	4.3	5/16	41/61	5.3	13/24	55/75	5.3	6/15	43/59	5.5
Strasbourg	0/4	32/39	6.5	5/15	41/59	8.5	14/26	39/79	8.5	6/14	43/57	6.8
Toulouse	19/26	66/79	6.3	7/17	45/63	3.8	15/28	59/82	3.8	9/19	48/66	5.5

TIME ZONES

France lies in the Central European time zone, which is one hour ahead of GMT. From Easter to Autumn, French time moves one hour ahead. Both switches occur about a week before such changes in the US.

MEASUREMENTS

France invented, and still uses, the metric system of measurement. The basic unit of length is the **meter (m),** which is divided into 100 **centimeters (cm),** or 1000 **millimeters (mm).** 1000 meters make up one **kilometer (km).** Fluids are measured in **liters (L),** each divided into 1000 **milliliters (ml).** A liter of pure water weighs one **kilogram (kg),** divided into 1000 **grams (g),** while 1000kg make up one metric **ton.**

MEASUREMENT CONVERSIONS

1 inch = 25.4mm	1mm = 0.039 in.
1 foot = 0.30m	1m = 3.28 ft.
1 yard = 0.914m	1m = 1.09 yd.
1 mile = 1.61km	1km = 0.62 mi.
1 ounce = 28.35g	1g = 0.035 oz.
1 pound = 0.454kg	1kg = 2.202 lb.
1 fluid ounce = 29.57ml	1ml = 0.034 fl. oz.
1 gallon = 3.785L	1L = 0.264 gal.

NATIONAL HOLIDAYS

The main national holiday is **Bastille Day** *(La Fête Nationale)*, July 14, which commemorates the anniversary of the storming of the Bastille in 1789. When a national holiday falls on a Tuesday or Thursday, the French often also take off the Monday or Friday, a practice known as *faire le pont* (making the bridge). Banks close at noon on the day before, or the nearest working day before, a national holiday.

DATE	HOLIDAY
January 1	Le Jour de l'an (also called la St-Sylvestre): New Year's
April 1	Le lundi de Pâques: Easter Monday
May 1	La Fête du travail: Labor Day
May 8	Celebrates the end of World War II in Europe
May 24	L'Ascension: Ascension day
June 4	Le Lundi de Pentecôte: Whit Monday
July 14	La Fête Nationale: Bastille Day
August 15	L'Assomption: Feast of the Assumption
November 1	La Toussaint: All Saints' Day
November 11	L'Armistice 1918: Armistice Day
December 25	Noël: Christmas

FRENCH PHRASEBOOK AND GLOSSARY

ENGLISH	FRENCH	PRONOUNCED
GENERAL		
Hello./Good day.	Bonjour.	bonh-ZHOORRH
Good evening.	Bonsoir.	bonh-SWAHRRH
Hi!	Salut!	sah-LU
Goodbye.	Au revoir.	oh rhVWAHRH
Good night.	Bonne nuit.	bonn NWEE
yes/no/maybe	oui/non/peut-être	wee/nonh/p'TEHT-rh
Please.	S'il vous plaît.	seel voo PLAY
Thank you.	Merci.	mehrrh-SEE
You're welcome.	De rien.	de rrhee-ANH
Pardon me!	Excusez-moi!	ex-KU-zeh-MWAH
Go away!	Allez-vous en!	Ah-LAY vooz on!
Where is...?	Où se trouve...?	oo s'TRRHOOV...?
What time do you open/ close?	Vous ouvrez/fermez à quelle heure?	vooz ooVRHEH/ ferhMEH ah kel'URH?
Help!	Au secours!	oh-SKOORRH.
I'm lost.	Je suis perdu(e).	zh'SWEE pehrh-DU
I'm sorry.	Je suis désolé(e).	zh'SWEE deh-zoh-LEH

OTHER USEFUL PHRASES AND WORDS

ENGLISH	FRENCH	ENGLISH	FRENCH
PHRASES			
Who?	Qui?	**No, thank you.**	Non, merci.
What?	Quoi?	**What is it?**	Qu'est-ce que c'est?
I don't understand.	Je ne comprends pas.	**Why?**	Pourquoi?
Leave me alone.	Laissez-moi tranquille.	**this one/that one**	ceci/cela
How much does this cost?	Ça coûte combien?	**Stop/Stop that!**	Arrête! (familiar) Arrêtez! (pl.)
Please speak slowly.	S'il vous plaît, parlez moins vite.	**Please repeat.**	Répétez, s'il vous plaît.
I am ill/I am hurt.	J'ai mal./Je suis blessé(e).	**Please help me.**	Aidez-moi, s'il vous plaît.

I am (20) years old.	J'ai (vingt) ans.	**Do you speak English?**	Parlez-vous anglais?
I am a student (m/f)	Je suis étudiant/étudiante.	**What's this called in French?**	Comment-on dit...en français?
What is your name?	Comment vous appelez-vous?	**The check, please.**	L'addition, s'il vous plaît.
Please, where is/are...?	S'il vous plaît où se trouve(nt)...?	**Je voudrais...**	I would like...
a doctor	un médecin	**the cash machine**	le guichet automatique
the toilet	les toilettes	**the restaurant**	le restaurant
the hospital	l'hôpital	**the police**	la police
a bedroom	une chambre	**the train station**	la gare
with	avec	**single room**	une chambre simple
a double bed	un grand lit	**double room**	une chambre pour deux
a shower	une douche	**two single beds**	deux lits
lunch	le déjeuner	**a bath**	bain
included	compris	**without**	sans
hot	chaud	**breakfast**	le petit déjeuner
cold	froid	**dinner**	le dîner
DIRECTIONS			
(to the) right	à droite	**(to the) left**	à gauche
straight	tout droit	**near to**	près de
north	nord	**far from**	loin de
south	sud	**east**	est
follow	suivre	**west**	ouest
NUMBERS			
one	un	**six**	six
two	deux	**seven**	sept
three	trois	**eight**	huit
four	quatre	**nine**	neuf
five	cinq	**ten**	dix
fifteen	quinze	**twenty**	vingt
twenty-five	vingt-cinq	**thirty**	trente
forty	quarante	**fifty**	cinquante
hundred	cent	**thousand**	mille
TIMES AND HOURS			
open	ouvert	**closed**	fermé
What time is it?	Quelle heure est-il?	**It's 11am**	Il est onze heures.
afternoon	l'après-midi	**until**	jusqu'à
night	la nuit	**public holidays**	jours fériés (j.f.)
today	aujourd'hui	**January**	janvier
morning	le matin	**February**	fevrier
evening	le soir	**March**	mars
yesterday	hier	**April**	avril
tomorrow	demain	**May**	mai
Monday	lundi	**June**	juin
Tuesday	mardi	**July**	juillet
Wednesday	mercredi	**August**	août
Thursday	jeudi	**September**	septembre
Friday	vendredi	**October**	octobre

Saturday	samedi	**November**	novembre
Sunday	dimanche	**December**	decembre

MENU READER

agneau (m)	lamb	**frais (fraîche) (adj)**	fresh
ail (m)	garlic	**haricot vert (m)**	green bean
asperges (f pl)	asparagus	**huîtres (f pl)**	oysters
assiette (f)	plate	**jambon (m)**	ham
aubergine (f)	eggplant	**lait (m)**	milk
bavette (f)	flank	**lapin (m)**	rabbit
beurre (m)	butter	**légume (m)**	vegetable
bien cuit (adj)	well done	**magret de canard (m)**	duck breast
bière (f)	beer	**maison (adj)**	homemade
bifteck (m)	steak	**marron (m)**	chestnut
blanc de volaille (m)	chicken breast	**fraise (f)**	strawberry
boeuf (m)	beef	**miel (m)**	honey
boisson (f)	drink	**moules (f pl)**	mussels
brochette (f)	kebab	**moutarde (f)**	mustard
canard (m)	duck	**nature (adj)**	plain
carafe d'eau (f)	pitcher of tap water	**noix (f pl)**	nuts
cervelle (f)	brain	**œuf (m)**	egg
champignon (m)	mushroom	**oie (f)**	goose
chaud (adj)	hot	**oignon (m)**	onion
chèvre (m)	goat cheese	**pain (m)**	bread
choix (m)	choice	**pâtes (f pl)**	pasta
choucroute (f)	sauerkraut	**plat (m)**	course (on menu)
chou-fleur (m)	cauliflower	**poêlé (adj)**	pan-fried
ciboulette (f)	chive	**poisson (m)**	fish
citron (m)	lemon	**poivre (m)**	pepper
citron vert (m)	lime	**pomme (f)**	apple
civet (m)	stew (of rabbit)	**pomme de terre (f)**	potato
compote (f)	stewed fruit	**potage (m)**	soup
confit de canard (m)	duck confit	**poulet (m)**	chicken
coq au vin (m)	rooster stewed in wine	**pruneau (m)**	prune
côte (f)	rib or chop	**rillettes (f pl)**	pork hash
courgette f)	zucchini/courgette	**riz (m)**	rice
crème Chantilly (f)	whipped cream	**salade verte (f)**	green salad
crème fraîche (f)	thick cream	**sanglier (m)**	wild boar
crêpe (f)	thin pancake	**saucisse (f)**	sausage
eau de robinet (f)	tap water	**saucisson (m)**	hard salami
échalote (f)	shallot	**saumon (m)**	salmon
entrecôte (f)	chop (cut of meat)	**sel (m)**	salt
escalope (f)	thin slice of meat	**steak tartare (m)**	raw steak
escargot (m)	snail	**sucre (m)**	sugar
farci(e) (adj)	stuffed	**tête (f)**	head
faux-filet (m)	sirloin steak	**thé (m)**	tea
feuilleté (m)	puff pastry	**tournedos (m)**	beef filet
figue (f)	fig	**truffe (f)**	truffle
foie gras d'oie/de canard (m)	liver of fattened goose/ duck	**viande (f)**	meat

FRENCH-ENGLISH GLOSSARY

Le is the masculine singular definite article (the); *la* the feminine; both are abbreviated to *l'* before a vowel, while *les* is the plural definite article for both genders. Where a noun or adjective can take masculine and feminine forms, the masculine is listed first and the feminine in parentheses; often the feminine form consists of adding an "e" to the end, which is indicated by an "e" in parentheses: étudiant(e).

abbaye (f): abbey
abbatiale (f): abbey church
accuiel (m): reception
addition (f): the check
allée (f): lane, avenue
alimentation (f): food
aller-retour (m): round-trip ticket
an (m)/année (f): year
appareil (m): machine; commonly used for telephone
appareil photo (m): camera
arc (m): arch
arènes (f pl.): arena
arrivée (f): arrival
auberge (f): hostel, inn.
auberge de jeunesse (f): youth hostel
autobus (m): city bus
autocar (m): long-distance bus
autoroute (f): highway
banlieue (f): suburb
basse ville (f): lower town
bastide (f): walled fortified town
bibliothèque (f): library
billet (m): ticket
billetterie (f): ticket office
bois (m): forest, wood
boucherie (f): butcher shop
boulangerie (f): bakery
brasserie (f): beer salon and restaurant
bureau (m): office
cap (m): cape
car (m): long-distance bus
carte (f): card; menu; map
cave (f): cellar, normally for wine
centre ville (m): center of town
chambre (f): room
chambre d'hôte (f): bed and breakfast room
chapelle (f): chapel
charcuterie (f): shop selling cooked meats (gen. pork) and prepared food
château (m): castle or mansion; headquarters of a vineyard
cimetière (m): cemetery
cité (f): walled city
cloître (m): cloister
collégiale (f): collegial church
colline (f): hill
comptoir (m): counter (in a bar or café)
côte (f): coast; side (e.g. of hill)
côté (m): side (e.g. of building)
couvent (m): convent
cour (f): courtyard
cours (m): wide street
cru (m): vintage
dégustation (f): tasting
départ (m): departure
donjon (m): keep (of a castle)
douane (f): customs
école (f): school
église (f): church
entrée (f): appetizer; entrance
épicerie (f): grocery store
étudiant(e): student
faubourg (m; abbr. fbg): quarter (of town; archaic)
fête (f): celebration, festival; party
ferme (f): farm
fleuve (m): river
foire (f): fair
fontaine (f): fountain
forêt (f): forest
fronton (m): *jai alai* arena
galerie (f): gallery
gare or gare SNCF (f): train station
gare routière (f): bus station
gîte d'étape (m): rural hostel-like accommodations, aimed at hikers
grève (f): strike, French national pastime
guichet (m): ticket counter, cash register desk
haute ville (f): upper town
horloge (f): clock
hors-saison: off-season
hôpital (m): hospital
hôtel (particulier) (m): town house, mansion
hôtel de ville (m): town hall
hôtel-Dieu (m): hospital (archaic)
île (f): island
jour (m): day
jour férié (m): public holiday
location (f): rental store
lycée (m): high school
madame (f; abbr. Mme): Mrs.
mademoiselle (f; abbr. Mlle): Miss
magasin (m): shop
mairie (f): town hall
maison (f): house
marée (f): tide
marché (m): market
mer (f): sea
mois (m): month
monastère (m): monastery
monsieur (m; abbr. M): Mr.
montagne (f): mountain
mur (m): wall
muraille (f): city wall, rampart
nuit (f): night
palais (m): palace
parc (m): park
pâtisserie (f): pastry shop
place (f): town square
plan (m): plan, map
plat (m): course (on menu)
pont (m): bridge
poste (f; abbr. PTT): post office
pourboire (m): the tip
puy (m): hill, mountain (archaic)
quartier (m): section (of town)
randonnée (f): hike
rempart (m): rampart
rivière (f): river
route (f): road
rue (f): street
salon (m): living room
salle (f): room; in a café it refers to indoor seating as opposed to the bar or patio
semaine (f): week
sentier (m): path, lane
service compris: tip included
soir (m): evening
son-et-lumière (m): sound-and-light show
source (f): spring
supermarché (m): supermarket
syndicat d'initiative (m): tourist office
tabac (m): cigarette and newsstand
table (f): table
télépherique (m): cable car
terrasse (f): terrace, patio
TGV (m): high speed train
thermes (m pl): hot springs
tour (f): tower
tour (m): tour
traiteur (m): delicatessen
université (f): university
val (m)/vallée (f): valley
vélo(m): bicycle
vendange (f): grape harvest
vieille ville (f): old town
ville (f): town, city
visite guidée (f): guided tour
vitraux (m pl): stained glass
voie (f): road
voiture (f): car

INDEX

A

INDEX

D

E

F

INDEX

INDEX

ABOUT LET'S GO

FORTY-TWO YEARS OF WISDOM

For over four decades, travelers crisscrossing the continents have relied on *Let's Go* for inside information on the hippest backstreet cafes, the most pristine secluded beaches, and the best routes from border to border. *Let's Go: Europe*, now in its 42nd edition and translated into seven languages, reigns as the world's bestselling international travel guide. In the last 20 years, our rugged researchers have stretched the frontiers of backpacking and expanded our coverage into the Americas, Australia, Asia, and Africa (including the new *Let's Go: Egypt* and the more comprehensive, multi-country jaunt through *Let's Go: South Africa & Southern Africa*). Our new-and-improved City Guide series continues to grow with new guides to perennial European favorites Amsterdam and Barcelona. This year we are also unveiling *Let's Go: Southwest USA*, the flagship of our new outdoor Adventure Guide series, which is complete with special roadtripping tips and itineraries, more coverage of adventure activities like hiking and mountain biking, and first-person accounts of life on the road.

It all started in 1960 when a handful of well-traveled students at Harvard University handed out a 20-page mimeographed pamphlet offering a collection of their tips on budget travel to passengers on student charter flights to Europe. The following year, in response to the instant popularity of the first volume, students traveling to Europe researched the first full-fledged edition of *Let's Go: Europe*. Throughout the 60s and 70s, our guides reflected the times—in 1969, for example, we taught you how to get from Paris to Prague on "no dollars a day" by singing in the street. In the 90s we focused in on the world's most exciting urban areas to produce in-depth, fold-out map guides, now with 20 titles (from Hong Kong to Chicago) and counting. Our new guides bring the total number of titles to 57, each infused with the spirit of adventure and voice of opinion that travelers around the world have come to count on. But some things never change: our guides are still researched, written, and produced entirely by students who know first-hand how to see the world on the cheap.

HOW WE DO IT

Each guide is completely revised and thoroughly updated every year by a well-traveled set of nearly 300 students. Every spring, we recruit over 200 researchers and 90 editors to overhaul every book. After several months of training, researcher-writers hit the road for seven weeks of exploration, from Anchorage to Adelaide, Estonia to El Salvador, Iceland to Indonesia. Hired for their rare combination of budget travel sense, writing ability, stamina, and courage, these adventurous travelers know that train strikes, stolen luggage, food poisoning, and marriage proposals are all part of a day's work. Back at our offices, editors work from spring to fall, massaging copy written on Himalayan bus rides into witty, informative prose. A student staff of typesetters, cartographers, publicists, and managers keeps our lively team together. In September, the collected efforts of the summer are delivered to our printer, who turns them into books in record time, so that you have the most up-to-date information available for your vacation. Even as you read this, work on next year's editions is well underway.

WHY WE DO IT

We don't think of budget travel as the last recourse of the destitute; we believe that it's the only way to travel. Our books will ease your anxieties and answer your questions about the basics—so you can get off the beaten track and explore. Once you learn the ropes, we encourage you to put *Let's Go* down and strike out on your own. You know as well as we that the best discoveries are often those you make yourself. When you find something worth sharing, please drop us a line. We're Let's Go Publications, 67 Mount Auburn St., Cambridge, MA 02138, USA (feedback@letsgo.com). For more info, visit our website, www.letsgo.com.

Will you have enough stories to tell your grandchildren?

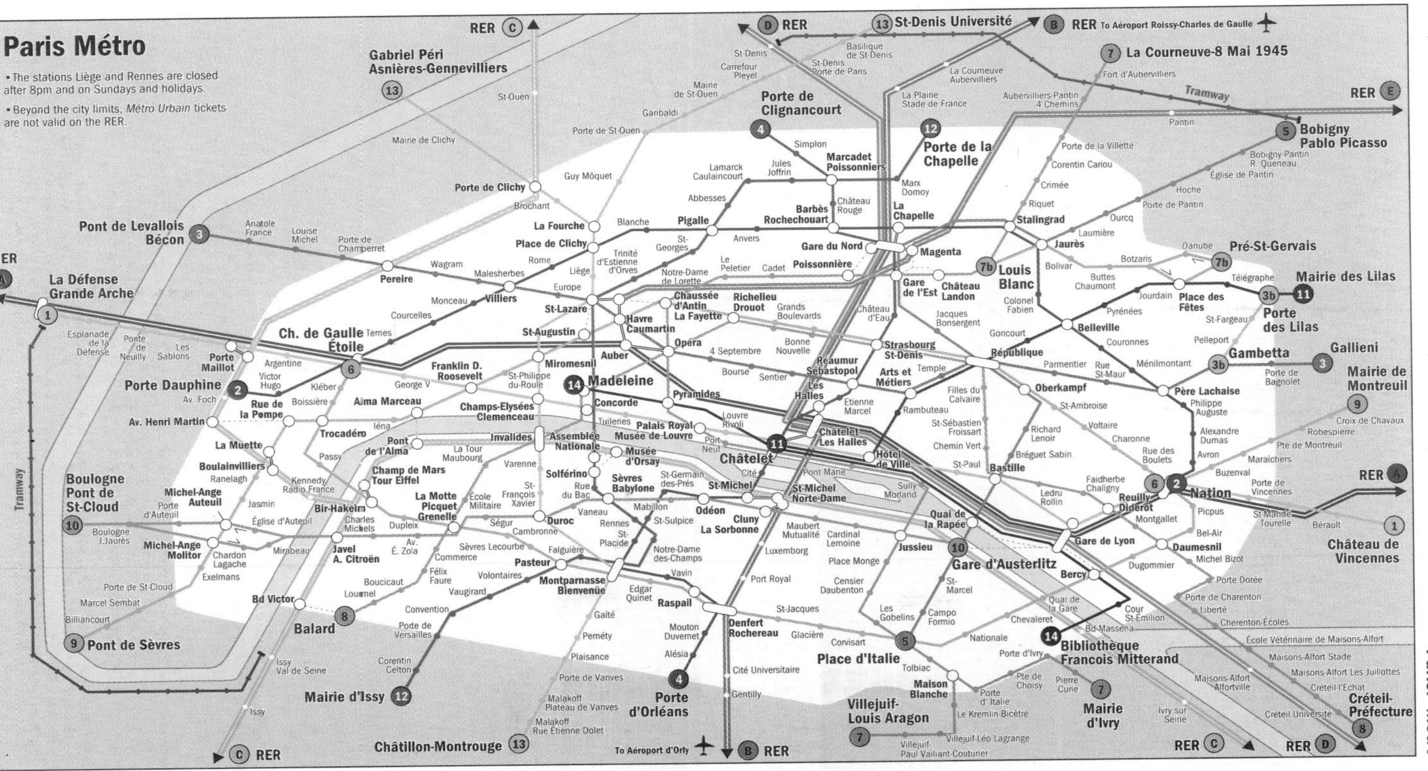
Paris Métro
• The stations Liège and Rennes are closed after 8pm and on Sundays and holidays.
• Beyond the city limits, *Métro Urbain* tickets are not valid on the RER.
RER A
La Défense Grande Arche
Pont de Levallois Bécon
Gabriel Péri Asnières-Gennevilliers
RER C
Porte de Clignancourt
RER D
St-Denis Université
RER B To Aéroport Roissy-Charles de Gaulle
La Courneuve-8 Mai 1945
RER E
Bobigny Pablo Picasso
Porte de la Chapelle
Pré-St-Gervais
Mairie des Lilas
Porte des Lilas
Gallieni
Mairie de Montreuil
Château de Vincennes
Créteil-Préfecture
Mairie d'Ivry
Bibliothèque Francois Mitterand
Villejuif-Louis Aragon
Porte d'Orléans
To Aéroport d'Orly
Châtillon-Montrouge
Mairie d'Issy
Balard
Pont de Sèvres
Boulogne Pont de St-Cloud
Porte Dauphine
Ch. de Gaulle Étoile
Madeleine
Châtelet
Gare d'Austerlitz
Place d'Italie
Nation
Tramway

Paris: Overview and Arrondissements
1 Cimetière de Montmartre
2 Sacré Coeur Basilica
3 Parc La Villette
4 Parc des Buttes Chaumont
5 Jardins du Trocadero
6 Palais Chaillot
7 Cimetière de Passy
8 American Embassy
9 British Embassy
10 Petit Palais
11 Grand Palais
12 Arc de Triomphe
13 Madeleine
14 Gare St-Lazare
15 Parc Monceau
16 Palais de la Découverte
17 Opéra Garnier
18 Galeries Lafayette
19 Printemps
20 Gare du Nord
21 Gare de l'Est
22 Opéra Bastille
23 Palais Omnisports de Bercy
24 Ministère des Finances
25 Gare de Lyon
26 Parc de Montsouris
27 Cité Universitaire
28 Cimetière Montparnasse
29 Gare Montparnasse
Bois de Boulogne
16e
17e
8e
7e
15e
14e
Seine
30 Bureau des Objets Trouvés (Lost and Found)
31 Louvre
32 Palais Royale
33 Forum des Halles
34 Musée de l'Orangerie
35 Central Post Office
36 Bourse
37 Bibliothèque Nationale
38 Ecole des Arts et Métiers
39 Archives Nationales
40 Musée Carnavalet
41 Musée Picasso
42 Centre George Pompidou
43 place des Vosges
44 Musée Victor Hugo
45 Notre Dame
46 Mémorial de la Déportation
47 Université de Paris (Sorbonne)
48 Ecole Normal Supérieure
49 Musée de Cluny
50 Museum Nationale d'Histoire Naturelle
51 Panthéon
52 Eglise St-Etienne du Mont
53 La Mosquée
54 Jardin des Plantes
55 Jardins du Luxembourg
56 Eglise St-Sulpice
57 Théâtre Nationale de l'Odéon
58 Eiffel Tower
59 Champs de Mars
60 Ecole Militaire
61 UNESCO
62 Hôtel des Invalides
63 Assemblée Nationale
64 Musée d'Orsay
65 Cimetière de l'Est du Pere Lachaise

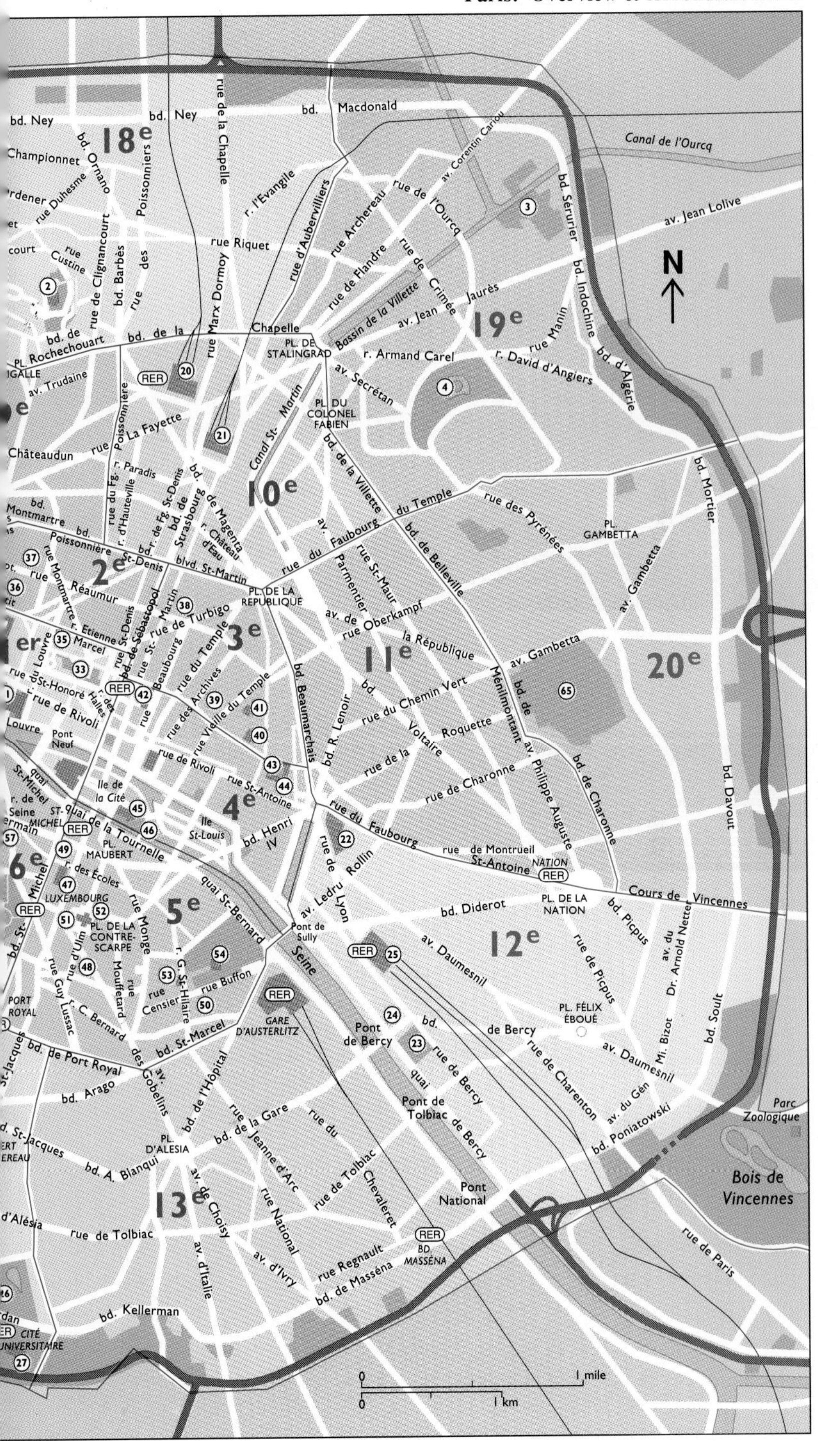
18e
19e
10e
2e
3e
11e
20e
4e
5e
6e
12e
13e
N
bd. Ney
bd. Macdonald
rue de la Chapelle
Canal de l'Ourcq
av. Jean Lolive
bd. Sérurier
bd. Indochine
bd. d'Algérie
bd. Ornano
Championnet
rue Duhesme
rue Custine
rue de Clignancourt
bd. Barbès
rue des Poissonniers
rue Riquet
rue Marx Dormoy
r. l'Evangile
rue d'Aubervilliers
rue Archereau
rue de l'Ourcq
av. Corentin Cariou
rue de Flandre
rue de Crimée
Bassin de la Villette
av. Jean Jaurès
bd. de la Chapelle
bd. de Rochechouart
PL. DE STALINGRAD
r. Armand Carel
rue Manin
r. David d'Angiers
av. Secrétan
PL. DU COLONEL FABIEN
Canal St-Martin
av. Trudaine
rue La Fayette
rue Poissonnière
Châteaudun
r. Paradis
rue du Fg. Poissonnière
r. d'Hauteville
r. de Fg. St-Denis
bd. de Strasbourg
bd. de Magenta
r. Château d'Eau
bd. de la Villette
rue du Faubourg du Temple
rue des Pyrénées
PL. GAMBETTA
bd. Mortier
bd. Montmartre
bd. Poissonnière
bd. St-Denis
blvd. St-Martin
PL. DE LA REPUBLIQUE
av. Parmentier
rue St-Maur
bd. de Belleville
av. Gambetta
rue Réaumur
rue Montmartre
r. Etienne Marcel
bd. de Sébastopol
rue St-Martin
rue de Turbigo
rue du Temple
av. de la République
rue Oberkampf
rue du Louvre
rue St-Honoré
r. des Halles
rue de Rivoli
Louvre
Pont Neuf
rue St-Denis
rue Beaubourg
rue des Archives
rue Vieille du Temple
bd. Beaumarchais
bd. R. Lenoir
rue du Chemin Vert
bd. Voltaire
rue de la Roquette
bd. de Ménilmontant
bd. Davout
quai St-Michel
r. de Seine
ST-MICHEL
St-Germain
Ile de la Cité
rue St-Antoine
rue de Charonne
av. Philippe Auguste
bd. de Charonne
Ile St-Louis
bd. Henri IV
quai de la Tournelle
PL. MAUBERT
r. des Écoles
LUXEMBOURG
bd. St-Michel
rue du Faubourg St-Antoine
rue de Montreuil
NATION
rue de Lyon
av. Ledru Rollin
Cours de Vincennes
PL. DE LA NATION
quai St-Bernard
PL. DE LA CONTRE-SCARPE
rue Monge
rue d'Ulm
bd. Diderot
bd. Picpus
av. du Dr. Arnold Netter
Pont de Sully
Seine
av. Daumesnil
rue de Picpus
rue Guy Lussac
r. C. Bernard
rue Mouffetard
rue Censier
r. G. St-Hilaire
rue Buffon
PORT ROYAL
GARE D'AUSTERLITZ
Pont de Bercy
bd. de Bercy
PL. FÉLIX ÉBOUÉ
av. Daumesnil
Mi. Bizot
bd. Soult
bd. St-Marcel
bd. de Port Royal
av. des Gobelins
rue de Bercy
quai de Bercy
rue de Charenton
bd. Arago
bd. de l'Hôpital
Pont de Tolbiac
av. du Gén
bd. Poniatowski
Parc Zoologique
bd. St-Jacques
PL. D'ALESIA
bd. de la Gare
rue Jeanne d'Arc
rue du Chevaleret
Bois de Vincennes
bd. A. Blanqui
rue de Tolbiac
Pont National
rue d'Alésia
rue de Tolbiac
av. de Choisy
rue National
BD. MASSÉNA
rue de Paris
av. d'Italie
av. d'Ivry
rue Regnault
bd. de Masséna
bd. Kellerman
CITÉ UNIVERSITAIRE
RER
0
1 mile
0
1 km

Paris: 1er and 2e

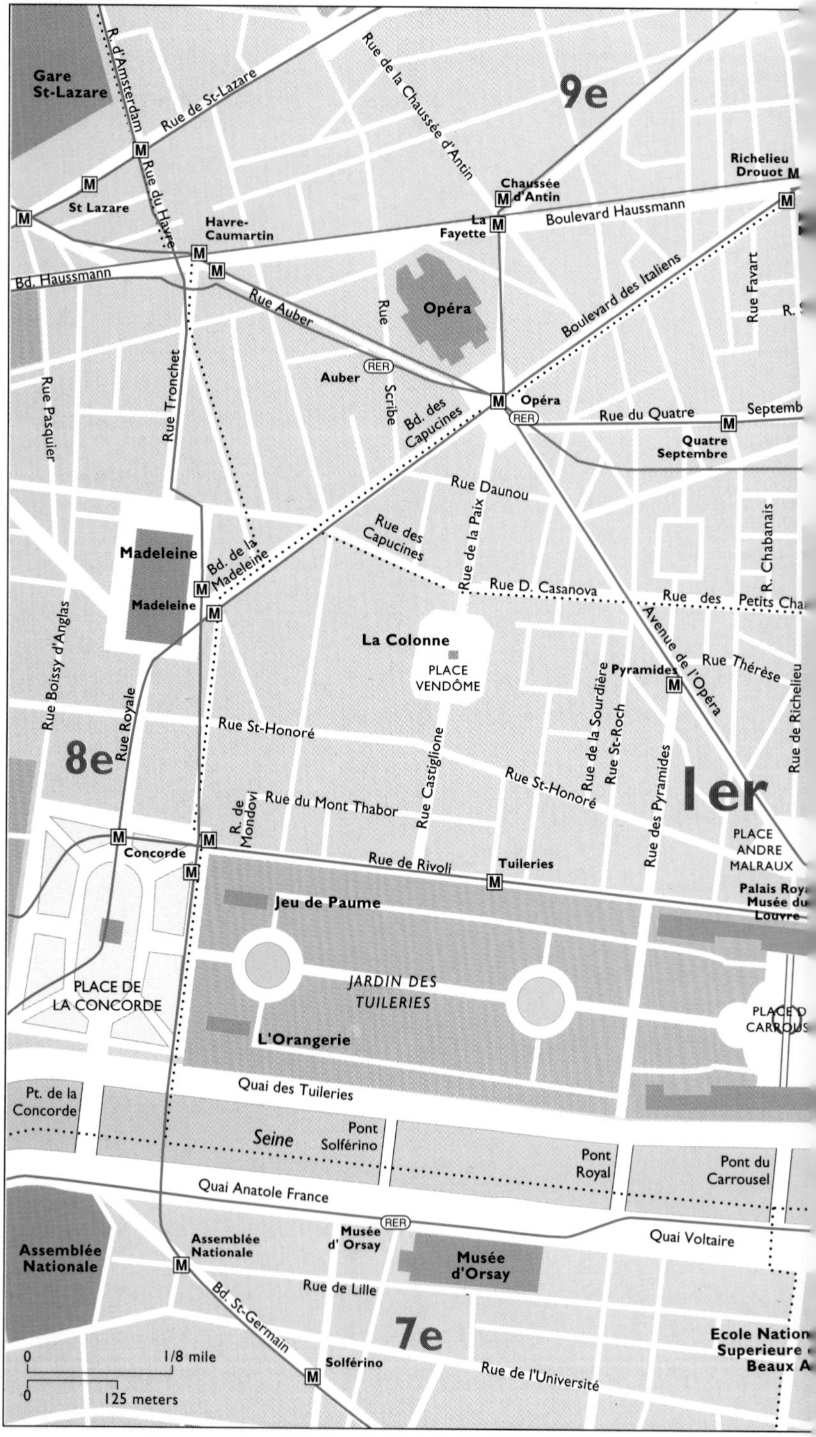

Gare St-Lazare
R. d'Amsterdam
Rue de St-Lazare
Rue de la Chaussée d'Antin
9e
Richelieu Drouot
St Lazare
Rue du Havre
Chaussée d'Antin
La Fayette
Boulevard Haussmann
Havre-Caumartin
Bd. Haussmann
Opéra
Rue Auber
Rue Scribe
Boulevard des Italiens
Rue Favart
Auber
Rue Tronchet
Rue Pasquier
Bd. des Capucines
Opéra
Rue du Quatre Septemb
Quatre Septembre
Rue Daunou
Rue des Capucines
Rue de la Paix
R. Chabanais
Madeleine
Bd. de la Madeleine
Madeleine
Rue D. Casanova
Rue des Petits Cha
Avenue de l'Opéra
La Colonne
PLACE VENDÔME
Rue Thérèse
Pyramides
Rue Boissy d'Anglas
Rue Royale
Rue St-Honoré
Rue de la Sourdière
Rue St-Roch
Rue de Richelieu
8e
Rue Castiglione
Rue St-Honoré
Rue des Pyramides
1er
R. de Mondovi
Rue du Mont Thabor
PLACE ANDRE MALRAUX
Concorde
Rue de Rivoli
Tuileries
Palais Roya Musée du Louvre
Jeu de Paume
JARDIN DES TUILERIES
PLACE DE LA CONCORDE
PLACE D CARROUS
L'Orangerie
Quai des Tuileries
Pt. de la Concorde
Seine
Pont Solférino
Pont Royal
Pont du Carrousel
Quai Anatole France
RER
Musée d'Orsay
Quai Voltaire
Assemblée Nationale
Assemblée Nationale
Musée d'Orsay
Rue de Lille
Bd. St-Germain
7e
Ecole Nation Superieure Beaux A
Solférino
Rue de l'Université
0 1/8 mile
0 125 meters